D1070970

HERMAN KLEIN
AND
THE GRAMOPHONE

Yours Sincerely
Hermann Klein

HERMAN KLEIN
AND

THE GRAMOPHONE

being a series of essays
on
The Bel Canto (1923)
The Gramophone and the Singer (1924–1934)
and
REVIEWS OF
NEW CLASSICAL VOCAL RECORDINGS
(1925–1934)

and other writings from
THE GRAMOPHONE
by
HERMAN KLEIN

Edited and with a Biographical Sketch by
WILLIAM R. MORAN

AMADEUS PRESS
Reinhard G. Pauly, General Editor
Portland, Oregon

ISBN 0-931340-18-7

Amadeus Press (an imprint of Timber Press, Inc.)
9999 S.W. Wilshire
Portland, Oregon 97225
Printed in Hong Kong

Library of Congress Cataloging-in-Publication Data

Klein, Hermann, 1856-1934.
    Herman Klein and the gramophone : being a series of essays on the
Bel canto (1923), the Gramophone and the Singer (1924-1934), and
reviews of new classical vocal recordings (1925-1934), and other
writings from the Gramophone / by Herman Klein ; edited and with a
biographical sketch by William R. Moran.
        p.   cm.
    ISBN 0-931340-18-7
    1. Vocal music--History and criticism. 2. Opera--England--London.
3. Sound recordings--Reviews.   I. Moran, William R.   II. Gramophone
(London, England) III. Title.
ML60.K527 1989
782'.009--dc20   89-36903
                                                               CIP
                                                               MN

CONTENTS

III. ANALYTICAL NOTES AND FIRST REVIEWS:

HERMAN KLEIN
AND *THE GRAMOPHONE*

By WILLIAM R. MORAN

That doyen of periodicals relating to the preservation and reproduction of sound, *The Gramophone,* was launched by the well-known British author and novelist, Compton Mackenzie, with the issue of Vol. 1 No. 1 in May, 1923. In his "Editorial Notes" for the issue of May, 1924 the following appears:

> Among other distinguished people who have promised to write for *The Gramophone* in the near future is Mr. Herman Klein, who, if anyone, is *the* authority on *bel canto.* Of course, he is many other things as well, a brilliant writer on musical matters as well as a brilliant teacher; and his recent essay on "Bel Canto,"* published by the Oxford Press is probably in the hands of most of our readers, who will appreciate the honour due to this review when Mr. Klein consented to contribute a series of articles on operatic records.

With no more introduction than this, the June 1924 issue of the magazine contained the first of the Herman Klein articles entitled "The Gramophone and the Singer". Under this heading the author produced a series of distinguished essays, on a monthly basis, (except for three in ten years) through the issue of March, 1934. In the issue for April, 1934 his obituary, written by Christopher Stone, appeared. The entire series of these articles is reproduced in the present volume.

From its first issue, *The Gramophone* featured reviews of the new records issued each month. Initially, these were grouped by manufacturer, but with the issue of October, 1925, the "Analytical Notes and First Reviews" section was presented in a classified format in which Klein's name is found as the author of the "Operatic" sub-section. In November, 1927, his review section was headed "Operatic and German Lieder", and in the following month, "Operatic and Foreign Songs", which title it retained through the issue of March, 1934. Klein also reviewed recordings in his areas of interest for the special October, 1931 supplement which listed the contents of the new HMV "Connoisseur Catalogue", the first "Decca-Polydor List" (April, 1932), and the new "complete" opera albums which flowed, one after another, from Columbia and HMV during the late 20s and 30s. Now and again he reviewed the new choral recordings, and at one time had an interesting exchange, through the correspondence columns, with Landon Ronald about the recording of Adelina Patti. All his contributions to *The Gramophone* for the last 10 years of his life have been collected here.

For the readers of 1924, Compton Mackenzie's brief introduction was perhaps enough, and while Stone's obituary of 1934 shows appreciation, affection, and expresses a real sense of loss, one wonders today if the editors of *The Gramophone* truly realized the historical importance of this unique man and his writings.

In a "Prefatory Note" to his *Thirty Years of Musical Life in London, 1870–1900* published in 1903, Klein writes:

> Not the least valuable asset of a life largely spent among artists is a good memory. From an early age, I cultivated the faculty of making mental notes; and, like most faculties, innate or acquired, it grew until it developed into second nature. During my quarter of a century's work as a London musical critic, I seldom found it necessary to more than jot down a word or two in the margin of a programme as a preliminary to the writing of an article. I accustomed my eye and ear to take records of what I saw and heard; and, where I happened to be sufficiently interested, those records assumed a more or less permanent form.

Klein's writings attest to his excellent memory, and reveal an educated and informed observer of the vocal scene in London from the 1870s onward; even his recollections before that time with respect to some of the singers he heard in his youth have merit. The circumstances under which he grew up, and especially his close association over a 10-year period with Manuel Garcia, the greatest singing teacher of his day, provided a unique opportunity for him not only to hear the great artists of the period, but to judge their technical work from an informed viewpoint, and eventually to get to know many of them on a close, personal basis. His years in the field of musical criticism and as a vocal teacher of stature in both London and New York spanned the closing years of the public appearances of many great singers who did not record for the phonograph, as well

*Reprinted in its entirety in this volume.

as the complete artistic careers of most of the great artists active during the early years of that machine. What other writer heard Nellie Mitchell Armstrong at Prince's Hall, Picadilly in 1886 before she went to Paris to study with Mathilde Marchesi to emerge a year later as Nellie Melba? Klein was also present at Melba's Covent Garden debut in 1888, and at her farewell in the same theater in 1926. What better authority can we today turn to when we ask the question: "How representative of the singer are their old recordings?" Klein's years with *The Gramophone* spanned the end of the acoustical era and the beginning of electrical recordings. He wrote hundreds of reviews of recordings to which the collector can still listen today. Thus, each of us can make our own evaluation of the opinions of a critic who heard just what we are hearing, and by extrapolation, we can judge on a personal basis, the validity of the opinion of this man who tells us in words what singers sounded like well over 100 years ago.

These then are the principal reasons Herman Klein's writings are important, and deserve to be collected and preserved, looking more closely at this man than Compton Mackenzie's 1924 introduction seemed to indicate was necessary.

Hermann (between 1910 and 1920 he dropped one "n") Klein was born in what he called the "musical city of Norwich," about 90 miles northeast of London, in 1856. His father was a teacher of languages; his mother directed a dancing school. An early desire to go on stage coupled with the opportunities provided by an uncle, who was editor of a local paper, to get to know the smell of printer's ink at an early age helped give direction to his career. Time was also allotted to study of the piano and languages. It was in Norwich, in 1863, that Hermann first heard Tietjens, Trebelli, Sims Reeves and Santley in rehearsal for the local festival; heard his first opera, *Il Trovatore;* and Jenny Lind:

> The voice, I remember perfectly, was as exquisitely clear and fresh as a young girl's; its sweet tones haunted me long afterward. Of the wonderous art of the great singer, I was too young to judge; but I shall never forget what she sang, of the rare wealth of religious sentiment with which she invested the prayer of *Agathe* in the favorite *scena* from "Der Freischütz." Upon the stage, of course, the heroine of Weber's opera always kneels while uttering her touching appeal for her lover's safe return, and Jenny Lind also knelt while singing the same passage upon the platform of St. Andrew's Hall on the occasion I am alluding to.

It was also at the time of one of the local festivals, that the young boy first met a man of music whose friendship was to open many doors:

> One of the proudest moments that I can recall of my early Norwich life was my being presented to Mr. (afterward Sir) Julius Benedict, who officiated as conductor of the festivals from 1842 until 1878. . . . By the light of subsequent experience, I learned to realize that Benedict was one of the worst conductors who ever held a baton. His head was invariably buried in his score . . . He rarely gave a cue until it was too late to be of any practical value; and he entirely lacked the magnetic power and the sense of ensemble that should be the primary gifts of a good conductor. But at the time I am speaking of these deficiencies were noted only by a few. The vast majority . . . including my youthful self, were satisfied to look upon Sir Julius not only as a great conductor, but as a musician whose coöperation brought honor and glory to the festival. Was he not the favorite pupil and friend of Weber? Had he not, when a young man of twenty-three, seen and shaken hands with the immortal Beethoven?

> I have been introduced to Verdi and Gounod; I have known and spoken with Wagner; but, great as those privileges undoubtedly were, I do not think they aroused in me the same feelings of mingled pride and awe that I experienced when, as a boy, I was first addressed by a man who had stood face to face with Beethoven. . . . It was at the suggestion of Malibran that Benedict left Paris and went to England in 1835 [where] he quickly made his mark as an operatic composer . . . Although such a mediocre conductor, he was an admirable accompanist . . . His reputation in this capacity was not a little enhanced by his association with Jenny Lind on her memorable tour of the United States (1850–52). . . . After his return to London, his services "at the piano" were in request at every kind of musical function, and he was practically the sole accompanist employed at the Monday Popular Concerts during the first twenty years of their existence.

Klein moved to London in 1869, where he continued his education, and at the same time managed to write musical columns for various journals. One of these featured interviews with well-known singers, contacts with whom were arranged through his continuing friendship with Sir Julius Benedict, a friendship which only ended with the composer's death in 1885. In 1872 he went to Liverpool to pursue a commercial career, but during his stay in London he had heard Patti in *Don Giovanni;* Christine Nilsson in *Faust* and *Robert le Diable;* Ilma di Murska in *Il Flauto Magico* and *The Flying Dutchman;* Tietjens in *Fidelio* and *Lucrezia Borgia,* and with her in the latter Trebelli as Maffio Orsini, and Italo Campanini (on the night of his début at Drury Lane) as Gennaro. Klein's stay in Liverpool seems mostly remembered by the musical events he attended. He returned to London in 1874 due to the illness of his mother.

> In the spring of 1874 there occurred an event which was destined to exercise an important influence upon my career. Manuel Garcia, the great teacher of singing, came to live under my parents' roof. We occupied a large house at the corner of Bentinck Street and Welbeck Street, Cavendish Square,—then, as now, the recognized fashionable quarter for London professional people,—and Signor Garcia took the entire ground floor for his "studio" and dwelling apartments . . . Fortunately, Garcia took a considerable fancy to me. He was fond of discussing politics, but having little time to read the papers, would generally ask me for the latest news. . . . About music I was afraid for a long while to talk to him. One day, however, he heard me singing in a distant part of the house, and told my mother that I had an agreeable light tenor voice. She at once asked him if he would be good enough to give me some instruction. He readily consented, and, within an hour, to my intense delight, I found myself taking my first lesson from Manuel Garcia.

Klein has described "The Teaching of Manual Garcia" in Chapter III of his *The Bel Canto,* reprinted in this volume. During this four year period of study with Garcia, he had kept busy with his literary endeavors.

> It was this increase of profitable journalistic labour that compelled me to arrive at a definite decision regarding my vocal career. I put the case frankly to Signor Garcia, and he advised me without hesitation to give up singing: "Your voice is not strong enough for opera; and as you do not care for concert work, why take the risk of exchanging the stalls for the stage? You have studied with me—how long?—four years; well, you know enough of singing to be able to write sanely about it, and that is more than can be said of some of the critics." My parents . . . were of the same opinion, with the additional argument that as a pupil of Garcia I should always be entitled, if I wished, to teach others the art of singing.

Klein's horizons continued to expand. Through his close relationships with Garcia, Benedict and others, he was able to form lasting relationships with impresarios such as Grau, Gye, Mapleson and Harris, as well as the elite of society who made up the local musical world. In addition to singers, he heard and got to know the famed instrumentalists of the day: Wieniawski, Vieuxtemps, Joachim, Clara Schumann, Wilhelmj, Sarasate, Saint-Saëns. Richter, Mottl, Mahler, Weingartner, Nikisch, Seidl, Strauss, Randegger, Pasdeloup, Colonne, and Lamoureux and Hallé were among the conductors with whom he became acquainted, some apparently to become close friends. His interest in the stage continued, and Ellen Terry, Sir Henry Irving, Edwin Booth, Ada Rehan, Sarah Bernhardt and Mrs. Kendal were among the actors and actresses he knew well. He was a close friend of Arthur Sullivan and Rupert D'Oyly Carte, and had a speaking acquaintance with W. S. Gilbert. He attended and wrote critical reviews on every first performance of a Gilbert & Sullivan operetta from 1878 to 1896. He attended the first performances in London of many of the now "standard" operas of Verdi, Wagner, Puccini, Massenet, Gounod, and of course many lesser works. He was present at the local debuts of such singers as Nordica, Eames, Calvé, De Lussan, Plançon, the De Reszke brothers, Lassalle, Cotogni, Tamagno, Minnie Hauk, Sigrid Arnoldson, and Francesco D'Andrade. He was also present for the debuts of Ternina, Tetrazzini, Sembrich. . . . The list could go on for pages.

Klein was apparently not just a distant voice of the press; he seemed to have a facility for getting closely involved in many musical happenings:

> When I went with Augustus Harris (Director of Covent Garden) to Paris to engage Jean de Reszke for the tentative season of 1887, he had attained just half his full span of life [and was] in the prime of vigorous manhood. Edouard, slightly his junior, had already sung for several seasons at Covent Garden. I had seen both brothers . . . and Pol Plançon (superb artist!) in the original cast of Massenet's *Le Cid* at the Opera in November, 1885. In that role Jean had proclaimed his right to be called a tenor . . . When Jean sang [the role of] Roméo with Patti in French at the Paris Opéra in 1888, Gounod, with tears in his eyes, declared in my hearing that his dream had at last been realized. He embraced Jean as the perfect ideal of Shakespeare's lover, and told him he was "finer than Mario because he sang Roméo so divinely in French."

> In those early days Edouard used to keep Jean in roars of laughter by caricaturing Wagnerian declamation *à la* Wotan, whilst I improvised a noisy orchestral din for him on the

piano. But even then he was studying Walther in *Die Meistersinger* . . . and laying the ground for Tristan and Siegfried to be sung in German. . . .

Klein also added the role of singing teacher to his other activities, taking a limited number of private pupils. In 1888 he joined the teaching staff at the Guildhall School of Music, where he continued to teach voice until 1901. In December of that year he made the move to New York, where, armed with letters of introduction from such notables as Adelina Patti, Manual Garcia and Jean de Reszke, he set up a school of singing on West 77th Street. Among his pupils he numbered Clara Clemens, daughter of Mark Twain, who had a distinguished concert career before and after her marriage to pianist Ossip Gabrilowitsch. With his ability to make contacts "pay off," Klein wasted no time in becoming involved in the social as well as the musical life of New York, and soon numbered many of that city's "Four Hundred" among his friends. He became a member of the famed Lotos Club, and as a member of its Entertainment Committee provided musical programs for its meetings. For a time he acted as Music Critic for the *New York Herald,* and developed a close friendship with James Gibbons Huneker of the *New York Sun.*

He managed to stay involved with matters operatic:

> When *Parsifal* was given in English in 1904-5 for the first time in America by Mr. Henry W. Savage, he asked me to undertake the duty of instructing his numerous artists in the proper use of our language. This was no light task, because most of them were foreigners who did not know a word of English; and no fewer than three separate casts were required for Wagner's sacred drama, in order that it might be played on tour eight times a week—which it actually was, for forty weeks. To make this practicable, the whole of the foreign singers were instructed to meet me in Berlin in July, 1904, and there, with two conductors in turn at the piano, they had to study the *Parsifal* text and music, under my supervision, for an entire month.

Back in New York, Klein renewed many of his London friendships: Melba, Ternina, Calvé, Tetrazzini, Gadski, Schumann-Heink, Nordica, Eames, Suzanne Adams all of whom he had known since their London débuts. He attended Sembrich's retirement, and remarked that he had been present at her Covent Garden début some 20 years before.

> I also met Geraldine Farrar, and saw her in some of her best characters; it is London's loss that she should never have been heard at Covent Garden.

In his first article for *The Gramophone,* Klein tells of his association with the Columbia Graphophone Co. and how he brought them his close friend, David Bispham, his pupil Ruth Vincent, as well as Van Rooy, Blauvelt, Gilibert, and of course Lillian Nordica. The story of Nordica's association with the recording horn is told in some detail in this writer's *Recordings and Lillian Nordica,* an appendix to Ira Glackens' *Yankee Diva: Lillian Nordica and the Golden Days of Opera* (New York, 1963). Klein was also marginally involved with the affairs of both the Metropolitan Opera and later Oscar Hammerstein's Manhattan Opera venture. More or less in passing he mentions:

> . . . Miss Mary Garden was a disappointment at Covent Garden, but well received in New York, thanks to her admirable performance as the heroine of Debussy's *Pelléas et Mélisande,* which she introduced there with other members of the original Paris cast. This engagement I helped to bring about at the joint request of the late Gustave Schirmer and Oscar Hammerstein, through M. Durand, the Paris publisher, in the summer of 1907. Miss Mary Garden hesitated some time before accepting the offer, having, it was understood, made up her mind never to go to America; and but for this opportunity she would probably never have gone there.

In May, 1909, Klein returned to London, where he took up residence at 40 Avenue Road, Regent's Park, and picked up the threads of his old life. His advertisement ran: "To Singers: Taught or Untaught/Mr. Herman Klein/may be consulted upon all subjects connected with/The Training of the Voice/and/The Art of Singing/by appointment at his Studio Residence." He became a frequent contributor to the *Musical Times:* In the December, 1911 issue he published an interesting article on Oscar Hammerstein's "The London Opera House", and on Hammerstein himself, and throughout the brief career of its existence, he supplied a series of other articles chronicling the ventures there attempted. The *Musical Times* volume for 1921, contains several long and interesting articles by Klein on the history of The Royal Albert Hall.

Throughout his life, Klein contributed material to most of the musical papers in London. His first major publishing effort was the annual *Musical Notes,* issued for the years 1886–1889. In 1894 he assisted his old teacher, Manuel Garcia, with his *Hints on Singing* (London, 1894: Ascherberg, Hopwood & Crew, Ltd.). His first "autobiographical" work, *Thirty Years of Musical Life in London, 1870–1900,* has already been mentioned: It was written during the author's stay in the United States, and first published in New York by The Century Co. in 1903, and the same year by William Heinemann in London. After his return to England came *Unmusical New York: A Brief Criticism of Triumphs, Failures & Abuses* (London & New York, 1910; John Lane). His next book-length work was the well known *The Reign of Patti.* (New York, The Century Co. & London, T. Fisher Unwin, 1920; reprint edition, with note on Patti recordings and Discography, Arno Press, New York, 1977). Klein noted that this was an "authorized" biography, written at Patti's request. His next work was *The Bel Canto* (London, Oxford University Press, 1923), which is reprinted in the present volume. It was followed by *Musicians and Mummers* (London & New York, Cassell and Company, Ltd., 1925), more or less a continuation of the author's *Thirty Years,* but with much fill-in data covering the period of the former work. In 1931 came *Great Women-Singers of My Time* (London: George Routledge & Sons, Ltd.) with a foreword by Ernest Newman, which gives biographical details and personal recollections of some 26 singers. His final book was *The Golden Age of Opera* (London, George Routledge & Sons, Ltd., 1933). This work is really a recapitulation of the author's life: it covers much the same ground as his previous works, but reflects much of his experience gained in the study and review of recordings during the period of his work for *The Gramophone,* collected in the present work.

In spite of the "biographical" format of some of Klein's works, the emphasis is on description of what he saw and heard, and there is very little to tell the reader anything of the author's personal life. It is by an incidental footnote or two that we pick up a few clues which have aided in further research. Hermann had at least five brothers: Max, whom he describes as "younger" took violin lessons from Louis Ries, later studied under J. T. Carrodus, and joined the orchestra of the Royal Italian Opera at Covent Garden. Later he went to America to become a member of the Mendelssohn Quintet; for three years he was principal second violin of the Boston Symphony Orchestra under Gericke and Henschel. In 1888 he accompanied composer-conductor Frederic H. Cowen to Melbourne as leader of the Centennial Exhibition Orchestra, and remained in that city until 1891. In that year he returned to London, and for a time resumed his place in the principal London orchestras, dying in Cairo in 1894.

Brother Charles (1867–1915) was a dramatist. He was born in London, but settled in the United States, where his first success was as author of the book for John Philip Sousa's operetta *El Capitan* in 1896. His plays, such as *The Music Master, The Lion and the Mouse,* and *Potash and Perlmutter* were produced by Warfield and Belasco. He went down in the *Lusitania,* together with his mentor, Charles Frohman, but was remembered nearly 30 years later by H. L. Mencken who recommended him for inclusion in a new edition of *Twentieth Century Authors.*

Hermann's brother Manuel Klein was a composer and conductor, born in London in 1876. He also found life in New York lucrative, as conductor for Belasco, the Frohmans, and the Shuberts at the Herald Square and Lyceum theaters and the New York Hippodrome. His list of credits for Hippodrome productions is long, beginning with *Mr. Pickwick* in 1902 and averaging almost one per year until his death in 1919.

Of Hermann's other two brothers we know little: Alfred was said to be a successful actor on the New York stage before the turn of the century. The remaining brother is nameless: he receives brief mention in *Thirty Years* because he had just fatally shot himself in the head a few minutes before the arrival of Camille Saint-Saëns to pay a call.

We know even less about Hermann's personal life: we know that he composed songs and piano pieces, including a Grand March for the Paris Exposition in 1878. He was active in Freemasonry, and at one time held the post of Grand Organist for the Grand Lodge in London. Once or twice in *Musicians and Mummers* he alludes to a wife who was present at some function or other, and in fact dedicates the book to her. In the same work there is a passing mention of "my older son," Adrian, who was born in 1892, and an even briefer mention of "my daughter Sibyl." Beyond this, nothing. No one seems to know what became of Klein's library and personal files after his death. Reference to them today could very possibly solve a number of long-standing puzzles, including the identity of Lillian Nordica's Manrico, given name Marcello, who appears on a 1905 Columbia test recording in the author's collection. Without doubt, he was one of Klein's pupils.

In the fall of 1931, The Gramophone Company issued a special-order list known as the *H.M.V. Connoisseur Catalogue.* This contained recordings selected from company lists around the world notable for their special artistic interest, but not deemed appropriate for the general record catalogs. Reviews of these recordings were presented in a special supplement to *The Gramophone* magazine for October, 1931, with discussion of most of the vocal recordings falling to Herman Klein. Klein's reviews have been included in this volume, but reviews by others of instrumental and orchestral recordings have been omitted. In addition, a few selected reviews of vocal recordings from other issues of *The Gramophone* have been included.

It is fascinating to listen to these same recordings today, with Klein's words in hand. Remarks in reference to the quality and style of singing are most revealing. His comments are usually gentle, yet still forceful. He manages to praise Göta Ljungberg, for example, for her "glorious resonant timbre," but takes her to task for her lack of "colour". "Her notion of *Vissi d'arte* . . . is not emotional enough," Klein remarks, "not sufficiently indicative of disappointment and torment." How true this evaluation is! He praises Dusolina Giannini for "sheer beauty of voice," but notes "One feels inclined to ask what the peerless Dusolina came to be doing *dans cette galère?*" in singing German Lieder. He is frank in his expression of dislike for John McCormack's Wolf songs . . . and explains why. He recommends that Maria Olszewska, whom he calls a "talented contralto," take a lesson from the records of Elena Gerhardt and Elisabeth Schumann. He approaches the art of Yvonne Printemps in just the correct way: not from the standpoint of "great singing," but rather as a talented French actress, a *diseuse*. "One is listening to Yvonne Printemps," says Mr. Klein, "and that fact covers a multitude of sins." His suggestion that Schipa's recordings should be an example to other singers is well phrased. His remarks about the recordings of Elisabeth Schumann should be read and heeded by a modern critic who claims that Schumann "was not capable in her Lieder singing, as Sembrich was, of charming us through singng alone without affectation, by purity of tone, smoothness of line and the simplicity of delivery." After giving the highest praise to Schorr for his oratorio work with "the tempi . . . in the Mendelssohn tradition handed down through Staudigl and Santley", Klein is frank in his dislike of the "funereal pace" of Schorr's Lieder. Who could take offense at criticism such as this? Klein always seems to point out what he feels is good first . . . then clearly states what he does not like.

At times, I find myself disappointed with the brevity of his comments about some recording I have lived with, one might say intimately, for some 50 years. How much more he could have written, with perhaps detailed comparison with the great interpreters of another generation! But we must take the brief reviews in context: these were first impressions after perhaps one playing, and there may well have been 20 more recordings to listen to before the month's deadline.

The Gramophone and the Singer series, on the other hand, make a continuous set of essays which allow the mellow, experienced critic a chance to relax, lean back, and chat with his readers. Often current events in the opera house or concert hall open the door to recollections of the past. His "current events" are now history, but a unique history which we are privileged to view from a very special base rarely accorded the conventional historian. When Klein describes a *Tristan* with Leider, Olszewska, Melchior, Helgers and Janssen, a *Walküre* with Lehmann and Melchior, or a *Siegfried* with Easton and Melchior, or what Schorr did with the rôle of Hans Sachs, we today have a very good idea of what he is talking about, and can renew our own memories and impressions at will by simply putting on the recordings. In this way we can form our own ideas of the validity of Klein's judgement of the voices of Ternina, Nilsson, Trebelli, De Reszke, Cotogni and those other legendary names which can only be described to us in words because we can not associate them with the phonograph. For those of us who have long enjoyed, but have sometimes been a bit skeptical about Bernard Shaw as a music critic, it is good fun to read what Klein thought of his writings, for he, too, attended most of the same performances about which Shaw wrote.

Two brief warnings: today's readers should be aware that Klein's manuscripts were in hand-written form when handed to the printer, and that deadlines did not always permit proof-reading and correction. Thus there are a good many typographical errors which went undetected. The editor has corrected a few of these . . . such as altering de Luca's name when de Lucia was clearly indicated, but there has been no attempt to correct every error. Dates should be verified (for example in references to Klein's usually very accurate books) before being quoted by modern authors: there are occasional errors, some perhaps typographical, or because our critic wrote from memory. Remember too, that Klein's record reviews spanned the change-over from acoustical to electrical recording. When he speaks of a newly released title as "Re-recorded" he does not mean a dubbing, but rather he is making reference to an electrically recorded version of a selection by a particular artist which was previously available as an acoustical recording.

So step back 50 to 60 years and see how our historical recordings were viewed, as they were published, by one who was eminently qualified to project his observations back a like number of years.

La Cañada, California
May, 1988

Part I
THE BEL CANTO

Oxford Musical Essays

THE BEL CANTO

With particular reference

to the singing of Mozart

By HERMAN KLEIN

OXFORD UNIVERSITY PRESS

LONDON: HUMPHREY MILFORD

1923

TO THAT GENUINE MOZART-LOVER
SIR THOMAS BEECHAM, BT.
WITH ADMIRATION AND ESTEEM.

CONTENTS

PREFACE

THERE are solid reasons why the art of the 'Bel Canto' should be associated in a particular degree with the name of Mozart. His vocal compositions demanded singers of the highest order, and the supreme technical excellence displayed by his chosen interpreters is generally conceded. It is doubtful, indeed, whether the 'beautiful singing' of the Mozart period has since been equalled; certainly it has never been surpassed. Hence the importance of preserving faithfully every feature and rule of the tradition which comes down to us from that period.

A record that may serve as a trustworthy guide in this matter seems to be especially called for at the present time, when the hold upon the true traditions of the 'Bel Canto' is no longer so firm as it was, and when, as it happens, the appetite for Mozart is growing keener every day. The demand to hear Mozart's operas is one of the few bright spots upon the horizon at a critical moment in the history of our lyric stage. Nothing, therefore, should be left undone that can help to renew and maintain the lofty standard of past performances.

Much of the material of this book was put together for a lecture which I gave at the Wigmore Hall last March under the title of 'How to Sing Mozart'.

H. K.

LONDON, 1923.

I

THE MOZART REVIVAL

It must have been in the late 80's, or perhaps very early 90's, of the past century when I began to notice in an unexpected quarter an attempt to revive interest in the operas of Mozart. The movement started at Munich, of all places; and its chief instigator was a man then regarded as a leading apostle of the 'Music of the Future'—Richard Strauss.

How far the movement was altruistic I was never quite sure. It could not have been intended merely to rescue the masterpieces of Mozart from undeserved neglect, because they had never actually been neglected. Nevertheless, it was true that their popularity had declined. They had only shared the fate of several other favourite operas of the old repertory that had been gradually shifting into the background to make room for the more exciting works of Richard Wagner.

It is more probable that the inauguration of Mozart-cycles at the Munich Opera-house, to follow upon the close of the summer Bayreuth Festivals, owed its origin to a clever business policy. Rich musical tourists from all parts of the world were on the spot with nothing to do, after hearing *Parsifal* and *The Ring*, but to 'take a cure' or go and listen to more music. The main thing was to furnish a contrast. If not Carlsbad or Marienbad (or even with them to follow), why not go to Munich for a couple of weeks just to take in, as a 'corrective', some of the simple but beautiful operas of Mozart? Already Strauss had attracted attention with his admirable revivals—well staged, well sung, carefully rehearsed—during the seasons when he was chief conductor there. It did not take long to organize a cycle and advertise it with Teutonic thoroughness on both sides of the Atlantic.

The success of the scheme was instantaneous. The Bayreuth pilgrims—British, French, American, Russian, Italian—in fact,

13

holiday-seeking Continental amateurs generally, not to speak of the music-loving German tourists themselves—flocked in thousands to these performances. They revelled in every moment of them. The older generation renewed and freshened their love for Mozart; the younger conceived a novel and pleasant liking for him. Gradually but surely the taste began to spread in other centres besides Munich, to other examples of the master's genius besides his operas. Before the end of the century it was evident that a big Mozart revival had come to stay.

It has stayed until now. The desire for Mozart pervades our musical life, no longer as a desire, but as a necessity. It is founded upon a rock; it is not to be swayed or moved by other revivals or other new loves. Once it had passed the perilous period of the Wagner craze, the musical excitements of a still later growth were powerless to stir it.

A recognized and universal art treasure may, however, for lack of worthy interpretation, fail to be displayed in its full glory. Mozart here is like Shakespeare. Both of them demand, in order to do them justice, interpreters specially gifted and specially trained. The plays of Shakespeare require *acting* of the highest order; the operas of Mozart *singing* of the highest order. There is barely enough of the former in the world. Of the latter I may say without hesitation that in this country vocal material for the perfect rendering of Mozart's operatic masterpieces has long been wanting.

In other words, our interpretative resources have failed to keep level with the renascence of public interest in these most exacting examples of lyric art. Something has been lost, or at least is in imminent danger of becoming lost; and it is the purpose of the following pages to show what has been lost and how it may be found again.

II

THE LINES OF THE MOZART TRADITION

Among the great masters Mozart stands alone. His universal genius made him pre-eminent in every sphere of music. I will not say that his achievements were nobler or loftier than those of Purcell, Bach, Handel, or of Beethoven; but as a whole they were unique.

The death of Mozart ended a great school, to which later schools proved incapable of adding aught that was peculiar to its particular character or type. Until Beethoven discovered his new paths, music was no more than dormant.

At the end of a period in Art, a 'pause', or even a 'full-close', is marked against the style which is the characteristic quality of that period. Just as you cannot surpass the product itself, neither can you improve upon the manner of rendering or representation which is germane to it. It remains in its purity the essential style of the period or of the master who invented it. It may be changed or modified; it may afterwards blend with some later style. But then it is no longer pure.

How long, then, can a style be said to be actually 'living'? Is its life limited to the existence of its creator? Certainly not; for when he dies his works do not, and his original interpreters may survive him for years. Rather, the living manifestation, that is, the immediate, direct, authoritative exemplification, of a style continues so long as its original exponents remain alive and active to embody and illustrate it. After that there remains only a Tradition.

In music the continuance of a tradition runs along two parallel lines—the instrumental and the vocal; and to-day, in my opinion, the instrumental tradition of Mozart remains as vivid, and as sure in observance and execution, as it was a hundred years ago. The

15

line of executive skill has been throughout of consistently equal merit, and has therefore remained unbroken.

With the vocal tradition of Mozart it has not been the same. There has been a perceptible deterioration in the executive level, a gradual weakening in the succession of interpreters, a growing loss of touch with the special qualities and attributes that marked the original realization of the master's ideas. This has been especially noticeable during the past thirty years, the very period in which the average degree of excellence in the performance of Mozart's orchestral and chamber music has, at any rate in this country, tended to improve.

The explanation may be seen in the following facts : first, that Mozart's vocal music is, on the whole, much harder to perform than his instrumental music. Much of it was written for exceptional voices and for the artists of exceptional capacity who lived in his time. Secondly, that its difficulty has often been increased by the gradual raising of the musical pitch to the modern level (it is nearly $\frac{3}{4}$ tone higher now than in Mozart's time). The higher the *tessitura* or texture of vocal music, the greater the demand upon the physical resources of the singer. This change, on the other hand, has not affected the instrumentalists at all. Thirdly, that the standard of singing is lower than it was, both upon the operatic stage and in the concert-room. The voices of contemporary singers do not compare for beauty with those of the past ; nor does their technical training, save in the rarest instances, nearly approach the same height of perfection. Fourthly, that this falling-off, which synchronized with the decline of Italian Opera and with the neglect of Mozart, has interrupted tradition, and has left us, just when the Mozart operas are regaining their popularity, with less vocal talent for continuing it.

The tradition itself has not been lost ; of that I am convinced. Nor will it be so as long as there are teachers who jealously guard it, who are capable of imparting it to gifted and industrious pupils, and who will insist that those pupils shall not follow the modern custom of curtailing the period of study and seeking their public débuts with undue haste.

III

THE TEACHING OF MANUEL GARCIA

To justify my claim of knowledge of the vocal tradition of Mozart, I point to the sources of my knowledge: my teacher, Manuel Garcia, and those singers of Mozart whom I heard in his operas at Covent Garden and Her Majesty's Theatres during the last thirty years of the nineteenth century.

Manuel Garcia (1805–1908) was in his seventieth year when he came to live at my parents' house in Bentinck Street, Manchester Square. There he carried on his private teaching for nearly ten years, before moving to his ultimate residence at Cricklewood. When he came to us I was a youth of eighteen, and I studied with him continuously during his first four years there. Whatever I did not learn from him personally, I had ample opportunity to learn through hearing his lessons to other students, amongst whom were many vocalists already before the public. Despite his years Garcia seemed still 'young', and was a wonderfully hard worker.

Among other things I learned the family history of the Garcias —about the wonderful Elder Manuel (father of my master, of Malibran, and of Pauline Viardot-Garcia), that stern Spanish martinet of the operatic stage, who took his son and his famous daughter to America in the twenties to introduce Italian opera and Rossini's *Barber of Seville* to New York.[1] Grove's *Dictionary* mentions this celebrated musician: 'Beginning as a chorister in the [Seville] Cathedral at the age of six, at seventeen he was already well known as a composer, singer, actor, and conductor.' The record is interesting, for it was only some ten weeks before

[1] The family of the Garcias was happily described by Chorley as one of 'representative artists, whose power, genius, and originality have impressed a permanent trace on the records of the methods of vocal execution and ornament'.

Manuel Garcia the Elder attained his seventeenth birthday (January 1792) that Mozart had died at Vienna and had there been interred in a pauper's grave. I was therefore the pupil of a man whose father had actually acquired his Mozart style at first hand before it had become a Tradition; in other words, during the lifetime of the composer.

When, therefore, my master used to speak to me, as he would occasionally, of the great singers of his younger days, and describe what they had accomplished with their glorious voices and their inimitable art, I listened to him with a feeling of awe for that golden period which seemed then so remote as to be surrounded with a halo of romance; especially when he spoke of the famous Madame Pasta, the particular object of his adoration—'an extraordinary woman, with not only a voice of haunting beauty but a nobility and grandeur of style that has never been excelled!'

Yet he who said this had himself, some five and thirty years previously, been the teacher who restored and properly 'placed' the voice of the great Jenny Lind; who had given many lessons to Christine Nilsson and Charles Santley, both still in their prime. Magnificent still were Adelina Patti and Theresa Tietjens; while the two matchless tenors, Mario and Giuglini, the famous soprano Giulia Grisi, and the great contralto Alboni (whom I had then just heard sing in private) had but recently retired from the scene. Could it be, I would ask my master, that the great artists of the seventies were really already so much lower in stature than the giants of half a century before? 'Unquestionably,' said Manuel Garcia.

But at the period I speak of the Tradition itself was very much alive—infinitely more so, of course, than twenty years later. In 1872 I heard *Don Giovanni* for the first time at Covent Garden with a cast that included Patti (Zerlina), Marianne Brandt (Donna Elvira), Faure (Don Giovanni), Nicolini (Don Ottavio), and Ciampi (Leporello). Three years later I heard the same opera at Her Majesty's with Tietjens, Christine Nilsson, and Trebelli-Bettini in the three female rôles. At about the same time I heard the *Magic Flute* with Tietjens as Pamina, Ilma di Murska (also

Marimon) as the Queen of Night, Santley as Papageno, and Foli as Sarastro; and the *Nozze di Figaro* with Tietjens as the Countess, Pauline Lucca (or Trebelli) as Cherubino, Marimon as Susanna, Cotogni (or Faure) as Figaro, and Graziani as the Count.

Most of these artists were the most distinguished Mozart singers of their time. Their manner of interpreting Mozart's operas tallied more or less exactly with the general rules laid down by Garcia, and were so far in accordance with the right Tradition. Their rendering of every phrase and every note was unforgettable.

In 1894 I helped my old master (then in his ninetieth year, but still astonishingly youthful) to prepare for the press his *Hints on Singing*,[1] the last text-book that he wrote. We worked together upon it for several months, and a very wonderful experience it was. Dealing with every characteristic point of the category of Italian ornamentation and embellishment, this little work leaves no doubt regarding the correct interpretation of the vocal problems of the eighteenth century.

It was in the preface to his *Hints on Singing* that Garcia uttered his famous words on the ' decline of the florid style '. One of its most important causes was, he thought,

> ' the disappearance of the race of great singers, who, besides originating this art, carried it to its highest point of excellence. The impresario, influenced by the exigencies of the modern prima donna, has been constrained to offer less gifted and accomplished *virtuosi* to the composer, who in turn has been compelled to simplify the rôle of the voice and rely more and more upon orchestral effects. Thus singing is becoming as much a lost art as the manufacture of Mandarin china or the varnish used by the old masters.'

Manuel Garcia rarely expressed an opinion upon the merits or failings of the more prominent artists who were singing Mozart

[1] Published by Ascherberg, Hopwood & Crew, Ltd., 16 Mortimer Street, London, W.

at the time I was studying with him. Indeed he very seldom went to the Opera. But I remember his telling me that he had heard Patti as Zerlina a season or two after her début (1861), and had admired her immensely, though he could not agree with one enthusiastic critic who had declared that her Zerlina was 'better than Malibran's'. He thought no one in the world ever compared with his sister except Pasta.

IV

THE VOCAL DEMANDS OF MOZART'S MUSIC

A DISTINGUISHED authority, Mr. Edward J. Dent, has recently stated [1] that what the London opera-goers and critics of the seventies 'liked best were Mozart's most obvious tunes'; and that this 'naturally led to the notion that Mozart's operas were nothing more than a string of pretty tunes, tunes so pretty that no one but Patti could ever be allowed to sing them'.

Nothing could be farther from the facts. Whatever our elders may have misunderstood concerning the growing complexities of modern music, they knew their Mozart well and listened to him with a degree of appreciation which their greater familiarity with the vocal art of their era made wholly trustworthy. To realize this it is only necessary to turn up the files of the old newspapers and read the operatic criticisms—often prosy, sometimes prejudiced, but always independent, fearless, and authoritative—of writers like Davison and Chorley.

Moreover, it is unfair to the memory of the other great singers of the mid-nineteenth century to suppose that Adelina Patti, because she was called the *diva*, enjoyed any sort of monopoly of the 'Mozart tunes'. In all her career she sang but one Mozart rôle, namely, Zerlina; whereas Tietjens was equally good, in the public estimation, in the three parts of Donna Anna, the Countess, and Pamina. Patti in later years essayed 'Voi che sapete'; but she had not studied it as she did Zerlina with Maurice Strakosch (her brother-in-law and 'coach', who had acted as accompanist for Pasta when the latter was teaching); and here Patti missed the right rendering. On the other hand, both Pauline Lucca and Trebelli were exquisite Cherubinos, and their delivery of the immortal air was absolutely without flaw.

Most of the traditional Mozart singers whom it was my good

[1] *The Nation and the Athenaeum*, 17 March 1923.

fortune to hear received their training from teachers whose memories, if not their actual instruction, dated back to those surviving artists who were actively working upon the stage either in Mozart's lifetime or during the years that immediately followed. They were thus the third generation of his interpreters. It may therefore reasonably be assumed that they did exactly what he intended, and I cannot but think that he would have approved their treatment of his music as surely as he would have admired their voices and their pure Italian method.

This method was the one then being taught by such Mozartians of the second generation as Garcia, Lamperti, Sangiovanni, and Nava (the teacher of Santley). It was the method which Wagner openly proclaimed to be indispensable for the satisfactory rendering of the trying declamatory music of his operas and music-dramas. Indeed, practically the whole of the experienced German artists who created the heroes and heroines of *Der Ring des Nibelungen* and *Parsifal* were trained in the Italian school.

So long as the notable singers of that generation lived and flourished the Tradition held its own. All so far was well; but when they began to retire from the stage in the final decades of the past century, it quickly became apparent that they had no worthy imitators. So gradually the succession of the Mozart tradition weakened, until lately it has broken completely, though an occasional demonstration may still be heard.

To re-discover the art of these old singers, it is necessary to know what demands were made on them by Mozart's music. Mozart was surrounded by such consummate vocalists that apparently he could never write anything too difficult or too brilliant for them. Anyhow, he was too wise to write beyond his artists' powers. But the difficulty of his vocal music did not lie solely in its *bravura*, its daring *fiorituri*, its flights into *altissimo*. It lay even more, perhaps, in its extreme simplicity.

For Mozart was one of the greatest tune-makers that ever lived; and there is nothing harder to sing beautifully than a simple tune. Other composers before him also wrote wonderful tunes—Purcell, Bach, Handel, Lully, Gluck, Haydn. But as a composer for the stage this tune-maker transcended them all. Mozart may have reeled off his tunes by the hundred ; but if he fitted the simplest of them to words, it never failed to embody in every accent and every phrase the full emotional content of the poet's lines. Alike as a piece of vocal music and as a vehicle for the expression of human feeling, it was complete, perfect in itself. The consequence is that it demands from the singer, besides a simplicity equal with its own, a purity of *legato*, a charm of style, a certain warmth of expression, a depth of sentiment and even of passion, which the music of Mozart's contemporaries and his predecessors (with the exception perhaps of Gluck) had never required. He was a man of strong temperament, and every bar he wrote for the voice overflowed with the essence of his own nature.

Many singers to-day fail, if for no other reason, to do justice to Mozart because they approach his music without the necessary warmth and intensity of feeling. They think that it suffices to sing him calmly and prettily. They could make no greater mistake, unless it be perhaps to treat him sentimentally and warble his ' pretty tunes ' as though there were nothing beneath their surface. In reality there is so much that every bar needs to be deeply studied and thoroughly understood. Above all, to do Mozart justice you must love him.

It is often said nowadays that beauty of vocal tone does not matter as much as musical knowledge, rhythmical accuracy, and clear diction. That may apply to liturgical Tudor music or the secular writings of the old English composers. Somehow loveliness of vocal quality and temperamental curves have not invariably been associated with these things. A tradition here is not directly to be traced at all. The right reading can, however, be sufficiently gathered from the printed page, and ' sound common sense ' may be trusted to supply the rest.

But of what avail would scholarship, historical erudition, or the cold process of reasoning be to the artist in the achievement of the right singing of Mozart? He may hate the so-called shackles of tradition as much as he pleases ; he may treat it with contempt, dispense with it, deny its authority or its very existence. But he will probably live long enough to see the operas of Mozart in even worse plight, for lack of adequate vocal skill and traditional handling, than they are even now.

To no other cause can be attributed the unquestionable deterioration that has already come about. It is certainly not that to-day human beings are not born with equally beautiful voices. It can only be because—here in England at least—modern conditions do not provide or insist upon the essential training, the essential technique, the essential knowledge of what Mozart really demands.

Mozart demands everything. To begin with, a beautiful voice controlled and directed by correct scientific breathing; ample resonance; an equal scale achieved by the perfect blending (or if you like it better, the obliteration) of the registers; a clean attack; a steady *sostenuto*; a smooth, pure *legato*; an elegant use of the *portamento*; a well-graduated *messa di voce* or management of *crescendos* and *diminuendos*; flexibility, agility, and brilliancy of execution; and, not least of all, the capacity to sing absolutely in tune.

With vocalization of this kind the obstacles of language should give no trouble. The right principles of articulation, diction, and accent, the distinct enunciation of every consonant, are more important than the question of the language in which Mozart is sung. My personal choice is for the language in which he composed his music. But naturally the text of his operas, to be comprehensible to an English audience, are best sung in English.

In the rare but necessary combination above described are to be found the chief material and technique of the singer's art. One voice may, of course, be less beautiful, less flexible, less extended in range than another; but those are merely individual limitations, . . . and Mozart has written for voices of every type and size. Apart from physical and technical considerations, there still remain the important questions of musical intelligence and culture, rhythmical sense, dramatic feeling, and the instinctive gift for interpretation. I will first deal, as briefly as I can, with the technical.

V

THE TECHNIQUE OF THE 'BEL CANTO'

I DO not propose to attempt here more than a bare description of the principal features of the so-called 'Bel Canto', or old Italian method of singing. A closer analysis, if required by the reader, must be sought for in pages specially devoted to the method itself, without reference to the interpretation of any particular composer.

Many people imagine that there is involved in the teaching of the Italian method something in the nature of a great secret. As a matter of fact, there is nothing more secret about it than there is about the characteristics of the tradition of Mozart.

In a recent review of a book of musical recollections, the complaint was made that it contained no suggestions for remedying certain vocal abuses and malpractices denounced by the author; the reason given for the omission was that probably the latter had thought it unadvisable to give away the 'stock-in-trade' of the teacher's art. The true answer to that suggestion is that if trade secrets of the kind ever existed they were divulged by Manuel Garcia years ago.

It is not easy, of course, to grasp and co-ordinate the various factors that make up the true art of singing from the printed page alone, nor can they effectively be put into practice save under skilful and experienced guidance. Art is a thing of imitation, and in the study of singing you require the aid of the living model and critic as absolutely as in the study of painting or dancing. Nevertheless, a clear record or statement of facts is essential, and the printed page may therefore be regarded as a valuable accessory to the work of the teacher.

Garcia recognized this when he published in this country an English translation of his famous *Traité complet de l'Art du Chant*, which first appeared in Paris in 1840; and again when he supplemented it fifty-four years later with his *Hints on Singing*, which embodied all the subsequent experience garnered during a lifetime of successful teaching.

The main essentials of the Italian system are the mastery of—

(*a*) BREATHING
(*b*) RESONANCE
(*c*) VOWEL-FORMATION AND ATTACK
(*d*) THE SOSTENUTO (SUSTAINED TONE)
(*e*) THE LEGATO (SLOW SCALE, REGISTERS)
(*f*) THE PORTAMENTO
(*g*) THE 'MESSA DI VOCE'
(*h*) AGILITY (COLORATURA, ORNAMENTS, ETC.).

This order of progression is natural but by no means invariable. For example, the formation of a vowel shape must necessarily precede the attack of a sound, but the study of its manifold variations would have to come later. So the slow *scale* will naturally proceed simultaneously with the *legato* ; whilst the quick scales form part of the acquisition of *agility*.

(*a*) BREATHING

Although scientific *Breathing* stands both at the base and the apex of the whole vocal structure, it is, nevertheless, the thing most neglected and most misunderstood in the average modern practice of this art. Correct instruction in respiration is, I think, the feature which chiefly differentiates the good teacher from the bad, the efficient master from the charlatan who misleads, cheats, and defrauds the innocent and unwary pupil. We cannot too frequently repeat the familiar saying of Maria Celloni :

Chi sa respirare sa cantare.[1]

But commonly the novice is told, if told anything at all about respiration, to take a 'deep breath'; to fill the lungs with air as though crowding the chest with ozone or inhaling the perfume

[1] He who knows how to breathe knows how to sing.

of flowers; to breathe in or out ' from the waist ' (wherever that may be), or even to expand the abdomen with a vigorous outward push of that obscure muscle, the diaphragm.

Obedience to these familiar rules must inevitably tend to guide the student in the wrong direction and lead to bad habits which, once acquired, are exceedingly hard to eradicate. The breathing taught by the old Italian masters entirely reverses the order and changes even the physical character of the usual processes of inhalation and exhalation which form part of our daily life. Singers proceed differently; hold their bodies differently; train their muscles and organs to act differently. And yet from first to last the whole procedure is normal, beneficial to the health, unfailing in its accomplishment of the right result.

One seldom hears talk of abdominal breathing. It is this filling of the lowest part of the lungs by the expansion of the stomach which not only flattens (and therewith locates) the hidden diaphragm, but prepares for its contraction when the stomach is drawn in and the ribs are raised, thus giving the necessary impetus for the expulsion of the breath by muscular pressure from below the middle of the body, not from the region of the chest.

This mode of inhalation is doubly beneficial: (1) because we are only able completely to inflate the lower part of the lungs by slowly introducing the air there first and filling the upper part during the same inhalation afterwards; (2) because, where we feel the breath go, thence shall we expel it; and, inasmuch as steadiness and purity of tone are only to be obtained by this *upward* pressure from between the lower ribs, just above the stomach, we thereby learn how to avoid all superfluous or ill-directed pressure; we learn how to control our breathing action from the region of the diaphragm; and how, finally, to keep the chest high and firm, utilizing it as a receptacle for air not inhaled directly into it from without, but pressed into it from the lung spaces underneath.

Thus concentrated, the breath virtually becomes ' compressed air ', that is, air possessing an inherent force of its own. Hence its greater power, moving always by muscular contraction in the upward (the necessary) direction, and so doing its work of creating tone in all degrees of loudness with the minimum of physical action or effort, and with a total absence of strain.

This I believe to be the old Italian system of breathing, as it was taught by Manuel Garcia, and as I have taught it myself for many years. The secret of its success lies primarily in the controlling power of the abdominal support and action. Much depends, however, upon a correct attitude of the body, the capacity for retention and expulsion of the breath in any required volume or degree, and the ability to perform the mechanical functions of the breathing apparatus either slowly or quickly, as may be needed, with the same subconscious, automatic accuracy, smoothness, and noiselessness of operation.

(b) RESONANCE

The old Italian teachers had no trouble in obtaining a bright, ringing tone. 'Resonance', therefore, may not have entered very largely into their theory, but was far from being ignored in their practice. Thanks chiefly to their 'open' vowels an easy 'forward' tone came naturally to the majority of their students, especially the native ones. If it did not, the masters opened their pupils' throats (temporarily at least) until the sound-waves had learnt to find their way to every facial cavity or space (besides the mouth) that was capable of 'reflecting' a vocal tone. The idea seems simple enough. The voice, in order to acquire its full vibrant power, must have the aid of a 'reflector', just as surely as the light burning in a lighthouse. The singer can no more dispense with its aid than the performer on the piano or the violin could dispense with that of a sounding-board.

As the act of singing is a natural organic function, common to the majority of civilized people, there is no need to discuss here the physiology of tone production. The point is, rather, whereabouts is that tone situated or sounding when it has left the larynx? The answer is that a clear note is, at the moment of its utterance, instantly ringing clear and true in its ultimate position, projected and maintained there by steady diaphragmatic breath-pressure, and enhanced in strength and colour by shape and other influences. To the singer the resulting sensation is that the tone is coming not from the throat at all, but existing ready-made in the area to which it is reflected.

Free, unobstructed access to these 'forward' cavities can alone enable the voice to obtain all the advantages of complete resonance. Properly directed and well supported by the breath, it can entirely escape the danger of a nasal quality and attain increased beauty of timbre, diversity of colour, and penetrative power.

(c) Vowel-formation and Attack

The formation of some vowel shape must necessarily precede the attack of a vocal sound—an act which involves the opening of the mouth. If we sing with the mouth shut we hum; but the act of humming is not without its use as a means for indicating where the vibration of the sound-waves may be *felt* re-echoing in the facial resonators when unable to make their exit by the ordinary route.

When we open the mouth to sing a note, it must be done by dropping the lower jaw, and without moving the head, which remains erect and still. The tongue flattens as the jaw descends, whilst the pharyngeal space at the back of the throat enlarges as the soft palate rises and forms the roof of the mouth into a dome or arch. The shape thus created gives us, without further preliminary action, the natural mould for the formation of the universal vowel sound 'ah'—that is, the first vowel of the Italian alphabet.

The formation of all other vowels, no matter what the language, is simply a variation on this fundamental process, although the sense of their location seems to the singer to be different with different vowels. In reality vowel sounds should all *feel* alike, to the extent that they feel so when we speak them. Only, some vowels create a more naturally 'forward' position than others, and those that do not must, by correct treatment, be made to acquire an equal degree of resonance.

The outcome of this assimilation is that the singer finds both tone and vowel impinging upon the same identical facial area, that is to say, in the 'mask'; and there alone, will their union be made perfect. In no other fashion and by no other mechanical means can 'speech and song' be resolved into a single function.

Garcia says (*Hints on Singing*, p. 12) that 'the Pharynx ought to be considered the real mouth of a singer'. The idea is not an easy one to convey in words, but I understand it to mean that, just as the mouth contains the organs of speech (with especial reference to consonants), so the right place for forming vowel shapes and originating tonal character is the passage leading from the throat to the mouth and the nasal cavities. I also believe the idea in question to have been an essential feature of the old Italian method.

Another idea was that the utterance of 'open' sonorous vowels in a natural manner ensured a free, elastic movement of the jaw, without the least muscular stiffness, leaving the tongue 'limp and motionless', yet not entailing an excessively wide opening of the mouth, which 'favours neither low nor high notes'. This, the true singing position, is a matter of the utmost importance, and it is peculiarly associated with the teaching of Manuel Garcia.

The assuming of the singing position as a mental and physical attitude corresponds to the spontaneous gesture of the speaker. It coincides with the inhalation of the breath, and is immediately followed by the act of phonation or *attack* of the sound. The old Italians were right in their location of the true source of attack when they said *respirare, e poi appoggiare*: inhale, and then support with the breath. An inflated air-cushion, once the screw is tightened, affords a firm and resilient support for the whole weight of the body. Similarly, the voice must rest easily and comfortably upon the solid column of air that holds it in position.

And it must do this from the outset. From the moment that the singing position is assumed and the vowel shape formed, the diaphragm takes control; the breath is impelled upwards into the chest, towards the throat, where it becomes tone, and towards the resonators, where it becomes a voice. The whole process is comprised in a single physical movement, in a smooth, even exhalation. Therewith, not in the throat nor with any perceptible action of the glottis, but in the ultimate 'forward' area to which it has been projected, does the attack of the vocal tone actually begin.

I need scarcely add that the misuse of Garcia's scientific definition, *coup de la glotte*, is no longer tolerated by the best teachers.

In vocal attack the intensity of the glottic action may vary according to circumstances. It depends largely upon the nature of the utterance or the emotion to be expressed. A perceptible glottic impetus is not in certain cases inadvisable. For the singer there must be but one aim—that the tone, whatever its character, is to be so *prepared*, mentally and physically, that it shall sound perfect from the start.

(d) The Sostenuto (Sustained Tone)

In the old Italian school of singing nothing used to be more admired and cultivated than an absolutely steady tone. To-day even in Italy a strong *vibrato* or a quivering *tremolo* is generally preferred. Consequently the modern Milanese 'maestro' encourages it.

Whether a trembling tone can ever furnish a satisfactory medium for the singing of Mozart is another question. We have evidence, both internal and external, that the voices for which Mozart wrote did not suffer from this particular drawback. The sin did not become common until some years after it had started at the Paris Opéra in the midway of the last century Meyerbeer, Auber, and Gounod openly expressed their detestation of it. In alliance either with a strain of pure melody or a declamatory passage, a trembling voice, no matter how pleasing its quality *per se*, has always sounded disagreeable to the ears of an English audience.

Intelligent use of the method of breathing described above practically obviates all danger of an unsteady tone. Instinct for the exactly right amount of breath-pressure should be natural to the good singer and made reliable by practice and experience. It contributes, moreover, to the liquid purity and clearness of timbre resulting from an undisturbed adjustment of the vocal cords.

This economy of breath and this adjustment are interdependent, since the muscles of the throat respond and resist automatically in exact proportion to the varying degrees of pressure from the lungs. Yet the need for care does not end there. The singer intent upon the tone must not think of the throat, but of where and how the tone itself is being reflected or placed : that is the true *point d'appui*.

It follows that a perfect *sostenuto* can only be obtained when the singer has the sensation of direct and uninterrupted breath support extending from the region of the diaphragm to the area of resonance.

The gradations of strength and varieties of tone-colour, like the cultivation of the *mezza voce*, are things that cannot be wholly explained or taught in books. They are best acquired by careful listening and clever imitation.

The value of a beautiful *mezza voce* ('half voice' never seems to convey the same idea) cannot be over-estimated. Every singer ought to possess it ; but, like the old *falsetto*, now happily discarded by most singers, it comes more easily to some voices than others. Learning the *mezza voce* is not unlike acquiring the knack of a stroke at golf or lawn-tennis ; and the ear must be kept upon the tone as the eye upon the ball.

The art of skilfully graduating a *crescendo* or *diminuendo* (dealt with later under the head of 'Messa di Voce') should be associated with a constant endeavour to purify the tone. It is the pure sound that travels farthest, not the merely loud one. The delicate *mezza voce* of a soprano or a tenor can provide an instantaneous contrast not less delightful than that of the most exquisite variation in nuances of colour. These are things that must be studied and worked at, for years if necessary, until they are definitely gained.

(e) THE LEGATO (SLOW SCALE, REGISTERS)

It is one thing to sing a single note well. To sing a group of notes all equally well, with a clean, direct transition from the middle of one to the middle of the next involves a good deal more than appears upon the surface.

It means, to begin with, command of the pure *Legato*, a term more readily understood on an instrument than in the human voice. The singing of the scale in the legato manner has often been compared to the stringing of a row of pearls. When they are perfectly matched they form the perfect necklace. The act of uniting notes identical in quality and colour with unbroken smoothness constitutes the perfect legato.

The first step is the management of the breath. Every note must be supported from the region of the diaphragm with the degree of pressure that it demands, not for itself alone, but in its relation to its neighbours and the true gradation of the entire series. The higher the pitch of the note the greater the degree of pressure required, and vice versa; the ear and the sense of volume must combine to secure and preserve the even gradation of the scale up or down. The great point is to make sure of the identity of the tone.

It is not necessary to begin either at the top or the bottom of a scale. The old Italians were wise enough not to enforce an arbitrary rule on this point. Their plan (adopted also in Paris by the great singer and teacher, Faure) was to find the best note in the middle of the voice and use it as the pivot on which to balance the two halves of the scale lying above and below it. In this way they had less difficulty in obtaining an even scale and a smooth legato.

This device is so effective that many years ago I invented for the study of it a form of rhythmical slow scale in three sections, each commencing on the dominant. The key must be varied so that the dominant in every case may afford the safest model for the succeeding notes :

This slow scale must be sung with the dark or 'closed' tone (*voix sombre*), whereas quick scales and runs are best executed in the bright or 'open' tone (*voix claire*), which lends itself more readily to passages requiring flexibility.[1]

Just as the dominant or initial note supplies the model for the others, so must the breathing of the descending scale be imitated in the ascending scale (not the reverse). The legato is always easier, neater, and to be employed with better gradation on the down scale—certainly at first.

The point is that, whether the voice be mounting or descending the scale, the same note shall always be sung in the same manner ; that the 'pivot' tone, when returned to or sung in passing, shall invariably sound quite the same.

The ability, however, to manage this depends also upon the correct blending of the registers, an important matter upon which I can only touch briefly here. Unless the differences of sensation and changes of mechanism which characterize what are known as the 'registers' of the human voice have so merged into each other as to create a harmonious whole, smoothness of scale or legato singing is out of the question.

The provision of registers, with their three different mechanical actions, enables the same vocal cords to produce a succession of sounds of extensive range. They thus add to what might otherwise be a relatively limited compass and provide for an infinitely

[1] Both formations are shown with diagrams and described in *Hints on Singing*, p. 11.

greater variety of timbres. Until Manuel Garcia discovered and invented the laryngoscope, the nature of these different mechanisms was not understood; the effect was known, but not the cause. From close observation, however, one fact appears—that we must not alter our manner of singing because we feel the mechanism to be in some subtle way altering its automatic procedure. Interference is bound to entail disaster.

The solution of the problem lies in uniformity—uniformity of breathing, of ' singing position ', of resonance—the last is perhaps the most important. So long as the voice is securely reflected in its ultimate forward position and is sustained there by the breath, supported from the diaphragm, the vocal cords will enjoy the elasticity and freedom essential for modifying their action, without that sudden change or ' break ' which is commonly heard. Otherwise the modification cannot be made imperceptibly, and the abrupt transition from one register to another will become audible. The blending tone, if properly graduated, extends over three or at most four notes, to which the French give the name of *voix mixte*.[1]

With the aid of this *voix mixte*, the union of the ' chest ' and ' medium ', of ' medium ' and ' head ' tones, proceeding either up or down the scale, the voice can be brought into line throughout its whole compass. Once the uniformity is achieved the secret of the legato, elusive as it may appear, becomes comparatively clear. The eclectic ear of the singer must do the rest.

(f) THE PORTAMENTO

The portamento resembles the legato, only in its execution the carrying of the voice is made audible over the interval separating the two notes.

[1] The finest exercise I know for obtaining clearness and uniformity of tone in the medium register is that which Garcia gave to Jenny Lind when she went to him in Paris in 1841 to ' mend her worn and uneven voice '. It will be found on p. 16 of *Hints on Singing*. It is not to be used merely as a remedy, but as a study for maintaining a ringing quality of tone on the descending scales, and at the same time preparing the way for a natural pure legato.

The mastery of the portamento is not more elusive than that of the legato; but its application to a musical phrase, the choice of a right mode of executing it, and various other considerations which musical feeling and experience alone can satisfy, combine to make it the more subtle and difficult device of the two. In the singing of Mozart both play an exceedingly important part.

The English word 'slur' is capable of too many interpretations, and has not the same precise significance as the Italian *portamento* or the French *port de voix*. These imply a mode of carrying the voice which, if employed gracefully and in the right place, always adds character, elegance, force, or intensity of expression, to the delivery of a phrase. Without one of these purposes in view it had better not be used. But, correctly to fulfil the traditions of the Italian school, it cannot be dispensed with.

To enhance the elegance of a phrase, the portamento should as a rule be lightly sung. Merely pushing the voice up or dropping it down from note to note deprives the device of all charm. The tone must be delicately poised and supported by the breath; it must likewise be carried without jerk or interruption over the whole of the interval, attaining its goal with perfect intonation and quality. Correct breath-pressure and intelligent anticipation of resonance will alone make this possible.

To impart declamatory force or vigour of sentiment, the portamento should be employed with an energy and directness that leaves no doubt as to its object, yet always with the greatest discretion. The intention of the composer must be carefully studied, and this in the case of Mozart will scarcely leave room for mistaken zeal or choice of the wrong place. The portamento is not invariably indicated, but where it is not, tradition and taste enable us to mark the spot.

.   .   .   .

As an ordinary device for adding sentiment to the music, the portamento has been exaggerated and overdone to an extent that has created a prejudice against its use at any point. That, of course, is absurd, like most objections that go to an extreme. Sixty years ago the excessive use of the portamento was unknown.

The great singers used it in just the right measure and no more; they made it rare enough for the ear to be grateful for its charm, never 'slurring' two or three intervals in succession or spreading the tone up and down with sickly heaviness. I remember the period when the exaggeration gradually set in. The song-writers of the eighties were as much responsible for it as the singers, one of the most popular of them, Grieg, suffering from an inordinate love of portamento, as his songs show.

Then began a reaction. The more cultivated English audiences became familiar with the Passion-music and cantatas of Bach, and learned to appreciate the proper reticence in this matter. They began to enjoy a final cadence without the customary upward or downward *glissade* to the concluding note. Musicians perceived that the artistic singers were imitating the grace, perception, and restraint of players of the violin or the violoncello like Joachim, Sarasate, Ysaye, Lady Hallé, Hollman, Hausmann, and Piatti, who were the right models from whom to acquire them.

(g) The 'Messa di Voce'

The English meaning of this curious term is naïvely but accurately defined by Garcia in *Hints on Singing*. The *messa di voce*, he says, stands for the process of singing 'swelled sounds', which should 'begin pianissimo and by degrees acquire increasing force till they arrive at their loudest, which should happen at half their length; then the process should be reversed'.

The apparently simple act of swelling and diminishing tone, not alone on single notes but on sentences or phrases, is the central characteristic of the old Italian school. The mastery of the 'straight line' must come first, as it would precede that of the 'curve' in drawing. But one does not suffice without the other—above all in the singing of Mozart, who demanded the *messa di voce* at nearly every turn of every piece that he wrote for the voice.

Here, once more, it is diaphragmatic breathing that enables the singer to accomplish the well-directed support of a steady tone while swelling or diminishing the strength and volume with perfect evenness and regularity of gradation.

The action of the *messa di voce* becomes, with practice, mechanical and subconscious. The utmost care is therefore needed in the exercise of a dynamic force that is liable to over-assertion and to produce a certain monotony of style. It may be constantly used, but only if guided by ease and economy of breath-pressure, coupled with musical intelligence.

A Mozart singer who does not possess this gift would, in my judgement, be an anomaly.

(*h*) Agility (Coloratura, Ornaments, etc.)

It is a common belief that only light voices are fitted by nature for the execution of florid or *coloratura* music. That is a misapprehension which has only grown up in recent times, and did not prevail among the old teachers, because their pupils, even those with the heaviest organs, were continually demonstrating the opposite. Bach and Handel, Mozart and Rossini, wrote many passages that are *tours de force*, it is true ; but, generally speaking, the former did not write their runs and ' divisions ', or the last-named his brilliant passages and cadenzas, for what they would have called exceptional voices. They wrote them indiscriminately for singers of every calibre—and for basses and contraltos as much as for sopranos and tenors.

The basis of all flexibility is the pure vocalization of the quick scale upon the bright tone, or *voix claire*. In order to be able to sing clearly, evenly, and rapidly an octave or more of notes, one must be able to do the same thing on two, three, or five notes. That means careful and constant practice with correct breathing and mechanism, adequate resonance, a true ear, freedom from muscular rigidity of the throat or larynx, and the natural impulse which imparts ease and abandonment to the steady, effortless flow of tone.

The free oscillation of the tone from note to note necessary for the preparation of the quick scale is also the right beginning for the practice of the shake or trill. But when more than two notes are attempted the larynx does not oscillate; the voice glides smoothly over the group with a slight accent upon each note, so that, no matter how rapid the movement, the singing of the scale becomes clear, definite, flexible, and of even strength throughout.

The main factor in the attainment of this lightness, elasticity, and accuracy is the supreme controlling action of the breath, working in complete accord with mind and ear. To sing scales crisply and clearly we must be able to *think* them in perfection.

Similar rules apply to the practice of runs (or ' divisions '), which form perhaps the most characteristic and persistent feature of Italian music of the seventeenth and eighteenth centuries. The mastery of these is the key to every branch of florid singing. They provide the groundwork for all vocal agility, for the ease and brilliancy of rendering which alone justifies the survival of this class of music.

Apart from smoothness and beauty of tone, a clear accentuation of the various rhythms is extremely important. Usually the accent falls upon the first note of a group of four, six, or eight notes, but the singer must be able to place it anywhere without interfering with the rhythm and clarity of the run. Nothing can be worse than triplets sung with a slurred and indistinct middle note, except perhaps a jumbled ' turn ' of which the final note is not audible.

In the singing of Mozart, correctly-marked rhythms—he has such an extraordinary variety of them—constitute a vital feature, notably in the concerted music of the operas and in the play between solo voice and orchestra. The ability to observe peculiar or divergent rhythms, in addition, is frequently essential in passages where agility is also called for. The study of one should therefore go hand in hand with the other; though naturally the scales and runs have to be mastered first.

With Mozart's special *ornamentations*, the point is that he treats the various types of ornaments, not as mere embellishments, but as integral parts of the composition. He thus enhances their dignity and makes their faultless execution of equal importance with that of the main melody.

The master had his favourite ' ornaments '. Grace notes simply abound in his music: turns (*gruppetti*), *appoggiature*, repeated and staccato sounds, shakes, slurred notes (*notes coulées*) constantly arrest the attention of the student. One and all demand the utmost purity and flexibility of voice and delicacy and finish of execution.

Mozart was especially fond of *notes coulées*, which are very difficult to sing really well. They belonged rather to the technique of the violin or the 'cello than of the voice. Two gliding notes to a single ' up or down bow ' are comparatively easy to play (compare the semiquaver passages in the *Tannhäuser* overture) ; but two notes to a syllable for a few bars in succession present a greater difficulty to the singer because of the certainty, smoothness, and grace that are demanded of the executant, who should here closely imitate the violin.

At the root of the matter lies the command of agility, and every student of this art who works diligently enough can be trained to become a more or less accomplished singer of florid music.

VI

LANGUAGE AND DICTION

To the code of laws that governs the Italian school of singing there need only be added a few words on the subject of enunciation and diction. Here the laws are again almost universal; but the rules for their application should be modified according to the language employed by the singer.

'Music,' as Garcia has said, 'though the language of the emotions, can only arouse them in a vague and general manner. To express any feeling or idea we must make use of words. Hence the importance for the singer of delivering these with the utmost distinctness, correctness, and meaning, under the penalty of losing the attention of the audience' (*Hints on Singing*, p. 45).

The mechanism of verbal utterance is the same in singing and in speaking. So far as the pronunciation of consonants is concerned, it must not be altered or varied, unless greater distinctness of articulation can be so obtained. For instance, what might be regarded as exaggeration in ordinary speech or drawing-room conversation seems perfectly natural in singing or stage elocution. I have generally found that, granted the vocal gift, the person who speaks well stands a better chance of making a good singer than the person who speaks badly.

The disparity between English and Italian as singing languages is greatly over-estimated and can always be overcome, although it seldom is. The advantage of the Italian lies chiefly in the more 'open' vowels—an advantage not to be despised, seeing that 'intonation, sustaining of the voice, expression or quality of timbre, tonic accent, and vocalization are all entrusted to the care of the vowel'.

But when the openness, the amplitude, the freedom of the Italian vowels are reproduced in the formation of the equivalent English sounds, together with a similar forward projection of the resultant tone, the disparity should almost entirely disappear.

The true explanation why this does not always happen lies in the fundamental obstacles presented by English consonants, as they are pronounced with half-closed mouth and tightened jaw by the vast majority of people to whom the English language is the mother-tongue. With their fixed 'singing position', their rigid facial muscles, their inelastic joints, and their rebellious tongues, their common habit is to allow syllable after syllable to slither out half articulated. Thus vowels which might otherwise be admirable for singing are badly shaped, inadequate, and impure.

I have tested and proved this in hundreds of instances, on both sides of the Atlantic, proving it most decisively by the facility with which foreigners can be taught to surmount the difficulties of English pronunciation. With their superior method of vowel-formation and enunciation, they invariably learn to make themselves better understood in singing than their English-speaking colleagues.

As a medium for beauty of speech and vocal sound, the language of Shakespeare is not less favourable than any other tongue spoken upon the earth. Patti could sing with equally irresistible charm in English, French, Spanish, Russian, German, and Welsh.

My preference for Italian in the singing of Mozart is where he himself employed an Italian text for his compositions ; and he employed it for most of his operas. He loved the language. Its softness, its sweetness, its poetic grace, its graphic force appealed to him ; and he knew how to set it to music with the maximum of racial flavour and rhythmic feeling. The least the singer can strive to accomplish is to do Mozart justice by a clear, refined utterance of the words to which he allied his ineffable melodies.

Singers with beautiful voices and moderate executive ability do not sufficiently recognize the tremendous influence of diction on their art. As a rule they think too much about their tone. On the other hand, those possessing only fair voices often do wonders by delivering the poet's lines with some peculiar charm of style, with distinctness, intelligence, refinement, and the requisite sense of contrast. But the proper combination is rare.

The mechanism for clear, emphatic, or rapid articulation is granted by nature to 90 per cent. of well-bred people; yet probably not one-twentieth of that number is so trained as to display their valuable faculty to advantage in either speech or song. The neglect of the former in childhood, crudities of dialect, and a slipshod mode of speaking that have not been corrected soon enough, are common obstacles to the would-be vocalist, and are exceedingly hard to overcome.

The old Italian singers were adepts in the art of 'patter'. They could rattle off their words at a rate that was simply astounding, and so distinctly that the audience could understand every syllable, which was perhaps the sole excuse for treating dialogue in opera, as Mozart did, in the form of *recitativo secco*, which I confess to finding extremely dull, with its eternal accompaniment of chords scraped by the principal 'cello and double-bass. But the art of the *recitativo secco* made it easy for the singers to pronounce the words of their airs with ease and clarity. The one was regarded as a preparatory study for the other.

A most remarkable illustration of this was the famous baritone, Cotogni, who used to sing Figaro to Patti's Rosina at Covent Garden in Rossini's *Barbiere*. His delivery of the 'Largo al factotum' was as quick and lively as that of the present-day Titta Ruffo, and certainly more distinct; and in the recitative of the Figaro of *Le Nozze* his clear utterance was beyond reproach. Yet it is a fact of which all his friends were aware that Cotogni suffered from an impediment in his speech which in ordinary conversation was painfully evident. He did not stammer—people who stammer badly but do not hesitate when singing or reciting are not uncommon. He made a whistling sound with the sides of his tongue against his teeth that was worse than a lisp. The moment he began to sing it entirely disappeared.

In Mozart we find the need for a quality additional to good diction—the quality of drama. Other composers before him made, indeed, a similar demand; but Mozart in some manner asked for a greater union of rare gifts than any of them.

The all-round development of the many rare talents here referred to constitutes what we now regard as the *sine qua non* for the interpretation of the classical Lied and the higher type of modern song, wherein poem and music are supposed to be brought absolutely into line with each other. Mozart was among the earliest of the great musicians to equalize the importance of both elements.

It was not as a writer of Lieder that Mozart displayed this gift. None of his songs is worthy of discussion here except that masterpiece 'Das Veilchen', the model of the felicitous treatment of a simple theme that was followed by so many illustrious song-writers. I mention it not in order to show how it should be sung; the song itself shows that; but because it stands apart from everything else that Mozart wrote. Otto Jahn, his biographer, says of it:

> 'The crown of all the songs, by virtue of its touching expression of emotion and its charming perfection of form, is unquestionably Goethe's "Veilchen".
>
> 'In other songs we discern musical genius divining and bringing to light the poetic germ which lie hidden in the words; here we have the impression made upon Mozart by true poetry. It may seem remarkable that so simple a lyrical poem should have been treated by Mozart as a romance, giving a certain amount of dramatic detail to the little story; and yet it must not be overlooked that the masterly touch which repeats the closing words: "Das arme Veilchen! es war ein herzigs Veilchen!" fully reasserts a genuine lyric element. Goethe's clear and plastic presentation of a simple image, true in every feature, could not fail to impress him deeply.'

The singer who can do justice to 'Das Veilchen' probably owns most of the qualities required for the interpretation of the Lieder of Schubert, Schumann, Brahms, and even Wolf and Strauss.

VII

TRADITIONAL INTERPRETATION

MOZART wrote easily and rapidly but never carelessly. His tireless industry for thirty years resulted in a prodigious output, which prematurely sapped his vitality. But he never put on paper a note or a sign that he did not want to be observed. Grace and symmetry were as natural to him as to a Greek sculptor; and he was one of the greatest masters of musical form that ever lived.

We can scarcely realize how marvellously original he was. At the time he lived and wrote a large proportion of his melodies, his peculiar rhythms, his turns of phraseology and expression, his cadences—his individual mannerisms—were things that must have sounded absolutely new.

When I was studying an air from *Don Giovanni*, I once asked my master how I could best improve my phrasing of Mozart's music and my rendering of his ornaments.

'Go to the "Pops" every week,' said Garcia. 'Go to St. James's Hall and listen to Joachim and Piatti and Norman-Néruda. Make a turn or a shake or an *appoggiatura* as they do; make your *portamenti* as lightly, as delicately, and with as much reticence. The great violinists and 'cellists have preserved that art much better than the singers. You can learn from them everything that you want to know about it, and you may imitate them without fear.'

This was said over forty years ago, and it stands good to-day, even though the vocalist has always something to add to the instrumentalist's clarity.

A close study of Mozart's operas shows his amazing aptitude for colour, for an individual quality of dramatic expression, peculiar not only to each character, but to every thought or feeling of that character. This aptitude is the more astonishing because it is obviously spontaneous, not the result of long reflection or laborious effort.

45

Observe, for instance, how in the two airs of the Countess in *Le Nozze di Figaro* 'Porgi amor' introduces the proud but neglected lady in a prayer for help to the god of love; while the first part of 'Dove sono' is rather an outpouring of vain regrets over a happy past that shows little promise of renewal. The music of each differs in character from the other; yet both are generally sung in the same monotonous key of misery and boredom, and with exactly the same vocal colouring.

The gramophone, had it been invented thirty years earlier, would provide evidence of Theresa Tietjens's reading of these two pieces, and prove how a great dramatic singer could infuse into each its full and individual qualities. Description cannot replace such evidence; but it may at least be said that, apart from her eloquent colouring of each utterance, Tietjens achieved not a little of her triumph by the purity and simplicity of her phrasing and the natural, unforced tragic grandeur of her style. To her the instinct for variation or contrast came without being sought, and it enabled her to realize Mozart's exact intention.

The same may be said of Patti's delicate differentiation between the two airs of Zerlina in *Don Giovanni*, which she made partly by instinct and partly because she had been trained in the right tradition.[1] Her singing of 'Batti, batti' was always marked by a mixture of coquetry and flattery obviously meant to coax Masetto into forgiving her for her flirtation with the amorous

---

[1] Adelina Patti is often belittled because of certain breaches of artistic taste that occasionally disfigured her concert career after she had left the stage. The younger generation who never heard her in opera could only judge her by what she did on her periodical appearances at the Albert Hall for twenty years with the *beaux restes* of a marvellously-preserved voice. At Covent Garden between 1861 and 1885 she had, at any rate as Zerlina, done something more than warble Mozart's tunes; she had established her fame as a genuine Mozart singer. One reason for this was, that she had studied the rôle with her brother-in-law, impresario, and 'coach', Maurice Strakosch, who previously acted for some time as accompanist for the great Pasta when she was teaching at Como. There Strakosch learned the tradition of the part of Zerlina from one who had sung Mozart in London less than twenty-five years after the composer's death. The tradition was therefore direct and (in the opinion of Garcia) correct.

Don. Zerlina knows, of course, that her simple sweetheart would never raise a finger to hurt her, but she offers to submit to corporal punishment all the same. On the other hand, in 'Vedrai, carino' one could instantly perceive, when Patti sang it, the tone of unaffected regret and anxious sympathy aroused by Masetto's physical suffering, even with the undercurrent of humour that accompanies the air.

Apart from tradition, however, the composer's intention was clearly conveyed by the nature of the vocal treatment revealed in these two airs. In 'Batti, batti' the repeated downward trend of the quavers plainly suggests a sort of caressing, insinuating motion, which the singer must render with an unbroken surface of legato, yet with scarcely a shade of portamento anywhere. This restraint imparts the greater effect to the delicate gliding of the *notes coulées* on the phrase 'E le care tue manine'.

In 'Vedrai, carino' there is more scope for an expressive portamento, very lightly graded on the slurred quavers; and no less important is a neat execution of the mordent on the word *carino*, which gives the cue, as it were, for Zerlina's attitude of real solicitude this time. As a musical indication of her *certo balsamo*, that run of three notes is a stroke of genius; and so, too, are the three taps when she places her hand upon her heart and slyly says, *Sentilo battere*.

Although portamenti as a rule are to be lightly sung, that is, when uttering 'moderate or tender sentiments', they must, when 'applied to expression of powerful feelings, be strong and rapid' (*Hints on Singing*, p. 63). Examples of the latter are frequently to be met with in Mozart, especially in *Don Giovanni*, where he uses the portamento again and again as a means for dramatic expression and indicates it (as in the opening phrase of the Don's serenade) in a manner that cannot be mistaken. The mastery of this vocal grace is essential and of the highest value to the dramatic singer.

The music of Donna Anna and Don Ottavio contains many similar instances—the former in 'Non mi dir', the latter in both his solo airs, notwithstanding the extraordinary contrast that they otherwise present. In 'Dalla sua pace' the word *morte*, sung without a strong portamento from the D to the G, would be ineffective; while in 'Il mio tesoro', which is as florid and declamatory as the other air is lyrical, there are similar points to be observed.

So again, in the part of Donna Elvira, Mozart has employed the same mode of heightening emotional fervour in music that is otherwise quite different in cast, like, for example, the opening of the trio 'Ah, chi mi dice mai' and the very difficult aria, 'Mi tradì alma ingrata'. The explanation of the disparity in Donna Elvira's case is, curiously enough, identical with that in Don Ottavio's, namely, that the two pieces were not written for the same artists. 'Dalla sua pace' was composed for a Viennese tenor, Signor Morello, who found 'Il mio tesoro' too much for him; whilst 'Mi tradì' was introduced into the opera for the famous Madame Cavalieri because there was not a show-piece brilliant enough for her liking.

Yet 'Mi tradì' is not difficult on account of its brilliancy. It has nothing in common with the vengeful outbursts of the Queen of Night. The strange mixture of contradictory feelings that besets Donna Elvira finds expression here in one long series of *notes coulées*, extremely difficult to sing with neatness and at the same time the right dramatic accent. The question has been asked why Mozart set the air in this manner. It was either because he wished to illustrate Donna Elvira's unbalanced, hesitant condition of mind (she was supposed to be a *ci-devant* nun, whose troubles had upset her mentally), or because Mme Cavalieri was an uncommonly good executant of Mozart's favourite *notes coulées*.

I once heard Christine Nilsson in this rôle (Tietjens being the Donna Anna and Trebelli the Zerlina); and although I saw many good Elviras subsequently, I never again experienced the same realization of the unfortunate lady's state of mental distraction or the same rare beauty of voice and method in performing the 'ups and downs' of 'Mi tradì'. It reminded me of the exquisite bowing of Sarasate. Even if the gift came to her by intuition, how hard she must have practised at first!

VIII

THE TREATMENT OF RECITATIVE

THE chronicles of opera in the eighteenth century show how much the composers owed to their stage interpreters. They had to provide tasks worthy of artists who possessed voices of incredible range, beauty, and flexibility—great singers who were likewise great actors and actresses, and not their least amazing gift was their capacity for declaiming the magnificent vocal and dramatic passages which carried on the stage action even more than the airs, the ensembles, and the choruses.

Those passages were embodied in dramatic *Recitative*, not the rapid *parlando* of the *recitativo secco*, which was merely a hurried explanatory dialogue, but the recitative on the grand scale, accompanied by the orchestra, the secret of which was no less natural to Mozart than was the method of delivering it to his interpreters. Unfortunately the gift of the master and the art of the singers have alike disappeared. In opera, though not in oratorio, this form of dramatic recitative has been superseded ; but nothing has ever surpassed it for energy, spirit, or power. It remains to this day the perfect model for all that vocal declamation can achieve.

Among the most extraordinary singers of Mozart's time was the capricious Aloysia Weber, with whom he fell in love. He never married her, but took her younger sister, Constanze, to be his devoted and famous wife. Aloysia, however, sang in many of his operas, and it was for her that he wrote some of his most exacting pieces.

Among these was a ' grand' aria ', composed in 1779, which was a setting of the recitative and air that Alceste sings on her first entry in Gluck's opera. It might have been regarded as a kind of challenge to the older master, whom, notwithstanding, Mozart knew and respected. It was a tremendous *bravura* piece bristling

49

with difficulties and *tours de force* of every description—with a compass extending to G in *alt*—such as Aloysia Weber alone could have done justice to.

The recitative was in its way a masterpiece. Nothing to equal it had ever been heard before. This is what Otto Jahn says about it:

> 'But the importance of this song does not depend alone on the brilliancy of its passages.... The recitative, undeniably the most important section of the composition, is second to none of Mozart's later recitatives in depth and truth of expression and noble beauty, and richly provided with un-expected harmonic changes ... if this carefully and minutely-elaborated recitative be compared with Gluck's simple *secco* recitative there can be no doubt that Mozart's is far superior both in fertility of invention and marked characterization.'

Aloysia, we are told, did justice both to the recitative and the aria; and in order to do this she must have been equally marvellous as a dramatic and a coloratura singer; and let me add that since Ilma di Murska no soprano within living memory has quite answered to that description.

In her dual capacity lies the encouragement to the singer.[1] Aloysia Weber was not the possessor of a powerful or even a robust organ. Jahn says 'the powerful rendering of violent and fiery passion was not her forte. A certain moderation seems to have been peculiar to her, which Mozart turned to account as an element of artistic harmony.' Another writer says that 'she performed marvels with her delicate throat, and her voice resembled a Cremona violin'. Yet she could declaim recitative magnificently! So much can a singer with a 'delicate throat' accomplish by means of genius, industry, and determination; and I believe Aloysia Weber must have had all three.

The singing of Mozart's recitatives calls for qualities far beyond the merely vocal. They require, to begin with, first-rate elocu-

[1] She took the part of Donna Anna on the first production of *Don Giovanni* in Vienna, May 7, 1788, when the opera was regarded as a failure.

tion, a freedom of balance and accent akin to that needed for the delivery of blank verse. The time not being strict, the notes are to be regarded as no more than an indication of the approximate length and weight of utterance to be accorded to the syllables. Yet every sentence must have its proper rhythmical swing and the sense conveyed by due emphasis and expression on every word and tone. The pauses, the silences are all eloquent; and the use of the *messa di voce* on a held note must contribute something real to the sentiment of the passage. Contrasts or sudden changes of feeling must be depicted by the colour of the voice no less than by the mode of delivery.

In that wonderful recitative, 'O quali eccessi', which precedes 'Mi tradì', a rapid transition has to be effected. Donna Elvira, in less than half a dozen bars, passes from a climax of rage to a flood of tender self-pity, followed by the feeling that her love is not yet dead.

There are numbers of recitatives in Mozart's operas calling for similar qualities and depicting every imaginable *nuance* of human emotion. They must all be treated in similar fashion—i.e. conceived in the right dramatic spirit, attacked with vigour, correctly accentuated, enunciated and declaimed with clearness, and sung without superfluous portamento or a vestige of vocal trickery.

A score that well repays study for this purpose is that of *Idomeneo* (produced at Munich in 1781), an opera which unfortunately is never heard in England. It was Mozart's first *opera seria* and marked the starting-point of his career as a dramatic composer. The treatment of the recitative in *Idomeneo* is in many respects quite original, and not less masterful than that of the orchestra. The opera is best known for the charming soprano air, 'Zeffiretti lusinghieri'; but another feature is its anticipation of the 'supernatural' effects in *Don Giovanni*, which was not produced until seven years later.

Mozart's versatility in writing recitative, as in everything else, was astounding. He could express every emotion and could even caricature his own serious style with a result that was genuinely comic. A notable instance of this occurs in *Così fan tutte*, when

Isadora (Fiordiligi) pretends to be furiously angry with the fickle lovers for breaking their plighted vows. Her manner in 'Come un scoglio' is that of a tragedy-queen, and in delivering her invective she skips over some tremendous intervals; but the whole number is obviously a clever parody of the real thing.

However, whether the sentiment be real or artificial, the art of the singer must be equally great. For clean attack, impeccable intonation, pure, neat phrasing, ample sonority, and strong accentuation must mark the declamation of every sentence.

IX

THE APPOGGIATURA

The appoggiatura has been much discussed and at times has led to more heated argument than it demanded. The rules pertaining to it were laid down (or gradually laid themselves down) on perfectly clear lines, and have only to be understood for mistakes or misinterpretations to be avoided. For these rules I have, where possible, found it better to consult tradition rather than text-books—excepting of course in the case of Garcia, who put the one into the other.

The *appoggiatura* dates back to the now remote period when composers left the choice of ornaments and graces to the artists who sang their music. It was a stupid fashion, but doubtless there were good reasons for it, until, over a century ago, Rossini gave it up on the sensible ground that he found himself better served by supplying his own ornaments.

But in music of a date earlier than Rossini's one has still to deal with the old custom that gives a loophole for wrong treatment to the ignorant, the ill-informed, or the bigoted; or to those who imagine that every note written by the old masters, in recitative or elsewhere, should be literally sung as it appears on the printed page; who imagine that because Bach does not require—nor should he indeed receive—the usual Italian interpretation of the appoggiatura, the same strict law must perforce apply to Mozart.

The master's obvious conclusion, according to Garcia, was that the appoggiatura ' must be introduced '. That is to say, ' when a sentence ends with two equal notes, in the Italian style, we raise the first a tone or a half-tone, according to the degree of the scale '. And he adds, ' the exception to this rule is when the two notes are both an essential part of an idea, when they belong to concerted voices, or when the harmony does not permit the alteration' (*Hints on Singing*, p. 67).

These exceptions have to be very carefully considered; but in the majority of cases their treatment has been made familiar by tradition. They rarely occur in recitative, where the intention is generally too plain to leave room for misconstruction. The need for the heightened accent afforded by raising the first note seems unmistakable. In the three sentences with which Susanna begins the recitative 'Giunse alfin', preceding 'Deh vieni', a literal rendering of the same notes on the penultimate syllables of *momento*, *affanno*, and *mio* would sound bald, ugly, unlike Mozart, although he wrote them so. In the aria greater latitude is possible; but it should not be left to the teacher or singer of no special knowledge to decide where the two notes are or are not 'an essential part of an idea', or where the appoggiatura is calculated to spoil the harmony.

There is another point—the *length* of the raised note. Should it be permissible to alter it? In my opinion, certainly not. When Mozart wrote a crotchet he did not mean it to be sung as a quaver. Susannas like Marimon and Sembrich did not depart from tradition in one regard, nor did they wilfully disobey it in another. Thus, in 'Deh vieni' they naturally sang the appoggiatura where it does and should occur, namely, on the last two notes of the first and fourth phrases, on *bella* and *tace*; also again on *l'aura* and *adesca*. But I never heard them convert the crotchet-quaver of these two syllables into two quavers, as the late Mr. Randegger gave them in his Novello edition of the arias of Susanna and Cherubino.

In concerted music the appoggiatura must *not* be introduced, above all where the voices are singing together. It brings in a note foreign to the chord and creates an effect that the composer did not intend. If Mozart wished for an appoggiatura in one of the themes of an ensemble he never failed to indicate it in the orthodox way by a small note (to be accorded the same value as a large one). Examples of this occur in the duet 'La ci darem' (*Don Giovanni*), where Zerlina has twice to glide down a whole fifth on *Mi trema un poco il cor*. But it would not justify her in raising the last note but one, as many a Zerlina has done, on the subsequent word *Masetto*.

Similarly with the two duets in *Le Nozze*: Susanna must sing the word *boschetto* in 'Sull' aria' without the appoggiatura, although the Countess sings it with one; the text of the music clearly indicates this in each case. In 'Crudel, perchè' the Count should never alter the C sharp on *verrai* and *mancherai*, since obviously the composer has never asked or meant him to do so. But I admit that every famous singer I have heard in the part has sinned by transgressing this rule, probably because it sounds rather prettier.

Here, for once, authoritative tradition exemplifies the fact that recognized laws may be broken by the people who as a rule accord them the most implicit obedience. But on the whole I prefer a sound, definite law to a doubtful tradition, however widely accepted.

X

MARKS OF EXPRESSION, BREATHING-PLACES, ETC.

In teaching I have found it convenient to make use of modern editions of Mozart's operatic airs because they are well printed and have fewer misprints than the old sheet-music copies published years ago. Many of the indications and substituted notes are correct and some of the marks of expression permissible ; those which are not one can always change.

But therein lies the danger. These 'edited' versions are too untrustworthy to be followed without question. The student should carefully think out the doubtful points and reject without hesitation all changes or embellishments which seem out of keeping with the true characteristics of the Mozart style of which I have endeavoured to indicate the salient features. For his own marks of expression—*p* or *f* ; *cres.* or *dim.*; the acceleration or slackening of *tempo* ; pauses, and so forth—it is necessary to look to the accompaniment even more than the voice part, for there they are mostly to be found.

It was not the custom of the day to indicate *breathing-places* otherwise than by rests, and then only in the rarest cases, except in recitative, where the natural accentuation and rounding-off of the phrase, as in ordinary spoken declamation, provided obvious opportunities. The latter were intended not so much to indicate silence as to serve the purpose of punctuation.

In the solos and concerted pieces the musical phrase dictates the best place for taking breath as well if not better than the text. The charm and symmetry of the musical effect needs to be the first consideration in the rendering of all Mozart's melodies, and the singer may, in this particular matter of phrasing, be as accurately guided by good taste and right feeling as by the most reliable tradition. On the other hand, I do not agree, where faulty English translations are the cause, with new breathing-places that upset the melody for the sake of badly-fitting sentences. The words are important, but in Mozart it must be the music, first and last.

Beyond a doubt Mozart wrote for singers who had a prodigious breathing capacity, as did Bach and Handel before him ; but only now and then did he call upon them to sing passages which we should to-day find impossible of execution in a single breath. There is no virtue in accomplishing these *tours de force* when the passage can be so much better sung with the aid of an extra breath, taken imperceptibly at the right moment and in the right way.

It is a serious question whether many of the trying passages, based upon a single syllable, that are so familiar to Mozart students, were invariably sung a hundred years ago in a single respiration. Manuel Garcia never expected it, for example, in the extended run that occurs in ' Il mio tesoro ', but at once marked the conventional breaths—the same that I heard Caruso take on the solitary occasion when he sang Don Ottavio at Covent
* Garden. Nor did the old teacher act differently in other cases, such as the long runs in ' Gli angui d'inferno ', ' Ah, lo so ', ' Non mi dir ', ' Zeffiretti lusinghieri ', &c.

* Caruso actually sang the rôle of Don Ottavio six times at Covent Garden: twice in 1902 (the first performance of July 19 was perhaps that heard by Klein); twice during the 1905 season; and twice in 1906. Battistini was the Don Giovanni in one of the 1906 performances. Since Klein resided in New York from December, 1901 to May, 1909, he can perhaps be forgiven for the error. Ed.

XI

UNION OF GRACE AND SKILL

GRACE of execution must distinguish the rendering of Mozart's *ornaments*. These *gruppetti* or turns, these quick *appoggiature* and *acciaccature* ('two rapid descending notes ornamenting a third note'), these repeated or staccato sounds, and, perhaps most important of all, the perfect shake or trill, must be at the command of the thoroughly-trained vocalist.

But to mechanical accuracy must also be added two things—entire ease of manner and constant unfailing obedience to the rhythmical accent of the bar.

In Mozart there is never occasion either to hurry or to drag the 'grace' notes. The ornament, whatever it may be, always has its precise place in the theme or phrase, and, if properly executed, there is always abundant time for singing it with smoothness, clarity, and distinction. Yet how seldom do we hear this done, especially where the *turn* is concerned. A violinist will take pains to make you hear the last note of the turn ; a singer will trouble less about it. Above all, every note of every ornament must be as perfectly in tune as the theme which it embellishes.

It is almost a crime to add to or take away from the literal text of Mozart's ornaments. They suffice as they stand. The great Italian singers used occasionally to insert a turn or a mordent after a pause on a long ending note. Mario did so in 'Il mio tesoro' on the words *a vendicar io vado* ; Patti sometimes on the *dove mi stà* in 'Vedrai, carino'. But these were among the later traditions not so strictly to be imitated. Mozart is best left alone.

Pasta invented more changes and additional ornaments than any other *coloratura* soprano of her time. But she reserved them exclusively for Bellini, who wrote *Norma* and *Sonnambula* for her ;

for Donizetti, who adored her Anna Bolena; and for Rossini, who thought her the ideal Semiramide. She never altered or added a note to Mozart. There the singer declared herself 'on holy ground'.

The *cadenza*, again, was a growth of the nineteenth century. It is out of place in Mozart's vocal compositions because the scheme of his design is complete without it; besides, when he wishes, they contain quite sufficient elaborate passages for display to serve the ambition of any average good singer. The cadenza belongs, properly speaking, to the school of the Italian composers above named, and to Verdi or Meyerbeer.

. . . .

I have now, I think, enumerated all the principal points involved in the application of Italian singing to the music of Mozart. The perfect union of the two is the goal that the student should have in mind from the start; and the conscientious labour required for its accomplishment can hardly fail to be rewarded, since the key to the 'Bel Canto' unlocks in Mozart the richest storehouse of vocal treasures that musician ever gave to the world.

Part II
THE GRAMOPHONE
AND
THE SINGER

THE GRAMOPHONE AND THE SINGER

By HERMAN KLEIN

IT must be well over twenty years now since I first began to realize what an important adjunct the gramophone might be made to the work and art of the singer. I make no claim to be the actual originator of a new idea in this connection; but I have reason to believe that I was among the first—if not the very first—to bring it to a practical test. I would like to tell you how it came about.

From 1902 until 1909 I made my home in New York, cutting only partially adrift from this, my native, land because I came over every summer for three or four months to teach singing and write criticism or articles for my old papers. So, whilst never losing touch here, I took an increasing interest in musical affairs and musical inventions in the United States, renewed old friendships with famous singers of the day when they came to New York, and made the acquaintance of many new and gifted artists whom I had never met in London. To give a list of these would occupy considerable space and serve no useful purpose. I will mention only a few whose names will be more especially familiar to gramophone lovers as the makers of the best records in the early days of the invention. They are worth noting, not only for their own sake, but in view of what I shall have to say about their singing and in the way of comparison later on.

At the time I speak of the only two firms of any importance that were manufacturing gramophone machines and records in America were the Victor and the Columbia. In 1902 the Victor had the pick of the leading opera singers and, I must add in all fairness, produced by far the most satisfactory disc-records. The Columbia had barely begun to make the latter; they were still doing nearly all their business with the primitive cylinders and the no less primitive music associated with them. One day I heard a Victor reproduction of an aria sung by my old friend, Madame Sembrich, and I thought it so good that I went off post-haste to her flat at the Savoy Hotel, in Fifth Avenue, to talk to her about it. "Yes," she said, "it is remarkably good; but you have no notion what an enormous amount of trouble we had, and how many times I had to sing it to avoid

HERMAN KLEIN

the 'blasting' and smooth over the uneven patches before we arrived at this result."

I gathered that her records were selling splendidly; that only Melba's could approach them in popularity (though a little later they were to surpass them); and that both prima donnas were at that moment tied by "exclusive" contracts to the Victor Company. I became deeply interested in the details of what was to me an entirely new combination of art and industry. I studied various records of these and other artists. I noted the clarity of Sembrich's tone, the ease with which she executed her *fiorituri*, the richer timbre of her voice compared with the silvery quality of Melba's, yet not excelling it in musical sweetness or flexibility or a clean articulation of every note in the brilliant passages. I found it very hard to choose between these two on points of excellence; I preferred them both, however, to another popular Victor soprano, Emma Eames, whom I had also known in London, a beautiful singer, but one whose slightly constricted method of production militated against the perfect recording of her true voice. Again I noted these differences, as well as certain points of similarity, in various kinds of exceptional voices that I had already studied thoroughly in the opera house or the concert room. At the time, though, I was unable altogether to account for them. As yet, too, I had made no move with the object of getting into contact with either of the firms I have mentioned. Incidentally I had learned that the way to the Victor offices was "blocked" by Mr. de Gogorza, the American baritone, who was acting as their musical adviser and securing the big artists for them.

I wanted to get Caruso, and was only just too late to land that valuable prize, as he frankly admitted when I first met him in New York, after having heard him previously at Covent Garden. I thought his marvellously clear, smooth tone—a miracle of *sostenuto*—would come out magnificently on the gramophone; and so it proved, as all the world was soon to know. He came to see me at my house in W. 77th Street on his way from California to London and gave me a highly realistic description

63

of the great earthquake at San Francisco. He had escaped, he said, by clinging to the window-frame in his bedroom, half in, half out of the window, whilst the ceiling and plaster were tumbling in masses about him; and he showed me exactly how he had stood shivering and holding on until the earthquake shocks had subsided. Had he been killed in that dreadful business there would not have been a tenth of the Caruso records that we possess to-day.

It must have been shortly after that visit that I was lunching one day with the celebrated prima donna, Lillian Nordica—delightful woman and delightful artist—perhaps the most accomplished singer that America has ever produced. We were old friends; for, long before she appeared here in opera, I had written about her début at the Crystal Palace with Gilmore's Band in 1878. Suddenly it occurred to me to ask her if she had ever made a gramophone record. She had not. I asked her why? "I can hardly tell you," she replied, "unless it is that the idea of it has always given me a nervous feeling, as though I should never be able to put my real voice into that dreadful horn. You have to sing into a horn, have you not? Well, I am sure I should never make a success of it." It seemed to me a strange thing for a beautiful singer to say. But, stranger still, I was ere long to prove that it was true. In 1906, when I became " musical advisor " to the Columbia Graphophone Company I introduced to them such artists as David Bispham (who made such amazing records), Anton van Rooy, Lillian Blauvelt, and my pupil, Ruth Vincent, who was singing in New York in " Véronique." I also took to them Madame Nordica, and, as usual, was present when she sang her records. It is a fact that neither on that nor on any subsequent occasion did she succeed in doing herself justice or producing a record—unless, perhaps, one of the air " Suicidio," from Ponchielli's *Gioconda*—that the public would be actually keen to buy. The voice sounded thin and " pinched " and even muffled in tone; in fact, so little like the original organ that one could scarcely recognize the timbre, much less the breadth and sonority, of one of the finest Elsas I have ever heard.

But Madame Nordica fully compensated for her deficiency, in my estimation, by a suggestion, entirely new to me then, which she made during our conversation at the luncheon already referred to. She asked me, " What do you think of the idea of using vocal exercises, sung by first-rate artists and made into gramophone records, for students to imitate either by themselves or under the guidance of their teachers? It seems to me that they ought to prove a real boon to both. Very few teachers are capable of illustrating their art to their pupils in the finished manner that it ought to be; and as singing is an art that can only be thoroughly learnt

by imitation, surely you have here just the right device for providing the necessary model. Think it over; and, if you will write the exercises, I have no objection to making an attempt to sing some of them." I did think it over—very long and very seriously; for I had seen at once the genuine utility and importance of the idea. What was more, I laid a complete scheme before the Columbia people and set to work to plan a system, which I denominated the " Phono-Vocal Method " for teaching or learning singing with the aid of the gramophone. I wrote out my exercises for all four voices (S.C.T.B.), and although unfortunately, Madame Nordica never got to the point of executing her share of them, I contrived, in spite of many obstacles and delays, to complete my task and get all but the tenor records ready by the time—literally on the very morning—that I sailed from New York to take up my permanent residence once more in the old country. I have not space to continue the story in detail. Enough that my " Phono-Vocal Method " was never efficiently exploited either in the U.S.A. or over here, in spite of much hearty encouragement from all who took the trouble to examine its working and test the records. The plain fact is that the world was not then ready for it. It was a good idea put into practice before its time. Besides, the Columbia Company of 1909 was not the Columbia Company of 1924, or there might have been a different tale to tell; also the vocal examples, admirably as they were sung, are now " dated "—they belong to the early days of the science of record-making. Two things, however, will endure: one is the idea itself, for which I shall always feel myself primarily indebted to Lillian Nordica; the other is the volume of instructions for vocal students which I wrote to accompany the set of ten double-disc records for each of the four voices. The latter was the first book on the art of singing that I ever had the courage to write.

My principal motive in relating the foregoing episode has been to make clear that I have had a lengthy as well as a fairly technical experience of matters connected with the Gramophone and its development; and, further, that I possess a deep-seated belief in the value of this popular instrument, as a means of enabling all who are interested in singing to study and copy what is good and right, or *per contra* to avoid that which is wrong or false or mistaken, in the methods of the leading vocalists of our day. For it is this experience, supplemented by this belief, that will enable me to fulfil the purpose which the Editor of THE GRAMOPHONE has had in view in asking me to write the regular series of articles whereto the present one serves as introduction. He wishes me to act as a kind of Mentor, to guide his readers to a closer understanding and livelier appreciation of the art that these famous singers of records employ—to describe what they do and how they do it; how they conquer their difficulties and how they occasionally miss their mark (for no singers, not even the very greatest, can invariably accomplish to perfection what they set out to do); and, moreover, to point out where and how they differ from each other in their modes of rendering the same piece or the same passage. The distinctions between the methods of one intelligent artist and another always repay observation. I am not personally interested in mere " changes " of vocal ornament; I am not now alluding to them, though I admit that the greater the artist the more musical and appropriate these " changes " are likely to sound to the cultivated ear. There are a hundred different ways of singing *Una Voce*, but you will listen to only two or three with the feeling that, had Rossini written variations on his own air, that was precisely the kind of thing he would have provided. Patti and Sembrich and Galli-Curci have given us *Una Voce* in this manner—the " grand manner " I might term it—and my only regret is that the celebrated *diva* was no longer in her prime when she made her sparse collection of records for the H.M.V. The differences of rendering to which I intend to draw attention are of a more subtle kind, and will probably be found to belong rather to technical and artistic questions that are of importance to the vocal student.

I regard the gramophone of to-day as a wonderfully truthful and accurate reflection of the voice and art of the singer. There was a time, not so long ago, when its performances had to be accepted with reservations, with constant allowances and excuses; when it tortured us with noises that we would gladly have dispensed with, and left to the imagination much that might have been beautiful had it only been there. But that stage, thank goodness, has long passed, and by comparison with the old machine which did me useful service for many years, the admirable Sonora model which Messrs. Keith Prowse & Co. have placed at my disposal is simply a gem. It is affording me a new education. I have, of course, had opportunities of listening to many up-to-date models and judging what they are capable of. But in this Sonora I have been trying some records belonging to a bygone, not to say prehistoric, period and the contrast, which is quite remarkable, demonstrates clearly enough that the improvement in the modern gramophone is due at least as much to the reproducing as to the recording mechanism. Anyhow I can confirm what was said last month by the Editor concerning the merits of this machine and its special " brilliancy " in bringing out the human voice. I feel, therefore, that I am adequately equipped for the task that lies before me.

In the meantime I am asked to give my impressions of two or three records of recent issue which have not yet been noticed in these columns. I gladly do so because, in more than one instance they illustrate the fact that an operatic excerpt, as heard on the gramophone, need not essentially be a specimen of the *Bel Canto* in order to interest and satisfy the listener. It may transgress some of the most prominent rules of the art and yet " get home " because it reproduces the character of the personage and the atmosphere of the scene. In this category I would place two efforts of Adamo Didur, whom I heard years ago at the Metropolitan Opera House, New York. They are both utterances of his Satanic majesty—one the *Veau d'or* from Gounod's *Faust;* the other the so-called *Whistle Song* (*Son lo spirito chi nega*) from Boito's *Mefistofele* (Pathé Actuelle, 10610). Their mood is not quite identical, but Didur achieves each in turn—the first gay, lively and vigorous in its irresistible swing; the second replete with irony, contempt, defiance, the " spirit that denies." But beyond this admirable realization of the Kermesse and the Brocken there is not a great deal to praise. The words are not distinct, the vowel tones are distorted, and the voice—no longer in its first youth—suffers from a decided *vibrato*. Yet, in spite of the faults, one feels the authority and *sang-froid* of the experienced artist. So again, one can overlook for the sake of its real Neapolitan feeling and rhythm, the lack of vocal charm in Tito Schipa's rendering of Tosti's *Marechiare* and the tuneful old *canto popolare* known as *Santa Lucia* (Pathé Actuelle, 10622). For there are life and jollity in both; you can hear every syllable; and, after all, you can easily forgive a rather noisy, open production when the tenor is a Southern Italian who might be singing to a sunburnt crowd in front of the San Carlo. I recommend, however, the use of a soft needle as a refining influence in both cases.

Our English tenor, Frank Mullings, is more discreet in volume (therefore acceptable with a loud needle) in the two Canio selections from *Pagliacci* viz., *Such a game* and *No, Pagliaccio, no more* (Col. D 1476), which he declaims with characteristic spirit and an abundance of dramatic sentiment. It is a pity the tone is not more steady at certain moments, for at the right place it can convey the veritable *cri de cœur*, which is then always worth hearing. Again I object to the " scoop " and to the exaggerated vowel-formation that spoil good English nearly as completely as do unsounded consonants. One would also have welcomed a stronger touch of irony in the first air, such as the Italians give it, especially on the return to the subject, which would thus have effected a better contrast. Canio in real life is no fool, and he wants his friends to know it. Still, on the whole this is an excellent record.

HERMAN KLEIN.

65

THE GRAMOPHONE AND THE SINGER

(Continued)

By HERMAN KLEIN

The Recording of *Una Voce*

THE thoroughpaced modernist would fain have us believe that the vogue of florid singing, or vocal fireworks, as it is sometimes derisively termed, has completely gone out. But actual experience proves him to be wrong. Let a light soprano who is really entitled to be called great appear at any leading opera house to-morrow, and I will wager that she will achieve a triumph more brilliant, a sensation more tremendous, than ever yet fell to a Brünnhilde, an Isolde, or e'en a Madam Butterfly or Aïda. Surely an instance of the kind was forthcoming seventeen years ago when, on a memorable evening, Luisa Tetrazzini made her début at Covent Garden. In spite of the fact that the Rossinian school was already being subjected to cheap gibes and sneers, on the day following her first appearance in London, after a career of several years' duration in Italy and South America, the new prima donna awoke to find herself famous, and has remained a popular favourite ever since It is proved more than ever to-day by the extraordinary and unparalleled celebrity that has attached itself to the name of Amelita Galli-Curci—an Italian *soprano leggiero* who has never yet appeared in this country, a singer whose reputation has been built up to such amazing heights through the medium of the gramophone, that it has been found possible to sell every seat eight months in advance for a concert which she is to give at the Albert Hall in October next. I need scarcely add that a feat such as this is entirely without precedent; and the reason it has never happened before is because the conditions which have rendered it practicable did not exist prior to the era of the gramophone.

I do not express any particular feeling or *penchant* of my own in this matter. I like good singing of every kind, provided it *is* good. My object is to point out the constant, undiminished partiality universally shown by the public for displays of brilliant vocal execution on the part of the popular prima donna. The more dazzling the " fireworks " the better the record seems to sell. The loftier the flights of scales, arpeggios, and cadenzas into the *altissimo* region, the stronger the fascination seems to grow. It is the same as in the case of the Caruso records—the demand is greatest for the pieces that display the largest volume of opulent tone, no matter how hackneyed the opera or the aria wherein they

occur. In short, the ear loves not only to hear the familiar melody, but to revel in these gushing streams of rich and penetrating vocal sound, authentically uttered by the recognised masters and mistresses of the art—that is to say, by those of them who are capable of producing the faithful replica of their beautiful voices in a gramophone record. It is the achievement of the great combination—theme, tone, and art—that alone spells success in the exploitation of this wonderful modern device. It is not given to every accomplished vocalist, as I pointed out in my article last month, to possess the faculty for making perfect records. The voices that succeed best are those which are most easily and naturally produced ; those which maintain the most perfect balance of breath-pressure and tone-vibration, with the maximum of unforced resonance. And this is in most cases, if not as an absolute rule, the outcome of a born gift rather than an acquired talent. Melba had it in the supreme degree ; so has Galli-Curci ; so, no doubt, have plenty of well-known singers. But there is also at the present time an operatic soprano who has not yet been heard in London, and whose popularity in America is scarcely, if at all, inferior to that of Mme. Galli-Curci, but whose reputation as a singer of gramophone records is practically negligible. I allude to Mme. Jeritza. I have never heard this famous Viennese prima donna, who, like her Italian rival, " skipped " our metropolis when she first went to the United States, and forthwith triumphed to an extent that made her infinitely too expensive for the limited pockets of the Grand Opera Syndicate. But where are Jeritza's records ? Let me candidly confess that I have never come across one. They exist, because at least two of them are to be found in the H.M.V. catalogue—excerpts, I fancy, from *Tannhäuser* and *Lohengrin*. But in this country there is no demand for them worth speaking of, and the probable reason is that they do not belong to the class of record that appeals to gramophone-lovers ; whereas if the same artist, with her extraordinary celebrity and her unquestionable operatic genius, had given us a dazzling version of *Una voce* or the Mad Scene from *Lucia* her records would be selling by the thousand in every part of the globe. One does not miss chances like this without good cause.

Hence, therefore, the number of sopranos of the *leggiero* type who continue to compete for these valuable prizes, and incidentally strive to surpass each other in the brilliancy and daring of their executive feats. I have been quite amused as well as interested of late, comparing a select collection from various sources of variations upon that evergreen popular theme, the *Una voce* of Rosina, from Rossini's comic masterpiece *The Barber of Seville*. It is an air which, because of its well-nigh inexhaustible opportunities for florid display—opportunities that, in spite of purist arguments to the contrary, were actually provided as well as tolerated by the composer himself—is a peculiarly apt specimen for the purpose in view. Everyone knows it, and most lovers of the old school of Italian singing adore it. Yet how few, even of the cleverest vocalists of to-day, can sing it really well! A veritable *aria d'entrata*, sung by the heroine (written for a mezzo-soprano) when the curtain rises on the second scene of the opera, it demands a certain grandiose dignity and assurance at the start, followed by an immediate transition to sly humour and coquettish caprice, in the expression of which the singer may employ every kind of ornament and showy device known to the *bravura* style. It is because these *fiorituri* have to be supplied by the interpreters (or, rather, by their teachers, for there is not a sign of any of them in the printed copies of the piece) that no two Rosinas will sing *Una voce* to exactly the same pattern. Consequently there is no limit to the extent and variety of the difficulties with which it can be amplified, provided they are made to fit into the framework fashioned by the composer. These " changes," as they are called, used to be regarded as the peculiar property of the singer, and she very rarely attempted to alter or improve them. I believe that Adelina Patti—the greatest of all Rosinas after Malibran, and the finest exponent of *Una voce* I have ever heard—sang the same " changes " all through her long career, except the last ten or fifteen years, when she took the trouble to learn a new set written for her by the conductor Enrico Bevignani, who always accompanied her at Covent Garden. I was staying with her at Craig-y-Nos Castle at the time, and was present when she sang them first at her annual charity concert at Swansea. The wonder of her rendering of this air was that she infused as much comedy into her vocalisation as into her acting of it.

I come now to the consideration of the records of *Una voce* by contemporary artists of eminence, and have before me a selection of five, which, in my opinion, will repay analysis and comparison. They are by Marcella Sembrich, Luisa Tetrazzini, Amelita Galli-Curci, Evelyn Scotney, and Celys Beralta. All are in the same key (F), or a semitone higher than the original; it is, therefore, almost always transposed, but anyhow the difference is very slight. The

opening part of the *cavatina*, as an aria in this form is termed in Italian, is marked *andante*; while the second part, known as the *cabaletta*, is somewhat quicker, being marked in this instance *moderato*. I regret to note, however (especially in the case of Mlle. Beralta), that the effect of the contrast has been spoiled through the undue hurrying of the *andante*. The object of this was, I imagine, to bring the whole piece within the necessary time-limit, but that is no excuse for spoiling the music. It is infinitely better to make a liberal " cut " than alter the character of the piece.

Mme. Sembrich's (H.M.V.—D.B. 341) is at all points the traditional Patti rendering, and sounds best with a loud needle, the recording not being quite so delicate as that of a subsequent date. The singer uses a rather open tone in the medium—a fault of which she was seldom guilty in the concert-room—and thus descends many times to the word *sarò*, with a quality which does not sound pleasing to the ear. But that is her only loophole for criticism. Her scales (and there are plenty of them in the ornamental passages) are simply beyond reproach, and her trill is no less perfect. Everything is of crystalline clearness; you hear every note, no matter how intricate the weaving of the vocal arabesques; and the high D in the cadenza, like the C at the end, is taken without effort. These things are largely due to Sembrich's admirable breathing, in which, as in the unusually rich quality of her " dark " tone, she always reminds me of her acknowledged model, the far-famed " Adelina." In the *cabaletta* the changes may be described as pretty and graceful rather than elaborate; they are not like so many complicated barricades in a vocal obstacle-race. Moreover, it is always pleasant to hear them so neatly and easily mastered by the singer. In this way we get a series of telling effects overcome and presented by simple means.

Mme. Tetrazzini (H.M.V.—D.B. 690) contrives a much more ambitious and imposing structure. The weak point in the armour of this distinguished singer is her *voix blanche*, or colourless tone, in the medium register. (It was probably of that type from the time when she first sang as a girl, and no attempt was made to darken it during or after the period of change to womanhood, as it ought to have been. Later on it becomes a more difficult if not, in some cases, impracticable operation.) Thus at the outset the tone in the *andante* is marred here and there by slightly harsh notes, but directly the melody or the ornamentation gets into the higher part of the scale, the quality of the voice is delightfully pure and sympathetic, the runs are brilliant, the much-used *staccato* is as clear and distinct as the chime of bells, and the descending chromatic scale is a marvel of smoothness and accuracy. The cadenza does not terminate as usual with the high C, but, after a moment's suspension, is carried on with an added series of *roulades*, which ultimately reach their climax upon a group that includes the E in *alt*. In the *cabaletta* Tetrazzini ascends comfortably yet another semitone and to even loftier heights of executive display, wherein the tone reveals a very remarkable natural resonance, due to a naturally more " forward " placing of the voice. Indeed, apart from an occasional abuse of the slur or *portamento* in the melodic passages, I have naught but praise for this portion of an extremely clever record, which I like best played with a soft needle.

The extreme attractiveness of Mme. Galli-Curci's *Una voce* (H.M.V.—D.B. 261) lies in its all-round merit. The rich, satisfying timbre, the essentially Italian quality of the voice, easily produced and managed with rare, unfailing skill, strikes the listener at once. With the very opening phrase you picture Dr. Bartolo's capricious ward in a confidential humour, telling you calmly and with a certain air of dignity what the " still small voice " is whispering to her heart—that she has fallen in love with " Lindoro " (the name assumed by Count Almaviva), and that she means to have him for her very own. A famous French critic once said that in his opinion " there was a great deal of assurance in the song of this persecuted youthful lady, but very little love." I do not agree with him. At any rate, it depends largely upon the manner in which it is sung, and in the Galli-Curci rendering I find something more than the mere " triumph of a beautiful voice." There sounds the pæan of an anticipated victory, followed by the suggestion of the " hundreds of tricks " wherewith the sly Spanish coquette intends to tease and worry her handsome suitor. One feels somehow that the vocalist is all the time acting the character in the old tyrant's study, and that, aided by Figaro, she will overcome with her wiles the safeguards that surround her. Her enunciation is so strong and clear that it makes every word distinct ; there is the same ease of delivery in each sentence that there is in the musical phrase which conveys it. In short, one perceives the effortless suavity that betokens the experienced and accomplished artist whose technique is on a par with her natural gifts, and who imparts a definite reading to whatever she interprets. The breathing is faultless, utterly inaudible, yet so deep that it results in a delightful sense of abundant support and reserve. The medium tone is full, rich, and sympathetic, the head tone lovely in its sweet, pellucid, bell-like clearness of quality. The *arpeggiando* and the *staccato* passages are alike wonderful for their neatness, their delicacy of touch, their impeccable accuracy. In course of these the voice reaches an exceptionally musical E flat in *alt*.

With the beginning of the *cabaletta* we note immediately a change in the colour of Mme. Galli-

Curci's tone. It inclined previously to the *voix sombre*, or dark quality, associated in her mind with Rosina's characteristic assumption of dignity and self-importance. It has now turned no less decidedly to the *voix claire*, or light colour, with all its potentialities of insinuation and sly innuendo. The effect is irresistible, the more so because one could not ask for more finished vocalisation. There is a sense here of dazzling, coruscating brilliancy that reminds me not so much of Adelina Patti as of her scarcely less gifted sister, Carlotta, whom I remember once singing this air at a Covent Garden concert. The *staccato* is particularly wonderful, and the scale passages are quite perfect—so perfect, indeed, that I feel I could never wish to hear anything better. This is all extraordinarily high praise, but the truth of the matter is that in the Galli-Curci record one finds the unmistakable evidence of a great singer, thus compelling the use of superlatives without any danger of falling into exaggerated or too-flattering encomiums. It is, therefore, with good reason that, as far as the singing of Rossini's air is concerned, I feel bound to award the palm to this particular record (best heard with a loud needle), and it makes it quite easy to understand why all who have listened to the famous prima donna on the gramophone are looking foward keenly to her appearance at the Albert Hall in October.

As already hinted, the version given by Celys Beralta (Aeol. Vocal.—C.01081), loses both dignity and charm through being too hurried. I find little to admire, either, in the actual singing. Careless breathing causes an unsteady tone and consequent untidiness in phrasing. The shake is distinct but too long, the *staccato* clear but employed to excess, the cadenza uninteresting because lacking in contrast. If the tempo is too quick at the start of the *andante*, it becomes wilder still in the *cabaletta*, which seems to pursue its course in a headlong chase for " home." The efforts of the orchestra to follow the soloist in this stampede are but too easily defeated ; there is no unity of rhythm between them. The voice rushes persistently on regardless of clean, precise execution or beauty of tone. The high C is not really an agreeable note, and it seems endless in duration. Altogether I arrive at the conclusion that Mlle. Beralta is a showy singer, but possesses no true charm of either voice or style.

On the other hand, there is much to praise in Evelyn Scotney's rendering (Aeol. Vocal.—D.02148), which interested me especially in view of her recent triple appearance at the Albert Hall Sunday concerts, a privilege not accorded to new artists unless they are possessed of exceptional talents. Well, Miss Scotney, who is said to be an Australian, has a lovely voice and has been exceedingly well taught. Her only serious vocal fault is a tendency to drop off the ending note of a phrase with a breathy *diminuendo*, which is the more noticeable because her tone, as a rule, is of limpid clearness and penetrating resonance. Her vocalisation is brilliant and sure, her intonation very true, her *staccato* bright and pure. She rises easily to the high E flat in her first cadenza, which is altogether a pretty bit of execution, while the total effect of the *andante* is quite satisfying. Again, in the *cabaletta* the various changes are neatly done; there is a good sense of rhythm, free from undue haste, and the Italian pronunciation is excellent. On the whole, therefore, this record is to be recommended as an example of good legitimate singing; it proclaims Miss Scotney to be a *soprano leggiero* eminently worthy of being heard and also of being imitated by the advanced student.

HERMAN KLEIN.

(*To be continued.*)

THE GRAMOPHONE AND THE SINGER

(Continued)
By HERMAN KLEIN

Two Famous Verdi Arias

I RECOMMEND an interesting job to some lover of statistics. It is to go through the catalogues of the leading British gramophone firms and tell us the total number of records that have been listed of all operatic pieces from every source, so that we may be able to see at a glance the order in which the composers stand in public favour. What proportion the figures would bear to actual sales could only, of course, be guessed, though according to the laws of supply and demand the result ought to prove much the same, if not absolutely identical. But my sole curiosity in the matter is to ascertain who, in the estimation of gramophone-lovers, is the most popular operatic composer at the present time and in this country. Personally, I have not looked into the question at all closely, and I possess no special information whatever in regard to it. I am therefore only stating an idea when I express my belief that it would be a very near thing in the contest for top place between Verdi and Wagner.

We have to bear in mind, however, that to a certain extent the directing or influencing of public taste in this important matter is in the hands of the singers. Their preference is naturally for the piece that shows them off to the greatest advantage; that is the primary consideration, I fancy, though obviously the popularity of the opera and the piece itself has also to be seriously thought about. Hence the fact that if one vocal celebrity records a certain aria and makes a success of it, half a dozen others will instantly follow suit in other *ateliers* (or perhaps in the same one), striving his or her hardest to outdo the achievement of No. 1, and very often, if the truth be told, succeeding in doing so. Then comes the purchaser of records, with one of two purposes in view : either he wants to buy the best obtainable record of a particular piece without regard to the personality of the singer, or he asks for the Galli-Curci or the Caruso or the Battistini or the Titta Ruffo record of that piece, maybe listens to it in the shop, or possibly doesn't, and anyway, departs perfectly satisfied with his bargain.

I recollect some years ago in New York being asked to pass judgment upon the relative merits of three records of the *Jewel Song* from *Faust*, each by a different singer. Of these I at once recognised two ; the voices were unmistakable. The third voice was new to me, and I declared without hesitation that I had never heard it before. Also I gave it as my opinion that the third record was by far the best, alike from the technical standpoint, as an example of the recording of that period, and for the rendering of the popular waltz-air, which a true artist could always present in beautiful and pleasing fashion, in spite of its being so hackneyed. Now I do not think it fair to mention names in connection with this story, but there is no reason why I should not state that the record which I thought so superior to the others was made by the Fonotipia Company, of Milan, and that it was sung in Italian. The outcome of my opinion was, I believe, distinctly beneficial to the unknown foreign firm, though I knew nothing about that at the time. The point is that we were enabled to discover fresh talent, to hear fine singing by artists whom we had never seen on the stage, to enjoy their rendering of familiar things, to learn to value gramophone records on their merits and not merely by the prestige attaching to distinguished names.

Did I not, like my Editor, detest *clichés*, I should apologise for this " digression," the object of which has only been to make clearer to the reader why I am fond of comparing the manner in which different singers treat the same composition. I want, moreover, to emphasise the fact that Verdi's music of his so-called second period—the period that gave to the world *Rigoletto*, *Il Trovatore*, and *La Traviata*—is, in a sense, as popular to-day as it was sixty years ago ; and that *Caro nome* and *Ah ! fors' è lui* are favourites strong and irresistible at this moment as they ever were, both to the public and the prima donna. So I have been busy studying a selection of each of these airs, and am prepared to deal with them on much the same lines as I dealt with *Una voce* in last month's issue of THE GRAMOPHONE. I wonder how many people think for a moment of the tremendous contrast that is embodied in these two Verdi arias—how far removed from the maidenly innocence and simplicity of the love that is awakening in Gilda, the exquisite glow of girlish infatuation as she dwells rapturously upon the echoing sound of the name, false as the lips that breathed it, which she has just heard for the first time—how strangely unlike to this is that other solitary confession at the end of the first act of the *Traviata*, when the notorious Dame aux Camélias makes the discovery, after all her hectic experiences, that she too has at last succumbed to a serious passion and determines (in vain, as we know) to resist it to the uttermost. Well, this extraordinary contrast has been caught and depicted in a way that is thoroughly worthy of the grand old musician of Busseto. He stamped them both with his hall-mark ; and yet two pieces of love-music could hardly differ more completely in the nature of their sentiment, in their mode of treatment, in the quality of the musical passion that pervades each.

The recitatives are quite dissimilar. That of Gilda is pensive and dreamy ; she reiterates the name of her student-lover with the restrained delight of one to whom its mere utterance is a new-found joy. So brief is this thrill of a few bars that one wonders by what process of reasoning it could have been omitted from the aria to which it so naturally and spontaneously leads us. Yet it appears in none of the records of *Caro nome* now before me except that of Mme. Galli-Curci ; they all start crudely and without preface (beyond the introduction for the two flutes) with the opening phrase of the aria. Another cut to which I object is the lopping-off of the delicate little coda which follows the final cadenza and without which the piece is incomplete. In it Gilda once again murmurs the beloved name and repeats the theme on the down-scale, then takes her lamp and, as she mounts the steps outside the verandah, finishes with a prolonged shake on the E–F sharp. The Melba record is the only one which contains this coda.

In *Ah ! fors' è lui* Verdi followed more closely the lines of the regular *cavatina*. The recitative is more elaborate, more dramatic than the *Rigolètto*, and winds up with a showy passage, expressive of Violetta's naturally joyous disposition, which every prima donna from Patti downward has always revelled in. But how few seem to reproduce in the gramophone the atmosphere of the air that follows ! —the surging tides of emotion as they rise and contend for mastery in that marvellous phrase, " A quell'amor ch'è palpito dell' universo intero," the intense yearning of the woman's soul to share in those purer joys of the world that have so far been denied her. The music realises it ; the singing rarely, even on the stage. The *cabaletta*, or final quick movement, fares better as a rule. " Sempre libera ! " she declares ; " I will remain free to enjoy my life of pleasure ; " and though she does not mean it, it sounds very genuine, very resolute, as she dashes off the brilliant *roulades* and ends (at least Patti did) with a trill on the G-A flat that lasts for twenty bars or thereabouts. Thus, when all is said and done, the contrast between these two airs is so profound and complete that it requires an accomplished actress as well as an accomplished singer to bring it into full and striking relief. I will not, however, pursue comparisons further, but proceed to describe each record on its merits and so leave my readers to draw their own conclusions. I begin with *Caro nome*.

The Melba example (H.M.V.—D.B.346) is notable for its simplicity and almost literal adherence to the text. We realise at once that this is not another *Una voce*, otherwise a sort of vocal *mannequin* to be loaded with an abundance of external decoration. The ornamentation is quite plain where there is any ; the shakes are faultless ; the recording is fairly good ; and the tone very characteristic, even to the constant use (or rather misuse) of the chest quality wherever practicable. Why could it not all have been made as lovely as that exquisite " Gualtier Maldè ! " when the singer warbles it in the coda ? But, for aught that is to be found here of real tenderness or depth of expression, Mme. Melba might just as well have been singing a *solfège* as a love-song. And *Caro nome*, being in point of fact a series of clever variations on the down-scale of E major, nothing more, is just one of those pieces that the vocalist can readily convert into a mere vehicle for mechanical display. Changes of tempo alone impart no variety, and those graceful " skips " from B natural to G sharp lose all their prettiness when the lower note is sung so jerkily as to be inaudible—a mistake of which nearly every Gilda is nowadays guilty.

I am sorry to have to say much the same things

about Mme. Sembrich (H.M.V. — D.B.431) and Mme. Tetrazzini (H.M.V. — D.B.536), so far as *Caro nome* is concerned. Both appear to have been too much obsessed with thoughts of the mechanical process to be able to project the right kind of tone or expressive sentiment into their artistry ; both are inclined to be serious and heavy, both indulge in the open chest quality where it sounds unpleasant, and, in short, both have done much finer work in far more exacting solos. On the other hand, I find little that is not deserving of praise in the Galli-Curci record (H.M.V.—D.B. 257), which, as I have previously noted, starts at the right spot and might easily, with a little extra care, have been made quite perfect by sustaining the long notes with true intonation and on a steady instead of a slightly tremulous tone. The tempo of the air at the outset is a trifle deliberate for *allegro moderato* (crotchet 76), and later on becomes even more dragged until after the *tenuto* on the G sharp (held on a lovely note) as marked by Verdi. Thence the time quickens, the intonation becomes faultless, the semiquaver skips are smoothly and evenly sung, and the slurred notes which succeed them are rendered with exquisite grace and distinctness. The following section on the quavers in C major, modulating back to E, gains by not being hurried ; and then comes the cadenza, which greatly resembles Mme. Tetrazzini's without being quite so extended and ends with a lovely if lengthy high B which might fairly be described as "linkèd sweetness long drawn out." This prolonged *messa di voce* is a favourite device of Mme. Galli-Curci's, but here possibly it adds to the charm of a very charming record, which comes out well on my Sonora Model.

Of the four Vocalion records of *Caro nome* the best is that of Evelyn Scotney (A.0191), conspicuous alike for neat phrasing, distinct enunciation, and excellent recording. The "skips" are hurried and uneven, but, as usual, this artist sings her cadenzas boldly without overdoing her effects, nor does she spoil her tone by any approach to forcing. As much can scarcely be said of Celys Beralta (C.01082) or Elsie Cochrane (C.01014), who betray plainly enough the sense of effort and the inability to imbue the music with something of its dramatic purport. The former, particularly, makes the mistake of employing excessive breath-pressure, and thus hardens her tone besides making it unsteady and disagreeable. The fourth, by Lucette Korsoff (C.01044) is sung in French to a piano accompaniment. Dreamy, sentimental, careful throughout, it is nevertheless taken too slowly and gradually engenders a feeling of dullness—a desire to yawn in sympathy with an obviously sleepy Gilda, so tired that she must be glad to light her candle and go to bed. Alas, that she should have to be disturbed so soon !

With regard to *Ah ! fors' è lui*, I may state at once that the earlier records are interesting mainly on account of the famous *prime donne* who sang them. We are not truly listening here to the voices of Melba (H.M.V.—D.B.346), of Sembrich (H.M.V.—D.B.434), or even of the slightly later Tetrazzini (H.M.V.—D.B.531) as those voices actually sounded when the records were made. I say nothing on that score, therefore, beyond advising a soft needle for the first, and a loud one for the second and third. The first two again cut out the recitatives entirely and so manage to include a brilliant but mutilated version of the *cabaletta*, "Sempre libera." That was how they contrived to compress and economise in the old days. On the other hand, the Tetrazzini is in two parts, on a double disc ; but commits the error of omitting the preliminary recit. " E strano " (for which there was plenty of room), and then on the other side, strangely enough, provides an entire " repeat " of the " Sempre libera," which I cannot remember to have heard done more than once or twice on the stage in all my experience. However, there are the familiar pure tone and smooth legato, the inevitable descending chromatic scale in the cadenzas, the queer liberties with the text, and the bright, animated reading with which Tetrazzini used to make us feel that the Dame aux Camélias was a rather, jolly, careless, joyous sort of creature after all. Really it is because Violetta in this air depicts so many moods that we want the whole of it, not merely snippets, and we resent the omissions accordingly. I have no particular criticism to offer on other grounds of Frieda Hempel's rendering (H.M.V.—D.B.294), except that it is quite conventional and not on the whole very interesting. But that of Graziella Pareto (H.M.V. —D.B.565) gains enormously by being in two parts, one on each side of the same disc, thus practically giving the entire air from start to finish. The voice is of delightful quality and the *sostenuto* tone well brought out in an admirable bit of recording ; though no additional pathos and no gasp on the *staccato* were needed to emphasise the melancholy feeling (ought it to be so extremely sad ?) with which Violetta realises that she has at last seen the man whom she can love. Every passage proclaims the musician, save that short cadenza leading from the " Follie " to the " Sempre libera,' which, by the way, Sullivan borrowed for Mabel's waltz-air, " Poor wandering one," in *The Pirates of Penzance*. In Evelyn Scotney's record (Voc. —A.O 156) the *cabaletta* is missing altogether ; otherwise I like it for its clear tone and neat vocalisation, though I suspect that the singer stood a little too close to the receiver.

I have left Mme. Galli-Curci's (H.M.V.-D.B.257) specimen of *Ah ! fors' è lui* for the last, because in my opinion this gifted artist again carries off the palm in almost every essential that goes to the making of a thoroughly satisfying record. Oddly enough, it is on the reverse side of the disc which contains *Caro nome*, while to obtain the *Sempre libera* you must purchase a separate 10in. disc (H.M.V.—D.A.216) with which is issued as companion piece the touching passage from *La Traviata* entitled *Addio, del passato*. However, with these two records you obtain complete versions of the pieces I have been dealing with, and, as it seems to me, at little more than the cost of one. Only one thing do I dislike in the Galli-Curci rendering and that is the hysterical laugh after the "Follie" episode. One might not object to it merely as a novelty were it not distinctly out of place—an effect that is all very well when done by the half-demented

Canio when calling himself contemptuously a "Pagliaccio!" Violetta wishes to forget, truly, but she is not precisely in the humour to vent her feelings in a mocking laugh. But never mind; the tone of this record is beautiful, the singing correct and full of contrast, the phrasing generally so artistic that one readily forgives the frequent *portamenti* and the long-held high notes in the sheer enjoyment of the sensuous charm of the whole thing. Another point : Verdi's text is reproduced with accuracy, the notes are as he put them down, and the awkward bits in the coda just before the end are not facilitated by alterations such as those which disfigure one or two of the records previously mentioned. In this respect Mme. Galli-Curci is a model for some of her rivals.

HERMAN KLEIN.

THE GRAMOPHONE AND THE SINGER
(Continued)
By HERMAN KLEIN
The Prologue to "Pagliacci"

HOW came there to be a prologue to *Pagliacci*? I had the answer to that question from Leoncavallo himself, when he visited London in 1893 to superintend the production of his opera at Covent Garden in May, 1893. "I wrote the prologue," he told me, "as an afterthought; as an inducement to a clever, but rather egotistical baritone whom I wanted to sing the part of Tonio, but who did not think the part, as it stood in the opera, quite important enough for an artist of his distinction. Perhaps he was right. Anyhow I thought the matter over and hit upon the idea that a prologue, sung before the curtain by one of the humblest characters, would prove something of a novelty and by no means out of place. Being, as you know, my own librettist, I quickly wrote the words and sketched the music. My baritone was delighted, both with the notion and the result, and I am bound to add that it proved one the most striking features of the opera when I brought it out at the Dal Verme, Milan, just a year ago." (e.g., on May 21st, 1892). Like his gifted countryman Boïto, the composer of *Mefistofele*, who curiously enough was also in England that same summer to receive his doctor's degree at Cambridge, Leoncavallo was a singularly modest man, and wanted no credit for a lucky hit which he had regarded in the light of a *pis aller*.

There was, I remember, great excitement in operatic London over the production of *Pagliacci*, which was given on the Friday of Sir Augustus

Harris's opening week—his sixth Covent Garden season. Only eighteen months previously *Cavalleria Rusticana* had created a sensation when performed here for the first time at the Shaftesbury Theatre, and the popularity of the newer opera had been reported equally great not only in Italy, but in Berlin and Vienna as well. Covent Garden was crowded from floor to ceiling and there was the air of expectancy that one associates with special occasions. Luigi Mancinelli was the conductor; calm, collected, but energetic as ever, just the man to throw all the necessary spirit into the animated prelude that precedes the prologue. An instant's pause, and the strange thing happened. The tableau curtains parted, and there stood before us, uttering his quaint, polite "Si può?" that singularly handsome man, Mario Ancona, made up into the ugliest of red-nosed Tonios, begging that he might lay before us the motive of this new version of an ancient domestic tragedy. Deftly, and with infinite feeling did Ancona heighten our curiosity and envelop the house with just the correct atmosphere for appreciating the picturesque force of the episode that was to be enacted. His rugged but sentimental clown prepared us for the rest of the actors in the drama—the strong, sympathetic *pagliaccio* of De Lucia, the sly, furtive columbine of Melba, the serious harlequin of Bonnard, the persuasive lover of the English baritone, Richard Green. The new-old story, when it did come, held us under a spell, and the music seemed to satisfy our expectation of something unfamiliar yet essentially Italian ; music with a clever technique underlying a wealth of melody ; music that, without being original, copied nobody's and answered its purpose, and, like Mascagni's, followed in the wake of Ponchielli and Boïto to strengthen the foundations of what we had begun to recognise as the Young Italian school. Such was the idea that Leoncavallo embodied and concentrated in the strain of this unpremeditated " ugly duckling " which, had it come at the end instead of the beginning, one might have called the swan-song of the opera. Great music it could never be designated ; but graphic and picturesque, spontaneous and well-contrasted in its descriptive force I have always thought it ; and, as such, by far the best that Leoncavallo ever wrote. I agreed with my old colleague, the late R. A. Streatfield, who, when he " measured " this composer for " Grove's Dictionary," said of him : " In operas of the type of *Zaza* and *Pagliacci* his strong feeling for theatrical effect serves him well, but his sheer musical inspiration is singularly deficient, and his more pretentious works are hardly more than strings of ill-digested reminiscences." His version of *La Bohème*, which I have never heard, was beaten out of the field long ago by Puccini's, and his *Medici* is generally admitted to be a terribly tiresome opera. But his *Pagliacci* has never looked back, in this country or any other, since that memorable night in 1893, when Covent Garden rang for ten minutes with frantic applause whilst the artists were searching for the composer, and Dame Melba dragged him from under a piece of scenery into the glare of the then newly-installed electric footlights. And now if you please we will go back to the *Prologue* and " Ring up the curtain ! "

Yet before dealing with the records I would like to say with Tonio " A word, allow me ! " First, then, this opera should never be labelled *I Pagliacci*. Leoncavallo called it simply *Pagliacci* without the definite article, which he always objected to if any one superfluously used it. But the mistake was often made, and it continues to be made to this day, by writers who ought to know better. Secondly, I have never liked the late F. E. Weatherly's translation of the libretto, and particularly that of the *Prologue*. It fails frequently to convey the true meaning of the Italian lines ; it has many false accents and little poetic quality. However, it is too late, I fear, to remedy this ; for bad operatic translations, once generally employed, are extremely difficult to dislodge. Another point. The *Prologue*—one of those universally popular things which every baritone regards it as a duty to sing—is far from the easy show-piece to do justice to that it appears to be. It does not " sing itself " by any means. Hence the fact that one so frequently hears it shamefully maltreated by the amateur and the incompetent professional. It calls for an extensive range both of voice and dramatic feeling. If not phrased with distinction and charm it can sound exceedingly commonplace, and it lends itself only too readily to exaggeration. Snatches of melody that have always reminded me of *Maritana*, and might certainly have been written by Vincent Wallace or our beloved Balfe, require the touch of an artist to raise them above the level of the obvious and the ordinary. (They may possibly never quite permit the achievement of that feat.) I am aware that certain altered notes and substituted high ones are now considered *de rigueur* in this piece, and will soon, no doubt, be regarded as traditional. But these, after all, are only so many added effects which the composer did not authorise, and, unless they can be executed without the smallest betrayal of effort, had better not be attempted at all. Unfortunately, the singer who dared omit the interpolated G's or A flats would be accused either of ignorance or of inability to sing them, so that he has very little choice in the matter. So far as the actual recording is concerned, the *Prologue* seems to present unusual difficulties to others besides the singer. I have yet to hear a perfect record of it. The orchestral accompaniment almost invariably comes out rough and blurred—worse, that is to say, than it sounds in the opera house ; while the fragmentary nature of the music, with its frequent violent contrasts, tends to produce marked inequalities of vocal timbre and a pervading lack of tonal smoothness.

Beginning with the English examples, I find most to praise in that of Peter Dawson (H.M.V., C.968), which fills both sides of the disc and is complete from the first note of the orchestral prelude ; it does not annoy you by a single cut anywhere. The instrumentation, notably the brass and wood-wind, also comes out better than in most cases. I like the strong accent and bold diction of the singer, though I wish his vowel tones were less variable in form and quality and the customary absence of sibilant sounds less noticeable. The breathing is good, and there was no need, surely, to interrupt the voice so long at the rest on the phrase " and he marked the time," a break for which the English words make no allowance. On the whole, too, the dramatic character is faithfully reproduced, and the recording excellent. After this I had to ask myself why another good baritone, George Baker, should have preferred the original text to his own native tongue (Voc. Red., C.01012). Not that the Italian is badly pronounced when it is audible, but for the most part it might as well be Greek or Chaldaic. The singing is also unequal and very spasmodic. The notes are vigorously attacked but invariably drop off with a diminuendo. One cannot help admiring the quality of the voice, especially in the phrase " Un nido," which is beautifully sung. The G at the end is taken with apparent effort. Altogether this record makes me wish the singer would have another try—in English this time.

The capital work that Mr. Frederick Collier has been doing with the B.N.O.C. led me to expect better results than are perceptible in Aco., F.33041. His vowels are not altogether Cockney, but they are distinctly of the colloquial order, without being too musical at that. Even more disappointing is the voice, which lacks the true *sostenuto* or continuity of smooth tone which this music demands. It is decidedly jerky in delivery and there is a sense of hurry that frequently mars the dramatic effect. It is as though Tonio had received orders to get back behind the curtain as quickly as possible. On the other hand, it is also true that the acceleration of the *tempi* has enabled him to squeeze his entire *Prologue* into one side of a disc without cuts. And yet, with all its faults, I prefer Mr. Collier's rendering to that of Mr. Thorpe Bates (Col., 486), the last of the English records of this piece with which I propose to deal here. A lengthy career in comic opera has not improved this artist's style, mellowed his tone, or added clarity to his diction, which on the concert platform used to be quite good. He now exaggerates most of his vowels. A " word " with him becomes a " war " ; " sends " becomes converted into " sands " ; and his " mem'ries " are naught but " mam'ries." Besides these and similar solecisms Mr. Bates is guilty of over-sentimentalising his utterances and charging them with more breath than a gramophone record can conveniently absorb. The latter error takes much of the " edge " off his tone, particularly in the longer notes and more sustained passages. Yet it is and always has been intrinsically a fine voice, even though this record proclaims that it is beginning to betray signs of wear and tear. So far as the recording is concerned, I am of opinion that full justice has been done alike to the singer and his theme.

In a very careful interpretation by Stewart Gardner (H.M.V., D.225) I seem to perceive the influence of a sound oratorio training. There is an air of solemnity about it which suggests the idea of " It is enough," yet not with sufficient dramatic energy and animation for " Is not His word like a fire ? " The voice is of pleasant baritone quality and well placed ; the English words are correctly pronounced, even when glossed over for the sake of the tone ; and, bar the cut, which was not really indispensable, the record is a good one.

I shall not surprise my readers when I express the opinion that, as a whole, the Italian records of the *Prologue* attain a higher level of declamatory merit than the native group above noticed. I do not say, of course, that they are all equally good ; but the best of them are superior in other features of excellence besides, such as sustained sonority and volume of tone and bolder attempts at characterisation.

Perhaps the earliest of these, in point of date, is that of Giuseppe Campanari, an artist not unknown to Londoners, although the greater part of his stage career has been spent in America. His voice in this record (Col., A.5126) still sounds fresh and bright and has a true baritone ring which I have always admired. His words, too, are notably clear, despite a tendency to let the final syllable die away. To-day, probably, he would not be asked to make the stupid cut which eliminates a salient passage almost at the outset ; neither would up-to-date recording have permitted the freakish variations of tonality which occur during the *andante cantabile* (" E poi "—" Ah think then "), lifting the voice gradually a whole semitone from D flat to D natural. This blemish quite spoils an otherwise smooth and interesting performance. More satisfactory results are secured in the Ricardo Stracciari (Col., 7355), in which there is no cut. Not only is the recording vastly superior, but the volume and balance of the orchestra show a distinct advance in the modern methods of this firm, being extremely rich and full. The singing is rhythmical, authoritative, and charged with ample sentiment ; even if the tone be slightly muffled at times and the G and A flat at the end a trifle shaky. But first and foremost Stracciari is a dramatic artist and one feels the intensity of his colouring in every detail of the picture. Altogether a very satisfactory record, this.

The chief point in favour of Ramon Blanchart (Col., A.5206), is that he makes no cut. In his singing there is much to criticise, had I the space for it ; but indeed the faults are sufficiently obvious— " a conspicuous tremolo ; a tendency to drag ; heavy, laboured declamation ; little real spirit ; not very pleasing high notes ; on the whole, a dull and uninspiring rendering." Such were my pencilled remarks as I listened to this record.

I have never seen Ugo Donarelli (V.F., 552), but he has a capital voice of rather heavy calibre, and plods steadily on, with little change or variety, as if he could keep at it like that all day. His style is vocal without being truly dramatic, broad and vigorous, but relieved by so little contrast that one fears he would make a tedious, common-place Tonio. Yet might one do worse than imitate his method of declaiming, which is more clearly defined than the actual enunciation of his words—a distinction worthy the attention of students. The high notes are well taken and held. The accompaniment, however, suggests a brass band, or at least strings so badly placed as to be inaudible. There is the usual absurd cut of the *meno mosso*, both in this and in the example of that fine artist, Pasquale Amato (Fonotip., 74142), which I like immensely in almost every respect, artistic and mechanical, save that the voice sounds low for the *tessitura* of the music. Amato gives the impression here of being a *basso cantante*, or next door to one; and the *Prologue* was not written for a voice of that type. Nevertheless, it has the advantage of displaying a broad, opulent tone, with ample scope for delicate gradations of colour and feeling, and never an approach to exaggeration, simply because Amato is too much of an artist to use undue effort or introduce high notes which he cannot sing easily. It is a pleasure to listen to such a smooth *sostenuto*, such pure, refined tone, such artistic phrasing. The music is exactly as the composer wrote it, and I, for one, do not miss the high notes even if I complain that the voice sounds heavy; there is a good high G on the "Incominciate," and that quite suffices. By the way, the very lowest Continental pitch seems to have been adopted by the Fonotipia people in this record, which may partially account for the singer appearing to be so far down in the depths. I found some difficulty in adjusting the pitch so that the voice vibrated well in the proper key, but it came out better when I raised it nearly a semitone. Another Fonotipia record (B.92293) is that of Ferrucio Corradetti, a baritone who evidently takes himself and his task very seriously. He begins dismally, then wakes up a bit, then becomes tragic again, and eventually brings his *Prologue* to a close without mentioning the curtain—perhaps because there was none to ring up. The whole thing sounds rather like a funeral "with maimed rites."

On the other hand, Renato Zanelli gives us (H.M.V., D.A.398) every note of the *Prologue*, from the start of the orchestral prelude, in a two-sided 10-inch disc which is technically quite first-rate. (There is a mistake in the nomenclature of the second label, because the *Nido di memorie* concludes the first section, whilst the second begins with the subsequent *Dunque (Come then)*; but this small error can esaily be corrected.) More important is the fact that this singer has a capital organ and is evidently an intelligent actor. Were his style a little less ponderous and deliberate, less marred by *parlato* effects where we look for voice, I should feel inclined to rank this effort very high indeed. And why, after all, should a "song of tender mem'ries," even if written with "sighs and tears," call forth such pathetic, lachrymose tones, almost, sobs, indeed, from Tonio in the *Prologue*? We are listening to the man, it is true; but there is an alarming tendency in these days to overdo the "sob-stuff."

With this I conclude for the present—having already exceeded my space tether—this review of the *Prologue* records, and in doing so I would like to thank the gramophone companies for their courtesy in placing them at my disposal. At the same time I have by no means exhausted the list, and it may be that I shall have to refer to a second batch later on.

P.S.—I gladly respond to the request of Mr. H. F. V. Little for a few words concerning Eugénie Bronskaya's *Una Voce* (Col., A.5209). It is certainly well worth hearing, alike for the beauty of the voice, which is sympathetic, flexible and musical, and the brilliancy of the *coloratur*, which includes a splendid shake, lovely scales, and a good *legato*. This soprano sings with conspicuous ease and certainty of style as well as impeccable intonation, and she should certainly go far. The faults I find are a tendency to pause too long on particular high notes and to pinch occasionally in the head register; also to over-elaborate "changes," which are not invariably appropriate to the Rossinian style. This version of the aria is more than full—it is running over.

HERMAN KLEIN.

THE GRAMOPHONE AND THE SINGER

(Continued)

By HERMAN KLEIN

"Celeste Aïda" and more "Prologue"

WE return to Verdi. Not, however, to the Verdi of the second or middle period, as represented by *Traviata* and *Rigoletto*, but to the great Egyptian opera which ushered in the third and final period of the illustrious Italian composer. I am one of those who recognise in his music the existence of these three separate and distinct " styles," as they are termed ; and I may add that I feel them almost as much in his writing for the voice as in the turn of the melody, the development of the harmonic structure, and the changes in the mode of orchestration. In some ways, indeed, *Aïda* seems to stand alone, as it were, in a period by itself ; for neither before nor after did Verdi write an opera of precisely the same type. Never before, certainly, did he provide for a quartet of leading characters music that maintained such a steady, continuous demand upon their voices for the maximum of stamina and resisting power (Wagner was the only composer who went further in this direction, and then it was in a different fashion). He had not been in the habit of letting his singers off lightly, it is true ; but *Aïda* opened up a new vista for them, and I formed the impression immediately on a certain hot night in June, 1876, as I sat in the gallery of Covent Garden listening to the first performance in England of this fascinating and original work.

I dare not linger to dwell at any length upon the memories of that wonderful night. It was a superb cast : Adelina Patti the Aïda, Scalchi the Amneris, Nicolini the Radamès, Maurel the Amonasro, and Bagagiolo the Ramfis ; and the striking *décor* sent over expressly by Ricordi from Milan seemed to convey one into the very heart of the Nile country, though I thought rather too much fuss was made of the new long shrill trumpets used in the scene of Radamès's entry. But if the opera was a revelation, so was the surprising experience that the delicate " little lady " who was wont to delight us as Rosina, Violetta, Zerlina, etc., should have proved fully equal to the task of sustaining without the slightest symptom of fatigue such an intensely dramatic rôle as Aïda. Patti had studied the music with Verdi himself, and he always said that no one but the original Aïda, the gifted Teresina Stolz (who created the part when the opera was first mounted for the inauguration of the

Khedivial theatre at Cairo in 1871), had ever sung the air *O cieli azzuri* with the same degree of charm. To the general astonishment, Patti acted it with a measure of emotional and dramatic fervour such as she had never previously manifested, while her voice sounded as clear and strong in the final duet as in the opening act. Her triumphs at that memorable *première* were, I may add, fully shared by the famous contralto, Scalchi, and by the French tenor who subsequently became her second husband, Ernest Nicolini. It was a remarkable achievement for a rather *petite* soprano of the *coloratura* stamp who had then been singing at Covent Garden for fifteen years (and before the public as child and woman for eleven more) ; and, as such, I have always held it up to my pupils as the paramount example of what a singer and artist whom men thought worthy to be called the " diva " was capable of accomplishing.

I cannot forget either how magnificently Nicolini sang *Celeste Aïda* on the same notable occasion. In spite of the persistent tremolo that always afflicted him (and his hearers), he declaimed with splendid vigour an air which I have generally regarded as the most awkward and trying that Verdi ever wrote for the tenor voice. It dwells in my mind as the model alike for phrasing and general rendering, and I only wish the invention of the gramophone had come in time for it to have been recorded by this elegant exemplar of the heroic French school. Jean de Reszke sang it no less beautifully on the night of his début (as. a tenor) in *Aïda* at Drury Lane eleven years later ; but he also never made records, though his brother Edouard did, unfortunately long after his noble bass voice had passed its prime. If memory may* be trusted, the first good record of *Celeste Aïda* that I ever heard was among a number sung by the famous tenor Tamagno, and played for me especially by the artist himself one summer afternoon, when I went over from Lugano to visit him at his *castello* on the outskirts of Varese. It was most interesting ; not merely hearing the records for the first time in the early days, but to watch Tamagno as he stood by his H.M.V. machine, at times leaning lovingly over it, listening all the while with profound enjoyment to the tones of his own robust, colossal voice. From time to time he would ejaculate with a broad smile " Che

*There is no such recording known today (Ed.)

bellezza!" or "Com 'è bello, non è ver?" And I could but agree that it did sound fine, though I was never quite sure whether Tamagno's admiration was mostly aroused by the sound of his voice, or his singing, or by the reproduction of both on the gramophone.

The short recitative before *Celeste Aïda*, with its repeated martial fanfare, embodies a quick *volte-face* from the warrior to the lover, and leads without break to the *romanza* in which Radamès pours out his adoration for the bewitching Ethiopian slave. This is largely based upon a simple tune of five notes up the scale from the dominant, skipping thence to the octave, and, thanks to that very diatonic simplicity, requires a good ear to sing it each time in perfect tune. (The interval of a fifth is too often slurred up, whereas Verdi meant it to be sung *legato*. The interval of a third he did intend to be sung with *portamento*, and has so marked it.) The style of the whole number is unlike that of any aria the master had ever previously penned. It demands the utmost suavity of delivery so as not to sound a trifle commonplace, but the sustained high *tessitura* makes this difficult to accomplish. The originality lies in the treatment more than in the music; and indeed it may amuse you to recognise in one little phrase—so simple is the notation —the extremely familiar bit of melody (accompanied here in the minor key) which goes to the second sentence of our National Anthem. The Italian words are "le dolci brezze del patrio suol," but in this country we sing the same tune to "Long live our noble King, God save the King." By the way, I am doubtful whether this absurd coincidence has been pointed out before; but there it is, and you can hear it for yourself.

If I am not mistaken, the oldest of these Italian records of *Celeste Aïda* is that made by Florencio Constantino (Col. A.679), an amiable and excellent tenor whom I met in New York years ago when he was singing for the Columbia Co. It is also one of the best. The voice is characterised by the ease and purity of a natural production, sympathetic in quality, delightfully in tune throughout, a welcome example of the perfect alliance of words and melody. There might be more contrast in the recitative and possibly a trifle more passion in the aria. But Constantino goes for beauty of effect, and there are plenty of singers who do the other thing. He regards his outpouring not so much as a safety-valve for the hidden volcano of his love

HIPOLITO LAZARO

as a suave poetic soliloquy to tell us his state of feeling; and he is right. After all, there is nothing Teutonic about this dusky but well-behaved warrior.

Another capital record is that of Giovanni Martinelli (H.M.V., D.B.335), a tenor whom I have always held in high esteem. His intonation is definite and beyond reproach; he keeps the sequences of scale-notes smooth and even, with a fine sense of continuity; his breathing is ample and noiseless; and he imparts not only distinctness but dramatic edge to his enunciation. One feels the authority and decision in his clear, ringing tone from the outset, while the aria is given out with sustained power and not a suspicion of strain. On the other hand, Martinelli has a better B flat than he displays here. He was probably told to "step back" when making it, and went too far. Nevertheless, a worthy record.

It is a curious but eloquent proof of the trying nature of this piece that nearly every singer of it shines to less advantage towards the end than at the start. Even the giant vocal physique of Hipolito Lazaro (Col. 7342) betrays a slight falling-off, his final B flat (not well approached) being decidedly inferior to that which occurs in the middle. What a huge tone!—the biggest I have heard since Tamagno's, and, like his, inclined to be nasal. But it is a genuine *tenore robusto*, and gives an impression of unlimited power in reserve. Now please note: when I tried this record first in the original key of B flat (hard needle) it sounded dull, wheezy; but when I played it again a semi-tone higher I found that was the right key for it. Evidently Lazaro sang it in B major, for the tone sounded clear and true at the accelerated pace—and again I say, what a tone! The high notes are of great power, taken with ease and held without effort, and, despite one or two moments of exaggeration, one appreciates the real Southern feeling of the artist, especially that sudden change to the *mezza voce* after the high B on the return to the principal phrase. His *portamentos* are ultra-liberal, but also quite traditional. Take him for all in all, Hipolito Lazaro is a singer to whom you can listen with a delightful sense of security and satisfaction, and his *Celeste Aïda* is decidedly the best of my more recent modern group.

Two Slavonic examples need not detain us long. Neither Vladimir Rosing (Voc. A.0187) nor Leo Slezák (Col. A.5396) possesses the essential joyousness of tone for expressing a happy Radamès. They anticipate his melancholy state of mind in the Nile scene. Rosing slurs up and down like a vocal switchback; his vowels are hazy and un-Italian; he trembles sadly on the long notes, and his hollow timbre smacks rather of the horn. The orchestral accompaniment, for a wonder, errs on the loud side, and the recording, on the whole, is not very satisfactory. The Slezák record owes its deficiencies entirely to the singer—mainly faulty breathing, a slow, dull delivery, an imperfect scale, and last but not least, inaudible consonants.

Of three records by Englishmen I prefer that of Thomas Burke (Col. 7347), which is sung in what Hamlet called "choice Italian," and with a no less choice quality of Italian voice. The head tone is especially brilliant, and, but for a tendency to get a shade sharp at times, there would really be little fault to find. Burke's declamation is admirable, and though he shares a common failing in finishing his big notes with a jerk, one forgives it for the sake of his dramatic sincerity and strong sense of climax. I cannot, unluckily, award the same meed of praise to Frank Mullings (Col. L.1349), whose energy is so often carried to the point of excess. Here the voice is too noisy for the weak accompaniment, and there is little balance anywhere. The singer uses a quaint translation by Paul England (something about "Celestial Aïda, daughter of heaven"), but really the language might just as well be any other as his own. The recitative promised better things. The tone in the aria is clear and pleasing enough until it begins to spoil the effect by getting sharp, and then the case becomes hopeless—fine notes here and there, truly, but the final B flat a mere shout. Why do some tenors exaggerate in this way, and so frequently go off the key in consequence? Another English record, by William Davidson (Aco. F.33045), suffers from the opposite blemish, namely, a style lacking in assurance and a voice more remarkable for sweetness than stamina. Parts of it are pretty and musically rendered, but, properly speaking, Celeste Aïda ought not to be sung with gentle touches only or finish up with a falsetto B flat.

It is sixteen years since Giovanni Zenatello made his début at Covent Garden, but I had heard him the previous winter at the Manhattan Opera House, New York, and then formed a high estimate of his powers. The more disappointing, therefore, because he was a splendid Radamès, is the evidence that he did not succeed in achieving a good record of Celeste Aïda (Col. A.5400), whenever that record was made. It positively groans under the weight of a persistent vibrato and a lachrymose, sobbing delivery. Nor does the trouble end there. The portamento is carried to an irritating excess, the phrasing lacks refinement, the voice sounds rough and emitted with jerks and apparent effort. In short, I can only repeat, Zenatello ought certainly to have done better than this.

An admirable specimen in every way is the Enrico Caruso (H.M.V. D.B.144), which I had the good fortune to hear on that well-constructed instrument, the Vocarola. The two things seemed to me worthy of each other; the purity of the singing was matched by the purity of the mechanical reproduction, and between them they revived agreeable memories of the greatest tenor that this century has so far seen. The effect of the whole was one of singular clearness, of notes clean cut as the facets of a diamond. It was thus that Caruso sang Celeste Aïda on the stage; without fuss or hurry, calm yet ecstatic, beautifully phrased, without ever a slur from the C to the F in the initial theme; the characteristic Caruso tone, velvety, liquid, mellifluous and unforced from the first note to the last. It was in this mood, too, that I liked him best. The task did not call for profound or passionate expression, which was never really Caruso's strong point.

The "Pagliacci" Prologue (concluded)

The four records with which I now complete my review of the Prologue must be included among the pick of the series, and I take them, as usual, in the order in which I happen to have played them on my Sonora model. First, then, comes the Emilio de Gogorza (H.M.V. D.A.485), a baritone whose reputation has been chiefly won in the American concert room. He was once (and for aught I know may still be) the "musical advisor" of the Victor Company in New York, and further distinguished himself by becoming the second husband of that talented prima donna, Mme. Emma Eames. I fear de Gogorza must be held responsible for the mutilated version of the Prologue, as rendered by himself and the two singers next mentioned in this article, for all three are exactly alike in this respect; the fourth is the exception, as we shall see in due course. But the de Gogorza label is wrong. It describes the piece as Parte I. If it be so, where is the Parte II.? Never mind, though; it is capitally sung, the dark, rich tone comes out with manly effect in broad, measured phrases, despite a certain hollowness that is apt now and then to suggest the influence of a megaphone. The high G at the end is clear and easy.

Antonio Scotti has not been heard in London for some years. I am told, however, that his voice is wearing well, even if it be no longer quite so fresh and resonant as it sounds in this record (H.M.V. D.B. 422). Still it is with the latter that I am for the moment solely concerned, and hasten to add that it renews a pleasant recollection of one of the best Tonios that ever filled the rôle either at Covent Garden or the Metropolitan Opera House. The tone is natural and sympathetic, particularly at the outset. Something of a tremolo, I admit, but scarcely enough to be objectionable. (I have known Scotti to be as steady as a rock, when he exercised sufficient control of his diaphragm; but when he is careless or "forces," as he does here towards the end of the *Prologue,* either his voice deteriorates or he sings sharp.) The rendering, what there is of it, is strictly traditional, and the balance between singer and orchestra quite good until one's attention becomes diverted by the reiterated twang of an E flat on the too-adjacent harp just before the close, which, by the way, shirks the "curtain" ending.

Pasquale Amato's (H.M.V. D.B.156) sounds less sepulchral than his Fonotipia described last month; it has more of the genuine baritone timbre and less of the basso. It reveals an equally admirable method and artistic interpretation, though I must qualify the latter with the criticism that the music is taken too slowly and becomes a trifle over-sentimental—faults which Leoncavallo would never have tolerated. Apart from these blemishes (and, of course, the cut), there is little to choose between the two records.

I conclude with Titta Ruffo (H.M.V. D.B.464), and this I can describe without hesitation as the finest record of the *Prologue* that I have ever listened to. Happily the division into two parts, one on each side of the disc, permits the whole piece to be included, from the first note of the introduction down to the very climax of the "Incominciate," which this singer, after having previously indulged in a ringing A flat, winds up

with a comfortable, long-sustained G. The orchestral prelude is brightly played, the characteristic qualities of the various instruments coming out more clearly than usual. This may be partly due to the fact, which I only discovered after going through the whole record, that the pitch was raised a semitone for the first side of the disc. But why the disparity? I can only guess at one explanation : the opening passages lie comparatively low for this singer; the later ones high; but not high enough to trouble Titta Ruffo, who revels in G's and A flats, or even A's. Hence the alteration. Compare the relative pitch of the two sides and you will find that, whereas *Un nido di memorie* is in the original key, the same speed gives the *Si può* exactly half a tone higher than it was written. Anyhow the voice sounds equally full throughout. It is a magnificent organ, properly produced, amazingly resonant, free from nasality or *vibrato,* and controlled by true diaphragmatic breathing. The power and opulence of the tone strike the listener from the instant he sings the "Signore, signori"; and you can even—rare event! —catch the hissing of the "s" as well. In each successive phrase there is an abundance of expression, ample contrast, and not a trace of exaggeration. To teachers who use the gramophone I would say, "Here is your perfect model!" I may even add my opinion that this is how Santley in his prime would have sung the *Pagliacci* Prologue. And praise can go no higher than that.

HERMAN KLEIN.

79

THE GRAMOPHONE AND THE SINGER

(Continued)

By HERMAN KLEIN

"Mon cœur s'ouvre à ta voix"

FEW operas have so romantic a history as *Samson et Dalila*. To tell it in detail here would take too long; but there are certain facts which came out recently in Jean Bonnerot's revised biography of Saint-Saëns that ought, I feel, to be related as preface to my own remarks on the work.

Was it originally intended to be an opera or an oratorio? That question, which has so often puzzled people, cannot even now be answered in a sentence. It goes back to the year 1867, when the subject was suggested to the composer by a friend who greatly admired the *Samson* of Voltaire, already set to music by Rameau, but never performed at the Paris Opéra owing to religious opposition.* Saint-Saëns jumped at the idea, and asked a young poet, Ferdinand Lemaire, to prepare an entirely new text based upon Judges XVI., which he proposed to treat as an *oratorio*. "An oratorio!" exclaimed Lemaire, ".why not make an opera of it?" And after some persuasion the musician agreed. Together they arranged the plan of the story, and as soon as the libretto was delivered Saint-Saëns set to work upon it with his customary enthusiasm. But it is important to note that he did not begin at the beginning. He started with the second act; and the initial impulse of his creative genius was directed to the setting of the love duet for the hero and heroine, whereof the particular gem is *Mon cœur s'ouvre à ta voix*. Soon it became known that he was writing a Biblical opera. His more intimate friends did not relish the idea and sought to discourage him. He played over portions of the second act to them at a soirée at which Anton Rubinstein was among the guests. They admired the music but still set their faces against the project. A little later he tried his "fragments" on another circle of friends, and with much the same result. That settled it; he put his score aside and determined not to persevere with *Samson* in any form.

Six years elapsed before he took it up again. With feverish haste he completed his second act, wrote the first, and sketched the third. It was no longer an opera, but an oratorio to be called simply *Dalila*; and it was still far from finished when, in March, 1875, the first act was performed at one of the Châtelet concerts under Colonne. The real encouragement, prior to this, however, had come from the famous singer Mme. Viardot-Garcia (the sister of Malibran and Manuel Garcia), who had given as a surprise a private stage performance of the second act, at the little theatre in her garden at Croissy, on August 20th, 1874. On that occasion Mme. Viardot herself sustained the rôle of Dalila, and it was from her lips that the beautiful melody of "Mon cœur s'ouvre" was first heard; which was only fitting, seeing that Saint-Saëns actually wrote the whole part for the great mezzo-contralto, and ultimately dedicated to her the work itself when he put his finishing touches to it in January, 1876. But neither as opera nor as oratorio did any manager want *Samson*. Halanzier, the powerful director of the Opéra, who was present at Croissy, had stealthily slipped away before the end and would have nothing to do with it. He had no use for Biblical opera, especially when composed by a "downright Wagnerian and a devoted partisan of Music of the Future" (*sic*).

Thus, in spite of Mme. Viardot's influence, *Samson et Dalila* was not destined to see the light first in its composer's native country. It was actually first performed on the stage in Germany, at Weimar, under the auspices of Liszt, on December 2nd, 1877. It took fifteen years more to find its way to Paris; two years, that is to say, after it had been produced for the first time in France at Rouen. The reception in each case was enthusiastic in the extreme. But what of London? There we were still indulging the innocent prejudices and habits of the Victorian era. *Samson* might be acceptable enough as a Biblical opera on the Continent; hither it could only be allowed to journey in the guise of an oratorio; and it was so given for the first time at a Covent Garden concert on September 25th, 1893, under the direction of Mr. (now Sir) Frederic Cowen. Never shall I forget that performance; it was a wonder the work ever survived it. Neither of the French singers engaged for the title-rôles was present to sustain it. The Dalila (Elena Sanz) had rehearsed the duet with Samson (Lafarge), with Saint-Saëns himself at the piano, in my studio at Temple Chambers. That was early in the preceding week. Then suddenly, two or three days before the concert—for some

---

* According to Félix Clément, Rameau never wrote the score at all, and Voltaire's tragedy was first set to music by Weckerlin and given in concert form at the Paris Conservatoire so recently as 1890.

reason that could never be ascertained—Saint-Saëns went off to Paris, accompanied by his tenor. Mme. Sanz followed to fetch them back, but, like them, failed to return. In this dreadful extremity the manager, Mr. Farley Sinkins, engaged two English singers (Miss Edith Miller and Mr. Bernard Lane) to do the best they could with two heavy, unstudied parts at 24 hours' notice; and under these trying conditions (with that fine artist Eugène Oudin as the High Priest) was *Samson et Dalila* introduced in oratorio fashion to a British audience. Only sixteen years later, in 1909, was it transferred to the Covent Garden boards in its proper operatic form and given nine times before crowded houses during that one season. It is now a popular item in every operatic répertoire.

From what I have said it will be seen that *Mon cœur s'ouvre à ta voix* was practically the first number of this work that Camille Saint-Saëns put on paper. He began with the duet of which it is not only the principal feature but the indubitable gem. (The air, "Amour, viens aider," although it precedes the duet, was written at a later period.) It should be observed that "Mon cœur s'ouvre" is largely built up both in its exquisite refrain, "Verse-moi l'ivresse," and in the accompaniment to the second verse, upon a descending chromatic passage of six notes, obviously intended to typify Dalila's deceitful nature, the false smiles and sinuous, serpentine movements that lure poor Samson to his ruin. Upon this insinuating theme much of the music of the whole duet is cleverly based. Saint-Saëns, who is so often sneered at by the "highbrows" of to-day, was one of the ablest and most original musicians that France has ever owned. Greatly as he admired Wagner, he never imitated him or his methods, and was extremely reticent in his use of the *leit-motiv*. It was that famous conductor and

CAMILLE SAINT-SAËNS
at the Khedivial Palace, Cairo.

pianist, Hans von Bülow, who, when *Samson* was done at Hamburg in 1882, declared that "Saint-Saëns was the solitary contemporary musician who had contrived to draw useful hints from Wagner's theories, without allowing himself to be upset by them." And how wonderfully he always wrote for the human voice! Like his intimate friend Gounod, he took a leaf in this respect from the rare example of Mozart. The reason for the universal popularity of "Softly awakes my heart," as the English version has it, apart from the suave elegance and sustained beauty of its melody, lies in the scope afforded by every phrase for the perfect display of the voice, the richness and texture of the tone, the purity and charm of delivery, the mastery of breath-control, and, finally, the pervading sense of that elusive quality which we call style. It is, therefore, an exacting piece to sing. The supreme art of Pauline Viardot-Garcia must have made it sound very marvellous. I know that Elena Sanz did so, though I heard her only in a room. The contraltos and mezzo-sopranos of to-day who have recorded it on the gramophone do not, I am bound to say, impress me as having the peculiar gift for conveying its message as a tremendous love-appeal, something overwhelmingly passionate and irresistibly seductive. For the most part they imbue it with an air of doleful misery and tearful upbraiding, rather than a promise of joy; and this, being fundamentally wrong, upsets the poetic musical values of the whole piece. It is a way that contraltos have.

I sat by the master's side in a box at Covent Garden at the performance of *Samson et Dalila* given as part of the London Jubilee Festival (which I had the honour to organise), in June, 1913, to celebrate the seventy-fifth anniversary of his artistic career. The Dalila on that occasion was Mme. Kirkby Lunn, whose fine voice was then, perhaps, at its very best. He was particularly pleased with her rendering of " Mon cœur s'ouvre," and exclaimed as she finished it, " Quelle excellente artiste ! " She did not hurry the tempo then as she did when recording it (H.M.V., D.B.509), for the ostensible purpose of squeezing both verses into one side of the disc. It is rather a scramble, but otherwise a good record. The tone is pure and characteristic, the French accent excellent. In the concluding bars, which nearly every singer alters to her own liking, there is no attempt to appropriate the high notes that belong to Samson—a device which Saint-Saëns objected to so strongly that he once, in my hearing, refused to conduct the air for a young contralto (who shall be nameless) unless she consented to sing the *coda* exactly as he had written it for Dalila's voice. But apart from the opera few artists are blameless in this matter, and I do not propose to refer to it again here. It is like the all-pervading dolefulness of the deep-toned appeal for " l'ivresse "—too universal to excite wonder or to produce the expected effect on the listener, be he Samson or a modest lover of the gramophone.

The execution of the peculiar throbbing accompaniment to this piece is another thing that suffers from varied treatment at the hands of different orchestras, so-called, in different *ateliers*. These palpitating semiquavers, which generally sound altogether wrong on the piano, undoubtedly present a problem in the recording-room. It is overcome best, I think, in the H.M.V., because there the treatment is tolerably legato and delicately rhythmical ; it does not, like some, suggest the laboured puffing of a goods engine toiling up an incline with half a mile of coal trucks. But in no single instance does the accompaniment to the second stanza (when it *is* included) afford an even remote notion of the effect intended by the composer with his descending chromatic *motif*, as he flings it swiftly from one wood-wind instrument to another. However, when all is said and done, it is not the orchestra but the singing that you are expecting me to talk about. I could wish, as a matter of fact, that some of that stood on a higher plane.

Two interesting examples, both Columbia, are those of Dame Clara Butt and Mme. Maria Gay. They illustrate the remarkable difference between scampering through to get in both stanzas and a comfortable, leisurely rendering of only one. For the moment I am content to prefer the latter, as given by Maria Gay (Col. A.5280), although it is not an excuse for an excessively slow tempo or for unduly long pauses on long notes, such as that endless C natural leading up to the " Verse-moi l'ivresse." Still the voice has a splendid timbre (in the chest register it sounds absolutely like a tenor), and the lengthy phrases are steadily sustained by admirable breathing, while the French diction is clear and beyond reproach. Equal praise cannot be accorded

to the popular English contralto (Col. 7318), who, besides undue haste, spoils her phrases one after another by using a heavy, breathy tone on over-closed French vowels that sound woolly and dull. Some of the medium notes are sympathetic, but the general effect is unmusical, loud, and exaggerated. Technically regarded, the recording does not, of course, compare with the beautiful work that the Columbia are doing to-day, especially, I may add, their instrumental achievements with the Mozart *Symphony in E flat* and the playing of the Léner Quartet, to which I have listened with real pleasure on the Grafonola. Yet another of their records of *Mon cœur s'ouvre*, sung in English by Muriel Brunskill (Col. 3328), is on a 10in. disc, which holds the one verse easily. It sounds to me as if transposed down a semitone, the sole advantage of which would be to lend a little extra sonority to some excellent chest tones. On the other hand, certain high notes do not come out well, notably that glorious G flat which is the climax of Dalila's imperious demand for love.

There is less of imperiousness than pleading grace and sweetness about the effort of that accomplished concert artist, Julia Culp (H.M.V., D.A.152). It is very pretty singing, the breathing is good, the French diction is neat. But not a solitary gust of passion disturbs the smooth surface of the vocal tone ; that want seems to be supplied by the puffing throbs of the accompanying engine, only it does not exactly provide the necessary human touch. Just the reverse occurs in the opulent, sonorous interpretation of Louise Homer (H.M.V., D.B.299), whose tones are so big and manly that they almost smother the attendant semiquavers. They are not quite so refined or so steady, either, as they were when the American contralto sang here twenty years ago, and the introduction of a noisy A flat at the end is wholly out of the picture. A rather aggressive and insistent Dalila this ! A still loftier excursion into the " ledger lines " is the B flat perpetrated by Sigrid Onégin (Clift., 518A.) at the same spot. Her sole excuse is that she is a high mezzo-soprano with a strong metallic tone that mounts up rather easily. Her name suggests a Finnish origin, but I have never heard the lady, and only know that the gifted Jeritza writes something nice about her in her recent autobiography, " Sunlight and Song " (published by Messrs. Appleton). So far as this record is concerned, I am of opinion that Miss Onégin, although her French is not particularly first-rate, enunciates very distinctly, sustains the *cantabile* melody (one verse only) with evident facility and discretion (bar that superfluous B flat), and also contrives to impart a suggestion of simulated passion whilst getting away somewhat from the lachrymose appeal of the deeper voices.

Finally, two English records, one by Ethel Hook

(Voc., D.O.2065), the other by Edna Thornton (H.M.V., D.282), each having features of merit to recommend it. Ethel Hook, younger sister of Clara Butt, possesses the unmistakable ring and amplitude of the family organ, with a smooth, even scale which she utilises for an over-generous display of *portamento*, both up and down. It is a good honest voice, albeit the method lacks distinction and the amorous Dalilean charm is missing, even when she declares " I love but thee." Both verses are here, with the consequent rush, and a harp is very prominent in the accompaniment. Edna Thornton has had the advantage of playing the part so often that the atmosphere of the scene and music is distinctly felt. She does not treat it as a mere concert piece, which is a notable gain for the listener ; moreover, her voice, when it is not too tremulous, pleases in virtue of a natural richness and musical timbre, and the notes are always perfectly in tune. Altogether I am glad to be able to say that these two records by native artists are by no means " out of the running."

P.S.—Since I wrote last month two of the greatest, if not actually *the* two greatest living singers of gramophone records have appeared in London upon the concert platform—Amelita Galli-Curci for the first time, John McCormack after an interval of ten years. I heard them both with very great pleasure and interest. It is good to know that time is treating the Irish tenor kindly ; good to listen once more to his own sweet, smooth tones, given out by his own masterful throat, and sustained in his own easy, assured, delicate way. It is a lovely quality, wholly individual in character, and the *mezza voce* still atones by its appealing charm for any lack of power or ringing force in the head register. McCormack's style has broadened considerably, and it was just as delightful to hear him in the old Italian airs as to enjoy the humour and grace that he put into his familiar Irish ditties. He had a magnificent reception.

The crucial question, " Is she as wonderful as her records make out ? " was, to some extent, answered by Mme. Galli-Curci in the affirmative. Indeed, how could it be otherwise, seeing that she herself made them ? Still, on the principle that selected samples are bound to approach perfection more nearly than the " goods " they exemplify, my chief feeling in the matter is one of relief at not having found myself disappointed. I have heard great coloratura singers who added a larger measure of personal charm to vocal gifts not less brilliant and assured than those of Galli-Curci. But, on the other hand, she is amazingly versatile ; she possesses *aplomb* and rhythmical sense in an extraordinary degree ; and if her tone-colour is a little monotonous, its warmth and purity of timbre in the medium is quite exceptional. For this, indeed, her records prepared us, even as they also led one to expect in the concert room a stronger, clearer enunciation of her words. But the rapidity and sparkle of her " patter " are astounding ; and it is an exaggeration to state in so many crude words that " She sings off the key." She does nothing of the sort. It might with truth be said that her tone does too frequently deviate a hair's breadth, if only a vibration or two, from the right pitch. *Voilà tout !* Still, it would be better were there no deviation at all.

HERMAN KLEIN.

THE GRAMOPHONE AND THE SINGER

(Continued)

By HERMAN KLEIN

Maria Jeritza—and Others.

THE two operatic sopranos who have won most popularity in America during the past few seasons are Amelita Galli-Curci and Maria Jeritza. Neither has yet been heard on the stage in this country, and goodness only knows how long it will be ere Covent Garden boasts sufficient affluence to afford us that privilege. Nowadays, however, the gramophone brings us voices long before we behold their owners; and, if we enjoy listening, we find an additional interest in endeavouring, with the aid of possibly flattering photographs, to form an idea of what the original is like. Still, even then it is only half the story. I understand from those who should know, that the Galli-Curci of the stage comes much nearer to the Galli-Curci of the amazing records than the Galli-Curci of the concert-room. That is quite comprehensible; and by a similar deduction I should form the opinion that the Jeritza of the stage approaches much more nearly to the level of her press notices than the Jeritza of the gramophone. The chief justification for this parallel reasoning lies in the fact that Galli-Curci makes perfect records and Jeritza does not. But the two prima donnas need not on that account come to fisticuffs. Their particular geniuses are wide as the poles asunder, and they do not cross each other's paths at any point unless when cashing huge cheques at the bank—a most unlikely contretemps.

Nevertheless, in spite of this phonographic disparity, there is something about the Jeritza records, some quality of atmosphere or personal magnetism, that makes them interesting. It also enables me to gather from their message the nature of the peculiar gifts that have permitted this artist to conquer in her own particular line the fastidious public of the United States, as well as that of Austria and Germany. Readers of these pages will remember my saying, not long ago, that I had never heard any of Mme. Jeritza's records; indeed, I could not state with certainty whether she had ever essayed the art of record-making. I even hazarded a guess that she had done so and failed to satisfy; but in that I was wrong. Since then I have not only listened to her records, but read her book "Sunlight and Song," a bright autobiography (translated by Frederic H. Martens and published by D. Appleton and Co.,

New York and London), which contains many charming portraits of the singer and an amusing chapter on "Singing for the Phonograph." Therein she admits at once that she would "rather sing through two rehearsals than make one record, at any time." Every artist would probably say the same thing; only some find it easier and less enervating than others. The point is, as Mme. Jeritza says, that the record "cannot (i.e., must not) represent the artist at anything but her best," and she found it hard to do that at first, especially under American conditions, which were new to her and "very distracting." "With the orchestra so close to the singer the sound of the instruments is so overpowering that it drowns the voice and I could not hear myself sing. It is the hardest kind of hard work, and very exacting. Yet it is something that can be done if intelligence and concentration are brought to bear on the task." Besides, "the phonograph, just like the camera, must be humoured; only if you adapt yourself to the machine and find the absolutely right conditions for allowing it to reproduce your voice to the best advantage, will it do so." The number of trials, the amount of patience that singers and operators have to go through in the attainment of the model record is fabulous, incalculable. I think Mme. Galli-Curci and Enrico Caruso must have been very patient and persevering at this business.

Maria Jeritza is a native of Brünn, an old town which she says an English friend of hers once described as the "Austrian Manchester." Her first operatic parts were Elsa and Marguerite; and she must have been remarkably gifted, for she had only sung these rôles and Violetta five months in Olmütz when she became straightway engaged for the Volksoper at Vienna, where she made her début in 1910 as Elisabeth in *Tannhäuser*. Her success seems to have been altogether exceptional, thanks to great personal beauty and intelligence, allied with rare vocal and histrionic talent, a glorious voice, and a degree of versatility that enabled her to shine to equal advantage in the most contrasted parts. She became an immense favourite with the Viennese, from the Emperor Francis Joseph downwards, and sang in a long string of operas besides creating several new characters. Among the latter was Marietta, the heroine of Korngold's *The Dead City*, wherein she made her first appearance at the Metropolitan Opera House, New York, on November 17th, 1921; and apparently it ranks among her finest impersonations. (An air from *The Dead City* is among the records I shall notice later on.) Mme. Jeritza's American début did not come, however, until after she had won a tremendous reputation, both before and during the War, in all the principal cities of Austria and Germany; but, for the story of these tours I must refer my readers to her book. I would only point out, as I did in a letter to *The Times* exactly three years ago, that, owing to there being no "international" grand opera at Covent Garden during such a long period, an event almost without precedent had occurred, namely, that a European operatic celebrity of the standing of Maria Jeritza had "skipped London" on her way to the United States without so much as opening her mouth in this country. It might be argued that Tetrazzini and Galli-Curci had done the same thing. But their cases were different, because neither had made a name for herself *before* crossing the Atlantic—Tetrazzini to make hers in Buenos Ayres, Galli-Curci hers in Chicago. How it happened that such a singer of the Strauss and Puccini operas as Jeritza was overlooked by our Grand Opera Syndicate both before and after the War is a circumstance that I do not pretend to explain. There is now no telling how long we may have to wait before hearing this greatly-lauded artist in person.

Meanwhile, what of her records? Well, as I have previously remarked, I doubt whether they actually do her justice; and yet they are well worth hearing; at least the later ones are, for I surmise that the *Elisabeth's Prayer* and *Elsa's Dream* were made when Mme. Jeritza first went to New York, and they are distinctly not so good as those which followed. She tells us herself in her book: "The process of making vocal records here in the United States, though not new to me, was novel. In Austria the phonograph is not as widely and generally distributed as here, and cannot be said to enjoy the same popularity." She was probably nervous and prone to "force" her voice by superabundant breath-pressure; anyhow she succeeded in making the tone so unsteady that the listener who had not heard the subsequent records might well be pardoned for accusing her of a tremolo. The timbre was also too dark and heavy for a perfect rendering of Elisabeth's *Allmächt'ge Jungfrau* (H.M.V., D.B. 306), or of Elsa's *Einsam in trüben Tagen*, which is on the reverse side of the same disc. Yet the sympathetic quality of the medium voice comes out agreeably, and one perceives in both efforts the fine resonant tone of the head notes. This I noted particularly when, after an unsatisfactory essay on the Sonora Model, I tried them again on my Columbia Grafonola, which imparted a splendid ring to the voice and far greater clearness and prominence to the orchestral accompaniment. The colouring was still too sombre, however, the text insufficiently enunciated, the vocal attack, if fairly clean, marred by a tendency to swell every accentuated note at the beginning. These faults of technique, curiously enough, are less conspicuous as the singer becomes more accustomed to her work and more at her ease in the act of recording. The rhythm and phrasing also tend to improve. But on the whole I observe that it is not given to the best of Wagnerian singers to imbue the master with exactly the same spirit (*Geist* is the word rather than *Stimmung*) on the gramophone that they do on the stage.

The Jeritza voice is a pure soprano of lyric rather than dramatic calibre, warm and musical in the medium, clear and ringing in the head tones; and she is never so much as a shade of a vibration off the true pitch. It is a pity, though, that she has not a better accent alike in French and Italian —the vowel sounds are faulty in both languages, possibly because she has never lived among people who speak either. The "a" and "o" are entirely wrong, for lack of proper teaching or correction. In *Divinités du Styx* (H.M.V., D.B.355) there are several bad mistakes of pronunciation: "transport" in French is not pronounced "trainsport," nor is "point" sung as if written "pouaint." On the other hand, the singer gets a far finer tone in this record, and also in the *Suicidio* from Ponchielli's *La Gioconda* which is on the reverse side, than she does in her German pieces—a curious but unquestionable fact. The quality in the Gluck air is distinctly superior, apart from the greater animation and rhythmical "go" which explain all the triumphs that Jeritza has won in the popular Austrian light operas. The fine *Suicidio*, however, sounded rather strident with a loud needle, and I preferred it with a "half-tone." What seemed chiefly lacking then was the sense of tragedy in the voice; beauty of tone certainly, but no great depth of expression, notably in the wonderful phrase, "Domando al cielo di dormir queta," one of the loveliest in this shamefully neglected opera. Here, again, I imagine the singer fulfils the dramatic idea in contrasts of vocal tone and colouring much more vivid in the theatre than those she gives in her record. Her American critics, at any rate, allow her credit for possessing this faculty.

On a third disc (H.M.V., D.A.524) are two more German items, namely, *Dich, theure Halle*, from *Tannhäuser*, and a harmless little air from Korngold's *Die tote Stadt*, entitled *Glück, das mir verlieb*. The former (too heavy with a loud needle) is on the whole somewhat wistful and sad for what should be a joyous greeting to the Hall of Song.

The line of melody is steadily sustained, and I like the magnificent ringing B even better than the oft-recurring G. The words, however, are not so good as one could wish. The Korngold song is graceful, if a trifle monotonous. It opens with a pretty orchestral introduction, which is capitally reproduced. The kind of folk-tune sung by Marietta should be very effective in the opera, for the semi-religious pattern of some of the phrases gives them a decidedly individual character. It all makes pleasant hearing, but somehow I doubt whether Mme. Jeritza delights her American admirers in this work to the extent that she does her Austrian. Anyhow, she must be an artist of superlative merit, and I once more express the hope that it may not be long before we have an opportunity of judging her in her native element in this country.

Turning now to another theme, I am going to speak of some records that I have quite recently heard on the New Edison. Concerning the machine itself, I fancy there is no need for me to write at length; its peculiar claims and characteristics are doubtless familiar to readers of this magazine. I have not, of course, personally applied its special test of placing the artist beside the machine, to continue the piece *vivâ voce* where the reproduction leaves off, and so compare the two. I could not do this because the recording artists did not happen to be handy for the purpose. But I understand that it has been done, and with results entirely satisfactory to Mr. Thomas Edison. In any case one must be thankful to him for his diamond point reproducer, which obviates the necessity for changing needles, even though it limits its functions to records made specially for the Edison machine. Twelve of these " Re-creations," as they are termed, I shall now proceed to comment upon, premising that the " Heppel-white " model which played them is said to be surpassed by several larger-sized models from the same laboratory.

The first of these Edison records that I took up was a *Caro nome* by Alice Verlet (82080R), remarkable chiefly for easy, assured singing and neat *fiorituri*. The clearness of the voice is interfered with somewhat by the " scratch," which can be still better overcome, I think, on such a good machine as this. The " scratch " is a nuisance that the listener cannot suppress; but he can avoid the highly-flavoured American description of the plot of *Rigoletto*, with its western pronunciation of Italian names and outside-showman's delivery, by the simple precaution of not playing the reverse side, which is simply wasted on such nonsense. Luckier, therefore, the purchaser of 83079 L., which gives you Carolina Lazzari with one of the big airs from *Samson et Dalila* on each side, in French, in a strong, clear,

sympathetic contralto, well produced and evenly sustained throughout. There is some rich chest tone in *Amour, viens aider*, though the appeal to the Philistine god of love, whoever he may be, is a trifle too *triste* for a Dalila. Both verses of *Mon cœur s'ouvre* are given, and if the G flat were as good as the rest there would be little fault to find. The accompaniments are sonorous, well-balanced, and nicely restrained in all these records. In another example (82213 R.) a not too refined rendering of the flower duet from *Madam Butterfly*, by Marie Rappold and Caroline Lazzari, is backed by Tosti's *Povera Mamma* as sung with characteristic Italian sentimentality by an excellent light baritone, Mario Laurenti. The voices blend agreeably in the duet and they are both well in tune; but there was no need for them to keep so consistently loud throughout. The xylophone effect in the orchestration is prettily done.

Several of the records are by that clever daughter of a clever father, Claudia Muzio, who now sings entirely in America, where, of course, the New Edison mechanical productions all originate. She has a pure soprano of light calibre, with a delicate musical quality that can develop strong dramatic feeling when occasion requires, yet without the slightest forcing or tendency to sharpen. There is a slight tremolo, undoubtedly, but only at certain moments; while the breathing is good, and the voice retains its evenness of texture and colour all through the scale. Being an accomplished vocalist, Signorina Muzio attacks every sort of piece with equal confidence and ability, but sometimes her endeavour to get off the beaten track leads her to very dull, uninteresting spots. For instance, there is little of the real Bellini whom we all love (or ought to love) in the aria *Sorgi, o padre*, from *Bianca and Fernando* (82267 R.), with its lengthy minor introduction for flute and harp accompaniment. This sort of thing can only be likened to *Sonnambula*-and-water. So again, the *Pace, mio Dio* on the other side of the disc, from *La Forza del Destino*, can only represent Verdi at his feeblest, no matter how earnestly and intelligently it be sung. Of the more modern school the singer gives us a familiar but beautiful example in Margherita's prison air, *L'altra Notte*, from Boito's *Mefistofele* (82305 R.), which rôle I have heard her sing with unalloyed pleasure. She sings the pitiful melody with infinite charm and, in conjunction with it the still more modern *Che me ne faccio di vostro castello*, from Giordano's opera *Madame Sans-Gêne*, which meanders on with saccharine sweetness and uninterrupted flow to very excellent orchestration. I prefer to the latter (82247 L.) an excerpt from Ciléa's *Adriana Lecouvreur* called *Io son l'umile ancella*, which begins almost *parlato*, with graceful flute passages supporting the voice, then broadens out into a most effective aria. It is extremely well sung, the enunciation of the words is particularly distinct, and the recording (as in most of the records of this selection) appears to me to leave little if anything to be desired. Similar praise may be bestowed on the duet from *Pagliacci—Silvio, a quest'ora*—which furnishes material for the reverse side (82247 R.), wherein the voices of Claudia Muzio and Mario Laurenti afford a delightful example of perfect blending and warm, passionate feeling. Neither, I think, could easily be excelled.

With the remainder I must be brief. The famous Lucrezia Bori displays her silvery light soprano with exquisite purity in *Ah! fors' è lui* (82539 R.). She sings faultlessly in tune, with admirably distinct, clear-cut phrasing; refined, not hurried, neatness itself save when there is too much *portamento*; and lacking only a trill and the *Sempre libera* to make it an ideal record.

A capital baritone, Arthur Middleton, imitates good models in a lively rendering of the *Largo al factotum* (82545 R.), executed with abundant spirit and contrast, clear enunciation and a crisp, *staccato* ending to every sentence. A very business-like Figaro, this! Finally, three instrumental records that do not really belong to my province, but assuredly deserve favourable mention, viz., a *Serenade* and a *Hungarian Dance* (82263 R.), played with splendid tone and execution by that fine violinist, Albert Spalding; two piano solos by Rachmaninoff (82187 R.), one the inevitable *Prelude*, from the gifted fingers of the composer and both admirable reproductions; and, lastly, two selections from *Madam Butterfly* (80633 R.), played with much animation, crispness of rhythm, and picturesque instrumental colour by the American Symphony Orchestra.

HERMAN KLEIN.

THE GRAMOPHONE AND THE SINGER
(Continued)
By HERMAN KLEIN
Mozart in Excelsis—" Deh vieni "

MOZART, and yet more Mozart! The ever-growing demand is one of the features of modern musical life. It rivals the appreciation of the Elizabethan composers as the greatest musical revival of our times. I would not degrade aught so deep and abiding as the renascent love of Mozart by describing it as a " craze." Besides, it started about a half a century ago—in other countries before this—and " crazes " are not, as a rule, things that come to stay. I merely quote the term as an indication of the rapidity, the intensity of the spread of this healthy artistic disposition; also because it is reaching places where it never penetrated before and taking new forms in order to do so. By " new forms " I mean, of course, the gramophone and, in a lesser degree, radio-broadcasting; for it must not be supposed that more is being done to-day to popularise Mozart in the opera-house or the concert-room than was done in the seventies and eighties of the last century. It is only that the concert area has widened and, thanks to the musical schools which teach thousands where they used to teach hundreds, the public has grown infinitely larger. When I was a youngster—*Eheu fugaces!*—I was plentifully nourished on Mozart symphonies at the Crystal Palace or the Philharmonic Concerts and Mozart quartets and quintets at the dear old " Pops " at St. James's Hall.

But what of the Mozart operas? Are we hearing them performed so much more frequently nowadays? On the whole I fear not. I have been looking through the lists of all the Covent Garden seasons so carefully drawn up by Mr. Richard Northcott in the recently-published revised edition of his charmingly illustrated book,* which covers the period from 1888 to 1924. Now I am quite sure that in the twenty years preceding this period the performances of the three great Mozart operas at Covent Garden and the old Her Majesty's Theatre reached as high a total as they did (allowing for the War) in these last thirty years. I have not space to prove it here and now; I can only state the figures as counted from Mr. Northcott's brochure, and they are as follows: *Don Giovanni*, 104; *Marriage of Figaro*, 28; *Magic Flute*, 12; *Il Seraglio*, 1; and *Bastien et Bastienne*, 3. Of course the disparity between *Don Giovanni* and the other operas, excluding the last-named, would be less striking if this calculation included the

* Covent Garden and the Royal Opera. By Richard Northcott. The Press Printers, Long Acre, W.C.

Beecham and B.N.O.C. performances at Drury Lane and His Majesty's, where the *Don* was omitted in favour of the other three named. Still, even then, *Don Giovanni* would continue to head the list, as it has always done. It is only quite latterly that *Figaro* and the *Magic Flute* have regained some of their former popularity. Whereas there was never a season at Covent Garden without *Don Giovanni* from 1882 to 1907, there were no fewer than 13 when the *Marriage of Figaro* was not given at all, while the *Magic Flute* was only remounted once in 1888 and not again until given in English by the B.N.O.C. in 1922. I think I am right, therefore, in asserting that, so far as opera is concerned, the modern growth in the love of Mozart has not been so remarkable as is generally supposed or, indeed, as one had the right to expect.

Mozart's operatic version of Beaumarchais' immortal comedy, *Le Mariage de Figaro*, is one of the masterpieces of musical art, and the aria, *Deh vieni non tardar*, is among the most brilliant gems scintillating in a glorious score. It is Susanna's great moment ; the one moment in the opera when she is really serious ; when she has something to sing that is the expression of her true self, that places her alone " in the limelight " as a woman and a vocalist. The music is the purest imaginable Mozart, and difficult for any but the perfect Mozart singer to do justice to. Hence the fact that there are few first-rate records of this piece, as I have lately discovered in trying over a collection of five or six, gathered, most of them, from the H.M.V. It can only be sung in Italian—the language to which it was composed—because unfortunately no other language renders it with equal beauty and no translator who has yet appeared can find an English equivalent that does not sound ridiculous. Another trouble is that if sung at the proper tempo it is rather long for one record ; so that either the exquisite recitative is omitted (which is a sin) or the few bars of orchestral introduction leading to the air are left out. In one case the whole thing is liable to be sung too slowly or, in the other, too fast ; and neither gives us the true effect. However, it is useless to be hypercritical on this point, and I will register my opinion of each record without regard to the question of tempo.

I begin with Marcella Sembrich (H.M.V.,D.B.433), one of the great Susannas of her day and probably the only one of them to leave a gramophone record of this lovely melody. I know not when it was made, but I do know that the famous artist was no longer in her prime when she sang it. She takes too many breaths ; the voice is occasionally doubtful in intonation and unsteady in tone ; some of the passages sound very laboured. There is no recitative ; but the air is most artistically phrased, and the interpretation, so far as it goes, is in accordance with the best traditions. Both this record and that of Selma Kurz (H.M.V., D.B.500) came out well on the Sonora Model, that is to say, with purity and clearness ; while the renderings are very similar save for the cadenza or interpolated turn leading to the B flat, with the scale down to C, which Mme. Sembrich would never introduce ; but the majority of Susannas do because it is pretty and effective. Selma Kurz does not maintain an absolutely steady line, and she becomes sharp on her head notes (particularly in that very cadenza), but her singing is expressive and betokens the experienced artist.

Graziella Pareto (H.M.V., D.B.567) gives us two good things—the recitative, *Giunse alfin il momento*, and the strictly correct ending. On the other hand, her over-enunciated consonants (rare fault !) destroy the tenderness of a Susanna in love, while her undue haste is not that of a wife burning to greet her lawful husband so much as anxiety to get her song over before he arrives. Her rhythm, too, is faulty ; her *legato* lacks the true *bel canto* of the Mozartian school ; and lo ! she sings not one solitary *appoggiatura*, but apparently makes a virtue of never raising the penultimate note, as if *Deh vieni* were from Bach's *Passion*. I like this clever singer much better in her modern Italian airs, which the Milanese teachers know a great deal more about than they do about Mozart. Almost identical criticism applies to the version of that excellent vocalist Lucrezia Bori (H.M.V., D.B.153) with the added remark that she is too free with her *portamento* and plays sad tricks with her *rubatos* and *rallentandos*—flighty little touches that this, of all music, positively will not stand. Otherwise both these last records are admirably made, and both sound wonderfully well on my Columbia Grafonola, which brings both voice and accompaniment into perfect relief.

Another, by Kathleen Destournel (Voc., C.01087), has many features to recommend it, notably a clear, resonant tone, exceedingly neat phrasing, and a bright musical style, with plenty of swing yet no lack of feeling. A trifle more suavity next time, greater smoothness in the vowel tone, with the recitative added and the cadenza omitted, and I fancy this singer could contrive to achieve a wholly delightful *Deh vieni*. When all is said and done, it is a very exacting as well as divinely beautiful air, and worth any amount of trouble in order that in the end the perfect result may be attained.

I have received from the Columbia Company a series of extremely fine records made by Cesare Formichi, the Italian baritone who created something very like a sensation on his début at Covent Garden last June. He came here with a big reputation, added to a reputation for " bigness," and the magnitude of his organ amply justified both. He compares in my mind with such tonal giants of the past as his compatriot Navarrini, the Frenchman Lassalle, the Dutchman Van Rooy, the Polish Edouard de Reszke, singers of the eighties and nineties who left no records of their phenomenal voices for the present generation to enjoy. It is striking evidence of the progress made with the gramophone that the recording instruments of to-day should be capable of " taking " voices of this calibre at full pressure and within normal distance. The result in Signor Formichi's case is a tone of such stentorian proportions that it needs to be modified in an ordinary drawing-room by the use of a half-tone needle ; otherwise it is quite powerful enough to fill a good-sized hall without extra enlargement. In fact, so extraordinary is the penetrating opulence of the solo voice that for bars at a time it completely obscures the splendid accompaniments conducted by Mr. Hamilton Harty and Mr. Albert Ketelbey, which could not very well be bettered. When the balance is right, however, it is very good indeed, and I advise Signor Formichi when he next sings for the Columbia to bear this point in mind.

The present series consists of seven double-sided discs, two 12in. and five 10in., the former comprising two excerpts from *Rigoletto*, one from *La Tosca*, and one from *Otello*. The *Cortigiani* and *Pari siamo* (L.1578) are both magnificent examples of the best school of Verdian declamation ; the breathing, the physical stamina, the alternating gusts of fury and tenderness are alike remarkable. All the traditional points are easily made, and if Signor Formichi did not frequently " scoop " up to his notes when he puts menace into his utterances there would really be little fault to find with his singing. But for this blemish, indeed, his rendering of Iago's *Credo* would be beyond criticism, and anyhow, it is a superb effort. The *Tosca* excerpt is from the finale to the church scene of Act I., and its effect with chorus, bells, and orchestra is one of immense sonority. There are two more bits from *Tosca*, both from the supper scene, *Ella verrà* and *Già ! mi dicon venal* (D.1489), these being perhaps the nearest approach to a solo that the wicked Scarpia was vouchsafed—and, I suppose, all that he deserved. Both are well sung and convey the necessary idea of villainous devilry. Concerning the *Pagliacci Prologue* (D.1487), it is only essential to emphasise the exceptional depth of contrast in the colouring of the familiar phrases ; so, too, with the still more hackneyed *Di provenza il mar* (*La Traviata*) (D.1488), with which is coupled the brief duet, *Signor? va, non ho niente*, in which Rigoletto is accosted by Sparafucile, here represented by Fernando Autori.

For the rest, I can distinctly recommend Signor Formichi's French records, not so much for his accent as for the sweetness which the language seems to import into his voice. One gets here a sympathetic " covered " tone which is often absent from his Italian. The two airs from *Thaïs* (D.1490) are well worth listening to ; and even finer is the *Légende de la Sauge* from Massenet's *Jongleur de Nôtre Dame* (D.1491), which record also provides a stirring delivery of the air for the High-Priest from *Samson et Dalila*.

HERMAN KLEIN.

✠ ✠ ✠

89

THE GRAMOPHONE AND THE SINGER

(Continued)

By HERMAN KLEIN

"Messiah" and "Elijah"

NOTHING is to be gained by wishing for or regretting the impossible. That fact I am bearing pretty constantly in mind as I pen these articles, because I am dreadfully tempted, when I listen to new records of old music, to become lachrymose over the absence of phonographic evidence of what great singing was like half a century ago. Mere comparisons are of so little value to those who have not heard *both* the things that are compared ; and it is my object in these pages to deal in comparisons that can actually be made by the reader as well as by myself. I hope it will be allowed by those who peruse me regularly that I am not exclusively a " praiser of times past." I have laid some rather thick laurels upon the heads of living opera-singers, whilst recollecting vividly how their predecessors sang the same pieces before them, and criticising them no less impartially on that account. But this month I am not going to write about operatic records. I am going for once to change over to oratorio ; and it is, I fancy, sufficiently notorious that the deterioration in oratorio-singing has been far steeper in its downward curve than that observable in opera. There are two very good reasons for the deterioration. One is that oratorio is no longer the tremendous popular attraction that it used to be ; the other, that the operatic star of bygone days, who was equally the star of oratorio, does not now find it worth while to master both branches. It may be some time yet before the true traditions of the *Messiah* and *Elijah* become lost, because these two masterpieces are still frequently performed, and, so far as vocal traditions of any sort can be conveyed by the printed page, they have been set down with tolerable clearness and accuracy by the late Mr. Randegger in his Novello editions. The pity is that no amount of " editing," however careful and conscientious, can register anything beyond dynamic effects, speed measurements, pauses, and the ordinary marks of expression. These things will not afford either the student or the amateur the remotest idea of how Jenny Lind, for instance, sang *I know that my Redeemer liveth* or *Hear ye, Israel* ; how Tietjens sang *Rejoice greatly* ; how Patey and Trebelli sang *He was despised* or *O rest in the Lord* ; how Sims Reeves sang *Comfort ye* and *If with all your hearts* ; how Santley sang *Why do the nations* and *It is

enough. These glorious examples of a fast-disappearing art lie buried either in the limbo of the past or in the memories of a few veterans in whose ears they are still ringing clear and strong.

But enough of the past. The question I would like answered is, why does the average quality of oratorio records to-day stand on an infinitely lower plane than that of operatic records ? Do the leading gramophone companies take the same trouble over the one that they do over the other ? They will probably tell you that it would not pay them to do so, much less to invest a similar amount of capital in each. The latter is a fair business argument, no doubt ; but it does not quite answer my question. I will put it another way. Is the talent now available, even if the gramophone companies were willing to pay the price for it ? Could they induce the operatic favourites of the hour to study and sing oratorio airs if they wanted to ? I doubt either proposition. So far, then, it is not their fault ; but still I cannot acquit them altogether, for the reason that the lists of oratorio records in their catalogues at the present moment are deplorably inadequate. Even those of the still popular works with which I am now dealing are neither representative nor anything like complete. They are, I suppose, sung by the best available native artists—the same who are usually engaged to sing them at the festivals, at the Albert Hall, at Queen's Hall, and elsewhere. But the omissions are such as leap to the eyes. Will it be believed that I have sought everywhere, and sought in vain, for a soprano solo from either oratorio ?

The only explanation of this serious *lacuna* that I can put forward is the unwillingness of any popular concert soprano to launch her vocal barque (no pun intended !) upon the troublous waters of *Rejoice greatly* or *I know that my Redeemer liveth*. Both are extremely hard to sing on the concert platform ; and to make a perfect record of the " divisions " of the one or the long-sustained phrases of the other would probably be harder still. Beyond this guess my baffled imagination refuses to soar. Our contemporary Handelian singers, male as well as female, are not, with very rare exceptions, reared nowadays on the exercises of the florid Italian school. They are not equal to attacking the awkward runs invented by the Saxon master with the beautiful precision, the delightful sense of certainty, smoothness, and easy control, the steady flow of pure, unruffled tone that distinguished the *coloratura* of our great English oratorio vocalists in the past. But these excuses do not apply in the case of *Hear ye, Israel* or the duet for Elijah and the Widow, which are really written on a straightforward vocal line, and therefore presumably not beyond the powers of the modern concert soprano. Why they should have been altogether overlooked passes my comprehension. Their absence intensifies my feeling of regret at the inadequacy of the selections I am about to notice, and I can only add a hope that ere long this state of affairs will be remedied. If it pays to bring out complete operas for the gramophone, so, in my opinion, will it pay to bring out complete sets of other oratorios besides *The Dream of Gerontius*, and especially of such perennial favourites as *Messiah* and *Elijah*. Perhaps in the meantime some of our budding sopranos (I need not mention names) will set to work to acquire the requisite flexibility and facility of technique for doing justice to these missing solos.

All I can do at present is to say a few words about each of such existing records as I have been able to obtain ; taking them in the order in which they would occur in a performance of the work. My object is, of course, to enable lovers of these two immortal compositions—or those desirous of playing selections from them—to form their own conclusions as to which discs it will best be worth while to procure. The accompaniments, I may add, are without exception orchestral.

" MESSIAH "

1. *Comfort ye* and *Ev'ry valley* (two-sided discs).

Tudor Davies (H.M.V., D.777) is robust rather than tender ; he menaces more than he comforts. His fine voice is over-covered and not steady enough. He delivers his message with authority and decision, if with a dead level of loud tone.

Lewis James (Voc. K.05070) is another Welsh tenor who enunciates well but darkens his vowels too much—a common fault with most of these singers. The runs are less accurate than those of Mr. Davies, but the intonation is never faulty, the rhythm always well marked. The style generally lacks distinction, and every " e " penetrates like an arrow into a target.

Frank Mullings (Col. L.1452). The recitative is better than the air, despite the absence of *messa di voce* on long notes. There is a welcome measure of restraint ; the quality is agreeable, the voice fairly steady, and the words are clear. The runs in the air are slurred and noisy, and one objects to the comical aspirate where there are two notes on the first syllable of " valley," converting the word into " va-hal-lee." Otherwise a creditable record.

2. *Thus saith the Lord* and *But who may abide*

Robert Radford (H.M.V., E.277, two-sided, 10in.) gives an admirable rendering in the traditional manner of both recit. and air. His diction is clear, his phrasing precise and clean. The only faults are over-closed vowels (with the resultant sombre tone) and a tendency to accentuate and dwell too long on final syllables.

Norman Allin (Col. L.1453, one side) does wrong to omit *Thus saith the Lord*, a pronouncement as vital to the meaning of *Messiah* as is Elijah's opening recitative to what follows. (It is to economise space and leave *Why do the nations* for the other side.) In the singing there is no restraint of any sort, but tone at all costs—i.e., rough tone, without religious sentiment or expression, *ff* throughout. I leave it at that.

3. *Behold a virgin shall conceive*, and *O thou that tellest good tidings*.

Louise Homer (H.M.V., D.B.303, one side) also does wrong to leave out the recit., but her delivery of the air is very fine. Here is a genuine contralto tone, and she puts rare nobility of style and expression into her oratorio work. The important A natural in the air comes out clear and strong, which is more than can be said for the English singers who follow. The whole piece is very smoothly given.

Edna Thornton (H.M.V., D.781, one side) includes the recitative, but her tone all through is strangely uneven and woolly, with no clear resonance anywhere. I tried it both on the Sonora Model and Columbia Grafonola with similar results.

Carrie Herwin (Col. 915, one side ; reverse *He was despised*) forces her powerful tone unnecessarily and often pays for it with a tremulous medium, but her singing has abundant life and spirit. She also takes the air at top speed, which matters less in this than other solos.

4. *For behold, darkness* and *The people that walked*.

Robert Radford (H.M.V., E.304, two sided 10in. disc) is irreproachable in the recitative and effective in the air ; dark enough for Hunding in the one and rollicking enough for Don Bartolo in the other. The excessive speed of the latter is its only blemish.

Norman Allin (Col. L.1446) devotes one side to this air, the reverse to *The trumpet shall sound*, whereof a word later. But, according to Mr. Allin's method of slurring Handel's quavers, the people did not walk, they positively *rolled* in darkness ! The *portamento* is pressed downwards and upwards with equally unrelenting force ; also with a huge amplitude of tone and vast nasal resonance, which a soft needle only slightly tends to modify. Balance with the orchestra is thus entirely lost. This is realism carried to excess.

5. _Then shall the eyes_ and _He shall feed His flock._

Kirkby Lunn (H.M.V., D.B.506) omits the recitative, but brings all the resource of her fine organ and ripe experience to the interpretation of the air. She sings it with a clear, bright tone, with few _nuances_ of light and shade, but in a broad, big style and expressive manner that well befits her theme. (N.B.—All the three contraltos who sing this piece begin the " He " with a penetrating vowel " e " that stands out like a splash of vermilion.)

Leila Megane (H.M.V., D.657) gains by vouchsafing the recit., and loses solely because she is made to hurry the lovely air, which, however, she sings beautifully. Her tone and words are quite admirable.

Louise Homer (H.M.V., D.B.301 one side ; reverse _He was despised_) is heard to great advantage in this record. Her rendering is complete, unhurried, and in the legitimate oratorio style. Very few American singers can command the Handelian phrasing with equal purity, and, bar some tremolo, the quality of the tone is rich and luscious.

Come unto Him is conspicuous by its absence.

6. _He was despised._

Louise Homer (H.M.V., D.B. 301) takes this ineffable melody at a faster tempo than tradition warrants, thereby lessening by a shade its wonderful pathos. Otherwise she sings it well. The words are distinct, save the ending consonants, particularly the " f " in " grief."

Carrie Herwin (Col. 915) adopts an even quicker pace, while the expression has little if any depth of religious fervour. The timbre of the voice is rich, but loud and a trifle unyielding where delicacy and refinement are called for.

7. _Thy rebuke, Behold and see, He was cut off, But Thou didst not leave._

Arthur Jordan (Col. 973 two-sided disc) is the only tenor who gives the whole of the Passion music ; and remarkably well he does it. A soft needle is necessary on the Grafonola to modify the power of his resonant tone, that is all. I have naught but praise for his poignant, manly expression, his well-balanced phrases, his unfailing sense of contrast. He has a pure tenor, and his vowel-tone is free from exaggeration.

John Harrison (H.M.V., E.55) sings _But Thou didst not leave_ with plenty of spirit, if with more vigour than discretion. He requires a soft needle or else the open air. The pressure never diminishes.

8. _Why do the nations._

Clarence Whitehill (H.M.V., D.B.435) is an excellent artist ; but Wagnerian and Handelian singing have little in common, especially where flexibility is needed. The tone is good, but the triplet runs are a mere scramble.

Malcolm McEachern (Voc. D.02087) is another scrambler, but a much rougher one. It is a fine voice with a slap-dash style. The runs are not only uneven, but the " rage " has no " g," and where breath is taken the vowel changes.

Horace Stevens (Voc. D.02145) succeeds fairly well in the runs and enunciates distinctly, despite the intemperate speed. He has a big voice, but does not overdo things, which is a good deal in favour of this record. There is rhythm, too, in his animation and vigour.

Norman Allin (Col. 1453) has ample opportunity here for his stentorian tone, and, were the triplets less slurred, the rest would count as this artist's best contribution to the present selection.

9. _He that dwelleth in Heaven ; Thou shalt break them._

Arthur Jordan (Col. 978) is again very satisfying here. The air demands ease of production, sureness of attack and intonation, bright ringing head notes. This singer has them all ; and he declines to interpolate the high A at the end which Braham and Sims Reeves were so fond of. Perhaps he is right ; still the tradition goes back a century.

John Harrison (H.M.V., E.55) is less reticent ; but, unfortunately, in getting up to the A, he rather smudges the passage. However, in this piece his natural energy is well placed, and he declaims it with just the right measure of spirit.

10. _The trumpet shall sound._

Norman Allin (Col. 1446) merits the exact criticism last used. What are faults elsewhere become excellences here, and the effect of the duet between the trumpet and the human voice is just what Handel intended—something that represents " waking the dead." But use a soft needle, unless your room is a hall.

Horace Stevens (Voc. D.02105) also gives his _obbligato_ a good race for power. Nevertheless, his fine bass voice remains clear and vibrant to the end, and his declamation no less solid and free. I append a list of the available choruses :—

Glory to God and _For unto us a Child is born_ (H.M.V., D.778).

Surely He hath borne our griefs and _His yoke is easy_ (H.M.V., D.779).

All we like sheep have gone astray and _Lift up your heads, O ye gates_ (H.M.V., D.780).

Hallelujah, Leeds Festival Choir (H.M.V., C.481).

Hallelujah, Sheffield Choir (H.M.V., C.930).

And the Glory of the Lord and _Hallelujah,_ New York Oratorio Chorus (Col. 451).

Glory to God in the highest and _Hallelujah,_ Sheffield and Leeds United Choir (Col. 331).

"ELIJAH"

1. *Ye people, rend your hearts* and *If with all your hearts.*

Walter Hyde (H.M.V., D.108) displays a sound oratorio style in this lovely tenor number. Over-pressure hardens his tone somewhat in the recitative, but not in the air, which he invests with the right degree of yearning, wistful expression. The contrasts of tone are unusually vivid.

Arthur Jordan (Col. 807) declaims and breathes so well that there is no need for excessive *portamento* or for the sentimentality which disfigures the return to the subject in the air. On the whole, however, an artistic rendering.

Hardy Williamson (Voc. K.05071) sustains very smoothly and with a nice tone. It is a pity his " dialectic " vowels have not been corrected.

Evan Williams (H.M.V., D.B.454) had such a glorious tenor voice that to hear it again in this record makes one grudge his omission of the recit. The air is too slow and drags ; but it is sung with intense sincerity and charm, and there is a wonderful touch of mystery in the " Oh, that I knew where I might find Him !"

2. *Lord God of Abraham.*

Clarence Whitehill (H.M.V., D.B.435) has precisely the nobility of tone and delivery for this broad strain of melody. It is a worthy effort, albeit the listener with a long memory will agree that it lacks the fervent appeal of Santley, who sang it rather quicker.

Robert Radford (H.M.V., D.267) has the right tempo and is altogether at his best here. A fine record.

Horace Stevens (Voc. D.02105) very properly begins with " Draw near, all ye people " and uses a more " covered " tone than usual. This, with the aid of a soft needle, brings out to advantage a superb quality of voice in a most impressive rendering.

Malcolm McEachern (Voc. K.05130) imparts an abundance of tone and sincerity of feeling to his well-sustained phrases, which require a large auditorium. It is a pity his English vowels savour so strongly of the West; they need refining.

3. *Is not His word like a fire ?*

Robert Radford (H.M.V., E.76) is again in capital voice in this record, and the tone is powerfully sustained to the end.

Horace Stevens (Voc. R.6145) gives a too staccato rendering. His voice is strong and resonant, and the words are distinct ; but one feels that the " hammer that breaketh the rock " also breaks the phrase " into pieces." However, the fault is not serious enough to spoil a good effort.

4. *It is enough.*

Charles W. Clark (Col. 1096) has a rather light baritone for the demands of this sublime air ; he also needs more distinction of style. But his voice is very steady, and in the middle section he displays adequate dramatic feeling.

Clarence Whitehill (H.M.V., D.B.438) is quite in his element in this touching farewell to earth, which reminds me, in many ways of his splendid *Wotan's Farewell to Brünnhilde.* Many vowels are over-closed, but the singing as a whole is finely dramatic and instinct with true pathos.

David Bispham (Rena, Berlin, 154) is the third American vocalist to provide a record of this air, with a voice that now, alas, is " still." I have had it in my possession several years, and am not certain whether it is now obtainable. But it is magnificent— a marvel of artistic singing and heartfelt expression.

Horace Stevens (Voc. D.02145) gives an original rather than a traditional reading. It is too full of *sforzandos* and *staccatos* for my taste, but in a large auditorium would doubtless sound well.

5. *O rest in the Lord.*

Kirkby Lunn (H.M.V., D.B.504) does not drag this inspired melody as so many contraltos do, but adopts just the right speed. It brings out the luscious quality of her medium to perfection, and she phrases it with true religious feeling.

Carrie Herwin (Col. 2626) hurries the tempo and employs a colourless but straightforward method. The voice itself is sympathetic.

Louise Homer (H.M.V., D.B.302) has somehow failed to achieve a satisfactory record of a piece that she can sing well. The voice sounds thin and pinched, the effect generally noisy and unsteady. I tried this on two machines and with several needles, but without improvement.

6. *For the mountains shall depart.*

Robert Radford (H.M.V., E.76) has, I fancy, transposed this down a semitone. Anyhow the voice is not at its best and the rhythm is dragged.

Horace Stevens (Voc. R.6145), more reticent than usual, employs the *messa di voce* here with admirable skill, and phrases like an artist a melody that is always trying for the departing Elijah.

7. *Then shall the righteous.*

Evan Williams (H.M.V., D.A.393) had an amazing *sostenuto* and a glorious tone, but neither did he display to good advantage in this difficult piece. It caught him at a moment when he was weak alike in accent and diction.

Hardy Williamson (Voc. K.05071) sings this with an excess of sentimentality and too slowly. It requires before all things manly vigour.

Choruses.—None. But I recommend an excellent record (H.M.V., C.481) of the overture to the oratorio, preceded by Elijah's opening recitative, finely sung by Peter Dawson. HERMAN KLEIN.

THE GRAMOPHONE AND THE SINGER

(Continued)
By HERMAN KLEIN

The Jubilee of "Carmen"—I.

WITH this article I celebrate the fiftieth anniversary of the first production of Bizet's *Carmen*, which took place at the Opéra-Comique, Paris, on March 3rd, 1875. It was an historic event, but not more remarkably so for British music-lovers than the Italian representation which introduced *Carmen* to this country at Her Majesty's Theatre on June 22nd, 1878, which I had the privilege of witnessing in the company of my teacher, Manuel Garcia. Between the two "receptions" of the opera, however, there was a great difference. Paris treated it coldly and even hissed it (thereby breaking Bizet's heart); London welcomed it with open arms. There were reasons—bad ones—for the former attitude, and I will explain them directly. Meanwhile, a word about the singers.

The original Carmen, Mme. Galli-Marié, was a charming artist. I heard her in the part when she came over and sang it at Her Majesty's eleven years later (1886) during a season of French opera directed by the late Mr. M. L. Mayer. Her voice was still fairly fresh, and I described her impersonation at the time as "a happy medium between the vulgar and the lady-like Carmens to whom we have been treated in turn. Her gestures are bold yet never coarse, her 'devilry' is neither too capricious nor too diabolical; as strong in her hate as she is in her love, this Carmen glories in her sense of power . . . She takes the *Habanera* much slower than anyone else, and when she dances for *Don José* she only sings an occasional bar or two of the tune . . . In the way of jewellery she contents herself with a pair of large gold ear-rings (such as gipsies wear), a simple necklace of oriental beads, and a brooch made of a large Burmese crystal." On this highly picturesque assumption every Carmen that we know has in effect been more or less based. No other member of the original cast appeared here with Mme. Galli-Marié; but at various times the chief ones—Lhérie (Don José), Mlle. Chapuy (Micaela), Bouhy (Escamillo), and Dufriche (Zuniga)—had been heard in London.

Our first Carmen—she of the Italian performance in 1878—remains, however, the most famous of them all. This was Minnie Hauk, a gifted American soprano who still survives and is residing somewhere in Switzerland, though some years ago she became totally blind and has since, I fear, fallen upon evil times. A native of New York, but of Austrian parentage, she was an artist of remarkable versatility and intelligence, and used her bright, resonant voice with admirable skill. She was a clever, subtle actress; her Carmen was a vivid, striking personality, more sensuous, more persuasive, in a word, more Spanish and panther-like than Galli-Marié's, whose creation, like Trebelli's and Calvé's, was more French than the type that Mérimée drew. The nearest approach to Minnie Hauk's unforgettable Carmen was, in my opinion, that of her still-living and talented country-woman, Zélie de Lussan, who therein certainly succeeded her in the estimation of English opera-goers. Both exercised the same fascinating charm, the same freedom from exaggeration; and both invented much new "business" that has since become traditional. What a pity that both retired from the scene before the day of the gramophone! Dozens of other Carmens have I seen and heard since those whose names I have mentioned—the superb Pauline Lucca, the graceful Marie Rôze, the attractive Lillian Nordica, the passionate Rosa Olitzka, the picturesque Giulia Ravogli—but outstanding vividly in my memory remain that unsurpassable perfect Carmen, Minnie Hauk, and her bewitching successor, Zélie de Lussan.

Practically all that we knew of Bizet before his opera was produced here was the lovely *Arlésienne* music (the No. 1 suite) and the *Habañera*, which Mme. Trebelli used to sing delightfully as a concert number. Once we had heard *Carmen* we really found it difficult to keep our tempers when we thought of the lovable genius who had given this work to the world, lying in his tomb at Bougival, near Paris, buried there at the age of 37, exactly three months after the night when the Parisians hissed his masterpiece at the Opéra-Comique. Even then time had taken its revenge; but too late, alas, to remedy a mistake that was unutterably stupid and inconsiderate, rather than vindictive or intentionally malicious. Swiftly as it came, the triumph of *Carmen* in France, in England, everywhere else, was powerless to re-animate the pen that had the originality and the courage to construct such a score.

But there is a fact to be noted that is too often forgotten or ignored in connection with the "five-minutes' failure" of *Carmen* in the city of its birth; and it is worth recalling now, after fifty years of success, as an example (like the Wagner example) of how careful critics should be in exercising their judgment upon arts that are in a state of transition. For it was not the daring of the musician alone that excited the anger of the Parisian purists. Besides objecting to Bizet's strange harmonies (that sound so simple and innocent to-day compared with those of Stravinsky and the Futurist " Six "), they were extremely annoyed, upset, even disgusted, with the operatic setting of Prosper Mérimée's story of *Carmen*, as laid out by those famous and experienced librettists, MM. Henri Meilhac and Ludovic Halévy. It simply demoralised them. They were utterly incapable of understanding how such wicked people as Carmen and Don José could possibly be allowed, much less tolerated, on the operatic stage. The Dame aux Camélias and the Garden Scene in *Faust* were bad enough, but this was positively shocking. (Such sinners as Santuzza, Lola, and Turiddu, as Nedda and Silvio, Tosca and Scarpia, or even Siegmund and Sieglinde and Tristan and Isolde, had not yet arrived within their purview.) Moreover, they openly denounced what they considered new and unpardonable liberties taken with the traditional rules for writing verse and rhymes (*sic*) in French opera. So, regardless of cruelty and its consequences, they simply went for the whole thing hammer and tongs !

Autres temps, *autres mœurs*, say the French. Perfectly true ; and, just to show how much ideas have changed since *Carmen* first withstood the attacks of the purists, I will quote for the first time in print a few oracular utterances made by one of the leading Parisian critics immediately after the *première* of poor Bizet's immortal opera. They will be few but funny, even as literally translated :—

" The opera contains some fine moments, but the strangeness of the subject has urged the composer into ugliness (*bizarrerie*) and incoherence."

The effect of the *Habañera* upon Don José is such that " from that moment, seized with mad passion for a vile creature, he will become during four acts—almost without remorse—successively a perjurer, a deserter, a brigand, a thief, a smuggler, and an assassin." Incredible !

" The scene at Lillas Pastia's tavern, as represented upon the stage of the Opéra-Comique, is in worse taste than any that I can remember to have seen enacted in the theatre. With the arrival of the bull-fighter, Escamillo, we behold Carmen providing herself with yet another lover (counting the officer Zuniga). Three of them in two acts ! —rather numerous."

Micaela's efforts to snatch José away from the temptress " afford some relief, though they are too obviously based upon analogous scenes in the opera of *Robert le Diable*. Truly a singular story for the libretto of an opera." (Why, oh why ?)

And as for the text and the rhymes, they are compared to " the worst that Scribe ever wrote for the operas of Auber," an insult to the memory of that great librettist which I would flatly contradict, even at this remote date, because I am familiar with them also. I have been guilty myself of an English adaptation of the book of *Carmen* (the score is published by Metzler and Co.), which has been sung at Covent Garden, and I can honestly say that the task of translating Meilhac and Halévy's delightful text was an unalloyed pleasure.

My final quotation from this angry criticism declares that Bizet was " too pre-occupied with seeking after picturesqueness and *couleur locale* "; that " he joined the apostles of the so-called ' music of the future ' (Wagner indeed !), and so broke with what had hitherto been regarded as the traditions of good taste, the satisfaction of the ear, of harmony in the concrete and special sense of the word. . . . Therefore, to correct the bad impression that has been created, it will be necessary to remodel the libretto, to remove its vulgarities, and its realism, to make Carmen a capricious gipsy, not a *fille de joie*, and to change Don José from a vile and odious fellow into a victim of sorcery."

So much for prejudice and bigotry. Nothing of all this has been done, and yet *Carmen* remains, after the lapse of half a century, one of the most popular, if not *the* most popular work in the whole repertory of modern opera. Neither in France nor anywhere else in the world would its admirers have it different from what it is. We love every note of it, and we forgive whatever may be repulsive in the character of its protagonists because we feel that they are true to life and that they faithfully reflect the masterful creations of Mérimée. In saying this I do not ignore the recent verdict of the B.N.O.C. supporters in Manchester. They have placed Wagner, Verdi, and Mozart in front of Bizet ; but I think I know the reason for that. They were asked to select the operas which they would soonest have performed by the B.N.O.C. during its forthcoming visit ; and, naturally, they gave the preference to those which they think the B.N.O.C. performs best—for example, the *Meistersinger*, *Tristan*, *Siegfried*, and *Aïda ;* these being followed by the *Magic Flute* and *Carmen*, which are not by any means the best. If this company could discover another great Carmen like Calvé or Zélie de Lussan, who years ago set the standard for this part all over the United Kingdom and America there would be a different story to tell—even in Manchester.

Anyhow, here we are celebrating this month the jubilee of *Carmen's* existence, and surely THE GRAMOPHONE could not do so in a more fitting manner than by presenting its readers with a portrait of Mme. de Lussan in her famous character, together with a review of a representative collection of the best obtainable records of the opera. This review I shall be unable to complete in the present issue, but I look forward to dealing with what is left over in the April number. Meanwhile, I am sorry that the law of progress has compelled the withdrawal of several records of *Carmen* numbers that were made too long ago for them to be acceptable now, those of Mme. de Lussan included. Perhaps the opportunities missed of worthily recording the great *Carmen* singers of the past will ere long be compensated for by one of those complete reproductions which are the pride of a newer generation. At present, of course, it is the connecting links that are chiefly conspicuous by their absence.

ACT. I.—*Prelude* and *Chorus*.

The solitary example of the orchestral *Prelude* is Col. D.5582, with which is combined on the reverse side the *Chorus of Cigarette Girls*. Both are rendered by the executive forces of La Scala, Milan, and therefore entirely adequate. The *Prelude* is especially clear and well-defined; the chorus, which begins with the preceding appeal for the men, is a trifle blurred in course of the modulations that constitute its main difficulty. Rarely, somehow, do Italian choristers, even now, manage to sing these in perfect tune, though it was worse by far in the old days, when they used to land themselves at this point a good semitone off the pitch.

The Habañera.

The place of honour in the rendering of this celebrated air belongs of right to Mme. Calvé (Pathé 5559), and, old as the record is, it is still passable enough to afford an idea of her treatment of it. Vocally we have here the essence of neatness, both in phrasing and diction, with no attempt at passion, but rather a gipsy-girl amusing her friends with a song of the people which they love to hear her warble. It was thought at one time that this *Habañera* was a genuine national tune, but it is nothing of the kind. Bizet merely provided his heroine with a clever imitation of the real thing; and it suits Carmen to perfection. Mme. Calvé allows it to tell its own tale. Her singing imparts all the necessary charm and is a spell in itself without the aid of further colouring or exaggeration.

It is extraordinary what a variety of readings the *Habañera* can inspire. No two of them are exactly alike; and in saying that I fancy I indicate the only important distinction between their respective merits. If it comes to choosing between them I will do so later on. A useful interpretation, because a faithful and complete one, is that given in Italian with the chorus of La Scala by Fanny Aniuta (Col. D.5583), who has a powerful mezzo-soprano and has done the whole opera for the

Columbia so far as the part of Carmen is yet recorded. She is evidently quite at home in it, gives you lots of chest-tone, and is very liberal with *portamento*. A capital record for a large auditorium.

In the matter of " atmosphere " the next three (all in French) are hard to beat. Each in turn cunningly contrives to convey the feeling, not only of the music, but of the dangerous gipsy-girl who, from the moment she set eyes upon José, has evidently been bent upon the conquest of that unlucky dragoon. Marguerite d'Alvarez (Voc. A.0200) may slur more than we like, but her fine voice is instinct with passion, and we feel it actually vibrating through the tone that she invests with so much life and colour. When she sings " l'amour " she utters the word as though nothing else existed for her ; and that is Carmen, no less than the little splashes of semi-vulgarity which she throws into her phrasing now and then. The castanets are a trifle over-loud, but I daresay they are intended to represent the chorus as well.

On a lower vocal plane stands the effort of Geraldine Farrar (H.M.V., DA.510), whose Carmen was yet non-existent when I heard her in New York. She is a wonderfully clever artist in parts that suit her, and I should imagine she would act the *Habañera* for all it is worth. As to her singing of it, she uses in this record what the French call a *voix criarde*, with a decidedly unpleasant nasal tinge that calls aloud for the use of a soft needle ; and she " blasts " quite unnecessarily on an E natural, a circumstance which age alone (in the record itself, I mean) can possibly excuse.

The third of the " atmospheric " renderings is that of Maria Gay (Col. A.5279), another Carmen of universal renown—one whom I have seen in the part and also admired in it. A born Spaniard, imprisoned in her girlhood for singing a revolutionary song in the streets of Barcelona ; who, when she was only 23, sang the rôle of Carmen (without having had a lesson in singing and at only five days' notice) at no less a theatre than the Brussels Monnaie, yet achieved a sensational success—for an artist with such a history as Maria Gay's one always feels what might be termed a favourable predisposition. (No doubt this was what the tenor Zenatello experienced when he married her just before the war ; but mine, which was more purely artistic, dates from six years earlier, when she sang at the Manhattan Opera House, New York.) It is quite remarkable how she concentrates the Carmenesque qualities in the singing of this record. It is brimming over with energy and vigour and rhythmical swing ; there are some exciting flashes of sparkling Spanish gaiety ; and yet as a whole the piece is really well sung, nothing is overdone. It shows us, if nothing else, that Maria Gay has a splendid voice and knows how to use it.

Tatiana Makushina (V.F. 590) is wrong in adopting for this music a jerky, staccato method. Nothing could be less suited to the character or the piece.

Duet—Micaela and Don José.

Under different titles I have three records of this graceful duet, which, by the way, a French critic once objected to because, he said, he had never heard of a mother sending a kiss to her son by his *fiancée*. How could the latter be so indelicate as to proffer such a " message "? Ah, well, that critic ought to have lived in the twentieth century ! In Italian, *Mi parla di lei*, Inez Ferraris and Luigi Bolis (Col. D.5583 ; reverse already noticed) give a very smooth and competent rendering—nice voices well in tune, style careful if without distinction. In English, *We had quitted the church* by Rosina Buckman and Maurice d'Oisly (Col. L.1062), suffers from a bigger cut than was really necessary, but has more life and go about it. The two voices blend well and are of sympathetic quality—a remark which also applies to the third example, *My mother I behold*, sung by Elsa Stralia and Frank Mullings (Col. 7332). Here the soprano records particularly well and the tone of both voices is very musical and resonant. Moreover, the orchestral accompaniment sounds just right.

The Seguidilla.

Here is another vivid specimen of the captivating dance rhythms that Bizet put into the mouth of Carmen. She may have gipsy blood in her, but her dance tunes are Spanish enough, and she evidently loves them as she loves fine clothes and cigarettes and the perfume of her crimson flower. But she cannot dance the *Seguidilla* tied more or less to a chair ; she can only sing it, and thereby worry the hapless José with every kind of suggestive touch—voice, look, gesture, accent—that she is capable of imparting to it. Two past-mistresses of the art have succeeded very well in doing this ; a third not so well ; while an Italian, Fanny Anitua

(Col. 5584), gives us only the shell, the musica. framework of her ditty, minus the life and soull A good voice and plenty of energy are not enough, even in a record. You feel the need of colour and contrast and an all-pervasive languorous charm. This last is abundant and convincing in the effort of Geraldine Farrar (H.M.V. DB.244), who gets true devilry into her " atmosphere," employs any amount of *rubato* and *rallentando*, and makes you hear every syllable of her French text. I think she transposed the whole piece a semitone higher (G major instead of F sharp)—anyhow it sounds better for her voice in the higher key, the *Carmen* music being a little low for her.

In this respect the piece is better suited to Marguerite d'Alvarez, whose French accent is also preferable (Voc. B.3102), but who would have made more effect had she hurried her *tempo* less. She is rather difficult to accompany, and gets a slightly flat F on " Voici la fin de la semaine " ; but her high B at the end is splendid for a contralto and altogether her record is to be praised. (By the way, I liked it best on the Sonora Model.) To conclude the group, and with it the first act of the opera, there remains an excellent rendering by the talented American singer, Olive Fremstad (in French, Col. A.5282, *Près des Ramparts*), whom I recollect as being a superb Carmen. The contrasts are less violent, but an abundance of colour and beauty in the timbre of the voice amply satisfies the ear until the last two notes—a jump of an octave, you remember—which are squeaked in the drollest manner.

P.S.—I have just received news of the death of Mme. Alwina Valleria, who was the incomparable Micaela in the first London performance of *Carmen*. An American by birth, she was an admirable singer and a great favourite both in Italian and English opera.

HERMAN KLEIN.

THE GRAMOPHONE AND THE SINGER

(Continued)

By HERMAN KLEIN

The Jubilee of "Carmen"—II.

BIZET is not easy to sing. His music, like that of Mozart and Gounod, has certain qualities, certain peculiarities of idiom and style, that demand from the vocalist technical gifts, both natural and acquired, of a high order. In this way it is very deceptive music. At first hearing, or even at first glance, it seems to be so melodious, so straightforward and rhythmical in its vocal line, that one feels inclined to say " Oh, if you are anything of a singer you can surely manage this ! " Yes, that is precisely the point ; it can be " managed " well enough, but to be sung in the polished manner that the composer imagined when he wrote those catchy tunes requires something more. He demands the " art which conceals art," and that, as we know, is the most exacting art of all.

Into the exact reasons for this hidden difficulty which pervades every page of *Carmen*, it would occupy too much space to enter at length here and now. But my experience both as a teacher and a critic has made me only too familiar with them. Indeed, I will admit without hesitation that I have heard even worse singing in *Carmen* than in *Faust*, which the humblest opera company will unhesitatingly attack, or *The Marriage of Figaro*, which the manager of any up-to-date troupe thinks fair game for his young people to exercise their talents upon. If the reader who judges by the contents of the gramophone catalogues cherishes any doubts upon this subject, let me point out, as a startling contrast, the disparity between the quantity of vocal selections from *Carmen* sung by the professional in the concert-room or the amateur in the drawing-room with the endless amount of Puccini that is purveyed in both by both. I am ready to wager that you will hear *Vissi d'Arte* or *Un bel dì* twenty times for one rendering of Micaela's song ; not because they are more beautiful, for they distinctly are not, but simply because they are infinitely easier to sing, and can more readily be made effective by the soprano who is not an accomplished vocalist. Your daring baritone will always be able, I know, to make the *Toreador's Song* go down (with a decent accompanist to aid and abet him), and the tenor with the necessary high notes will do as much, *perhaps*, with the *Flower Song*. After these things, however, what is there that you are likely to have offered you from *Carmen* ?—positively nothing ; unless it be in the form of a gramophone record.

Therefore, I say, let us realise from the outset that the *Carmen* music is not easy to sing, and that its value on the gramophone is not only enhanced by that fact, but to be counted proportionately to the credit of the artist who performs it. Bearing this in mind, both in retrospect and with regard to what is to come, let us now proceed with the consideration of our published records of the opera.

ACT II.

It is in this act that we get the two most popular numbers for solo voice, viz., the *Toreador's Song* and the *Flower Song* ; and, as a matter of course, both are very numerously recorded. Even with seven of the former and eleven of the latter I am by no means confident of having secured the whole of the available material, but—we have done our best. If there are others they are probably of " a certain age," and are now withdrawn from circulation—a contingency that collectors should always reckon with in these cases. And here I may mention that a set of three new Parlophone records which reached me too late last month comprise half a dozen instrumental selections that should be found very enjoyable. They are executed by the orchestra of the Berlin Opera House, under Dr. Weissmann, and have a sufficiency of full-bodied tone as well as rhythmical spirit and go, though the quality of the instruments is not quite up to ours. They consist (E.10245–6–7) of the following : *Introduction* to Act I. and *Chorus of Boys ; Entr'acte*, Act II. and *Smugglers' Chorus*, Act III ; *Intermezzo*, Act III ; and *Ballet Music*, Act IV. On the other hand, not quite so recent are the solitary Columbia examples of the

Gipsy Dance,

upon which the curtain rises in the scene at Lillas Pastia's, and of the subsequent

Smugglers' Quintet.

Both, however, are deserving of praise for great liveliness and energy besides precision of ensemble. The dance is numbered (D.5585) and on one side only, while the quintet is in two parts (D.5587–8), a sensible arrangement with so long a piece. Fanny Aniuta takes part in all, and her clear, powerful tone rather throws into relief the thinner notes of two girls and, still more, the rough, raucous voices of the two men. Vocally, therefore, the balance is not satisfactory, though the general effect is inspiriting. I have for convenience' sake taken these together, though in their actual order they are divided by the

Toreador's Song.

This is the number which won the greatest popularity in Paris in course of the thirty-seven representations of *Carmen* given during the first year it was produced. It is not with the swinging march refrain, however, that the singer finds any difficulty, but rather the extended compass, the swift, sudden contrasts, the whirl and animation of the descriptive narrative depicting the bull-fight in song. The nature of the task is proved by the fact that although the crowd loves and applauds and encores it, the *Toreador's Song* very seldom creates the impression of being sung with ease and elegance by a true *espada*, a typical Spaniard, a man to whom the danger of a pretty face is far more serious than the rush of an Andalusian bull. That was how Del Puente and Lassalle and Plançon contrived to make you feel. But not very often, I am sorry to say, can you feel so nowadays, even amid the excitement of the theatre, much less the cooler atmosphere engendered by the sound of a gramophone. Never mind ; here are some very good records, especially three by Italian baritones, who are on the whole the best Escamillos we have to-day. Mario Ancona (Pathé 5259) no longer sings on the stage, but he shares with Riccardo Stracciari (Col. 7355) and Cesare Formichi (Col. D.5586-7) the merit of putting a *legato* style and breadth of phrasing into this music, besides mere strepitous declamation. Stracciari's rendering is particularly telling, well sustained and powerful ; and so, for that matter, is Formichi's, which covers both sides of the disc. Emilio di Gogorza (H.M.V. D.B.625) sings his in French with excellent voice and style, supported by a chorus, and I prefer it to that of Gaston Demarcy (Imperial 1334), of the Monte Carlo Opera, who is breathless and hurried and trembles a good deal. In this last a predominant fault is that the music is declaimed rather than sung, without any vocal charm whatever ; and I make the same complaint concerning the English records of Norman Williams (V.F. 530) and George Baker (Voc. J.041200), both of which are extremely spasmodic in utterance. They try to be realistic and overdo it. An interesting link between the two big solos for the bull-fighter and the dragoon is the

Duet—Don José and Carmen,

which, so far as I can perceive, is wholly neglected by English gramophone artists. Of the two that are available there is most dramatic colour in the one which begins with the *Halte-là* (H.M.V. D.K.108), by Geraldine Farrar and Giovanni Martinelli. The latter trolls forth his ditty *f* throughout with the opulent tone of which he possesses such an abund-

ance. I think a gradual crescendo would have been better. The dance is sung by Miss Farrar with a rather excessive assumption of vulgarity, which she effects by a liberal mixture of open chest and medium tone ; while the castanets and the distant bugles sounding the retreat furnish the correct background. An Italian version by Fanny Aniuta and Luigi Bolis begins with José's entry (*Alfin sei giu*, Col. 5588) is less agitated, but on the whole not less effective. Both lead directly to the

Flower Song.

Six of the eleven records are Italian, two French, and three English, and I will refer to them briefly in this order. Between the first-named there is really little to choose ; they are typically Italian in the modern sense, as though cut out of rolls of the same quality and pattern, nearly identical in timbre, breathing, phrasing, and expression. Dino Borgioli (Col. D.1503) is more tasteful, but less robust and pure than Luigi Bolis (Col. 5589), who is very clear and telling. Manfredo Polverosi (Fonot. 69224) has a voice that wavers and becomes tremulous under pressure ; his words are a " cross-word puzzle," his reading an irrelevant fragment, his B flat feeble. *Per contra*, Michele Fleta (H.M.V. D.B.524) is extremely slow and sentimental ; he gives you the real " sob stuff," to which the listening Carmen must perforce succumb as soon as his mighty and prolonged B flat will permit him to add " io t'amo." Less lachrymose but more love-sick still, is the Don José of Armand Tokatyan (Voc. A.0224), who declares his feeling with much scooping and portamento, but as a matter of fact has a very agreeable voice. Best of all among the Italians is the Greek tenor, Ulysses Lappas (Col. D.1463), whose organ is not only of fine quality and power but artistically displayed, with a splendid high note at the end.

Of the two French records, I like that of Lucien Muratore (Pathé 5204) for charm of delivery and diction ; that of Florencio Constantino (Col. A.692) for its purely vocal attractiveness, and old Italian suavity of tone-production. The English " varieties " are acceptable too in their way : Frank Mullings (Col. L.1443), manly and vigorous ; Frank Titterton (Voc. D.02134), emphatic and in deadly earnest ; and John Perry (*V.F.* 1024), clear, smooth distinct, and effortless.

For the remainder of the act we have to rely mainly on the series (Col. D.5590-1), sung in Italian by Fanny Aniuta and her colleagues, which may be described in simple language as " rough but honest." The only other number is *Là-bas dans la montagne*, a continuation of the duet already noticed (H.M.V. D.B.244), and sung in French by Geraldine Farrar. This, unlike the Italian, does not include the whole of the finale, with the other solo voices and chorus.

ACT III.

Here, to my thinking, Bizet is at his finest, excelling in originality, romantic splendour, and dramatic characterisation either of the previous acts. The ensembles are enriched with exquisite harmonic colouring and astonishing contrasts of rhythm; the climaxes grow with a delicacy of graduation and a sense of power that betray the master hand. Some day, perhaps, they will be reproduced for us on the gramophone with the perfect balance and beauty of tone that they deserve —the voices all equally good, the nuances of light and shade carefully studied, the handling of crescendos and diminuendos as skilful as it would be in a Mozart quartet or a Beethoven symphony. As it is, scarcely anything so far recorded rises to the level of the music. The ten-inch Columbias continue to fill in certain gaps, sometimes creditably, sometimes crudely, but always with Italian fluency and efficiency; as, for example, in the ensemble *Il nostro affar è il Doganier* (Col. D.5592), which follows directly after (Col. D.5591–2) a complete reproduction of the inspired episode known as the

Card Trio.

In this scene, where Carmen's superstitious foreboding of death at the hands of her despised lover is first revealed, the cue arises from the merry duet of the gipsy-girls, Frasquita and Mercedès, whose piquant repartee, whilst they tell their fortune with the cards, is not a bit less important as a background than the tragic fatalism of Carmen which provides the main issue. The trouble is that in this record, even more than on the stage, the heroine takes the centre to a degree that relegates the other fair smugglers to absolute obscurity; while another actually obliterates them altogether. Nevertheless, Fanny Aniuta manages to be impressive with the aid of a large supply of chest tone; and so does another Milanese mezzo-soprano, A. Parsi-Pettinella (Fonot. 92037), though this lady over-accentuates her words at the expense of a resonant dramatic voice. The best individual rendering is that given in French by the talented Maria Gay (Col. A.5279), who cannot help being intensely dramatic and realistic or putting the true atmosphere into her Carmen, whether in the theatre or the recording-room. But it is realism without exaggeration, an effort not merely of voice and speech, but touched with the *afflatus* of born genius. What we have here may not be a veritable picture in sound of the *Card Trio*, but it is at least a graphic and moving delineation of Carmen's presentiment as she turns up the cards and reads " death " in her book of fate. For so much let us be thankful and pass on to

Micaela's Air,

which I have in Italian, French, and English. The first (Col. D.5593) is beyond the capacity of Inez Ferraris, who may be good enough for Frasquita, but is quite unequal to this really difficult air, which so many sopranos believe easy—till they try it. The 'cello obbligato is missing, and replaced by chords for the strings both here and in the excellent English record of Elsa Stralia (Col. 733), the tone whereof is clear and the text commendably distinct. For all-round merit, however, highest praise must be awarded to an original French version of Alma Gluck (H.M.V. D.B.279)—a delightful commingling of musical, expressive tone, clear diction, and artistic phrasing. The sole flaw in the whole thing is the superfluous " turn " and high B flat at the concluding bar.

In the succeeding

Duet—Don José and Escamillo,

the latter is represented (Col. D.5593–4) by Cesare Formichi, who henceforth holds his place in the Italian series to the end. He lends it both dramatic value and rich vocal colour, though it must be admitted that the tenor, Luigi Bolis, is quite his equal in the scene of the encounter, which begins at *No, non m'inganno*. In fact, I prefer this to the record (H.M.V. D.B.554) starting with *Ho nome Escamillo*, sung by Bernardo de Muro and Roberto Janni, which has a less spirited swing to it. The finale to the act follows, and is completed (Col. D.5594–5) on three sides of the two discs. There is no other rendering, but this is sufficiently adequate.

ACT IV.

With a reminder that the charming dance music of the last act (one number of which Bizet appropriated from his earlier opera, *La Jolie Fille de Perth*) occurs in the Parlophone group already noticed, there remains only to mention the two duets. The first of these is the

Duet—Carmen and Escamillo,

the tune of which many good judges consider the melodic gem of the opera; certainly it is one of those heavenly strains, " of purest ray serene," that one finds only in the pages of the great masters. The French version starts from the chorus acclaiming the entry of the Toreador and his radiant sweetheart, and the delicious *Si tu m'aimes* (H.M.V. D.K.107), admirably sung by Pasquale Amato and Geraldine Farrar, fills only the latter half of the record. On the other hand, Cesare Formichi and Fanny Aniuta (Col. D.5596) start at once with their duet (voices well balanced), and the rest comprises the captivating bit of musical dialogue wherein the two girls warn Carmen that Don José is lurking in the neighbourhood. The latter excerpt is the better of the two because it leads naturally into the

Duet Finale—Carmen and José,

which forms the climax of the drama. The Italian (Col. D.5596–7) cover three sides of two discs, sung by Fanny Aniuta and Luigi Bolis. The French are complete in two sides, namely, *C'est toi, c'est moi* and *Je t'aime encore,* sung respectively by Helen Sadoven and Fernand Ansseau (H.M.V. D.B.784) and by Giov. Martinelli and Geraldine Farrar (H.M.V. D.K.108). This last is not quite so satisfactory as the record of *Si tu m'aimes;* still the tone of both singers is very big and dramatic—Martinelli intensely pathetic in its despairing appeal, Farrar's fearless, defiant, contemptuous as ever. Helen Sadoven, another mezzo-soprano owning a lovely but tremulous voice, joins that excellent French tenor Ansseau, with irresistible emotional force. And so two fine records bring out all that is vocally so touching, so impressively tragic, in the concluding scene of this wonderful opera.

If Bizet had not been one of the greatest lyric composers, he would have been one of the greatest pianists of his time. Liszt considered him as a boy one of the most amazing prodigies he had ever come across. But he was too full of music of his own, and its well-springs had perforce to overflow through broader, nobler channels than fingers and a keyboard could provide. HERMAN KLEIN.

❦ ❦ ❦

THE GRAMOPHONE AND THE SINGER

(Continued)
By HERMAN KLEIN
"Madam Butterfly"

IN Puccini's own estimation *Madam Butterfly* was his best opera. I agree with him that it was, and I am also inclined to believe that it brought him a larger income in royalties than either the *Bohème* or the *Tosca.* The strange part of it was that when first produced in its original shape at La Scala, Milan, in 1904, it was as good as hissed off the stage. The audience hooted and booed in true Italian fashion, as though they had hated Puccini instead of loving and admiring him; they would not have his Japanese opera at any price. Obviously there was something the matter with it, beyond the mere question of unfamiliar atmosphere and personages, but exactly what it was difficult to say. Puccini was not to be discouraged, however. He talked it over with his friend, Tito Ricordi, then the head of the famous publishing firm, and between them they decided that certain scenes needed to be shortened and remodelled; otherwise there was surely nothing wrong with either the story or the music. It must have been very early in 1905 when I heard from Luigi Mancinelli (who had then conducted at Covent Garden for sixteen years) that *Madam Butterfly* had been tried again in its revised form at Brescia, and with so much success that he looked forward to introducing it to London in the following season. But *l'homme propose,* etc.; for Mancinelli was not well enough to conduct after the *Bohème* performance on June 24th, and his successor, Cleofonte Campanini, had the privilege of directing the new opera on July 10th, with Destinn, Caruso, Scotti, and Gabrielle Lejeune in the principal parts. Puccini himself was present, and that splendid performance has always remained in my mind the perfect model for the rendering of this opera. Needless to say, it was received with the utmost enthusiasm.

The first English performance that I heard was in the following year in New York, where I was then living, and for which Mr. Henry W. Savage engaged me to train all his artists—two complete casts—in their diction studies. Tito Ricordi came over to put the finishing studies to the production, which took place at the Garden Theatre on Nov. 12th, 1906. At the Metropolitan Opera House *Madam Butterfly* was not given until the following February; Caruso and Scotti being associated this time with Geraldine Farrar, while Louise Homer was the Suzuki. In both languages the opera was splendidly sung and always rapturously applauded. I shall never hear it better given. Puccini went to America expressly for the productions of this and his *Manon Lescaut,* which was also a novelty there, and his reception when he entered the huge opera-house was one of the finest tributes that the popular composer ever received.

It is not inappropriate to recall these facts, because it was to an American magazine-writer (Mr. John L. Long) and the play founded upon his story of *Madam Butterfly* that Puccini owed the material for the libretto of this opera. How much of it all was due to the genius for stage effect of that arch-producer, Mr. David Belasco, has also to be borne in mind, notwithstanding the failure, comparatively speaking, of Puccini's second attempt to borrow from the same source—namely, in *The Girl of the Golden West*. But never mind; one *chef d'œuvre* from a single field is not a bad harvest; and there can be little doubt that in the opinion of the world at large *Madam Butterfly* is a veritable masterpiece. The music is extraordinarily melodious, original, curiously and cleverly harmonised. Its suggestion of Japanese colour, like that of Sullivan's *Mikado*, owes little if aught to national tunes, but it does suggest them very often in a wonderful degree. It is grateful music for the singer; it contains many strong dramatic climaxes; the orchestration is masterly in its variety and its use of clever devices; the ensembles are interesting, and one chorus at least—that based upon the letter *motif* and sung at the back with *bouche fermée*—is as haunting as it is ingenious. Altogether I know no opera from the same pen that boasts the same fertility of resource and characterisation, or that palls so little upon the ear, no matter how often it be heard.

My task as reviewer differs in the present instance from that which confronted me in the case of *Carmen*, in that I am not dealing with a heterogeneous collection of records from various sources, but with an entirely novel product in the shape of a single series of gramophone records covering the whole opera of *Madam Butterfly*. This product, enclosed in a handsome, elegantly-bound album, consists of fourteen double-sided 12in. discs, and comes from the *ateliers* of His Master's Voice. It reflects upon that firm's infinite credit, involving as it does a much less easy proposition than the recording of the Gilbert and Sullivan operas, which just preceded it. *Madam Butterfly* is not divided up into "numbers," but is a continuous affair; and the points for breaking off have been well selected, while very few cuts have been made. We have here practically the music of the entire work, and the cast of English singers employed is as follows :—

Madam Butterfly (Soprano) ..	Rosina Buckman.
Suzuki (Mezzo-Soprano) ..	Nellie Walker.
F. B. Pinkerton (Tenor) ..	Tudor Davies.
Kate Pinkerton (Mezzo-Soprano)	Bessie Jones.
Sharpless (Baritone)	Frederick Ranalow.
Goro (Tenor)	Sydney Coltham.
Prince Yamadori (Baritone) ..	Edward Halland.
The Bonze (Bass)	Edward Halland.
Conductor ..	Eugène Goossens.

It is nobody's fault, I suppose, that the English adaptation of Illica and Giacosa's libretto used here is that published in the Ricordi vocal score, and necessarily sung in English performances of the opera. It is not one of those translations which will tend to foster the admiration and love of the British public for opera in the vernacular. Like those of the *Bohème* and *Tosca*, it is undistinguished, lacking in poetic grace, too frequently stupid and commonplace. Nor is it very singable either. In America I was obliged to alter many of the words and eliminate others that are superfluous, as, indeed, I find Mr. Ranalow has wisely done with his part in the present version. The pity is that, once the damage is done, there is no real remedy for this sort of thing. Messrs. Ricordi are rather obstinate in such matters and perhaps a trifle too indifferent at the outset. The cost of reprinting scores and bringing out new editions is, of course, far too heavy to be contemplated, even if artists can be persuaded (which they cannot) to put themselves to the trouble of learning improved versions of operas that they already know. Consequently, the H.M.V., and with them Mr. Eugène Goossens, and after them the vast community of gramophone lovers, must, like myself, perforce be content with the verbal gifts bestowed upon them by the gods of Milan!

But the music remains unaffected, reproduced as it is with a measure of spirit and accuracy that is truly delightful to the critical ear. The undercurrent of orchestration flows throughout with pellucid clearness, neatly and delicately executed, and almost as easy to follow as in the theatre. Seeing what a part it plays in the score of the opera, this means no small achievement. If it is occasionally rough, happily it is not so at the moment when the voices are in evidence. Thus at the very beginning of Act I. the noisy prelude dies down directly Pinkerton and Goro start their conversation in No. 1 anent *The Walls and the Ceiling*, and the words come out fairly well. (By the way, I am not quoting the catalogue number of each of these 28 records. Enough that they begin with D.893 and run on regularly from Nos. 1 to 10, on five discs, these containing the first act.) Even at this stage I perceive by my Columbia Grafonola that the voices of Mr. Tudor Davies and Mr. Coltham will benefit by the use of a soft needle; there is no need for Goro to be quite so explosive, or for Pinkerton's narrative to Sharpless to be so strongly emphasised.

The duet between the two Americans is continued in No. 3, *Is the bride very pretty?* Here Mr. Ranalow's tone is excellent and his diction incisive and smooth. Here, too, the girls arrive. In No. 4, *What a sky, what a sea!* Butterfly's voice should approach gradually, but Miss Buckman is already "on the spot." She is especially loud on syllables with "e" or an "a" in them—a disparity that might have been guarded against; but when she sings *piano* her tone is very sweet and sympathetic. It sounds well later on in the colloquy with Pinkerton, when she shows him her "girl's few possessions," and in that with Sharpless in No. 5, *What might your age be*, which Mr. Ranalow sensibly reduces to "What is your age?" (Also he brings out the fact that Butterfly is eighteen, not fifteen; a wise precaution, seeing that the stage baby appearing in the next act is generally half his mother's age.) Then comes the ensemble with the relations and officials who gather for the wedding, and here Mr. Ranalow's voice dominates the scene. No. 6, *I should like to*, continues the music down to the end of the marriage ceremony and makes a remarkably effective record. In No. 7, *Dear Madam Butterfly*, that harsh personage, the Bonze, comes in with his fierce denunciations of poor Cio-cio-san, leading up to the departure of Sharpless and the relations, all of which cleverly suggests the stage atmosphere. Finally, in Nos. 8, 9, and 10, we get the whole of the love duet for Butterfly and Pinkerton. It is, on the whole, capitally sung by Miss Rosina Buckman and Mr. Tudor Davies, despite the stress laid by the former on her favourite "forward" vowels, and there is abundant passion in this concluding episode of the first act.

Apropos of Miss Buckman, I would mention that her inequalities of resonance are considerably modified by the use of a soft needle, and also by playing her records on the Sonora Model. At the same time, this can only be done at the expense of the orchestration, which comes out best, I find, on the Grafonola—information which will only be valuable to those who can choose between the two. Happily, however, our Butterfly improves as she goes on; that is to say, after No. 11, in which she scolds poor Suzuki with jets of penetrating tone that really hurt. Being now in Act II., No 12, *And with his heart so heavy*, promptly brings us to *Un bel dì*, and there, somehow, the inequalities are so much less perceptible that one can enjoy the most hackneyed piece in the opera without reservation. What follows is equally good. Sharpless comes upon the scene for the next six records and his singing is simply splendid; in fact, I fancy I am right in surmising that Mr. Ranalow inspires Miss Buckman as much here as he might on the stage. After No. 13, *Come, she's here*, we have the entrance of the love-sick Yamadori and the subsequent confab between him, the Consul, and Butterfly, extending to No. 14, *We were saying*, and No. 15, *You hear me*.

The fine bass voice of Mr. Edward Halland tells well all through here, and the picturesque bits of orchestral colour stand out in strong relief. Where Butterfly is emotional Miss Buckman is quite admirable; the lovely quality of her voice comes out in its true beauty. In the letter scene and in No. 16, *How on earth can I tell her*, Mr. Ranalow's alternate touches of humour and pathos enable us to visualise the whole picture. Then No. 17, *Look here, then!* introduces the wonderful baby, that should be two years old, and on the stage always looks

(thanks to the law) seven or eight. Butterfly's fantasy and the departure of Sharpless fill the remainder of this and most of No. 18, *'Tis late, I must be going*. The succeeding scene with Suzuki (No. 19, *Look, 'tis a man of war*) carries us on to the first part of the Cherry-blossom duet, which ends in No. 20, *Not a flower left*. Miss Nellie Walker, an artistic singer with a sympathetic contralto timbre, is quite equal to her share of the task, and the two voices blend admirably. So it goes on to the close of the act, the quaint incident of the "make-up" and the preparations for the all-night vigil (*Bring me now my wedding garment*, No. 21), followed by the Letter melody, which the distant voices sing *bouche fermée* with all the accustomed effect.

The third act is the shortest, and it has less interest both dramatic and musical, than the other two. To me poor Butterfly's tragedy, with its inevitable climax of desertion and death, is always distinctly painful; I resent the presence of Mrs. Pinkerton the Second as an unwarrantable intrusion, and her request for the child as a downright piece of cruelty. Anyhow, there it is; we must accept it as one of those unpleasant *dénoûments* whereof operatic stories afford too many examples, and be thankful that at least it proceeds swiftly to its close. The orchestral introduction is contained in No. 22 and flows on into No. 23, *'Tis daylight*, with the distant snatches of choral song and the *reprise* of the pretty cradle lullaby to which Butterfly takes away her child. Both records are well made, and enhance our admiration for the alertness and skill that Mr. Goossens has bestowed upon the whole of the instrumentation. In the trio for Suzuki, Sharpless and Pinkerton (No. 24, *Who is it?*) the composer is at his strongest, and the two men put plenty of energy into it; but the Suzuki (who in this act is Miss Gladys Peel, not Miss Walker) sounds weak by comparison. After No. 25, *Is it not as I told you?* —well-merited reproach!—the American men make room for the two wives, whose pathetic encounter also fills No. 26, *He is here!* Mr. Tudor Davies delivers his full-voiced farewell without stint (it is his most generous deed), and Miss Buckman infuses genuine dramatic power into the concluding passages of her act of renunciation, as set forth in the last two records, No. 27, *Ah, can you not forgive me?* and No. 28, *You! You!*

On the whole this final climax is not unworthy of an opera that is replete with emotional outbursts and pathetic situations, nor is its rendering inferior in this new gramophone setting to the best that has gone before. Once more let me offer my tribute of sincere and hearty eulogy to all associated in what must have been an extremely difficult task, and also to the enterprising house at whose instance that task was undertaken.

THE GRAMOPHONE AND THE SINGER

(Continued)

By HERMAN KLEIN

The Royal Opera Season

ONCE more, for all too brief a space, does the Spirit of Grand Opera rule over an active working establishment within the honoured walls of Covent Garden. It resumed its neglected duties, for the benefit of a long-starving aristocracy, on May 18th, a date which unfortunately fell too late for any notice of the actual performances to appear in the present issue of this magazine. But, whilst postponing criticism until our next number, there is no reason why something should not be said beforehand concerning published records of certain of the less familiar operas that are down for revival—no real novelties whatsoever being underlined for production.

First of all, though, a word about the enterprise itself. It has been launched by a body called the London Opera Syndicate, whereof Lieut.-Col. Eustace Blois is the managing director, Mr. Percy Pitt the musical director, and Mr. Charles Moor the *régisseur*, with the customary personnel of the older syndicate working in the background. I need scarcely say that Covent Garden in the middle of the London season remains, despite its vegetable and floral surroundings, the ideal house for what we now term "international" operatic undertakings of this brilliant but evanescent type. Neither in shape nor holding capacity does it resemble the kind of national opera-house that is being projected, for instance, by Mr. Isidore de Lara. The auditorium of the latter would not be designed for showing off dresses and tiaras, or for society celebrities to meet and stare at each other. In that respect the two places would be so unlike in purpose that if both were standing in the same parish there would be no real reason for their clashing. Still, if opera at cheap prices cannot possibly be made to pay at Covent Garden, it is so eminently suited for high-class expensive opera that one is extremely glad to see it occupied for this purpose, if only for a couple of months, at the present time of year. *Dum vivimus, vivamus*, and, so long as it stands, the old house in Bow Street has every claim to be recognised and utilised as the legitimate home of grand opera (so-called) in the capital of the Empire.

In accordance with latter-day custom, the season started with a spell of German opera, omitting for once, however, serial performances of *The Ring* in its entirety. There were good reasons for this, an especial one being the very short time for preparation that was found to be available. Hence, moreover, the frank confession made by Colonel Blois at the outset that in the planning of this season operas had been "fitted to artists rather than artists to operas." Under the circumstances the repertory announced in the prospectus was sufficiently interesting. Wagner and Strauss supplied the works for the German month; Verdi, Donizetti, Rossini, Puccini, Giordano, and possibly Ponchielli, the wherewithal for the Italian month that is still to come. The revival of *Der Fliegende Holländer* was particularly welcome after an absence of twelve years from the bill. It is one of my favourites, and all true Wagner-lovers listen to it with pleasure, not only for its own melodious sake, but because it embodies the first unfolding of the master's new ideas and style after he had begun to cut adrift from the conventions of Spontini, Weber and Meyerbeer, as manifested in his earliest big opera, *Rienzi*.

The Flying Dutchman was the first of Wagner's stage works to be produced in English by Carl Rosa, under whose own direction it was brought out at the Lyceum Theatre in October, 1876, with the unforgettable Santley as Vanderdecken. Curious is it to recall how strange and exotic the music sounded to our ears at that time—even, perhaps, to those who had already heard it in Italian at Drury Lane six years previously; though not, of course, to the privileged few (myself *not* among them) who had just been listening for the first time to the *Nibelungen* at the opening of the new Bayreuth Theatre. Another six years were to elapse before (1882) we were to hear Wagner's colossal tetralogy in this country at Her Majesty's Theatre, with a complete German company and some of the original cast, at which time, it must be admitted, we were barely ready for it. In the self-same season, too, we were granted at Drury Lane Theatre, under Hans Richter, the initial hearing in London, also in German, of *Tristan und Isolde*, which glorious music-drama, it is interesting to note, had its 100th performance at Covent Garden on the second night of the current season.

Of Strauss's brace of operas *Der Rosenkavalier*, with last year's cast, evoked a much brisker box-office sale than *Elektra*, and for the best of reasons. *Elektra* is a work to see once, for the satisfaction of sheer curiosity; and perhaps a second time, in order to confirm one's first impressions concerning its supremacy as an agglomeration of dramatic and musical horrors. I like it even less than *Salome*, and that is saying something. On the other hand, I have a considerable admiration for the *Rosenkavalier*, despite the pungent Viennese flavour of its libretto and the over-lengthy attenuation of interest of the story in the restaurant scene of the last act. But the latter you are compelled to sit out, because you would not on any account miss the superb trio which is one of the great musical moments of the opera—perhaps the greatest. Had he written naught else for the theatre, the reputation of Strauss as an operatic composer of distinction might rest with perfect security upon this achievement. Were it of equal merit all through, it would suffice to stamp him for posterity as the legitimate successor of Wagner. I believe Germany, or at least Austria, already looks upon him in that light. In the meantime the world in general regards with infinitely greater favour the operas of Giacomo Puccini.

And mention of Puccini brings me to a consideration of the Italian half of the season now in progress. Truly, as I have said, there is little here that is not familiar, save in the personality of the artists to whom it will be entrusted; and with them I must perforce deal later on. But the moment seems favourable for saying something about two operas that are down for revival, and which have not been heard at Covent Garden for eighteen years: I refer to Giordano's *Andrea Chénier* and *Fédora*. Both are exceedingly popular in Italy, where I suppose Umberto Giordan, since the death of Puccini, has been regarded as the greatest among native living composers. His gifts fairly entitle him to be so considered. Born at Foggia in 1867, he was educated at the Naples Conservatoire and competed for the Sonzogno prize which Mascagni gained with *Cavalleria Rusticana*. But if his one-act opera *Marina* did not win the prize, it was nevertheless much commended by the judges, and brought the commission for his opera, *Mala Vita*, produced at Rome in 1892. Four years later success came to Giordano in full measure with *Andrea Chénier*, which remains so far his masterpiece. Brought out at La Scala, Milan, in 1896, it was first given in England by the Carl Rosa company at Manchester in 1903, and at Covent Garden, in the original Italian, during the autumn of 1905, with Zenatello, Sammarco, and Febea Strakosch in the principal parts. It was also performed twice in the summer of 1907, but since then has not been repeated here. During the latter year I heard it

for the first time at the Manhattan Opera House, New York, and formed a favourable opinion of its merits.

The story of *Andrea Chénier* is founded by Luigi Illica upon incidents in the career of the talented young poet who flourished and faded during the tempestuous period of the French Revolution. The last three acts take place in Paris, but the scene of the first is laid at the castle of the Count of Coigny, where Maddalena, only daughter of a proud and wealthy house, comes under the poet's influence and they fall in love. The whirligig of the revolution reveals another admirer in the *ci-devant* lackey Gérard, who was once Chénier's friend, but is now his rival and enemy, being, moreover, a powerful official in the service of the Republic. Upon the situation thus brought about an interesting plot is constructed, and some highly dramatic scenes are contrived. The best of these are the lengthy episode of Chénier's trial before the revolutionary tribunal and the final interview which the repentant Gérard secures for the lovers in the prison before the poet is led out to execution. These scenes occupy the third and fourth acts respectively, and in both instances the music gradually grows in intensity until it rises to the fullest heights of passionate feeling. Great music it may not be; original in the true sense it is not either; but it bears the characteristic stamp of the modern Italian school—of Mascagni and Leoncavallo, perhaps, rather than Puccini—and beyond a question it is melodious, dramatic, picturesque, effectively written for the voice, boldly and cleverly scored for the orchestra.

Qualities of much the same order distinguish the score of *Fédora*, though, for reasons that must be attributed in part to the libretto of Arturo Colautti, it does not make quite so good an opera. Giordano has himself described how he came to choose the subject of Sardou's play. He had, when a student in Paris, seen Sarah Bernhardt in it (as did the present writer on the first night it was performed), and was so fascinated both by the play and the great actress that he begged Sardou to grant him permission to make an opera of it. This was duly accorded, but Giordano admitted that he found difficulty in getting his librettist and converting *Fédora* into a first-rate operatic story. However, when it was given in Paris in 1905—one year before it was produced at Covent Garden with Giachetti and Zenatello—Sardou was present. He liked the opera so much that he invited Giordano to his villa and forthwith offered to write a new " book " expressly for him; which he did, calling it *La Fête du Nil*, and dealing with Napoleon in Egypt, the scenes being laid in and near Cairo. Only, there was to be no music for Napoleon, who was seen but once in the second act, near the Pyramids, at nightfall. Giordano, when in London in 1906, said that he hoped to complete this opera for production in Paris in the following year, but I cannot discover that it has ever been produced anywhere. He also hoped that his *Siberia* would be done here. It still awaits that honour; but I saw the New York performance in 1907 and found it, I am bound to say, extremely dull.

When *Fédora* was first mounted in Italy at the Teatro Lirico, Milan, the two chief rôles were splendidly sung by Bellincioni and Caruso—the former the original Santuzza of *Cavalleria Rusticana*, in which part and also in *Carmen* I heard her at Covent Garden in 1895. Caruso must have been a magnificent Loris Ipanoff; while probably the most attractive Fédora of past days was Lina Cavalieri, who invested both the character and the music with an infinite degree of charm. The setting of Sardou's story is fairly forceful and coherent, seeing what a quantity of dialogue of a conversational sort is contained in it; but on the whole the strength of the plot and the dramatic intensity of much of the music save it from dullness. The former is too familiar to call for narration here. Other famous actresses besides Sarah Bernhardt helped to make Fédora a famous character; for it contains tremendous opportunities, and the situation alike in the play and the opera are among the most effective that the resourceful Sardou ever invented. A well-known London critic once remarked concerning Giordano's work, " You cannot go to sleep when listening to *Fédora*." And if you understand what the story is about you need certainly find no difficulty in keeping awake.

The majority of the records from *Andrea Chénier* at my disposal are by the H.M.V., and the dramatic incidents which they illustrate are briefly set forth in the admirably-arranged manual published by that firm under the title of *Opera at Home*. (A cheap and useful volume that ought to be in the possession of every gramophone-lover.) They must be described as excerpts rather than " numbers," for there are no set lyrics in *Andrea Chénier*; the action is continuous, and only interrupted by the fall of the curtain at the end of each *quadro* or tableau. In point of fact, it is as essentially a music-drama as if it were by Wagner or one of his many imitators. Giordano pays little heed to questions of " form "; he is content to ignore all the old-fashioned rules and conventions of operatic writing. He takes a phrase as it comes; sets it to music for what it is worth; expresses its meaning in a passage that exactly fits it, after the rich, rare, and racy modern Italian style; then passes on to the next one. But it is all very effective; for there is abundant colour and variety in the vocal treatment, in the alternation of melodic charm with declamatory vigour, in the accompanying flow of orchestral device. In short, it is the kind of thing—highly individualised, of course, for Giordano has an

unmistakable hall-mark of his own—that Italian opera of to-day has gradually developed through the successive stages indicated by the works of Ponchielli, Mascagni, and Puccini. Only these we know a great deal better than we know Giordano.

The gifted baritone, Titta Ruffo, has made a splendid record of the soliloquy, *Son sessant' anni* (H.M.V. D.A.351), sung by the discontented lackey, Gérard, almost at the opening of the opera. It embodies his angry reflections as he watches his old father toiling with his broom in the winter garden of the Coigny castle. Needless to say how Titta Ruffo makes the most of such an opportunity as this, declaiming every phrase with broad vowel tones and unrestrained ardour of expression, emphasizing the value of every consonant and the weight of every syllable. Later in the same scene comes the well-known " improvisation " of Andrea Chénier, beginning *Un di all 'azzurro spazio*, of which I find three excellent examples. It demands a plentiful supply of powerful sustained tone throughout; and of this there is no lack in the modern operatic tenor. Ulysses Lappas (Col. L1514) may be a Greek by birth, but he is undeniably Italian by adoption, and therefore does not spare himself here. At the same time he is very intelligent, his sharp contrasts are very striking, his delivery and diction well controlled. The recording, too, is extremely good. In Beniamino Gigli (H.M.V. D.B.670) the same typical qualities emerge, but the rendering differs at certain points. I admire particularly the imposing crescendo where the poet depicts the sun flooding with golden light " il firmamento," and leading to the outburst which exasperates the assembled " aristocrats " whilst kindling love in the heart of Madalena. More resonant than either of these is the rendering by Bernardo de' Muro (H.M.V. D.B.553), whose voice and style remind me not a little of Tamagno—penetrating, passionate, and powerful, yet occasionally quite subdued and tender in feeling.

From Tableau II. there is nothing; but from the third there are three, beginning with what is, I believe, the most famous passage in the opera, viz., the *Nemico della patria ?*—wherein Gérard signs the lying document that ultimately sends the poet to the guillotine. Declaimed by Titta Ruffo (H.M.V. D.B.242) in his finest manner, this is from every point of view a magnificent record. The second is Elisabeth Rethberg's *La Mamma morta* (Bruns. 50054A), from the tremendous scene where Maddalena confronts Gérard and promises him anything, everything, if he will only save Andrea. In this a well-executed record reveals a fine voice of true dramatic soprano timbre, clear, pure, and pathetic, save only at moments when over-pressure makes it a trifle hard and unsteady. The change of the closing G to an octave higher than it is in the score is fully justified by the effect. The third is Chénier's appeal to the tribunal, *Si, fui soldato*, by Bernardo de' Muro, which fills the reverse side of the record by that artist noticed above. It is an equally telling bit of declamation and ends on a notably fine phrase —" You would kill me ? Be it so. But do not deprive me of my honour."

In the concluding tableau we have a beautiful version by Enrico Caruso of the poet's touching monologue, *Come un bel dì di Maggio* (H.M.V. D.A.117), the last poem that his pen is to indite as he awaits death in his prison cell. Here in a faultless record is to be found the same wonderful tone of old ; dark, strong, manly, pathetic in a singular degree, yet not marred by over-many sobs. It is an effort worthy of the great tenor, and the high B flat inserted between the two G flats in the last bar but one seems to be a customary effect, doubtless introduced with the composer's consent. The same thing is done by Ulysses Lappas (Col. L1514) in his exceedingly dramatic rendering of this piece, which some readers may be glad to possess in addition to the Caruso. It is well worth hearing. The final duet, *Vedi ? la luce incerta del crepuscolo* (Parlo. E10122), is an outburst of ecstatic passion for the hero and heroine just before they are led out to execution. It is sung by A. Cortis and Z. Fumagalli with any amount of strenuous energy ; and with it the opera comes to an end.

The yield from *Fédora* is ridiculously small for a long opera in three acts. The reason, however, is explained by the fragmentary nature of the musical setting, due to the conversational method employed by the librettist. The sole approach to an air is the passage wherein Loris Ipanoff declares that Fédora's awakening love for him will assert its sway in spite of her efforts to extinguish the flame. The title, *Amor ti vieta di non amar*, appears on records by three singers, namely, A. Bonci (Col. D8086), B. Gigli (H.M.V. DA225), and Ed. Johnson (H.M.V. D.A.166), and on the whole there is not much to choose between them. Gigli has a fine organ and sustains the long-drawn phrases without a semblance of effort. His fault is that he carries to excess his imitation of the Caruso " sob," especially in the second excerpt from this opera, *Vedi, io piango*, which appears on the reverse side of D.A.225. For artistic restraint and contrast of colour, Bonci presents a preferable reading, to an orchestral accompaniment in which the harp is very prominent. This able singer is beginning to develop a slight tremolo, but his tone in the head notes is still extremely pure, and unforced. I cannot say the same for the Johnson record, which conveys without mitigation the maximum of energy and force.

HERMAN KLEIN.

THE GRAMOPHONE AND THE SINGER

(Continued)

By HERMAN KLEIN

Opera at Covent Garden

IT has been a very busy season—so busy, in fact, that I fear I have had no time to spare for the legitimate gramophone work which I owe to the readers of this magazine, and comparatively little for the collection of really interesting material concerning the first or German half of the performances at the Royal Opera. The fact which stands out in clearest prominence with regard to the latter is that its financial success has far surpassed the most sanguine expectations of its backers, and has put into the shade all experiences during the regular grand season at this house since before the War. Night after night, for five nights in the week, the demand for seats has been extraordinarily large—large enough, indeed, to fill the big theatre very nearly or quite to " capacity." The public appetite for the

German representations seemed to grow with what it fed upon, and, when they reached their allotted span by the middle of June, I imagine the new *entrepreneurs* must have felt some qualms of regret that they had not opened their campaign a fortnight or so earlier. For all that, it must not be too readily assumed that they had so far succeeded in making ends meet. Opera on the " international " scale is a vastly expensive business ; the outlay that has to be incurred for so short a period, with artists all demanding tip-top terms, makes the idea of profit practically out of the question. To cover expenses under such conditions is really an achievement, and the most that can be hoped for.

What the future may have in store is another question. I am quite prepared for a big develop-

107

ment next year. As America has plainly shown us, unlimited capital and a direction with a clearly-defined policy can accomplish wonderful things where opera of the international type is concerned. After the encouragement vouchsafed the present Covent Garden undertaking we may confidently expect a considerable extension next year—probably twelve or even sixteen weeks instead of only eight. If so, it is to be hoped that there will be no unnecessary economy in any particular department, especially one that has given rise to much adverse criticism during the recent German performances. I allude to the dearth of good German tenors.

By a happy chance, I was seated next to Herr Bruno Walter at the annual dinner of the Critics' Circle, held at the Trocadero Restaurant on June 7th. Like the new musical knight, Sir Hamilton Harty, and many theatrical celebrities, the gifted conductor was among the distinguished guests whom the critics " delighted to honour " on that occasion, and I did not lose the opportunity to ask him a few questions. For instance, I wanted him to tell me whether, in his opinion, the Wagnerian tenors whom we had heard this season provided a fair sample of the best that Berlin, Vienna, Munich, or Dresden could supply at the present stage of Continental reconstruction? His reply was given without the slightest hesitation :

" By no means. How it has come about is not for me to say ; but the fact remains that there are at this moment at least three, and possibly half a dozen, splendid *Helden* (=heroic) tenors in Germany and Austria, any one of whom is superior to those whom London has lately been hearing." And then he went on to mention names ; but as Herr Bruno Walter is a man whom I esteem for his personal qualities and charm no less than his outstanding ability as a great conductor, I have too much regard for him to violate his confidence beyond this point. Doubtless, too, the mistake will not be repeated another year. Herr Walter told me he had never had a better orchestra to conduct in all his career, or one that answered so quickly to the helm : " It was simply amazing what your English players accomplished in the short allowance of time for rehearsal at our disposal." He was also warm in his admiration for the gifted sopranos and baritones of the company, and I agreed with him that they, most of any, preserved the high level of the great Continental artists who used to visit this country in the past to impersonate the leading characters in the operas of Wagner, Strauss, and other modern composers.

There is nothing to say here about the Strauss operas that has not been said before. I have no patience to write about *Elektra* and its horrors, and the cast of *Der Rosenkavalier* was virtually identical with that of last year. But one revival there was which, although the work itself was probably the most familiar of the lot, interested me in an especial degree because of the very pleasant memories that it brought back. I allude to that of *Lohengrin*. To begin with, it was the fiftieth anniversary, almost to a day, of the first production of Wagner's opera in this country and at this very house. The coincidence appeared to have escaped general notice ; but it did not escape mine, for perhaps I was the only person—certainly the only critic—in the house who could claim to have been present on both occasions. Never can I forget that warm May night in 1875, when I sat perched up in the gallery, sharing my Novello octavo score with friends on either side, and yielding for the first time to the enchantment of music that sounded at once so new, strange, and beautiful. It was sung in Italian, the conductor was an Italian (Vianesi by name), and the cuts were huge. But what did that matter ! The Italian chorus did not wander so much further from the key than the German one did now ; nor was the French Lohengrin of yore, the gallant Nicolini who was to become the second husband of the incomparable Adelina Patti, nearly so disappointing as the tenor from beyond the Scheldt whom the Covent Garden swan (was it the same, I wonder ?) tugged on to the scene in 1925. And our first Elsa ?—none other than Dame Emma Albani, the talented French-Canadian songstress, who was then our most versatile and musicianly prima donna and soon to be the daughter-in-law of the eminent impresario of Covent Graden, Mr. Frederic Gye, and whose friends of to-day, by celebrating (without knowing it) this interesting jubilee with a supplementary benefit concert, had secured her tardy admission to the list of Dames of the Order of the British Empire at the good old age of 72 !

Well, speaking without prejudice, I think I can honestly say that the fair Lotte Lehmann—lovely of voice, winsome of aspect, dignified of mien, admirable in her art—was not more wonderful in all these things than the Emma Albani of half a century ago. I preferred listening to this music in the original language, of course ; and Lotte Lehmann is a singer who lets you hear every word that she has to utter ; also, thanks to the absence of cuts, she gave us more of the part of Elsa than we are accustomed to hearing nowadays even at Covent Garden. But enough of comparisons, otherwise I shall go on indulging in them *ad infinitum*, even to the extent of contrasting the various members of the recent German casts and, regarding *Lohengrin*, of complaining because one of the greatest of Ortruds, Marie Olczewska, should have had to give way to a less gifted in the person of Bella Paarlen. That's precisely where the shoe pinches—as Eva is supposed to say to Hans Sachs—in the short-season distribution of operatic rôles. The artists you would like to hear may all be in the company, but you cannot contrive to hook them all at once and include them in the cast of your own particular choice. I say no more about the Knight of the Swan, but, on the other hand, I have rarely heard since Edouard de Reszke a King Henry so smooth and sonorous, so dignified and imposing in delivery, as Otto Helgers. The way he led off the prayer in the first act, with that magnificent bass of his, was quite exceptional. Emil Schipper is another artist of the first rank, and his Telramund, like his Wotan, reveals notable individuality of thought and style. I like studying his facial expression; it is, as it should be, the faithful index to the processes of his mind, and you can see (when the stage is not too dark, as at the opening of the second act of *Lohengrin*) the precise effect upon his disposition of scolding wives like Ortrud and Fricka. Moreover, he takes his " medicine " bravely, even though his resistance be weak, and so carries out Wagner's intention to the letter.

Another unpremeditated anniversary of the German season was the hundredth performance of *Tristan und Isolde* at Covent Garden on May 19th. The pity was that it should not have been more wholly worthy of the occasion; but with such an inadequate Tristan as Laurenz Hofer proved himself to be, the rare merits of artists like Gertrud Kappel (Isolde), Friedrich Schorr (Kurwenal), Maria Olczewska (Brangäne), and Richard Mayr (King Marke) could scarcely be enjoyed at their full value. I cannot put it better than did the able critic of *The Times* when he wrote of this tenor as very much below the average, and added that " the man who can sing the intimate melodies of the love duet and the monologues of the last act as though he were addressing a public meeting is not the Tristan we want to hear." On a subsequent night his place was taken by another " inadequate " tenor named Soot, who had been hurriedly brought over for the purpose by aeroplane; even so he was not to be inspired to great deeds by that superb Isolde, Frida Leider, than whom no more inspiring singer of this part has been heard since the famous Milka Ternina. To the constant *habitué* it was doubtless a no less constant source of interest to watch the respective methods of the two conductors, Herren Bruno Walter and Robert Heger, who divided pretty equally the labours of leadership. I had not previously seen the latter in the conductor's chair, and, truth to tell, I think he proved himself a most reliable and alert occupant thereof.

For instance, it was Robert Heger who directed the repetition of *Die Walküre* on June 3rd, and the amount of spirit that he infused into his beat produced a corresponding effect from those under him, especially in the more exciting moments of the second and third acts. The preliminary scene in Hunding's dwelling began a trifle slowly. Here one could feel that the cool, calm, but beautiful Sieglinde of Delia Reinhardt was taking an un-usually long time to awaken to the touch of passion. In the end, however, she responded warmly enough to the call of a strange Siegmund, who was beginning to wake up at about the same psychological moment. He was no other than that fine English tenor Morgan Kingston, who, called upon at short notice, did himself and his country immense credit. His clear, ringing tones and experienced art stood him in good stead in the love duet; and I admired him even more in the scene with Brünnhilde (Gertrude Kappel), where, apart from his poetic phrasing, the timbre of his voice conveyed just the right sombre feeling and sense of fatality. It was exactly the kind of " white " voice that one wants from Siegmund at the moment when the heavy hand of destiny is laid upon him. This was consequently a scene worthy of association with those between Wotan and Fricka and Wotan and Brünnhilde, whose admirable exponents I have already named.

The revival of *Der Fliegende Holländer* was worth the trouble, for the same reason that actuated Bayreuth years ago—because it embodies the most significant turning-point in the early Wagnerian development. But it is not one of the master's great works, and does not repay too frequent hearing. Not even a Frida Leider can sustain the interest of Senta beyond the limits of her big opportunity throughout the second act, where it both begins and ends. Still it is a privilege to hear a Dutchman with the wistful, romantic spirit of Emil Schipper, and to enjoy another proof of the rich versatility of Richard Mayr in a part so *ennuyant* as that of Daland. I cannot speak personally of *Die Meistersinger*, and I say this with genuine regret for more than one reason. I am told that the performances of it which came during the final fortnight afforded—save as to the part of Walther—well-nigh unalloyed delight.

THE ITALIAN SEASON.

On Monday, June 15th, Covent Garden began a brilliant display of new *prime donne*—new, that is, to us, but by no means new to contemporary fame in countries that spend more on opera than we do. Society was ready to acclaim the fresh arrivals, and did so in serried ranks, at any rate on the first two nights of " Ascot Week," which is as far as circumstances will allow this chronicle to extend. Well, after all the wonderful things that have been said about Toti dal Monte at La Scala, and Jeritza at Vienna and the New York Metropolitan, it was certainly interesting to see and hear them in the flesh; by which I mean to indicate, otherwise than through the medium of their gramophone records. The first-named, making her début in *Lucia di Lammermoor*, challenged every sort of comparison. She also made sure of a rich opportunity; every point was scored with the certainty and accuracy that come of ample experience. She has a pure soprano voice of fairly extended compass, with clear but occasionally hard head notes, and sings like an Italian born and trained. In the *Regnava nel silenzio* we heard a smooth *legato*, a delicate *cantilena*, a crisp, pearly scale (not so perfect in chromatic as in diatonic passages), and brilliancy alike in the staccato and the shake. This air brought down the house ; but somehow the sextet failed to do so, perhaps for lack of a big climax in the voices to match that of the brass and the big drum. Here, if anywhere, Lucia should wake up to the awful cruelty of her brother's deception, and depict the anger and despair that precede her insanity. But Toti dal Monte took the situation, so to speak, " lying down," sang prettily, and never attained an exciting moment. On the other hand, her " Mad Scene " was from first to last an elaborate conception, slow and deliberate in execution, replete with clever and often touching vocalisation, if not with brilliant flights or *tours de force* that could exactly be termed thrilling. She acted it well—indeed, acted well throughout—and altogether proved herself a highly accomplished stage artist. This, and not a great singer, is what I must describe her as being. The support was, on the whole, moderate. The tenor, Dino Borgioli, was without charm ; he could not compare with the Edgardos of past days, who used to sing with Patti and Nilsson, Albani and Melba. The Enrico, Badini, was admittedly suffering from a cold, and the others were tolerably efficient. The conductor, Antonino Votto, acquitted himself ably of an easy task.

The triumph of Maria Jeritza in *Tosca* on the following evening was due as much to a winning personality and magnificent acting as to the effect of her ringing, powerful tones and genuinely dramatic singing. Here, as I fully expected, was an artist who could produce in the opera house a far deeper impression than that created by her gramophone achievements ; therein differing from Toti dal Monte, who resembles Galli-Curci (and most other *coloratura* singers, I imagine) in that her records attain a higher level of vocal perfection than when she is facing an audience. But what a Tosca !

What a combination of all the qualities, human and artistic, that go to the making of that many-sided creature ! Jeritza is not exactly like any one of her great predecessors in this rôle. She unites, though, some of the strongest characteristics that distinguished each, and she brings them into sharp contrast with the adroitness and skill of a mistress of her art. Thus by turns she gives you the feline touches of Sarah Bernhardt, the feminine devotion of Ternina, the tempestuous passion of Destinn, the shrinking fear of Emma Eames. Tenderness alternates with jealousy in the church scene ; anxiety, alarm, and resentment with burning rage, despair, and gloating, satisfied vengeance in the terrific duet with Scarpia. Then, after the prolonged physical struggle, whilst she is lying full length on the ground, her face distorted and her wonderful hair all dishevelled, she half murmurs, half weeps the bitter plaint of *Vissi d'arte* with an intensity of emotion such as no Tosca off the stage has ever yet dared to put into a gramophone record. It was not in this air that she " forced " her tone, as has been suggested ; but if she did so at all it was at certain moments in the tremendous episode when it was far more pardonable to over-stress the *fortissimo* than do the reverse. At such a climax it seems wonderful how a singer with a temperament like Jeritza's can keep control of her forces as she does ; for she makes you feel that the vocalist is not being studied in the least—that all physical power is being reserved to meet the demands of the actress. Altogether, then, her Tosca is an intensely striking and superb performance. Beside this display of sheer genius the Scarpia of Benvenuto Franci was tolerably impressive, but nothing more. He has a fine voice and used it well in isolated passages, but as a rule his declamation was too rough and noisy. Cavaradossi had a competent representative in an American tenor named Aroldo Lindi. The new Milanese conductor, Sergio Failoni, was probably too nervous to do himself justice, but he improved as the opera went on. The warmth of the enthusiasm and the number of recalls must have reminded him of the Scala at its liveliest. HERMAN KLEIN.

THE GRAMOPHONE AND THE SINGER

(Continued)

By HERMAN KLEIN

Record Singers at Covent Garden

ON the whole, I fear, they were rather a disappointing lot, for singers of "international" repute. Quite good they were, of course; but not altogether up to the old standard. That is the worst of the present-day system of "booming" new-comers and lauding them to the skies in the most exaggerated language. It makes you expect too much. All the inflated nonsense that the press agents get into the newspapers constitutes a bad preparation for sensible criticism, because it leaves the ordinary person in bewildering doubt as to which of the two is likely to be true and correct. Speaking for myself, I may be *désillusionné*, but I am far from being *blasé*. I still retain my precious faculty for admiring and enjoying the beautiful in art, even with a lifetime of glorious memories and rare musical experiences behind me. I can still appreciate the singing of a first-rate artist without the kind of rejuvenating aid that Mephistopheles accorded Faust—in his case for a consideration. (True, Faust was not a musical critic, nor even until he somehow became engaged in opera, a regular student and professor of the vocal art, being merely, as we know, a philosopher tired of life.) No one, as a matter of fact, could have been readier than the present writer to be delighted by the celebrities who appeared at Covent Garden in June and July.

Experience has now proved that it is the exception rather than the rule for singers to live up to their gramophone reputations. In other words, their records are generally several degrees nearer perfection—by which I mean what is *their* very best—than their *viva-voce* achievements before a public audience. It was so in the case of Galli-Curci; it is so in the case of Toti dal Monte. In both there can be no question to my thinking that the gramophone listener gets the best of it. In the recording-room the influence of nerves may be almost, if not quite, left out of calculation; and there, again, imperfections can be removed by the simple process of repeating the piece as often as may be necessary until the best result is attained. Galli-Curci has not been heard here on the stage, but she probably would not come much nearer to doing herself justice at Covent Garden than at the Albert Hall. Toti dal Monte is slightly more self-possessed before an audience than her famous rival, and she is also far more deliberate. She did better at the Albert Hall, in the opinion of many good judges,

than she did at the Opera. She was also infinitely to be preferred in the comedy of *Il Barbiere* to the sentimental tragedy of *Lucia*. But her technique, as I said last month, is quite wonderful; it is only the quality of some of her head notes and the accuracy of her chromatic scale that are open to criticism—apart from that irritating pause which precedes every cadenza, as much as to say, "Now listen; you are about to hear something marvellous!"

With Maria Jeritza it is the other way about. She is heard to much greater advantage in the opera house than on the gramophone; and in any case, notwithstanding the warmth and richness of her voice, it is her fascinating personality and her clever acting that interest you more than her singing. Exaggeration apart, her striking impersonation of the Tosca will dwell in one's memory long after her rendering of Puccini's music has faded into oblivion. Herein, therefore, one suffered only a partial disappointment. In *Fedora* the balance was about even. The 10in. disc of two excerpts from this opera recently given out by the H.M.V. (D.A.579) supplies a wholly truthful reflection of Jeritza's voice and style, and they make of the music about all that there is to be made of it. *Son gente risoluta* is a trifle too strident, especially on the "e" sounds; but as regards animation and emphasis the rendering is just right. The *Dio di Giustizia* on the reverse side is the shorter but more interesting of the two. The plaintive tones come in with welcome sweetness after a charming orchestral introduction, and the snatches of melody are touchingly phrased.

Come we now to Elisabeth Rethberg. I found her voice in *Aïda* exactly as I described it in the June number of THE GRAMOPHONE after hearing her *Mamma morta* (Bruns. 50054A) from *Andrea Chénier*. It is a lovely organ, skilfully managed, only rarely hardened by over-pressure; and her singing is marked by exemplary steadiness of tone as well as purity of style. But it was not the right voice for Aida. It sounded too light, too thin in volume, lacking in the richness and power that had satisfied me in the gramophone record; in short, no more impressive to the ear than I found her infelicitous "make-up" as Amonasro's daughter to the eye. The Southern warmth of her slightly ochreous complexion was not adequately reflected either in her singing or her acting—the latter more restless, more suggestive of the aspen leaf in human shape, than I care to see in the most apprehensive of Aïdas. Now, unluckily, I could not see Elisabeth Rethberg as Madam Butterfly, which rôle must unquestionably suit her much better. But her performance in Verdi's opera added one more proof to my growing conviction that the gramophone record, however perfect and pleasure-giving in itself, must not always be regarded as a reliable indication of the effect that the singer will produce either in the piece or the part inside an opera house. I must say, however, that Rethberg's Aïda gained immensely, vocally speaking, by comparison with such a consistently noisy, strident Amneris as Georgette Caro, and also with that more justifiably stentorian baritone, Benvenuto Franci, who does not often seem to remember the meaning in his own language of the words *piano, mezza voce,* or even *messa di voce.* Finally, for a great conductor, Leopoldo Mugnone might have kept his orchestra down much more.

Elisabeth Rethberg's *Ritorna vincitor* was one of the best things she did in the opera—smooth, full of contrast, well phrased, dramatic in conception and feeling. She was thinking then of her singing, not wasting effort on starts and shivers and physical contortions. I do not remember to have heard her record of that piece (assuming that she has made one) ; but what I have heard and enjoyed quite as much is her rendering of Schubert's *Serenade* (Brunswick 15069A.), sung in the original German, with an orchestral substitute for the original piano accompaniment. This is a wholly delightful interpretation of the familiar *Lied,* clear, appealing, *fairly* steady in tone and faultless in intonation. The Dresden soprano is scarcely so satisfying in *Solveig's Song,* which occupies the reverse side of this record, because she takes it too slowly and thus limits herself to one verse only. Besides, her medium register is not invariably so sympathetic as usual, owing to excessive breath-pressure. But the quality of the *mezza voce* is lovely, and her tone in the refrain exquisitely musical.

Whilst on the subject of records by the Covent Garden stars, I may as well complete my brief survey with a word about two by Toti dal Monte and Jeritza. The former's *Deh vieni non tardar* (H.M.V., D.B.831) is given minus the recitative, and with a cheerful Italian disregard for the *appoggiature.* One looks in vain here for the true Mozart style, for the immaculate purity of phrasing and avoidance of mere effects which that style entails. Yet on the whole the immortal melody is neatly and agreeably sung ; it has considerable vocal charm, and the admirable *sostenuto* that Toti dal Monte owes to her correct breathing. Nevertheless, I am quite sure that her delivery of this air at the Albert Hall concert was in a purely artistic sense superior to her record of it. On the other hand, Maria Jeritza's *Vissi d'Arte* (H.M.V., D.A.565) is as unquestionably a better vocal achievement here than the realistic reading which she gives whilst gracefully but anxiously reclining upon the floor of Scarpia's apartment. It may not be free from harsh tone on the more acute vowel sounds (a common fault with the German singers), but it is sustained with a finer *cantilena* and a more convincing sense of Tosca's right to complain of the poor reward she gets for all her good deeds. On the reverse of the same disc is the Austrian soprano's very careful but not particularly " atmospheric " rendering of the romanza *Voi lo sapete,* from *Cavalleria Rusticana.*

Having already dealt in my June article with the principal records of *Andrea Chénier,* there remains only to say a few words about the Covent Garden performance. It did not disappoint me because I knew the opera well enough not to expect great things. It was all very picturesque, lurid, and revolutionary, and so forth ; but, all said and done, how little of it got over the footlights—or past the noisy orchestra—that filled the soul with joy or imagination ! I was certainly not troubled by direct comparisons of any sort. The only one I found myself making was between the juvenile Margaret Sheridan of six years ago—the pretty little promising Irish Iris of Mascagni's opera— and the more mature—the almost portly—Maddalena of this ugly tragedy of '89. But even that comparison was very faint ; for I failed to recognise the one in the other, and speedily forgot that I had gazed upon an earlier figure or heard an earlier voice. If Miss Sheridan is to be regarded as a specimen of the Italianised British soprano of one's dreams, then I can only say that some people's taste in these matters must be extremely curious. It is always a pity when expectations are raised above the normal, and in this respect Miss Sheridan's case is one that calls rather for sympathy than blame. But she has in reality a pleasing, musical voice, and if she will refrain from forcing or from the further cultivation of a *vibrato,* she has still every chance of becoming an excellent artist. I have no intention of going through the cast of *Andrea Chénier* seriatim. The new tenor, Giacomo Lauri-Volpi, has a voice of great resonance and power, capable of some variety of colour and depth of expression ; and, save that he now and then lost his hold on the pitch, his singing left few loopholes for criticism. Moreover, he maintained control in his louder outbursts, which was more than could always be said of Benvenuto Franci—otherwise a fine baritone and a capable artist—in his dramatic portrayal of the vacillating flunkey-revolutionist, Gèrard. As in Aïda, the ensemble of orchestra and stage showed the talent of the veteran Leopoldo Mugnone in a more favourable light than that of the new-comers who had preceded him in the conductor's seat. The young conductors at La Scala are not all up to the level of Toscanini, though they go forth equipped with credentials from him.

There was much that was interesting, and not a little that was instructive in the manifesto issued towards the close of the season by Lt.-Col. Eustace Blois, the managing director of the London Opera Syndicate. It was something of a surprise to learn that, in spite of the improvement on 1924, the eight weeks' season had resulted in a "steady substantial loss." Perhaps it would have been wiser to deny at once, instead of leaving uncontradicted, the periodical announcements that the house had been sold out in advance and that no seats for the cheaper parts were obtainable for days beforehand. The promise to publish in due course a summary of the actual financial results was extremely welcome, as being likely to shed a useful light upon future possibilities. But what sensible person does expect " grand opera " to be self-supporting in this or any other country ? As regards the repertoire chosen for the Italian representations, I do not quite agree that the best was done that was possible in the circumstances, even allowing that first thought had to be given to the requirements of the artists engaged. We could have done perfectly well without Strauss's *Elektra* ; we could have done with less Giordano, or even with none at all ; and no one was exactly dying to hear *Lucia* again or any other of the old prima donna operas, unless there was time to rehearse them adequately and mount them to perfection. And if the old school was to enjoy a revival where, oh where was Meyerbeer ? Only that is another story, and one in which I shall have something to say, I hope, ere very long.

The complaint that too much criticism has been directed at the *mise en scène* commands my entire sympathy. Everyone knows that Covent Garden is years behind the times in this department. It possesses neither the resources nor the inventive genius of Vienna, Berlin, Prague, or half a score other Continental opera houses in capitals that are

not supposed to own a hundredth part of London's wealth. It is scarcely reasonable to expect a modest Syndicate coming into Covent Garden for barely two months in the year, to accomplish things which require an enormous systematic outlay, and must either be provided for by the State in support of a national institution or be justified by big advance subscriptions for virtually the whole of the private boxes and stalls that the house contains. It is precisely this last guarantee that Lt.-Col. Blois tells us his Syndicate means to make sure of before next December, prior to determining its plans for another season in 1926, with a better programme that shall suit the artists to the operas and not the operas to the artists. I wish him all success in his creditable effort.

P.S.—Among operatic records recently issued by H.M.V. I would assign a high place to those of Dinh Gilly. They are out of the common as to choice, artistic in execution, and up to the loftiest mark as examples of up-to-date recording. Two bits of Puccini (D.A.559) represent the lamented *maestro* in his earliest and latest manners—viz., *Scorri fiume* from *Il Tabarro* and *Vecchia zimarra* from *La Bohème*—and both are excellently sung. The *Legende de la Sauge* from Massenet's *Jongleur de Notre Dame* (D.B.693) comes out well because of its refinement and grace, just as the deeper note of tragedy permeates the big air *Il est venu*, from that extraordinarily bizarre opera, *La Coupe du Roi de Thule*, by *Eugène Diaz* (D.A.558), which has been justly forgotten since its production at the Paris Opéra in 1873. More welcome than these things will be the duets from *Butterfly*, sung by Dinh Gilly with Joseph Hislop, and which fill two sides of one disc (D.B.743) under the respective titles of *Amore o grillo* and *Dovunque al mondo*. Both artists are heard to the greatest advantage. I wish I could say as much for Mr. Murray Davey's delivery of *Pogner's Address* from *Die Meistersinger* (Voc. A.0234), but unfortunately I find it dull and monotonous in the extreme.

HERMAN KLEIN.

THE GRAMOPHONE AND THE SINGER

(Continued)

By HERMAN KLEIN

The Treasures of Meyerbeer—I.

FOR some years now Meyerbeer has ceased to be a fashionable composer. When Wagner came into favour his old rival slowly but surely made his exit from a scene where there was apparently not room for both at the same time. I say "apparently" because in reality, as was proved by certain exceptions, there was ample space for the two masters in the affections of opera-lovers who could see good in each. Thus in France, where Meyerbeer was nurtured, so to speak; where his most important operas were first given to the world; where the greatest dramatic singers of their time devoted themselves to the study and exposition of his music —in France, I say, he is nearly as popular to-day, with certain sections of the public who support their operatic institutions, as he was fifty years ago. In America, too—South as well as North—they still go to hear him occasionally, when visited by tenors of that heroic order to whom Jean de Reszke, Tamagno and Caruso belonged (alas, there are now only a few second-rate imitations of them available) and where the Meyerbeer traditions have not yet wholly faded into oblivion. But these places are only the exceptions. In most countries that I am acquainted with, including more particularly this tight little island of ours, the chauvinists and the highbrows have taken excellent care so to discredit Meyerbeer and all his works in the minds of their fellow-men that there would seem to be little chance of reinstating him in their favour, as one of them has just said, this side of the year 2020.

It is the highbrows who are chiefly responsible. As in the case of the celebrated Dr. Fell, the "reason why they cannot tell"; but they hate Meyerbeer, and they have hated him this many a year, with a hatred that is almost fanatical in its intensity. It started in a gingerly sort of way in the 'eighties among the disciples of Stanford and Parry, victims of *trop de zèle*—critics and others whose onslaughts gathered strength as time went on, and the object of their dislike grew less and less recognizable under their continuous mud-slinging. But managers like Augustus Harris and Carl Rosa did not share the views of these young men. They liked Meyerbeer, and continued to revive and mount his operas to the end of their careers, to the entire satisfaction of the British public, side by side with their memorable productions of the whole of the Wagner repertory.

So long as these two great impresarios survived there was ample room, most assuredly, for both Wagner and Meyerbeer; but when they died it did not take long for the highbrows to get the upper hand. The example of Bayreuth, of Munich, nay, even of Dresden, proved too powerful for the newly-educated minds of the rising generation, and it quickly became impossible for the one school to tolerate the other. If you loved Wagner, you must necessarily desire to send Meyerbeer to the bottomless pit ! Only let me point out that, so recently as the opening year of the present century, a great operatic centre like Vienna was still able to tolerate and enjoy the much derided combination. When I was there in 1901 I was present at one of the finest performances of *Le Prophète* that I ever witnessed. And who should be the Jean de Leyden (the pseudo-Prophet) on that occasion but the famous tenor Winkelmann, who had succeeded Niemann at Bayreuth, and created Tristan and Lohengrin and Walther in German in London at Drury Lane, under Hans Richter !

A few months ago I was moved to write a couple of articles for a leading American daily paper on the subject of "The Singing of Meyerbeer," wherein I think I made it clear that the main trouble about his music was not its "insincerity" or lack of beauty, but the technical difficulties which it presented to the average opera singer of to-day. For years one has heard that parrot-cry of insincerity *à propos* of Meyerbeer. According to the purists, he could do nothing right—probably because he did not slavishly follow in the footsteps of others. If he showed originality he took liberties; if he wrote melodies he was commonplace and sought only to please by writing down to the level of a vulgar taste. His gifts may have been great,—but he himself was not a great man ; in short, he never had the will or the courage to express himself, and consequently was never sincere. Well, I do not agree with all this because I know that it is based upon a warped and prejudiced judgment; also because I am too well acquainted with Meyerbeer and his works to heed such one-sided diatribes. The latest of them was an article in the July number of *Music and Letters*, bearing the title of "The Tragedy of Meyerbeer," and signed A. E. Brent Smith, a name with which I do not happen to be acquainted. It contains the customary stream of abuse and depreciation, the main theme of which is that Meyerbeer was a spiritual coward and " prepared to barter his soul for a mess of admiration." It interested me solely because it appeared just at a moment when I was making ready to write a series of articles quite in the opposite sense for this magazine. For aught I can tell, it may have been called forth by my American articles already referred to. But I am not going to repeat those arguments now ; indeed there is no necessity to to so.

The best defence, the strongest justification for Meyerbeer, lies in his music. If we cannot at present get his operas, we can get the next best thing in the form of gramophone records of his finest and most popular airs. They are not among the latest items in the leading catalogues, for the obvious reasons that they have not been in such demand recently as when the Meyerbeer works were being more universally performed. Nevertheless, they are mostly by first-rate artists, as indeed they had to be if they were to be sung with adequate skill ; for the calls that this music makes upon the singer are as exacting in their way as those of any music in existence. On what grounds it can honestly be charged with " insincerity," it passes my comprehension to perceive. Take the big operas scene by scene, from *Robert le Diable*, which has scarcely been heard here within living memory (I heard it at Drury Lane, when a boy, with Nilsson, Ilma di Murska, Mongini, Gardoni, and Foli in the cast), down to *L'Africaine*, which Augustus Harris revived magnificently at Covent Garden in 1888, his first season there. The airs are remarkable for their inventive skill, their sense of appropriate feeling, their rare power of graphic illustration, whether of the bizarre or the beautiful, the tragic or the comic, the trivial or the grandiose. Their form and treatment, like that of the ensembles and choruses, may be what is now termed old-fashioned ; but do we complain of this in the operas of Mozart and Gluck, of Beethoven and Weber ? Can any of them show us examples of gorgeous lyric splendour, of tonal combinations more dramatic and imposing, than the great ensembles in the second and fourth acts of *Les Huguenots*, the coronation scene in *Le Prophète*, and the ship episode in *L'Africaine* ?

It is all a question of taste, I admit. It was a matter of taste when we began to love Wagner ; to prefer the later to the early Verdi ; to enjoy Mascagni, Leoncavallo, and Puccini rather more than the eternal round of Bellini, Donizetti, and Rossini ; to admire the Russian operas of Moussorgsky and Rimsky - Korsakov ; to place Debussy and Charpentier on a level with the best of Gounod, Massenet, Bizet and Saint-Saëns. But the supreme question, to my mind, is the same that occurs to me when I enter the National Gallery or any other choice collection of great masters—*Why not love and enjoy what is beautiful in them all ?* It matters not one jot that they represent different or even opposing schools, that they do not resemble each other in detail and execution or even in many of their underlying art principles. Good heavens ! how monotonous and wearisome pictures and plays would be without the joy of contrast and infinite variety. Then, by the same rule, why decry and belittle a master like Meyerbeer, and strive to ostracise his superb music-dramas, and shed crocodile tears over the pretended " tragedy " of his refusal to compose tunes and harmonies to a recognized pattern, in obedience to arbitrary ethical laws and in accordance with certain narrow individual views ?

There are of course, a few juvenile operas by Meyerbeer, that have never been seen or heard in this country, and never will be. Those are the works that excited the anger of his fellow-student, Weber ; they did not deserve to succeed. But it is unfair to confound them with the *chefs-d'œuvre* that came later, after he had taken up his residence in Paris and found his ideal librettist in Eugène Scribe. In these, as one of his biographers has said, " we see that to the flowing melody of the Italians and the solid harmony of the Germans, he united the pathetic declamation and the varied, piquant rhythm of the French. Never before had such operas been seen upon the stage, and their popularity during a period of forty years was simply enormous." The finest of them I have always thought to be *Les Huguenots*—" the most vivid chapter of French history ever written . . . depicted and endued with life and reality, while the whole is conceived and carried out on a scale of magnificence hitherto unknown in opera." I was candidly gratified, therefore, to read in recent numbers of *The Musical Times* and *Musical Standard* a letter from Mr Algernon Ashton concerning the neglect of Meyerbeer's masterpiece. He said, " Why this world-famous opera, one of the most glorious ever written, has of late years fallen into disfavour, is an absolute mystery to me. I know that Meyerbeer's detractors, in their stupid ignorance, are never tired of maintaining that this illustrious composer sacrificed his magnificent abilities for the sake of ' effect.' As if Wagner, and indeed every other opera composer, did not always strive after ' effect ' ! It was Berlioz who said that there was material for ten operas in Meyerbeer's *Huguenots*, and, considering the endless wealth of delightful melodies which this work contains, the great French composer was not far wrong."

A revival not only of this but of the whole series, not omitting *Robert le Diable*, *Dinorah*, and *L'Etoile du Nord*, would be a source of genuine pleasure to thousands of opera-goers ; but I doubt whether these are times in which to expect such an enterprise. It might, nevertheless, be worth while for Colonel Blois—if the plans of the London Opera

Syndicate should materialise—to consider the advisability of re-mounting *Les Huguenots* at Covent Garden next season. If a strong cast—a " star cast " it was invariably called—could be got together once more, I am quite convinced that we should find this opera drawing overflowing audiences just as it used in the old days. The great thing is to give it really well. There are seven principal parts of about equal prominence, each requiring an artist of the first order, besides three or four minor rôles that require to be competently rendered. Then extra rehearsals would be essential, because the *Huguenots* is no longer in the current repertory sufficiently to be familiar to a company drawn from various theatres. Allowing that the solo work and the duets for Valentine with Marcel and Raoul may be safe, there are still the great ensembles— the scene where the Catholic and Huguenot noblemen take the oath and the " Bénédiction des Poignards "—requiring especial care, apart from the items in the Pré aux Clercs scene, such as the " Rataplan " chorus, the ballet of the gipsies, the duel septet, and the grand entry of Queen Marguerite de Valois (on horseback) to honour the espousals of Raoul de Mangis and Valentine, daughter of the Comte de St. Bris. These are all scenes and incidents demanding elaborate stage as well as musical preparation ; moreover, they repay all the trouble that can be lavished upon them. The orchestration is far from easy, and it is replete with solo touches for the various instruments of the kind that Meyerbeer was especially fond of, and which exhibit with peculiar felicity and force his inventive genius in this direction. They are quaint, bold, and ingenious, and for fresh listeners they have all the charm of the unexpected.

Before dealing with the collection of records from Meyerbeer's operas, which has so far come into my hands (it is not yet nearly complete), I should like to devote the remainder of this preliminary article to mention some of the famous singers whom I heard in the great rôles with which they were associated. At that time they sang here in no other language but Italian, and, although the original libretti were French, I cannot recall hearing any of Meyerbeer's works so sung except in France or Belgium— certainly never in London. The features of the performance of *Robert le Diable* (referred to above), which have most dwelt in my memory, were the exquisite voice of Christine Nilsson in the tuneful aria *Quando lascio la Normandia*, and Ilma di Murska's brilliant rendering of the then-hackneyed *Roberto, tu che adoro*. Both were unforgettable ; while no less impressive, to my mind, was the ghastly scene in the cloisters where, at the demon's invocation, the nuns arise from their graves, youthful once more, and execute a fascinating ballet.

It was three or four years later (1875) that I heard *Les Huguenots* for the first time at Her Majesty's Theatre in the Haymarket. Apart from the joy of it, I have good cause to remember the event from the fact that the ticket was sent to me by no less a person than the great Tietjens herself, this being two years before the memorable occasion (October, 1877) when I attended her funeral at Kensal Green Cemetery. She acted Valentine in a vein of high tragedy, and her noble voice sounded sublime in the love duet of the fourth act, where she was worthily partnered by the silvery-toned Fancelli. Then, too, I heard the glorious tones of Trebelli-Bettini for the first time in opera as the page, and got an idea of the real charm of the air, " Nobil signor," when sung by an irresistible artist. In the other parts I was to hear better singers at Her Majesty's later on. For example, Marie Marimon as the Queen, Rota as St. Bris, Del Puente as De Nevers, and Foli as Marcel ; or at Covent Garden Bianca Bianchi, Bagagiolo, Cotogni, Graziani, or Maurel, with the superb contralto, Scalchi, as the page, Nicolini or Gayarre as Raoul, and just once, for her annual " benefit," Adelina Patti as Valentine. It was not one of the *diva's* greatest rôles ; it was rather too heavy for her ; but, marvellous to relate, she had sung it when a girl of seventeen at New Orleans, and had its traditions at her finger-ends, and she sang the music magnificently.

The Meyerbeer heroines wherein Patti was unapproachable were Dinorah and Caterina (in *L'Etoile du Nord*), parts in which she drew packed houses to Covent Garden scores and scores of times. In the former she was simply delicious—her *Shadow Song* was a dream. In the Russian opera, especially with the illustrious Faure for her Peter the Great, she won every heart in every scene ; first in the touching farewell, *Vegli dal ciel* (a truly sublime melody, sung when she bids good-bye to home) ; then with the pathetic cry that awakens the drunken Czar out of his stupor ; and lastly, with the brilliant air with two flutes in the final act, where Caterina recovers her lost wits. But *Dinorah* particularly owed a great debt to the amazing art and captivating personality of Patti ; for, as the distinguished critic Eduard Hanslick truly declared, she was the first and almost the only singer to reveal the full beauty of the music sung by the demented heroine and bring into clear relief the intentions of the composer. Quite otherwise was it with her attempt in later days (1879 to be exact) to rival the picturesque and gifted Pauline Lucca as Selika in *L'Africaine*. Here we had a classical illustration— *Carmen* afforded just such another—of the fact that even the greatest prima donna cannot succeed entirely in parts for which she is not fitted by temperament or disposition. Patti could sing any music that was ever written, from Handel down to Gounod, but she could not realise an impulsive, passionate, half-savage creature like the African queen, whereas the fascinating Pauline Lucca could actually make her live for us in the flesh. As Selika she was absolutely irresistible. Wonderful men, too, have I heard in this opera—as Vasco di Gama, the Frenchmen Naudin and Nicolini, the Spaniard Gayarre, and Jean de Reszke; as Nelusko the incomparable Lassalle, Maurel, Faure, and Graziani; as Don Pedro that fine basso, Bagagiolo.

At Covent Garden *L'Africaine*, like *Les Huguenots*, was constantly given for twenty years (1865–1885); but during the same period, for reasons hard to explain, *Le Prophète* was allowed to lie upon the shelf, despite its uninterrupted popularity in Paris. Ultimately in 1890 it was revived by Harris for Jean de Reszke, who had long before won great success in the title-rôle in Paris, and now sang and acted it here with a nobility and charm that reminded *habitués* of the celebrated Mario in the part. It was a *reprise* to be remembered—admirably mounted, splendidly sung. Together with Jean de Reszke there was his brother Edouard as one of the three Anabaptists, Mme. Richard as the Fidès, and

Mlle. Nuovina as the Berthè, and, by the way, now I come to think of it, I fancy *Le Prophète* on this occasion was sung in French. Five years later it was given here for the last time with Tamagno the Robust as Jean de Leyden and Giulia Ravogli as Fidès, and that, too, was an excellent performance. All this time, of course, *Les Huguenots* was regularly done every season at least twice, and sometimes more frequently, being kept in the active repertory until 1912, when it was given four times with a cast that included Destinn, Tetrazzini, Donalda, Paul Franz, Marcoux, and Sammarco.

So much for Meyerbeer in the past. For the moment he is certainly under a cloud; but it is my firm belief that his day will come again, and that, perhaps, ere very long. Treasures such as he left to the world cannot remain buried and hidden for ever, no matter how loudly the highbrows may scream; and next month I shall begin my task of bringing the best of the record-specimens to light again.

HERMAN KLEIN.

❧ ❧ ❧

THE GRAMOPHONE AND THE SINGER
(Continued)
By HERMAN KLEIN
The Treasures of Meyerbeer—II.

MUCH to my regret, it is not in my power to pass in review the whole of the existing records taken from the operas of Meyerbeer. And even if I could do so it would be of small advantage to the readers of this magazine, for the simple reason that about half of the records in question were manufactured by the Odeon and Fonotipia Companies, and are practically unobtainable in the United Kingdom. I have also been unable to procure all that I could wish of the Polydors, while the Vocalion and the Parlophone seem to be limited to half a dozen specimens, not more.

In my last month's article (the proofs of which I did not see, being on holiday in Ireland—hence some uncorrected printer's errors) I pointed out that certain of Meyerbeer's operas were still in the active repertory of many of the leading Continental theatres where up-to-date works are naturally in chief request. It is a further indication of the force of my argument that so large a proportion of the gems from those operas should have been recorded in Germany, Austria, and Italy. At about what date most of them were made I cannot say, but

even worse in a book that is intended primarily for educational purposes; and such I take to be the *History of Music* by Charles Villiers Stanford and Cecil Forsyth, published by Macmillans in 1916. On pages 274–6 of this useful book occurs a short account of Meyerbeer which, I am sorry to say, teems with abuse, misrepresentation, and obviously prejudiced opinions. I have not the space to quote all of it here, but a few sentences will give a sufficient idea of its general character. Apparently, then, Meyerbeer was " clever to his fingertips, opportunist of the deepest dye, cultivated, ambitious, and a master of his craft; a composer with great conceptions to his credit, who nevertheless has never gained the respect of great musicians, because he never hesitated to sacrifice principle to gain success." This statement is not true. It was his astonishing success that fanned the hatred of Meyerbeer's rivals; and I cannot help feeling that his old fellow-student, Weber, was just a wee bit under the influence of the green-eyed monster when his heart " bled to see a German composer of creative power stoop to become an imitator in order to win favour with the crowd." But Meyerbeer was no guiltier surely it was not many years ago, while the Polydors that I have heard must have been comparatively recent. Anyhow, our English houses have not been equally enterprising where Meyerbeer is concerned. Both the H.M.V. and the Columbia have limited their efforts to the sprinkling of popular pieces that the " international stars " are in the habit of including in their concert programmes—for example, the *Shadow Song* from *Dinorah*, the *Page's Song* from *Les Huguenots*, and the even more inevitable *O Paradiso* from *L'Africaine*. But there are so many lovely airs and ensemble pieces besides these that have no place in the English catalogues; and, what is more, I really believe there are the singers capable of recording them in adequate fashion if they can be induced to take the trouble to learn them. How much more welcome such examples of vocal writing would be than the eternal round of latter-day Italian and French operatic excerpts that we have to listen to! To some of those Meyerbeer " treasures " I am coming directly.

But I have not quite done yet with the adverse propaganda; and since poor Meyerbeer lies buried under a sea of it, a return to the subject is not so superfluous as it may appear to be. Unfair criticism is bad enough in a newspaper, but it is than Handel or Mozart because of his " dalliance with Italian methods." What crime was there in that? The Italian touches in his music improved it, and there was absolutely no reason for asserting that he introduced them—" a concoction made to order "—so as to achieve " popularity at all costs," any more than there was for accusing him of working assiduously to assimilate French methods to please the habitués of the Paris Opéra.

How about Rossini? He, of course, being an Italian, had a right to adopt any style he pleased— lazy genius!—as he amply proved in his *Stabat Mater* and *Guillaume Tell*. But, according to Stanford and Forsyth, " the Italian carried con- viction, the German Hebrew did not "; which statement is neither truthful nor elegant, though quite on a par with the unkind gossip about the claque and the scene-shifter, which the same writer has retailed on the authority of Mme. Viardot. And this all to discredit Meyerbeer in the eyes of the world, in spite of his " great work in developing the constructive side of opera and showing how great effects of climax can be attained," " because of his disregard of high ideals and lack of self-sacrifice in the nobler interests of his art." What rubbish! Naturally the German highbrows and patriots were angry because Meyerbeer did not stay at home to write operas for them (surely, though, Wagner tried hard enough to please the Parisians, and failed!). Nevertheless, when those same operas, those same artificial and amazing " conglomerations of fine music, trivial detail, masterly orchestration, and striving after effect," were transported to the

German stage, they were at once taken to the bosom of the Teutonic public, and in a certain degree remain there to this day. *Hinc illæ lachrymæ.*

The term " grand opera," as well as the chain of lyric dramas that gave rise to it, may be dated from the production of Meyerbeer's *Robert le Diable* at the Paris Opéra (then called the Académie Royale de Musique) on November 21st, 1831. The libretto, by Eugène Scribe and G. Delavigne, was based upon a mediæval legend crowded with picturesque personages and supernatural incidents. It embodies the struggle for the soul of the wayward hero, Robert of Normandy, between Bertram, the spirit of evil, actually his father, and Alice, the simple peasant girl who was his foster-sister; the latter being ultimately successful. Its highly-coloured plot and dramatic situations offered just the right oppor- tunity for the development of young Meyerbeer's romantic disposition and faculties. It was hailed as an extraordinary example of originality and musical power; and there has never been the smallest reason for questioning the truth of that verdict. The supernatural magic of *Robert le Diable* is not more stupid or childish than that of *Tann- häuser* or *Lohengrin* or *Der Freischütz*. The musical treatment is of a different type, that is all— a type not less new and strange or less beautiful of its kind, but illustrating earlier forms rather than the novel continuity of orchestral flow and line of vocal phrase to be presented shortly after in the early works of Wagner. In short, Meyerbeer's style was his own, just as Wagner's style became his; the former owed no more to Spontini and Grétry than the latter owed to Beethoven and Marschner and Weber. For many years the public preferred its Meyerbeer to its Wagner; then it reversed the order of things; finally, everywhere but here, it found that there was room for both.

Robert le Diable was, I admit, an unequal opera, but it was replete with variety of character, of rhythm, of melodic charm. It revealed an astound- ing sense of contrast and vivid dramatic effect. Unfortunately I have not enough records at my disposal to illustrate these features, but I was pleased to come across, in the H.M.V. catalogue, the magnificent Evocation, *Voici donc les débris*, de- claimed by Chaliapine (in Italian, D.B. 106) in his grandest manner. This is a truly worthy specimen both as to singing and recording. The energy of the former is amazing, and towards the end it grows literally diabolical in its force. No wonder this music wakes the poor nuns from the dead and con- verts them temporarily into a youthful and attrac- tive ballet! Another excellent record of the same passage is that sung by Michael Bohnen (Polydor, F. 2206, in French), whose strident tones are admirably adapted for it. He has not, however, the unique breathing capacity of Chaliapine, though just as capable apparently of " waking the dead."

118

Yet another up-to-date example from this opera is the *Valse Infernale* (H.M.V., D.B.310) superbly declaimed in Italian, *Demoni fatali, fantasmi d'orror*, by Marcel Journet. The famous French basso is here thoroughly in his element, revelling in the revelry of the demons who echo him with their sardonic chorus, emphasising the thunderous rhythm of music in which he is evidently at home. The French singers know their *Robert*, so to speak, from the cradle. Yet here is also a German favourite, in the person of Frieda Hempel herself, giving us a faultless rendering of the familiar *Robert, toi que j'aime* (H.M.V., D.B. 297). She sings it with exquisite tone and taste, smoothly accompanied by orchestra; and her elaboration of the final cadenza is so discreet, so well in keeping, that no one can complain of her introducing into it a lovely high C.

There are several gems besides these in *Robert le Diable* that ought to be recorded on the gramophone, but are not. The ballad, *Jadis régnait en Normandie*, is one; another, Alice's air with a similar title, *Quand je quittai la Normandie*, which Christine Nilsson formerly sang with such delicious grace; and yet another the duet for Bertram and the villagers, *Ah! l'honnête homme*, which someone has described as " a masterpiece of high musical comedy." The fine Evocation already mentioned has been recorded in New York by that inimitable artist, Pol Plançon (Victor, 6371), but I have not had the advantage of hearing it. Plançon has been dead a long time, and he must have made this record nearly twenty years ago.

The second of the Meyerbeer *chefs-d'œuvre*, and on the whole the greatest of the six, was *Les Huguenots*, produced on February 29th (Rossini's birthday), 1836, at the Paris Opéra. My sole criticism of Scribe's libretto (certain lyrics were written by Emile Deschamps) is that, in place of a coherent plot, it gives us in its five acts what may rather be termed a string of highly picturesque and dramatic episodes, founded upon that fearful blot on French history, the Massacre of St. Bartholomew. The last part of the story, after the blessing of the daggers is overheard by the Huguenot nobleman, Raoul de Nangis, and his effort to warn his friends is prevented by Valentine (daughter of the Catholic leader, St. Bris), thanks to the discovery and avowal of their mutual passion—this wonderful scene, with all its glorious music, leads up coherently enough to the final climax of the fifth act, where the two lovers, together with the faithful old Huguenot soldier, Marcel, are shot side by side in the churchyard amid clouds of gunpowder smoke. Only unfortunately the opera is so long that this concluding act is now seldom, if ever, performed. The curtain finally falls, therefore, on the scene where Raoul, tearing himself away from Valentine, leaves her insensible on the ground, and rushes, too late, through a bay window to tell his people of their danger. But, in spite of the drawbacks I have indicated, it makes a magnificent opera, and the crescendo of musical and dramatic interest is overwhelming. As a distinguished French critic has said, " The chief merit for this is the musician's; for the interpretation develops in proportions infinitely more vast than the theme." It is nothing less than a sin that beauties such as this work abounds with should be withheld from the present generation of opera-lovers.

Of available records from *Les Huguenots* the first to be noticed is the air sung by Raoul in Act I. after the banquet of which he partakes in a mixed company of Catholic and Huguenot nobles. It is a favourite, because of its remarkable combination of poetry and imagination, being the description of a vision of feminine loveliness that Raoul has been privileged to behold. It is a suave and sensuous melody, with a viola obbligato for its well-nigh sole accompaniment; and it is exceedingly difficult to sing. In the Italian version it is known as *Bianca al par di neve alpina*, and the most perfect record of it is that of Enrico Caruso (H.M.V., D.B.115). One artist alone in my experience sang it more ravishingly than Caruso—that was Jean de Reszke; and he never, so far as I am aware, made a record of any sort. But this of the great Italian tenor's is a jewel in every sense of the word—for luscious opulence of tone, for charm of elegant phrasing, for beauty and ease of the big head-notes, for admirable breathing— in short, everything that constitutes a superb artistic vocal effort. It was obviously done when Caruso was just in his prime. More than this there is no need to say. An earlier specimen, but a welcome one, is that which Florencio Constantino sang in New York for the Columbia (A.5204), and which is even now quite worth hearing. The voice is pure and sympathetic, the style very refined and pleasing. He takes a superfluous breath occasionally (as for instance at the opening of the recitative, *O qual soave vision*, between the *soave* and the *vision*); but on the other hand he never " scoops," and his attack is neatness personified. A much later record (H.M.V., D.B.470), by Antonio Paoli, will not compare with either of the above. The voice sounds pinched and tremulous (I tried it with two or three different needles, too), and the robustious manner of the singer is quite out of place in an elegant dreamy narrative such as this. The graceful viola obbligato fairly puts him to shame.

The rugged ditty of the old soldie·, Marcel, which he trolls forth to amuse his master's friends, the famous *Pif, paf, pouf* (H.M.V., D.B.307), is in an entirely different vein; it shows Meyerbeer in his most characteristic mood. The energetic swing of the whole thing is irresistible, and in the solitary record of Marcel Journet are to be found the sonorous volume with the freedom and vigour essential for the traditional delivery thereof. It is, perhaps, a shade too *parlato*—almost shouted, in fact—but after all the style is that of the piece, and what more need one say?

Three examples of the celebrated *Page's Song*—probably the most familiar number in the opera—and not one of them beyond criticism either for rendering or recording. But *que voulez-vous*? It is rarely sung with the right mixture of distinction and raillery, of graciousness and self-importance even on the stage; and who to-day can reproduce the manner of the glorious Alboni or the ingratiating Scalchi? The best of the trio is Louise Homer (H.M.V., D.B.665), though she is rather rough with her rich tone, while her Italian is very faulty. In Bettina Freeman's (Col. A.5215) there is bright vocalisation, but not sufficient real animation—the self-assertive spirit of the Queen's messenger. Still less of either emerges from the effort of Katharine Arkandy (Polydor, B.24154), feebly recorded in a thin, small voice, with neat execution but absolutely no distinction of style, and sung in all but inaudible German. The cadenzas in each case are singularly ill-chosen. There are no other solos in the first Act. I wish, however, that the final ensemble could be heard on the gramophone. It includes a curiosity of rhythm not unknown to modern ears, yet rarely identified for what it is—viz., a bit of chorus that was utilised many years ago by the late Lieut. Dan Godfrey, bandmaster of the Grenadier Guards, for the Slow March in the "Trooping of the Colour." It is known to the Guards simply as the tune from the *Huguenots*, and I hope you have seen them execute that wonderful slow, dragging march to it, one step to each bar, as I have on the Horse Guards Parade and at Wembley. Its "trio," by the way, is a tune from Halévy's opera *La Juive*, and another theme sometimes used is Figaro's air from *Le Nozze*. But for this inimitable example of perfect drilling the tune from the *Huguenots* has the others "beaten to a frazzle." You may recognise its origin next time you hear it.

The charming music of the Queen, whilst she is awaiting the arrival of Raoul in the Gardens of Chenonceaux, is all that I have from the second act. Not a trace of the *Chœur des Baigneuses*, of the melodious duet for the Queen and Raoul, or of the superb ensemble when the nobles swear their oath of fidelity. The solo for Marguerite de Valois, *O beau pays*, is imperfectly rendered in French by Frieda Hempel (H.M.V., D.B.276), the quality of the more acute notes being at times more than a trifle shrill, and the intonation of the chromatic passages decidedly inaccurate. The cadenza, over-elaborated, compares unfavourably with the sweetness of the flute obbligato. It is a pity the other side of the record is not used for the quick portion of the air, which is incomplete without its *Cabaletta*. This omission is not imitated in the German version (Polydor, 943360–1), sung under the titles of

O glücklich Land and *Dies einz'ge Wörtlein Liebe*, by Käte Herwig. Both sections are excellent; the first very prettily phrased, neat, and musical in execution; the other extremely brilliant and effective and marked by clever vocalisation. A third record of *Dies' einz'ge Wörtlein* (Parlophone E10362) is sung with elegance and finish by Margarethe Siems, the gifted original Marschallin of *Der Rosenkavalier*; while on the reverse side Fritzi Jokl gives a delightfully spirited account of the *Page's Song*—both well accompanied by orchestra.

The real drama of this opera begins with the third act, where the opposing forces of Huguenots and Catholics are for the first time brought face to face. The salient features of their bitter struggle are brought out with wonderful force of contrast in things like the "Rataplan" and "Curfew" choruses, the fight between the students (interrupted by the ballet of *bohémiennes*), the duel septet, the *grand duo* for Valentine and Marcel, and finally the State entry of Marguerite de Valois to honour the espousals of the Comte de Nevers and Valentine. Of these I have but one German record to speak about—namely, that of the duet by Barbara Mickley-Kemp and Paul Knüpfer (*Welch ein Schreck* and *Ach, dies Herz*, Polydor, 044279–80), which I have always thought to be the *clou* of the scene in the Pré aux Clercs. The soprano is not altogether on a level here with the artistry of Knüpfer, whom we have so often heard at Covent Garden—in music of a different kind. But on the whole it is a competent rendering and verifies my statement that Wagnerian singers abroad are still quite at home in Meyerbeer, simply because it forms part of their regular work. Unfortunately the other *grand duo*, that between Valentine and Raoul in the fourth act, does not seem to be recorded. It will be some day, I am quite sure; but, meanwhile, all that we have from the stupendous scene of the *Conjuration* and the *Bénédiction des Poignards* is a much mutilated version of the famous passage in which the Comte de St. Bris makes his fanatical declaration to the assembled conspirators, monks, nuns, nobles, etc., and binds them all to secrecy. This is finely sung in German by that admirable Wotan, Friedrich Schorr (*Schwur und Schwerteweihe*, Polydor, B.22083), supported by a capable ensemble; and in French by Marcel Journet (*D'un sacro zel*, H.M.V., D.B.307), with supporting chorus only. Both give a capital idea, brief as it is, of the grandeur of this episode and the masterly nature of its musical handling. It brings to a close for the present my task of resuscitating the Meyerbeer operas, which I hope to complete in the November number.

HERMAN KLEIN.

THE GRAMOPHONE AND THE SINGER

(Continued)
By HERMAN KLEIN
The Treasures of Meyerbeer—III.

I HAVE been agreeably surprised at the number of good judges who have spontaneously come forward with assurances of their full sympathy and agreement in my crusade on behalf of Meyerbeer. They hope something will come of it; so do I; but whether that something will take the practical form of stage revivals remains to be seen. I appreciate, beyond all, the approbation of my accomplished Editor, whose keen perception of the beautiful in music has enabled him to see and feel the charm of Meyerbeer's style and to grasp, as I have done, the true inwardness of the present boycott of his operas. This boycott—for it is nothing less—is bound, sooner or later, to come to an end. It is too stupid and unfair to last for ever. But at least it will have had one beneficial result (and this is somewhat in the nature of a prediction): when Meyerbeer is sung again he will come to the rising generation and to the majority of current opera-goers so fresh and unfamiliar, practically so new, I may say, that they will be able to listen to him with wholly unbiased ears and enjoy him as they would any other strange master —for precisely what he is worth. Meanwhile, the gramophone alone serves as substitute for the opera-house, and, were the supply of selections only larger, a very good source of propaganda in favour of revival it would be.

With *Robert le Diable* and *Les Huguenots* I have already dealt. *Le Prophète* was the third of Meyerbeer's grand operas to see light at the Paris Opéra (then called the Théâtre de la Nation), where it was produced on April 16th, 1849. Again the libretto was by Scribe, who, taking more than the usual number of liberties with historical detail, presented a plot more remarkable for spectacular opportunities than sympathetic personages or powerful dramatic interest. The genius of Meyerbeer secured an equal balance and grandeur for all, in one of the longest scores he ever wrote. The hero, Jean de Leyden, is transformed by three fanatical Anabaptists from an inn-keeper (he was actually a tailor) into a prophet, whom we see crowned with great state in the cathedral at Münster, after leading an army and winning battles like the heaven-sent Messiah that he proclaims himself to be. In course of his upward progress the false prophet deserts his fiancée, Bertha, and renounces his faithful old mother, Fidès; and these sins cost him both his throne and his life, for in the end he commits suicide by having his palace blown up with himself and his enemies inside it. This last offers a fitting climax to a series of superb stage spectacles, which include in the third act the picturesque Skating Ballet (one of the stage wonders of the time), and in the fourth the famous Coronation Scene where the prophet denies his mother and pretends he does not know her. The music of the latter episode is the finest in the opera, while the imposing Coronation March is, of course, familiar all the world over.

It was the Coronation Scene that provided the great tenors of the French stage—from Roger (the original Jean) and Gueymard and Duprez, down to Jean de Reszke—with their hymn of triumph, their stentorian show-piece, *Roi du ciel et des anges*, known in the Italian version as *Re del cielo*. Of this we have three interesting records, two of which were probably made at about the same period, say twenty years ago, viz., by Florencio Constantino (Col. A.848) and Francesco Tamagno (H.M.V. D.R.104). All I can say of the Constantino record is that it is smooth, clear, and bright, without impressing you particularly by the robustness of energy and *entrain* which such a piece requires. The other was done too late to represent Tamagno at his finest; it betrays signs of waning power and his besetting sin of nasality, together with moments of the old heroic nobility and force. I am, however, fond of it because, for me it is associated with two pleasurable recollections. When Tamagno first sang in *Le Prophète* at Covent Garden, in 1895, I sat most of the evening in a grand tier box facing the stage with Sir Augustus Harris, who loved this opera even more than I did. The excitable impresario, when Tamagno had filled the house with his magnificent notes in *Re del cielo*, was so delighted that he led the demand for an encore, and, what is more, he got it. That was only a year before Harris died.

The second recollection concerns Tamagno himself. Happening to be at Lugano in the summer of 1904, I thought I would run over to Varese one afternoon and fulfil an old promise by visiting the famous tenor at his *castello*, situated on the outskirts of that town. After a hot, dusty walk from the station, I found that he was out driving; but in half an hour he was back, and offered me a hearty welcome. He showed me round the castle, and took particular pride in a valuable collection of butterflies and moths which he had brought from South America and arranged in a room lined on every side with handsome mahogany drawers. (I wonder what became of the lovely things!) But still prouder was Tamagno of something else —namely, his new gramophone, just sent by " His Master's Voice," with a parcel of his own records. Would I like to hear some of them? Certainly. Well, he played them for me himself, and never shall I forget the signs of intense enjoyment which he displayed in doing so, or the undisguised delight with which he listened to and commented upon the sounds created by his own voice. He leaned over and caressed the instrument, just like a child with a new plaything or a mother holding her baby to the keyboard of a piano. They were sounds worth hearing, too, and Tamagno was very happy when I told him I thought them a splendid reproduction of his wonderful voice. Among the first of the records he played, curiously enough, was this from *Le Prophète*; and I may add that on the reverse side of it is the *pastorale* sung by Jean de Leyden in the second act, a charming air known as *Sopra Berta, l'amor mio*. A trifle nasal in timbre, perhaps, but marvellously restrained and delicately graceful —for Tamagno! A much later rendering of the Inno Trionfale, *Re del cielo*, by Antonio Paoli (H.M.V., D.A.409), is sung with chorus and completes it to the end of the act. The solo voice is extremely resonant and powerful, and the ringing high notes are of good quality.

The famous contralto air, *Ah! mon fils*, was never, unfortunately, to be recorded by the illustrious original Fidès, Pauline Viardot-Garcia. There is, however, an excellent version extant by Ernestine Schumann-Heink (H.M.V., D.B.414), now somewhat *passé* as a record, but otherwise very sweet and tender; a more up-to-date, but badly executed, effort by Maria Olzewska (in German, Polydor B.24115), whose rich beauty of tone is completely absent, in spite of the poignant pathos of her expression; and, finally, a really magnificent rendering in German by Sabine Kalter (Odeon XX.72661), not only of this air, *Ach! mein Sohn*, but of the immensely difficult aria sung by Fidès in the last act, *L'ingrato m'abbandona*, or, rather, so much of it as the disc could provide room for. It is extremely long, and no one nowadays can sing it without cuts, if at all. Nevertheless, this performance of Sabine Kalter's is alike vocally and dramatically superb. I can also commend a French record of *Ah! mon fils* made for the French H.M.V. by Suzanne Brohly (W.441). It is welcome as a faithful example of the true Meyerbeer school, sung by a member of the Opéra-Comique, who imparts to it without effort the dignity and dramatic quality that it demands. Voice and diction are alike admirable.

L'Etoile du Nord belongs to the répertoire of the Paris Opéra-Comique, where it was first given on February 16th, 1854. The sole record available from its delightful pages is the prayer and barcarolle, *Veille sur eux toujours*, which I mentioned under its Italian title in the first of these " Treasure " articles and was one of Patti's most inspired achievements. It is here sung by Amelita Galli-Curci (H.M.V., D.B.597), who is, I think, more successful in the florid barcarolle than in the pathetic melody of the prayer, which she overloads with *portamenti*. As usual, her *coloratura* is brilliant and accurate, but the cadenza with flute which she introduces at the end is not in the opera and sounds banal here.

Dinorah, originally called *Le Pardon de Ploërmel*, was also produced at the Opéra-Comique (April 4th, 1859), the libretto being by MM. Barbier and Carré, the authors of Gounod's *Faust*. Would that the story were equally attractive, instead of being undeniably dull and stupid! The skill and resource of the musician, coupled with the art of the singer, have alone availed to preserve from oblivion one of the cleverest scores that have come to us from Meyerbeer's pen. Yet little of it is heard now beyond the two excerpts that survive in the gramophone catalogues, to wit, the *Shadow Song* and the baritone air, *Sei vendicata assai*. The former is sung by Dinorah in the second act, where the distraught maiden, vainly seeking for her lost goat, suddenly comes upon her own shadow in the moonlight and, for lack of another companion, invites it to join her in dance and song. The outcome is one of the most graceful and fascinating waltz-airs ever written for the voice—and one of the best-known.

Yet, hackneyed as it is, the *Ombra leggiera* is seldom faultlessly sung. Why cannot gifted sopranos like Mme. Galli-Curci (H.M.V. 260) be satisfied to sing it straight through as it was written, without altering and cutting out whole passages— not because she cannot do them perfectly, but merely to leave room somewhere for one of those long, eternal interchanges with the flute which seem (ever since David composed *Charmant Oiseau*) to form the essential *tour de force* of every " international " artist's cadenza? But the ease and fluency of the scale work, the elegance of the ornamentation, the rhythmical flow of the waltz-tune—all this and more simply delights the critical ear, for it is Galli-Curci at her best. Selma Kurz (Polydor J.24014) makes fewer cuts, yet adopts a slightly slower tempo and sings her phrases with a clean attack and well-marked rhythm. She is not quite so brilliant as her Italian rival, but is neatness personified; which is more than can be said for the orchestral accompaniment. Luisa Tetrazzini (H.M.V., D.B.534), with her characteristic tone, her sure and effective execution, her admirable trills and *staccati*, trips gaily and lightly through the well-worn dance, though to my ear, her cleverness sounds just a trifle mechanical.

This is a fault not to be found with the alert, joyous rendering of Eugénie Bronskaya (Col. A.5210), which, by the way, sounded particularly good for pure vocal quality on the Sonora Model. I liked this record better and better on closer acquaintance.

All the prominent baritones of our day have a try in the concert-room at *Sei vendicata assai*, but only two or three seem to have recorded it. Best among these is Pasquale Amato (H.M.V., D.B.636), whose style is very *legato*, with suavity of manner and unaffected sentiment to match. His fine voice suggests exactly the kind of remorse that Hoël in the opera is supposed to feel when he addresses the insensible form of his deserted Dinorah. On the other hand, Titta Ruffo (H.M.V., D.B.178), intelligent singer as he is, uses his colossal organ as though the reproaches ought to come from him ; or is it really that he wants to show how angry he is with himself ? Enrico de Franceschi's (Parlophone E.10221) is a good average rendering, in very dark tone, marked by little colour or variety. And so much for *Dinorah*.

L'Africaine was truly Meyerbeer's " swan-song." Scribe handed him the libretto in 1852, but the score was not entirely completed until 1864, the year of his death ; and it was only produced at the Opéra on April 28th, 1865. The fact that he did not live to witness its performace is doubly regrettable, because, in the opinion of many, this posthumous work was the greatest of Meyerbeer's masterpieces. Personally, I love every note of it. I have enjoyed precious opportunities for hearing it to the highest advantage. It was my good fortune to hear at Covent Garden the original Vasco de Gama (Naudin) and the original Nelusko (Faure), together with the finest of all Selikas, Pauline Lucca ; while in 1879, in Paris, I saw also that incomparable Nelusko, Lassalle, with Vergnet as Vasco and Mme. Krauss as Selika. The records of the opera available to-day are not by singers of this calibre ; none the less, a few of them are very good and I will briefly point out their merits in their order as they occur in the score.

The first and the only one from the opening act is the romance for Inès, sung in German by Käte Herwig (Polydor O.943019), which I did not find satisfactory until I had tried it with the softening effect of the Sonora model, which always favours the voice rather than the instrumentation. This piece begins, however, with long unaccompanied phrases, followed by a strain of graceful melody (*Adieu, mon beau rivage*), and Fr. Herwig delivers both with a suitably sweet *legato*. Her cadenza, though, is not Meyerbeer's. From the prison scene of Act II., where Vasco de Gama is detained with his two slaves, Selika and Nelusko, I have the lovely *berceuse* or *air du sommeil* sung by the African queen to her sleeping hero (*Figlio del Sol*, Col. D.8076). Half of it is cut, however, to get it on a 10in. disc, and the singing of the fascinating tune by Eugenia Burzio has no special charm. The number for Nelusko which succeeds it is one of the gems of the opera, and is known in the German as *Dir, o Königin* (Polydor B.22054), which, sad to relate, is the sole version at my disposal. It is fairly well sung by Heinrich Schlusnus, but the orchestra, one feels, ought to be in the prison and the Nelusko at liberty. The succeeding septet (unrecorded) is another " treasure " ; and, oddly enough, the principal theme of it is almost identical with that of *The Minstrel Boy*.

The third act takes place on the deck of Vasco's Portuguese galleon—a marvellous picture illustrated by marvellous music, with Nelusko as the leading figure in each. He it is who causes the vessel's course to be changed, whereby she is wrecked and at the mercy of his barbaric brethren. Titta Ruffo has a splendid though brief record of the stirring call (*All'erta, marinar*, H.M.V., D.A.164), wherewith Nelusko arouses the sleeping sailors. But even more striking is his famous ballad, *Adamastor, roi des vagues profondes*, one of the most original things of the kind ever written. Each of the four examples I possess of this has good points to recommend it : for example, the amazing energy and fine tone of Titta Ruffo (H.M.V., D.B.406) ; the clear coherent declamation of Pasquale Amato (H.M.V., D.B.637) ; the sonorous voice and vigorous rhythm of Giacomo Rimini (Voc. A.0202) ; and, last but not least, the very excellent rendering in French by Roy Henderson (Voc. K.051585), bold and vivacious in style, resonant in tone, and declaimed with plenty of contrast. In fact, I am inclined to admire the Englishman's effort as much as the Italians', which is saying a good deal.

In what part of Africa the fourth act is located, Scribe never disclosed, and no one has ever discovered. But it must be a kind of tropical paradise ; for thus the joyful Portuguese explorer apostrophises it in the great tenor air which is the best-known piece in the opera. No fewer than fifteen records of *O Paradiso sorti de l'onde* have come to hand, and there are doubtless as many more, though not all of similar quality. It is a noble bit of music and very exacting for the singer. Space compels me, however, to deal briefly with my material. Finest of all is Enrico Caruso (H.M.V., D.B.117), for its glorious tone, ease, reserve of strength, sense of triumph and joy. Giovanni Martinelli (H.M.V., D.B.336) gives a melancholy tinge and his timbre is thin. Beniamino Gigli (H.M.V., D.B.109) has animation and power, a well-covered tone, but drags the tempo—as indeed do most of them. Bernardo de Muro (H.M.V., D.B.549) is resonant and clear, but pinches his head-notes. Fernand Ansseau (H.M.V., D.A.427) uses to advantage the dark French vowels, phrases broadly, and has a strong, steady tone. Evan

Williams (H.M.V., D.B.443), on the contrary, loses by tight English (Welsh) sounds and has no distinction of style. Florencio Constantino (Col. A.5109) is robust, yet refined and artistic. Hipolito Lazaro (Col. 7343) displays an easy *sostenuto* and telling B flats, but his tone is unequal. Charles Hackett (Col. 7366) sings splendidly, combining taste with power and opulence of tone. V. Rosing (Voc. A.0209) suffers from a persistent vibrato and dull, lugubrious style. Armand Tokatyan (Voc. A.0224) also trembles slightly and his " white " timbre is monotonous. Alfred Piccaver (Polydor J.22015) impresses very favourably with his strong steady voice and notable breadth of style. Lenghi-Cellini (Parlo. E.10044) displays some good points. Mario Chamlee (Bruns. 15040A) sustains big tone without effort and does justice to his theme. Nicola Fusati (Velvet-Face 607) has a capital organ, but his tremolo is disturbing and he drags terribly.

From Act IV. there remains to note a rather feeble record of the *Marche Indienne* (Polydor O.40844), and a rough but effective one of Nelusko's cavatina (*Wie hat mein Herz geschlagen*, Polydor B.22088), by Heinrich Schlusnus on the reverse side of the *Dir, o Königin*. But the cavatina, without the chorus, is also recorded by the inimitable Battistini (*Averla tanto amata*, H.M.V., D.B.210) in a manner that I can only describe as magnificent. Finally, the touching scene of Selika's suicide beneath the poisonous upas tree in Act V. receives delicate treatment from Lilly Hafgren-Dinkela (Polydor B.24000), in the German version, of course, and very sweet and tender in sentiment without any strong sense of pathos or tragedy.

With this I conclude a task which I have regarded both as a duty and a labour of love. If I have interested my readers in Meyerbeer and pointed the way for a renascence of some of his operas I shall indeed be content. HERMAN KLEIN.

🦉 🦉 🦉

THE GRAMOPHONE AND THE SINGER
(Continued)
By HERMAN KLEIN
The Supremacy of Mozart—I.

TO-DAY, as 150 years ago, Mozart stands supreme in his comprehension of the capacity of the human voice, alike as a mechanical instrument and as a medium for musical expression. Without his rare understanding of the art, although he might always have written melodies of ineffable charm, he would never have been able to compose music for his singers that was so absolutely " vocal " in its nature, so rich in the qualities that call forth the highest feelings of the interpreter, so invariably true to the emotions that have to be expressed. In this immense gift he outshone all his giant rivals of the eighteenth century, including both Handel and Gluck ; and, if equalled by one or two in the nineteenth it was only in certain branches of the art—as, for instance, Schubert, who was essentially a song-writer, which Mozart was not. Then, again, the amazing all-round ability of Mozart was fully on a par with that extraordinary originality which was one of the miracles of his time. Not only did he write beautiful music, but he wrote music the like of which had never been heard before ; operas entirely new in their construction, treatment, and character.

Listen to what Fétis, the famous French musical historian, said about *The Marriage of Figaro*. Writing sixty years ago in his " Biographie Universelle des Musiciens," he remarked, " The proportions of this score are colossal. It abounds with airs, duets, ensemble-pieces of different kinds in which the wealth of ideas, the taste, and freshness of the harmonies, modulations, and instrumentation unite in forming the most perfect combination. The two finales alone are equal to entire operas, more abundant in beauties of the first order than any other lyric production." Nothing heard or known before *The Marriage of Figaro* had given the idea of such a work. It aroused enthusiasm everywhere, and, of all Mozart's operas, it was the one best understood from the outset. It obtained its greatest triumph in Prague, where a year later (November 4th, 1787) the first performance of *Don Giovanni* took place. The public there instantly recognised what a masterpiece Mozart had written for them and declared it to be " the finest, the most perfect opera that had ever been performed." The Viennese were slower to perceive this. As Fétis says, " Too many beauties were accumulated in the score, and those beauties were of an order too novel to be understood at first by the public; only a few musicians were capable of grasping the fact that Mozart had here attained the highest degree of invention and of the sublime. Opinions were divided, therefore; but ere long wiser counsels prevailed, and the whole country became enthusiastic over this immortal work of genius."

One hardly knows which to marvel at most, the extent or the variety of the strenuous and increasing labour that Mozart accomplished, whilst delicate and ailing, during the concluding years of his unparalleled career. Such activity, such slavery, was never equalled by any musician before or since. After *Don Giovanni* other great works were still to come, treading on each other's heels; operas such as *Cosi fan Tutte* (1790) and *The Magic Flute* (1791), with that miraculous final achievement, the *Requiem*, written and very nearly completed on his death-bed in 1791. But, enormous as was the quantity of that feverish output, it was not more astonishing than the development of style and the constant growth in the masterful handling of ideas that were pervading it all. No opera was exactly like its predecessor, though each in turn was pure Mozart.

The originality of *Il Seraglio* (1782) is said to have taken aback the Viennese tremendously. Said the Emperor Joseph II. to the composer: "It is too lovely for our ears; in fact, there are too many notes in it for me." "Precisely as many as are wanted," replied Mozart, who had only received 50 ducats for writing the opera! But four years later the music of *The Marriage of Figaro* sounded newer and more original still. For the treatment of the Beaumarchais comedy was entirely different; whilst another phase in the master's manner became manifest in *Don Giovanni*, and yet another in *The Magic Flute*. I do not say that these distinctions are palpable to every ear; but unquestionably they are there, and they help to account for the perennial freshness and charm that lift these operas of Mozart above all danger of sameness or monotomy. Hence it is that one seems never to listen to them without an abiding sense of unalloyed enjoyment and satisfaction. Would only that the whole of the series that I have named above could be heard in London regularly every year! Perhaps a couple, not more, will be given at Covent Garden next season.

The available collection of Mozart gramophone records can scarcely be termed a truly representative one, so far as the voice is concerned. Neither does it do justice to the glorious opportunities afforded by even the more familiar operas to which I have been referring. They do not nearly cover the ground. It is useless for one to begin to enumerate the vocal numbers and the many wonderful ensembles—essential features, of course, of any stage performance—that you may search for vainly in the current catalogues. Why is this? Are we to suppose that the interest of the buying public has become centred entirely in the symphonies and quartets and instrumental items generally? Or is it that during the period that these long-neglected gems have been receiving attention, the operas have been allowed to recede into the background? But anyhow, it is an unquestionable fact that the latter have never yet been recorded on a scale that nearly approached completeness. I do not go so far as to suggest that the time has come for recording any of Mozart's operas from the first note to the last. It would not pay to treat *Don Giovanni* or *Le Nozze di Figaro* in similar fashion to *Madam Butterfly* or *Faust* or the Gilbert and Sullivan operas. In any event, of course, it would be quite unnecessary to include the arid wastes (musically speaking) of *recitativo secco*, which embody the copious dialogue of the Abbé da Ponte; but of all the rest not a single number that is habitually heard in the theatre ought to go unrecorded. The only question on which I do entertain some doubt is whether the right singers are to be had for the purpose—singers, that is to say, of sterling ability, who have been trained adequately and correctly to interpret Mozart. And that is a very big question indeed.

"LE NOZZE DI FIGARO."

I propose to deal in this number with the two great operas which Mozart composed to Italian libretti; or rather I should say, perhaps, to discuss the merits of such records from these operas as have been deemed worthy of consideration. Most of them are new to me; though a good many, no doubt, have been in their various catalogues for many a season. With here and there an exception, they give me the impression of being executed by artists who were not completely at home in this kind of music; in some cases by artists who had never actually played the part under contribution, or had forgotten, whilst recording it, the dramatic situation in which the piece occurred. For instance, I cannot definitely state that Amelita Galli-Curci has never played Cherubino on the stage; but I can safely declare that her *Non so più* (H.M.V., D.A.214) contains no more evidence that she knows what she is singing about in her language than the same air, *Neue Freuden, neue Schmerzen* (Poly. 65654), rendered by Elisabeth Schumann who has certainly sung Cherubino, gives any indication that she does so in hers. The former is too staccato, the latter too slow and melancholy; they may be capital records, but they are incredibly unlike Mozart. We get more of the real thing in the *Non più andrai* of Mattia Battistini (H.M.V., D.B.736) and Mario Sammarco (H.M.V., D.B.607), both of which are lively and full of spirit. Each has such distinctive merits of its own that I do not care to praise one more than the other. As to the treatment of the *appoggiatura* they are entirely at variance; and I think the same may be said of practically all the other Mozart records that I have come across, Italian and German alike. The literal rendering is quite wrong, of course, and it is this alone that spoils, for my ear, the otherwise charming record of *Porgi amor* (alias *Heil'ge Quelle reiner Triebe*, Polydor 72910) made by that admirable soprano, Lotte Lehmann. It is the tender prayer for a return of happier days, uttered by the Countess at the opening of the second scene, and is followed almost immediately by the Page's Song, familiarly known to all the world as *Voi che sapete*.

I have yet to hear a perfect record of this inspired air. Frieda Hempel's is too pallid in tone, too suggestive of a choir-boy, too devoid of real warmth (H.M.V., D.A.675), or I should gladly say, "Here is the latest and best setting of a precious gem." But it is delicately phrased and free from liberties or exaggeration; which is more than can be said for Elisabeth Schumann's spasmodic, over-sentimentalised version (Poly. 65654.) in the German tongue. It is also included in the Patti group referred to below, but the part of Cherubino was never sung by the great prima donna. For the remainder of the first act, with its magnificent finale and all the smaller *bonnes bouches*, gramophone lovers must wait as patiently as I shall.

From the next or third scene we have refined and beautifully-balanced renderings of the two duets, viz., *Crudel! perchè*, by Geraldine Farrar and Antonio Scotti (H.M.V., D.K.118), and *Che soave zeffiretto*, by Emma Eames and Marcella Sembrich (H.M.V., D.K.121). Both bring back agreeable recollections of these artists and delightful bygone performances of the opera. I admire Scotti's suave *legato* pleading as the Count, and Farrar's sly, spirited repartee as Susanna. The other voices, in the "Letter" duet, are rather dark and sad, but for all that they furnish a fascinating record of two famous singers. The *Dove sono* of Claire Dux (Polydor 72890) is scarcely an outstanding example of pure vocalisation by one whom we know to be an excellent Mozart singer (though she is now, I understand, appearing on the operetta stage in Vienna). Nevertheless, and in spite of the German (*Nur zu flüchtig bist du entschwunden*), it is all very smooth and pleasing; the two sections are well contrasted; and in the round tone-colour there is a just expression of the Countess's unbearable *ennui*. Those who would like to hear more of Claire Dux and Lotte Lehmann can do so by procuring their *Deh! vieni* or *Rosen-Arie*, as the Germans call it, which is my final excerpt from *Le Nozze*. The former (Poly. 72890) gives us the recitative but not the *appoggiature*; the latter (Poly. 72910) reverses this proceeding. So you can pay your money, etc., and be sure that whatever your choice you will have no regrets. Claire yields the lovelier timbre, perhaps, and is not quite so *triste* as Lotte; but the singing of both is tasteful and delicate in a very delightful degree.

"DON GIOVANNI."

From the opening scene of this opera there is nothing. The grumbling air for Leporello and the dramatic duet for Donna Anna and Don Ottavio are both missing. So, too, is the trio of the second scene where Don Giovanni and his loutish valet come across the hapless Donna Elvira. We make a notable start, however, with the next number, which is the famous catalogue song, *Madamina*, sung in Italian by Chaliapine (H.M.V., D.A.555, in two parts). Individual and unconventional, a *tour de force* of speed and patter, brimful of realistic humour, it represents the Russian singer in a highly characteristic mood. The *allegro* is really too quick to be distinct; it sounds more like an exercise than an attempt to deceive a poor ill-used lady. But the *andante* is wonderful—a rare piece of subtle colouring and writ "Leporello" all over. The varied repetition of the *la piccina*, even where it is so *pp* that the breathy tone fails to register the first time, is quite masterly, and the ending may fairly be called comical. After this one feels a certain amount of sympathy for Peter Dawson's clever effort to do the same air justice in English (H.M.V., B.1202); he takes it much slower, however, and is consequently easier to follow than the gifted "celebrity," while the orchestra is also more audible. Where the vowels permit, Mr. Dawson yields ample tone and suggestive colouring, especially in the *andante*, which is again the more satisfying side of the disc.

From *Madamina* it is not a far cry to *La ci darem*, a good example whereof is supplied by Geraldine Farrar and Antonio Scotti (H.M.V., D.K.111). The exquisite old duet is well sung by both artists; the Don on the whole a trifle more prominent than the coquettish Zerlina, but not exuberantly so, while the timbres mingle agreeably and the *legato* is never disturbed by a "wobble." Thence we pass to a German version of *Dalla sua pace*, one of the most trying airs for tenor that Mozart has written. I cannot say that I care for it in German or that I find anything to admire in this rendering by Herman Jadlowker (Polydor 72538), which is sentimental to tearfulness and badly disfigured by slurs and scoops. Pity 'tis that a fine voice should not be better used. Don Giovanni's aria in praise of wine, which follows, is quite another affair. It chiefly needs voice, and of that it receives enough and to spare from the ever-generous Titta Ruffo in *Fin ch'an del vino* (H.M.V., D.A.357). It is delivered, moreover, with immense *brio*, or what we term "go."

126

After this comes the irresistible *Batti, batti*, in which Zerlina wheedles Masetto, her clownish peasant lover, until he forgives her for her flirtation with the amorous Don. Once upon a time the perfect model for realizing the fascination of this delicious air was the incomparable Adelina Patti, who included it among the group of records which she made at Craig-y-Nos Castle not many years before her death. Alas, these efforts came too late to afford more than a pale reflection of the diva's marvellous voice and faultlessly pure Mozart style ; yet there is a something that she alone could have given us in the specimen that survives (H.M.V., 03055), and for her sake I for one shall always treasure it with all its faults. (By the way, it is sung much too fast and the piano accompaniment is a mere scramble, while the once glorious Patti tone is only present in miniature.) In the same piece you may also listen to Marcella Sembrich (H.M.V., D.B.428), Luisa Tetrazzini (H.M.V., D.B.537), Frieda Hempel (Polydor T.24006), and Elisabeth Schumann (Polydor 65655) ; this last only sung in German. I like them best in the order in which I have here written them down. Bar a misplaced high note at the end, the style of the Sembrich record is irreproachable ; but, oddly enough, the German sopranos, despite their more recent recording, do not achieve the true Mozart reading of *Batti, batti*.

Nothing from the wonderful ball-room scene—not even the tuneful minuet that everybody used to hum ; not a sign of the trio of maskers, so horribly difficult to keep perfectly in tune ; and, of course, not a bar from the immortal finale to the first act. The second is mainly represented by the piquant serenade with the pizzicato string accompaniment which Don Giovanni (impersonating Leporello) sings beneath Donna Elvira's window. Several eminent baritones have, of course, done this for the H.M.V.—for example, Maurice Renaud (D.851), Antonio Scotti (D.B.668), Emilio Gogorza (D.B.184), and Titta Ruffo (D.A.357). Of these I like best the Gogorza, not only for its vocal

qualities, but because the tempo and general interpretation are in accord with tradition. Being too short to fill the whole side, each artist provides the requisite full measure with a little extra contribution ; thus Renaud repeats the last verse in Italian ; Scotti adds the *Quand'ero paggio* from *Falstaff* ; Gogorza appropriately gives the serenade from Berlioz's *Faust* ; and Titta Ruffo—but no, I am wrong, Ruffo adds nothing ; he takes the whole thing so slowly, makes so many pauses, that he adds naught save a long high note to finish with, and so completes his *ad captandum* version.

Of Zerlina's second air, *Vedrai carino*, I have two capital records, the better of which is by Lucrezia Bori (H.M.V., D.A.130), a charming singer with a neat and pretty style that just fits the piece. The other, by Elisabeth Schumann (Polydor 65655), is in the German translation, *Wenn du fein fromm bist*, certain sentences of which remind one rather of a clucking hen. But apart from the consequent lack of suavity there is little fault to find, the tone being clear and musical, the words well enunciated, and the recording excellent. There remains only to speak of Don Ottavio's great air, *Il mio tesoro*, as rendered by John McCormack (H.M.V., D.B.324) and Herman Jadlowker (Polydor 72538, see above). The former is worthy of the Irish tenor in the purity and smoothness of its phrasing and *sostenuto*, in the admirable control that enables him to execute the extended run in a single breath, and its textual accuracy throughout. Personally, I prefer in this air a more heroic manner and a dark tone, rather than a *voix blanche*, but that shall be my sole criticism of an extremely artistic record. Anyhow, I prefer it to the robust illustration given by the German tenor, who has no idea of contrast, and is heavy and tremulous, with his *Tränen vom Freund getrocknet*, where he should be light and graceful and steady. No ; decidedly these masterpieces sound best in the Italian to which Mozart wrote them.

HERMAN KLEIN.

THE GRAMOPHONE AND THE SINGER

(Continued)

By HERMAN KLEIN

Some Operatic Records of 1925

AT my Editor's request I am interrupting the sequence of my comments upon the Mozart operas, in order to interpolate a few seasonable suggestions regarding the pick of the operatic records issued during the past year. Apart from a natural readiness to obey orders, I comply the more gladly because this proceeding has enabled me to make acquaintance with a good many records that I had not had occasion to listen to before. Either they had come out prior to my quite recent pages on new operatic records, or they had not come within the scope of my regular articles ; or, if I have dealt with them already, I can now mention them again in briefer fashion.

1925 was, I think, a wonderful year in the history of the gramophone—wonderful not so much for the mechanical developments and improvements in the instrument itself, though they were extremely important, as for the growth of its utility and popularity, the scope of its functions, and, above all, perhaps, the ever-widening field of its instrumental repertory. The continued progress in the department of orchestral recording naturally had a good effect upon the quality of the vocal accompaniments, which have now reached a far higher level of excellence than ever before ; and in this, as in many other respects, the English houses have definitely shown that they have nothing to fear from comparisons with the American and Continental *ateliers*. Wonderful, again, has been the ease with which the gramophone has held its own in the face of the severe competition from other quarters, old and new. The piano-players are doing it no harm ; the wireless is positively helping to magnify its blessings and spread its message. When I was broadcasting last spring from 2 L O for the first time, I think nothing done in the studio struck me more forcibly, as evidence of this, than when the announcer, to fill in time, connected a Grafonola or an H.M.V., I am not sure which, with the microphone and sent out a Kreisler solo to the two or three million listeners who were patiently waiting for my remarks on wireless diction.

There has been a distinct increase in the number and variety of the selections from the better-known operas, and not a few from operas that are anything but familiar to our general public. I wish I could say that they embody an equally satisfac-tory proportion of good singing ; but to state that would, I fear, be indulging in flattery. However, novelty counts for a good deal, especially when it marks a step towards greater completeness. Artists need not be afraid of a lukewarm reception for the many beautiful passages in opera that have been ignored hitherto by record-makers simply because they do not form part of some detached number or piece. There are still plentiful bits of Wagner that are easily separable from their surroundings, not to mention Puccini, the modern French operas, and those Meyerbeer gems to which I have lately been drawing attention. Among the Wagner possibilities one 1925 example is that glorious passage in *Tannhäuser* where Elisabeth intercedes with the outraged Knights for the life of her sinning hero. It comes in the midst of a big finale ; but Emmy Bettendorf has done it as a solo (*Elisabeth's Pleading*, Parlophone, E.10219, with the *Prayer* on the reverse side), and it would be impossible to desire a more sympathetic or touching interpretation. Well sung and well recorded throughout, the concluding phrases are particularly lovely.

It is a good idea, this commingling of the un-familiar with the hackneyed ; so, while I am about it, I will bestow credit upon two other Parlophone efforts, to wit, Zita Fumagalli-Riva's (E.10240) conjunction of *Sul fil d'un soffio etesio* from Verdi's *Falstaff* with *Vissi d'arte* ; and Zinaida Jurjevskaja's (E.10278) *O du mir einst Hülfe gab* from Gluck's *Iphigenie auf Tauris*, together with Pamina's air *Ach ! ich fühl's*. Each of these has excellent points to recommend it. Fumagalli has a fine voice, replete with tender sentiment, and fairly enhances the charm of the delightful *Falstaff* excerpt ; while the fanciful orchestral accompaniment is admirably played. Jurjevskaja's delivery of Gluck's tragic air is full of intense feeling and distinguished by exceptional beauty of voice and style, yet with a rare simplicity and nobility of phrasing. Concerning her air from the *Magic Flute* I will write another time. (Meanwhile a special interest attaches to the records of this gifted young soprano, whose body was reported to be found in the river Reuss near Andermatt in Switzerland on the 6th December last, under conditions that seemed to afford evidence of her having committed suicide. She was a member of the State Opera

House in Berlin.) Yet another hit from the same source is Emmy Bettendorf's finished rendering of two selections from the exquisite music of the Marschallin in the first act of the *Rosenkavalier*. The Mirror solo, *Kann mich auch an ein Mädel erinnern* (Parlophone, E.10341) is quietly and sweetly warbled in a *mezza voce* that is very cleverly managed ; but even more entrancing is the soliloquy that follows, *Er soll jetzt gehen*, after the departure of Oktavian. That final ending of the scene, when so deliciously sung as this and including the fascinating dreamy passage for the two violins, is one of the most inspired things that Strauss has ever written. It is worth going a long way to hear.

I will glance next at a few of the additions to the H.M.V. catalogue, beginning with Frieda Hempel's "faultless rendering," as I have already termed it, of *Robert, toi que j'aime* (D.B.297), which is here bracketed with the Dell' Acqua *Villanelle*—the latter brilliantly sung with any quantity of additional ornaments and *fiorituri*. Noticed already are Maria Jeritza's *Dio di giustizia* and *Son gente risoluta* (D.A.579) from *Fedora*, both excellent in tone, atmosphere, and recording. Two duets from the first act of *Tosca*, *Chi è quella donna bionda* and *Ora stammi a sentir*, by Gota Ljungberg and Browning Mummery (D.B.752), are given with the necessary brightness and animation. I do not care, though, for the Aïda-Amneris duet (*Fù la sorte* and *Pietà*, D.B.728), as rendered by Tina Pola-Randacio and Maartje Offers. Regardless of balance, the contralto is too loud throughout, and the singing of both is undeniably rough. In the fine air, *Selva opaca* from *William Tell* (D.B.831), Toti dal Monte imparts much grace to the one verse that she sings, but takes it too slowly and with a curious combination of timbres, clear and well " covered " in the head register, open and " white " in the medium. (I often wonder why Italian sopranos use their musical vowels in this variegated manner ; but they do.) A more interesting record is that made by Mary Lewis in French (D.B.810) of two excerpts from *Thaïs*. This singer, whom I recollect hearing in Vaughan Williams's opera *Hugh the Drover*, has a pleasing, well-trained voice, neat florid execution, and an unfailing rhythmical accent. She omits the recitative, *Je suis seule*, although that is the title here employed, and begins with the showy air, *Dis-moi que je suis belle*, which piece of pure Massenet she gives with all the Mary Garden effects. The other *morceau* is really Thaïs's part in the final duet with her monk-lover, Athanaël, which has for violin *obbligato* the famous *Méditation*, used also as an *entr'acte* and as such the chief hit of the opera. Here it accompanies the opening phrase, *Te souvient-il* ; hence the use of that title.

A growth in the demand for records by Russian opera singers has been created and met principally by the H.M.V. As I have previously observed, ignorance of the language proves no obstacle to a complete enjoyment of them. It suffices to get the fine voice, the broad, masculine style, the declamatory power, the intelligent phrasing—all these qualities in combination with the melodious theme, the unwonted, exotic atmosphere of strange but haunting music. When we are listening to Chaliapine it matters not whether he is singing one of his native songs or something from one of his countrymen's operas, we yield wholly to the spell that he creates. We cannot help ourselves, nor do we want to. Chaliapine's contribution last year was from the collection of songs that he draws upon—being his own quaint announcer—at his Albert Hall recitals ; and if I am not mistaken, he has been heard there both in Tchaikovsky's *Nightingale* and that terribly sad song by Alnaes, *The Last Voyage* (D.B.757). Thanks to this capital record, they can be heard to equal advantage on your own gramophone. Quite as valuable in its way is the selection of two duets from *Boris Godounov* (D.B.765), sung with all the customary Slav characteristics by Pimen and Gregory, as represented by two excellent artists, Smirnoff and Kaidanoff. The former of these also displays his resonant tenor in a still newer record (D.B.753), giving us the melody *Pourquoi mon triste cœur* with the cor anglais in a delightfully refined *mezza voce* ; and on the other side the rarely-sung duet with the soprano (Maria Davidoff) known as *O Tsarevitch, I implore thee*—both from *Boris Godounov*—which alternates between angry emphasis and passionate appeal, interesting from first to last.

Some other good additions to the H.M.V. operatic list may also be noted that I have not already dealt with. For instance, enthusiasts for the Italian tenor will not pass over Beniamino Gigli's sweet warbling of *M'appari* on the same disc as the *Paradiso* from *L'Africaine* (D.B.109). Nor will admirers of early Wagner sung in English overlook the bridal chamber love duet from *Lohengrin* (D.931), when recorded with such rare smoothness and ample volume as it is by Florence Austral and Tudor Davies. Then lovers of sheer baritonal sonority who possess a wide choice of needles, will revel in the Granforte rendering of the air *O Lisbona* from Donizetti's *Don Sebastiano* (D.B.834) —an opera that makes a poor pudding, but contains excellent plums. Yet again, the early Wagnerites will probably find enjoyment in the long air *Gerechter Gott* from *Rienzi*, as executed in two parts (D.B.756) by Maartje Offers, whom I like better in this than in the *Aïda* duet. Her declamation is first-rate, though her tone is frequently unsteady. Tudor Davies's English (or Welsh) versions of the two Don Ottavio airs from *Don Giovanni* (D.957) somehow got omitted from my retrospect of last month. Both might be steadier and less throaty, but they are delivered with welcome animation, and the singer's breathing capacity is amazing.

The additions for 1925 have further included several already noticed, both in these articles and in the reviews of new operatic records for October, November, and December, to which I must refer readers who have not been regularly studying the pages of THE GRAMOPHONE Magazine. It is not worth while merely to enumerate them again, nor do I feel that there is anything fresh to say about them. There remain only three or four that have quite recently come into my hands, the best of these being a 10in. Columbia (X.320) made by Riccardo Stracciari. On one side is Scarpia's soliloquy at the supper table, *Già.mi dicon venal*, declaimed in a broad, sonorous manner and with considerable subtlety of inflection; on the other a *triste*, contemplative air from Catalani's opera *La Wally*, *T'amo ben io*, not vastly interesting on first hearing, but very popular, I believe, in Italy. On the whole, a record full to the brim with rich, generous tone. Students of *coloratura* will find a useful model for technique in Luella Paikin's clever treatment of two old-fashioned bird ditties (Vocalion 0236), viz., *Lo, here the gentle lark* and *La Capinera*, by Benedict, which Lemmens-Sherrington and Liebhart sang in the seventies under the title of *The bird that came in spring*.

In another Vocalion record (K.05167) Roy Henderson has attempted Schubert's *Serenade* and the *Erl-King*, succeeding best in the former, in spite of over-darkened tone and excessive breath-pressure that result in a slight tremolo. The *Serenade* needs a lighter touch; and, by the way, the "mordent" should precede the triplet on *one* beat of the bar, not convert the whole into an ordinary "turn." For the *Erl-King* the singer requires three tone-colours, and here I find only two. There is too much of a family resemblance between the voices of father and son; while the Erl-King (whom Mr. Henderson calls the "Oil King") suggests rather the child. In the climax a sense of terror and the supernatural are lacking. Stanley Chappell's playing of the accompaniment is creditable, but one hears little of it whilst the voice is there.

HERMAN KLEIN.

❧ ❧ ❧

THE GRAMOPHONE AND THE SINGER

(Continued)

By HERMAN KLEIN

The Supremacy of Mozart—II.

"THE MAGIC FLUTE."

IN an article by the Italian writer, Alfredo Casella, recently published in the *Christian Science Monitor*, the following passage occurs: "It is interesting to see the extent, in the case of Wagner, to which symphonism introduced into the theatre hurt it [the latter]. Whereas Mozart did just the opposite and introduced the theatre into the symphony, into chamber music, even into oratorio; with the result that the operas of Mozart seem younger than the dramas of Wagner. The fusion, dreamt of by the latter, of *all the arts* (my italics) is a pure Utopia which has already disappeared from the horizon. In the musical theatre music alone reigns." This is eminently true; and it is here that we find the secret of the permanence and the perennial attraction of an opera like *The Magic Flute*, which depends for nine-tenths of its charm upon the undying melodies of Mozart. The remaining tenth is quite adequate for the story and char- acters invented by the egregious Schikaneder, though, to be just, one has come across librettos even more difficult to understand that his.

I believe the present generation flatters itself on being the first to appreciate Mozart's operatic swan song at its true value. In a footnote in Mr. Francis Toye's clever book, "The Well-Tempered Musician" (lately published by Methuen and Co.), I read that it was "an amateur performance of *The Magic Flute* at Cambridge (and also one of Handel's *Semele*) that enabled us to realise the potentialities, more or less unrecognised at the time (*sic!*), of each of these masterpieces." I can assure my youthful friend that so far as the Mozart opera is concerned he is quite mistaken. Whatever its "potentialities" may precisely signify, there can be no question that the general meaning and the hidden subtleties of the plot (such as it is) were as aptly appreciated in the last century as they are in this; while the music was far more beautifully sung by the artists of that epoch than it is to-day. When I first heard *Il Flauto Magico* in the 'seventies, with Tietjens as Pamina, Ilma di Murska as the Queen of Night, Sinico as Papagena, Santley as Papageno, Bettini as Tamino, and Foli as Sarastro—a cast never to be replaced or matched!—other leading singers of the company did not disdain to fill the small secondary parts, such as the Tre Damigelle, or the Tre Geni, and so complete a perfect ensemble. The opera, thus performed, was invariably given to a crowded and enthusiastic house, and not only enjoyed but understood.

Still, this had not always been the case. *Die Zauberflöte* was first produced at Vienna on September 30th, 1791; three months later Mozart died, leaving behind a triumphant success for his music, but a very bad name for Schikaneder's libretto. Ten years afterwards the directors of the Paris Opéra wanted the former and refused to have the latter at any price. What did they do? They effected a compromise by producing under the title of *Les Mystères d'Isis* a *pastiche* containing musical plums from the whole of Mozart's operas and even fragments of Haydn's symphonies! This precious mixture had such a big success that it held the stage in Paris for several decades; and, indeed, with the exception of some performances in 1829 by a German troupe, the opera in its original form was never heard in France until it was produced at the Théâtre-Lyrique in 1865, with a new translation, under its present title of *La Flûte enchantée*. Meanwhile, in Austria and Germany the puerilities of the plot had never formed an obstacle to its popularity, seeing that the original text was German, and that Mozart, in wedding his wonderful music to it, had achieved the amazing feat of moulding a masterpiece as purely German in its nature and essence as the *Nozze di Figaro* and *Don Giovanni* are purely Italian. In no stage translation, be it Italian, English, or French—and I have heard them all—does the music of *The Magic Flute* sound so sublimely beautiful and grand, so supremely expressive, as does the German to which it was composed. For this reason, and for this alone, I would under all circumstances advise my readers to lend a willing ear, and even to accord their final preference, to gramophone records of this opera sung in the German language. Fortunately, they comprise the pick of the whole series that have come under my notice.

Thanks to latter-day demand, *The Magic Flute* has been almost, if not quite as, extensively recorded as either of the other favourite operas. (The overtures and instrumental excerpts I have left, of course, to the able pen of Mr. Francis E. Terry.) The first available item is Tamino's opening air, *Dies Bildniss ist bezaubernd schön*, sung in German by Leo Slezák (Polydor 65773) and in English by Tudor Davies (H.M.V., E.401) as *Loveliness beyond compare*. The former is hard and strident, sustained with effort;

the latter easy, but throaty and indistinct, not so good altogether as the air with the flute, *O voice of magic melody*, which occupies the reverse side. After these the Queen of Night claims attention, and, I may add, arouses conflicting emotions, her records being, like the curate's egg, good in parts. The two great airs must, for convenience sake, be considered together. No. 1, sung in Italian by Frieda Hempel, *Infelice, sconsolata*, (H.M.V., D.B.331), does not rise to the dramatic heights that Christine Nilsson and Ilma di Murska used to touch; but the runs are exquisitely neat and the staccato notes in *alt* delightfully clear and musical. No. 2, *Der Hölle Rache*, given in German, reveals stronger declamation together with the same faultless florid singing, and therefore is the finer effort of the two (H.M.V., D.B.365). Recording as perfect as this would, perhaps, have done greater justice to the rendering of the same airs (on one disc, Polydor 65634) by Sabine Meyen, an excellent high soprano, though not yet the finished vocalist that Frieda Hempel is. She starts with the recitative, *O zittre nicht, mein lieber Sohn*, but the tone is not well managed—it continues rough and is marred by scratchiness and blasting, while the runs sound hurried and anxious. Much better altogether is the *Hölle Rache*, more grandiose and regal in style, with a superb climax in the loftier regions. No. 1 is also carefully sung, but without distinction or character, by Evelyn Scotney (H.M.V., D.1035), and No. 2 by Luella Melius (H.M.V., D.A.723), who transposes it down to E flat and shines most in her staccato passages. Both these are in Italian. Perhaps the latest recording of the Queen of Night airs is by Maria Ivogün (Polydor 85310), the same disc containing them both in full, and sung in German. It compares favourably with the best of the others, alike for tone, dramatic accent, and brilliancy of vocalisation. The staccato runs sparkle brightly and are well in tune. Any inequality in the declamatory passages is entirely due to the " pinching " of the more acute vowels, and that is a fault from which scarcely a single one of these Central European artists—even the most distinguished—can be pronounced wholly free.

The delicious quintet, the trio, and the finale of the first act, alas! are missing. All that we have in compensation from this scene is the ever popular duet, *Là dove prende*, or *Bei Männern welche Liebe fühlen*, whereof I can cite four capital examples. The Italian one by Emma Eames and her husband, Emilio Gogorza (H.M.V., D.K.121), was probably made some time ago, but it could scarcely be beaten for smoothness of *legato* and accuracy of intonation. One hole only can I pick in the rendering, and that is the pause made by the soprano on the B flat— merely because it happens to be a high note—in the cadence towards the end. This un-Mozartian reading is not to be found either in the admirably-blended and balanced version by Lotte Lehmann and

Heinrich Schlusnus (Polydor 72932), or in the very tasteful and bright one by the same baritone with Selma Kurz (Polydor 85301)—both such pleasing records that it is hard to choose between them. The German artists unquestionably have the right tradition in this matter, as can be perceived, moreover, in the authoritative reading of two other fine singers, Emmy Bettendorf and Friedrich Schorr (Polydor 65646). The balance here may be less perfect, because Schorr's full voice is of vast sonority, but when he moderates its power and gives Emmy a chance with her captivating warble, the effect is charming enough.

The second act brings us straightway to the sacerdotal surroundings of Sarastro and his good priests of Isis, whose benevolent task it is to overcome the evil machinations of Astrifiammante, the Queen of Night. Both of his noble bass airs are recorded in welcome profusion, the first in all four languages. They form, truly, the most magnificent pillars of Mozart's imposing musical structure, and gramophonists will find them not unworthily represented. Robert Radford's *O Isis and Osiris* (H.M.V., E.78) recalls his voice at its freshest and strongest, resonant and telling down to the deepest note of the compass. Marcel Journet (H.M.V., D.A.259) spreads his amazing breadth of tone with the most exemplary diction over the phrases of the French version, known as *Isis, c'est l'heure où sur la terre*. Paul Bender (Polydor 62304) is a shade less impressive because in *O Isis and Osiris* the salient notes lie a trifle low for him. But the gem, in spite of a piano accompaniment and a " vintage " that must date from twenty years at least, is the Italian *Grand' Isi, grand Osiri* left us by the inimitable Pol Plançon (D.B.657). I could not listen without emotion to my old friend's beautiful singing of this air. The record possesses in a wonderful degree the singular individuality and charm of timbre that were peculiar to his voice, and I shall henceforth regard it as a rather precious souvenir. Scarcely less glorious, however, is his delivery (reverse side) of the more familiar *Quì sdegno*, which I am happy to be able to describe as, in my opinion, very nearly on a level with the finest vocal recording of to-day. Anyhow, it is a perfect model for all basses to utilise if they are wise. Journet, singing in French (*La haine et la colère*, D.B.613) had to hurry to get in both verses, but, bar the tempo, his is a splendid specimen too. Paul Bender, singing in German (*In diesen heil'gen Hallen*, Polydor 62304), profits by singing only one verse and yet achieves a very unequal effort, the falling-off in resonance towards the end being very marked. Alfred Jerger, also in German (Polydor 62368), has the right kind of voice for this air and a first-rate low E ; but he rolls out phrase after phrase as if it were an old drinking song, and in so doing uses altogether too much *portamento*.

The common Teutonic fault just mentioned is the sole blemish on Elisabeth Schumann's tenderly expressive rendering of *Ach, ich fühl's* (or *Ah, lo so*, Polydor 65811), that little *chef d'œuvre* of tragic grief wherein Pamina pours out her soul over a Tamino whom she imagines to have lost for ever. (When I was a youngster, people were willing to travel miles to hear the famous Tietjens sing this, and hers was indeed a very beautiful and touching performance.) Another, by Delia Reinhardt (Polydor 72776) drags it a little, notably in the slow scale passages, and lacks the highest degree of elegance requisite for perfection—a big word, I know. Yet a third approaches this more nearly than either. It is by Zenaida Jurjevskaja (Parlo. E.10278), who spins her enchanting tone slowly, securely, without the slightest dragging of the tempo, not so intense in feeling, perhaps, as faultless in execution ; on the whole a first-rate record. Finally, there remains Papageno's immortal song with the bells, simplest of ditties if you like, but lovable as the simple bird-catcher himself. We have it traditionally correct in German by Friedrich Schorr (*Ein Mädchen oder Weibchen*, Polydor 65646), who gives it the necessary swing and lively lilt, with a manly, robust tone in the bargain. The Italian reading (*Colombo o tortorella*, Columbia D.1522), by Ernesto Badini, makes a too solemn thing of it, being much too slow and sustained. All one can say is, here is a fine singer out of his element ; and yet—shades of Santley, Graziani, Cotogni, Del Puente, and a few more that I could name !

" IL SERAGLIO."

This was the opera which the Emperor Joseph II. satirically complained of as being too *lively* for Viennese ears (not too " lovely " as the printer made me say in my December article). Although it was written to a German book, I employ the Italian title because it is the shortest. When it was produced on July 12th, 1782, Mozart was only 26, and the world hailed it as a masterpiece. For every reason it ought to be heard oftener in this country. The excellent Beecham revival at His Majesty's promised to lend it a new lease of life, but, unfortunately, the stimulant soon lost its force, and the only reminder of that event preserved by the gramophone is Robert Radford's admirable record of the two airs for Osmin (H.M.V., D.114), known respectively as *When a maiden takes your fancy* and *Ha! My pretty brace of fellows*. The doleful self-pity of the one contrasts effectively with the crisp, clean-cut vivacity of the other, while the voice shows no sign of wear and tear. The two songs for Constanze are done on a single disc by Sabine Meyen (Polydor 65747) ; and of these the *Ach ich liebte, war so glücklich*, if far from easy, is still child's play compared with the stupendous *Martern aller Arten*, one of the most elaborate florid airs that Mozart ever

132

wrote. Both pieces are marked by neat execution and natural agility, and the customary big cut in the second still leaves a crowded disc. The same exacting aria is also sung in German by Maria Ivogün (Polydor 85303) with a stricter adherence to the text and more musical charm; and in Italian (*Che pur aspro il cuore*, H.M.V., D.B.331) by Frieda Hempel, who likewise conquers its difficulties with unfaltering ease. Blonde's two airs, *Durch Zärtlichkeit und Schmeicheln* and *Welche Wonne, welche Lust*, prettily sung by Elisabeth Schumann (Polydor 65580), complete the slender selection.

"COSÌ FAN TUTTE."

Another of Mozart's Italian operas—very nearly the last of them—and among the finest. Why not, then, heard more frequently? Because Da Ponte for once contrived a rather tiresome plot—story and characters of the kind that we now call overdrawn or improbable, or both. In England, too, we don't know how to translate the title without making it misleading. The word *tutte*, being the feminine of " all," indicates that it is here the girls, not the men, who are the perennial flirts. Literally, therefore, it should be " The girls all do it " ; only that suggests the title of a comic song rather than a Mozart opera, so I prefer to leave it as it is. Anyhow, Isidora and Dorabella are a couple of charming coquettes, and their waiting-maid, Despina, is a delightful embodiment of seventeenth century intrigue and mischief. The latter's two principal airs, *Una donna a quindici anni* (or *Schon als Mädchen*, Polydor 19132) and the still better known *In uomini, in soldati*, are recorded on one disc by Vera Schwarz, who imparts the needed sprightly touch to both. A prettier tone and greater distinction is, however, discernible in Lucrezia Bori's rendering of the second of these (H.M.V., D.A.132). The famous tenor song, *Un' aura amorosa*, finds a sound, traditional interpreter in Hermann Jadlowker (Polydor 72663), though I confess that this artist arouses in me more admiration for his technical ability than the quality of his voice. *Et voilà tout !*

MISCELLANEOUS OPERAS.

On the other side of the record just mentioned is a still more notable effort—nothing less than the excessively trying air from *Idomeneo* (*Nöch tönt mir ein Meer im Busen*) written nearly ten years earlier than *Così fan Tutte*, but marvellously foreshadowing the later style in its elaborate florid treatment of the voice parts. This is, perhaps, the most exacting and arduous piece ever written for a tenor, and Jadlowker really does it tolerable justice, which is saying a great deal.

To a still earlier date (1775) belongs *Il Re Pastore*, only remembered to-day for the poem of Metastasio and the soprano air, *L'amerò*, with violin obbligato, which Melba used to sing with Joachim. Her record of it (H.M.V., D.K.112), done with Kubelik, forms a pleasant souvenir, but that is all. More up-to-date

is that of the Hungarian soprano, Hüni-Mihactek (Polydor 65636), who possesses a wonderfully pure tone and displays it with equally pure art. In fact I fancy I prefer hers to Maria Ivogün's (Polydor 85311), though there is really nothing to be said in the way of adverse criticism against this either.

Less known, but still more beautiful, is the air *Ruhe sanft, mein holder Leben* (Greta Stückgold, Polydor 19238), from another early opera called *Zaïde*, which I happen to know Sir Thomas Beecham had serious thoughts of reviving a few years ago. It rather resembles in character *Il Seraglio*, the production of which seems to have eclipsed it for ever. Nevertheless, it was mounted at Frankfort in 1866, and maybe one day we shall hear it in London.

Lastly, there is another half-forgotten opera entitled *La Clemenza di Tito*, produced at Prague three weeks before *The Magic Flute*, and which, like the works just previously referred to, appears to be saved from total oblivion by a solitary piece. In this instance it is the lovely air *Non più di fiori*, whereof Kirkby Lunn some years ago made a splendid record (H.M.V., D.B.517). I recommend it to the notice of all true Mozart lovers. And the opera itself—a miracle of grace, replete with charms of every type, yet never heard in this country !—was composed, written, scored, rehearsed, and placed upon the stage all within a period of eighteen days. Three months later, or a little over, the incomparable master lay buried in an unknown—some say a pauper's—grave !

TWO OPERA BOOKS.

Even with the preliminary aid of scores and gramophones, helping on the musical side, it is hard to take in all the salient features of an operatic representation—as eye and ear combined ought to take them in. As a rule a great deal is missed ; but there will be less fear of this for amateurs who have been wise enough to possess themselves of Mr. Paul England's book entitled " Fifty Favourite Operas," just published (12s. 6d. net) by George G. Harrap and Co. They will find in it everything that is worth knowing about almost every opera that is worth hearing—remarks about the composer, a vivid account of the plot, references to the music—all written in an easy gossipy fashion that is the very antithesis of pedantry. The plan of the book is original and consistent without being in any sense cut-and-dried. One feels throughout, " here is an experienced cicerone who knows his subject from *a to z*, and who can therefore save me an infinity of search and study, as well as prevent me from passing unnoticed the beauties and the points that might otherwise escape me." It follows, naturally, that Mr. England has succeeded in writing not only a useful compilation but an exceedingly interesting book.

With regard to his opinions, which he allows

unusually copious sway for a volume of this nature, the student ought perhaps to be a little cautious. It is obvious that the author has his likes and dislikes; he expresses both freely and can even be apologetic at having to include certain operas that he does not much care for. I am sorry I cannot see eye to eye with him in some of these cases—notably *Les Huguenots*, the only one of Méyerbeer's operas that is described in full (by the way, there ought to be a separate index for the "favoured fifty"). I cannot, for my part, understand why Mr. England's positive adoration of Wagner, whose works he writes about so sensibly, and his equally wise admiration of the Italian school, especially Verdi, should be incompatible with any sort of tolerance for Meyerbeer or even the Rossini of *Guillaume Tell*. For him there exists no sincerity here, no honest emotional expression; all is artificial; the great scene of the Benediction of the Daggers is " mere violence and volume of sound," and " here, at least, Meyerbeer deserves the hardest things that have been said of him. Yet," says Mr. England, " it contains perhaps the best melody that Meyerbeer ever wrote, of a kind which finds an echo in Gounod and Saint-Saëns " (oh, disgrace !); and then, on the very same page, we are told that melody was " always Meyerbeer's weakest point " (*sic !*). But, apart from a curious viewpoint here and there, or an odd omission now and then (for example, Lilli Lehmann was a fine Norma, but why on that account leave out Tietjens,

who was by far the finest Norma that came after Grisi ?), this is eminently a book to buy and keep close at hand. The illustrations, too, are of the highest interest. (N.B.—There is a slip in the maiden name of Mozart's sister-in-law, the phenomenal soprano for whom he wrote the music of the Queen of Night in *Die Zauberflöte*. It was not Josepha, but Aloysia Weber.)

Different in plan and size—also somewhat in character—from the above volume is the new and enlarged edition of the late Gustav Kobbé's " Complete Opera Book " (price 15s.), published by G. P. Putnam's Sons. I shall, however, express no preference for either ; I like both. The latter takes in double as many operas and quotes over 400 of their leading airs and motives ; hence its justification of the adjective used in the title. It is ably written ; the various operas are grouped under the names of their composers ; the stories are concisely told ; and the music gets its full share of the general analysis. I have detected only one or two errors worth mentioning. For instance, when the *Di quella pira* in *Il Trovatore* is transposed down from the key of C major to that of B flat, it ought scarcely to be asserted that the high C descends to a note " a tone and a half lower." A welcome feature of this edition is the new section, consisting of modern Russian and English operas, contributed from the able pen of Mr. F. Bonavia.　HERMAN KLEIN.

134

THE GRAMOPHONE AND THE SINGER

(Continued)

By HERMAN KLEIN

Gems from Half-Forgotten Operas—I.

MANY operas there are of comparatively modern date that have failed in this country, or perhaps have never been heard here at all, but which are still occasionally revived—perhaps as a tribute to the memory of their composers—in the land of their birth. I need not give a list of these semi-failures; but their names will readily be recognised in the operatic catalogues of the various gramophone houses, where they occupy a modest place in virtue of the fact that they have yielded a certain amount of grist for the mill of the busy singer in search of effective material.

Needless to say, these interesting *trouvailles* afford no real criterion of the merit or attractiveness of the opera as a whole. One can enjoy listening to a piece, or even to a selection, from an opera by an eminent musician like Verdi or Gounod, Bizet or Massenet, whereas sitting out a three-hour performance of the whole work may prove, for various reasons, little short of an infliction. I have tested this for myself in not a few cases where duty compelled, and, like the individual who was buttonholed by the Ancient Mariner, I had no choice but to obey. None the less, recollection of the cumulative result need never detract from the pleasure of listening to a bit of good music apart from its original surroundings.

I propose, therefore, to act as cicerone *after the event*, and ask my readers to stroll with me for a while along these unfrequented avenues, where our friends the opera-singers have been industriously performing the labour of excavation and rescue. As with a visit to Pompeii, we shall not be able to do it justice in a single promenade; but if the task prove in its way equally " repaying " as Baedeker puts it, we shall not think the time wasted.

EARLY VERDI.

Until he began to write the successes of his " second period," Verdi shared the responsibility for many failures with his librettists. They supplied him with " blood-and-thunder " plots; he wedded their highly-coloured language to music equally strenuous with the din of brass and vocal fortissimos. One of the earliest, *Nabucodonosor* (1842), was one of the noisiest, but at the time, one of the most successful. Titta Ruffo found in it an air for the Assyrian king which he thought good enough

for the gramophone; however, I have not yet heard it. It is probably not so effective as the one for the Babylonian priest, *Tu sol labbro de'veggenti* (H.M.V., 6434—A), sung by José Mardones, which I have listened to with a good deal of pleasure. This Spanish bass has an organ of sonorous volume and the kind of pontifical delivery that suits this music. If *Nabucco* drew attention to Verdi's talent, *I Lombardi*, in the following year, excited Italian admiration still more, and I am surprised that out of its many fine numbers only two or three have survived. I can only speak here of the splendid trio *Qual voluttà trascorrere* (H.M.V., D.M.126), magnificently sung by Frances Alda, Caruso, and Journet—a record that any collector might be happy to possess. Caruso dominating the entire piece, starts it with a sobbing *cantilena*, full of tears, touching and beautiful; then, towards the end, a succession of thrilling high C's from him and Frances Alda, as if winding up with a cascade of brilliant fireworks, with Journet booming in the background.

After *I Lombardi* came a real success in the shape of *Ernani* (1844), still popular with Latin audiences, though many years have slipped by since I heard Patti singing *Ernani, involami* at Covent Garden. Another opera, *Luisa Miller* (1849) was also given here for the *diva* in 1875, but did not meet with equal favour. A third, which came between the two, was *I Due Foscari* (1845), and, having proved a downright failure at Florence and Paris, never got so far as London. Nevertheless, an air from it figures in more than one list under the title of *O vecchio cor che batti*, and, as a specimen of the true Verdi style, I rather admire a sentimental rendering of it by Pasquale Amato (H.M.V., D.B.636), which may suggest to some how Caruso would have made it sound had he been a baritone. Others will prefer, maybe, to hear the illustrious tenor himself in a tremendous declamatory air, *Ah, la paterna mano*, from the later opera of *Macbeth* (1847), which he trolls forth with astonishing energy and in his characteristic flamboyant manner (H.M.V., D.B.118). It was precisely, as we shall see, in these half-forgotten Verdi operas that Caruso achieved some of his finest records.

The three triumphs of the master's second period were *Rigoletto* (1851), *Il Trovatore* (1853), and *La Traviata* (also 1853); and after these we come to the first opera that Verdi wrote for the French stage, *Les Vêpres Siciliennes* (1855), which was never a real success either in Paris or Milan, where it was given at La Scala in 1856. It embodied an advance in many ways—notably greater refinement of style in declamation and orchestral scoring. The libretto, by Meyerbeer's *collaborateurs*, Scribe and Duveyrier, recalled " one of the bloodiest episodes of the ancient wars between France and Italy," and the two principal parts were created by two great singers, Sophie Cruvelli and Gueymard (the former of whom made a nine-days' sensation by disappearing from Paris with her future husband, just prior to the production, but turned up again in time for it). Still, neither the genius of Sophie Cruvelli, whom Adolphe Adam had admired so much in *Ernani*, nor that of Verdi, whose skill in writing the vigorous and passionate music demanded by his countrymen, the same able composer-critic had frankly pointed out,* could save *Les Vêpres Siciliennes* from the fate earned by an over-lengthy and tedious opera.

With the exception of the *bolero* in the last act, recorded, I may say, by Tetrazzini, the only big fish caught by the gramophone net from this much-debated score has been the famous bass air, *O tu Palermo*, the *cheval de bataille* of every popular *basso* whom I have encountered in my long experience of the Italian stage. The most notable records of it that have come under my notice are the following : by José Mardones (Victor–H.M.V., 6434—B), powerful, telling, always in tune ; by Alexander Kipnis (Polydor, 65724), resonant, a trifle unwieldy when not agitated, but effective and provided with an elaborate final cadenza ; by Malcolm MacEachern (Voc. K.05130), suave, sympathetic, restrained ; and, in English, Norman Allin (Col. L.1553), sustained with a good body of tone and smoothly sung. Each of these has merit, but the MacEachern omits the necessary recitative. On the reverse side of the Kipnis disc is another well-known bass air, *Il lacerato spirito*, taken from Verdi's very next opera, *Simon Boccanegra* (1857), which obtained at Venice and elsewhere no more than a *succès d'estime*. In addition to the German basso, who makes an admirable record of it, creditable in every way to Polydor workmanship, I may mention with no less unqualified praise the efforts of José Mardones (Col. A.5201), noble alike as to amplitude of voice and phrase ; Virgilio Lazzari (Voc. A.0222), rather dejected in tone, but broad and massive ; Ezio Pinza (H.M.V., D.B.699), who uses a well-covered dark organ with poise, deliberation, and power ; and, finally, Nazzarene de Angelis (Fono. B. 92440), who, on two sides of a 10in. disc, sings the whole piece with excellent feeling and dramatic colour.

---

* Arthur Pougin's *Life of Verdi*.

During the sixteen years that elapsed between the production of the *Vêpres Siciliennes* and the revelation of *Aida* (Cairo, 1871) three operas besides *Simon Boccanegra* issued from this prolific pen. Each was notable, but only one, *Un Ballo in Maschera*, continues in the active repertory to-day. This period of Verdi's career was transitional —one that had left behind the second, in some degree at any rate, but had not yet attained the third, that amazing epoch of maturing styles which opening up with *Aida*, advanced with *Otello*, and culminated in *Falstaff*. By far the best of these transitional operas was undoubtedly *Un Ballo* ; and its survival is doubly interesting, because of the fact that its book is not a whit less open to criticism than those of its contemporary works, *La Forza del Destino* (1862) and *Don Carlos* (1867). In both these cases it may be truly said that the exaggerated melodrama and violent situations which gave them birth also contributed largely to their speedy degeneration. Mr. J. H. Mapleson proudly declared in his memoirs that the first production in England of *La Forza del Destino* (originally written for St. Petersburg), was the principal feature of the season at Her Majesty's in 1867. I do not observe that he had much to say about it beyond that ; though I remember being present (and very little amused) at one brief revival of it at the same house a few years later, when a well-known prima donna, Caroline Salla by name, and, I think, the tenor Fancelli, appeared in the chief rôles.

Now, despite its liberal sprinkling of attractive numbers of up-to-date Verdian flavour, the Paris Opéra refused to have anything to do with *La Forza del Destino*. On the other hand, the director resolved in 1865 to arrange with the composer to write another opera expressly for that house. Hence *Don Carlos*, given for the first time at Paris in March 1867, the year of the great Universal Exhibition, and mounted at Covent Garden in the following June. It was well received, but its success was shortlived. Once more the composer had no luck with his French librettists ; it was the experience of the *Vêpres Siciliennes* over again. The fact was that he was never happy when writing to a French text, and, though he had made a decided advance in his art in twelve years, the general musical plan of *Don Carlos* lacked cohesion and consistency of style. Still, the score contained many beauties which could please separately, whilst the opera as a whole made a favourable impression nowhere save in the composer's native land. So much for the two failures that just preceded the brilliant triumph of *Aida*.

That *La Forza del Destino* has recently been revived on the stage in America, I am quite aware, and I attribute this more to its gramophone reputation than anything else. It is a magnificently recorded opera. In this fashion the most gifted and best-paid singers of the day have done it ample justice with far greater profit to themselves than they could have ever gained by performing it in the theatre; nor has it been their fault if many gramophonists have not yet realised to the full what a treasure of superb tone and declamatory art lies concealed in these unexplored regions. So far as I have played them for myself on my excellent Grafonola and Sonora Model, they have afforded me a great deal of pleasure; and I would even, had time permitted, have tried some of them again (at the office of this magazine) on the new H.M.V. machine, whereof I have only made a passing acquaintance at the Oxford Street establishment. Generally speaking, they seem to be fairly recent examples of the recording art and mostly first-rate at that. I note these things because I am now dealing with operas that have not been heard here by Londoners of the past two or three generations.

Those who love Verdi's earlier and more familiar operas will need no assurance that *La Forza del Destino* contains many melodious and intensely dramatic moments. After *Rigoletto* and *Un Ballo* he simply could not write a score which did not include a large proportion of such passages. You have only to listen to the Caruso records of this opera to feel that the singer simply adored it. He did not spare himself; he lavished his golden notes—" golden " in every sense—upon each phrase that afforded scope for his inexhaustible resources, and with a degree of generosity unequalled in any other opera. More especially is this apparent in the duets—the *Invano, Alvaro* (H.M.V., D.M.106) with Pasquale Amato comprising also *Le minaccie, i fieri accenti*, both wonderfully dramatic and exciting; and, again, in the *Sleale! il segreto fie dunque violata* (H.M.V., D.M.107), with De Luca, immense in volume and power, in stormy abusive declamation and the shower of high C's towards the end. Again, in another duet (H.M.V., D.M.105) the better-known *Solenne in quest'ora*, the famous tenor is associated with his old colleague, Antonio Scotti, and, though the latter has less to do, their voices go splendidly together. This piece begins with a long solo passage for the higher voice (" big guitar " accompaniment), the repeated " Addio " at the close being curiously reminiscent of that in the first act of the *Traviata*.

I have several additional examples of it, varied in their quality as records, but ably interpreted. The best all round are the two German ones, by Robert Hutt and Heinrich Schlusnus (Poly. 72735) and by Schubert and Scheidl (Poly. 65592); particularly the first-named. That by Constantino and Blanchart (Col. A.5184) is toneless and veiled; that by Garbin–Corradetti (Fonot. B.92254) very nice and agreeable, no more; and that by Lenghi-Cellini and Geo. Baker (Voc. 04105) likewise of average merit. None of these will be preferred to the Caruso–Scotti.

The most important tenor solo in *La Forza del Destino* is the *O tu che in seno agl'angeli*—made up of characteristic Verdian themes and effective points, but with no real climax to carry it off. Caruso put all that was possible into it (H.M.V., D.B.112), scoring wherever there was a chance; but I must confess that Tudor Davies's effort (H.M.V., D.707) gains nothing from the English version, *O thou that now with angels*, to which it is rather mildly rendered. Another English example is furnished by Florence Austral in the prayer, *Virgin Mother, hear me* (H.M.V., D.798), a broad melody of the well-known type, to which her opulent tones lend the fullest value, after deducting something for the absence of a choral background, such as Verdi loved to lend his leading soprano in her pious moments. We get the effect of this support and of the restless violin accompaniment in the Italian interpretation of Celestina Boninsegna, *Madre, pietosa Vergine* (Col. D.8081), although the thin solo voice, compared with that of Florence Austral, actually constitutes a loss on balance. However, on the other side of her 10in. disc Celestina readjusts matters with an artistic and pleasing performance of *La Vergine degl'angeli*, which air, with choral and harp accompaniment, is also recorded by Rosa Ponselle (Col 7340) and Emmy Destinn (Col. A.5398). This last may be the oldest record of the three, but for beauty of tone it is infinitely the best; it reproduces a voice that one recalls with enduring admiration. Destinn was a great singer.

Two baritone airs, *Urna fatale del mio destino* (H.M.V., D.B.738) and *Egli e' salvo* (H.M.V. 189), are both sung by Mattia Battistini in his usual masterful way. Those who enjoy vengeful or jubilant outbursts will choose the first; those who prefer a graceful and tender *cantilena* will want the latter; each is good of its kind. Finally, in this opera, there is to speak of the soprano air known as *Pace, pace, mio Dio!*—the title whereof ought, I think, to be *A te, mia figlia*, seeing that the whole piece is practically built up on these words. The theme consists of three snatches from *Il Trovatore*, commencing with the chromatic descent that forms the *coda* of *Il balen* (happily the grand old Italian was only utilising his own property over again). This charmingly devised mosaic is not well suited to Luisa Tetrazzini (H.M.V., D.B.538); it demands a richer, darker medium than hers. Not at all satisfactory, either, are the efforts of Ester Mazzoleni (Fonot. B.69189) or Georgina Caprile (Fonot. E. 74151), which are too tremulous; nor can I speak highly of Zita Fumagalli-Riva's (Parlo. E.10296), which is spoilt by excessive slurring and complete absence of articulate utterance. On the other hand, there is much to be said in favour of two others, viz., the sweet individual timbre and smooth phrasing of Celestina Boninsegna (Col. A.5199), and the more powerful, delicately - nuanced rendering of Rosa Ponselle (Victor–H.M.V., C.440). These are among the desirable items that, thanks to the gramophone, will help to keep alive *La Forza del Destino*.

Don Carlos is less rich in separable excerpts. But one or two are worthy of Verdi at his best, and particularly so the fine baritone air, *Ella giammai m' amò*, which, to my thinking, is nearly, if not quite, equal to *Eri tu*. There need be no fear that it will share oblivion with the opera, though one wonders why it has not been more recorded than it is. Columbia has never done it at all; and H.M.V. provides only one example, with the inadequate French title *Elle ne m'aime pas* (D.K.127) occupying the reverse side to a duet from the same score, *Dio che nell'alma infondere*. Marcel Journet is not so impressive as usual in this air; he does not recall in it the superb art of his countryman, Faure. I should almost prefer Alfred Jerger (Poly. 65648) for his sympathy and refinement, if he were not a shade too lachrymose. I like *les larmes dans la voix*, but not when they are overdone. Murray Davey (Voc. A.0245) is at any rate resonant, clear, and enunciates well. Alexander Kipnis (Poly. 65723) displays manly vigour in a pure baritone voice and shines to advantage in the higher range; his scale is even, and the orchestra, with its viola obbligato, accompanies smoothly. But then he sings in German and the needful bass quality is missing. So I am still waiting for the ideal record of this beautiful solo.

The duet already referred to, *Dio che nell'alma*, is sung by Martinelli and de Luca, but not with so much heroic *élan* and martial energy as by Caruso and Scotti (H.M.V., D.M.111). After the introductory tenor solo, it runs into fluent "thirds" and becomes a kind of Italian "Lord is a man of war"—*à la* Verdi, of course; and thereafter in the matter of blending and precision there is little to choose between the two records. Concerning Dame Clara Butt's familiar delivery of the well-known air, *O don fatale* (Col. 7316), it would be superfluous to offer comment; she has sung it, I fancy, ever since her Royal College days, but, truth to tell, it lies very high for a pure contralto. The baritone solo, *Per me giunto è il dì*, is cast somewhat in the same hackneyed mould and

tells us nothing in a musical sense, that the master had not told us a hundred times before (happily he told us much more original things later on). Yet, for a typical Battistini effort (H.M.V., D.B.148), one could hardly choose a finer record of its class—superb tone, sustained throughout with the utmost artistry. De Luca (H.M.V., D.B.218) also has a warm, rich baritone (with an occasional suspicion of tenor quality) and displays it to advantage when it is quite steady in the same piece.

He manages his low notes—as does Battistini—with greater adroitness than Titto Ruffo (D.B.178); but otherwise the latter pours out a lovely tone with any amount of pathos and sobs galore. De Luca I like much better in the air *O Carlo ascolta* (H.M.V., D.A.190), which he sings in excellent *cantabile* style. Nor must I omit a final word of appreciation for the tenor air *Io l'ho perduta*, as given with abundance of robust tone by Bernardo de Muro (H.M.V., D.B.554); and with which I end my retrospect of the recorded quasi-failures of Giuseppe Verdi. You will agree that they are too good to deserve oblivion.

P.S.—It was interesting recently to compare Elisabeth Schumann as an interpreter of Lieder with the operatic and gramophone singer whom one had already studied. In my estimation she came out as well at Wigmore Hall as at Covent Garden, where her Oktavian was excellent; and at the same time she exhibited a warmth of style that is frequently missing from her records. These I find, as a rule, coldly correct, but devoid of characterisation. She brings to the concert platform an atmosphere that suggests the influence of the stage and the feeling for the dramatic situation in an air like Mozart's " Deh vieni." Her finished technique and sense of tone-colour enable her to invest her Schubert and Strauss songs with the right qualities of facile ease, contrast, and authority. In short, she is a singer to be listened to with interest and pleasure.

Elena Gerhardt should now confine herself at recitals exclusively to her native Lieder. She is, I fear, developing an occasional tremolo; and it shows most when she attempts as she did at Queen's Hall on Feb. 2nd, less familiar songs by Marcello, Gluck, and Purcell. These things are not quite in her *genre*, and they are unwelcome when sung in the garbled German versions which mutilate and defy every genuine tradition.

HERMAN KLEIN.

THE GRAMOPHONE AND THE SINGER

(Continued)

By HERMAN KLEIN

Gems from Half-Forgotten Operas—II.

GOUNOD.

COMING now to the French school, let me begin by reminding readers that here especially we find a large number of operas which are only forgotten or neglected outside of France. There, belonging as they do to the native répertoire, they enjoy prescriptive right to occasional revival, and can even, some of them, claim unbroken popularity. In London nowadays we hear Gounod, for instance, only through his *Faust* and *Roméo et Juliette ;* but there are other operas of his worth hearing that we have either never listened to or are unlikely ever to hear again.

Such, for example, are his *Reine de Saba,* tabooed at Covent Garden because its story is Biblical (!), and his *Philémon et Baucis,* which Augustus Harris mounted with a success that for a few seasons was quite remarkable. *Philémon,* indeed, is a gem of melody and grace, and in connection with it I always think of Pol Plançon's exquisite performance as Jupiter and Santley's superb rendering of the *stances* of Vulcain, *Au bruit des lourds marteaux,* which he first introduced at the old "Pops." I am surprised that the air just named should not be recorded more frequently ; it is well known, full of energy and *entrain,* and a piece that will live. Gounod's *Mireille* is another charming work, but like his *Polyeucte* (founded upon Corneille's tragedy), the story does not lend itself to operatic treatment, and the beauty of the music gets, so to speak, submerged beneath uninteresting details. I remember witnessing one revival of *Mireille* at Covent Garden, but *Polyeucte* has never been done here ; while the *Reine de Saba* I never saw abroad on the stage, though I have heard it in concert form under the title of *Irene* according to the English version of the late H. B. Farnie.

La Reine de Saba, which followed *Faust* at the Paris Opéra after an interval of three years in February, 1862, furnishes another case of a beautiful score rendered useless by a stupid libretto. But the accomplished master was in his prime, and half a dozen numbers at least deserve to survive. Of these one of the best known is the soprano air, *Plus grand dans son obscurité (Far greater in his lowly state),* which, strangely enough, does not appear to have been recorded. The noble tenor air, *Inspirez-moi (Lend me your aid),* was made famous in this country by Edward Lloyd, who used to sing it magnificently. (Would that he had made a record of it !) Somehow, no one else seems to have surmounted its lofty *tessitura* or sustained its lengthy phrases with the same consummate ease and undeviating smoothness of luscious tone. No, not even Enrico Caruso, for all his marvellous reserves of power and *sostenuto.* The best that may be said of his interpretation (H.M.V., D.B.145) is that it was unusually suave, unforced, and polished. It was evidently not the sort of thing that imparted the inspiration he was asking for, nor was he perhaps over-familiar with it. Another French performance, by Maurice Oger (Voc., O.41042) is dramatic enough and achieves certain vocal effects, but lacks dignity and breadth of style. Less distinguished still, though sufficiently solid and suggestive of stamina are the two English examples by John Harrison (H.M.V., D.234) and John Perry (Parlo., E.10220), the latter's being spread over the two sides of the disc. Both singers have capital voices, and it seems a pity that their diction — the vowels particularly — should not reflect the true, unaffected refinement of cultured British speech. Another familiar item from the same opera is the fine bass air, *She alone charmeth my sadness (Sous les pieds),* once the *cheval de bataille* of the celebrated " Signor Foli," whom his friends all knew as Jack Foley—born not a very long way from Tipperary, me bhoy ! He, too, was a splendid singer, and I am glad to be able to say that worthy reproductions of his reading of this piece have been made by Robert Radford (H.M.V., D.269) and Norman Allin (Col. 756). Both artists are exceptionally commendable in this instance, alike as to colour and quality of timbre, enunciation, and musical phrasing generally. The recording is also good.

Mireille is thought by some French critics to be one of Gounod's "most remarkable and best-inspired scores." At any rate it should have yielded a richer harvest to gramophone artists than is actually in sight. Where is Mireille's big air, *Mon cœur ne peut changer*? where Andreloun's pastoral song, *Le jour se lève*? Chiefly in request, of course, is the well-known waltz air, called in Italian *O d'amor messaggera,* whereof I can mention four attractive examples, viz., Luisa Tetrazzini (H.M.V., D.B.703), Frieda Hempel (H.M.V.,

D.B.373), Maria Barrientos (Col. 7338), and the French Mlle. Brothier (H.M.V., P.397). To which of these the palm should be awarded it is hard to say, for each has its own particular charm. Tetrazzini atones by a round, delicious quality and faultless intonation for an excessive use of the *rubato* in her *bravura* passages ; the fascinating Frieda is consistent in rhythm and brilliancy, and runs her scale up to the E in *alt ;* while la Barrientos challenges both her rivals with the exceeding prettiness and delicacy of her execution, including a wonderful *staccato*, and only teases you once with an unduly prolonged high D at the end. The record of the waltz made by Mlle. Brothier, of the Opéra-Comique, gives the idea of being sung by a soprano who is in the habit of singing the rôle. She renders it prettily, if with no great animation, and executes her runs with the utmost neatness ; at the same time there is no effort, no straining to make effects, and the tempo is very leisurely. On the reverse side of this is another air from the same opera, *Si les filles d'Arles sont reines*, done by M. Bauge, a high baritone also engaged at the Opéra-Comique. He has a bright, telling voice, and imbues this characteristic air with all the necessary rhythmical spirit.

Ambroise Thomas.

I have been slightly in doubt whether to include among my " half-forgotten " collection the *Hamlet* of Ambroise Thomas. On the other side of the Channel it would assuredly be thought high treason to do so ; but how many people, I wonder, recall the solitary revival at Covent Garden sixteen years ago, let alone the earlier scattered *reprises* given for the sole purpose of preserving the performing rights at that house ? I heard it there in my youth, with the incomparable Faure in his original character of Hamlet, less than a decade after he had created it in 1868 at the Paris Opéra. I heard it again in 1890 with Lassalle as Hamlet, Melba as Ophélie, and Richard as the Queen. I enjoyed portions of it immensely, but, as a whole, the work made no stronger appeal to me than it did to London operagoers generally. It never struck me as embodying Shakespeare's tragedy, even to the extent that Gounod suggests in his *Romeo and Juliet*, or Verdi, still more finely in his *Othello* and *Merry Wives of Windsor (Falstaff)*. But, whilst I object to Hamlet trolling forth a drinking song in the theatre, I am not in the least averse to listening to the same spirited piece in my studio, especially when sung by such distinguished gramophonists as Battistini or Titta Ruffo. Of course, they both use the Italian version, *O vin, disaccia la tristezza ;* and both give you on the reverse side the touchingly sad air, *Come il romito fior*, which the melancholy Dane sings in the last act. Battistini (H.M.V., D.B.202) is delightful in each, his manly tone

fitting the sparkling tune and jolly refrain of the one no less perfectly than the tender sweetness of the other ; while Titta Ruffo (H.M.V., D.B.569) imparts in turn his never-failing gusto and a measure of expressive, restrained emotion that is less usual with him.

Ruffo's versatility is also displayed in another record (H.M.V., D.A.352) illustrating Hamlet's first encounter with the Ghost. He gives us on one side, in *spoken* declamation, the speech on the castle platform which is not in the opera at all ; and, on the other, the so-called " invocation," *Spettro santo*, wherein Hamlet implores his father's Ghost to speak to him. Both are well done and impressive, and in the *Apparizione* the artist shows that if he had not been a splendid singer he might have followed in the footsteps of Salvini and Rossi. I must not omit to mention also a particularly fine rendering in French by Maurice Renaud (H.M.V., D.857) of the air noticed above, here entitled *Comme une pâle fleur*. It recalls that famous baritone at his best. He sings it with exquisite pathos, and the rich effect of his native tongue imparts an added charm to the tender melody.

There remains the Mad Scene. It is sung now by every ambitious soprano ; and it deserves to be. To my thinking it is far more interesting and characteristic than the display of vocal *feux d'artifice* which sudden lunacy engenders in Donizetti's unlucky heroine, Lucia di Lammermoor. It is more varied, richer in contrast, of far greater intrinsic musical value. It is also much more difficult and the fact that it is considerably shortened for the gramophone is perhaps not a disadvantage. The three examples I have tried are by Dame Melba (H.M.V., D.B.364) in French, by Tetrazzini (H.M.V., D.B.543) in Italian, and by Evelyn Scotney (H.M.V., D.968) in English. The first is extremely brilliant, and suggests a heroine really distraught, sweeping onward to an exciting climax that terminates with a glorious trill. The second is remarkable for beauty of tone and execution all through ; the third for singularly clean, clear-cut phrases and neat *fiorituri*, with a dazzling chromatic run up to *altissimo* to end with. Hence, I recommend each in turn, leaving the choice of singer and language to the reader.

Massenet.

The half-dozen operas by this composer which are neither successes here nor failures in France, but whereof records are available, comprise *Don César de Bazan* (1872), *Le Roi de Lahore* (1877), *Hérodiade* (1881), *Le Cid* (1885), *Le Jongleur de Notre Dame* (1902), and *Cléopâtre* (1914). To these ought, perhaps, to be added *Werther* (1893) and *La Navarraise* (first produced at Covent Garden, 1894) ; but at the Opéra-Comique the former almost shares popularity with *Manon* (1884), which is generally regarded as Massenet's *chef-d'œuvre*. I limit my selection, therefore, to the half-dozen first named, reckoning *Thaïs* (1894) likewise among the category of operas too successful for the present purpose.

Massenet was just thirty when he wrote *Don César de Bazan*, the subject being drawn, like that of Wallace's *Maritana*, from the more or less historical drama of Victor Hugo. But where Wallace succeeded amazingly with his much-derided ballad-opera, Massenet registered a literal fiasco in 1872, which he only obliterated five years later with *Le Roi de Lahore*. Two years after that we were hearing *Il Rè di Lahore* in Italian at Covent Garden, and never shall I forget the impression created in it by Lassalle, who then made his début in his original part of Scindia. His golden voice and finished art secured for the opera whatever favour it won, notably in the beautiful air, *Promesse de mon avenir* (*O casto fior del mio sospir*), which is about the only number in the score that the gramophone has preserved. Other baritones have sung it since, but not with Lassalle's enchanting tone or height of sensuous charm. Nearest to him, perhaps, comes de Gogorza (H.M.V., D.B.627) with much amorous tenderness and many *rallentandos*. Next I am inclined to place a very expressive rendering by Eric Marshall (Voc., I.04109), whose French may not be immaculate, but whose style here is both impassioned and sincere. Frankly, the Italians Battistini (H.M.V., D.B.150) and Titta Ruffo (D.B.401) lack the caressing touch for this song. The latter, who sings it in Italian, overloads it with sheer energy and emphasis, to an accompaniment that is super-thin.

The music of Jules Massenet makes up by its charm for what it lacks in originality, and it demands above everything, charm from its interpreters—the one predominant feature of the French school. Without that it fails to rivet the ear. Take *Hérodiade* and *Le Cid*. It was the inimitable genius of Jean de Reszke that first won for them those triumphs in Paris which they have never gained elsewhere out of France and Belgium. Yet both operas contain delightful music, when sung by the right artists. The best thing in *Hérodiade*, the baritone air, *Vision fugitive*, holds no fascination as sung in Italian by Campanari (Col. A.5127); but de Luca (H.M.V., D.B.221), in inferior French, makes a decent thing of it; whilst de Gogorza (H.M.V., D.B.627) certainly shows, as he ought, that it is the spasmodic apostrophe of a madman under the nocturnal influence of a drug. The well-known soprano air, *Il est doux, il est bon*, I have heard much better sung than it is by Mary Garden (Col. A.5289); her tone is unsteady and her portamentos seem unending. In a word, this piece (unlike the air in *Thaïs*) does not suit her any better than the lovely *Pleurez, mes yeux*, from

Le Cid, can be said to suit Dame Melba (H.M.V., D.B.711), or, for that matter, than the tenor air from the same opera, *O souverain, ô juge, ô père*, suited Caruso (H.M.V., D.B.123). The consequence is that they did not call forth the finest qualities of the gifted vocalists who attempted them, and the results are unsatisfactory.

I return for a moment to *Don César de Bazan*, in order to mention the *Sevillana*—its solitary legacy—as recorded by Melba (H.M.V., D.B.711) and Galli-Curci (H.M.V. 611). This is one of those clever imitations of the Spanish idiom for which Massenet was at one time celebrated, and both artists have striven to realise its picturesque rhythms with maximum effect. There is a strong similarity between the two renderings, as though the one done first had been copied in the other. But that does not matter. I prefer the Galli-Curci for many reasons : its liveliness and tremendous rhythm ; its sense of enjoyment and *joie de vivre* ; its *staccato*, clear as a bell and as penetrating ; above all, its genuine Spanish flavour and *couleur locale*. What a pity Massenet could not give us anything as spontaneous as this in his *Cléopâtre* forty years later. Here, again, is a solitary legacy—the *Air de la Lettre*, from the second act, recorded by Marcel Journet (H.M.V. 259), replete with pathos and deep feeling, phrased in a noble tone by a great artist. But what a dull piece apart from its context !

So with the much-recorded *Légende de la Sauge* (*Fleurissait une rose*) from *Le Jongleur de Notre Dame*. It does not transplant well. In its place in in the opera, sung by the warm-hearted monk who cooks for the monastery, it sounds extremely quaint and archaic, in fact, like an old French folk-song, simple and full of character. Separated from the life and colour of the stage, I find it rather tedious music, despite the distinction of the artists who have seized upon it for the gramophone. The happiest effort is that of Dinh Gilly (H.M.V., D.B.693), who combines with an old-world grace a certain amount of vigour and unaffected sentiment, such as the piece calls for. Equally appropriate is the rendering of M. Rouard (French H.M.V., W.408), done like Dinh Gilly's on two sides of the disc, and apparently a Parisian product in every sense. In these there is at least a touch of poetry that is conspicuous by its absence from Cesare Formichi's (Col. D.1491)—an Italian version with little but " voice " to recommend it. Even Journet (H.M.V., D.B.313), although a Frenchman, is too heavy a singer for this kind of thing. When I saw *Le Jongleur* produced at New York in 1908, at Oscar Hammerstein's Manhattan Opera House, the part of Jean, originally written for a tenor, was undertaken by Mary Garden, who certainly gave an effective performance of it. But she can make nothing on the gramophone of the provocative drinking song,

Liberté (Col. A.5289), which gets him locked up in the monastery. In fact, it is even more tiresome than the *Légende*.

So much for Massenet. Next month I shall conclude this series of " Half-forgotten Operas " with selections derived from other French and Italian sources.

THE COMING OPERA SEASON.

By Easter we can form, as a rule, a pretty accurate idea of what the London season is going to bring forth in the way of grand or international opera. This is, therefore, the right moment for a forecast. Happily, the directorate of the London Opera Syndicate, headed by Lt.-Col. Eustace Blois, consists of a small, but compact, body of resourceful people possessing the courage of their opinions. And, naturally, they have been additionally encouraged by the success of last year's preliminary venture ; also their timely announcements for 1926 were of a nature to deserve and receive a highly satisfactory response. Both the German and the Italian seasons—beginning on Monday, May 10th and lasting altogether eight weeks—contain such an abundance of attractive features that they seem bound to excite interest in the various classes of opera-lovers whose combined support is needful.

These are matters that concern the readers of THE GRAMOPHONE Magazine, for the reason that opera on the grand scale and of a high order must necessarily appeal to their musical instincts ; and because only the best of its kind can possibly satisfy a taste that becomes ever more and more fastidious. The admirable first-class records of opera that now abound in such unlimited quantities have been educating the modern ear even more than actual stage performances, which have latterly been both limited in supply and variable in quality. In reality the appetite for first-class opera can only grow by what it feeds upon, whether it be presented through the medium of the gramophone or in its complete and living form with all the resources of a great operatic establishment. The point is that the ear so prepared—with the further valuable assistance of the eye—seems more than likely to find a satisfying, if not an ideal, realisation of its most exalted yearnings in course of the campaign that is shortly to start. The repertory is chosen, the leading singers of the day are engaged, th. orchestra will be led by conductors of supreme talent. More than this it would be superfluous, at the moment, for me to say.

HERMAN KLEIN.

THE GRAMOPHONE AND THE SINGER
(Continued)
By HERMAN KLEIN
Covent Garden Opera and Gems from Half-Forgotten Operas—III.

IF starvation whets the appetite, and it inevitably must, then surely London should be very hungry indeed for the operatic feast that lies before it. Here in this gigantic metropolis of ours we have had no opera to speak of since the last international season ended nine months ago. The fact is rather discreditable, but no good will come of dwelling upon it now. The remedy lies in the future—in the realisation of somebody's scheme—Mr. Isidore de Lara's or another's—for providing London with a large opera-house at which opera can be given at cheap prices and mainly in English all the year round. Anyhow, we ought not to go on being starved as we have been of late.

Meanwhile there is distinct compensation for our long abstention in the high order of the artistic menu laid before us by the London Opera Syndicate for the coming eight weeks at Covent Garden ; and there is also solid ground for satisfaction in the generous advance support—the largest known in recent times—that has been accorded to the present undertaking. I think we may take for granted that, whatever may happen, Covent Garden and its " grand " season are in no imminent danger of extinction. The market and its purlieus may disappear, but the opera-house will not go with them so long as society and the wealthier patrons of high-class opera continue willing to pay the necessary prices for the international article, as the Americans do. No one has the right to complain on this score. The two things—expensive opera and good cheap opera—are as distinct from each other as are luxuries and the ordinary necessaries of comfortable living. Costly singers are for those who can afford to pay to hear them ; and, seeing that they help to keep up our standard, I should be the last to grumble if conditions permit of their visiting us occasionally.

Among the fifty odd artists engaged for the season which begins on May 10th, not more than a dozen are unfamiliar to connoisseurs of the gramophone. All the prominent musical nationalities are represented, from Italian to Scandinavian, from Russian to British—quite an unusual proportion indeed of the last named. Yet very few are absolutely newcomers, and of these the most interesting, I imagine, will be Mariano Stabile, the young Sicilian baritone, of whose Don Giovanni report speaks so highly. Personally I am extremely curious to hear him in this important rôle, for it is many years since the " perfidious Don " has had a truly great delineator in London. As for the final quintet, which Bruno Walter has determined to revive for us, I should hardly think it has been done here within living memory—certainly not in my own.

Another interesting début will be that of the Belgian soprano, Fanny Heldy, one of the favourites of the Paris Opéra-Comique, who is to appear as the heroines of Massenet's *Manon* and Ravel's *L'Heure Espagnole*. According to all accounts she is a lively actress and a charming singer. Her Des Grieux in *Manon* will be that splendid tenor Fernand Ansseau, who returns heavily laden with New York laurels. In connection with the Italian and French operas a third important début will be the conductor's. Vincenzo Bellezza was the friend and accompanist of Caruso and was with him when he died. He comes here with a wonderful reputation, won first of all as a prodigy, then as a conductor at the San Carlo at the age of 20, and subsequently a brilliant career with the bâton all over Italy, Spain, and South America. I hope Bellezza will prove as gifted as he seems to be, and there will be no lack of opportunity for proving it. It is when a conductor has to do with big artists that he proves his strength, and the chance will be forthcoming when he faces Chaliapine in the *Barbiere di Siviglia* and *Mefistofele*, not to mention Jeritza in *Thaïs* and the *Gioielli della Madonna*. He is likewise to direct Dame Melba's farewell performance in opera as Mimi in *La Bohème*.

Most of the German protagonists were here last season—the ladies, at any rate ; and some of them will be heard in the revivals of *Figaro* and *Don Giovanni*. The principal airs they have already recorded in their own language (which is the one they are to use in *Figaro* now), and I have duly noticed some of them in my monthly review column. It will be doubly interesting, therefore, to listen to Lotte Lehmann as the Countess and Donna Elvira ; to Elisabeth Schumann as Zerlina and Susanna ; to Frida Leider as Donna Anna ; and to Richard Mayr as Figaro. Even more notable, in a sense, will be the return after several years' absence of that fine bass singer, Marcel Journet, in his old part of Leporello. His début at Covent Garden in 1897 was little noticed, eclipsed as he then was by Edouard de Reszke and Plançon ; but as the seasons rolled on he succeeded to more important rôles, and rose steadily in public esteem, until the war came and America monopolised his winters, France the rest of his year. Since then he has made more records, I suppose, than any other Frenchman singing in either of those countries, while recently he has been winning additional fame at La Scala. Journet must now be in his prime. Another welcome return will be that of Giovanni Zenatello, the famous tenor who married Maria Gay. He appeared here first in 1905 and last in 1914, when his Otello was greatly admired. He is now to sing this part with Lotte Lehmann for his Desdemona and Mariano Stabile as Iago—a strong combination.

The solitary cycle of the *Nibelungen*, which starts on the second night of the season, will be performed without cuts, and Gertrude Kappel will be the Brünnhilde. It will perhaps introduce a new Siegfried in another New York favourite, Rudolf Laubenthal, who is, we are told, a " young and handsome man." He will also sing Tristan, with Leider as Isolde, Olczewska as Brangäne, and Richard Mayr as King Marke. In the *Meistersinger* we are to have Fritz Krauss as Walther, Lotte Lehmann as Eva, Emil Schipper as Hans Sachs, and Eduard Habich as Beckmesser. Altogether the German casts promise to be exceptionally strong, and, under the able guidance of Bruno Walter they cannot fail to yield some splendid performances.

Some good Russian artists were heard at Covent Garden in the performance of a concert version of Rimsky-Korsakoff's opera, *The Sacred City of Kitesh*, given by the B.B.C. on March 30th. Under the conditions it was extremely well rendered, but without stage action and accessories one cannot fairly judge a mystical lyric play of this type. Anyhow, little if any of the music would lend itself to gramophonic purposes, nor would the characters themselves possess the least attraction unless interpreted by artists of Russian nationality and of the same calibre as these. I should like to hear more of Mme. Smirnova, who is an admirable singer, despite her tremolo ; of Pozemkovsky, a fine dramatic tenor ; of Popov, a serious comedian and clever singer who by sheer facial art depicts a strange fantastic figure ; and, above all, Mosjourkin, a real *basso profondo* with the style of a Chaliapine.

In resuming — and concluding — my "Half-forgotten" series, I would like to make it clear, in order to save correspondents trouble, that I do not pretend to make these retrospective articles of mine exhaustive. I cover the ground as well as I can in my endeavour to give information concerning operas and records that have found a place in the various catalogues. But, for one reason or another, there are bound to be missing items that have escaped the meshes of our net; and I would add that whatever slips through this office is not likely to be easily procurable by the general reader. Criticism in such cases can hardly serve any very useful purpose.

During the early spring of 1914 there was revived at Covent Garden (concurrently with the first production of *Parsifal* in this country) an opera which had not been heard there for 73 years, and then only in the form of an oratorio—a fate that it shared with Saint-Saëns's *Samson et Dalila*. The opera in question was Méhul's *Joseph*. Not a great masterpiece by any means, but an interesting example of lyric writing during the Napoleonic era—1807, to be exact—and always a favourite at the Opéra-Comique, where I heard it well given in 1883. In London we had to listen to it in German, and somehow the elements did not seem to mix, although the dose was thrice repeated. The gem of the score is the tenor romance for Joseph, *A peine au sortir de l'enfance*, the only number reproduced on the gramophone, although the soprano solo for Benjamin is scarcely less charming and ought to be recorded by a Frenchwoman. By a curious caprice the air first named appears in the H.M.V. catalogue under the misleading title of *Champs paternel*, and as such is ably sung by Fernand Ansseau (D.B.482) and John McCormack (D.B.634). Styles more utterly different it would be difficult to imagine—the former full of life, vigour, and contrast; the other smooth, pleasant, and insinuating, but quite colourless. Both sing in French, and language counts for a good deal. On the whole, for every reason I greatly prefer Ansseau's rendering.

Only one fragment from *Joseph*. Only three from another religious (not Biblical) opera, Halévy's *La Juive*, which far exceeded Méhul's in popularity during the middle of the nineteenth century. Brought out at the Paris Opéra in 1835, frequently performed in London in French, Italian, and English, it has grown too frankly old-fashioned to hold the stage here, though the travelling opera companies still, I believe, find it pay for revival. Quite a fuss was made because the original production cost the unheard-of sum of 150,000 francs (then £6,000); but we think in higher figures nowadays. The bass air for the Cardinal, *Si la rigueur*, is very familiar. Excellent records of it have been sung by Mardones (Col. A.5202), Richard Mayr (Pol. 65652), and Ezio Pinza (H.M.V., D.B.698), the first in Italian being the most impressive in volume, the second in German the most lugubrious, and the third, also in Italian, the richest in colour and sentiment. The big tenor air, which Edward Lloyd often used to sing, is reproduced in French by Caruso (*Rachel, quand du Seigneur*, H.M.V., D.B.123) with that manful, robust tone, and animated accent so characteristic of him. German audiences seem to prefer a more tearful manner of the "sob-stuff" order, at any rate in these religious apostrophes; and such are the two Polydor records by Leo Slezák (*Recha, als Gott dich einst*, 65769) and Richard Schubert (65618), though both are of decided mechanical excellence. Quite on a musical level with the above is the Meyerbeerian soprano air, *Il va venir* (*He will be here*), a first-rate record of which is made by Florence Austral (H.M.V., D.798) with exemplary clearness of tone and diction. More dramatic and emotional are the German versions of Lotte Lehmann (Pol. 72905) and Vera Schwarz (Pol. 15884); but neither is quite so satisfying in effect. The former's tone is very veiled, especially in the medium, and the latter drags nearly every phrase.

An interval of half a century separated the opera just referred to from Edouard Lalo's *Le Roi d'Ys*, a charming work—half romantic, half miracle-play —which has never had a fair chance in this country. It is not big enough for Covent Garden, where it was given in 1902 with Plançon and Journet in the cast, but it contains some delightful music. The *clou* is the simple, diatonic *aubade* for the tenor, Mylio, which I find exquisitely rendered by the Opéra-Comique favourite, M. Clément (Victor 6062), and also nicely sung by Beniamino Gigli (Victor 906), the Frenchman's being, of course, quite the real thing. But what I cannot recommend "at any price" is an H.M.V. example of this piece by Dame Melba. Surely there is plenty of soprano music in the world, without popular prima donnas needing to lay piratical hands on tenor solos just because they happen to be beautiful.

Patrie! is an opera by Paladilhe (who died quite recently), founded upon Sardou's moving spectacular play, and was produced in Paris in 1886 with a cast that included the incomparable Mme. Krauss, Jean Lassalle, and Edouard de Reszke. It was a magnificent performance, but I found the work dreadfully tedious. It is still given occasionally in France, but all that immediately concerns us are two H.M.V. records of some interest, chiefly for the personality of the singers—one Emil de Gogorza's *Air du Sonneur* (D.B. 625), the other Titta Ruffo's *Pauvre martyr obscur!*—and of these I can only say that each exemplifies good singing and good recording. Side by side with these may be coupled two more records of a favourite excerpt from a more than half-forgotten opera, to wit, the *Bourbonnaise*, otherwise *L'Eclat de Rire*, alias *C'est l'histoire amoureuse*, from Auber's *Manon Lescault*, made for H.M.V. by Galli-Curci (D.A.215) and Evelyn Scotney (D.968). Although both display clever technique, the result is no longer the infectious laugh intended by the composer. It sounds more like a staccato study ; and as such one grows rather tired of it. But is this really all there is for gramophonists to enjoy from Auber's extensive output of fascinating melody ? Putting aside *Fra Diavolo* as being his quite unforgotten masterpiece, has no one yet fished for gems in *Masaniello* (*La Muette de Portici*), *Les Diamans de la Couronne*, *Le Domino Noir*, or even *L'Ambassadrice* ?

MODERN ITALIAN OPERAS.

Reckoning the nineteenth century—all Verdi, for instance, previously dealt with—as part of this category of modern semi-failures, the same question arises. I am, I know, omitting excerpts from many bygone favourites that are not yet consigned to oblivion elsewhere, if they are in England. But even so, can it be that the exploiters of the gramophone have no use for the splendid vocal pieces interred in the neglected scores of Bellini, Rossini, and Donizetti ? Surely not. A few, but only a few, of Donizetti's have been rescued, at any rate—thanks chiefly to the industry of Caruso and Battistini ; and I have listened to them with genuine enjoyment. The famous tenor has left a superb record of *Deserto sulla terra*, which Gayarre used to introduce in *La Favorita*, but entitled *In terra solo* in the H.M.V. list (D.B.700). It occurs in *Dom Sebastiano*, an opera which owed its failure to one of Scribe's very worst libretti, written for the French stage in 1843. A record of the same air by Alfred Piccaver (Pol. 72877) can only be described as a slavish imitation of Caruso's. Finer still is the latter's rendering (and the music) of the air, *Angelo casto e bel*, from *Il Duca d'Alba* (D.B.640), a smooth *cantilena* cast in the purest Donizettian mould, sung with rare emotional fervour and rising with a big *crescendo* to a glorious climax. Battistini has recorded extracts from *Maria di Rohan* and *Maria di Rudenz* ; but the best of his is also from *Dom Sebastiano*, namely, the celebrated *O Lisbona* (H.M.V., D.B.207)—suave, elegant, and refined—other records of which have been admirably furnished by Granforte (D.B. 834) and Eric Marshall (Voc. K.05143). With mention of these I take leave of the type of opera that was in vogue during the " palmy days " of Covent Garden and Her Majesty's.

What was termed the " Young Italy " school, began to forge ahead soon after the advent of *Aïda*. The real impetus dates from the production of the revised version of Boito's *Mefistofele* at Bologna in 1875. Five years before that we had also heard of a new opera called *Il Guarany*, by a youthful

Brazilian, Carlos Gomez, of whom great things were expected by the *habitués* of La Scala. However, when the work was mounted at Covent Garden in 1872, it failed to catch on, notwithstanding the efforts of such singers as Faure, Nicolini, Cotogni, Bagagiolo, and the fascinating Mlle. Sessi. Struggles between Spanish and Portuguese adventurers in the wilds of Brazil could not, after all, greatly excite European audiences before the days of the cinema-film, however picturesque the music. Nevertheless, the Fonotipia provides several reminiscences of an opera that is still to be heard in South America ; while H.M.V. has an excellent record of the melodious duet, *Sento una forza indomita* (D.B.616), sung with immense spirit and vocal beauty by Caruso and Emmy Destinn. The former has also done ample justice to the well-known song *La mia piccirella* (H.M.V., D.B.144), from *Salvator Rosa*, another opera by the same composer—which song Mme. Albani introduced over here many years ago. It is a tenor piece by rights, but can be no less effectively sung by a soprano.

Another twenty years and Mascagni and Leoncavallo had arrived. But, alas, the brilliant triumphs of *Cavalleria Rusticana* (1890) and *Pagliacci* (1892) were never afterwards approached by either maestro. The tale of half-successes henceforward grows too lengthy to be followed. What is it that is just missing in some of these operas, scattered with charming *morceaux*, that would maybe have converted failure into the other thing ? Almost always, of course, it is the crass stupidity of the libretto that is to blame. Yet not invariably. The poetry of Mascagni's *L'Amico Fritz* and his *Iris* is quite on a level with his music ; and the former —done at Covent Garden in 1892, with Calvé, Giulia Ravogli, and the tenor De Lucia—ought to be as popular as *Cavalleria* is to-day. On the other hand, his second opera, *I Rantzau*, proved to be one of the most tedious affairs that a poor critic ever had to sit out ; it was done once in 1893—and never again. But, apart from the little Sicilian masterpiece, I have no records of anything out of these operas. So far as the gramophone is concerned, Leoncavallo has been luckier. His *Zazà* and his *Bohème* have been plentifully and faithfully recorded, the former in particular. Caruso, as usual, working in America, did not overlook the talented compatriot who had inspired him with *Vesti la giubba*. He lavished his opulent resources upon two airs from *La Bohème* (both on H.M.V., D.B.122), duly imitated by Piccaver (Pol. 70768). Again, Martinelli excelled himself in two from *Zazà* (H.M.V., D.A.329) ; while the delightful *canzone popolare*, known as *Zazà, piccola zingara !* has been recorded in turn by Titta Ruffo, Stracciari, Amato, Sammarco, De Luca, and the Germans, Scheidl, Schlusnus, and Schwarz, which ought to be about enough, without mentioning the duet *Il Bacio* (no connection with Arditi's celebrated waltz), sung by Geraldine Farrar and De Luca (H.M.V., D.A.209). Yet, in spite of all this, Leoncavallo's *Zazà* has never been thought worthy of production in London. There are doubtless excellent reasons for it.

RUBINSTEIN AND TCHAIKOVSKY.

The great pianist, Anton Rubinstein, has yet to be appreciated at his true worth as an operatic composer. The simple truth is that we were not ready for Russian music of any sort 45 years ago, when his opera *The Demon* was produced in Italian at Covent Garden. In common with most other people who heard it then, I thought it over-heavy and monotonous, albeit splendidly sung by Albani, Trebelli, Lassalle, Marini, and Edouard de Reszke. With a cast like that I might think differently now, though I am not altogether sure. The music, at any rate, or some of the best of it, has been preserved for us by Chaliapine and Baklánov, and I unhesitatingly commend to my readers their respective records (H.M.V., D.B.611 and D.A.465). Both contain on either side magnificent specimens of vocal and recording technique. No less praiseworthy are two Italian reproductions from Rubinstein's *Nero*, an opera very different in character to Boito's, which it preceded by many years, although designed at about the same period—the late seventies. These comprise a sorrowful air with a pretty harp accompaniment, sung by Caruso the tireless (*Ah mon sort*, H.M.V., D.B.127); and a declamatory *Epitalamio* (D.B.211), rather explosive for a wedding chant, vigorously given by Battistini. A word of praise must also be accorded Baklánov's dramatic render-ing of the air, *I am he whom you called*, on the reverse side of D.A.465, noted above.

I conclude with a Tchaikovsky item. It is not, of course, from *Eugene Onégin*, because that is not a forgotten opera, nor likely to be one yet awhile (though I may mention that Lensky's air, finely sung by Caruso, is on the same disc as the *Nero* extract just referred to). The record which must typify Tchaikovsky here is the tenor solo, *Forgive me*, and *What is my life* (H.M.V., D.A.569) from his *Pique Dame* (*Queen of Spades*), perhaps the most attractive vocal number in the work which Oscar Hammerstein gave at the London Opera House, Kingsway, in 1915. One section is tearful, the other martial; while both are more or less tuneful and sung with abundant expression by Smirnoff, an excellent artist who has, I fancy, been heard here. But the story by Pushkin on which the book is framed is rather far-fetched and violent, and I doubt whether the opera will ever win lasting favour out of Russia.

HERMAN KLEIN.

* * *

P.S.—I am glad to say that henceforward I shall be able to test a due proportion of the records that I write about through the medium of the latest His Master's Voice gramophone. That will be an inestimable advantage, for I already perceive it to be a very wonderful machine—the " last word," in fact, in every detail that makes for reproductive perfection. As time goes on I shall learn to know it still better and continue, I hope, to chronicle my growingly vivid impressions in these pages.

THE GRAMOPHONE AND THE SINGER

(Continued)

By HERMAN KLEIN

Opera at Covent Garden: The Weber Centenary

MOST of us are anxious, I fancy, to forget as soon as possible the terrible inconveniences that were inflicted upon us by the General Strike. I will make no attempt, therefore, to depict the difficulties of transport that had to be overcome during the opening week of the Royal Opera season. Fortunately for the London Opera Syndicate, the house had been sold out in advance, and the audiences—those who did not possess cars —managed for the first three nights as best they could, while lorries were provided by the directors to convey the chorus, orchestra, and the whole of the stage workers to and from the theatre. I need not say how thankful they all were when things became normal once more. It was wonderful, under the circumstances, that there should have been such a brilliant gathering as there was for the initial representation of the season on Monday, May 10th, when Mozart's *Figaro's Hochzeit* was given—for the first time in German, if I am not mistaken, at this house.

As my readers must by now be aware, I am of opinion that *Le Nozze di Figaro* is heard to greatest advantage with the Italian text to which it was composed. That opinion did not undergo modification at any moment of the performance under notice; on the contrary, it was confirmed by the impression of ponderousness that prevailed generally in the diction of the singers even at their most fluent. One could, of course, perceive the reason why the opera, if it was to be given at all, must be sung in German this time. Only the German artists were there to do it at the outset of the season; and the Italian, when they did arrive, would have quite enough to do with preparing, rehearsing, and singing *Don Giovanni*. But this would not justify me in attempting for a moment to compare the performance with those given here by the Italians in bygone years. It was no better in some respects than the best of those given under Sir Thomas Beecham, though I am glad to be able to add that the *tempi* adopted by Bruno Walter were much more sane and correct; they did not ruin every quick movement in a reckless endeavour to take things faster than they had ever been taken before. Also I noted with pleasure that the absurdly exaggerated hoops and crinolines of the Beecham period had disappeared, or very nearly so; and now there only remains to dispense with his fanciful *décor*, consisting of angular apartments quite unsuitable for this opera, especially Susanna's, which opens at the back to a wide staircase with an exposed doorway accessible to everybody, as well as to Cherubino and the Count. This, of course, spoilt the comedy of the scene.

And now as to the singing. I derived both interest and satisfaction from listening to the *viva voce* rendering of the music by artists whose gramophone work I have so often been called upon of late to judge in these self-same airs. It makes a difference, certainly; but not precisely in a vocal sense. What we get with the theatre, as I have said before, is the atmosphere of movement and gesture, of facial expression and living drama. Otherwise I am not prepared to say that Mmes. Lotte Lehmann, Elisabeth Schumann, and Delia Reinhardt gave the music of the Countess, Susanna, and Cherubino respectively with any greater charm of voice or art than we can discover in their records. They sang well—the first two even beautifully— and that should suffice. Better actresses than these it would be hard to find. The fact that the opera was given without cuts involved rather too much " dry " recitative and also the restoration of the small part of Barberina, which was sung in sprightly fashion by Katherine Arkandy.

But I cannot quite admit that Richard Mayr was the right choice for the part of Figaro. Splendid and versatile artist as he is, the ideal Baron Ochs of *Der Rosenkavalier* may not essentially be able to delineate for us the immortal Sevillian barber of Beaumarchais. His lightness and humour are not of that calibre; for between the two types, the Viennese and the Spanish presented by these two characters, there is a wide gulf fixed; and Richard Mayr cannot span it. Nor does the music of Figaro altogether suit him, though he sings it glibly enough. Allowing that it was written for a low and not a high baritone, my experience is that it ought never to be attempted by a *basso cantante*, which is precisely what the Count Almaviva of *Le Nozze* ought to be and what Josef Degler was not. Thus we had a Figaro whose voice was too heavy and a Count whose voice was too light; and yet, for physical and histrionic reasons, it would not have done for them to have changed places. The Basilio of Albert Reiss and the Bartolo of Norman Allin were both familiar and excellent, and it was good to see the English bass in this company.

147

I heard first-rate accounts of the *Meistersinger* performance, but could not attend it myself, nor can I say anything about the earlier sections of the *Ring*. I can, though, speak from personal knowledge of the truly magnificent way in which *Tristan und Isolde* was given on Thursday, the 13th ult. No such rendering of Wagner's masterpiece has been heard at Covent Garden within recent recollection, and I doubt whether the parts of the two protagonists have been so supremely well sung as they were in this instance by Frida Leider and Rudolf Laubenthal, since Jean de Reszke and Lillian Nordica sang them here first in 1896. It is so rare to hear those glorious duets in the first and second acts sung perfectly in tune by voices well-matched and well-balanced, with refinement and delicacy, in addition to passion that rose occasionally to the highest climaxes of abandonment and power. At moments like these Frida Leider's voice never loses an iota of its pure musical timbre, thanks to her perfect breath-control. The admirable capacity for reserve that one notices in her records was put in evidence here by the delicate gradations of strength with which she managed her crescendos, while never ceasing, meanwhile, to realise the exact meaning of the dramatic situation. Altogether I consider her the greatest Isolde on the stage to-day.

Laubenthal, without being an equally great Tristan, is undoubtedly a good actor, and he expresses the tremendous emotions of passion aroused by a love-philtre, not alone with sincerity and force, but with a voice that is of sweet quality and as steady as a rock. Imagine, therefore, the joy of listening to a Tristan and an Isolde neither of whose voices " wobbled "; a Brangäne with tones so rich and method so irreproachable as those of Maria Olczewska; a König Marke so dignified and pathetic as Richard Mayr; a Kurwenal of merit who can sing and act as impressively as Herbert Janssen; safe artists in the minor rôles; and a clever conductor like Robert Heger, with a fine orchestra to follow his beat—imagine an ensemble such as this, and you have some idea of the reasons that have provoked me to unwonted enthusiasm over this memorable *Tristan* performance.

Of the *Ring* performances I can speak here only of the third, which took place on Monday, May 17th. If I can call any section of the tetralogy my favourite I think it is *Siegfried*, but, truth to tell, I can give it but a shade of preference over *Die Walküre*, which I may mention was the first to become known and popular on the Continent prior to the production of the complete series of music dramas at Bayreuth in 1876. In the present *reprise* at Covent Garden, the parts of Siegmund and Siegfried were assumed, in accordance with Wagner's intention, by the same singer. The father and son, thus embodied, give

colour to the idea that one has grown up the image of the other, and that some twenty years have elapsed since Brünnhilde was put to sleep by Wotan, when the moment comes for her to be awakened by Siegfried's kiss. The disobedient Valkyrie does not apparently recognise Siegfried at once, since her first salutation is addressed to the sun and the light—" Heil dir Sonne, heil dir Licht "—and not to the youth who has aroused her from her trance. But a little later she emphatically congratulates herself upon the fact that it *is* Siegfried, who has successfully defied the flames surrounding her couch and thus become entitled to possess her. It is, perhaps, worth mentioning that Laubenthal, and not Melchior, was the Siegfried in *Götterdämmerung* a night or two later. But that fact does not weaken my argument, nor did the change trouble Brünnhilde in any way.

It was the marvellous climax of the story that provided the musical and dramatic triumph for Gertrude Kappel, and also in a slightly lesser degree for Laurentz Melchior, in *Siegfried*. Both sang magnificently, and, had the tenor attained the same heights of poetic charm and nobility of expression as his fair companion, it would have been a case of honours divided. As it was, he proved himself a satisfying representative of the fearless hero—alert, sympathetic, spirited, and vocally competent—without creating the profound impression that I can recall in some of his predecessors. As for Gertrude Kappel's Brünnhilde, I take it to be about the finest, on the whole, now before the public. She has all the traditions, her gestures and acting are superb, and there are the tones of joy and tragedy alike in her pure, vibrant voice, so that she can call upon either at will, just as Rosa Sucher and Ternina could. The music of Wotan the Wanderer received no more than justice at the hands of Emil Schipper; beyond that, in point of dignity and distinction, he failed to go. At the stormy moments his voice was not under perfect control, and when suavity (not tenderness, mind, as in the *Abschied*) was required he became prosaic and dull. Nor could he always fill the house above the din of the brass in Bruno Walter's powerful orchestra, which, however, very properly allowed the disappointed Wanderer to fend for himself in the duet with Erda, whilst diminishing its force to a real *pianissimo* whenever Olczewska's lovely notes had to be in the foreground.

The masterful Mime of Albert Reiss has not altered a jot in the thirty years that it has been known to habitués of Covent Garden. It is as clever, as subtle, as humorous and unforced in its comedy as ever. Habich's Alberich is not less meritorious than his Beckmesser, and that is saying much. This artist's enunciation is so clear that he gives you every syllable distinctly; and, despite the megaphone, Fafner the dragon enjoys a similar privilege, thanks to Otto Helgers. I wish I could say the same of the representative of the Forest-bird, but, as she sounded extremely nervous, it may be that she will be heard to better advantage another time. The conducting of Bruno Walter displayed an amazingly intimate knowledge of the score. He has it not only by heart, but he obtains an unfailing realization of Wagner's ideas and therein proves himself a worthy successor to Hans Richter, Anton Seidl, Gustav Mahler, and Arthur Nikisch. Can I say more?

Of the return of Chaliapine and his first appearances in London as Mefistofele and Don Basilio I shall perforce have to defer notice until next month. I witnessed his début in Boito's opera at the Metropolitan Opera House, New York, in 1908, and his incomparably fine impersonation appeared to me to excel in grandeur even the conception of the Italian Master.

THE WEBER CENTENARY.

A hundred years ago this month since Carl Maria von Weber died at 91, Great Portland Street! It seems strange now for me to remember that his favourite pupil, Sir Julius Benedict, was my intimate friend; that when I was a youth in my 'teens I used to sit with Sir Julius in the drawing-room of his house in Manchester Square, and chat with him about his master's operas and the difficulties under which they had been composed. His love and admiration for Weber were unbounded. He, Julius Benedict, whose hand had trembled when it shook that of Beethoven, who had accompanied Jenny Lind on her tours in England and America; who had met nearly every great musician of the nineteenth century, was wont to declare that the composer of *Der Freischütz* was the greatest genius he had ever encountered. The true founder of German opera, all who had come after him, Wagner included, owed him an enormous and incalculable debt. Had there been no Weber, the entire history of German lyric art after *Fidelio* would have been different to what it was.

In the light of this fact (for it is more than a mere opinion) it is interesting to recall that Weber's fellow-student under the Abbé Vogler at Darmstadt was no other than Giacomo Meyerbeer. The two young men were close friends, but strongly-contrasted types, and we know well to what a singular degree their respective talents pointed in different directions. Nevertheless, I do not agree that, because Weber adopted the highest art-models, Meyerbeer must naturally have pandered to lower tastes and so departed from the true canons of his art. Why, Weber himself drew the line at Beethoven, whose ideas and his own, he felt sure, were too far apart ever to meet. He acknowledged Beethoven's power, but would only accept his early works; the later ones, he wrote, "are to me a bewildering chaos, an obscure straining after novelty, lit up, it is true, by divine flashes of genius, which only serve to show how great he might be if he would but curb his riotous imagination." Weber was mistaken, of course, and even his faithful disciple, Sir Julius Benedict, admitted to me that he had lived long enough to perceive this. On the other hand, he would contend that Weber was a more original, a more resourceful composer of romantic opera than Beethoven, and as great an inventor and master of the romantic style as Wagner, whose development of the music-drama could be largely traced to Weber's influence. And now I myself have lived long enough to see that Benedict was perfectly right.

Then if that be so, the reader may ask, why are Weber's operas not more popular in this country—the land that he loved to visit, where he died and lay buried (in Moorfields) for eighteen years, and for which he wrote his last opera, *Oberon*? Frankly, I do not know exactly how to answer this question. It is many, many years since I heard *Oberon* in London with Tietjens and Trebelli in the cast; it must be a long while (never mind the dates!) since I witnessed a revival of *Euryanthe* by the pupils of the Royal College of Music; and I can quite understand what a terrible obstacle the libretto of the second, if not also the first, of these operas must present to the modern point of view. One deals too much with spirits of air, earth, and water; the other is too utterly stupid. Yet there is music in both that is undeniably and irresistibly beautiful. But what is there to complain of in *Der Freischütz*? Is the story too childish, the form too Mozartian, the spirit too purely German? If so, why do we welcome *Hänsel und Gretel*, why do we cherish the delicious absurdities of the *Magic Flute*, and why do we revel in the mediæval Nurembergities of *Die Meistersinger*? I make no comparisons between Weber and Mozart or Weber and Wagner; and I leave Humperdinck out of the question. But I do assert that *Der Freischütz* is one of the operatic masterpieces of all time; a score scintillating with gems " of purest ray serene," rich in captivating melody, replete with sublime expression and the most deftly-woven patterns of orchestral texture. We used formerly to hear it here in Italian and English, and though it naturally sounds best in German, I would like nothing better than a fair test for *Der Freischütz* by reviving it at Covent Garden in English, with good singers, a first-rate conductor, and an up-to-date *décor* by Max Reinhardt or his British equivalent—if we have such a thing.

For the gramophile I am afraid that Weber does not yield a very bounteous harvest. It consists principally of records of numbers from *Der Freischütz* made in Germany and sung by German artists. The noble air known in the English version as *Softly sighs* and in the original as *Leise, leise,* has provided the Polydor with material for two complete discs; one by Marcella Roesler (65692), the other by Lilly Hafgren-Dinkela (65608). Of these the first-named is a good average rendering, nothing more; but the second reveals a big tone of satisfying quality, a genuine dramatic soprano that does ample justice to a worthy task. Two incomplete excerpts, giving only Agatha's Prayer —the opening portion of this air—are sung by Delia Reinhardt (72787) and Claire Dux (72889); only I consider it a great pity that artists of their calibre should have restricted their efforts to the *Gebet,* with its preceding recitative, *Wie nahte mir der Schlummer.* On the reverse side Delia Reinhardt at least sticks to the same opera with a charming delivery of Agatha's second air, *Und ob die Wolke sie verhülle*; while Claire Dux offers her admirers a little contrast in the shape of *The sun whose rays are all ablaze,* from *The Mikado*! But here somehow neither cloud nor sunshine seems to fit the case quite accurately. Lotte Lehmann, on the other hand, leaves the big air out altogether, and sings *Und ob die Wolke* (72916) with all her finished art and purity of expression —a tribute which I can pay almost in equal measure to Hüni-Mihacsek (65637), who displays a lovely soprano timbre and tender feeling. The accompaniments generally are fair.

With her remarkable opulence and natural beauty of tone, Florence Austral makes a record of *Softly sighs* (H.M.V., D.775) that is effective rather than grand or striking. Her reading of certain passages is not accurate; of others it is lacking in signs of careful study. The *allegro* part needs more brilliancy and life, and unfortunately half of it has had to be omitted for want of room. (As will have been seen, the German artists would not think of cutting this air.) I advise Miss Austral to make another record and give the whole thing complete on two sides of the disc. She can then

JERITZA as SIEGLINDE

also make sure of correcting the faults that disfigure this effort, including the "fading away" and breathlessness of the final coda.

From Polydor likewise I have the sparkling duet, *Schelm! halt' fest,* with which the second act is opened by Agatha and Aennchen. As sung by Birgitt Engell and Elisabeth van Endert (14391, 10in.) it has no great distinction but plenty of brightness and "go," while the two voices blend nicely, despite their rather dull timbre. Years ago the two favourite airs in *Der Freischütz* were Rudolf's tenor solo, *Through the forest,* and the drinking-song for Caspar, which everybody could whistle or hum. The former is splendidly recorded by Tudor Davies (H.M.V., D.932); the latter is done with characteristic vigour by Richard Mayr (*Hier im ird'schen Jammertal,* Pol., 62389), who gives all three verses on a 10in. disc. Apart from these items I may mention an admirable performance of the famous overture by the Minneapolis Symphony Orchestra under Henri Verbrugghen (Bruns. 50055), on two sides, 12in.

While *Euryanthe* foreshadows *Lohengrin,* it is interesting to note that *Oberon* was the romantic source wherefrom sprang conspicuous passages in Schumann (*Paradise and the Peri*), Mendelssohn (*Midsummer Night's Dream*), and Wagner (*Die Walküre* and *Siegfried*). Weber was practically a dying man when he was setting Planché's English libretto to music of the most original and glorious kind. The opera was produced at Covent Garden in April, 1826, and he died in the following June. Its neglect in this country is for every reason indefensible; for, say what one may about the inanities of the book, I think our opera-loving public would imitate their forbears and ignore that, for the sake of music so exquisitely beautiful and fascinating.

The glorious overture, which for just a century has been a feature of every classical instrumental répertoire, has been finely recorded for the H.M.V. by the Royal Albert Hall Orchestra and the Coldstream Guards Band (D.154 and C.115); by the New Queen's Hall Orchestra under Sir Henry Wood (Col. L.1677), a very fine performance on two sides of a 12in. disc; by the band of the 1st Life Guards (Voc. K.05051); also in a shortened version by the Sutherland Orchestra (Beltona, 489). Then there is that magnificent soprano air, *Ocean, thou mighty monster!* *Ozean, du Ungeheuer!*), worthily recorded by two Polydor artists, viz., Frida Leider (65625) and Helene Wildmann (72804). Both are exceptionally good, but the former especially so for its splendour of tonal and dramatic treatment, the recording and accompaniment being also highly praiseworthy. Moreover Mme. Leider lays-me under a personal obligation by proving here that I am right and all the other German singers wrong when they ignore the *appoggiatura* and treat Weber literally, as if he were Bach or Palestrina.

She sings this air exactly as Tietjens used to, and a closer adherence to the composer's intentions it is impossible for me to conceive. At the same time I must confess that I like hearing the big airs from *Oberon* sung to the original text, and for this reason, if for no other, I would draw special attention to the excellent rendering of Elsa Stralia (Col. 7328), wherein voice and text alike come out with clearness and effect. Finally, the long and trying tenor solo, *O 'tis a glorious sight* (H.M.V. D.932) receives ample justice from Tudor Davies, albeit minus the concluding passage, which in this instance can fairly be dispensed with. Few singers, probably, could lend equal dramatic power and robust spirit to this piece, and in saying so much I intentionally pay the Welsh artist a high compliment.

HERMAN KLEIN.

THE GRAMOPHONE AND THE SINGER

(Continued)

By HERMAN KLEIN

The Opera Season : the Handel Festival

CHALIAPIN was here and gone again almost before we knew it. He stayed just long enough to show London that he was still a great opera-singer, to replenish his wardrobe before sailing for the Antipodes, and to pay a visit to the H.M.V. offices in Oxford Street for the purpose of talking over records and royalties. He accepted no social engagements worth speaking of, and, when I tried to secure him as our guest at the annual dinner of the Critics' Circle, he politely assured me that there was no chance of his coming, as it fell on the Sunday between his appearances in *Il Barbiere* and *Mefistofele* (second performance), and he was going out of town to make it a genuine day of rest. Would he come back next year? He could not say definitely, but he might. At any rate, he wanted to, if it was possible.

Certainly his reception here was flattering enough to make him anxious to return. I do not pretend to know exactly what fee —*cachet* is the proper word —he was paid for his three performances, but I do know that the house was sold out for each at something like double prices, and that consequently there must have been a substantial profit for the Syndicate on the engagement. (Incidentally, if Chaliapin is not too extravagant in Savile Row and the Rue de la Paix he ought to retire a wealthy man.) But, truth to tell, Covent Garden has been filled to overflowing nearly every night this season, and the financial success will probably be the biggest there has been since the days of Augustus Harris. The *Barbiere* performance (on May 28th) was described by more than one critic as remarkable for the excellence of the acting rather than the singing. On the whole I consider that a just verdict; for, anxious as I am not to be playing for ever the part of *laudator temporis acti*, I cannot help admitting that I have heard the three principal singing parts better rendered at this house, not once, but dozens of times. I preferred Toti dal Monte, the *soprano leggiero* of last year, to Mercedès Capsir, the Rosina of the present occasion. The latter's voice is a most unequal organ, with pleasing moments, much agility, and a really pretty staccato, as against other moments of positive shrillness and a timbre as hard as steel. Her *Una voce* was extremely clever, but without true charm or the smallest appreciation of its comic significance; and in the duet, *Dunque io son*, she was no less mechanical, studied, and conventional. She made, however, a graceful stage picture, and smiled archly behind her Spanish fan. The Almaviva, Mr. Charles Hackett, sang as an American tenor of experience might be expected to—with the assurance and competence of an artist who has learnt his part well. But, unlike his Roméo, it did naught to captivate the ear. Ernesto Badini was too heavy and noisy for an ideal Figaro. Excellent actor and satisfactory singer in rôles that suit him, he was not honestly entitled this time to many of the superlatives that critics of short memory bestowed upon him. Battistini and Titta Ruffo, to name no others, can show us even now that *Largo al factotum* may—nay, should—be sung with lightness and *finesse* as well as alertness and dash.

Apart from Chaliapin's adroit management of the wonderful crescendo in *La Calunnia*, his Don Basilio presented no vocal features of particular interest ; indeed, the part is almost without any. But what a conception or, rather, what a development of the traditional concept of a quaint comic character ! At the back of it I could see plainly enough the impression created by Edouard de Reszke as the same personage—the tall gaunt figure, the long-striding, gawky music-teacher imagined by Beaumarchais in his immortal comedy —sly, cunning, subtle, yet apparently stupid, always open to a bribe. There was nothing that gesture, facial expression, exaggerated make-up could do to realise these characteristics that the gifted Russian left undone ; all his " business " was quite amazingly clever, yet so artistic and natural that it never introduced a false note even when it lifted Basilio to a prominence that he never enjoyed in this opera before. So much can a great artist achieve without detriment to the balance or the consistency of a dramatic ensemble. His treatment of the famous exit after the " Buona sera " was entirely new. He is supposed to go out, then return, repeat the " buona sera," and finally depart. Instead of this, Chaliapin quietly remains in the room unperceived by the others and, sitting down behind the door, begins humming a note like the buzzing of a drone. Naturally the noise suffices to interrupt Figaro once more in his attempt to shave Don Bartolo, until eventually they discover the cause and expel the miserable intruder with the *reprise* of the " Presto al letto " that Rossini provided to end up the joke.

Vincenzo Bellezza strikes me as being one of the best Italian conductors of recent years. His dynamic control is a blessing for the singers as well as for those who listen to them. There were some points in *Mefistofele* which differed from the composer's own reading, but they were not serious ; and he brought out strongly all the salient features which made this opera sound so original and striking when it first came out. It sounds so still in my opinion, and mild attempts to belittle it are really misplaced. Together with *La Gioconda* it forms the main basis of the whole modern Italian school. Verdi, of course, stands in a temple of his own and has many worshippers, but few imitators capable of reproducing his later methods, which were those of a consummate genius. The revival of *Mefistofele* was worth while, therefore, not for the sake of Chaliapin alone—and dramatically his portrayal of its Satanic central figure was of unique if repellent grandeur—but because the opera has qualities of enduring interest and strength. The other chief singers, Bianca Scacciati and Francesco Merli, were neither better nor worse than their records had led me to expect.

Of greater interest, though, in a purely vocal sense, was the revival of *Otello* on June 1st. To begin with, it served for the eagerly-awaited début of Mariano Stabile, the young baritone who has lately been arousing to an unwonted heat of *fanatismo* the exacting audiences of La Scala. Well, I can now understand their enthusiasm. Stabile only requires more experience to become a very great artist ; for, apart from youth, good looks, height, intelligence, alertness of gesture, and nobility of feature, he possesses a baritone voice that is round, powerful, steady, and of a fine resonant quality. He has been well trained and has mastered the part of Iago sufficiently to invest it with the necessary picturesque force, albeit I imagine that Shakespeare intended his arch-villain to be a man of maturer years. In the great scene with Otello in Act II. Stabile displayed a subtlety and variety of tone-colour more remarkable than the actual volume of his voice, which seemed to need greater amplitude for things like the *Credo* or the *Brindisi* of the opening act. Still, his power sufficed to give effect to the music and adequate support to the Otello of Giovanni Zenatello, whom I have frequently heard in this rôle and am glad to find still fairly in possession of the resources that brought him fame 20 years ago. The tone does not invariably ring so true and clear as of yore, but his declamation, like his acting, remains superb. Only one objection have I to offer regarding Zenatello's Otello, and that is that he gives the Moor a mottled complexion of *rouge et noir* which I am convinced no Venetian *grande dame* would ever have looked upon with favour. That illustrious actor, Salvini, knew better than to make Otello an ugly blackamoor. It was not for such a specimen that Desdemona told the Doge she " perceived a divided duty " as between father and husband.

And this brings me to Lotte Lehmann's exquisite delineation of the gentlest and most persistent of wives, the sweet generous lady whose anxiety for the welfare of Cassio proves her downfall and destruction. I may have seen in this opera a Desdemona as sweet and as gentle ; but never before have I heard a singer of Verdi's music so ideally perfect, so completely and utterly satisfying. Individual comparisons with other Desdemonas would be uncalled for, even untimely ; but it is as I say—and I have heard nearly all of them—the performance of Lotte Lehmann will remain a fragrant and delicious memory. The *Salce* may have been as beautifully sung by Albani, by Melba, by Emma Eames at their best ; I assert naught to the contrary. But the *Salce* is not everything, nor are the duets with Otello beyond the easy reach of sopranos such as these. It was in that most difficult scene of all, the elaborate ensemble that follows after the Moor has struck Desdemona before his whole court—it was in this trying episode that Lotte Lehmann did so magnificently both as singer and actress, that she rose to heights never attained here before, at least in my experience. Taken altogether, the representation was an admirable one, conferring an added prestige upon Vincenzo Bellezza and his forces, and therefore upon the present Covent Garden management.

With the *reprise* of *Don Giovanni* on June 7th, after an interval of twelve years, I must confess to have been ever so little disappointed. Perhaps I expected too much ; perhaps those troublesome recollections of past glories would come urging me to comparisons again. Anyhow I will dwell lightly upon the shortcomings because I think many of them were attributable to lack of a few more rehearsals, and even the inclusion of the final quintet, which converts the opera from a tragedy into a comic opera, was duly accomplished at a later performance. Why a conductor so reasonable and full of common-sense as Bruno Walter, whose tempi are exactly what they ought to be, should have refused to make a single cut and then insisted on leaving out Elvira's fine aria *Mi tradì*—merely because Mozart added it to the score *after* the first performance at Prague—was an instance of puritanical pedantry that passed my comprehension. I wanted so much to hear it sung by Lotte Lehmann, for with it she would have completed one of the most satisfying embodiments of Donna Elvira that has been heard in recent years. I enjoyed it even more than Frida Leider's Donna Anna, whose dramatic qualities were for once on a higher plane than her vocal artistry—notably as to *Non mi dir*, where her phrasing and *coloratura* left just a little to be desired. The Zerlina of Elisabeth Schumann suggested the *deutsches Mädel* rather than the Spanish peasant-girl, but her singing was neatness itself. I was told that these three ladies were all singing their parts in Italian for the first time.

I can well imagine that with further experience Mariano Stabile will be able to give us a magnificent Don Giovanni. Even now he is well above the average. His manner of making love is engaging, impulsive, even fascinating, and he cuts a handsome figure in doublet and hose; but he does not yet sing Mozart with the same elegance that he acts. In time, though, I think he will. Fritz Krauss is too throaty to be more than a passable Don Ottavio; and I did not grieve over the excision of *Dalla sua pace*. I failed to discover in Jean Aquistapace's Leporello the amount of humour that some other writers did, but he has a good voice and uses it well.

Melba's " Farewell to Covent Garden " (on June 8th) was of necessity a sad and touching occasion, with not a note of joy, except the wealth of lovely flowers and the eager cheering at the close, to relieve an atmosphere of unmitigated gloom. The King and Queen, by their gracious presence, only emphasised the sense of almost national loss at this parting from the singer who for forty years has been the acknowledged representative of our far-flung Empire in the world of operatic art. Who could help feeling sorrowful now that the moment had arrived to say good-bye to Melba? I, for one, was bound to feel it keenly, since I had witnessed her début on these same boards and her triumphs from first to last, in other lands besides our own, always excepting those she won in the country of her birth. She sang wonderfully still, with the old *voix d'argent* bright, silvery, clear as ever, especially in the Balcony Scene from *Roméo et Juliette*, which began the programme. It brought back instant memories of the first time she sang it with Jean de Reszke thirty-seven years ago—a well-nigh miraculous instance of perfect tone-preservation, wherein the bright voice and refined singing of Mr. Charles Hackett now helped her to keep up the illusion of eternal youth. Why, you ask again, should such an artist have to bid us farewell? The answer to that question came before the end of the evening. It is the lack of vocal stamina, the inability to last out against the strain of long operas that is the conclusive test in these cases. As it was, Dame Melba did exceptionally well to sing with so much freedom and fullness of volume in the scene from *Otello*; indeed, she has never sung the *Salce* better, save perhaps as to the A flat at the end of the *Ave Maria*. But the last two acts of *La Bohème* proved rather trying, even though genuine feeling and expression in every phrase made up largely for declining strength and ring in the carrying-power of the voice. It seemed all too appropriate when Mimi's notes died away into silence. Still, happily the word *finis* has not yet been written. Melba's incomparable voice will be heard again, I am sure, at other " farewells " besides this and the Albert Hall.

Jeritza continues to be a safe draw. She followed up a sensational *rentrée* as Sieglinde with a no less sensational appearance as Thaïs. She is the greatest melodramatic opera-singer of our time; only she does not make your blood run cold; quite the reverse. For sheer physical loveliness her portrayal of the Alexandrian courtezan has never been approached, and neither Mary Garden nor Louise Edvina ever imagined that teetotum spin with the back fall at the conclusion of the second scene with Athanaël. I don't think Sybil Sanderson, the original, ever did anything like it, or that she, more than the others, sang the air with the mirror, *Dites-moi que je suis belle*, in an entirely recumbent attitude, stretched upon a kind of high pink velvet catafalque (you could hardly call it a sofa) in a diaphanous crimson robe with a vast train of cloth of gold covering it—the catafalque, not the recumbent figure—with its glistening folds. So much for that. Nor is the rich, warm timbre of Jeritza's voice or her ability and resourcefulness as a singer to be gainsaid any more this year than it was last. Her tones may not electrify or haunt the spectator as the picture does, but at least she always rises to the occasion. She was well supported in *Thaïs* by an impressive Athanaël, new to London, in Tilken Servais and a tuneful Nicias in Alfred Legrand, both French artists with capital voices Massenet's opera was conducted by Vincenzo Belezza.

Again, in Wolf-Ferrari's opera, *I Giojelli della Madonna*, we had another striking display of Maria Jeritza's histrionic powers, in conjunction with just so much effective singing as the rôle of Maliella allows scope for. The quality of her voice at its finest undeniably gives pleasure to the listener, and saying this reminds me that I may congratulate H.M.V. on having completed contracts last month, not only with Jeritza, but with another popular Covent Garden artist in Elisabeth Schumann. The cast of *I Giojelli* was efficient, without bearing comparison (bar the Maliella) with that of 1912, when Martinelli and Sammarco were in it. Giuseppe Noto as Rafaele proved only a moderate substitute for the latter; while Francesco Merli sang agreeably as the unhappy youth who steals the Madonna's jewels.

A triumph of French art was achieved in Massenet's *Manon* by Fanny Heldy and Fernand Ansseau. Such superb singing by artists of the Paris Opera has not been heard in London for many years. The soprano is young, comely and an accomplished artist; her voice of clear, ringing quality and delightfully even throughout. That Ansseau has improved immensely both as a singer and an actor is as much a matter of congratulation for the public as for himself. He is now one of the world's few really great tenors. The duet in the St. Sulpice scene was gloriously sung, and roused the house to veritable enthusiasm.

THE HANDEL FESTIVAL.

It would be interesting to make lengthy comparisons between the first Handel Festival which I attended as a youthful critic, in 1874, and that of last month; but, for reasons of space, I must resist the temptation. I will say only this: the choral singing as a whole has improved; the orchestra is of far finer quality; but the soloists do not, either individually or collectively, stand in the same category. As regards the last item the very names will be sufficient evidence; in 1874 I heard in the centre transept of the Crystal Palace Tietjens, Sinico, Lemmens-Sherrington, Trebelli, Patey, Sims Reeves, Edward Lloyd, Cummings, Vernon Rigby, Foli, and Santley. Such a list could not, of course, be equalled to-day anyhow—not for a million of money. One's sole compensation lies in the thought that it is not, after all, the solo singing which forms the primary attraction of this great triennial event, but the choir—the magnificent concatenation of thrilling choral effects which you can procure under no other conditions, and therefore nowhere else in the world. So once more, drawbacks notwithstanding, I enjoyed the Festival immensely—as indeed, any genuine adorer of Handel, celebrating his " jubilee " thereat, as did the Earl of Balfour and my humble self, was more or less bound to.

The Handel Festival has had four conductors—viz., Sir Michael Costa, Sir August Manns, Sir Frederic Cowen, and, lastly, Sir Henry Wood. Their methods have all differed according to their respective natures and temperaments, and, after Costa had accomplished the spade work with an ability and masterfulness never to be ignored, the others, each in turn, has tried to introduce improvements with more or less successful results. Sir Henry Wood has carried his reforms even farther than Manns and Cowen, and obtained a much better balance between the choir and the orchestra. On the other hand, in the endeavour to assert his individuality he has, in my opinion, unduly interfered with the tempi of Handel's music in choruses like those of the *Messiah* and *Israel in Egypt*; he has sought to quicken the pace wherever there was a chance, though frequently at the cost of clearness and steadiness; he has tried to prove that you can move mountains and armies with the same facility that you can shift sand-dunes and platoons. His efforts to improve the enunciation of the words, the accuracy and unanimity of rhythm, the truth and beauty of expression, have deserved great credit, but in the end they have achieved results little in advance of those attained by his predecessors. The colossal grandeur and noble breadth of the rendering of those old Handelian choruses to the ample swing of Costa's beat has never been surpassed, and I fancy never will be.

It was, of course, a feather in Sir Henry Wood's cap that he should have contrived to furnish some interesting novelties to add to the attraction of the miscellaneous selection on June 8th, the opening day of the Festival. The old " Selection Day " used to come between the *Messiah* (Monday) and *Israel in Egypt* (Friday); but that arrangement had outlived its utility and the present plan proved in every way more convenient, offering as it did two Saturday afternoon and two evening concerts. It also deserved a far larger measure of patronage on the part of music-lovers generally; but, owing to the stupid clash of other musical events in the same week and the adverse condition of affairs still troubling the country, there was no lack of .excuse for keeping away. The fresh choral items above referred to were culled from five of Handel's least-known operas, viz., *Admeto, Rinaldo, Deidamia, Lotario,* and *Atalanta;* and delightfully tuneful and full of grace, charm, and ingenuity they proved. Sir Henry Wood was responsible for arranging them, and took especial pains to get them sung and played in a manner that was practically faultless. The orchestral pieces were better chosen than the organ concerto (executed by M. Marcel Dupré), which was not one of Handel's most inspired examples of the kind. The vocal soloists were Miss Carrie Tubb, Miss Margaret Balfour, Mr. Walter Widdop, and Mr. Robert Radford, while the organ accompaniments were safe in the experienced hands of Mr. Walter W. Hedgcock.

The *pièce de resistance* of the Festival, *Israel in Egypt*, which used to come on the concluding day, was now combined with a second selection on the Thursday. It was in the choruses descriptive of the plagues and the great double choruses, *The Lord shall reign* and *Sing ye to the Lord*, that the best work was done. Whatever improvements had been wrought, through Sir Henry Wood's satirical scolding and the choir's increased familiarity with his intentions, became apparent in these inspired numbers, the result being a memorable treat for those who listened. In imitation of the Albert Hall practice, the duet " The Lord is a man of war " was sung by the first and second basses of the choir. The solos were effectively rendered by Miss Florence Austral, Miss Muriel Brunskill, Mr. Ben Davies, and Mr. Norman Allin.

A noble performance of the *Messiah* brought the gathering to a worthy termination. The wisdom of giving it on the last day was demonstrated by the supreme excellence of the choral work, which betrayed no symptom of fatigue, but, on the contrary, increased power and all the benefit consequent upon so much practice together. Everyone worked hard, not least of all, of course, Sir Henry Wood, who concluded his heavy task amid thunders of applause, shared with the admirable solo artists, Miss Flora Woodman, Miss Margaret Balfour, Mr. Joseph Hislop, and Mr. Horace Stevens. Artistically the Festival was quite a success. HERMAN KLEIN.

THE GRAMOPHONE AND THE SINGER

(Continued)

By HERMAN KLEIN

Why "International" Opera?

I HAVE grown to dislike the word "international." It has been much abused of late years, and, whether applied to musical celebrities or to Communistic Trade Unions, its precise meaning is no longer easy to determine. Originally, I believe, the substantive form of the word was used to indicate the secret societies that seek " the assertion everywhere of the sovereign rights of the working man." As an adjective it signified all things pertaining to the intercourse between different nations, diplomatic relations, athletic contests of the Olympic order, exhibitions and so forth. But with music in a general sense, or with musical artists in particular, it had absolutely nothing in common. In art, as I am never tired of repeating, there ought to be no such thing as nationality, whatever the native land of the individual professing or practising it. How, then, can it be reasonably claimed that there is such a thing as musical " internationality " ?

In seriously asking those concerned—excepting the circus proprietors and other demonstrative showmen for whom it may still have a positive value—to abandon the use of so ambiguous a term, I am appealing not alone to certain high-class concert *entrepreneurs*, but to the management of " opera on the grand scale," who may be tempted after recent successes to employ the word "international" permanently as a guarantee of super-excellence. For my part I regard it as nothing of the kind, and, what is more, I consider it as being in a degree derogatory to the dignity of all great artists, who are thus by inference declared to have the right to appear in first-rate company solely in virtue of the fact that they are foreigners. I trust, therefore, that the London Opera Syndicate will not perpetuate this error. It has now shown us for two years in succession what it is capable of doing. It has fairly established a high reputation for its manner of carrying on opera at Covent Garden. It has admitted English singers to its *personnel* to undertake such parts as they were capable of performing with credit to themselves and to the advantage of the ensemble. When another Albani or another Melba becomes available it will even resume the engagement of British " stars." Meanwhile, the " grand " season at Covent Garden, which sins only by its brevity, is not a whit more "international" to-day than it was fifty or a hundred years ago.

It may be taken for granted that the London Opera Syndicate is going on. The season just ended was not only a genuine artistic success, but it probably went as near to paying expenses as any big operatic undertaking in the metropolis is ever likely to. It began splendidly and it ended as it began ; no novelties, and only one or two singers whom we had not heard before, but a steady succession of fine, efficient, satisfying performances. There was no chance to grow tired of anybody or anything. I have no recollection of such frequent changes of bill, such a variety of casts, or such brief appearances of first-class artists. That kind of campaign can only be carried out, of course, when an impresario can afford to pay big terms to famous —not merely " international "—artists to sing three or four or half-a-dozen nights ; in fact, as few or as many as may be required, backed beforehand by the comforting assurance that the house will be sold out at high prices and that the season's subscription for boxes and stalls is already secured with the money in the bank. In such fashion alone are these operatic miracles to be worked.

I left off last month with a brief reference to the revival of *Manon*. That was a particularly good performance of an opera that is seldom well done here. You can count perfect Manons seen in London on the fingers of a single hand ; and, oddly enough, I was thinking of one of the best of them when the news came of her death in Paris. I allude, of course, to Marie Rôze, a French artist of rare charm, who was the first to sing the part in this country. She was most popular, perhaps, in *Carmen*, though I thought her too " ladylike " (like Trebelli) to be an ideal representative of Bizet's heroine. But her Manon, whether she sang it in Italian or English, was an embodiment replete with grace, elegance, and womanly tenderness, and I must say I have heard no better until Fanny Heldy appeared upon the scene. I am not sure whether she has yet recorded any of the music, but anyhow I hope that when she does she will have Fernand Ansseau for her companion, as at Covent Garden, and that the pair of them will record their scenes together as delightfully as they did at Covent Garden.

Two nights after that came the diverting double-bill consisting of *L'Heure Espagnole* and *Gianni Schicchi*, neither of which provides any material worth mentioning for the gramophonist, but which certainly furnish between them a capital evening's entertainment. The two short operas form a perfect contrast, and I scarcely know which is the more difficult, the cleverer, or the more characteristic of its composer. I only wish that Ravel would write another opera or two of the same calibre as *L'Heure Espagnole*, with a libretto rather better suited for universal degustation. It might not be so amusing, but it would probably be easier to understand than the meaningless nonsense set forth as a plot in the Covent Garden programme. The conception of Fanny Heldy was extremely fascinating, but vocally not on a par with her Manon, which was more adapted to her Conservatoire training. Maguenat as the muleteer was again simply perfect, and the other male characters, with one exception, were in familiar hands.

It was due to the masterly skill of the new Italian *régisseur*, Giovacchino Forzano, that the comedy of *Gianni Schicchi* was carried out with so much spirit and energy. The drollery of the situations, wherein the cunning Schicchi so completely outwits the greedy relations who are waiting to pounce upon the dead man's property, has never been so quaintly realised here. Equally new to many ears was the quaint scherzo-like appropriateness of Puccini's music, every note of which seems to be spontaneously evolved from the humours and emotions of the dramatic flow of ideas. Italian and English artists filled the cast between them, and Ernesto Badini showed himself in the name part an actor of consummate ability as well as a master of clear-cut, sparkling diction. Here, too, let me pay another tribute to the skill of the new conductor, Vincenzo Bellezza, whom I consider a genuine " find " for the Covent Garden management. He knows exactly what latitude to allow his singers ; he accompanies without overwhelming them ; his orchestra is under absolute control ; and he knows his scores thoroughly. I hope we shall be having Bellezza here again next year.

For the wind-up of the season we had a real *bonne bouche* in the shape of Verdi's *Falstaff*, that marvellous product of the old age of a great master. Welcome the revival was in every sense ; for creditable as are the occasional performances that we get from academic sources, they are at best but makeshifts, and afford only a faint notion of the wealth of ingenuity and technical resource, of creative power and skill of delineation, concentrated in the pages of this amazing work. Obviously, mature artists alone can grapple with the difficulties presented here—by Shakespeare's superbly-drawn character and by Verdi's highly elaborate settings of each and every scene. A youthful Falstaff, no matter how cleverly made up, must be something of a square peg in a round hole, and the fact that Mariano Stabile seemed a trifle young for the part

was the solitary fault that I had to find with his otherwise superb impersonation. It lacked the mellow ripeness of the older Italians and, of course, the Shakespearian quality of the English actors who have been associated with the rôle of the amorous knight. Yet, when all has been said, Stabile's was a wonderfully finished and satisfying performance, and I was quite able to understand, after witnessing it, the enormous reputation that it has won for him in his native land. The vanity and conceit of the old coxcomb were portrayed in a thousand adroit touches, combining as a whole to produce a highly humorous and amusing portrait. He also sang very finely in the exacting scenes at the Garter Inn —everything except the exquisite little passage, *Quand ero paggio del Duca di Norfolk*, in which his *mezza voce* diction disappointed me after Maurel's miracle of delicacy—a joy never to be forgotten in this zephyr-like breath of song.

My critical colleagues were curiously at variance in their estimation of the work done by the Italian ladies who represented the " Merry Wives." Some thought them excellent, some the reverse. My own opinion did not go to either·extreme, because I thought they acted well whilst singing on the whole with too little refinement, too noisily, or, as they would say, with too much *brio*. Their ensembles with the men also needed toning down, and would have been the better for another rehearsal or two ; yet for my own part I prefer in this complex music an excess of spirit to doses of dullness—such, for example, as the two lovers, Fenton (Charles Hackett) and Nannetta (Aurora Rettore), permitted themselves to indulge in. Sweet Anne Page ought to be sentimental, I allow, but surely never dull. Bellezza was again the conductor, and I thought he brought out all the beauty without overdoing the vigour of Verdi's masterful orchestration.

With a repetition of *Falstaff* on the last night, the subscribers and the general public turned their backs upon Covent Garden in the healthy condition known as " wishing there were more." That ensures their looking forward to next year, and also suggests the wisdom of a slightly longer season. Another ten or fifteen performances would, I feel sure, be welcomed, and might surely be ventured upon without financial risk. This could be done by starting on or about the 1st of May and continuing until the middle of July. It would then be practicable to give at least two cycles of the *Ring*, instead of only one, and more repetitions of the Wagner operas for which the house is said to be, and generally is, " sold out."

HERMAN KLEIN.

THE GRAMOPHONE AND THE SINGER

(Continued)

By HERMAN KLEIN

Some Columbia "Celebrities"—I.

IT was rather over two years ago—in June, 1924, to be exact—when I told the readers of THE GRAMOPHONE, in the first of these articles, the story of my connection with the original Columbia Company as organized in the city of New York at the beginning of this century. I mention it again now with no purpose of recapitulation—that being quite unnecessary—but merely to explain why I feel a personal interest in some of the artists and the records that fall under the category of Columbia "Celebrities." Most of them I knew well personally, and in the making of certain of their records it was my privilege to take an active part.

My sole regret is that it should have been found requisite to expunge so many of both from the latest Columbia catalogues, either because some of the recording of fifteen or twenty years ago has not stood the test of time, or because of the failure of the artist to attract sales, or, most likely of all, the loss of or irreparable damage to the original master matrix. But it is good to see that so many of these earlier "celebrity" records still justify their existence—in their actual recording qualities as well as, presumably, in their sales. Speaking of recording qualities, a goodly proportion of the forty-two records of my own "Phono-vocal Method" for learning singing by the aid of the gramophone are even now quite acceptable specimens. So, I think, were many others worth preserving for the sake of the singers and the singing, which no longer figure in the Columbia list (or, at any rate, in the "Celebrity" section) that were recorded by such gifted artists as Lillian Blauvelt, Ruth Vincent, Edouard de Reszke, Anton van Rooy, and David Bispham.*

The last-named baritone more especially had the voice and the faculty for recording magnificently; and, since he was one of the most versatile, clever, interesting singers that America ever produced or

LILLIAN NORDICA

English audiences ever loved, it seems to me a thousand pities that the whole of his splendid Columbia records should now be relegated to the limbo of a bygone era. Perhaps, however, a small but choice selection of David Bispham records may, in spite of all their prehistoric defects, yet be included in the October article on this subject, which will deal with the sterner, even as the present is to deal with the fairer, sex. Meanwhile I may mention that Bispham was by far the most successful of the group of new record-makers whom I introduced to the Columbia *atelier*; things like his wonderful renderings of Schubert's *Hark, hark the lark !* and Walter Damrosch's setting of *Danny Deever* have for years had a huge sale in the United States and Canada.

But the first real (soprano) Celebrity to sing for Columbia was the talented and lamented American prima donna, Lillian Nordica. How I had the good fortune to bring that about was related in detail in the article already referred to. Admirable alike in opera and oratorio, she was a no less versatile singer in her way than was Bispham in his ; and both were equally distinguished as interpreters of Lieder and of leading Wagnerian rôles. Nordica was perhaps less successful than her countryman in overcoming the difficulties of record-making which then prevailed, but I am convinced that this would not have been the case if she had had the advantages conferred by the electrical developments now existing.

Her voice, it may be remembered, was of a very unusual and individual quality, something between a dramatic soprano and the rather lighter kind known as the lyrical or, as the Italians term it, *mezzo-carattere*. Hence her rare capacity for singing music and rôles of the most varied and widely-contrasted types. When I first heard her at the Crystal Palace, as soloist with Gilmore's American band in 1878, her vocal education had not been half completed, but the telling resonance of her

---

* *Note.*—I am, however, informed that in all these cases the records were withdrawn because of matrix breakdown and failure.

bright, youthful notes was such that they could be heard throughout the building. Then nine years later she made her real début in London both in opera and oratorio, and behold, the inexperienced girl had been metamorphosed into a finished Italian vocalist, a clever actress, and a charming woman. Well do I recollect her first appearance on the opening night of a season of Italian opera at cheap prices, given by Mr. Mapleson at Covent Garden, singing Violetta in Verdi's *La Traviata*. She was destined, as I wrote later on " to play a conspicuous part in the operatic history of the season (and of many seasons to come), and all her efforts were distinguished by invariable intelligence and earnestness." Subsequently we heard her as Gilda and Marguerite, as Donna Elvira (one of her best), as Aïda, and even as Carmen, which did not really suit her. But it was only after another dozen years of added experience and ceaseless study, when she took up the Wagner rôles and won success as Elsa even at Bayreuth, singing that rôle and Isolde superbly in German and Brünnhilde as well, that Lillian Nordica entered upon the most brilliant stage of her career. Alas ! it was not to endure to a natural close, for she was still singing admirably in public and touring the world when, in 1914, she was submitted to terrible exposure during the wreck of a steamer on which she was travelling in the Far East and died from its effects. I saw a great deal of her during my stay in New York, and counted her among my warmest and staunchest friends. At about that period, too, she had the courage to wed her *fourth* husband, Mr. George W.

MARIA BARRIENTOS

Young, the banker, who, I believe, survived her.

I have been listening to the eight Columbia records made by Mme. Nordica, numbered from 74021 to 74029, and omitting 74023. All have pink labels and are made on one side of the disc only ; and I take them now in the order in which they stand in the catalogue. That of the *Suicidio* air from Ponchielli's *La Gioconda* is of peculiar interest to me, not merely because I heard it made, but because the part was one of the most picturesque and dramatic in Nordica's répertoire (her romantic Selika was another) and her rendering of this particular air was not surpassed even by the original Covent Garden Gioconda, her compatriot, Maria Durand. It is sung with orchestra, as are those of *Isolde's Liebestod* (in German) and the

Polonaise from *Mignon* (in Italian) ; and I cannot refrain from saying how infinitely better they sound on the wonderful H.M.V. machine of to-day than when I heard them two or three years ago. In fact, the improvement is so extraordinary that I must unreservedly withdraw my criticism of 1924 and declare that I can now recall perfectly the well-remembered *timbre* of the voice and the characteristic features of the singer's style. These are quite amazing in the Hungarian air by Erkel, *Hunjadi Laslos*, where you may hear a faultless staccato and a beautiful shake on the high C–D flat in the cadenza, with a real *legato* in all the difficult intervals. There is true " atmosphere " in the animation and natural sentiment that pervade each of these records—in Debussy's graceful *Mandoline*, in *Annie Laurie*, in the American ditties of Cadman and Nevin, more perhaps than in the *Serenade* of Richard Strauss or even the *Liebestod* itself. But, were I asked which I think the two best of the lot, I should not hesitate to name the *Suicidio* and the *Polonaise*, which are, vocally speaking, as good as anything you can listen to to-day.

The fame of Maria Barrientos began to spread over Europe and America (South more than North) in the earliest years of the present century. I heard of her first, as being a *soprano leggiero* of the highest order, at the time when the Columbia Company (in a creditable endeavour to improve the artistic standard of the phonograph, or rather the graphophone, as they preferred to call it) were introducing into the U.S. the product of the Milanese Fonotipia Company. The pick of these bore the Portuguese name of Barrientos, who had by then become a tremendous favourite with the audiences of Buenos Ayres, Mexico, and Rio de Janeiro. Then, while I was in London in 1903, I witnessed her début at Covent Garden as Rosina in *Il Barbiere*, and wrote about her in the *Sunday Times* of July 5th. I described her as extremely young (only nineteen) and an extraordinary singer for her age, " a phenomenal mistress of the school of acrobatic vocalisation." Yet, in spite of her astounding agility, she was not then the finished artist that she became later or that she proved herself in the records to which I am about to draw attention. Why she never returned here is more than I am able to explain. She was at least the equal of every one of those so-called " international " celebrities who have displayed vocal

* Klein is mistaken here: the published version of the Suicidio was recorded in New York 2 Feb.,1911, after the author had returned to London. The recording session at which he was present was that of 3 Apr.,1906. The Gioconda recording made at that session was unpublished until a dubbing of a test pressing was released by the IRCC in May, 1946. Ed.

acrobatics in London or New York during the twenty-three years that have elapsed since her solitary visit to this country.

Her four double-sided records, numbered 7336–9, do not include *Una voce* ; and I ought not to regret its absence, seeing that I described her variations (or changes) as " more clever than graceful or pretty " when she sang it in the part of Rosina. On the other hand, her encore in the Lesson Scene, where she " displayed a brilliancy and *entrain* that evoked well-deserved applause," was the self-same *Waltz* from *Mireille* that I couple with the *Bell Song* from *Lakmé* as the two finest examples of this Columbia group. The quality of the tone is exquisitely musical and pure ; the execution of the *fiorituri* absolutely faultless ; the adherence to the text exact to a degree that would have filled either Gounod or Delibes with joy. No less perfect than these is her *Caro nome*, in which she holds a remarkably clear, strong D sharp in *alt*, including a lovely cadenza. But I care less for her *Deh vieni non tardar*, on the reverse side of the same disc. It is distinctly dull, and the intention of Mozart is defeated by her avoidance of the *appoggiatura*. I find comparatively little scratching in these records, while the voice comes out singularly bright and clear. So again with *Regnava nel silenzio* and *Charmant oiseau*—you get the same marvellous Barrientos agility and ease combined with the same superlative breath-control and impeccable intonation. Her attack of high notes I consider a model for any singer, whether artist or student, to strive to imitate ; it is altogether exceptional. And nowhere does she exhibit these gifts more amazingly than in the sparkling old vocal waltz of Johann Strauss, *Voci di Primavera*, which dazzling display of *feux-d'artifice* is coupled with an Italian version *à la* Flötow of *The Last Rose of Summer*. How few foreign singers,—charming Marthas though they be—understand the simple, unaffected art required for the perfect delivery of that dear old ballad !

There are, of course, more " celebrities " on the Columbia list than it will be convenient to include in the present selection. It is better, however, to write about a few who are or should be interesting to gramophonists generally, than to provide an anthology, as it were, of stars whose records, like themselves, one only hears about as distant planets that hardly ever come within our ken. Those whom I deal with now have all, at one time or another, been heard at Covent Garden.

Lina Cavalieri has had a truly romantic career. In recent years she has been singing chiefly at the Chicago Opera House, and it was whilst there, I fancy, that she married the well-known tenor, Lucien Muratore. But it is as long ago as 1892 since this soprano, then a lovely Roman girl of 14,

began making her living by warbling *canzonette* at café-concerts. Her voice and her beauty alike attracted notice everywhere, but her method was not thought good enough for the operatic stage until she had undergone a careful training at the hands of Mme. Mariani-Masi. Then in 1901 she made her début at the Teatro Real at Lisbon in 1901 as Nedda in *Pagliacci*, and scored an immediate success. Afterwards she appeared at all the big opera-houses of the world in turn, including the Metropolitan and the Manhattan in New York, where I heard her (1908)

LINA CAVALIERI

in *Tosca*, *La Bohème*, *Fedora*, *Manon Lescaut*, and *Adrienne Lecouvreur*. She sang in most of these the same year at Covent Garden, doing best on her début with Zenatello and Scotti in Puccini's *Manon*; but on the whole there can be no question that Cavalieri won the chief triumphs of her later career in the United States. In Milan and Paris her great part was Thaïs, but in that I cannot remember to have heard her.

As an artist of the theatre it seemed to me always that Cavalieri was somewhat mechanical and cold ; neither her singing nor her acting held the same fascination as her physical charm, which, despite her thinness, was on the purest classical lines. She could be dramatic, though never with the ring of real passion. As you can perceive in her *Vissi d'arte* (A.5178), she delivered her phrases at a long-drawn, measured tempo, while the same inclination to drag is to be observed in the short excerpt (reverse side) from *Manon Lescaut*, known as *In quelle trine morbide*. Yet there is a certain vibrant quality in the tone that you cannot help admiring, together with the unforced clearness of her Italian diction, which compares favourably with her French in the *Habañera* from *Carmen*. The latter (A.5179) I somehow missed in my articles on Bizet's opera, but, except for a tendency to over-slur, it is a capital record and the better worth having because on the other side is one of those catchy Neapolitan airs, entitled *Maria ! Mari !* which Lina Cavalieri used to sing, as Caruso did, with the genuine spirit and swing of the Southern Italians. Here she became lively and really let herself go.

Come we now to the Garden—not Maud, but

160

Mary ! I have written before concerning this clever but capricious prima donna, and even criticised (in our April number of this year) one of the two discs that bring her under the heading of Columbia Celebrities. She is a composite creature—one-third Scotch (born in Aberdeen, you may remember) ; one-third American (brought up in the U.S. from the age of six) ; and one-third Parisian, having studied mainly in the French capital, where she first sang at the Opéra-Comique in *Louise* in April, 1900. This was, on the whole, her best part —stronger, more arresting even than her Thaïs, albeit perhaps not so poetic or touching as her Mélisande or so daring as her Salomé (Strauss's). I am aware that her Manon was always much admired, and it was as the heroine of Massenet's opera that she first sang at Covent Garden in 1902. I heard her in it there in the following year, but her voice all those years ago was neither so round, full, or pleasant as it sounds to-day in her records, which, by the way, include two (the *Hérodiade* air and the *Liberté* drinking-song from *Le Jongleur de Notre Dame*) that have already been noticed in these columns. I mention them again with pleasure, because I am glad to say that they come out with immensely enhanced effect on my new H.M.V. machine. The portamentos in *Il est doux* are still there, it is true, but the tone seems steadier and sweeter, while the drinking-song is distinctly less dull. A two-sided disc of *Ah, fors è lui*, by Mary Garden, is rather a useful curiosity because of the fact that it is sung in French, in which language one seldom hears it. Here, again, the voice emerges with unsuspected power a n d clearness, and the whole air is given with singular care and animation though one rather misses the familiar long shake at the end.

The above do not by any means exhaust the roll of feminine " Celebrities " attached to the Columbia banner ; but I do not propose to re-traverse ground which I have previously covered. For example, on one occasion or another I have already praised the records of that great artist, Emmy Destinn, comprising *Aïda*, *La Forza del Destino*, and *Cavalleria Rusticana* ; of Olive Fremstad, from *Tannhäuser*, *Lohengrin*, *Carmen*, *Tosca*, and *Die Walküre* ; of the extensive Italian collection made by the Russian soprano, Eugénie Bronskaja ; of Maria

MARY GARDEN

Gay from *Carmen*, *Samson et Dalila*, and the duets with her husband, Giovanni Zenatello ; also of Rosa Ponselle, Eugenia Burzio, Celestina Boninsegna, Elsa Stralia, and Rosina Buckman, and not forgetting our own Dame Clara Butt.

I would, finally, make special mention — not having done so before— of the graceful and sympathetic Russian soprano, Lydia Lipkovska, whom we first heard at Covent Garden in 1911 with Sammarco in the production of Wolf-Ferrari's delicious little opera, *Il Segreto di Susanna*. She also returned in 1912 and sang in *Rigoletto*, *La Bohème*, and *La Traviata*, with John McCormack for her leading companion. We then admired her immensely, alike for her voice, her art, and her individual charm ; but after that the " almighty dollar " seems to have taken entire possession of her, and since the war she has been heard here no more. Unluckily, too, her Columbia contribution consists only of a share in familiar duets by Mozart, Rossini and Verdi with two well-known baritones, George Baklanoff and Ramon Blanchart. The pick of these is, I think, the scene between father and daughter from the third act of *Rigoletto* (*Figlia ! Mio padre !* A.5296), dramatically rendered by the two Russian singers. The quality of Lipkovska's voice in these duets is simply exquisite.

HERMAN KLEIN.

LYDIA LIPKOVSKA

161

THE GRAMOPHONE AND THE SINGER

(Continued)
By HERMAN KLEIN
Some Columbia "Celebrities"—II.

I INTEND to be just as exclusive in my selection from the masculine as I was last month in choosing from the feminine side of the Columbia super-catalogue. It sounds a trifle invidious to make these distinctions, but, after all, how are they to be avoided if one wants only to deal with real "celebrities," unmixed with the would-be's, and, further, to avoid covering the same ground twice, writing about records that have already been dealt with? This latter risk is the more difficult to escape in the present instance because the number of men and their records is larger. I shall get out, however, by truthfully confessing that to me they are all less interesting—the men, I mean, not the records; the individuals, not the artists. I know less about them, and, consequently, can dismiss them with fewer words.

CAMPANARI

For instance, take the tenor with the longest list to his name—Florencio Constantino. I never saw this excellent singer upon the stage, though I met him more than once at the Columbia *atelier* in New York. He made his reputation much more in South than in North America, and I think he never sang at Covent Garden. This did not, however, prevent his being the possessor of a fine voice and an admirable exponent of the legitimate Italian school, as exemplified in the past by Campanini and Tamagno. Proof of which statement is to be found in the fact that, although it must be nearly twenty-five years since Constantino first sang for the Columbia, the majority of his records—I am not sure whether he re-made any of them or not—are as good to-day as they were then. He was the first operatic tenor of any distinction to sing for this company. He gave them the *fine fleur* of a wide repertory, which has since been faithfully imitated and repeated by every tenor associated with the gramophone, from Caruso downwards. Truth to tell, Constantino was one of the pioneers at the game; and for many reasons

I feel a particular respect for any artist who was clever and persevering enough to overcome the difficulties and obstacles that beset the recorder of those early days.

I have on previous occasions said all that it was necessary to say about Constantino's records of the more hackneyed solos. In many of them (see Columbia list) he is quite good; in others he does not, I allow, compare with the pick of the younger tenors. His tone is "whiter" than theirs, he takes more breaths, and he sometimes gives the impression of being tired; though next moment he will wake up and come out with a ringing high note—witness his top C at the end of *Di quella pira*—that scouts the very notion of fatigue. But perhaps the point that strikes you most is the variety of his phrasing and the skill with which he adapts his style to the music he is singing. This faculty he illustrates notably well on a 10in. disc (A.848), with on one side the *Inno trionfale* from Meyerbeer's *Le Prophète*, and on the other the air, *Deh! non mi ridestar*, from Massenet's *Werther*. A similar contrast occurs in A.706, where he gives the *Ecco ridente* from *Il Barbiere* and Buzzi-Peccia's lively serenade *Lolita*.

A tenor for whom I entertain a genuine admiration is Alessandro Bonci, a contemporary and rival of Caruso and Constantino, and perhaps the most finished vocalist of the three. I often wonder why he has not done more work for the gramophone. Now well on in the fifties, he has had a busy career in every part of the operatic world, including Covent Garden, where he made his début

GIOVANNI ZENATELLO

with Melba in *La Bohème* in 1900, and three years later again appeared with Maria Barrientos and Titta Ruffo in *Il Barbiere*. He was also here in 1907–8, winning especial success as the Duke in *Rigoletto* and as Faust, but since then he has sung chiefly in New York or Chicago. Bonci's total contribution to the Columbia collection amounts to a mere half-dozen discs; but they are all first-rate of their period and well worth hearing. The fine "covered" quality of his tone is displayed with delightful musical effect in every instance—in the *Rigoletto* airs (D. 8083), in the usual *Tosca* numbers (expression without exaggeration), and the excerpts from *Manon Lescaut*.

Next on my list comes Giovanni Zenatello; but about that powerful *tenore robusto* I

RICCARDO STRACCIARI

have nothing fresh to say, except this. His records undoubtedly sound to better advantage on my new H.M.V. machine than they did when I wrote concerning them in THE GRAMOPHONE two years ago. I have listened carefully once more to *Celeste Aïda* and *Cielo e mar* (A.5400), to *Vesti la giubba* and the *Siciliana* from *Cavalleria* (A.1235), and to the splendid duets with Emmy Destinn and Maria Gay, and I have been well rewarded for my pains. There only remains to suggest that before it is too late Zenatello had better make a few records of choice passages from Verdi's *Otello*, in which opera, now that Tamagno is gone, he is indisputably without a rival. In the recording-room he would probably be more careful to preserve the even quality of his voice than he is on the stage, when carried away by the excitement of the dramatic situation; and he could certainly dispense entirely with that mottled make-up which at Covent Garden last June rather spoilt the effect of Otello's most serious moments. Why not record the big duet of the second act with Mariano Stabile?

Another revised impression that I would like to chronicle, since it comes into this same category, is Hipolito Lazaro's record of the *O Paradiso* from Meyerbeer's *L'Africaine*. There is still, and always will be, an excessive amount of *vibrato* in the last part, but in all the rest of it the tone is so superbly rich and the startling power of the high B flats so brilliant that I must now place Lazaro's rendering of this air among the very best that the gramophone can boast. On the other side, too, he gives a rendering of the difficult aria, *A te, o cara*, from Bellini's *I Puritani* (7343), which is almost

equally meritorious. When one listens to this magnificent organ one can only regret that its owner has not yet paid a visit to this country. He would not regret it, I am sure, if the chance came his way; and he might do worse than add a few more records to the Columbia catalogue whilst winning the enthusiasm of the new Covent Garden *clientèle*. There is no need for me to dwell afresh upon the efforts of Ulysses Lappas, Tom Burke, Frank Mullings, or the other well-known tenors whose names further grace this honoured roll. I will come at once to the deeper voices.

From the harvest of the baritones one misses the formerly conspicuous work of Giuseppe Campanari, among the earliest of Columbia "celebrities." I understand that with few exceptions his records are now all withdrawn. There remain, nevertheless, his two airs from *Le Nozze*, *Se vuol ballare* and *Non più andrai* (A.740), just to remind one what a splendid Figaro he was. This was the character (only it was in Rossini's, not Mozart's opera) that he made his début at Covent Garden so long ago as 1898. But I fancy he sang here no more after that season, when his Amonasro also won high eulogy. Campanari's career unfolded itself chiefly at the Metropolitan Opera House, New York, almost concurrently with that of Marcella Sembrich, with whom he was constantly associated. He had a voice of extremely sympathetic quality, and was a talented, conscientious artist. He was, moreover, a worthy comrade of Constantino among the pioneers who helped to lift the Columbia work out of the rut of cylindrical comic songs and cheap negro minstrelsy.

In the latest issue of the catalogue Riccardo Stracciari is set down as "One of the world's few great grand opera baritones." It all depends, of course. Allowing the "few" to be correct, I will not be critical enough to deny the justice of con-

NORMAN ALLIN

sidering Stracciari amongst the elect, provided he does not object to being judged by that standard. His voice records well, and he is unquestionably a sound artist, as I have often declared when

163

writing about his work; but beyond that I do not feel inclined to go. Let us therefore avoid comparisons with Battistini, Titta Ruffo, and one or two more of that class, and simply admit Stracciari to a place among the "celebrities," because he can hold his own in first-rate company and because his singing always gives pleasure. That is quite sufficient. Another baritone, Ramon Blanchart, has set himself no less ambitious tasks without achieving a similar measure of success. The trouble is that his voice is unsympathetic and of very ordinary quality, allied to a style completely devoid of charm. Anyone who may consider this judgment harsh is hereby requested to listen to his *Eri tu* (A.5207). He has also done

a large number of duets with other artists, the best of which is the one from Verdi's *Forza del Destino* (*Solenne in quest'ora*, A.5184), because seven-eighths of it is sung by Constantino and the remaining eighth by Blanchart. The records by Cesare Formichi have been amply reviewed already.

Among the basses José Mardones and Norman Allin must be accorded an equal right to share the leading place; the former in virtue of adequate examples of the old Italian school, the latter for his consistent meritorious work in the various departments of opera, oratorio, and song-recording. Norman Allin's industry is remarkable; and when he is good he is "very, very good."

HERMAN KLEIN.

THE GRAMOPHONE AND THE SINGER
(Continued)
By HERMAN KLEIN
A Plea for Light Opera

WE have no equivalent in this country for the French State-subventioned theatre known as the Opéra-Comique, an institution that has been in existence for rather over two centuries. It is there regarded as the home of all opera which is not "grand" (in the sense that tragedy, drama, and massive musical effects make it grand opera), which does not include a ballet on an important scale, or in which as a rule the dialogue is spoken, not sung in the form of recitative. Its repertory may and does include examples of what we call light opera; but not what the French themselves distinguish by the term *opéra-bouffe*, to which classification most of the pieces written by Offenbach belong. The question is, what precisely is "light opera"? Assuming that it cannot be opera founded upon a serious subject and seriously treated (like *Carmen*, for instance, or *Roméo et Juliette*, both of which were originally produced at the Opéra-Comique), is there any distinction to be drawn between the kind of comic opera that we should call "light" and the *genus* to which the Opéra-Comique varieties of Boieldieu, Donizetti, Auber, Adam, Hérold, Massenet, and one or two of Messager may be said to belong?

Such a distinction undoubtedly exists; but it is not easy to define. You will best recognise it, perhaps, by pointing to the comic operas or *opéras-bouffes* which have *not* been admitted to the stage

of the Paris Opéra-Comique. I mean the French compositions of Offenbach, Lecocq, Audran, Planquette, Hervé, and the average Messager; the German of Johann Strauss; and last, but not least, the English of Gilbert and Sullivan, Alfred Cellier, and Edward German. These may all be reckoned, properly speaking, in the category of light opera, for the simple reason that, whilst they are the reverse of "heavy," they are yet the work of cultured musicians and artistic both in material and structure. Their spirit is more or less the spirit of comedy, of humour and fun, or even in certain instances of parody and burlesque. For all that, light opera cannot be said wholly to exclude certain of the bright, happy examples belonging to Opéra-Comique school. Consequently, it constitutes a fairly comprehensive type; and I have no hesitation in adding that its most ordinary specimens are distinctly superior to the kind of production which here goes by the name of musical comedy.

This brings me to my point. I want to see light opera restored to its former popularity as a high-class musical and theatrical entertainment. I think the time for that revival has come. Most people are sick and tired of the inanities and trivialities of musical comedy and the vulgarities of revue. The talent that is wasted on these up-to-date musical shows could be so much better employed on pieces that are infinitely more amusing because

164

they have head and tail, rhyme and reason. Has not this been amply demonstrated in the case of the Savoy operas? Ten years ago you could never hear the D'Oyly Carte Company anywhere nearer than some distant suburb; and I think I was the first London critic to draw attention (in the *Saturday Review*) to the absurdity of that fact. Now the annual season at the Princes Theatre draws packed houses from beginning to end. It is my firm belief that light opera, similarly placed upon the stage, only with even better singers, would meet with the same success. What a blessing it would be if the taste of our audiences that love music in the theatre could be diverted from the sickly rubbish and the eternal jazz that they now have to pretend to enjoy, and elevated once more to the level of the enchanting melodies, the graceful and spirited dance tunes, the bright choruses and ingenious ensembles that delighted the far more exacting public of the 70's and 80's!

The change can be brought about; I have no doubt whatever as to that. But it is not to be done " in the twinkling of an eye." The chief factor in the process must be the musical one, and that should be a task for the gramophone companies. Sudden revivals of bygone triumphs—*La Fille de Madame Angot*, for example—will accomplish nothing, as we saw at Drury Lane just before the production of that creditable and astounding modern gold-mine, *Rose Marie*. In course of time all or most of the old favourites, from the *Grande Duchesse* and *La Belle Hélène* down to *Madame Favart* and the *Cloches de Corneville*, might pay for re-mounting on a costly scale, but it will have to be led up to gradually. There can be no question that people are ready to welcome real plots, with clever lyrics and dialogue containing witty repartee and some pungent satire—witness the everlasting freshness of Gilbert's librettos. But it is not so absolutely certain that they will hum or whistle the old tunes of Offenbach or Lecocq, comparatively unfamiliar as they now are, with the same obvious enjoyment that they repeat and hear repeated the well-worn numbers of Arthur Sullivan, whose freshness never can and never will fade.

But to these last the gramophone recorders have already done abundant justice; as they have also done more than justice to every hackneyed air that the grand opera scores could be made to yield. And not without good reason; for the music is mostly beautiful and the product has helped to earn good dividends for shareholders. But for the real gems of light opera you will search their catalogues, as I have done, in vain. And the reasons for that, too, are pretty evident. When light or comic opera of the legitimate sort was at its apogee in this country the gramophone was non-existent. A marvellous popularity of thirty or forty years' duration was already on the wane when the new invention came along, and the light opera artists —irresistible in their day—were either disappearing or turning to pure comedy, after the fashion of that wondrous survival, Marie Tempest. Thus there was no connecting link, as in the case of serious or grand opera, to perpetuate (or at least prolong) the love for a type of music that was equally unsurpassable in its fascination and *entrain*. Let us suppose that there had been, only ten years ago, a Hortense Schneider, a Florence St. John, a Selina Dolaro, or even a Kate Santley, to make records of their famous songs from the pieces with which their names are indissolubly associated. The link with the past would never have been severed, and there would have been no room for the solitary doubt which may arise to-day—that the individual style of singing many of these things may have become lost, " mislaid " or forgotten.

It is my belief, however, that if the need existed the requisite vocal talent would quickly be forthcoming. There is, beyond all doubt, a vast quantity of delightful music awaiting resuscitation from among the old light operas that would be easily within the means of the capable artists now at the disposal of the gramophone firms. It is only for the latter to decide when they will dip into the opulent store which has lain so long untouched that it is now literally and legally free for all to partake who choose. There will be no royalties to pay on any of the gems from the French composers I have named above, with the exception of Messager, who is still living. As to the question whether the music is worth the trouble and outlay, I can only express the opinion once more that we are getting nothing of the kind to-day to equal it for originality, charm, and wealth of musicianly resource. Look up some of it and try it, out of the cheap second-hand scores if you can get hold of them, and you will perceive the truth of my argument.

Of course, if the gramophone were ever to popularise the unknown and neglected Offenbach —not to mention the forgotten Auber, the despised Lecocq, and the rest of them—sufficiently for stage revivals to appear worth while, we should then have to proceed as the Germans have done with *Orphée aux Enfers* and *La Belle Hélène*, *i.e.*, re-write the books, remount them with modern scenery and up-to-date effects *à la* Max Reinhardt, and render them alluring to the youthful as well as the grown-up audiences of the present day. There would be no necessity to adhere religiously to the original text, as in the case of Gilbert and Sullivan, whom change of fashion can no more improve than it could improve the Bible or Shakespeare. Which reminds me that one or two privileged jesters in Mr. D'Oyly Carte's troupe at the Princes Theatre *do* take liberties that would never have been permitted in the old days at the Savoy; and for the life of me I cannot see that there is the least occasion for it. There the sole object is, or should be, to maintain the old standard and preserve every known tradition. So far as the mere singing of light opera is concerned, I see no reason why the gramophone houses should not entrust it to the same vocalists that now record grand opera. As I have said, plenty of good material awaits their attention; but should they not come across it easily nothing will give me greater pleasure than to aid the record-makers in their search. Anyhow, the experiment I have suggested should be worth trying.

Before leaving this subject let me once more emphasise the value for our stage of the many neglected *chefs-d'œuvre* that are lying *perdus* in the repertory of the Opéra-Comique. Many of them are works for all time. They are no more old-fashioned in their way than the operas of Mozart or Rossini. So with the masterful operettas of Johann Strauss; *Die Fledermaus* is the classical model of its type, and its recent revival at Salzburg was one of the hits of the big Festival held there this summer. Whilst these things are being absolutely neglected in England, it is amusing to see our amateur operatic and choral societies making futile attempts to do justice to an opera like *Carmen*, which is very difficult for the stage and a mere travesty when done in concert form. (The latter result is only aggravated when the book and the score are both mutilated, as in the version just published by Messrs. Novello.) Such mistakes could be wholly avoided by an enlargement of the right repertory, through bringing real light opera into favour once again. There would be no need then for either amateur or professional bodies to ring the same eternal changes on Gilbert and Sullivan and one or two others that they now do. Again, I say, it is for the gramophone to lead the way!

VIDELICET—"LOVE ADRIFT"?

No, not with this. I cannot, with hand on heart, declare that I thought the ill-fated new "comedy opera" at the Gaiety a typical specimen of the kind of light opera that would bring joy to British audiences or grant a new elixir of life to this captivating form of stage art. It was an interesting experiment, an essay far above the average for cleverness of idea and executive merit. But it had the unpardonable weakness of gradually letting your interest dwindle, by not sustaining curiosity or enjoyment to the end; and that, to my thinking, was the fatal defect.

At first glance *Love Adrift* seems to be compact of very weird, strange material. Weird it may be, certainly; but it is not altogether so strange as it looks. The whole might fairly be described as Gilbert and Sullivan topsy turveydom treated after the manner of a Hungarian *goulasch*. One can trace the Gilbertian model clearly enough in this idea of a wedding feast eaten by the wrong guests; of a snowstorm that blocks the road for the bridegroom and his friends, but drives an unknown crowd to shelter in their place; of gaudily uniformed Magyar officers and enterprising students who dance the *lassan* and the *frishka*; of demure damsels in the mild crinoline skirts of 1830; and quite a number of grotesque *opéra-bouffe* servitors drilled to perform ridiculous evolutions in the approved Savoy fashion. All these features might be diverting enough if set forth to Gilbertian dialogue or utilised as adjuncts to a strong, intelligible plot; but, unfortunately, there is neither one nor the other to help the halting action along, while the characters are neither adroitly conceived nor amusingly drawn. The serious father and mother are utterly out of place in such a *galère*. They seem to have stepped out of some Wagnerian music drama—Wotan and Fricka having their quarrels over again in nineteenth century dress, with declamation and gestures to match. Then, again, two pairs of lovers leisurely sitting down at opposite tables, singing about goodness knows what in a quartet inspired, like so much else, by stray bits of *Die Meistersinger*.

The character of the quarrelsome, irascible mother, with her Fricka-like attitudes and her menacing gestures *à la* Ortrud, is even more of a mistake than the hen-pecked Telramundic father, with his genial tones and Pogneresque beard. Their music, like everyone else's, is of a complexity that outdoes the worst efforts of Richard Strauss, and consequently is horribly difficult to sing. Hence the engagement of Eva von der Osten, now a matured declamatory artist of the first order, who naturally instils everything but comedy into a part that might conceivably have been intended for Rosina Brandram or Bertha Lewis. No one would recognise in her the dapper, youthful Rosenkavalier of the pre-war decade; nor is the voice what it once was; but her execution of the most trying intervals is quite amazingly accurate. She has worthy English coadjutors in Frederic Collier, Andrew Shanks, and Jack Wright. The chorus is, without exception, the liveliest, the best-trained, *and* the loudest that has been heard in a London theatre in recent years. It also has some of the only tuneful stuff in the opera to sing.

And what of the music generally? I can only say that it strikes me as being an extraordinary misfit. Again and again one asks, "What is this elaborate score, after the style of Humperdinck in his *Königskinder* (only infinitely more complicated and less rich in rhythmical melody) doing in the domain of comedy opera?" Some of it sounds very Hungarian, and when it is we are thankful. One is also aware of an occasional glimpse of Sullivan in the tramping choruses; but that is all. The remainder is either serious music meandering without a pause for speech, or else providing unvocal hard nuts for unlucky singers to crack.

166

A lot of it is really clever good music, too, and quite agreeable to listen to. By the way, the composer's name is Poldini, which sounds Italian, but I believe is not so. Anyhow he is fortunate to have found such faithful, hard-working interpreters as Mr. Hubert J. Foss, the conductor, and the rest of the present Gaiety company. I may mention in conclusion that the young critic who stated that the term " comedy opera " had to be invented for this piece was mistaken. The name was actually adopted by the Comedy Opera Company that D'Oyly Carte *père* started in 1876, to perform the first of the Gilbert and Sullivan operas at the old Opera Comique Theatre in the Strand.

P.S.—It will be appropriate to add here a line of approval for Mr. H. Saxe Wyndham's biography of *Sullivan*, lately published by Messrs. Kegan Paul. What I like about this book is that, without being the smallest bit pretentious, it tells us in clear, succinct form and with sufficient detail all that the general student needs to know concerning the life and works of the gifted British composer. It has been written chronologically and with a careful regard for accuracy ; it should therefore prove a useful little work of reference.

P.P.S.—The fair editor of *The Sackbut* does not quite agree with the views I expressed in the August number of THE GRAMOPHONE about the use of the word "international," as applied to opera. But I think she has not quite correctly construed my words ; at any rate, in quoting them she has omitted two important ones at the beginning of the first sentence and changed another at the end of the second. By missing the former—viz., " In art "—Miss Greville has unwittingly been led into doing me an injustice. To say that people should not " profess or practice nationality " would be sheer nonsense. The qualities of artistic work may be national ; but I repeat that it is erroneous to describe them as " international."

HERMAN KLEIN.

THE GRAMOPHONE AND THE SINGER

(Continued)

By HERMAN KLEIN

The Year's Best Operatic Records

VIEWED from the mechanical side, 1926 has been a year of such remarkable progress as to make it outstanding in the history of the gramophone. It would be idle to pretend that vocal art has contributed in any measurable degree to that advance ; but, on the other hand, it is undeniable that gramophone singing has been facilitated and improved by it in more ways than one. The job of making records is no longer the experimental, doubtful, nerve-wracking one that it was a little time ago. The reviewer never knows, of course, any more than the public, how many essays and repetitions have gone to the making of the record that is passed, or, as they call it, " released " for sale. Speaking generally, however, I would give it as my opinion that the purely vocal achievement to-day bears evidence of greater spontaneity and ease, of less trepidation and strain, and even of a stronger dramatic atmosphere, than it has done heretofore. This alone should and does represent an enormous gain.

Some 25 or 30 records seem to me to stand out prominently among these which I have reviewed in THE GRAMOPHONE magazine during the year now drawing to a close. Each month in turn yielded one or more of these extra-meritorious examples, and I begin with one from a foreign *atelier* (January, p. 391) that was really very good indeed. It was a rendering in German of the two duets for soprano and baritone from *Don Giovanni* and *Le Nozze di Figaro* by Lotte Lehmann and Heinrich Schlusnus (Polydor 72933). This was not, of course, a specimen of the wonderful new electrical recording, which has only lately been adopted by the Polydor Company. But the method was, *sui generis*, of the best ; and the two voices were as delicately balanced as the style of the singers was pure Mozartian. The diction, too, was refined and clear above the average.

In February I gave especial praise (p. 444) to the work of two distinguished baritones, Michael Bohnen and Riccardo Stracciari. The former, a Wagnerian artist of the first rank, gave on a two-sided disc (Polydor 85277), a singularly fine rendering of Wotan's farewell to Brünnhilde in the closing episode of *Die Walküre*. He has his faults, judged by the highest vocal standard, but his voice is little if aught inferior to that of Heinrich Schlusnus, who enjoys about the same measure of fame in Germany ; and until I have heard them both on the stage I shall not venture to compare more closely these popular Polydor stars. I repeat the opinion that Michael Bohnen possesses an organ of exceptional beauty, and his record of the *Abschied* is perhaps the finest there is. Stracciari's records of the two solos for Mephistopheles in Berlioz's *Damnation de Faust* (Columbia X.333) were extremely good and quite deserve a mark of distinction. Nevertheless, I find him even more in his element in the two lovely airs from *La Favorita* (Columbia X.334), which he made at the same time and were noticed by me the following month (p. 487). His admirers cannot afford to be without this well-laden 10in. disc. Another gem issued in March was the splendid American record by Rosa Ponselle of Ponchielli's *Suicidio* and the *O patria mia* from *Aïda* (H.M.V., D.B.854). It made an immense impression on me, alike for the beauty, freshness and power of the voice and the intensity of its emotional appeal. I hope we are going to hear Ponselle at Covent Garden before she approaches the "sere and yellow" period. It is years since an Italian dramatic soprano of her calibre sang here.

Emmy Heckmann-Bettendorf is another soprano, of different nationality, it is true, who would receive a very warm welcome whenever the powers that be care to introduce her to London audiences. Her voice is of an exquisite timbre and it reproduces with a fidelity that is extremely rare. I commented upon several of her records during the year, but upon none more favourably than the two melodies from Strauss's *Ariadne in Naxos* (Parlophone E.10421), noticed in the March number (p. 489). The music may not be familiar, but the record is a gem. Again, a month later (p. 530), the same artist's recording of the two airs for Amelia in *Un Ballo in Maschera* (Parlophone E.10431) claimed similar admiration ; and together with it I placed the fine, if not wholly faultless, effort of Maartje Offers in the great contralto air from Bach's *St. Matthew Passion* (H.M.V., D.B.907). In April there also appeared the first of Gertrude Kappel's magnificent records (Polydor 66099–66100) of Brünnhilde's closing scene from *Götterdämmerung*, which I consider the most successful example of sustained vocal declamation yet achieved from this music-drama. Worthy to rank with it in its way is Marie Olczewska's poignant and tragical delivery of Waltraute's message from the same section of the *Nibelungenring* (Polydor 72982), only the task was less exacting. (The whole of this very desirable group were noticed on pp. 530–1 and the second Brünnhilde portion in August, p. 125). The April review further included an interpretation of the duet from the last act of *La Bohème* by L. Bori and T. Schipa, which, I think, I fairly described at the time as "complete and absolutely adequate."

The difficulty of discovering operatic novelties grows more and more evident. Different artists caracole upon the same old "battle horses,"

regardless of the opportunities that they afford the critic for more or less damaging comparisons. They even display a *penchant* for identical excerpts upon the same disc, witness, for example, the two Columbia issues (May and October) of *Celeste Aïda* and *Cielo e mar* sung respectively by Francesco Merli (D.1546, p. 576) and by Ulysses Lappas (L.1762). I had to praise both because both deserved it ; but I positively refuse to risk my personal safety by minutely comparing them now. Suffice it to say that lovers of these airs will find in each some magnificent tenor tone. Another May contribution (p. 575) of rare excellence was the duet for Hans Sachs and Eva from Act II. of *Die Meistersinger*, as interpreted (Parlophone 10443) by Alfred Jerger and Emmy Bettendorf. A better than this it would be difficult to imagine.

The first of the summer records done by Chaliapin with chorus was not from Covent Garden, though doubtless the outcome of electrical recording. It was the selection from *Boris Godounov* by the H.M.V. symphony orchestra and chorus (D.B.900), and I select it for mention again here, because, as already stated (Vol. IV., No. 1, p. 35), it has all the "life, vigour and *élan* of a stage performance." Later on came the reproductions of the real thing in the shape of the *Mefistofele* records noticed in August (p. 125) and October (p. 203). These two discs (H.M.V., D.B.942 and D.1109) were even more amazing in that they were obtained *in situ*, and so convey the very elements of a rendering upon the stage itself. On that account I regard them as gramophone records possessing a historical value because the first of their kind and therefore especially worthy of preservation. In June (p. 35) I also drew attention to a remarkably good 10in. disc (H.M.V., D.A.759), of airs from Berlioz's *Faust* and Bizet's *Jolie Fille de Perth*, sung by Marcel Journet. They accentuated regret that the celebrated French basso did not revisit, as promised, the scene of his former glories at Covent Garden. Somehow I fear that we are not going to hear him again on this side of the Atlantic, and if so his latest records will possess a peculiar interest for those who heard him in bygone days. In the same issue came an exceedingly good record by Elda di Veroli (Duophone G.S.7007) of *Caro nome* and the *Proch Variations*.

Two great *coloratura* singers and a clever Wagnerian prima donna provided exceptional material for comment in July (p. 77). From Amelita Galli-Curci we had the Mad Scene in *Hamlet* (H.M.V., D.B.297), and from Selma Kurz the *Ah, non credea*, with the *Ah, non giunge* from *La Sonnambula* (Polydor 72953). The charm of the former lies in ease and grace rather than pronounced characterisation, but the singing throughout is intensely individual and interesting—in fact, Galli-Curci of the best type. The second is equally worthy of

Selma Kurz in its vocal finish and purity of style; while the third, by Elsa Alsen (Parlophone E.10453), furnishes an unusually careful and authentic rendering of *Isolde's Liebestod* by first-rate executants.

My re-review is nearly done. September was, for me, drawn blank. In October was noted (p. 203) the splendid record of duets from *La Forza del Destino* and *La Bohème*, by Joseph Hislop and Granforte (H.M.V., D.B.939), which I understand has won general admiration. I must not forget, either, a special word for Fritzi Jokl's *Una voce*

(August, p. 203, Parlophone 10461), because it was decidedly above the average. Finally, in November, came a large and rather choice collection, the pick whereof comprised (pp. 247-8) the *Walküre* duet by Göta Ljungberg and Walter Widdop (H.M.V., D.B.963); the *Aïda* duet by Rosa Ponselle and Giovanni Martinelli (H.M.V., D.A.809); and the Wolfram pieces from *Tannhäuser* by Heinrich Schlusnus (Polydor 66408). All these were virtually beyond criticism.   HERMAN KLEIN.

THE GRAMOPHONE AND THE SINGER
(Continued)
By HERMAN KLEIN
The Singing of Lieder—I.

CUTTING adrift for a space from the fascinations of opera and oratorio, I propose devoting some attention to the more restricted product represented in modern gramophone catalogues under the heading of "Lieder." Would that it occupied a larger place there, for to me it embodies a subject infinitely absorbing and replete with interest. The word *Lied* is the German for "song"; but in the mind of the musician it means a good deal more than that. It signifies either a simple ditty, a pure folk-song or *Volkslied*, the derivation of which may or may not be traceable; or it can be a song of a much higher type, cast more or less in an art form of classical design; a setting in which the music is not merely repeated for each verse of the poem, but expresses and illustrates every turn or phase of its meaning until the end is reached.

In the original instance the term *Lied* was applied to "a German poem intended for singing" (Grove, Vol. II., p. 725), and not to a musical composition. It is rather odd, therefore, that the first *Lieder* I can remember hearing should have had no words at all. I refer, of course, to the *Lieder ohne Worte* of Mendelssohn, which, as everyone knows, are pianoforte pieces cast in the *Lied* form. At the time I speak of, the *Songs without Words* were much

more familiar in this country than the German songs *with* words. The latter were only to be heard at the so-called classical concerts, when foreign or English vocalists of distinction were taking part in them, and generally as a relief to the instrumental chamber works—then gradually coming into favour with the musical public—which constituted the major portion of the programme. Songs by Schubert, Schumann, Liszt, Franz, Lassen, or Brahms were, with a few rare exceptions, still too advanced for general audiences. They were still "caviare to the million," and the founder of the London Ballad Concerts, Mr. John Boosey, if he allowed Mme. Arabella Goddard to play some of the *Lieder ohne Worte*, would never have dreamed of mixing up a few real *Lieder* with the British ballads, old and new, that furnished the indigestible material for his weekly feasts at St. James's Hall.

But the period of transition had even then begun to set in, and it is interesting now to note the fact that the same honoured institution which was to change the course of musical taste among the community at large did so in the direction of vocal as well as of instrumental compositions. The oft-derided mid-Victorian era it was that witnessed

169

the actual beginnings of that slow but steady renaissance of good music in England which has not yet by a long way attained to its full fruition. I do not refer now to the work of the defunct choral bodies, such as the Sacred Harmonic Society (is not oratorio said to be—though I do not believe it—*in articulo mortis?*), or to the still struggling Philharmonic, whose sole partiality for vocal " relief " was formerly indicated by the engagement of a prima donna with suitable selections from favourite operas. No, the institution I speak of was the Monday and Saturday Popular Concerts, best known as the " Pops ", and carried on by the old house of Chappell for over forty years, from 1859 until the first decade of the present century, at the St. James's Hall which that firm built on the ground between Regent Street and Piccadilly where the Piccadilly Hotel now stands.

Here it was, far back in the seventies, eighties, and nineties, that I had the privilege of listening to some of the finest singers of the day, both British and foreign, in the choicest treasures of the masters named above. I have often recalled but seldom described those experiences. I have often traced the powerful influence of the " Pops " and their illustrious performers on the growth of the love for chamber music in this country, even though, not possessing the gift of prophecy, I failed to foresee the day when the Columbia Company would publish complete records of Schubert's *Quartet in D minor* and Mendelssohn's *Trio in C minor,* or H.M.V. give us Schubert's superb *Trio in B flat,* Op. 99, played by Cortôt, Thibaud, and Casals, to be listened to in one's own drawing-room. What would not some of us not give to be able to hear anew these lovely masterpieces, played by the old Pop quartet, Joachim, Ries, Straus, and Piatti, or, in the trio's, the first and last of these artists with the unforgettable Madame Schumann! But that was not to be. The gramophone as we now know it came a few years too late—not so very many, but just sufficient—to enable us to preserve and reproduce the performances of those giants when in their prime. It is a great pity. They would not alone have afforded music-lovers of a younger generation much joy, but they would have averted many ignorant and futile comparisons.

Nor have I set out to institute comparisons of my own on this matter, much less to attempt to set right people who never had the inestimable advantage of hearing great players of the past as well as those of to-day. I would speak, as I said before, of the *singers* who used to appear at the Pops, the kind of music that they sang, and in what fashion they placed their efforts upon a level with those of the instrumental artists and the pianist. The string players varied in number, naturally, in accordance with the works that had to be performed ; but except on rare occasions there was never more than one pianist and one vocalist. The programme invariably opened with a string quartet (or quintet), followed by the first vocal selection, after which came the pianoforte solo—generally a sonata by one of the great masters. Then ensued an interval of eight or ten minutes—a genuine *entr'acte,* as we used to call it—put to practical use by the subscribers, including not a few of the most famous painters, poets, and *littérateurs* of that time, who would stand up or leave their stalls, as the case might be, to enjoy a brief chat with their friends and talk over the gorgeous treats of the evening. (Among the dozens of celebrities whom I thus grew to recognise as *habitués* in the early days the most constant and conspicuous were Robert Browning, Swinburne, Tennyson, G. F. Watts, Alma Tadema, Whistler, Horsley, and many eminent lawyers, doctors, and other professional men who really loved the best music.) After the interval came the ensemble works bringing in the pianist ; then the vocalist once more, and finally as a rule some trio or sextet, or the Beethoven septet or Schubert octet, or very often a simple but delightful Haydn quartet to wind up with. The whole concert was over by 10 o'clock or a few minutes past.

It was in 1872, when I was a boy in my teens, that I first went to a Monday Pop and heard Santley sing Schubert's *Erl-King.* He gave it in English, and it was a magnificent piece of characterization, each individual in the drama being differentiated without the slightest shade of exaggeration. I remember that the audience simply loved it, but was too well-trained to insist upon an encore after two recalls. Two or three years later I heard our famous baritone there again in Schumann's *Ich grolle nicht.* This time he sang in German and with a very fair accent ; but generally he preferred a translation, as, for example, in Mendelssohn's forgotten *Hirtenlied* (*The Shepherd's Lay*), of which he was particularly fond. The democratic and intensely musical Pop audience did not care a bit what language it was so long as the singing proved worthy of the piece, and it always did. It was the fashion then to sing Beethoven's *Adelaïde* in Italian, and the interpreter *par excellence* of that beautiful *lied* was the great tenor, Sims Reeves, who invariably drew a big crowd when he sang it at the Pops. I must have heard him in it there on at least half a dozen occasions, and, although his voice was beginning to lose something of its power, the quality was still exquisite and the phrasing finished and elegant beyond compare. The wonderful accompaniment was played for him at different times by Sir Julius Benedict, Sir Charles Hallé, and Sidney Naylor ; Henry Bird only came later.

Another glorious tenor—still happily living—who helped to insert the thin end of the wedge for the love of *Lieder* at the same place was Edward Lloyd. He gave with exquisite charm two songs in particular—Schubert's *Serenade* and Mendelssohn's melodious setting of Tom Moore's stanzas *The Garland*, better known by the opening line, *By Celia's Arbour*. His voice sounded divine in the *Ständchen*, as it did also in Wagner's *Preislied*; but nothing could induce him to sing either in German. The first time I heard the Schubert song in the original was from the lips of the "Swedish Nightingale," Christine Nilsson herself, one afternoon at the house of Madame Balfe, and on that occasion it was the present writer who had the honour of accompanying her on the piano—an imperishable memory for me, I can assure you. I cannot now recall half the distinguished male singers whom I heard at the Pops in those early days, but I have a vivid recollection of a February night in 1877, when a new German baritone made his début in London and incidentally added a fresh foundation to the structure which *Lieder* were helping to build up.

The still-living artist who brought this impetus with him from the land of *Lieder* (he was born at Breslau in 1850) was that versatile musician—singer, pianist, conductor and composer—Sir George Henschel. His instant success induced him quickly to settle down here, and three or four years later he married his gifted American pupil, Lillian Bailey, a soprano with a voice of such beautiful timbre that it would even blend with her husband's and compensate for the peculiar crudeness of his quality. Thanks to their supreme art it was always a delight to hear these two sing duets, but at the Pops they did not appear together so regularly as at the vocal recitals which they were among the first to make a successful form of entertainment. Certainly, Mr. and Mrs. Henschel did more than any other married couple of their day—more, perhaps, than any other two singers whom I could name individually—to popularize the art of *Lieder*-singing in this country. They took their well-chosen and fascinating programmes into the farthest corners of the provinces, and taught the uninstructed amateur (with a soul above the royalty ballad) how to appreciate and enjoy the gems of their unfamiliar repertory. They won admirers wherever they went; they took part in all the leading festivals; they sang as delightfully in French and Italian as they did in German and English. A brief illness deprived us of Mrs. Henschel just 25 years ago last month, but Mr. Henschel went on singing and conducting for a long while (he received his knighthood just before the war), and he still carries on his teaching. His clever daughter, Miss Helen Henschel, reflects the distinguished talent of both parents and has done her share towards fostering the growth of *Lieder*-singing.

Two other gifted bass-baritones who visited London and made their mark alike in opera and *Lieder*, but did not remain here, were the famous Eugen Gura, a Bohemian by birth, and the equally celebrated Anton van Rooy, who was a Dutchman. The former sang all the leading parts in the first German season under Richter at Drury Lane in 1882; van Rooy, after his sensational début at Bayreuth, appeared during several seasons at Covent Garden under Augustus Harris. Both were superb artists and both gave recitals here subsequently—one at St. James's Hall, the other at the Bechstein (now Wigmore) Hall. Gura was especially fine in Schubert and the Loewe ballads, in which Henschel also shone; while van Rooy was at his best, in my opinion, as an interpreter of Schumann, particularly of the *Dichterliebe*, which, it is announced, may soon be recorded as a series—and worthily too, I trust—for one of the leading gramophone houses.

To return to the Popular Concerts. It was not to the sterner sex alone that the early advance of the *lied* in the esteem of Arthur Chappell's supporters ought to be attributed. I recollect a Monday evening in November, 1875, when a rather small, unimpressive *Mädchen* came upon the platform of St. James's Hall for the first time. She sang some Schubert songs with a purity of voice and perfection of style that made her fastidious hearers literally "sit up," stare, look at each other, then applaud the new singer with might and main. That was practically the beginning of the English career of the celebrated Thekla Friedländer, of whom Grove truly says: "The possessor of a sympathetic soprano voice of great delicacy and refinement, she excelled in old Italian airs and the *Lieder* of her own country, viz., Schubert, Schumann, and Brahms." During the ten years that she remained here before returning to her native land, she did splendid work that never ought to be forgotten. Among other things she used to be heard frequently in duets with her compatriot, Fräulein Redeker, a most artistic contralto with a voice of delicious quality, who became the wife of the well-known throat surgeon, Sir Felix Semon, and who still survives her husband. The treat of hearing Frls. Friedländer and Redeker together was one of the joys of the Pops for many seasons, and, if my memory does not err, it was they who, together with Mr. William Shakespeare and Sir George Henschel in 1877, first introduced the *Liebeslieder-Walzer* of Brahms to a London audience. The demand for Brahms was just spreading (that was the year of his first symphony at Cambridge) and amateurs had fairly begun to realize the inspired loveliness of his songs.

After the departure of Thekla Friedländer the Pops were for a time without a really first-rate *Liedersängerin*, but not for long. In 1889 there appeared another soprano of the highest order in the person of Marie Fillunger, a native of Vienna and a pupil at the Conservatoire there of the famous Mathilde Marchesi, though subsequently, on the advice of Brahms, she went to finish her vocal training at the Berlin Hochschule. She was, I wrote at the time, " an artist of exceptional dramatic feeling and intelligence and the possessor of a powerful, well-cultivated organ." Her readings of the three great masters of German song were tremendously interesting and full of colour—in fact, quite on a par with anything we have since heard from the lips of Elena Gerhardt and Julia Culp. Marie Fillunger was also a great favourite with the Crystal Palace audiences, and I, for one, shall never forget her rendering there of Beethoven's *Ah perfido !* and Schubert's glorious song, *Die Allmacht*, on the occasion of her début at Sydenham. Besides her wonderful Brahms she was an extremely fine Bach singer. Her career was influenced for good by her intimate friendship with Sir Charles and Lady Hallé, whom she accompanied as vocalist on their tour through Australia in 1891 and again through South Africa four years later. On her retirement as a public singer in 1904 she accepted Hallé's invitation to become a professor at the Manchester College of Music. She was then only 54 and her voice still fresh enough for her to have made some valuable records if fortune had so willed it.

With the turn of the century came the end of the Pops—the 1602nd concert of a series that had gone on unbroken from February 14th, 1859. Personally, I am glad that I was not then in England to witness the melancholy demise of an institution which, as I have often declared, ought never to have been allowed to become extinct. When the house of Chappell passed into other hands, with St. James's Hall pulled down and " Uncle Arthur " no more, the purely artistic interest ceased. The centre of operations was transferred to Queen's Hall and the Promenade Concerts, which have done a tremendous lot for orchestral but less than nothing for vocal music. Happily, before the new era set in, the seed sown on the old ground had already begun to bear such good fruit that there was no possibility of its being wasted. The taste of the younger generation had been definitely formed and the knell of the ballad era was already sounding. The rubbish commonly known as " pot-boilers " may not have been entirely done with; indeed, plentiful examples thereof continue to shoot up and flourish commercially even now. But to-day real music-lovers will have none of it, while the less cultivated public has learnt how to distinguish between ballads and ballads, between songs which have some sort of merit in them —whether harmonic, melodic, or both—and the vulgar sentimental or jazz ditties that have not a single good quality to recommend them.

Yet, side by side with the poster that announces some fast-expiring enterprise associated with the ballad entertainments of old, we may read announcements of vocal recitals galore, programmes filled to overflowing with the *bonnes bouches* of the gigantic catalogue of *Lieder*, of gems of the Elizabethan epoch, and, yes, of that first half of the nineteenth century when even the much-derided British ballad yielded occasional examples of good music. That the singers are always worthy of their theme I would not dare to assert ; far from it ; but the average, at any rate, reach a higher standard than that which prevailed when their less ambitious compeers of fifty years ago were not only content but proud to take a place in the ranks of the leading oratorio choirs. Nowadays, of course, every budding vocalist, whether professional or amateur, aspires to sing classical *Lieder* of every period and even prefers them, as a rule, to the operatic aria or the solo from some surviving oratorio. Interpretative intelligence rather than sheer good singing is what shows the best advance ; and that is a quality which certainly counts for a good deal, though by no means for so much as some people would have us think, where *Lieder*-singing is concerned. The only great exponents of this branch of art are those—male or female—who can combine the noblest qualities in fullest and richest measure. And of that precious type there are very few examples indeed.

In next month's article I shall commence a review of the best available records of *Lieder* sung by the foremost contemporary artists. The largest number by far stands, naturally enough, to the credit of the Polydor Company. Still, quite a goodly collection has already been made by the H.M.V. and the Vocalion in this country, and I hope ere long to see all our leading gramophone firms waking up to the national needs in the same direction as thoroughly as they are doing in the vastly more expensive departments of orchestral and chamber music.

P.S.—I note with pardonable satisfaction a distinct wave of feeling in several quarters in favour of a Meyerbeer revival. It is obviously in response to the articles which appeared in this magazine during the autumn months of last year, for until then no one had dared to advocate what would look like a challenge offered to the " boycott " criticisms of the ultra-modern highbrow. Fortunately, the timely visits to New York (in a professional capacity) of Mr. H. C. Colles and Mr. Ernest Newman served to modify their views on the subject. Those two able critics found that Meyerbeer at the Metropolitan Opera House was not altogether so *ennuyant* as they had expected. Anyhow, among the interesting productions now promised at Covent Garden for the coming season I am happy to observe a *reprise* of *Les Huguenots*.

HERMAN KLEIN.

THE GRAMOPHONE AND THE SINGER

(Continued)

By HERMAN KLEIN

The Singing of Lieder—II.

I AM glad to find that my promise of a series of articles on *Lieder* has met with general acceptance. The subject evidently interests those who feel, as I do, that the appreciation of good music entails the study, or at least the effort to understand, every class of composition (vocal or instrumental) that comes within the highest category of this art. In using this distinction I cast no slur upon music of less exalted types; how could I, when they include so much that we all love and admire? Yet the lower levels have had to be reached from those which lie lower still, or even from the rock-bottom of sheer musical ignorance; and if the taste of the humble but earnest and industrious amateur can be gradually trained to understand and enjoy better things, surely there is no reasonable ground for limiting at any stage the progress of that growth. Would the gramophone companies have believed me if I had told them twenty years ago that in 1927 they would be selling electrically-recorded discs of quartets and trios, sonatas, symphonies, and the like by the hundred and the thousand every week?

I ask this of them now because I venture to predict, without fear of losing my reputation as a prophet, that the time is near at hand when they are going to do similar trade with *Lieder*. My sole stipulation (in case this prediction of mine should ever be brought up as evidence against me) is that the songs shall be wisely chosen and that they shall be recorded only by the best obtainable singers. By the "best" I mean not only those with the finest voices, but with the particular gifts that are most suitable for the true and correct interpretation of the piece. How often have I found the rendering of certain *Lieder* completely spoiled because the artist, with the blindness due to the natural vanity that afflicts the majority of the race, has not possessed either the voice or the style or the temperament that was indispensable to the composition. This sort of adequate performance, intelligent but indistinguished, musical but not in the slightest degree inspired, electric in the mechanical sense but no other, will never result in making a record popular or help to sell it for the simple pleasure of listening to it. For this reason it will be wisest to "go slow"; to see that the singer knows how to make his or her selection; not to fix upon the piece until the artist is available who can do it justice. In this way I feel convinced we shall soon be offering incontestable proof that we have first-rate *Lieder*

singers of our own in this country. Meanwhile, I am going to give a glance at what has so far been done.

I begin with Schubert because he was the first of the great *Lieder* writers. When Beethoven lay on his death-bed and Schubert was just thirty, a volume of his songs was placed in the master's hands. He expressed the utmost admiration and astonishment at their exceeding beauty, then added : " Truly, Schubert possesses a spark of the Divine fire ; some day he will make a noise in the world ! " Well, he lived and died a poor man, but his " noise " included hundreds of beautiful songs which will live for ever. It is related that his friend, Johann Vogl, thought he wrote whilst in a state of clairvoyance and confirmed his theory by the following incident : " Among some songs recently composed was one to which Vogl took a special fancy, but finding it too high for him he had a copy written in a lower key. A fortnight later he tried over the song in Schubert's presence and the composer exclaimed, ' H'm ! Pretty good song. Who wrote it ? ' He composed so much that he had not recognised his own handiwork. He was, after Mozart, the greatest master of melody that ever lived, and he knew to perfection the art of writing for the voice. Poetry lay deep in his soul, and his gift for expressing it was so stupendous that he conveyed the poetic idea as eloquently in his accompaniment as in the voice-part. Hence it was that every note of his songs helped to ' tell the story.' "

Taking the original German titles in their alphabetical order, we make a start with *An die Musik* (Elena Gerhardt, Vocalion A.0220), and a very good beginning too, for there is an individual beauty both in the song and the rendering that makes one very glad to be listening to it. Just a tinge of nervousness it may be that is responsible for the over-pressure of breath which causes a slight trembling in the tone ; but it does not prevent one's enjoyment of the familiar Gerhardt quality and phrasing in this sublime melody. It comes out clear and well-defined, with faultless intonation, in an excellent piece of recording. (On the reverse side of *An die Musik* is another song, which I shall mention in its proper place, putting *an asterisk against the name or number to show it has been quoted already.* The name of the singer will generally indicate pretty accurately the type of voice for which the song was written—high, medium, or low ; but nearly all of

Schubert's favourite songs are to be had in transposed keys.) By the way, *An die Musik* was composed exactly a hundred years ago, to words by Schubert's steadfast friend, Franz von Schober, who wrote the libretto of his opera, *Alfonso und Estrella*.

Der Atlas (Leo Slezák, Polydor, 62422) belongs to the set of 14 songs known as the *Schwanengesang* (swan-songs), written in August, 1828, three months before he died. The poem, by Heine, illustrates the sufferings of Atlas, the Mauritanian king, who was fabled to have supported the world upon his shoulders. The music gives wonderful realism to the idea, the heavy bass octaves toiling heavily under the *tremolando* chords of the treble ; while the singer, although a tenor, imparts just the right sense of weariness and semi-exhaustion, even pitying himself because he has to bear all the sorrows of the world. To lend this clever bit of drawing greater force, Slezák has on the other side done an exquisitely delicate rendering of *Der Neugierige (No. 6 of the Schöne Müllerin* cycle of twenty songs, composed in 1823 to words by Wilhelm Müller), the inquirer who asks the brooklet whether his sweetheart truly loves him. The comparatively " white " tone and the soft *cantilena* enhance the contrast, and, even though the singer's German vowels be not over pure, the general effect is undeniably delicious.

The dainty ballad, *Auf dem Wasser zu singen* appears in two catalogues. Written in 1823 to the words of Count Leopold von Stollberg, its flowing semiquaver accompaniment suggests the sound of the gurgling water as the boat floats past it towards the setting sun ; while the singer depicts the colour and feeling of the picture with equal grace of rhythm. The rendering of Elena Gerhardt, with Paula Hegner at the piano (H.M.V., D.B.916), is remarkable for its lightness and delicacy, both as regards the even smoothness of the " slurred notes " and the easy flow of the German words. She also lends it variety by the *rubato* at the beginning of certain bars, albeit the pause on the first note is occasionally over-accentuated and compels her to hurry the remainder. The same device is adopted by Olga Haley (Vocalion, K.05122), though with a still more marked dwelling on the note and a misplaced slur that somewhat spoils the rhythm. Still, all credit is due to the English vocalist for the neatness of her phrasing and style and the purity of her tone.

Miss Haley also gives a good account (Voc. K.05257) among many others of the famous *Ave Maria*, which Schubert set to a German translation of the verses in Walter Scott's *Lady of the Lake*. The style here is duly prayerful and the voice sounds sympathetic. Both are happily free from the interference of *obbligatos* for violin or harp, or both, which disfigure the records of Claire Dux (Brunswick Clifto, 10249A), of Emmy Bettendorf (Parlo.

E.10205), and of John McCormack (H.M.V., D.B.578). Why this should have been thought necessary I cannot imagine—as if the melody and the singer did not suffice without such meretricious additions, which really amount to a vandalism. When such artists as those named are allowed to make their voices audible, amidst the din of the instrumental flourishes (there is a Müstel organ poking its nose in in the Bettendorf), these records are satisfactory enough. Claire Dux is always artistic ; Emmy Bettendorf always attaining sensuous beauty even when she, as here, overdoes the pathos ; and McCormack always sweet and tuneful, especially in enunciating the original English text. (The others are all sung to the German.) But I prefer to any of the above group the examples provided by Elisabeth van Endert (Poly. 13277) and Julia Culp (Poly. 70531), or even the contralto version by Emmy Leisner (Poly. 72838), not only because they give you (like Olga Haley's, I admit) the *Ave Maria* " pure and undefiled," as Schubert wrote it, but because they contain the best singing. The pick of the whole bunch is the Julia Culp, against which I have written—" rich mezzo-soprano like a clarinet ; the voice admirably sustained ; singularly clean phrasing ; grief and penitence without profound or abject misery."

Du bist die Ruh' belongs to 1823, the *Schöne Müllerin* year, and is an exquisite song. It depicts the wonderful peace and joy that a woman's loving presence and care can instil into the grief-worn heart. Its beauty is matched by its absolute simplicity. The three records received of this, all in German, are utterly different in character : Eric Marshall (H.M.V., D.1055), the essence of lassitude, tearful, sob-stricken, and vocally thin ; John McCormack (H.M.V., D.B.766) the soul of happiness and contentment, lively and tender by turns, charmingly sung ; and Leo Slezák (Poly. 65774), manly, full of deep, strong feeling, particularly well varied in treatment and therefore interesting. After saying which, I leave the choice between the three to the reader.

That immortal song, *Der Erl-König*, composed to Goethe's words in 1816, passed through more than one version before its final completion, but I believe the final one is preserved in the State Library in Berlin. It is Schubert's masterpiece in the *Lied* form, as perfect in its way as Mozart's " Das Veilchen," and as vivid a setting of a legendary story as is the other of a dainty allegory. It is because the *Erl-King* presents a whole drama in three minutes, with a narrator and three characters for its *dramatis personæ*, that it is so hard to sing and interpret adequately. It is hard to accompany well because the rattle of triplets is as rapid and uninterrupted as that of the horse's feet. To make the picture complete each voice must sound like that of a different person, and this is what so

174

many singers strive in vain to accomplish. In the four attempts before me each sensibly uses his or her own language as being the easiest, but not one is absolutely convincing as a piece of characterisation, so I will not pursue that point further. The most successful of the four, anyhow, is Elena Gerhardt, who has the advantage in this case of being a German. Her record (Voc. A.0215) reveals exceptionally clear, strong tone and distinct enunciation, with a tempo at top speed and a singularly good accompaniment. The ending, "In seinen Armen das Kind war *todt!*" is splendid. Muriel Brunskill (Col. 9088) is very dramatic, her voice resonant, her diction easy to follow. Roy Henderson's (Voc. 05167) I have noticed before; it has many admirable features—tonal especially—to recommend it. Robert Radford's (H.M.V., D.257) has considerable variety, plenty of dramatic impulse, and a good sense of contrast. I certainly like it best of the English group.

Die Forelle (Schubert's poem, 1818) is celebrated for its sprightly accompaniment, suggesting the sudden flash of the hungry trout as he leaps out of the stream into the sunlight or darts hither and thither beneath the surface. The singer tells how the fish gets caught, and the little scene seems enacted before our eyes. Crisp, neat singing is required here and a strong rhythm. Elisabeth van Endert (Poly. 14673) gives both, together with a pretty tone and delicate *staccato*, and also with lots of *rubato* for those who like it. Olga Haley (Voc. X.9528) treats it in much the same fashion, though with a heavier, more abrupt *staccato*; she takes no liberties, however, and the spirit of the *lied* is manifestly there—in good German, too. In an exactly opposite mood is the setting of Mayrhofen's tragic verses entitled *Freiwilliges Versinken* (1820), sung with fitting dignity and feeling by the gifted contralto, Sigrid Onegin (Poly. 72921), who, I am glad to see, is to be heard at Covent Garden this season. This song is not familiar to many, and the awkward intervals make it difficult; but the artist overcomes them with ease, and the timbre of her fine voice enables her to realise every passage with dignity and a certain grandeur. The tremendously long pause on the C natural on the second " Wohin " makes a very weird effect in what is a generally fine record.

The masterly setting of the *Gretchen am Spinnrade* (or, as we say, " Marguerite at the Spinning Wheel ") from Goethe's *Faust* belongs to the year 1814. It deals with the later period of the girl's unhappy existence and her reflection on the lover of bygone days. Elena Gerhardt, accompanied by her friend Paula Hegner (*H.M.V., D.B.916), takes it unusually fast and the whirring wheel positively tears round. There is something very dramatic and touching, however, in her agitated, breathless sentences and the intense yearning that they express.

Olga Haley (Voc. K.05257) sings it less hurriedly and in a lower key (B flat minor), using a dark tone which only gathers strength in the two climaxes. An artistic rendering, nevertheless.

Heidenröslein (literally " Little Heather-rose ") was composed in Schubert's most prolific *Lieder*-year,† 1815, to words by Goethe. It is a gem of daintiness and grace, requiring none of those " aids to beauty " that are associated usually with fading charms. Imagine, then, my astonishment on finding that an artist like Claire Dux (Clifto. 15061A) should have permitted herself the abomination of a vamped-up orchestral accompaniment, as though her own bell-like soprano were not good enough without such supplementary decoration. The excessively slow speed—another mistake—makes a dull song of *Heidenröslein*, and this is the only fault I find with the rendering of Emmy Bettendorf (Parlo. E.10388), for she sings it delightfully to the proper piano accompaniment. (Even more satisfying is the sprightly *Wohin* which completes one side of the disc.) Another by Ernestine Färber-Strasser (Poly. 62372) is also painfully slow and depressing. Is the new German idea about this song going to take permanent root? I hope not.

Der Hirt auf dem Felsen is a very long *Lied*, written just before Schubert died to a poem of Schober's, with accompaniment for piano and clarinet. It embodies the reflections of a lonely shepherd (*à la Tannhäuser*, Scene 2) in some melodious themes for voice and clarinet, the former being here interpreted by a clever Viennese singer, Gertrude Foerstel, with truly remarkable breathing capacity. She fills both sides of a 12in. disc—not, of course, all with one breath, but about half as many as most people would take.

Hark! hark! the lark (1826) is too familiar to need discussion. The setting of the lines from *Cymbeline* is simply ideal, and of the three records before me Frieda Hempel (H.M.V., D.A.382) provides the perfect one. Alma Gluck spoils hers (H.M.V., D.A.238) by employing an orchestra and a funereal voice; while poor Evan Williams (H.M.V., D.A.383) eliminated all the joy and animation by adopting a dragging tempo and sentimental style. The superb record of *Hark! hark! the lark* made several years ago for the Columbia by David Bispham, has, I fear, been taken out of the catalogue. Could it be re-recorded, I wonder? There are so few *Lieder* sung—and well sung—in English among the collection I am reviewing, and yet the only way to make them appreciated is to make them known. Take, for example, a little gem like *Der Jungling an der Quelle* (1815), which no one but Claire Dux seems to have thought of recording (Poly. 70688). It ought to have been done here

---

† In 1815 Schubert wrote no fewer than 138 songs, in addition to a vast number of concerted instrumental works, symphonies, Masses, etc.

long ago. I care less, much less, for *Der Kreuzzug* (1827), but I allow that Sigrid Onegin (Poly. 72714) makes an even more lachrymose ditty of it than Schubert could have foreseen. On the other hand, nothing could be sweeter or more ingratiating than *Das Lied im Grünen*, as warbled (it is the only word!) by Elena Gerhardt (H.M.V., D.A.706), which was composed in the same year. If this will not inculcate the taste for *Lieder* nothing will.

It is inexplicable to me that so many of Schubert's most beautiful and popular songs should, so far as I am aware, be still unobtainable either in England or the land that gave them birth. Anyhow, only a few have been recorded by more than a single artist. In Austria and Germany everyone knows *Der Lindenbaum* and it appears in two or three lists; but the sole example that I have of this jewel of the *Winterreise* cycle (1827) is one by Leo Slezák. He sings it nearly all through in his charming *mezza-voce* and with a rare depth of yearning sentiment—just the right way, in fact. The delicious accompaniment is well played. Slow and solemn is the rendering of the impressive *Litanei* (Litany written in 1816 for All-Souls' Day, Poly. 66143) by a low baritone named Schobl; but the piano here is too heavy. In direct contrast is Elena Gerhardt's *Der Musensohn* (1822, Voc. 3112), which no one sings as she does. I might call it a *cri de joie* in two keys, the happiest thing imaginable, with a dashing accompaniment and ably recorded.

The sublime song, *Nacht und Träume*, is a setting of words by Schiller published in 1825, and worthy of it in every way is the record by Emmy Bettendorf (Parlo. E.10399), who supplies the glorious tone and slow sostenuto that it demands. Less successful is Leo Slezák (Poly. 65773), who takes it slightly faster, yet in a somewhat depressed mood. A much earlier *lied* called *Seligkeit* (1816) does not strike me as at all noteworthy, though tuneful enough and pleasantly sung by Elisabeth van Endert (*Poly. 14673).

Then come we to two magnificent specimens of Schubert's genius, viz., the *Ständchen* or *Serenade*, forming No. 4 of the *Schwanengesang* (inspired by Rellstab's words not long before the master's death) and the no less renowned setting of the *Who is Sylvia?* from Shakespeare's *Two Gentlemen of Verona*. A soprano, three tenors, and a baritone have recorded the *Serenade*, and each is open in some manner to criticism. The English versions are good, but those of John McCormack (H.M.V., D.A.458) and *Evan Williams (H.M.V., D.A.383) are not enhanced by the use in one case of a violin obbligato by Fritz Kreisler (naughty!) and of a full orchestra in the other. Roy Henderson uses a feeble American translation, but sings well (Voc. K.05167), bar the usual exaggerations; *Charles Hackett (Col. 7367) employs pure tenor tone and phrases neatly, but introduces an unwarrantable "turn" instead of the *mordent*; while Elisabeth van Endert (Poly. 19110) uses the original German text with her accustomed charm of voice and expression. Beyond this I can offer no decided preference. Again, in the case of *Who is Sylvia?* I fear I must leave the choice to the reader, whilst suggesting the unmistakable merit of Miss Olga Haley's and Mr. John Thorne's efforts. Emmy Bettendorf's is spoilt by an exaggerated slowness that makes only for sickly sentimentality. My complete list of records of this melodic gem is as follows :—

WHO IS SYLVIA?

*Charles Hackett	.. ..	Col. 7367.
Dora Labbette	.. ..	H.M.V., D.1553.
Arthur Jordan	.. ..	Col. 3832.
Herbert Thorpe	.. ..	Beltona 6017.
John Thorne	.. ..	Aco G.15980.
*Emmy Bettendorf	..	Parlo. E.10388.
Hubert Eisdell	.. ..	Col. D.1419.
Derek Oldham	.. ..	H.M.V., E.395.
Olga Haley ..	.. ..	Voc. X.9561.

The remainder of the Schubert collection I must perforce leave until next month. It is about three-fourths finished in the present article, and at the end of it I shall begin on the Schumann.

HERMAN KLEIN.

THE GRAMOPHONE AND THE SINGER
(Continued)
By HERMAN KLEIN
The Singing of Lieder—III.

SCHUBERT (*concluded*).

N.B.—It may be well to repeat that these pieces are being dealt with in alphabetical order, and that an asterisk after a title or number indicates that the disc has already been mentioned when noticing the record on the other side.

I resume the Schubert *Lieder* with *Der Sieg*, a fine example (Polydor 62519) of the composer's early manner, written in 1814 to words by Mayrhofer. It requires dignity as well as feeling, and both are supplied by Josef Groenen, the chief basso at the Vienna Opera House. His voice has an uncommon quality and it records exceedingly well.

Der Tod und das Mädchen is best known, perhaps, as the song upon which Schubert based the slow movement of the lovely quartet in D minor, which he wrote in 1826, two years before he died. It ought to be equally well known for its own sake, having regard to the beauty of the soothing, hymn-like theme (it accompanies Death's reply to the Maiden's protest) and the weird atmosphere of this simple setting of Claudius's lines. As for its interpretation, the principal effect lies in the strong contrast that has to be made between the two voices—the pleading urgency of the Maiden followed by the consoling and anything but alarming assurance that she will soon be asleep in the arms of Death. The contrast should be felt in the manner of the singer more even than the tone, for, of course, the female voice cannot be made to sound exactly like a man's. In this respect the effort of Leila Megane (singing in English) is discreet and intelligent (H.M.V., E.396), while her voice is very pleasing. On the other hand, Klara Czery (Polydor 62527) attempts the precise impossibility I have indicated by bringing her " open " chest notes into play immediately after a weak start on the medium. Best of a group of three is another German rendering by Elena Gerhardt (Vocalion B.3107), who simply broadens out for " der Tod " and makes no attempt to overdo or falsify her tone anywhere. Altogether the record is quite artistically done.

Dem Unendlichen, a noble, dignified setting of Klopstock's lines, belongs to Schubert's " banner " song-year (1815), and excellently well is it sung by Jenny Sonnenberg (Polydor 66081), who enters thoroughly into the spirit of it. No less worthy of praise is Sigrid Onegin's reading of *Verklärung* (*Polydor 72921), the words of which were by Pope, translated into German by Herder and set to music in 1813. The sole blemish here is an excess of *portamento* ; the singer's tone is wonderfully luscious and expressive.

We come now to that glorious song *Der Wanderer*, the music of which Schubert, greatly inspired, wrote down *in a single night* to Schlegel's fine words in 1819. It was the first of his *Lieder* that I ever accompanied —perhaps ever heard—and I venerate it accordingly. Nothing could depict more graphically in the simplest phrases the unsatisfied longing of a weary soul for peace and companionship in the lost native land. I have only the English versions here sung by Eric Marshall (H.M.V., D.1022) and Robert Radford (H.M.V., D.272), whereof the latter comes nearest to realizing both vocally and spiritually the disappointment and despair of the Wanderer who has gone astray. It suits his genuine bass voice, and, though a little hurried in the slower passages, is marked by broad phrasing, clear enunciation, and a resonant descent into the ledger lines below the bass clef at the end. This is precisely what the baritone singer is unable to manage, and his effort fails to come off in consequence. Besides, his voice sounds dreary and miserable, and that, after all, is not essentially the quality that conveys the idea of yearning so much as of fatigue after a long journey. Why not have expressed both by a judicious admixture of animation and colour ?

The charming *Wiegenlied* (*Cradle Song*), words by Claudius, Op. 98, No. 2, was written in 1816, and must not be confused with the later one, Op. 105, published in 1828. It is generally sung by a mezzo-soprano and suits Olga Haley perfectly (Vocalion X.9727), though her tempo is too fast. Her German, as usual, is irreproachable ; but next time she records the *Wiegenlied* she might do so in her own tongue, and if so try a simple version that I know of in the series of *Lieder in English*, published by Metzler. It has been very sweetly done by Emmy Bettendorf (Parlophone E.10399), who takes it at just the right speed ; but unluckily the record is a feeble thing, with a piano accompaniment that emulates the proverbial tin kettle. The exceptional tone of Josef Groenen comes out with the same impressive effect in *Das Wirtshaus* (*Polydor 62519) as in the song above noticed on the same disc, This is one of the *Winterreise* group and better known on the continent than here.

Who, though, is not acquainted, if a Schubert-lover, with the delicious *Wohin?*—one of the gems of the *Schöne Müllerin* series, Op. 25 (1823)? The literal translation of the title is *Whither?* and it begins "I heard a brooklet rushing." The five records I have tried are all from what I may term "aristocratic" sources, and it is a somewhat invidious job to differentiate between them, for each has a special quality of some sort to recommend it. The Frieda Hempel (H.M.V., DA.634) is fluent, fresh, bright, and clear, like the "rushing brooklet" itself; tempo traditionally just right. Elena Gerhardt (H.M.V., DA.706) is quicker, but not much; also singularly neat and crisp—perhaps a trifle too crisp. There is a *hiatus* between the notes that makes them staccato, which the composer does not seem to have intended. Claire Dux (*Polydor 70688) adopts the same brisk tempo as Frieda Hempel, with greater volume of tone and a smoother *legato*, very distinct enunciation, ample contrast, and a nice *diminuendo* at the end. Altogether as good a record as she has made that I know of. Olga Haley (Vocalion R.6143) sings in English here, a very careful, easy, precise rendering of the tripping melody, with faultless rhythm. The vocal tone is pure and musical, though a shade too sad for the song, which is surely meant to reflect brightness and sparkle in the voice-part as much as in the "rushing" accompaniment. Emmy Bettendorf (*Polydor E.10399) does likewise in her German version, which is very graceful and flowing and full of yearning, but without much tone.

With this I conclude my review of the available Schubert *Lieder*. I have since received a record by Fritz Soot (Polydor 62551) of *Die Forelle* and *Der Musensohn*, which, if not of the very highest class, comes very near to that category. The young Berlin tenor gave, I remember, a capital impersonation of one of the *Nibelungen* heroes at Covent Garden two years ago. His agreeable voice comes out well in both of these songs, particularly in a vivacious and rhythmical delivery of the "Trout" melody. He makes it "snappy" but not too staccato.

I thank R. W. S. (Hull) and R. E. G. (Victoria Street) for their appreciative letters on the subject of these *Lieder* articles and am sorry that I have not space to deal separately with the Schumann-Heink and other fine records, now practically unobtainable, that they name.

SCHUMANN.

Born at Zwickau, in Saxony, on June 8th, 1810, Robert Schumann wrote for the piano only, bar one unedited symphony, until he was thirty. Then he courted and married Clara Wieck—best known to us as the gifted pianist, Mme. Clara Schumann—and forthwith turned his attention to song-writing. Just as 1815 was Schubert's most prolific year, so was 1840 Schumann's. In it he composed at least one hundred songs, therewith carrying on and developing the Romantic side of the art of *Lieder* composition that had had its foundations in the genius and lifework of the Viennese master. So much did he enjoy this kind of work, so closely did he devote himself to it for the twelvemonth in question, that he then lay down his pen and said, "I cannot promise that I shall produce anything further in the way of songs, and I am satisfied with what I have done." But after a while impulse and inspiration were rekindled, and he was yet to achieve some of his best things in this direction. The extent of his total product was, indeed, amazing, and, as regards its beauty, its originality, its precious musical value, one feels that it would be an impertinence to add another word. My sole desire is to see the gramophone become the medium for making the Schumann *Lieder* far more familiar to British ears than they are at the present time. As yet, the number of records available for the purpose is ridiculously small.

Schumann wrote his finest, most moving songs at the time when he was most deeply in love; which was, perhaps, no more than natural. The spirit of Romanticism was strong within him, and it pervaded all that he wrote—music, essays, criticism, everything. Hence the Schumann hall-mark, which you do not see but hear, and can no more mistake in his pianoforte and vocal compositions than you could mistake the distinguishing mark (once you know it) upon a piece of old silver plate. Keeping to alphabetical order, I begin with the calm, suave *Abendlied* or *Evening Song*, words by Heine, which Joachim helped to make known by his paraphrase for the violin. But I confess to being unacquainted with the arrangement for soprano, violin *obbligato*, and organ presented by Claire Dux (Cliftophone 10205) in the high key of D flat. It differs in many respects from the original song, and only a singer of this calibre could safely tackle it or make it sound so beautiful in such lofty regions. She sings only one of the two verses, but, all said and done, I prefer to hear it rendered by a contralto or a low baritone. For instance, it would exactly suit Theodor Scheidl, who displays just the right quality of sadness and restrained emotion in *Auf das Trinkglas eines verstorbenen Freunde* (Polydor 66143). This embodies the reflections of one who gazes upon the drinking-glass of a dead friend—a rather morbid song, the latter half of which atones by its profound mysticism and harmonic beauty for the dulness of the first part. Both these are good records.

Heine's famous poem, *Du bist wie eine Blume*, has no lovelier setting—and there are many—than this of Schumann's in the series of 26 songs entitled "*Myrthen*," Op. 25. It has been recorded by Otto Wolf and Josef Groenen, but at the moment I have only that of Eric Marshall (H.M.V., E.433), which leaves much to be desired alike for the German accent and the colourless vocal concept of the music. It is also transposed from A flat down to E flat, which is a trifle too far away. But what a heavenly melody it is! *Du meine Seele* (or *Widmung*) is the first of the same "*Myrthen*" set, written to words by Rückert in 1840, and justly enjoys its reputation as a glorious song. Frieda Hempel (H.M.V., D.A.557) takes it a semitone higher and a shade slower than usual, but sings it with all the essential warmth and more than her customary richness of tone. It stands among her most artistic efforts, and it makes me wonder whether she has ever thought of recording that most delicious *Lied*, *Aufträge*, which should suit her to perfection. Has anyone done it?

Among the song-cycles, we are promised the *Dichterliebe* complete (and I hope it will be sung as it deserves to be), but meanwhile the only available set is the masterly one known as *Frauenliebe und Leben*, Op. 42, which Schumann wrote in the same productive year (1840) to the text of A. von Chamisso. The eight songs are recorded by that gifted mezzo-soprano, Julia Culp (Odeon, X.52948–55), one on each side of four 10 in. discs. All are so artistically sung that I can hardly praise one more than another. The only serious blemish on the perfection of Julia Culp's art concerns neither tone nor phrasing, but the audible gasp with which she takes a quick breath. She realises with rarest feeling the intensity of the woman's love, and her limitless adoration for the miraculous kind of man—truly the *herrlichste von allen*—whom the poet has here depicted, which makes the touching finale doubly sad. The voice comes out well in all this, but I regret to say that the accompaniments are badly played on a dreadful piano; one vibrates with human happiness, the other with a jarring sound of thin wires.

Frühlingsfahrt, one of the *Romanzen und Balladen*, Op. 45, neatly sung by Fritz Soot (Polydor 62551), must of course not be confused with the well-known *Frühlingsnacht* nor with the less familiar *Frühlingsgruss*. The former is one of the *Liederkreis*, Op. 39, words by von Eichendorff, and can be recognized at once by its extraordinary contrast between the rapid triplets of the accompaniment and the subdued passionate melody of the air. It is sung in the original key by Sigrid Onegin (Polydor 70638), whose tone is always enchanting, but here loses the necessary passion through the tempo being too slow. The *Frühlingsgruss* is a song rather of the *Volkslied* description in the *Lieder-Album*, Op. 79, No. 4, all three verses being alike. Its simple character doubtless appealed to poor Evan Williams (H.M.V., D.A.395), who often sang it in English (as he does here) under the title of *Return of Spring*. His pure tenor sounds charming in it. By the way, Sigrid

Onegin also records (*Polydor 70638) *Ins Freie*, from the "Sechs Gesänge," Op. 89, a jubilant setting that fits her exactly. But it is a pity that, with that easy tone of hers, she is so much inclined to slur and "scoop."

Die Lotosblume ("Myrthen") is one of those gems wherein poetry (Heine) and music alike create the perfect alliance, and several artists have recorded it abroad. Here it is associated by Eric Marshall (H.M.V., E.433) with *Du bist wie eine Blume* and is on the whole the better interpreted of the two. For sheer beauty of tone, however, I recommend Sigrid Onegin (Clifto-Brunswick 10213B.), who understands the art of modulating her opulent chest and medium notes even more than probing the depths of Heine's verse. With the aid of an orchestra she enlarges her lotus-flower into a huge magnolia blossom. *Love when I gaze* is an English version of *Wenn ich in deine Augen seh*, and No. 4 of the *Dichterliebe* or story of the Poet's love as told by Heine. It is nicely sung by Roy Henderson (Vocalion K.05250) and shares a disc with Henschel's effective *Morning Hymn*. Some day the singer will infuse into it that deeper tinge of pathos which his fine organ at present lacks. Just the contrary is the case in Elena Gerhardt's rendering of the lovely *Der Nussbaum* (*Vocalion A.0215)—another "pearl of price" from the "Myrthen." Here I find the gifted *Liedersängerin* putting into the song more emotion than it calls for; gracious and suave it certainly is, but surely a trifle over-sentimentalized for the simple secrets that the walnut-tree imparts to the maiden! Otherwise it is beyond criticism. There are half a dozen other German records of the *Nussbaum* concerning which I am unable to speak, but only a single English version that I can mention here, viz., *The Hazel-tree*, sung by Elsie Francis-Fisher (Aco G.15937). This is so like Elena Gerhardt's in its solemnity and deliberation that I could almost vow the one had been made a model for the other. In any case I do not think either manner correct; but apart from that there is no fault to be found. The English singer has an uncommonly sympathetic voice, and sings the *legato* phrases in graceful fashion.

I come now to another "adaptation" bearing the seal of approval of that arch-transgressor, Claire Dux. Schumann wrote some hundreds of songs—none of them "unvocal" in the hands of an artist—and it is simply unpardonable, to my thinking, that any German singer should go out of her way to record "arrangements" which the composer himself would never have tolerated for a moment. Everyone knows the beautiful *Träumerei*, of course, and hitherto I have always thought it to be one of the seventeen "Albumblätter" for piano alone. (If I am wrong I apologize, but I don't think I am.) Anyhow, it is here presented by Claire Dux (*vide* the *Abendlied*) in the form of a song, with specially-written words and brought out in that illegitimate form by the Brunswick-Cliftophone (*10249A) without a word of explanation on the label. To make matters worse, the melody of *Träumerei* is not really suitable for vocal purposes; some of the intervals are badly slurred, and the singer is projected into her head register too frequently and too long. Altogether it is not an achievement to be proud of.

The Two Grenadiers (*Die beiden Grenadiere*) is in this country the most popular of all Schumann's songs. Composed in the supreme vintage-year of 1840, it is No. 1 of the set of "Romanzen und Balladen," Op. 49, and I scarcely need add that the words are from the pen of that extraordinary genius, Heinrich Heine. I presume it was the musician who first conceived the idea of wedding the last part of the poem to the tune of the *Marseillaise*; anyhow, it was assuredly a "happy thought" and has no doubt contributed largely to the universal acceptance of this celebrated *ballade*. Records of it are to be had in five or six languages, and there is not one of them that does not appeal to the ear by its martial ring, its lofty note of patriotism, and the touch of true pathos that underlies the talk between the two veterans as they wearily wend their way back to France. Not a word or a note seems wasted in the telling of the story; from start to finish the thread is never lost for a moment; it grows in excitement as the dying soldier utters his last wishes to his comrade, anent the mode of his burial with hand on the sword that is to defend his Emperor even in death. No finer climax than the *Marseillaise* to such a theme could possibly be imagined. Well do I remember how magnificently Pol Plançon used to declaim that imperishable refrain, and I have a notion that he once recorded Schumann's song, but if he did I fear the record is no longer in circulation.

To-day its most striking interpreter is Theodor Chaliapin, who as a matter of course sings it in Russian, and, like most others, with the assistance of an orchestra. (Schumann thought the piano good enough, and so I daresay would most singers if a misguided public were not in the habit of refusing vocal records without orchestral accompaniment.) Chaliapin has done two versions of *The Two Grenadiers*. The earlier one (H.M.V., D.B.102) was acceptable enough until the second (H.M.V., D.B.933) took its place, and the vast superiority of the latter makes choice easy. The tone-colour and style are characteristic in the extreme, while the orchestra under Eugene Goossens gives admirable support. The life and energy of this rendering and its sense of contrast are what one misses in the otherwise adequate and precise performance of George Baker (Parlophone E.1050), one of the several English versions procurable in London music-shops. I give Roy Henderson credit (Vocalion K.05250) for contenting himself with the piano; also for the manly quality of his dark tone and the strong emphasis of his diction. He ought, however, to have accelerated more just before approaching the *Marseillaise*. Clarence Whitehill (H.M.V., D.B.438) is powerful but uninteresting and uninspiring—probably because he uses a wretched translation. The Italian version employed by Titta Ruffo (H.M.V., D.B.242) seems to contain too many syllables, consequently upsetting the conciseness of the rhythm and to some extent the sonority of the voice. Still, it is an exceedingly realistic bit of work and can hardly fail to please the immense crowd of Titta Ruffo's Italo-American admirers.

There are other creditable English examples. Harry Dearth (H.M.V., D.215) was quite at his best when he recorded this song—well in tune, a free, vigorous style, unmistakable diction; Thorpe Bates (Columbia D.1043) plenty of virile tone, artistically managed, effective contrasts, and excellent enunciation (these both with orchestra, the second a semitone up); and, finally, Harold Williams (Columbia 3547), a bright, animated bit of singing, especially in the higher part of the *tessitura*, good clear diction, and a satisfactory piano accompaniment.

In addition to the above there are some twenty-five current records of Schumann *Lieder* in the latest Polydor catalogue, but these have not reached me in time for notice in the present article. Those of Brahms, Strauss, Liszt, and perhaps Loewe will, I trust, provide the main material for my concluding article on this subject next month. In the meantime I may renew the expression of my hope that a genuine demand may spring up for British records of the great German *Lieder*, whether sung in the original or to an English text; and this can only be done if the leading gramophone houses will promptly take the job in hand, engage the right artists to sing for them, and carry out the whole thing as thoroughly as they are building up their operatic and symphonic répertoires. In the end, I am convinced, it will pay them equally well.

HERMAN KLEIN.

(*To be concluded.*)

THE GRAMOPHONE AND THE SINGER

(Continued)

By HERMAN KLEIN

The Singing of Lieder—IV.

I FIND I have not yet finished with available records of Schubert and Schumann. Since last month the Polydor company have sent over a large parcel of *Lieder* of their own selecting that includes a good many by these composers which were not at my disposal in time for the reviews in our February and March numbers. It is only fair that I should deal with them now before going on to other masters; they will help to make this study of the subject more complete, though even so, I cannot hope that it is anywhere near exhaustive. Naturally the Germans are ahead of us in this important department. Not alone are they satisfying a demand created by long and widespread familiarity with the songs themselves—the manifestation of an art which they had made their own decades before we as a musical nation began thinking about it—but they have at hand the right interpreters for the purpose, the singers specially trained in the difficult and superfine art of *lieder* singing. I trust that ere long it will be in our power to say and do as much.

(Where the number only is quoted in this article it will be understood that the record is a Polydor.)

HERMAN KLEIN

SCHUBERT (*supplementary*).

Two things this retrospect has enabled me to perceive: first, that the portions of the Continent now called Central Europe yield many more *lieder* singers of the first rank than we have yet heard in that capacity in England; and, second, that it is quite immaterial to which sex the singer belongs—a particular *lied* is not regarded as the particular property of either. I do not say we have not followed the latter custom to a certain extent, but I have frequently noted the existence of a dividing line where there is no need whatever for it. The question is at least as much one of

vocal suitability. For example, there is no reason why Fritz Soot (62550) should not appropriate *An die Musik* as rightfully as Mme. Gerhardt (already reviewed); only unluckily in this case the tenor is not heard at his best, the voice being rough and the sentiment overdone, while doubtful intonation and a poor piano do the rest. The *Erl-König* again offers another "neutral" theme, though I confess to liking it best in a man's voice; and it would be hard to find a smoother rendering than this of H. Rehkemper's (66006), a high baritone of unusual merit. Besides being dramatic, he displays admirable diction with a tone of pleasing quality, and happily is favoured with a first-rate accompanist. On the reverse side he gives an equally good account of *Orpheus*, one of Schubert's comparatively unknown songs (composed 1816, words by Jacobi), wherein the master-lutenist informs the unwilling Furies how much nicer things are on earth than in the infernal regions. His melody, being nearly as persuasive as that in Gluck's opera, deserves to be as universally familiar as a good record can make it.

Two gems, *Heidenröslein* and *Die Forelle*, are presented both on the same disc, in German by Jenny Jungbauer (62478) and in English by W. F. Watt (Columbia 4220). The combination is rather a coincidence but not unwelcome, for both singers have pretty voices. I vote for the lady's as the better performance. Lovely tone and exquisitely tender feeling are associated with a scratchy record and a metallic pianoforte in Maria Olczewska's beautiful delivery of the *Kreuzzug* (72814). Leo Slezák I have always admired in opera for his intelligence, his romantic feeling, and the dramatic significance of his impersonation. These qualities stand him in good stead as a *Lieder* singer, and in my estimation he now stands as high in the one sphere as in the other, while his popularity is partly evidenced by the extent of his output. For my part I do not want to hear a more perfect or more poetic diction, better phrasing, an apter sense of colourful contrast, clearer rhythm, or greater depth and purity of expression. His Schumann records come later; meanwhile, the attributes just named are abundantly displayed in the wonderful song entitled *Trockene Blumen* (62423), the 18th of the *Schöne Müllerin* cycle. English basses who love *Der Wanderer* will discover an ideal model in Paul Bender's fine example (65575), though few will be able to imitate his rich deep tone, or sing it in the key that he does, taking him down at the end to a splendid low D flat. Rehkemper's *Wohin?* is notable for its neat, clean enunciation, vivacious manner, and an unimpeachable *legato*.

SCHUMANN (*supplementary*).

Der Hidalgo, with its bold *bolero* rhythm, breathes in tuneful melody the Spanish atmosphere of Geibel's poem—a picture of the real old Sevillese life before the builder and the taxi-driver began their nefarious modern crusade. This kind of thing suits F. Soot (*62550) much better than *An die Musik*, and with plenty of *verve* and swing he makes a capital record of it. The same song is done in a lower key by H. Rehkemper (62476), who imparts to it a rather more varied style generally; but both are good. Another difficult choice, which perhaps the question of sex—contralto or tenor— will best decide, lies between the *Mondnacht* of Maria Olczewska (70653) and that of Leo Slezák (65775), who both make the famous little song sound like what it is—a lovely work of art.

The former adds to the value of hers by giving on the other side a superb rendering of the equally famous *Frühlingsnacht*, taking it at terrific speed as though suddenly letting loose the rush of an emotional torrent. There is only one drawback: these records already " date," and they are undeniably scratchy. Less open to criticism on the same account are Leo Slezák's *Der Nussbaum* (*62423) and *Die Lotosblume* (62424), which I have never heard surpassed for sheer delicacy and beauty of treatment. Poetry and music alike stand out in classic relief. Finally, I have listened with approval to yet another German record of *Die beiden Grenadiere* (66007), by the basso, Theodor Scheidl, whose sonorous tones bring the story out with convincing ease and sincerity. His tempo may drag somewhat (a Teutonic fault of the day), but one feels the deep sentiment and, even better, the definite marching step.

BRAHMS.

Johannes Brahms—born at Hamburg in May, 1833, died at Vienna in April, 1897—worthily carried on the line of the great German song-composers in succession to Schubert and Schumann.

Like them, he was a prolific and masterly writer for the voice, an inspired melodist, and the inventor of a thoroughly original style. You cannot mistake the music of Brahms, once you have grown familiar with and learned to love his strongly-marked mannerisms, his delightful harmonies and modulations. He can be, and for the most part is, alternately rugged and tender, ponderous and soulful, dreamily poetic and energetically virile. Whatever the words, they bring out the music which fits them and which expresses precisely the emotion that they " yearn for," as Wagner put it. Very few of his songs have been recorded in this country, but, thanks to the Polydor parcel, I can now proceed to deal briefly with what may be considered on the whole a fairly representative collection of the Brahmsian output.

First, then, *mirabile dictu*, a creditable English record of *An eine Aeolsharfe* (*To an Aeolian harp*, Columbia 3364), by Glanville Davies, a light baritone with a tenor quality. He pours out the stream of gracious melody with freedom and apparent enjoyment. The song belongs to a set of five written in 1862 and marked Op. 19; it is a characteristic early example. Much better known and infinitely lovelier is the *Feldeinsamkeit*, Op. 86, written twenty years later to a poem by Hermann Almers, depicting the sensations of one lying prone and gazing skywards amid the summer heat in a grassy meadow at midday. There are three records of it—by John McCormack (H.M.V. D.A.635), rather *blanche* but sweetly phrased; by Elena Gerhardt (Vocalion A.0216), with a wonderful smoothness and even *sostenuto* revealing the singer at her best; and the other, not so faultless, by Leo Slezák (*Polydor 65775), rather tremulous and lacking in the sense of utter repose, but a model of perfect diction. Of the three, the Gerhardt is the one to have.

Immer leiser wird mein Schlummer is a cry from a death-bed, a despairing appeal for the loved one to come before it is too late, glorified by music of exquisite sadness. Composed in 1889, Op. 105, to lines by Hermann Sing, its pessimistic cry of anguish is truly reflected in a fine record by Maria Olczewska (*Polydor 72814), the tone and effect being absolutely perfect, save for a slight " hooting " on certain vowels in the medium, intensified, maybe, by the recording horn of prehistoric days. The rich low notes are a joy. The accompanist however, hurries the intervening piano passages.

In *Komm bald* we find one of those simple tunes which Brahms apparently took from an old *volkslied* and harmonized after his own inimitable manner. It is, however, entirely original, and peculiar to his later period (1886, Op. 97), while John McCormack (*H.M.V. D.A.635), imparts to it more real charm than to *Feldeinsamkeit*, which is on the same disc. He is better still, though—using a darker, more manly tone—in (H.M.V. D.A.628) the enchanting *Die Mainacht*, Op. 43, which was written to Hölty's poetic lines in 1868. The latter disc also includes the Irish tenor's excellent rendering of *In Waldeinsamkeit*, another long-drawn melody (Op. 85, published in 1882), with a delicious coda about the *Nachtigall*. But singers love *Die Mainacht*, and no wonder Muriel Brunskill (Columbia 977), puts heart and soul into every note of it, an orchestra supporting, though not necessarily improving her effort. Sigrid Onegin (Polydor 72687), a gifted mezzo-contralto with a splendid organ, also sings it with admirable breath-control and deep feeling. She shines to advantage in tearful *lieder*, and one of these, *Nicht mehr zu dir zu gehen* (Polydor 70615), I have to thank her for hearing; it breathes the very spirit of desolation and is an early song, Op. 32, to words by Daumer.

Sandmännchen (*The Sand-Man*), is still earlier, being one of the *Volks-Kinderlieder* composed in 1858 and well known here. It is nicely sung by Constance Willis (Vocalion X.9526) and Vera Devna (Beltona, 6042). Next comes the glorious *Sapphische Ode*, Op. 94, written in 1884 to lines by Hans Schmidt. This gem of poetic melody is recorded by five famous singers, each in a different key, viz., Elena Gerhardt (Vocalion A.0220), Kirkby Lunn (H.M.V., D.A.597), Schumann-Heink (H.M.V., D.A.525), Sigrid Onegin (Polydor 72714), and Frieda Hempel (Polydor 85299). The most satisfying to my ear are the second and third; both admirable in tone-colour, diction and restrained passion. No. 1 is too slow, No. 4 is over-slurred, and No. 5, though very sweet, lacks breadth. The *Ständchen* or *Serenade* (Op. 106, published 1889), is vigorously rendered by Leo Slezák (Polydor 62424); while the more humorous and clever *Vergebliches Ständchen* (1882, Op. 84), a delicious setting of a Lower Rhine folk-song, is warbled with infinite grace and spirit by the diligent Elena Gerhardt (Vocalion B.3115).

Towards the close of his busy life, Brahms composed (April—May, 1896), his *Vier ernste Gesänge*, Op. 121 (*Four Serious Songs*), to biblical texts, " of which three treat of the universality and bitterness of death, only yielding to consolatory thoughts in that death appears as the angel of deliverance from poverty and all affliction." It is not true that they embodied a presentiment of his approaching end; for when showing the MS. to a friend he remarked simply, " This is what I have given myself for my birthday." Anyhow, they are extremely beautiful. Properly speaking, they should be restricted to the bass voice for which they were written; but there is no reason why a contralto should not sing them, and as recorded by Sigrid Onegin (Polydor 72919–20), I must say they are profoundly moving. The gifted artist obtains all the necessary contrasts of colour and feeling so remarkable in these songs, ranging as. they do from deep devotional expression to moments. of sheer dramatic power and quaint outbursts of sober joyousness unlike all the rest. This fine achievement might well be imitated—closely imitated, I mean—by any British basso able and willing to undertake the task of recording the *Serious Songs* in English. The orchestral accompaniments are capably handled.

The magnificent *Von ewiger Liebe* is, I suppose, among the best known of Brahms's *lieder*. I was quite a young man when I heard it sung at the old " Pops " for the first time in this country, and shall never forget the impression it made on me. The poet, Joseph Wenzig, provides a simple picture of a man and a maid comparing notes, as it were, about the significance of " enduring love " as they each understand it. It is just the difference of viewpoint that life has portrayed since the struggle betwixt constancy and " free love " first began. Brahms wrote his masterly setting in 1868 (Op. 43), and the two available records are by Elena Gerhardt (*H.M.V., D.B.848), and Sigrid Onegin (Polydor 72687). I prefer the former for its greater brightness, variety and clarity of dramatic perception. Frequent changes of tempo and tone-colour, together with strongly articulated syllables and effective characterization, combine to make it a genuine piece of interpretation. The recording of voice and accompaniment is excellent.

If I am not mistaken, the popular *Wiegenlied* (1868, Op. 49) was first sung in London by Mme. Albani. Present records of this most soothing of cradle-songs are those of Elsie Francis-Fisher (*Aco. G.15937), which is quite nice; of Ernestine Schumann-Heink (*H.M.V., D.A.525), which glows with maternal warmth; and of Julia Culp (H.M.V., D.A.151), which gently deposits you in the land of dreams. You must take your choice.

Considerations of space compel me to leave over my concluding article on *lieder* until next month.

HERMAN KLEIN.

THE GRAMOPHONE AND THE SINGER

(Continued)

By HERMAN KLEIN

The Singing of Lieder—V.

MY task is nearly done. By far the heaviest part of it was completed when I finished with the records of the three great classical song-writers, Schubert, Schumann, and Brahms. Any further choice does not rest with me ; it must be guided entirely by the nature and extent of the available material. To take up isolated examples by this or that composer, even illustrious masters like Mozart, Beethoven, or Mendelssohn, forms no part of the purpose of these articles. There are certainly in existence excellent records of *Das Veilchen*, of *Adelaïde*, of *Auf Flügeln des Gesanges* ; but these *Lieder* are, after all, only beautiful specimens belonging to the school or schools already dealt with, and their very isolation shows that if we would find what attracts the recorder of *Lieder* and his public in Germany to-day we have to look elsewhere. In other words, I must perforce come at once to the product of the leading moderns, Richard Strauss and Hugo Wolf. If there is space left when I have done with them, I promise that I will utilize it to the best advantage.

RICHARD STRAUSS.

This composer is now in his 63rd year. He wrote his best songs when he was in his thirties, and latterly he has written scarcely any. In this, as in every other branch of composition, he is remarkable for the inequality of his work : now rising to heights so exalted that they almost merit the term " sublime " ; now descending to a level of banality and emptiness incredible in a musician of such genius and resource. With Strauss, somehow, I always feel that I am lucky if I have not grown weary or mentally exhausted long before he has said all that he had to say, especially when he is relying upon the orchestra alone—as in the *Sinfonia Domestica* or the *Alpine Symphony*— for the exposition of his vast crowd of nebulous ideas. But when he is brief he is almost invariably interesting ; while he is simply a master of the art-song form, with the added merit of knowing perfectly how to write for the voice. His piano accompaniments, for the most part terribly difficult and intensely descriptive, are the work of one who is himself a consummate executant, without mercy for those who are not.

Some twenty songs represents the total recorded by the Polydor Company. Of these I have about half, and when the number alone is quoted it belongs to their catalogue. First in alphabetical order stands *Cäcilie*, the second of the fine group, Op. 27, which includes gems like *Morgen*, *Ruhe, meine Seele*, and *Heimliche Aufforderung* (see below). A striking contrast is afforded by two records of *Cäcilie*, each first-rate in its way, viz., by Elena Gerhardt (Vocalion B.3115) replete with movement, passion, and impulse ; and by Lauritz Melchior (66440), who supplies the Wagnerian declamation and phraseology which it demands and so makes a rather big thing of it. The latter is aided by an orchestra, but the former, with pianoforte only, comes nearer to Strauss's intention. Again in the *Freundliche Vision* there occurs similar opportunity for contrast. The man in this case is Josef Schwarz (70598), a baritone with a poetic tone and a quality that seems to lie between a *mezza-voce* and a *falsetto*, which he sustains with just the right effect for this dreamy song. The lady is Tatiana Makushina (Velvet Face 1106), a very intelligent singer with a sympathetic voice and artistic style, whose dreaminess, however, is a shade too measured and metronomic. I admit a preference for Josef Schwarz also in his *Heimliche Aufforderung* (*70598), as compared with Heinrich Schlusnus (70796), whose voice is here very nasal and his enunciation indistinct. This restless song requires more resolution, clearer definition, a more manly tone ; which are precisely the qualities that Schwarz imbues it with in a particularly fine record. The accompaniment stands out well.

Ich liebe dich, words by Detlev von Liliencron, Op. 37, No. 2, is another fiery song, having nothing but its title in common with Grieg's familiar little *chef d'œuvre*. For my own part I think it rather dull, in spite of its vivacity of movement and the almost violent outbursts of the singer, a tenor named Karl Oestvig (70665). A better song by many degrees is *Ich trage meine Minne*, words by Karl Henckell, Op. 32, No. 1 ; and of this you can make a choice between two records—H. Jadlowker (70512) and Leo Slezák (62427). Both are admirable tenors and as regards the singing there is little to choose between the two ; but Jadlowker's is the vastly superior record alike for clearness and purity of tone, and I have no hesitation whatever in recommending it. *Morgen* deserves its popularity, for it is a lovely song. The poem, by John Henry Mackay, is a tender outpouring expressive of hope and peaceful anticipation; not the kind of sob-stuff that some singers put into it, as for example, Ernestine Färber-Strasser (62372), a mezzo-soprano, who always seems to be literally in tears. Like Jadlowker (*70512) and John McCormack (H.M.V. 644), she makes use of an effective violin *obbligato*—suggested by a counter-melody in the piano accompaniment—which in the case of the Irish tenor is played by no less an artist than Kreisler. On the other hand, this adventitious bit of " make-up " is dispensed with by Elena Gerhardt (Vocalion B.3112), who depends solely upon the support of Harold Craxton in a very sweet and touching display of artistry. Jadlowker's is also a splendid record, with clean, manly tone admirably sustained.

Ruhe, meine Seele, which belongs to the same set (Op. 27), is a thoroughly Wagnerian setting, *à la* Erda in *Siegfried*, of lines by Karl Henckell and fascinates one the more because of the obvious source of its inspiration. Hence, too, the fact that it fits that ideal Erda, Maria Olczewska (70651) like a glove—the veil of mystery, the significant phrases, the restrained half-voice unfolding the hidden secrets of her soul—a sort of spiritualistic medium with a glorious contralto voice, badly in need of eternal repose after an unusually trying *séance*. Doubly welcome as a contrast is the delightful *Ständchen*, the best known of all Strauss's songs and, as many opiné, the most original and most spontaneous of the whole collection. There is no need to describe anything so familiar. It is an early effort (Op. 17), but has always sounded to me like a fully-fledged little masterpiece. (Van Schack's spirited lines have been well adapted by Paul England.) Apart from the Polydor records of Claire Dux, Jadlowker, and Leo Slezák, which I have not heard, there are others by Frieda Hempel (85296)—light, airy, joyous—by Elena Gerhardt (Vocalion A.0216)—darker, but full of happiness and charm—and by E. van Endert (19110), which, as an elegant and ecstatic outburst of impatient love, I consider the " pick of the bunch," and one of the most perfect examples of modern recording that has yet come my way.

A fantastic song called *Schlechtes Wetter* (" Bad Weather ") was unknown to me until I heard the record by Heinrich Schlusnus (*70706). It sounds most interesting, with its touches of cynical humour, its sinister vocal effects, and its background of clever descriptive accompaniment, and distinctly adds to the value of the disc. *Traum durch die Dämmerung*, the well-known setting of Otto Bierbaum's words (Op. 29, No. 1), ranks among the most poetic and original of this composer's songs. A record of it by Friedrich Schorr (62379) is quite excellent—full of colour and expression, finely-modulated tone, and no sense of monotony such as one often hears in it. Another by Leila Megane (*H.M.V. E.396) is sung in English, rather indistinctly, it is true, but with pure, fairly steady tone and artistic feeling. I conclude my Strauss review with two tenor examples of that ingenious *lied, Zueignung*. Neither is in the first class, but on the whole I prefer Karl Oestvig's (*70665), despite his open tone, because it is simple, straightforward, and free from tremolo; which is more than can be said for Otto Wolf's (62515), the effect whereof is further spoilt by the orchestral embellishments.

HUGO WOLF.

The understanding of Hugo Wolf is indispensable to a complete appreciation of the latest developments in the domain of the German *lied;* and it is among the chief merits of the gramophone that it can enable the student to attain that understanding with comparative facility. The greatest songwriter—as many hold—since Schubert, near whose grave at Vienna his body lies, Hugo Wolf (born 1860, died 1903) was too much of a genius, too brilliant an exponent of his art, to make the smallest allowance for lack of technique either in the singer or the accompanist. To do him all-round justice is harder, in my estimation, than in the case of either Wagner or Strauss. But the reward is proportionately as great to the performer as is the view of the Alps to the climber who has toiled his weary way to the top of Mont Blanc; and it is the privilege of the gramophonist, through this interpreter, to enjoy the sublime scene as easily and readily as though he had been conveyed to the summit in an elevator or an aeroplane—in fact, far more easily and inexpensively than either. At the present moment the songs of Hugo Wolf are very little known to general concert audiences in this country. They are not much sung by our native vocalists, and as a rule rather badly when they are. I trust it may prove to be the function of the gramophone so to widen the knowledge of these songs, that the demand for them will grow and spread as it is doing for the vocal masterpieces of Schubert, Schumann, and Brahms. The need for brevity must be my excuse for the utter inadequacy of the following criticisms. Most, if not all, of these records deserve close analysis and are distinctly worth having.

First comes a favourite, *Auf dem grünen Balcon* (*H.M.V., D.A.715), exquisitely sung by Elena Gerhardt, the artist who has helped more than anyone else to make it known here. As Ernest Newman (Wolf's biographer and champion) has justly said, this song " is instinct with delicate and fragrant poetry; for sheer loveliness there are few things of his to compare with it." Its subtle inflections are skilfully conveyed by the accomplished singer. A fine baritone monologue is *Biterolf* or *The Crusader's Song*, as it is sometimes called, sung by the home-sick warrior in the Camp of Akkon, 1190. Different as they are in style, there are good points about both the English and the German records—the first by John Thorne (*Aco, G.1598-0), and the second by Friedrich Schorr (*62379); but the latter has more variety of tone and poetic colour. *Er ist's* (or *Song to Spring*) overflows with life and energy. Grete Stückgold (20083), a soprano whom we are to hear this month at Covent Garden, throws plenty of vivacity into it, and the effect, I am bound to say, is enhanced by a sparkling orchestral accompaniment, which sounds more clean-cut than the piano original used by H. Schlusnus (*70705). In either case the song is a joy. The baritone just named is also commendable in *Der Freund* (*70658), and again in *Fussreise* (*70705), where he seems inspired by the wonderful Schubertian swing and rhythm of the " tramp, tramp, tramp." Otto Wolf (62449), on the contrary, loses the rhythm of the tramp and sounds thin and unconvincing in his ditty.

Weyla's Song may be popular in Germany, but, to my thinking, it does not compare with some other settings of the Mörike poems ; besides, the harp arpeggios are not intended to be played by violins. Otto Wolf (*62449) sustains the melody well ; but Grete Stückgold (*20083) is unluckily made to " blast " and sound scratchy. *Heimweh* is one of the most attractive of the *Mörike-lieder* and there are four records of it, viz., by E. van Endert (13982), Julia Culp (70531), F. Windgassen (62498) and O. Wolf (*62515). The awkward modulations are smoothly managed by Julia Culp, whose nostalgia is tenderly expressed, whereas van Endert's is a trifle too sentimental. Both ladies, however, sing better than the men. Heinrich Schlusnus is again to the fore in two superb songs, *Der Musikant* (*70658) and *Der Rattenfänger* (70660) ; the one full of lightness and humour, the other characteristic, rich in graphic touches suggestive of Berlioz, and cleverly orchestrated. I cannot imagine these better interpreted, and no less may be said of Heinrich Rehkemper's (66004) magnificent rendering of the great setting of Goethe's *Prometheus*. The tremendous dramatic power of this music, which recalls so vividly the tirades of Wotan in the *Nibelungen*, is realised in noble declamatory passages that rise again and again to epic grandeur. The record is in two parts and admirably free from flaw. The whole thing makes one want to hear Rehkemper himself. He must be a great Wotan.

A quiet, contemplative song is *Ueber Nacht*, made fairly interesting by F. Windgassen (*62498), who has a broad, manly style. But much better known, of course, is *Verborgenheit* (*Secrecy*), one

of the Mörike-*lieder* and among the most individual. It suggests a world of hidden grief and sorrow, and the voice of Elena Gerhardt (H.M.V., D.A.715) is perhaps a shade on the bright side for it. Nevertheless, she sings it beautifully. *Au contraire*, the contralto tone of Klara Czery (*62527) expresses the grief and misses the sustained beauty of the phrases and the climax. She slurs to excess and pronounces badly. Of another well-known lovely song, *Verschwiegene Liebe*, excellent records are forthcoming from Leo Slezák (62425) and H. Schlusnus (*70660). Both are imbued with intense poetic feeling and rare distinction of style. It is indeed hard to choose between them, but, if compelled to give a verdict, I should pronounce in favour of Schlusnus, on account of his exquisite *mezza voce* effects and the irresistible charm of his phrasing. On the whole, it is the best record I have yet heard by this singer, whose efforts invariably reveal profound sentiment. What a blessing it would be if he could lend a little of his dark timbre to John McCormack ! The rendering by our Irish tenor of *Wo find ich Trost ?* (H.M.V., D.B.766) might then possess real significance in addition to a sweet voice and a fluent method. At the same time it is not one of Wolf's great songs, and perhaps there is little more to be done with it.

I had originally intended to include Franz and Lassen in the purview of these articles, they being representative composers of a certain type of popular art-song which enjoys more or less permanent favour in German musical circles. But after all, I find that they yield little for the edification of gramophonists, and as they are sung even less in this country—much less, certainly, than they were towards the close of the last century—there is nothing to be gained by pursuing my comments further in that direction. As for *Lieder* of the ultra-modern type, I am not sure that any of them are recorded ; and if they are I prefer to leave them to speak for themselves. Meanwhile, I propose to conclude with a few examples by two composers whose vocal works have very properly been thought good enough for reproduction, namely, Franz Liszt and Carl Loewe.

LISZT.

This extraordinarily versatile musician, the most conspicuous link between the classical and the modern schools of composition, did not write a large number of songs ; but some of them were of notable originality and interest, and a good many survive. As one authority has well said, " One may doubt whether Liszt possessed real creative gifts, yet his high culture, his extensive knowledge of literature, and his warm enthusiasm for ideals which make for progress (refusal to be tied by rules, aim after characterisation) have, at any rate, given to his works the stamp of originality." We may perceive these qualities more readily perhaps,

186

in his big works for the orchestra and the piano than his oratorio, *The Legend of St. Elizabeth*, which I heard performed in his presence at St. James's Hall on his last famous visit to London, in 1886. That was distinctly a trying experience. On the other hand, I shall never forget the almost supernatural charm of his playing, to which it was my good fortune to listen on three different occasions—once at Mr. Henry Littleton's house at Sydenham, once at the Royal Academy of Music, and once at the old Grosvenor (now the New) Gallery at the soirée given in his honour by his pupil and champion, Walter Bache.

His best-known song is, I fancy, the dramatic setting of the mediæval *Volkslied*, called *Die Loreley*, which is generally supposed to have been written for a soprano voice. However, as chance will have it, the only record that has come to hand is an H.M.V. (D.1098) made by Tudor Davies, and I am sorry to add that it is not a very good one. The important accompaniment sounds both mechanical and slovenly, while the words give the impression of being a Welsh, not an English, translation. The voice comes out well enough, but wholly without variety of colour or interpretative power. In short, the piece does not really suit the singer. Another of Liszt's favourite *lieder* is *Es muss ein Wunderbares sein*, a love-song with a strain of ravishing melody to which a singer like Leo Slezák (62428), when at his best, knows how to impart the full measure of fascination. He uses the *mezza voce* almost throughout and the smoothness of the tone is astonishing. Less inspired as a composition is *O komm im Traum*, though the voice and art of Josef Schwarz (72537) would almost persuade us to the contrary. You can see by this how much the singer has to do with it, for the same song as rendered by Otto Wolf (62516) would probably bore you to tears. However, this again may be the fault of the voice—a rough, " open " tenor—as much as of the method. I do not like Mr. Wolf's spasmodic, unrefined style any better in the graceful *lied* from the same pen which he has recorded on the reverse side of the same disc.

To be quite candid, Liszt requires first-rate artistry from his vocal no less than his instrumental interpreters. I have always been aware of this, and acquaintance with these few records of his songs has not tended to modify my opinion. Only one more instance : the well-known *Liebestraum* (whether originally composed for the voice or the piano matters not) can be made, by the art of a Paderewski or a Godowsky, to sound just as delicately poetic as an ordinary pianist can make it sound vulgar. But neither the co-operation of a string quartet, nor a solo pianist to throw in the firework cadenzas where they occur in the piano arrangement, suffice to raise the effort of Mario Chamlee (Bruns. 30113B.) to the requisite artistic level. It all sounds poor stuff, really ; very long and extremely tedious—everything bar the text, which escapes criticism for the best of reasons : it never " gets over." An Italian version of the same piece, sung by Tito Schipa (H.M.V., D.B. 873) is more acceptable vocally, and should please those who are familiar with the melody, and prefer a tenor voice to a pianoforte. So much for Liszt.

LOEWE.

The celebrated art ballads of Carl Loewe were written during the first half of the 19th century. It was well on in the second before they began to trickle through into this country, and even now they remain undeservedly neglected by singers, who protest a fanatical admiration for the Tudoresque and the folksong. As descriptive stories in song they are unique. They have a distinct musical value of their own, a character that cannot be mistaken, and even composers like Wagner and Schumann have been influenced by them. The complete collection was published in Germany (in London by Weekes & Co.) in 1891, edited by Albert E. Bach, of Edinburgh, who prefaced the eight volumes with an instructive introduction in both languages. Loewe, who was born in 1796 and died in 1869, was a friend of Goethe, a splendid musician and a widely-cultured man. *Edward* (effectively recorded by Norman Allin, Col. L.1466) and *Archibald Douglas* are the best known of his ballads, but there are others equally fine, if not finer. " The Ballads of all nations inspired him, and scarcely any composer has succeeded like Loewe in representing in tone mysterious, ghostly, eerie, and gloomy subjects." The high esteem in which they are held abroad is shown by the seriousness, the concentration of thought and feeling, with which they are approached by the most distinguished male singers. I remember how they were interpreted years ago by Gura, by Henschel, by David Bispham ; and I am glad to have the present opportunity of praising a few Polydor records as a completion of the task I set myself in the New Year, namely, to interest the readers of THE GRAMOPHONE in the Singing of Lieder.

And the Loewe singers, who are they ? Nothing less than the very pick of to-day's German operatic basket. Most industrious of them all is Theodor Scheidl, a past-master in the art, a truly Protean delineator of every shade of human emotion set forth in these old historical and legendary narratives. He simply fascinates and holds you like some ancient mariner, whether he be hurling at you verse after verse of *Archibald Douglas* (65509—two parts) ; or executing the weirdest runs and ornaments in *Der Nöck* (66142—two parts) ; or trolling a Hungarian-like *volkslied* in *Prinz Eugen, der edle Ritter* (66001). Then Emil Schipper positively makes your blood run cold with *Herr Oluf* (70703—two parts) so characteristically " tuppence-coloured " is it, so repellent in tone and manner, so full of fear and menace and tragedy. I would that I had space to describe it in detail. Atmosphere, indeed! These records positively teem with it. Again another consummate artist, Paul Bender, in *Der Mummelsee* (65575), displays an unsuspected phase of his genius in the quaintest florid ornamentation *à la* Handel, extremely difficult to execute, but all clearly, crisply, elegantly done. Next Leo Slezák, most versatile of modern tenors, in the wonderful setting of *Tom the Rhymer* (*Tom der Reimer*, 62431—two parts), replete with sharp contrasts of full and half-voice, affording a masterly study of vocal colouring in every imaginable dramatic shade. And, finally, two delightful bass records on one disc (66371) by L. Schützendorf, one of the aforesaid *Tom*, and the other of the naïve, melodious ballad known as *Die Uhr*, which in English ought to be entitled *Once round the Clock*.

Dear old warm-hearted Loewe. How pleasant it would be to find his interesting Art-ballads getting popular in our midst! But, as you will have perceived, they are not merely for beginners; and they really take some singing.   HERMAN KLEIN.

✦   ✦   ✦

THE GRAMOPHONE AND THE SINGER
(Continued)
By HERMAN KLEIN
German Opera at Covent Garden

IN accordance with the custom established by the London Opera Syndicate, the early weeks of the summer season at Covent Garden have been devoted to German performances, including two complete cycles of *Der Ring des Nibelungen*. Beyond notice of these, it will be impossible to extend the present article; and even so, my story cannot well be completed without overflowing into the August number, inasmuch as the Italian half of the season will be continuing until too late in June to be wholly dealt with in our following issue.

I take it that the interest of GRAMOPHONE readers in London's too brief annual festival of opera on the " grand scale " is mainly directed to what is done— may I say in the flesh ?—by those eminent foreign artists whose records are reaching us by monthly instalments all the year round. For this reason more particularly I account it a privilege that so many of these eminent ones should come (thanks to lucrative contracts) and be heard here—collected " stars," in well-disposed constellations—even for so short a period as eight consecutive weeks. (Would that it were for longer! I have already suggested that a three months' season can be made to pay quite as well; and, since writing that, I have ascertained that Lt.-Col. Blois is veering round to the same opinion,

in view of the increased subscription and the very big attendances this year.) It is hardly necessary to repeat that these rare continental visitors are extremely expensive. To expect performances of the same class at any " national opera house " carried on in the ordinary way, even with the aid of a State subsidy, would be manifestly absurd. Society and the wealthy patrons of the art, with the humbler lovers of opera to fill the cheaper parts (which they gladly do), constitute the only reliable support for the " grand season " as we are now getting it, thanks to the enterprise of the London Opera Syndicate.

This distinction is not sufficiently borne in mind. You may found a permanent home for opera if you can procure the necessary million or two for the purpose (if, mind!); and you may even fill the house fairly well for ten or eleven months out of the twelve. But, with all that in favour of the institution, it would be impossible to give performances approaching in quality, in all-round perfection of ensemble, those which are now sustained for a couple of months at Covent Garden by the *élite* of the lyric stage. There would be advantages of another kind, of course, and of the two things—permanent national opera or periodical luxurious grand opera—I have little doubt that the former would ultimately prove of greater value to musical art and education in this country. In the meantime, however, we ought to be thankful for what we are getting. It is the best that is to be had; and in opera, as in everything else, the best was never too good for London. It is on a par with the standard that has been maintained here for the last 150 or 200 years. The operas have changed, the the taste has changed, the quality of the vocal performers has changed; but in principle the nature and class of the entertainment remains the same. If prices are double what they were, it is only in proportion to the universal rise in values and the increased terms demanded by artists, orchestra, chorus, stage-carpenters and everyone else engaged in the undertaking. In the operatic, as in every other business, you are obliged to cut your coat according to your cloth.

These and other cognate thoughts crowded into mind as I took my seat on the opening night of the fiftieth season of Royal (or erstwhile Royal Italian) Opera that I have attended at Covent Garden in the capacity of professional critic. The scene alone had undergone no change: the same brilliant picture; the same well-dressed crowd; different personalities, fewer distinguished notabilities, certainly fewer Royalties—that was all. Yes, the same old glorious National Anthem to inaugurate the proceedings at what in by-gone days would have been considered the unearthly hour of 7.15. The very early commencement had been necessitated by the choice of that inordinately long opera, *Der Rosenkavalier*, which, including two 20-minute *entr'actes*, occupies exactly four hours in performance. It should not be more trying on that account than *Tristan* or *Götterdämmerung* or *Les Huguenots;* and yet somehow it seems to be, because the incidents of the final act are unduly spun out and reach a degree of attenuation that leaves the dramatic interest very bare indeed. One grows tired, not of the music, which includes that magnificent trio for the women, but of the Baron Ochs von Lerchenau and all his Falstaffian " goings on."

If not the best performance of *Der Rosenkavalier* that has been heard here, it did not fall far short of it. Certainly the singing could not have been finer, nor the acting of the principal parts. Mme. Lotte Lehmann was an ideal Marschallin, alike as to appearance, manner, and every sort of vocal attribute. Mme. Delia Reinhardt, though she never makes me forget Eva van der Osten, improved upon her Oktavian of a year ago; and Mme. Elisabeth Schumann remained the Sophie of one's dreams. To assert that the Baron Ochs of Richard Mayr was on a level with these embodiments is to pay him the highest possible compliment; he seemed once more to have been " resurrected " bodily from the naughty Vienna of 1750. No wonder this is a costly opera to produce. There are twenty characters, and even the smallest require artists to do them justice; while

certain of the " supers " must have special training for the comic scenes at Faninal's House and the business at the restaurant.

The performances of *Tristan und Isolde* and the first cycle of *The Ring* resembled in detail those of 1926 so closely that it would be equivalent to repetition if I even touched upon them now. Enough that the work done by Frida Leider, Maria Olczewska, Sigrid Onegin, Lauritz Melchior and Friedrich Schorr was worthy of artists whose names have for some time been familiar to readers of these pages. The potency of the Wagner spell shows no signs of diminishing, for the house has been uniformly sold out and the enthusiasm generally up to fever-heat. For my part I venture to doubt whether the existing operatic public will ever grow tired of these all-absorbing music-dramas. At the same time it is worthy of note that German audiences, who certainly do not love them less than we do, always turn from them with pleasurable relief to the purer atmosphere of Mozart. The example for this, as a change after Bayreuth, was set years ago at Munich; and we had the same experience more or less at Covent Garden in the revival on May 4th of *Il Seraglio* (*Die Entführung aus dem Serail*).

I am under the impression that it was the first time the opera had ever been given at this house in German, that is to say, the original text. I remember it there in Italian so far back as 1881, when it was revived for Marcella Sembrich: and also as recently as the winter season of 1922-3, when it was given in English under Eugène Goossens by the B.N.O.C.: but never between these years, save at His Majesty's in 1910 by the Beecham Company. One can enjoy its humour, delicacy and Mozartian lightness of touch best in a small theatre. I candidly confess that I always feel a shiver when I hear the performers suddenly dropping into spoken dialogue at Covent Garden, although I really prefer it elsewhere to the Italian patter of the *recitativo secco*. Either one or the other is, of course, indispensable for the rapid speech of the comic characters and the scenes wherein Osmin, the major-domo (or chief eunuch) of the harem, is so pleasantly fooled. These semi-farcical incidents afford a delightful contrast to the serious side of the story, which concerns the rescue of Constanze, the lovely captive of Selim Pasha, by her faithful adorer Belmont, with the aid of the sprightly pair, Blonda and Pedrillo. Most wonderful of all is the inimitable and well-nigh miraculous art with which the master-hand has fitted music of exactly the right kind to both aspects of the plot. Each in turn holds you under a spell—the Mozart overflowing with light-hearted jollity, and the Mozart expressing tragic emotion through flights of grandeur and *fioriture* for Constanze, as he was afterwards to do for Donna Anna and the Queen of Night.

Only an artist of the first rank can do real justice to this part, and it was rather disappointing to find that

189

Maria Ivogün, who is justly entitled to be considered to the tip-top category, was not in her best form. It was only a passing indisposition, no doubt (she proved that, I was told, when the opera was repeated a few nights later), but sufficient to prevent the clever vocalist from adding brilliancy and truthful intonation to her skilful rendering of the long and difficult aria *Martern aller Arten*. It will be remembered that I have already had occasion to eulogise her fine record of this piece. At Covent Garden the florid passages were beautifully executed, but unluckily the tendency of the artist most of the time was to sing sharp. She was much better, however, in the quartet that concludes the act. On the other hand, the Blonda, Elisabeth Schumann, was throughout up to the level of the best achievements credited to her alike on the stage and on the gramophone. The tone was under perfect control, its quality exquisite, and the spirit of every bar and every scene reflected in singing and acting worthy of the *vraie comédienne*. Her teasing coquetry and skittish fun in the episode with Osmin found a splendid foil in the impersonation of Paul Bender, which was simply ideal. The tenor airs for Belmont were made the most of by Karl Erb, who signalized a promising début; while Wilhelm Gombert no less accurately followed tradition in the lively rôle of Pedrillo.

Both the performances above noticed were conducted by Bruno Walter, a musician and a *chef-d'orchestre* of supreme ability, whose sole weakness is that he is occasionally apt to obscure his beat instead of marking the rhythm with the utmost clearness. It is true that his men understand him, but for perfect orchestral playing it does not do to take too much for granted. The fault, if it can be called one, was more conspicuous in the *Rosenkavalier* than in the vastly less complex score of the *Entführung*, which was interpreted with irreproachable refinement and grace. The other German conductor, Robert Heger, has fully confirmed the favourable impression he created here last year.

It was pleasant to watch the "serried ranks" of a packed house listening, silent and absorbed, to the long performance of *Parsifal*. The scenes of the Flower Maidens' Enchantment and the Good Friday Spell were as beautifully done as any I have ex-perienced since Bayreuth; but elsewhere it was possible to pick holes. Headed by Elisabeth Schumann, the damsels entrusted with the vain task of fascinating Parsifal warbled and glided with exceptional grace and charm, whilst lending all possible effect to the lovely music—the most grateful for the voice in the whole sacred drama. Truth to tell, all the cream of this marvellous score is allotted to the orchestra, concentrating therein the whole essence of the spiritual idea and its dramatic development. For the principal characters there are only rare moments of vocal beauty, such as Wagner furnished in his pre-*Nibelungen* days or even in the tetralogy itself. That Gurnemanz can be an inveterate bore no impartial critic will deny; and I confess that Richard Mayr was unable, with all his art, to prevent a repetition of this impression. In the first act the Ancient Mariner was nothing to him, and for the Good Friday music he had not the sustained power. Lauritz Melchior as Parsifal was also better in the later scenes, but nowhere was he up to the level of many Parsifals I have heard. He was too ponderous, anyhow, for the "pure fool" at his youthful stage. On the other hand, Goete Ljungberg is an almost ideal Kundry. Tall, refined, restrained in feeling, she acts that difficult character admirably, and sings it with much beauty of voice, significance of inflexion, and clearness of diction. I thought her scene with Parsifal in the magic garden greatly improved by her moving about and not remaining the whole time like an invalid on her couch. Her voiceless facial expression and her gentle, deliberate movements in the touching episode where she imitates the Magdalene by washing Parsifal's feet and drying them with her hair—all this was exquisitely done with the utmost reverence and with genuine feeling. The other parts were in safe hands, and the orchestra under Robert Heger achieved better results on the whole than the worthy Knights in their Grail scenes.

The revivals of *Fidelio* and *The Huguenots* I look forward to writing about next month; also the production of *Turandot*, which is expected before the middle of June. Meanwhile, I may say that the financial results of the season so far are exceeding all expectations.

HERMAN KLEIN

THE ROYAL OPERA SEASON

By HERMAN KLEIN

THE " promise of May " held out by the prospectus of the London Opera Syndicate, should warm the hearts of our opera-loving readers—a brand whereof my Editor declares that this journal possesses a large and growing proportion. I trust also that we can direct a quite special appeal to those with large pockets and rich friends in Society, who may have the means for subscribing to the pit-tier boxes at Covent Garden, the disposal of which, as we are assured, will involve either a debit or a credit balance at the end of the season. Personally, I should like to see the whole lot subscribed for, not only for the financial reason, but because the pit-tier was always in the old days, and can be still, the prettiest, the most sociable and ornamental, the most comfortable place for seeing and hearing well, in the whole house. Meanwhile it is good to know that applications for seats are coming in quickly ; also to learn that the results last year showed such a substantial improvement.

The list of artists for the season of eight weeks, which opens on Monday, May 2nd, is already a strong one, and most of them are well known to readers of THE GRAMOPHONE as among the leading record-makers. They comprise (in alphabetical order) *inter alia* the following :—

Sopranos.—Katherine Arkandy, Maria Ivoguen, Maria Jeritza, Lotte Lehmann, Frida Leider, Goete Ljungberg, Delia Reinhardt, Elisabeth Schumann, Lotte Schöne and Helene Wildbrunn.

Mezzo-Sopranos and Contraltos.—Evelyn Arden, Maria Olszewska, and Sigrid Onegin.

Tenors.—Fernand Ansseau, Luigi Cilla, Hans Clemens, Karl Erb, Wilhelm Gombert, Fritz Krauss, Rudolf Laubenthal, Lauritz Melchior, John O'Sullivan, and Aureliano Pertile.

Baritones and Basses.—Paul Bender, Eduard Habich, Alexander Kipnis, Richard Mayr, Dennis Noble, Albert Reiss, Emil Schipper, Friedrich Schorr, and Mariano Stabile.

Conductors.—Vincenzo Bellezza, Robert Heger, Bruno Walter.

Apart from two cycles of the *Ring*, instead of one, the Wagnerian music-dramas will include *Parsifal* and *Tristan*, *Fidelio* will be revived to honour the centenary of Beethoven's death, Mozart's *Seraglio* remounted after a long interval, and *Der Rosenkavalier* again performed. The Italian *répertoire* is to be interesting, comprising as it will *Aïda*, *Otello*, *Rigoletto*, *Il Trovatore* and *Tosca* ; while the only novelty—an important one—will be Puccini's posthumous opera *Turandot*, the first records of which have just reached this country and are reviewed in an adjoining column.

Finally, I take especial pleasure in again drawing attention to the promised revival of *Les Huguenots*. The undeserved neglect of Meyerbeer, which I ventured to stress with emphasis in this journal more than a year ago, is at last to cease, and I am glad to see that this sensible move on the part of Lt.-Col. Blois and his co-directors has been warmly welcomed by Mr. Ernest Newman and other of my more prominent colleagues. The great thing is to mount the opera with first-rate singers and to have it carefully rehearsed, which will no doubt be done. Should a fine performance be the outcome, I have no fear whatever as to the verdict of the real lovers of opera. Their opinion in this matter will follow that of the present-day public in America, France, Germany, Austria—yes, and the Baltic States and Czechoslovakia !

THE GRAMOPHONE AND THE SINGER

(Continued)

By HERMAN KLEIN

The Royal Opera Season

LOOKING back for a moment at the earlier half of the season which has just come to a close, two points occur to me that are worthy of attention. One is the extraordinary hold that German opera still possesses over a certain section of the London public ; the other is the variable merit, according to current criticism, of performances which are costly enough alike to the management and the opera-goer to attain the highest level of perfection. For four solid weeks, bar Saturdays and Sundays, Covent Garden was crammed to repletion by audiences that displayed frenetic enthusiasm whenever the rules permitted them to do so. Apparently the house could have been sold out twice over on a sufficient number of occasions to have justified the addition of at least another fortnight to the German campaign of a month. So far results showed a clear and substantial step in the right direction.

As regards the question of excellence, I am of opinion that such shortcomings as were emphatically stressed in a few leading organs of the Press were due less to the lack of capable artists than the inadequate time for preparation and rehearsal, which is the permanent curse of these annual assemblages of heterogeneous executive elements at our principal opera house. The same artists on their respective " native heaths " would be allotted as many weeks for rehearsing the big works of Wagner and Mozart as they get days here. It is unreasonable, therefore, to expect an equivalent degree of polish from the ensemble, with or without the co-operation of an orchestra which is variable in itself, thanks to the constant abuse of what is known as the " deputy " system. That is precisely the difference between representations of *The Ring*, *Der Rosenkavalier*, *Tristan und Isolde*, etc., as we hear them at Covent Garden and the same works as given with practically identical casts at Bayreuth, Munich, Dresden or Berlin.

Take, for example, the performance of *Fidelio*, Beethoven's great and only opera, which was supposed to shine in the reflected glory of a Centenary observance. I have witnessed so many which were superior to it from almost every point of view that I am not sure whether it is worth while to say anything about it now. But, dealing only with the vocal side, I still feel inclined to ask if it was really impossible to bring over a less ordinary Leonora and Florestan than Hélène Wildbrunn and Fritz Krauss. The soprano, according to " information received," was formerly at Stuttgart, but now " divides her time between the Stadtsoper at Vienna and the Stadtische Oper in Berlin, where Herr Bruno Walter is the conductor " and who conducted the performance to which I am now referring. She owns a good voice certainly, and displays dramatic feeling both in her singing and acting; but she has no real power, no magnetism, no impressive accents of tragedy such as were revealed by the great Fidelios of the past—Tietjens, Lilli Lehmann, Ternina, Thérèse Malten, to name only a few of the illustrious ones I have myself seen. It would not have been fair, of course, to expect genius like theirs; but I was disappointed for all that, because the magnificent climax of the prison scene— one of the grandest moments in the whole range of opera—evoked no sort of thrill beyond that inherent in the drama itself and the noble music which illustrates it. It must be rather a poor Fidelio who cannot " send cold shivers down your back " at that crucial instant when the devoted wife points her revolver at Pizarro's wicked countenance, and the sound of Beethoven's marvellous trumpet-call is heard from beyond the castle walls.

The tenor has difficult music to sing in this opera, I admit, but too frequently does one find it entrusted to artists who are barely equal to the task of getting through it; and I am bound to confess that Herr Fritz Krauss was one of these. I wonder whether an accomplished singer like Léo Slezák has ever thought the part of Florestan good enough for a refined specimen of the *Heldentenor*. If not, why not? The feature of the evening for me was the quartet " in canon " in the opening scene—that sublime yet simple piece of inspired music which always sets my heart off beating " pit-a-pat " with the same suppressed excitement that pervades the feelings of the four singers. Hereabouts I began to discover that Lotte Schöne had a very sweet, charming voice and delightful personality for the part of Marcellina; also that Wilhelm Gombert sang well and did not offend by his persistence as the damsel's lover, Jaquino. On the other hand, the voice of Otto Helgers was not really heavy enough for the bass music of Rocco (shades of Carl Formes and Foli!), while Gotthold Ditter merely achieved the conventional shouting in the outbursts of that angry gentleman, Don Pizarro. The German chorus was competent; the English orchestra up to the average, but no more. Bruno Walter is an admirable conductor, but he cannot work miracles in the time at his disposal; and that limitation, I fear, is nobody's fault in particular.

THE " HUGUENOTS " REVIVAL.

Meyerbeer still has his enemies, and they are mostly of the implacable sort. I did not expect them to respond very gracefully, if at all, to the movement that was initiated in THE GRAMOPHONE so long ago as September, 1925, with my articles on " The Treasures of Meyerbeer." Nevertheless, their attitude, whether negative or positive, could not prevent the ultimate working of the leaven. The good that men do lives longer after them than the evil. The unfair, because untruthful, attacks of Wagner on the brother composer who had striven to help him began to be seen through at last; and, although the libel had had a start of fifty years, its influence was too false to endure for ever. Last year some of the leading musical writers began openly expressing the opinion, confirmatory of my own, that Meyerbeer ought now to be given another trial in this country. The result was the reappearance of *The Huguenots* in the current Covent Garden prospectus after an absence of 15 years, and in due course its revival before a curious and expectant audience, which included the King and Queen, on May 30th, the opening night of the Italian half of the season. Owing to this latter circumstance, and also to the fact that the cast was almost entirely from the fair land of Italy, the opera was given under its once-familiar but not very euphonious title of *Gli Ugonotti*.

The Fates, however, were not kind. As things turned out, the test was not made under satisfactory conditions. It will be remembered that in my articles I alluded more than once to the executive obstacles with which Meyerbeer's music bristles; the command of the important traditions that are a *sine quâ non* for its proper rendering; the need for many stage and orchestral rehearsals (in Paris and Berlin they used to devote at least six months to putting on a Meyerbeer opera); and finally, the presence and control of a conductor possessing all the experience and sympathy necessary for his task. To anticipate a full realization of all these essentials would, of course, have been to indulge in Utopian fatuity. I was not quite sanguine enough for that, knowing as I do the difficulties under which luxurious grand opera labours in our midst. But, doubts notwithstanding, I had ventured to hope for a better performance than this. I will be perfectly frank about it. It was almost from first to last a grievous disappointment; and perhaps its most serious shortcoming was its consistent dullness, its lack of verve, spirit and inspiration. Where it should have been ruthlessly cut—as, for instance, in the first Act, which is always considerably shortened —a great deal too much was left in. On the other hand, in the second Act, beneath the Castle of Chenonceaux, the chorus, with dance of *baigneuses*, was omitted, together with the trio for the Queen, the Page and the Dama d'Onore, and also a large part of the finale. The third Act was somewhat livelier and more coherent; but even there inadequate stage management made certain incidents appear ridiculous. Alas for the value of youthful present-day criticism! One or two of the notices that I read in our sensational evening papers made poor Meyerbeer responsible for all these and other *lâches*, complaining *inter alia* that the operatic treatment of such a big historical subject was beyond his powers (*sic*). One of these gentlemen, indeed, went so far as to declare that my friend, Dr. Vaughan Williams (who was there as the guest of another critic, by the way), would have been able—witness, *Hugh the Drover!*—to make a far better job of it. Well, well!

As regards the purely vocal side of the representation, the plain truth is that only two members of the long cast actually rose to the level of the occasion— one a German artist, one an Italian. I will not say that Alexander Kipnis (whose splendid record of Wotan's *Abschied* I reviewed last month) has quite the deep *basso profondo* notes for a perfect Marcello; but he sang the *Piff, paff* air with immense vigour and character, while the richness of his voice told with fine effect in the *Pré aux Clercs* duet with Valentina. He also looked his part well, as did that other fine singer, Mariano Stabile, in the rôle of de Nevers, to which only a baritone of high class can impart the requisite distinction. It enabled Signor Stabile to show how remarkably versatile he is, for an embodiment further removed in character from either Falstaff or Iago it would be hard to imagine. He sang admirably and acted the noble-minded Count to the life.

The earliest (and also latest) of the evening's disappointments was the Raoul di Nangis of John O'Sullivan. His records had prepared me for a tremolo, but not for a tone so thin and unsympathetic in all but the highest register. His high B flat and C are vibrant, clear, ringing notes, and yet the " bridge " leading from the medium to the head is distinctly dull. Perhaps nervousness interfered with his rendering of the *Romanza* in the first Act, because he sang so much better in the duel septet and the final duet with Valentina; but he is a poor actor, anyhow, and in the scene with the Queen his comedy was as lifeless as his singing. The ladies were also palpably nervous on making their débuts. Bianca Scacciati proved an efficient Valentina but not a great one; dramatic but lacking in charm; a clever singer whose organ will not stand the slightest forcing. In the duet with Marcello she omitted the high C with the descending scale. As Urbano, Albertina dal Monte betrayed a throaty production, and I found nothing to admire in either of the Page's songs. Anna Maria Guglielmetti did tolerable justice to the music of Marguerite de Valois in a technical sense, but without the added value of distinction or finish; while Fernando Autori put fitting energy into the rôle of San Bris. To Bellezza's conducting I have already referred, and about the general performance there is no need to say more.

" AIDA."

After Meyerbeer, Verdi once more. The choice of operas for a season like this, as I have often observed, is largely dictated by the presence or calibre, or both, of the available artists. Wagner, of course, requires his own particular interpreters; and the great German singers who can do him justice can generally do justice to Verdi as well, though it is far from being the same thing the other way about. Thus, when the Teutonic portion of the season had reached its close, quite a number of its protagonists remained here for a few days to help to carry on the labours of Part II. (I could not help wishing that there had been more of them in *The Huguenots*, but—enough said.) I did not hear *Rigoletto* at all, though reliable opinion would have it that Maria Ivogün was still out of form and out of tune, too, pretty frequently. The non-appearance of Formichi was strange but not altogether surprising. It was also disappointing for a good many people who love a huge voice in a Rigoletto, and who cannot perceive that Mariano Stabile is a fine interpreter of other rôles besides Falstaff. Some found nice things to say about both the Dukes, Dino Borgioli and Tom Burke, especially the latter, who is probably a much better vocalist to-day than he was when he made his rather sensational début with Melba in 1919 as Rodolfo in *La Bohème*. The new Italian conductor, Fornarini by name, made a highly favourable impression; but he was not entrusted with *Aïda*. The rendering of this masterpiece made amends for a good many shortcomings. It was the finest we have had at Covent Garden in recent years. What is also of importance to my readers as well as myself, it served to confirm opinions already expressed in these columns concerning three or four prominent singers of gramophone records whom I had never listened to through any other medium. First and foremost, Sigrid Onégin. In voice, in dramatic instinct, in physique and personal charm, she is all and more than I pictured her; while her attractive qualities made one marvel even more than usual at Radamès's strange taste in preferring Aïda to such an Amneris. The slight blemishes of style noticeable in her records disappeared altogether on the stage. The critical verdict concerning the Swedish mezzo-contralto was unanimous. She left all the slurring tendencies to Grete Stückgold, who indulged them with much generosity whilst presenting an Aïda of considerable originality—a veritable " child of the desert " in a constant state of fright, a primitive creature with startled eyes and hair permanently on end. She used her sympathetic voice artistically, but without any notable power. This last quality was, however, sufficiently demonstrated by Sigrid Onégin and Aureliano Pertile, who made Covent Garden ring with the same gigantic tone-vibration that one hears in their records. The new tenor also justified his reputation as a genuine *robusto* with a pleasing, unforced tone and broad, manly style. I admired his acting less, but altogether he stands far above the current Italian level. Emil Schipper shared with Pertile and Grete Stückgold the honours of the Nile scene; he was a picturesque and forceful Amonasro. Alexander Kipnis also gained distinction as the High Priest. I will not say that he approached Edouard de Reszke in this part any more nearly than as Marcel; but he certainly has a splendid organ, and I endorse every word I wrote about his singing in his record of Wotan's *Abschied*. Bellezza, conducting finely throughout, made the *ensemble* of the second Act a tremendous thing; and the dancing of Karsavina in the ballet of that scene was a gem of Egyptian posturing and quaint Eastern grace. Altogether, then, a very memorable *Aïda*.

THE PRODUCTION OF " TURANDOT."

There were three performances of Puccini's post-humous opera; and I was present at the second, on June 13th. That was one more than poor Maria Jeritza was able to attend; for, as ill-fortune would have it, she was not well enough to fulfil her engagement to come to London. She was to be replaced by the Turandot of the first performance at Rome, Bianca Scacciati, whom I had expected to share these performances with Jeritza. But at the second we had, quite unexpectedly, a soprano with a finer voice than either of these in the person of Florence Easton, an Englishwoman who—married to the American tenor, Francis Maclennan—has lately been working her way

up to the top of the tree at the Metropolitan Opera House, New York. Her success in the new opera amounted to a positive triumph. A striking figure in her gorgeous Chinese robes, she enacted the repellent Turandot with power, and skilfully portrayed the nuances of the gradual change that love effects in the nature of that unnatural princess. Above all, she displayed a far finer voice and more resourceful art than those of the Florence Easton whom I heard in *Butterfly*, both in New York and at Covent Garden, nearly 20 years ago. How she now holds her own with the giants of the Metropolitan it is easy to understand. I especially admired her beautiful high notes.

Turandot is in some respects Puccini's finest work. I would say the very finest if the libretto enfolded fewer horrors and if the composer's pen had not " dropped from his hand," as Toscanini put it, before the completion of the final duet, which I find tiresome as shaped by Signor Alfani. But the stage tableaux are magnificent and some of the ensembles very striking, while the clever music allotted to the three ministerial worthies, Ping, Pang, and Pong, afford alike relief, amusement, and subject for admiration. These were splendidly acted and sung by Ernesto Badini, Luigi Cilla, and Giuseppe Nessi. As the Unknown Prince, the tenor Francesco Merli even improved upon his record singing of this music. He gave a capital rendering of the soliloquy *Nessun dorma* in the third Act, and sang well also in the scenes with the unhappy slave-girl Liù, who had a sympathetic delineator in Lotte Schöne. Altogether *Turandot* was adequately cast, lavishly mounted, and worthily performed under the able direction of Vincenzo Bellezza; and whenever it can be equally well given the opera will be sure of a no less enthusiastic welcome. The production, which owed much to the picturesque lighting and stage management devised by Mr. Charles Moor, was a big feather in the cap of the London Opera Syndicate—by far the biggest they have yet earned.

" IL TROVATORE."

Early Verdi has come into fashion again, and so much the better for all concerned. Until June 14th the once hackneyed and despised *Trovatore* had not been sung in Italian at Covent Garden since 1905, on which occasion Riccardo Stracciari made his début as the wicked Conte di Luna. I had not heard it there myself (being in New York) since ten years before that—Augustus Harris's last season but one; so no wonder it came almost as a novelty to contemporary opera-goers. The present revival owed its excellence to careful all-round preparation and the exceptionally good interpretation of the three leading characters by Frida Leider, Maria Olczewska, anod Aureliano Pertile, who used their fine voices with irresistible effect in the music of Leonora, Azucena, and Manrico. The Count of Armando Borgioli stood upon a somewhat lower plane. He has a good telling baritone, with great power in the middle register, but sings without much control or command of colour and refinement. Pertile is by a long way the best Manrico I have heard since Tamagno, and perhaps the best Italian tenor that has sung here since Caruso. He may be less " electrifying " in *Di quella pira* than either of those departed stars, but I think neither of them could have phrased *Ah si, ben mio* with more intelligence, grace, and charm. It is a real pleasure to listen to him. The Ferrando (not Fernando, as they spelt it in the programme) of Autori was un-

usually dramatic, and the Ruiz (Cilla) and Inez (Kathlyn Hilliard) were also worthy of a strong cast. A gratifying feature revealed itself in the work of the chorus. Instead of shouting everything in the customary manner, they positively sang *p* and *pp* where they had to, and thus produced some delicate effects that invested the choral writing of Verdi's first " manner " with an entirely novel character. For this and the crisp, spirited playing of the " big guitar " accompaniments Vincenzo Bellezza deserved all praise. It was quite a delightful evening.

HERMAN KLEIN.

❦ ❦ ❦

THE GRAMOPHONE AND THE SINGER

(Continued)

By HERMAN KLEIN

Problems and Prospects of Opera

I AM thankful to the Editor of THE GRAMOPHONE for allowing me to exercise the privileges of a " free lance." This enables me to escape now and then from the thrall of the recording siren and take up for discussion cognate subjects like Opera, in which I feel somehow that the average reader of these pages is almost as deeply interested. I bear in mind the fact that much space has already been devoted thereto. I am aware that opera generally has been more discussed in the public press of late than it ever was in its history. But the last word has not been said; nor is it likely to be so long as we remain *in statu quo* and make no real advance towards the goal which well-meaning mentors who can talk much but do little else kindly continue to point out for us.

The goal itself is, or ought to be, easy enough to perceive. What we are wanting, as it seems to me, is a new opera-house with about twice the holding capacity of Covent Garden, in a central part of the metropolis, and attached to it a strong all-round company to perform opera—light as well as serious—during the greater part of the year. When it is not performing in London this company should be touring in the provinces and making money, as it assuredly would, in the dozen principal towns of the Kingdom where they do not support a permanent opera troupe of their own. Such a plan is practically the one that was projected by the late Carl Rosa some forty years ago, when ill-health and death stepped in and prevented its fulfilment. It stands equally good for to-day, because in the main conditions have not changed, except that we are now even worse off for

opera of the right sort than we were in those days. Stay!—I forgot; there is one thing more we had then which we do not possess now, and that is—the right man to organize, govern, and administer the whole enterprise upon truly national lines.

For of course it has to be a national undertaking, in the sense that the people of this country, the legitimately musical population of the British Isles, shall look upon it as their own and take a pride in its welfare accordingly. That this kind of pride is not easy to arouse I am perfectly aware. It involves outlay in the form of subscriptions and capital, and the experiences of the past year or so do not encourage a belief that the requisite " million," or whatever the wherewithal be assessed at, will be secured by preliminary meetings and public appeals. I do not pretend to foreshadow the financial jugglery whereby National Opera will ultimately be set going and kept going until it is solidly established; but that it can and must be accomplished somehow there can be no question. Maybe—who knows?—the occult scheme of Sir Thomas Beecham is destined to succeed where the somewhat naïve and too sanguine proposals of Mr. Isidore de Lara were doomed to failure. A definite opinion on this point cannot be expressed until the former is fully disclosed, and at the moment of writing it is not. I wish it were. It is not good policy, in my opinion, to keep the public on tenterhooks too long in a matter of this sort. Curiosity quickly dies out, and people get tired of hearing about operatic projects that are to achieve wonders, yet never arrive within hailing distance of a start.

At the present moment there appears to be serious danger of our falling between the two stools—that is, between cheap good opera, as exemplified in the great Continental cities of Europe (which is primarily what we are in need of), and expensive luxurious opera upon the grand scale, as exemplified during eight hectic weeks of the year at Covent Garden. The product of the London Opera Syndicate may be very fine, but when all is said and done it can benefit only the few. It is opera for the " classes," not for the masses. Nearly every night of the recent season all the expensive seats were sold; not a reserved seat was to be had at the box office for the amphitheatre, stalls or dress circle, unless purchased days beforehand or else at a heavy premium at the libraries; the gallery was invariably packed. In the aggregate some thousands of opera-lovers were turned away hungry and unsatisfied because the house would not accommodate them. And, in spite of all this evident yearning for well-performed opera generally and German opera in particular, we are told that it may not be worth while to go on because the business entails risk, because the expenses are so terribly heavy and are barely covered by the receipts, or may even result in a loss for the Syndicate.

But who expects to make opera pay? Read the autobiographies of the Great Impresarios (such as there are) and judge for yourself whether operatic management is one of those favoured occupations, like building cheap motor cars or running cinema combines, which, if adroitly " taken at the flood, lead on to fortune." It is quite certain that, *au fond*, our Beechams and our Courtaulds, who genuinely love good opera, do not dabble in it with any idea of profit; neither, on the other hand, ought they to complain when the balance is on the wrong side. I always think in this connection of something that was said to me by the late Sir Joseph Beecham (father of Sir Thomas) during his first season of Russian opera at Drury Lane. It is a true story and has never yet been put into print. We were chatting in the dress circle corridor during one of the performances—I think it was of *Boris Godounov*, with Chaliapin in the title-rôle.

" A horribly expensive business," I remarked, " giving opera on such a scale as this, with no subscription to back you! "

" Yes," said Sir Joseph. " The money goes out a good deal faster than it comes in."

" You don't seem to worry much about the losses," said I.

" No," said Sir Joseph, whom I knew to be a millionaire. Then a pause before I framed another sentence:

" Are you very fond of opera, Sir Joseph? "

" I am," was the reply.

" Fond enough to be doing this? "

" I don't know." Another pause, and then the truth came out: " You see, I regard it as a splendid advertising medium. It helps to keep the name before the public, both on the hoardings and in the papers." We smiled and parted.

That was some fifteen years ago, and since then much water has flowed under the bridges. But opera has become a dearer instead of a cheaper luxury. For one thing, the Syndicates, labouring under the disadvantages that a costly, unremunerative theatre like Covent Garden imposes upon its lessees, have found it impossible to give opera under economical conditions. Their public refuses to put up with any but expensive foreign artists and conductors. It will only subscribe in advance for what it considers to be the best talent, regardless of the utter impracticability of attaining equal merit in the performances themselves, owing to the inadequate allowance of time for rehearsing. In a word, the public which supports Covent Garden is utterly spoilt for eight weeks in May and June, and during the remainder of the year it is content to have nothing. As for opera sung in English, it will tell you plainly that it does not want it at any price, no matter how first-rate the quality. All of which points to a very unsatisfactory state of affairs.

But is the operatic history of this country—a history not lacking in its glories and triumphs—to end here? Surely not. There must be a remedy of some sort against a *débâcle* that would mean disgrace in the eyes of all the neighbouring nations, to whom opera is part of their daily artistic life.

May I humbly suggest that the first step to be taken in the direction of that remedy should be to interest London in the idea of a new opera-house? We must have that to begin with. If the money can be found for cinemas and greyhound race-courses, on the supposition that they will pay in the long run, assuredly there must be capital available for erecting a simple large building on some accessible spot, say after the design of the Volkstheater in Vienna, and where the experiment of performing opera on attractive but economical lines could be fully put to the test. That there is nothing novel in this proposition I am fully aware. It sounds like the Isidore de Lara scheme over again; it may even be the root-idea of the long-delayed new Beecham scheme for which, as I write, the world is still patiently waiting. But the resemblance cannot be helped, for the reason that the essential preliminary to any great metropolitan plan for opera must be the provision of a new home for it. Isidore de Lara was right when he talked of an auditorium to hold 5,000 people at reasonably low prices (I would put them at 7s. 6d. down to 1s. 6d.); but he was unpractical when he talked about a capital of a million to be subscribed by the public in single pound shares.

The public—by which I mean the whole community—must be interested somehow in the scheme, of course; but the money for the building, which ought not to exceed £100,000, must come from five or six rich men, ready and willing to found a great musical institution as they would be to endow a new college for a university or a new church for their native city. There must be no debt or encumbrance of any sort on the new opera-house. It must belong to London, and the opera-lovers of London must meet the cost of its upkeep, which they will effect by the simple act of filling it every time there is a good performance. And there should never be any *bad* performances. Somehow I fancy it will be found that Sir Thomas Beecham's idea, when it emerges from his resourceful brain, will be found to include a plan for making the public part-shareholders in the undertaking. But has not the B.N.O.C. tried something of that kind already, and without success? Well, *nous verrons*.

POLYGLOT OPERA.

The experiences of the past season at Covent Garden were not such as to recommend either in the near or distant future the employment of mixed nationalities for the casts of popular operas. I say this in relation to the Italian or French, not the German representations. The term " polyglot opera " came into use during the régime of the late Sir Augustus Harris; but it did not, as is often supposed, imply the singing of more than one language in the same work, such as is occasionally heard abroad when " guest " celebrities appear who are not familiar with the language of the country. It meant simply that operas were being sung in the texts to which they had been originally composed. This wholly artistic proceeding was accompanied, in Harris's time, by an especial degree of care to secure the correct pronunciation of the particular language, whatever it might be. I do not say that exceptions to the rule did not occur; but they were extremely rare, particularly in the French répertoire, which was then much larger than it is to-day. The American prima donnas might worry us now and then, though not more than a certain Australian *diva* who shall be nameless; while the incomparable brothers Jean and Edouard de Reszke, whose French was like that of born Frenchmen, did not escape criticism when they declaimed Wagner in German with a soft Slavonic accent.

I cannot, however, call to mind a single polyglot example or an instance of mixed nationalities from out of those bygone days when the consequences were so disastrous as in the recent Covent Garden revivals of *Les Huguenots* and *Carmen*. The number of square pegs in round holes on those two occasions was simply astonishing. Concerning Meyerbeer's opera, I have

personally nothing more to say; I only hope that the youthful critics who are still belabouring a vulnerable libretto may all live long enough to hear the music adequately interpreted. But the *Carmen* performance —as yet unnoticed in these columns—was on the whole let off a great deal too lightly; albeit I admit that in certain quarters certain features thereof did receive the verbal castigation that they merited. Some of the shortcomings were due to insufficient rehearsal, which our present system unfortunately renders inevitable, and which in a permanent operatic establishment can always be prevented. To my ears, though, an even worse shock was the French accent of the German singers. It was the living verification of a defect that I have frequently had occasion to point out in their records of French operatic pieces.

Maria Olczewska, a great artist in the parts that fit her, proved an almost wholly disappointing Carmen. The music did not suit her rich, heavy voice and noble style; nor did the Spanish character seem to strike a sympathetic chord in her direct, un-subtle, even if coquettish and temperamental, nature. For a Pole her French accent ought to have been more free from the solecisms which one expects in the case of the Teutonic singer, whereof the charming Delia Reinhardt—the joyous Ocktavian and the irresponsible Cherubino of our dreams—gave such a coruscating display in the music of Micaela. The constant substitution of the closed *é* or *et* for the broad *è* or the still more open *ai* was positively exasperating, and it was not less so when done *vice versa*. Besides, there should be a simple spiritual appeal in Micaela's wellknown air, *Je dis que rien ne m'épouvante*, and this the fair Delia seemed to miss altogether in her search for a dramatic rendering. The smugglers' ensembles could have been sung much more crisply, with greater polish and *entrain;* and I agree with the critic who pointed out the sin of omission committed by Vincenzo Bellezza in leaving out the three women's repetitions of the word " l'amour " at the end of the *Toreador's Song*.

But let me close on a note of praise. Both Fernand Ansseau (Don José) and Marcel Journet (Escamillo) justified their high reputations, won alike on the operatic stage and the gramophone. I reckon Ansseau to be the finest French tenor of the day, and only wish that others could successfully imitate the steadiness and virility of his magnificent tone. The veteran Journet, whose début at Covent Garden I witnessed thirty years ago, is as sturdy and reliable now as he was then.

HERMAN KLEIN.

197

THE GRAMOPHONE AND THE SINGER

(Continued)

Modern English Songs—I.

By HERMAN KLEIN

WHEN I was asked a short time ago to deal with existing records of our best "art songs," upon the same lines as in my articles on German *Lieder*, my thoughts naturally turned at once to the collection of *Fifty Modern English Songs* published a few years ago by Boosey and Co. for the Society of English Singers. I said to myself, "Here is a recent selection from the songs of the best British contemporary composers, chosen by a body of experts and brought out at the reasonable price of 7s. 6d. net. It is, what it claims to be, a representative set of songs, guaranteed as intrinsically good, and there is no fee or licence of any sort attaching to their public performance (beyond, I suppose, the customary demands of the Performing Rights Society). Surely, then, I shall find that by this time most of these songs have been recorded and have assumed their proper place in the catalogues of the gramophone companies." But I appear to have been utterly mistaken. My Editor tells me that only one or two—certainly not half a dozen—out of the fifty ve as yet been honoured in the fashion that I had ken for granted. So much for the backing-up that the Society of English Singers and Messrs. Boosey have received from the British vocalists who sing for gramophone! The question is, Who are wrong—the experts who selected the songs or the artists who might have been expected to sing them?

In any case I am driven to the conclusion that I was obliged to form with regard to the *Lieder*, namely, that these "art-songs" are still too good for the buying or spending musical public of this country. The demand is not yet widespread enough for them to be worth an extensive investment on the part of the gramophone houses. Where money-making is the primary consideration, I fear that the subtly-harmonized but essentially commonplace modern ballad still holds sway. Delighted that the Promenade Concerts had been rescued from perdition and carried on by the B.B.C., I carefully scrutinized the prospectus for the season which began at Queen's Hall on August 13th, only to find that the vocal selections were as incomplete as usual, and consisted chiefly of the operatic arias that grace the first part of the programme. Whether the items in the second part were to be of better class than heretofore I was

unable to discover. I sincerely hope that they were. Meanwhile, it was only too evident that modern "art-songs," if sung by the vocalists engaged for the Promenade Concerts, were not regarded as a draw, or as calculated to induce amateurs to subscribe for season tickets on the strength of an attractive prospectus. Sir Henry Wood is an adept in constructing orchestral schemes as well as conducting them. He is less interested, I fear, in the vocal side of things, unless it be where their preparation is concerned, and there probably he can be induced to take a good deal of personal trouble. The real question at issue is, Who are to be considered responsible for the quality of the British songs that we hear at the Proms—the B.B.C., Messrs. Chappell and Co., or Sir Henry Wood?

The history of the English "art-song," as distinguished from the now-despised ballad, goes back about 40 years, not more. It started with the efforts of Frederic Cowen, Villiers Stanford, Hubert Parry, Goring Thomas, Arthur Somervell, Maude V. White, and one or two others, to reflect more closely in their music the emotional or dramatic content of the poem. I recall especially the first books of songs or "lyrics" put forward by Cowen, Parry, and Goring Thomas, also the song-cycle *Maud* by Somervell, not to mention Stanford's Irish songs. All of these are still happily in demand to-day in virtue of their refined melodic charm, and because their beauty is of a type that does not easily fade or tire, thanks to its unity of expression with words that live likewise. Their appeal is irresistible because, as with that of the *Lied*, it is a double one, poetic and musical, complete and satisfying. In fact, they were in many respects superior to the more elaborate, dissonantic product of certain present-day writers, with their *cherché* cleverness of harmonization, their eternal "suspensions," and their unvocal vocal line.

Among these last I am not, assuredly, meaning to classify the recorded specimens of modern English songs that I am about to place before the reader's notice. Nor do I for a moment pretend to making more than a limited selection from the vast total of songs of one kind and another that are to be found in the gramophone catalogues. I cannot, either, say exactly when they were recorded, though only a small proportion, I fear, are recent enough to have been done by the new electrical process. I shall merely endeavour to write about the pick of them *per se*, with apologies in advance if any song that I may occasionally suggest as too good to be omitted from the lists should turn out to have been included in them somewhere already.

Taking them as far as I can in the alphabetical order of the composers' names, I begin with Granville Bantock, one of our most thoughtful, individual, and resourceful musicians, who has been Professor of Music in the Birmingham University since 1908. His marked *penchant* for Eastern subjects has been indicated alike in operas, cantatas, and shorter vocal pieces; while his command of rich harmonic colouring and rhythmical idiom has enabled him to give full effect to the themes of his chosen fancy. These qualities are conspicuous in two of the " Songs of Egypt," well recorded by Leila Megane (H.M.V. D.973, 12 in.), and called respectively *Invocation to the Nile* and *Lament of Isis*, filling one side of a 12 in. disc with *Amour, viens aider* on the other. There is haunting melody in both songs, and Miss Megane's sympathetic mezzo-soprano sounds steadier in them than usual. The orchestral accompaniment enhances the effect—as one can tell by a comparison with the piano version of the *Lament of Isis* used by Clara Serena (Vocalion K.05252). Here the voice starts on a " hoot," but settles down quickly to a pleasanter timbre, and then delivers the lament with an abundance of rich tone and appropriate mournfulness. But it needs the orchestra, whereof Prof. Bantock is an acknowledged master. (There are, of course, other records of this composer's songs, as indeed there are of most of those whose names will now follow. But at the moment of writing, the work of collecting all the available material is not nearly complete. I may, therefore, be compelled sooner or later to return and begin a second alphabetical list in order to include the items that may now have to be missed. The more I delve into the past of English song-records the more I perceive the magnitude of the task that I have undertaken. But never mind; there is no hurry, and I am told to take over this job all the time that its importance warrants.)

Arnold Bax has shown greater industry, perhaps, in the direction of song-arranging than of song-writing, and his piano accompaniments, despite their exotic flavour of atonality, are always characteristic and interesting. His peculiar methods of treatment are aptly exemplified in the *Three Irish Songs* (H.M.V. E.410, 10 in.) sung by Anne Thursfield. They exhale a curious sweetness, particularly the *Cradle Song*, which is now better known in another setting—Herbert Hughes's *Men from the Fields*. Mrs. Thursfield is an artist of infinite taste, and if these old songs are worth hearing at all, it is as much as anything for the delicacy and refinement of feeling and vocal charm that she puts into them.

In Frank Bridge we boast one of the most versatile of living musicians; one of the most modest and most capable; one who excels in every branch of his art that he chooses to handle, and not least of all that of the song-writer. His style is modern without being aggressively so, and pleasurable because it connotes a constant eye to beauty. It is paying him a high compliment to declare that his songs are on a level with his chamber compositions. Conspicuous among them is *Love went a-riding*, a strain of joyous, triumphant melody with a piano accompaniment that requires skill—one representing the " Love " and the other the " Riding." The former is expressed by Tudor Davies (H.M.V. E.414*, 10 in.) with a vigour that would be more convincing if more evenly sustained, and I fancy that the new recording would also do his voice better justice. A record of *Love went a-riding* (Col. L.1825, 12 in.) by the late Gervase Elwes is notable for the beauty of the voice and the refined elegance of the whole rendering. It is taken rather too slowly and lacks joy, but as a fine piece of singing and model diction it could not be beaten. On the other hand, the feminine version of Ethel Kemish (Beltona 787, 10 in.) not only has the requisite life and go, but the tone and words are unusually clear, and the piano comes out well. The same happy conjunction distinguishes Carmen Hill's rendering of *O that it were so* (H.M.V. E.370, 10 in.), a song which I should enjoy even more than I do if the musical accent fell on the penultimate instead of the last syllable of the title; it should not be on the adverb but the verb. I care less for *Isobel*, as sung by Leila Megane (H.M.V. E.361, 10 in.); first, because the song itself is more ordinary, and secondly, because the words in this record are indistinct. Another of Frank Bridge's, *Go not, happy day* (Vocalion, X.9195, 10 in.) is quite in a Schubertian vein, with an *arpeggiando* accompaniment that persists throughout. The tune is simple and pretty, and Frank Titterton sings it neatly; but the high note at the end is superfluous.

By the way, the question of hearing the words, which brought a challenge for my opinion last month in a long letter from the Rev. W. Arthur B. Clementson, Keremeos, British Columbia, presents exactly the same difficulties through the medium of the gramophone as it does when one is listening to a singer in the theatre or the concert room. The intervention of the mechanical process makes the problem neither better nor worse. When the vowel-formation is true and unmistakable; when the union of the tone and the syllable is effected by one correct, spontaneous action, as in natural speech; when the enunciation of all consonants is clear, definite, and incisive—then I think one ought to make out every word of the poem (without the aid of the printed page) with the same ease that one can grasp the pitch and quality of the notes to which the voice is uttering them.

199

I ought to say here, *par parenthèse*, how much I regret that space will not permit me to refer to the words of these modern English songs, as I did in the case of the German *Lieder*. There is consolation, however, in the fact that if anyone is sufficiently interested to wish to study the poem, or compare the text with the singer's effort at reproducing it, nothing can be easier or more beneficial than to send for a copy of the song. This will be an advantage which I have not always enjoyed myself; nor do I seek to, because I always like, in listening to a gramophone record, to see how far the singer is capable of making the whole thing clear and comprehensible to the ear.

In Samuel Coleridge-Taylor, English music lost a composer remarkable for what he achieved no less than the promise of still greater things to come had he lived to perform them. He was only 37 when he died exactly fifteen years ago, and his *Hiawatha* was concrete evidence of the originality and strength that lay in his genius. His songs varied a good deal in musical value, but some of them were beautiful, even if cast in the mould of the higher type of English ballad, rather than that of the veritable *Lied*. Among these I should, for instance, classify the well-known *Eleanore*, which in my opinion eminently deserves its popularity. It is well sung by John Coates (Vocalion, A.0246, 12 in.), in that the tone is finely sustained, the phrasing intelligent, the diction faultless, and the contrasts telling. Two Columbias, one 10 in. by Arthur Jordan (3565), the other 12 in. by Edgar Coyle (9070), are neither of them on the same level, although both have their good points; the tenor voice is mostly " white " in colour, the baritone marred by a diction without charm and apparently American. A first-rate example of *Eleanore* is that by Tudor Davies (H.M.V. D.696), which exhibits the oft-variable qualities of the Welsh tenor in their best light. The tone is singularly pure, the feeling manly and expressive, the style spirited and vigorous. The song is also done by Frank Titterton (Vocalion K.05026, 12 in.), but not quite so smoothly or so free from ejaculatory fervour as it ought to be. Finally, there is an orchestral performance with solo by Cecil Sherwood (Pathé 5571, 10 in.) which has artistic merit, vocally and mechanically, to recommend it.

Another good song by Coleridge-Taylor, *Thou art risen, my beloved*, has two capital interpreters in Tudor Davies (H.M.V. E.414*) and John Thorne (Aco G.16064, each 10 in.), both employing an appropriately dark tone and the passionate sadness that the melody asks for. More in the vein of a folk-song is *She rested by the broken brook*, relieved by modern touches, and on the whole admirably treated by John Thorne (baritone, Aco G.15915, 10 in.). There is more character still in *Sons of the sea*, more dramatic spirit in its minor strain, with a bold, rugged style that reminds one rather of *Hiawatha*. It is effectively sung by Idris Daniels (yet another Welshman!) a baritone with a pleasant but not over-steady voice.

Mention of *Hiawatha* reminds me that the wonderful lines, *Onaway, awake, beloved*, were set to music by Frederic Cowen long before Coleridge-Taylor touched them, and published with several volumes of other high-class songs that deserve to be better known by the public of to-day. I do not include the *Hiawatha* setting here because it belongs to a choral work and is familiar to everyone.

Sir Frederic Cowen's treatment does not suggest the persuasive lover so much as the impulsive Indian warrior. Its swing is rapid, irresistible; and it has tremendous " go "—qualities that are fully recognised in a record by Roy Henderson (Voc. X.9513, 10 in.). The vocal tone is especially pure and clear, and the words emerge fairly well, even if the sibilants are weak. This is a better rendering than Howard Fry's (Beltona 6061, 10 in.), in which I find no continuity of phrasing, much distortion of vowels, and an altogether incorrect method of diction. I can also conceive of a much less sentimental, drawling delivery than Sydney Coltham's in another song of the same series, *At the mid hour of night* (H.M.V. B.2323, 10 in.), which must be considered as among Sir Frederic's most charming inspirations of a notably inspired period. Less known, perhaps, is his song *An Idle Poet*, with its lazy, dactylic rhythm and graceful melody, suavely warbled by Dame Clara Butt (Col. X.325, 10 in.), quite in her most engaging manner. This is, by the way, done to orchestral accompaniment. The same composer's *Border Ballad* is a successful imitation of the martial Scottish ditty of the traditional type—quick, jaunty, and full of fire—too familiar to call for description. It receives all the necessary energy and liveliness from Charles Tree (orchestral accompaniment, Pathé 5742, 10 in.), but the delivery is very spasmodic and jerky, and the voice lacks inspiration. Many other songs from the same source are to be found in the gramophone catalogues; but things like *The Swallows*, *The Better Land*, and *The Chimney Corner* scarcely belong to the present selection.

Frederick Delius contributes nothing like the share that is his by right of talent and eminence; and yet the explanation seems simple. His efforts do not attract the ordinary ear. Not his the gentle art of improvizing ingratiating tunes and fitting them with honied harmonies to verse with a fascinating lilt. Yet surely he might write more such graceful songs as *Sweet Venevil* and *To Daffodils*, both of which are charmingly sung and admirably recorded—the former by Leila Megane (H.M.V. E.430, 10 in.), a quaint, *triste* sort of folk-song, well pronounced; the latter by Muriel Brunskill (Col. 3876, 10 in.), a sad, touching *Lied*, highly poetic, and conveyed in a tone of infinite mellowness. One day, before it is too late, I hope, the more discerning amateur will do better justice to the great gifts of the Bradford musician.

HERMAN KLEIN.

THE GRAMOPHONE AND THE SINGER

(Continued)

By HERMAN KLEIN

Modern English Songs—II.

I CONTINUE this month with Thomas F. Dunhill, now a man of fifty; one of the early pupils of the Royal College under Villiers Stanford and Franklin Taylor; and a composer whose orchestral and chamber works should have brought him even greater fame than he enjoys. His songs, too, are of the best type, and there ought to be more of them. Perhaps the one most widely known is *The Fiddler of Dooney*, a clever and picturesque setting of Yeats's poem, chiefly supported by a tripping piano accompaniment in the shape of an Irish jig. The voice part is exceedingly tuneful and characteristic, a delightful Irish strain wherein humour plays its fitting share with a touch of sentiment here and there to set it off. Two interesting records do justice to *The Fiddler of Dooney*, one by a tenor, W. F. Watt (Col. 4296, 10 in.), with a pleasing voice and lively manner; the other by Peter Dawson (H.M.V. B.2139, 10 in.), who finds plentiful scope in it for Hibernian flavour, robust humour and painstaking diction. Still more contrast, however, distinguishes *A Sea Dirge*, a fine setting of Ariel's song from *The Tempest, Full fathom five thy father lies*. The lines were, of course, set to music by Purcell in his own incomparable way, but Mr. Dunhill has also succeeded in his, the burthen of the " ding-dong bell " being cleverly treated in a double fashion. (By the way, the Shakespearian text is not " These " but " Those were pearls that were his eyes," as Purcell wrote it.) It is a great privilege to be able to hear the splendid rendering of this " ditty," as Ferdinand calls it, left to us by the lamented Gervase Elwes (Col. L.1398, 12 in.), who imparted to it all the richness of his broad, manly tone and cultured style. First, the solemn tread of the dirge, then the bell-like ding-dong bright and clear, and then the dirge again—the effort of a singer who knew how to get to the heart of a song! On the other side is Ley's *Lake of Inisfree*, so the record is well worth having.

I come now to the recorded songs of Sir Edward Elgar. For so prolific a composer—down to the last few years, at any rate—it is strange that they should not cover a wider territory. Still, quality is preferable to quantity, and the latter could be increased by the inclusion of items from choral works or *Land of Hope and Glory*, which nevertheless do not enter into this category. Some of the best music that Elgar has written for the voice is to be found in his song-cycles, or what might be more accurately called his group-

settings. The first of these, *Sea Pictures*, came just before *The Dream of Gerontius*, and was introduced at the Norwich Festival by Dame (then Miss) Clara Butt. It made an impression which I for one shall not readily forget. The individuality of the musician is stamped upon every bar; the whole thing is *spirituel*, detached in feeling, poetic and original in conception. The complete work is admirably recorded by Muriel Brunskill (Col. 9170-2, three 12 in. discs), with orchestral accompaniment. The words are not always clear enough, but the tone is full and sympathetic and every note is in tune. An unconscious tendency to imitate Dame Clara is amusingly apparent in *Where corals lie*, which the famous contralto has also recorded (Col. 03299, 12 in.) in her sweetest and most soothing *mezza-voce*. On the other hand, Miss Brunskill's idea of *The Swimmer* is all her own, and, despite rather thin head notes, is as emphatic and dramatic as one could desire.

Another group, less familiar, but no less worthy of recollection, formed part of the incidental music to *The Starlight Express*, a delightful fantastic play by Algernon Blackwood, mounted some years ago at the Kingsway Theatre. This comprises four 12 in. discs (H.M.V. D.455-8), most of them sung by the late Charles Mott, an excellent baritone and an artist whose premature death in the Great War aroused widespread regret. His singing of the Organ-Grinder's Songs acquires a double pathos, so full is it of tenderness, repose, and sustained charm. Such gems as No. 1, *To the Children*; No. 2, *Blue-Eyed Fairy*, with its graceful waltz measures; and No. 4, *The Curfew Song*, wistful, expressive, deeper in feeling—all these are far too good to be lost. For that matter it is lovely music throughout, and real enjoyment is to be had likewise from listening to Agnes Nicholls (now Lady Harty), at a younger stage of her career, singing *Tears and Laughter* and the *Sunrise Song* with poetic feeling and restraint; or, again, *The Laugher's Song* with its bizarre effects, and in the finale with Charles Mott, which has a theme reminiscent of Sullivan. The recording (old process) of all these numbers sounds smooth and musical.

Quite in a different vein, yet no less suited to the nature of the theme, are the settings of Kipling's verses entitled *The Fringes of the Fleet*. Sung by Charles Mott and other competent artists (H.M.V D.453-4, 12 in.), they breathe the spirit if not the very air of the " briny," and, in their simple, rollicking character, might almost be described as up-to-date sea-chanties. In *The Lowestoft Boat* and *The Sweepers* poor Mott suggested the veritable breezy, salt-water touch; while in *Submarines* the music is of the right mock-mysterious sort, with the swish of the waves outside to complete the illusion.

Among other songs of Elgar's may be named *Like to the damask rose*—with a faint odour of Wagner—nicely rendered by Harold Williams (Col. 3547, 10 in.), but rather palpably old recording. A far finer example of the *Lied* than this is *Speak, Music*, which evinces both poetic treatment and romantic feeling. It is exquisitely sung by John Coates (Voc. A.0229, 12 in.), who understands the art of giving it noble expression and the requisite tone colour. Gladly would I say as much for Eric Marshall's interpretation (H.M.V. E.425), but here an acceptable tone is frittered away in a tearful exaggeration of the manly sentiment at which the composer aimed. A similar contrast is to be remarked in two versions of that clever song *The Pipes of Pan*. It would be hard to improve on the Horace Stevens (with orchestra, Voc. K.05176, 12 in.), so bright and crisp in diction, overflowing with life and vigour; whereas the same composition is scarcely to be recognised in the Harold Williams (Col. 3232, 10 in.), which is so dull and unconvincing that I am sure the singer could do much better with it. Finally we have in *The River* a sample of Elgar in the folk-music mood, speaking through his own idiom. It is a song that depends largely upon the aid of the words, and these I defy anyone to distinguish through the ebullient declamation of that impulsive singer, Tudor Davies (H.M.V. D.1098, 12 in.). Otherwise it is a sound performance.

Edward German is by birth a Shropshire man, and his music seems generally to remind us of the fact by its straightforward tunefulness, its strong sense of rhythm, and its pure British flavour. He has stuck to his guns without fear or favour from his Royal Academy days until now, when he by no means looks his sixty-five years; and British his music will always remain. That, I suppose, is why I like to include his songs in a collection that typifies to-day nearly as much as yesterday, and only shuts out comic opera of the Savoy species because it has to draw the line somewhere. The hand of the cultivated and skilful musician never fails to manifest itself in the compositions of Edward German; hence the quality that always distinguishes his songs from the trashy imitation. There are one or two, such as *Sea Lullaby* (published by Chappell's), that have somehow escaped the notice of the " recording angel "; but no doubt the pick of the basket are before me, and I will briefly mention them. The prime ballad favourite seems to be *Glorious Devon*; next to that *Rolling down to Rio*; and capital records of one or both of these are provided by Jamieson Dodds (Pathé), John Thorne (Vocalion), Rex Faithful (Aco), Kenneth Ellis (Vocalion), Robert Radford (H.M.V.), Peter Dawson (H.M.V.), and Thorpe Bates (Columbia).

Listening to the later songs from the same fluent pen, one is struck by the individuality of their melodic inspiration and rhythmic feeling; also the evidence of musicianship which, as in the case of Sullivan, invariably saves the simplest tune from the sin of sounding merely commonplace. Take, for instance, the hornpipe lilt of *Four Jolly Sailormen* so well realised both by Robert Radford (H.M.V. E.379, 10 in.) and John Buckley (Voc. R.6004, 10 in.), bringing out so vividly the " Old English " atmosphere of the whole song. And this atmosphere is the all-pervasive joy of *Love the Pedlar*—perhaps the best-known favourite of the lot—neatly and prettily rendered by Kathleen Destournel (Voc. K.05207, 12 in.). Somewhat of an identical pattern is *Dream o'day Jill*, with its tuneful flow and catchy lilt, nicely caught by Dora Labbette (Col. D.1555, 10 in.), though without a trace of the joyous ring that it cries aloud for. Sentimental yet not sad is again the motive in *Charming Chloë*; and of this graceful ditty I have two equally charming examples—the soprano by Elsie Suddaby (H.M.V. E.421, 10 in.) and the tenor by Leonard Gowings (Aco G.15570, 10 in.), both so good that it is hard to choose between them. Another excellent Aco is that of *My Song is of the sturdy North* by John Thorne (G.15611)—a good song well sung and well recorded. Lastly, a wholly Germanesque, lively, and pleasing song entitled *Love is meant to make us glad*, into which plenty of substantial tone and animation are infused by Marion Beeley (Col. 2640, 10 in.).

Sir George Henschel, if German by birth, is English by adoption and naturalisation. He has lived in London for half a century, and during that period has played a conspicuous part in our musical life, being in his particular domain an Admirable Crichton, if ever there was one. Among other things he has published (John Church Company) a book of *Fifty Songs*, many of which (often sung in days gone by by his gifted wife) deserve to be more widely known. Yet in this interesting collection I do not find *Spring*, one of his happiest efforts and perhaps the most original. It is also one of the only two that have as yet been recorded, the other being the popular *Morning Hymn* (*Soon night will pass*). The latter, fortunately, was sung by Gervase Elwes for H.M.V. (B.322, 10 in.), and remains a splendid souvenir of his fervid, earnest style. *Spring* is delightfully done by Elsie Suddaby (H.M.V. E.381, 10 in.), the quaint imitation of the cuckoo, with its *acciaccature* and trill, being executed with especial neatness and grace, while the quality of the voice is exquisite. Herein Alice Richardson (Beltona 820) is only partially successful, because she lacks an easy, rapid shake, the prime essential for this song. She makes it sound too mechanical and not a bit bird-like.

Only one song, but that a good one, represents the eccentric genius of Josef Holbrooke—composer (born

202

1878) of every kind of music, from Welsh operas, dramatic symphonies and tone-poems down to military band *potpourris* and serenades for five saxophones. I like his songs better than his chamber music (bar his *Folk-Song Quartet*, recorded by the London String Quartet), and one of them, *A Lake and a Fairy-boat*, ought certainly to be done. Another, the setting of Tennyson's *Come not when I am dead*, is positively beautiful; nor does it suffer aught at the hands of either John Coates (Voc. A.0232, 12 in.) or Arthur Jordan (Col. 3832, 10 in.), albeit as a " reading " the former singer presents the finer argument.

Gustav Holst, senior to Holbrooke by four years, has written even less material for the solo voice. His four songs for voice and violin (1916) are justly admired for their chaste elegance and the contrapuntal skill which they share with everything that comes from this pen. They are most artistically recorded by Dora Labbette and W. H. Reed (Col. L.1590, 12 in.), the mingling of the sad, wistful voice with the pure violin tone of the counter-melody being ideal in intonation and smoothness. Two songs by W. Y. Hurlstone, the gifted and promising Royal College student, whose death at the early age of thirty will always be deplored, are recorded on a single disc by John Thorne (Aco G.15962, 10 in.). One, *Wilt thou be my dearie?* is a sweet wooing song, a gracious melody alternating with a more urgent pleading passage; the other, *The Derby Ram*, a countryman's song of characteristic English type. Both are endowed by the singer with robust feeling, and make a very pleasant record.

John Ireland has the natural bent for song-writing, and a few years ago gave the impression of being likely to go far in that direction. Of late, however, he has been less productive—I know not why—and most assuredly he has yet to write another song combining simplicity with nobility and breadth in the degree shown by the setting of Masefield's *Sea Fever*. Still, there is yet ample time before him. He has only just turned 48, and his fine sonatas for piano and violin continue to demonstrate his capacity for fresh creative work. The intense yearning spirit of *Sea Fever* is well conveyed in an early record by Fraser Gange (H.M.V. E.3, 10 in.), a naturally talented baritone who deserted these shores for the Antipodes several years ago. It is also admirably interpreted by Kennerley Rumford (Col. D.1532, 10 in.), who conveys the sense of longing in a manner closely resembling that of Fraser Gange. The similarity even extends to the same clipping of the syllables on the two short notes of the prevailing phrase, and they are more quickly sung, I fancy, than the composer intended, the rhythm being strengthened at the cost of clear enunciation. A third record is one by Norman Williams (Velvet Face 1118, 10 in.), rather more matter-of-fact perhaps, but sung with resonant tone and the right kind of sentiment. A characteristic but not very effective setting of the well-known lines,

If there were dreams to sell, stands upon a lower plane than *Sea Fever*; it is not conceived quite in the same lofty vein, though the melody is flowing and provides material for a sympathetic rendering by George Baker (H.M.V. B.2317, 10 in.). Different, again, are two jolly ditties sung by Norman Williams (Velvet Face 1118 and 1120, 10 in.), entitled respectively *Hope the Hornblower* and *I have twelve oxen*. These are frankly folk-tune ballads of the Edward German type, and none the worse for that; on the contrary, so genuinely British in idiom and lilt that they are bound to please British ears.

The words just written also describe with entire appropriateness the vocal compositions of Frederick Keel, which have of late come into considerable favour with baritone and bass singers. The family likeness that runs through them is no doubt one of their chief recommendations. These easy tunes are the invention of one who was a singer himself before he was interned at Ruhleben, and therefore knows to a nicety what will please a mixed audience. But, being a good musician, he also has the art of setting off his tunes—Elizabethan and otherwise—to peculiar advantage by adroit harmonic treatment and variation in his accompaniments, thus preventing repetition from engendering monotony. He has, we are told, made a special study of old and traditional songs, and there is evidence of the fact in his own settings of traditional and other verse. A conspicuous example of this knack, if I may venture so to term it, is *Helen of Kirkconnell*, as neatly if rather tamely recorded by Dale Smith (Col. 3833, 10 in.). The tendency to melancholy starts here with a minor mode that is seldom absent for long from Mr. Keel's melodies, though fortunately his talent for striking up a " lively gait " makes them sound just as bright in the minor as if their mode were major. I notice this faculty also in the *Four Salt-Water Ballads*. From these Topliss Green in *A Sailor's Prayer* and *Cape Horn Gospel* (Col. 3607, 10 in.) contrives to squeeze out the last drop of sentiment; while Watcyn Watcyns in the complete set (Voc. K.05131 and X.9432, 10 in.) relieves them with a manly touch and a swinging jog-trot that seem to tumble out naturally with his genial tones. In another line of his " traditional " researches Frederick Keel furnishes a *trouvaille* with his setting of *Bonnie George Campbell*, and I am bound to admit that it sounds equally well in the contralto of Catherine Stewart (Beltona 6041, 10 in.) and the baritone of Andrew Shanks (H.M.V. B.2202). The latter, however, scores extra marks for his first-rate diction. In *To-morrow* Lewis Endersby (Aco G.15679, 10 in.) secures the necessary contrast between the two " modes "; and a distinctly Elizabethan version of *Sigh no more, ladies*, John Thorne (Aco G.15678), gives picturesque effect to a catchy flowing tune.

HERMAN KLEIN.

203

THE GRAMOPHONE AND THE SINGER

(Continued)

By HERMAN KLEIN

Modern English Songs—III.

ONE particular source of pleasure that I am deriving from my present task is the opportunity for re-hearing songs by living English composers that I like and have not heard for some while. It is surprising how quickly good songs get laid aside when others come along to take their place in the singer's stock repertory. They may not become altogether forgotten; but, if taken up only from time to time, they are liable in the end to gather more dust upon the title-page than the merit of their musical content would warrant. So again, very many standard songs of modern date have already found their way into the gramophone catalogues, and helpful courtesy is enabling me to include what I believe to be the pick of them in the collection under notice. But more remain to be recorded; and it also has to be constantly remembered that many ought to be re-recorded. For we are going through the most important transitional period in the history of the instrument, and the listener is growing accustomed to such perfect mechanical results that neither the song nor the singer will satisfy unless the record itself provides a faultless reproduction for both. No doubt the question is receiving attention already in the right quarters.

The vocal compositions of Gerald Graham Peel are widely known, and some of them have attained popularity. These do not, however, seem to include his best, which are in the form of song-cycles and have yet to be favoured by the recording world. A Manchester man and a pupil of Dr. Ernest Walker, he has the gift of neat construction, conciseness of form, and appropriate expression; can write an interesting accompaniment and preserve a straightforward vocal line. His fault lies chiefly in a tendency to sacrifice variety and contrast to a given mood or a persistent musical figure. His *Early Morning* is not long enough to suffer from this, and it makes a fascinating little song in consequence. So does the bright, tripping setting of *I will make you brooches*, included by Vaughan Williams in his *Roadside Fire*. Both are sung on one record by Anne Thursfield (H.M.V. E.404, 10 in.) with her customary sweet voice, delicate sentiment, and refinement of utterance.

In Summertime on Bredon stands in a yet higher class, a welcome example of English poetry set to music in the vein of pure English folk-song and relieved here and there by a touch of realism that strongly colours the simple pastoral narrative. It has been recorded by several singers. George Baker (H.M.V. B.1957, 10 in.) marks the rhythm in a slightly staccato manner, with distinct enunciation and sympathetic tone. His feeling, however, is so detached and impersonal that it comes as a surprise when, instead of singing the line " Oh noisy bells, be dumb ! " he shouts it in a violent *parlato* far noisier than the bells themselves. Should it not be in the nature of an entreaty ? So, at any rate, thought Gervase Elwes (Col. L.1101, * 10 in.) in his straightforward rendering of the story, replete with deep, unaffected sentiment, yet by no means monotonous. I would recommend his natural way of pronouncing the word " Sunday " to singers who are so fond of accentuating the literal sound of the *second* syllable (where there is no accent to mark), and who habitually turn every gar*den* into a zoological one. Among these, I am afraid, I must include Harry Drummond (Beltona, 1007, 10 in.) and John Thorne (Æolian, 15823, 10 in.), though in other respects there is little to find fault with in their excellent records of this song. By the way, there is a second rendering by George Baker (Pathé, 5233, 10 in.) in which the *parlato* effect is happily absent altogether. I prefer it because here we get a " noisy bell " sounding the knell in actual fact, and so lending realism to the singer's request. There are good points also in a *Summertime on Bredon* by Edgar Coyle (Col. 598, * 12 in.), notably the tone-colour, general feeling, and clear diction. What cannot be praised, however, is the use of vowels that one only expects in common colloquial speech, and then from what I term a " Middlesex mouth." It is a dialect like any other, and should be eschewed by refined singers.

With other art songs by Graham Peel I confess to being less familiar, perhaps less favourably impressed on a first hearing. Yet there is musical interest in them, and they will doubtless repay study. " Wild Ettrick," named *Ettrick* for short, a tuneful 3-4 setting of W. H. Ogilvie's ballad, suggests a woman's rather than a man's interpretation; but Dennis Noble (Col. 4073, 10 in.) puts into it easy grace and model diction with a charming tone, so why care ? In the *Song of the wooden-legged fiddler* (Col. 1603, 12 in.) and the *Ballad of Semmerwater* (Col. D.1513, 10 in.) Peel displays his fastidious taste in the choice of words; but in both there is considerable dreary repetition, which Norman Allin, despite his assumption of bizarre, growling character, scarcely succeeds in counteracting. The first-named is a queer imitation of an old-fashioned roundelay. Just such another quaint narration is embodied in *The Emigrant*, with an *arpeggiando* accompaniment, and carefully sung by John Thorne (Vocalion, 15848, 10 in.); the same baritone being also vocally responsible for *The Lute Player* (Aco, 16085, 10 in.), which most listeners will probably find a vastly inferior setting to that of Frances Allitsen. The latter song may not be of modern type or boast much of what Cavaradossi terms *recondita armonia*; but it is far more picturesque and effective than this of Graham Peel's.

The art songs of Roger Quilter call for especial attention on this first of November, because it happens to be the Brighton composer's fiftieth birthday, which falls three months after that of Graham Peel. The anniversary was not needed, of course, to stimulate appreciation of songs so keenly and universally admired, but it is just one of those coincidences that ought to be noted. It was in America that I first came across a song of Roger Quilter's—in 1906, I fancy—and the singer who showed it to me was that rarely-gifted artist, Lillian Nordica. She made me go over it five or six times in succession, and the more I played it with her the more I liked it. That song was *Now sleeps the crimson petal*, a delicious little *romance* (to use the French term for once), fragrant with the odorous charm of the East called forth by Tennyson's lines. Many vocalists attempt it; few succeed in giving it perfect expression (as Mme. Nordica did), or in conveying something of its elusive beauty through the medium of the gramophone. The one who comes nearest, perhaps, is Browning Mummery (H.M.V. B.2355, 10 in.), only unfortunately its value is somewhat discounted by a particularly aggressive and " thumping " piano accompaniment which never ought to have been " passed." Next I place Gervase Elwes (Col. L.1055, * 12 in.), wherein there is true *cantabile* elegance, and Kirkby Lunn (H.M.V. DA.434, 10 in.), who faithfully preserves the fine contralto timbre and reveals much care and delicacy in phrasing, if little variety of colour or significance. In the effort of Harry Brindle (Beltona, 6003, 10 in.) a stilted diction detracts from the essential dreamy quality; while in that of Watcyn Watcyns (Vocalion 9419, 10 in.) a lugubrious, mournful style produces a similar result. For the stupid violin *obbligato* introduced by the Hilda Nelson Trio (Aco G.15240, 10 in.) there is positively no excuse. Why commit these enormities?

But I must be briefer in my dealings with the prolific Roger, or I shall never have done. He is at his best, of course, in his Shakespearian settings; though whatever he writes bears its hall-mark plain and clear—the easy melodic flow of the voice-part, with the incessant play of contrapuntal themes and harmonies in the accompaniment, and a wonderful grace about it all. It is music, too, that demands good singing—such, for instance, as one does not get

from Derek Oldham either in *Autumn Evening* or *Land of Silence* (H.M.V. E.426, 10 ins.), thanks to faulty breathing and a tremolo. The latter, again, mars Frank Titterton's *Come away, Death* (Vocalion K.05251,* 12 in.); while over-darkened tone shuts out contrast in *Damask roses* and *Brown is my love*, both on the same disc. *My life's delight* is admirably sung both by Olga Haley (Vocalion K.05308, 12 in.) and George Baker (H.M.V. B.1967, 10 in.); the former coupled with that splendid song, *Fair House of Joy*, the latter with *Damask roses*.

Most valuable, to my thinking, of all the Roger Quilter records is that which Gervase Elwes made of *Fair House of Joy* and the popular *O mistress mine* (Col. L.1119, 12 in.)—not electrical recording, naturally, but singularly clear, vibrant, and pure for all that. I prefer the former in a male voice, and poor Elwes with his lovely emotional quality simply made a gem of it. Besides his version of Shakespeare's song, eloquent in its enthusiasm and tender feeling, I have others that are more or less worth hearing. Frank Mullings (Col. D.1537, * 10 in.) sings it neatly and adds with telling resonance an animated *Blow, blow, thou winter wind*. So does Barrington Hooper (Velvet Face 563, 12 in.), using good diction and a sympathetic voice. Leonard Gowings (Aco G.15720, 10 in.) warbles it in his smooth tenor together with *The Maiden Blush*. Frank Titterton includes it on the disc already noticed (Vocalion * K.05251), infusing into it plenty of life and vigour. Of *Blow, blow* the two best are by Gervase Elwes (Col. L.1055 *) and John Coates (Vocalion B.3119, 10 in.), each a delightful rendering and a striking contrast in style to the other.

The song-cycle, *To Julia*, is of unequal merit. The words, by Robert Herrick, belong to the Quilterian type, and they are daintily treated by the musician, who for gramophone purposes has provided an interesting accompaniment for piano and string quartet. The whole set of seven songs is recorded by Hubert Eisdell (Col. D.1460, 3 10 in. discs) with artistic care and spirit, if with rather inadequate vocal skill. He attacks things boldly enough, but grows weak as he proceeds, while his enunciation is indistinct. Happily the best song gets the best handling; that is, *To Daisies*, a really charming lyric which fully deserves its popularity. On the other side of the third disc is a somewhat colourless setting of Edmund Waller's exquisite poem *Go, lovely rose*, also sung by Sydney Coltham (H.M.V. B.1766, 10 in.); but both renderings have in them too much of the love-sick sentiment to please me. *To Daisies* is recorded separately by other singers. Gervase Elwes (H.M.V. B.321, 10 in.) imparts to it a strong, manly touch, and couples it with the *Song of the Blackbird*—a sparkling, passionate trifle. Frank Titterton (Vocalion X.9476, 10 in.) is also robust and animated, though he might do with fewer breaths. Yet another Elwes success was obtained in *Love's Philosophy* (Col. 1055, * 12 in.), a bright and joyous setting of " The fountains mingle with the river "; and, finally, in *Fill a glass with golden wine* (Col. L.1101, 12 in.), a capital song, also recorded by George Baker (H.M.V. 1967, * 10 in.) and by Percy Bilsbury (Aco G.16063, 10 in.). I like these best in the order that I have set them down. The singer last named has likewise done a pleasing record (Aco G.16108, 10 in.) of *Moonlight*.

That nearly completes the Roger Quilter collection so far as male singers are concerned. There remain to be mentioned only two short Shakespearian settings, viz., *Take, oh take those lips away* and *Hey, ho! the wind and the rain*, both pleasantly and artistically sung by Edgar Coyle (Col. 9097) on one side of a 12 in. disc. That this composer's melodious outpourings should not have attracted the ladies more— I mean the ladies who sing—is partly explained by the nature of their prevailing poetic content, which is mostly addressed by the stronger to the softer sex. A welcome exception is offered by Olga Haley in *Music, when soft voices die* and *In the bud of the morning* (Vocalion K.05308, * 12 in.), one tender with wistful expression, the other extremely dainty and full of charm. Secondly and finally, there is a suave, rhythmical performance by Edna Thornton of *Over the mountains* (H.M.V. E.365, 10 in.), an old-fashioned melody of Irish tinge, with a pretty, flowing accompaniment.

After the two portentous groups just noticed, one turns with pleasant anticipation to the next name on the alphabetical list—Cyril Scott—only to discover in the vocal branch an almost entire blank. How comes this, I wonder? The clever North of England musician has written a goodly quantity of interesting, original songs, some of which have been undeniably successful. His reputation as a pianist and a composer of orchestral and chamber music is world-wide. Consequently it is not easy to explain a measure of indifference that limits his vocal output in the eyes of the gramophone companies to exactly two songs. However, there it is; and I can only hope that amends will soon be made for what is obviously an instance of undeserved neglect. It would be superfluous to dwell here upon the technical peculiarities of Cyril Scott's writing—features of " modernism " which were much more novel and strange when he first came to the front 15 or 20 years ago than they are to-day. What sounded very complex then appears quite simple now, and, as has been said, his music possesses " a strangely exotic charm; he has a horror of the obvious." Of the two songs alluded to I prefer *My lady sleeps*, with its graceful curves in the voice-part and piquant dissonances in the accompaniment; but would prefer a less languishing, slurring delivery than Sydney Coltham's (H.M.V. B.1968, 10 in.), a suggestion of physical torment that would be calculated to disturb my lady's slumbers. On the contrary, one perceives both earnestness and conviction in Eric Marshall's rendering of *Immortality* (H.M.V. E.425,*

10 in.). The tone is steady and strong, and one feels genuine force in the fine utterance, " There is no death; there are no dead ! "

The vogue which the songs of Martin Shaw have enjoyed in recent years may be set down to the very qualities that lend them distinction and lift them clear out of the ruck of the ordinary ballad : they are musicianly and uncommon without being dry; they are tuneful and catchy, whilst being " tricky " and difficult enough to require adroit handling. In short, they please and interest as much as they " intrigue " the ear; and because of that, I suppose, I am very fond of them. Not long turned fifty, Martin Shaw (native of London and a pupil of Stanford at the Royal College) has been exceedingly industrious throughout his career of organist and composer of church music, light opera, incidental music, and vocal pieces of every description. As a matter of course, he is inadequately recorded; but what there is is good and worth having. If memory serves correctly, one of his most notable efforts, *The Song of the Palanquin-bearers*, was first introduced by John Coates; yet I have not so far been able to trace a record of it by him, and indeed the sole specimen available is by Arthur Jordan (Col. 3564, 10 in.), who preceded it on the same disc with *So sweet is shee* and (other side) added one of the *Songs of the Hebrides*. Unluckily the palanquin-bearers in this instance convey the idea of having a heavy burden to carry, for their song is distinctly miserable. Yet their words do not suggest rude complaint, since, if my ears deceive me not, the cry which they reiterate is " Lightly, *politely*, we bear her along." What a charming inspiration it is !

Cargoes is another of the same characteristic sort, and like it, too quickly ended. Peter Dawson (M.M.V. B.1930, 10 in.) infuses into it abundant spirit and swing. He is again excellent in his colouring of *Wood Magic* (H.M.V. B.2154, 10 in.), a more elaborate song containing quick contrasts of feeling and rhythm, now mysterious, now full of fear that is dispelled by trust and loving prayer, a broad melody succeeded by a colloquial touch. This is as well recorded as it is well enunciated and sung. The quaint *Old clothes and fine clothes* goes well with a clever setting of *Full fathom five* (Vocalion X.9502, 10 in.), and both are sung with evident relish by John Buckley, who ably realises the measured tread and old-time " burden " of the former no less than the grave, vivid, deep-sea picture and splendid " ding-dong bell " of the *Tempest* ditty. Yet another clever piece of writing, the *Bubble Song* from the music to *The Cockyolly Bird*, is a genuine example of the Martin Shaw style. Frank Titterton has caught its spirit and inflections to a nicety (Vocalion X.9118, 10 in.), the quick changes all admirably done with due light and shade and welcome crispness of diction. So much for a most enjoyable series of songs from the pen of a delightful composer.

The songs of Dr. Arthur Somervell, Principal Inspector of Music for the Board of Education, form but a small proportion of the total creative output of this busy, industrious man. Yet there are many more, written and published, than are to be found in the gramophone catalogues. Some of them are of a high order of excellence; some are widely known; and all are good. I remember how grateful I felt when I first made acquaintance with Somervell's early songs when he was a professor at the Royal College in 1895; for he had the right stuff in him, and he had studied under Stanford at Cambridge, at the Berlin Hochschule, and under Parry at the R.C.M. Two in particular were the tuneful *Shepherd's Cradle Song* and the thoughtful setting of Tennyson's *Tears, idle tears*, which last is not recorded. The former, a translation from the German, is really the *Shepherdess's Cradle Song* (by the way, was it not once so called?) and the words sound rather *malàpropos* in a man's mouth, because " father " is supposed to be " guarding his sheep," not rocking baby's cradle. This fact has not deterred Edgar Coyle (Col. 598,* 12 in.) from warbling it prettily. Muriel Brunskill (Col. 3987, 10 in.) sings it in two voices, a suitable *mezza voce* and a heavy contralto; but the two change too suddenly and do not fit. Paula St. Clair (Vocalion X.9581, 10 in.) spoils her rendering by inequalities of another sort and by wrong diction and vowel sounds.

Somervell's song-cycles exhale the essence and the perfume of the poems which they reflect in music. The most deservedly popular of them is the one based upon Tennyson's *Maud*, two numbers from which are included in Boosey's *Fifty Modern English Songs* (" Birds in the high hall-garden " and " Come into the garden, Maud "); but neither of these appears to have been recorded so far. For the Vocalion, Horace Stevens has, however, done four songs, all of them absolutely first-rate, viz.: *A voice from the cedar tree* (K.05186) on one side of the disc; and, on the other (a) *O that 'twere possible*, (b) *O let the solid ground*, and (c) *Go not, happy day*. I commend the first as a composition as well as for the singer's artistic juxtaposition of energetic emphasis, tenderness, and strong gusts of passion. In the shorter triad we also get fine contrasts of broad, noble tone with quick passages in a more lightsome mood. To conclude the present selection I make mention of *The Gentle Maiden*, one of Arthur Somervell's happy inspirations in the old folk-song manner—the " Drink to me only " sort. It is sung by Frank Mullings (Col. 2695, 10 in.) with wondrous self-restraint and a somewhat muffled tone that makes is resemble a baritone rather than the most robustious of all our tenors.

HERMAN KLEIN.

P.S.—I have received for review the first volumes of the new *Grove* and of Sir Henry Wood's book on *The Gentle Art of Singing*. In a subsequent number I hope to say something about both; and meanwhile I would like to congratulate Mr. H. C. Colles, the latest Editor of the famous *Dictionary*, upon what seems to be the most complete and well-arranged issue of the work that has yet been compiled.

THE GRAMOPHONE AND THE SINGER

(Continued)

By HERMAN KLEIN

Recent Musical Literature*

I LEAVE over until the New-Year the fourth and final contribution to my series of articles on "Modern English Songs" in order to offer some comment upon three or four books of notable musical interest that have lately made their appearance. First among these, by virtue alike of its importance and value, is Vol. I of—

GROVE'S DICTIONARY,

a review of which was included in last month's GRAMOPHONE. To that I would only add a few general observations upon the vocal features of the work, using the qualifying term "general" advisedly because, in the space at my disposal, anything like detailed criticism is out of the question.

The new editor, Mr. H. C. Colles, has improved upon the achievement of his predecessor because, being a man of greater all-round musical sympathies, he has spread his net more widely, seen to the revision of many old articles, had them brought up to date, and added several that were previously conspicuous by their absence. Of such, for instance, is the article on *Accompaniment*, by Mr. Colles himself, which eliminates all the superfluous historical matter and provides an account of the subject that is really illuminating and instructive. The concluding paragraph is well worth quoting :—

The art of accompaniment, then, at the present day, whether it is the art of the conductor in directing his orchestra in combination with singers and solo instrumentalists, or of the pianist collaborating with a singer in a recital of Lieder, is the same. The conductor or pianist cannot be content to "follow" the soloist. His function is really to control the *ensemble*, to preserve the right relation of all the parts which make up the whole, in quality and volume of tone, in rhythm and in *tempo*.

To the new article from the same pen on *Additional Accompaniments* similar remarks may be applied. In the extended account of *Albéniz* I notice that a former error is repeated. The year of the production of his opera, *Pepita Jiménez*, at Barcelona, should not be

---

Grove's Dictionary of Music and Musicians. Third edition. In five volumes edited by H. C. Colles, M.A. Vol. I. (A to C). (London : Macmillan & Co. 30s. net.)

The Gentle Art of Singing, by Henry J. Wood. In four volumes. Vol. I. (London : Oxford University Press : Humphrey Milford. 21s. net.)

Sir Arthur Sullivan, his Life, Letters, and Diaries, by Herbert Sullivan and Newman Flower. (London : Cassell & Co. 21s. net.)

Some Memories and Reflections, by Emma Eames. (London : D. Appleton & Co. 21s. net.)

1895 but 1896. Franklin Taylor's notes on the *Appoggiatura* remain as before, minus some illustrations ; but, having regard to the varied treatment of this early ornament by modern singers, I am sorry that someone with authority did not add a few lines laying down more definitely the rules either for observing or ignoring it. The present state of affairs is simply chaotic.

The article on *Balfe* has been improved, and appreciation may be offered for the newly-added list of his principal operas, with the dates of production. It is this kind of information that makes *Grove's Dictionary* so immensely useful to musicians. I am again amused by the definition of the word *Ballad*; it is—" as applied to certain kinds of English songs, a composition of the slightest possible degree of musical value, nearly always set to three verses (neither more nor less) of conventional doggerel." The practically new article on *Ballet Dancing* is most interesting, and of course winds up with the story of the Russian revival. Among the fresh short biographies of distinguished modern singers is one of *Mattia Battistini*, by the late Sydney H. Pardon—one of his great admirers. It ends as follows :—" His vocal recitals at Queen's Hall caused quite a sensation. Time had left his beautiful voice almost untouched, and he could sing all his favourite songs without transposition. No listener, ignorant of his identity, would have guessed he was a man of sixty-five." Regarding *Sir Thomas Beecham*, one learns that he has produced in all some 120 operas, of which about half were " new to this country or revived after a long period of neglect." The notice of *Bizet* is correct (except that Minnie Hauk's name is spelt *Hauck*); but, considering the world-wide interest in the composer of *Carmen*, it might have been more liberal as to details of his works. Four times as much space has been devoted to *Boïto* and more than double as much to *Bruneau*.

Among the other improvements with which this new edition of Vol I abounds, I would signalise one more—the article on *Comic Opera* which replaces the long-winded, out-of-date compilation by the late John Hullah. It is signed by Nicholas C. Gatty, and compressed into about 30 lines; and I agree with every word of it, notably this :—

Since the days of the ballad operas the English public have always welcomed the association of light music with plays of a light and amusing character. But unless there is real workmanship and invention in both text and music such works are ephemeral and reflect merely the taste of the moment.

208

Sir Henry's "Gentle Art of Singing."

When a famous conductor takes to writing books on singing it is well to be prepared for something out of the ordinary. Get ready for some surprises and even for some shocks. Do not be alarmed at the size of the first volume and the fact that it costs a guinea. Do not wonder that three more volumes are to follow it, or whence the material is coming from to fill them withal. When you open these preliminary pages and grasp the system whereby all the hundreds of exercises are evolved and repeated with variations, you will merely ask, Is there any reason why this kind of *moto perpetuo* should ever come to an end? But, as a matter of fact, neither the surprises nor the shocks will be found in these exercises, all of which have been used in "singing tutors" ever since the old Italian teachers began writing such things.

If you would seek to discover monuments of fresh and electrifying wisdom on this ancient topic, it is rather to Sir Henry Wood's text that you must turn. There you will speedily find that his art is not quite so "gentle" as his title might lead you to expect. Nor am I inclined altogether to blame him on that score, since the bad singing and bad teaching of the present era are the targets at which he aims his most pointed shafts; and continues doing so all the time. To use another metaphor, he hits out from the shoulder from first to last. There is nothing particularly novel to be discerned either in the evil or its remedy. We knew all or most of it before. But this is probably the first time that the impeachment has been uttered in such plain, strong language: "You must pause, fathers and mothers, before you let that girl of yours, who is always singing about the house, have her voice trained. . . . As a rule, it is the teacher who is blamed for the inevitable failure by parents who have spent hundreds of pounds on the vocal training of their offspring, with no outcome except bitter disappointment and reproaches, wailing and gnashing of teeth."

I disagree, however, on many points with Sir Henry Wood's general remarks in his opening chapter. His exhortations to hard work and study, to care in the choice of a teacher, not to come out before the student is ready or prematurely to accept engagements, and other warnings of like nature are obviously right enough. But negative instruction alone never yet made a good singer, nor will mere description enable the pupil to create the tone that is wanted.

At one juncture Sir Henry asks why more singers did not go to hear Battistini and imitate him. Next moment he says, "Never imitate gramophone tone." Why not? "Gramophone records," he says, "have done a great deal of good and some harm to the modern student of singing. If he would only listen to the phrasing, to the diction, particularly of foreign languages, and to the general interpretation, not to the tempo, which is always too fast, he might learn much from them." But why not the tone as well, provided it is the perfect model that it ought to be and one has the real gift of imitation? Again, why not copy the cadenzas and the ornaments (omitting the " tricks ") if the singer be advanced enough to execute them? It is frequently hard to know whether our author is addressing himself to beginners, to advanced students, or to those " quarter-baked " singers whom he very properly despises and denounces. On the other hand, there can be no mistaking his quarry when he goes for the " tone-deaf " teacher who works twelve hours a day, or the public which is " the root of the evil " because it gets singing " exactly as good as it desires." Quite true, this!

The one thing I look for and do not find in these pages is a clear, simple definition of the way a singer should breathe. In fact, there is next to nothing here dealing with the subject in a practical, scientific manner. What is a " deep breath "? How and where is it taken? How and whence is it expelled from the lungs? These are questions that we should expect to find answered in a work of this calibre. The eye encounters, instead, all sorts of new and strange expressions, such as " kick at the larynx," " normal teeth-gap," " downward will-pulse at the throat," the " vowel cavern," or—as distinguished from good fundamental tone—the " thin, bleaty, nasal, white, dark, hooty, hollow, teethy, even throaty tones " that " have their place and use in dramatic singing." What, one asks, will the ordinary, everyday individual, with a vocal complex and sincere yearning for instruction, be able to make of these and similar terms? Then the exercises—900 odd of them. Can it be that, as Sir Henry imagines, the student " who will devote daily practice for even five years to such graded and logical exercises as are in these volumes is bound, by ear and rhythmic training alone, to acquire a vocal technique which will equip him for most vocal difficulties "? Well, everything is possible. but perhaps the remaining three volumes will explain better how the feat is to be accomplished.

Life of Sir Arthur Sullivan.

There are two frontispieces to this—the veritable standard work on Sullivan. The first (inside cover) is a photogravure of the last seventeen bars of the "Christe eleison " in *The Golden Legend*, reproduced from the autograph full score. The other is a reproduction in colour of the clever but not wholly successful portrait of the composer by Millais, now in the National Portrait Gallery. Another striking illustration, vivid with the scarlet and gold of a Chapel Royal boy, is taken from a painting of Sullivan at the age of about 14, in the costume which he was always proud to have worn. The early part of the book, which describes his youthful trials and experiences until he was safely landed on the high road to fame and fortune, betrays the graceful pen of Mr. Newman Flower at its best.

The historical facts, if I may term them such, are tolerably familiar, yet not devoid of fresh interest, thanks to the letters from the boy to his family that now appear in print for the first time. The correspondence, however, which is of greatest value and, indeed, lends highest importance to the whole book, is that between composer and librettist, which extended over most of the years that they were working together. It sheds a flood of new light upon the conditions of their partnership, and ought to be read by everyone who loves the Savoy operas. It will leave little doubt behind, I fancy, concerning the natures of the two men, the differences in their temperaments, or who was sinned against and who the sinning. Personally speaking, I may say, as one who knew them both well, that these letters absolutely confirm what I have always believed, namely, that Sir William Gilbert's wilful, cross-grained disposition and bad temper made him an extremely difficult man to get on with. Knowing, as he did, the martyrdom that Sullivan was undergoing, through his physical sufferings during the latter portion of his life, Gilbert might have exercised greater restraint in many ways, seeing that *au fond* he generally meant well.

Another feature of interest is the story of the musician's friendship with that beautiful and delightful woman, Mrs. Ronalds, whose photograph at the period when I first made her acquaintance (1889) is also given. Their life-long devotion to each other was quite wonderful. The unique Sunday afternoon *musicales* that Mrs. Ronalds used to give at her house in Cadogan Place formed, it is stated, a " feature of London's life. All musicians appeared there, all lovers of music in the highest walks of life [including the chief Royalties of the time] were her guests." It was my privilege to be frequently among those thus welcomed. Nor is it forgotten that for Mrs. Ronalds it was that *The Lost Chord* was written, that she it was who sang it for the first time and, what is more, that in later years (my italics)

"*the first phonograph record ever played in England was that of Mrs. Ronalds singing this song*, and it was performed in Sullivan's drawing-room. When the instrument scratched its way into the first notes of *The Lost Chord*, and the voice of the singer rang through the room, clear, resonant, nearly a hundred people stared at each other in blank amazement. They might have been early Britons stained with woad, and somebody, some magician, had by a freak dropped down among them the first motor-car. No one spoke. The song—yes, it was clearly Mrs. Ronalds singing, and yet she stood there smiling at them. The song finished on the grand ' Amen.' A man went up to her and said, ' God gave somebody a brain to invent this instrument so that we should never forget your singing. But it was quite unnecessary.' "

I would like to correct here an impression that, because he wrote contemptuously in his diary about the characters in *Rheingold* or the *pièces d'occasion* that were unworthy of the true Wagner, Sullivan felt aught save the deepest admiration for the great music in the representative works of the Bayreuth master. Again and again did he express that admiration in my

hearing, and I have mentioned in one of my books how I found him one night at Covent Garden all alone in a pit-tier box listening to *Die Meistersinger* and poring over the full score of the opera between the acts or (when the lights were high enough) during the performance. I should add that the impression I allude to was conveyed not in this book, but in a review of it written by Ernest Newman in the *Sunday Times*. The biography as a whole affords an exceedingly truthful account of Sullivan the man and the musician.

EMMA EAMES'S " MEMORIES AND REFLECTIONS."

The retired prima donnas continue to write their autobiographies. The world has waited some time for Emma Eames's, but without doubting for a moment that it would come sooner or later. A woman of her ready wit, with her rich vein of pungent satire, her haughty outlook, and her unusually fluent pen, was bound ultimately to follow the example of her less literary sisters. Her pages give evidence that she has forgotten none of them, even when she does not mention them by name. Nor has she omitted to pay back in plain language the grudge owing to her famous teacher, Mathilde Marchesi, now deceased. She has even remembered one or two of her English critics, myself more especially, though the proper way of spelling my name has escaped her memory, like those of MM. Gevaert and Gailhard—also deceased. But I, who am still living, fear I must be rude enough to contradict her statement on page 95 regarding my talk with her in the wings at the Metropolitan Opera House. No British journalist could ever have been so stupid, so lacking in self-respect, as to eat his own words in that way, even to please so remarkable a woman and artist as Mme. Eames. She boasts in this book that she never read what the critics said about her. Whether that was so or not, the policy was a mistake. Good criticism would have helped her to improve her already admirable art. Anyhow, I should have liked for her to have read what I wrote in the *New York Herald* about her Tosca. It got me into trouble with my editor, because the notice was so eulogistic that he had to utilize the head-line (or sub-head, rather) to make the writer doubly responsible for praise that went beyond the *Herald* limits in the matter of superlatives.

And now, dropping the personal, allow me to assure our readers that the wife of that eminent singer of records, Emilio de Gogorza, has written a very quaint sort of book. The many photographs add to its interest and do ample justice to her famous good looks. She writes about many well-known people; and her " Memories," despite the tendency to slips already noticed, throw at least as curious a light as her " Reflections " upon a brilliant operatic epoch, the like of which, I fear, we shall never see again.

HERMAN KLEIN.

210

THE GRAMOPHONE AND THE SINGER

(Continued)
By HERMAN KLEIN
Modern English Songs—IV.

SIR CHARLES V. STANFORD was the most prolific and one of the most gifted writers of our modern musical Renaissance. He was also one of the most versatile musicians and ablest teachers of his art that the land officially styled Great Britain and Ireland has ever produced. Had he been more fortunate in his libretti, his serious operas would have lived ; he knew how to choose his subjects and how to handle them ; but there was not in them the dramatic stuff essential for endurance. He composed nearly a hundred songs, many of them quite beautiful ; and he arranged a vast number of Irish folk-songs and edited all Moore's Irish Melodies. He wrote for the voice, with sympathy and understanding ; his accompaniments were distinguished by skill, variety of treatment, and imaginative character. But I am sorry to say that the gramophone output of his music, both vocal and instrumental, is distinctly inferior to its deserts—wherein I include the charm that it is capable of exercising over the listener. The list comprises in all no more than twelve or fourteen pieces.

A Carol of Bells—a sort of vocal *potpourri* of chime-tunes familiar to the nursery—shall begin my selection, not because it represents Stanford at his best, but because it was well recorded by Gervase Elwes (Col., L.1152, 12 in.). The tone of it is remarkably fine, although it belongs to a period when the letter " s " was conspicuous by its absence ; while the diction could scarcely be improved. As for the chimes, the regretted singer rang them out as though he loved them. A simple Irish ditty may fitly describe *John Kelly* (Aco, G.15697, 10 in.), which is sung by Stella Murray with a languishing tone that recalls Dame Clara Butt in one of her softer moods. The actual resemblance will not escape notice. The better-known *Boat Song*, which never fails to please, is given to perfection by Louise Kirkby Lunn (H.M.V., D.A.438, 10 in.). Its graceful melody, effectively set off by the flowing accompaniment, is sung with soothing sweetness and a rare degree of steadiness.

Of the popular arrangement of *Father O'Flynn* I have altogether nine examples, and the place of honour must be assigned on all accounts to that incomparable baritone, Sir Charles Santley (Col., 373, 12 in.), who, according to the catalogue, recorded it " not long before his death in September, 1922." Anyone might be proud and happy to possess this touching souvenir of the well-remembered voice, wonderful still in old age, and replete with that unique, indescribable quality that, but for the gramophone, we should never have heard again. Every word comes out clearly, with the quiet humour that we used to relish so, and with the quaint Irish flavour which pervades the smiling tone as well as the smooth, gliding diction. (I may add that, as an illustration of Santley's talent as a " quick change artist," you have only to turn this disc over and you can play his no less amazing rendering of *Simon the Cellarer. Eheu! fugaces!*) Details as to the remaining *Father O'Flynns* are hardly called for, but, briefly adjectived, here they are :—Robert Radford (*H.M.V., E.420, 10 in.), robust, vigorous, distinct ; Reginald Whitehead (Parlo., E.10575, 12 in.), sonorous, pure bass, fair Irish accent ; Thorpe Bates (Col., 2454, 10 in.), persuasive, rhythmical, spirited ; Stephen Langley (Aco, G.15380, 10 in.), good tone, but staccato and jerky ; Harry Brindle (Velvet Face 653, 12 in.), too slow, but resonant and humorous ; Robert Howe (Regal, G.6303, 10 in.), right tempo and swing, telling voice ; Tom Kinniburgh (Pathé, 1334, 10 in.), lively, pleasant ; Manuel Hemingway (Beltona, 995, 10 in.), sympathetic, tuneful. All but the first three of the above and the last are with orchestra.

The *Songs of the Sea*, five in number, belong to Stanford's middle period and represent a much higher type than the ordinary nautical ballad, though imbued, where necessary, with the true salt-water spirit. The complete cycle is ably recorded by Watcyn Watcyns (two discs, Voc., K.05211-2, 12 in.). This singer does not possess great variety either of tone or style, but he is thoughtful and convincing. He reflects the quiet mood of *Homeward bound* best of all and is tender in *Outward bound ; Drake's Drum, Devon O,* and *The Old Superb* are spirited, but need more *entrain.* The requisite " go " is forthcoming in two separate records of *Drake's Drum,* one by Harold Williams (Col., 3312, 10 in.), the other by Thorpe Bates (Col., 2464, 10 in.). I must, however, point out that in neither are the vowels beyond criticism, though they do not include the Welshman's mistake of saying Ply*mouth* and Eng*land* ; and I would also ask Mr. Williams if he ever heard a British sailor say Cap*tain*? These are affectations.

In the interpretation of that interesting song, *The Pibroch* (Voc., X.9597, 10 in.), I find a far more satisfying display of contrast on the part of Watcyn

Watcyns. After the merry Irish opening, wherein the piano accompaniment plays such an irresistible part (thanks here to Stanley Chapple), the effect of the lovely sentimental passage is wonderful. Moreover, it is admirably sung, and makes one feel all the tragedy of the ending. In *Molly Brannigan* (Col., 3799, 10 in.), we have another Irish ditty of abnormal length, yet so redolent and racy of the soil that no true Hibernian would wish it to be shortened by a line. The vocalist is a tenor with a very nice voice, named W. F. Watt, who is likewise responsible for the rendering of *Trottin' to the Fair* (Col., 4120, 10 in.), a setting of A. P. Grave's familiar poem. No less acceptable is Elsie Suddaby's *Cuttin' rushes*, a delightfully pretty and tripping tune set to Moira O'Neill's words from " An Irish Idyll."

So much for the recorded songs of Villiers Stanford. And now, if you please, who is prepared to get on with the good work? Who will make a study of—if nothing more—the selection that is to be found in Boosey's *Fifty Modern English Songs?* It includes, apart from *Cuttin' rushes* and the *Boat Song*, such gems as *The Fairy Lough, Ochone when I used to be young!* and the haunting air from Stanford's opera, *The Veiled Prophet*, set to Tom Moore's familiar lines, *There's a bower of roses*. It is simply astonishing that this last should never have been recorded.

Twenty, nay, ten years ago, I should have approached the turn of Sir Arthur Sullivan with fear and trembling—or something very much like it. In the decade antecedent to the London revival of the Savoy operas the name of the composer was distinctly out of favour. The highbrows of that epoch had not a good word to say about him; for the crusade started against him by a certain clique, which shall be nameless, was bearing good fruit, and a kind of " boycott " of his music, as stupid as it was fanatical, was having the effect of keeping his name as much as possible in the background. This I always take to be the reason why Mr. Rupert d'Oyly Carte was afraid to bring his touring company to town for years, until at last he took his courage in both hands, and made the " Great Discovery " which in turn made his fortune. To-day you cannot enter a bookseller's shop the shelves of which are not lined with Sullivanesque literature—biographies of the two Savoyards, stories of the Savoy operas, and so forth. There is now no more popular musician in the world. Positively his " Irish " symphony was performed the other day, and nobody uttered a protest.

He wrote a goodly number of songs, but I grieve to say that many of them were of the purely ballad type and not worth recording for the benefit of a later generation. These songs do not, either, appeal to present-day singers, who may do more difficult things better, and yet do not cultivate the particular qualities that enabled the great vocalists of the late Victorian era to impart charm and attractiveness to a simple Sullivan ballad. Instances of this are vouchsafed in *Once again* (which people used to rave over when Sims Reeves and Edward Lloyd sang it), in *Edward Gray, My dearest heart*, and *Mary Morrison*. But, honestly, I do not feel in the same way about these songs as presented on the gramophone—*Once again* by Derek Oldham (H.M.V., D.1136, 12 in.), Wm. Heseltine (Col., 3424, 10 in.), and Walter Hyde (H.M.V., D.107, 12 in.); *Edward Gray* by Sydney Coltham (H.M.V., C.1094, 12 in.); *My dearest heart* by Clara Serena (Voc., K.05252, 12 in.); and *Mary Morrison* by Alexander MacGregor (H.M.V., D.976, 10 in.). Old recording may have something to do with the tone, but not with the style. It is the style that is palpably not there.

It is the same story, to some extent anyhow, with two of the superior songs. And here I would utter my protest against the new fashion of altering the phrasing that was obviously intended by the composer, for the sake of taking breaths in accordance with the punctuation. It is a growing habit, and it is utterly wrong. If you do not hold with the composer's manner of setting the words to music, there is no need to sing his song at all; leave it alone. But you are not entitled, as an artist, to join lines of verse or sentences together by omitting breaths and then introducing them at will later on where the first chance occurs. The effect on those who knew the song of old is deplorable, and, on those who did not know it, misleading. In *Thou'rt passing hence, my brother* Horace Stevens (Voc., K.05147, 12 in.) is more than once guilty of this device, not to mention the fact that he hurries the *tempo* and uses un-English vowels.

The other and more celebrated song is *Orpheus with his lute*, the most difficult Shakespearian piece, with the exception of Desdemona's " Willow Song " (Verdi's *Otello*), written for a soprano voice. Each of the four records that I have of this is more or less open to serious criticism. Here are my notes: Doris Vane (Voc., K.05075, 12 in.), *tempo* too slow, in *coda* too fast; final cadence (despite lowering the key a semitone) imperfectly sung; words excellent. Théa Philips (Aco, F.33064, 12 in.), lacks lightness, grace, and contrast; words in one place repeated by mistake; numerous incorrect breathing-places; piano accompaniment spoilt by excessive *rubato*. Dora Labbette (Col., L.1442, 12 in.), nice tone; words often indistinct; little attention to *nuances* or marks of expression; needs more contrast. Florence Austral (H.M.V., D.1042, 12 in.), like previous example, accompanied by orchestra; voice sounds small (perhaps recorded long ago); faulty intonation here and there (rare thing with this artist); tone and style lacking in animation; inexcusable change of words in cadence at close—sings it on " fall asleep " instead of " or hearing die." Now I wonder what my old friend Arthur Sullivan would have said to these young ladies !

To Arthur Goring Thomas I have so often made allusion that there is little to add now, beyond expressing a hope that more of his singable music will yet be recorded. Has no one ventured to attempt *O my heart is weary*? It awaits, albeit hackneyed, a first-rate dramatic contralto, and I wish that either Maria Olczewska or Sigrid Onegin would have a shot at it in the German text, to which it was originally composed for the Berlin performance of *Nadeshda*. From the book of *Twelve Lyrics* I find only two, namely, that fine song *The Willow*, extremely well done by Doris Vane (Voc., K.05075, orch. acc., 12 in.); and *Time's Garden*, a quiet, reposeful melody with 'cello obbligato, sung with luscious tone by Edna Thornton (H.M.V., E.88, 10 in.), and by Dame Clara Butt (Col., 7310, 12 in.), associated with W. H. Squire. The latter disc also contains the well-known *Summer Night*, originally *Nuit de Mai* in the French, to which language Goring Thomas always preferred composing. In this way he wrote his finest song, *Le Baiser*, which we call *A Memory*. It was intended for a mezzo-soprano but is not recorded by one. Louise Kirkby Lunn does full justice to the lower notes, but her climax lacks *abandon*, though her singing is artistic (H.M.V., D.A.434, 10 in.). *A Memory* is also adroitly sung by Edgar Coyle (Col., 9070, 12 in.), but here again the final passage is disappointing.

If Maude Valérie White is less popular than she used to be, it is not for lack of good and enduring qualities in her songs. They have always revealed, first and foremost, the gifts of a musician; also a goodly measure of Lied inspiration and poetic feeling. They might, perhaps, have conveyed a greater depth of passion and colour of the kind manifested, for example, by another woman composer in her setting of *A Persian Garden*. Still, they are well constructed, refined, and full of melodic charm, and a good many have yet to be recorded that are worth doing. So far *To Mary* and *King Charles* are the favourites, and, of course, *The Devout Lover*, a great song in its class and one that will live. The long-drawn theme of the former requires economy of breath and a good *sostenuto*. It receives both from the well-preserved veteran, Ben Davies (H.M.V., D.100, 12 in.), and should be kept as a faithful replica of his beautiful tenor voice. *To Mary* is also artistically sung in a lower key by Rex Palmer (Col., 3988, 10 in.), whose sombre quality and clear enunciation it brings out to especial advantage; while a third singer of the same song is John Adams (Regal, G.6716, 10 in.), who also gives it in bright, manly style. Four records of *King Charles* run each other close in most respects, all being spirited and stirring in character, as befits the ballad. They are by Jamieson Dodds (Pathé, 5447, 10 in.); Horace Stevens (Voc., R.6009, 10 in.); Norman Allin (Col., 2693, 10 in.); and Peter Dawson (H.M.V., B.1242, 10 in.). A fifth, by Rex Palmer (Col., 4487, 10 in.) is of later date than these, and

reaps the full benefit of superior recording, apart from the merit of firm diction, clean, strong tone and rhythm, and telling sense of contrast.

The Devout Lover was, thirty years ago, *par excellence* the sure road to success in the drawing-room, in spite—or perhaps because—of the fact that it was a cut above the ordinary specimen of its *genre*. It has a particularly fine tune, strong and sincere as the words that inspired it, and works up to an irresistible climax. Being an exacting song, if properly rendered, I am not surprised at discovering weak points in each of the four records I have tried over. Stephen Langley (Aco, F.33050, 12 in.), is one of the best, though I could wish he were a trifle less staccato and impulsive. Thorpe Bates (Regal, G.7163, 10 in.), is quite good until the last verse, where something seems to have " happened " either to the singer or the orchestra, or both. Stewart Gardner (H.M.V., D.222, 12 in.), is careful and effective, very distinct, but lacks vigour. Hubert Eisdell (Col., L.1136, 12 in.), not being a baritone, is out of his element here; besides, the " Devout Lover " was assuredly not meant to be a " Society " youth, with a mincing accent and manner. A fifth record, by Percy Heming (H.M.V., B.2514, 10 in., just issued) realizes the composer's intention and, if a shade too fast, works up well to a strong finish. I complete this composer with first-rate records of two of her most Schubertian songs, viz., *When the swallows homeward fly*, sung with wistful charm by Olga Haley (Voc., R.6144, 10 in.); and *Absent yet present*, whereof a passionate outpouring " rises in tumult " from the well-remembered voice of Gervase Elwes (H.M.V., B.321, 10 in.).

It seems strange that so able a musician as Dr. Charles Wood, who died not long ago and was Professor of Music at Cambridge University from 1924, should have written one glorious song like *Ethiopia saluting the Colours*—and no more. He did write other songs, of course; but they are never heard, while his more important compositions are suffering neglect. His setting of Walt Whitman's lines affords scope for a contrast of tones that can be made almost weird and uncanny in its effect. The change of voice and manner when the old slave speaks, after the martial trend of the main theme, is wonderfully touching, and will give you a thrill such as you may experience, for instance, in Schubert's *Death and the Maiden*. This effect is obtained with skill by both the singers who have recorded the song, and I must award equal praise to Stuart Robertson (H.M.V., B.2407, 10 in.) and Norman Allin (Col., L.1612, 12 in.). Nor is there aught to choose between either so far as excellence of recording is concerned.

With the name of Ralph Vaughan Williams I come to the end of these " Modern English " articles, and, —*finis coronat opus*; for to-day we have no sturdier exemplar of all that is best in the English school of lyrical composition. His noble setting of the song-cycle, *On Wenlock Edge* (from A. E. Housman's poem, *The Shropshire Lad*), was fortunately written in time for it to be recorded by Gervase Elwes (Col., 7363-5, three 12 in. discs), for whom it was composed and whom I heard sing it at, I think, the Æolian Hall. It stands here a monument alike to musician and artist, with the original accompaniment played by the London String Quartet and piano. I need say no more. On the back of the third disc (7365) is the same singer's superb rendering of *The Roadside Fire*, now familiar and dear to all who take pleasure in a perfect song. This is also admirably done by Horace Stevens (*Voc., X.9693, 10 in.) with broad phrasing and a rich quality of timbre. By Peter Dawson (H.M.V., B.1375, 10 in.) it is given much more quickly and with blithe, rather careless spirit; by Harold Williams (Col., 3232, 10 in.) in quite the opposite manner again—slow, measured, no happiness, altogether too doleful—yet with an abundance of telling tone.

The popularity of *Linden Lea* is denoted by six recordings, including one by a lady, Catherine Stewart (Beltona, 6031, 10 in.), who trips lightly and rapidly through three verses and then fortunately trips off. This is essentially a man's song, and as such is robustly handled by George Baker (H.M.V., B.2396, 10 in., orch. acc.) with sustained tone and strong consonantal enunciation; likewise by John Coates (Voc., B.3118, 10 in., piano), who imparts the right bucolic touch and a pungent West-country dialect. Edgar Coyle (Col., 3211, 10 in., orch. acc.) adopts an easy-going air of lassitude; Norman Williams (Velvet Face, 1119, 10 in., piano) is masculine and smooth as usual; while John Thorne (Aco, G.15503, 10 in., piano) sings *legato* with a dash of sentiment. No lack of variety, you see, in the treatment of this quiet folk-tune! *The Vagabond*, a bigger song in every way, is finely realised by Peter Dawson (H.M.V., B.2297, 10 in.), with more care than is his wont both in tone and emphasis; and a well-contrasted performance is that of Horace Stevens (*Voc., X.9693), whose tone here is exceptionally dark and closed, yet never monotonous. In *Silent Noon*, Rossetti's words caught Vaughan Williams in one of his most characteristic moods—peaceful, diatonic, contemplative, solemn. The song is impressively rendered by Norman Allin (Col., L.1760, 12 in.), and very smoothly by Glanville Davies (Col., 3682, 10 in.). Better still, from a poetic standpoint, is an interpretation by J. Dale Smith (Col., 9245, 12 in.), though there are moments when the tone needs stronger support to enhance the value of its refined quality. On the other hand, despite welcome tonal charm, Clara Serena (Voc., K.05309, 12 in.) fails to convince me that *Silent Noon* attains its full significance in the female voice. In *Bright is the ring of words* R. L. Stevenson was not quite so felicitously treated, though the tranquil melody could indicate no other pen; and it was suavely recorded by Edgar Coyle (Col., 3946, 10 in.). HERMAN KLEIN.

THE GRAMOPHONE AND THE SINGER

(*Continued*)

By HERMAN KLEIN

The New H.M.V. Operatic Records—I

NO great stretch of the imagination is required to realise what a tremendous affair it must be, this business of recording anew the old popular items of the operatic repertory. For a long time we have known perfectly well that it had to come—indeed, that it was on the way. But the H.M.V. alone could have told the world when the regular issue of the new operatic supplement would begin. I am very glad to have the privilege of demonstrating in turn to our readers that it has actually commenced, and the experiences I have been enjoying in listening to the first batch.

I am told that most, if not all, of these new recordings have been made by the Victor Company in America. The fact is of interest for two reasons: first, because it explains how they came to be sung by operatic singers of distinction who have not been in England for a long while; and secondly, because it enabled me to find out, by putting the question direct and obtaining a frank reply, the nature of the *locale* in which the new records are sung. This latter point has puzzled me not a little of late; in fact, ever since the electrical process began to allow of record-making anywhere save in an ordinary *atelier*. One perceives instantly the effect of increased space for the spreading of sound-waves, of unconfined surroundings imparting the same quality of resonance that one would get in a large, lofty, empty room. I have wondered, indeed, if it was a room, or a hall, or an empty theatre; and no doubt it is sometimes an actual opera-house, like the Scala at Milan, the Opéra at Paris, or the Staatsoper at Berlin that is providing the *locale* as well as the performance.

But I was not aware until now that the Victor Company of New York had bought or leased for its purposes a *disused church*. That did come rather as a surprise; and yet, what a capital notion, seeing that the main idea is to provide the necessary space for big musical sounds, vocal and instrumental, to " travel " without confusion, without echo (worth speaking of), and without the piercing effects that produce blasting. I was told something about " division into compartments," though whether this applied to the floor or the ceiling I am not quite sure. Anyhow, one can understand how those noisy, acute soprano high notes, which used to be the despair alike of singer and operator, can get harmlessly away, and either be at once absorbed or else float gently aloft amid the arching rafters of a " disused church." Certain it is that they can now be fearlessly attacked and held with full voice and come out splendidly on the matrix. The clearness of the detail, too, is by the same device rendered simply amazing. You can recognise the individual timbre of every instrument in the orchestra, so that the accompaniments, instead of being a source of irritation, are a delight. I daresay my *confrères* have long drawn attention to this advance in other pages of The Gramophone. I have done so, truly, in my own monthly reviews. But I did not know until now that the highly-paid stars of the American operatic stage were spending their spare moments so profitably in a " disused church."

So much by way of preliminary. Coming now to the new records, I may without hesitation express the belief that they will signalize a fresh era in the history of the gramophone. They surpass my wildest expectations in the completeness of their victory over every defect and every weak point that has hitherto tarnished the mechanical purity of the finished product. Viewed from the old standpoints, all the customary faults and blemishes have gone by the board, disappeared from the picture. It is very much like the cinematographic film of to-day compared with that of ten years ago : there is no comparison possible.

And yet it must not be supposed from this that " Othello's occupation's gone." There may still be loopholes somewhere for the diligent and persevering critic to discover. Let him raise the already lofty standard of his criticism—somewhat, I suppose, in the theoretical way that the British Navy was suspected by certain transatlantic politicians of " elevating its guns " (whatever that may portend)—and there will yet come into view quite sufficient to afford him useful occupation. I say this in order to reassure my generous readers, they having a right to expect from me something more than string after string of superlatives. I warn them, nevertheless, that in matters of pure reproduction, as distinguished from those of interpretation, there is going to be much less room for fault-finding than formerly. The tendency henceforward, as it seems to me, will be to *flatter* the human voice instead of failing to do it justice. The gramophone will not only increase its volume by many degrees but improve its timbre and cover up many of its blemishes. In these respects I think it is going to approximate more closely than it ever has done to the art of photography, with its modern facilities for enlargement and touching-up. As for orchestral accompaniments to the vocal piece, there is no longer, of course, the slightest reason why they should not sound as perfect in tone, balance, and colour as they can be made to in the opera house or the concert room. The era of synthetic or *ersatz* gramophone bands and incomplete instrumentation has passed for ever.

Dealing critically with the first lot of new H.M.V. records rather suggests to my mind meeting a number of old friends who had been getting rather shabby, and, having come into some money, have visited the most fashionable places in the West-end and decked themselves out in the most expensive clothes they could buy. I cannot help recognizing them, of course, because I should know them under any disguise; but it is almost surprising that they should condescend to recognize me—except that I haven't changed as they have. Happily, however, the alteration is only in externals. *Au fond* and underneath the polish our old friends remain the same—greatly improved by their West-end process. They are, in every sense, worth a lot more money than they were.

Among these metamorphoses, if I may so term them, will be found a limited number of re-recordings by the artists who made them in the original instance. I begin my review with an example of one of them, viz., Toti dal Monte's *Mad Scene* from *Lucia*, which replaces DB.712 in the old list. It is now numbered DB.1015 (in two parts, 12 in.), and embodies an immense improvement in the vocal as well as the mechanical sense. Obviously, the singer rejoices in her new-born feeling of freedom (they all do more or less), and one remarks at once the ease and serenity with which she attacks the *Splendon le sacre faci*. Her voice has greater roundness in addition to an increased sonority and power. The new " atmosphere " will not escape your notice any more than the wonderful silent surface, which you paradoxically find conspicuous because of the absence of all scraping. The vocalization is worthy of Toti dal Monte at her best, and I cannot say more. The duets with the flute are flawlessly executed; but even more astonishing to my ear are those two long, gigantic E flats in *alt*, one at the end of each cadenza, the like of which I can safely say has never been approached by this medium before. Who until now ever dared to emit such a note? The same singer is responsible for a new *Regnava nel silenzio* from the opening act of *Lucia* (DB.1040), coupling with it *Convien partir* from the same composer's *Figlia del Reggimento*. The latter is particularly welcome because a beautiful air seldom sung; and both, I may add, place in a favourable light Toti dal Monte's admirable *legato* and sustaining capacity, the sobriety of her ornamentation, and her unusual blending of dark tone with smiling Italian vowels.

As a recent H.M.V. recruit, Margaret Sheridan naturally contributes to the new list. Her two discs are interesting without being irreproachable. On one (DB.988) she combines Elsa's Dream, *Sola ne' miei prim'anni* with *Si, mi chiamano Mimi*; on the other (DB.1084) *Ancora un passo*, from *Madam Butterfly*, with the scene with Sharpless, *E questo*, from the same opera. Her tone, lovely in quality but never quite steady, serves best in the Italian music of Puccini, where one feels that she is at home. She lacks the poetic diction for *Lohengrin*, and also the variety of colour; but Mimi's air comes out quite well. The chorus of girls in the first scene from *Butterfly* is a trifle too heavy, and shows that great care and restraint are necessary with choruses taken by the new process. They can easily drown the solo voice. The orchestral details in both instances are amazingly clear.

Hitherto the Italian dramatic soprano, Hina Spani, has been heard only in duets. She now becomes a fully-fledged soloist in *Tacea la notte* (*Il Trovatore*) and *Ma dall' arido stelo* (*Ballo in Maschera*), the latter appearing almost for the first time in the H.M.V. catalogue (DB.1045). She strikes me as being a typical Verdi singer, emotion and tremolo included. The voice is unquestionably a fine one, and if quite steady would sound magnificent under these conditions. Curiously enough, it grows in opulence as each piece goes on. Göta Ljungberg, a Wagnerian artist of the highest order, shows the versatility of the school in which she was trained by also attempting Verdi. Her two airs from *La Forza del Destino* (D.1352) are replete with intense expression and telling quality of tone. The *Madre, pietosa Vergine*, sung with chorus, is extremely effective and a splendid piece of recording. In the *Pace, pace* the singer is inclined to slur *à l'Italienne* more than she is wont to do in Wagner or Strauss. It is a natural proceeding, I admit, but the singer who can phrase perfectly the difficult passages of Kundry in the " Herzeleide " scene from *Parsifal* (also recorded by H.M.V.) has no need to indulge in vocal tricks of any sort. Her unbroken steadiness of resonant tone is a sheer delight. Altogether Göta Ljungberg is a valuable acquisition, and I hope we shall hear many more of her records.

And now, if you please, *place aux messieurs!* Here we become more than ever aware of the extraordinary developments brought about by the new system. There are, apparently, to be no more masculine voices

of moderate proportions. *Laissez aller* is the word, and hey, presto! they blossom forth with a sonority and amplitude that any decent machine will suffice to fill your biggest local hall with. The *grand jeu* of the old harmonium was tinkling child's-play compared with it. A genuine *tenore robusto* of the stamp of Giovanni Martinelli makes no more than his normal amount of effort, and instantly he is obliging you with an *n*th degree of power. I feel sure that his voice never sounded so fresh and strong and broad—in a word, so vast in its proportions, as it now does in the *Addio alla madre*—the most strenuous bit of singing that Turiddu has to do in *Cavalleria Rusticana*—which he now records for the first time for the H.M.V. Red Label section (DB. 1089). On the other side of the disc is another happy example of the same art and mechanism combined in the recitation and aria, *O tu, che in seno degli angeli* from *La Forza del Destino*. There is a certain nobility and repose of style in this which perfect arrangement of the breath alone can ensure, and I must say the line of smooth, even tone is very wonderfully sustained throughout. All the high notes sound easy and true; not one is shirked and not one is forcibly overdone. And here, at any rate, is no evidence of the " flattery " that I was speaking of. It is simply the gramophone reproducing the real Martinelli for the first time.

About Miguel (or Michele) Fleta I am unable to make up my mind quite so readily. I have never heard him on the stage. I know that he made his début at Trieste in 1919, and since then has sung with great success all over Italy and in Spain, his native country. For me he has been exclusively the clever gramophone artist associated with *Ay, Ay, Ay* and kindred ditties. Now, however, we discover him among the elect of the H.M.V. supplementary list, doing work of the Caruso-Martinelli type, and we have to criticise him accordingly. Well, I find him very clever. His is not a " big " voice, nor can the new process make it one. But it has big moments now and then, when it diverges from the sempiternal *mezza voce* which Fleta, imitating his famous prototype and countryman, Gayarre, indulges in so persistently. I could do with a trifle less of it, for instance, in the great Gayarre air, *Spirto* (not *Spirito*) *gentil*, from *La Favorita* (DB.986), although quite fitting in the *Sogno* from *Manon* (same disc). The sudden transitions from one kind of voice to the other pall after a while; they make the phrasing too spasmodic, too violent in contrast. To a certain extent a similar objection applies to the farewell and narration from the third act of *Lohengrin* (*Cigno fedel* and *Da voi lontano*, DB.976); only in these the *sostenuto* is somewhat better maintained—in a more or less *affettuoso* manner. The singer is altogether better suited, however, by airs like *O Paradiso* (*Africaine*) and Nadir's Romance, *Mi par d'udir ancora* (*Pescatori di Perle*) (DB.1071), the former proving that he has really a vein of dark tone for use when he wants it.

In fact, his records run in couples like that, one side light tone, the other dark, as he again demonstrates in *Che gelida manina* and *Vesti la giubba* (DB.1034). Taken in this order they balance each other very well, and, being superbly accompanied, you end up by rather enjoying your Fleta recital!

Armand Crabbé, the Belgian baritone who before the War appeared frequently at Covent Garden, is remembered as an artistic singer rather than the possessor of a remarkable voice. He has already recorded for H.M.V., but only insignificant pieces of an unfamiliar kind. Now his organ acquires augmented power under the improved conditions and appears quite sonorous in the drinking song from *Hamlet* (*O vin, dissipe la tristesse,* DB.1043) and the *Largo al factotum* from *Il Barbiere.* He sings both, of course, in French, and with plenty of rhythmical energy as well as dramatic character, while his diction is clearness itself. The new recording makes it an added pleasure to greet these old friends once again in fresh Gallic attire.

Connoisseurs will not find it easy to make a choice between the latest renderings of the *Pagliacci Prologue.* Apollo Granforte (DB.1044) contends henceforth against a doughty rival in Laurence Tibbett (DB.975), the new American baritone who has recently been enjoying such a " good press." There can be no doubt about it. Tibbett may not strike you as a very formidable name in an opera bill, but be assured that his voice, once you hear it, will impress you mightily alike by its size, its quality, and its carrying power. In other words, it will compare very favourably with the Polyphemic tones of Granforte, who, as you are doubtless aware, possesses an organ of abnormal volume. I am rather glad to have heard these records as it were side by side, since only by comparison could I have ventured to estimate the true magnitude of Laurence Tibbett's at what I may call its " face value." I should have felt inclined otherwise to imagine that it was due to the miracle of the new process, whereas now I can feel sure that the latter has not " flattered " one more than it has the other; and certainly it has imparted to Granforte a tonal grandeur that he never displayed in any previous record—perhaps also more steadiness, more freedom, more *abandon.* Another " best on record " for the Prologue is the wonderful sonority and clarity of the orchestral performance, this being of identical excellence in each case. Where Granforte is vastly

superior to the American artist is in his enunciation; there he is strong and convincing, while the other lacks grip and decision. But let us hope time will remedy that; and meanwhile you can enjoy **Mr.** Tibbett's dark Italian tone and that sense of reserve power which you recognise when he lets go *fortissimo* in the final passage. On the whole, then, two extremely fine records of the *Prologue!*

From that mine of recording wealth, *La Forza del Destino,* many gems are bound to be extracted and polished afresh by the new method. To begin with, here is the popular duet for tenor and baritone, *Solenne in quest 'ora,* first made familiar by Caruso and Scotti. It is now sung by Beniamino Gigli and Giuseppe de Luca (DB.1050), two scarcely less eminent exponents of the modern Italian school. Between them they produce a body of tone incredibly vast and yet withal of superb quality, sustaining it with a comfortable *ff* level of ease that betrays absolutely no misgivings on the score of blasting. (This word will soon, indeed, have to be omitted from the gramophone vocabulary, as having no further use except for dynamite purposes.) The result is huge but not exactly noisy tone, though I admit that in two or three places the voices contrive without apparent effort to drown the palpably extensive orchestra. Another duet fills the reverse side, to wit, the *O Mimi, tu più non torni* (*La Bohème*), which occupied a similar place on the Caruso-Scotti record just mentioned. I have no hesitation in saying that the present example far surpasses the older one. It is intensely charged with " atmosphere," and one might actually be listening to it at Covent Garden or the Metropolitan Opera House.

I conclude this review for the present month with a word of praise for Tito Schipa's two light arias (10 in., DA.885), one the favourite *Questa o quella,* from *Rigoletto,* the other the lesser known but in its way equally charming melody, *Sogno soave e casto,* from *Don Pasquale.* Both are sung with the young tenor's customary refinement and grace, together with a firmness and sonority of *mezza voce* which the old process rarely if ever vouchsafed him.

Next month I look forward to reviewing the new edition of *Opera at Home,* which the H.M.V. has for some time had upon the stocks. It ought, now more than ever, to be a very interesting and valuable compilation.

HERMAN KLEIN.

THE GRAMOPHONE AND THE SINGER

(Continued)

By HERMAN KLEIN

The New H.M.V. Operatic Records—II

I AM coming to the conclusion that the limits of the universal craze for achieving " records " will be reached ere long. I allude, of course, to records of speed, height, distance, endurance, and so forth, more especially those connected with mechanical movement or transport by land, sea, and air. Progress by new methods will always be going on; progress in art is ever a thing devoutly to be wished for. But the terrific struggle for pre-eminence in power where human capacity is concerned—the receptive capacity of the senses of sight, touch, and hearing, I mean—must ultimately be limited by what ordinary eyes, ears, etc., will bear.

Applying this law to gramophone records (not to the other kind of records, where it bears a different signification), I find there a tremendous tussle going on at the present time for the attainment of the maximum of loudness, and that sooner or later it will have to come to a stop because the human ear, as devised by nature, will refuse to stand anything louder. I have already touched upon the fringe of this subject, and given it as my opinion that mere sonority and volume do not represent the *Ultima Thule* of phonographic development and enterprise. The prevailing consideration from first to last ought to be the achievement of the highest perfection of musical beauty. Beyond that the functions of the microphone or the loud-speaker, or for that matter the megaphone, have no right whatsoever to carry us. Merely to magnify the size of the voice is not to render it more beautiful or more desirable. It is not lovelier because it will " travel " further or " split your ears " if you stand close to your machine. It may be very marvellous; but if it exceeds the original in amplitude and penetrating power, you will speedily become fatigued by it. I utter this warning for the reason that in my belief, granted a normal medium for the reproduction of the new electrical records, the limit of comfortable aural endurance has been reached.

Let me now hasten to add that my admiration for the other improvements involved in the new process remains exactly where it was. In continuing my review of the H.M.V. re-recordings, I shall make no further reference to the above question, unless by way of emphasizing my appreciation of the benefits of maximum sonority where it happens to produce the right and proper effect. I will begin with an example—the Storm scene in the first act of Verdi's *Otello* and the finish of the duet between Otello and Iago in the second act as rendered by Zenatello and Granforte with chorus and orchestra (DB.1007).

No one who has heard the opera will need to be told that these are places where the entire body of sound-producing instruments, from the singing voice down to the percussion of the big drum, has perforce to be let loose. Well, this record gives it with a degree of realism that has never been approached. It simply reproduces Verdi's calculated effects with an exactitude that makes you feel you must be listening to it in some large opera-house; in short, the ensemble sounds precisely as it ought to sound. Zenatello's *Esultate* is a supremely fine bit of declamation, and in the scene with Iago he has a worthy coadjutor in Granforte, both singing fearlessly at the top of their voices.

Some splendid records by the talented Roman singer, Ezio Pinza, are going to attract of lot of attention. Apart from their mechanical excellence, they are welcome because they bring to our notice a voice of noble proportions and a dignified, artistic style; for this *basso* (*cantante* or *profondo*, each in turn) stands straight in the line of Edouard de Reszke and Plançon. He created a rôle in Boito's *Nerone*, and is said to be the best Italian artist of his type now before the public. He is young, evidently very dramatic, and displays the correct traditions in Verdi pieces like *O tu Palermo* and *Ella giammai m'amò* or *Dormiro sol* (DB.1087); also in the *Possente Numi* (*Flauto Magico*) and *Donne che riposate* (*Roberto*) (DB.1088); and two airs in French from *La Juive* (DA.907, 10 in.), which last replaces a 12 in. Italian disc cancelled last year. His voice sounds finest in his native tongue, but he has made an exceptionally good record of the celebrated *Air du Tambour Major* from Ambroise Thomas's neglected light opera, *Le Caïd* (DB.1086), which, together with the lullaby from *Mignon*, forms a specimen worth having.

Fernand Ansseau, who ranks high among French tenors, if not actually at the top, has performed a useful work by replacing his old *Werther* disc, *O Nature* and *J'aurais sur ma poitrine* (formerly DB.485, now DB. 1085) with something stupendous in tone and beautifully sung. Also admirable are his two *Tosca* airs (DA.898, 10 in.), whereof *Lucevan le stelle* worthily cancels the old 12 in. disc. Another first-rate tenor, Beniamino Gigli, has done the same for his *Dai campi* and *Giunto sul passo*, from *Mefistofele*, which now wear an entirely different aspect in DA.883, 10 in. A similar improvement distinguishes the re-recording of Maria Jeritza's Wagner excerpts from the two early operas; only unluckily it is in this kind of music that I care for her least. She needs strong drama wherein to let herself go, and the outpourings of Elsa and Elisabeth (DB.1092) demand more of a poetic vein. Yet I doubt whether she will ever sing better records than these.

Writing not long since of Giovanni Martinelli, I had occasion to remark upon the care that he takes of his voice, which has shown no sign whatever of deterioration since I first heard him at Covent Garden nearly sixteen years ago. Evidently he imposes no more strain upon his constitution than upon his throat. Perfect ease is the distinguishing characteristic of his method, notably in his higher register, and he has in consequence been one of the first robust tenors to profit by the new recording facilities. His tone, entirely unforced, is remarkable for its sweetness and purity as well as its great power in things like the airs from *Fédora*, *Amor ti vieta* and *Mia madre* (DA.861, 10 in.), which have never previously been heard to such advantage. Martinelli is not a model French singer, any more than Ansseau is irreproachable in Italian; but I agree that it is best to sing operatic pieces in the original language and can therefore unreservedly recommend the former's two airs from *La Juive* (DB.865, 10 in.), *Rachel, quand du Seigneur* and *Que ma voix tremblante*. The flow of tone in both is wonderfully clear, rich, and smoothly sustained. He is delightful, again, together with Rosa Ponsella, in the final duet from *Aïda*, here given in two parts (DA.861, 10 in.), entitled respectively *La fatal pietra* and *Morir si pura e bella*. The tone of the soprano is singularly full and luscious, and the more I hear of her gramophone work the better I like it.

Antonio Cortis is a tenor of Spanish birth or extraction who has, I understand, been leading man at the Chicago Opera House for the past two or three seasons. He has not yet appeared at Covent Garden, nor has he previously sung for H.M.V.; but his name may be remembered in connection with some Parlophone work, though I cannot at this moment say exactly what. The point that matters is that he is the owner of a remarkably fine voice and that his robust style is commendably free from the usual modern blemishes. There is not a scintilla of " wobble " or " bleat " at any time; one can thoroughly enjoy the manly ring of his tone and the palpable absence of effort that marks his production

of it. It has, moreover, that covered quality so often neglected by the imitators of Caruso. I have only praise for the new Cortis record of the air from *La Favorita* (*Una vergine un angiol d'amore*, DA.757), so full is it of power that does not overstep the mark; also for a charming rendering of Rodolfo's *Mimi è una civetta* on the reverse side. But even more striking as a novelty, as well as a splendid sample of *sostenuto* declamation and dramatic energy, are the two excerpts from Giordano's opera, *La Cena delle Beffe* (DA.919). The music is fine, while the singer's fresh young voice, his command of high notes and tone colour, his power of characterization and his sardonic touches in the *Ah! che tormento*, combine to make this one of the most interesting records in the present list.

I spoke well last month of a record of *Vissi d'arte* and *Voi lo sapete* by Dusolina Giannini, a pupil of Mme. Sembrich, who has already been heard in London besides making a considerable name for herself in her native United States. Now comes a later effort in the shape of *Ritorna vincitor!* and *O patria mia* from *Aïda* (DB.1093), for which I must confess to slightly less admiration. Pleasing the voice assuredly is, but, if vocally agreeable and pretty, it sounds, for music of this type, dramatically insignificant. The *Ritorna vincitor* is hurried, mechanical, and affords but a poor notion of the conflicting emotions that the unhappy Ethiopian princess is undergoing. The other familiar selection is more satisfying, though it still lacks spontaneity and real impassioned feeling. Thus the phrasing, while technically correct, remains cold and uninspired. The conclusion is that Dusolina Giannini still needs time and experience to achieve all that is possible with her rare vocal gifts.

Does the quality of the voice undergo material change as singers get older? That is a question of some interest that has often presented itself to my mind. It is not to be answered with a " yes " or a " no," but rather with both; for some voices alter a good deal in course of the years—others not at all. I could give many instances out of the past, only it would take up too much space to illustrate this variableness; and also some—Melba's, Battistini's, Sembrich's, Gerhardt's—where the timbre has retained the identical quality that it had when I heard the singer for the first time. Happily, too, these are voices that can be heard to-day through the medium of the gramophone. Another—that of Marcel Journet —challenges comparison as one that remains strong, steady, and musical after a stage career of 35 years, more than thirty of which have come under my own observation. But in this instance I note an alteration. I noted it last year at Covent Garden, and now I note it again in the new record which Marcel Journet has recently made for H.M.V. (DA.771, 10 in.). It is not the singing that has changed, nor is the tone less resonant and sympathetic; but somehow it is different, and I am not sure that I should have recognized the voice as Journet's without certain characteristic touches that he has always put into *Vecchia zimarra* (*La Bohème*) and *Chi mi dirà* (the " John Barley-corn " song) from *Martha*. Both are sung with all the old point and rhythmical vigour (note the shakes in the latter), and it is evident that both gain by the new recording.

Yet more tenor débuts (both Italian), concerning which not a word was inserted in the H.M.V. cata-logue for 1928. The name of Angelo Minghetti, like those of Antonio Cortis and Lomelino Silva, pre-sumably owes its appearance in the Supplementary List to his presence in America, the home and refuge of all expensive singers. Minghetti, like Cortis, is a valuable *trouvaille*. His voice has not the same ring-ing quality, and indeed at moments is inclined to become dull and muffled (not the fault of the record-ing, however), but on the whole reveals a fine, big body of tone and an extensive range right up to a powerful high C. This last emerges in the duet from the garden scene of *Rigoletto*, *E il sol dell'anima*, wherein he has the support of Luella Paikin, the (? English) possessor of a beautiful soprano voice and more perfect in intonation than her companion. On the other side the tenor gives *Che gelida manina* (DB.952), and sings it very well indeed. His *Questa o quella* (DA.800, 10 in.) is commendably vivacious and distinct, and the tone in that is much brighter and solid than in *La donna è mobile*, where the before-mentioned muffled notes again occur. Yet another disc (DA.801, 10 in.) also arouses mingled feelings : a commonplace Italian ballad by Donandy, *Vaghissima sembianza*, has no interest or charm whatever, whereas the *Recondita armonia*, smooth and nicely phrased, has both.

Lomelino Silva is not in the same category, vocally speaking, with either Cortis or Minghetti. His is the authentic " bleat," with accompanying *vibrato*, that has disfigured the voices of too many Italian tenors during the last half century. In the two *Rigoletto* airs (DA.798, 10 in.) he displays few points of ex-cellence, while the flourish which concludes *La donna è mobile* is very suggestive of a caricature out of a Savoy opera.

As a gramophone artist Maartje Offers is now what I may term a familiar figure. Rarely does a month pass without my having to criticize some of her work in the review columns of this magazine. That fact is evidence that her records are in demand—or are ex-pected to be—both perhaps. She is not without faults ; but, reckoned as a whole, her balance is decidedly on the credit side. Were her method of breathing correct, her superb organ and chaste, artistic style would place her among the leading con-traltos of the present time. As it is, I will not say she is unreliable ; but she varies more than she ought. In her latest record (DA.825, 10 in.) she is steadier than usual, and Mozart's *Ave verum* receives from

her a rendering replete with broad tone and religious feeling. The accompaniment, executed by string quartet and organ (Herbert Dawson) is too heavily played, and tumbles into the new-process pitfall of occasionally drowning the soloist. On the reverse side, in quaint contrast, we get *Stride la vampa* from *Il Trovatore*, sung with bold rhythm and abundant spirit, but depreciated in value to my ears because many of the dotted quaver and semiquaver groups are blurred. With a little more care this blemish might have been avoided.

Two well-known items from her recital programmes provide material for what is perhaps the most perfect record yet made by the gifted Elisabeth Schumann. Both are by Mozart (DA.845, 10 in.) and sung with an orchestral accompaniment that is worthy of the singer, which is saying much. The *coloratura* of the *Alleluia* is flawless and the breath-control so complete that the tone remains at the same level of purity and resonance throughout. I should like to see this used as a model by every teacher and student in the country that owns a gramophone, and not only for the above qualities but for life, vigour, smoothness, and agility as well. The *legato* of *Vedrai carino* is more faithfully reproduced and the exquisite diction better main-tained than is the dramatic reading of the piece. Zerlina's shy humour and wheedling manner in this wonderful little song are scarcely realized. As it seems to me, Frau Schumann takes the whole thing *au grand sérieux*, which was obviously not what Mozart meant it to be. But despite that, it is a glorious record.

Tito Schipa reminds me of no living tenor so much as Bonci—less by his voice, which is neither so round nor ringing in timbre as Bonci's was twenty years ago, than by his art, which I admire more and more every time I hear him. There is no need to particu-larize over again concerning his technique. But Schipa's is a singularly individual talent ; he seems to imitate nobody ; he phrases in accordance with his own ideas as much as with tradition ; there is no seek-ing after effect. He knows he has a delightful *mezza voce*, and he takes care to make all possible use of it, which is readily done in the two Almaviva airs from Rossini's *Barbiere di Siviglia* provided the *piena voce* be also forthcoming now and then. The record of these two airs, *Se il mio nome* and *Ecco ridente il cielo* (DA.874, 10 in.), reflects all the above merits *plus* the advantages of the new recording, viz., admirable clearness, volume, and atmosphere. Everything else is there as well. The most hypercritical listener could not ask for more even, more accurately sung scales or ornaments executed with greater flexibility and grace. The chromatic scale in the *cabaletta* has never, in my experience, been so crisply and correctly given in a gramophone reproduction, and very seldom so well sung in an opera house. This may sound high praise, but it is not higher than Tito Schipa deserves.

HERMAN KLEIN.

THE GRAMOPHONE AND THE SINGER

(*Continued*)

The New H.M.V. Operatic Records—III
By HERMAN KLEIN

AS the termination of my present task is reached with this article, I ought perhaps to preface it with a few impressions regarding the new H.M.V. recordings as a whole. Well, only one verdict is possible. There cannot be the slightest doubt that the records comprised in this Operatic Supplement have raised enormously the level of average merit associated with the vocal section of the H.M.V. catalogue. For the recording itself no words of praise would be excessive. Thanks to the electrical process, it has become such a true and faithful reflection of the original presentation that the whole ensemble, no matter how vast or complex its component parts, seems to be actually and actively in progress in our very midst, focussed within a perspective that the ears can grasp as easily as the eyes can take in a picture.

That further improvement will be made is certain; but it will depend more, in my opinion, upon the executants or the conductors than upon the mechanism. What is required is a more perfect balance between the dynamic forces that constitute the "blend." As things stand now, the ideal balance is too frequently a matter of chance—much the same as it is in a wireless broadcast performance, only not so "rough and ready" or so blurred and noisy. Obviously more pains will have to be taken by singers and instrumentalists alike; pieces will have to be gone over and again, with unrelaxing patience on everybody's part, and under the watchful supervision of a capable, experienced listener. Particularly in choral ensembles there must be increased care not to allow principals to blot out choristers, or *vice versâ*; or to let both together obliterate the supporting orchestra. The position of the various forces in front of the microphone is doubtless an important factor, and often enough the effect on my ears seems to indicate that it is all wrong. But that it can be remedied and the proper balance obtained is equally certain.

Another warning—addressed this time to English male soloists. They are too much out for volume. Perhaps it is because they are mildly jealous of the foreigner, with his bigger voice and freer production. Anyhow, their tone sounds a great deal louder on the gramophone than it does as a rule in the concert-room or even in the opera house. They appear to be standing quite close—much too close—to the microphone, and, by using excessive breath-pressure, they either detract from the natural beauty and purity of their voices or else they set up a *vibrato* which is not a normal feature of their singing. In this matter, as I think I have observed before, the microphone is more relentless than a highly-polished mirror. It shows up every defect to which the human voice is liable; and I regret to add that the habit of making the tone unsteady by careless or unskilful breathing is one of the commonest of those defects. Otherwise electrical recording is a grand discovery, and, so long as its facilities are not abused and its dangers avoided, it is going to prove a permanent blessing for what Americans are still pleased to call the "talking-machine world."

And now to continue with the H.M.V. records. Hilda Spani, to whose advance to solo rank I drew attention in the first of these articles, makes yet another forward step with a 10 in. Puccini disc of surpassing excellence (DA.879). It would be difficult to imagine a more delicate and refined rendering either of the *Addio di Mimi* or the charming page, *In quelle trine morbide*, from *Manon Lescaut*. This singer offers a lesson in naturalness, sweetness, and steadiness of tone to many English sopranos I could name—above all the naturalness, which induces the best possible quality for recording purposes. If vocalists could leave their nerves behind them and forget themselves as well as their little mannerisms when they approach the microphone, what a gain it would be for all concerned!

Even an artist with all the *savoir faire* of Walter Widdop, whose fine tenor sounds so free in the theatre (and will, I hope, do so at Covent Garden very shortly), fails to do himself complete justice when it comes to recording. An element of muscular constriction and consequent throatiness creeps into his timbre. He sustains well, but he uses his chest instead of his ribs and diaphragm to propel the upward exhalation of breath, and instantly the voice takes on a slight yet perceptible *vibrato* which pervades the entire piece. What a pity this is! For positively it is the only fault I have to find with the excerpts from *Prince Igor* and *Lohengrin* upon a single disc (D.1353, 12 in.). Better declamation and diction one could hardly wish for; dreamy romantic feeling suffuses the delightful air *Daylight is fading*, from Borodin's opera; while the *Narration* from the final scene of *Lohengrin* is given with an unusually smooth, elegant *legato*, even though the tone trembles a little all the time. The intonation, too, is faultless, showing that the singer has a perfect ear, which is by no means always the case in this glorious Wagnerian *mélo*. So, having begun with a criticism, I find myself ending this paragraph on a note of high praise.

With a contribution of two splendid discs, the distinguished German baritone, Friedrich Schorr, makes a noteworthy début with H.M.V. It would seem, nevertheless, that the work was done in Berlin, not at Hayes—though of course the *modus operandi* was the same, and probably the mechanical *personnel* as well. But what concerns us is the result; and, happily, that is irreproachable. The orchestra is that of the State Opera, conducted by Leo Blech, whose exceptional ability and experience are made manifest in an admirable balance and clarity of instrumental tone. We have first of all the finale to the last act of *Die Meistersinger* done in two parts (*Verachtet mir die Meister* and *Was deutsch und echt*, D.1354, 12 in.). This is all splendidly sung by Herr Schorr in his own rich, sonorous, powerful tone, with the noble ending supported by an excellent chorus. The other disc yields more familiar pages from earlier operas of Wagner, viz., the *O star of eve* (in German *O du, mein holder Abendstern*) from *Tannhäuser*, and the opening solo of the duet (*Wie aus der Ferne*) between Vanderdecken and Senta from *The Flying Dutchman* (D.1355, 12 in.). Both are gems and both most poetically interpreted; still, I especially welcome the beautiful passage from the *Dutchman*, not only for its haunting melodic charm, but because the singer so exquisitely realizes the composer's indication that it shall be sung "*mezza voce e con molto portamento.*" The true effect of this is seldom attained by a heavy voice like Schorr's; yet here it is, " beyond all possible manner of doubt."

My previous advice on the subject of loud recording I particularly commend to Mr. Browning Mummery, together with a concentrated study of the record noticed in the preceding paragraph. This talented countryman of Dame Melba has still a great deal to do before his technique will compare with hers on points such as vowel-formation, tone gradation, refinement of expression, and other of the *nuances* that proclaim an artist. He either shouts at the top of his voice as in *The whole world over*, or he changes from a splashing outburst to a display of artificial tearful grief, as in *Yes, in one sudden moment* (C.1425, 12 in.). These samples from *Madame Butterfly* represent, as it were, the head and tail of Pinkerton's offending; his reckless rushing into a solemn engagement, and the " crocodile tears " that precede his escape from the scene of the tragedy. The same loud voice lies thickly over both; a voice whose ring is much more honest than the young lieutenant's conduct. The whole costs only 4s. 6d., orchestra included, so that you get plenty for your money.

I come now to the final group in this long selection. It consists of six choruses from the old operas, all but one Italian; and four choruses from *Carmen*, besides three instrumental excerpts from the latter. The whole are comprised in this order in three 12 in.

discs, B.2622-4 and C.1422-4, priced respectively at 3s. and 4s. 6d. My tastes being of the all-round type, I can enjoy some of the things at which the modern highbrow looks askance. Let me, therefore, candidly confess that I took a sober pleasure in listening to the tuneful numbers sung by the choristers of La Scala under Carlo Sabajno; and no less, certainly, in the well-known *Carmen* items, as rendered at Covent Garden under Vincenzo Bellezza. They are, almost without exception, clear, restrained, musical, and rhythmically vigorous. I disagree, though, with Signor Bellezza's *tempo* in the opening scene from *Carmen*, because it is altogether too fast for either the music or the singers, and therefore altogether wrong. In happy contrast to this, the Cigarette Chorus on the reverse side is taken at Bizet's Opéra-Comique speed, and, delightfully sung both by men and girls, strikes one at once as the perfect thing. The solo bits in the earlier chorus are done by Katherine Arkandy and Octava Dua, and, but for being so badly hurried, would sound better than they do. Bellezza's extra " notch " makes everybody gabble their words.

Personally, I enjoyed the Scala choruses in a special degree, because they brought back recollections of old Covent Garden days when they used to be sung at the Saturday afternoon operatic concerts in the Floral Hall—now (let me whisper it) the Potato Market. The choristers, clad in their best Sunday Italian garments, occupied two long rows at the back of the platform, and had to sit there all through the concert, listening (if not asleep) to the illustrious " stars," headed as a rule by Adelina Patti, who shared the operatic programme. Those were the occasions when we got these very choruses—most of them unisonal, if not in thirds and sixths—out of *I Lombardi*, *Nabucco*, *Ernani*, etc., even when the operas themselves were not being given. And, thanks to the Floral Hall and the Italian organ-grinders, you would hear these old tunes being whistled all over London. One of them, *O fosco cielo*, took me still further back to the juvenile parties at which I used to dance to the *Sonnambula* Quadrilles, arranged from the opera by Dan Godfrey or Charles D'Albert, I forget which. Only of course it sounds very differently, properly sung, on this record; being, indeed, the narrative set to music by Bellini in his inimitable manner wherein the simple villagers relate to the Conte Rodolfo, their lord and master, all about the horrid spectacle of the nocturnal ghost that haunts their mountain retreat—none other than poor Amina, who walks in her sleep! I apologize for the reminiscence; but you will agree that it appropriately winds up this long story.

So much for the H.M.V. Operatic Supplement bearing date January 15th, 1928. It will, I imagine, be supplemented by others in turn. Of the lot so far issued is would appear that seven discs only have replaced old recordings, the remainder being new.

Hina Spani and Dusolina Giannini have been advanced to the rank of " celebrity artists " (operatic); while Luella Paikin, Antonio Cortis, Angelo Minghetti, Lomelino Silva, Lawrence Tibbett, and Friedrich Schorr have made their first appearance in this Company's catalogue. Altogether a highly interesting showing. With regard to Miss Luella Paikin, I have been asked to clear up any doubts that a remark of mine may have created as to her nationality. I do so with pleasure. She is a born Manchester girl, and her father is a resident in that city at the present time. Before going abroad she sang with the Carl Rosa Company eight or nine years ago, and it was whilst appearing at Southport in *Rigoletto* that the Secretary of a Manchester Male Voice Choir engaged her for one of their concerts. That engagement was cancelled, however, in consequence of her leaving for Italy, where, of course, she acquired both the art and the experience that have since been admired in London in her concert and gramophone work.

Gramophone Stars for Covent Garden

Almost I feel that I ought to offer excuses for associating operatic " stars " *per se* with the gramophone; for in reality this grand invention is essentially democratic in its nature, and therein differs wholly from " grand opera," whose exponents are divided into distinct classes. I know all about celebrity lists and coloured labels, and so forth (if I did not the prices would soon inform me); but still I hold that " stars " are not " stars " before the microphone until they have proved their ability to make a good record; therefore, *vis-à-vis* of that formidable test, all singers should be reckoned as equals. Moreover, every one of them, whether eminent or not, is independent of the other, and is working primarily on his or her own account. Hence the democratic basis.

Yet naturally we find among the list of international stars (so-called) compiled for the forthcoming Royal Opera season many of what may fairly be termed the pick of the gramophone operatic performers. They are not there because they are " best sellers," or anything like it. (I miss, for instance, Mme. Galli-Curci and Master Lough.) But they have been engaged because of their world-wide reputations; because they have abnormally fine voices, and can be relied on to do their particular job, whatever it may be, as nearly to perfection as 20th-century grand opera entitles us to expect. Let it be remembered that they have to act as well as to sing, to move and gesticulate as well as study dynamic effects. There is a good deal more to do on the stage before the footlights than when standing in front of the indulgent microphone, which so many singers needlessly tremble before or shout at—or both. Nowadays, too,

they may be fulfilling the two functions in the opera house at the same moment—singing for their audience and for the recording angel who is taking them unawares. Nor is the day far distant when television will step in and complete the miracle, giving us the picture as well as the music, bringing the aural and the visual reproduction of the opera to our very fireside. Being a bit of an optimist, I am confidently hoping to live to witness that amazing achievement.

Meanwhile I congratulate Lt.-Col. Eustace Blois and the directors of the new Covent Garden Syndicate upon the high level of the vocal talent that they have secured for the season that opens on April 30th. Somehow I do not think we shall greatly miss Jeritza, who is apparently too busy elsewhere, or too unreasonable in her demands, or something. Anyhow, she dwells in our memories as an exotic rather than a hardy annual, and I admit that for my own part I can at any time dispense with orchids without a pang. On the other hand, we are to have the felicity of welcoming a genuine best-seller in Theodor Chaliapin. I am not sure how long he will stay here, but he has not been a regular member of a London opera company for many years, and it will be good to see him again in his old part of Boris Godounov, the superb embodiment wherein he made his début at Drury Lane in 1913.

It would be idle to attempt a forecast of the operas in which the different artists will appear. A list of the rôles with which they are individually acquainted is inserted in every contract, but it does not follow from that that they will play the lot for which they are set down as *disponibles*. The customary overlapping is bound to occur; but the experienced impresario is aware of it, and also knows that it is better to have too many than too few performers available. Only in a *saison de luxe* such as this, however, will you see a collection of red-label aristocrats, including such as Lotte Lehmann, Frida Leider, Göta Ljungberg, Maria Olczewska, Fanny Heldy, Dusolina Giannini, Eva Turner, Margaret Sheridan, Jane Bourguignon, Fernand Ansseau, Rudolf Laubenthal, Lauritz Melchior, Aureliano Pertile, Clemens, Thill, Widdop, Ivar Andrésen, Mariano Stabile, Emil Schipper, Marcel Journet, and others whose names are either new or less familiar. The two principal conductors will be Bruno Walter and Vincenzo Bellezza.

With these forces engaged, one need not hesitate to predict some very high-class and interesting performances. I was alone in suggesting last summer in THE GRAMOPHONE that it would be found both wise and profitable to extend the season beyond six or even eight weeks, and I am glad to note that this year it is to last for ten weeks. I only hope that the Syndicate will be in a position, when July 6th arrives, to justify my advice by paying a dividend.

HERMAN KLEIN.

THE GRAMOPHONE AND THE SINGER
(Continued)
The New Columbia Operatic Records—I
By HERMAN KLEIN

*E*PUR *si muove*! What Galileo said of the earth is equally true of the big gramophone houses: they do keep on moving. (So, I am told, do their shares on the Stock Exchange; but that concerns me not in the least.) Each is progressing steadily as a good, well-behaved planet should in its own orbit, and shedding new light *en passant* upon familiar objects that needs a little brightening up. Really the New Process is a godsend. It has come in the nick of time, to stimulate the activities of creation and renewal in this section of the world's business, at the very moment when the world itself was beginning to realize the vast artistic potentialities of a great mechanical product. The result seems to be, amazingly enough, that the demand for machines and records is for the moment greater than the supply.

For the last three months I have written about the H.M.V. Operatic Supplement. This month I come to Columbia's newly-issued list of grand opera records, and I am very glad to be able to deal with them forthwith. The opening words of our Editor's brilliant article on " Re-recordings " in last month's GRAMOPHONE prepared me for this eventuality, while his subsequent reassuring remarks about my notices of the H.M.V. supplement, if too modest concerning himself, afforded me a great deal of pleasure. We both feel, I think, that even though opinions may sometimes differ slightly in the evaluation of identical material, our main purpose is the same, namely, to enable the reader to choose the best out of the multitude of records that are constantly being issued. I also agree that it doesn't matter if many of the re-recordings are of hackneyed operatic arias, as well as of other and fresher numbers, so long as the singer does them well and imparts new interest to them under the improved conditions yielded by the electrical process.

This reflection leads me to another which is not less important, and that is the actual *provenance* or source—perhaps I ought to call it the nationality—of these re-recordings. I refer, of course, not to the artists who sing them, but to the country in which they are made. How are these countries—America, Germany, Italy, France, and England—comparing with each other in the race for supremacy, if there be one? At the present moment, as it seems to me, there is a considerable disparity between them in point alike of musical quality and artistic merit. I do not propose—not being actually called upon at this par-

ticular juncture—to differentiate between the five countries I have named, much less to award the palm in a contest that is as yet far from over. At the same time I feel that it is part of my critical duty, at the period of vital and rapid transition which we are passing through, to make one or two comparisons, and also one or two suggestions, that might prove to be of a useful kind.

My impressions may be founded to a certain extent upon guesswork; and yet somehow I know that I cannot be far wrong in my surmise as to the places where the new records are being made. As often as not the label tells us by giving the name of the opera house or the orchestra or the chorus; these being, indeed, part of the legitimate attraction that the up-to-date disc is supposed to hold out to the interested purchaser. But then there are also a large proportion, I might even say a majority, that tell us nothing about the *lieu de provenance* beyond the style or title of the manufacturing firm, which is, after all, as it ought to be, the main guarantee of excellence. I need scarcely add that these observations (like all that appear above my signature in this journal) have reference exclusively to vocal records.

In my recent review of the new H.M.V. operatic records I took occasion to express the belief that many of them were manufactured in America; nor did that detract from my high opinion of their quality. How could it? I have no prejudices in this matter, and it is my custom to judge things purely on their merits. But I do know from experience that the American makers of records are at least the equals of the English in the capacity for taking infinite pains which someone (it wasn't Carlyle) once gave as the definition of the word " genius." They have, in addition to improving their instrumental accompaniments, gone far along the road to a correct balance of dynamic strengths and the reduction of tonal force to its proper limits. We are doing creditably in the same direction, though not quite so well as we ought. The Germans vary a great deal. Their recording of the Wagner scores has improved, and in Lieder they are succeeding, in spite of their childish *obbligati*, in preserving a better sense of unity and delicacy coupled with the individuality of the singer. Occasionally in Wagner the solo voice is much louder than it need be; but, on the whole, it is steady, in tune, and of splendid quality. As a rule the piano accompaniments to the Lieder sound as bad as those to the operatic excerpts sound good. The comparatively few French records that I hear sound like faithful and accurate reproductions of the original, whatever it or they may be.

I come now to the Italians, and therewith to the new Columbia " grand opera " list. I may as well confess that it is entirely responsible for my odious behaviour in instituting these comparisons. The simple truth is that the Columbia lot—a representative collection of pieces from no fewer than thirty-six operas—is, with but two or three exceptions, the work of purely Italian singers and originally sung in Milan. Now, *primâ facie*, they should be all the better for that; since the artists are justly announced as " world-famous," are most of them well-known to the *cognoscenti* of the gramophone, and include exactly half-a-dozen of the ever-growing list of foreign celebrities who are to appear at Covent Garden this season. Leaving aside for the moment the question of individual merit, I feel bound to say that the interest of these records lies chiefly in the voices and the singing—hardly ever in the effect of the ensemble, the beauty of voices and instruments in combination, such as we should expect in the opera house under the magic wand of a Toscanini or a Bellezza. It is precisely here that I feel that Italy is behind the other nations. Its best singers sound to my ears as though they were getting careless in front of the microphone. They are also judging indifferently the power and the quality of their own voices. The studio orchestras are inferior to the Americans', the Germans', and our own. The whole arrangement is apparently supervised with less meticulous care and due observance of light and shade, of cause and effect. This impression is by no means a new one, and, despite exceptions, it is inescapably confirmed in the series I am now dealing with.

There is nothing wrong, so far as my ear can perceive, with the recording itself. In fact, it is as clean and clear in definition, as penetrating and powerful in tone, as are recordings by electrical process done anywhere else. What I find inferior in the Milanese output lies in the musical generalship, or, rather, the absence of it, and the mistakes committed in the disposition of forces. The balance between voices, between soloists and choristers, or between these and the orchestra, is seldom accurately adjusted; and, although the fault is a common one, it seems to be a trifle more conspicuous here than elsewhere. It betrays itself more frequently in a cascade of blurred sounds, which in the big ensembles degenerates into mere noise. Then, again, the instrumentation of the accompaniments to some of the old operatic pieces—especially those which used to be denominated the " big guitar " sort—are by no means deftly handled. A glaring illustration of this is the vamping bass, marking the bar with a single staccato note, in several of these pieces, by an obstreperous brass instrument, either a tuba or still more ancient ophicleide, after

the fashion of the pre-war German band. Such a thing should never have been tolerated. How much better work can be done is shown in the treatment of the Puccini items—notably an admirable record of the final duet from *Tosca*, which I shall speak of again in its turn.

Happily the singers, knowing the particular *genre* that suits them best, are as much at home in the older as in the modern operas, though not invariably in both. The Italian vocalist of to-day is trained upon a certain model or pattern. Tenors resemble each other so closely both in timbre and style that very often the expert listener finds it hard to distinguish between them. (I might suggest to my Editor that it would be great fun to start a competition for guessing the right names of the various tenors who oblige us so frequently with *La donna è mobile* or *Lucevan le stelle*, the test to be applied with brand-new records.) I quote as an example of this resemblance Pertile and Lazaro in the selections from *Andrea Chénier* and *Turandot*. Most of the popular sopranos at the Scala and other big Italian theatres nowadays are cast in the same identical mould, albeit their voices may differ in quality and degrees of steadiness. The contraltos, baritones, and basses can be more readily distinguished from each other.

To sum up, the position of Italy among the leading record-making countries is by no means all that it ought to be. It should, of course, be on a level with the best of them, and until that goal has been arrived at a heavy responsibility will rest upon the shoulders of those concerned. Meanwhile the other countries are not likely to stand still. America will grow more painstaking and give us a more polished product. Germany will be striving after stronger and ever-stronger realism, dramatic atmosphere, and clever tonal effects. We shall, I hope, continue to lead the way in the reproduction of oratorio and choral mass-ensembles, as well as in the great instrumental departments where, it appears to me, England is now running a pretty even race with the other two countries just named. Italy's " job " is clear. You have only to compare the quality of the records sung by the same Italian artists in Milan with those sung by them in New York to see exactly what I mean.

I take the new Columbia records in their order on the printed list, and after what has been said I can deal more briefly with those in which the prevailing defects occur, preferring as I do to dwell at greater length upon the good points. Most of the individual efforts, indeed, call for favourable criticism. The first disc on the list (L.2048, 12 in.) ought not to be solely attributed to G. Arangi-Lombardi (in large caps.) because she only takes part there in the *Easter Hymn* from *Cavalleria*, whereas the ensemble from the supper scene of *La Traviata* " features " Maria Gentile, another fine soprano, and the tenor Allessandro Granda. But all these are quite first-rate, even if the chorus is too clamorous. Arangi-Lombardi is still more satisfying in the two *Trovatore* airs, *Tacea la notte* and *D'amor sull'ali rosee* (L.2049 12 in.). Her voice is steady here and rich in quality, while her breathing capacity seems abnormal and she phrases artistically, though in her cadenza she loses control for a moment. Again in the duet for Santuzza and Turiddu (L.2075, 12 in., two parts) her voice is well matched with Francesco Merli's, and between them they do full justice to Mascagni—which is more than can be said of the orchestra.

Maria Gentile has a sweet voice, a very pure soprano, with clear, musical head notes and a good staccato. It is a pity her technique is not more polished and brilliant (also more accurate in her *coloratura*), because if it were she might fairly be placed at the top of the tree. Her *Caro nome* (L.2050, 12 in.) is pleasing but not impeccable, and the same disc gives the garden duet with the Duca, the latter being Dino Borgioli. On two 10 in. discs Maria Gentile has done some excellent Bellini and Donizetti (D.1061-2), but I object to the omission of the *cabaletta*, or quick second part, from some of these arias. If the whole of *Regnava nel silenzio*, why not the whole of *Quì la voce*, instead of supplementing the latter with *Come per me sereno* from *La Sonnambula*? Otherwise I commend both records as capital value.

We know our Guglielmetti now; and one can take her or leave her as one pleases. She is an acquired taste, a human musical-box replete with flights of vocal mechanism. Her *Una voce* in two parts (L.2051, 12 in.) is sung much too slowly and deliberately, with exaggerated pauses between phrases and tremendously long *points-d'orgue*. I prefer to this her *Mad Scene* from *Lucia* (L.2052, 12 in.), not alone because it is, on the whole, more neat and correct in execution, but because the tone is less " white." The same light soprano, after presenting these things in their entirety, gives us *Ah! fors' è lui* (D.1603, 10 in.) minus the *cabaletta*, and substitutes for it *Tutte le feste al tempio*, from *Rigoletto*, the only excuse being that for once she descends from her mechanical pedestal and sings it charmingly.

Come we now to Bianca Scacciati, the dramatic soprano, whose appearance at Covent Garden in the *Huguenots* will not have escaped recollection. Personally I liked her best in *Turandot*, she being a delightful Puccini singer, both sentimental and temperamental, though apt to overdo her *portamenti*, as, for example, in *Vissi d'arte* (L. 2053, 12 in.), which suits her to perfection. I also find points to admire in the air from *Un Ballo in Maschera*, *Morrò, ma prima*, which is on the other side. But by far the most satisfactory contribution from Bianca Scacciati is her share in the beautiful duet, *O dolci mani* (L.2078, 12 in., two parts), sung with Alessandro Granda, the possessor of a remarkably fine tenor voice. Altogether, as stated previously, I consider this disc,

alike for singing, accompanying, and recording, the gem of the collection now under notice. I hardly think that the atmosphere of that tragic final scene in *La Tosca* has ever been so well transferred to the gramophone before.

Rosetta Pampini is engaged for Covent Garden, and will probably be making her début soon after these lines appear. Her voice is a genuine soprano of warm, round timbre, with scarcely any tremolo and always well in the middle of the note. She is somewhat too vigorous for Mozart, and her rendering of *Voi che sapete* (D.1605, 10 in.) is not improved by the coarse attentions of the bar-marking tuba who follows her through all her pieces. He is especially palpitating in Rossini's *La Danza* (same disc), which receives rough treatment all round, but fortunately less prominent in the two airs for Liù from *Turandot*, which suit this singer admirably and will most likely be part of her approaching work in London. She ought likewise to be heard in *Madam Butterfly* (so many of these Italian sopranos are only at their very best nowadays in the Puccini operas)—that is, judging from her fine rendering with Francesco Merli of the passionate love duet which concludes the first act (in two parts, L.2076, 12 in.).

Another and still more beautiful love duet—that from Gounod's *Faust*—is sung by Maria Zamboni and Dino Borgioli (L.2077, 12 in.), filling both sides of the disc. Their voices blend agreeably in a typically suave *legato*, and they achieve a good average performance. The tenor also contributes a couple of solos (L.2054, 12 in.) in the same characteristic manner, viz., *Una furtiva lagrima* (*L'Elisir d'Amore*) and *Se il mio nome* (*Il Barbiere*). The voice is sympathetic when dark enough in colour, and the phrasing tender and refined at one moment, jerky and spasmodic the next. But with the *tenore leggero* of to-day we have to make up our mind to this constant alternation of what are termed *affettuoso* and *smorzando* effects, which are well enough in their place until overdone. The *Habañera* from *Carmen* and Mignon's *Connais-tu*, both in Italian (D.1604, 10 in.), are nicely rendered by Ebe Stignani, who has a well-trained mezzo-contralto voice.

I conclude for the present with some really first-class records by Ippolito Lazaro, a robust tenor who already fills a conspicuous place in the Columbia catalogue. He has a bright, manly tone, free from *vibrato*, rich and pure in quality, and quite even all through the scale, with high notes remarkable for their ring and the ease with which they are produced. He is essentially a vocalist of the modern school, and his fine declamatory gifts are vividly exemplified in these selections from *Andrea Chénier*, *La Fanciulla del West*, and *Turandot* (L.2055-7, 12 in.). There is practically nothing to choose between them, and once more I may mention that they recall Pertile at his best. They certainly increase one's desire to hear Lazaro at Covent Garden. HERMAN KLEIN.

THE GRAMOPHONE AND THE SINGER
(Continued)
The New Columbia Operatic Records—II
By HERMAN KLEIN

THE index to the list of new grand opera records recently issued by the Columbia Co. comprises thirty-six operas, all sung in Italian. Of these I noticed about half in our May number, and the remainder I am going to deal with now. Of the singers just half-a-dozen are due to appear at Covent Garden this season; but at the moment I am writing none of these had done so, for the simple reason that their services were not required until the Italian performances began, which was not long before the German series had been completed. All the names mentioned in the Columbia circular as belonging to the " World-famous " collection are familiar enough, or should be, to readers of these pages. As yet, however, Maria Gentile, Rosetta Pampini, Joseph Rogatchewsky, and Georges Thill are, I fancy, strangers to Covent Garden; while Dino Borgioli and Mariano Stabile have been heard here previously. In either case, I am happy to have the privilege of giving early reviews of their gramophone work as their records come out from time to time, and so help to make their names and their vocal ability known to our opera-loving readers long before the singers themselves arrive in London to display their gifts *in propriâ personâ*.

Enzo de Muro Lomanto is a new name to me. It has a Spanish ring about it that probably indicates the artist's nationality more accurately than his vocal style, which is distinctly Italian and very much up to date. Despite a slightly nasal and open tone, his tenor voice has some attractive qualities, the most fascinating of which is a *mezza voce* of exceptional sweetness and charm. This he employs, of course, at every opportunity, and swells from it to the full voice or *vice versâ* with practised breath-control, the *diminuendo* being especially well done. Between the two extremes, however, he has little to offer. The solitary 10 in. disc that discloses these facts contains such suitable items as the *Sogno* (dream) of Des Grieux from Massenet's *Manon* and Elvino's exquisite aria, *Prendi l'anel ti dono*, from *La Sonnambula* (D.1607), and I recommend it as an example of unusually smooth, level singing. Francesco Merli has a bigger voice than this but a more ejaculatory method. He displays both in the *Brindisi* and *Addio alla madre* from *Cavalleria Rusticana* (L.2061, 12 in.) as well as in two airs from *La Forza del Destino* (D.1068, 10 in.). There is no particular distinction about the singing of either, but the tone is good and the recording beyond reproach.

From the ultra-Italian school to the traditional French is almost as far as the road to Tipperary. Joseph Rogatchewsky exemplifies the Opéra-Comique style with a fidelity that in no wise betrays his Polish origin or birth (I can't say precisely which of the two it is). The purity of his tenor voice is in any case quite equal to his French accent, and he uses it with a suavity and sustained ease that makes him delightful to listen to. His rather sentimental and deliberate method is not objectionable, because he is intelligent and artistic, and he knows how to make his words very distinct. A pleasant *mezza voce* is made good use of in the *Romance* of Nadir from *Les Pêcheurs de Perles*, as well as in the graceful *Aubade* from *Le Roi d'Ys* (L.2062, 12 in.). It is prominent again in the somewhat overdone *Rêve* from *Manon* (L.2063, 12 in.), but on the other side of this is a curious contrast in the shape of the French version of *Che farò* from Gluck's *Orphée*, which we, of course, associate with a contralto, not a tenor. However, it suits him well enough and reveals the fact that he can sing with life and vigour and plenty of resonance. His Polish tearfulness comes in useful here, and, if he calls on Euridice in a strident tone, he makes the balance right by mourning her in a breathy one. It is a good record.

The Paris Opéra is represented in this list by Georges Thill, an excellent tenor whose records have won from me well-deserved praise. I place him in the same category with Paul Franz and Fernand Ansseau, and more than that need not be said. His ability as an actor and stage singer will be put to the test at Covent Garden very shortly; though not in Massenet's *Werther*, the opera and the rôle that apparently display his talent to especial advantage. Two of the airs are included in the present selection, but not on the same disc. One, *O nature pleine de grâce*, is coupled with the fine *Invocation* from Berlioz's *Faust* (L.2064, 12 in.); while the other, *J'aurai sur ma poitrine*, goes with *Siegmund's Spring Song* (*Chant d'amour*, D.1610, 10.). In both of these the singer satisfies with his broad, powerful *sostenuto* and elegant phrasing, his clear-cut diction and perfect intonation, and, last but not least, his entire freedom from tremolo. Whilst manly and robust in the *Valkyrie* excerpt, he is there slightly wanting in poetic feeling; still, passion is abundantly reflected in his vocal energy. In selections from *Pagliacci* and *Tosca*, given under their French titles (D.1609, 10 in.), but familiar enough even so, Georges Thill displays similar characteristics of the right sort, and I feel particularly safe in advising my readers to invest in his admirable records.

Formichi the Formidable has been endowed by nature with a tone-volume so sonorous that he has no need to take advantage of the new process for the purpose of increasing it. He always reminds me of the giant Polyphemus, as depicted by Handel in *Acis and Galatea*. The music does all that is necessary to make us realize what a huge personage he must have been. Whether in the chorus, *Wretched lovers*, or in his own wonderful ditty, *O ruddier than the cherry*, the intensely descriptive strains suffice to indicate the vast magnitude of that legendary or mythological creature by whom poor Galatea was persecuted. So with Cesare Formichi—he emits enormous sounds without a trace of exaggeration, and so cleverly does he colour them that they can be harsh and strident for one character, and as soft and melting as you please for another. The present disc (L.2065, 12 in.) furnishes precisely this contrast: on one side Gérard's *Monologue* (*Andrea Chénier*) in the manner of the merciless fanatic; on the other the splendid scene, *Pari siamo*, wherein Rigoletto recites (to himself) all his wrongs, hopes, and dreams of vengeance. Formichi's accent and diction in the latter lift him far above the level of the ordinary Rigoletto, while the vocal effect of his declamation is imposing and dramatic in the extreme. Altogether I consider this in every sense an exceptionally fine record.

TANCREDI PASERO

Continuing with the baritones, I find nothing remarkable in Carlo Galeffi's record of the *Toreador's Song* (D.1611, 10 in.), given, as usual, with chorus; but in an *Aïda* excerpt—Amonasro's eloquent passage in the scene where he is dragged on a captive—his combination of appeal with menace is cleverly conveyed by a mixture of broad tone and stentorian *parlato*. Still better art than this characterizes Mariano Stabile's singing of two notable pages from *Don Giovanni*, viz., the *Serenade* and the air in praise of wine, *Fin c'han del vino* (D.1612, 10 in.). Both are models of clear articulation and rhythmical energy, while the tone and the recording are also admirable. The opening phrase of the *Serenade*, however, is still spoilt by Stabile's literal insistence on the two B naturals, which Mozart so obviously intended to be treated as an *appoggiatura*; that is,

the first to be sung a C sharp. But some people are very obstinate in these matters.

A capital *basso cantante* is Nazareno de Angelis; a dramatic singer of the old type that used to vacillate, as he does, between extremes of the tender and lachrymose and the declamatory "tuppence coloured." His realism is always bold and earnest; his acquaintance with conventional points is profound —for which reason I prefer him in the older operatic music. He is quite good in *Ella giammai m'amò* (Verdi's *Don Carlos*, L.2071, 12 in.), done in two parts. He is less impressive, less convincing, in *Son lo spirito che nega* from *Mefistofele* (L.2072, 12 in.), which hardly deserves to be entitled the *Aria del fischio* because the whistle is so feeble. He snarls a good deal without reminding us much of Chaliapine, either in this or the *Ave, Signor*, from the same opera, which is on the other side. The *Calunnia* air from the *Barbiere* and the drinking song, *Viva Bacco*, from *Der Freischütz* (L.2073, 12 in.) are better in every way. All are well accompanied.

Finally we have some first-rate modern recordings by another *basso cantante*, Tancredi Pasero, who has a strong, telling voice of agreeable quality. He does facile justice to things like the *Vecchia zimarra* from *La Bohème* (D.1616, 10 in.) and the *Infelice!* from *Ernani*, though occasionally his tendency to indulge in overpressure hardens and unsettles his tone. Still, his style can always be dignified and dramatic, as he proves in the two airs from Gounod's *Faust* (D.1617, 10 in.), called in English the *Calf of Gold* and *Serenade*. Other favourites dug out from bygone collections are the air sung by the arch-Druid, Oroveso, in the first act of Bellini's *Norma*, and Ferrando's narrative, *Di due figli* from that of Verdi's *Trovatore* (L.2074, 12 in.). One seldom hears these old things so well sung, or indeed sung at all for the gramophone; and if for that reason only they are welcome items in this variegated list.

Opera at Covent Garden

In an article which I wrote in the *Radio Times* of April 27th I endeavoured to stress the great value of the tradition of "grand opera" which is bound up with the history of Covent Garden Theatre. I paid a compliment to the new Syndicate by declaring that it was imitating its predecessors in the effort to carry on that tradition. The first month of the season has passed with little beyond the annual sacrifices at the Wagnerian altar. It is too early, therefore, to say now whether the effort in question has been successful. One only knows that the German performances have been up to the customary level, that they have been splendidly attended, and that for the two cycles of *Der Ring des Nibelungen* the house was completely sold out.

Amid these signs of continued loyalty to the sacred lamp of Bayreuth, it seems strange that there should be any talk about a " New Anti-Wagnerism " which is to supplant the works of the master with operas of a still more modern type. Frankly, I do not believe either in the idea or the early advent of the genius who will carry it into execution. At present the latter has not so much as foreshadowed his existence. " Anti-Wagnerism " is a cry as stupid to-day as it was half a century ago before his music was properly known or understood. The new Covent Garden Syndicate is aware of this, and, like the sensible commercial body that it professes to be, exploits the surviving craze for Wagner as fully as circumstances will allow. One notes, of course, the absence from this season's repertory of *Tristan und Isolde, Parsifal,* and *Lohengrin.* Perhaps it is as well; all three had been rather overdone of late, and they will return the fresher to the scene another year. We have had instead *Tannhäuser* and *Die Meistersinger,* both of which demonstrated their popularity in the most conclusive manner.

At the same time I cannot help feeling—and I point this out as evidence of the inherent weakness of the operatic situation in England—that the choice of the current repertory at Covent Garden is too much dictated by the *personnel* of the artists who are engaged for the season. The argument seems to be, " We want to give only the operas which are a certain draw, or which are so when given with the singers whom we have engaged. We cannot give certain of the older operas because we have not the artists who are able to sing them, or would not be attractions in them if they could. Besides, the pick of those older operas (so far as we are acquainted with them) have been tried during the past three of four years and, from a box-office point of view, found wanting. Our present notion is to run no greater risks than we can help with our extended ten weeks' season."

Here is, I fancy, the answer to the letter from Mr. Eric Stuart Bruce, which appeared in *The Times* of May 8th, reminding folks of the bygone days at Covent Garden, when great singers like Patti, Albani, Melba, Christine Nilsson, and Tetrazzini " held the audience spellbound by the charm of the human voice." The writer pleaded for the revival of the older classics, as he called them—those of " Mozart, Rossini, Gounod and others "—for the sake of the " voices which seemed the most important part of the performance." Naturally, I have been pleading to

the same purpose myself, asking for a fair share of operas of this character to be included in the programme of every season. But what is the good of it, you are asked, if those operas do not draw with such " stars " as there are available in the world to-day, and who are capable of doing them justice? Do the subscribers or the public really want them? The gems of florid song may still be popular with the purchasers of gramophone records, but would the Toti dal Montes and the rest of them be capable of filling Covent Garden if they appeared in the operas from which the gems are extracted? Experience has rather proved the contrary. The chance for the " older opera classics " will only occur when something like the Imperial League of Opera materializes or a higher artistic spirit stimulates the enterprise of the Syndicates that run Covent Garden during the London season.

The revival of *Armide* was doubly welcome—for the work itself to begin with, and for the instructive comparisons that it evoked between the systems developed in the drama of the stage by Gluck and by Wagner. Into these I cannot enter now or here, but the subject is intensely interesting, and *Armide* illustrates it more vividly than any other opera that Gluck wrote. He composed it to a French libretto for the Paris Opéra, and it was sung in that language 22 years ago when mounted at Covent Garden for the first time. It was now sung in German, and the change grated on me to a corresponding degree—as much, in fact, as Wagner does when sung in French. Nor was this lack of harmony improved by the accent of the English singers who took part in the performance. Walter Widdop, for instance, has acquired a certain facility without mastering the subtle peculiarities of German pronunciation, and his English vowels stood out prominently in alliance with a roughness of tone and angularity of phrasing that compared badly with the singing of Herbert Janssen as Hidraot and Wilhelm Gombert as the Danish Knight. In truth, however, the art of Frida Leider overshadowed that of all the other singers except Maria Olczewska (Hate) and one British girl, Marion McAfee, who gave the lovely air of the Naiad with exquisite taste. The *première danseuse,* Ninette de Valois, is also of English birth, I understand, and she led the various *divertissements* with the *aplomb* of a born dancer. Robert Heger was the conductor.

It was Frida Leider, again, whose impassioned singing as Venus stood out in the *Tannhäuser* revival even more prominently than the calm, plastic display of Göta Ljungberg as Elisabeth. The cast altogether was a much stronger one, and I was glad to note the presence in it of a young English soprano, Annette Blackwell, whose unusually pure voice and method have not escaped notice among the records reviewed in these columns. She delivered the quaint passages in the Song of the Shepherd with notable sweetness and faultless intonation. It was a joy to hear the glorious organ of Ivar Andrésen in the dignified music of the Landgrave; and another fine Parlophone artist in Lauritz Melchior proved himself very nearly, if not quite, a great Tannhäuser, with Herbert Janssen a sympathetic Wolfram.

In connection with the first cycle of *Der Ring* I want to say a few words about the performance of *Götterdämmerung* and the Brünnhilde of Elisabeth Ohms. Not for a long while have I enjoyed the final section of the tetralogy so much, and this experience was in large measure due to the superb acting of the artist just named. I say acting advisedly, because it was that even more than her singing which raised her embodiment so distinctly above the ordinary level. Her voice is of very rich, refined quality, her declamation artistic and intelligent, but I have heard many Brünnhildes of greater power and capable of coping more easily with the vocal demands of that colossal rôle. On the other hand I can remember none since Milka Ternina who threw such tragic force and depth of pathos into the tremendous scene where the apparent perfidy of Siegfried is first revealed to her. Her by-play and facial expression throughout this touching episode could not have been surpassed. Again in the closing scene, where she mourns the fate and descants upon the glorious career of her great lover, she bore herself with superb dignity and seemed to tower head and shoulders above the humiliated Gutrune of Göta Ljungberg. Altogether the Brünnhilde of Elisabeth Ohms will dwell long and pleasantly in my memory. Rudolf Laubenthal once more invested the part of Siegfried with admirable spirit, alertness, and energy, notably in the delivery of the long narration just before he is killed by Hagen. As usual, too, that accomplished singer Maria Olczewska made a fine thing of Waltraute's poignant message in the opening act, while Odette de Foras, Theresa Ambrose, and Gladys Palmer successfully doubled the parts of the three Norns and the three Rhinemaidens. Herbert Janssen, Otto Helgers, and Eduard Habich impersonated the repellent male creatures who completed the cast; and the orchestra, magnificently

conducted by Bruno Walter, did ample justice to its important share of the production.

I am sorry I did not hear another new gramophone artist, the Swedish tenor, Carl Martin Oehman, except in a wireless presentation of the second act of *Die Meistersinger*, which, I regret to add, did not strike me as being remarkable in any sense. The cast was distinctly a moderate one. Far above this level, according to all accounts, were the gems of the second cycle—to wit, Frida Leider's Brünnhilde, Lotte Lehmann's Sieglinde and Gutrune, and Ivar Andrésen's Hagen, which was said to be " *Kolossal.*"

The performance of *Samson et Dalila* which opened the French season on May 22nd was perhaps the dullest, the most uninspired that I can remember. It ambled gently along from start to finish, punctured by waits of inordinate length that brought more than one protest from an impatient gallery. The best singing came from Fernand Ansseau, who was in capital voice. A new Dalila, in Mme. Georgette Frozier-Marrot, brought ripe experience and a rather throaty mezzo-soprano of fair compass to bear upon her part, but little in the way of real charm or fascination. The other rôles were not more than adequately filled, and Percy Pitt conducted. Altogether I was forced to the conclusion that Saint-Saëns's *Samson* is an opera requiring as much care in preparation and skill in handling as any other difficult stage work. If this cannot be vouchsafed at Covent Garden, it had better remain on the shelf there for another fourteen years. But it can and ought to be done. I retain a vivid recollection of the revival of 1913, when the opera was given on a special occasion in honour of the 75th anniversary of Saint-Saëns's musical career. The composer was present, and I had the privilege of sitting beside him in a grand tier box. The principal parts were sustained by Franz and Kirkby Lunn, and he was simply delighted with the whole representation under the guidance of the Italian conductor, Polacco. Why should we not be able to do equally well nowadays?

HERMAN KLEIN.

THE GRAMOPHONE AND THE SINGER

(Continued)

By HERMAN KLEIN

Opera at Covent Garden

PUCCINI was in request from the start of the Italian season; and with good reason. The public wants him—whether for good or ill it is hard to say—and the management has no alternative but to supply the kind of opera that yields the largest returns. At present I see no sign of fading favouritism either in the direction of Wagner or Puccini, though there has been rather strong evidence this season that the supporters of the Royal Opera are not exactly pining to hear masterpieces of the French school, such as *Carmen, Louise,* and *Samson et Dalila.* The real trend will show itself in due time, of course, and I think I know the conditions that will most help to decide it; but in that matter we still have to " wait and see." Much depends upon the quality of the singers. For French opera at Covent Garden we require the finest French artists, nothing less; and with them it would be practicable to give the operas of Gluck to much greater vocal perfection than was found possible when performing such a work as *Armide* in German with a mixed cast of German and English artists. *Armide* was given three times altogether, but on no occasion did it draw a crowded house.

On the other hand, there was a big audience for the performance of *Madama Butterfly* on the night I was present, and under the vigorous guidance of Vincenzo Bellezza it went with plenty of spirit. Its most attractive feature by far was the embodiment of the Japanese heroine by Rosetta Pampanini, the soprano whose records recently won unqualified commendation from the present writer in course of an article on the new Columbia recordings. (Unfortunately her name was spelt Pampini instead of Pampanini, but I hope the slip was pardoned.) Her voice in the theatre came out with the same sympathetic musical timbre that had pleased me on the gramophone—the same faultless intonation, steadiness and purity. Her *Un bel dì* was exceptionally praiseworthy because it epitomized the dramatic sense of Butterfly's vision and made us realize the vividness of the illusion. Her variety of tone-colour and contrasted *nuances* of feeling were evinced not only here, but in the many other emotional touches that Puccini's clever music calls forth in the unfolding of this poignant drama. There was lightness in her comedy with Sharpless (Ernesto Badini) and there was scorn in her refusal of her suitor Yamadori; above all, there was genuine passion in the love scene with Pinkerton (Dino Borgioli), whose singing I found nearly as uninteresting as his acting.

Foresight and a keen appreciation of artistic values in advance of public opinion is not the strong point in the " make-up " of either operatic impresarios or gramophone talent-seekers. Not in this country, at any rate. When a little boldness or real courage is displayed by either of this class of *entrepreneur,* how seldom it is that a prize turns up. They all want to wait until the good thing has been discovered for them or made palpably worth what they call the " risk " by a huge public success; then, when the chance for displaying their acumen or securing a bargain is absolutely lost, they make a simultaneous rush for the treasure and have to pay a heavy price for it. This was not always so. When Frederic Gye made his first contract with Adelina Patti and Augustus Harris his with the lady who is now Dame Melba, to mention only two instances, they got hold of vocal money-spinners, as yet unknown to fame, on terms that to-day would be considered ridiculously inadequate and cheap. Mapleson must have secured dozens of similar bargains. Are they to be had now? Certainly; both for the opera house and the gramophonic *atelier,* if the individuals who are supposed to be on the look-out for first-rate vocal talent or genius, or both, can only recognize it when it is brought to their notice. They need a little more *flair* for their business, a trifle less regard for the financial side of the question, that is all. Why wait always for the Continental verdict before making a decision, particularly where British artists are concerned?

Nearly if not quite a twelvemonth has elapsed since GRAMOPHONE readers began to learn that an English soprano named Eva Turner was achieving an unwonted series of genuine—not press-agent or manufactured—successes at all the big Italian opera houses, including La Scala. There were also printed in these columns reviews of new records sung by the same artist (abroad), and drawing attention to the manifest improvement wrought in her voice, her style, and her dramatic intelligence, by her diligent studies and practical experience on the operatic stage in a country where these advantages are to be procured, and where there is a fair chance for any singer, of whatever nationality, to work her way up to the top of the tree. It may not be pretended for a moment that Eva Turner's useful years with the Carl Rosa Company would alone have sufficed for her to attain the same altitude in her profession. When she left England to study in Italy she was simply not good enough. Yet

231

those who could recognize the exceptional quality and power of her voice (if she would only keep it pure and free from tremolo) might have perceived that she had in her the makings of a great dramatic soprano. Only did they? Did they say, " Let us invest some money in this gifted young woman, not only helping her to attain fame and fortune, but very likely obtaining for our opera house or our 'Celebrity List' a star that will recoup our outlay over and over again"? No, they preferred to wait for the reports from Milan and Rome; and if those were all right they would be willing to spend any amount to procure the services of the clever Bristol girl.

Her splendid records of *Cieli azzuri* and *Suicidio* afforded the first indication over here of Eva Turner's remarkable advance in her art. They justified every word that had been written about her singing in the Italian papers; and that rather opened my eyes to future possibilities, because as a rule I have little faith in their criticisms of foreign artists. Anyhow, taken in combination with the details of enthusiastic receptions and re-engagements everywhere, it caused me no surprise when I came across the name of Eva Turner in the list of artists down to sing at Covent Garden this season. The rest of the story needs no telling. Everyone now knows the kind of sensation that she created in the hardest rôle to be found in modern Italian opera—that of the frozen-souled Princess in Puccini's *Turandot*. It was Eva Turner's privilege, after her long absence, to reappear before an audience of her countrymen and women in a rôle that no one else had proved capable of filling so satisfactorily since the opera was written; and it was her further good fortune to awake on the following morning to find herself famous. This happy result, now a matter of history, no one can possibly grudge her. Rather must we all rejoice that a singer of English birth should have attained at a single bound the eminence and popularity that Eva Turner now enjoys. The feat should constitute a welcome, an encouraging, a stimulating precedent.

I have received from the Oxford University Press a copy of the vocal score of the new-old version of Moussorgsky's opera, *Boris Godounov*, admirably printed on thick paper, and altogether perfectly arranged and brought out. I am sorry that the revival at Covent Garden, with Chaliapine in his great impersonation, came too late in the month for notice to be possible here.

Così fan Tutte, etc.

My special " Plea for Light Opera " was made in THE GRAMOPHONE a couple of years ago, and the response materializes more slowly than it ought, considering the strength of the arguments that were brought forward in favour of the idea. However, I regard as a step in the desired direction the season of light opera in English, carried on during June and part of July at the Court Theatre by Mr. W. Johnstone-Douglas in conjunction with Sir Barry Jackson. If it has not included any of the light works of the French school which I was, and am still, anxious for the present generation to become acquainted with, it has done the next best thing by reviving classical comic masterpieces like *Così fan Tutte* and *Il Matrimonio Segreto*, and combining with them an admirable triple bill of short operas by Vaughan Williams, de Falla, and Schubert. Here, surely, is light music of the purest and most attractive kind—a perfect antidote of the poisonous post-war stuff that we have been afflicted with for far too long. Besides, it is opera in which young British artists can exploit their talent and appear to even better advantage than in that of the French school, which demands a special training and experience. Let us, therefore, be thankful for this creditable effort.

For my own part I found the *Così fan Tutte* a delightful performance. It was broad farce, if you like, but none the worse for that. To take the other view and treat da Ponte's amusing story of the lovers' wager as high comedy seems to me to be a pure mistake—as wrong in its way as converting *Don Giovanni* into serious drama. Mozart may not have conceived the situations altogether as farce, but beyond a doubt that is the spirit in which they ought to be enacted. One laughs at the absurdities and enjoys the delicious music, that is all; and I certainly did both on the occasion of my visit. The singing was not perhaps first-rate, but it was good enough for justice to be done to the duets and ensembles, while the acting, taken all round, was extremely bright and amusing. Candidly speaking, the girls needed to look a trifle younger, especially in their old-fashioned flounces and furbelows. The Despina especially appeared to be afflicted by age and clumsiness of movement to a degree utterly out of keeping with the lightness and grace of her utterances, tuneful and otherwise. But the men were excellent. Mr. Steuart Wilson artistic as usual, Mr. Johnstone-Douglas putting real humour into his acting and singing, while Mr. Arthur Cranmer made a subtle and clever Don Alfonso. The small but efficient orchestra, under Dr. Adrian Boult, played the accompaniments delicately throughout.

THE GRAMOPHONE AND THE SINGER

(Continued)

By HERMAN KLEIN

The Operatic Situation

THE close of another season leaves the position of Opera in England as dubious and unsatisfactory as it has been at any period within recent memory. In fact, I rather doubt whether it has ever been quite so bad. We are constantly being assured, not by one Mr. Micawber, but by three or four Mr. Micawbers, that something is on the point of " turning up." Yet nothing ever does turn up. The grandiose scheme for an Imperial League of Opera, sprung upon a waiting world by Sir Thomas Beecham over a year ago, still remains, if not " in the air," at least without signs of fruition. Every now and then a statement in the papers informs us that the League is alive—very much alive—but unable as yet to make a start. The nearest approach to a precise definition of the state of affairs was contained in last month's *communiqué*, to the effect that between a third and a half of the number of subscribers needed to provide opera in London had been found; but outside London not more than a quarter of the requisite number had come forward. Nevertheless it was hoped (of course) that if the League succeeded in establishing itself in London it must inevitably extend to the big provincial centres. Then followed the usual re-hash of the big things that foreign countries are doing for opera that this country does not do, together with an expression of opinion that " If the League were not somehow brought into being he (Sir Thomas Beecham) believed the efficiency of British musical life would suffer," and that anyhow " not for a very long period of time could the State be expected to take an interest in serious musical institutions."

Such for the moment is the expectant attitude of Mr. Micawber No. 2; and I refer to Sir Thomas as " No. 2 " because obviously he came second to Mr. Isidore de Lara in the quest for millions wherewith to set opera permanently on its feet in this benighted land. That too proved a disappointing wait for something to turn up. At any rate, what did turn up was considerately returned to the contributors. There was yet a third Micawber in the person of poor Paget Bowman, of the B.N.O.C., whose untimely end was sincerely regretted—the more so because it came at a moment when the practical value of the claim that the British public really wants opera in the vernacular was being put to its ultimate test. Perhaps I ought not to say "ultimate," because the test in a way is still being carried on by the inheritors of the B.N.O.C. stock-in-trade, a basis which continues

to represent something solid in the way of scenery, costumes, and prestige. But what has really come, I would like to know, of all the high-sounding promises and predictions, and the declarations of faith, both in English Opera and the public's love for it, that were heard when the undertaking was first set upon its feet with insufficient capital and inexperienced or inefficient artistic directors?

Let the fact be clearly stated—it has been plainly demonstrated in the London suburbs and in a dozen different important provincial towns :—the desire of the British public for good opera at cheap or fairly reasonable prices is limited to a period of a month (in some cases no more than a fortnight) in the whole year! Attempts have been made to interest musical communities like Manchester (I am not sure that there is more than the one unless it be the neighbouring city of Liverpool) in seasons of longer duration; and they have nearly always resulted in failure and loss. What, then, is the use of pretending any longer that we are *au fond* an opera-loving nation? What is the use of employing the Beechamsque extremes of appealing eloquently now for financial support and the next moment riddling the unfortunate unmusical population of Great Britain with darts of fiery scorn or contempt, because they compare dreadfully with the inhabitants of other civilized countries? Either proceeding produces equally little effect, when the appeal or the quick-firing round of invective is let loose upon the nation at large; for where opera is concerned the difference between the metropolitan and the provincial habit of thought is as the difference between black and white or day and night. In his latest manifesto Sir Thomas Beecham tells us exactly what he wants. He decides to omit Glasgow altogether, but to enable the League of Opera to close its subscription list he requires the following :—

From London at least a further 15,000 subscribers.

From Manchester a further 3,000 subscribers.

From Birmingham a further 1,500 subscribers.

From Edinburgh and Bradford each a further 1,000 subscribers.

From Leeds and Liverpool each a further 1,500 subscribers.

Operatic Conditions in London

Here we approach the other side of the picture. I say advisedly, we *approach* it; we do not completely attain or realize it. We have been told, and with perfect truth, that opera at Covent Garden this year has been at once extremely successful and distinctly inferior in quality to that of the preceding two or three seasons. In other words, it has been flourishing upon a reputation gained at the cost of heavy outlay and much arduous labour. The reasons why the Covent Garden Opera Syndicate has failed to maintain the standard reached by the London Opera Syndicate are somewhat obscure, and I do not pretend to be able to explain them. They would, however, appear to be closely connected with the rehearsal question, which in turn is always a question of willingness to spend extra money lavishly for the purpose of putting a finer polish upon the performance of difficult operas. It is not enough merely to have available expensive artists and a large orchestra. It is necessary to allow time and money for plentiful rehearsals, to give the conductors ample opportunity for building their forces so that the very finest results can be obtained from the ensemble. It has not been necessary to read very closely between the lines of last season's criticisms to perceive evidence of a falling-off in this respect.

Personally, I confess, I did not attend so many performances as I generally do—for the excellent reason that I was not invited. Nor am I betraying a secret when I mention that the new Syndicate began its régime by making an inroad upon the Press list and cutting it down in various directions, even to the extent of reducing on repetition nights the seats allotted to the leading critics. This proceeding was brought to the notice of the Critics' Circle, whose Executive Committee at once sent in a protest, pointing out that treatment of the sort was apt to recoil upon those responsible for it, if not now whilst the "opera boom" was on, then later on when the Syndicate might be in need of all the support that the press could furnish. To which protest I would here add that the warm reception recorded the German artists during the earlier weeks of the recent season was in part due to the constant publicity their names have received in a journal like THE GRAMOPHONE— not just prior to their arrival, but all through the year. In recommending their records we have recommended them to the favourable attention of our readers and so facilitated the task of the Covent Garden management. How this good work has been requited I have shown, and nothing more on the subject need be said now beyond pointing out the futility of displeasing or quarrelling with the critics. It is a "penny wise and pound foolish" plan and has never been known to pay. Doubtless the commercial gentlemen who form the Covent Garden Syndicate are more accustomed to the economic methods of the City than the running of a big opera house; but I can assure them that the few guineas they may have saved by reducing privileges which have been earned by right and custom during a long period of years will, in the end, prove to have been a loss and not a gain.

Opera *de luxe* has been well supported this summer; there can be no doubt of that. The people who willingly paid Bond Street prices for seats already too expensive, formed up in *queue* in Bow Street to buy them at the box office, got exactly what they wanted. They did not ask for novelties. They did not much care if they got no Mozart, much less Meyerbeer or Wagner, Rossini or Donizetti. They bargained for the *Ring* without "cuts"; but they were not particular about perfection or finish of detail in the various performances, so long as they heard the artists whose records they admired. So with the Italian operas. The selection was a matter of indifference to the majority, provided the singers were the ones they wanted to hear. It was like the bookmakers on a racecourse waiting for the punters to "make a favourite" before the betting really began. No sooner was it discovered that Eva Turner was a star of the first magnitude than there was a rush to hear her in whatever opera she might sing—whether *Aïda*, *Turandot* or *Cavalleria Rusticana* mattered not. Happily this triumph of a British singer coincided with views previously expressed in these columns and was therefore in no sense a surprise to the writer. Similarly, my gratuitous advice as to increasing the length of the season was proved to be absolutely sound; while the extra week-end at so-called cheap prices further demonstrated the fact that London can be definitely counted on to support grand opera of the right sort for at least three months in the year—May, June and July. The visit of Chaliapine also proved a financial success, although in the general opinion a decided disappointment artistically. No one seemed to be impressed by the Mephistopheles, in Gounod's *Faust*, and only a few would allow that any comparison was to be made between the Boris Godounov of to-day and the phenomenal impersonation we saw at Drury Lane fifteen years ago.

But what, after all, is the good of comparisons? It is very well for an accomplished amateur critic like Lord Wittenham (formerly Mr. George Faber, owner for a time of the Covent Garden lease) to write a long letter to *The Times*, as he did early in July, comparing the present with the past to the advantage of neither, and finding features to admire and praise in the work of both régimes. I am by no means sure that Lord Wittenham was right in saying that the successful season just ended revealed "fewer diamonds, fewer familiar faces, but more music lovers." I grant the diamonds and the faces; but the young folks whom I saw thronging the foyer looked to me more like would-be high-brows, keen for musical excitement of any sort, than genuine lovers of opera for opera's sake such as were seen there in the old days—minus the crush and the loud conversation and the clouds of cigarette smoke. On the other hand, Lord Wittenham was perfectly just in his lively panegyric concerning the beauties and the acoustics of our dear old opera house : it is certainly unique in its way. The history of his family's and his connection with it was interesting. It had suffered financial difficulties from its start in 1858; but luckily it had had some rich patrons. His relative, "the late Andrew Montagu, a friend of Disraeli, had two loves, music and politics, and during the last half of last century he was faithful and munificent to both. The Grand Opera Syndicate, which bought the lease of the house, with certain reservations, from them in 1899, numbered rich supporters, and gave many distinguished seasons until the War came; that seemed to be the death blow of the Opera House, but even as its two predecessors went through the fire, so, though differently, this veritable 'Phoenix' rose from the ashes of the War" and seems in its latest manifestation, "to afford good hopes that the great Opera House may still be able to carry on its fine traditions for some time to come."

It will, too, provided these traditions be not forgotten or betrayed, and if wisdom and discretion be shown in the direction of the enterprise. There yet remains to be considered the question of adequate rehearsals for every difficult opera that is mounted. These *must* be provided, no matter what the cost, if the artistic standard of the house is to be maintained. Lord Wittenham seems to imagine that the critics have not shown sufficient indulgence and made full allowance for the conditions under which the grand season labours. He said in his letter : " These difficulties are sometimes not quite realized by comfortably-seated critics who complain about perhaps trivial defects." His lordship is altogether mistaken. There can be such a thing as over-indulgence, and I venture to assert that the leading musical critics have been consistently shutting their eyes to the "trivial defects," whilst treating all the various production in turn with conspicuous fairness. Lord Wittenham was on safer ground when he declared that " One still waits for the great French singers. Where are the successors of Faure, Maurel, Lassalle, Plançon, and Alvarez ? " Echo answers : Where indeed ?

Light Opera in English

In an artistic sense Mr. W. Johnston-Douglas's season at the Court Theatre, which reached its allotted close on July 14th, was an unequivocal success, and right glad am I to hear that there is every prospect of its being repeated next year. The undertaking will be more likely to prosper in full measure if not attempted amidst the counter-attractions of mid-season, and if the theatre can be obtained, I suggest early spring as a more favourable time. There is undoubtedly a public for this sort of high-class light musical entertainment, only it wants urging to a sense of combined duty and pleasure to make it yield the necessary support for a run. As a matter of fact the people who call themselves music-lovers— people who patronize the stalls if they go to the opera or theatre at all—were the class most conspicuous by their absence and their lack of interest all through the season at the Court, and I hardly need add that that fact was highly discreditable to them. Instead of going to hear *Così fan Tutte* or *The Secret Marriage* on the nights when they could not get into Covent Garden, they doubtless repaired to the Coliseum or the Alhambra, or one of Mr. Cochran's revues, and honestly enjoyed something on a level with their mental and musical standard of culture. Anyhow they missed a treat. I do not say there were no shortcomings nor a solitary square peg in a round hole. I should like another time, for instance, to see the female characters in more capable hands and hear them sung with greater charm and finesse. But for the rest I admit that I enjoyed Cimarosa's masterpiece thoroughly from beginning to end. And I had not heard it since it was given at the Lyceum when I was a boy.

HERMAN KLEIN.

   ☯   ☯   ☯

THE GRAMOPHONE AND THE SINGER
(Continued)
By HERMAN KLEIN
About New Musical Books

I WONDER sometimes where the readers come from for the flood of musical literature that is more or less continuously descending upon the bookshops. In my experience there has been nothing to compare with this year's output, and I can only hope, for the sake of authors as well as the trade, that the sales have been proportionately large. The one thing to be desired is that books of this description should be cheaper than they are. They help, most of them, to instruct and educate the community, and goodness knows we have need, now perhaps more than ever, of sound musical literature to cultivate the understanding of the rising generation of music lovers, to elevate their taste and improve their standard by reading and study as well as by the vast amount of ear-training that they are getting through the gramophone and the wireless or radio.

It ought not to involve the question of what the subjects should be. My advice is—read everything that is worth reading. Do not saturate your mind with one class of literature in particular. Above all, do not believe that you have to go through an intricate course of preparation, mental and scientific, in order to learn how to appreciate great music at its full worth. Try to gain a little knowledge of form certainly; the meaning of marks and indications; the values expressed in the staff notation which all the famous composers used, even though the tonic sol-fa be your own individual medium. But, believe me, if you have it in you to love and enjoy music for its own sake, for its abstract beauty and charm as well as for its fascinating illustrative power when allied to poetry and drama, you will derive from it all imaginable pleasure and interest without special lessons in the mysterious arts of " How to listen " or " How to appreciate." For my own part I confess that I do not read from cover to cover half the musical books that come my way. But I do like dipping into them and trying to discover the " plums " in what I consider to be the salient chapters; and in that way I find that I can form a pretty accurate notion of the worth of the whole book. Afterwards, if I think I can profit by it, I can always read it through without missing a word.

As in searching for precious stones in Brazil or South Africa, one can never tell when the gem is going to turn up. A little time ago I was looking through a thick volume entitled simply *Music*, by a professor of Columbia University named John Redfield (published by Alfred A. Knopf), and I came across a chapter on " Tone Production." The writer being strictly a scientist, dealing with what he calls the "scientific approach to music," I was not surprised to find the greater part of this chapter in the nature of a technical essay on the formation and construction of wind and stringed instruments. Then, towards the end, my interest was suddenly aroused by some observations on the human voice. After reading (what I knew well already) about the chief influences in determining the tone-quality of the voice, viz., the size and shape of the air passages, I lighted upon this bold statement:

All music, in the final analysis, is singing ; or, at least, singing and dancing. We construct musical instruments to furnish us with a voice when we have no natural voice, to supply us with a more powerful voice when our voice is weak, or to provide us with a voice more to our liking in compass or tone colour. And with these artificial voices, we sing in such a manner as our natural voices would never permit. Or if our feet are too clumsy to dance as we would like, we become percussion players and dance to our hearts' content with sticks on our drum heads.

Well this, I thought, is one way of explaining the evolution of the orchestra, even though it may not exactly account for the prehistoric use of harps as an accompaniment to the voices of the celestial choir (or choirs). But I liked the phrase, "All music is singing," because in very truth it is so, though I do not remember to have seen it in cold print before. Other "gems" are to be found in this book; but you have to look for them. Parts of it are rather dry.

Again, in a privately-printed book bearing the curious title of *Long-Haired Iopas*, or *Old Chapters from Twenty-five Years of Music-Criticism*, by Edward Prime-Stevenson, of Florence, Italy, I found (apart from one chapter courteously dedicated to myself) the following notable excerpt from an address delivered by the Italian statesman, Gaetano Negri, during the Rossini Centenary Commemoration in the Scala Theatre at Milan, on January 23rd, 1892 :

Let us not speak lightly, let us not become ungrateful, as regards that Italian music which for so many years was *the* voice by which Italy said to other nations that she was not yet dead. Everything passes, transforms itself here below. But we ought not to forget that, during more than half a century, the Olympian smile of Rossini, the Virgilian elegy of Bellini, the romantic drama of Donizetti, the Shakespearian tragedy of Verdi, filled all the world and kept fixed upon the head of Italy at least a ray of ancient glory.

In the chapter above alluded to Mr. Prime-Stevenson quotes George Sand (*Consuelo*) as saying of music, through the mouth of Porpora, " The great, the beautiful, in the arts is—the simple ! " And then he proceeds, like Mr. John Redfield, to demonstrate that what we regard as new in music is "inherently but the antique. Take, for example, our contemporary concert-orchestra. The string, the pipe, the drum— after all is said, we have merely improved on their early models. We have not invented ; we have only amended and complicated." Thus do great minds think alike. I wonder, though, what both these authors think about the gramophone; that they do not deign to tell us. Perhaps they would say (and if they did I should agree with them) " The gramophone is not strictly speaking a musical instrument at all, since it does not create sound, but reflects and reproduces it. It is not, therefore, a development from the antique." But in one respect at least, now that it is perfected, it does resemble great music. It is simple.

Everyone interested in the renaissance of opera in this country may be advised to read carefully (rather than merely "dip into") Professor Dent's informative book, *Foundations of English Opera* (Cambridge University Press). I cannot overpraise the author for the amount of trouble he has taken to get right down to the roots of his subject and trace the growth of opera from its earliest beginnings. After all his researches he can still give us no clear, satisfactory definition of what an opera really is or ought to be, " although there is no lack of tradition and experience to guide those whose only object is financial success." Mr. Dent's conclusion appears to be that the principle underlying modern opera is essentially distinct from the normal musical principle or the normal dramatic principle; it must, therefore, be a combination of the two, wherein one may influence the other in a greater or lesser degree. Anyhow, to its history during the 17th century—hitherto sadly ignored—he has devoted special attention, and in this book, which was begun so far back as 1914, he has laid the whole story plainly before us. The eighth chapter, dealing with " French Influences," is of particular interest. It shows how Purcell at one period "endeavoured conscientiously to assume a more Parisian manner," notwithstanding his faithful adherence to the more modern Italian methods of which he was already a master, and "which made the composition of *Dido and Æneas* possible." The descriptions of this and other operas by Purcell form a large, interesting and valuable feature of this extremely useful and ably written book.

Mr. Dyneley Hussey made an acceptable addition to Kegan Paul's *Masters of Music* series when he contributed to it his thoughtful study on *Mozart*. I may not find myself in agreement with him on all points, but I certainly do on a good many; for it seems to me that, unlike certain contemporary writers, he has taken a fair and accurate view of Mozart's character and has not misjudged him either as a musician or a man. The tendency of late has been all too general to enquire into the private life and domestic affairs of the great composers, just as if that could possibly aid us to understand them and their creative achievement better than we do. This author has avoided the objectionable pitfall and contented himself as well as the reader with a careful and not too enthusiastic appraisal of Mozart's music—of those beautiful works which the whole world loves and admires now more than ever. Not the least instructive section of the book is that entitled " Conclusion," where we find argument and speculation concerning what Mozart was and what he might have been had he lived on into the nineteenth century:

He would have been only seventy-one when Beethoven died. Of that age—the age of the Wagner of *Parsifal*—it might have been reasonable to talk of an exhausted mind, a well dried up, a vein worked out . . . But of thirty-five it is ludicrous. On the other hand, a distinguished critic has suggested that, had Mozart lived on, the face of musical history during the last century would have been fundamentally changed. . . It is not quite idle to speculate about this, because now, looking back over what has been essentially Beethoven's century of music, it is quite clear that something was lost from music at the beginning of it which may be fairly attributable to Mozart's untimely death. The loss seems to account for some at least of the vague groping of twentieth-century music.

Again, I believe with Mr. Hussey that had Mozart lived longer " he would have developed his new [*i.e.*, his latest] manner in a way which we cannot indeed imagine, but which would have added to his great works in the branches of symphony, of chamber music

and of opera, others which would have stood level in the same class as the great works of Beethoven." But I cannot agree with the opinion that there is " little sustained melody in Mozart's music compared with that of Haydn or Schubert, and even of Beethoven or Wagner." The arguments in favour of this view are not convincing; and in one instance where he tells us that Mozart wrote nothing comparable with the *Preislied*, yet contrived to achieve "the flowing and unbroken line of *Deh vieni non tardar*," Mr. Hussey only succeeds in flatly contradicting himself. For, as an example of sustained melody, one is not more beautiful that the other, and each is unique of its kind.

A British musical figure around whom controversy has raged with ceaseless clamour almost as long as I can remember—Arthur Sullivan, to wit—found a new defender not long ago in Mr. Thomas F. Dunhill. His able analyses of *Sullivan's Comic Operas* (published by Edward Arnold and Co.) proved that a writer of good music (which everyone knew him to be) could also write strong, sound English, when sufficiently roused, to do justice to the talent of one whose many friends secured for him an equal number of powerful enemies. Mr. Dunhill puts the matter in a nutshell:

If Sullivan's detractors had been people of little account in the musical world their judgments might have been ignored. But this, unfortunately, is not the case. In many instances they were significant. Contemporary musicians who, perhaps rightly, considered their own aims more lofty than his. And so, fully convinced that Sullivan ought never to have had the success which he achieved, they have been at great pains to explain to the public how accidental, how undeserved, how thoroughly discreditable to the musical taste of this country, that success was.

How utterly wrong they were has been amply demonstrated; but this author has thought it "of high importance that a more just sense of perspective should be established;" hence his book. I am glad to see that he has not hesitated to name and to quote some of the bilious individuals whose hatred for Sullivan music was scarcely less intense than their personal dislike of the man himself. I knew the majority of them quite well and must admit that they formed an ardent, implacable coterie (or should I say, phalanx?) of determined adversaries. Mr. Dunhill has the courage to mention the worst of them, including two or three who are still alive; but I shall not repeat their names here, and will leave the curious to discover them for themselves by perusing the opening chapter of the book. Injustice, like all other sins, brings its own punishment and I am quite convinced that the enemies of Sullivan have undergone real torment by having to witness the recent triumphant revival of the Savoy operas. It is to the latter, of course, that the book under review is chiefly devoted. The task of analyzing them has obviously been a labour of love to Mr. Dunhill, and I advise all who take pleasure in them to read his book.

Clara Butt, her Life-Story, by Winifred Ponder (publishers, George G. Harrap & Co.), is a curious compilation of biographical details, personalities and small-talk. As a chronicle of the singer's career it hardly stands upon the plane of dignity that might have been anticipated from one who appears to have always been highly sensitive in all matters affecting her "rights" both as a woman and an artist. From the very outset she was ever ready to stand up for these; ever ready to pick up the glove if she thought herself unfairly treated, and have it out with her aggressor. What is more, she generally got the best of the many tussles recorded in this book; indeed, I have failed to discover a single case in which her *quid pro quo* was not counted equal to a " win."

The story of Clara Butt's successful struggle for the Bristol scholarship at the Royal College of Music and her early life while studying there makes amusing reading. One wonders, though, whether her first teacher at the College, Henry Blower, did really understand how to train that wonderful contralto organ in the right way. I formed my own opinion about it when I heard her for the first time as Orpheus in the students' performance of Gluck's opera, given at the Lyceum in December, 1892. I thought the breathing method was incorrect and the blending of the registers into a perfect scale far from what it ought to have been. That opinion was shared by Mrs. Ronalds, the beautiful amateur singer for whom Sullivan wrote *The Lost Chord*, and the hostess and friend through whose kind offices the budding favourite was enabled to break off her public work and proceed to Paris and Berlin for a year's further study under Bouhy and Etelka Gerster. Certainly she came back from that expedition a far more capable singer, with her magnificent voice under much better control, her scale, her phrasing, her diction all immensely improved.

Still the " life-story" does not dwell at any length upon its heroine's difficulties or the vocal obstacles that she had to surmount and the manner in which she strove to overcome them. One reads only that Bouhy, a splendid artist and teacher (like Etelka Gerster, who had been trained by the old Mme. Marchesi), was impressed not only with her voice, but with her artistic gifts, and used often to say, " Why do they speak only of the wonderful *voice* of Clara Butt, and not of Clara Butt the artist ? " The simple answer to this would have been that she went to M. Bouhy, not because she was an artist, but because she wanted to be made one; otherwise why did she need to go to him at all ? The tale about the visit to Saint-Saëns reads slightly exaggerated, especially his remark, " Never till now have I found my Delilah." The composer once said to me, " I never had but one perfect Delilah, namely, Elena

Sanz," who created the part on the revival of the opera at Rouen, and also at Covent Garden when it was first given there in oratorio form, at which performance I was present. The Lord Chamberlain's refusal to license the Biblical story for the stage was, of course, long anterior to the period when, according to Dame Clara Butt's biographer, " M. Saint-Saëns went back to Paris an angry and disappointed man, and the world was deprived of the perfect Delilah " (*sic*).

Apart from this misleading sort of thing, there is a great deal in the book that will probably interest and amuse Dame Clara's myriads of admirers in all parts of that globe which she and her lovable husband, Kennerley Rumford, have "trotted" with such unalloyed and invariable success.

Turning once more to serious literature, let me join most heartily in the chorus of welcome that has been extended to Professor Charles Sanford Terry's splendid biography of Sebastian Bach, bearing the simple title *Bach*, and published (at a guinea) by Humphrey Milford of the Oxford University Press. It is now 44 years since Novello & Co. brought out the first volume of the English translation of Spitta's famous treatise dealing with Bach's "work and influence on the Music of Germany, 1685-1750." Ever since, it has been regarded as the standard work on the subject; but I very much doubt whether it will continue to be so henceforward. Professor Terry has, after infinite study and research, given the world a genuine biography of the great Leipzig Cantor, and not merely "a critical appreciation of his music," which is what Dr. Spitta supplied. It tells us virtually everything that is known or discoverable about his life and career—details hitherto unchronicled because the writers who lived nearest to Bach's time never took the trouble, or else did not envisage the need, to set down the simple facts which we, who understand and love him better, now consider of such paramount interest. He is here the vivid central figure in an absorbing story, not what Professor Terry justly describes as "a nebulous figure in an eclipsing frame obliterated under a pitiless avalanche of exposition." The upshot of these remarks will be, I trust, to induce all of my readers who revel in Bach's genius and value his glorious music at its true worth to invest a guinea in this singularly well-written and complete volume. It is a brilliant exposition of a remarkable life, based apparently upon incontrovertible facts. It will help the student to follow the course of the master's long and busy existence, and, as claimed in the preface, the large appendix of photographic illustrations enables one "to visualize Bach's surroundings from the beginning to the end of his career."

HERMAN KLEIN.

THE GRAMOPHONE AND THE SINGER

(Continued)

By HERMAN KLEIN

Schubert Centenary Records

APRÈS moi le Déluge! Little did I imagine, when not so very long ago I was appealing to the Recording Angels who sit aloft on Olympus to give us fewer ballads and more Lieder, that the veritable deluge of good things was so near at hand. I feel very happy about it, of course; not only because my oft-repeated prayer on this subject has been heard, but because the nature of the response denotes a definite and complete change, an amazing growth, in fact, in the musical taste of the nation. A comparison between the gramophone catalogues of three or four years ago with those now in course of preparation or issue will illustrate better than can any words of mine the extraordinary period of transition that we are passing through. It is, I am aware, only one phase of the vast general development that is converting our communities on all sides to the love of what used to be called " classical " music. The Lied is only sharing in the glorious demand for the symphonic and chamber works of the great masters. Still, it has come far more quickly than I have ever dared to hope; and seeing how important the influence of good vocal music can be, how effectually it can rid us of the rubbish we hear sung, whistled and broadcast from morning till night, I feel that we have genuine cause for thanksgiving.

An important factor in all this, curiously enough, has been the Schubert Centenary. It has had a most extraordinary effect upon the public imagination, and has aroused a desire to become better acquainted with the compositions of the Viennese master among a class of music-lovers who had previously known barely half-a-dozen of his songs. Another thing: the observance of this

HANS DUHAN

centenary has been the most prolonged in my experience. It has been going on, not for twelve months, but for something like twenty, accompanied by sensational and exciting features like the Columbia Company's big prizes for the " completion " of the *Unfinished Symphony.* The duration of the so-called anniversary has given it time to " soak " into the uninstructed mind, and to make the world understand that Schubert was really something more than an every-day song writer or the amiable little man portrayed in *Lilac Time*—another factor, perhaps, in this remarkable " vogue." Moreover, it has given time for the mechanical accomplishment of the Schubertian deluge; that is to say, for the re-recording of such songs as had already been in the principal lists and for the addition of a great many more that had never hitherto been thought of in connection with the gramophone. This month it has come upon us not from one but from two or three quarters, and the heaviest contribution so far is that of His Master's Voice.

It was in every sense appropriate that H.M.V. should mark the occasion, to begin with, by issuing an Album (No. 68) of Schubert songs by that distinguished Schubert interpreter, Elena Gerhardt. Here tradition and individual feeling go hand in hand. The art of this singer has lost no iota of the " cunning," to use the Psalmist's words, that characterized it long ago in the days when she profited by the teaching and the accompaniment of Arthur Nikisch. The voice may not be altogether so fresh, so resonant, so reliable as it then was—indeed, how should it be? But it is still infinitely to be preferred to scores of others belonging to public singers whom one could name (under compulsion); while in every other respect Mme. Gerhardt still stands in her particular *genre* alone and unsurpassed. Concerning the nature of those qualities I need not particularize, any more than I need to define, or attempt to define, the beauties of the exquisite examples of Schubert's genius to which they are here allied. There are eighteen songs in the Album, sung on eight discs (only two of them 10 in.) and including as many numbers from the superb cycle known as " Die Winterreise." These last will be found on the three 12 in. discs (D. 1262-4, price 6/6) and the single 10 in., (E. 460, price 4/6), which comprises *Die Post* and *Die Krähe* because they are short. All the accompaniments are very beautifully played by Mr. Coenraad v. Bos, and I am thankful to say that they have not been tampered with in any way, but are played as they were written for the piano alone. The sole *obbligato* is not an *obbligato* at all, being merely a transference to the violin (Marjorie Hayward) of the delicious bit of melody that occurs *between* each verse of the *Litanei* and therefore does not interfere with the voice. A pamphlet containing new " free " English translations of each of the songs goes with the Album, but, as the name of the author is not mentioned, nothing need be said about them.

A second Schubert Album brought out this month by H.M.V. is devoted entirely to the cycle of songs, *Die schöne Müllerin* ("The Maid of the Mill"). It is curious that, in the Introductory Note, the poems should be apparently attributed to Rellstab instead of Müller. They consist of twenty songs done on ten discs, three of them 12in. (price 6/6) and the remainder 10in. (price 4/6). This collection represents the cream of the master's productive genius at its prime (1823) and includes some of his best-known efforts as a songwriter. No matter how he came by Müller's poems, and the story has several variations, his music unquestionably raised their artistic worth far above their level as poetry. I have never cared for the original title. It would have been far more accurate to call the story of the love-sick Miller *The Miller and the Brook*, or even *The Miller and the Maiden*. It is he, not the maiden, who is the hero and the singer. The latter in the present instance is Herr Hans Duhan, a light baritone engaged at the State Opera Vienna, and obviously a lieder-artist of no mean ability. It is also plain that he has made a close study of these songs and mastered them alike as a musician and a vocalist. Were his mastery of vocal colour equally thorough, his rendering would have been great in the highest sense. As it is, his singing attains an unusually exalted level. The voice is always pleasant and steady, the attack neat, the intonation absolutely sure, the diction beyond praise except for a slight lisp such as one notices in so many German singers nowadays.

The faults of style are trifling, the chief one being a tendency to over-stress the accent and use a *marcato* effect that separates the syllables and hammers them out too much. Yet Herr Duhan can be delightfully *legato* when he likes. His *Wohin*, for instance, is quite smooth enough, if it were only as quick relatively as his admirable *Ungeduld;* whereas the *Das Wandern* and *Eifersucht und Stolz* could be done with less energy and imitation of drum beats. In *Am Feierabend* he hits the exact happy medium for what is frankly a joyous Viennese waltz-air with a reflective alternative passage. I prefer Leo Slezák's *Der Neugierige;* but the *Mein!*, *Pause*, and *Der Jäger* could hardly be improved upon, the *Morgengruss* is smooth and pleasing, the *Müllers Blumen* very gracefully phrased. The contrast between the *böse* and the *liebe Farbe* does not appear sufficiently in the voice; but the singing does them both justice, as it does, indeed, to the two or three remaining songs, notably *Trock'ne Blumen*, where the strongly-marked rhythm is just what the artist enjoys. I would add that the accompaniments are all played with exceptional skill, taste, and delicacy by Herr Ferdinand Foll. The new recording, as in the case of the Gerhardt Album, marks a vast improvement upon previous productions of this type. Everything is clear and distinct, and one can enjoy the voice in all its pristine purity. The characteristic timbre of the singer is always there.

Of the Columbia contribution of Schubert Lieder for mid-September the German assortment is so good that one wishes it had been on a larger scale. The six songs sung by Alexander Kipnis are so wonderful that they not only whet the appetite for more of the *Lieder-Kreise*, for example, like that of Herr Duhan just noticed—but they utterly put in the shade the modest attempts by English artists which emerge in the same issue. The standard set by Herr Kipnis is so high that it is rather hopeless to expect Liedersinging of similar calibre from our own people; nor would I willingly discourage singers like Roy Henderson and Frank Titterton in their efforts to popularize the Schubert gems in decent English. Comparisons being, therefore, quite out of the question, I will not be unkind enough to make them. I will only tender a piece of advice which I have more than once offered already, namely, that British vocalists who aspire to do this class of work should make a point of first studying the right models for their purpose; and I cannot conceive of any better than the records of the same songs made by the leading foreign artists. Through these, if they will listen with sufficient care and intelligence, they will obtain the true idea of how the masterpieces of Schubert and the other great Lieder writers should be interpreted. Imitation may be the sincerest form of flattery, but there is nothing in that sort of flattery for any artist to be ashamed of.

Alexander Kipnis, a shining light of his art, whether it be exemplified in the opera house or the concert room, simply enriches the Columbia store by such noble offerings as these. They are not only beyond criticism, but they baffle description. I have heard nothing so perfect, at any rate since electric recording began, and that is really to say everything. A range of two full octaves enables Kipnis to spread his voice easily over the compass of *Der Wanderer* (L2134, 12in., 6/6), just as his control of dynamic strength, from a *piena voce* of immense volume down to the most delicate *mezza voce*, gives him a truly remarkable command of tone colour and contrast. Hence the spirit of weariness, of misery, of yearning, that pervades this wanderer's soliloquy with an effortless intensity of expression which is enhanced by the rare refinement and clearness of the singer's diction. He sings it in F, not in E, the usual bass key, presumably because the higher semitone at the end is the better note; anyhow, it is a fine one. On the other side of the same disc is a poetic yet robust, tender yet masculine rendering of *Der Wegweiser*, no less perfect in its way and a delight to listen to.

Avoiding further superlatives, I will content myself with pointing out as regards the other two discs (L2135-6), that Kipnis has thoroughly realized the sweet simplicity of *Der Lindenbaum*, with its affectionate longing and regrets for the peaceful happy hours of youth; and also the sad touching, dreamy, melancholy of *Am Meer*. Again, please note in *Der Doppelgänger* how wonderfully he preserves the tempo and rhythm of music that is quasi-recitativo, whilst depicting all the varied emotions of the being who gazes at his own form standing outside his former sweetheart's dwelling. Finally, with this is paired a splendid rendering of *Aufenthalt*, an almost genial greeting to a familiar resting-place, less varied but not less noble than the *Wanderer*, and ending upon a phrase with an F in it two octaves higher. The accompaniments to all these songs are admirably played by Mr. Frank Bibb upon a piano that sounds like a piano—and a good one.

There is a run on *Der Wegweiser*. After Gerhardt and Kipnis comes an English version (9433) by Roy Henderson, who couples with it that much less familiar but superb song, *Gruppe aus dem Tartarus*, and does it much better justice. The four songs selected by Frank Titterton were not very wisely chosen. Despite the co-operation of a pianist like Leff Pouishnoff, the *Erl-King* (9431) does not really suit a tenor, for he cannot impart to it the necessary variety of *timbres*; while in no case ought the *Ave Maria* (9432) to be appropriated by a male singer, being the prayer of a maiden, not a naughty boy. *Auf dem Wasser zu singen* is handled with lightness, but requires for its *notes coulées* a more delicate and finished vocalization. For the correct reading of *Am Meer* (By the Sea) refer to Kipnis.

A selection of Polydor records comes from Mr. H. L. Wilson, with a special Schubert supplement of some forty vocal items, including, however, a good many that are not by Schubert and which consequently do not interest me so much as they would

at any other moment. To begin with I see that that excellent tenor, Fritz Soot, combines *Der Doppelgänger* with Schumann's *Der Nussbaum* and the latter's *Hildalgo* with *An die Musik* (respectively No. 66434 at 6/6, and No. 62550 at 4/6); but as yet I have heard neither record. The same singer displays a pure tone, natural, easy delivery, and good rhythm in *Der Musensohn* and *Die Forelle* (No. 62551) though his trout is inclined to be too staccato in its jump. These and the following records are, I am glad to say, made with piano accompaniment only, the piano itself being also an improvement on the rattling metallic one of which I formerly complained, while the electric recording naturally exhibits a corresponding advance on older models.

Herman Jadlowker's version of *Der Lindenbaum* (No. 66634) should be supplied with a " lachrymal bottle," to catch the tears as the Egyptian women were wont to do. It is over-emotional and saddens the sentiment to the degree of sickliness and exhaustion. I prefer the life and spirit—the happy-to-be-off sort of spirit—that informs *Abschied* (reverse side). The singer does not sound so tired and miserable here, and the robustness of his fine voice comes out effectively. The *Doppelgänger* of Heinrich Rehkemper (No. 66537) is a masterly portrayal of ineradicable grief and haunting fear. But why is the innocent " double " described in the English title as *The Counterfeiter*? The other side provides a beautiful rendering of *Gute Nacht*; while on the same level of rich tone and rhythmical feeling are those two characteristic songs, *Die Post* and *Die Krähe* (No. 66611). A profitable three-shillings' worth is Franz Völker's excellent tenor rendering of *Ungeduld* (No. 20899) and associated with it is an equally satisfactory one of Hugo Wolf's splendid song *Heimweh*. Heinrich Schlusnus gives a highly poetic delivery of the *Serenade* or *Ständchen* (No. 62605) together with a smooth and gentle *Sei mir gegrüsst*, though he always makes me wish that his method were a trifle less inclined to nasality. His *Musensohn* (No. 62623) is likewise welcome, and none the less so for being coupled with Schumann's *Ich grolle nicht*, which he sings magnificently—high A included. The sympathetic contralto and clear diction of Lula Mysz-Gmeiner are agreeably displayed in *Frühlingsglaube* (No. 62534), which goes plus a charming sing of Mahler's in the *volkslied* manner, *Wer hat dies' Lied erdacht?* Another contralto, Jenny Sonnenberg, gives a good account of *Der Tod und das Mädchen* (No. 62604), bracketed with a couple of gems by Brahms, viz., *Das Mädchen spricht* (not the same one, I imagine) and the *Wiegenlied* or *Cradle Song*. A choral version of *Der Lindenbaum* done by the Berlin Lieder-Chor (No. 62636) may please those who care for such eccentricities. It is well sung.

A Parlophone record by Franz Steiner (baritone, E.10758, 12-in., 4/6) of *Der Neugierige* and *Der Doppelgänger*, scarcely rises to what may be called

Centenary level, if indeed it can be said to rise above mediocrity. The voice is slightly throaty and veiled, albeit possessed of a certain richness of quality and the pleading tone is calculated to ingratiate the listener. Moreover, clipped syllables do not tend to clarify the singer's enunciation. Another disc (Parlophone, R.20063, 12-in., 6/6) is scarcely worth the higher price. Herr Tauber may be very popular in Germany, but he will not persuade us that his light tenor is the right voice for *Der Wanderer* or even for *Am Meer*. Imagine having not only to transpose the *Wanderer* to a higher key, but to alter and hack about the whole of the marvellous final phrase to suit the unsuitable voice of the singer!

P.S.—Appropriate to this article will be the addition of a few lines concerning the best biography of Schubert that has yet appeared in our language—I allude to Newman Flower's *Franz Schubert, the Man and his Circle* (Cassells, 15/-). I will pay it the further high compliment of saying that it is as good as the same author's life of Handel and superior to his *Sullivan*. Admitting that he had an enormous amount of material to work on, one cannot but admire the skill and industry with which Mr. Flower has reduced to order what might have remained partial chaos. He presents at any rate a clear insight into the artistic career and domestic existence of one of the most interesting and lovable personalities that music has ever known. He has done it, moreover, in his own smooth, readable, distinctive manner, so that all who peruse the book and gaze upon its many well-made and well-chosen illustrations will come away from it feeling that they really do know something about the heaven-sent genius who wrote all those glorious *Lieder*, and the *Unfinished Symphony*, and the rest of the treasures that we have learnt to cherish so dearly.

HERMAN KLEIN.

THE GRAMOPHONE AND THE SINGER

(Continued)

By HERMAN KLEIN

Impressions of the Leeds Festival

AT the last concert but one of the series held in the Town Hall, Leeds, during the first week of October, I was assured by the secretary, Mr. Charles F. Haigh, that the recent Festival had met with the average amount of local support. I was glad to hear that because it had struck me that the audiences as a whole were not quite so crowded as usual, and I was rather anxious to discover whether the Executive Committee had in some degree lost touch with its public or not. Apparently it had not, even when it had adopted the strange policy of constructing a Festival programme without including in it a single new work. When I first glanced at the scheme in the summer I had formed the opinion that this was a risky as well as a wrong proceeding; there was no precedent for it; and, after all, one of the primary objects of these meetings is to encourage native talent by giving commissions to our leading composers. What was the reason for it? Was it because we have no British composers at the present time who can be trusted to write new works with the necessary drawing power? Or was it felt that it would be safer to rely upon the enduring attraction of the Yorkshire chorus in certain more or less familiar works and the popularity of the London Symphony Orchestra as utilized under the conductorship of Sir Thomas Beecham? Anyhow, as the event proved, the artistic question was alone involved; there was no ground for any other doubts, and, to be frank, if I had considered them in the light of history, I might have arrived at that conclusion before I did.

The Leeds Festival organizers have always had a reputation for the independence of their views, wrong or right, wise or unwise. I possess a copy of a book entitled *The History of the Leeds Musical Festivals*, published in 1892, and jointly compiled by Alderman Fred Spark, the late hon. secretary, and Joseph Bennett, the famous music critic of *The Daily Telegraph*, who used to write the analytical notes (and most of the new librettos) for each meeting. Now this book, which covered the years from 1858 to 1889, or rather less than half what would now be the total period of the Festival's existence, is a standing monument to the spirit of determination, the vigorour, not to say stubborn energy that marked the labours of the original Executive Committee and its successors past and present. Its correspondence

with the eminent composers who wrote for it (or refused to) is not only interesting in itself but forms an eloquent commentary upon the methods and ideas of the period. The superb way in which these Yorkshire gentlemen politely dictated their wishes, once they had formulated them, to the various distinguished musicians and others who came under their influence or sway provided an object lesson such as neither Birmingham nor Norwich nor the Three Choirs could possibly have excelled. I would I had the space to quote only a portion of some of the letters from both sides, for, as the preface truly says, they revealed some amusing secrets:

" Now, for the first time, the musical public have an opportunity of going behind the scenes of a Festival, noting for themselves the intricacy of the machinery, the many difficulties to be encountered in working it, and the cares and anxieties which beset those who make themselves responsible for results. It may be that readers who take advantage of the opportunity will be more ready than ever to judge with charity what may seen to them the shortcomings of the Festival management." Which sounds a trifle apologetic, but doubtless represented the feeling of Joseph Bennett rather than that of his Yorkshire friends.

One fact which emerges clearly illustrates the extraordinary change that has come about of recent years in the relative positions of Festival committee and conductor. Formerly it was the conductor who received his orders; now he practically gives them. The executive in many vital matters relies upon him absolutely for guidance and advice from the moment the ball is set rolling. Sir Arthur Sullivan, who was the conductor at Leeds for seven Festivals (1880 to 1898), was frequently consulted, but he used to complain because his appointment was delayed every time, and he retaliated by refusing to write a new work, if asked for one, until he knew whether he was to wield the bâton or not. Thus in January, 1888, he addressed the following letter to Mr. Spark:

I hold to the principle that one of the very first steps to be taken in the organization of the Leeds or any other Festival should be the appointment of a conductor... I cannot undertake to write a new work for a Festival until I know who is to be the responsible authority for its production. You will not appoint such an authority until you have selected the new compositions. So we are at a standstill. I

243

still am of opinion that it is a grave mistake to delay the appointment of a conductor until the musical matters are more than half arranged. There are many cases in which his advice might be sought and his influence used with advantage. It is also possible that errors may have been committed which a little discussion with a responsible musical adviser would have avoided. I wish you and the Committee could be induced to come round to my way of thinking. What say you to it?

Yours sincerely, ARTHUR SULLIVAN.

Ultimately, as we know, they did get round to his way of thinking, and a very important victory was thereby won for the coming race of Festival conductors. The new work in question, by the way, was *The Golden Legend,* one of the greatest successes ever produced at Leeds or any similar gathering; and that was forty years ago. Unfortunately conditions have so changed in other respects that it is not considered necessary, for the time being at any rate, to place novelties in the forefront of the scheme; but I have very little doubt that they will sooner or later be restored to their rightful position again. Meanwhile the Leeds authorities would be well advised to remember the duty that they owe to the art which they are supposed to foster in its creative as well as its executive aspects.

Coming now to my impressions of the recent Festival, I cannot too warmly express my satisfaction that the latest Leeds choir should have proved so completely worthy of its name and fame. Only by comparison with its own past achievements was it possible to measure the super-excellence of this wonderful body of singers. The tone remains as glorious now as it was in the year I first experienced the joy of hearing it, which was the year when Sullivan was first appointed and conducted his new cantata, *The Martyr of Antioch,* with Albani, Patey, and Edward Lloyd (*Come, Margarita, come*) in the chief solo parts. The beauty and intelligence of the singing as a whole, the amazing purity of attack, the extraordinary perfection of the intonation, the even *sostenuto* and gradation of *crescendos* and *diminuendos,* the unfailing staying-power under the most strenuous tests—all these points were just as remarkable and unique as heretofore. Nothing had altered either for better or worse in the quality of the material, unless it be that the sopranos were just a shade more musical, more bell-like, in the production of their acute head notes than ever before in the Beethoven *Mass.* The basses, as usual, were superb; but then so too were the contraltos and the tenors, so I honestly feel that it would not be fair to praise one section more than another. Happily, circumstances did not permit of my reaching Leeds on the first day—happily, I mean, because I was thus able to avoid the dire necessity of listening to Sir Thomas Beecham's caricature of Handel's *Messiah,* which inaugurated the proceedings. It afforded me further relief to read on the following day (October 4th) what my friend Dr. Herbert Thompson said about

it in the columns of *The Yorkshire Post.* After pointing out that " even the practised, highly-trained Leeds chorus could hardly sing some of the choruses at Sir Thomas Beecham's excessive speed, and maintain clearness of articulation," this able critic observed :—

With one of the features of Sir Thomas Beecham's arrangement of *Messiah* it is difficult to have patience, and that is the removal of the " Hallelujah " from its context, placing it at the close, instead of the " Amen." If an ordinary conductor had done this one would style it " a confounded impertinence," and leave it there. But when a responsible musician does such a thing one inquires what his object can have been, and it is difficult to find any other than that of making a brilliant finish to the oratorio. There is, however, the less excuse for this iconoclasm since the " Amen " chorus forms the grandest and most impressive finale imaginable. The fugal form has suggested a gradual climax, culminating in a splendid ending, the entry of the sopranos in the last few bars on their high A giving a thrill which not even the longest and closest familiarity can dull. To sacrifice this for even the " Hallelujah " seems a surprising thing for a musician of repute to do, even to Handel, whose great oratorio has been mauled by conductors and editors for many generations.

On the miscellaneous selection at the second concert and the Bach programme given on the Thursday morning there is no need to dwell here, beyond mentioning that Sir Hugh Allen made his entry with the latter and at once showed himself to be on excellent terms with the Yorkshire choristers. His methods as a conductor offer an interesting contrast to those of Sir Thomas Beecham, but they are marked by no less energy of physical action and they certainly produce the intended results. In other words, Sir Hugh was quite as successful in his way with the choir as Sir Thomas was in his with the London Symphony Orchestra, and that is saying a great deal. The only occasion when it struck me that the orchestra was not quite at its best was on the Thursday evening, when the romantic qualities of Schumann's E flat symphony were brought out with less masculine strength and more feminine sentimentality than seemed desirable. On the other hand, the magnificent performance of Brahms's *German Requiem* was big in every sense, climax after climax of grandeur such as I have never previously heard attained in this noble work. Here, of course, I allude to the combined choral and instrumental interpretation. The rendering of vocal solos was not upon the same level. It was a mistake to entrust Miss Dora Labbette with the dramatic soprano part, short as it is. Her voice was well placed in an earlier item, viz., Debussy's delicate setting of *The Blessed Damozel,* which was rendered in very doubtful French both by Miss Labbette and the female voice choir; but her presence for this was no excuse for asking her to sing in the Brahms, since at Festivals there should never be a suspicion of economy in the disposition of the available vocal talent. As a matter of fact, the soprano in the *Requiem* ought to have been Miss Florence Austral, who was only called upon to sing on the opening day. The baritone solos were creditably undertaken by Mr. Harold Williams.

The labours of Friday morning were shared by both conductors, and in my opinion it was a case of "honours divided." The resolute spirit wherewith Sir Hugh approached Beethoven's colossal *Missa Solennis in D* showed how fully he appreciated the importance of the occasion. He succeeded, moreover, in keeping his forces well together and obtained some very fine effects, even though it was beyond his power to secure a satisfactory balance from his quartet of soloists. Miss Dorothy Silk was artistic as ever but weak; Miss Muriel Brunskill was overpoweringly loud, squandering her beautiful tone where it was not needed; Mr. Parry Jones, excited by the opposition, threw out his chest and shouted; and Mr. Norman Allin, who could have overwhelmed all his companions, contented himself with a moderate exhibition of strength in the lower *tessitura*, for which he duly earned my gratitude. The mistake, to my thinking, lies in not rehearsing the solo quartet beforehand carefully and assiduously, and so bringing them to a right sense of proportion in the use of their varying tonal powers. This, of course, should be done at or even prior to the London rehearsals. An example of what good preparation can accomplish was forthcoming in the great C major symphony of Schubert, which occupied the post-lunch portion of Friday's work.

In the evening came a good performance of Parry's oratorio *Job;* in fact, the best I have heard since it was produced at the Gloucester Festival of 1892. Few then present have forgotten Plunket Greene's masterly delivery of the *Lamentations of Job*, now rendered by a clever and promising young baritone, Mr. Keith Falkner, who is, I understand, studying for opera at Vienna. He has a fine organ, for which further cultivation should do much, and with experience he should develop into a first-rate artist. Both Mr. Parry Jones and Mr. Dennis Noble acquitted themselves well, while Miss Elsie Suddaby lent charm to the air of the Shepherd Boy. The choruses went splendidly, especially the tremendous outburst of the fourth scene, which Sir Hugh Allen worked up very finely indeed. Then the Protean Sir Thomas took the rest of the concert upon his shoulders, giving us the "Spring" section of Haydn's oratorio *The Seasons*, sandwiched between the ultra-modern Stravinsky and Richard Strauss—respectively represented by movements from the ballet-suite "Apollo" and the "Heldenleben." The latter was a most brilliant performance and deserved every bit of the ovation that it awakened.

Instead of one big choral work as usual lending distinction to the Saturday morning—something big enough to fill the entire concert—we had, as it were, to wade through a selection suitable for the "Proms," before arriving at Berlioz's *Te Deum* and feeling ourselves landed upon firm Festival ground. *A qui la faute?* I am not able to say, although I might hazard a fairly accurate guess were I so inclined. But I do know that the hotch-potch drew the poorest attendance of the week and probably the least enthusiastic. Oh yes, it included some solid Brahms, in the shape of the part-songs for female voices and the double concerto for violin and 'cello (May and Beatrice Harrison); and it began with Vaughan Williams's *Pastoral Symphony*, a work of beautiful moments and dull quarters-of-an-hour. Quite out of place, however, were such fanciful, up-to-date *jeux-d'esprit* as the Sitwell-Walton burlesque entitled "Façade," and the "Temptation" Pipe March of Mr. Henry Gibson.

I may have been mistaken, but I certainly thought I saw the solemn faces of Edward Baines and the other statues in the Town Hall turn a rosy pink whilst they listened to such trivial strains as these. Still, I did not gather from Mr. Haigh, who sat near me, that such was actually the case; indeed he seemed rather to enjoy the jokes, which Sir Thomas Beecham certainly did. The popular conductor subsequently proceeded to furnish (after lunch) a stirring performance of the *Te Deum*, one of Berlioz's most remarkable compositions and (as I remarked when it was first introduced at the Crystal Palace in 1885) one whose effects, save at two or three points, are by no means commensurate with its difficulties. Nevertheless, it is in the ability to surmount such obstacles and make them appear easy that the extraordinary powers of the Leeds choir are best displayed. It is then that their stamina seems more than human.

Unfortunately the extra effort proved just a shade too trying for Sir Thomas. He had conducted the whole week long, rehearsals and Festival in succession, without having a single score before him, save that of the Vaughan-Williams symphony. It was perhaps the most arduous task as well as the most tremendous feat of memory ever recorded in the annals of Festival gatherings. I may not have admired it for its wisdom so much as for its combination of valour and skill. But when the final concert arrived Sir Thomas was sensible enough to "draw in his horns." He took the Wagner selections and Tchaikovsky's fourth symphony himself, but handed over Parry's "Blest Pair of Sirens" and Arnold Bax's unaccompanied choral work, *Mater ora Filium*, to the able chorus master, Mr. Norman Stafford; while Mr. W. H. Reed conducted the air, *Il lacerato spirito*, from Verdi's *Simon Boccanegra*, which Mr. Norman Allin declaimed in his most vigorous style. And therewith ended this highly diversified Festival. Whether it will be regarded as a model for the next no one can say; but my private opinion is that the Leeds people will try to do something better.

HERMAN KLEIN.

THE GRAMOPHONE AND THE SINGER

(Continued)

By HERMAN KLEIN

Columbia Complete Opera Albums

ACHIEVEMENTS that not very long ago would have been looked upon as impossible, or next door to it, are nowadays taken for granted. Which sounds like a truism where the capture and transportation of musical sounds are concerned; for the developments in that direction are so constant, so incessant, that we barely have time to turn round and say "Hullo! here is something new," before our admiring gaze is challenged by something newer still. For my own part, however, where the gramophone is in question I take nothing for granted, in the sense of treating with indifference any real fresh forward step. To do that—so rapidly are we moving in these times—would be to run the risk of missing some valuable link in the chain, or failing to appreciate the important bearing that some novel idea, not essentially a mere mechanical "gadget," may have upon the future of the whole industry.

For example, when the new electrical process became practicable there were predictions on all hands as to the beneficial effects that must accrue from it. But I do not remember any one particular person being sufficiently gifted with prophetic vision to foretell for us the whole of the wonderful things that it was going to render possible. I suppose that if I had known or guessed it myself, and, on the strength of that conviction, had gone in for wholesale speculation in gramophone shares upon a large scale, I should by now have been a comfortable British millionaire. Still, I do not regret having missed that chance of a lifetime; no, honestly I do not. If I feel anything at all about it, it is that, knowing the infinite power of good music to delight and stimulate the emotions of the human race, I ought to have had the courage to venture upon a bold and fairly accurate prediction as to the enormous and world-wide developments that must ensue from this relatively cheap and easy extension of a popular mechanical invention. Still, from any but the Stock Exchange point of view such a prophecy would have been interesting rather than valuable, and might have forestalled some of the pleasure of surprise that we now experience as each new outgrowth unfolds itself.

Among these nothing has astonished me more than the extraordinary readiness of gramophone-lovers to absorb all the complete recordings of famous works, operatic, choral, symphonic, and chamber-music, that come within their reach. I believe, moreover, that the ever-increasing facilities for bringing this great music to our firesides has done less harm than the wireless to the public enterprises of the opera house (where it exists) and the concert room; though to what extent even the wireless performances may be inimical to the actual is still, and must remain for some time, a moot point. Of one thing we may feel certain, namely, that with the growing demand for whole works—and without the demand the supply would not augment as it does—there is going on among the rising generation an amazing growth in the appreciation and understanding of high-class music in its finest manifestations. It is pervading every stratum of our social organization, and my firm belief is that ultimately, without losing an iota of its own individual attractiveness, this mechanical music *in excelsis* will exercise a splendid influence in favour of the real thing, as we can hear and enjoy it from the artist in person.

Coming now to the question of recording operas in their entirety, one stumbling-block only stands in the way of the literal accomplishment of this in the case of the older favourites. I allude, of course, to the recitatives. Being the equivalent of the spoken dialogue, which in certain instances and certain theatres is still employed, recitative is essential to an understanding of the plot, at any rate in a stage performance. We have to put up with it on that account; and, when I say "put up with it," I refer to the dry specimen known as the *recitativo secco*, which was for so long in use in Italian opera, from the time of Handel and Mozart down to the period when Wagner's ideas of reform began to find imitators. (The gradual working of the change can be clearly perceived by comparing the earlier with the later operas of Verdi.) Now to attempt to reproduce this kind of musical conversation on the gramophone would be an obvious waste of material and patience, besides unnecessarily adding to the cost of what is called an "album." Fortunately it can be dispensed with, without creating a sense of loss, where the characters in the story are not seen as well as heard. What will happen when television becomes part and parcel of the gramophone the future alone can decide. In the meanwhile, it may safely be assumed that the recordings of operas which are now being placed upon the market contain every note of the score that it is important to hear. In most of them,

I may add, so far as present observation enables me to speak, nothing essential is omitted. Naturally the music-dramas of Wagner ought, properly speaking, to be recorded without leaving out a note, despite the inordinate length of many passages; but I venture to doubt whether this will be found practicable yet awhile.

The latest and by far most important of the Columbia Albums is a recording of *Tristan and Isolde* made in the Bayreuth Theatre during the Festival of last summer. This is an achievement the value of which it would be impossible to over-estimate; nor can I speak too highly of the enterprise that rendered practicable this presentation to the world of something hitherto attainable only by dint of a long and tedious journey, considerable outlay, and no slight physical exertion. My point is not, however, to argue that the gramophone can here replace all the peculiar delights of a Bayreuth performance, with its unique stage effects and every accessory that the eye can take in. It suffices to realise that there is now available an amazingly perfect musical reproduction of this great music-drama, which goes forth clothed with all the authority of the Bayreuth hall-mark, replete with all the superlative qualities of execution and finish that differentiate it from the product of any other theatre in either hemisphere. I need not dwell upon the privilege that it is to be able to hear Bayreuth in this fashion, to repeat Bayreuth *ad infinitum* as we please, and to command its utterances in the solitude of our own homes. But I cannot help wondering what Richard Wagner would have thought of it all—whether that high and mighty potentate in his own domain would ever have consented to this transfer, even for the weighty consideration that we may be sure his " exors, admors and assigns " exacted (and rightly too) for the precious right in question. Anyhow, there it happily is for the gramophone universe to welcome with open arms and to rejoice over, I trust, with the same degree of pleasure that I have done.

In the thirty-eight records (19 two-sided 12-in. discs) that contain the master's masterpiece I have been able to discover few, if any, loopholes for criticism, either in the interpretation of the music or the excellence of the work done by the mechanism of the electric process. It stands from first to last upon the highest level of artistic merit, and, knowing Bayreuth as I do, I am led to wonder more and more at the resources of the mechanical agency that have made the whole thing possible. The cast was as follows:—Tristan, Gunnar Graarud; Isolde, Nanny Larsen-Todsen; Brangäne, Anny Helm; King Marke, Ivar Andrésen; Kurwenal, Rudolf Bockelmann; Melot, Joachim Sattler; Shepherd, Hans Beer; Seaman, Gustaf Rodin; conductor, Karl Elmendorff. Of these names the most familiar by far is that of Ivar Andrésen, the Danish basso whose records won

high praise in these columns some time before his début at Covent Garden last season. I have also had occasion to admire Mme. Larsen-Todsen's gramophone work, and may say at once that her present performance more than justifies her reputation as a superb Isolde. The Scandinavian tenor, Gunnar Graarud, has a fine organ and evidently possesses the heroic qualities essential for an imposing Tristan. I prefer him, however, in the tender love music of Act II., where his softer tones blend delightfully with those of the Isolde. His declamation is apt to be too vigorous at times, and then " forcing " hardens his tone. The voice, sweet, sympathetic, yet powerful, of Anny Helm as Brangäne comes out with especial beauty in the warning utterances of the night scene. The other parts are competently filled and the little that the male chorus has to do could hardly be better done. But, when all has been said and written, the individual features of this magnificent recording that remain most vividly in my memory are two—the glorious tones of Ivar Andrésen's King Marke and the simply gorgeous playing of the Bayreuth Festival Orchestra. Of the few " cuts " that time and space imposed (and none worth mentioning occur until the last act, where there are three that the most ardent Wagnerian ought not to grumble at), I am glad to say that Marke's " ineffable reproach " has been allowed to escape; for anything more touchingly beautiful and pathetic than Andrésen's delivery of it has never surely been heard. The exquisite purity of the orchestral tone is marvellous throughout—above all, perhaps, in the *Prelude*, the accompaniments to the love duet and the *Liebestod*, and the characteristic Introduction to the third act. Altogether this faultless rendering of an incomparable score reflects the utmost credit upon Karl Elmendorff, who " sounds " to me as though he were a conductor of the highest ability.

Cavalleria Rusticana forms an Album of ten 10-in. discs, as recorded for Columbia by the British National Opera Company with the following cast :— Santuzza, Miss May Blyth; Lola, Miss M. Parry; Lucia, Miss J. Griffiths; Turiddu, Mr. Heddle Nash; Alfio, Mr. Harold Williams; conductor, Aylmer Buesst.

This English recording of Mascagni's famous one-act opera I must briefly review on its merits, and without instituting comparisons, favourable or otherwise. It is only fair to remember that *Cavalleria* demands an atmosphere as strongly Sicilian as *Carmen* requires one strongly Spanish; and, for our native singers, the former is even more difficult than the latter to achieve by vocal means alone. I have always found it so on the stage, and am therefore not in the least surprised to note the same traces of British handling in a product of the B.N.O.C. At the same time it has this redeeming feature : you can follow the course of the drama without the aid of a translation and, so plainly does the text come out, without the loss of a single important word. (Whether the diction might be purer is another question; at any rate, it is so clear that you must hear everything the characters say and sing.)

Mr. Heddle Nash gives an admirable performance. His style has dramatic freedom and energy all through the opera, starting with a bold *sostenuto* rendering of the Siciliana which punctuates the Introduction, and ending with a not too tearful delivery of the final farewell to Mama Lucia. His is at least a manly-sounding Turiddu, whatever his moral conduct in the actual story which poor Santuzza relates to the sympathetic mother. The girl herself, as represented by Miss May Blyth, suggests one of those matter-of-fact creatures who blurt out the sad truth to everybody that comes along; that being, indeed, the sort of person that Santuzza actually is depicted as being—and hence all the trouble. When a singer takes this view one scarcely needs to look for the tonal contrasts and subtle inflections of an Emma Calvé. Miss Blyth gives you honest, straightforward vocalisation, and that must suffice. If it does not do so in the *Easter Hymn* it is because here the chorus needed a stronger lead; the general effect is bright and harmonious without being sonorous and impressive enough. All the other choruses, however, are given with the requisite animation and vigour. The Lola of Miss Parry is just the " bright spot " that it ought to be; while Mr. Harold Williams appropriately attains a best on record for speed in Alfio's song, where I can assure you the revengeful waggoner does not boast of his " horses fleet " for nothing. He is at his best, nevertheless, in his more serious passages with the innocent and guilty parties who cause all his misery. The orchestral work in this Album is extremely clear and refined throughout, and altogether the opera has been recorded with a painstaking care that cannot be too highly praised.

MATTIA BATTISTINI

The news of the death of this great baritone at Rieti, in Italy, early in November, came as a sad surprise to the many English admirers who had looked forward to seeing and hearing him again. Still more did it awaken regret in the few who, like myself, had known him well all his artistic life. Exactly how old he was does not appear to be quite certain. The second edition of *Grove* did not mention him. The third says that he was born at Rome in 1857, which is probably correct, though others give the year as 1858, on what authority I know not. But I do know that my old friend Sydney Pardon was seldom wrong about dates, though he made the mistake in his *Grove* account of attributing to the overshadowing triumph of Jean de Reszke the fact that Battistini did not win a greater success when he first returned to London and sang under Sir Augustus

Harris at Drury Lane in 1887. I may also claim to know something about that season, seeing that I helped Harris to organise it and was with him in Madrid when he engaged Battistini, who was then thirty. He had a lovely voice, and was a more polished singer than when he had sung here at Covent Garden four years before. But baritones do not compete for public favour with tenors. One might as well declare that the genius of Scalchi, the famous contralto, had been submerged by that of Patti, or Trebelli's by Tietjens. There never was and never could be any question of comparison between Jean de Reszke and Battistini. Only in the following year (and for many subsequent seasons) the former was re-engaged and the latter was not; the reason being, I believe, that during the intervening nine months the baritone had won triumphs in Italy which made it better worth his while to sing there than in England.

I first heard Battistini in Madrid as Figaro in *Il Barbiere*, and admired him immensely. The pure, silky quality of his tone in a delicate *cantilena* was a joy to be stored up in the memory; yet he lacked neither vigorous energy nor the vibrant power and depth of expressive colour that go to the make-up of a convincing dramatic singer. The flexibility of his organ and his rare vocal agility made him a complete master of the Rossinian *roulades* and *fiorituri*. He was even then a most excellent actor, as merry and amusing in his comedy as he was impressive and strong in his more tragic parts. As Rigoletto, his first part at Drury Lane, he was simply magnificent, and he made an instant hit in it. His Don Giovanni, however, could not then have borne comparison with that of another member of the company —Victor Maurel—although it won deserved admiration when he sang it at Covent Garden in 1906, nearly twenty years later.

It was precisely during the long interval prior to his *rentrée* in London that the main development of Battistini's artistic talent was going on. Not satisfied merely to impersonate operatic villains, jesters, barbers, valets, *e tutti quanti*, he conceived a sincere desire to earn distinction as an interpreter of higher examples of the vocal art, including the gems of the German *Liederbuch* and the pick of the song *répertoires* of the French and Italian schools. It is by these, no less than by his numerous operatic selections, that his wonderfully preserved voice enabled him for so long, and until quite recently, to secure the unstinted admiration of gramophone-lovers in every part of the world. He had brought to a fine point the gift of making records, and has left behind him some most interesting and valuable examples of his finished art. Their utility as specimens of perfect singing amply atones, in my opinion, for their not having been made by the new process.

HERMAN KLEIN.

THE GRAMOPHONE AND THE SINGER

(Continued)

By HERMAN KLEIN

Covent Garden and Some Records

THERE is a reason why the opera season at Covent Garden this year is being held about a month earlier than usual. Berlin, it appears, is anxious to recapture the operatic prestige among foreign visitors that it enjoyed before the war; and it cannot hope to do this without the co-operation of its principal conductor and artists in a proposed " festival season " of formidable proportions to run through the early summer months. Hence the necessity for the German " celebrities " (as Mr. Lionel Powell would denominate them) being through with their London work by the end of May or thereabouts, with a consequent commencement on the 22nd of April, or a fortnight after Easter, and a complete finish of the whole season of ten weeks by June 28th. The transposition will probably not interfere with anybody; on the contrary, it will be emphatically welcomed now—as it used to be when Messrs. Gye and Mapleson did the same kind of thing fifty years ago—by those who hold that the London season is virtually over by the end of June.

At the same time, I cannot remember having ever before seen the Covent Garden opera prospectus, even in its most preliminary form, so early as the last week in November. The object of that, no doubt, was to give people plenty of time to study what Lt.-Col. Blois described in his covering letter as one of the salient points, namely, the all-round raising of prices for the subscription and other tickets. This also will not matter much to the patrons and lovers of luxurious opera. They can afford, and are therefore willing to pay, whatever they are asked for the privilege of hearing during ten weeks of the year the particular operas and artists of their predilection. Nor is this the kind of competition that is going to interfere in the slightest degree with schemes like Sir Thomas Beecham's Imperial League of Opera, which is or ought to provide exclusively British performances for the British people. The two undertakings stand wide apart in every sense, save that both are concerned with opera in its finest forms, and that the *Gramophone Magazine* will continue to help both by appraising (directly and through their records) the merits of the singers, foreign and native, who are likely to take part in their proceedings.

* * * * * *

I have been reading with much amusement Mr. Isidore de Lara's *Many Tales of Many Cities* (Hutchinson and Co., 18s. net), and can emphatically recommend the book to all who care to while away an occasional hour in the company of that lively *raconteur*. The tales are brightly and wittily related, with an abundance of detail and *vraisemblance* that indicates an adequate substratum of actual fact and also a tolerable average of originality. Now and then, of course, an old friend crops up in a new disguise; as, for example, the story of the amazing breathing capacity possessed by the famous tenor Gayarre, who could hold a note whilst you were walking round the piazza outside the Scala at Milan, smoking a cigarette, and find him still holding it (the note) when you re-entered the theatre. The same anecdote has been current for years about Dame Albani, whose passion for long-sustained head notes was such that there was said to be time for the first trombone player to absent himself from the orchestra and get a drink " at the corner," whilst the prima donna was resting neatly poised upon her high A. Concerning Mr. de Lara's personal experiences, their romantic nature and so forth, there is no need to insist; they can be read with as vivid an interest as the intriguing pages that are devoted to his various operatic productions, and to the " procession of princes, patricians, and prima donnas " referred to on the front page of the " jacket."

I have also been perusing a little volume entitled *The Mechanics of Singing* (Dent and Sons, 6s. net), by E. T. Evetts and R. A. Worthington, respectively a teacher and a laryngologist, " who found themselves in agreement—that the tradition of voice production and the modern methods of teaching singing are wrong." I seem to have heard something like this before, and am rather inclined to endorse the opinion myself. The important question is, Have these earnest collaborators discovered a remedy for the deterioration of which they complain? Admitting that they have, does their discovery evolve any ideas that are really fresh or have not been enunciated a hundred times before? The answer to this second question is, No. I have failed to light upon anything new in these pages; but, on the other hand, I do find there a clear and intelligent statement of recognised facts that may prove useful to students, and even more to teachers whose minds are open to conviction. They are reminded, and properly so, not to rely too much upon science, but to extend a closer observation to the workings of Nature in establishing a fundamental basis for the culture of the human voice. And was not this, after all, what the old Italian masters did? I agree that " the less a singer knows of vocal physiology the better for his voice," but I do not agree that such things as registers can be ignored as non-existent because perfect resonation *ought* to obliterate them. Neither do I think that " more good singing and agreeable quality of tone " is to be heard in the variety halls " than in opera, oratorio, or concerts."

I often wonder whether it is thought best, in these days of recording actual performances in the opera house, to warn singers that the microphone is " working " and demands their special attention, or whether it were wiser to leave them in total ignorance of the fact. For my own part I should think the latter the better course of the two, unless the mechanical needs of the situation require it to be otherwise. Operatic artists are quite self-conscious enough as it is, without adding to their precautionary struggles for " safety first." In a word, they are not all Chaliapines. They cannot become so utterly absorbed in their task as to completely forget their audience and—themselves. Most people get nervous in front of a microphone (though only impromptu speakers have a real excuse for doing so), but I have yet to learn that anything on earth could make M. Chaliapine perform a part or sing a note differently from what he intended. He is and he does always exactly what he means to.

These reflections have been aroused by a study of the records taken by H.M.V. at Covent Garden last July during an actual performance of *Boris Godounov*. I was not present to see and hear it, but I am familiar enough with Chaliapine's Boris to be able, with the aid of these records, to enjoy his performance as thoroughly as if I had been there; and, even had I never seen him in the part, I think I could still derive the same extraordinary pleasure from a reproduction so life-like of sounds that seem to breathe out the very soul of the conscience-stricken creature who alternately declaims and whispers, murmurs and ejaculates, but only occasionally *sings* them. For one never ceases to realise that this is the true Boris, not merely the voice, but the one and only possible Boris of Moussorgsky's opera as created by Theodor Chaliapine. You may not be able to understand the Russian words, but with the Oxford score in front of you it is possible (with a little trouble) to follow the course of the music and the meaning of the English and French texts so admirably printed therein. You feel, moreover, that here is the authentic model for whomsoever may attempt to pourtray this same Russian Czar when Chaliapine shall have ceased to represent him.

There are now issued in all three double-sided discs (12 in., DB, 1,181-2-3, 8s. 6d. each), embodying in succession the two scenes from Act II.—*I have attained the highest power* and *Heavy is the hand of retribution*; the wonderful *Clock Scene* and the choral ensemble, *Come, let us vote*, from Acts II. and IV.; and, thirdly, the selections from Act IV. only, *It is a pity Prince Shuisky is absent*, and *Farewell, my son*. After what has been already said, I do not propose to analyse them in detail. Enough that their technical quality could not be improved and that they convey the concentrated essence of a fine performance—one that will be especially interesting to those who have heard the opera, yet not without attraction and fascination for those to whom it is unknown. The above excerpts were all conducted by Vincenzo Bellezza.

Another item of the same supplement is taken from a performance of Gounod's *Faust* given at Covent Garden on June 22nd, under the guidance of Eugène Goossens. On one side is James Hislop's " chaste and pure " rendering in excellent French of *Salut, demeure*, very manly in style and of splendid ringing quality; on the other is the dance portion of the *Kermesse*, beginning at the point where Mephistopheles replies to Valentine with his sardonic *Nous nous retrouverons* (DB, 1,189, 12 in., 8s. 6d.). It may pleasantly surprise the listener to recognise in this, apart from the robust utterances of Hislop, the even more unmistakable tones of Chaliapine, for neither artist's name is printed on the label. The record is, therefore, a valuable one.

From the same source come three Italian souvenirs of last year at Covent Garden, comprising *Gira la cote* and *O giovinetto* (the Funeral March) from the first act of *Turandot* (C 1,566, 12 in., 4s. 6d.); four selections on two discs (C 1,567-8, 12 in., 4s. 6d.) from Acts I. and III. of *Boris Godounov*; and the *Bell* chorus and opening chorus of Act II. from *Pagliacci* (B 2,837, 10 in., 3s.). These are all sung under Vincenzo Bellezza with admirable *verve* and are very clearly and faithfully recorded.

HERMAN KLEIN.

THE GRAMOPHONE AND THE SINGER

(Continued)

By HERMAN KLEIN

A "Carmen" Album and Other Topics

IN my notice in December of the Columbia Albums of *Tristan und Isolde* and *Cavalleria Rusticana* I had something to say about the difficulty of omitting recitative from reproductions of those operas where it is bound up with or merges in and out of the musical setting. It forms in them such an essential link in the chain of dramatic events that if the flow of the music be continuous it cannot be dispensed with. The case of *Carmen* is somewhat different. Here the dialogue is indispensable in the theatre, and would be missed by others besides those people who care for the clumsy wit and Cockney humour incidental to the late Henry Hersée's adaptation. As it happens, many of the recitatives are quite independent of that sort of thing; the majority of them, having been composed by Bizet subsequent to the completion of his original score, are exceptionally dramatic, interesting, and full of character. It is a pity if they have to be omitted, but what is to be done if excessive length is to be avoided? The responsibility for answering this question has happily been assumed, so far as the Columbia album is concerned, by the composer's own compatriots, since it has been made in Paris by the company regularly in the habit of performing the opera. Substantially the whole of the music is there; not a number that we are accustomed to look for is missing; the continuity is sufficiently unbroken for us to feel that we are listening to a coherent and complete reproduction of the score.

What is equally important, it is throughout imbued with a wonderful degree of atmospheric spirit and sung with an amount of *entrain* that imparts quite unusual realism to the gramophone performance. I need not enlarge upon the value of this. For my own part I would sooner listen to a perfectly trained ensemble such as the Columbia *Carmen* provides here from the authentic French source than the best haphazard collection of unrehearsed stars (so-called) that Covent Garden can put forward in the grand season. For one thing, I know that Bizet's music will receive, as it certainly does in the present instance, a traditionally accurate interpretation, and not be tampered with or experimented with or taken at ridiculous tempi by conductors anxious to show off their capacity for improving upon a composer's intentions.

Having generalised to this extent, I will now endeavour to indicate how the *Carmen* score has been laid out in the new Album. There are in all 15 (12 in.) records, and the cast is as follows: Carmen, Raymonde Visconti; Michaela, Marthe Nespoulous; Frasquita, Andrée Vavon; Mercédès, Andrée Bernadet; Don José, G. Thill; Escamillo, Guenot; Remendado, Roussel; Dancairo, Mathyl; conductor, Elie Cohen; with chorus and orchestra of the Opéra-Comique.

The overture (or, rather, introductory prelude) and opening chorus proclaim at once the merits of the electric process in the resonant timbre and clear definition alike of instrumental and vocal parts. Every note comes out distinctly, and so does every word; no confusion, no noise, no disregard for balance or proportion. Anyone who has seen the opera will at once be able to visualize the scene in Seville outside the cigar factory and picture the various leading characters as they arrive in turn. I find Mme. Nespoulous a particularly sympathetic Michaela, and she encounters an unusually good brigadier in M. Guenot, who is also to sing the rôle of the Toreador. (It is, of course, the privilege of the gramophone to allow of parts being " doubled " in this way, though I rather doubt the wisdom of its effect upon what may be termed aural characterisation, either here or in wireless performances.) The *gamins* and the cigar-girls (not cigarette-girls, mind) are strictly on the key, and Carmen introduces in Mme. Visconti an artist whose decision, reliability, and rhythmical feeling compensate amply for the occasional hardness and open quality of her voice. She evidently embodies Carmen to the finger-tips, and both in the *Habañera* and the *Séguidille* suggests the genuine Spanish swing of the hips. In Don José we recognise one of the finest French tenors of the day; indeed, M. Thill's records are by now familiar to the readers of this journal. He is splendid in the duet with Michaela, where we find restored the passage referring to the demon which is invariably cut over here.

The reverse side of the disc containing the finale to the first act gives the gipsy trio that opens the second scene in the tavern of Lillas Pastia. The latter is not over well sung, the semiquaver turns being hurried and slurred. M. Guenot scores heavily, however, in the *Toreador's Song*, the original ending of which (so often pleaded for in vain from the Italian conductors at Covent Garden) is here found in its proper place and welcomed accordingly, in spite of a slight trip in the toreador's intonation, which, if the bull had noticed it, might have cost him his life. On the other hand, no single flaw can be pointed out in the smugglers' quintet; it is taken at a reasonable pace and sung in the sprightliest, crispest fashion. I do not object to the cutting of a portion of Carmen's castanet dance, because I find Mme. Visconti's phrasing of the tune wrongly accentuated. Anyhow, amends are quickly made for this by a very dramatic rendering of the duet as well as by M. Thill's magnificent singing in the *Flower Song*. The choral finale winds up the act in brilliant fashion.

I ought to say that the playing of the entr'actes forms a notable feature of interest. The flute and harp duet in the pure Spanish style which precedes Act III. is charmingly given, as is also the introduction to the last act. The ballet is left out for the simple reason that it does not properly belong to the Opéra-Comique version, being (as I have pointed out before) an afterthought constructed out of numbers taken from *La Jolie Fille de Perth* and *L'Arlésienne*. The music of the whole scene in the smugglers' mountain retreat occupies only nine sides of the next five discs, and excellently done it is too. Here occur some of the most " tricky " portions of the opera, and M. Elie Cohen makes manifest in the remarkable precision of the ensembles all the qualities of a first-rate conductor. I observe again that the customary cut in the duet with which Don José and Escamillo precede their interrupted fight is not made. MM. Thill and Guenot sing the whole of that difficult bit of syncopation. Michaela's song is exceptionally well rendered by Mme. Nespoulous, her tone being less inclined to harden here than in the opening act. And so we go on to the final incidents outside the bull-ring, where the processional music and choruses are given with abundant animation, while the recording remains throughout at the same lofty level. The tragic duet between Don José and Carmen is also unusually well sung. The tenor, at any rate, does not evince the slightest sign of fatigue, and his delivery of all the big phrases is truly superb.

*   *   *

The more I hear of modern Italian singing, the more I grow convinced that the Italian teachers are shaping their pupils upon an identical pattern. The evidence of it stands out clearly in all the latest operatic records. With the tenors in particular it is really becoming difficult to distinguish one voice from another, for the production of the majority is emphatically nasal—which makes it easier for them to imitate each others' timbre—whilst one and all are obviously striving to carry off the palm for amplitude of volume. This is a polite way of saying that they don't care a jot what kind of tone they produce so long as it creates the maximum of noise; which, it may be remembered, is precisely the danger that I predicted in the making of gramophone records when the electric process first came in. There is a

round dozen of tenors at the present moment who are so completely " tarred with the same brush " that I would defy you to make sure of recognizing them from the sound of their voices. Indeed, were the London Editor of this journal to arrange a prize competition for guessing the names of the various Italian tenors (most of them unknown to Covent Garden) who oblige you with the hackneyed airs of Verdi and Puccini, he would, I am sure, provide his B.B.C. listeners with a much more amusing " stunt " than those recently attempted at 2 LO with " talkers " and other tiresome people.

But it is not, of course, the tenors alone who are working on this mistaken plan. The baritones are as bad; they are as much inclined (like their Teutonic rivals, for that matter) to indulge in what the American engine-drivers call " opening the throttle " to the uttermost. They also try to exercise at every opportunity the stale device of shouting a note at the top of their lungs in order to diminish it as slowly as possible to the proportions of a thin *mezza voce*. This the sopranos also do, though not with the same annoying persistence, the consequence being that singing in these cases resolves itself into the extremes of *ff* and *pp*, with rarely anything like a beautiful sustained *mf* or *p* between the two. Moreover, sopranos cannot with impunity submit their voices to a constant and unvarying application of nasal resonance. It is bad enough—that is to say, ugly and destructive to sweetness—in the case of the tenor voice, especially when done to excess. But to the more delicate soprano or contralto it can prove harmful in an even greater degree, and ultimately deprive the organ of all or much of its freshness and charm.

Mind, it is the method and not the music that produces the result every time. In the days when Wagner was just coming into fashion one heard warnings from Italy louder and more insistent than from any other country as to the dreadful consequences that must ensue from singing the " Music of the Future." Yet nothing of the sort happened. The great singers of that epoch did not take long to prove that the Wagnerian school of declamation, correctly employed, need not place an undue strain upon a well-trained human voice. It should be the same to-day with the operas of Puccini, Giordano, or the other modern Italian composers. Yet in the case of *Turandot* I would have you compare the records of Eva Turner with those of a Bianca Scacciati or any of the Italian sopranos who have essayed that trying music. The difference in the amount of effort, as well as in the quality of the tone, is hardly believable. The constant high *tessitura* does not trouble the Englishwoman in the least; she does not employ her nasal resonance to excess; she does not screech or scoop, neither does she scream whole phrases at her loudest. From first to last of the most trying part ever written for a soprano she gives you naught save genuine singing to which it is a pleasure to listen. All these noisy *tours de force*, these spells of *fortissimo* shouting, these dreary because oft-repeated tricks, such as dropping the voice suddenly from a trumpet-blast to a thread, do not really come within the domain of true vocal art.

I am the more sorry to see these horrid exaggerations—above all, the shouting contests among the leading tenors, with two or three exceptions—encouraged by the public of the Italian opera houses, because I know it to be their applause which is primarily responsible for the transfer of the same methods to the gramophone disc. Just as it began years ago with the *vibrato* and the *tremolo*, so is it making strides to-day in the growing favour accorded these other vocal " atrocities " of the operatic stage. If they are practised and accepted, who is to escape them when the operas of the old school or the classics of Mozart and Gluck are brought forward for revival? Who?—maybe a Toti dal Monte, a Mariano Stabile, and two or three others. But positively you can count the whole lot of this class upon the fingers of a single hand. The worst of it is that the style mostly exemplified by the gramophone is bound to be the one most widely imitated by singers in every part of the globe. And that style is in certain of its features identical, not alone because of the teaching, but because the singers themselves, if they do not actually listen to their rivals in the opera house, take good care to possess themselves of their records and reproduce their characteristics to the best of their ability. Imitation being their *forte*, I am sorry to say the majority of them succeed only too well. The pity is that they do not know better how to select the good from the bad, besides having sense enough to spare their listeners' ears by ceasing to take undue advantage of the latitude granted them by the electric process.

I read with very great interest Mr. John Thorne's short but pithy article in last month's GRAMOPHONE, entitled *The Fallacy of the " Recording Voice,"* and would like to state that I agreed with every word of it. The important point is that the new process makes it possible for the voice to be amplified " after it has passed the microphone." This is, indeed, a fact of tremendous significance, since it seems to me to account in the simplest possible way for the plague of excessive loudness which is becoming the subject of increasingly wide complaint. I uttered a warning about it in these pages a long time ago, only in my ignorance I addressed that warning to the singer instead of to the operator or " engineer," as Mr. Thorne calls him. (Had I known I should have warned them both.) Truth to tell, I have for some time been expecting something of the sort. Again and again I have asked myself how it could come about that two voices I knew well, one of decidedly inferior strength to the other, should be able to change places, as it were, as the effect of standing in front of a microphone. Technique may have much to do with the quality, as Mr. Thorne says, but surely it cannot greatly affect the volume, and a positive effort on the singer's part to exaggerate the size of the voice would almost certainly result in a certain amount of distortion. That result I had already noted, and yet had not found myself able wholly to account for the metamorphosis which made that small tenor, Signor X., appear to have as big a voice as a Martinelli or a Pertile.

Of course, the device, in one sense, is unfair; yet not so unfair as the opposite effect, which I take to be quite practicable, namely, of producing the kind of tone that answers the description of a *non*-recording voice, or voice that does not record upon the matrix a pure, true, natural reflex of the human organ, with all its inherent characteristics of individuality and power. I may not be able to go so far as Mr. Thorne and assert my belief that " there is no such thing as a ' recording voice,' " because that would be to deny that one voice may be so constituted as to yield a more faithful record than another, which the experience of pre-electric days has scarcely led me to credit. On the other hand, I quite admit that good technical training is a factor of overwhelming importance in the attainment of the right result; and I fully agree with all that Mr. Thorne had to say on this subject in the course of his too brief article. Moreover, it is certainly a " terrifying state of affairs " for the performer to be aware that it is in the power of the operator who is controlling the " reception " to alter, modify, reduce, or enlarge the voice according to his will. This power is particularly dangerous where tests are concerned. Otherwise it is difficult to conceive that, in the case of singers of reputation, there could be anything to gain by minimizing the excellence and value of their gramophone product, or endeavouring to persuade them that they do not possess a " recording voice."

P.S.—I went to the Royal College the other night to hear the students of Mr. Grünebaum's opera class in scenes from *Aïda* and *Samson and Delilah*. There were some good voices among them, particularly that of a South African mezzo-soprano who sung Amneris, Miss Betsy de la Porte. But, like her companions, she has still a long way to go before she will be ready for a real operatic career. The voices can and must be brought under fuller control, the gestures made more graceful and intelligent, the diction improved, the sense of the stage strengthened and developed. It has to be remembered by those in charge of these classes that nothing which smacks of " amateurishness " is likely to be tolerated either by the B.N.O.C. or by Sir Thomas Beecham when he is engaging artists for his Opera League Company. The material is undoubtedly there. HERMAN KLEIN.

THE GRAMOPHONE AND THE SINGER

(Continued)

By HERMAN KLEIN

Opera Prospects: Voice and Verse

THREATENED men generally live long; so do threatened buildings. There was talk of the Covent Garden Opera House coming down not long before Sir Augustus Harris went over from Drury Lane forty-one years ago next month and founded the fortunes of the Royal Opera, as carried on by himself and the various " Syndicates " that succeeded him. Yet the theatre in Bow Street still stands where it did, and, for aught we can tell, may continue to remain standing there much longer than the two years now supposed to represent the extreme limit of its existence. If it does so continue, however, I take leave to doubt whether it will then be found alone in its glory, amid an ever-widening sea of fruit and vegetables, as it is at the present time. I have been told (but I cannot vouch for the truth of what may, after all, be no more than a rumour) that a site has been secured and plans are being prepared for the erection of a large opera house capable of accommodating an audience of 5,000 to 6,000, at prices ranging from six shillings to eighteenpence.

I can only say that I hope my information is correct, for this is really the thing that is wanted if we are ever to get out of the present operatic *impasse*. I care not who does it, but the right opera house must be built in the right part of London before the great body of opera-lovers in this country can be persuaded that all the talk and all the promises on the subject stand for something substantial and permanent. The public is sick of theories about opera. It wants to see the place where it will be expected to go and enjoy itself before it will provide the necessary capital to support and fulfil the idea. James Mapleson knew this when, fifty years ago, he started building an opera house on the Embankment where Scotland Yard is situated to-day. But he had no money, and he was not the man to command the confidence that would bring it; besides, the site at that time was hopelessly out of the way. Thirty years later Oscar Hammerstein, imbued with the same ambition, the same right notion as to how to begin, erected with his own capital the London Opera House in Kingsway, now the Stoll Picture Theatre. But he in turn paid the penalty of choosing the wrong spot to suit the aristocratic patrons for whom he catered; and, as we all know, *force majeure* compelled him to fix his prices much too high for the pockets of the general public.

Two such warnings were too much for the courage of the penniless National Opera Trust, which went up like a rocket—and came down like one—a few years ago. Moreover, the ability to think and act in a practical manner was never placed in evidence by the promoters of that ill-devised project; they knew neither how to raise the money nor build the theatre that poor Paget Bowman longed to handle and direct. Then comes the League of Opera (for we will pass over the de Lara scheme in respectful silence) with, for its protagonist, a man who lacks neither courage nor public admiration and esteem—a musician who has won his spurs alike as a manager and a conductor of opera. His powerful and almost heart-rending appeals in the cause of the League meet with a response which he himself declares to be lukewarm, inadequate, even a trifle disgraceful. It is most disappointing, of course, especially after the sanguine assurance uttered during the Leeds Festival last October that things were going well and the League would be started before the end of the year. Why has that bold prophecy not been fulfilled? That is the question, coupled with the fixing of personal responsibility, that has been creating some journalistic stir and commotion.

The Times began the skirmishing with an article entitled " The Opera Movement," which drew attention to a certain expression of sympathy by the Chancellor of the Exchequer, in reply to a question put by Sir Martin Conway concerning " the educational importance of a permanent opera." This was very well; but the article also went on to point out that the League of Opera was " not yet an opera-producing institution," and that its cost to members of 10s. a year did not bring in return the " immediate and constant benefit " that accrued from the similar yearly charge made by the B.B.C. The B.B.C., with its enormous field of publicity, had obviously been at a much greater advantage than the League of Opera, but the latter had so far failed for other reasons—two other reasons, in fact, to wit: (a) the inadequacy of the organization and (b) the unfortunate circumstance that the name of Sir Thomas Beecham alone did not " command entire confidence." If, indeed, the League was to get any farther, it would have to be " lifted out of a position in which it could be regarded as ' a one-man show.' It must obtain a body of leaders, including men and women who are known for their sense of responsibility towards art, education, and social advancement generally." Finally, the article suggested that the B.B.C., without taking " any financial responsibility for the permanent opera " (heaven forbid that it should!), might promote the cause of the League by giving " very much more active encouragement to the spread of the idea than it has given up to the present."

This last suggestion aroused no sort of comment that I have seen. But the personal reference to Sir Thomas Beecham and the accompanying proposal about " leaders " at once gave rise to excited and angry rejoinders. A letter from Lady Cunard appeared on February 9th reminding the writer of *The Times* article of the fate of the National Opera Trust and declaring that the founder of the League of Opera had " a fair chance of succeeding wholly if he be given the opportunity, unhampered by unnecessary criticism, of continuing this great work in peace." On the following day, in the *Sunday Times*, Mr. Ernest Newman took up the running with characteristic energy, denouncing the suggestion of social leadership as a " cool proposal " to bring in the autocrats of the " academic world " and place in their hands the funds and the authority now possessed by Sir Thomas Beecham. In this manner a nice little controversy was started. How it progressed does not greatly signify, nor is the present writer, happily, called upon to express views of his own concerning the merits of the argument. My wish under any conditions is to see the League of Opera a success, no matter through whose mechanical or clerical agency that result be accomplished; and I cannot doubt that such is also the desire of the eager but insufficient thousands who have so far put down their money to become members of it.

In the meantime, the solitary supremacy of the Royal Opera, under the ægis of the Covent Garden Opera Syndicate, remains unchallenged. I understand that Lt.-Col. Blois and his co-directors are quite satisfied with the response to their early request for prompt applications; the list of subscribers is already as big as last year's, and, thanks to the publicity accorded in the Press, interest in the " international " season—the German portion of it at any rate—promises to be unabated. As these lines are written the identity of the hoped-for " entirely new opera " mentioned in the prospectus remains undisclosed, and, although a little bird persistently whispers in my ear that it will be the great Continental success, Krenek's *Johnny spielt auf*, I have no authority for making a definite statement to that effect. Since I last wrote on this topic several additions have been made to the list of artists

engaged by the Syndicate, and really I do not see, as it now stands, how a stronger team could well have been collected. Among the thirty-eight artists announced in the February list are the names of most of the favourite gramophone singers whose work is constantly being placed before our readers. I miss those of a few who have appeared during the last two or three seasons under the auspices of more or less the same management, but all of real importance are there, including, of course, the irresistible Feodor Chaliapine. As already stated, the season opens on Monday, April 22nd, and the first *Nibelungen* cycle will follow almost immediately. By the way, there was not the least ground for the fright that ensued among the new directorate upon the recent announcement that the Grand Opera Syndicate had gone into liquidation. No sensible person could have imagined for a moment that the affairs of the old Syndicate formed after the death of Harris, and which carried on for so many years under the chairmanship of the late Mr. Harry Higgins, were in any way connected with those of the actual Covent Garden Opera Syndicate. Presumably the recent death of Mr. Higgins was the main, if not the sole, reason for the liquidation.

* * *

Some weeks have elapsed since the issue by the Oxford University Press (London, Humphrey Milford; 7s. 6d. net) of Mr. H. C. Colles's book entitled *Voice and Verse*; but inasmuch as the Cramb Lectures upon which it is based were delivered by the author at Glasgow University so long as a full twelve-month ago, I scarcely feel that it is too late for discussion here and now. As a matter of fact, the subject of the alliance between music and poetry is one of perennial interest; and it becomes doubly interesting when approached, as it is in this case, from a practically fresh point of view. To put it in his own nutshell, the premise set forth by the accomplished music critic of *The Times* is " that instrumental music is merely an extension of vocal music." It is this simple statement—that the whole development of great music, whether it be symphonic, operatic, oratorio or church, can be traced back through its various periods to *melody* that had its origin in the ancient tunes chanted by the human voice, in the outpourings of the Eastern singer, in the community singing of the men and women who prayed together " with one accord," as related in the first chapter of the Acts of the Apostles. In other words, the voice originally did it all. The instrument, although it existed, did virtually nothing to aid in the foundation of harmony, much less the invention of common chords, counterpoint, the key system, and all the rest of the musician's working paraphernalia.

In this statement I can see nothing awry, nothing that Mr. Colles does not demonstrate the truth of in the course of nine chapters of well-reasoned argument. (There is a tenth, but that was remodelled after the lectures had been given, and may be regarded rather as an up-to-date summing-up of modern musical conditions.) The question is whether, in his anxiety to prove his case, he has not in the aggregate overstated it. That is the exception that I have seen taken to the book in more than one review; and yet, all things considered, I would not have had it otherwise. Better a bold, clear thesis, vigorously handled by a sane thinker and profound student, than all the complex, cloudy abstractions that a pedagogic pen can evolve, to show the true relationship between voice and music. One method can never convince; the other can and does. What could be plainer or truer than this?—

Music is often spoken of as a language. My contention is that the vocabulary, the grammar, and the syntax of that language have been brought into being by the expression of human feeling through the human voice; that, strictly speaking, there is no such thing as pure instrumental music, since instrumental sounds only become intelligible and sensible when they refer the mind of the participant to vocal experience of some sort.

At the present day there is a desire among certain composers to break with the vocal language. They are trying to make music independent of vocal associations. They would scrap the key system in favour of "atonality"; invent new scales and intervals, think in the equal temperament of the keyboard, dividing the octave up arithmetically. They claim to be inventing a new language and their experiments are interesting. They have only to go on talking their new language long enough to discover whether other people can enter into it, understand it, and talk it with them. At present it must be regarded as a musical equivalent to Esperanto, the universal tongue which nobody talks.

Into another nutshell Mr. Colles puts the minor premise of his argument, which " is simply that song depends for its existence on words as well as music, and that it is as natural to mankind to sing words as to speak them." This is absolutely indisputable —more so, perhaps, than the subsequent assertion " that it is only by an effort of virtuosity that mankind can arrive at singing without the aid of words." I am not so sure of that; but I do know that the " minor premise " is unassailable in itself, and that it is clearly and wisely illustrated in the succeeding chapters dealing with the life and contemporary appreciation of Purcell (a masterly exposition), also in " Handel in London " and " Towards English Opera." The chapter on " The Nature of the Case," from which the above quotations are drawn, is only equalled in its cogency, conciseness, and argumenta-

tive skill by the last one (the re-written one), called " Open Questions," wherein among other things the libellous statement, " English is so bad for singing, isn't it ? " comes in for severe castigation. Altogether, then, I consider *Voice and Verse* one of the best efforts, if not *the* best effort, to discuss a difficult subject from a new and adventurous viewpoint that has yet been written. It deserves to be widely known and carefully studied.

As I have made mention of Mr. Colles in his capacity of music critic of *The Times*, it may be as well if I point out that it was not he, but one of his " young men "—which of the brilliant group I do not venture to guess—who was responsible for the extraordinary article under the heading " The Musician's Gramophone " that recently spoke in disparaging terms of the Columbia-Bayreuth album of *Tristan und Isolde*. It had scarcely a good word for the whole thing, and from first to last was so obviously written in a spirit of *parti pris* that it may be said to have defeated its own object. The chief ground for complaint was the undue prominence— the " disjointed and displeasing prominence "— accorded to the voices and the " virtues " (*sic*) of the soloists at the expense of the orchestra. There was no musical continuity (presumably because there had to be 20 records); the Bayreuth auditorium was unfavourable to gramophonic reproduction; " the reception soon becomes fluffy and nasal "; the dramatic interest ought not " to pass from voice to voice," the singers being merely " frail vessels tossed on the waves of a great sea of sound "; in short, the recording only served " to exaggerate what is worst in Wagner," producing, finally, a " result more than fatiguing—it is ridiculous."

" Ridiculous " is perhaps too mild a word to apply to destructive and unveracious criticism of this sort. The only power for harm residing in such stuff was the influence of the journal in which it was printed, and which is my sole reason for drawing attention to it in these columns. One cannot hold Mr. Colles responsible for its insertion, any more than for the prejudiced opinions which the article expressed; but it was a pity, all the same, that it did appear, and, stranger still, that it should so completely have misrepresented the views of the author of *Voice and Verse* regarding the position taken by the human voice in the ideal adjustment of things musical in this world.

HERMAN KLEIN.

THE GRAMOPHONE AND THE SINGER

(Continued)

By HERMAN KLEIN

A New Prose Translation: "Traviata"
"Parsifal" and "Götterdämmerung" Albums

THE subject of translations has been more discussed during the past few years than at any period within my recollection. I would even say that it has been discussed *ad nauseam* were I not aware of its great importance and of the fact that we have still a long way to go before the ground is cleared of all the printed rubbish which the music publishers still continue to watch over as part of their " sacred rights." The old translations of the more familiar Lieder were bad enough (at least they were none too good); but those of the old operas were incontestably worse—they were, and most of them still are, an absolute disgrace to English musical literature. The development of the gramophone has helped, by creating a wider demand for these things, to display their poverty in a still stronger light, and I may truthfully add that this journal has done far more than any other to ameliorate the state of affairs, alike by trenchant criticism and by the provision of sensible substitutes (chiefly from the pen of Mr. H. F. V. Little) for the inadequate versions in common use.

It is necessary, of course, to mark the distinction between free translations, which are all that the gramophonist actually requires, and the singable adaptations which have to be made to fit the music exactly. The latter take much longer to do and constitute the more difficult task; but unfortunately these very difficulties—these restrictions on the freedom of the translator in the shape of time, rhythm and rhyme—have been the main source of the linguistical inanities which have been handed down to one generation after another in the operatic libretti and the foreign song albums. The worst obstacle of all was the supposed, the wholly imaginary, need for verse that rhymed.like the original. There existed a mistaken notion that the music required it, and, in order to follow that misleading will-o'-the-wisp, the loyal translator was wont to perpetrate nonsense and solecisms of the worst kind. Line after line of doubtful English bore only the faintest resemblance to the sense and meaning of the Italian, German or French text. It just fitted the music and that was enough, no matter how colloquial or commonplace the equivalent might be, no matter how high-falutin' or far-fetched the language.

But the advent of the gramophone-album is putting an end to this despotism. All that is needed for the thousands of listeners who do not understand the words that are being sung (and might be unable to distinguish them clearly if they did) is to be able to place in front of them a text which supplies in plain, simple language the meaning or purport of the original; which will enable them to follow without possibility of error the progress of the dramatic action and the changing emotions of the characters concerned in it. This is what the gramophone companies have at last begun to realize, without regard to the nature or quality of the stuff provided for them by the publishers of the score.

The latest—and best--example of such endeavours to compensate for the disadvantage of being unable to visualize the scene of the story is the new version of the libretto of *La Traviata*, which accompanies the complete album of the opera issued this month by Columbia. It is from the versatile pen of our Editor, Mr. Compton Mackenzie, and, if I may be permitted to say so here, affords yet another illustration of his practical sympathy with and understanding of all matters that tend in the direction of gramophone advancement. I need scarcely say that it is an immeasurable improvement upon the kind of translation that did duty as an aid to the feeble-minded in the eighteen-penny opera books sold in the old days at Covent Garden and Her Majesty's. The Italian libretto was bad enough—so bad, very often, that one marvelled at the genius which enabled Verdi and other 19th century composers to evolve their beautiful music from such stupid colloquialisms and trashy, stilted verse. But here you will find the familiar stuff presented under a new guise. If you have never read *La Dame aux Camélias* you will feel as though you were for the first time reading the play (not the novel) of Alexandre Dumas *fils* in some-thing like the literary form and style that it was written in. His personages are talking sense and expressing real human feelings in grammatical fashion in combination with the touching melodies that we know so well. Their actual medium may still be the original Italian of the opera, but we are no longer condemned to grope for its meaning through a translation that is ten times more flaccid and obscure.

It is quite true, as stated in the short account of the career of *La Traviata* which precedes Mr. Compton Mackenzie's new prose version, that " its popularity shows no signs of waning. *Traviata* is still one of the most frequently performed of Verdi's works—only his *Rigoletto* and *Aida* are as often to be heard in the great European opera houses." If we hear it less in London than we used to, it is not because of the music, but because of the paucity of great Violettas. I remember when every famous lyric soprano looked upon this and Marguerite in *Faust* as their biggest parts, as their inevitable and indispensable *cheval de bataille*. The exquisite Piccolomini was, of course, before my time; but I can well recollect Adelina Patti and Christine Nilsson singing the *Traviata* in their prime, not to mention Marcella Sembrich, who also brought her delightful art to bear upon the character of Violetta Valéry and upon the undying melodies that Verdi has bound up with her sad romance. Naïve though it may be reckoned by the highbrow, this music is still irresistible to millions, and I do not wonder that the Columbia Company has seen fit to confer upon it the latest *cachet* of universal appreciation.

The cast engaged for the Milan recording was as follows: Violetta, Mercedès Capsir; Flora and Annina, Ida Conti; Alfredo, Lionello Cecil; Germont, Carlo Galeffi; Gastone, Giuseppe Nessi; Doctor, S. Baccaloni; Baron, A. Baracchi; Marquis, N. Villa; with the chorus of La Scala and a competent orchestra under the able direction of Cav. Lorenzo Molajoli. Such a group of experienced executants alone would not have found it feasible to complete the whole opera in fifteen records (Col. 9629-9643), without either undue acceleration of tempi or spoiling the music by a sense of haste. I will not say that certain numbers are not taken rather fast, but in almost every case the music seems to stand it well, because it consists mainly of the dance rhythms which Verdi lavished so freely upon his Parisian subject. Evidently the conductor had rehearsed his company with adequate care, for the *prestos* are just as neatly done as the *andantes*, and, as we all know, their pace could not have been mechanically altered without interfering with the pitch. On the other hand, I fancy the voices have undergone the customary enlargement in sufficient measure to make the use of a soft needle desirable in all save large rooms and halls.

In an opera so full of action as *La Traviata*—as, indeed, with most of Verdi's operas—the necessity for being able to follow every line of the libretto is paramount. We may know every note of the music by heart, but that is no particular gain (especially if it be hackneyed music) unless we know exactly how and why it fits into its place in the general scheme. Even when we hear it in an opera house we may not be able to comprehend what is going on upon the stage, or understand more than a portion, if that, of the words that are being uttered; and, in these days of darkened auditoriums, following with the printed text is, of course, out of the question. Here precisely is where the gramophone comes in. Bar the action, the entire opera is presented for your artistic appreciation in the most complete and comfortable manner. The Italian words that are being sung are before you (you know the story already), and side by side with them is Mr. Compton Mackenzie's flowing English equivalent, so clear and straightforward and at the same time so vividly expressed, that you imagine you are conjuring up the play from the pages of one of his own novels. This is a new experience, anyhow, and one that I can warmly commend to your notice. The combined result provides one of those exceptional instances where the helpful prose translation of the text is bound to increase the demand for an excellent Columbia opera album. As regards the singing, I have only to add that it is characteristically Italian; that the voices are typically bright, clear, and emotional, well adapted to their duties, and employed throughout with alertness and intelligence. The crispness of the orchestral playing is particularly creditable, and as a whole the performance reveals distinct merit on the part of Cav. Molajoli and his forces.

* * *

The third act of *Parsifal*, sung in German and performed with the co-operation of the Berlin State Opera Orchestra under the direction of Dr. Karl Muck, forms a notable addition to the fast-growing group of Wagner albums published by H.M.V. Nearly four years have elapsed since the Gramophone Company gave out the first of its series of records reproducing the more salient scenes of the master's swan-song; but this is the first one to be executed abroad on a large scale, and it deals exclusively with the final act. The foreword to the synopsis of the story, printed on the inside cover of the present album, reminds us that those earlier selections, " apart from their musical interest, were important as being the *first* electrical recordings of a work of any size ever to be made and issued." They had and still have their value in that sense. Nevertheless it can hardly be doubted that before very long we shall be having the first two acts in the same complete form as the third; and, when it does so materialize, it will be possible to claim that the recording of the music-drama is a magnificent achievement.

I have often been asked which of Wagner's great works for the stage I consider his masterpiece. As yet, however, I have been unable to find a satisfactory answer to that " poser " of a question. It is like asking which of Shakespeare's plays or Mozart's operas or Beethoven's symphonies one prefers. Somehow I cannot make up my mind about the order in which I place my musical favourites. I feel very much as the owner of a picture gallery must feel when asked to name the greatest of the *chefs-d'œuvre* in his collection; he loves them all and admires each in turn so much that he cannot choose between them. If I have an overweening partiality for *Parsifal*—and I frankly confess that I have—it is not because in my humble opinion it is greater than *Tristan* or the *Meistersinger* or contains finer music than the *Nibelungen*, but simply and solely because of its associations. It is bound up in my mind with some very notable recollections which it would take too long to narrate or even briefly refer to here. Enough that I love it because it was the first work I ever heard at Bayreuth, after hearing a very wonderful concert performance at the Albert Hall under Barnby; I love it because Hans Richter familiarized me with all its choicest moments; I love it because for weeks at a stretch I was teaching gifted foreigners at Berlin and New York to sing it in English, thus mastering every note of the marvellous score; and, finally, I love it because its beauty is of a type that never, never palls.

The recording of the glorious third act has been carried out on eight double-sided discs (D 1537 to D 1544), with the three principal singing characters —Titurel being at this juncture dead and Kundry mute—sustained as follows: Parsifal, Gotthelf Pistor; Gurnemanz, Ludwig Hofmann; and Amfortas, Cornelis Bronsgeest. All these artists have splendid voices, especially the bass, who is another amazing specimen of the incomparable group of deep-voiced singers possessed by Germany at the present time. The name of Dr. Muck, who used to be a constant visitor to London, and under whose bâton I heard *Parsifal* twice at Bayreuth, is a sufficient guarantee that the tempi and general interpretation of the music are in strict accord with the true Wagnerian traditions. The playing of the Berlin Orchestra is indeed superb throughout. I can conceive of none finer; neither can I imagine recording that would have done it better justice. The ceaseless flow of masterful instrumentation, now an undercurrent, now predominant and supreme, produces all the grandeur of sonority and effect identified with one's experience of a first-rate opera house— nay, almost of Bayreuth itself. The scenes of Parsifal's return, of the feet-washing episode, of the Good Friday's Spell, of the transformation to the Hall of the Grail, and the tremendously impressive episodes which there bring the drama to its close, including the difficult choruses for the male and female voices—these are all reverently and faithfully portrayed, nor can the result fail to fill the most exacting Wagnerite with surprise and delight.

* * *

"It never rains but it pours," and, in the matter of Albums, this is a month not merely of showers but of torrents. To the foregoing I have now to add something about the two albums of *Götterdämmerung*, which have just reached this office. Each contains eight double-sided discs (D 1572 to 1579 and D 1580 to 1587), upon which it is specially stated that "A series of representative passages" is recorded. I quote this of set purpose as an answer to the disgruntled Wagnerite who, in his insatiable demand for "no cuts," fails to assimilate the idea that the H.M.V. collections of the moment make no pretence at being complete, or anything like complete, recordings of any section of the *Nibelungen*. He finds fault because this bit or that is missing; then immediately contradicts himself by expressing delight at the discovery of something he did not expect (one of his favourites, of course); and, generally speaking, devotes his extensive leisure time to discovering loopholes for criticism either in the H.M.V. plan or the critic who deals with it in the pages of this journal. I repeat that, whilst we are waiting for the very solid thirteen hours' production involved in the complete recording of *The Ring*, I for one shall be content to accept these generous excerpts at their face value, describing them as such to the best of my ability and endeavouring as far as I can not to mislead my readers either on the main issue or on any point of minor detail. I would also add, follow them with the score, if you will, but do not complain afterwards that a scene or a passage which *you* regard as essential was omitted, or smacks of an "arrangement," or, let us say, was described as a scene for Wotan alone when the voices of the Rhinemaidens might positively be discerned towards the end amid the orchestral crash of the entry into Valhalla.

The *Götterdämmerung* records have been sung in German by British as well as foreign artists, whilst the instrumental work has been shared by the London Symphony Orchestra, under Albert Coates and Lawrance Collingwood, and the Berlin State Opera Orchestra, under Drs. Karl Muck and Leo Blech. The selection opens with the confab for the Norns (Noel Eadie, Evelyn Arden, and Gladys Palmer), after which most of the salient episodes in the first scene duly appear, with Florence Austral and Walter Widdop as Brünnhilde and Siegfried, down to the hero's journey to the Rhine; all very smoothly done. From that point Goeta Ljungberg takes up the running as Gutrune; while Ivar Andrésen (Hagen) divides work with Emmanuel List and Arthur Fear; Walter Widdop is succeeded by Rudolf Laubenthal; Desider Zador shares Gunther with Frederic Collier; Maartje Offers being the Waltraute and De Garmo, Kindermann and Marker the three Rhinedaughters. So much for a distribution of rôles which I cannot describe as other than satisfactory, both as regards the cosmopolitan and the artistic results thereby accomplished. The titles aptly bestowed upon the sixteen records afford a clear indication of the purport of each and the general progress of the action, which, in a case like this, is about as much as can be expected.

It would not be a difficult task, either, to differentiate between the various qualities or degrees of merit exhibited in the contents of this album. But to do so would scarcely be worth while, even if space allowed me. For sonority and slow, gradual approach to the climaxes I feel that I must award the palm to the Berlin Orchestra and its gifted conductors. In all other respects there is naught to choose between them and our own L.S.O. under Albert Coates; his reading of the earlier passages is almost complete down to the end of Act I., interrupted only by Karl Muck's fine handling of the " Dawn " prelude and Siegfried's parting from Brünnhilde, and again by Leo Blech's accompaniment of the Hagen soliloquy. Perhaps the most striking achievement in the two albums is Karl Muck's magnificent treatment of the Funeral March; nothing more grandiose

or imposing, more gorgeous in tone or colour, has been heard from the gramophone. Similarly, for sheer vocal and declamatory volume, Ivar Andrésen surely surpasses all previous Hagens in the big scene where he summons the vassals to Gunther's domain. His was undoubtedly the colossal organ for the purpose dreamed of by Wagner. Another ideal voice for this kind of work was that of Florence Austral, who sings the music of Brünnhilde throughout, her closing monologue being especially grand. Of the two tenors, Widdop acquits himself well, but Laubenthal has the more difficult task and characterizes the Narrative superbly. Another admirable individual effort is the splendid singing of Maartje Offers in the Waltraute scene, which extends through no fewer than three records of some of the noblest music in the music-drama. There only remains to say that the recording throughout is a model of clarity and technical excellence.

HERMAN KLEIN.

❦ ❦ ❦

THE GRAMOPHONE AND THE SINGER
(Continued)
By HERMAN KLEIN
A "Norma" Revival: "Aida" Albums
The Opera

INTEREST in Bellini's once-popular opera *Norma* has been re-aroused by the fact that it is shortly to be revived at Covent Garden for the Italian-American prima donna, Rosa Ponselle, whom we have not yet heard here except through a few records made presumably by the Victor Company in New York. These have certainly won admiration, though I cannot recollect finding in them all the phenomenal qualities attributed to the singer herself by certain New York critics. It may be, of course, that she is a " real wonder," the " queen of the Metropolitan sopranos," an artist who " makes Golden the Age in which she lives," and so forth. But on the whole it will be safer not to judge her by her gramophonic efforts, brilliant though they be, and wait until we have heard and seen the lady herself, which will be very soon indeed now. For one thing, I am unfeignedly glad that she is causing this *reprise* of *Norma*. I shall be interested to compare her with two great Normas of the past—the greatest that have been heard in my time—namely, Theresa Tietjens and Lilli Lehmann. Of these, the latter sang the part at Covent Garden during her ultimate visit

(June, 1899), when I wrote in the *Sunday Times* as follows :—

" She presents a wonderfully dignified yet pathetic embodiment of the erring priestess, and rises in the fullest degree to the tragic situation of the last act. Her rendering of *Casta diva* was in many ways quite untraditional, being sung for the greater part in a delicate *mezza voce* that suggested in a striking degree the idea of mystery and awe ; while the sudden change to a broader tempo at the climax, if not what Bellini intended, was at least very imposing in effect."

Now, as most people are aware, the air *Casta diva* is the very *crux*, the supreme test of vocal art, not alone of this opera, but every other opera of the school to which it belongs. Its extraordinary difficulty, despite its comparative simplicity musically speaking, may be estimated by the exceedingly small number of sopranos who attempt it. It is not more frequently heard to-day than it used to be fifty years ago, when few singers had the courage to challenge comparisons with Tietjens's magnificent rendering— a triumph of vocalisation that baffles my descriptive powers just as much now as it did then. Adelina Patti's genius was first revealed when, as a child of seven, who had never had a lesson in singing, she was stood upon a table to sing *Casta diva* in imitation of what she had heard her mother do. But, except at that period, she seldom sang it in public, and in England during the lifetime of Tietjens, never! It is true that she included it among the precious if inadequate records which she made late in life for H.M.V. That, however, must not be regarded as a fair specimen of what Patti could do with *Casta diva*, much less what she might have done with it twenty years previously; or even, say, what Dame Emma Albani contrived to achieve with it on the concert platform in *her* prime (which was a shade less satisfying). There is also, by the way, a Columbia record of it sung by Celestina Boninsegna (old process), but upon the merits of that particular example I can express no opinion.

Norma dates back to what we should term the Boxing Night of 1831, and is therefore within hail of its centenary. Within six years of seeing the light at La Scala it was produced in turn at London (both in Italian and English), Paris, and New York. The original cast will be remarkable for all time because of the fact that the part of Norma was created by the illustrious Pasta, for whom Bellini wrote it; while the rôle of Adalgisa was filled by the famous Giulia Grisi, who was afterwards in this country to exalt that of Norma to the high level of tragic grandeur at which it was taken up and maintained by Tietjens. But the opera itself did not become popular in a night, nor did the phenomenal voices of Rubini, prince of tenors, or Lablache, the great basso, not to mention the divine Malibran, enhance its attractions until after the work had become an established favourite. Chorley tells us in his *Recollections* that " the critics of the hour flouted *Norma* as a poor work," that being when it was first mounted at the King's Theatre in 1833 and Pasta (whose final season it was here) betrayed signs of waning glory by, among other things, beginning " her evening's task half a tone too flat " (*sic*).

Three years later it was Grisi's turn, and " *Norma* set itself in its place, once for all." The new *diva* (it was for Grisi that the term was invented) was then " in all the splendour of her beauty of voice and person, and mounted the throne of her predecessor with so firm a step that the world of the moment might be well beguiled into doubting which of the two was the greater queen." Soon after this the historic *liaison* between Grisi and Mario began, and Lumley relates in his *Reminiscences of the Opera* the pitiable difficulty that he was in one night when *Norma* was announced for another prima donna, and " Signor Mario refused to sing Pollione with any other Norma than Madame Grisi, and his refusal seemed particularly unreasonable, as the lady in question was at this time unable to perform. The denunciations against him were heavy. Scarcely a London newspaper refrained from attacking the recalcitrant tenor in explicit, not to say harsh, terms."

But tenors are like that, so what was the use? Mario did not appear again that season, and he stuck to his pledge never to sing Pollione with any but his one and only Norma. Hers must have been an amazing performance! Chorley goes into ecstasies over it, even though he admits that it was modelled on Pasta's—" perhaps, in some points, was an improvement on the model, because there was more of animal passion in it. . . . There was in it the wild ferocity of the tigress, but a certain frantic charm therewith which carried away the hearer—nay, which possibly belongs to the true reading of the character of the Druid priestess, unfaithful to her vows. I think this must be so [adds Chorley] from recollecting how signally the attempt of a younger Norma to colour the part differently failed; I allude to Mademoiselle [Jenny] Lind. . . . Her failure was something as entire, as aimless, as it is possible for so remarkable an artist to make. The actress and the play had no agreement, yet in Germany . . . I have heard this ' maidenly ' reading of Norma by Mlle. Lind lauded as among the master-strokes of never-sufficiently-to-be-wondered-at thoughtfulness. So that Madame Grisi's reality kept the stage, and swept Mlle. Lind's novelty from it as with a whirlwind of fire."

I can add, of my own knowledge, that the Norma of Theresa Tietjens, if modelled upon anyone's, followed the impassioned conception of Grisi, not the " pale, weak, maidenly " delineation of Jenny Lind, to which Chorley took such strong objection. It will therefore be doubly interesting to me, and I trust to the reader now also, to note the precise line adopted in this respect by Mme. Rosa Ponselle when she gives us her view of the character. It will be found, I fancy, that she has not imitated one of Jenny Lind's " strange mistakes," and " consulted her own personality rather than the play." Nor is it necessary that she should prove her fitness for the rôle by repeating the realistic observance gone through by another celebrated Norma, Henriette Sontag, when in 1849 she was on a concert tour in England, in company with Lablache and other singers and the brilliant pianist Thalberg. For Mapleson records in his *Memoirs* that " On one occasion, after giving a concert at Salisbury, the whole party paid a visit to Stonehenge, where Sontag sang *Casta diva* and Lablache a portion of Proveso's solo music among the Druidical remains so suggestive of the opera of *Norma*." By the way, mention of Sontag reminds me that it was the combination of that glorious soprano with Bellini's heroine that first awakened Wagner's enthusiasm for this opera. He simply adored Sontag's voice and singing, and he looked upon *Norma* as a delicious fount that had gushed forth from the eternal spring of Italian melody. You see, Wagner could always be moved by beautiful melody beautifully rendered.

One more Norma story—this also told by Mapleson. " Giuglini had been playing the part of Pollio to the Norma of Mlle. Titiens (then spelt that way); and in the scene where the Druid priestess summons by the sound of the gong an assembly which will have to decide as to the punishment to be inflicted upon a guilty person unnamed, Mlle. Titiens, on the point of administering to the gong an unusually forcible blow, threw back the drumstick with such effect that, coming into violent contact with the nose of Signor Giuglini, who was close behind her, it drew from it, if not torrents of blood, at least blood in sufficient quantity to make the sensitive tenor tremble for his life. He thought his last hour had come, and, even when he found that he was not mortally wounded, still nourished such a hatred against the offending drumstick that he swore a special oath (duly described) never to sing in *Norma* again, besides requiring that the drumstick should never more be brought into his presence. If not destroyed, it was at least to be kept carefully locked up." So that made two distinguished tenors declining to appear any more as Pollio. Later on there were others, until at last I think the true explanation began to offer itself, viz., that the Roman officer who caused Norma's ruin and made love to her dearest friend was such an unutterable cad that no respectable Italian tenor wanted to impersonate him. Obviously Bellini ought to have written the part for a baritone.

*   *   *

The early appearance of *Aida* in album form was inevitable. Someone asked me the other day if I did not think it had become the most popular of all Verdi's operas, not excluding the three favourites of one's boyhood, to wit, *Trovatore*, *Traviata*, and *Rigoletto*. My answer was an unhesitating affirmative, for the reason that *Aida* bridges the gap between the old and the " advanced " styles of Italian opera and so satisfies the lovers of each. It unites the best attributes of Verdi's second and third " periods "; it traces clearly the course of the wonderful development that was going on in the nature and working of his ever-growing genius, whilst owing nothing, or next to nothing, to the influences (Wagner more especially) that were revolutionizing the musical world at the time. I never was among those who claimed to perceive that Verdi had derived the inspiration for his Egyptian opera from *Lohengrin* or *Tannhäuser*. To-day one asks what sort of resemblance there was, beyond the newness and the strangeness to our ears of their modern harmonies, to justify such a conclusion? Not even in his orchestration, in my opinion, did Verdi owe aught to Wagner—not nearly so much, certainly, as both owed to Berlioz. Yet the sheer novelty, not alone to the ear but to the eye, that *Aida* presented to the audiences of Covent Garden and Her Majesty's in the summer of 1876 would be scarcely conceivable by the present generation; nor was it the least of its

many charms. The spectacle, enhanced by the startling garishness of the scenery painted in Italy and sent here as actual replicas of the original *mise en scène* used at Cairo and La Scala, has long ceased to take our breath away as it did then. But the joy of Verdi's glorious music remains a fresh and unfading delight, and I for one warmly welcome it on behalf of gramophonists to the increasing store of operatic albums.

This present month of May sees both the leading companies ready with remarkably fine examples in electric recording of as difficult an opera as there is in the modern Italian repertory. Puccini with his *Turandot* may impose a heavier strain on the voice, but he demands neither the *finesse* of technique nor the pure line of *cantilena* that Verdi does in *Aida*. In the whole part of the imperious Chinese princess there is not a page calling for real *bel canto* in the same degree as do passages like *I sacri nomi*, *O patria mia*, and *Si schiude il ciel* respectively in the first, third, and fourth acts of this exacting work. Dusolina Giannini, who fills the title-rôle in the H.M.V. cast, has all the requisite delicacy and finish for the task, while her tone has the right ring of pathos and sweetness in addition to a power that is never forced. And these, after all, are the good qualities that were perceived in her *Aida* when she sang the part at Covent Garden, just as robust strength and easy control of a splendid organ distinguished Pertile's Radamès on the same occasion—his début here. But I had better give the whole cast, viz.: The King, Masini; Radamès, Pertile; Amonasro, Inghilleri; Ramphis, Manfrini; Messenger, Nessi; Amneris, Cattaneo; Aida, D. Giannini; conductor, Carlo Sabajno; with the chorus and orchestra of La Scala. The opera is contained in 19 double-sided 12-in. records, D 1595-1613.

It would serve no useful purpose to enter into minute or detailed comparisons between the H.M.V. performance and that of Columbia, which I shall deal with directly. Truth to tell, both are so far superior to anything gramophone recording could have furnished even a year ago that I find myself less inclined to criticise than to express my gratitude that such things can be. The listener, indeed, has less and less difficulty in imagining himself sitting at the back of a box at the Opera with eyes closed and enjoying every instant of a faultless musical representation. Finer voices, better singing, a more perfect ensemble and balance, added to a mechanical reproduction attaining the maximum of excellence, it would be unreasonable and absurd to expect. I will not choose between artists in this H.M.V. collection beyond saying that I think Dusolina Giannini, Pertile, and Inghilleri " head and shoulders " above their companions, even as I consider the third act distinctly the most completely satisfying of the four. This is not to say a word in disparagement of the other three; only that in the Nile scene, which many deem the finest in the opera—the most original, the richest in melody, tragic beauty, and intensity of poignant feeling—we do indeed get the greatest moments, the highest level of vocal achievement. Alike in the *O cieli azzurri* and the sublime passages of the duet with Amonasro, Dusolina Giannini stands out as a soprano of exceptional merit endowed with a voice of haunting charm. The orchestral playing, no less than the work of the chorus, is consistently good.

The Columbia version has also been executed in Milan and sung in Italian by Italian artists. The latter in the present instance are Giannina Arangi-Lombardi (Aida), Maria Capuana (Amneris), Aroldo Lindi (Radamès), Armando Borgioli (Amonasro), Tancredi Pasero (Ramphis), Salvatore Baccaloni (The King), and Giuseppe Nessi (Messenger). The conductor is Cav. Lorenzo Molajoli. Taken as a whole, the performance maintains a high standard of merit. Its vocal quality does this in a notable degree, the singers being not merely artists of ability and experience, familiar with every point and tradition in the opera, but thoroughly at home in up-to-date gramophone work. I am glad, also, to be able to say that I find here no evidence of excessive amplification, the result being that the parts stand out clearly in all the ensembles, while that of the great finale to Act II. is particularly good, in spite of the huge body of combined musical timbres. I tried the solos with various needles, and a Columbia " de luxe " is what I recommend for this album.

By way of detail there is not a great deal to be said. Inasmuch as every note of the score is included in the 36 records (18 discs, 12 in., Nos. 9726-9743), it is scarcely surprising that the tempo as a whole should err slightly on the side of speed. However, that is a prevailing fault of the modern Italian school, which has tended to grow more marked since it started with the efforts to " brighten up things a bit " that characterised the sway of the bâton by Luigi Mancinelli. Now all movements, slow as well as fast, must be made to feel the uplift of the accelerator, lest they run the risk of being thought tedious or inclined to drag. Besides, when it comes to recording whole operas for albums—even when there are two, as in this case—it is quite evident that, like another Major Segrave driving over his measured mile, your conductor has to make good time from the start and not lose a moment till it is all over. Perhaps an opera heard under such conditions does not suffer so much as some other music might ; and, if you listen to the whole of it at one sitting as I did, you will probably share my impression, when half-way through, that it is less of a strain upon your faculties than when the drama is being unfolded before you at the same time.

As I have already suggested, the most notable feature of the Columbia *Aida* is the equality of its execution. If I were to select any special artist for

praise it would be Signora Capuana. Her voice and style both remind me in their consistent purity and smoothness of Scalchi, the first and finest Amneris I ever heard. In the duets with Aida and Radamès she sings with splendid dramatic force, yet without in the least exaggerating or spoiling the timbre of a lovely tone. Arangi-Lombardi is also a fine singer, and if she takes rather longer to get into her true stride she happily does so in time for a worthy rendering of *Ritorna vincitor*, while the high notes in the *Cieli azzurri* sound exceptionally beautiful. Aroldo Lindi does full justice to the robust demands of the part of Radamès, and is at his best in the final duet with Aida. For the other soloists and for the chorus and orchestra unqualified admiration may be expressed. Moreover, for the clarity and skill shown in the recording no praise could be too high.

The Royal Opera Season

Wagner and Strauss have divided between them the honours of the opening fortnight of the season, and Covent Garden has been sold out for the whole of the ten performances embraced in that period. Doubtless there will be the same story to tell all through the piece, and in the face of it I once more dare to ask, Who says that we do not hunger for good opera in this country ? The inaugural performance on April 22nd was devoted to *Der Rosenkavalier*; a wise choice, for the reason that the experience of the past six years has conclusively proved it to be the most popular—as it is also the most interesting and attractive—opera written by a German composer since Wagner died. It drew, as a matter of course, a brilliant audience—the kind of representative gathering that Covent Garden can only surpass on a " gala " night. The chief rôles were in familiar hands, with the exception of Sophie von Faninal, in which Gitta Alpar, of Budapest and Berlin, had the unenviable task of following Elisabeth Schumann. Her voice is bright and does not lack power, but is not remarkable for sweetness or charm. She proved to be a vivacious actress, and looked in her pink and silver costume like a merry doll off a Twelfth Night cake. Lotte Lehmann, as the Marschallin, was simply a delight ; Delia Reinhardt once more a capital Oktavian ; Richard Mayr the ideal Baron Ochs ; and under Bruno Walter the whole opera went with a snap and a swing that made it intensely enjoyable. The orchestra is fully on a level with that of last year.

On the second night began the first of the two *Ring* cycles (still in progress), with a cast including Ivar Andrésen, Hans Clemens, Eduard Habich, Alexander Kipnis, and Frederick Schorr—a splendid combination. Between *Die Walküre* and *Siegfried* came *Tristan und Isolde*; while a performance of *Lohengrin* on the third night of the season introduced a new tenor in Fritz Wolff, of whom I shall have more to say anon. Altogether things have begun well.

HERMAN KLEIN.

263

THE GRAMOPHONE AND THE SINGER

(*Continued*)

By HERMAN KLEIN

The Royal Opera Season

I AGREE most heartily with my Editor upon every point of his argument last month in favour of the standardization of record prices, and having said so much, I feel that it would be presumption on my part to add a word to what he has said. If I cannot equally support his views concerning the nomenclature of symphonic and chamber works it is not because I fail to perceive the utility of the idea, but because I doubt its practicability. I don't see how it is to be applied to every recorded masterpiece in existence and without in the end making " confusion worse confounded." However, my opinion on this subject comes less definitely within the scope of these articles, and I only offer it because it affords me an opportunity of expressing my respect for the motive, which is surely to help the ever-growing multitude of music-lovers to identify more easily the works that they are now, for the first time, learning to know and love. The identification of operatic records is an easy job because each must of necessity carry its title upon its face, and I re-echo the hope that ere long we shall find a similar advantage to the buyer manifesting itself in the matter of standard prices.

The chief trouble in regard to first-rate operatic records, as in the case of first-rate operatic performances in this country, is that they are too costly. I prophesied years ago that the " stars," with their huge salaries, would ruin the market for opera at reasonable prices ; and they have done so. America, North and South, began the process of demoralization, and its effects are now being sorely felt in Europe, more especially in this capital, which insists on having the best whilst possessing little native talent of its own that the public will accept as first rate to replace or even to re-inforce the select expensive group known as " international " artists. The terms now asked by these privileged performers are, I understand, so incredibly high that they may be said in certain instances to border upon the extortionate ; and, whether it be to sing in opera or sing records, the result of the competition for their services is that the ultimate charge to the public is far above what it ought to be. Seats at Covent Garden, which cost more every season, have reached very nearly double the price (at the Bond Street Libraries they are more than that) at which they stood in the " palmy days "

of the Victorian era. This has made opera on the grand scale a luxury and an extravagance. Of course, for the ten weeks that the undertaking is carried on by the Syndicate at the height of the London season, the miracle of nightly crowded houses is regularly accomplished. But that does not prove the system to be a just and beneficial one, either for the public or the art whereby it is exploited. It simply makes one wish with all one's heart that the long-awaited period of reform had arrived. When will it arrive ? Comparatively soon, I think. Writing in the midst of an unusually uncertain General Election, it would be foolish on my part to indulge in deliberate predictions. But I have a notion that out of the new Parliament, with a good constitutional Government in power, it will be found possible to extract the subsidy for a National Opera House that this country ought to have been provided with a century or so ago. The times are eminently ripe for State intervention and support in this important direction. The success of the B.B.C. proves it ; and, if the Government can nationalize an enterprise like that, it can just as well appropriate an incomplete venture such as the Imperial League of Opera, build a real opera house for it, consolidate Sir Thomas Beecham's position as the head of it, and convert an uncertainty into the most glorious certainty imaginable. For if it is an assured fact that the nation wants broadcast music and is going to want " talkie films," it is not a whit less certain that it wants opera of the highest class at prices that everyone can afford to pay and sung as a matter of course in the language that everyone can understand.

I may confess without blushing that I did not closely follow the two cycles of the *Ring*. To sit religiously and watchfully through Wagner's colossal tetralogy now constitutes a somewhat fatiguing strain upon my powers of concentration. I love it and admire its miracles of beauty and achievement as much as ever, but am content to leave criticism of its interpretation to my younger colleagues. I take a pleasure, nevertheless, in reading their opinions especially when they deal at close quarters, as it were, with the German singers whose work has been made familiar either in previous seasons or by their gramophone records as reviewed from time to time in these pages. Taking the whole of the recent performances in perspective, it struck me that the casting of the various characters this year had not been very carefully thought out. It was lacking in the unity and consistency that ought to be aimed at in complete cycles like these. It appeared to have been arranged rather with a view to convenience—to allot certain characters to the artists who happened to be available at the moment. This may, of course, have been due to the irregular demands of Berlin or other centres upon the time of their leading artists, who are now able to go backwards and forwards by air in a few hours as they may be called upon at either end, though I cannot say positively of my own knowledge that this was done. In any case, it is always a distinct disadvantage when important parts like Wotan and Brünnhilde are allotted to different singers during the course of the same cycle, as was apparently necessary in these instances.

For example, Friedrich Schorr and Frida Leider gave place after the first *Die Walküre* to Rudolf Bockelmann and Elisabeth Ohms in *Siegfried*; while the latter in *Götterdämmerung* once made way for Frida Leider. The incongruity did not affect me personally because of those three performances I only witnessed the middle one ; but I know that it was doubly a mistake inasmuch as Elisabeth Ohms was not nearly at her best in the third act of *Siegfried*, whereas last year she was simply splendid in the second act of *Götterdämmerung*, though not nearly so fine as Frida Leider in the closing scene. There were other square pegs in round holes. It is hard to understand a singer with a confirmed wobble like Frau Anna Andrassy being entrusted with the part of Erda, whose music demands steadiness and breadth if ever music did, and again, with that of Magdalene, which is very nearly as exacting. A tremolo like hers may be tolerated in the role of the restless *intrigante*, Annina, in *Der Rosenkavalier*, where it doesn't really matter, but not surely in the later Wagner. The handsome Marie Olczewska, with her no less beautiful voice, can sing any music, as we are well aware. She is a delightful Waltraute, incomparable in the touching long message to her erring sister, Brünnhilde ; and she also makes an impressive, though not perhaps equally convincing, Ortrud in Lohengrin ; but her essentially emotional qualities, ever evincing the human touch, are not precisely well adapted to the shrewish scoldings of the goddess Fricka whose icy moral temperament they cannot begin to depict. On the other hand, her winning tones have never sounded more enchanting than they did in Brangäne's long-drawn notes of warning.

By the way, the second act of *Tristan* made manifest a curious variety of Teutonic values as provided by several different nationalities. The Isolde of Frida Leider, peerless in its moments of delicate restraint as in its outbursts of tempestuous passion, was sadly marred at times through the inadequacy of one of the weakest Tristans that has ever been heard at Covent Garden. Herr Erik Enderlein's voice sounded dull and uninteresting throughout, and during the greater portion of the great love duet he sang with a palpable effort and uncertainty of intonation that betokened not only nervousness but an unreliable method. Yet again did Herbert Janssen's rather light baritone prove insufficiently weighty for the part of Kurvenal ; but in revenge for this one could intensely enjoy Ivar Andrésen's superb delivery of König Marke's rebuke, which has never been surpassed in my experience. What a wealth of glorious tone and what welcome clarity of dignified declamation ! It is curious how, as a rule, these men's voices begin to sound more powerful relatively on the gramophone than they do in the theatre, thanks no doubt, to the liberal amount of amplification now in vogue. Alexander Kipnis (Hunding and Hagen) was another case in point, but I did not notice the difference so particularly in that of Lauritz Melchior, whose Siegfried has never come out so powerfully at Covent Garden before. In the Forging Songs I thought him simply magnificent, while the exquisite poetry of the forest scene likewise lost nothing at his hands.

The other chief successes were won by the newcomers Rudolf Bockelmann (Wotan and Hans Sachs) and Fritz Wolff (Lohengrin and Walther von Stolzing). The former has a singularly smooth quality of voice for a genuine *basso cantante*, and he sings with a suavity of manner that matches it. Power and sonority impress less than real beauty and refinement of style in this artist's intelligent delivery of Wagner's "infinite melos." It was a pleasure to hear a Wanderer of his type in the subtle confab with Albert Reiss's Mime. This favourable impression he confirmed subsequently in *Die Meistersinger* (of which I heard the third act, and that by wireless) ; on the whole, enough to justify interest in the name of Bockelmann whenever any of his records may reach these shores. They ought to prove exceptionally musical and artistic. The new tenor equally won golden opinions. The purity of his timbre and its very quality reminded one of that splendid tenor, Winkelmann, the first Walther ever heard in London ; while the long high notes of the *Preislied* were sustained in the final act without the slightest trace of effort. Altogether Fritz Wolff must be accounted a valuable acquisition, though it must be allowed that he needs further study to add perfect finish to his method alike as actor and singer. But he has youth as well as the voice on his side and they count for a great deal. Another excellent tenor, in Hans Clemens, lent strength to the ensemble both as Loge and David, his remarkable ability as a delineator of character being once more conspicuous. The Pogner of Alexander Kipnis proved, so far as voice was concerned, an even greater disappointment than his efforts in the *Ring*.

265

It was generally surmised that he must have been off colour during his recent visit. *Per contra* the gifted Lotte Lehmann lived up to her exalted reputation in the fullest degree. She is the ideal Elsa and Eva of our time, and those who heard her in either part are not likely to forget the treat that her accomplished vocal art afforded. The tones of her higher register as they soared above the other singers in the wonderful quintet of *Die Meistersinger* will haunt the memory for many a day.

The increased number of broadcasts from Covent Garden during the German season was, I am certain, enormously appreciated by listeners-in. I took full advantage of it myself on those occasions when the directorate in its wisdom omitted to request my presence at the overcrowded opera house. From many quarters I was told that a remarkable advance had been noted in the purity of the transmission, and such was undoubtedly my own experience. Much, however, depends, and quite naturally, upon the particular spot or part of the stage from which the voice is being projected. (It is not, for instance, to be compared either for equality or regularity of tonal flow with the effects that our London Editor contrives to obtain with those interesting gramophone recitals of his as recorded every week in *The Radio Times*.) But the *actuality* of the opera house broadcast is now equalled by the clearness of its definition, especially, as I have said, when the voices are favourably placed. Take for an example the first act of *Lohengrin*. In his farewell to the swan the new tenor, Erik Enderlein, obviously suffered through standing so far up-stage, the impression created being that of a pretty but diminutive voice; but immediately he came down to the front the sonority of his tone was at least trebled and its unquestionably tenor quality enhanced in due proportion. Our British Herald, in the person of Dennis Noble was, I fear, made to sound less trumpet-toned all through than he really was. On the other hand, the effect of different positions in the case of Ivar Andrésen was simply magical. So long as King Henry was discoursing beneath his primeval oak it was his declamation rather than his voice that engaged your attention; but when he strode forward a few yards and began pouring his luscious notes into the broad melody of the Prayer it was quite another story. The body of sound was so huge, so noble and imposing, that I said to myself: " Now I am listening in actual fact to the real voice of Ivar Andrésen, far removed from all possibility of artificial amplification, and I know I am right in my opinion about its extraordinary magnitude and beauty throughout a scale of exceptional compass. It is the finest bass in the world at the present time." Altogether the Prayer came over wonderfully well. I could plainly distinguish the lovely tones of Marie Olczewska creeping in when Ortrud opens her mouth for the first time in the opera; and another fine voice was clearly audible in the new Telramund, Wilhelm Fassbinder, who was much better liked in this part than as Wotan, which he sang the same week in the second *Walküre*. It was in the latter section of the *Ring*, by the way, that that delightful soprano, Meta Seinemeyer, filled the grateful role of Sieglinde. She elicited unqualified praise from all sides except one, but, as the regular critic of the paper in question happened to be away that night attending the Dvorak Festival at Prague, there was no necessity to pay much heed to the isolated opinion of his deputy.

To what has been said about this year's *Ring* cycles and of the German performances generally, I would add that the evidence of more frequent and thorough rehearsing was among the features that gave chief satisfaction both to habitués and critics. It would be too much to assert that the stage business is up to the level that we were used to in the old days, and I realize that the end of Covent Garden is too near for it to be worth while to provide a new *mise en scène* in place of the worn-out " sets " now in use. Still those drawbacks may well be endured if we can hear such supremely fine artists as have appeared here this season, and in conjunction with them such polished orchestral playing as was secured by Bruno Walter and Robert Heger. The talented Berlin conductors have never worked harder or, perhaps, with such completely satisfying results. When they went back to Germany for their Festival it was amid a unanimous chorus of critical praise. They happily left their superb orchestra behind them, but their native choristers (who had put more refinement into their efforts than usual) they thoughtfully took home with them.

I fear I cannot get beyond the German season in these notes. The Italian campaign began just too late to allow of my dealing with any part of it this month. Only one or two points connected with the former remain to be mentioned. A welcome feature of the last two performances of *Der Rosenkavalier* was the return of Elisabeth Schumann. Her superiority in the part of Sophie stamped its *cachet* not only on the second act but on the whole of the opera wherever she was *en scène*. The only wonder was that she should have been dropped even temporarily in favour of a singer who was untried and of uncertain merit. When the perfect representative of a part is to be had for the asking, and at a reasonable salary, why look farther? Extra performances of *Die Walküre* and *Götterdämmerung*, given after the completion of the *Ring* cycles, were made notable by the co-operation of a couple of native artists in Florence Austral and Walter Widdop, with Albert Coates as conductor, but with the remainder of the casts much as before. I was glad of this, because it is always beneficial for Covent Garden audiences to be made to realise that what Sir Thomas Beecham has so often said in this regard is true, namely, that we have singers of our own capable of holding their own with the pick of the Cont nental stages. In fact, the higher the standard of their associates the more credit they seem capable of earning for their own efforts.

It may be said with some exactitude that the intervention of the Great War had made most of us forget that Lilli Lehmann was still alive. When news came of her death, at Berlin last month, quite a number of her English friends of the prosperous days suddenly sat up and remembered that they had not previously heard of her decease. Only a very few were aware that the last two decades of her life had been spent in something like poverty. How that came about I do not pretend to explain, though doubtless her country's troubles helped to heighten her own. In her time she earned a very great deal of money, but it was always by her singing, not her teaching, that she did so. After she had retired from the operatic stage at the beginning of the century, she completed her well-known book *Meine Gesangskunst* (called in the English version *How to Sing*) and settled down in Berlin as a teacher. Yet it was neither this book nor the successes won by her pupils that brought her pupils; it was purely the enduring fame of her splendid career as an opera singer. Her voice when she was young had a delightful bird-like quality and she was a most accomplished vocalist. She was only thirty-four when I first heard her at the production of *Der Ring der Nibelungen* at Her Majesty's Theatre in 1882, when she sang the part of Woglinde, one of the Rhine-daughters. As time went on her organ developed into a dramatic soprano, while her rare gifts alike as actress and singer rose to the highest eminence. She was great in many parts, and greatest of all, in my opinion, in that of Leonora (*Fidelio*), one of the half-dozen outstanding roles, including Norma, that she sang at Covent Garden during her last visit to London in 1899.

HERMAN KLEIN.

P.S.—I have received from MM. Durand, the well-known Paris music publisher, a copy of their newly-issued vocal score of *Tristan and Isolde*, beautifully printed, with a French text fitted to the music by M. Gustave Samazenilh. This last is really a remarkable piece of work, and it is the more interesting because the greater part of it is from Wagner's own pen, being taken from the *Quatre Poèmes d'Opéra*, which he published in 1860, at the time when he was producing *Tannhäuser* in Paris. He himself, therefore, made most of the alterations in the music that the use of the French language rendered necessary; or, rather, he did so with the assistance of his great political friend and admirer, M. Challemel-Lacour; thus ensuring, in combination with the piano transcription of Hans von Bülow, an edition that is in every sense authoritative. Still, it would not have been the perfect thing that it is without the powers of skilful adaptation brought to bear upon it by M. Samazenilh, who was obviously the best man that MM. Durand could have selected for the task. The pride that Wagner took in everything connected with *Tristan* is evidenced in the *Lettre sur la musique* that he addressed to Frédéric Villot and printed as a preface to the *Quatre Poèmes d'Opéra*. In it he says, among other important passages, " This work may be estimated according to the most severe laws that govern my musical theories. . . . Believe me, there is no greater happiness than complete spontaneity in the work of creation, and that spontaneity I knew when composing my *Tristan*." His spirit, therefore, reigns actively here alike in the verbal and the musical lines of the new French score, and that is why I take exceptional pleasure in recommending it to the notice of all who know and love the language and are willing to enjoy the wonderful music through its fascinating medium.

H. K.

THE GRAMOPHONE AND THE SINGER

(Continued)

By HERMAN KLEIN

The Art of Rosa Ponselle: Hail to "The Radio Critic."

HISTORY'S habit of repeating itself is sometimes extremely irritating. The circumstances attending the début of Rosa Ponselle at Covent Garden last month bore an almost absurd resemblance to those associated not long ago with the coming of another celebrated gramophone artist—to wit, Amelita Galli-Curci. The earlier event, it is true, took place at the Albert Hall, thus giving a rather unfair idea of what an opera singer could do to justify (or mar) her reputation on the concert platform. Whereas the more recent débutante challenged criticism on the loftier plane of the stage, where acting comes into the picture as well as singing, especially when exhibited in a rôle supposed to be susceptible of the grandest imaginable tragic interpretation. There remains, nevertheless, the fact that both *prime donne* were made an enormous fuss of on the strength of American, not European, fame; that, moreover, both were of Italian birth or parentage, and that, but for their gramophone records and the advance trumpeting thereby secured, both might have had to wait heaven knows how much longer before gaining the concentrated attention of the British public. But their London impresarios were, of course, in both cases well acquainted with the situation, and could be trusted to take full advantage of its opportunities. It was very different in the days when singers came to England to make a name before crossing the Atlantic to make their fortunes. Then we got just a trifle nearer, I fancy, to appraising them purely on their merits. We did not run the risk, anyhow, of being influenced by the " puff preliminary," to which we took care not to pay the smallest attention; while the glamour of piled-up superlatives boldly flaunted in gramophone advertisements did not yet exist to throw us off our balance by raising our expectations too far above the normal pitch. Nor were there then the records themselves to take us by storm well in advance, through demonstrating beyond cavil what a marvellous *coloratura* soprano Galli-Curci really was, and what a celestial quality of voice, what supreme vocal artistry, were actually possessed by the amazing Rosa Ponselle. The critics at least could not be " knocked out " before the fight had practically begun and before they had had time to strike a blow. Are they now? I wonder.

Speaking for myself, I may say that my ability to form a calm, dispassionate judgment concerning the powers of the new American soprano was materially aided by the absence of first-night excitement. In other words, I did not hear her until her second appearance in the part of Norma. One trifling disadvantage resulted from that, namely, that she happened to be suffering from a slight cold, contracted, so I was told, midway between the two performances.

The trouble was plainly perceptible in the medium register. It was also responsible, I fancied, for the extraordinary extent to which Mme. Ponselle relied upon her *mezza voce*. Very rarely indeed did she allow herself the indulgence of declaiming a passage with the full voice demanded by the nature of the utterance and the music. During the greater part of the opera, in fact, she was singing everything in this subdued, quiet manner, so utterly unlike the impetuous, unrestrained Norma of one's early recollections and probably quite unlike the one depicted by Pasta or Grisi. There were moments when it sounded not only beautiful (it was always that) but particularly appropriate. Such, for instance, was the long-drawn phrasing of the wonderful opening to *Casta diva*; no singing could possibly have been lovelier under any conditions. Again, in the famous duet for the two women, *Mira, o Norma*, where Adalgisa stands pleading for the lives of the two children, holding each one by the hand, whilst Norma reclines on a couch with her head buried in the pillows, the living embodiment of grief and remorse.

You might wonder whether she has even heard the appeal addressed to her in the so-familiar melody; and then, without a movement or gesture to indicate its source, you suddenly hear the distant echo of an exquisite tone answering in softest *pianissimo* with the same notes sung to the words, " Ah, perchè, perchè la mia costanza vuoi scemar con molli affetti ? " (" Why seek to bend my resolution with gentle words ? ") The effect of that soft entry was intensely pathetic, indescribably beautiful, and I could not remember to have heard it done exactly in that way before. But I cannot help thinking that it would have been more wonderful still had we not been already treated to a long evening of persistent *mezza voce* pervading alike *aria* and *caballetta* and occasionally even declamatory recitative. Again and again did I feel that I would have given anything to hear a magnificent outburst of tone, rich, glorious, and powerful, to match one of Norma's overwhelming torrents of indignation and injured pride. What I did hear was deliciously pure and sweet, delivered with the perfection of vocal art and an impeccable refinement of style (which is, after all, something rare enough to listen to with joy and thankfulness); but it was not the outpouring of the soul of Norma in magniloquent volume and thrilling grandeur, filling every corner of the theatre as I could remember to have heard Tietjens fill it.

I am told that Mme. Ponselle on her first appearance had evinced more of this requisite power, especially in the great scene of the final act. If so, it would have been only right in fairness to her if the management had made an announcement on the second night to the effect that she was suffering from slight indisposition. As it was, I daresay there were not twenty people in the audience who noticed that there was anything the matter. Like the accomplished technician she is, she conquered her difficulties with masterful skill; resonance and the ring of a tragic accent in the middle of the voice were alone lacking to lend dramatic significance to her clear, incisive *coloratura*. Her timbre is of a quality that never fails to satisfy the ear, her scale is a model of purity, her intonation quite faultless. Her gifts as an actress are also exceptional, though whether completely suited to a part like Norma, which requires classic dignity and a noble breadth of stride and gesture that seem to sweep the whole stage in a single movement, I must take leave to doubt. Her facial expression, too, despite unusual alertness and intelligence, just misses that withering glance of scorn and contempt which should appear to sink creatures like Pollio and Adalgisa to the level of worms grovelling at Norma's feet. Yet all this, and more, will I willingly dispense with any day for the joy of hearing *Casta diva* sung as Rosa Ponselle—cold or no cold—sang it on the occasion I have been describing.

For the rest, enough that Bellini's opera seemed to be wearing well, and extracted notes of admiration from quarters where least expected. It suffered as usual from the inferiority of the tenor, since no decent tenor will consent to impersonate the obnoxious Pollio; and that matters more than some people think. On the other hand, Sgra. Cattaneo used her fine mezzo to good purpose in the music of Adalgisa, and Vincenzo Bellezza treated the old-fashioned score with the same sedulous care that he would have done a Puccini or a Ponchielli. *Apropos* the latter, ample evidence was forthcoming a few nights later when *La Gioconda* was revived; only one thing is certain: this splendid opera needs cutting down to about two-thirds of its present

length. The long conversations and monologues in recitative, however essential to the plot, are disastrously tedious in a musical sense. To be candid, the best music is either to be found in the gramophone selections, including the delightful *Ballet of the Hours*, in the two big ensembles and the "sea-shanty" chorus, which, of course, requires the stage. Personally speaking, I would sooner hear Francesco Merli's record of *Cielo e mar* than behold him in the act of singing it. He is, I think, one of the "stickiest" actors that Italy has sent us for a long time. Happily there was compensation here in the strong and consistent by-play of Giovanni Inghilleri as that double-dyed villain, Barnaba; while Fernando Autori and Irene Cattaneo made a lively "tuppence-coloured" Venetian married couple of the period; and Maria Castagna sang her *Voce di donna* very soothingly, amid a pin-drop silence that apparently encompassed the entire population of Venice. One only encounters these strange samples of mass hypnotism in the domain of opera.

Rosa Ponselle was, I thought, more truly in her element in a picturesquely melodramatic rôle such as La Gioconda than as the statuesque, impressive Norma. She was also, I was glad to find, in complete command of her vocal resources and thus able at the right moment to project her penetrating head notes clear above the din of the competing sounds. The effect in the ensemble was superb, though not perhaps more striking than that of her rich middle and lower notes in those descending cadenza-like *bravura* passages whereof Ponchielli was so inordinately fond. Best of all, however, was the requisite combination of voice and art displayed in her attack and holding of that glorious B flat, immediately following the *Voce di donna*, where, as the crowd is dispersing, La Gioconda gives expression at once to her gratitude for her mother's release and her absorbing passion for her disguised prince, Enzo the Reckless. Here, methought, was nought of melodrama; here nought that owed a tittle of its effect to those restless ever-changing shades of facial expression (too constant to be natural); nought to account for the thrill save the sheer loveliness of a single long-held note, a miracle that the human voice properly directed could alone achieve, and worthy in its loveliness to linger in one's memory with that exquisite *mezza voce* entry in the *Mira, o Norma*, which I have already referred to. Summing up the combined reflections, one could come to but a single conclusion: Rosa Ponselle, apart from her born natural gifts, is unquestionably endowed with the qualities and the art that constitute a great singer.

* * *

I am anxious for many reasons to take this early opportunity of bestowing my whole-hearted blessing upon the scheme set forth last month by our tireless editor for starting his new periodical, *The Radio Critic*. Such a paper as this, long urgently needed, has now been made an absolute necessity by the recent unprecedented developments at Savoy Hill. Not only has the B.B.C. taken root in the life of the nation as the provider and dispenser of every phase of art, science, and literature that can be transmitted by wireless broadcasting, but it has grown into the largest and most powerful monopoly that music has ever possessed in this or any other country. It likewise owns its own journals, its own literary staffs, its own critics—ready and able to criticise anything under the sun with the exception of the work done by the people whom it engages to carry out its programmes. This missing link it is that *The Radio Critic* is intended to supply; and everyone who realises the importance of fearless independent criticism for the maintenance of a high artistic standard in any branch of this vast undertaking must instantly have perceived the value of the idea projected by Mr. Compton Mackenzie in the June number of THE GRAMOPHONE.

It appealed to me in a special degree, because, as it happens, I have in this matter already enacted the rôle of prophet and lifted up my voice in the wilderness on more than one occasion. At a period when I was permitted to talk before the microphone more frequently than I am now, I was the first to raise my voice in protest against the faulty diction, the bad pronunciation, the inaudible consonants, the husky, over-noisy or over-faint specimens of vocal tone that speakers used to afflict us with before Sir Oliver Lodge and Sir Walford Davies came along. I was the first to begin a crusade against the plague of singers with a tremolo who afflicted us three or four years ago, even more numerously and egregiously than they do to-day. Finally, I was the first, in my capacity as chairman of the Music Committee of the Critics' Circle, to bring Sir (then Mr.) John Reith into personal contact with my colleagues of that body, and to warn the latter that the day was at hand when, whether they liked it or not, they would have to deal with B.B.C. performances in the columns of their various journals. This prediction has been partially fulfilled, but to nothing near the extent that it ought to be and sooner or later will be.

Meanwhile, for the salvation of all parties concerned, and more especially, as I take it, for the ultimate benefit of the B.B.C. itself, here comes our versatile and ingenious Editor, bringing along with him the promise of *The Radio Critic*, the very thing that is wanted to guide aright the judgment of the huge, ever-growing multitude of wireless listeners. Is there any need for me to repeat that I think it a splendid idea? Surely not—any more than I need apologise for foretelling its instantaneous and unequivocal success.

HERMAN KLEIN.

THE GRAMOPHONE AND THE SINGER

(*Continued*)

By HERMAN KLEIN

"Judith": Covent Garden and Provincial Opera

FRANKLY, I was disappointed with *Judith*. Arnold Bennett's libretto had struck me as being picturesque and vigorous in its handling of a difficult Biblical story. Less gruesome than von Hofmannsthal's ending to *Salome*, because it dispensed with the actual head of Holofernes (or a papier mâché imitation of it) either upon a charger or in a sack ; it gave opportunity, nevertheless, for a fairly dramatic *dénouement*. This was unfortunately missed, alike by the musician and the producer, the curtain being allowed to fall upon a tragedy so carefully concealed within the tent of the Assyrian general that no one knew for certain what had happened either to his head or his body. It was generally supposed that Göta Ljungberg had killed him in his drunken sleep, because he made no attempt to detain her when she was quietly walking off in the direction of Bethulia with his head (presumably) in the sack carried by Gladys Palmer. After this, I shall always be able to appreciate Mr. Dick's *idée fixe* concerning the head of Charles I.

If Miss Ljungberg was melodramatic and indistinct in the part of Judith, I am afraid Walter Widdop was entirely at sea in his conception of that of Bagoas, the Chief Eunuch. He declaimed less jerkily than the Israelitish heroine, but his blustering manner was altogether too military for the kind of individual he was supposed to be portraying ; there was no subtlety of colouring whatever in his impersonation. In the case of Holofernes, the absence of this particular quality mattered less, because he enacts a plain, straightforward soldier of the period, and on the whole Arthur Fear adequately realized that aspect of the character, albeit the passionate and sensual side was neither vivid nor convincing. As for the ballet, I can only say that it was no more absurd or out of place than dozens of other ballets which have been introduced into romantic opera from time immemorial, notably on the French stage, where it is regarded as a *sine qua non*. In this instance the dancing and posturing were sadly inappropriate (even though done by Russian *coryphées*), the only gain to the story being that they gave Holofernes reasonable time to get tipsy and Bagoas a chance of displaying his authority over the nice young ladies who followed the Assyrian camp. But as usual with these fanciful shows, the personages

for whom the ballet was thoughtfully provided at such short notice were the ones who paid it the least attention.

Now as to the music of *Judith*. Thanks to the courtesy of Messrs. J. and W. Chester, I had had the advantage of being able to go carefully through the vocal score before going to hear the opera, and the conclusion I arrived at was that it might more accurately have been termed an "unvocal" score. That impression was fully confirmed by what I heard at Covent Garden, and I may add that it constituted by far the principal ingredient in the disappointments of the evening. I had always had a firm belief in the creative talent of Eugène Goossens the Younger. I was talking about him not long before to an American musical friend who knew much better than I did what splendid work he had been accomplishing in Rochester, N.Y., under the generous patronage of Mr. Eastman, of Kodak fame. I asked my friend whether he intended going to hear *Judith*. He replied : "I am sorry to say I shall not be in London ; but if I were, I would not look for too much." "Why ? " I asked. "Oh, not for any personal reason," was the answer, "but merely because my experience is that good conductors as a rule can't write good operas." And, allowing that Wagner and Strauss were composers first and conductors afterwards, I dare say my friend was right.

If asked to describe *Judith* in a sentence, I should call it an orchestral drama, or drama for orchestra, with dialogue sung by the various characters in a sort of unrhythmical declamatory recitative. It is a case of "Instruments first and the voice practically nowhere "—a case far from being without precedent in modern opera, I am sorry to say. But however numerous the examples, there can be no excuse for the system when it results in mere ugliness and cacophony, as it unquestionably does in the present instance. Personally, I am rather tired of hearing that the word "beauty" has no definite meaning ; that it must be discarded henceforth because it is only a relative term. In its application to music, and more especially to what is generally spoken of as melody, even in its most developed forms, I think everyone wants to know what is implied by the use of the adjective "beautiful." Well, after very careful and anxious search of Mr. Goossens' score, followed by no less careful and anxious attention at the performance, I failed absolutely to discover any such moment in the whole of *Judith*; nothing, that is to say, which gripped the ear and mentality of the listener as music depicting and enforcing the action of a stage drama inevitably must if it is to fulfil its purpose at all. That it was cleverly put together I am not prepared to deny; but what is the use of the cleverness if the total outcome is an agglomeration of sounds without logical sequence and consisting for the most part of harmonic monstrosities? It was not with such material as this, whether atonal or polytonal, that Stravinsky earned admiration when he wrote *Petrouchka*; still less do we find it in the inspired pages that at one time earned for Wagner's efforts the title of "Music of the Future." True, Richard Strauss once perpetrated an opera called *Electra*; but who ever hears it mentioned to-day?

In conclusion let me express the hope that Mr. Goossens will not feel discouraged, but rather profit by the criticisms that have been levelled at *Judith*, and try again. His talent is beyond question, and it may be that the illustration of Biblical tragedy is not his *forte*; also that, Mr. Arnold Bennett's skilful book notwithstanding, the story of the events which led up to the decapitation of Holofernes does not furnish an extremely suitable subject for an opera.

* * *

It is only too true that opera sung in English has never made a fortune for anybody at Covent Garden, either before or since the old theatre was destroyed by fire in 1856. (For that matter, the giving of opera is not under any circumstances to be regarded as a money-making proposition; quite the contrary, in fact.) But that is no reason why opera in English sent into the provinces under the *ægis* of a Covent Garden management should not fare very well indeed. The name stands for something—I might say a good deal—in other eyes, besides those of London's fashionable amateurs; and, if the present Syndicate is without experience in this particular kind of enterprise, it has taken care to place the practical direction of affairs in tried and able hands. A month ago, when the announcement was first made by Colonel Blois, scarcely any details were given beyond the interesting circumstance that the Syndicate had arranged to take over the autumn dates and virtually carry on the provincial work of the B.N.O.C., which was on the point of giving up the ghost. That talented and energetic young conductor, Mr. John Barbirolli, has since been good enough to give me some details.

JOHN BARBIROLLI.

There is no need, of course, to relate the entire story now and here; it will suffice to give such portions as are essential to a correct understanding of the mutual relations between the parties concerned.

Putting two and two together, it is easy to see that, but for the intervention of the Syndicate, the collapse of the B.N.O.C. must have been followed by a sort of interregnum, during which the old members of that body would have found themselves facing idleness and (possible) starvation. The company had failed; no one was coming forward to assume its functions and carry them on. There was the remote contingency that Sir Thomas Beecham might be in a position to start his venture this year; there was the more likely one that he would be unable to make a beginning before the summer of 1930. What were the artists, the choristers and the orchestra to do for a living in the meantime? Could they hope to find employment suddenly in London concert halls, at the seaside, or, least of all, in the cinema theatres at a moment when the latter were ridding themselves of all or nearly all their musical staff? The result of delay must then have been disaster for them. And yet there was the goodwill of the B.N.O.C.—that is to say, such prestige as it had gathered during years of variable artistic success, mismanagement, and evil fortune—awaiting the bid of the first-comer, together with its erstwhile Beecham scenery and costumes, and a few remaining assets, including the dates for the provincial autumn season, which had had to be abandoned for lack of capital. It was when matters had reached this crisis, somewhere in May or early June, that the idea occurred to Colonel Blois of proposing that the Covent Garden Syndicate should take over, not the B.N.O.C., either as a going concern or as a concern *in extremis*, but such of its workable resources as could be said to possess a market as well as an artistic value. The suggestion was, I understand, promptly welcomed, and taken up by his co-directors.

At this point it would be appropriate to say something biographical about Mr. Barbirolli, who has been appointed Musical Director to the touring company; but to readers of THE GRAMOPHONE any such formal introduction would be quite superfluous. You all know, I fancy, the story of this British-born musician's career, his education as a 'cellist at the R.A.M., the revelation of his unusual gifts as a conductor of opera and orchestral music generally. The compliment, no less unusual, of being invited whilst so young a man to conduct a Philharmonic Concert was not bestowed without good cause. He has also been tried and not found wanting during the regular season at Covent Garden ; while his experience with the B.N.O.C. has perhaps testified more than anything else to his fitness for the position he will be called upon to fill. He seems to have the talent not merely for conducting works, but for guiding the musical temperament aright, for reconciling to the good of the common cause the desires and caprices of the artistic dispositions that come under his direction. He has strongly developed in his nature that human sympathy which enables him to perceive the first fruits of the Syndicate's intervention, the providing of immediate employment for the personnel released by the collapse of the B.N.O.C.

It was clearly in no spirit of opposition to the League of Opera or Sir Thomas Beecham, or of competition with the League (as Lord Wittenham suggested in his letter to *The Times*), that this important move was made by Colonel Blois and the Covent Garden Syndicate. But human mouths have to be fed, and families provided for, and musicians cannot wait longer than other people for big schemes to fructify and rolling snowballs to attain their projected size. Young and old alike, these workers require the continuation of their weekly salary to be able to go on living. When the League of Opera becomes a *fait accompli*, as I heartily trust it soon may, it will, like the League of Nations, embody a very noble and grandiose achievement ; when that happy hour arrives, no doubt a fresh adjustment of some kind will have to be made. In the meantime, Colonel Blois has given us plainly to understand that " there is no ' combine ' or ' link ' with any other body "; that his company had had "no connection of any kind with the B.N.O.C., or any other organization ; and that the tour which opens at Halifax on September 23rd will be recruited, rehearsed, produced and managed entirely by the Covent Garden Opera Syndicate."

There are two or three things to be said in addition. I gather that the performers and instrumentalists of the new troupe are in the main to be British ; but that will not prevent the engagement of " guest " singers, whenever convenient or advisable, on the system that has obtained for years in Germany,

where municipal opera is established in every important town. In this way we shall probably be seeing very shortly the names of artists like Lotte Lehmann, Elisabeth Schumann, Inghilleri and others in conjunction with those of well-known British artists. The question of nationality does not enter in here. There is great value to be derived from the co-operation of singers of the first rank with opera companies where the " star system " is prohibited ; where the supreme merit of the ensemble is a primary consideration ; and where the field provides a training ground for the bigger organization which will some day become our central national institution of operatic art. The prices for these performances must obviously be no higher, either in London or the provinces, than those charged (thanks to State support) at the big Continental theatres. Smoking in the auditorium where opera is being sung must not be allowed on any account. (I understand that it was permitted duing the recent Carl Rosa season at the Lyceum Theatre, as it invariably is at the Old Vic ; but smoking is none the less objectionable and harmful wherever singing is in progress, and is, therefore, wholly unpardonable.) The public will only be taught to love and long for opera when it is taught at the same time to show consideration and respect for those who interpret it. It is a form of art that requires understanding and appreciation in the highest degree. Above all it needs the constant help of encouraging and instructive criticism, free from all trace of vulgarity, ridicule and caricature. Opera has too many enemies, conscious and unconscious.

The repertory selected for the forthcoming tour is uncommonly attractive. One particularly interesting item will be the first performance in English of *Turandot*, and I hope that both the version of the text and its enunciation will contribute to a better comprehension of this fascinating Chinese puzzle than has hitherto been accessible to the majority of opera-goers. The works underlined, in addition to *Turandot*, are *The Mastersingers*, *Lohengrin*, *Falstaff*, *Trovatore*, *Tosca*, *La Bohème*, *Madame Butterfly*, *The Barber of Seville*, *Faust*, *Cavalleria Rusticana* and *Pagliacci*.

THE GRAMOPHONE AND THE SINGER

(*Continued*)

By HERMAN KLEIN

The Gramophone in Fiction.

THE place and value of the gramophone in the psychology of the modern novel is a subject which our esteemed Editor is infinitely more capable of discussing than I am. I would not venture to touch upon the fringe of it even now, but for a lurking suspicion that his modesty causes him to refrain from mixing up the two things—that is to say, writing about novels in this journal or about gramophones in his novels. That he thinks about each in totally different terms is sufficiently obvious to all who, like myself, read whatever he writes and listen-in to whatever he discusses per radio. At the same time, having come across something entirely new to me—new, I mean, as an illustration of this particular topic—something, moreover, which is purely musical in its essence and character, I feel that I shall not be taking an unwarrantable liberty if I venture to deal with it as a holiday subject under the now-familiar caption that heads these articles.

The leading motive, or *leit-motif*, as Wagner christened it, is a musical medium for exercising a psychological influence upon the ear and mind of the spectator. A particular theme can be associated with a particular person or event so definitely, so inseparably, that its mere repetition suffices to recall either or both vividly and instantaneously. Wagner did not actually invent the device of employing these " references," as Sir Arthur Sullivan preferred to call them ; but he used it more than any other composer, and developed it to the fullest degree that it has ever reached. Its enormous psychological influence must have been felt by all who have listened attentively and with musical apprehension to the scores of *Tristan und Isolde, Der Ring des Nibelungen, Die Meistersinger*, and *Parsifal*. Wagner built up the whole edifice of his dramatic and musical structure upon the foundation created by this plan. He knew, as Gluck and others had known before him, the effect of *mélodrame*, a system of introducing through the orchestra of the theatre musical themes, often played in a certain manner, to accompany leading characters and incidents, and thereafter at given moments used again to recall and emphasize the precise emotion that they originally helped to arouse.

The experience itself, then, is as old as the hills. There is no need to dwell upon it further as an illustration of the subtle influence that a strain of music can exercise for re-awakening emotions with which it has at some time or other been associated. It has happened in my own case again and again ; and, what is more, it has never taken me more than a few seconds of reflection to recall the exact circumstances—the place, the period, the performer—connected with my first hearing of that particular theme. Often enough one short phrase has sufficed to produce this result ; and I daresay there are thousands besides myself whose musical ear in this respect is not a whit less retentive. But what, I hear you ask, has this to do with the gramophone or the novel ? I will explain. The whole idea, depicted with admirable skill, I found the other day embodied in a few pages towards the end of a new story called *Erromango*, from the pen of the gifted French novelist, Pierre Benoit. And the interest lay not merely in the mention of music and a gramophone (which one can read about incidentally, and, as a rule, with any amount of inaccurate detail in most modern novels), but in the fact that they are here made to illustrate the power of suggestion under rather remarkable circumstances and in an exceedingly dramatic manner. The gist of the story is as follows :—

A young Frenchman named Fabre (an Australian by birth) has been sent by a development company in Sydney to experiment in sheep-rearing on a lonely island among the New Hebrides, in the Southern Pacific. Steamers call there rarely, and many of the native inhabitants are still in the cannibalistic stage. On landing at Erromango, Fabre takes over the solitary bungalow that was occupied by his predecessor in the service of the company, who forthwith departs by the same steamer, after giving Fabre some useful information about a couple of white people who dwell on the island. One of these is a dealer in copra named Jeffries, a morose individual of misanthropic habits (and a dead shot) who lives alone in a neighbouring bay and refuses to allow visitors to come near him. His wife is dead ; but she had come over from Sydney with Jeffries, and her tomb lies concealed between his house and the shore. Fabre does not succeed in making friends with this hermit ; they scarcely ever meet. The new-comer is a scientist of some reputation, and does not object to a lonely life so long as the climate remains favourable and the island beautiful. He amuses himself occasionally with a gramophone.

So the months pass until the date comes round for the steamer to call at Erromango again. Fabre goes on board and joins the captain, the officers, and the few passengers at a convivial lunch. Jeffries is also aboard, supervising the loading of his copra for Sydney, but takes no part in the festive gathering. The fact that he is within hearing has, however, to be noted because it so happens that Fabre, over the whiskey and cigars, regales his companions with a story of certain *bonnes fortunes* that had come his way some years before his departure from Australia. The hospitality of his villa at Rose Bay had been accepted for several days by a charming lady who also hailed from Sydney, but whose name he had never succeeded in learning. She was musical; she played the piano and sang; and her favourite song was an English ballad, the title of which she had never mentioned, but the tune?—that Fabre could remember. And, as he wound up his story, he hummed to his friends the refrain of the ballad that his fair visitor had loved to warble to him.

It is from this point that tragedy begins slowly to creep into the story, and its progress is described with great ingenuity. One small detail in particular we are not allowed to miss. Although the misanthropic Jeffries was not present at the lunch, he came down to the adjoining smoking-room to write some letters, and could not, therefore, have avoided overhearing Fabre's merry tale or the graceful melody which he quoted at its conclusion. Well, did it matter if he did hear it? That is precisely the question which Fabre is asking himself during all the dreary months that follow upon the awakening in his mind of a suspicion—the alarming and probably well-founded suspicion—that his guest at Rose Bay and Jeffries's dead wife were one and the same woman! Was it really so? We are never informed in so many plain words. But, that Fabre should believe it; that Jeffries should have overheard the half-tipsy story which he so bitterly regrets having related to amuse his friends; these and other matters amply suffice to bring about a tragic *dénouement*.

To begin with, the rainy season sets in. The climate changes; a cyclone occurs and nearly destroys Erromango, besides killing most of Fabre's sheep and ruining his bungalow. He loses his servants; he takes to drinking too much whiskey; his health gradually becomes undermined, and his reason affected. Then one incident happens which bowls him over altogether. (It may be termed the central feature of this narrative.) Seated on his untidy verandah, imbibing liberal doses of neat whiskey, he listens one day to his gramophone whilst his native servant, Gabriel, changes the discs and (let us hope) inserts the new needles. Suddenly he hears a tune that makes him sit up with a start and open his eyes wide with astonishment. He had heard it before—too well did he know and instantly

recognise it; but not out here at Erromango. How had Gabriel come across that strange disc? Where had he found it? The explanation comes quickly! he had discovered it among a parcel of old gramophone discs left behind by Fabre's predecessor, and somehow had never chanced to play it before. It was, as we guess, the fatal tune that he had heard sung by the lady of Rose Bay. The words—" I have opened wide my lattice, Letting in the laughing breeze, That is telling happy stories, To the flowers and the trees "; and then the refrain, with its " *trilles stridents*," " Spring is coming." Yes, out in the New Hebrides, out on the broad Pacific, here was the ballad that he had listened to ten years before on the outskirts of Sydney, the melody that was doubtless familiar on every continent in the Old and New Worlds. He had never known its name, any more than he knew hers.

First he sends away his servant. Then he drags himself slowly to the gramophone, and, seizing the disc, manages to decipher the almost illegible words printed in gold on its well-worn label!

The Swallows, sung by Alma Gluck, words by Clifton Bingham, music by Frederic H. Cowen.*
But staring ever so hard at the disc could tell him nothing more; it might increase, but it could not silence his fears. Jeffries must know that song well; must have heard him hum it on board the ship. He might even have heard it played from this same disc before Fabre came, though Gabriel had declared it was one with which he was not familiar. Here was the long arm of coincidence with a vengeance: —out on a lonely island like Erromango, to come across the husband of the " only woman he had ever really cared for," yet not be absolutely sure that she and the anonymous one were the same identical person. Then to hear the song she used to sing (and which he had foolishly repeated for the benefit of other men, though he had forgotten the words) brought to life again by a discarded gramophone at a spot where it might be heard by the man who was waiting for just such evidence of his guilt!

As will be seen, the gramophone incident is made to form an integral part of the plot. It adds immensely to that quality of tense atmosphere and dramatic realism which characterises all Pierre Benoit's stories, and which makes him resemble Maeterlinck in method and style more than any other living French author. I will allow that the idea may be a trifle far-fetched, but imagine its effect, if cleverly utilised,

---

* This record is catalogued in the H.M.V. list for 1928 as D.A.239, the only other of the same song being one by Tetrazzini numbered D.B.526. With the Italian soprano it was a favourite for encore purposes, and may have been made by her at Hayes, Middlesex. On the other hand, Alma Gluck probably made hers in New York; and either there or in Sydney it might have been picked up by the author of *Erromango*, who goes to all the places that he writes about. *The Swallows* does not rank among Cowen's best songs, but it is pretty and catchy; and to me, personally, it is of interest because a pupil of mine was among the earliest to sing it publicly when it was first published in the 'nineties.

in a talkie-film, where the refrain of *The Swallows* might be actually heard whilst Fabre is seen seated in his *chaise longue*, listening in agony to its joyful lilt. One can understand why, after locking the disc in his safe for the night, he takes it out next day, carries it down to the beach, smashes it into a thousand atoms, and carefully buries them in the sand deep below the surface.

The rest of the story is quickly told. Upon a mind less disordered than Fabre's—it must be admitted that he is something of a coward and a weakling for the hero of a novel—this unpleasant combination of events might not have produced such serious consequences. But the poor fellow feels that in the mysterious Jeffries he is "up against" a terrible menace and an unknown quantity at that. One afternoon Jeffries comes over to see him, but nothing comes out during their talk; it only heightens the

impression that the " widower " knows all and is biding his time—waiting for the answer to certain inquiries that he has set on foot in Sydney. During the long interval of waiting for the steamer to return with the mail, the atmosphere of uncertainty and anxiety becomes more and more exciting and the condition of Fabre grows worse every day. He sees no way out of the tangle, no loophole for escape from that avenging bullet. And so the end comes—not in such a way that we see the deed actually committed or recognise the individual whose finger pulls the trigger. Indeed it is possible to form the notion that poor Fabre commits suicide. Anyhow the friends who come to fetch him to the ship find him seated at his office table, his head resting on his arms, his body cold and stiff, and a bullet-hole in his right temple.

HERMAN KLEIN.

THE GRAMOPHONE AND THE SINGER

(*Continued*)

By HERMAN KLEIN

"*La Bohème*" and Henschel Albums.

THE career of *La Bohème* in this country has been a curious one. When produced in English by the Carl Rosa Company at Manchester in the spring of 1897 it was received with favour, but with nothing like the enthusiasm—despite the presence of the composer—that would mark any ordinary performance of it to-day. When the same company opened its season at Covent Garden with the new opera in the following winter little increase of warmth was displayed, though people evidently liked the music. Until then Puccini had only been known to Londoners by his *Manon Lescaut*, which Sir Augustus Harris had nearly killed (as he virtually *did* kill himself) by including it as "overweight" among the eight novelties that he mounted during the extraordinary season of 1894. But it was not until some five years later that the Puccini vogue really set in. It may be dated from two events—viz., the production of *La Bohème* with Melba as Mimi in 1899, and that of *Tosca* with Ternina in the title rôle and Scotti as Scarpia in 1900; both operas given at Covent Garden and sung in Italian.

Now I think I am right in attributing this hesitant attitude of the British public vis-à-vis of *La Bohème* to the extremely bad English translation in which it was sung. People would tell me that they could not make head or tail of the plot, while the greater part of the dialogue was so stupid and inane that it positively annoyed them. Unluckily this was true. The task of adapting Giacosa and Illica's libretto had been too much for the two estimable Englishmen who had shared it. (One died, if I remember rightly, after he had finished the first two acts, and the other completed the remaining two.) Probably neither of them was entirely conversant with the delicate subtleties of the Italian language or, at any rate, capable of finding suitable English equivalents to fit Puccini's music. I do not say the job was altogether easy. The characters drawn by Henri Murger in his *Scènes de la Vie de Bohème* were quite ordinary personages. It would have been a mistake to put flowery or high-falutin language into their mouths, and clever librettists like Giacosa and Illica knew better than to do so. At the same time they had to bear in mind that they were dealing with the abusive epithets and decent—I mean not precisely vulgar—argot that French bohemians were in the habit of using in 1830 or thereabouts.

It was just the free, careless nature of these folk, their wonderful vivacity and their generous hearts, that had attracted the young Puccini. Of coherent story there was no more than there had been in Murger's book; how could there be without upsetting its balance and over-colouring the simple vivid truth of scenes and incidents that tell their own tale? But it appealed to the composer as none of his earlier libretti had done, and he determined to set it to music line by line, word by word, with a closeness of touch and feeling that should reflect every *nuance*, every detail, in the progress of the action. He accomplished this, moreover, with an amazing degree of originality and skill, touching in the high lights of comedy and pathos, the sudden outbursts of emotion and the moments of high-spirited burlesque, with a masterful ingenuity worthy of the genius that was his acknowledged model—the genius that brought forth *Die Meistersinger*. Hence the supreme importance of a translation that should enable the spectator to follow the meaning of every idea and if possible every sentence in the text. Imagine the disappointment in store for the critic and the problem that awaited the average opera-goer of thirty years ago when it was found, if not impossible, at least extremely difficult to take in the gist of a quarter of what was being said and done by the protagonists of a wholly novel type of opera like *La Bohème*.

I have more than once told the story of my trip to Manchester to witness the Carl Rosa production of 1897 and my return to London on the following day in the saloon carriage that also brought Puccini back to Euston. I had found him in low spirits when I went down; he was even more unhappy as we were coming back. He could not speak a word of English, and understood very little more when he heard it spoken; consequently he had only the vaguest notion how much of the meaning of action and text had got across the footlights. When he asked me I told him regretfully that I feared "Very little." "That is a pity" (*E peccato*), he said, "because half the pleasure is lost when only half the humour of the words can be grasped. But I rather doubt," he added, "whether it will ever be grasped except when *Bohème* is sung in Italian." In after years I reminded him of this opinion of his and admitted that it had been partially proved, yet not entirely, seeing how enormously popular his opera had grown in every part of the English-speaking world. A quarter of a century had sufficed to make everyone who really wanted to understand familiar with the general import of the text.

And now, years after that, another stage has arrived in the process of popularizing *La Bohème*. It has been added to the " Columbia Masterworks " in album form, with a brand new prose translation from the pen of Mr. Compton Mackenzie, whose handling of the *Traviata* libretto met, it will be recollected, with unanimous approbation. His present effort deserves even warmer appreciation ; first, because it was in itself a far more difficult thing to do well, and, secondly, because, for the reasons that have been stated in this article, it confers an even greater benefit upon the work and all who listen to it through the medium of the gramophone. It meets the case precisely in the manner that Puccini foreshadowed in his talk with me. It enables you to grasp the flow and humour of story and music simultaneously, whilst being presented to you in the original Italian tongue and by accomplished Italian singers. There is no need for you to miss a solitary point because there stand the English words before your eyes, showing you with admirable fidelity and vigour, as well as with the skill and ease of the practised writer, exactly what meaning you are to attach to what is being said. Happily the difficulties of mild slang and mock-serious abuse hurled at each other by the Parisian *bohémiens* have been overcome by Mr. Mackenzie with characteristic cleverness ; the insults

SIR GEORGE HENSCHEL
in his Inverness-shire home.

are of the good, strong colloquial order, without being either coarse or silly, and reveal all the linguistical appropriateness and force that might have been expected. The only pity is that so splendid a translation cannot be sung whenever the opera is given on the stage in English.

As I have already hinted, this album comprises in its thirteen records mechanical results of a very high quality. The recording is on a par with the artistic labour that has been concentrated upon the interpretation of one of the most "tricky" scores I know. It will repay careful and reiterated study, because there is in it such an accumulation of orchestral detail that rarely if ever comes out clearly in the opera-house. It is just this surprising clearness that I find so peculiarly welcome—the constant interplay between voices and instruments without disturbing factors due to the necessarily constant fussiness of the movements on the stage. The second act in particular gains enormously from this musical isolation, and not even the interruptions for changing records can be said to obscure or interfere with its

pleasure. The chorus here is excellent, the sudden changes of tempo and rhythm, the contrasts of orchestral colour depicting the *va et vient* of the motley crowd, the ensembles wherein Musetta is the central figure, and in fact the whole scene appeal to the ear with wonderful force.

The characters are represented as follows :— Rodolfo, Luigi Marini ; Schaunard, Aristide Baracchi ; Benoit and Alcindoro, Salvatore Baccaloni ; Mimi, Rosetta Pampanini ; Parpignol, Giuseppe Nessi ; Marcello, Gino Vanelli ; Colline, Tancredi Pasero ; and Musetta, Luba Mirella. These are names familiar enough literally to speak for themselves and make up a genuinely strong cast. The studio pranks of the four men are indicated with an animation that is free from noise or confusion ; they shout at each other without deafening you, and their vocal repartee can be followed without difficulty. As regards vocal merit in the solo parts I like best the superb tone and fine singing of Rosetta Pampanini. She improves as usual with the demand for increase of dramatic intensity ; there is a note of unforced pathos in her scenes with Rudolph that brings its thrill every time. Would that Marini's voice were as pure and steady as hers or Vanelli's, especially in the scene outside the inn at the Barrier d'Enfer ! When the trio become a quartet Mirella's Musetta proves quite exceptionally good ; while the noble quality of Pasero's tone imparts the needful touching effect to Colline's adieu to his " ancient garment." So there ! After all this optimistic appreciation you will require no further assurance from me to realize that the Columbia *Bohème* is an exceedingly elegant and perfect production.

SIR GEORGE HENSCHEL ALBUM.

Sir George Henschel is a unique example of the well-preserved veteran musician. He does equally well to-day all that he did to the admiration of the world over half a century ago. As a singer he was supposed at one time to have retired from the active arena and limited himself to teaching. Yet here he is, giving short recitals over the wireless (therewith renewing old experiences in a *métier* that he was practically the first singer to popularise in this country) and crystallizing his art in an album group for Columbia that will stand for ever, let us hope, a monument to his triple ability as *diseur*, vocalist, and self-accompanist. I can only repeat concerning these efforts what I have said more than once already about the recent records of other great artists : it is a blessing that the gramophone of the electrical epoch exists to create and establish models which may be equalled but can never be surpassed. I dare say

Sir George Henschel wishes as much as I do that the thing had been invented and available when he was a young man. It would have preserved for us not only the incomparable voices of other singers, but it would have enabled the present generation to hear how delightfully he used to sing duets with that accomplished lady who was his first wife. Still, we may well cry content with such admirable specimens as are contained in this album.

They include nine records (four discs, two 10 in., two 12 in.) of Lieder that have always been closely identified with his art as an interpreter—viz., *Der Leiermann, Das Wandern, Lachen und Weinen*, and *Gruppe aus dem Tartarus*, by Schubert; *Ich grolle nicht, Lied eines Schmiedes*, and *Die Zwei Grenadiere*, by Schumann; and Carl Loewe's ballads, *Heinrich der Vogler* and *Der Erlkönig*. Of this small but representative collection the first two and the last one bring out the voice with most adequate strength and the greatest measure of colour and effect. All alike, however, are sung with the old variety and truthfulness of dramatic perception, power of characterization, fervour of expression, and, last but not least, smoothness coupled with the utmost distinctness of enunciation. As a model example of this ultimate gift I can cite nothing more remarkable than the half-whispered flattery poured by the Erlkönig into the ears of the frightened boy as he clings to his father on their terrible ride.

HERMAN KLEIN.

THE GRAMOPHONE AND THE SINGER
(Continued)
By HERMAN KLEIN
Some Radio Experiences—and Some Advice

NOT long ago I put on the headphones attached to my crystal set, at an hour when it is not my custom to do so—it was somewhere about lunch time, I fancy—and found myself listening to a remarkably fine rendering of a well-known Puccini aria. I recognised the voice at once (but don't intend for a reason to mention here the name of the singer), and decided at the same instant that it could not possibly be proceeding from an actual performance at 2LO. Then came to my ears the sound of ever so slight an undercurrent of buzzing tone, not loud enough to interfere with the music, but palpable and continuous enough to make me realise that what I was hearing was the well-manipulated outcome of a gramophone record. Until that moment I had positively not suspected the presence of any such intermediary, and I tried all I could to go on listening in the pleasant belief that, inasmuch as the singer had originally made the record, she was as good as on the spot at Savoy Hill singing to me now.

Somewhat to my surprise, I discovered that it was not at all difficult to assume this oral or mental attitude; and therewith was born another pleasant conviction, namely, that I would much rather listen to a good gramophone-radio performance like this than to many of the " actual " efforts to do justice to—or should I say avoid misinterpreting ?—the same piece which were habitually emanating from the B.B.C. studio.

Yet I am not sure that this illusion would always have been practicable; *i.e.*, that the transmission of a gramophone record by wireless two or three years ago would have been equally pure and unimpeded. If not, it is only one of the many improvements that have been wrought of late in the direction of microphone operations. We know, of course, to what extent these ingenious advances have tended to help both singer and speaker since the early days of the radio era. There is no comparison to be made between what was done then and what can be done now. The amplifying process and the rest of the mechanical gadgets that the intervening engineer can bring to bear have completely altered the aspect of the entire operation. Experience " on both sides of the microphone " has also done a great deal. The same old excuses for blemishes and blunders are no longer frequent. Voices do not " fade " or tremble or tumble off the key to anything like the extent that they used to.

Nevertheless, and despite all these ameliorations, I am bound to confess that most of the radio singing heard under the present régime is far less satisfactory than it ought to be—certainly far below the level of excellence attained on the best gramophone records. Why is this? Admitting that we cannot expect to be listening all the time to first-rate artists (who are rare as well as expensive), it appears to me that when serious or exacting music is in the programme the choice of vocalists is not so felicitous or adequate as it should be. The changes are rung too frequently upon the same names. The parts in an opera or an oratorio are not invariably allotted to the right voices. Phrases and passages are misread with the same nonchalance that characterises the utterances of certain announcers, whose acquaintance with their own as well as foreign languages (notably as regards proper names) is obviously incomplete. On the whole the diction in singing has improved; it is much more audible than formerly. But it is still wofully blurred and unrefined, marred by the ridiculous sounds which certain vocalists imagine to be the vowel tones of the English language; while the consonants are still too much left to take care of themselves.

The trouble is that there is no central authority appointed by the B.B.C. to deal with these cases—no one with the right, the knowledge, and the ability to prevent their happening. It might be done, of course, at rehearsal; few programmes are rehearsed with a sufficient margin of time allowed for interruptions of any kind, much less for those connected with technique. In reality, therefore, the only remedy, the only means for guarding against the occurrence of errors of every sort, is to *correct them beforehand*. The B.B.C. is the sole institution possessing the power to accomplish this great and necessary reform. Will it exercise that power? I wonder.

In the relatively insignificant critical notices that the papers condescend to spare for broadcast music, stress is often laid on the disadvantage of listening to singers without being able to see them. I admit it. You lose the magnetic influence of personality, of facial expression, of the more delicate and subtle shades of vocal nuance. But in the case of these last qualities, does not the fault arise very often from the inability of the singer to supply them? I complained long ago of this lack of " atmosphere " in the singing of gramophone records, and, thanks partly to the aid of the electrical process, its absence is not nearly so frequent as of yore. In broadcasting from the studio the same results ought to be obtained, and there are two distinguished examples to prove it in Sir George Henschel and Sir Walford Davies. When you listen to them—the one singing, the other speaking—you feel as if they were there actually with you; nay more, they seem to be exclusively addressing themselves to you and you do not lose a syllable that they utter.

Naturally it is not so easy to convey this impression or illusion (for it is both) from the concert-room. We know that; and we know, moreover, that one concert-room can serve a great deal better than another for broadcasting purposes. But neither excuse will explain the immeasurable difference between one singer and another when heard on the same occasion from the same room. I mention as a case in point the performance of Mendelssohn's *Hymn of Praise*, radioed from the Bishopsgate Institute one night early in October. While Mr. Frank Titterton came over distinctly and strongly in all respects, Miss Isobel Baillie was merely distinct; her pure soprano sounding singularly thin and, as it seemed, incapable of giving power to the head notes or rising to the necessary climaxes of religious fervour. Skill in characterisation and variety of tone-colour are things that I never expect from the average wireless singer. Anyhow, I very rarely encounter them.

Then there is the question of the programmes—that eternal problem which worries musical listeners in almost as badly as the unemployment problem troubles the nation. It is one of the subjects on which we cannot possibly all think alike, since it depends entirely upon the taste of the individual. Consideration for others besides ourselves is therefore requisite. Personally I dislike vaudeville as a rule exceedingly, and, like His Majesty the King, " I hate jazz." But this does not blind me to the fact that there are hundreds of thousands of people who are extremely fond of both, and whose *penchants* have to be catered for by the B.B.C. They are probably the same people who did not rejoice over the generous and beneficial allowance from the Promenade Concerts that I enjoyed by radio during the recent season. Well, I am sorry for them. I also regret, however, that the opening up of another new station for the London region has not yet resulted in a better subdivision of the evening programmes, so as to avoid the simultaneous supply of selections of the same type and to secure the requisite alternative schemes for suiting as far as possible both extremes of taste.

Finally, I would like to register an emphatic vote at Savoy Hill against the unlimited quantity of right-down bad voices and bad singing that are permitted to assault the ear in course of a week's broadcasting. I would say, " Allow vaudeville by all means, if you must; but please do exercise some sort of discretion as to the kinds of vocal noise that you accord the liberty of sheltering under it." I know something about the music hall, and have done ever since I was a youngster. I heard every " lion comique " we had, from George Leybourne and the Great Vance down to Albert Chevalier, who was, in his line, a greater artist than any we have to-day. But never have I heard such shouting, such howling, such hideous attempts to imitate the American *artiste*, coloured or white, as I have endured through sheer curiosity from 2LO. Where these people come from I have not the vaguest idea; but I do know that there can be no need to employ their services in the sacred name of vaudeville. They should be banished forthwith and for evermore. An ugly or discordant voice is a bad example for young people, and should never be tolerated by a body that sets out primarily to educate and improve the taste of the masses.

THE SAVOY PRODIGALS' RETURN.

After all "there's no place like" the Savoy Theatre for the Savoy operas. They sound more at home there than anywhere else. Not even the metamorphosis that lavish outlay has wrought both in structure and *décor* can alter one's sensation that this is truly the theatre which witnessed the birth of all, or nearly all, the delightful progeny of W. S. Gilbert and Arthur Sullivan. Mr. Rupert D'Oyly Carte's company was long overdue ; but when it did come back it came surrounded by an atmosphere and a halo of glory. I was present at the opening of the original Savoy in 1881, and remember thinking it the prettiest, richest-looking modern theatre that London had had up to that time. I remember, too, the first production of *The Gondoliers* in December, 1889, and can never forget what a dream it was of bright, handsome *mise en scène*, of bewitching lilts

à la Vénitienne, and delightful acting and singing by a glorious cast of Savoyards that included Courtice Pounds, Rutland Barrington, Frank Wyatt, W. H. Denny, Geraldine Ulmar, Jessie Bond, Rosina Brandram, and Decima Moore, with the composer as usual at the conductor's desk.

But the revival of 1929, for the opening of the rebuilt house, will go down to history as a still more gorgeous affair. Indeed, I am not sure that any Gilbert and Sullivan production in the whole chronicle of half a century has ever been endowed with "scenery, dresses and properties" on a par for magnificence with those designed for this latest *reprise* of *The Gondoliers* by Mr. Charles Ricketts, R.A. As for the house itself, I can only re-echo the general opinion that it far outshines in sheeny loveliness and jazzy satin comfort the refined interior designed by the late Charles Phipps for D'Oyly the First. But beyond that comparisons need not be carried. The singers of the 'eighties were hard to equal, much less to beat.

HERMAN KLEIN.

THE GRAMOPHONE AND THE SINGER
(Continued)
By HERMAN KLEIN

Columbia Album of "Madame Butterfly"

FORTY years ago, come next April, there was performed at the Duke of York's Theatre a Japanese play, founded by David Belasco upon a magazine story from the pen of J. Luther Long, which had already won success in New York. Its title was *Madame Butterfly*. Someone—I fancy it was Comm. Tito di Ricordi—brought the little drama the notice of Giacomo Puccini, then in London for the production of *La Tosca*. It interested him enormously. He was looking out for a subject for another opera, and he quickly made up his mind that here was what he wanted—something quite novel, a dramatic plot that appealed to him, and just the right group of characters for an opera. The affair was soon arranged with Belasco and the script of the piece handed over to Puccini's able librettists, Illica and Giacosa, who were equally delighted with it.

The composer made up his mind from the outset to lend "local colour" to his treatment of the story by imitating the method employed (if only slightly) in the score of *The Mikado* by Sir Arthur Sullivan and

introducing into it some genuine Japanese tunes. For this purpose, as we are reminded in the H.M.V. publication, *Opera at Home*, he made use of some early gramophone records. "To this end the Gramophone Company presented him with a set of the first records ever made in Japan," and in addition he also borrowed, as we know, the theme of *The Star-spangled Banner* to typify "that devil of a Pinkerton," as the U.S. Consul Sharpless so accurately describes him. But I do not agree with the writer of the Puccini article in *Grove's Dictionary* when he says that the composer of *Butterfly* "had not the genius of the symphonic writer which can turn a common tune into a thing of tragedy or pathos"; or that "the American and Japanese tunes in *Butterfly* remain to the end foreign elements." In my opinion Puccini utilized those elements with a fine perception of their possibilities and blended or merged them into his own music with consummate skill. On the other hand I do agree that he was less successful in accomplishing a similar purpose in the score of *The Girl of the Golden West*, which opera he also derived from a play by Belasco.

No mystery attached to the failure of *Butterfly* on its first production at La Scala in February, 1904. The Milanese were simply unprepared for anything so strange, so quaint and original. Besides, in its initial form—two acts—it was unwieldy and over-long. The revised version, done at Brescia three months later, brought a complete reversal of the first verdict and with it a triumph that has proved lasting. I remember well the enthusiasm that marked its reception at Covent Garden on July 10, 1905, when the principal parts were sustained by Emmy Destinn, Gabrielle Lejeune, Caruso, and Scotti; and, again, at the Metropolitan Opera House, New York, when the same famous Italians sang it with Geraldine Farrar and Louise Homer. Between those two productions it fell to my lot to train the double cast of singers for the (English) first performance in America under the management of Henry W. Savage, which took place at Boston in November, 1906, and was followed by a tour of the States that lasted a year or more. Puccini came to America with Tito di Ricordi for the Boston performance and expressed himself delighted with it. It was conducted by Walter Rothwell—then a newcomer—and the Butterfly was a charming Hungarian named Elza Szamosy, whom I subsequently heard at Budapest in 1913 in *The Girl of the Golden West*.

So much for the general history of this fascinating work. For my own part I prefer it to all Puccini's other operas, though many good judges, I am aware, now consider *Turandot* to be his masterpiece. The dazzling orchestration and immense cleverness of the posthumous opera are wonderful; but there is no humanity, no pathos, in the Chinese story, whereas the Japanese is full of both. The latter yields a melodic line that is delightfully vocal, besides being supported by new and alluring harmonies in an inexhaustible variety. *Turandot* at times seems to me very boring, but there is scarcely a dull moment in the whole of *Butterfly*. Hence is it that I welcome with unqualified pleasure the appearance of a Columbia album of this familiar score, executed in Milan by Italian artists, orchestra and chorus, on precisely the same model as the *Traviata*, *Aida*, and *Bohème* albums that were recently issued from the same *atelier*. It consists of fourteen discs (28 records) numbered from 9784 to 9797.

The cast is as follows : Madama Butterfly, Rosetta Pampanini ; Suzuki, Conchita Velasquez ; Mrs. Pinkerton, Cesira Ferrari ; Pinkerton, Alessandro Granda ; Sharpless, Gino Vanelli ; Goro, Giuseppe Nessi ; The Bonze, Salvatore Baccaloni ; Yamadori, Aristide Baracchi ; Commissioner, Lino Bonardi ; with the Milan Symphony Orchestra, conducted by Cav. Lorenzo Molajoli.

This is an excellent vocal and instrumental combination, equipped at all points to do justice to a difficult theme. One perceives, from the very start of the busy introductory bars, the requisite sense of life and energy. More vital still, one can feel, as the opening episodes proceed, that peculiar *entrain*, that unbroken continuity—apart from the changing of records—which can alone be infused by stage artists of experience, ready with and for their " cues," in fact, working together with the same easy realism as though they were actually going through the business. I know none better than Italians, if so good, for introducing this atmospheric element into the operation of recording dramatic music ; and it is another good reason for my argument that gramophonists do well to put up with the foreign language so long as they can gain more of the composer's original colour and hear (as they can here) every syllable of the text. The translation this time has not been specially provided, being the one printed in the Ricordi vocal score. Cav. Molajoli evidently has the Milanese traditions of *Butterfly* in his veins—*presto, e sempre più presto !*—a game which our own drill-Sargents are also fond of indulging in. But in this instance it does no harm to the music and enables the opera to be recorded with fewer cuts. These, by the way, I find on comparing them with my New York copy of the score, are very nearly identical with those made by Tito di Ricordi, which had probably been approved by Puccini himself.

Those of us who have heard Rosetta Pampanini sing *Butterfly* at Covent Garden will recognize at once the salient features in her treatment of the part in these records. She is brimful of emotion and intensely dramatic, without ever losing the unexaggerated artistic touch. Only one trifling blemish strikes me at the outset : she does not graduate from a *pp* to a *ff* her tender melody (afterwards the main love theme) when she climbs the hill to Pinkerton's dwelling, but starts off at her loudest, as if she had already reached the top. Her friends and relations ought also to enter a shade more delicately ; though they are perhaps a little less assertive—relatively. The only other fault for which I hold Sgra. Pampanini responsible is her failure to rise a full major third to the F natural when she describes her tiny dolls as " the souls of my forefathers." This leaves the key for a moment in doubt. On the other hand, she sings *Un bel dì* better than any other soprano I have heard since Destinn ; but none of her achievements is really cleverer than her almost startling contrasts of tone as she embodies in turn the joyous, irresponsible geisha-girl of the first act ; the anxious yearning of the waiting Butterfly ; the defiant pride of the mother in her and Pinkerton's child (happily out of sight and therefore no older or bigger than that he ought to be) ; and, finally, the tragic disillusioned creature who commits *hari-kari*. I find all these phases quite admirably depicted.

The marriage scene, with its Japanese bells and quaint orchestral touches, comes out more clearly than it does as a rule on the stage. The love duet at the end of the first act also receives its due, for Alessandro Granda has a fairly steady voice of considerable charm, and almost persuades us that Pinkerton means to prove a constant lover. (It would be difficult, moreover, to pick holes in the recording either here or elsewhere in this album.) In the second act the tendency to hurry rather robs the passages between Butterfly and Suzuki of some of their mournful and poignant sweetness. But it does not affect the subsequent rapid passages in which Sharpless and Yamadori are concerned; there we get broad, sympathetic tone from Gino Vanelli and Aristide Baracchi—good artists both. Throughout the act, which includes the graceful flower duet, the voice of Rosetta Pampanini stands sharply outlined against the others; while its dark timbre and the undercurrent of sobs lend a peculiar presentiment of sorrow to the Japanese tune wherein Butterfly predicts her baby's future destiny. In addition to all this, a distinct success is scored with the highly original finale, where the two women (in the opera) post themselves before the *shosi* whilst the chorus hum, *bouches fermées*, the haunting melody of the Letter theme. Is this, too, pseudo-Japanese? I shouldn't wonder.

The second part of Act II—which we generally consider the third act—is preceded by an Intermezzo founded upon some of the main themes of the opera.

It is not an inspired bit of music, however, and in the opera-house is mostly played amid the disturbance caused by people returning to their seats. It sounds better in this tranquil form, as played by the Milan Symphony Orchestra, and is in a measure indispensable to the completeness of Puccini's design. Not so Mrs. Pinkerton. She has been ruthlessly reduced to a few bars; which is about all she is worth, poor lady! Her appearance upon the scene and her confab with Butterfly have always struck me as a piece of hollow sentiment, utterly superfluous and about as hypocritical as that final cry of Pinkerton's, heard outside just before the curtain falls upon the tableau of his victim's suicide. As it is given here on a single disc, we get quite enough explanation to render the situation clear. After which the events of the tragedy move swiftly, as they should, to their climax, with all the best of the music always in evidence. Rosetta Pampanini does not spare us quite so many sobs and ejaculations as I should like her to in a gramophone performance, but she is otherwise splendid to the end. The Suzuki, too, improves immensely in this act; she seems to gather confidence as she goes on.

On the whole, therefore, I may congratulate Columbia upon an excellent production of this exacting opera.

HERMAN KLEIN.

THE GRAMOPHONE AND THE SINGER

(Continued)

By HERMAN KLEIN

A Parlophone Celebration (1904—1929)

PARAPHRASING Shakespeare's immortal Juliet, one might aptly inquire, " What's Parlophone ? " and then proceed—

it is nor hand, nor foot—
Nor arm, nor face, nor any other part—
Belonging to a man. O, be some other name !—
What's in a name ?

Ay, there's the rub! " What's in a name ? " Why, in these days of bold advertisement, the name, once earned, is everything. And so no doubt it was in Juliet's time, when young ladies went shopping under the arches of a colonnade at Verona to buy themselves new rosin or lute strings; for they knew even at that epoch how to ask for what they wanted. The importance, then as now, lay not so much in the name itself as in what it implied; and that is why I think that record-buyers who attach a

certain value to the Parlophone mark may be glad to learn something about the inner history of the enterprise that gave birth to it. After reading this article they will probably be ready to agree with me that the name, whilst neither Romeo nor Montague, has a very great deal in it.

The opportunity arises out of an anniversary celebration and a handsome book compiled in connection therewith, this last taking the form of a highly interesting historical survey of the business from its inception in 1904 down to the present day —in point of fact, just a quarter of a century. The volume, which is nearly of sheet-music size, is copiously illustrated with photographs of the appropriate persons and places, taken in every part of the world, besides numerous coloured plates reproducing special drawings by J. C. Turner, and designs, trade-marks, labels, etc. It is beautifully printed on thick paper, in clear roman type, and the get-up of the whole thing is perfect. The title-page indicates (by what it omits rather than by what it states) that our friend " Parlophone," is the British Associate of the Berlin firm of Carl Lindström Aktien-Gesellschaft, or, more briefly, C. L. & Co., Ltd., a combine of talking-machine businesses that started in 1904 on the third floor of a small factory in the Brückenstrasse.

Who was Carl Lindström ? A Swedish mechanic who, after having made a study of the *fin-de-siècle* phonograph, began manufacturing machines and records on his own account at Berlin in 1897. It was the period of semi-ignorance and half-hearted enterprise ; .when only a few had got beyond mere dreams of the future possibilities of the gramophone business, and not a soul had as yet pictured in imagination the potentialities of its artistic development. (Five or six years later the whole idea had progressed. I was living then in New York, and acting as musical adviser to the Columbia Graphophone Company. The flat disc was gradually replacing the tubular roll, and the old talking-machine giving way to new methods of reproducing the human voice. I was more or less an eye-witness of that unforgetable transition.) But the Germans were not far behind the Americans, though the world was hearing much less about them. On the banks of the Spree, Carl Lindström and his co-optimistic allies were slowly but surely extending their operations, their personnel, their buildings, and making constant advances in their methods. After the manner of their nation, they imitated everything good that they dared to imitate, and then—proceeded so far as they could to improve upon it. Admirably is the perfected outcome of their processes in the making of *Schallplatten*, or flat discs, described in the earlier pages of the book now before me. It represents in word and picture alike the incredibly gigantic growth of what is now one of the great industries of the world.

The principal co-founder of the undertaking with Carl Lindström was Dr. Max Straus, who in 1928 received from the Technical High School of Breslau the honorary degree of Doctor-Engineer in recognition of his services as inventor and leader in the *Sprechmaschinen* and disc industry. Associated with Dr. Straus in the directorate we find other groups of clever-looking faces—those of Richard Seligsohn, Max Thomas, C. M. Goldstein, Max and Alfred Gutmann, and Paul Offenbacher. Then among the photographs of the Committee of Supervisors and Advisors we come across two familiar names and countenances—those of Sir George Croydon (now Lord) Marks, and Mr. Louis Sterling, the chairman and managing director respectively of the Columbia Graphophone Company. What does that mean ? you ask. Shall I tell you ? I will ; but I only heard it myself the other day. Well, it means that at the present time the Lindström group form part of the Columbia International Company. You would have hardly thought it possible, any more than· I did, but it is so. In these days of mergers and millions money can buy any limited company, *Société Anonyme* or Aktien-Gesellschaft, on the face of the earth.

But recover your breath, turn over another few pages, and what do you see ? A familiar dark-blue placard illuminated with the " sterling " device, " £," and the word " Parlophone," indicating as plainly as anything can that the English branch both for the manufacture and the distribution of these well-known records is associated with the same powerful organisation. I could almost believe that to be another surprise for you, had you not probably guessed (or heard) it by now. It seems that the English Parlophone Company which was formed in October, 1923, is nevertheless an entirely independent concern, preparing and marketing its own records as we know in this country, and also dealing here with the product of the Odeon, Fonotipia, Beka, and other associated foreign companies. To know this is to understand the ever-widening sweep of the nets that have of late drawn the pick of the leading Continental artists and orchestras into the Parlophone catalogue. Moreover, the quality of its work has improved in proportion, and, speaking in the critical sense, I am bound to acknowledge on the part of Mr. Francis and his recording staff willingness to show a ready acquiescence in the occasional suggestions contained in my reviews elsewhere in THE GRAMOPHONE.

There are a few other features of the souvenir album that are deserving of notice. Following upon the lengthy description of the Berlin factory, some sixty pages are devoted to a really remarkable series of photographs showing exterior and interior views of the Lindström branch establishments all over Europe (not forgetting 85, City Road, E.C. 2) and every part of the tropical and antipodean globe. The nature and far-reaching extent of this well-managed business could not be better demonstrated. I have no notion of the combined value of the myriads of gramophones, loud-speakers, records, and mechanical musical appliances of every description on view in this vast collection of stores, but it must amount to something enormous.

Next comes an article, ably written by Dr. Franz M. Feldhaus, giving a history of the various instruments for reproducing, imitating, and amplifying the human voice from the sixteenth century down to the present era. This is illustrated by facsimiles of old wood-engravings, some of them very amusing, which clearly show how definitely the ideas of to-day had started in the minds of men so long as three or four hundred years ago. From primitive transmission by speaking-tube—invisible where mystery was sought—to the model of Edison's first phonograph of 1878, reproducing speech, to the first flat disc of Emile Berliner (1888), and so on to the apparatus in use to-day, the whole march of progress is plainly traced. Then follow testimonials from prominent men and musicians, a scientific essay by Dr. Wilhelm Heinitz, and an entertaining dissertation on babies and the gramophone from the pen of Fred Hildenbrandt.

Further on, Herr Hans Lebede tells of the artists whose supreme merit and distinction on the operatic stage and concert platform on the Continent have brought them under the Lindström banner. Their pictures border this article for several pages, and among them I recognise, of course, the names, if not the faces, of all our Parlophone friends. Coming in the order in which they made their records and covering the whole period of a quarter of a century, they make a very interesting collection of photographs, numbering altogether over two hundred. There is more material still, all of it appropriate, before one gets to the end of this wonderful book. But I have said enough to show what it is like, and will end by saying how much I wish I could send a copy of it to every one of our readers, with my best wishes for a Happy New Year !

THE GRAMOPHONE AND THE SINGER
(Continued)
By HERMAN KLEIN

A Festival of Old Opera Revivals

THE good work done at the New Scala Theatre during the month just ended will not be forgotten. The promoters of the London Opera Festival may be assured of that. If they lost money—and probably they lost a considerable sum— they can take consolation from the fact that they lost it in a splendid cause. To say as much is to remove in advance the harsh edge from whatever criticism I may have to utter concerning the particular feature of the performances which most interested me—I mean, of course, the singing. As a whole it was unquestionably bad. But now that it is all over, does it really matter ? It was the glorious chance of listening to such a series of strange old masterworks, some of them for the first time in one's life, that actually counted. Oddly enough, too, it coincided with the opening of the Exhibition of Italian Art at the Royal Academy, and, with greater perfection in the rendering, might equally have been regarded (by lovers of old music) as a privileged opportunity for making acquaintance with things long read about but never seen (or heard). Only, Burlington House was thronged from the outset and the Scala wasn't ; in spite whereof I can truthfully declare that I enjoyed each of my visits to the theatre ; for the " beggarly array of empty benches " did not disturb me, while the greater part of the music was as beautiful as it was unfamiliar.

One question that I kept asking myself I would like to set down here : Will the day come, I wonder, when some of these unknown vocal pieces will, for the sake of their sheer musical beauty, be recorded and put in the lists of the leading gramophone companies ? To record them at all would no doubt be a purely artistic venture ; yet it might, I think, prove worth while. When one hears so much as we are now hearing of what the gramophone is accomplishing for instrumental music, one feels that it might do much more for vocal music of the older classical schools that stands upon exactly the same exalted level. I refer to the operatic music of Purcell, Gluck, Handel, Mozart, and other eighteenth-century masters, unhackneyed because comparatively unknown, but nearly always lovely and grateful to the ear. If these gems were recorded they would at least be competently sung, which would be a gain in itself ; and during the Scala Festival I more than once caught myself feeling ashamed as well as sorry that practically none of them could be listened to and enjoyed through the medium of the gramophone. To particularise now would take up too much space, but I have made a mental note of several airs that I hope to include in my waiting list when the scores become available to the outside world.

Monteverde's *Orpheus* lent a peculiar distinction to the opening of the season. Strictly speaking, it was less of a revival than a resuscitation, and as such should have excited far more curiosity than it did. This 300-year-old opera may not command the popularity that has fallen to Gluck's more richly inspired work, but, as the masterpiece of a great innovator, it should have opportunities of being heard from time to time. Gratitude to Mr. Robert Stuart and his Oxford associates for rescuing it from oblivion ought to have been substantially demonstrated ; though for my own part I had not anticipated a better showing from the Covent Garden and Queen's Hall highbrows, whose musical tastes still remain singularly limited. The professional musicians on this occasion were either unable to afford the Scala prices (which were, it must be admitted, rather high, even for members of the Imperial League of Opera), or else they were, like the god Baal referred to by Elijah, " peradventure in a journey "—to conferences at Chester or The Hague or elsewhere. Well, it would have been worth their while to travel even farther to hear some of those wonderful choral madrigals, or to listen to Mr. Norman Allin for three minutes in his very touching rendering of the divine passage (not of the Styx) allotted to Charon. They would likewise, I am sure, have enjoyed Mr. Dennis Noble's pathetic delivery of the music of Orpheus.

Apart from the numerous " square pegs in round holes " that marred most of the casts, one unfortunate mischance, due to inexperience, was that of the second night, when Purcell's glorious *Dido and Æneas* was mutilated and squeezed into the final fifty minutes to make room for practically the whole of the Locke and Gibbons masque, *Cupid and Death*. One hour of this interesting curiosity of the Cromwellian period would have amply sufficed. As it was, it lasted nearly an hour longer, and just that much of it proved extremely tiresome. The solo-singing on that evening was particularly moderate; but, on the other hand, I thought the seated choristers, who lined either side of the stage, did their work excellently, and the dancing was the most fancifully grotesque and graphic that could well be imagined.

To hurry the tempi of *Dido and Æneas* or abbreviate it by a single bar—on the rare occasions when it is performed—is to my thinking nothing less than a crime. Cut Handel or Mozart if you must; one could have done with even less of *Julius Cæsar*, and (after that amazing first act) with about two-thirds of what was actually given of *La Finta Giardiniera*. But such a miracle of symmetrical grace and perfection like the earliest flower of English Opera was surely not to be made to suffer for anything. Well, let that pass. I could have forgiven the lapse more readily had there been a different Dido. No one would deny Miss Denne Parker the possession of intelligence or artistic feeling; but Dido needs to be young and beautiful; neither too tall nor too stout; above all, she requires, in addition to a fine voice, the breadth and sonority of tone essential for noble declamation, for the dramatic power of a first-rate actress. None of these qualities did Miss Denne Parker command in satisfying measure. Yet for some reason or other she was entrusted, not only with the rôle of the Carthaginian Queen, but with one or two prominent parts in the classical works that preceded Purcell's. I will only add that the lively, reassuring Belinda, Miss Annette Blackwell—now growing into a very charming singer—proved far more equal to her task than her solemn mistress.

The dressing of *Julius Cæsar* provided capital fun, and that, to my thinking, was the best excuse for attempting it. Combined with the humours—the " heroics and absurdities,"—of the high-falutin' dialogue, the fantastic garments of the early Georgian epoch displayed upon the backs of Roman warriors and Egyptian kings and queens, went a long way towards atoning for the *lâches* of the singers. Nor was it only the costumes and the lines that made the audience rock with laughter. Some of the characters, notably the Egyptian villains, went " all out " for the manners of the transpontine drama, and burlesqued one incident after another to their heart's content. It was, in fact, amusing to see Ptolemy and his blood-thirsty general, Achillas, strutting behind Julius Cæsar, with their drawn daggers ready to stab him in the back had they only dared; which of course they did not. And to behold Cleopatra herself, dancing about the stage in a crinoline skirt of huge dimensions, for all the world like a Parisian grisette of the ante-Balzac period—that was also good fun. But I fear these feasts for the eye diverted one's attention a good deal from the Handelian side of the show. What of the music, indeed? I confess I went to the Scala knowing only two or three of the arias in *Julius Cæsar*—one of which, the beautiful *Piangerò la sorte mia*, was unfortunately omitted by Mr. Arthur Fear after he had given us the whole of the recitative—and I went away feeling every bit as unfamiliar with the remainder of its " lovely music " (to quote Mr. Stuart) as when I entered the theatre. One reservation should be made, however, and that applies to the admirable work of Mr. Gervase Hughes, both in arranging the score and conducting the efficient orchestra, including the faultless accompaniments played upon the harpsichord by Mr. Boris Ord.

This experience with *Julius Cæsar* has not tended to heighten my confidence in the revival of Handel's operas as a regular feature in the *curriculum* of the lyric stage. They may serve for an occasional *succès de curiosité* but nothing more. Whatever the beauties contained in the scores, they do not repay either the time or the outlay that has to be expended upon a whole evening's entertainment. The species, *quâ* opera, is virtually as extinct as the North American dinosaur whose skeleton was recently discovered in Morocco, and nearly as far removed from its original habitation. Moreover, I feel bound to repeat, because the fact cannot be over-emphasised, that we no longer have stage singers capable of doing even moderate justice to this music, and only a few who can sing it properly upon the concert platform. Still less would it appear that our modern vocalists are being trained, as they were in bygone days, to be able to combine both *métiers*. In this matter Handel is much worse off than Mozart, as was plainly illustrated in the next of the Scala reproductions.

For *La Finta Giardiniera* was by no means badly sung. It was entrusted to an entirely distinct group of interpreters, three or four of whom could act as well as sing, and, being treated in the genuine *opera buffa* spirit, remained fairly amusing until the inanities of the plot became involved to an extent that bordered upon mere go-as-you-please clowning. I give Mr. Nugent Monck, of Norwich, all credit for what he did for the " production " of Mozart's youthful opera. It was through no fault of

286

his that its absurd puerilities proved too much for him long before the end. The impression made by the music was really extraordinary in its anticipation of the maturer Mozart. Again and again did I find myself listening to phrases in the various voices and ensembles, to passages in the orchestration, that occur almost note for note in *Don Giovanni*, *Le Nozze*, and *Il Seraglio*. That Mozart should have already imagined and fashioned these things in his mind when little more than eighteen years old seems as much of a miracle as the feat achieved by Mendelssohn with the music to the *Midsummer Night's Dream*. But in *La Finta Giardiniera* there is too much music, with no Shakespeare to keep your interest alive. The airs and finales are dragged out to regulation Mozartian length, whilst you are all the time resenting the total absence of real comedy or of the smallest rational excuse for interrupting, let alone explaining, the action. Yet, as I said earlier in this article, the first act is a delight—pure, sweet, delicious Mozart from beginning to end—and, were the rest only as good, the opera would not to-day be the " unknown quantity " that it is. Miss Noel Eadie sang nowhere else with the pathos and the unaffected charm that she did in this scene ; the rich timbre of Miss Marjorie Parry's voice there made its fullest effect ; while Mr. Edward Leer and Miss Doris Lemon both showed good art and the right spirit in their work. Apart from these young people, the hero of the performance stood on the other side of the footlights, in front of the harpsichord, which he manipulated himself for the recitatives. I refer to that clever and accomplished conductor, Mr. Leslie Heward.

Considerable regret, but no surprise, was felt when it was announced that the projected revival of Gluck's *Alcestis* would have to be abandoned. If nothing else had caused difficulties—and there were doubtless many—the complete indifference of the opera-going public to this Scala enterprise was quite sufficient to account for this. Opera is an expensive luxury even in Charlotte Street, and you cannot go on playing to comparatively empty houses for a fortnight without feeling the financial strain rather acutely. I felt glad, therefore, when Sir Thomas Beecham saved the ship by conducting *Der Freischütz* for five nights instead of three, and so allowing time for a more profitable wind-up. This was precisely what happened. As soon as the " follow-my-leader " crowd heard how well Weber's opera had been put on, and that the aristocratic highbrows had at the last moment taken up the show, there was quite a respectable rush for seats, and the concluding performances drew crowded audiences.

Whilst not altogether agreeing with Mr. Robert Stuart that *Der Freischütz* is to the Germans what the Savoy operas are to us, since they belong to types too dissimilar for such a comparison, I fully admit that its irresistible appeal to the national love of sentimental romanticism, apart from its delightful music, is the true secret of the extraordinary popularity that *Der Freischütz* has enjoyed in Germany for some 110 years. It had its day—as Weber in person also had—in this country, too, where it was heard in English so long ago as 1824, or two years before the composer died almost in the act of bequeathing us his beautiful English opera *Oberon*. Having heard both these operas magnificently sung as a youth, I am naturally very fond of them ; hence my ability to enjoy *Der Freischütz* whilst retaining vivid memories of Tietjens and Pauline Lucca as Agathe, not to mention Foli and Faure as Caspar, or Nicolini and Bettini as Max. Perhaps I laid less store in those days upon the historic importance of Weber's masterpiece ; for it was too soon in the 'seventies to estimate its tremendous influence upon Wagner or upon the development and evolution of German romantic opera. Nevertheless its neglect in recent times has to me been utterly inexplicable. It has been so complete that I have failed to find even a mention of the title in the H.M.V. *Opera at Home*—an omission that I feel sure will be speedily remedied now.

One valuable feature was certainly brought out by Sir Thomas Beecham's reading of the score, in conjunction with the staging and production of Mr. H. Procter-Gregg : and that was the unmistakable atmosphere, the genuine Teutonic spirit, of the whole revival. It pervaded the work of every member of the cast and chorus, not to mention an orchestra that was really worthy of the alert baton which directed it. Mr. Arthur Fear's Caspar was a vast improvement upon his Julius Cæsar ; in the famous drinking-song and the splendid music of the casting of the magic bullets he was wholly admirable. Mr. Tudor Davies seemed not at his ease in the part of Max. Miss Thea Phillips made an imposing personage of Agathe and, acting with sincerity, displayed a fine voice and artistic method in *Softly sighs*. The Aennchen of Miss Nora Gruhn was sprightly and vivacious ; in her long scene with Agathe her resonant if slightly hard tone and neat technique told exceedingly well.

Altogether, then, *Der Freischütz* lent unexpected glory to the termination of this artistically interesting, if financially disastrous, operatic venture. Once more let me say that Mr. Robert Stuart and his friends had my warmest sympathy. They laboured with a whole-hearted devotion that merited a far more adequate reward. They have also earned some experience of a kind that practical work under adverse conditions can alone bring out. May it prove of equally practical value to them in the future should they ever be induced to try again ! Perhaps we shall see some of the real harvest in the early proceedings of the Imperial League of Opera.

HERMAN KLEIN.

THE GRAMOPHONE AND THE SINGER

(Continued)

By HERMAN KLEIN

The Columbia "Tosca" Album.—Destinn, Sammarco and Kirkby Lunn

AFTER a *Bohème* and a *Butterfly*, the issue of a *Tosca* Album might fairly have been anticipated. The race for popularity between the three operas is pretty even; and, if the first two are at this stage making something like a dead heat of it, it would scarcely be true to say that the other is a "bad third." Chronologically speaking, *La Tosca* came after *La Bohème* and before *Madama Butterfly*, the exact order of places and dates of production being as follows: *La Bohème*, Teatro Regio, Turin, February 1st, 1896; *La Tosca*, Teatro Costanzi, Rome, January 14th, 1900; and *Madama Butterfly*, La Scala, Milan, February 17th, 1904. I may add that the identical interval of four years between these was increased to nearly seven before Puccini completed his next opera, *The Girl of the Golden West* (New York, December 10th, 1910), which has proved in the literal sense a very bad fourth, if not already beaten for that position in the public esteem by the posthumous *Turandot*.

As everyone knows, the libretto of *Tosca* (originally so called without the *La*), was founded by Illica and Giacosa upon the melodramatic play written for Sarah Bernhardt by Victorien Sardou. Puccini, always thirsting for a strong emotional story to serve as subject for an opera, was absolutely right in his instinct about this play, just as he was wrong about *The Girl of the Golden West*, which he would never have selected but for the authorship and influence of David Belasco, the adroit producer who had converted *Madame Butterfly* out of a magazine story into a successful stage play. I had seen Sarah Bernhardt in *Tosca* several times both in Paris (on the night after the *première*) and in London, so I felt fully justified in congratulating Puccini upon his choice of a subject as soon as I heard he was working upon the score. He was right again in selecting that gifted Wagnerian soprano, Milka Ternina, to create the title-rôle at Covent Garden in July, 1900 (with Scotti as Scarpia, De Lucia as Mario, and Gilibert as the Sacristan), albeit at the time the critics, unacquainted with her all-pervasive genius, were doubtful about her suitability for the part. The opera made a hit here from the outset, and Ternina shared with the composer a series of triumphant recalls such as I have never known to be exceeded for enthusiasm on a Covent Garden first-night.

Notwithstanding this and the universal success that follows, the late R. A. Streatfield wrote in his article on Puccini in the second edition of *Grove's*

Dictionary (mostly reprinted in the third) some rather funny things about *Tosca*—things that I should hardly have expected from such a reliable judge, in fact, an exceptionally able writer of books on opera. He says, *inter alia*, that the libretto "is a prolonged orgy of lust and crime, which lends itself but ill to musical illustration"; adding that "Much of *Tosca* is hardly more than glorified incidental music," and that "the passions treated in it are often crude and sometimes monstrous," while allowing that Puccini, in the airs for Cavaradossi and Tosca and in the whole of the last act, showed that his "power of expressing certain aspects of emotion was maturing in a very remarkable manner." I need scarcely say that I regard this criticism of the opera as sheer exaggeration—a wholly mistaken view of the nature of Sardou's drama, and an opinion so isolated and absurd that I would not have drawn attention to it here and now but for the fact that *Grove* is justly looked upon as a world-wide authority, and that "R. A. S.," when dealing with opera, was supposed to know what he was writing about. In this particular case, however, poor Streatfield was clean off the target.

In one respect the preparation of the Columbia *Tosca* album has brought to light a distinction for which it is probably unique: that is, the extraordinary profusion of stage indications and directions crowding every page of the libretto. This is not surprising when one remembers its Sardouesque origin; but it makes rather an effort the task of following the text quickly enough whilst the gramophone is reproducing the music, and to meet that difficulty the "free" translator has suggested in a special note the advisability of reading the libretto through beforehand. The advice ought certainly to be followed, even at the expense of half-an-hour (or less), because a previous acquaintance with the plot and dialogue cannot fail to enhance the interest of the opera as a whole. In a darkened opera house nowadays there is no possibility of following a performance with the book or the score. (And a good thing too. It is bad for the eyes and detrimental to the enjoyment of the acting and stage effects.) But your true opera-lover takes care, at least, to know all about the drama in advance, and the same rule may properly apply to listening to the music at home.

The new Columbia recording of *La Tosca* has been done with the co-operation of the Milan Symphony

Orchestra, under the direction of Cav. Lorenzo Molajoli. The chief parts are allotted as follows : Floria Tosca, Bianca Scacciati ; Mario Cavaradossi, Alessandro Granda ; Scarpia, Enrico Molinari ; Angelotti, S. Baccaloni ; The Sacristan, Aristide Baracchi ; and Spoletta, Emilio Venturini. The complete opera is reproduced on fourteen 12in. discs (two sides each, Nos. 9930 to 9943), and is, of course, sung in Italian. Careful thought has evidently been given to the division of the various episodes, with a view to meeting the exigencies of the music and the capacity of the disc. Experience teaches ; and I am bound to say that the interruptions for changing the records seem more timely and less irritating than they used to be. Indeed, until mechanical ingenuity is equal to the achievement of a device equivalent to the " non-stop " of an express train, I fail to see how the inevitable breaks could have been better glossed over than they are in this instance.

Where modern operas are concerned, little if any systematic division into " numbers " is practicable (*tant mieux !*), and consequently little is to be gained from an attempt to criticise the series of records one by one on individual merits. Well-known and popular excerpts have naturally separated themselves from their environment, both for convenience sake and other cogent reasons. Yet it is hardly essential for me at this hour to describe in detail how Alessandro Granda has meted out entire justice to *Recondita armonia* and *Lucevan le stelle* ; or with what dramatic intensity Bianca Scacciati has realized the vocal and histrionic potentialities of *Vissi d'arte*. Enough that these familiar friends do stand out the more vividly because they are led up to amid their legitimate surroundings and can be the better appreciated in the light that is thrown on their actual meaning and significance. So, again, with the fine passage, *Se la giurata fede*, wherein Scarpia assumes an air of offended dignity when Tosca asks him his price for letting her lover go free. Only one sort of reward, he declared, and that not coin of the realm, can induce him to forswear his oath of fidelity. This striking passage has been recorded separately before, but never, I am sure, with the splendid dramatic effect that Enrico Molinari contrives to infuse into it here.

And *Se la giurata fede* is only one among several incidental episodes that you may not know so well, but that grow upon you the more you hear them. Tosca's " Idyll " (as I myself christened it for Ricordi's publication some years ago) is another delightful bit of music that might easily escape notice, among the cross-currents of passion that flow through the love duet of the first act. It is charmingly sung by Signora Scacciati ; and the sympathetic quality of her voice is not so apparent throughout as it is in this case, though on the whole I must concede her Tosca to be a very admirable performance. The Church scene from first to last is exceedingly well done. Its musical importance speaks for itself, but its dramatic purport, even on the stage, cannot somehow be said invariably to emerge with entire clarity. More particularly, the relations between the fugitive Angelotti and the painter Cavaradossi ; how the face of the former's sister comes to be in the latter's picture of Mary Magdalene, thus awakening the jealousy of Tosca and the suspicions of Scarpia ; why the discovery of the Marchesa Attavanti's fan should furnish the fatal clue that leads to Cavaradossi's arrest, torture, and death—these are all points extremely difficult to bring out in the ordinary way, while yet being vital to an understanding of Sardou's skilful plot. It is all to the good, therefore, to find the sequence of events clearly depicted and musically so well presented. The imposing *finale* of the first act is, as usual, a gorgeous combination of voices, bells, organ, orchestra, and distant firing of cannon, when the Cardinal is blessing the assemblage and gracing with his presence the *Te Deum* for the victory that never occurred. But the real connection of Scarpia with this scene is also made apparent.

In a sense, the so-called " horrors of the torture scene " in Act II. may be better read and heard about than witnessed ; but, as a matter of fact, they are of a kind that the present generation accepts with greater equanimity than did Victorian or even Edwardian opera-goers. Personally I would be content to ignore the realistic side of the whole business and regard it as I should a " close up " of that terrible young woman, the Jungfrau of Nuremberg. One can also enjoy to the fullest extent the orchestral delineation of the tragic episodes of Scarpia's death (with the crucifix and candle incidents), and all the powerful realism of the scenes winding up with the shooting of the unlucky Cavaradossi. The singing throughout these long-extended climaxes is uniformly excellent, the diction and the recording quite first-rate. The playing of the Milan Symphony Orchestra could scarcely be improved upon. The prelude to the final act is beautifully done.

* * * * *

The death of Emmy Destinn at Budweis (Bohemia), on January 29th, at the comparatively early age of 52, awakened keen regret in all who had heard her in her prime during the decade of grand seasons —1904 till 1914—when she regularly came to Covent Garden. The *Times* obituary notice was wrong in giving 1902 as the year of her début here, though stated correctly enough in *Grove's Dictionary* as 1904. She had then had four or five years' experience at the Berlin Opera, where she sang Salome on the production of Strauss's work at that house—and was probably too sensible ever to sing it anywhere else. I fancy, however, that I heard her in every one of her other important parts ; and

I would not readily have missed her in any. Her magnificent Senta, first seen at Bayreuth in 1901, I can never forget. It was the pure ideal of Wagner's concept, and it was that achievement which started her world-reputation. Next to it I would bracket her Aïda and her Donna Anna—the rôle wherein she made her London début under Hans Richter. With Ternina here, she refrained from attempting Elisabeth, but did well as Elsa and Nedda ;—less well, however, as Carmen in 1905, the year in which she scored her great triumph as Madama Butterfly on the first production here of Puccini's opera. At that memorable *première* she sang superbly, with Caruso as Pinkerton, Scotti as Sharpless, and Campanini conducting. Fine actress no less than fine singer, her genius demanded parts with broad and ample scope ; hence her impressive Valentine and her sympathetic Santuzza.

In America (1910) Destinn created the heroine of Puccini's *Girl of the Golden West*, but could not command in it a striking success either for the opera or herself. A similar verdict awaited the Covent Garden production in the following season. She did more, to my thinking, for Baron d'Erlanger's opera, *Tess*, produced here in the same year (1909) that we saw her with Sammarco in a revival of *La Tosca*, in which she was very fine indeed. In point of fact there was no one superior to her in the melodramatic Puccini rôles. Her voice was remarkable for the depth and intensity of its ringing timbre, its individual and sympathetic quality, its smoothness and carrying power, and its easy, effortless *sostenuto*. She was a singer of rare intelligence and obvious sincerity, and most schools came alike to her when the music suited her organ.

Like a good Bohemian, she strongly advocated the cause of her compatriot, Smetana, the composer of *The Bartered Bride*, whose operas she admired immensely. As I have previously noted, Emmy Destinn made some excellent gramophone records, especially from the Verdi and Puccini operas, and they include interesting duets in Czech with Dinh Gilly, besides others with Caruso, Martinelli, McCormack, and Kirkby Lunn. Unfortunately these were made (for His Master's Voice) prior to the days of electrical recording ; but they are nevertheless well worth having, as living souvenirs of a gifted and beautiful singer. She last visited London in the summer of 1919 to sing at the Czechoslovak Festival at Queen's Hall, and also appeared at Covent Garden in a couple of her favourite characters.

Another singer much admired in the world of opera and the gramophone, Mario Sammarco, also died last month. Born at Palermo in 1873, he was a close contemporary of Emmy Destinn, having made his début at Covent Garden as Scarpia during an Italian autumn season in the same year that she first appeared here, namely, 1904. The rôle was one in which he was often to sing with her, though not,

I fancy, for the succeeding four years, when Scotti was available for his incomparable impersonation. Of these two baritones Scotti was the finer Scarpia, while Sammarco—in a vocal sense, at least—was by a long way the superior Rigoletto. That was his best character, and, indeed, at the period in question Sammarco may be said to have shared with the Frenchman, Renaud, the distinction of being the finest Jester to be heard in Verdi's opera. His Marcello (to Melba's Mimi) is another fragrant memory ; likewise his Tonio in *Pagliacci*, his Barnaba in *La Gioconda*, his Count Gil in *Il Segreto di Susanna*, and, of course, his Gérard in Giordano's *Andrea Chénier*, a part which he created at La Scala and also here in 1905.

Sammarco had a voice of singular purity, breadth, and vibrant power, always in tune, well controlled, and capable of deep as well as varied expression. He was a capable actor, and invariably imparted to his embodiment a sense of adequacy and dramatic intelligence. He made only a few records for H.M.V., all of them pre-electric ; and the sole example from *Rigoletto* was the quartet sung with Melba, McCormack and Edna Thornton.

In Louisa Kirkby Lunn, who, to the general regret, also died last month, there passed from this busy scene the best English singer that our lyric stage had possessed during the first two decades of the century. I remember well her début in a performance of Schumann's tedious opera, *Genoveva*, given by the Royal College students at Drury Lane, in December, 1903. This is what I said about her in the *Sunday Times* : " Still more conspicuous was the success won by a Manchester student, Miss Louisa Lunn, in the character of the witch Margaret. Thanks to the broad declamatory method and impressive style of this youthful mezzo-soprano, the wicked old beldam was elevated into a personage of the first importance. Miss Lunn has a remarkably fine voice and she is evidently gifted with true dramatic instinct." The accuracy of this estimate was abundantly verified during the years of good work and experience that followed with the Carl Rosa Opera Company and subsequently at Covent Garden, where, of course, Mme. Kirkby Lunn reaped her proudest laurels. An inclination to abuse the chest register was by then more or less overcome, and the rich quality of her timbre gradually spread to the head register, where it resounded powerfully in declamatory passages. After her training under Visetti she studied for a short time under Bouhy in Paris, and, later still, was coached by Jean de Reszke for the parts of Amneris and Dalila, wherein she achieved the most brilliant triumphs of her career. She had musical intelligence and imitative gifts ; she was a born actress ; and, as I found when she studied Kundry with me in New York, she was a genuinely hard worker.

HERMAN KLEIN.

THE GRAMOPHONE AND THE SINGER

(Continued)

By HERMAN KLEIN

The Improving Operatic Outlook: A Suggestion

IN the middle of February there appeared in *The Times* a most unusual phenomenon, in the shape of a leading article headed "Operatic Production." I found on reading it that the immediate motive thereof lay in another column of the same issue of the paper, to wit, a long contribution from its Milan correspondent all about the "Economic and Artistic Difficulties" of "Opera in Italy." It appeared that the well-known journal, the *Corriere della Sera*, had sent round a questionnaire to the composers, conductors, critics, singers, impresarios, and music publishers, asking what they thought about operatic affairs generally; and the answers had in the main afforded rather unpleasant reading. The three great opera houses of Milan, Rome, and Naples were in the same boat as the 24 other first-class opera houses in Italy; for "All these theatres, although in the past they have never made great profits, are now run at a loss." The causes of this common deficit were said to be various; yet the explanation was practically the same in every case. Expenses were largely in excess of income, thanks to the high fees that had nowadays to be paid to artists, the heavy cost of mounting new operas which did not attract the public, the costliness of the *mise en scène* generally, and the Government taxes on entertainments; and thanks also to counter-attractions like the cinema, the wireless, etc.

The remedies proposed were, like the grievances, "various." But, as the *Times* leader pointed out, "Genius is not to be commanded," and composers like Verdi and Puccini, who can fulfil their own artistic aspirations whilst proving that they merit the big expenditure, are not forthcoming very often either in Italy or any other country. The composers of to-day have "little or no sense of responsibility towards their audiences;" yet they claim their right to a hearing where there is really no right in the matter. The remainder of this sensible article was devoted to an appeal for further subscribers in support of Sir Thomas Beecham's Imperial League of Opera; nor is it to be denied that the two branches of the subject—opera abroad and at home—have enough in common, despite their different conditions, for us to be able to profit by the mistakes of others. Financial difficulties are being encountered at the great operatic establishments of Berlin, Vienna, and even Paris. The only country that escapes entirely, because it can afford to spend what it pleases, is wealthy America.

Very soon after the *Times* exposé of the Continental operatic situation had appeared, I paid Sir Thomas Beecham a visit and had a long chat with him. As usual, he gave utterance to some quaint and interesting observations. To begin with, he could not see that the state of affairs on the Continent need interfere in the slightest with the progress of the operatic crusade in this country, which, so far as he was concerned, appeared to be making slow but sure progress. The League would have no subsidy from the State to help it (at any rate at the outset) but only the support of its subscribers and the public; and that looked like proving adequate enough for a punctual start to be made next autumn. Should a preliminary season take place in London under his direction between May and July, the responsibility for such an undertaking would be exclusively his. As to the lines contemplated for the artistic working of the League, he had two policies in view, but exactly what they were he preferred not to say until he knew for certain which of them would be adopted. He had made up his mind, however, not to perpetuate the old mistake of selecting his repertory to suit the capacity and individual ability of his company. On the contrary, he meant to settle upon the operas first and then proceed to engage the artists best fitted to interpret them. "My idea," he said, "is that we should labour neither for the work nor the singers, but for the establishment."

Other matters of interest that emerged in course of our interview included a plan for dividing the personnel of the League into two separate units—one for London, the other for provincial or touring purposes, both of them to work during most of the year and thus afford continuous employment for the best available talent. It was desirable that London should remain the centre of International Opera, because the greater its prestige in that respect the greater would be its prestige as the centre of National Opera, and the League might become the parent organization of similar establishments which, Sir Thomas hoped, would gradually spring up in the leading provincial centres. Finally, he unfolded a project, to which he attached particular importance, for organizing a periodical exchange of complete companies between the League and certain Continental opera-houses like, for instance, the National Theatre at Prague. There the fine operas of Smetana and Dvorak were sung only in the Czech

291

language, neither of which we had heard over here, any more than the inhabitants of Prague had ever heard an opera sung in English. By the interchange of entire troupes during a brief period, unprecedented facilities would be afforded for enjoying perfect manifestations of the lyric art of the various countries who entered into this mutual arrangement.

So much for the League and its founder's intentions. Let us now consider for a moment one or two important correlative questions which, at the moment I am writing, still remain unsolved. The first of these is the problem of an opera-house, which seems to me to be no nearer solution to-day than it was when the project of forming the League was originally started. You cannot give opera on a large scale, or indeed on any scale worth mentioning, minus a theatre that is adapted for the purpose; and what that entails I have discussed too often for it to be necessary to say more about it now. But, supposing the suitable locale to be available, what about artists, chorus, scenery, costumes, and all the rest of the indispensable accessories? How are they to be collected and got into working order within the space of a few weeks or even months?

Even allowing, as regards *mise en scène*, that Sir Thomas Beecham might have at his disposal the valuable material that passed from his hands to those of the B.N.O.C., there still remains the matter of the singers—singers capable, experienced, and distinguished enough to be fit for the high-class performances expected from the Imperial League of Opera. Can these be obtained in a moment, as it were, by the waving of Prospero's wand or the rubbing of an Aladdin's lamp? Do we not know for a certainty that all the best suitable artists are already engaged for long periods in advance in different parts of the world? They are not so numerous that we can expect it to be otherwise.

Then a yet more weighty question looms up: How far is the leader of the new enterprise taking into consideration—as so skilful a strategist must assuredly be doing—the effect of the very strong position that has now been assumed by the Covent Garden Opera Syndicate? There can no longer be the smallest doubt about the success of the move that was inaugurated in the provinces last autumn. Excellent performances were given in English by the powerful company gathered under the able leadership of Mr. John Barbirolli, which earned the warmest praise from the local press and drew consistently crowded audiences in most of the large towns. The impression thus created is not going to be quickly forgotten and we may expect it to be repeated every time Colonel Blois chooses to send his forces upon a similar expedition. What is more, I understand that this year's autumn tour is to be preceded by a season of a month at Covent Garden, beginning in September, in course of which

Don Giovanni and *Rosenkavalier* will be the chief new productions of the Anglo-Italian company.

Meanwhile the opera-house in Bow Street will be fully occupied with the proceedings of the "grand season" which commences on the 28th of this month. Most, if not all, of the preliminary details were announced some time ago, together with the names of the lengthy list of celebrities that have been engaged—the most imposing by far that the present Syndicate has put forward. We know, moreover, that the campaign will open with the customary Wagner selection, including two complete representations of *The Ring*, and that the additions to the active repertory will comprise (in German) *Die Fledermaus* of Johann Strauss, and (in Italian) Flotow's *Marta*, Giordano's *Andrea Chénier*, and Montemezzi's *L'Amore dei Tre Re*. Among the revivals we are to have Gounod's *Roméo et Juliette*, Debussy's *Pelléas et Mélisande*, and *La Traviata*—this last with Rosa Ponselle as Violetta and the famous tenor Beniamino Gigli as Alfredo.

Such, then, is the outlook which I have ventured in the headline of this article to characterise as "improving"; and in that roseate light I would fain have my readers justified in regarding it. But—and now comes my final irrepressible query—what I want to know is, will there be room in Central London this year for both these undertakings to be profitably worked at the same time? I doubt it. The ground has not yet been sufficiently prepared. We shall be finding ourselves at the end of the struggle (and a struggle it cannot fail to become) in a position very much akin to the *impasse* they are now encountering in opera-bred, opera-loving Berlin, with their problem of having to support three opera-houses where they only need two. The result will be as bad as the effect of the railway train was to be upon Stephenson's "coo." It strikes me, therefore, that prevention in such a case would be infinitely better than cure, and I suggest that the best plan in the circumstances will be to avoid the struggle by merging the two enterprises into one.

There is no reason that I can see why this friendly "combine" should not be effected. These are days when amalgamation is in the air; when opposing concerns find it to their advantage to join forces, instead of wasting their strength upon deadly competition with each other. A simple course is open to the Covent Garden Opera Syndicate and the Imperial League of Opera as personified in Sir Thomas Beecham. The objects they have in view are practically identical. Let them avoid fighting and benefit their mutual cause by pooling their interests and operations. *L'union fait la force*, and by joining forces they will both stand a better chance of achieving complete success. The other course can hardly fail to bring disaster to one of them.

HERMAN KLEIN.

THE GRAMOPHONE AND THE SINGER

(Continued)

By HERMAN KLEIN

Elijah : Crucifixion : and Siegfried Albums

THE Columbia Company issues this month a new album of Mendelssohn's *Elijah*, made recently at the Westminster Central Hall under the direction of Mr. Stanford Robinson, the trainer and conductor of the B.B.C. National Chorus. It will be taken for granted that it represents the " last word " in the art of recording by the electrical process ; and so, indeed, it is. The only serious criticism I have to point in that direction is the mistake which appears to have been occasionally made of amplifying sound where the extraordinary degree of resonance obtainable from the big hall itself made further amplification entirely superfluous. I may be told, of course, that the empty hall was responsible for this effect ; but I hardly think it can have been, because the same relative degrees of strength do not pervade the whole of the recording ; and, curiously enough, I generally find in these cases that the solo voice which needs least reinforcement—the insistent tenor, for example—gets most of it. Well, I have always set my face against overamplification ever since it started, and I always shall. It lessens the beauty of the tone by distorting the natural timbre and lending it a fictitious volume and power that sometimes render the singer unrecognisable.

Let me hasten to add that the fault I am complaining of is not so conspicuous in this *Elijah* album that it cannot be easily counteracted by the use of a soft needle ; neither is it on the whole employed to the extent that marks the H.M.V. recording of Stainer's *Crucifixion*, which I have to speak of directly. I daresay gramophone-lovers are becoming used by now to the " abuse of power " manifested in the modern record ; and, as it does not actually spoil voices, but merely reduces their measure of charm—a result that the singers themselves ought to be the first to protest against—I will content myself with hoping that the matter may ere long satisfactorily adjust itself to the satisfaction of all parties, myself included.

Taken as a whole, this performance of Mendelssohn's great oratorio gives a wonderfully vivid idea of its dramatic beauty and grandeur. I do not say I agree with all Mr. Robinson's tempi. Many of them are a good deal quicker than the composer's traditions, as handed down to conductors who knew him personally, would be thought to have justified. But there can be no questioning the value of the atmosphere of briskness and vigour that the B.B.C. conductor imparts to the livelier choruses, or the unforced spirit and energy which he has extracted to the last ounce from his highly intelligent singers. For instance, the Baal choruses, the *Thanks be to God* and the *Be not afraid*, are so strong, clear, and impressive that I doubt whether a finer effect could have been obtained herein from any oratorio choir in the Country, not omitting the Leeds Festival Chorus itself. The values in the dramatic scenes are brought out with singular fulness and precision, the balance with the well-trained orchestra being admirably preserved.

Coming to the execution of the solo parts, pride of place as well as the warmest tribute of praise must appropriately be allotted to Mr. Harold Williams for his splendid interpretation of the rôle of the Prophet. One hears much in these days of the demand for " Security." Well, there is no need to clamour for it here. From the first phrase of the significant opening recitative, Mr. Williams makes you feel absolutely sure of him, that he is literally " in the skin " of his part and probably singing every note of it into the microphone without the aid of a score. What is more, his control of tone-colour is masterly, and enables him to characterise quite definitely the varying emotions that Elijah has to portray in course of the drama. Contrasts like that between *Lord God of Israel* and *Is not His Word like a fire ?*, between the scenes with the Widow and the Youth, and the lovely *It is enough*, and the sarcasm of the remarks addressed to Ahab and his people, do one good to listen to. It would have been well had Miss Clara Serena imbued with equal truth of contrast her *Woe unto them* and her *Rest in the Lord*. They sound too much alike in feeling ; the deprecatory vein of reproach in the former is missing, while in the latter there are too many slurs. Miss Isobel Baillie is excellent in the soprano solos, her *Hear ye, Israel* being extremely artistic, and her voice is heard to great advantage in the ensemble numbers. Mr. Parry Jones owes more than he needs to owe to the amplifier ; but the right needle can subdue him.

Taken for all in all, then, the Columbia *Elijah* is well up to their accustomed mark, and a most welcome addition to their list. I should mention that it is recorded on fifteen 10in. double-sided discs, numbered DB49–63, which strikes me as being a noteworthy economy of material, whilst preserving everything that is essential to the completeness of the oratorio. On this point a note in the first page of the text accompanying the album explains that a slight abridgement has been deemed essential (very wisely too), and "only such excisions made as competent judges have agreed as permissible." Further, that "In all cases the omissions are indicated, and comparison with the vocal score will show the exact passages not here included." Little is to be gained from making these comparisons, though I am aware that certain sticklers for "no cuts" enjoy themselves in their own fashion by doing that sort of thing. I can perhaps save them the trouble by assuring them that nothing has been omitted which it was really important or worth while to retain in any ordinary concert version of the oratorio.

When, a year ago, I reviewed the Columbia album of Stainer's beautiful Easter oratorio, I told the story of my visit in the composer's company to the St. Marylebone Parish Church to hear the first performance. I laid stress, moreover, upon the extraordinary world-wide popularity that *The Crucifixion* has won during the forty-odd years of its existence. It is music intensely imbued with religious spirit and with a descriptive power that loses nothing on account of its simplicity and unaffected melodious sweetness—on the contrary, it gains everything from those very qualities that differentiate it from modernism, and make it as easy of comprehension as the tunes of Handel and the chorales of Bach. Such music enters into the hearts of the people and lives there.

Small wonder, then, that H.M.V. should now have followed in the wake of their doughty rivals, after the lapse of a twelvemonth, and brought out *The Crucifixion* in album form. They have also imitated a wise precedent by reproducing what is evidently a church performance of the work—so much so that one can visualise dozens of small places of worship in out-of-the-way districts where the congregation can be provided by means of a gramophone with the genuine Easter treat contained in these records. The six discs, by the way, are two-sided 12in., numbered D1817–22 ; and they are also available coupled in sequence (D7219–24) for use with H.M.V. automatic models. The full text is not supplied, presumably because for the greater part any copy of the New Testament or, better still, the cheap Novello vocal score, will serve for that purpose. Instead, there are pasted on the inside cover some useful descriptive notes, signed A. R., dealing with

each of the twelve sides.* The analysis concludes with the statement that "This well-balanced and faithful recording will prove a source of infinite pleasure to those who have sung in or listened to Stainer's *Crucifixion* and who have always hoped to possess it in this permanent and intimate way."

On the whole I find this anticipation justified by the merit of the achievement. The two soloists are Richard Crooks (tenor) and Lawrence Tibbett (bass), and very excellent singers they both are, besides being the possessors of exceptionally pure, sympathetic voices. Alike in their tone and the manner of their delivery may be perceived that rare touch of reverential awe which their task called for, as well as a quality of English diction that is redolent of the best traditions of church singing. Had Mr. Tibbett attacked his words with the same strong consonants that he sounds in the middle and at the end of the syllables ; and had Mr. Crooks, with his admirably steady tone and delicate *mezza voce*, managed to avoid a slight lisp and a tendency to over-"refane" certain of his vowels, there would be absolutely no fault to find with these soloists. No less deserving of high eulogy is the rendering of the choruses by the Trinity Choir and the quite first-rate work done by Mr. Mark Andrews at the organ. Of the former both voices and words come through with remarkable clearness allied to unusual unanimity and purity of utterance. That "sturdy piece of writing," the chorus *Fling wide the gates*, is particularly spirited, and the lovely unaccompanied quartet, *God so loved the world*, is exquisitely sung.

Readers of THE GRAMOPHONE will have been prepared by the preliminary article which Mr. H. L. Walters wrote last month for the appearance of the album of five remarkable *Siegfried* records now being issued by H.M.V., and I draw particular attention to that article because it set forth very concisely all the necessary details connected therewith, and therefore spares me the duty of repeating them here. All the same, I find it hard to resist the temptation to describe in full my impressions as I followed the course of the three great scenes— one from each act of the most picturesque of all Wagner's music-dramas—that are embodied in this latest manifestation of the perfected science of record-making. Some, nay much, of the ground has been covered already. But I intend making no comparisons of the kind that Mr. Walters indulged in, though I feel justified in confirming every word that he uttered concerning the extraordinary merit of the collection as a whole. Experience teaches,

---

*It may be noted that the original recording of this Album is the work of the Victor Company at New York. The Trinity Choir is that of the famous Trinity Church, Broadway, where Mr. Mark Andrews presides at the organ. Both soloists are well-known vocalists, and some excellent records by Mr. Lawrence Tibbett have been noticed in THE GRAMOPHONE. The diction of these American singers might well be emulated by many engaged on similar tasks on this side of the Atlantic.—H. K. [Actually, this recording was made (on 27 & 28 May, 1929) in Victor's "Church Bldg. Studio" in Camden, N.J. The "Trinity Choir" was Victor's regular house group, which also recorded as the "Victor Light Opera Co." &c. Ed.]

even as resources expand and proficiency reaches higher levels. One begins to look for nothing less than perfection in this science; and in the present instance I am bound to admit that the acme of perfection appears to have been attained.

What we get here is neither more nor less than a faithful reproduction of a Covent Garden performance or, rather, such features of it as five two-sided 12in. discs will contain. Save that Mr Albert Coates is the conductor, and the orchestra the London Symphony—a distinction without a difference in aught but personnel—you could easily imagine yourself seated in, say, the fifth row of the stalls listening to last season's quartet of singers, viz., Lauritz Melchior (Siegfried), Albert Reiss (Mime), Rudolf Bockelmann (Der Wanderer), and Nora Gruhn (Der Waldvogel). It would be useless to open your eyes and look for Brünnhilde and the rest of them, because they are not included in this "show." I fancy, however, that you will find yourself sufficiently content for a single séance with the feast spread before you by this more limited banquet. To me it seemed just long enough, and I enjoyed it amazingly. What is more, I derived an extra amount of pleasure from being able to follow

it with the companionship of the score—a privilege that can never be enjoyed at the Opera, because there the lights are rigorously extinguished whilst the curtain is up, and one's visual attention, very properly, is wholly restricted to the business of the stage.

Lauritz Melchior is superb throughout. It is not alone his voice, his declamation, and his splendid freedom that you admire, but the contrasts of tone-colour wherewith he characterises the different phases of Siegfried's development—the fearless youth forging his sword " Nothung "; the tender yearning of the monologue in the forest and the colloquy with the bird; the daring spirit of defiance in the scene where he splits the Wanderer's spear in twain and dashes up the rocks to find his sleeping goddess. Albert Reiss, more musical than he sometimes lets his voice sound, is the same wonderful dwarf that he has been to my personal knowledge any time these thirty years. Rudolf Bockelmann and Nora Gruhn are so good in their respective parts that one wishes they had more to do, and from first to last the orchestral work is a marvel of clearness and beauty.

HERMAN KLEIN.

THE GRAMOPHONE AND THE SINGER

(Continued)

By HERMAN KLEIN

Opera : Its Advocates and its Enemies

ONCE more are we in the very midst of the opera season, and apparently no nearer to the fulfilment of all our wonderful ideas and schemes regarding operatic enterprise on a national scale than we were a year ago. Again I say, *plus ça change, plus c'est la même chose.* Miracles of reform and development are projected; nothing is actually accomplished. The one definite conclusion that can be arrived at without fear of its being delusive is the fact that where opera is concerned London and the provinces are at loggerheads. They are not of the same opinion upon any single feature of the question. Yes; they like opera well enough when it comes their way. But if you ask them what they want done about it, they will no more agree than any two music-lovers of one's acquaintance will agree as to the precise method that the B.B.C. ought to adopt in the matter of programmes and performers and regional organisation.

Now tastes differ more concerning music—as well the gramophone companies know—than anything else in the world except, perhaps, matters relating to the *cuisine* and, I might add, the heart. It is useless, therefore, to talk of providing entertainment for one type of cultured class in the hope of therewith pleasing all. It simply can't be done. There are as many varieties and degrees of appreciation for opera as there are for the drama, the music hall, and the cinema. In this country we are not brought up on opera as are our neighbours on the Continent, and maybe we are not yet quite ready for the kind of League opera house where a stock company can regale us every night of the week with a miscellaneous repertory ranging from the classical of Monteverde and Gluck down to the modern of Debussy, Krenek, and Milhaud. There is a time and a place for everything, and for none more than in operatic affairs.

Some people would argue that because Covent Garden is sold out night after night for these annual " star " shows that the Syndicate offers every May, June and part of July, the same amount of patronage could be safely counted on for as many weeks in the autumn, winter, or early spring; that is, supposing it were possible to collect the same artists and personnel at any other period or periods of the year. Yet let me assure all who are of that belief that nothing could be further from the truth. This wonderfully prosperous summer season is a delicate yet sturdy operatic plant of many years' growth and standing; in reality, however, it is an exotic that, in spite of its having been so long acclimatised, will not bloom at any other time of year save the present. Sir Augustus Harris and the Grand Syndicate tried opera at Covent Garden in the autumn for a good many years, but from a commercial point of view they never found it really worth while, and from the artistic they never reaped the smallest measure of gratitude.

That experience at least the Syndicate actually in control to-day does owe to the past. Together with the Covent Garden prestige (kept alive by the London press), it has inherited the statistics and the business records which show clearly what has to be avoided as well as what has to be done if the necessary interest on capital is to be earned. Hence its accurate choice of the right moment, the right material, and the right programme. It makes no mistakes. It knows exactly what London wants; hence the nightly crowds in the auditorium and the solid phalanx of cigarette smokers between the acts in the foyers and the corridors. Nothing like it was ever seen (or inhaled) within those stately walls before. But the same Syndicate is far too clever and wide-awake to take this same programme into the provinces when it goes there. When it gives its short season at Covent Garden in September and October it will show us precisely the class of operatic entertainment that it thinks suitable for London out of the season and for provincial audiences at any time. It will not include the *Ring* or the lofty joys of the German répertoire or the most precious and costly gems of the Italian. But it will be opera, and good opera at that; consequently well fitted to the requirements of the public for whom it is designed. I will add my sincere belief that, so far as it goes, no organisation working within these music-loving isles could do the job better.

Having attended very few of the German performances this year, I have been perusing the current criticisms in the daily and weekly papers with tolerable regularity, as well as with more than the usual amount of sympathy for those of my colleagues who find it hard to avoid repeating themselves. Not being so bold as Mr. Hubert Foss or so daring as Mr. Harvey Grace, I will not venture to mention various critics by name or complain of the manner in which they carry out their functions for their respective journals. Indeed, such is not the object of my reference to them. But I do want to take this opportunity of saying that in my opinion there is too much deliberate endeavour nowadays on the part of certain highbrow writers to discredit opera and operatic art in the eyes of the rising generation. These clever people never tire of pointing out what they consider the weaknesses and fatuities of the lyric drama as an art form. They proclaim its inconsistency and make-believe; they love to dwell on the abstract merits of music *qua* music and drama *qua* drama, but they will not allow that you can make an æsthetic combination of the two.

And pray why not? Does it never occur to these purists that the " conventions " peculiar to the stage and inseparable from it are not a whit less artificial and unlike real life when accompanied by speech only than when further illustrated through the medium of music and vocal utterance? If they object to opera, common sense demands that they should object just as much to plays—Shakespeare included. As it is, they affect to despise a type of work which they are obviously incapable of estimating at its true worth and in its true perspective. I was reading the other day in F. Bonavia's new book on Verdi* how some of the early critics of *Otello*—

praised the force and point of its dramatic style, but took exception to the lyrical parts, which seemed to hinder the development of the action.

Commenting upon this the author goes on to say—

Lyrical expression—it must be admitted—invariably retards action. Yet drama consists not merely of action, but of character as well, which lyrical expression may often present under a new aspect. Othello's farewell to the " pride, pomp, and circumstance of glorious war "—most frequently quoted as an unwarranted break of dramatic continuity—has a definite purpose, to show how Othello's mind is affected by Iago's plotting, how all that Othello loves best in the past is shattered by the knowledge of Desdemona's supposed treachery. It is lyrical poetry in the original, and could only be rendered by lyrical music. We understand the action all the better because Othello, having looked for a moment into his mind, gives expression to the gathering darkness.

Wagner has, of course, done the same thing in a different way in hundreds of instances, but Mr. Bonavia very justly refuses to allow that Verdi owes anything vital to Wagner for the methods which he developed in *Aida* and *Otello*. Nor is there anything in Verdi's interesting letters, which furnish the basic material for this study of his career and his operas, to warrant the belief that he ever had the least idea of imitating anybody. On the contrary, soon after he had completed and produced *Aida* he wrote to a friend—

*"Verdi," by F. Bonavia, Oxford University Press, London Humphrey Milford. Price, 7s. 6d.

Melody and harmony are merely the means which the artist has at his hand. If one day a time comes when there will be no longer any question of melody and harmony, of Italian and German schools, of past and future and the rest, then the kingdom of art will begin. . . . You tell me that I owe my success to the blending of the ideals of two schools. *I never gave a single thought to it.*

Precisely. The marvellous visionary powers possessed by these people who object to opera because they see in it things that they dislike also enable them to perceive intentions that neither librettist nor composer had in mind. They do not resent the intrusive yet explanatory comments of the Greek Chorus (which they tolerate, maybe, as a necessary evil), but they do object very noisily to the presence in an opera of a crowd of persons simultaneously giving utterance to a single thought in identical language. Well, Wagner himself took both sides in this argument, though he showed us what he really thought about it in *Die Meistersinger* and *Götterdämmerung*, where he manifested in the most emphatic and masterly manner his appreciation of what might be accomplished by a good operatic chorus.

But Wagner is Wagner. The critics of opera will seldom level their shafts at *him*—except to confess that he sometimes bores them sadly. Then why go to hear him? Because, I suppose, he is fashionable and all the best people go to listen to him as interpreted by the best artists. Besides, they feel somehow that they can put up with dragons, talking birds, and ladies who can swim and sing under water because the music is Wagner's—and rather fine music at that. I am convinced that the personality of the composer has a lot to do with it. Even Mr. Bonavia " sees red " when he brings in Meyerbeer, which he does in his book for the sake of proving how much " more reasonably Verdi's conspirators behave " in *Ernani* than do Meyerbeer's in *Les Huguenots*. In the latter, he thinks, " the loud shouts and the catlike tread of the conspirators are worthy of the stagecraft of Vincent Crummles." And pray, I would ask, is there nothing of the " tuppence-coloured " about those nocturnal abductors in white silken hose who carry off poor Gilda, to the whispered refrain of *Zitti, zitti*, in the second act of *Rigoletto*?

I am afraid it is true that opera—particularly of the old-fashioned Rossini-Bellini-Donizetti type—is rather thickly sprinkled with the conventional absurdities and fatuities that arouse the ire of the moderns. But ought they really to matter sufficiently to give opera a bad name? For my own part I find that, after more years of it than the majority have had, I am still capable of enjoying the flavour of my favourite *morceaux*, provided they are served up with the artistic elegance and finish that is their due. The only trouble is that the requisite *maestria* in the handling is not often there.

HERMAN KLEIN.

THE GRAMOPHONE AND THE SINGER

(Continued)

By HERMAN KLEIN

Old Friends at Covent Garden

WHEN the Italian season begins at the Royal Opera there are always notable changes on both sides of the curtain. The German element dissolves into thin vapour; Wotan and his entourage cease from troubling; the Valkyries and the Gibichungs are at rest for another year; the "Fledermäuse" have fled back to their native soil, and the tones of the Viennese turtle are no longer heard in the land. Equally startling is the metamorphosis of the audiences. The corridors and foyers are less crowded and noisy, and, yes, less smoky too. The Teutonic has somehow given place to a more mellifluous sound of speeech; criticism by word of mouth is less emphatic and perhaps a trifle less harsh; the Walter that was entirely Bruno has changed into the Vincenzo that is a very dream of Bellezza.

All this is to be expected and well enough in its way. It were better still, though, if with the German operas there vanished less of the German discipline and the true German art spirit. Why must some—I do not say all—of the Italian stars reintroduce their bad old custom of coming out of their characters to bow and acknowledge with "wreathed smiles" the applause that greets their arias and *tours de force*? The new tenor, Beniamino Gigli, was a conspicuous offender in this repect. Why, again, should these privileged mortals have the right to dictate the particular operas in which they shall make their débuts or rentrées? For years, season after season, the illustrious Adelina Patti insisted on effecting her re-entry in *La Traviata* in preference even to her more favoured rôle of Rosina in Il Barbiere the reason being, I presume, that Violetta shows off her wonderful jewels and her latest Parisian gowns to such supreme advantage. In the same manner it would seem that we are to have Mme. Rosa Ponselle reappearing regularly in her admirable impersonation of Norma, oblivious to the fact that, despite its undeniable beauties, a little of Bellini's masterpiece, minus the tragic genius of a Grisi or a Tietjens, may be found to go a very long way.

For my own part, I have no objection whatever to listening to the still-popular "chestnuts" of the Italian répertoire, provided they are worthily sung and made interesting by artistic treatment of a high order. In other words, the opera house, with its attendant trouble and expense, must furnish something beyond the mere pleasure of hearing hackneyed selections or favourite airs sung by the most admired vocalists of the day. That much you can get out of any gramophone, and can still further amuse yourself by comparing at your will the various methods of interpreting the same pieces. The reader must be nearly as familiar with the pick of the records and the ever-growing album collections as I am myself. At Covent Garden last month I felt literally as though I were in the midst of a crowd of vocal friends whose little manneristic peculiarities I knew from A to Z. It even occurred to me that their efforts would give me nothing to criticize because I had carefully described and dealt with them all before. It might be true that I had never seen my friends Gigli or Zanelli *in propria persona*; yet I seemed to know them both intimately and, in a purely musical sense, could anticipate to hear what they would do with the *chevaux de bataille* of *Andrea Chénier* and *Otello*.

Now I say "musical sense" advisedly, since it is precisely when the operatic stage gives us the combination of the artist in person, the magnetic qualities of the living individual, the impressions which affect eye as well as ear, that we get something from the theatre beyond what we can derive from gramophonic reproduction, no matter how perfect. Speaking as an old critic who still loves a fine gramophone record much better than he does the best radio transmission yet vouchsafed the human voice, I am yet bound to confess that I feel safer in my judgment of a singer at first hand, as it were, with all the accompanying attributes of facial expression, gesture, histrionic power, and so forth, than I possibly can when listening only to the vocal reflection contained in the mechanical reproduction. The verdict delivered under these latter conditions ought always, I feel, to be handed in with a certain measure of reserve.

Hearing Mme. Ponselle's Norma once again suggested to me the likelihood of her being one of those artists who never alter their way of rendering a piece. Also that it is just as delightful to hear her *Casta Diva* from the H.M.V. record as when she is clipping the mistletoe from the primeval Covent Garden oak. Hers is indeed a lovely voice, and with it she makes an ideal record; but in reality she presents little variety of expression, and still fewer contrasts of tone-colour wherewith to enhance the effect of her unceasing restlessness of facial movement. To give examples: Ternina possessed this manifold power; Melba and Tetrazzini never had it. The Pollione of the *Norma* performance was the kind of tenor one is only too glad to forget; but the Oroveso should be mentioned for two reasons. First, he was Ezio Pinza, a real bass with a magnificent organ and a growing list of records; secondly, his tremolo is much less aggressive in the opera house than it sounds in certain of his gramophone efforts. If you like the latter (and I do), be sure you do not miss the next chance of hearing him.

I do not consider that Beniamino Gigli was well advised in choosing the rôle of Andrea Chénier for his English début. We are not exactly fond of Giordano's opera here; we find it rather heavy and noisy, and we are tired of stories of the French revolution in any kind of setting. In the United States, where Gigli has earned his fame and fortune, there are more Italians than there are in this country; hence their demand for modern Italian opera alike on the stage and in the recording *atelier*. So Gigli " fancied himself " in *Andrea Chénier* and it was duly revived for him—a specific case of the artist dictating the opera. Well, his clear, bright, ringing voice sounded extremely well in the *Improvviso* and in the duets with Maddalena (though no better than it does in the records), whilst at times when the drama became exciting he did a good deal of literal shouting. He ought never to be compared with Caruso; yet he often is. There are in reality very few points of similarity between them. Caruso's was a much darker, heavier tone, and it mounted with greater ease, smoothness, and sustained power to the high B flat, B, and C. Miss Margaret Sheridan showed improved head notes in *Andrea Chénier*, and Giovanni Inghilleri put to his credit some admirable singing as Gérard. But I cannot honestly declare that I enjoyed the opera.

Gigli's " second choice " was the part of Lionello in Flotow's *Marta*, and therein he hit the mark more accurately. The tuneful old opera, which had not been heard at Covent Garden for 34 years, was thoroughly enjoyed, despite an alteration in the cast, throat difficulties, and need for more rehearsal of the ensembles. The tenor was quite the best that has sung *M'apparì* in London since the days of Campanini and Ravelli; for his smooth, easily-held head register enables him to do entire justice to these sustained melodic phrases, so that he really gives you in his singing as well as in his acting just the right idea of the love-sick farmer. As I have previously indicated, his record of *M'apparì* is the gem that indirectly brought about the revival of Flotow's opera, which, I may now add, ought to be heard here as regularly as it is Germany and America. Miss Edith Mason, who was the Lady Enrichetta, has a charming light soprano voice and a no less charming stage presence, with a sprightly, vivacious manner to match. Owing, no doubt, to a lingering cold, her medium notes did not tell well in the concerted music, but such was the resonant quality of her head tone that no matter how delicately sung, it made itself audible against the other voices and in every part of the theatre.

I did not hear Miss Mason in *Madama Butterfly*, while Miss Maggie Teyte, who succeeded Miss Sheridan as *remplaçante*, sang so well in the third act, which we were privileged to hear broadcast, that I regretted not having listened to the whole opera from the auditorium. It struck me that Miss Teyte's voice had gained considerably in volume, and also that it possessed a new ring of dramatic fervour which might be capable at times of approaching the tragic. A relay of the third act of *Aida* on a subsequent evening proved less satisfactory. The voices never stood out quite clearly and the trio suggested the clang of noisy bells. Still, one could appreciate the beauty of Miss Eva Turner's high C as well as the growing richness of her low register. Similarly, imperfect transmission failed to cloud the splendour of Inghilleri's animated declamation as Amonasro, or to disguise the evidence of excessive effort in Francesco Merli's singing as Radamès, whose name the unlucky announcer at Savoy Hill gave out with the accent on the second syllable.

No one can complain that the operatic world is badly off for robust tenors, and among the best of them is Renato Zanelli, despite a certain throatiness or woolliness of texture in the higher register that is due to slightly faulty production. But for this his head notes would ring out with the same amazing power that distinguished those of his great model, Tamagno, and enable him to impress as *he* used to at the tremendous moments provided for him by Verdi in the part of Otello. Neither in his records nor in the opera can Zanelli be said to do this; and yet his performance leaves behind no sense of insufficiency, because, first of all, he sings the music with a wonderful command of colour and feeling, and, secondly, he is an actor of the very highest order. Long before hearing Tamagno as Otello, I had seen the two celebrated Italian tragedians, Salvini and Rossi, in Shakespeare's play, and I am fairly acquainted with the potentialities of the character. I can only say that I think Zanelli's conception and treatment of it masterly in the extreme. Without exaggerating aught, he depicts superbly the growth of jealousy in the Moor from the start to the climax of its delirium when, after striking Desdemona before the assembled Venetians, he falls prone upon the palace pavement. By contrast his tenderness in the last act was most touching, as a recent record of his clearly indicated it would be.

The Iago of Mariano Stabile remains the best we have had since Maurel's. He *thinks* his *Credo* in addition to singing it with a remarkable variety of nuance; and his *mezza voce* when relating Cassio's supposed *Dream* is just perfect as a *suggestio falsi* from the villain who fabricates his lie as he goes along.   By the way, the action of Stabile in placing his foot on Othello's chest when he lies prostrate on the ground is absolutely traditional, notwithstanding the assertion of a leading critic to the contrary.   It was done by Maurel at the Scala with Verdi's approval and at Boito's suggestion.   Iva Pacetti's Desdemona revealed many good points, but her voice is strangely uneven—beautiful in quality when she sings softly, harsh when she presses it; steady for bars at a stretch, then suddenly quite tremulous.   The same uncertainty of mood, or whatever it is, displays itself in her recording.   But neither as singer or actress is she " big " enough for the exacting ensemble of the third act of *Otello*.   This opera was splendidly conducted by Vincenzo Bellezza.

Much as I admire *Pelléas et Mélisande*, and greatly as I appreciated the merits of the performance given under Giorgio Polacco on June 17th, I am reluctantly coming to the conclusion that Debussy's only opera is not wearing well.   Maybe it ought to be heard in a theatre half the size of Covent Garden; maybe its poetry, its weird mystical charm, requires a certain intimacy and sustained delicacy of treatment that cannot be imparted to it in a big auditorium.   Whatever it was, I am bound to say that by the time we got to the third act I began to experience unmistakable symptoms of tedium and monotony such as I cannot remember having felt, for instance, when I first heard *Pelléas* sung at the Manhattan Opera House, New York, with the three members of the original Paris cast—Mary Garden, Jean Périer, and Henri Dufranne.   Nor can I altogether blame the artists of last month for this seeming deterioration, if such it were, in the psychological influence of this curious commingling of fantasy and unreality, of human weakness and brutality, of exotic harmonies and dialogue half-spoken, half-sung.   It is a combination that somehow does not grow upon one as one knows it better, and all the art in the world will not in that case prevent it from becoming wearisome to the ear and the soul.   I found Miss Maggie Teyte even more delightful in the part of Mélisande than when she sang it here years ago; she has grown perceptibly in artistic stature since then.   A new tenor, Roger Bourdin, displayed all the requisite mastery

of the traditions, without the charm of his predecessor; and John Brownlee as Golaud—pronouncing his French with ease and distinction, as became a reigning Parisian favourite—did wonders with a rôle that must always at best be difficult and ungrateful.   The orchestra was often too loud both for the music and the singers; as a whole, however, the delicate score was interpreted with infinite care and *spirituel* insight.

The revival of *La Traviata*, like that of *Norma*, was exclusively at the behest of Mme. Ponselle.   Her Violetta might not claim equality with the great ones of Patti, Nilsson, and Sembrich, but it was clever, well thought out, beautifully if fantastically gowned—in a word, attractive enough to have pleased instantly, which it did.   Musically speaking, the American soprano's reading of the part was extremely original; too much so at many points for the liking of those who knew how Verdi wanted his music to be sung.   He would not, for example, have approved the trick of starting every salient passage with the same subdued *pp cantilena*—audible thanks only to the telling timbre of a marvellous *mezza voce* —working up with a long, slow crescendo to the full voice.   This process the singer repeated again and again (generally commencing from a half-recumbent position if the dramatic situation permitted) at the approach of every climax, where, however, the power and volume of the tone frequently proved disappointing.   These features were noticeable more particularly in the duet with Germont *père* (finely impersonated by Inghilleri) and the concerted finale of the third act, where Angelo Minghetti (a capital Alfredo, by the way) considerably flung, not notes and gold, but an innocent-looking purse at Violetta's feet.   This ensemble was taken by Vincenzo Bellezza at an absurdly fast tempo, as the *Sempre libera* had also been, after an *Ah! fors' è lui* that was the most unconventional in my experience. Somehow I felt that an overweening desire for making new points was the keynote of Mme. Ponselle's clever delineation, and this fact lessened my admiration for it, whilst not blinding me to its many excellences. Anyhow, it drew several crowded and enthusiastic audiences.

HERMAN KLEIN.

THE GRAMOPHONE AND THE SINGER

(Continued)

By HERMAN KLEIN

The Story of my "Phono-Vocal" Adventure.—I

IT is a quarter of a century or thereabouts since the thing happened, and though I have made allusion to it at various times, I have never yet told the whole story. The reason why I propose to do so now is that people are beginning to talk about learning how to sing with the aid of a gramophone as though the idea were something new—actually believing, for the first time perhaps, that the notion is a practicable one. As a matter of fact, I developed and put it to the test myself, whilst living in New York in 1908-9, and can unhesitatingly attest to its entire efficacy. Only at that period the gramophone was in its infancy and commanding the suffrages of a very restricted public. The electrical process of recording had not yet been invented. In many ways I was disastrously before my time.

To-day there is talk of the possibility of useful vocal instruction by means of wireless lessons, reinforced by " living " examples of how to sing and study exercises. For the Radio teaches us many things connected with the art of music, besides languages and other educational blessings. But singing, it would seem, is not admitted to the curriculum of the B.B.C. as an educative factor—chiefly for the reason that it is an art which is not also a science; its rules are not definitely fixed; and there are too many opinions extant as to the correct way of imparting the right method (or methods.) Hence, a likelihood of occasions for those displays of righteous indignation and anger to which vocal teachers are so peculiarly prone when they find the " man in authority " enunciating views that happen to be opposed to their own.

So much by way of preamble. I come now to my story. I was lunching one day late in 1907 with the famous American soprano, Mme. Nordica, in her New York apartment, when she first broached the question of singing what she called " exercise records " for the use of vocal students. Good singing, she thought, was largely a matter of imitating good models, and these she was very anxious to provide with her own voice; if she were willing to sing them, would I provide the exercises? After due reflection, I saw Mme. Nordica again and told her that, in my opinion, if the device was to obtain a universal and not a limited value, the exercise models would have to be sung not by one voice only, but by four; and, moreover, that it would be essential forthwith to secure the co-operation of one of the leading manufacturers of gramophone records.

It happened that I had for a year or more been in close alliance with the Columbia (then called the America) Graphophone Company as its musical adviser; for that was the epoch of its bold and ultimately successful attempt to escape from the shackles of the early cylinder record and the trite, vulgar, popular Yankee tune and ditties to Sousa marches which then held the field. Already the round, flat disc was coming into use; the Columbia was emulating the example of the Victor Company in securing first-rate opera singers to make records of the principal arias from all the favourite operas. An orchestra was just beginning to be employed in addition to the piano for accompanying purposes; and very wonderful were some of the substitutes that were invented to replace the ordinary stringed instruments. The players would all crowd round the singer, in front of the solitary horn that communicated the sound-waves to the engraving needle as it inscribed its message (on the other side of a wooden partition) upon the revolving waxen matrix; and the whole business was about as uncomfortable, as uninspiring, as enervating, as anything you can possibly imagine.

I need scarcely say that my mission on behalf of Mme. Nordica was welcomed with open arms. I interviewed first one of the Vice-Presidents of the company, then the President himself (no need to recall names now); but it was chiefly with the former, an astute American lawyer for whom I was never a match in any respect, that negotiations were carried on. It was eventually arranged that Mme. Nordica should not only sing the proposed " exercises," but make some operatic records, for which generous royalties were to be paid. I was to engage the three other singers—contralto, tenor and bass—teaching them my exercises, when ready, the company paying them a lump sum each for their services; while my reward was to be in the shape of a small royalty on the records sold and a fixed sum on each of the accompanying instruction books, whereof I was to furnish the complete text. These were to be twenty in number more or less identical, but in different keys to suit the different voices; and they were to be sung on ten two-sided discs, the whole collection bearing my name and the title of " The Phono-Vocal Method." So far so good. Contracts were prepared and signed, the astute legal Vice-President having drawn them up himself, and at this point in the history of the affair things looked extremely promising. The troubles did not begin until later.

During the winter of 1907-8 I wrote the music for what I termed the "Exercise Records," also extensive preliminary instructions on technique and separate guiding observations for the study of each record as played upon the gramophone. The whole was based upon Manuel Garcia's *Hints on Singing*, which wonderful *résumé* of the principles of the art I had had the privilege of helping my old master to bring out when he was living at Cricklewood in 1894. Mme. Nordica thoroughly approved of my plan and liked the exercises, which were pretty comprehensive—too much so, in fact, and not quite so simple as I had really meant to make them for the ordinary self-training student. However, they were certainly varied, and covered the whole ground, from breathing, vowel formation, and attack down to phrasing, tone-colour and expression as exemplified in selected passages from oratorio, opera, and recitative.

Up to this time it had still been Mme. Nordica's intention to sing the soprano records herself. But fate willed that it should be otherwise. Her repeated attempts to do her voice and herself justice under the old primitive conditions still necessarily in vogue at the Columbia *atelier* (as at any other, for that matter) were proving more or less of a failure. One or two turned out well—for example, the *Suicidio* from *La Gioconda*; but with the majority she had been so dissatisfied that she openly confessed to me that she was growing too disheartened to try again.

This was rather a severe disappointment; the more so because I had not yet come across a tenor whose style—above all, one whose pronunciation of English—seemed pure enough to serve as a model for imitation by the rising generation of this world's singers. For the contralto and the baritone (or bass) records I had engaged respectively Miss Janet Spencer, a well-known and talented American singer; and a clever pupil of my own named Frederic Weld, who was just beginning to make a name for himself as a church singer in New York. Both of these were entirely familiar with the special kind of work that I was calling upon them to perform. Quickly mastering their task, they were soon ready for the further ordeal of proving that their voices recorded well and that neither vocal nor recording obstacles had terrors of any sort for them.

I was beginning to discover that the business was not such an easy one as I had imagined. It was not only good voices that I needed, but faultless production, perfect style, the ability to illustrate with unimpeachable accuracy every branch and feature of the art of singing. The search for a first-rate English tenor I decided to postpone for a time, or at any rate until my next visit to London. But how about a good soprano? True, sopranos were plentiful as blackberries in the United States; but the right one for the job proved extremely difficult to find. Find her at last I did, however, in the person of a clever Dutch artist, Mme. Jeanne Jomelli, who had recently come to America, and made a hit as Giulietta in *Les Contes d'Hoffmann* at Oscar Hammerstein's Manhattan Opera House.

Mme. Jomelli had a pure soprano voice of singularly clear, steady, musical quality, and she was an accomplished vocalist. She came to me to study English diction and generally to extend her *répertoire*. During the winter of 1908-9 we arranged that she should replace Mme. Nordica as my soprano model, and right well (being an artist of uncommon intelligence) did she conquer the details of her task. On the other hand, she found the process of making records less easy to carry out. Indeed, I repeat that the kind of operation which it constituted at that period made it neither pleasant of fulfilment nor certain as to its results even for the most experienced singers. It proved a long and tedious business. The able technical staff at the Columbia establishment showed the utmost good-will with the comparatively primitive means at its disposal. We thought ourselves fortunate, nevertheless, if we succeeded in completing three or four satisfactory records at each *séance*; and by the three voices there were sixty altogether to be done. To test the quality of the recording, we invariably re-played the first and sometimes the second rendering direct from the wax, which, of course, made those particular matrices useless; still, they served as a guide for correcting faults and improving details until we arrived at the best that could be done. This required great patience and concentration on the part of everybody—especially the singers.

But, strive as we would, the spring of 1909 was upon us with only the contralto and the bass records finished; the tenor, as I have explained, entirely untouched; the soprano, owing to certain difficulties for which Mme. Jomelli was not wholly responsible, going along very slowly. Another and much more serious trouble loomed upon the horizon: my time in New York was growing short. I had made arrangements for bringing my long 7½ years' sojourn in that city to a termination, and had booked passages for myself and my family to return in May to England, where I was going once more to take up my permanent residence. There was also to win my four sets of text-books from the clutches of the slowest music-printers that I had ever encountered in my life, and, not least of all, to settle certain delicate matters connected with the fulfilment of my rather one-sided contract with the American Graphophone Company. How these and other obstacles to the successful launching of my " Phono-Vocal Method " were ultimately overcome, I shall relate next month in a second article.

HERMAN KLEIN.

THE GRAMOPHONE AND THE SINGER

(Continued)

By HERMAN KLEIN

The Story of my "Phono-Vocal" Adventure.—II

BEFORE resuming this narrative I would like to to say something about the exact plan of a method which, although tentatively put forward twenty years in advance of its time, may yet prove to be of practical value to teachers of singing, as well as a guide and model for those whom circumstances compel to study the art without an instructor's direct aid.

In my preface to the text-book I began by saying that I had always refused to write a book on singing, " because of the extreme difficulty of offering effective instruction to would-be singers through the printed page alone, without the aid of the voice to illustrate my meaning." I added that the gramophone had supplied the missing link. The exercises provided in the records were " not supposed to be easy "; but they were essentially progressive in character, and each was to be studied only a few bars at a time, " not practised in entirety until every section had been mastered." Finally, I said, " The Graphophone reflects the voice as faithfully as the mirror reflects a face. The student who can hear both words and voice aright will find the key to the magic portal, and enter the Temple of Music that *rara avis*—a good singer ! " Some thirty pages of the book were devoted to preliminary instructions and concluding advice.

Then, in Part II., came directions for the use and study of the " Exercise Records." The music of each was printed on two staves, the top one showing the notes to be sung and the lower one simple chords to serve for the piano accompaniment, both corresponding exactly with those heard in the record. A series of " Notes for Study " followed the music in each case, referring the student to the correlative sections in the preliminary instructions and adding further advice of the kind that a teacher might give whilst showing his pupil what to do and what to avoid when practising. *Apropos*, let me here add that my idea for this method from its very inception was to make it serve not merely as a substitute, but as an actual and ever-reliable aid to the teacher in person. Teachers are liable to grow physically weary ; their voices are apt to lose freshness ; so it is not a bad plan to have at hand a machine such as the gramophone to help one at any moment with the labour of supplying the necessary illustrations.

To return now to my story. I had to leave New York, as I have said, in the May of 1909, and by the Easter of that year the soprano records were not nearly ready. The books were still coming in slowly from the printer, and I was making no further effort to find my suitable tenor. In the midst of these anxieties I was called upon by the A.G.C. to furnish a considerable cash payment for a large quantity of the records and text-books, as soon as they became available, in order therewith to secure the selling rights of my " Phono-Vocal Method " in Europe and all British Dominions excepting Canada, the product to be delivered after my arrival in England. The advance payment was duly completed long before the records were. Mme. Jomelli's share of the work went on so slowly and so many of her discs had to be done over again that my day of sailing actually arrived without the last one or two having been passed as satisfactory. (It should be remembered that I had had personally to supervise the preparation of the whole series and play all the accompaniments myself.) We managed to get through by the " skin of our teeth." I met my singer at the Columbia *atelier* on the way down to the dock on the morning of my departure, and her last note was sung just in time for my brother Manuel to rush me down in his car and enable me to catch the steamer.

I was sorry in a sense to be leaving the States without having assisted actively in the exploitation there of my scheme. But it could not be helped. I suggested to the Columbia people everything that I could think of in the way of suitable "publicity," and I am bound to say that they did their best, when the time came, by arranging demonstrations in various cities (notably Boston) and obtaining testimonials from well-known opera artists and teachers, speaking very highly of the new method. From the London branch of the Columbia—then a tiny organization in comparison with what it is to-day—I also received every assistance and encouragement in the completion of my task. The tenor difficulty proved nearly as formidable on this side of the Atlantic as it had been on the other. Ultimately I decided to overcome it by employing two tenors instead of one —an Italian and an Englishman—the former for the solfeggi and operatic examples ; the latter for the sustained tones, scales and divisions, and the oratorio selections. Thus allotted, with the willing co-operation of Signor Lenghi-Cellini and a Lancashire tenor who was studying with me at the time, we contrived to compile a very creditable score of model records. Just then, or soon afterwards, the first consignment of records and books arrived from America and was duly stored in the Columbia factory at Bendon Valley, Earlsfield. I began to breathe more freely. Surely, I thought, nothing further can happen to prevent the successful launching of my " Phono-Vocal Method."

But I was over-sanguine. While in the midst of my plans for giving a public demonstration at Wigmore Hall, to which I intended to invite the leading teachers of singing and members of the vocal profession, I was greeted one morning with the interesting news that the Columbia factory at Bendon Valley had been burnt to the ground. Of course the whole of my precious stock of records, etc., had been involved in the fire, and, to make the disaster still worse, I had not insured it for a single penny. I am not quite sure of the date when this conflagration occurred, but it was certainly a year or two before the War, though not much more than that, for there had been considerable delay in completing the preliminary work. Fortunately the matrices had been kept in New York together with the stereotyped plates for the books ; so the disaster was not, from one point of view, absolutely beyond repair.

Nevertheless, I will admit that I was beginning rather to lose heart over my project. I have never been a great believer in what is called " luck " ; but I could not help feeling that if such a thing existed it had so far been dead against me—certainly at no point had it been on my side. Again and again I asked myself whether it was worth while to go on. Gladly would I have discussed the question with my good friend Mme. Nordica, whose ingenious fancy had imagined and suggested the whole idea. But, alas, she was just then away touring in the Far East, where her valuable life was shortly to be prematurely sacrificed through exposure during the wreck of the steamer that was bearing her to Batavia. (As a matter of fact she died there on May 10th, 1914, a few weeks before the War broke out.)

Yet so strong was my belief in the benefits to singing mankind that would accrue from the aid of the gramophone that I ultimately resolved, notwithstanding the intervention of the world-war, to place an order with the Columbia Company for a further supply of the records and books to replace those which had been destroyed by the fire. I did so ; and

waited very patiently—I cannot now recall exactly how long, but it seemed like years—until the new stock had been safely packed away (and duly insured this time) in the new building at Bendon Valley.

Then came the final blow. It is hardly to be credited, and, as I look back on it now with even less of superstition in my nature than I had at that troublous epoch in our lives, I cannot help wondering what evil genius was waiting to inflict further injury upon me and my well-meant experiment. Be that as it may, the extraordinary fact remains that one morning early in 1918, on taking up my paper to read the latest news from France, I caught sight of an interesting paragraph which informed me that history had once more repeated itself. There had been another disastrous fire at the Bendon Valley works and, for the second time, the flames had reduced to ashes the European material of the invention known as the " Phono-Vocal Method."

Well, that was the end of it so far as I was concerned. I neither could nor would make another attempt to " carry on." As before, the Columbia directors over here showed me all possible consideration and sympathy, but naturally they could do no more. I heard subsequently that the New York company—probably as suspicious of an unkind Fate as I was myself—had disposed of their rights, together with the entire available stock of records and books, to a firm known as the " Music Phone Method," which was then dealing in language and other educational gramophone systems. What it managed to do with my poor unfortunate ewe-lamb (twice roasted, I might almost say) I was never able to ascertain.

There remained, and there remains still, one consolatory reflection. All the events above related occurred during the period of ante-electrical recording. The forty discs or eighty examples, over which I took such infinite pains and spent so many anxious moments, would be utterly useless in a commercial sense to-day. Every one of them would have to be made over again ; and, though I know perfectly well that the task would be a much less difficult one under existing conditions, I am by no means sure that I should care to face it once more. If I did, I would unquestionably facilitate it by re-writing the exercises themselves, with a view to rendering them easier for beginners, more gradual and less concentrated in content for the ordinary student. Perhaps someone else would now like to " take on the job ? " It will certainly be done one day.

HERMAN KLEIN.

THE GRAMOPHONE AND THE SINGER

(Continued)

By HERMAN KLEIN

Some Effects of Operatic Pessimism

IT is useless endeavouring to disguise the fact that, where opera is concerned, we are suffering at the present time from an acute " inferiority complex." Let us admit that there may be some reason for it; that we are entitled to feel in rather low spirits when we realize how far behind other great nations we are in the pursuit of this form of musical recreation, and how regularly all our best laid plans for its amelioration "gang agley." Yet ought we really to allow ourselves to become so terribly downhearted over our operatic status? Ought we to be so hopeless and pessimistic as we are about the future of this art in our land, just because it is less capable here of resisting the effects of the world-slump than it is in countries where it rests upon stronger and deeper foundations?

My reply is an emphatic negative. It is my fixed opinion that the love of opera is as firmly ingrained in the hearts of British musical amateurs as it is in those of any other civilized people; that it only needs to be wisely, sensibly, unselfishly exploited to flourish as greatly in our midst as it does anywhere in Europe. Glance through the pages of the Index to Volume VII. of THE GRAMOPHONE, and judge for yourself whether, in the list of works arranged under the names of composers, the proportion of operatic selections is not representative and adequate. That only indicates, of course, that it held its own, from June, 1929, to May, 1930, with the rest of the sources from which the gramophone companies culled its popular and profitable collection. But it does not mean that the tremendous increase in the numbers of high-class instrumental recordings—the vast growth in the demand for symphonic, orchestral, and chamber music of the finest type—has lessened in any degree the appreciation of the glorious gems of the lyric repertory. Comparison between the respective qualities of the execution in these different departments is another matter and does not enter into the pros and cons of the present discussion. I am wanting only to demonstrate that, if the outlook for operatic enterprise seems worse than it was a year or two ago, there is still the same interested public ready to support opera, provided opera is put before it in a systematic manner and not in the confused, hydro-headed, higgedly-piggedly fashion that it has been of late.

There have been, and there still are, too many Richards in the field. I pointed this out six months ago, just before the London opera season began, when things looked more promising than they look, or are supposed to be looking, now. In the April number of this journal I made the suggestion that the Covent Garden Opera Syndicate and the Imperial League of Opera (otherwise Sir Thomas Beecham) should merge their interests, instead of wasting their energies by opposing each other. It may be that we shall learn before these lines appear in print that they have done so; but at the time I am writing no announcement to that effect has been officially made. Meanwhile, it must be confessed that the " Improving Operatic Outlook " which I ventured to depict in the article referred to was not precisely realized by the events that followed; nor was my anticipation so much in the nature of a prediction as of a fervent expression of hope. Somehow, I am always inclined to take an optimistic rather than a pessimistic view where opera is in question, hence my particular unwillingness to subscribe to the latter when the trade of the Empire is bad, when over-taxation is rife, when people have no money to spare for luxuries that they will not miss or cannot easily dispense with.

One must not, of course, be blind to facts. If the German season at Covent Garden was a brilliant success (and is, in consequence, to be longer next year), it is equally certain that the Italian season was a brilliant failure. Nobody really wanted to hear *Martha* or the *Traviata* or *L'Amore dei Tre Re*, or even *Norma* and *Andrea Chénier*; but people went to them for the sake of the artists who sang in them, without filling the house for the second performance. To submit to the bygone usages and customs of the " star system " is not the way to restore Italian opera to its place in the favour of the British public, whatever its efficacy with the American. Then, on the other hand, what is the good of recommending new operas by English composers as a means of attracting Promenade Concert audiences to the opera house at a delicate juncture like this, when musical tastes are, so to speak, in the melting-pot and the whole future of opera as a national concern is at stake? Yet that is what I saw advocated in the *Musical Times* for August, in the form of an " open letter " to an imaginary English opera composer. It was, in point of fact, a lengthy editorial from the pen of " Feste," containing, amid much justifiable criticism and contempt for present-day operatic methods, a distinctly chauvinistic appeal on behalf of the stage works of Vaughan Williams, Gustav Holst, and others (including incidentally Eugene Goossens). As if these were the men—however consummate their ability or their readiness to take Feste's jocular advice and write down to the level of Covent Garden musical tastes—to rescue operatic enterprise in this country from its present *impasse*! *Hugh the Drover, The Perfect Fool, At the Boar's Head*, and *Savitri* may be masterpieces if you like; they might even " make admirable wireless operas." But it has been conclusively shown that they need, like delicate plants, a favourable atmosphere as well as a special soil to foster their drawing powers. Fifty years ago Carl Rosa tried a like experiment under much more advantageous conditions with new operas by Cowen, Goring Thomas, Mackenzie, and Villiers Stanford. Some of those works were actually beautiful, and for their beauty I loved them. But what did they permanently accomplish for English opera; and where are they to-day? No, it is not to the composers and their works, any more than to the singers, the conductors, or the impresarios, that we have to look for the final establishment of opera upon a firm and lasting basis, but to the British people themselves. And by the people I naturally mean the State. I was not always a believer in the virtue of State support for opera. On the contrary, I opposed it years ago because I feared that it involved interference with artistic freedom and progress. Now I think otherwise, because I know that opera on a worthy representative scale cannot possibly be made to pay in England without a subsidy from the State, if it will not do so in those countries where it forms an essential part of the lives of the people. As we have lately seen, it cannot be made to escape some loss even in Italy, France, Germany, and Austria, where

the yearly aid from State or Municipality is fairly generous. The heavy costs of production and the comparatively low prices charged for admission (not so much the salaries paid to the artists, chorus, and orchestral players) are mainly responsible for the deficit in those cases. A few thousand pounds per annum, guaranteed to one big central organization carrying on opera under the right direction in London and the provinces all the year round, would secure at any rate a practicable working scheme and possibly an enduring institution.

But is there any chance, you ask, of such aid being forthcoming at the hands of a British Government? That is a very important question, and one that cannot be answered off-hand. It is, to a certain extent, involved in the working out of the political situation and in that return of national prosperity which presents by far the most vital problem of the moment. I have lost faith in individual schemes, not merely because they have hitherto spelt failure and stopped short of success at the critical moment, but because somehow the personal element has been too conspicuously in evidence and the motives at the back of such projects have not invariably seemed to be free from the taint of selfishness. But, meanwhile, there have been of late one or two little signs of good augury for the cause of opera; as, for instance, the efforts of the gifted wife of the Chancellor of the Exchequer in presenting special operatic programmes at her " At Homes " at Downing Street with Covent Garden and Carl Rosa artists, and pleading eloquently by word of mouth for the better support of opera in our benighted land. Nothing definite can be said, of course, but influences such as this, pointing in the right direction, may turn out to have a very real value when the time comes.

HERMAN KLEIN.

THE GRAMOPHONE AND THE SINGER

(Continued)

By HERMAN KLEIN

The Apotheosis of Carl Rosa

THE name is familiar enough, but how many people nowadays know anything about the man or what he did? They are able, if asked, to tell you that he formed an opera company which is still doing active business. They may even be aware that the Company was started in 1875, and that Queen Victoria, who "commanded" it to Windsor several times, gave it permission in 1897 to use the prefix "Royal." But since Carl Rosa died in 1889 the undertaking has passed through so many hands and had so many ups-and-downs that the personality of the original founder can be but vaguely recalled, save by the few who, like myself, knew him well. Yet the work that he accomplished for English Opera during the brief space of fourteen years was of the most remarkable kind. It was to have a lasting influence upon musical progress in the direction of the cause for which Carl Rosa may truly be said to have sacrificed his life.

His posthumous rewards have not been great. For one thing, he has never enjoyed the advantage of an adequate biography. A few years ago Mr. H. B. Phillips, whose energetic wife is now carrying on the administration of the troupe, approached me with a view to my writing the story of Rosa's amazing activities in this country: but somehow the project fell through and a good idea came to nothing. It may, however, be revived ere long, for now a society has been formed to honour and perpetuate the name of Carl Rosa as well as to foster the labours of the company which bears that name; and, of course, one of the first things that such a society is bound to do is to see that some authoritative account is provided of its hero's life-work. It was, perhaps, regrettable that the new edition of *Grove's Dictionary* should have furnished such an incomplete supplement to the short paragraph written by "G" himself for the first edition. For the time being that is all the history of Carl Rosa that is available.

In my book *Musicians and Mummers* (published by Cassells in 1925), I have related what Carl Rosa told me at his house one evening in 1882, a few months before he began his fruitful connection with Sir Augustus Harris at Drury Lane Theatre. By then he had already won the affection and esteem of the public with his splendid productions of opera in English, dating from the memorable opening season of 1875 at the Princess's Theatre in Oxford Street, when he mounted among other things Mozart's *Marriage of Figaro*, with Santley in the part of Figaro. In the following year he had given the first English performance of an opera by Wagner (*The Flying Dutchman*), with the same eminent artist in the title-rôle, and a new opera by Cowen; while later on came versions of Nicolai's *Merry Wives, Lohengrin, Tannhäuser, Rienzi, Manon, Carmen, Mignon*, and *Aida* to swell the new repertory. But down to 1883 he had done nothing, or next to nothing, directly to encourage the British composer, and it was of his intention to embark upon this fresh policy that Carl Rosa gave me confidential information upon the occasion I have alluded to. In the Easter week of that year he produced, in conjunction with Harris, Goring Thomas's *Esmeralda* and A. C. Mackenzie's *Colomba*. In the succeeding spring he brought out Villiers Stanford's *Canterbury Pilgrims* and Mackenzie's *Troubadour*. Subsequently he commissioned and mounted Goring Thomas's *Nadeshda*, Cowen's *Thorgrim*, Corder's *Nordisa*, Hamish MacCunn's *Jeanie Deans*, and other operas.

But he overworked himself. He travelled all through the provinces with his company; he conducted most of the operas himself; he personally superintended their production; he attended to the business management of the concern. His heart and soul were in the task of raising English opera to a level of excellence and a degree of popularity that it had never reached before. He succeeded, but at the cost of his health. I remember his paying an unexpected visit to London, in course of which he informed me that he had had a nervous breakdown and the doctors had ordered him not to hear a note of music for three months—if possible for half a year. It looked very serious; doubly so because his partner, Augustus Harris, was then also embarking upon big operatic ventures on his own account (he took Covent Garden in 1888) and doing more work than was good for him. Nevertheless, Rosa regained some of his strength and temporarily returned to the post of duty. He transferred his enterprise to a limited company and engaged assistant conductors, among them Eugene Goossens, senr. Although the London seasons became less regular, the business continued to be prosperous; but the improvement in the chief's condition did not last. In the April of 1889 he was staying in Paris, and there, on the morning of the 30th he died, to the intense regret of all his friends and of the many communities that had regarded him as the only champion of opera in the vernacular. I wrote at the time, "Thanks to his courage and enthusiasm, native musicians were brought to the front as opera-writers, the works of Wagner and other modern composers were given for the first time in the English language, and the lyric stage in the provinces was raised to a higher level that it had ever before attained."

Such was the man who bequeathed to his art the valuable tradition that has led to the foundation of the "Carl Rosa Society." At a meeting held at Claridge's on the last day of September it was resolved, not only to perpetuate his memory, but to aid in encouraging by every possible means the success of the company that has so long borne his name. Membership of this society (offices at Steinway Hall, George Street, Hanover Square) costs only the modest sum of half-a-crown per individual, or one guinea for a school or college; while a fee of five guineas is required for the privilege of being enrolled as a Life Associate member. To all who join the society and keep up their yearly subscriptions certain rights will accrue, and, considering the extent of the ground that the Carl Rosa Company covers on its provincial tours, the membership ought soon to become a very large one. Opera-giving, as we all know, is a costly business, even when done upon an economical scale; and, when theatre prices only can be charged, it can scarcely be carried on—much less made to pay—without some sort of additional help from outside sources.

Apart from this practical purpose, the formation of the Carl Rosa Society brings into being a new symbol, a fresh stimulant, to secure the maintenance of the old tradition. I referred to that when speaking at the meeting mentioned above; but I did not (as reported) declare that the high standard set by Carl Rosa himself had *invariably* been upheld. On the contrary, it marked at one time a distinct downward curve, and the repute of the troupe suffered extensively in consequence. But that is a long story, and nothing would be gained by relating it now. Indeed, it may well be forgotten at this important turn in the affairs of the company. The main point is that in recent months the improvement discernible in the performances has been quite remarkable and the good name of Carl Rosa has been saved. I say this without in the least depreciating the good work done in the past under the auspices of the late Mrs. Rosa and the brothers Walter and Alfred van Noorden; but I must add that responsibility for the present recovery rests entirely with the actual manageress, Mrs. Phillips, and to her all credit must be given.

The immediate future of provincial opera would appear to involve the prospect of severe competition. Yet from the strongest opposition I fancy the Carl Rosa Company has nothing to fear. There is room for more than one first-rate organization in the country, provided they can contrive to keep their visits to the same places sufficiently far apart. Love of opera is an appetite that grows. like its modest reproducer, the gramophone, by what it feeds upon. The more one hears of it in any satisfying artistic form, the more one wants to go on hearing. And, in this particular Carl Rosa case, the British public of to-day is not only supporting something from which it derives a direct benefit, an ample *quid pro quô*, but it is at the same time helping to keep alive the good name of one who served its immediate forefathers faithfully and well.

The Opera Fusion

It is six months since I first suggested that the Imperial League of Operas should amalgamate with the Covent Garden Syndicate. I suppose it is nobody's fault in particular that most of that time has been practically wasted on negotiations. One might blame the reticence of the public in its response to Sir Thomas Beecham's appeal for a bigger membership; but then, had the response been entirely adequate it is doubtful whether the proposed fusion would ever have been sought. The members themselves were said to be twenty to one in favour of the proposal, and the majority would assuredly have been larger (and the replies more prompt) had the famous post-card questionnaire been more carefully drawn up. No person of ordinary intelligence ought to have imagined that the Covent Garden International season was to be included in this scheme; but people are apt to rush to pleasant conclusions unless they are definitely warned not to. Still they had a right to complain very seriously at the withdrawal of the privilege as to priority of booking granted to all members of the League. That was for many one of the principal inducements for joining. It is a too common experience that good seats and tickets for the cheaper places are unobtainable at the box office. They are invariably snapped up beforehand by the libraries and the "speculators."

I could not altogether agree with the "Doubtful Subscriber," whose letter appeared in the *Observer* of October 19, that the member who might want to buy an extra seat for his wife should expect to obtain it without subscribing for her to join the League also. He failed to remember how many male members under such circumstances would temporarily discover that they were married men. On the other hand I felt quite touched by the same correspondent's appeal for an extension of the notorious Covent Garden press list; which he described as "narrow and based on an obsolete principle"; adding, "Can we be assured that Sir Thomas's will be wider—and especially that musical journals will be invited to send their critics to his performances?" But this, again, has reference to the International season, not the operations of the combine.

HERMAN KLEIN.

THE GRAMOPHONE and THE SINGER

(Continued)

By HERMAN KLEIN

The Distortions of Over-Amplification

THESE are of various kinds; but they all proceed from the same generic cause—miscalculation either of human needs or of artistic requirements. I do not wholly blame that unconscious medium, the microphone. It has not yet become a perfect instrument, as no doubt one day it will; and when that day arrives I am sure it will, among other things, automatically refuse to aid and abet the chief culprit—to wit, the amplifier—in splitting our ears or transmuting the voice into something utterly unlike its original. Let me offer an example.

At a public luncheon given recently, one of the speakers began by directing his speech away from the microphone, so that all you could hear were the agreeably mild tones of his natural voice. Someone then moved the microphone-stand nearer to him, so that he could not elude it. Immediately there issued forth a noisy din devoid of all human charm and bearing not the slightest resemblance to the voice that we had been listening to a moment before. The words, when we grew accustomed to the change, became a little more distinct, that was all. Later in the proceedings two other speakers declined (apparently) to avail themselves of the microphone's friendly reinforcement. One jerked out some faint sentences, which were quite inaudible to everybody except those quite near him. The other, a famous actor, had no need of help. His glorious speaking voice and faultless elocution enabled him instantly to throw tone and words to the farthest corner of the big room. One experienced the delight of feeling that it was to the man himself one was listening, not a robot. In large places like the Albert Hall, the Connaught Rooms, or the Kingsway Hall, where bad speakers hold forth only too frequently, the amplifier may be very useful, if not necessary; but the distortion is always present. Words are blurted out by the dozen that never get understood.

I do not often go to a cinema theatre, but I take an interest in the talkie-film, just as I do in wireless broadcasting, as a phase of modern progress that is more or less allied to the arts I love and practise. My impression is that the control of voice reproduction has latterly made a much more decided advance in the direction of the radio than in that of the speaking voice which accompanies the movement of pictures on a film. The vocal quality may have improved somewhat. I noted that not long ago in the *Song of My Heart* film, which "features"

John McCormack. Evident pains had been taken to reproduce the peculiar timbre of the popular tenor's voice; and, since it could be done in his case, I was set wondering why it could not be accomplished equally well for others. Why should it not have been as easy to bring out the same truthful replica of the spoken sounds—including, I may add, those of Count John himself, whose speech seemed to my ears far more nasal and coarse than it is in reality.

This opinion was confirmed so recently as the end of October, when I visited a cinema house not a hundred miles from Piccadilly Circus to see an American film that was supposed to have had embodied in it all the latest improvements. This had certainly been done with flawless results in every respect save the quality of the talking. The timing of sound and action was absolutely right; as the lips moved so the words came forth. But such dreadful voices, such horrid types of unrefined American accent, such slithering slides up and down the scale of the commonest New York dialect, I have rarely heard. Worst of all, the megaphonic attentions of the amplifier had obviously helped to exaggerate the loudness and ugliness of the whole thing, including the dance music and the inane ballad-warbling that filled up the quota of the marginal programme. I asked myself a hundred times how such Hollywood atrocities as this could attract and amuse certain sections of the British public. But evidently they did.

Rather a different affair from those I have been writing about is the new sin of over-amplifying a singer's voice in the making of a gramophone record. That is surely an avoidable offence, and therefore not pardonable in the same sense that you can pardon an error which is unintentional or the innocent outcome of a mistaken idea. For I cannot help regarding the process of enlarging or exaggerating the human voice as a deliberate act of deception. It is not akin to the enlargement of a photograph or a picture. It is not the same excusable device as that employed for increasing the volume of vocal, spoken, or instrumental sounds for the purpose of filling a large auditorium. It is done simply in order to make the organ of the singer appear bigger, more resonant, more imposing and impressive, than it is in reality. In other words, it is a system unfair to everybody concerned. It is unfair to the artist, whom it renders liable to all sorts of comparisons, both as represented on other records and, worse still, when heard in the concert-room or the theatre. It is unfair to the public because it creates a wrong estimate of the size of the voice, alters its whole character, deprives it of its natural charm, and, as a rule, exaggerates whatever faults there may be of enunciation, accent, and diction. In short, it converts the gramophone from a true witness into a false one.

I think I know how this amplifying business has been allowed to creep in. Most people will remember that in the old pre-electrical days, when there were only half-a-dozen firms in the world making gramophone records, there used to be shocking degrees of variety in the quality and *strength* of their products. Gradually one feature after another of the process underwent improvement, until at last the horn gave place to the microphone and the way was cleared for a free, normal musical performance. The effect of this, whether vocal or instrumental, was at the outset wholly delightful in its realistic purity and faithful adherence to the original. One observed with the keenest satisfaction the steadier course of the recording needle as it traced its circles in the wax and the consequent diminution of the amount of wavering and scraping in reproduction. The weakness and faintness of the softer tones that we were wont to complain of in the earlier records had all but disappeared. We were beginning to feel that the era of actual truth to nature had at last arrived. And so in a very large measure it had.

Then came the amplifier—the instrument and also the man behind it; and with their advent some of us proceeded to bid a regretful adieu to our peace of mind—and ear. My earliest experiences of the new gadget were not, so far as I was aware, strictly derived from records of solo singing. At any rate, the increasing loudness, when I first noticed it, was emitted by a Columbia record of an oratorio chorus that had been taken at the last Handel Festival at the Crystal Palace in 1928. Well, I thought, that is an extremely fine body of tone; and I promptly attributed it to the abnormal magnitude of the sound created by the 3,500 performers in the Centre Transept. It was splendid to find that such a conglomerate mass could be accurately conveyed and reproduced by the gramophone. But I did not imagine then, nor do I think now, that amplification was at the root of that experience or even a main factor in it. A more convincing illustration of the latter followed shortly after in the shape of a new H.M.V. record of Boëllman's *Suite Gothique* for organ, taken from a splendid performance by Herbert Dawson. I considered this as nearly as possible perfect, whatever its secret might be. It was not until some months later, however, that the amplifying of voices began to grow noticeable, and at first there seemed nothing objectionable about it; in fact, rather the contrary.

Here, let me say, I found myself—and to a certain extent find myself still—in something of a quandary. To what is the augmented volume of modern recording primarily to be attributed? Is it to the action of the amplifying mechanism alone? No. It is also due to two other influences—one, the clarifying effect and consequent reinforcing of the timbre when converted into electric waves by the microphone (I hope my scientific definition is correct); the other, the increased freedom of delivery which permits the singer to use unrestrained vigour in the strongest parts of the voice and, if he or she so wills it, to shout every note of a piece without incurring the old danger of "blasting." You will say that the amplifier (or the man behind it) should be able to regulate and counterbalance these excesses. Partially, perhaps; but it can only be at the risk of interfering with the quality, just as may be done by over-magnifying. In either case the result must be an impure tone and therewith its regrettable concomitant—an ugly, faulty, and perhaps inaudible enunciation of the words. Whatever the cause, therefore, the outcome is bad, and, if it be the fact that the stentorian would-be Carusos, Eva Turners, and Ivor Andrésens are as much to blame in this matter as the *mécanique*, I can only say that they will continue to receive in these columns the criticism they deserve. Feeling as I do about this abuse of force and the whole question of over-amplification, I was greatly delighted when I read what our Editor had to say on the subject in the last number of THE GRAMOPHONE. What he writes is always attentively as well as widely read, and I sincerely hope that his warnings will be taken to heart. He is right in every way. There is serious danger of the public taste being "irreparably spoilt" should the average vocal disc continue to be "but little removed from an infernal row." He is right when he says that one should not have constantly to be changing needles to suit the various discs in order to procure "some mitigation of this row." He is right in his opinion that "every great singer has lost something by electrical recording," and that it should be easy to get better results. Finally, the closest heed must be paid to his observations concerning the distortions of the microphone; the absolute necessity for greater care on the part of recorders and recorded alike; and, in regard to the Talkies, the duty of the gramophone to correct their tendency to bring about the "complete debasement of the human ear."

I hope for all our sakes that a drastic reform of this abuse will now be effected. I put it in the plural because there is not a soul possessing a decently sensitive musical ear who does not suffer through it. Remember the fate that befel the creator of the soulless monster, Frankenstein! There comes a time when these "many inventions" of man pass beyond control.

HERMAN KLEIN.

THE GRAMOPHONE and THE SINGER
New "Mikado" and "Patience" Recordings:
The Opera Crisis
By HERMAN KLEIN

I CONFESS to a wholesome dislike of the word "potted," as applied to music, and I never use it in that connection. The dictionary gives it as something "preserved in a pot or a cask"; but you cannot preserve music, properly speaking, in either of those vessels. How the French came originally to apply the term "pot-pourri" to a heterogeneous collection of tunes from an opera I am not altogether sure. In reality it is not much more appropriate than the English word, but its use has become hallowed by time, and the *Dictionnaire National* of Bescherelle furnishes as among its meanings either a "Morceau de musique sur une suite d'airs différents et connus," or "Chanson dont les couplets sont sur différents airs." Here the actual meaning of the word *pourri* (i.e., rotten) is obviously not implied at all, *pot-pourri* in its literal sense being the term employed for a "ragoût or stew of different kinds of meat, vegetables, etc., seasoned and cooked together, and served at table in the pot in which it was cooked." Anyhow, whether referred to as food or music, this is something wholly different from what we describe in English as a "potted article," whether purchased at Burgess's "fish-sauce shop," or at Jackson's in Piccadilly.

Now the Columbia "Portfolio" of 16 selections from *The Mikado*, which has called forth these prefatory remarks, is something infinitely more important and extended than a *pot-pourri*, without being a reproduction of the complete opera like the usual Album. It lies, in fact, rather more than half-way between the two, and, from the economical standpoint, will probably be welcomed as serving pretty well the same purpose as the more expensive product. It is effected in a series of six 10-inch records, numbered DB321-6, sung by the Columbia Light Opera Company and conducted by Mr. Joseph Batten. The following is the cast: The Mikado and Pooh Bah, Robert Carr; Nanki-Poo, Dan Jones; Ko-Ko, Appleton Moore; Pish Tush, Randell Jackson; Yum-Yum, Alice Lilley; Pitti Sing, Joan Cross; Peep Bo and Katisha, Nellie Walker.

I have heard too many casts of this most popular of all the Savoy operas to dare allow myself the indulgence of comparisons; they would carry me too far. Neither are they really called for in the present instance. Memory and imagination combined can very well serve to supply whatever is missing—even what a note in the accompanying book of words describes as "Gilbert's almost immortal wit and satire, heightened by the attractive Japanese setting." The Savoy fan of to-day does not look for the spirit of an original that he never knew and that can never be recaptured. But he can at last sit back and listen with pleasure to the liberal allowance which he will glean from this series of excerpts, representing as it does the absolute pick of Sullivan s ever-fresh, ever-green, ever-fascinating melodies. They are melodies so magical in their exhilarating charm that they even have the power to defy (where the gramophone is concerned) any lapses from the high level of vocal intelligence and refinement of phrasing which the composer foresaw when writing them and insisted upon in person when rehearsing them. That was just five-and-forty years ago last March.

The new Portfolio omits the overture and starts with the opening choruses (capitally sung), followed by *A Wandering Minstrel I*, which Mr. Dan Jones delivers in plain, matter-of-fact fashion, dwelling lovingly upon his vowel tone and quite ignoring the consonants. Disc No. 2 is devoted to the Lord High Executioner, Mr. Appleton, who exchanges the Welsh method for that of the West-countryman, and enunciates his Gilbertian lines with a clearness and humour that fully atone for his dialect. Then arrive the *Three Little Maids from School*, crisp, quaint, and sprightly; after them the duet, *Were you not to Ko-Ko plighted*; and so on to the famous trio anent a pestilential prison, with a life-long lock,

Awaiting the sensation of a short, sharp shock,
From a cheap and chippy chopper on a big black block.

From the second act we have Yum-Yum s song, neatly rendered by Miss Lilley, with, on the same disc, the exquisite madrigal, *Brightly dawns our wedding day*, ending merrily "in tears," as tradition rightly demands. The latter, very smoothly sung, is succeeded by the patter trio, *Here's a how-d'ye-do!* and, of course, the Mikado's popular song with chorus about the "object all sublime" that is to "let the punishment fit the crime." The rest of the familiar gems follow in due order, all excellently recorded, and worthily rounding off a selection that gives full prominence to the wealth of ensemble contained in Sullivan's sparkling score.

Patience came after *The Pirates of Penzance*, four years before *The Mikado*; and when its long run was at its height people used to wonder whether a piece that caricatured a passing craze could possibly out-live the so-called æsthetic movement which it helped to kill. With what success it has done so there is no need to tell. The laughter that greets its amusing quips at every revival is as loud as the applause awakened by the wonderful music whose interest can never fade. Small wonder, then, that H.M.V. has seen the advisability of re-recording the complete opera, to replace the Album which was made before the electrical process came in, with Violet Essex, Edna Thornton, Nellie Walker, F. Ranalow, George Baker, and Peter Dawson for principal singers. It may be doubted whether the new cast will be considered quite as strong, part for part; but as an ensemble it is even better, because it has brought to its work the authority and constant co-operation of the sempiternal D'Oyly Carte Company, under the experienced guidance of Dr. Malcolm Sargent; and that, of course, is a combination not to be beaten by the finest "scratch" team ever put together. Here is the distribution: Col. Calverley, Darrell Fancourt; Major Murgatroyd, Martin Green; Lieut. the Duke of Dunstable, Derek Oldham; Reginald Bunthorne, George Baker; Archibald Grosvenor, Leslie Rands; Lady Angela, Nellie Briercliffe; Lady Saphir, Marjorie Eyre; Lady Ella, Rita Mackay; Lady Jane, Bertha Lewis; Patience, Winifred Lawson. The Album consists of ten 12-inch records, numbered D1909 to D1918.

It may go without saying that the technique of the recording shows an incomparable advance upon that of the ten-year-old series that preceded it. The delicacy and refinement of the instrumentation stand clearly forth all through, together, I am glad to say, with a precision of execution and accuracy of tempi that the careful François Cellier would assuredly have approved. Another welcome feature is the quality of the choral tone, alike in girls and men; for I can fairly say that it is quite up to the best Savoy standard, new as well as old. Neither is rhythm or spirit lacking, while the words of the "twenty love-sick maidens" impinge upon the ear as incisively as those of the "heavy dragoons." Of the principals, Mr. Baker and Miss Lewis strike me as carrying on the true traditions most faithfully. It is better under these conditions to listen to a Reginald Bunthorne, who can sing as well as he acts, than merely to have a good comedian in the part of the "fleshly poet." If, as a gramophile, I had to choose between the late George Grossmith, Sir Henry Lytton, and Mr. George Baker, I would not hesitate to take the last-named. He is an accomplished vocalist, and knows how to sing his music, besides lending it the necessary character and touches of humour. His patter is superb because, no matter what the speed, every syllable comes out as clear and neat as if he were talking. This, too, is where he surpasses that clever artist, Mr. Darrell Fancourt, whose method is too explosive for microphonic purposes, and he is consequently indistinct. On the other hand, Miss Bertha Lewis, with her imperturbable *sostenuto* and pellucid enunciation, offers a model that the whole company might profit by imitating in the more sedate passages of the opera. To some extent Miss Briercliffe seems to achieve this; but the tones of Miss Lawson's thin soprano voice only grow more acidulated as time goes on, and her recording timbre, which may recommend itself to some judges on account of its penetrating quality, sounds to my ears so pinched as to be at times positively unpleasant. In the theatre it is certainly less so, thus proving that a singer of this type has little reason to be grateful to the amplifier. On the whole, however, it must be allowed that the last-named, whether instrument or individual, has obtruded only to an infinitesimal degree in the making of this admirable version of *Patience*.

The Opera Crisis

At the moment of writing it looks as though the proposed amalgamation would definitely fall through; the Covent Garden Syndicate pulling one way, Sir Thomas Beecham with his League of Opera the other. In spite of political opposition, the subsidy will probably be granted, and the public will benefit by it, as should also the B.B.C. in the end. One good result will be a long season of Opera in English at Covent Garden during the autumn of 1931; another, I hope, an understanding between the Syndicate and the Carl Rosa Company for organising their provincial tours in such a way that they do not clash. To contrive this, the visits to the big towns must be fairly apportioned; while the Carl Rosa management must be granted an annual sum out of the subsidy, otherwise it will go to pieces, which no one ought to desire.

I do not pretend to foreshadow the ultimate attitude of Parliament towards Mr. Snowden's project for helping opera in this country, though I cannot help wishing that it had been brought forward in a less happy-go-lucky, piecemeal fashion. Nor can I agree with Sir Alfred Butt's economic view of the question or his aspersions upon the operatic tastes of the British public, which have nothing to do with their alleged love of musical comedy or their passion for pastimes. Instead of discussing these matters in the papers, Sir Alfred would be doing his metropolitan constituents a greater service if he were seriously to consider the possibility of providing the League of Opera with a home for six months in the year. Would Sir Thomas Beecham be ready to pay a fair rental for Drury Lane if he could get it? If not there, or at a theatre like the Palladium, I do not see much chance of the League getting a show in London for a long while yet.

HERMAN KLEIN.

312

WHEN OLD ARIAS SHOULD *NOT* BE "CUT"

By HERMAN KLEIN

THE intriguing problem of cuts continues to annoy and baffle the musical world as persistently as it has done ever since I can remember. It is one of those things on which there is not a general understanding, much less universal agreement, and I doubt whether a Round Table Conference between delegations from every conservatorium on earth, sitting for a whole year, would ultimately succeed in arriving at a unanimous decision on the subject. Yet it seems to me to be, in the main, a comparatively simple question. If we try to make a piece of music shorter by eliminating a portion of it, the object as a rule must be to reduce the length of the time that it takes to perform. Then, again, it may also be because it is sought to avoid repeating a certain section or sections of the piece, and thereby averting a danger which the innocent composer, no matter how illustrious, may not have dreamt he was incurring—the danger of monotony, or taxing the patience of the listener.

But there may be yet a third purpose to be served, which applies more particularly in the case of singers, namely, where the piece is so long and exacting that it might, if performed in its entirety, impose undue fatigue or strain upon the vocalist. About such as these I shall have a good deal to say presently; for the moment I would merely remark that the risk just referred to would not appear to be so imminent in these Wagner-Strauss days as it was, for instance, in the halcyon period of Rossini, Bellini, Donizetti, or early Verdi, when some (not all) opera singers had more beautiful voices and used and guarded them with greater care. In other words, I do not believe that the practice of abbreviating vocal pieces would have been started at all under present conditions. It originally came into fashion in the concert room, to save time, when the miscellaneous programme was

HERMAN KLEIN
whose "Great Women Singers of My Time" will be published by Routledge this month.

nearly twice as long as it is now and lasted from $2\frac{1}{2}$ to $3\frac{1}{2}$ hours (*vide* the old Philharmonic programmes at the Hanover Square Rooms and St. James's Hall).

On the operatic stage an aria was rarely if ever cut; neither was an oratorio shortened by omissions and cuts as it is in a modern performance, or has been until quite recently—on special occasions. During the last half of the nineteenth century it became the custom in fashionable London, though not abroad. to cut down the long operas of Meyerbeer until they had disappeared from the active repertoire, and those of Wagner until the younger generation refused to be deprived, if they could help it, of a single bar of the score. It was purely a question of time—not of consideration for the singers— where the whole work was being given. The composers would never have thought of allowing cuts (or allowing *for* them) in the ordinary way; they could have devised them much better themselves than conductors could. Indeed, so greatly did they object to them that Rossini and Verdi used purposely to arrange their keys and "returns to the subject" in such a way as to make a respectable *coupure* extremely difficult, if not practically impossible.

Where actual "repeats"—as indicated by the usual dots—are concerned, different considerations arise, and, in so far as they apply to symphonic or chamber music, I do not propose to touch upon them at any length here. Besides, I fancy they have already been amply dealt with in the editorial pages of THE GRAMOPHONE. The old masters down to Beethoven's time, and even later, based their opening allegros strictly upon the regular sonata form, which definitely required the repetition of the first section of the movement; and the same with the scherzo. Contemporary conductors and many quartet players ignore the former direction and obey the latter—wherein I quite agree with them. As regards the airs of Bach and Handel, the considerations are again somewhat different. In these the need for going back and singing the first part through once more is largely determined by the necessity for finishing the air in the right key or the key in which it was begun. It is there, in the course of that repeat, that the customary cut is ordinarily effected with least disturbance to the music or sense of deprivation to the listener. For let it be admitted that in certain of the big works of Handel and Bach the solos, beautiful though they be, are very numerous and very long, and if some of them could not be abbreviated they would have to be left unperformed altogether.

Having said so much, I think I have shown that I am not averse to the introduction of cuts where they are justifiable. Where I do not consider them justifiable, in nine cases out of ten, is in a gramophone performance of an operatic aria. I have recently had occasion in my reviews of new records to complain of the inordinate extent to which this process of abbreviation is being carried; and it grows worse instead of better. I have received no explanations or apologies from the sinners, nor am I likely to be favoured with any. But I know perfectly well what the replies would be if my criticisms were answered. I should be told various things: that the cuts were the conventional or traditional ones; that certain Italian airs as they stood were too long; that there was not room for the whole air on one side of a disc, and it was not thought saleable enough to occupy both; or else, perhaps, that the public did not know the piece well enough to miss what was omitted. To any or all of these excuses I should retort that they were not good enough to hold water and would not bear argument. Yet for the reader's sake I will state here and now what I feel about them.

So-called traditional cuts are not always the best, being frequently, as I have pointed out, awkwardly effected so as to overcome awkward key structures. The form of the aria had much to do with it. The Rossini type, which the later Italians followed, was always assailable in the *cabaletta*, or quick final portion, by omitting the "repeat," and thereby leaving a truncated, top-heavy piece of music. You will find this plan nearly always followed in such things as *Bel raggio* (*Semiramide*), *Tacea la notte* (*Trovatore*), *Ah! fors' è lui* (*Traviata*), *O mio Fernando* (*Favorita*), *Casta diva* (*Norma*), *Ah! non credea* (*Sonnambula*), *Quì la voce* (*Puritani*), and—less extensively because too valuable for display—*Una voce poco fà*, the *Mad Scene* from *Lucia*, *Caro nome*, and the waltz from *Roméo*, the last two being too short to allow of cutting. With certain other solos the liberties taken are even more serious. How seldom does one hear on a record a complete rendering of the *Jewel Scene*! It is generally hacked about dreadfully, until reduced to about half its real length. (I was glad to see that Elizabeth Rethberg's fine H.M.V. record, reviewed by me last month, was spread over both sides of the disc; yet even then part of the recitative was missing.) But what shall one say concerning certain recent mutilations of the *Shadow Song* (*Dinorah*), of the *Polonaise* from *Mignon* and the *Freischütz* air, *Softly sighs*? These were daring enough to have made the composers turn in their graves, if such miracles ever happened.

It would take up too much space to quote further examples of the popular operatic items that are subjected to this sort of crude curtailment, which has nothing in common, of course, with the kind of compression exercised in the abridged portfolio versions, where it is inevitable. My protest is intended for the protection of the public as well as of the composer, dead or living. I consider it absolutely unfair and misleading to label with its ordinary title an excerpt from an opera or an oratorio (as exemplified in *I know that my Redeemer liveth* and *With verdure clad*), unless the whole of the piece be included in the record. Excuse on the ground of excessive length would seem obviously silly when we can see that the record would hold much more—nay, that it is frequently not half covered, and that the piece is short by comparison with the lengthy symphonic movements and the gargantuan selections from Wagner that are recorded from the edge of the disc to that of the label in the centre.

There was a time, not many years back, when cuts on a liberal scale were to be looked for as a matter of course, alike in the opera house and the theatre. Not so much, though, in the concert room. Beethoven's *Ah! perfido* and Mendelssohn's *Infelice!*—long vocal *scenas* very frequently sung—were never curtailed by a single bar. To-day, I am glad to say, cutting down masterpieces to save a few moments is beginning to be looked upon almost in the light of a crime. Italian arias may not all be precisely masterpieces, and thousands of ascetic amateurs would doubtless not mind if they never heard one again. On the other hand, we know quite well that if such things were not in large demand they would not be extensively recorded in every prosperous *atelier*. What is more, if worthily sung and properly accompanied, they are works of art capable of affording as much pleasure in their way as the smaller objects in the Persian Exhibition or the South Kensington Museum. Why not, therefore, present them in complete form; ask the singers to desist from the abominable old habit of making cuts at the same old places; and encourage gramophiles to look for an interpretation as correct and unmutilated as the composer intended it to be?

HERMAN KLEIN.

The Gramophone and the Singer

HOW TO IMITATE GOOD RECORDS

By HERMAN KLEIN

THERE was once a clever performer of conjuring tricks named Dr. Lynn, whose proud boast it used to be that in the end he always let his audience into the secret of how his deeds of legerdemain were accomplished. After each of his tricks—and very mystifying ones they were as a rule—he would remark with a humorous twinkle in his eye, "And that's the way it's done!" Needless to say, the spectators, who had been carefully watching his proceedings, were not a bit wiser than they had been as to the exact method by which the quickness of his hand had deceived their eye. Some mystification of a similar kind is what occurs when the "average listener" to a vocal gramophone record endeavours to discover, by diligent hearkening to every note, the exact means, technical, artistic, and otherwise, by which the so excellent rendering of the piece has been brought to fulfilment by the singer. That "average listener," possessing no personal or special knowledge of the art of singing, will say, generally speaking, "Well, I don't know in the least how it was done. I only know that it was lovely (or some other adjective suitable to the occasion) and that I enjoyed it immensely (or the reverse, as the case may be)."

So much for appreciation pure and simple. But when it comes to something beyond that, and the listener is desirous of utilising the record as a model to be studied and imitated in the practical sense, then knowledge of a closer kind is requisite; in other words, one needs to be a bit of a *prestidigitateur* in order to grasp how the trick is done. The root idea of this utilisation of gramophone records for the purpose of study was, of course, the creative basis of the experiment which I essayed myself in New York twenty-five years ago, and the story of which I set forth in the pages of this magazine last August and September, under the title of "My Phono-Vocal Adventure." That scheme was more comprehensive, however, in that it included its own expressly-made records, and showed the possessor of a voice how to use his or her voice—*i.e.*, how to guide, train, and develop it, with or without the aid of a teacher—so as to be capable of imitating the singing of my exercises as executed by the suitable type of organ. The experiment was made public at about the time when the method of learning languages with the aid of the phonograph was being tried; and it would, I believe, have been equally successful but for the obstacles which I fully described in my articles. As

it was, I accepted defeat and said to myself, "*Che sarà, sarà.*"

At this juncture, a quarter of a century later, there steps into the field another Richmond*. His scheme is a good deal less ambitious (and expensive) than mine was, and it differs from it in many important details. Indeed, I doubt very much whether the author, Mr. Dawson Freer, has had an opportunity of so much as glancing at the text which I wrote to guide the student in the understanding of the technique of the art and the records. I conclude this from the fact that he makes no reference to any former effort in the same direction, but proceeds gaily to his task as though no one before him had ever lighted upon such an idea as he states in his foreword, namely, that "This study of the means by which artistic results are obtained can be greatly assisted by the aid of the gramophone." In fact, the attitude adopted in Mr. Freer's brochure is that of an amiable guide who has arrived at conclusions of his own as to the best way to reach the North Pole, and is quite willing to impart his particular knowledge to those who will follow him.

On the other hand, there is an essential difference between Mr. Freer's plan and the earlier one. He does not provide specially-designed models, but asks his readers to employ some of the best available records in the post-electric H.M.V. catalogue, indicating the main characteristics of each and their usefulness as illustrating a particular feature of vocal equipment and skill. He points out that there may be others in the same list that they have a preference for, and justly adds that "it is by analysis and by comparison that a high standard is set up, which cannot but act as an incentive to the listener." He then proceeds to defend Tradition in a few sentences that deserve quotation :—

> "It is no exaggeration to say that the Gramophone has already become the living voice of tradition. To despise tradition in connection with the singer's craft is foolish. An enduring tradition does not depend upon the arbitrary and obsolete dicta of bygone pedants. It was evolved from the nature of the singer's instrument. The capabilities and limitations of the voice are not subject to the dictates of fashion. They are fixed by physical laws that cannot be disobeyed without detriment to the possibilities of vocal development and preservation. To study the tradition of the singer's art is to find out the legitimate capabilities of the voice from the examples of great singers, who, in their turn, have emulated their predecessors."

---

* *The Student of Singing and the Gramophone*, by Dawson Freer. London : The Gramophone Co., Ltd. Price one shilling.

This is all true enough, though to some ears most of it may sound like "dicta" that have been heard before. The same impression will be gathered from the main body of **Mr. Dawson Freer's** book; for he has a way of setting forth certain commonplaces of his "craft" (as he calls it) with the air of one who has made new discoveries of his own and is now giving the world the benefit of them. Verily, there is nothing new under the sun. The point is, I suppose, that the majority of the people who love good singing and have heard many singers (not all of them good) imagine that they know a vast deal more about it than they actually do, and that the facts contained in these pages, whether fresh or not, will be of equal value as a guide to the systematic accumulation of a little useful knowledge. I agree; and because I approve of the motive and the system I cannot help regretting a certain looseness of language in the author's mode of defining many of his dicta. He has considerable facility, not to say fluidity, in his use of the pen upon subjects connected with singing, but I fear he is not always quite careful enough in his choice of the words wherewith to express his thoughts. For instance, in the classification of voices, after saying that timbre and not compass "is the principal factor that enables a correct decision to be made," he admits this quality cannot be described in words any more easily than one can "define the taste of an apple or a pear. The flavour of a fruit can only be known by tasting it, and the quality of a sound can only be recognised by the ear." It will be admitted that about all this there is nothing very original or informative or helpful.

Dealing with the sub-divisions into which "the soprano voice is sometimes split up" (and badly too), Mr. Freer is no more accurate when he speaks of Rosa Ponselle's as a "heavy" voice than when he differentiates it from "the more bird-like quality of a light soprano"—to wit, Galli-Curci. The art of executing brilliant *coloratura* is not limited to the *soprano leggiero*; neither is the "lyric" soprano to be limited to the style or styles here suggested, reflective, flowing, *cantabile*, or otherwise. Patti, Nilsson, Albani, and Melba were all lyric sopranos; yet they were supposed to appeal by their "dramatic fervour," whilst their "brilliant execution" was assuredly equal to that of the most dazzling *coloratura* artist. Jenny Lind belonged to the same category; and Tietjens, who was a great declamatory singer, could infuse the utmost dramatic feeling into the rendering of her *fiorituri*, whether Handelian, Mozartian, or Rossinian. The truth is that this question of nomenclature as applied to different voices is fraught with many dangerous pitfalls, and, albeit Mr. Freer has attacked it with characteristic daring, he has not escaped the inevitable fate of those who "rush in where angels," etc. The gramophone student who follows him on these topics must be careful, though

tenors at least will have no excuse so long as they exercise the discretion that he wisely counsels.

The records recommended for study are on the whole well selected, and two lengthy lists of them are provided, one at the beginning of the book, the other as an appendix. In both cases the catalogue numbers, names of the singers, and prices are given, together with a brief descriptive *résumé* of the dramatic idea contained in the piece. It is a pity, however, that in some instances the printers should have contrived to separate these; the title, etc., being given on one page and the descriptive matter on the next.

In a little volume so closely packed with aphorism and epigram as this, it would be easy to draw attention to dozens of phrases that strike one by their cleverness rather than their actual instructive import. Some of them, too, have a humorous ring that is obviously unintentional. For example (from the chapter on "Interpretation"): "The singer is the artistic middleman between the composer and the public." "An ascetic attitude cannot produce an æsthetic result." "The artistic singer's task does not merely consist of observing rules of the game; the game must be played for the purpose of reaching some desired goal." "The colour of Melchior's heroic voice may be likened to polished bronze." "Personality is paradoxical; it expresses individuality and, at the same time, it stands for the common humanity we all share." And finally (in a concluding section): "It may be said that the connoisseur's enjoyment begins at the point where the average listener's powers of hearing ends (*sic*). The most precious gems of beauty are only revealed to those who take the trouble to seek for them."

Evidently the average listener needs to take more trouble.

The International Opera Season

Thanks to the gramophone in general, and this GRAMOPHONE in particular, the names of the best artists engaged for the coming Covent Garden campaign have a familiar ring. The full list comprises altogether between fifty and sixty singers, fifteen or so of them British-born, I am proud to say. Among the foreigners the majority of the names speak for themselves; notably, for instance, those of Lotte Lehmann, Frida Leider, Rosa Ponselle, Elisabeth Schumann, Maria Olczewska, Dino Borgioli, Benj. Gigli, Lauritz Melchior, A. Pertile, Gotthelf Pistor, Ivar Andrésen, Eduard Habich, Gerh. Hüsch, H. Janssen, Richard Mayr, Fried. Schorr, and Mariano Stabile. The repertory, apart from the usual two cycles of the *Ring*, contains fresh features in the shape of *La Forza del Destino*, *Francesca da Rimini* (Zandonai), and *Fedra* (Romani), in addition to revivals of *Die Zauberflöte*, *Falstaff*, and *Gianni Schicchi*. Altogether there is promise of a brilliant season.

HERMAN KLEIN.

316

The Gramophone and the Singer

PRECIOUS VOICES OUT OF THE PAST

By HERMAN KLEIN

WHAT the late Sir Frank Burnand used to call a "happy thought" occurred to our London Editor early last month, in connection with the broadcasting work that he does so well. A bare forty minutes, in the Regional evening programme, was all that the B.B.C. had placed at his disposal, and yet he contrived within that short interval to arouse a stronger emotional interest and stir deeper memories than I have experienced for many a day. Somehow the intensity of the treat was heightened by the consciousness that I was not enjoying it all by myself, but sharing it with thousands of other listeners; by which I mean others who were as familiar (or nearly so) as I was with the voices out of the past thus wonderfully resuscitated for us. Never yet since gramophone and wireless became close allies have I known such a vivid realisation of the miracle wrought by their united power, or of the privilege and value—so easy to foretell when I first wrote about these things—that would be accorded future generations by the availability of records sung or spoken by famous people.

One feature that surprised me as much as any on this notable evening of March 5th was the clearness and strength with which these pre-electric recordings came over the radio. Happily my reception was perfect, and although, of course, some came through better than others—some, too, more promptly after the cheery remarks of Christopher Stone had ceased to "announce" the coming record—the average quality was surprisingly good. The consequent speed and continuity of the whole demonstration, coupled with the aptness of the accompanying information, resulted in an entertainment that was not only interesting but positively exciting for old stagers like myself. Let me add that, as there was not time for the programme to be prepared and inserted in *The Radio Times*, the London Editor has consented, by my request, to have it printed in the present issue of this journal—an advantage to our readers which I am sure his modesty would not otherwise have allowed him to contemplate. It will be found on page 552.

Reference to that list shows that nearly the whole of the remarkable group selected for presentation was taken from the H.M.V. Catalogue No. 2 (1930), which comprised *Records of Unique and Historic Interest*. To the speakers, wisely enough, was accorded pride of place, and the name of the first I did not hear, nor do I think it was given out, beforehand. The gruff, toneless voice, talking in something that sounded more like German than English, was that of Count Leo Tolstoi, speaking in 1907, at the age of 79: a mere "curiosity of literature," as Disraeli's father would have called it. But then came a delicious treat—the real voice, the actual *voix d'or* of Sarah Bernhardt's reciting a passage from Rostand's *La Samaritaine*, an excerpt all too brief and touching that made us all alive in an instant to the significance of the moment and the strange joy it was bringing. Did anyone in this world ever, I wonder, put into the word *"Amour"* the wealth of ineffable beauty that the divine Sarah did? How marvellous to have heard it from her very own lips once more! Next came the *Hamlet* speech, "To be or not to be," gently murmured in the familiar manner of Sir Herbert Tree, the halting cadences awakening a no less familiar smile of welcome from at least one old friend.

It was followed by another great Shakespearian quotation, the "Quality of Mercy" speech, delivered in the exquisite voice of Ellen Terry so recently as 1911, when she was 63 years of age. No halting there; but that amazing continuity of tone, that beautiful *legato* whereof no actress of to-day seems to have caught the secret. As in a dream, the incomparable Portia was with us once again—and as quickly gone. And then more Shakespeare, this time like a refreshing breeze, the address of Henry V to his army at Harfleur, given by Lewis Waller, with the characteristic crescendo of excitement that used to take our breath away (though he was never really breathless himself), flooding his audience with the wave of emotion and patriotic sentiment that never, never failed. It brought to my mind, oddly enough, a wireless actor of to-day, yet not an actor in the true sense, but a spontaneous elocutionist, if I may so term him. I refer to Captain Allison, the well-known describer of football matches, whose rapid crescendos on the approach of a likely goal so often recall the rising exaltation of the departed Lewis Waller.

From the histrionic our cicerone passed to the political section of his collection. It was not less remarkable either for interest or the extraordinary acoustic excellence of the old recording, but space compels me to dilate upon the individual specimens with less detail. First we had President Roosevelt speaking in his strong American staccato on "The Farmer and the Business Man," and dealing in 1912 with conditions of living in terms that apply as forcibly to the present day. Then one of the addresses by Lord Roberts of Kandahar on "National Service" just before the Great War; another in Hungarian by Admiral Horthy Miklos (Regent of his country), followed by one in French by the late M. Jean Bratiano, a third in Spanish by General Primo de Rivera, and a fourth in Greek by M. Venizelos—all astonishingly plain in utterance even to ears that could not grasp their meaning. Finally, in this group we heard a perfect example of Italian diction from the Duce, Mussolini in person as it were, talking in his calm, self-possessed way to the people of North America and the Italians on that Continent, very instructive and very edifying.

Then back to the stage—the music-hall stage this time—for a few moments of Dan Leno and Albert Chevalier. Of these inimitable comedians the former, as belonging to a slightly earlier generation, had provided the earlier record, so far back as 1900, in a voice admirably clear and penetrating. I remembered his song and patter about *The Huntsman*, and wondered how he had refrained from improvising one of his ready jokes on the horn that he was facing. He so seldom missed a chance, dear old fellow! *My Old Dutch*, now ætat 20, scarcely seemed to represent Albert Chevalier in his best singing mood; but there was the melting tenderness, the pathetic sweetness that no one has since achieved, coupled with the true and sustained *mezza voce* of the vocalist, who, whatever his mood, was an artist to the finger-tips. After these came a record that gave me a surprise. I had never heard Fernando de Lucia save on the operatic stage, and I had known him well in the days when he was with Sir Augustus Harris at Covent Garden, singing strenuous parts like Turiddu and Canio, the latter of which he created here. The marked tremolo he then indulged had now quite disappeared in a charming rendering of the since-hackneyed *O sole mio*. Doubtless the record was one that had helped to spread the popularity of the song; but as it happened, I had never heard it before, nor had I altogether associated my old acquaintance, except by name, with the tenor whom the H.M.V. list justly described, I see, as "a delightful and consummate artist in his rendering of Neapolitan songs." So listening to this afforded a double pleasure.

Cleverness of arrangement was not the least distinguishing feature of the recital which I am describing. It was free from the incongruities of contrast which often, I am told, disfigure gramophone programmes, and, what is more, by dint of just appreciation in the matter of quantities, it gave us just enough of each record to secure the necessary impression, whilst making room for a singularly full forty minutes' worth of absorbing souvenirs. Hence an easy transition from the Neapolitan to the pure *bel canto* of the illustrious Adelina Patti—a portion of *Voi che sapete*, one of the best of the records made at Craig-y-Nos Castle in 1906, with Sir Landon Ronald at the

piano. I knew it well, for it was my privilege to give the first public performance of most of these records in illustration of a lecture on the art of the great singer at the Wigmore Hall soon after I came back from America. Like the unforgettable voice that it brought back to us, its "state of preservation" seemed next door to a miracle, and I feel sure it must have yielded to very many of my fellow-listeners the same inexpressible joy that it did to me. I often wonder whether the millions of gramophiles who never heard the great singer realise what it means to be able to recapture, even in diminished power and pre-electric recording, the unique tones of the famous *diva*. After it the duet *La ci darem*, sung by Battistini and Emilia Corsi, sounded just a trifle disappointing. In this the gifted baritone had been too loud all through, while his fair partner had remained too consistently in the background; literally, no doubt, too far away from the horn.

The last of the *bonnes bouches* took us back—those of us who had been there in the flesh—to that night of farewell on June 8th, 1926, when Melba bade adieu to opera at Covent Garden, to her admiring public, and to the beloved theatre where she had been singing for, off and on, very nearly forty years. Her speech from the footlights was, you may recollect, one of the first of its kind to be successfully recorded from the front of the house, and every inflection of the sad, tearful voice, every spasmodic variation of the goodbye theme, down to the final irrepressible outburst of audible weeping, was faithfully chronicled through the microphone. Curiously enough, the memory of that scene had recurred to me only a few days previously, when the news of her death reached England, and I had thought of her words whilst she lay dying in far-off Sydney (her native land, but not her native city)—the farewell words of regret, "I love this place. It is so hard to think I shall never sing within these beloved walls again." Truly, it was another of our cicerone's happy thoughts, before winding up on this sorrowful note, to give us the lovely record (H.M.V.054129) *O soave fanciulla*, from *La Bohème*, sung in brighter days by Melba and Caruso. They made a wonderful pair in Puccini's opera, and we may be thankful for the invention that enables us to resuscitate at will, not only the voices, but the distinctive vocal qualities of two such beautiful singers.

HERMAN KLEIN.

Listeners' Corner

Early in March I attempted to broadcast some records of "Famous Voices," to which Mr. Klein is devoting his article this month; and in order to cover as much ground as possible in the time at my disposal I was allowed to use a special fading in and out device that the B.B.C. engineers had gallantly, if rather reluctantly, prepared for me. Their chief objection to it was that a certain amount of induction was inevitable; but I doubt whether nine out of ten listeners noticed this. The advantage of the system was that I could play excerpts from records without abruptness in starting and stopping each of them, and could superimpose any comments or details that I had to give without breaking the continuity of the programme.

On the other hand, it was a nerve-racking job, since while sitting with my script in front of me and a turntable on each side and the fading apparatus between my knees, I had to change the records, wind up the motors, change the needles, and start or stop the records, at the same time manipulating the three knobs which controlled the microphone and this or that turntable; and all with my two hands. There were some anxious moments, and I was glad at the end to escape into the Savoy Theatre next door and to forget all about it in the diverting environment of "Wonder Bar" and its vivid cabaret drama.

The "Famous Voices" programme turned out to have been a success, and many listeners besides Mr. Klein (who would have done it so much better himself) wrote appreciatively and even asked for an encore. One or two, however, took the view which in advance I had expected; as, for instance, the writer (anonymous, of course) who said, ". . . I am unable to hear your mid-day recitals and I was annoyed and disgusted with the abominable atrocities which came over the ether to-night. As a friendly criticism I fail to see how this will enhance either your reputation or that of the Gramophone Company. If such records must be played, would it be possible to torment mid-day listeners instead of tired workers who require pleasure, not torture?" A constructive as well as a friendly critic, you see.

Here are the details of the programme, all the records being

H.M.V., those in the No. 2 Catalogue marked with an asterisk. The records of foreign statesmen, marked with two asterisks, can only be obtained from The Gramophone Co., Ltd., Hayes, Middlesex.

(1) E158*, Tolstoi; (2) E326*, Sarah Bernhardt, a passage from Rostand's *La Samaritaine;* (3) E162*, Sir Herbert Tree, *Hamlet's Soliloquy;* (4) 2.3535*, Dame Ellen Terry, *The Quality of Mercy;* (5) E164*, Lewis Waller, *Henry V at Harfleur;* (6) D825*, Theodore Roosevelt, *The Farmer and the Business Man;* (7) D367*, F.M. Lord Roberts, *National Service;* (8) AM1281**, Admiral Horthy; (9) AM1000**, M. Jean Bratiano; (10) E520**, General Primo de Rivera; (11) G.K.4**, M. Venizelos; (12) S4800**, H. E. Benito Mussolini; (13) C545*, Dan Leno, *The Huntsman;* (14) D373*, Albert Chevalier, *My Old Dutch;* (15) DA335*, Fernando de Lucia, *O Sole Mio;* (16) 03051*, Adelina Patti, *Voi che sapete;* (17) DB228, Battistini and Corsi, *La ci darem la mano;* (18) 054129, Melba and Caruso, *O soave fanciulla;* (19) DB943, Dame Nellie Melba, *Farewell Speech.*

Some of these records are marked in the catalogue "below 78" and others "above 78," so that it was necessary to attend to the speed indicator with every disc.

A pleasant result of the broadcast was the arrival of a box containing seven of the ancient Berliner seven-inch single-sided records which were still playable. The earliest of them was dated January 16th, 1896.

Have you ever tried the Winner record (5206) of *John Peel* on the dog? Listeners write to tell me that their dogs responded violently to the music of John Peel's pack as devised in the Edison Bell studios, when I broadcast the record last month.

The Gramophone and the Singer
THE TURN OF THE OPERATIC WHEEL
By HERMAN KLEIN

ONCE more we stand at the threshold of the London summer opera season, with minds expectant and appetites freshened for the coming feast. The menu, save as to a few details here and there, might almost be described as a repetition of last year's. There will be the same equal division of International repertories and scarcely any changes worth mentioning in the personnel of the leading foreign artists. The latest engagement was that of Maria Nemeth, the talented Viennese soprano, whose singularly perfect records obtained instant recognition in these columns when first issued by Parlophone last year. As in many other instances, Maria Nemeth's was a case of gramophone *réclame* first, followed by a London engagement and, as I sincerely hope, a London success. It is fully expected that she will prove to be a delightful artist. Another addition to the list of singers announced in March is a particularly good robust tenor from Belgium named René Maison. I do not remember to have heard any records by him, though I am told he has begun making some; but he is said to have a fine voice and already enjoys a reputation in certain Wagner rôles. We shall soon see.

I had a most enjoyable talk with Colonel Blois at Covent Garden one afternoon not long before the opening of the season. From this I gathered that the prospects, in spite of the world-depression, were surprisingly promising. The general subscription stood round about the average mark, and even at that juncture the house for the two cycles of the *Ring* was practically sold out. It was then the director's intention to make the revival of Mozart's *Die Zauberflöte* the earliest feature of the German campaign, and long before these lines appear the date of the event and the full cast will of course have been announced. For my own part I am looking forward greatly to this *reprise*, and later on I hope not to miss (as I did last year) the performance of *Die Fledermaus*, which I regard as one of those light masterpieces which the connoisseur can only enjoy thoroughly when sung by Viennese-trained artists in their own native tongue.

The famous impresario, Mapleson, states in his *Memoirs* that "the London season of 1867 was remarkable for the first performance of Verdi's *La Forza del Destino*." He does not mention that it was given at Her Majesty's Theatre on June 22nd, neither does he recall that it was a complete failure; for he never does draw attention to the failure of a production of his own. Now at that time the opera had only been given at St. Petersburg, Verdi

having written it expressly for the Imperial Theatre there. Its reception (November 10th, 1862) had been comparatively cold, thanks neither to the music nor its interpretation, but to the nature of the story, which, says Arthur Pougin, "was too sad, too sombre, too melancholy (the three principal characters perish simultaneously of a violent death, one in a duel, the other assassinated, the third by suicide), and so appeared to the audience a little too deep in colour." Then, two years after it had been heard in London, it was mounted at La Scala with a libretto partially revised by Ghislanzoni (the author of *Aida*) and a score considerably touched up by Verdi. These improvements secured for the opera a much more favourable verdict from the Milanese, even though it did not encourage the rulers of the Paris Opéra to try it there. They preferred to have Verdi write *Don Carlos* for them; which he did.

But in these Grand-Guignol days we object less to melodramatic horrors than did our opera-going parents. Hence am I in agreement with Colonel Blois and his co-directors that, having regard to its success wherever it is now done, the time has come for a revival of *La Forza del Destino* upon a scale that will make it one of the features of the Italian portion of the "International" season. It will certainly be a novelty for contemporary opera-lovers in every respect but where those musical excerpts are concerned which the gramophone has done so much to make popular. It is interesting, moreover, to note that the splendid duets to which I drew special attention in my operatic reviews last month were sung by at least two of the principal men who are to figure in the Covent Garden cast. This will be as follows: Don Alvaro, Aureliano Pertile; Carlo, Benvenuto Franci; Leonora, Rosa Ponselle; Guardiano, Tancredo Pasero; Melitone, Ernest Badini. The conductor will, of course, be Tullio Serafin, who, assisted by John Barbirolli, is to be in charge of the forthcoming Italian performances. Yet another revival to be awaited with curiosity is that of Zandonai's clever opera, *Francesca da Rimini*, which I may remind readers was produced at Covent Garden in July 1914, with Mme. Edvina, Martinelli, and others in the cast. Romani's *Fedra*, also down for production, has not yet been seen here, nor do I think I have heard a note of the music.

All things considered, it must be allowed that the prospects for the season just started are exceedingly bright, and that the position of the Covent Garden Opera Syndicate is at the moment an uncommonly enviable one. It is looking forward with tolerable certainty to the lion's share (if not the whole) of the promised Government subsidy, the granting whereof is not an actual *fait accompli* as I write these lines, but regarded by most people as a fairly sure proposition. Whether this will in any event prove an unmixed blessing remains to be seen. Something depends upon the manner in which it is going to be distributed and employed; something upon the question whether the amount is really large enough to be of solid and permanent value to the cause. I can hardly conceive of a State subsidy for opera which does not gather within its beneficent folds the purely British undertakings represented by the Carl Rosa Company and the Old Vic. The educative value of these institutions, one in the provinces, the other in two great London suburbs, cannot by any possibility be overlooked. Each has a strong claim to share in the spoil, if I may so term it; nay, more, each needs the support in order to be able to carry on without constant financial worry. It was matter for general regret when the Carl Rosa Company found itself compelled recently to bring its operations to a premature close, first of all in the country, afterwards at the Lyceum, just when it was giving some of the best performances in its history. I sincerely hope that the stoppage is only temporary.

Meanwhile, Sir Thomas Beecham, aided and abetted by Mr. Lionel Powell, has sprung upon us a veritable surprise. The present sojourn of *Bitter Sweet* at the Lyceum is to be followed by a six weeks' season of Russian opera and ballet, beginning on the 18th inst. It has nothing to do, apparently, with the still dormant activities of the Imperial League of Opera; nor does one see at first glance how it very well could. The *fons et origo* of the new speculation springs from the same adventurous source, that is all, and in the result it may prove to have been quite a good idea. Russian opera and ballet is a combined form of entertainment with which the name of Beecham has been long and honourably associated. Father and son exploited it at Drury Lane—at considerable personal outlay, it is true—nearly twenty years ago, with the co-operation of that same redoubtable Diaghilev who had previously introduced his Russian company for the first time at Covent Garden in 1911. The Beecham seasons of 1913 and 1914 were remarkable not, as Mapleson put it, for a novelty that failed, but for a series of successes that dazzled a new generation and set up a new fashion. The intervention of the war modified the course of events in that direction, as it did in so many others. Nevertheless, none who then witnessed *Boris Godounov* and the triumph of Chaliapin can possibly have forgotten it, and for them at least it will be good news that the famous singer is coming over to sing twice a week during this unexpected season at the Lyceum. He will also be welcome to the much larger circle of those admirers who have heard him in

one guise or another at the Albert Hall, but have never yet seen him on the legitimate operatic stage.

Chaliapin will, it is said, appear on the opening night in one of his favourite operas, namely Darjomisky's *Roussalka*. It should prove an attractive item in the repertory of this Russian company, which has been performing more or less regularly at the Théâtre des Champs Elysées, Paris, for the last three years. The artists, with the exception of Chaliapin, are unknown here even by name, but they are said to be a capable and well-trained troupe and the ensemble should by now have been brought to a high degree of efficiency. There will be an orchestra of seventy, with a Russian conductor, while Sir Thomas Beecham is to direct certain of the operas. The list of these includes, besides *Roussalka*, Rimsky-Korsakov's *Sadko*, Glinka's *Russlan and Ludmila*, Rimsky-Korsakov's *The Bride of the Czar*, Borodin's *Prince Igor*, and Moussorgsky's *Boris Godounov*. The ballets will comprise *Petroushka* (Stravinsky), De Falla's *L'Amour Sorcier*, Prokofiev's *Les Bouffons*, and Moussorgsky's *Le Mont Chauve*, all of them arranged by M. Boris Romanoff. For the cheaper parts of the house popular prices are to be charged, and, as the Lyceum Theatre holds 3,000 persons, full houses should comfortably pay expenses and leave a substantial profit.

To what extent the Russian season will affect Covent Garden, if at all, remains to be seen. Certainly not more, in my opinion, than Covent Garden will do harm to the Lyceum venture; and neither Sir Thomas Beecham nor Mr. Lionel Powell seems to have entered upon this "surprise" undertaking with any particular fear of the strongly entrenched opposition higher up the street. It has happened again and again in days gone by that the regular London opera-houses (two of them, both supported by a large roll of aristocratic subscribers) have been suddenly threatened in mid-season by the menace of a visit from a powerful foreign company, without suffering in the end to a disastrous extent. Such was Sir Augustus Harris's experience in 1889, when, during his second Covent Garden season, a strong Italian troupe from Milan, backed by Ricordis, turned up unexpectedly early in July and gave us our first performances of Verdi's *Otello* with the original Otello and Iago, Tamagno and Maurel, at the head of a powerful cast and conducted by the celebrated Faccio, who was the Toscanini of his day. Curiously enough, too, it was at the old Lyceum (Irving's theatre, I mean) that that very opposition rose up; and I remember we thought, among other things, that an orchestra of seventy was rather too big for the theatre. But the present auditorium is a good deal larger than the old one. Anyhow, in less than three weeks the struggle will be on, and it ought to prove exciting.

HERMAN KLEIN.

321

The Gramophone and the Singer

THE GERMAN SEASON

by HERMAN KLEIN

FORTY years ago exactly the "overflow" from Covent Garden was so extensive at the start of the London season that Sir Augustus Harris, whom I often quote (though I was never his "secretary," as my old friend Robin Legge stated in a charming article last month, but only his *unpaid adviser*),—Sir Augustus, I say, had the temerity to open up Drury Lane Theatre for the German, whilst reserving the opera house for his regular subscribers and the Italian and French performances. This went on six nights a week for two months or more at each house; and the *Ring* cycles, conducted by Gustav Mahler, were instanced as the finest ever heard outside Bayreuth, the company and the orchestra being, indeed, well-nigh unsurpassable. To expect such a record to be beaten in this present year of grace would be wholly unreasonable. Let us be thankful if, in point of artistic merit, the achievements of Bruno Walter and Robert Heger can be declared on a level with those of their famous predecessor. Without carrying comparisons any farther, I am fain to admit that the singing of Lotte Lehmann, Frida Leider, Elisabeth Schumann, Maria Olczewska, Lauritz Melchior, Friedrich Schorr, Herbert Janssen, and Ivar Andrésen was, as a whole, equal to the best that has been heard here in the works of Wagner and Strauss.

Another thing I must admit. It was not possible for me to hear all the German performances given last month. Thus I had to miss the *Rosenkavalier*, though I listened to the broadcast of the first and last acts from my arm-chair, and enjoyed them immensely. Lotte Lehmann and Richard Mayr sounded as inimitable as ever in their customary rôles, and it seemed to me that I had never heard any Italian tenor "oblige" the Marschallin so admirably as Heddle Nash did in the boudoir aria. In regard to the newcomer, Margit Angerer, I feel I ought to suspend judgment until I can see as well as hear her Oktavian. One could not thoroughly relish either her feminine vivacity of style or the musical ring of her voice so long as the tone had to suffer the infliction of a decided tremolo. Some of it may have been due to nervousness; not all, I fancy. Anyhow, most of it may disappear in another part.

The *Walküre* performance in the first cycle attained the peak of supreme excellence; as to this the general verdict was singularly unanimous. The *Siegfried* was equally free from blemish until the moment came for the awakening of the new Brünnhilde. The credentials of Juliette Lippe were almost as obscure as her Valkyrian descent, and I knew not whether to regard her as a German or an American, or both. The fact remained that she was better suited to the part in a physical than a vocal sense. The prolonged arm-stretching led up to none of the thrills, declamatory or otherwise, that Siegfried was so anxiously looking for. When he had recovered his breath he outsang the lady at every point, for, truth to tell, her head notes were palpably ineffective, and only a few in the medium fell gratefully upon the ear. The timbre had neither richness nor resonance, and not a suspicion of the essential tragic timbre. The plaudits at the end of the duet were obviously all for Lauritz Melchior.

That we should have had an exactly similar experience in *Götterdämmerung* was due to what the Lord High Executioner described as "a set of curious chances." By rights the superb Frida Leider should have resumed her proper rôle in the final episodes of the tetralogy; but, owing to the foot trouble that very nearly kept Lotte Lehmann out of *Die Fledermaus* and *did* keep her out of the *Rosenkavalier* on the following night, Frida Leider had to take her place as the Marschallin, and was thus (wisely objecting to appear three nights in succession) prevented from impersonating the pathetic Brünnhilde of the closing drama. So much the worse for us—and also, probably, for the German-American soprano, who was called upon at short notice to replace the missing (and sorely missed) Frida. It was the same story over again: plastic beauty marred by jerky gestures and attitudes shorn of real dignity, together with a complete absence of inspiration or vocal thrills. The Conspiracy and Oath scenes went for less than usual; or, rather, would have done so but for the admirable work of Lauritz Melchior, Herbert Janssen, and Ivar Andrésen, whose Hagen was the finest that has been heard since Edouard de Reszke's. In the same category stood the beautiful Waltraute of Maria Olczewska—by far the best since the days of Schumann-Heink—and the extraordinarily clever and subtle Mime of Heinrich Tessmer, who relieves the horrid little dwarf of all the exaggerated helplessness and unvocal squeakings that Albert Reiss had gradually developed, to the entire detriment of Wagner's conception.

322

The stage setting for the revival of *The Magic Flute* was exquisite in design and colouring—by far the loveliest I have ever seen of Mozart's fantastic masterpiece. Much of the singing was quite excellent, without being precisely *hors ligne*. The new Pamina, Margarethe Teschemacher, has a sympathetic quality that stood her well in *Ach, ich fühl's (Ah, lo so)*, without attaining the plane of a Claire Dux. The Tamino, Marcel Wittrisch, rather lacked the requisite smoothness of tone. Gerhardt Hüsch made a delightful Papageno; his lightness of touch was just right for the music. Fluency without brilliancy, accuracy with too little dramatic power, marked Noel Eadie's rendering of the airs of the Queen of Night. Those of Sarastro were nobly phrased by Ivar Andrésen, but the low notes were disappointing. All the trios were neatly sung, while Herbert Janssen and Heinrich Tessmer were simply perfect in minor rôles. On the whole Bruno Walter kept his orchestra under admirable control in what came near to being a memorable revival.

The splendid qualities, both vocal and dramatic, of Friedrich Schorr are too well known for it to be necessary to lavish fresh praises on his Wotan or his Kurwenal. I would like instead to thank him here for the fine examples of his artistry with which, through the hospitality of Mrs. Imhof, he enchanted a number of his admirers at the little concert room in New Oxford Street one afternoon last month. Comparisons between the real voice and the gramophone reproduction are interesting as well as profitable; but in this case I need do no more than say that if it is a pleasure to listen to Herr Schorr's records it is a double joy to hear the same music from the lips of the man himself. It was delightful to watch his intelligent and expressive countenance as he depicted the changing reflections of Hans Sachs whilst musing over the *Wahn, wahn* soliloquy; as he poured forth the devotional ecstasy of Wolfram's *Star of Eve*; as he enforced the contrasting emotions, the pathos, and the patriotic fervour of the *Two Grenadiers*. He reminded me more than once in these things of the art of his gifted countryman, Eugen Gura, and I thank him for recalling so gifted an interpreter, even as I thank Mrs. Imhof for affording me the opportunity of listening *en petit comité* to so accomplished and perfectly equipped a singer as Friedrich Schorr.

A remarkably fine performance of *Lohengrin* was that which terminated the series of German productions on May 18th. Happily the strength of the ensemble owed as much to the commanding presence and poetic singing of the new Belgian tenor, René Maison, as to the consummate art of Lotte Lehmann—the best Elsa since Rosa Sucher—and the highly-coloured Ortrud of Maria Olczewska. The other men, too, were unusually good, while the conductor, Robert Heger, had rehearsed his orchestra and chorus so as to bring out in absolute perfection the finest details of Wagner's glorious score. Having to be elsewhere as well, I concentrated on the first act and the bridal duet. In the latter René Maison displayed some really beautiful high notes and sang and acted with quite impressive dignity, while Elsa's mental struggle was magnificently depicted by Fr. Lehmann.

The Russian Season at the Lyceum

Some notes in the adjoining column cover the ground so far as the repertory is concerned. The opening opera, Dargomijsky's *Roussalka*, was immediately followed by a second novelty in Rimsky-Korsakov's *Fiancée du Czar*, while on the third night came an old acquaintance in the shape of *Prince Igor* —a sufficiently interesting start. The feature of *Roussalka* was—what it always has been—Chaliapine's phenomenal impersonation of the too-confiding old miller whose daughter's misfortunes ultimately drive him insane; and it was the extraordinary realism and histrionic power, added to the incredible vigour that the great singer exhibited in these scenes of *démence*, which made his whole effort so amazing. I did not find great variety in the opera on first hearing, nor an abundance of musical charm in the Russian melodies. But so long as Chaliapine was on the stage there was no lack of interest or excitement. He proved himself, indeed, as wonderful as ever.

What *Roussalka* lacked in musical values and gained from Chaliapine's personal achievement was counterbalanced in Rimsky-Korsakov's *La Fiancée du Czar* by a far more interesting score and an individually strong ensemble. But oh, how long-drawn everything seems! The librettist, with a good dramatic idea to work on, never contrives a scene that is concise or a character that is clear-cut. The composer never avoids monotony by knowing when or where to stop. Were it otherwise the *Fiancée du Czar* might be deemed another *Boris* or *Bartered Bride*. The concerted music is splendid, the local colour marvellous; and the performance, on the whole, was up to the best Russian mark. With two such capital novelties the season at the Lyceum began well.
                                        HERMAN KLEIN.

Notes on the Russian Operas

The season of Russian opera at the Lyceum gives an opportunity of hearing a few works for the first time. The names of Glinka and Dargomijsky are of great importance in the history of Russian opera, and the former wrote the first important national work, *A Life for the Tsar*, in 1835. This was the first attempt to write in the Russian style, and it came as a welcome change from the hybrid Italian work of his predecessors, deriving its inspiration from Russian folk-music. Glinka's next work was *Russlan and Ludmila*, now being given at the Lyceum. The story concerns the rivalry of three suitors for the hand of Ludmila, the daughter of Prince Svietozar. Of these the Princess loves Russlan. A sort of Caliban, Chernomor, falls in love with Ludmila, and by means of magic arts carries off the bride from her wedding-feast. Prince Svietozar sends the three knights to rescue his daughter. The rest of the plot concerns their adventures, and the ultimate success of Russlan. The libretto is weak, but the beauty and force of the music entitle it to respect. Berlioz wrote of it, "The work is fantastic and half Oriental, as though written under the double inspiration of Hoffmann and the Thousand and One Nights. It has a beautiful harmonic web, and is skilfully scored." Liszt was also impressed by the beauty of the music. There are some Eastern dances in the work which foreshadow the later Russian ballets. (Overture, H.M.V. D1808.)

Turning to Dargomijsky, the aim of this composer was to make "the sound represent the word," and he was a pioneer of what may be called "melodic recitative," an effort to impart truth to operatic music by giving it verbal verisimilitude. His first opera, *Esmeralda*, was conventional; his next, *The Roussalka*, which is in the Lyceum repertoire, was his masterpiece, and the third, *The Stone Guest* (or Don Giovanni under another name), was an effort to carry his ideas to their ultimate range of realistic expression by means of a mezzo-recitative. The Roussalka, or the Water Sprite, combines "dramatic feeling with fantastic colouring." Natasha, a miller's daughter, is in love with a young prince, who deserts her after receiving her love, in order to marry in his own station. Natasha drowns herself in the mill-stream and becomes a Roussalka, seeking the downfall of mortals. Her father, the miller, is driven mad by misfortune. The Prince, meanwhile, is unhappy in his marriage, and driven by remorse revisits the mill, now in ruins. The crazy miller appears, and

in revenge hurls him into the stream. Chaliapine gives one of his finest performances in the part of the miller. Cui says of the work: "On the dramatic side it reaches a very high level, while the recitative is equal to the best that has been written." The other two unfamiliar operas in the Lyceum are the *Tsar's Bride* and *Sadko*, both by that master of the fantastic in music, Rimsky-Korsakov. *The Tsar's Bride* is a brilliant and melodious work, richly orchestrated. The Oprichnik Gryaznoy loves to distraction Martha, daughter of a merchant, but she is engaged to the Boyard Lykov. Nevertheless, the Tsar, Ivan the Terrible, sees her by chance and chooses her to be his bride. The whole plot is too complicated to be given here. This is one of the most popular of Rimsky-Korsakov's operas, and it had an instant success after its first performance at Moscow in 1899. Pougin says, "The strings, and especially the violins, have a prominent part, and are handled with a fine sense of richness and sonority." *Sadko*, A Legendary Opera, in seven tableaux, was produced in 1897, and was received with tremendous enthusiasm. Sadko is a poor minstrel, who wagers that he will catch goldfish in the Lake of Ilmen by means of his singing and playing. He has many adventures, some of which take place at the bottom of the sea. The music is full of picturesque and brilliant effects, and contains many beauties, including the famous Chant Indou. The other two operas given, *Prince Igor* and *Boris*, are, of course, well known.

RICHARD HOLT.

The Gramophone and the Singer
THE ITALIAN SEASON:
"La Forza del Destino" and Other Operas
by HERMAN KLEIN

HEARING *La Forza del Destino* for the very first time on the opening night of the Italian season at Covent Garden, I sought in vain reasons for altering opinions expressed in these pages on the strength of a study of the vocal score and the gramophone records of Verdi's transitional opera. I had grown up in the belief that the music—much of it worthy to rank with the best in *Trovatore*, *Rigoletto*, and *Traviata*—must inevitably be more or less "killed" in the opera house by a story of irremediable improbability, absurdity, and incoherent melodrama. And so it proved, at any rate in my view. I enjoyed a great deal of what I heard, for how could one fail to listen with pleasure to the numbers that gramophonists know so well, when presented in person by such thoroughly competent singers as Rosa Ponselle, Aureliano Pertile, Benvenuto Franci, and Tancredi Pasero? I observed with curiosity, not unmingled with amusement, the strong early Verdian flavour of the choruses and dances in the scene at the inn, which recalled the corresponding episode in *Un Ballo in Maschera*, the customary contralto fortune-teller with a "wobble" and the gipsy ballet in *Traviata*. I noted an opening act similar to that of *Don Giovanni* —the angry father pierced (accidentally) by the sword of his daughter's innocent (not profligate) lover; and, later in the opera, the initiation of the heroine (in

male attire) into a Franciscan convent (*sic*) where, so far as I could perceive, only monks took part in the ceremony. However, the choicest ensemble bits occurred hereabouts; while virtual experience proved to one's entire satisfaction how the sorely-wounded hero came to have voice enough to join his arch-enemy (or best friend, I forget which) in a long and dramatic duet like *Solenne in quest' ora*.

What struck me most, however, in the familiar pieces for the two men was their unnecessarily loud, strident tone. It was so big in its sustained fortissimo as to suggest that I might have been guilty in their case of finding fault with the amplifying operator for what was really due to their own shouting. I cannot for the life of me see what object singers with magnificent organs like Pertile and Franci can have in keeping them at full pressure the whole time their mouths are open. Tancredi Pasero, whose tremolo seems to disappear entirely on the stage, carefully avoided this abuse of force, and his voice as the Guardiano sounded peculiarly rich and noble. Rosa Ponselle's, though not at its very best, exhibited its accustomed sweetness and charm in all *mezza voce* passages, besides conveying whenever necessary a wonderfully subdued yet intense expression of fear and mental suffering. She has this gift in a singular degree. I should have preferred the Curra (Nadia Kovaceva) in the part of the gipsy girl (Gianna Pederzini), and vice versa, had the voices permitted. But Ernesto Badini as the serio-comic Fra Melitone was the right man in the right place; and equally so was Maestro Tullio Serafin at the head of an excellent orchestra. The *mise en scène* was extremely artistic.

It is frequently my lot, as readers of THE GRAMOPHONE are aware, to have to criticise prominent Continental singers on the strength of their records before they make their débuts in this country. Maria Németh is a case in point. So long ago as February of last year I noticed her remarkable rendering of a couple of airs from Goldmark's opera, *The Queen of Sheba* (H.M.V. D1720), describing how, against a background of female voices, "her pure, steady soprano, with its limpid, translucent timbre, floats easily and with dominant power above them all." It was precisely this clear, penetrating tone, that can be sustained at its loudest and highest for minutes at a stretch without losing its musical quality, which proved Maria Németh to be the ideal soprano for the hard, cruel, but brilliant part of Turandot. But not only that. She also infused extraordinary significance into her acting, and depicting with an absorbing mastery of vocal *nuance* the gradual change from furious rage and aversion to passionate love for Prince Calaf. The latter rôle was played, as it should be, with combined simplicity and resolution by Antonio Cortis, a Spanish tenor of youthful mien, and the final duet was admirably sung by both artists. A delightfully sympathetic and tender Liù was forthcoming in Eidé Norena, whose capital record of the *Mad Scene* from *Hamlet* (Parlophone R20145) I had occasion to praise last month. The minor parts were in capable hands; the bâton in those of John Barbirolli, who warrants his growing reputation in Puccini's posthumous opera more than in any I have seen him conduct, bar *Gianni Schicchi*.

With the Verdi "boom" at its height, such an admirable Italian revival of *Falstaff* as we had on the third night of the season ought rightly to have drawn a crowd. Still, the Derby and Russian counter-attractions may have accounted for a diminished attendance. I am not willing to believe that the professed lovers of truly great music, whether in its operatic or its symphonic forms, can wish to treat with indifference—merely leaving posterity to appreciate, as it undoubtedly will—so superb a masterpiece. They will rarely, anyhow, have a better opportunity of relishing the marvellous wit and humour, the incredible technical skill, of Verdi's delicious score, as interpreted in the language to which the libretto was written, than was offered in this instance. The fruity Falstaff of Mariano Stabile improves with maturity, and I know no finer than his to-day. Indeed, all the men in the cast were efficient —much better, in fact, than the women, though the

shortcomings of the latter were trifling, and perhaps concerned their sartorial more than their musical make-up. The Dame Quickly of Elvira Casazza was an exception to the rule, but I have also, I admit, heard the lovers' duets better sung than they were by Dino Borgioli and Aurora Rettore. The orchestra, under Tullio Serafin, played with delicacy, if guilty of a few slips.

Traviata and *Rigoletto* in the second week completed the Verdi selection; and quite enough, too, for one season. *Aida* and *Otello* have received pretty regular attention in recent years, and will come all the fresher, when revived, for their omission this time. In the general opinion the performance of *La Traviata* equalled that of 1930, when Rosa Ponselle also filled the rôle of Violetta. She was well supported now by Dennis Noble and Dino Borgioli as the Germonts *père et fils*—a firm for whom I have never felt any particular admiration. For *Rigoletto* I could have spared more eulogies but for a disagreeable sensation that the Italians, knowing possibly that half the opera was being broadcast, were out for noisy tone all the time, and at last got so completely out of hand that Maestro Serafin quite lost control of balance in the famous quartet. This part of the opera I heard at home by radio, after witnessing the first and second acts at Covent Garden. The experience, as usual, enabled me to institute some interesting comparisons. If the singing of Dino Borgioli and Benvenuto Franci seemed to lack restraint in the theatre, their voices came over louder still by wireless, despite what I conceived to be a normal reception. In the quartet they very nearly submerged Noël Eadie's Gilda and completely obliterated Gianna Pederzini's Maddalena. In the scene with the courtiers and his hapless daughter the Jester indulged in an immoderate use of *parlato*, and positively shouted many of the execrations that Verdi meant to be declaimed to notes. Altogether Franci's Rigoletto struck me as being exceedingly melodramatic, which is, of course, what it should be, but at certain moments decidedly overdrawn.

As to the true ability of the new Gilda it was rather difficult to judge. She was far too nervous in the first act to be able to do herself justice, though happily her voice is naturally so steady that nervousness does not manifest itself by a tremolo. At first it sounded weak and veiled, but as she gained confidence it improved, and when the time came for *Caro nome* it was clear and strong throughout its compass. Miss Eadie has an exceptionally pure soprano tone, a well-equalized scale, and much facility of execution, together with impeccable intonation. The long-sustained high notes after the cadenza were of a bird-like clearness, the shake was an easy, natural trill. The success of the young artist under such trying conditions was most encouraging.

A notable revival of *Tosca*, with Stabile, Pertile,

and Iva Pacetti in the principal parts, was followed next night by the new opera, *Fedra*, by Romano Romani. Covent Garden owed this novelty to the kindly offices of Rosa Ponselle, who justly perceived in the title-rôle a magnificent opportunity for the display of histrionic powers beyond any that we had yet suspected. True, her Norma and Gioconda had in a measure prepared the way; but not until now had there been legitimate ground for acclaiming her as a great tragic actress. I take for granted that everybody has a notion of the purport of that dreadful Greek story which forms the subject of Racine's immortal tragedy. Not since Sarah Bernhardt enacted the unhappy Athenian queen who fell in love with her stepson have I seen anyone, actress or singer or both, save Rosa Ponselle, possessing the requisite dramatic genius for the portrayal of this character. It was not merely her realization of the woman's physical torment and mental anguish, ended only by death, that impressed me as wonderful, but the tremendous all-round art that enabled her to cope triumphantly with the colossal scene where the horrid truth stands revealed and Theseus murders both wife and son. Splendidly did the singer sustain the test of this extended *tour de force*; and no less splendid was the support that she received in its delineation from the new Spanish tenor, Antonio Cortis, and from Cesare Formichi, who, having created the part of Theseus when the opera was first done in Italy in 1915, came over expressly to undertake it here, or at least stayed for that purpose on his way home from America.

Lucky musician, you will rightly say, this "Roman of the Romans," to have such devoted friends! Certainly his opera, which has not even yet acquired the dignity of a printed vocal score, might never have been given at Covent Garden but for their potent aid. Yet the music—clever enough in its way, highly coloured, intensely emotional, competently put together and ably scored—needs only greater originality and more distinctive character to make the work a powerfully descriptive rendering of the story. Anyhow, it will always serve to show how amazingly well Rosa Ponselle can act and declaim, even though it be no sort of medium for the exhibition of the finer qualities of her vocal art. By the way, the new opera was preceded by *Gianni Schicchi* —the conductor in the one case being Tullio Serafin and in the other John Barbirolli, who presented a remarkably vivid study of Puccini's subtle little musical comedy.

The return of Beniamino Gigli again brought into actual hearing one of the rare tenor voices of our time—perhaps even of all time. He counts one for Italy; and, if I be not mistaken, I fancy the world will soon be counting another young tenor—Antonio Cortis, to wit—as one for Spain. What a voice, to be sure!

The Russian Season

The Russians, like the Italians, have come and gone. Both have left us something to think about, and too many months to do the thinking in. Of the two companies, the one at the Lyceum showed us the more vividly how much ground has yet to be covered before this country can legitimately claim to have a national opera of its own. Will it ever? I am not sure; but I can at least predict that we shall never, never equal the Russian musicians or the Russian singers at this particular game. With the aid of subsidies our Covent Garden Touring troupe and our Carl Rosa Company may continue to perform the operas of other nations in acceptable or even brilliant fashion. But that will be all. As yet, the British composers who can yield us works like *Sadko*, *Boris Godounov*, *La Fiancée du Czar*, *Prince Igor*, or even *Roussalka* and *Russlan and Ludmila* are not in sight. Nearly as invisible, I may add, are British singing actors and actresses and inspired choral masses, all of them trained and drilled to a miraculous degree of precision, of the type that we have just been seeing and hearing at the Lyceum. In this latter regard I do not say the thing is impossible; I only stress the likelihood of its taking long years to achieve, and even then it will be in the masterpieces of any school but the Russian.

Of all those I have named I liked *Sadko* best, even as it is conclusively the finest of Rimsky-Korsakov's operas. Coherent in form, replete with dramatic interest and picturesque detail, it is richer in contrast than the rest of the group, and so counteracts the effect of monotony and naïveté which these fantastic stories of folk- and fairy-lore of Russian and Scandinavian origin almost always present. In *Sadko* we saw not only wonderful pictures, but listened to some delightful melodies and capital singing. The sole disappointment, curiously enough, was the rendering of the piece that everyone knew best. The tenor who sang the *Hindoo's Song* to the crowd at Novgorod would have done well to study Kreisler's record in order to imitate the clarity needed for those descending semiquavers. The two heroines embodied vocally just exactly the opposites needed for the difference between the human and the supernatural, while the heartlessness of the hero—surely the tallest personage ever seen in an opera—was no less aptly revealed in his bright, hard, declamatory tones.

From a choreographic point of view the ballets were not of outstanding merit and could not compare with the glories of the Pavlova-Nijinsky period. There was a decided sameness about most of them, while the music, with the exception of De Falla's, had little individuality or charm. As a specimen of old-fashioned opera-ballet, *Russlan and Ludmila* was welcome; but the school of Glinka has outlived its day, and I for one can only regard it as a curiosity.

HERMAN KLEIN.

The Gramophone and the Singer

THE LILLI LEHMANN RECORDS

by HERMAN KLEIN

WE are constantly hearing vain regrets that the gramophone was not perfected in time for the great *fin-de-siècle* singers to leave behind permanent manifestations of their genius. Or else, that the records which some of them did make were taken in pre-electric days, and consequently were valueless for present or future utilization. It is this last contention which is going to be seriously combated. The question is a simple one: would you rather possess some semblance of a precious original, whether it be a voice or a face, or a script of some sort—even if reproduced by an imperfect method, so long as it emanated directly from that original—or would you prefer to have nothing at all? I have very little doubt as to what the answer of the majority would be; but, on the other hand, I am not altogether certain whether the response would be backed up by sufficiently widespread purchases to make it worth the while of the older gramophone companies to bring out all their " historical " records and put them on the market.

This danger of commercial risk has been the reply proffered by the companies for the last twenty years whenever they have been advised to keep the early records by famous singers in their current catalogues instead of relegating them to the limbo of things unattainable or forgotten. I have never ceased to insist in these pages on the value of such records, not merely for their sentimental associations or as living proof of what the actual voice was like, but for their availability as priceless and incomparable examples of perfect singing and ideal interpretation. It would be useless to pretend that they are beyond criticism; for they were executed under great difficulties, with inferior or makeshift accompaniments, and nearly always by artists who had had no special training or born adaptability (as in the cases of Marcella Sembrich, Melba, Caruso, and Battistini) to fit them for the task of gramophone recording. Nevertheless, there are to be found in these old records features of artistic beauty belonging to a school which, if not completely lost and gone, is rapidly disappearing beneath our ordinary horizon. Here, at any rate, are innumerable points to be studied and, if possible, imitated by young singers, to be listened to and enjoyed by all who love good singing. Glad am I, therefore, nay delighted, to find that a start has just been made on the road of resuscitation by the Parlophone Company with a collection of old recordings made by that very

gifted German soprano, Lilli Lehmann, who died in May, 1929, at the age of 81.

They were sung by her in the months of June and July, 1907. Consequently she had then just turned fifty-nine, and the fact is worth bearing in mind when you come to admire the extraordinary youthfulness of the tone, its well-preserved clarity and ringing timbre, and the remarkable energy and vivacity of the style. Let it be here noted that Lilli Lehmann's was one of those voices known as a " soprano sfogato," having in the head register a thin yet ethereal quality which she used to bring down into the medium as well, until it dropped naturally and often suddenly into the chest tone. This equalization of the scale *downwards* explained her ability to sing for long periods without fatigue and also to undertake the heaviest as well as the lighter soprano rôles. Thus her *coloratura* was exceptionally smooth and brilliant, whilst at the same time she could declaim to perfection the most dramatic of Mozart's recitatives. She was thus directly in the line of Jenny Lind, Tietjens, and Ilma di Murska, and happily equipped to illustrate in an enduring form the art which they practised so superbly without having the privilege of leaving the evidence of it behind them. That is why I declare that the world has reason to be grateful for the re-discovery and re-issue of these Lilli Lehmann records.

They are, indeed, despite their subdued volume, their old-time scraping, and their quaint orchestral devices, nothing less than a series of gems. My sole regret is that they do not include a reminder of the fact that this amazingly versatile woman was among the celebrated Isoldes of her time; but unluckily Wagner recording on the grand scale had not begun in 1907. As compensation, however, they afford irrefragable evidence on two points that have frequently been insisted upon by the present writer: first, that Wagner preferred his interpreters to be singers who had been thoroughly grounded in the principles of the true Italian school; and, secondly, that in the operas of Mozart (as in the oratorios of Handel), the use of the *appoggiatura* must be adhered to in accordance with the customary rules of the period—not in the academic literal way now taught in Germany and imitated with servile accuracy in this country. If anyone thinks I have been too dogmatic on the subject, let him carefully study these records of a great authority on the art of vocal interpretation.

In the matter of mechanical excellence they do not vary much, if at all; while, as for the question of accompaniments, it really does not signify whether they are orchestral (of the old *Ersatz* description) or pianistic. Everything centres in the voice and the rendering, and these are wonderful. As enumerated in the Parlophone " Special Edition " list (1931, Odeon Red Label) the group consists of seven 10¾-inch double-sided records and two 12-inch ditto, the price of the former being 7s. and of the latter 8s. 6d. each. Three sides—one small, two large—are worthily devoted to Leonora's great air, *Abscheulicher*, from Beethoven's *Fidelio*, in which opera I heard her several times prior to her final appearance in it here in 1899. Again does the interpretation stand out as a classic model in every possible respect, the ideal rendering of one of the most difficult pieces ever written for a dramatic soprano. Others of the same type, and no less exacting, are the two airs for Donna Anna from *Don Giovanni*, wherein the distinguished singer also appeared during the same farewell visit; yet another being *Norma*, which is, of course, represented by the opening melody of *Casta Diva*, in addition to the passage known in the German as *Empfange diesen Schwesternkuss*, from the scene with Adalgisa. But, after all, the most glorious examples are the Mozart. Besides the *Don Giovanni* they comprise the two trying florid airs from *Seraglio* (*Ach, ich liebte* and *Marten aller Arten*), both sung not merely with faultless purity of style and execution, but with a sustained power that can only be described as astounding. Then there are likewise the soprano duets from *Così fan tutte* and *Le Nozze di Figaro*

(*Sull' aria*), in which Fr. Lehmann was joined by Hedwig Helbig, who was, I believe, a pupil of hers. Anyhow, the two voices are so remarkably alike in quality that you can hardly distinguish one from the other, while as regards freshness there is absolutely nothing to choose between them.

Finally, there are on a separate 10-inch record two notable excerpts from *La Traviata*, the opera wherein the famous soprano made her début at Her Majesty's Theatre in the summer of 1880. Well do I recollect her gay Violetta—a tall, handsome woman in her early thirties, clever actress and charming singer, with a technique that could surmount Verdi's cadenzas as he wrote them (not as changed or facilitated in the Marchesi manner) and a voice like Adelina Patti's, that could take on the more sombre hue essential for the emotional episodes of the opera. Precisely that contrast is what we get here in the records of *Ah, fors' è lui* (much abbreviated) and the finale of the third act, where Violetta's touching appeal, *Alfredo, Alfredo!* is continued by the concluding ensemble, the solo voice alone being reproduced. I wish she had enriched the souvenir by recording the Polonaise from *Mignon*; for Filina was the part in which she followed up her initial success as Violetta, winning her triumph in the lighter rôle side by side with a memorable group that included Christine Nilsson, Trebelli, Campanini, and Del Puente. That was a cast worth hearing! But we can afford to be satisfied with this gramophone collection as it stands, and I sincerely trust that its reception will be such as to justify the rescue from oblivion of other " precious voices from the past."

The Gramophone and the Singer

A SEVEN YEARS' RETROSPECT

by HERMAN KLEIN

IN obedience to the Editorial behest, I have been busily engaged during recent days in preparing for this centenary number a catalogue that will, we trust, prove useful as well as interesting to our readers. It is a list representing the pick of the choicest vocal records from among the thousands (yes, it must be thousands) that I have written about since I began work for THE GRAMOPHONE in June, 1924. The magazine was then not quite a year old, and I have always somehow had a feeling of regret that I was not privileged to write for it from the start. On the other hand, I am always grateful to my Editor-in-Chief and to my London Editor for having given me the opportunity to do so as soon as they could, as well as for the unfailing support and moral encouragement which they have never ceased to accord their devoted contributor.

When I wrote my first article under the new heading of THE GRAMOPHONE AND THE SINGER, explaining therein the circumstances of my twenty years' previous experience in connection with the instrument and its product, I little dreamed that another seven years of such progress and development lay before me as those which are more than completed with the 100th number of this journal. It has indeed been a marvellous period of advance, alike in regard to the perfecting of the process through the invention of the electrical method of recording the human voice, the vast improvement in the truthfulness and quality of the reproduction, and the superiority of the material in which modern records are preserved. For the singer it has represented an enormous gain in facility and comfort, through being allowed a fair chance to do oneself justice whilst facing a sympathetic microphone in place of a resentful and distorting horn. What that change has meant to the operator no less than the performer can only be known to those who have " gone through the mill." You would hardly credit what hours of positive torment, of suspense, vexation, and disappointment, had to be endured before the passable result was arrived at. Still less would you believe how many first-rate artists with recognized vocal talent were ruthlessly rejected and wasted because their " tests "—often not real tests of actual merit at all—failed to earn the approval of self-satisfied committees whose solitary consideration was the achievement of certain commercial results. And, knowing what I do, I am not prepared to assert that

considerations of a similar kind are not continuing to exist under the easier conditions of to-day. Anyhow, one thing is certain; it is now a comparatively simple matter for vocalists of the second rank to make better commercial records than those accomplished with infinite difficulty by the greater artists of a day gone by. The amplifier is largely responsible for this illusion.

For these reasons, apart from their enormous personal interest, the old pre-electric records which I first wrote about in THE GRAMOPHONE possess a measure of sentimental value that I fancy will be shared by many of my readers. They cannot be duplicated; but it may be that spare copies of the majority of them are still to be had. Remember, those included in the following list were what I consider to have been the choicest from every point of view, the artistic no less than the mechanical and technical; and some of them were extraordinarily fine—far finer than the noisy, over-amplified specimens that we too often hear now. I have not been listening to them over again for the purpose of making this catalogue; nor was it necessary to do so. But I have carefully re-read every article and review that I have written in this connection—a labour of duty, mind, not of love—and I think I may say that I have found I had a more or less distinct recollection of every record.

Those of earliest date include many that are of quite remarkable interest. It should be borne in mind that my group-articles, dealing with various composers, various schools and periods of opera, oratorios, lieder, and so forth, were spread over a very wide area and enabled me to gather in my net all the gems of a then-untouched mass of treasures. As time went on the older stock gradually became exhausted until, in 1926-7, the new electrical recording began by degrees to replace everything else. And a very wonderful crescendo has been the result.

A SELECTION OF NOTABLE RECORDS

(with references to " The Gramophone and the Singer " and Monthly Reviews)

1924

Sembrich, *Una voce,* H.M.V. DB431	...	...	July
Galli-Curci, *Una voce,* H.M.V. DB261	...	...	,,
Melba, *Caro nome,* H.M.V. DB346	...	...	August
Galli-Curci, *Caro nome,* H.M.V. DB257	...	...	,,
Galli-Curci, *Oh! fors' è lui,* H.M.V. DB257	...	...	,,
Scotney, *Caro nome,* Voc. A0191	...	...	,,

1924

Dawson, *Prologue to Pagliacci*, H.M.V. C1259 ... September
Ruffo, *Prologue to Pagliacci*, H.M.V. DB464 ... ,,
Stracciari, *Prologue to Pagliacci*, Col. X328 ... ,,
Amato, *Prologue to Pagliacci*, Fonotipia 74142 ... ,,
Formichi, *Prologue to Pagliacci*, Col. 1487 ... ,,
Zanelli, *Prologue to Pagliacci*, H.M.V. DA398 ... ,,
Constantino, *Celeste Aida*, Col. A679 ... October
Martinelli, *Celeste Aida*, H.M.V. DB335 ... ,,
Hipolito Lazaro, *Celeste Aida*, Col. 7342 ... ,,
Caruso, *Celeste Aida*, H.M.V. DB144 ... ,,
Onégin, *Mon coeur s'ouvre*, Brunswick 518 ... November

1925

Formichi, Two *Rigoletto* airs, Col. L1578 ... January
Radford, Two *Messiah* airs, H.M.V. E277 ... February
Homer, *O Thou that tellest*, H.M.V. DB303 ... ,,
Lunn, *He shall feed*, H.M.V. DB506 ... ,,
Homer, Two *Messiah* airs, H.M.V. DB301 ... ,,
Jordan, *Messiah* recits, Col. 973 ... ,,
Allin, *Why do the nations ?*, Col. 1453 ... ,,
Stevens, Two *Messiah* airs, Voc. DO20145 ... ,,
Whitehill, *It is enough*, H.M.V. DB438 ... ,,
Lunn, *O rest in the Lord*, H.M.V. DB504 ... ,,
Calvé, *Habañera* from *Carmen*, Pathé 5559 ... March
Maria Gay, *Habañera* from *Carmen*, Col. A5279 ... ,,
Farrar, *Seguidilla* from *Carmen*, H.M.V. DB244 ... ,,
Formichi, *Toreador's Song*, Col. D5586–7 ... April
Lappas, *Flower Song*, Col. D1463 ... ,,
Muratore, *Flower Song*, Pathé 5204 ... ,,
Gluck, **Alma**, *Micaela's Air*, H.M.V. DB279 ... ,,
Buckman, **Davies**, **Ranalow**, etc., *Madam Butterfly* (first Opera Album), H.M.V. ... May
Ruffo, *Nemico della patria*, H.M.V. DB242 ... June
Rethberg, *La Mamma morta*, Brunswick 50054 ... ,,
Caruso, *Come un bel di*, H.M.V. DA117 ... ,,
Bonci, *Amor ti vieta*, Col. 8086 ... ,,
Hislop and **Gilly**, *Butterfly* duet, H.M.V. DB743 ... August
Chaliapine, *Voici donc les débris*, H.M.V. DB106 ... October
Hempel, *Robert, toi que*, H.M.V. DB297 ... ,,
Caruso, *Bianca al par*, H.M.V. DB115 ... ,,
Journet, *Pif Paf*, H.M.V. ... ,,
Tamagno, *Rè del cielo*, H.M.V. DR104 ... November
Kalter, *Ah, mon fils*, Odeon XX72661 ... ,,
Galli-Curci, *Shadow Song*, H.M.V. DA260 ... ,,
Tetrazzini, *Shadow Song*, H.M.V. DB534 ... ,,
Amato, *Sei vindicata*, H.M.V. DB636 ... ,,
Ruffo, *Adamastor*, H.M.V. DB406 ... ,,
Caruso, *O Paradiso*, H.M.V. DB117 ... ,,
Piccaver, *O Paradiso*, Polydor J22015 ... ,,
Battistini, *Averla tanto amata*, H.M.V. DB210 ... ,,
Dux, *Dove sono* and *Deh vieni*, Polydor 72890 ... December
Battistini, *Non più andrai*, H.M.V. DB736 ... ,,
Chaliapine, *Madamina*, H.M.V. DA555 ... ,,
Farrar and **Scotti**, *La ci darem*, H.M.V. DK111 ... ,,
Patti, *Batti, batti*, H.M.V. O3055 ... ,,
Sembrich, *Batti, batti*, H.M.V. DB428 ... ,,
Hempel, *Batti, batti*, Polydor T24006 ... ,,
Schumann, *Batti, batti*, Polydor 65655 ... ,,
Gogorza, *Serenade* from *Don Giovanni*, H.M.V. DB154 ... ,,
McCormack, *Il mio tesoro*, H.M.V. DB324 ... ,,

1926

Jurjevskaya, *Air from Iphigenie auf Tauris* (Gluck) and *Ach! ich fühl's* (Mozart), Parlo. E10278 ... January
Bettendorf, *Marschallin airs from Rosenkavalier*, Parlo. E10341 ... ,,
Chaliapine, *Russian Songs*, H.M.V. DB757 ... ,,
Gigli, *O Paradiso* and *M'appari*, H.M.V. DB109 ... ,,
Lehmann and **Schlusnus**, *Mozart duets*, Polydor 72933 ... ,,

1926

Ivogün, *Queen of the Night aria*, Polydor 85310 ... February
Bettendorf and **Schorr**, Duet from *Magic Flute* ... ,,
Plançon, *Airs from Magic Flute*, H.M.V. DB657 ... ,,
Radford, *Airs from Magic Flute*, H.M.V. E78 ... ,,
Schumann, *Ah, lo so*, Polydor 65811 ... ,,
Ivogün, *Martern aller Artern*, Polydor 85303 ... ,,
Hempel, *Martern aller Artern*, H.M.V. DB331 ... ,,
Bori, *In uomini, in soldati*, H.M.V. DA132 ... ,,
Lunn, *Non più di fiori*, H.M.V. DB517 ... ,,
Bohnen, *Wotan's Abschied*, Polydor 85277 ... ,,
Alda, **Caruso** and **Journet**, *Trio from I Lombardi*, H.M.V. DM126 ... March
Pinza, *Il lacerato spirito*, H.M.V. DB699 ... ,,
Caruso and **Scotti**, *Solenne in quest' ora*, H.M.V. DM105 ... ,,
Destinn, *La Vergine degl' angeli*, Col. A5398 ... ,,
Rosa Ponselle, *Pace, pace, mio Dio*, H.M.V. DB1275 ... ,,
Battistini, *Urna fatale*, H.M.V. DB738 ... ,,
Bettendorf, Two airs from *Un Ballo in Maschera*, Parlo. E10431 ... ,,
Caruso and **Scotti**, Duet from *Don Carlos*, H.M.V. DM111 ... ,,
Ruffo, *Per me giunto*, H.M.V. DB178 ... ,,
Allin, *She alone charmeth* (Gounod), Col. 756 ... April
Barrientos, *Waltz from Mireille*, Col. 7338 ... ,,
Melba, *Ophelia's Mad Scene* (Thomas), H.M.V. DB364 ... ,,
Galli-Curci, *Ophelia's Mad Scene* (Thomas), H.M.V. DB927 ... ,,
Gogorza, *Vision fugitive*, H.M.V. DB627 ... ,,
Gilly, *Légende de la Sauge*, H.M.V. DB693 ... ,,
Kappel, *Closing Scene* (*Götterdämmerung*), Polydor 66099 ... ,,
Olszewska, *Waltraute* (*Götterdämmerung*), Polydor 72982 ... ,,
Caruso, *O Rachel* (*La Juive*), H.M.V. DB123 ... May
Austral, *Il va venir* (*La Juive*), H.M.V. D798 ... ,,
Destinn and **Caruso**, *Sento una forza*, H.M.V. DB616 ... ,,
Baklanov, *Air from The Demon* (Rubinstein), H.M.V. DA465 ... ,,
Melchior, Two *Siegfried* pieces, Parlo. E10442 ... ,,
Leider, *Ozean, du Ungeheuer*, Polydor 65625 ... June
Tudor Davies, *O 'tis a glorious sight*, H.M.V. D932 ... ,,
Journet, *Calunnia* and *Serenade* (*Faust*), H.M.V. DB921 ... July
Kurz, *Sonnambula* airs, Polydor 72953 ... ,,
Nordica, *Suicidio*, Col. 74021 ... September
Barrientos, *Bell Song* (*Lakmé*), Col. 7338 ... ,,
Cavalieri, *Vissi d'arte* and *In quelle trine*, Col. A5178 ... ,,
Lipkovska and **Baklanov**, *Rigoletto* duet, Col. A5296 ... ,,
Chaliapine, *Airs from Mefistofele*, H.M.V. DB942 ... October
Bonci, *Airs from Rigoletto*, Col. D8083 ... ,,
Zenatello, *Celeste Aida* and *Cielo e mar*, Col. A5400 ... ,,
Hislop and **Granforte**, *Solenne in quest' ora*, H.M.V. DB939 ... ,,
Ljungberg and **Widdop**, *Walküre* Love Duet, H.M.V. D1322 ... November
Ponselle and **Martinelli**, Final duet, *Aida*, H.M.V. DA 809 ... ,,
Schlusnus, Two airs from *Tannhäuser*, Polydor 66408 ... ,,

1927

Galli-Curci, *Shadow Song*, H.M.V. DA817 ... January
[First allusion to electrical recording.]
Bettendorf, *Ocean, thou mighty monster*, Parlo. E10525 ... February

1927

Rethberg, *Ritorna vincitor* and *O Patria mia* (*Aida*), Brunswick 50084 ... ... February

Bettendorf and **Melchior,** Bridal duet, *Lohengrin,* Parlo. E10515, 10527, and E10540 ... ... ,,

Culp, *Ave Maria* (Schubert), Polydor 70531 ... ,,

Gerhardt, *Erl-könig* (Schubert), Voc. A02125 ... ,,

Hempel, *Hark! hark, the lark,* H.M.V. DA382 ... ,,

Slezák, *Du bist die Ruh'*, Polydor 65774 ... ,,

McCormack, *Serenade* (Schubert), H.M.V. DA458 ,,

Haley, *Who is Sylvia ?,* Voc. X9561 ... ... ,,

Dux, *Wohin ?,* Polydor 70688 ... ... March

Culp, *Frauenliebe und Leben,* Odeon X52948–55 ,,

Onégin, *Du bist wie eine Blume,* Brunswick 10213 ,,

Chaliapine, *Two Grenadiers,* H.M.V. DB933 ... ,,

Rehkemper, *Erl-könig* and *Orpheus,* Polydor 66006 ... ... April

Slezák, *Der Nussbaum,* Polydor 62423 ... ,,

Slezák, *Lotosblume* and Brahms's *Ständchen,* Polydor 62424 ... ... ,,

Onégin, *Vier ernste Gesänge* (Brahms), Polydor 72919–20 ... ... ,,

Schumann-Heink, *Sapphische Ode,* H.M.V. DA525 ,,

Iunn, *Sapphische Ode,* H.M.V. DA597 ... ,,

Gerhardt, *Von ewiger Liebe,* H.M.V. DB848 ... ,,

Zenatello and **Noto,** *Otello* duet, H.M.V. DB953 ,,

Eva Turner, *Vissi d'arte* and *Voi che sapete,* Col. L1836 (recorded at Covent Garden) ,,

Van Endert, *Ständchen* (Strauss), Polydor 19110 May

Schorr, *Traum durch die Dämmerung,* Polydor 62379 ... ... ,,

Gerhardt, *Auf dem grünen Balcon* and *Verborgenheit* (Wolf), H.M.V. DA715 ... ,,

Rehkemper, *Prometheus,* Polydor 66004... ,,

Scheidl, *Archibald Douglas* (Loewe), Polydor 66009 ... ... ,,

Allin, *Edward* (Loewe), Col. L1466 ... ,,

Stabile, *Onore* and *Quand ero* (*Falstaff*), Col. L1970 ... ... ,,

Kipnis, *Wotan's Abschied,* H.M.V. D1225 June

Jeritza, *Il est doux* and *Adieu, forêts,* H.M.V. DB1041 ... ... July

Fleta, *Celeste Aida* and *Una vergine,* H.M.V. DB1053 ... ... August

Spani and **Granforte,** *Pagliacci* duet, H.M.V. DB1046 ... ... ,,

Gervase Elwes, *Love went a-riding* (Bridge), Col. L1325 ... ... September

John Coates, *Eleanore* (Coleridge-Taylor), Voc. A0246 ... ... ,,

Megane, *Sweet Venevil* (Delius), H.M.V. E430 ... ,,

Eva Turner, *Ritorna vincitor,* Col. D1578 ... ,,

Gervase Elwes, *Full fathom five* and *Lake of Innisfree,* Col. L1398 ... ... October

Brunskill, *Sea Pictures* (Elgar), Col. 9170–2 ,,

John Coates, *Speak, Music* (Elgar), Voc. A0299 ,,

Suddaby, *Charming Chloe* (German), H.M.V. E421 ,,

Elwes, *Morning Hymn* (Henschel), H.M.V. B322 ,,

Labbette and **Reed,** Songs for voice and violin (Holst), Col. L1590 ... ... ,,

Fraser Gange, *Sea Fever* (Ireland), H.M.V. E3 ... ,,

Chaliapine, *Boris Godounov* re-recordings, H.M.V. DB934 ... ... ,,

Martinelli, re-recordings, H.M.V. DA891, DB979 ,,

Lehmann, L., *Ozean, du Ungeheuer,* Parlo. R20024 ,,

Horace Stevens, *Four songs* from " *Maud,*" Voc. KO5186 ... ... November

1928

Santley, *Father O' Flynn,* Col. 373 ... ... January

Ben Davies, *To Mary,* H.M.V. D100 ... ,,

Elwes, *On Wenlock Edge* (V. Williams), Col. 7363–5 ,,

Dale Smith, *Silent Noon,* Col. 9245 ... ... ,,

1928

Dal Monte, *Mad Scene* (*Lucia*), H.M.V. DB1015 February

Ljungberg, Airs from *Forza del Destino,* H.M.V. D1352 ... ... ,,

Gigli and **de Luca,** *Solenne in quest' ora,* H.M.V. DB1050 ... ... ,,

Schorr, *Sachs Monologue,* H.M.V. D1351 ... ,,

Schumann, *Alleluia* and *Vedrai carino,* H.M.V. DA845 ... ... March

Schipa, Two airs from *Il Barbiere,* H.M.V. DA874 ,,

Tauber, Schubert's *Winterreise,* Parlo. RO20037– 42 ... ... ,,

Lehmann and **Kiepura,** Duets from *La Tosca,* Parlo. R20048 ... ... ,,

Widdop, Airs from *Prince Igor* and *Lohengrin,* H.M.V. D1353 ... ... April

Heldy and **Ansseau,** Duet from *Carmen,* H.M.V. DB1115 ... ... ,,

Scacciati and **Granda,** *O dolce mani,* Col. L2078 ... May

Schoene, Airs of *Liù* (*Turandot*), H.M.V. E503 ... ,,

Olszewska, Card Scene (*Carmen*), H.M.V. D1363 ,,

Formichi, Airs from *Andrea Chénier* and *Rigoletto,* Col. L2065 ... ... June

Stabile, Airs from *Don Giovanni,* Col. D1612 ... ,,

Bettendorf, *Senta's Ballad,* Parlo. E10706 ... ,,

Galli-Curci, Homer, Gigli, de Luca, Pinza and **Bada,** Sextet from *Lucia* and Quartet from *Rigoletto,* H.M.V. DQ102 ... ... ,,

Henschel, *Das Wandern* and *Der Leiermann,* Col. D1621 ... ... ,,

Branzell, Airs from *Gioconda* and *Trovatore,* Parlo. E10719 ... ... July

Burg, baritone airs from *Tannhäuser,* Parlo. E10721 ... ... ,,

Eva Turner, Airs from *Turandot* and *Aida,* Col. D1619 ... ... August

Kipnis, *Der Wanderer* and other Schubert songs, Col. L2134–6 ... ... October

Chaliapine, *Vi ravviso* and *Ave Signor,* H.M.V. DA962 ... ... ,,

Larsen-Todsen, Closing Scene (*Götterdämmerung*), Parlo. E10756 ... ... ,,

Austral, *Ocean, thou mighty monster,* H.M.V. D1504 ... ... November

Leider, *Abscheulicher* (Fidelio), H.M.V. D1497 ... December

Inghilleri, *Prologue* and *Largo al factotum,* Parlo. RO20070 ... ... ,,

1929

Hislop and **Chaliapine,** *Faust* at Covent Garden, H.M.V. DB1189 ... ... January

Peter Dawson, *Song of the Flea,* H.M.V. C1579 ,,

Martinelli, Two *Pagliacci* airs, H.M.V. DB1139 ,,

Dal Monte, *Carneval di Venezia* Variations, H.M.V. DB1001 ... ... ,,

Onégin, *Che farò,* H.M.V. DB1190 ... ... February

Piccaver, *Ah! si ben mio,* Brunswick 50115 ... ,,

Lehmann, *Ave Maria* (Bach-Gounod), Parlo. RO20076 ... ... ,,

Leider, Airs from *Don Giovanni* and *Armide,* H.M.V. D1547 ... ... March

Ponselle, Martinelli and **Pinza,** Trio from *Forza del Destino,* H.M.V. DB1202 ... ... ,,

Borgioli and **Gentile,** Duets from *La Traviata,* Col. L1639 ... ... ,,

Andrésen, Airs from *Magic Flute,* H.M.V. C1625 ,,

Giannini, *Madre pietosa,* H.M.V. DB1217 ... April

Seinemeyer, *Liebestod* (*Tristan*), Parlo. E10829... ,,

Seinemeyer, *Vissi d'arte* and *Cantate* (*Tosca*), Parlo. E10851 ... ... June

Bettendorf and **Branzell,** Duets from *Lohengrin,* Parlo. E10852 ... ... ,,

Lucky the man who has all these treasures in his library. Very many of them are collectors' pieces, long withdrawn from the catalogues, owing to lack of public support : a few have been re-recorded electrically with new numbers.

HERMAN KLEIN.

The Gramophone and the Singer

The English Opera Season : Its Lessons

by HERMAN KLEIN

THE six weeks of opera in English at Covent Garden should have taught its promoters some valuable lessons. Will they, I wonder, be pondered and profited by ? If so, one of the first things to be done is to get rid of the idea that the attitude of the critics, on the whole, was either prejudiced or unnecessarily harsh because it happened to be severe. I should be among the first to deny this ; and I ought to know. Nay, more, I honestly believe that the faults and shortcomings—and there were many of them—were pointed out in the friendliest possible spirit, without *arrière-pensée*, in a whole-hearted desire to benefit the cause. After all, it is the duty of newspaper criticism to insist upon a high standard ; and you cannot give opera at Covent Garden, any more than you can listen to it there, without keeping that standard pretty constantly in view. I may be told that what was good enough for Manchester and Liverpool in the spring ought to be good enough for

London in the autumn. But is this so when the *locale* is Covent Garden ? Aye, there's the rub ! Even companies like Sir Thomas Beecham's and the B.N.O.C. have tried it in the past and found that there is a difference.

To begin with, there is the vast alteration in physical environment imposed upon young native singers by the increased size of the auditorium—not its holding capacity, but the larger area, the more extended focus and the unwonted gulf that divides the performers from their audiences. To singers who are not accustomed to this separation, there seems to be no *rapport* between them and their public. The result is that they consistently raise their voices and use them too loudly. The *mezzo-forte* does not exist ; the *piano* is rarely heard ; during most of the time we get only *fortes* and *fortissimos*, chiefly the latter. My objection to excessive loudness is not being lessened by the amount of it that

I hear from up-to-date records, and I find it no less objectionable on the wireless because there it cannot be modified without detracting from the true quality of the voice. The fault was less in evidence when the German and Italian artists were singing last spring than on most occasions during the recent season, and I noticed it as much when I went to the theatre as when listening to a broadcast.

An even bigger trouble, because it will be less easily remedied, is that of the words. Very few artists in this company knew how to make them heard. I should award first prize to Mr. Percy Heming, for he was not only distinct, but showed what an improved and versatile artist he has become by attacking successfully several strongly-contrasted rôles, and singing them admirably into the bargain. His really clever impersonation of the marriage-broker in *The Bartered Bride* takes me back to what was one of the most interesting productions of the season which it inaugurated. Smetana's masterpiece, when performed in a theatre of the right size for its *opéra-comique* subject, may command the same popularity in London as *The Barber of Seville* and *Die Fledermaus*. These are operas that have to be treated with a light hand, acted with the right spirit and verve, sung with delicacy and finesse. How can such comedies be intelligently followed and enjoyed from a distance when most of the lines are getting lost en route ? The ubiquitous Mr. Heming plainly showed the way, with Miss Thea Phillips and Mr. Francis Russell running a dead-heat for second place. Mr. Octave Dua in his delightful character studies conquered his Italian accent to such good purpose that his Wenzel, the stammerer in *The Bartered Bride*, was more audible than most of the fluent speakers.

There were other artists whose diction was also creditable—occasionally, though not as a rule. The reason for these variations was the absence of a guiding mentor (during the early rehearsals with piano) to stop the vocal malefactors and tell them when their words were undistinguishable. Distorted vowels, dropped consonants, weak enunciation, mispronounced words are blemishes that simply ought not to be tolerated in a good English opera company. They contribute to the inequality of the representation quite as seriously as mistakes or slips in the orchestra, and an overworked conductor cannot be expected to correct everything. Mr. John Barbirolli was under manifest pressure and did remarkably well considering the minimum space of time allowed him for preparation. He had reason to be proud of his *Tosca* performance. It was full of go, and the right melodramatic spirit prevailed with particular effect in the second act, where I thought Mr. Percy Heming made a forcible and forbidding Scarpia and Miss Odette de Foras a highly picturesque Tosca. *Carmen* was conducted by a new-comer, Mr. Frederick Hay, who did not seem very familiar with the traditions of the opera, notably as to tempi. He allowed Miss Enid Cruickshank too many liberties—and she took them, whilst thinking infinitely more of her vocal effects

than her diction. It was, perhaps, as well that most of Hersee's funny old version should be hidden, as it was, amid a continuous cloud of gabbled words. As *The Times* and the *Observer* truly pointed out, the only exceptions to the rule of " Jabberwocky " were the Remendado (Octave Dua) and the Micaela (Thea Phillips) The latter never allowed her beautiful voice to stand in the light of her lingual task ; she sang really well, albeit, like others in this opera, the victim of faulty stage-management. The Toreador, whose name was Escamillo, seemed to instil Mr. Arthur Fear with prospective doubts about his approaching *corrida* at Granada. He was extremely nervous, and unluckily his song was further spoilt by the inability of the Mercédès to tackle her G sharp in an otherwise meritorious attempt to reintroduce Bizet's long-neglected *coda*.

On the whole, I should feel inclined to say that the heavy operas came off better than the lighter ones in a season that was somewhat of a *frittura mista*. Certainly more praise than blame was awarded for the general rendering of *The Mastersingers*, *The Valkyrie*, *Aida*, *Lohengrin*, and even *Parsifal*. After all, these are works of the calibre that the stage of Covent Garden is rightly fitted to display and for the house to enable one to hear to advantage. As for *The Wreckers*, which likewise belongs to the heavy brigade, I can only reassert what I have previously said somewhere about Dame Ethel Smyth's opera. With its massive choruses, its tricky ensembles, and its wealth of declamatory recitative and choice, sturdy Cornish recrimination, it is vastly more likely to succeed as a dramatic cantata in the concert room than as an opera. The story may be what is commonly called picturesque ; the final catastrophe in the cave may recall (with a difference) the last act of *Aida*, where the lovers are immured, not drowned, together. But too much of the action is repetitive and futile ; a sense of dullness reigns supreme. To call it an attractive musical entertainment would be sheer flattery.

The performance of *Parsifal* suffered from a lack of that wonderful repose for which Bayreuth alone seems to set the shining example—one more proof that the precious brilliant ought never to have been torn from its original setting or, should I say, reproduced in vulgar paste. Some individual figures stood out well : for instance, the wisely abbreviated and stately Gurnemanz of Mr. Norman Allin ; the pitiful, pathetic, yet dignified Amfortas of Mr. Percy Heming (another amazing metamorphosis) ; the sonorous, sinister Klingsor of Mr. Hubert Dunkerley ; and, in lesser degree, the efficient but undistinguished Parsifal of Mr. Parry Jones. Mere singing cannot realize characters like the last-named, much less the difficult and complex rôle of Kundry, for which Miss Odette de Foras has had neither the experience nor the severe training. *Parsifal* is a work that must, if played at all, be approached, dealt with, and judged only by the loftiest standards. You may " get away " with *The Mastersingers* and *The Valkyrie*, but there can be no half-measures with Wagner's swan-song. The conductor, Mr. Hay, obviously knew his score ; but in his reading there was no intellectual breadth, just as in his beat there was none of the quiescence, the calmness and cohesion, that the whole interpretation demanded. The first Grail scene has departed in many details from the Bayreuth model, and should be re-copied at headquarters. Everyone moved too quickly, except the boys (who could not, however, keep step) ; worst of all, the Esquire who leads the procession bearing in his hands the Holy Grail, and who should take only one long trailing step to the others' two. Well do I recall Pauline Cramer, the soprano, whom Wagner selected for this silent rôle. She looked the living embodiment of some ethereal, spiritualized youth, serene and angelic of countenance, utterly absorbed in his proud duty. The same ineffable impression, never to be experienced again, was created by the unforgettable voice of Schumann-Heink, singing from the heights the inspired theme of the " Durch Mitleid wissend der reine Thor."

The second provincial tour, which was to open on October 26th with a fortnight's visit to the Theatre Royal, Glasgow, will be chiefly notable for a new English production of *Der Rosenkavalier*, underlined for the 29th. The cast includes Miriam Licette as the Marschallin, Norman Allin as the Baron Ochs, Marjorie Parry as Oktavian, and Norah Gruhn as Sophie, with John Barbirolli conducting. Following Glasgow come fortnights in succession—and, I hope, success—at Edinburgh, Liverpool, and Birmingham.

P.S.—I hear that the Carl Rosa Opera Company is not going to Canada after all—not, at any rate, for the present. Instead, a contract has been entered into for a tour in the United States, opening at Boston on December 28th and to last for twelve weeks. After that the company will return to England. Meanwhile, it will continue with its home activities for six weeks at various provincial towns. All this is much better than talk of enforced idleness and premature dissolution.

⧫   ⧫   ⧫

The Gramophone and the Singer

Sims Reeves: "Prince of English Tenors"
by HERMAN KLEIN

IT was a Scotsman and a Glaswegian, David Baptie, who bestowed upon Sims Reeves the above appellation in his *Musical Biography*, published in 1883. He was right enough in so doing, though he was wrong about the date (as were other dictionaries at the time) of the famous tenor's birth, which was not October 21st, 1822, but, as shown by the register of Woolwich Church, September 26th, 1818. Our " prince of tenors " always had a pardonable weakness for wishing to appear young ; and he certainly looked it when I last heard him sing in public at the Empire Theatre, 36 years ago— even also when I visited him at his bedside at Clapham not long before his death, which occurred at Worthing, October 25th, 1900. There were then people living who could remember his illustrious predecessor, John Braham (according to Baptie " one of the most wonderful tenor singers of whom we have any record "), whose career of sixty years he equalled, and whose age of 79 he beat by three years. The voices of great singers often last an amazingly long time ; and Sims Reeves was a great singer in every sense of the word. I do not think,

however, that he was a great teacher. I never heard a really remarkable pupil of his, and he gave lessons in the room next to mine at the Guildhall School of Music for several terms. One of them was his second wife, Miss Maud René.

Let me quote from my obituary notice in the *Sunday Times* of October 28th, 1900 : " I heard Sims Reeves for the first time in Costa's oratorio *Naaman* at the Norwich Festival of 1866. He had just turned forty-eight, and was still, comparatively speaking, in his prime. What a beautiful voice it then was !—so peculiarly Italian in its clear, pure timbre and its ' velvety ' yet resonant quality, so wonderfully capable of the tenderest expression, so tinged with that poetic sadness which was one of its rarest charms. . . . When Sims Reeves went to Milan to study in the 'forties, the art of the *bel canto* was still in its meridian there, and the glorious traditions of the Italian school were quickly and easily imbibed by a young singer whose genuine tenor voice so readily lent itself to music and method alike. On his return to London in 1847, Sims Reeves was able

334

to shine to advantage by the side of those vocal giants of the 'palmy days.' In a word, beauty of voice and style, high artistic intelligence, and rare distinction of manner and bearing combined to justify his being at once hailed as the leading English operatic tenor of his time. His triumphs as an oratorio singer began soon afterwards, and, although he did not desert the lyric stage for many years, it was in the concert room that he was destined to achieve the most lasting and memorable of the brilliant successes identified with his career."

If he died a poor man, it was largely because of two things : he had not the knack of saving, and he lost as much as he earned (he himself once calculated that the total amounted to £80,000) through the throat troubles —real or imaginary—that so frequently prevented him from keeping his engagements. The relief and joy when he actually appeared upon the platform were almost amusing; yet he commanded what were for those days very high fees. Sometimes there were other reasons for his non-appearance. He refused to sing at the Handel Festival of 1877 on account of the British high pitch then in vogue. He had long protested against it as being injurious to the voice, and in 1868 wrote a long letter to the *Athenæum*, confirming Chorley's complaint that the pitch in this country was half a tone higher than that of most foreign orchestras, and a whole tone higher than it was in the time of Gluck. Happily, in the end, the arbitrary dictum of Sir Michael Costa was overcome, and Reeves lived to see the *diapason normal* universally adopted.

As it was, however, I often had the good fortune to hear him in oratorio in my young days, and an immense treat it was to listen to his superb declamation in pieces like *Thou shall break them*, *The enemy said*, and *Sound an alarm* ; or to admire his wonderful delivery of *Deeper and deeper still*, which remained, " almost to the last, a miracle of tragic pathos." And then (again quoting from my memoir of him), " his rendering of *Adelaide* was one of those ideal efforts that entitle Sims Reeves to a place among the few great classical singers of his time. Somehow all his finest qualities both of nature and art seemed to be concentrated in the interpretation of Beethoven's immortal romance ; and the result was a something that lingers with undying fragrance in the memory of all who heard it. As a ballad-singer he was for many years without a rival. The mantle of Braham fell upon his shoulders, and he wore it worthily even down to those darker moments of his life when necessity compelled him to descend to a sphere beneath that whereof he had so long been a shining light."

In 1889 he published his reminiscences under the title of *My Jubilee ; or Fifty Years of Artistic Life*. As proof that he was a good musician he wrote :—

Besides being taught the piano and soon afterwards the organ, I learnt at a very early age to sing. When I was a boy of ten I could play all Handel's organ accompaniments from the original figured basses ; and at the age of fourteen I was appointed to the post of organist, or at least performed an organist's duties, at North Cray Church. I also trained the choir.

He had, he recorded, been first trained as a baritone, and it was not until he had sung for some time on the operatic stage that " Nature and my own self-consciousness taught me that I was a tenor. There have been instances, as I have elsewhere remarked, of singers coming out as tenors and finding afterwards they had baritone voices. . . . But apart from my own case, I never knew any instance of a singer beginning as a baritone and afterwards becoming a tenor until a few years ago I found that the eminent vocalist, M. Jean de Reszké, had gone through precisely the same experience." Besides reiterating in his book his views about pitch, he also penned some sane remarks about the miserable English translations of Italian opera libretti and the martyrdom that the " worthless doggerel " inflicted upon singers. Likewise, he denounced the " star " and the " encore " systems, the latter of which so long constituted the bane of his artistic existence. People were constantly asking, " Why won't Sims Reeves give encores ? " His answer was, " Because I am not paid to sing them, and I wholly object to them on principle."

Lastly, let me print once more what he said to an interviewer from the *Pall Mall Gazette* long before he wrote his book :—

You ask me how I have been able to put such pathos and feeling into a song and make a great success of it, when other singers would fail altogether. It is because I have always studied my words. I have read them and phrased them in every possible way, asked myself what they meant, and interpreted them according to my own feeling. I walk up and down, trying this line and that, until I feel I have struck the right idea. But I am never satisfied. Nowadays singers do not study elocution sufficiently, if at all. In a recitative, for instance, the words are sacrificed to the music. In my method they are of equal importance.

And yet, after the great tenor had died, one critic remarked that in his opinion Sims Reeves used not to enunciate with sufficient distinctness—a libel that attested either to the critic's unconscious deafness or his lack of truthfulness. Anyhow, the words that he spoke to the *Pall Mall* reporter in 1884 come down clearly, strongly, and appropriately enough to the present day, nearly fifty years later, when we are informed by certain sapient folk that the diligent and meticulous study of song-words by singers is an entirely novel development. There is where ignorance about *tempi passati* can create false beliefs.

The pity is, of course, that the modern gramophone came just too late for Sims Reeves to leave the world any records of his indescribable voice and incomparable art. Unfortunately, too, he never had a successor ; for neither Edward Lloyd nor Ben Davies (a hale and hearty veteran still) ever laid claim to that distinction. Like the other great 19th century singers whom a few of us heard and perhaps knew, Reeves is just a memory, no more. Among the latter is the well-known choral conductor, Mr. Arthur Fagge, who remembers him distinctly because he acted as his accompanist during the closing years of his career; and it has been left for Mr. Fagge to devise a scheme whereby the gramophile can obtain some notion, at second hand, of those characteristics of treatment and phraseology that were prominent features of what may be termed Sims Reeves' ballad style. This idea has been carried out (under Mr. Fagge's supervision and with his own pianoforte accompaniments) by Mr. Frank Titterton, who has sung for the purpose eight records manufactured and just brought out by the Decca Company.

On the face of it the experiment may be deemed a laudable one. To what extent it has succeeded is a question that must be answered exclusively in the light of what we have a right reasonably to expect. It is obvious that a singer, however intelligent, however ably "coached," cannot give an exact imitation of something or someone he has never heard. He cannot reproduce the peculiarities, the mannerisms, the individual inflections, much less the inimitable timbre and expressive quality of voice that was as unique as it was beautiful. Would that he could! But, to Mr. Titterton's credit be it said, he has not attempted the impossible. I would not even be sure that, in his heart of hearts, he lays claim to the possession of all the qualifications for his difficult task that are set forth in the Decca note for publication which I have received with these records. Mr. Titterton, like a modest man, probably wishes them to be judged at their face value, and, so far as the present writer is concerned, precisely that and no more shall be done. I shall take leave only to point out here and there a few deviations from the exact Sims Reeves readings which careful attention and a good memory have enabled me to observe. But after this lengthy preamble I shall have to be brief.

The four double-sided Decca discs are numbered K614 to 617, and I would like to take them here in their order of importance, beginning with *Deeper and deeper still* and *Waft her, angels* (K616). Mr. Titterton sings the recitative with genuine feeling, though his pathos would have more closely have resembled his prototype's had he broken up the phrases more, as punctuated by Handel, instead of preserving such even continuity, save of course in the outburst, " 'Tis this that racks my brain." The *appoggiature* are correct, except one in "Gilead hath triumphed," which I fail to recall. Too many s's are lisped; too many are quite inaudible— a pity where there is such a number of them. Some of the accompanying chords sound too weak. I think Reeves used to make Sidney Naylor play them with greater firmness and strength; he liked delicacy, but he also knew how to appreciate support. The pathetic ending, where the voice dies away with a sigh, " I can no more," is well portrayed both by singer and player.

In *Waft her, angels*, there is a hint of the robust tenor of earlier days, though none of that wonderful *legato* on the " slurred notes " with which Sims Reeves made us hold our breath as his lovely notes soared into the heights. Here, again, I feel that the crescendos on the piano scarcely balance with the vigour apparent in each rising vocal phrase.

With Braham's famous nautical ballad, *The Death of Nelson* (K617), we are transported to another and no less familiar region of Sims Reeves' varied repertory. Here he was wont to be boldly descriptive and frankly realistic, yet, at the right moment, like Nelson himself, tender as any woman. Mr. Titterton has caught the spirit, even though he occasionally misses an effective contrast. He has not lost a single chance, however, in *The Jolly Young Waterman*, which fills the other side of the same disc and is the most satisfying of the whole group. In *Tom Bowling* the rhythm should have been more marked; while, if the s's are clear enough here, never once do we catch the final consonants either in the " aloft " or in any of the words that rhyme with it. Much better in regard to enunciation is the rendering of *The Bay of Biscay*; it shares the same disc (K615), and goes with plenty of swing. But was Mr. Titterton really told to pronounce Biscay with an equal stress on both syllables, making the second rhyme with the letter K ? I never heard it sung so before. Reeves used to give it the same sound as " whiskey " (whether Scotch or Irish mattered not). On the other hand, his Scots accent in *Macgregor's Gathering* (K614) mattered very much when he sang for his friend Ambrose Austin, at St. James's Hall, on a St. Andrew's Eve. It was, indeed, excellent; which I am sorry to say Mr. Titterton's is not, albeit he throws abundant *verve* into his singing of the old ballad.

There remains only to speak of a record of *The Last Rose of Summer* on the reverse side of the last-named disc. I find difficulty in dealing with this, for the reason that I never heard Sims Reeves sing the air. However, the question has been put to Mr. Arthur Fagge, who informs our London Editor that it was first sung by Reeves as an encore at a concert given in Newcastle, and it went down so well that he subsequently repeated it in other programmes. But if he sang it to Mr. Fagge's accompaniment, did Reeves approve of the ornate harmonies here employed or the extra flourishes introduced by Mr. Titterton ? In any case, I would observe that it was not Reeves' habit to sing what was regarded in his time no less than ours as a woman's song. To my thinking, it would have been far more appropriate to have included, in place of *The Last Rose*, such a characteristic example as *My pretty Jane* or *Come into the garden, Maud*, which will ever be associated with the name of our " Prince of English Tenors."

HERMAN KLEIN.

The Gramophone and the Singer

"RUDDIGORE" IN RETROSPECT

by HERMAN KLEIN

IT will be forty-five years on the 22nd of this month since *Ruddigore, or the Witch's Curse*, a comic opera in two acts, by W. S. Gilbert and Arthur Sullivan, was produced at the Savoy Theatre in the presence of the most brilliant and distinguished audience that I ever saw at one of those wonderful first nights ; and I remember them all from *The Sorcerer* onwards. The interest in *Ruddigore* was of a special kind, because it was known that the author was making something of a new departure in this parody of transpontine melodrama. The nucleus of the idea he had taken from his own clever little sketch, *Ages Ago*, which I must have seen at least three times during its long run at the German Reed's Entertainment in Regent Street. He gave this the topsy-turvy touch peculiar to all his creations, while the dialogue and lyrics were quite up to the customary Gilbertian mark. Yet at the outset the cleverness of the whole thing escaped appreciation. It took more than one revival to bring home to a rather dense public the subtle humour of a plot concerned with the curse that compelled the wicked Sir Despard Murgatroyd and his descendants to commit a crime every day, coupled with the device of bringing to life the family portraits and making them the instruments to enforce the fulfilment of the family curse.

This last naturally proved the pivotal scene of the story, and, had the rest been equally good, all would have been well. But, although the dénouement was quickly altered, the second act has always remained scrappy and incoherent, leaving as the sole weight to balance the other side of the scale—what ? Some of the most charming, original, and delightful music that Sullivan has put into any of his Savoy scores. True, it never acquired the popularity of its near neighbours in date, *The Yeoman of the Guard* and *The Gondoliers*, much less of the earlier favourites such as *Pinafore*, *The Pirates of Penzance*, and *The Mikado*. Yet even then the first run lasted for ten months, and good judges were consistently echoing my opinion that the music "was certainly not a whit inferior in tuneful grace, humorous character, picturesque fancy, and masterly knowledge of effect" to the best of the composer's efforts. It belonged to what many consider his finest period—that of *The Golden Legend*, first heard at the Leeds Festival of the previous autumn—and, indeed, we read in the excellent biography of Herbert Sullivan and Newman Flower that " From the superb numbers of the *Legend* he could return, completely attuned, to compose the lightest of music in *Ruddigore*. He always considered

that this Opera contained some of the best of his light opera composition." (? compositions.)

It is interesting now to note (thanks to the same biographers) the circumstances in which *Ruddigore* had been first discussed by the two famous Savoyards just a year previously :—

. . . "a January of snow. One morning, in the midst of a blizzard, a snow-covered figure battled his way against the driving sleet up to the steps of Sullivan's house. It was Gilbert, who brought with him the outline of an entirely new plot. So pleased was he with the theme, that he had hurried off to Sullivan before he had begun to work his story out. It was Sullivan who let him in, who tried to brush a mountain of snow from his overcoat. Gilbert appeared as a veritable visitor from the North Pole. They went to their chairs and the fire . . . Gilbert had brought the idea for *Ruddigore*.

" They sat there, these two, the windows banking up with snow, scheming out the story. Lunch-time came, was announced, and passed. Who wanted lunch ? The twain were absorbed by the theme. An hour later the manservant announced lunch again. They went on talking, they talked as they ate, and *Ruddigore* was a practical entity by the time they had finished the meal."

Such was the inception of the piece which His Master's Voice now adds to the list of its Savoy Albums electrically recorded under the supervision of Mr. Rupert D'Oyly Carte. If not exactly familiar, the plot is probably as well known to the readers of these pages as it is to most of the members of that healthy young body, the Gilbert and Sullivan Society, whereof I confess that I know nothing beyond its name—and I am not even sure that I have got that right. In any case, " Not mine to sing the stately grace " of the crafty but criminal Murgatroyds as they step from their full-length frames in the picture gallery at Ruddigore Castle ; or to recall the quaint conceits uttered by that fascinating lunatic, Mad Margaret. Permit me to do something more useful by quoting—at full length—the original cast, if only because it contained certain honoured names that were not expected subsequently to reappear in a Savoy playbill; thus, as Percy Fitzgerald put it, "The loss of Grossmith was impending . . . Rutland Barrington had seceded . . . Durward Lely, that finished tenor, was soon to depart ; his successor, Courtice Pounds, was to follow. Jessie Bond, after a long service, was to go also." But of these Barrington, Pounds, and Jessie Bond were to remain for a time longer ; whereas one favourite then singing in her last opera was the delightful Leonora Braham, who, sadly neglected, poor thing, survived in retirement until her death a few weeks back. What an admirable vocalist and actress she was! Well, here was the cast —

Robin Oakapple...	Mr. GEORGE GROSSMITH
Richard Dauntless	Mr. DURWARD LELY
Sir Despard Murgatroyd	
	Mr. RUTLAND BARRINGTON
Old Adam Goodheart ...	Mr. RUDOLPH LEWIS
Sir Roderic Murgatroyd	Mr. RICHARD TEMPLE
Rose Maybud ...	Miss LEONORA BRAHAM
Mad Margaret ...	Miss JESSIE BOND
Dame Hannah ...	Miss ROSINA BRANDRAM

I omit the seven Ghosts, but if they are still " walking " they will, I am sure, forgive me. I do not intend making any comparisons between the galaxy of talent enumerated in the original Savoy cast and the group of artists collected by the present Mr. D'Oyly Carte for the H.M.V. performance ; it would obviously be unfair to do so. Enough that it is the best now available. The actual distribution is as follows :—

Robin Oakapple...	Mr. GEORGE BAKER
Richard Dauntless...	Mr. DEREK OLDHAM
Sir Despard Murgatroyd	Mr. SYDNEY GRANVILLE
Old Adam Goodheart	Mr. STUART ROBERTSON
Rose Maybud ...	Miss MURIEL DICKSON
Mad Margaret ...	Miss NELLIE BRIERCLIFFE
Dame Hannah ...	Miss DOROTHY GILL

Conductor, Dr. MALCOLM SARGENT.

The Album is completed on nine double-sided discs (numbered DB4005 to 4013), and on the inside cover is provided a full synopsis of the plot corresponding in sequential order with the series of records as played. It would be still more satisfying, of course, if these reproductions could include Gilbert's witty dialogue, which is necessarily missed by all who love its clever " quips and cranks " and scintillating repartee. In compensation for its absence, one ought to be able to distinguish with ease every line of the lyrics; but that, I fear, is more than could be said with truth of most of the singers, notably those of the fair sex and the tenor, Mr. Derek Oldham, who swallows too many consonants, and puts tone too exclusively in front of language. One may well ask, where is the famous Savoy diction gone ? Only three or four of the men seem to have caught a glimpse of the old tradition. For example, Mr. Baker, Mr. Robertson, Mr. Granville, and Mr. Darrell Fancourt, who happily crops up in some of the second-act records, named on the labels if not in the cast. Miss Dickson's

enunciation is especially faulty ; it lacks refinement and comprises too many superfluous diphthongs. Miss Nellie Briercliffe is better in these respects, and her singing of Mad Margaret's scena, *Cheerily carols the lark*—a masterpiece of verbal and vocal humour—rises well on the way to the Jessie Bond level.

But the patter of the girls (always excepting the chorus) is nothing like so clear as it ought to be. There is an unusual quantity of Sullivan's rapid-fire patter in *Ruddigore*, and too few of these singers appear to have the secret of it. Mr. Baker, for one, sets the right example, and when he says to Mr. Derek Oldham, " My boy, you may take it from me," it would be well if his injunction were literally obeyed. Does anyone look after these things, I wonder ? Mr. Carte is responsible, of course, for the " supervision " ; and so in a sense, I suppose, is Dr. Malcolm Sargent, though I don't exactly see how the conductor can be expected to tackle problems of enunciation when his forces are gathered before the microphone. At the same time, it seems to me that the same preparatory polish ought to be imparted to the work of the principals that one perceives so plainly in that of the chorus and orchestra. The voices of the former are delightfully fresh, their words crisp and distinct. The accompaniments are played to perfection, and it is a treat to hear the Sullivanesque overture, with its sustained vivacity, its weird suggestions of the supernatural, its lightning runs for the violins, and its amazing mastery of form, so splendidly rendered. The ensembles and the two finales go with capital spirit, and I look forward to the day when television as applied to the gramophone will enable us equally to enjoy the dances, the stage gestures, and the picturesque costumes.

To return for a last word as to the singing. If some of the solos and duets are disappointing, no fault can be found with the majority of the numbers ; while in things like the madrigalian section of the first finale there emerges a degree of precision and a quality of tone that bring back memories of bygone days. Again, I congratulate all concerned upon the advancement of a worthy Savoyard and successor to the lamented Bertha Lewis in the person of Miss Dorothy Gill. Her voice, a genuine English contralto, reminds me more of Rosina Brandram's than of Bertha Lewis's, which showed a growing tendency to force up the chest register ; but, on the other hand, Miss Gill needs to equalise the upper part of her scale, and also to cultivate with greater breadth of style more dignity and repose of delivery. I have only to add that the recording of the entire Album is up to the highest H.M.V. standard.

HERMAN KLEIN.

The Gramophone and the Singer

KEEPING OUT THE FOREIGN MUSICIAN

by HERMAN KLEIN

A YEAR or so after the Incorporated Society of Musicians was formed, I was asked whether I would like to join it. I did not refuse outright, but said I would prefer to wait a little and see what line the Society was going to take regarding certain professional matters in which I happened to be particularly interested. Time passed, and I began to notice that the matters in question were either ignored, or else discussed in a very casual way at the annual conferences. Unfortunately, I do not possess copies of the Society's proceedings, and have not the time to refer to them wherever they are to be found ; nor is it necessary to do so for the purposes of this article. But of one thing I am quite sure, and that is, that the Incorporated Society of Musicians has never done all or nearly all that it should have done for the protection of the British singer and the advancement in this country of the art of singing generally. It has never, for instance, tried to get an Act of Parliament passed, making it illegal for an uncertified person to ruin young voices by bad teaching, or to call oneself a teacher of singing at all without first passing a formal examination similar—though less severe—to those required of a doctor or a dentist. In this vital matter it has preferred a neutral attitude, if indeed it has considered it at all.

Yet we find this same Society, at its recent annual conference, taking a very active part in an exceedingly foolish and shortsighted agitation for making this land of ours a sort of Tom Tiddler's ground that shall be unapproachable to the foreign musician, from the most eminent specimen down to the humblest restaurant fiddler. What a brilliant idea, to be sure ! True, the initiative in the business was taken by the landing authorities at our various ports, acting under the powers granted by the Aliens Act, which, of course, goes back to the period of the war, when we were compelled for our own safety to keep out suspicious characters, and to intern all persons of enemy birth. The only excuse for exercising such powers to-day, where musicians are concerned, is of an entirely different kind. It cannot possibly be meant for the protection of the few, but of the many ; in other words, like the Orders in Council to stop " dumping," the application of the old law can and ought to be only with the object of keeping out a crowd of mediocre foreign performers, instrumental and vocal, when we have such a multitude of our own—on an average, of superior calibre—who are quite unable to make a living under existing conditions.

Had the taboo stopped there, no one would have objected ; but it did not. Unluckily, it went so far as to prevent the entry into England of solo artists of recognized eminence—singers, pianists, violinists, and others who stand in a special category of their own, " far from the madding crowd." And the president of the Incorporated Society of Musicians, instead of deploring a course of action that could not be of the slightest benefit to our native performers, but, on the contrary, only tend to arouse resentment and anger, seems to have actually applauded it. His pronouncement was quickly followed by the resignation of one of the society's most talented and representative members, Mr. Harold Samuel, who had vision enough to perceive that all this ill-judged agitation for keeping out the foreign artist of distinction was bound to result in retaliatory measures against our own travelling musicians. Then Mr. Harold Samuel's action was in turn applauded by Mr. Samuel Courtauld (carrying on the bold bid for freedom in art that was made by his lamented wife shortly before her death), in a letter which rightly declared it to be " intolerable that in a so-called civilized country, music, or ideas in any form, should be classed with material imports and subjected to restrictions impeding their untrammelled flow. England makes herself a laughing-stock by such measures." Truly she does.

The fact that exceptions have to be made leads inevitably to unfair discrimination between one artist or class of artists and another. One wonders who the individual (as distinguished from the Government department) may be who is vested with the final authority to settle these questions. What does he know about singers, instrumentalists, and orchestras in other countries than his own, to be able to decide whether their reputations or abilities justify their admission here for a particular period, short or long ? He may, of course, be guided (i.e., influenced) by the managerial source from whence the application reaches him. Yet even that will not prevent him from making mistakes or displaying partiality. Was there not a case soon after Christmas where no less a body than the B.B.C. was refused permission to employ the services of a famous French lady violinist, who had previously delighted listeners with her playing on I know not how many occasions ; whilst in the very same week the coveted permit was granted to a lieder-singer, possessing a title but little talent, to whom I listened with no pleasure whatsoever ? That shows clearly enough that the working of the system, apart from its utter stupidity as a device for helping native musicians, is altogether wrong.

I have been seriously asked by Chauvinistic reformers whether, in my opinion, the cause of British opera might not be materially assisted by dispensing with the International season at Covent Garden and replacing it with exclusively English performances, given by the company which appeared there in the autumn and has lately been touring the provinces. My answer to this question has been an unqualified No. It would be in every sense a retrograde step. It would mean cutting ourself adrift from the last anchor that holds our operatic ship to the traditions of a great and glorious past. It would be on a par with the nonsense preached by the advocates of false economy who confound the slogan of " Buy British " with a refusal to buy anything in the domains of art, science and literature that did not originate, like clothes or furniture, in the neighbourhood of Regent Street or Oxford Street. Even allowing that first-class international opera is a luxury, that it never does and never can " pay " those who run it, still, it represents a form of musical art which we cannot afford to abandon or neglect, and which well-to-do music-lovers have not so far refused themselves during the London season on the ground that it was expensive. When opera-goers keep away from Covent Garden or Russian opera at the Lyceum, on account of the high prices, it will be time to talk about dispensing with more or less ideal German performances (possibly leaving out the Italian) when they enable our stage to maintain the loftiest standard now attainable. We need something of this quality to remind our artists and public of what opera in English is supposed to be striving for.

Meanwhile, Viscountess Snowden has reminded us of something else. She has told those who object to the subsidy (a quite inadequate sum, in my opinion) that it is repaid, and with something to spare, by the amounts which the Treasury, after deducting it from B.B.C. earnings, recoups from the Entertainments Tax on the receipts, and from the Income Tax levied upon the salaries of the foreign artists. So that the paltry £17,500 a year, instead of imposing a burden on the nation, costs absolutely nothing ; and the dreadful foreigners who keep the bread out of British mouths (according to the president of the Incorporated Society of Musicians) are actually mulcted in a quarter of their London earnings before they are allowed to depart from these shores. What, then, would be the excuse for preventing them from entering the country ? There could only be one—that we have singers of our own as good as they are, and as capable of doing justice to works that our public wants to see and hear. That, I venture to say, is not the case. Without solid artistic support, the whole edifice of serious opera as we know it would crumble to the ground.

Another question arises. In what measure does the elimination of non-British artists affect the making of high-class gramophone records ? I have been glancing once more through the titles of that amazing compilation, *The Connoisseurs Catalogue*, and have said to myself : How fortunate that all these celebrities from abroad were here, on the spot, and able to get through their work at Hayes before the difficulties on the score of nationality began to interfere with free intercourse between the musical centres of England and the Continent—yes, and America ! A capable Hungarian quartet, a Viennese prima donna, or a new Italian tenor (hot from La Scala but unknown to the Ministry of Labour) might as readily be stopped at the frontier as the newest dance band from New York or the most up-to-date balalaika orchestra from Budapest.

Public anxiety on these points was to a certain extent relieved by the announcement made from the Ministry of Labour on January 8th, following upon a conference between the officials and the representatives of the B.B.C. and various interested musical bodies. It cleared up some of the doubts and promised, at any rate, not to prevent (thanks so much !) the free entry of " artists of first-rate international standing." It also indicated that obstacles would not be put in the way of foreign artists coming here " to give a recital or recitals on their own account," or " less well-known artists who, *by their record or on the evidence of competent opinion*, can claim to be able to contribute something new, distinctive, or original in the way of musical performance or interpretation." At the same time, it did not satisfy my curiosity as to the identity or capacity of this new Censor of Musicians.

The real problem is how to couple common sense with knowledge and experience in the adjudicating officer who regulates the taboo ; and, mind, I am all for exercising the right of exclusion where the foreigner is not definitely superior or there is a unique combination of some kind that we do not possess. In any case, we may be sure that the payment of income-tax is as rigorously enforced in the matter of gramophone royalties as it is in that of operatic earnings. Neither is deducted " at source," nor are the gramophone companies, I understand, called upon to furnish Somerset House with a list of the performers and the amounts paid them in royalties every year. But the worthy gentleman known as the Inspector of Taxes keeps a lynx-eyed watch on all these musical money-spinners from overseas, and, if they make any attempt to go back home without settling up for their British " schedule D," so much the worse for them.

On the whole, then, we may regard it as certain that the interests of the country are pretty well looked after where musical art is concerned, and especially so in the financial sense. As to the situation in which the musical profession of to-day finds itself, I agree that it could not well be worse. The trouble is that, like unemployment in the industrial trades, it is on such a vast scale. If I may be allowed to repeat a truth that I openly gave out as a warning twenty years ago, the supply of musical talent in every branch is infinitely bigger than the demand, thanks chiefly to the excessive number of teaching institutions and the ridiculous cheapness of musical training, good and bad alike. So long as students continue to be turned out by the thousand, with the expectation of making a living—perhaps a fortune—by means of their musical abilities, so long will this glut of professional skill clamouring for its reward be bound to persist. Of amateurs trained to enjoy and understand good music, and with a soul above the prevalent inanities of vaudeville and jazz, there cannot be too many. The greater their numbers the greater will be the demand for first-rate music and first-rate executants, whether on the radio or the gramophone, in the concert-room or in the music-hall. When the craze for the wretched drivel that comes to us from across the ocean ceases like the wicked " from troubling," then and then only will the weary be at rest. Anyhow, there will be no occasion for any more talk from responsible quarters about barring the way against front-rank foreign musicians, for the ostensible purpose of making more room for second-rankers of our own.

HERMAN KLEIN.

★   ★   ★

The Gramophone and the Singer

COWEN AND ELGAR
by HERMAN KLEIN

TO my great regret, I was unable to be present at the dinner of the Musicians' Club, which honoured the 80th birthday of Sir Frederic Cowen. But, although prevented on that notable occasion from paying a personal tribute to one who was during long years a close and intimate friend, my thoughts were nevertheless with him and busily bringing up all the while a host of pleasant recollections. I seem to have been hearing and writing about Frederic Cowen all my life. He and his compositions (the early ones) were popular long before I took up my critical pen. He has never ceased work in one direction or another ; and here he is, still active and vigorous, besides being the same inveterate punster that he was when I first came across him in the late 'seventies.

To me this seems the more wonderful because, properly regarded, Sir Frederic Cowen's splendid capacity for holding his own is less in the nature of a survival than a *revival*. For, truth to tell, it struck me when I came back from New York in 1909 that he had begun slightly to lose his hold on the suffrages and affections of the music-loving public. Younger men had come into prominence. There were plenty of newcomers at that particular epoch who " knew not Joseph " ; and fashions as well as passions in the musical world of that period were running high. It was the custom to depreciate with huge doses of undisguised scorn everything that did not glorify the school of the moment. The hundred Cowen successes that had followed the *Rose Maiden* of the youth of eighteen ; all the other cantatas and oratorios, the symphonies and operas, the orchestral pieces and the high-class songs, that had aroused our admiration and hopes a couple of decades previously—these seemed to be gradually sliding into the limbo of things neglected or forgotten. Then suddenly the *descensus Averni*

was stayed. Mr. Cowen's marriage to a charming woman rejuvenated him. The triumph of his fine cantata, *The Veil*, at the Cardiff Festival of 1910 made people open their eyes. The knighthood which came in the following year acted as an encouragement and an incentive to renewed effort. By the time the Great War was on us, Sir Frederic was himself again, and doing good work as conductor and teacher at the Guildhall School into the bargain.

Now I look upon this as what we call in cricket an " amazing recovery." Certainly you will find few instances to be compared with it in the annals of music or, indeed, any other art. The miracle will only be complete, however, when the present generation and the next have fully realized (and recognized) Frederic Cowen's true standing as a composer. They can afford, if they please, to leave aside the question of his doughty deeds as a conductor, who was directing the Promenade Concerts at Covent Garden when Henry Wood was a boy of eleven ; who was conductor of the Philharmonic Society, of the Scottish Orchestra, the Cardiff and the Handel Festivals for many years ; and who took out the English Orchestra that played at the Melbourne Centennial Exhibition of 1888–9. Conductors, like singers and players, of the Victorian era left behind them no enduring traces of their talents. Not so the composers. Their works remain ; and such as are worth rehearing can always be revived. Some of Cowen's finest lyrical efforts may have been wasted upon operas like *Thorgrim*, *Signa*, and *Harold*, because of their dull, spineless librettos (the curse of the British music-drama !) ; but the same obstacle will not prevent our choral societies from performing with advantage to themselves and their audiences such fine cantatas as *The Sleeping Beauty*, *St. John's Eve*, *Ruth* (an oratorio), *The Veil*, *The Water-Lily*, and

341

John Gilpin, or even the early but clever *St. Ursula*. I predict also renewed life for the *Scandinavian* and the *Welsh* symphonies, two masterful works practically unknown to this generation. These and many other orchestral compositions from the same pen will be heard long after the craze for " contemporary " ugliness has decayed and sunk into well-merited oblivion.

The justification for this prophecy was stated by Sir Frederic Cowen himself, at his birthday banquet, when he contended that " melody was the basis of all music." He had an especial right to utter that word of truth, being himself one of the most prolific creators of beautiful melody that this country (to put it modestly) has ever possessed. It may be melody that varies in type and quality. It began putting on new colour and flavour in *St. Ursula* when the young composer returned in 1880 from his Scandinavian tour with Trebelli. But, alike then and since, it was always melody that you could instantly recognize as " Cowenesque "—stamped, that is to say, with an individuality of character that you could no less readily perceive than if it were Sullivanesque or Elgarian ; melody which constitutes the very essence of that personal touch that distinguishes one musician (or one painter) from another. And perhaps the Cowenesque has had this particular advantage over the others—that it is the kind of melody most exquisitely adjusted to the idiosyncrasies and needs of the human voice—in a word, it is the most *singable*.

It was eminently fitting that Sir Edward Elgar should have been entrusted, at the function I am referring to, with the duty of proposing the health of his octogenarian friend. This enabled him to recall the fact, of which few people were aware, that when he had entered the London musical world in 1884, " an utterly unknown person," Fred Cowen was the only one of the reigning conductors who had complied with his request that they should " look over his compositions." That, he said, was the beginning of over 45 years of unbroken friendship, and he went on to seal the bond with the warmest tribute to Sir Frederic's outstanding gifts as a conductor that has been uttered by any living musician. The public expression of gratitude from such a source was peculiarly welcome, tardy though it might appear to be. Perhaps—who knows ?—Sir Edward was inwardly comparing the long years that it had taken his old friend to obtain a coveted distinction at the hands of Royalty with his own unprecedentedly rapid rise to fame and all imaginable social honours. As a rule those disparities are not easy to explain, and to make the attempt in the present instance would involve too long a history. Let it suffice to say that, whereas Sir Frederic Cowen belonged to the Victorian era, Sir Edward Elgar had the good fortune to blossom in the Edwardian.

I have thought it right in this article to sing at some length the praises of the Victorian because I feel that my readers ought to appreciate now—as well as or even better than later on—the estimate held of him by one who has known him for the best part of his career. To do the same with the Edwardian would be superfluous, though I have known him, too, ever since I heard his first oratorio, *The Light of Life*, produced at the Worcester Festival of 1896 ; for no English musician has ever, in his lifetime, had so much written about him or his music, and the story is far too familiar for repetition here and now. Neither would any detailed comparisons between the Victorian and the Edwardian serve a useful purpose. That is a task that writers of a later day will be much better able to perform, especially after the verdict of posterity shall have been ascertained and registered. Meanwhile the advantage rests, as it naturally must, with the more modern composer, whose style, whose idioms, whose very mannerisms, have formed part and parcel of the musical growth of the twentieth century. But the good music, the " beautiful melody," be it Cowenesque or Elgarian, produced in all ages has its equal right to immortality, and we may be sure that that claim can never fail sooner or later to assert itself.

Sir Edward Elgar's frank expression of gratitude was, like his presence at this feast, a notable sign of the times. Musicians too commonly forget what they owe to those who have helped them to obtain a footing on the first rung of the ladder. They are inclined only to remember failures and adverse criticisms in the Press. For my own part I cannot recall that Sir Edward Elgar, unlike his old friend Sir Frederic, ever achieved such a thing as a palpable failure—nor even an approach to one, despite the oft-repeated erroneous statement that *The Dream of Gerontius* was coldly received on its production at the Birmingham Festival of 1900. On the contrary, I can emphatically declare (and I was there) that it was received with enthusiasm ; while the critics, without exception, lavished upon it their warmest superlatives. (How, indeed, could they honestly have done otherwise ?) To prove this, once for all, I will quote here some of the opinions that they wrote :—

The Daily Telegraph : " There is nothing for it but to lay before Mr. Elgar the homage due to a very striking and brilliant effort, the more remarkable because he barred himself from other than occasional use of melody, as apart from chromatic progressions determined by harmonic ends. . . . *The Dream of Gerontius* advances its composer's claim to rank among the musicians of whom the country should be proudest."

The Times : " If we look back to the sugary inanities of the oratorios of Gounod, which nearly twenty years ago were so loudly admired in Birmingham, we may well be grateful for the solidity and the sincerity of feeling which are apparent on every page of Mr. Elgar's score."

The Standard : " *The Dream of Gerontius* is a work of more than ordinary importance. It has occupied Mr. Elgar for over eight years, and the result may unhesitatingly be pronounced to be one of the finest choral writings of recent times. . . . In short, it is a composition in which are revealed very great qualities, imagination, and poetic feeling, besides a remarkable capacity in dealing with the resources of the orchestra."

The Daily Chronicle : " It is as notable for its melodic beauty and sustained loftiness of tone as for its elaborate construction."

The Manchester Guardian : "Comparison with Berlioz is simply inevitable—for Edward Elgar's dramatic power admits of comparison with the great masters."

Pall Mall Gazette : "Mr. Elgar has produced a genuine masterpiece. Since the death of Wagner, no finer composition has been given to the world."

So much, then, for the instant verdict of the leading critics. It does not read like a "comparative failure," does it ? Yet that is how the chronicler in *Grove* has described it. On the other hand, looking back at my own criticism of the Birmingham performance (*Sunday Times*, October 7th, 1900), I find I said that "A more perfunctory rendering of a new work it has never been my lot to listen to at a big Festival." In a word, it was permeated by a spirit of hesitancy, apart from flat intonation, uncertain attack, and "a grating harshness of tone that wrought material harm at its birth to a composition which demands in a peculiar degree the absence of those distracting influences which accompany a faulty interpretation." Still, there was no approach to disaster such as the composer had feared at the final rehearsal, when he had "lost patience with the chorus and told them, in good plain English, that they neither knew nor understood his music." The simple truth was that the Birmingham Choir that week was a mixture of youthful incompetence, inexperience, variableness, and lack of stamina. At the same time it would have been impossible to have had three more perfect soloists than Edward Lloyd, Marie Brema, and Plunket Greene, or a greater conductor than Hans Richter. The composer, when he appeared, received an enthusiastic ovation.

Finally, of the *Dream* itself I wrote : "If this cantata does not belong to the type of works that live and flourish in the full light of day, then am I greatly mistaken concerning the present trend of musical feeling and opinion in this country. Cardinal Newman's poem is a *chef-d'œuvre*, and, to pay Mr. Elgar the

highest compliment in my power, I consider his music worthy at all points of association with it." The realization of the true grandeur of his conception soon followed upon the fine performances that were heard in London and elsewhere. Meanwhile the present writer went to New York and helped to spread the Elgarian propaganda there. From that period of revelation success upon success, triumph after triumph, honour after honour, fell to the new master with a rapidity never before experienced in our musical annals. Such examples of genius meeting with quick and abundant reward are rarely encountered. And so, in the time of harvest as in the time of sowing, there was constant and unending reason for the expression of gratitude.

HERMAN KLEIN.

P.S. The above was written before I had seen the account of Mr. Basil Maine's "Elgar Lecture" at the Royal Institution. The address seems to have brought out some thoughtful and instructive points. I was interested to note that Mr. Maine had applied the term "Edwardian" to Elgar and his work in precisely the same manner that I have done in this article. I am not sure whether the idea had previously occurred to any publicist of the moment ; but, if not too late, I shall be pleased if my brother East Anglian (we were both born in Norwich) will permit me to share the honour of it with him. I would like also to congratulate him on his way of putting the case with regard to Professor Dent's indefensible disparagement of Sir Edward Elgar some time ago in a German *Handbuch*. In a sense, one might say that the Professor had been sufficiently sat upon already. In another it could be urged that the objectionable article has never been withdrawn from circulation. There may be justification sometimes for "flogging a dead horse."

★ ★ ★

The Gramophone and the Singer

NEW ADVOCATES FOR MEYERBEER

by HERMAN KLEIN

BETWEEN six and seven years ago—to be precise, in September, October, and November, 1925—there appeared in THE GRAMOPHONE a series of three articles, entitled " The Treasures of Meyerbeer," which formed part of a larger series dealing with the masterpieces of the leading operatic composers and the gramophone records taken therefrom that were then published. From evidence forthcoming at the time, I have reason to think that I succeeded in my twofold object so far as was practicable. Not having been quixotic enough to imagine that I could remove at one 'fell swoop the indefensible and unfair prejudices created concerning Meyerbeer and all his works at the beginning of the century—in this country at least—by an unscrupulous clique, I was content to have done what I thought my duty. I had aroused a certain amount of interest; I counted on time and the example of countries like France, Germany, Austria, Belgium, and America to do the rest.

I have no intention of repeating my arguments now; but I would like to recall just a few details connected with the gramophone side of them. Furnished by the leading companies through the office of this magazine with 63 records of pieces taken from Meyerbeer's six representative operas, I was able to show with more or less exactitude what had been done by H.M.V., Columbia, Parlophone, Polydor, Vocalion, etc., in the pre-electric days to skim the cream off milk still marvellously fresh, though it had been standing in the operatic dairy for over half a century. The collection was not nearly so large as it ought to have been, but it was adequate enough to make manifest the value placed upon Meyerbeer's music as a medium for the display of the art of vocalization by the best singers of the gramophone epoch. I tested, criticized, and wrote about them all in turn, and an analysis of my articles provides curious reading. Compared with the ceaseless Verdi-hunt, the albums, the long selections, the constant search for material among the old half-forgotten operas of the composer of *Il Trovatore*, the result of our Meyerbeer gleanings amounted numerically to a mere trifle. Besides, there was a notable disparity in the choice; it left untouched many of the most notable " treasures." There were 4 from *Robert le Diable*, 14 from *Les Huguenots*, 9 from *Le Prophète*, 1 from *L'Etoile du Nord*, 7 from *Dinorah*, and—mark this—28 from *L'Africaine*. This last lot included no fewer than 15 records of *O Paradiso !*

All things considered, however, I suppose it was not such a bad harvest. One thing that my review led

to (so I was told) was the revival of *Les Huguenots* by the Grand Opera Syndicate at Covent Garden. But unfortunately that did more harm than good, inasmuch as an extremely mediocre performance gave a sceptical public a wholly incorrect impression of the opera, and only helped to show how completely the Meyerbeer tradition had become lost here. Since 1925, the demand for Meyerbeer records has diminished almost to the vanishing point. H.M.V. have brought out four, Columbia three—seven altogether; and that is all. One or two of these I may have reviewed already; for instance, Valente's *O Paradiso !* (H.M.V. B3141, not very good) and Gertrude Johnson's *Shadow Song* from *Dinorah* (Col. 9707, sung without taste in doubtful English). Then there are an electric reproduction of Caruso's fine *Deh ! ch'io ritorni* from Act 4 of *L'Africaine* (H.M.V. DB1386); a magnificent re-recording of Titta Ruffo's wonderful *Adamastor* from the same opera (H.M.V. DB1397), to which our Editor referred in such eloquent terms last month; a glorious *O Paradiso !* by Beniamino Gigli (H.M.V. DB1382); another, much less glorious, because badly pronounced and phrased in inferior English, by Heddle Nash (Col. 9104); and, lastly, a phenomenally sonorous rendering of Marcel's *Ein' feste Burg* from *Les Huguenots* by Ivar Andrésen.

So much for the effects of world-depression, fanatical prejudice, and other deleterious influences upon the humble Meyerbeerian propaganda that I started six and a half years ago. It failed then for lack of support am I over-sanguine in thinking that it might not do so now ? There are signs at this moment that the seed may not have fallen upon barren ground, that it may have taken root upon unexpectedly fruitful soil. Can it be that my arguments were just, and that Meyerbeer was not altogether the " spiritual coward prepared to barter his soul for a mess of admiration " that Mr. Brent Smith described him as being ? Is it possible that I was right when I described as absolutely unfounded and untrue the garbled masses of abuse and misrepresentation teeming in that precious *History of Music* by C. Villiers Stanford and Cecil Forsyth, published in 1916 ? I had, I remember, one firm believer in the accomplished and outspoken Editor of this journal, who expressed his satisfaction at my crusade in his customary clear, plain English. But that was in the October of 1925. From that date I had read nothing on similar lines until February of this year, when there appeared on the Saturday music page of *The Daily Telegraph* two articles from the pen of Mr. Bernard van Dieren, headed " In Defence of Meyerbeer."

Now I have read these articles with very great pleasure, for they came as a complete surprise. I had no idea that this gifted Anglo-Dutchman (who writes English as well as he composes music) had felt strongly enough about it to enter the lists on behalf of Meyerbeer. I had never compared notes with him upon the subject, not having even the pleasure of knowing him by sight; though I am convinced that he must possess " all those van Dieren young charms " characteristic of his mother's—the French—nation ! Space will not allow me to quote to the extent I should wish from his admirable defence of a great, if by no means immaculate, composer ; but one part of it in particular strikes me as furnishing a complete answer to the accusers :

> Perhaps there are grounds for the reproach of " insincerity " that is with monotonous regularity hurled at Meyerbeer. But surely it cannot mean that he wrote music which he knew to be quite different from what he should and could have written. If we judge Beethoven, Wagner, Strauss, or Verdi by this standard, can we be so sure that their " sincerity " will bear close scrutiny? Are their purple patches always completely justified? Do not all composers grasp the glorious opportunities to " let go," and is it not just that which makes opera immeasurably more than a musical illustration of a favourite novel ! Meyerbeer committed the same crimes against literature that all opera composers have to if they are to appeal to our musical sense. But no one has surpassed him in the building of imposing ensembles from the simplest motives, closely-knit structures with massive effect and superb melodic embroidery, or in his power to dwarf the most towering musical edifices by emotional summits that, with modest means, achieved a climax through sheer lyrical intensity.

In concluding, Mr. van Dieren says : " Let musicians get to know Meyerbeer's works, and not accept groping adaptations of them, and they will discover that they have long been neglecting a master who, unjustly maligned for a time, can again give them much that they are vainly seeking in modern music which, however impeccable in its literary susceptibilities, lacks the robustly healthy qualities our fathers appreciated in *Les Huguenots, Robert le Diable, L'Africaine, Le Prophète, L'Etoile du Nord, Dinorah,* and, not least, the astonishing overture and incidental music to *Struensee.*" At present, of course, this excellent advice can only be carried into effect through the study of the vocal scores. The doors of the opera house where these works once received their most lavish and adequate interpretation will only be opened this season for a four weeks' Wagner Festival beginning on May 9th ; and, seeing that inferior singing is the one thing that Meyerbeer's music will not stand—in fact, does it more harm than good—the less we hear of it in the concert room the better.

Meanwhile, Mr. van Dieren's articles have achieved palpable good in another direction by attracting the powerful advocacy of Mr. Ernest Newman. In the *Sunday Times* of February 28th, that eminent critic gave his readers an exposition of the Meyerbeer situation that was full of illuminating commonsense. He began by expressing his belief that " A properly sung, properly played, properly staged performance of one of the operas would presumably be as successful in London as in any Continental or American town." After telling us that he " heard *Dinorah* and *L'Africaine* in New York some years ago, and was strangely impressed by them," he goes off on his favourite tack to examine the mind that conceived and gave them birth. He was " repelled " by that mind, " yet paradoxically unable to get away from it and the psychological problems that it called up ; the music seemed to me like those strange scents that create a faint nausea in us, but for some reason or other make it difficult for us to escape their unpleasantness by the simple process of keeping away from them." Like Mr. Newman's New York colleague, I agree with him that this effect may well be produced in certain cases on the musical ear of to-day ; on the other hand, I cannot agree with his surmise that Meyerbeer may have " affected his contemporary audiences to some extent in somewhat the same way— whether some people did not find the odour of the man's mind just a little unpleasant, but were still unable to shake themselves free of its curious fascination."

My memory goes back to the period some ten years after Meyerbeer's death, which occurred in 1864, when his operas were still in the enjoyment of their great popularity, in London as elsewhere, and I can declare with absolute certainty that I never heard or read any criticism of them which even hinted at an experience of the kind. Apart from this I am in the fullest agreement with all that Mr. Newman says. He has done a service by recalling Heine's estimate of Meyerbeer and his earliest big opera, *Robert le Diable* ; also the interesting comparison drawn by Heine between the " predominating factors " of his music and that of Rossini. Each, truly, was a "man of his epoch," though not more so that I can see than Bizet, Puccini, Mascagni, and Leoncavallo were men of theirs ! Again, Chorley was right in pointing out that certain strongly-drawn characters, such as Marcel and John of Leyden and the three Anabaptists, had never been treated in opera until Meyerbeer (thanks to his librettist, Scribe) had introduced these and analogous figures into the *Huguenots* and the *Prophète.* " In each of his operas," says Mr. Newman, " Meyerbeer gave his audiences the delighted feeling that they were being brought into touch with real life, that the characters they saw on the boards were men and women such as they might meet any day themselves, men and women caught up in such problems of morality or politics or social life as they themselves were interested in."

Here, again, is an irrefutable statement. It is just as true as the argument that another " man of his epoch," Wagner to wit, went for his stories and characters to the old sagas and legends in order to escape as much as possible from the realities of contemporary existence. But no one has justification for asserting that because one master was right the other was wrong, and it is because I venture to perceive this impartial attitude in Mr. Newman's timely essay that I hereby express my gratitude to him for it. In this Metropolis, opera, like everything speculative or risky that requires capital at its back, will have to wait for the return of prosperous times before it can indulge again in the "grand seasons" of old or experimental revivals of masters who have gone out of fashion. Then, again, if such good luck were to befall us, if the incredible were to happen and opera-lovers were clamouring once more for Meyerbeer, where are the artists to come from to sing his music, unless we import complete foreign companies to do the job ? But the I.S.M. need not be afraid. The contingency is not likely to come about. A new race of British singers specially trained for the purpose would be the best solution of the problem ; and undoubtedly we have the voices. Will not one or two millionaires oblige ?

HERMAN KLEIN.

✷ ✷ ✷

The Gramophone and the Singer

The Gramophone as a Vocal Instructor
by HERMAN KLEIN

THIS is not a new subject—far from it. But, like many another well-worn theme, it has to be taken out of its cotton-wool or tissue-paper occasionally if only for the purpose of answering those youthful enquirers who imagine they have discovered something new. How can there be any doubt about it ? Just as surely as imitation is the most important factor in the study of every form of art, so is it certain that the use of a good gramophone record may be as valuable to the vocal student as is, say, the employment of a suitable model by the painter, the actor, or the ballet-dancer. Models, as we know, date back to the times of the ancient Greeks, and a great deal farther. The Egyptians and the Chinese had need of them from 2,000 to 3,000 years B.C., though whether they always used *suitable* ones is a question which depends somewhat upon the appropriate canons of taste. That, nevertheless, is the question that has to be asked now, in the twentieth century, when considering the choice of a model from the vast agglomeration of published vocal records for imitating in the course of one's regular studies.

Nor is it a matter of choosing one model at a time. Record discs are not so expensive as living models. They are comparatively cheaper—cheaper now, in fact, than ever ; and, if one wishes to contemplate, analyze, and listen over and over again to a dozen reproductions of an identical theme, it can be done at no very extravagant outlay of cash. Only it may be here, in this very multiplicity of models, that there resides a certain element of risk, against which it will be well to be prepared. When I am asked, as I frequently am, to make comparisons between this and that record of a certain piece, or to give an opinion as to the best record that has been made of one, I always feel myself in a difficulty—that of knowing whether it is wanted merely for enjoyment's sake or for self-educative and imitative purposes. If for the latter, I feel I should like first to be informed on these points : (1) whether it is the singer's voice that is to be imitated or (2) the peculiarities of phrasing ; (3) the style generally or (4) the diction ; (5) the verbal accent or (6) the musical and artistic interpretation as a whole. It may, of course, be for guidance on all of these points ; but, if so, I would warn the "seeker after truth" that the model which can combine the whole of them is as much a *rara avis* as the all-inclusive human model sought by the painter or the sculptor. It may exist ; but it is very hard to locate.

My diffidence in this task of recommending the right examples out of the various gramophone catalogues has not been lessened by the developments of recent years. Let me explain more fully what I mean. As most of my readers are aware, I was in the early days of this century a very strong believer in the value of the gramophone as a medium for acquiring—either without or, better still, with the aid of a teacher—a certain proficiency in the art of singing. In fact, I invented and co-ordinated the material for what I believe to have been the first method ever prepared with that object. My ideas concerning the feasibility of the system have undergone no change. I still think it can be of great practical utility to students who are unable to avail themselves of the help of a teacher, more especially in those distant parts of the country or the globe where reliable teachers are not easily to be had.

But I have confessed before, and I confess again, that the original *format* of this "Phono-Vocal Method" had its drawbacks. It attempted too much, because it tried to squeeze the practice of the entire art of singing into twenty records. No matter how perfectly the patterns may have been executed—and it was never denied that they were of copybook super-excellence—they suffered under the serious disadvantage of being too comprehensive and concentrated, in a word, too *difficult*, for the early gramophone fan of 1907.

To-day, of course, they are of no practical value for commercial purposes, because they were not electrically recorded; and in this shortcoming they share the fate of hundreds, if not thousands, of records intensely interesting *per se*, inasmuch as they were made by "celebrities" who are either no more or who have now relinquished their active labours. They are desirable just as curiosities, nothing more. And yet—stay! This very reflection brings me to a point that has probably escaped the attention of most people, if, indeed, it has been noticed by anyone apart from the present writer. I allude to the conclusion, which has forced itself upon me after long and close observation, that the human voice as recorded in pre-electric days was much easier to *hear* and, therefore, to imitate accurately than the more artificial and manipulated kind of sound that proceeds from the modern combination—be it the outcome of the record, the sound-box, the instrument, or all three working together.

In saying this I put forward no claim to having made a discovery. Readers of THE GRAMOPHONE need not be reminded that our senior Editor has more than once, nay, often, expressed his decided preference for the older records of particular pieces as compared with the new, and I cannot remember a single instance in which I have been of a different opinion. Now, to what might that superiority, when it does assert itself, be attributed? Partly, no doubt, to the greater art brought to bear upon the earlier performance; for it will not be questioned, I suppose, that the actual gramophone singing of the distinguished bygone recorders, such as Sembrich, Melba, Louise Homer, Caruso, Constantino, Battistini, and de Gogorza, has never been equalled, much less surpassed, *quâ* singing. But it was also partly due to something else: something in the nature and quality of the tone engraved upon the surface of the waxen matrix as an exact and truthful reflex of the singer's voice. That it was always more beautiful in effect, or that it achieved a finer acoustical result, I am not prepared to argue. But those are not the points I am wishing to make, any more than I am concerned for the moment with the improvements due to the uses of the microphone, better sound-boxes and needles for reproducing, or the virtues (and vices) of amplification.

What I have found, however, is that the older recorded voice, thinner, smaller, apparently more distant though it sounded, was truer to the original, besides being of a nature that made its timbre easier for the ear to grasp and the singer to imitate with some measure of success. The idea is not easy to convey in words, but what I really mean, I suppose, is that you could hear the tone itself more definitely in its pure, pristine quality. The difference is similar to that between the old, untouched photograph, which gave you the face just as you knew it, wrinkles and all, and the modern work of art, which places before you a picture imagined by the toucher-up (excuse the word!) as what the person photographed ought really to look like. And,

to strengthen the analogy, I may add that in former days a painter, working upon a portrait of an individual he had never seen and was never likely to see, would frequently produce an admirable likeness. Nowadays an attempt of that kind is, as a rule, a dire failure, for the reason that the photo which is being copied has been so carefully "improved" that it provides little more than a resemblance, with features changed and distorted, to the dead or distant original. In some degree the voices that we hear over the wireless come to us through similar disturbing influences. We recognize them (sometimes); we can also enjoy them (sometimes); but, as with listening to the gramophone, we can hardly fail to perceive the difference between that and the experience of listening to the living singer in the opera house or the concert room. There likewise it is a question of degree.

So much by way of warning. But there are two sides to every question. Modern records, if they do not invariably facilitate the imitative process, can be helpful in directions where latter-day improvements in mechanism have wrought an acknowledged advance. Among these, for example, are increased clarity of tone; elimination of extraneous noises; a more accurate definition of pitch; stronger because more effortless enunciation of consonants; a closer-sounding voice; and variations of power and volume that the microphone is capable of transmitting with almost miraculous fidelity. These, of course, are improvements the value of which it would be impossible to over-estimate. Possibly they may be thought to outweigh whatever disadvantages I have deemed it advisable to point out in the modern record, so far as its utility as a model is concerned; and, after all, it must be frankly admitted that from first to last I have not suggested that aught which is positively inimical to good singing lurks in the endeavour to imitate the new records made by first-rate artists. A good ear is half the battle; a gift for vocal mimicry will do the rest. Besides, the old records of which I am thinking are not, many of them, included in current catalogues and may most likely cost a good deal more to purchase. In any case, even when they do exist, they cannot be so easy to procure.

Apart from the element of tone, the whole of this problem is, in my view, a simple one. I have already enumerated the remaining features of vocal excellence that the student may be anxious to acquire by imitating a gramophone record. Of these the peculiarities (or characteristics) of good phrasing are by no means the least important. The term "phrasing" is rather wide in its meaning and application, and, as these are things fully comprehended only by the few, it can do no harm if I repeat for the benefit of the youthful student of technique a recommendation that I have often made before, viz., to read with close attention the wonderful section that Manuel Garcia wrote (when in his 90th year) upon this subject in his *Hints on Singing*. The primer, which is published by Ascherbergs, can be obtained through any music-seller. One attribute of the art of phrasing that immediately distinguishes the accomplished vocalist is the correct employment of the *portamento*, both in the upward and the downward movement of the voice. Another is the smooth, even management of crescendos and diminuendos (swelled sounds or *messa di voce*) on notes and phrases of the melody or *cantilena* that have to be so treated. The " general style of the piece " comes under the same

category; and almost any modern record by an artist of high standing may be trusted to afford beyond peradventure the proper and reliable manifestation for the purpose in view. It is the imitation of the tone alone that demands the exercise of very special care and discretion, for there it is that the most serious mistakes can be made.

HERMAN KLEIN.

The Gramophone and the Singer

GERMAN OPERA AT COVENT GARDEN

by HERMAN KLEIN

IT was doubly fortunate that Sir Thomas Beecham got back from America in time to conduct *Die Meistersinger* on the opening night of the so-called Wagner Festival at Covent Garden. Not only did his co-operation heal unnecessary wounds and lend valuable prestige to the occasion, but invested with something more than *routinier* interest the otherwise familiar features of the cast. Then again, he contrived to extract with his personal magnetism certain qualities that the orchestra rarely if ever yields under the baton of the best foreign conductors. It would take too long to describe them; I only know that he achieved a combination of delicacy and strength, of Hans Richter and Anton Seidl, such as no other Englishman has ever brought about in this opera. Never mind if many of the tempi were too fast. It did less harm to Wagner than it does to Handel; and the worthy baronet—seated for once and with the score in front of him—always knew how to slow down when necessary.

From the overture onwards it was a definitely-planned, coherent reading of *Die Meistersinger*. The climaxes were big without being thundered out with deafening sonority; and I refuse to find fault with the balance of the quintet, which, together with the final scene on the Pegnitz, I raced home to listen to by wireless. I mention this because it seemed to me that the voices in that wonderful ensemble were not evenly caught or distributed by the microphones. And yet there Mme. Lotte Lehmann's tones sounded no less clear, musical, and fresh than at any time during the evening; indeed, I have never enjoyed her Eva so much. Friedrich Schorr was in his best voice, which means that the music of Hans Sachs received a wholly perfect interpretation; while Fritz Wolff, if not a very handsome nor elegant-looking Junker to those who remembered the Walther of Jean de Reszke (oh, those irritating souvenirs!), certainly sang with spirit and " stayed the course." Thus on the whole we entered upon the season (an enthusiastic crowd), too, enjoying

our gramophone friends with eye as well as ear, feasting on the beauties of a glorious opera, and appreciating the intelligent efforts of the native artists who, besides acquitting themselves ably, benefited by their association with the stars from the Continent.

On the second night came the preamble to the *Ring*—first of two promised cycles—and therewith some disappointment. I can call to mind many a better *Rheingold* than this. Robert Heger, excellent conductor as he is, could not maintain the " driving force " that had inspired *Die Meistersinger*, and more than one scene fell flat. The best thing of the performance was the Alberich of Eduard Habich; it was better even than his Beckmesser. Alike in the depths of the Rhine, the fogs of Nibelheim, and the vision of Valhalla he was simply superb. No gramophone records had preceded the new Wotan, Ludwig Hofmann—why, I cannot exactly say, for one is reviewed elsewhere in this number. His voice sounded somewhat thick and throaty in the theatre, but he is a good declamatory singer, and has all the needful stage traditions for the part. On the other hand, the singing of Fritz Wolff entirely satisfied, whilst the requisite lightness of touch and variety of fantastic posturing were lacking in the difficult part of Loge. The giants Fasolt and Fafner were sonorously and subtly portrayed by Otto Helgers and Norman Allin; the former might even have had a little tone to spare to help Rispah Goodacre, what time her un-Erda-like head was exposed above the top of what looked like her own gravestone. The lovely picture presented by Maria Olszewska, together with her classical attitudes and fine facial expression, lent due importance to the rôle of Fricka; but it was not in the power of Josephine Wray to bring similar qualities to that of Freia. Anyhow, both are most ungrateful parts and not nearly so interesting as those of the three Rhine maidens, whose singing in the distance happened to be particularly moderate.

The *Tristan* of the following night came very nearly,

if not quite, to the level of the *Meistersinger* performance, and I suggest that the presence of Sir Thomas
Beecham in the conductor's chair again had much to
do with the smoothness and unity of the entire interpretation. I should have to go back many years to
remember a better—in fact, to one that Toscanini
conducted at the New York Metropolitan in 1909, or else
one that Jean de Reszke and Ternina sang in at Covent
Garden in 1898. Both of those were ideal, unsurpassable.
The differentiation in the present case would take too
long to explain, nor is explanation really required.
Enough that Frida Leider, Maria Olszewska, Lauritz
Melchior, Otto Helgers, and Herbert Janssen, all at the
very top of their form, furnished a quintet of convincing
merit and distinction, and perhaps as strongly equipped
at all points as any that the lyric stage of to-day could
offer. In their duets the first three singers preserved
with supreme art the pure quality of their tone (as all
true gramophone artists should and must) whilst
varying its strength from passages of the softest
pianissimo to the loudest fortissimo. Perfect examples
of the former were forthcoming from Frida Leider and
Melchior in the prolonged love scene of the second act ;
while the voice of Brangäne floating above them from
the watch-tower—beautifully sustained by Olszewska
in her richest notes—created just the exquisitely
ethereal effect that Wagner intended. For me this was
the great moment of the performance. Nowhere did
Sir Thomas Beecham's beat falter. He contrived, with
marvellous judgment, to keep the tension of both
singers and orchestra at its maximum from *Prelude* to
Liebestod ; and in the actual music-drama that represents a " lap " which takes some doing.

The place that *Die Walküre* holds in the esteem of
amateurs was evidenced by much enthusiasm and
genuine gratitude for a performance of superlative
excellence, whereof every prominent feature was familiar. There is no more need at this time to tell how
Lotte Lehmann and Lauritz Melchior acquitted themselves as Sieglinde and Siegmund than to describe the
Fricka of Maria Olszewska and the Hunding of Norman
Allin, or to bestow fresh eulogies upon Frida Leider and
Friedrich Schorr for their truly magnificent singing in
the glorious duet of the last act.

The derogatory remarks made in one or two quarters
about Frida Leider's voice after the *Siegfried* were
wholly unmerited. After all, her high notes were never
her most beautiful, and her " Hei-yo-to-ho " may not
be as impeccable as some we have heard. But I would
not for either reason wish to dispense just yet with one
of the grandest Brünnhildes that has adorned the
Wagnerian stage. In *Götterdämmerung* her medium
and lower head registers sounded as beautiful as ever
and her declamation was, from her first entry with
Siegfried down to the last note of the closing scene,
worthy of the finest Bayreuth traditions. I agree that
the final section of the cycle ought not to have been
taken out of the hands of Herr Heger and placed in
those of Sir Thomas Beecham. It is bad enough to find

the principal characters in different hands, as we
sometimes do, but to change the conductor of *The Ring
en route* is even worse than swopping horses whilst
crossing a stream. Nevertheless, taken for all in all,
the first cycle may be said to have gone exceedingly
well, and there can be no questioning the fact that it
drew demonstrative crowds from start to finish.

A long-standing engagement prevented my hearing
Tannhäuser, but I may say a few words, chiefly of
praise, concerning the representation of *Der Fliegende
Holländer* on May 18th. The best thing in it was the
rendering of the duet between Senta and the Dutchman
in Act II by Odette de Foras and Friedrich Schorr,
and I can congratulate the Canadian soprano upon the
skill with which she here overcame the difficulties
attendant upon an incipient head cold. In the Ballad
she was less successful, the attack of the G in the
opening phrase being hard and forced, while just previously the same note, sung pianissimo, had refused to
make its exit from the singer's throat. Still, she did very
creditably for a first appearance in a big character
during the German season.

New " *Connoisseur* " Issues

Under editorial instructions, I propose to review here
month by month, until completed, the new records
just added by H.M.V. to their " Connoisseur's Catalogue." Speaking of them as a whole, I may say now that
these supplementary records fully maintain the standard
of the first collection. One might, indeed, have expected
as much.

The first items calling for notice are four Russian
songs by the Balalaika Orchestra and Chorus (B4129–30,
two discs, 10in.). These are of the usual strongly-
marked character, and fortunately the solo voice, having
much to do, is a good one. I need not give the titles.
Four ballads by Carl Loewe, including *Heinrich der
Vogler* and *Tom der Reimer*, are welcome because sung
by that admirable baritone-bass, Rudolf Böckelmann
(B4115, 10in., C2376, 12in.), and well accompanied
on the piano (as written) by Clemens Schmalstich. A
rival effort by Cornelis Bronsgeest, with *Archibald
Douglas* in two parts (C2396, 12in.) and two less
well known (D2390, also 12in.), will also repay careful
listening. Here is a first-rate singer, and only on that
account may his *Archibald Douglas* be pardoned the
use of an orchestra.

Four new recordings by Theodore Chaliapine form a
notable addition to this list. Most remarkable, and
therefore most valuable, because of their freshness and
vigour at this advanced stage of the artist's distinguished career, are two excerpts from *Boris Godounov*
(with orchestral accompaniment conducted by M.
Steimann), viz., the *Clock* scene and the famous
Monologue from Act 2 of Moussorgsky's opera (DB1532,
12in.), the former of which, if I am not mistaken, appears
in the H.M.V. catalogue for the first time. It is scarcely
necessary to add that they embody Chaliapine's fullest
art of dramatic expression and characterization. The

English title, *I have attained the highest power*, seems to be an indication of the artist's achievement quite as much as a reflection of what is passing in the mind of the conscience-stricken Tsar. Anyhow, it is a wonderful bit of singing. Two airs, *Doubt* and *Stenka Rasine* (DB1469, 12in.), are also welcome from the same source. The first-named, by Glinka, has a charming *obbligato* for 'cello played by Cedric Sharpe, with Ivor Newton at the piano.

The choir of the Berlin Singakademie contributes an extremely fine performance of Brahms's *German Requiem*, conducted by Professor Georg Schumann. It is done on four 12in. discs, numbered C2377 and C2381–3. To descant upon the beauties of such a well-known masterpiece would be superfluous, for it has been a favourite in this country for more than forty years. The voices are well-balanced, refined, and admirable in their regard for light and shade. The intonation, too, is faultless, while the tempi are just right and the orchestration comes out splendidly. High praise, but thoroughly well deserved.

HERMAN KLEIN.

The Gramophone and the Singer
THE GENII OF BROADCASTING HOUSE
by HERMAN KLEIN

AMALGAMATION of forces and fusion of interests are among the commonplaces of the age. They are almost the sole remedy for wasteful competition and unnecessary trade friction. Two or three seasons ago I formed the opinion that the only chance for operatic enterprise in this country lay in a union of the existing organisations, in a cessation of the policy of endeavouring to cut each other's throats ; and I said as much in these columns. The fusion of the Covent Garden interests with those of Sir Thomas Beecham (the League of Opera), the Carl Rosa Company, and the Old Vic-Sadler's Wells combination, could not fail to have an enormously beneficial effect upon the cause of opera alike in London and the provinces.

These thoughts came into my mind with vivid force the other day when, by the courtesy of Sir John Reith, I was for the first time shown over the new headquarters of the British Broadcasting Corporation in Portland Place. Whilst gazing upon the inexhaustible wonders and surprises of that amazing building I was saying to myself : " Here in this working home of the B.B.C. is now situated, for good or ill, the real mainspring of the musical life of the British Empire. No matter how important and all-embracing its other branches of activity, there is none that it has taken in hand with such executive completeness, with such commanding influence and power, as the provision of the material appertaining to the art of music."

There is no need to speak of the exterior of Broadcasting House. That everyone can see for himself and inspect without the aid of an assiduous and attentive cicerone. To my thinking, it is frankly plain ; perhaps unnecessarily devoid of beauty. The interior is also plain and utilitarian, though not, I am given to understand, quite so convenient in arrangement as it might be for the co-ordination of the various elements and sections of an ultra-heterogeneous staff. But the 22 studios contained in the central tower and the offices and waiting-rooms in the external structure, so far as I was enabled to visit them in course of a two hours' tour, all seemed to me to be elegantly appointed and comfortable—especially the easy-chairs, which I sampled frequently. The inset communicating windows and doors also seemed to me cleverly planned for facilitating the necessary understanding where combined or ensemble work is required. The degree to which the studios are sound-proof is amazing ; and, while the silence can be actually oppressive, the atmosphere never can be so, for the ventilation is such that fresh air greets you everywhere from the sub-basement to the eighth floor above street level.

It was to the latter that we first mounted by a noiseless lift and entered what was for me one of the most interesting apartments in the whole establishment—to wit, the Control Room. It was the one place that I felt I would like to stay in for hours, nay, days, until I had mastered the working of its elaborate equipment of switchboard and amplifiers and exquisitely delicate electrical indicators. I wanted to put on earphones, like those young engineers seated at their six tables or desks ; to judge the relative acoustic strengths of the talkers and the actors whose transmissions and rehearsals they were so smoothly regulating ; to increase or diminish to the proper focus the sounds that were going out or coming in, or both. The long apartment was the " Dramatic Control " room ; the " Musical " room, if I am not mistaken, occupied a smaller area. I was also shown an invaluable " Mixing Board " contrived to bring about the correct timing and combining of speech and incidental music ; also meters fixed to a required level and a marvellous instrument called the " potentiometer " that has, I believe, much to do with the process of amplifying. Here it was that I encountered my friend Sir Walford Davies, not in person, but discoursing in his familiar confidential manner about the Bells of St. Martin's, and, with the aid of two peals of bells, a pianoforte, and that powerful adjunct the amplifier, projecting his cheery tones lustily in the nursery songs of old for transmission to every corner of the radio world. I should mention, however, that the " Musical Control " room is actually situated on the floor below (the seventh); and so is the Production studio, with its atmospheric devices for imparting either indoor or open-air qualities to spoken dialogue.

Naturally, I did not enter half the studios (though most of them were unoccupied in the afternoon) nor did I intrude into any of the dozens of busy offices. Thus I did not come across many of the 750 *genii loci* who frequent this extraordinary hive of industry. I should have liked to see more of them. I should have liked especially a nice quiet chat with certain members of the Worshipful Company of Announcers, in order to impress upon them the necessity for a more careful study of the pronunciation of the French language, a more careful regard for the peculiarities of their own (unimproved so far by the notorious B.B.C. vocabulary), and the general avoidance of incoherent mannerisms in their distribution of the news bulletins. Some of these gentlemen are too painstaking; others not half painstaking enough. One office that I certainly enjoyed visiting was that of Major Gladstone Murray, the ubiquitous and able Director of Publicity, who thoughtfully invited me to join him and a friend or two in a welcome cup of tea. But of the Director-General I saw nothing on this occasion, nor were the Governors at work in their conference room or council chamber, whichever it is; neither was a religious service being conducted in the singularly remote and beautiful Religious Studio designed by Mr. Ed. Maufe, which I admired immensely. But if I missed the *genii* in person I was able, nevertheless, to appreciate the accommodation provided for their well-ordered tasks.

I was glad to see working the Blattnerphone recording equipment of which I had heard so much. It appeared to be a very simple machine, winding and unwinding its wheels of steel tape, to be reserved for reproduction if and when required. It is also connected with the Control Room so that any programme may be recorded or fed back for re-transmission. The device is doubtless less simple than it looks, like many other new inventions utilised in this up-to-date establishment, but then I am not pretending to give more than a layman's impression of a gigantic technical achievement. The electrical equipment alone could not be described in more than double the space at my disposal; nor dare I begin to enlarge on such topics as microphones, with their carbon or condenser types, the acoustic treatment of the studios, the qualities of loud-speakers,

the various kinds and uses of amplifiers, and so on. Then, again, how could I hope to do justice to the miracles accomplished in the " Effects " Room, provided as it is with a myriad mechanical appliances for imitating every sort of sound to be heard on land and water. The marvel is how these can be provided and transmitted to any studio at the precise instant they are required.

On one floor below, the fourth, I visited in turn a band studio (where a sectional comic opera rehearsal was in progress), the Religious studio already mentioned, and the commodious Vaudeville studio, where, I believe, preparatory work never ceases, and where, by the way, a numerous studio audience can be accommodated. But this last is tiny by comparison with the big Concert Hall which rises from the lower ground to the top of the first floor and is situate in the centre of the building. In shape it reminds one of the stern portion of a huge galleon cut in halves, with space for a choir at one end, for an audience of about 750 seated on a slope at the other, and the orchestra on the flat floor surface between. It is to be provided later on with a fine organ, and certain of the performances given here will, it is expected, be open on payment to the public. As to the acoustic qualities of the hall I am unable to offer an opinion, beyond the fact that—judged by my own brief vocal experiments—it produces no echo and will serve splendidly for purposes of wireless transmission. Neither will the loudest musical sounds within be audible beyond its walls. And here again the complex ventilation is perfect, the air being extracted from under the seats by fans situated somewhere on the distant roof.

I must not omit to mention the two admirable rooms where members of the Press (particularly musical critics, of course) can listen in comfort to transmissions from any British or foreign regional station or from the studios. There are also two small " News " studios on the fourth floor, from whence are communicated those concise " weather and news " bulletins which, at 6, 9, or 10.15 p.m., depend so much for their charm upon the culture, the intelligence, the accuracy of accent and speech of the inaccessible and unassailable gentlemen who read them. Would that—but never mind ! I will merely observe that, if the mechanism in the Control Room can " check the quality " of the transmissions, it might also be so contrived as to improve the French, German, and Italian accents of the Medes and Persians who are privileged to do the announcing. Do *they* ever listen, I wonder ?

It will be noted, I hope, that among the more active *genii* of this modern dream-palace are many of vast ability and importance whom I would gladly have beheld in the flesh had time and opportunity allowed. I would have loved to describe to the reader some candid interviews with " monarchs of all they survey," such as the Directors of Programmes, of Talks, of Music, of Vaudeville, *et hoc genus omne*; not forgetting either those omniscient gentlemen, the Editors of the *Radio Times*, the *Listener*, and *World-Radio*. I am not vain ; but I fancy that if I could have quietly button-holed them in their new sanctums I could have told them a thing or two. Yet let me admit that, after completing the tour of this magnificent place, I had a distinct feeling of pride and delight that London should be the possessor of a treasure so amazingly unique— a gem of untold value that is even now radiating its glorious light and spreading its beneficent influence to every corner of the civilized globe.

It did not occur to me until I had left the new building and was some distance up Portland Place that I had not caught a glimpse of our Junior Editor, or of the studio from which he broadcasts his popular gramophone recitals. I should have liked to see him at work ; but it was not his hour, or one of them—for, like his records, they are numerous and varied. (By the way, on page 371 of the current *B.B.C. Year Book* there is a picture of the American apparatus for providing an hour's continuous transmission of an electrically-recorded programme ; but I do not think this is in use here.) Let there be no question about it, it is to Christopher Stone that the radio world pays tribute for the recent extraordinary development in the use of gramophone records for the provision and distribution of wireless music. His commentaries are inimitable ; but his methods have found imitators in every country, to the advantage, no doubt, of their exchequers as well as their resources for entertainment-supply. Just think how easy it is now to turn on the gramophone for a vacant half-hour and, thanks to electrical recording, furnish first-class orchestral or vocal music so true to the original that only the expert ear can detect the difference between it and the real thing.

But it is the new recording that "does the trick." The contrast between the new and the old is such that when, for example, Mr. Stone gives us one of his valuable recitals of precious and obsolete records made thirty years ago, as he did on June 6th, one almost fears the effect of the wrong impression which they give of the quality, the volume, the resonant power, of the voices that sang them. They serve for a sweet and welcome reminder, to those who heard them in actual life, of once-familiar beautiful tones that will ne'er be listened to again, together with certain indivi-dual characteristics of style (for those who are capable of appreciating them) that are fast fading into the *Ewigkeit* of the vocal art. Above all, perhaps, they serve as a vivid illustration of the difference between the natural, easy, and perfectly distinct enunciation of bygone days and the wretchedly slipshod, inaudible utterance of the words that we are condemned for the most part to put up with now.

But for every reason, I would thank Mr. P. G. Hurst for the loan of the delightful collection of old records that enabled our Editor to awaken such exquisite memories on the occasion I refer to. I had no idea that some of them were in existence or in a condition to be heard. One of the greatest surprises was Edward Lloyd's *Preislied*, to which I lately referred ; it was made, apparently, after his series of farewell concerts in 1900, when he was living as a gentleman farmer near Worthing. But his voice was still clear as a bell, and the "thrice happy day" in the last strophe of the *Preislied* never rang out more clearly. Emma Calvé's *Seguidilla* was extremely good, and Battistini's *Largo al factotum* amazing for its rapid diction, though not for actual tone. I did not care much for Albani's *Angels, ever bright and fair*, but Suzanne Adams's *Jewel Song* was everything that was claimed for it—a model for purity of Gounodian style. Ancona in Tosti's *Mattinata* and Melba in Bemberg's *Chant hindou* both proved excellent examples and recalled pleasant recollections of their respective personalities. Fainter than either of these was the reminder of Edouard de Reszke's glorious organ in the *Infelice* from *Ernani*, but the matchless phrasing was there sure enough, with something of the timbre into the bargain. Best of the whole group, though, for vitality and realistic repro-duction, was the last, namely, Victor Maurel's recording of *Quand' ero paggio*, from Verdi's *Falstaff*, which rôle (like Iago) he originally created at La Scala. Too short to fill the entire side of the disc, the delicious little air was spun out by two repetitions, one in response to a well-staged Fonotipia studio encore—the first ever known—and the other sung over again to the French text. In these, Maurel's voice seemed to improve as he went on, and what his artistry was like I leave you to guess. Again many thanks !

The Gramophone and the Singer

G.B.S. AND MUSIC IN THE 'NINETIES

by HERMAN KLEIN

GEORGE BERNARD SHAW may not have been a musical critic in the ordinary sense of the term, but he wrote about music in a very unconventional and amusing manner and with a certain amount of *connaissance de cause*. When I first knew him he was, I think, writing for *The Star*, and his trenchant style attracted the notice of Edmund Yates, who very soon appointed him to replace the clever but venal Louis Engel and act as musical colleague to William Archer on his—Yates's—powerful sixpenny weekly, *The World*. These criticisms, which appeared during 1890–94, have now been collected and reprinted in three volumes as part of the standard edition of the author's works*. I used to read them regularly as they came out, and invariably enjoyed them so much that their re-perusal has been doubly interesting. As for the events which they chronicle, I may say that I was representing the *Sunday Times* and other papers at nearly every one of them and can remember them all.

A good idea of the enormous area covered by this retrospect may be gathered from the copious index of thirty-odd pages printed at the end of the third volume. It comprises the name of every celebrity, every singer good or bad, every executant great or small, who flourished under our musical sun during those four years. Not only that. It guides you to the pages that will tell you exactly what G.B.S. thought of every composer, dead or living, whom he happened to write about, without regard to their place in popular esteem. These views of his are amusing as well as edifying, because he was then, what he is still, a man of strong prejudices, who rejoiced in the expression of opinions differing from those held by other people. He liked to be looked upon as the rampant Fabian that he was. He would come to concerts at St. James's Hall in a light tweed suit and a flaming red tie, and he never donned dress clothes unless absolutely compelled to. Yet I always found his manner amiable and conciliatory, and in his smile there was the same gleam of mischievous humour that it radiates to-day. Let me confess, however, that I was never admitted to his favourite " seventh circle " of close or intimate friends. Perhaps I was not enough of a Fabian.

Now although there are hundreds of opinions in the course of these pages that are diametrically opposed to those expressed by myself at the time, I feel no more inclined now than I was then to challenge or discuss them. The task would be far too colossal. Besides, it might not prove amusing for the reader, who will prefer, I fancy, to cull the gems *en passant* and savour them *cum grano salis*. To start off with, in May 1890, Miss Zélie de Lussan was singing Carmen. Thus G.B.S. : " Miss de Lussan is no more like Carmen than her natty stockings are like those ' with more than one hole in them ' described by Mérimée. . . . I miss the tragic background of ungovernable passion and superstitious fatalism to the levity and insolent waywardness which Miss de Lussan makes so much of. The truth is she cannot act the tavern scene nor sing the prophetic episode in the fortune-telling trio, to anything near conviction point." Nevertheless, it is generously allowed that she " shows remarkable cleverness " in the part. And at any rate she did not wobble—a cardinal sin to which G.B.S. was not alone in objecting. " The more we show by our encouragement of Miss Nordica, Miss (Ella) Russell, and Miss Macintyre, and by our idolatry of Madame Patti with her eternal Home, Sweet Home*, that our whole craving is for purity of tone and unwavering accuracy of pitch, the more our operatic visitors insist on desperately trying to captivate us by paroxysms of wobbling. Remonstrance, in English at least, is thrown away on them." Which only confirms my oft-repeated statement that matters in this respect were much the same forty years ago as they are to-day, if not rather worse.

During the same Covent Garden season we read that " The Huguenots, admirably rehearsed (note that !), goes without a hitch. . . . In the absence of a first-rate basso profundo, Edouard de Reszke was forced to repeat the double mistake of relinquishing the part of St. Bris, which fits him to a semitone, and taking that of Marcel, which lies too low for him. He has to alter the end of the chorale, and to produce the effect of rugged strength by an open brawling tone which quite fails to contrast with the other bass and baritone voices as Meyerbeer intended." With this I certainly agreed : Edouard was a splendid St. Bris, but by no means a first-rate Marcel. Again, referring to the ill-advised return visit of the clever but overrated Hungarian soprano, Etelka Gerster, who, in a physical but not a vocal sense, " has grown mightily since June 1877. Her columnar neck and massive arms are now those of Brynhild rather than Amina. . . . But the Ah, non giunge fell equally flat in 1877 ; and her Astrifiammante (spelt Astriffiamante) in that year showed exactly the same want of the delicate tintinnabulation which was so enchanting in Di Murska's singing of Gli angui d'inferno."

Music in London, 1890–94, by Bernard Shaw. In 3 vols., price 6/- each. London : Constable and Co., Ltd.

*It is to be noted that G.B.S. used neither italics nor inverted commas to distinguish titles of operas or names of pieces.

To turn for a moment from singers to pianists. When Paderewski first came out G.B.S. thought him " a man of various moods, who was alert, humorous, delightful at his first recital ; sensational, empty, vulgar, and violent at his second ; and dignified, intelligent, almost sympathetic, at his third." (Later on he found in him more to admire and less to blame.) " Sapellnikoff is never at fault in the domain of absolute music ; but when the music begins to speak, his lack of eloquence is all the more startling. . . . His playing of Chopin's Polonaise in A flat was stupendous. Stavenhagen, on the whole, is the finest, most serious artist of them all. . . . Of course there is the inimitable Sophie Menter, with the airs of an invalid and the vigour of a Valkyrie, knocking the breath out of poor Schumann at the Crystal Palace, laughing Weber's delicate romance out of countenance at the Philharmonic, playing everything like lightning, and finishing always with a fabulously executed Liszt rhapsody for which all her sins are at once forgiven her. Madame Teresa Carreño is a second Arabella Goddard (!) : she can play anything for you ; but she has nothing of her own to tell you about it. Playing is her superb accomplishment, not her mission." Well, well ! I could go on quoting, but have not the space this month.

Of all the composers of the period G.B.S. disliked none so heartily as Brahms. He even went one better than Wagner, who, it is said, called Brahms his *bête noire*. Here is a sample of his style in polishing off Brahms's symphony in E minor (No. 4) : " The spectacle of the British public listening with its in-churchiest expression to one of the long and heavy fantasias which he calls his symphonies always reminds me of the yokel in As You Like It quailing before the big words of the fool. Strip off the euphuism from these symphonies, and you will find a string of incomplete ballad tunes, following one another with no more organic coherence than the succession of passing images reflected in a shop window in Piccadilly during any twenty minutes in the day. . . . His symphonies are endured at the Richter concerts as sermons are endured, and his Requiem is patiently borne only by the corpse." Again, with reference to the latter work, we read : " I am sorry to have to play the ' disgruntled ' critic over a composition so learnedly contrapuntal, not to say fugacious ; but I really cannot stand Brahms as a serious composer. It is nothing short of a European misfortune that such prodigious musical powers should have nothing better in the way of ideas to express than incoherent commonplace. However, that is what is always happening in music : the world is full of great musicians who are no composers, and great composers who are no musicians." This epigram sounds well ; but I wonder how far the Promenade Concert *habitués* of to-day will feel inclined to echo it. I admit, however, that it was written for their fathers and not for them.

It is curious to note how many interesting people made their débuts in the year that our mentor began writing for *The World*. On the whole he sized them up with tolerable acumen and fairness. A few of them are dead and gone, but many are still alive and active. He rather ignored Mr. Isidore de Lara as a singer, but criticized him as a composer " who avoids academics and simply gratifies his turn for writing voluptuous lyrics, which are none the worse for a little opium-eating orchestration heightened by an occasional jingle of the *pavillon chinois*." Concerning the Albéniz of the early days we read, " A. will find the professors inclined to dispute his right to call his spontaneous effusions ' sonatas ' and ' concertos ' ; but if he sits tight and does as he pleases in this respect, he will find himself none the worse. He is, so far this season, the most distinguished and original of the pianists who confine themselves to the rose-gathering department of music." Again, a graphic pen-portrait of the last of Mme. Schumann's pupils making her début at the " Pops " in the New Year (1891) : " A wild young woman named Ilona Eibenschütz made her first appearance, stumbling hastily up the stairs, and rushing at the piano-stool with a couple of strange gestures of grudging obeisance, as if she suspected some plot among us to be beforehand with her, produced an unmistakable impression on the matronhood of the stalls. Backs were straightened, elbows drawn in, lips folded : in that moment Ilona, it seemed to me, was friendless in a foreign land. But when she touched the first chord of Schumann's Etudes Symphoniques, the hand lay so evenly and sensitively on it, and the tone came so richly, that I at once perceived I was wasting my sympathies, and that Ilona, however ingloriously she might go to the piano, would come away from it mistress of the situation. And she certainly did." I may add that this same Ilona, after becoming a tremendous favourite, married the late Mr. Carl Derenburg and settled down in London, where she still resides, a happy grandmother and quite a figure in society.

But for the present I must draw to a close. In another article I hope to make a further selection from these volumes, showing especially what G.B.S. thought of the more prominent operatic singers of this particular epoch.

The Gramophone and the Singer

HOW G.B.S. CRITICIZED FAMOUS SINGERS
by HERMAN KLEIN

AS I have already hinted, the circle of readers to whom Mr. Bernard Shaw addressed himself in the columns of *The World* was an extremely limited one. How they reacted to his opinions I cannot say, but he undeniably amused them, and the more his pin-pricks hurt the artists—as when the bull is shivering under the neat attacks of the banderilleros—the better they enjoyed reading him. "Criticism," he says (Vol. II, p. 156), " of course knows no gratitude and no regret ; but I must say that if all the artists of the Titiens epoch had been as good as Trebelli, my occasional references to that dark age would be much less ferocious than they generally are." This remark, àpropos of Trebelli's death, 15 years after that of Tietjens, contains the right adjective for an unwarrantable, because unjustifiable, onslaught upon a really great singer whom G.B.S. happened to have ceased to admire. I will quote it at length :

"What I am not so sure of is whether Sir Augustus Harris ever found Titiens out—whether he ever realized that in spite of her imposing carriage, her big voice, her general intelligence, and, above all, a certain good-hearted grace which she never lost, even physically, the intelligence was not artistic intelligence ; the voice, after the first few years, was a stale voice ; there was not a ray of creative genius in her ; and the absurdity of her age, her pleasant ugliness, and her huge size (which must have been to at least some extent her own fault), the public got into a baneful habit of considering that the end of opera-going was not to see Lucrezia, Leonora, Valentine, or Pamina, but simply Titiens in these parts, which was tantamount to giving up all the poetry of opera as a mere convention, which need not be borne out by any sort of artistic illusion."

No, G.B.S. Neither Sir Augustus Harris nor anyone else, bar your own imaginative self, ever " found this out." A discovery so contrary to the facts was never, indeed, lighted upon by any other living soul whose experiences actually went back to the " Titiens epoch." But such specimens of " sensation at any price," if pardonable in the nineties, need not have been reprinted forty years later.

Reading the criticisms of one man week after week is a vastly different thing from re-reading several years' of them *en bloc*. The collection is liable to show up his inconsistencies and self-contradictions. In his attitude towards certain artists one can thus trace a degree of prejudice that amounts almost to positive antipathy. He writes a great deal about Jean and Edouard de Reszke, and nearly always in the same satirical, condescending vein. He says little, if anything, about the quality of their voices or the beauty of their singing. He cannot forget that Jean was once a baritone, and prefers the recollection of his Don Giovanni and Valentine to any of his tenor rôles, with the exception of Walther von Stolzing. In his *Faust* and *Roméo*—yes, and his *Lohengrin* as well—he can not only find nothing to admire, but objects to them because in these Gounod parts he is " still vaguely romantic rather than intelligent in his acting," which he elsewhere describes as " lifeless and unimpassioned." In plain English, when it comes to dealing with the Polish brothers, if there is nothing to be said against their singing, *qua* singing (though Jean might shirk a high C or Edouard over-indulge in " bawling "), this critic could always find something unpleasant to say about their acting or the conception of their parts.

These pages afford ample evidence of a critic's right to change his mind about people and things. He sometimes grew to admire exceedingly artists whom he had handled with his customary severity on first acquaintance. Take, for instance, the famous contralto, Giulia Ravogli, who became Mrs. Harrison Cripps and is happily still living and residing in London. After dwelling at the outset on her and her sister Sofia's " unheard-of *naïvetés*," " their Tuscan full of nasal and throaty intonations abhorred of the grand school," their way of " trusting to luck rather than to skill for getting over florid difficulties," their " untrained metrical sense, and their scales with the accents hardly ever on the right notes "—after this, it is refreshing to find, a few pages farther, a delightful eulogium of a truly great and memorable achievement, the wonderful Orfeo of Giulia Ravogli, about whom, our critic here says, " I now confess myself infatuated. . . . Her success was immense. Nobody noticed that there were only two other solo-singers in the whole opera, both less than nothing beside her. She—and Gluck—sufficed."

Moreover, it is interesting to note how some singers get the superlatives, others the crushing obloquy ; or, again, how they are praised in certain parts and pulled to pieces, often quite justly, in others. On the whole, G.B.S. felt a tremendous admiration for Patti, even when getting old and " deprived of her enchantments as a wonderful florid executant," and, despite that " senseless hotchpotch programme of the miscellaneous order that always rubbed musicians the wrong way. . . . Though Patti has never been convincing or interesting as a dramatic singer in the sense in which, for instance, Giulia Ravogli excels [*sic*], yet in the old days we could not help wanting to hear those florid arias of the old school on that wonderful vocal instrument, with its great range, its birdlike agility and charm of execution, and its unique combination of the magic of a child's voice with the completeness of a woman's."

Again, the intellectuality of Victor Maurel was always his most prominent attribute, both as actor and singer.

His Don Giovanni, one reads, " though immeasurably better than any we have seen of late years, is not to be compared to his Rigoletto, his Iago, or, in short, to any of his melodramatic parts. Don Juan may be as handsome, as irresistible, as adroit, as unscrupulous, as brave as you please ; but the one thing that is not to be tolerated is that he should consciously parade these qualities as if they were elaborate accomplishments instead of his natural parts. And this is exactly where Maurel failed. He gave us a description of Don Juan rather than an impersonation of him. . . . When all is said, the fundamental impossibility remains that Maurel's artistic vein is not Mozartian." Nevertheless, the startling fact emerges that the creator of Iago incurs serious criticism in the most famous of all his rôles :

"The chief objection to Maurel's Iago is that it is not Iago at all, but rather the Cæsar Borgia of romance. As far as it is human, it is a portrait of a distinguished officer, one who would not be passed over for Cassio when he was expecting his step. . . . A certain bluffness and frankness, with that habit of looking you straight in the face which is the surest sign of a born liar, male or female, appear to me to be indispensable to ' honest Iago ' ; and it is the absence of these, with the statuesque attitudes, the lofty carriage of the head, and the delicate play of the hands and wrists, that makes the figure created by Maurel irreconcilable with any notion of the essentially vulgar ancient who sang comic songs to Cassio and drank him, so to speak, under the table. There is too much of Lucifer, the fallen angel, about it—and this, be it remarked, by no means through the fault of Verdi, who has in several places given a quite Shakespearean tone to the part by *nuances* which Maurel refuses to execute, a striking instance being the famous Ecco il leon at the end of the fourth act, when Iago spurns the insensible body of the prostrate Otello. . . . His performance is to be admired rather as a powerfully executed fantasy of his own than as the Iago either of Verdi or Shakespeare. If his successors in the part try to imitate him, their wisdom will be even less than their originality."

Maurel once gave some lectures in London on a new vocal method of his own which was to supersede in many details the laws of the old Italian school. Unfortunately, Maurel could never find language in which to define his ideas, and as a result, through never being revealed, they remained lost to the world. With these effronteries G.B.S. dealt indulgently, if rather amusingly ; but at the same time I think he took too much for granted where the technique of singing was concerned. He certainly did so in his obituary remarks on Emil Behnke, the voice specialist, with whom he himself studied for a time. Behnke was a great friend of mine and an excellent laryngologist ; but it would have been better for some of his pupils had he not allowed (or taught) them to make their attack of a vocal tone with so violent a glottic action based upon the utterance of the guttural consonant " K." Mr. Shaw says that " he at least did no mischief." I am not quite so sure about that.

Our candid critic had singularly little to say about Harris's colossal double opera season of 1892. He notices only a few of the performances and scarcely mentions Gustav Mahler, even when praising his orchestra. " The orchestra played Wagner just as the Manchester band played Berlioz ; it knew the works [taught by Mahler] instead of merely spelling through them at sight in the London fashion, and everybody must have been struck with the difference this made." He goes on to compare the various principal tenors and pays a handsome tribute to a handsome man—Max Alvary :

" Among the leading artists the one whose success is likely to have the greatest success is undoubtedly Alvary. . . . Van Dyk's eminence as a tenor is explained at once by his exuberant force and brilliancy, as Jean de Reszke's is by his romantic grace and distinction both of voice and person. . . . Alvary's voice is serviceable, but by no means beautiful ; and in plucking Nothung from the Branstock, or forging it anew on Mime's anvil, he has no superfluity of physical power with which to exult and play the Titan. And yet he held the attention and interest of the house whenever he was on the stage, and made a smart Loki, a pathetic Siegmund, and a remarkably handsome and picturesque Siegfried. . . . I attach immense value to the competition of artists like Alvary, who could not retain his place on the stage at all if he had nothing but his lungs to recommend him. The career is now opening to the talented ; and the demand for artists of the Alvary type will increase with the number of our music dramas."

G.B.S. was right in this, as he was in a few other of his prophecies, though he was too astute to make many. However, these reprints are not going to be read for the sake of what they forecast, but because of the fact that they furnish a diverting picture in the undiluted Shavian style of an interesting musical period. Viewed from that standpoint, and bearing in mind the spirit of irresponsible free-lancedom that pervades every line, they reappear as characteristically fresh to-day as in the years when they first came out.

The Gramophone and the Singer

PAST AND PRESENT RECORDS COMPARED—I

by HERMAN KLEIN

I AM setting out upon the task of comparing certain records of the new era with those of the same pieces that were executed in the pre-electric days, and as such reviewed by me in the pages of THE GRAMOPHONE. To do this will not incur altering opinions previously expressed, and for that I am devoutly thankful. When, in the course of looking over the old volumes, I come across some of the things that were said about the gramophone and the wireless, I cannot help fancying that the writers, if not heartily ashamed of their lack of vision, must cordially regret having ever given utterance to their early prejudices. It is all very well for these gentlemen to claim the right to alter their minds ; but have they now the right to set themselves up as authorities on either gramophone or wireless questions ? Hardly. At any rate, since consistency is precious, I would venture most especially to exclude from the above category both the Editor-in-Chief of this magazine and his regular critical staff, not forgetting the present writer.

No, I am not going to compare opinions, but records : and my object is to help the contemporary reader to discover the choicest and best among post-electric reproductions of those same selections which, at the time I first wrote about them, I considered the finest that were to be had. It goes without saying that improved recording has not necessarily brought greater artistry ; neither has it invariably happened that a re-recording of the same piece by the same singer has been equal in sheer vocal merit to the earlier one. But that, after all, is not the point. The present-day purchaser of gramophone records, unless on the look-out for " curios," is not wanting to spend his money on the pre-electric article at any price. Hence the probable utility of this endeavour to aid him in arriving at the pick of what in book-shop lore would be called the later modern editions. I shall now proceed to deal with them item by item as I originally wrote about them, and I begin with the subject of my second article, July 1924 (Vol. II, page 40), which concerned

THE RECORDING OF *Una Voce*

The examples here reviewed were by Marcella Sembrich, Luisa Tetrazzini, Amelita Galli-Curci, Evelyn Scotney, and Celys Beralta ; and, after a careful summing-up, I had little difficulty in awarding the palm to that by Mme. Galli-Curci (H.M.V. DB261), which, I may add, still figures in the latest H.M.V. general list. It is, however, practically superseded by the same artist's re-recording, now included in the Connoisseur's Catalogue and numbered DB1355 ; which

is in all respects superior and still, in golfing parlance, leads the field. I have also had occasion to speak in laudatory terms of an *Una voce* recently sung by Valeria Barsova (Parlo. E11128), and another by Anna Maria Guglielmetti (Col. L2051). Both of these are in two parts on a 12-in. disc ; but with the Galli-Curci you have on the other side her no less brilliant rendering of the *Polonaise* from *Mignon*. In two parts, again, are the renderings of Rossini's cavatina by Conchita Supervia (Parlo. R20074), by Margherita Salvi (Parlo. E10669), and Olga Olgina (Decca M92) ; and very excellent efforts they are. The Supervia was the first record by the Spanish singer that came under my notice (February 1930), but, clever as it is, I cannot rank it among her very best. Happily the pronounced *coup de glotte* that disfigured it quickly disappeared, and experience has since made Conchita Supervia one of our best gramophone vocalists. The Salvi record is brilliant in the extreme ; while with Olga Olgina's there is no material fault to be found—indeed, it is to be admired for a pretty tone and easy, graceful vocalization. But, as I said before, the new Galli-Curci yields to none of these for purity and beauty of tone or all-round technical excellence.

My article for August 1924 was headed

TWO FAMOUS VERDI ARIAS,

namely, *Caro nome* and *Ah ! fors' è lui*. I chose them because they were as popular then as they had been sixty years before ; and beyond question that observation still holds good to-day, eight years later. Here, again, as in *Una voce*, the work of Galli-Curci clearly demonstrated that as an exponent of the art of gramophone recording she was already definitely ahead of her compeers, if the paradox may be permitted. The group comprised in this instance Melba, Sembrich, Tetrazzini, Evelyn Scotney, Frieda Hempel, Graziella Pareto, Celys Beralta, Elsie Cochrane, and Lucette Korsoff. Of these Graziella Pareto's (H.M.V. DB565) was not only a delightful performance of the *Traviata* air, but actually the first, I think, to record it on two sides of the disc. It has not been done since then by Galli-Curci ; but her *Caro nome*, as I scarcely need remind my readers, is one of the gems of the Connoisseur list (DB1477), where it seems likely to shine unchallenged for many a day. Next to it I should feel inclined to place that of Margherita Salvi (Parlo. E10691, one side, with *Tutte le Feste*), which won eulogy for its vocal freshness and charm together with rare purity of intonation and neatness of execution. The same artist's *Ah ! fors' è lui* (Parlo. E10731, two parts) likewise pleased immensely, and on re-hearing it has just claims to be considered the finest rendering of this air yet recorded by the electrical process. Not for a moment to be compared with it is the mutilated version by Guglielmetti (Col. D1603), which for some unaccountable reason omits the *cabaletta*, *Sempre libera*, as though it had no connection with the piece. It is, however, brilliant enough so far as it goes, and perhaps one day when the artist is in London she will be allowed to repair her omission and furnish the missing link, in place of the *Tutte le Feste* which occupies the reverse side. By the way, an artistic *Caro nome* that ought not to be forgotten is that by Eugénie Bronskaja, which figures in the latest Columbia list (A5193) in conjunction with Gounod's *Ave Maria*. On the other hand, her *Una voce*, which my colleague Mr. Little and I agreed in thinking rather good, has disappeared from the current catalogue—presumably for the reasons connected with the law of supply and demand that really govern all these questions.

In September 1924 I took in hand the task—still more formidable to-day—of dealing with

THE PROLOGUE TO *Pagliacci*

The average quality of the five English and seven Italian recordings of this hackneyed piece was by no means first-rate ; but, on re-perusing my necessarily severe criticisms of some of them, I have perceived that they were largely evoked by blemishes which more modern mechanical methods would have tended to eliminate, though faults of style are not, of course, counted among these. The following were the singers, as noticed :—Peter Dawson, George Baker, Frederick Collier, Thorpe Bates, Stewart Gardner, Giuseppe Campanari, Riccardo Stracciari, Ramon Blanchart, Ugo Donarelli, Pasquale Amato (Fonotipia 74142), Ferrucio Corradetti, Renato Zanelli. In the succeeding month I had four more records of the *Prologue* to write about, all in Italian, sung by Emilio de Gogorza, Antonio Scotti, Pasquale Amato (H.M.V. DB156), and Tita Ruffo. They were as a whole superior to the previous lot, and Tita Ruffo's represented then, as it still does (H.M.V. DB464), my ideal rendering of the most variously-treated composition ever written for baritone voice. Knowing as I do Leoncavallo's intentions in regard to what he prefaced as an after-thought to the score of *Pagliacci*, I have no hesitation in saying that the Ruffo record cannot possibly be improved upon.

Peter Dawson (H.M.V. C1259) and Stracciari (Col. D1626) have both re-recorded theirs alike wisely and well. In each instance a distinct improvement in tone and enunciation is made manifest. In addition to these, four other records, one English, one French, and two Italian, appear in the H.M.V. catalogue, sung respectively by John Brownlee (D1385), Armand Crabbé (DB1128), Apollo Granforte (DB1044), and Lawrence Tibbett (DB975). In each of this group I have found something to praise, but definite choice must be left to personal inclination in the matter of language, voice, or what not. If I had to pick one from the half-dozen to please my own taste, I think I should choose the Granforte. And, àpropos, I should mention that all post-electric examples of the *Prologue* are given on two sides of the disc.

The Columbia series now consists of four, viz., Stracciari's above noted, one by Armando Borgioli (5248), and one each by Mostyn Thomas (DX213) and Harold Williams (3843). I liked Borgioli's immensely. In my review of it (April 1929) I said that I was ready, " nay, glad, to listen to the sempiternal *Prologue* as often as may be necessary, provided it be sung as artistically and with the same vocal finish as Borgioli delivers it in this record." I considered it then, and I consider it still, second for all-round artistic merit only to Tita Ruffo's much earlier effort, and second to none among the more recent recordings. Excellent, too, was the pre-electric specimen of Cesare Formichi's (Col. 1487), now no longer in the Columbia collection, although I had the temerity to include it in my list of " Notable Records " published in the 100th number of THE GRAMOPHONE a year ago. Of the two sung in English that by Harold Williams is to be preferred. It has the right distinction coupled with the right distinctness and a satisfying measure of the right dramatic feeling. The Mostyn Thomas, as I observed in my review of it, rings clear with a fine voice, but also with a strong Welsh dialect that might grate upon the general ear. Another which misses its mark for different reasons is by Eric Marshall (Brunswick 20082) ; but there were many good points about an unpretentious effort of Sydney de Vries (Piccadilly 5008), not the least being that it cost only a florin. In the current Parlophone list there are two—one by Giovanni Inghilleri (R20070), the other by Fausto Ricci (E10733). Of these the former is superior both for beauty of voice and breadth of style, and, though a trifle hurried so as to manage the whole of it on one side, there is the compensating fact that the reverse side provides a splendid *Largo al factotum*.

I hope to continue these comparisons between past and present in future articles, at any rate down to the end of the year. I will endeavour to leave out nothing of value in either category, but of course the task is rather an extensive one, and I shall have to be forgiven if I omit much in order to keep it within bounds.

An Important Discovery

I read an interesting account given recently in the *Christian Science Monitor*, by Volney D. Hurd, of a successful experiment made in the *ateliers* of the Victor company at New York, that may have the effect of reviving both artistic interest and commercial value in some of these old records *de luxe*. It seems to me to be very wonderful and very practical. Here are some bits of the story :

" One often hears the complaint, ' Isn't it too bad that Caruso and some of the other great artists were not recorded electrically so that we could get the same full effect from their records that we get from the modern ones?' Taking Caruso, for instance . . . It was primarily in the deep accompaniment that the old records were deficient. The first step was to go into some of the original records and it was found that with modern electrical apparatus there was more to be taken from these records than had ever been heard in the original machine. This meant that the recording of the voice itself was quite good. . . .

" The next idea to suggest itself was to record a new accompaniment electrically and blend this with the original voice of Caruso. Nathaniel Shilkret, the popular Victor conductor, was called in. He had conducted for one of the last records made by Mr. Caruso. . . .

" The final result was probably one of the strangest things that has ever happened. An orchestra played a perfect accompaniment to an operatic score without hearing the singer in any way. Before this orchestra stood Mr. Shilkret with headphones clamped to his ears. Through these headphones he was listening to the original Caruso voice recording. Thus he heard Caruso's voice and in turn directed the orchestra, although the men never heard the slightest vocal sound. Then the new recording was electrically blended with the old to produce a single new record. . . .

" It is now stated that some six of Caruso's records have been worked over this way so that we can listen to that great voice with a deep resonant background of the latest in orchestral accompaniment. It will be interesting to have an opportunity of trying these records to see how nearly they really achieve their objective."

I agree, it will; especially if the voice itself can be amplified into exact proportion with the volume of the instrumental sound.

P.S.—I have been asked to point out an error in the Columbia catalogue. The Jewish record by Cantor Joseph Rosenblatt, E2819, should appear under the letter Y, not the letter T. The Hebrew title of the chant, written in English, should be *Yisgadal V'yiskadash*.

HERMAN KLEIN.

PAST AND PRESENT RECORDS COMPARED—II

by HERMAN KLEIN

BEFORE continuing my comparisons I would like to say, in reply to enquiries, that the change-over from the old process of recording to the new began in the summer of 1925. It was not, of course, effected in a day, like that of the *Times* printing type. The gramophone companies found themselves face to face with a welcome, long-sought solution of one of their most vital problems, an improvement in the science of recording which they had neither excuse nor desire for putting off a day longer than they could help, but one which might at the outset involve them in heavy loss unless they acted warily and with foresight. In other words, as owners of enormous stocks of records, they required time for the disposal of the old and the necessarily gradual introduction of the new. In some cases, they found, it took only months to work off the old ; but in others it has taken years whilst new records and recordings of old ones that were in demand were slowly filling the vacant places on the shelves.

During this period there has been in progress the work of building up an instrumental section the like of which never existed, never was dreamt of, in pre-electric days. It is at the present time, I imagine, quite as large as, if not larger than, the vocal, and it has been occupying the machines and their workers no less constantly. It has also been marked by a greater advance in executive merit than that shown, on the whole, in the singing of the post-electric records. The new process may have resulted in finer vocal effects, especially where large masses of sound are focussed in the microphone ; in greater clarity of reproduction, in increased purity of the tone generally, in ability to amplify the volume of the voice without resorting to the extremes that produce distortion. But, as against all these advantages, there remains the incontrovertible fact that the art of the singers who made the earlier records was superior to that of to-day, excluding only the interpretation of *lieder* and the quality of Wagnerian declamation. The beauty of the work in the two branches just named has risen to a standard level with that attained in orchestral and chamber music ; which is saying a great deal.

A month ago I found myself constantly putting the question, When exactly did the change-over begin ? I could not be quite sure, and I did not want to content myself with merely guessing, but since then I have obtained the required information and can pass it on to my readers with certainty, giving the actual month of issue in two cases out of three. The first electrical

record issued by H.M.V. came out in June 1925 ; but it had not been made at Hayes—it was actually manufactured by the Victor Company in New York, which had even then stood in long and close business relationship to the Gramophone Company of London. The first electrical issue of the Parlophone Company was the record E10508, which was placed on sale in November 1926. It was the *Prelude and Liebestod* from *Tristan and Isolde*, and all 12-in. records thereafter in the catalogue are electrical. In the Parlophone-Odéon series the new process began with R2008 and, excepting in one minor instance, all later numbers belong to the same category. With regard to the Columbia I am only in a position to state they began issuing the new records in the same year as the H.M.V., namely, 1925. This, it may be added, was only about eighteen months after I first started my articles in THE GRAMOPHONE.

And now to resume. The choice for my next review of records in retrospect (October 1924) was the tenor air

CELESTE AIDA.

I found that there were about a dozen records of this piece to be dealt with, and, after going over them with considerable care, concluded that not more than half of them were likely to prove of lasting interest. They were those of Caruso (H.M.V. DB144), Hipolito Lazaro (Col. 7342), Martinelli (H.M.V. DB335), Constantino (Col. A679), and Frank Mullings (Col. L1349). The remainder were by Thomas Burke, Wm. Davidson, Vladimir Rosing, Leo Slezák, and G. Zenatello. The whole of them have disappeared from current lists with the exception of the Caruso, concerning which I wrote : " The purity of the singing was matched by the purity of the mechanical reproduction, and between them they revived agreeable memories of the greatest tenor that this century has so far seen. The whole effect was one of singular clearness, of notes clean-cut as the facet of a diamond. It was thus that Caruso sang *Celeste Aida* on the stage." My estimation of the high quality of this record holds good to-day.

Martinelli's re-recording (H.M.V. DB979) was coupled with another of *Che gelida manina*, and I considered it a distinct improvement upon the older one—in fact, that it would bear comparison with the best of the post-electric specimens. (The *Bohème* excerpt elicited equal praise.) That was in October 1927, and a couple of months before then I had bestowed a favourable criticism upon the *Celeste Aida* of Michele Fleta, which was associated with *Una vergine, angiol divina*, from

La Favorita : " Both, I admit, are slightly nasal, but not disagreeably so, and the singing is robust and tender by turns ; while the recording is wonderfully clear." In February 1929 came a good record by Francesco Merli (Col. L2208), and two years later that by Alessandro Valente (H.M.V. B3682), which I did not care for particularly : " As to the beauty of the voice and the declamation there can be no question, but it is a beauty of volume rather than of charm or expression." Meanwhile there appeared simultaneously in May 1929 the two complete *Aida* albums of H.M.V. and Columbia, with Pertile's *Celeste Aida* in the former (D1596), and in the latter that of Aroldo Lindi (Col. 9726). Between these two it is very hard to choose, but if I must admit a preference it is a slight one in favour of Lindi's ; at the same time I have no hesitation in saying that I consider Martinelli's re-recording, mentioned above, definitely superior to either. It is the one that approaches most nearly to the old Caruso record.

The article for November 1924 was devoted to

Mon cœur s'ouvre à ta voix,

now better known to most people, I suppose, under its English title of *Softly awakes my heart*. This beautiful air, which has unfortunately become decidedly hackneyed—since every mezzo-soprano or contralto on the surface of the singing globe has it in her repertory—is not only the gem of Saint-Saëns's *Samson et Dalila*, but furnishes the thematic and melodic basis of the entire scene in which it occurs. It was, indeed, the first number in the opera that the composer put on paper. It was chiefly built up, both in the refrain, *Verse-moi l'ivresse*, and the accompaniment to the second verse, " upon a descending chromatic passage of six notes, obviously intended to typify Dalila's deceitful nature, the false smiles and sinuous, serpentine movements that lure poor Samson to his ruin." The most perfect rendering of it that I ever listened to was by Elena Sanz, who created the part of Dalila at Rouen when the work was first done in France, and was to have sustained it at Covent Garden (in concert form only) in 1893, under Mr. F. H. Cowen. She duly came to London with a tenor named Lafargue and rehearsed her part with the *maître* in my studio one unforgettable September morning ; then—went back to Paris again in search of Saint-Saëns, who had previously rushed over to find his tenor, who had mysteriously disappeared. Thus all three failed to appear, and the opera was (badly) sung for the first time in England as an oratorio on the 25th of the same month. All that remained to me thereafter was my memory of Elena Sanz's exquisite singing ; nor has that faded yet !

The records of *Mon cœur s'ouvre* available in 1924 were ten in number, and of these I reviewed nine, viz., by the late Kirkby Lunn, Dame Clara Butt, Maria Gay, Muriel Brunskill, Julia Culp, Louise Homer, Sigrid Onégin, Ethel Hook, and Edna Thornton. The tenth, which I somehow missed, was by Carrie Herwin (Col. 343), and it still retains its place in the current list. Others also to be had yet are those of Muriel Brunskill (in English, Col. 3328), Kirkby Lunn (French, H.M.V. DB913), Dame Clara Butt (French, Col. 7318), and Edna Thornton (English, H.M.V. D282). The last two are the oldest ; in fact, they are pre-war, having been sung about 1913-14 ; but both are well worth hearing and owning even now. Oddly enough, the Sigrid Onégin was the first record by that artist I ever heard (it was a Cliftophone-Brunswick, 518A), and I liked it extremely, save for an intrusive high B flat at the end, which struck me as being very much out of place.

I turn to the electrical recordings of this exacting air—for exacting in a rare degree it undoubtedly is—with the regretful conviction that not one of them would have wholly satisfied the musician who wrote it. Certainly I cannot point to any that I consider beyond criticism from a purely vocal standpoint. How comes this ? The *cantilena* is straightforward enough, and the intervals are singable as well as graceful. Yet how rarely is that rising seventh in the *Verse-moi l'ivresse* sung with a faultless *portamento* combined with impeccable intonation and breathing and the right intensity of simulated passion ! Again, how many singers bear in mind that the Dalila of this air is a siren, not a woman pleading for the adoration of the man she genuinely loves ? For sheer beauty of steady tone I am not sure that I admired any among the new recordings more than the English one by Marion Anderson (H.M.V. C2047) ; but surely a colder, less demonstrative Dalila never came out of Gaza ! On the other hand, those presented (in French) by Maartje Offers (H.M.V. DB912) and by Marguerite d'Alvarez (H.M.V. DA1000) were both disfigured, if not spoiled, by the same blemish—an incessant tremolo. It was a great pity, for in the matters of style and expression there was no fault to be found with either, though in that of pitch Mlle. d'Alvarez left much to be desired.

Finally I come to the " pick of the bunch," namely, the record issued in October 1928 by Maria Olczewska (H.M.V. D1465). I described it at the time as " a thoroughly artistic performance and quite free from the customary exaggerations." It is perhaps something more than that, albeit not attaining quite to the ideal that I fancy we should have been enchanted with had Elena Sanz flourished in the gramophone epoch.

P.S.—I am reminded by a reader of two excellent records which I omitted from my article of last month— one the French *Caro nome* of Eide Noréna (Parlo R20162, listed in the Supplementary Index since the complete Catalogue) ; the other the *Ah ! fors' è lui* of Mercédès Capsir (Col. 9632) in the *Traviata* Album for which Mr. Compton Mackenzie wrote the new English version (April 1929). Both these records stand in the first class, and I am not disinclined to agree with my correspondent that Capsir's is fully equal to Margherita Salvi's. Another of the same air which I also left out was the delightful effort of Olga Olgina (Decca K570), which I reviewed in March 1931. I hope I am forgiven for these omissions ; they are not quite easy to avoid.

HERMAN KLEIN.

The Gramophone and the Singer
PAST AND PRESENT RECORDS COMPARED—III
by HERMAN KLEIN

I FIND that I shall now have to deviate somewhat from the course marked out by my earliest articles. The last two for the year 1924 became more general in character and dealt with oratorio as well as opera. Besides, the selections made for me were by no means exhaustive, and did not nearly cover the whole of the ground as they probably would if I were beginning the same task over again to-day. Thus in January, 1925, I talked about Mozart, and dwelt upon the shameful neglect of his operas that had been shown in this country during the thirty years preceding the War, and even during the period 1888–1924 covered by the late Richard Northcott's brochure, *Covent Garden and the Royal Opera*. The total number of performances therein set down was as follows : *Don Giovanni*, 104 ; *Marriage of Figaro*, 28 ; *Magic Flute*, 12 ; *Il Seraglio*, 1 ; and *Bastien et Bastienne*, 3. These figures did not, of course, include the Mozart operas given elsewhere by the Beecham Company, by the B.N.O.C., or by the Carl Rosa Company in the provinces ; but, even with these added, it would have been a poor showing compared with the totals reached abroad.

Happily our interest in Mozart has vastly increased since then ; though I doubt whether the demand for the gramophone records of his music has extended to the operas in nearly the same proportion as to the symphonies, the concertos and the quartets. To enlarge the demand for operatic records there exists only one potent incentive, and that is to perform the operas themselves. The effect of the constant succession of concert and wireless performances upon the instrumental section can be judged by a glance at the gramophone catalogues. Mention of the latter, by the way, reminds me that in my recent searches for the newer Mozart records I have been struck, not to say puzzled, by the variety of the English titles bestowed upon the same pieces. I ask, how is the uninitiated or uninstructed tyro to recognise one from the other, or, if they be identical, to discover the fact ? The main cause of the trouble is that our native artists use at their discretion any one of three versions, viz., the Novello, the Boosey, or the American Schirmer editions, or perhaps for *Le Nozze di Figaro* the translation of Professor Dent, which I fancy is not yet published. The only way to avoid this confusion is to identify each piece by adding in brackets its familiar Italian title. The German titles give no help in this matter, and very often they differ as well.

The solitary Mozart number that I reviewed in my article for January, 1925, was Susanna's aria, *Deh vieni non tardar*, the singers being Marcella Sembrich (H.M.V. DB433), Selma Kurz (H.M.V. DB500), Graziella Pareto (H.M.V. DB567), Lucrezia Bori (H.M.V. DB153), and Kathleen Destournel (Voc. C01087). Of these not one remains for sale in the ordinary way now—perhaps for the sufficient reason that all were more or less open to criticism, through one fault or another which modern recording methods would have helped the singer to avoid. In the interpretative sense Marcella Sembrich or Selma Kurz could not possibly have been improved upon in the rendering of this " very exacting as well as divinely beautiful air." On the other hand, infinitely better tonal results have been obtainable in the up-to-date recording of Elisabeth Schumann (H.M.V. DB1011), of the late Meta Seinemeyer (Parlo. E11130), or, in English, of Isobel Baillie (Col. 9373). I have already spoken in high terms of each of these.

Nearly a year slipped by before I returned to the subject which I had so much at heart, and then I treated it fairly exhaustively in the articles which appeared in THE GRAMOPHONE of December, 1925, and February, 1926, under the title of " The Supremacy of Mozart." That is to say, I did my best with the available material, for the whole collection, as I complained at the time, was anything but a representative one and did not nearly cover the whole of the ground. Needless to say, it consisted entirely of pre-electric work, some of it what we should now regard as mere antiques of the art of reproduction and interesting solely on account of the artists who made them. Taking first *Le Nozze di Figaro*, I found the *Non so più* of Amelita Galli-Curci and Elisabeth Schumann " incredibly unlike Mozart " and the latter's *Voi che sapete* " spasmodic and over-sentimentalized." I liked Frieda Hempel's reading of the page's song, also the *Dove sono* of Claire Dux and Lotte Lehmann, both of whom sang *Deh vieni* delightfully enough to make one regret that their efforts are *passés*. There is still, however, consolation to be had in Lotte Lehmann's *Heil'ge Quelle* (*Porgi amor*) (Parlo. R20054) and Elisabeth Rethberg's ditto (Parlo. RO20115), both of which stand in the first rank of post-electric singing, together with the *Dove sono* in two parts of Meta Seinemeyer already referred to. The *Non più andrai* of Battistini and Sammarco were quite good enough to have deserved a better fate ; and so were the duets *Crudel, perchè*, and *Che soave zeffiretto* sung respectively by Farrar and Scotti and by Emma Eames and Sembrich.

By far the best new record of *Voi che sapete* is the one sung in German (*Ihr die ihr Triebe*, Parlo. R886) by Louise Helletsgrüber, noticed by me in April, 1931. It is quite perfect in its way. This soprano has done equally well on the reverse side with *Non so più*, but not in Italian, for which language I admire in about the same degree either Elisabeth Schumann's (H.M.V. DA844), which has coupled with it the lovely *Venite*, *inginocchiatevi* ; or Conchita Supervia's (Parlo. R20077) ; or Gitta Alpar's (Parlo. R20082). Of the old lot, the *Voi che sapete* of Frieda Hempel (H.M.V. DA675) is still listed ; but I did not care for its pallid tone and lukewarm expression before, nor do I like it any better now. It is hard to choose between the *Porgi amor* of Florence Austral (H.M.V. D1446) and that of Miriam Licette (Col. DX130), for both are excellent in tone and phrasing ; while the latter singer is impeccable in *Dove sono* (Col. 9436). Again, the choice between the *Voi che sapete* of Rosa Pampanini (Col. D1605) and that of Isobel Baillie (English, Col. 9373) may be guided chiefly by lingual considerations. If you feel any particular desire to hear the same familiar air sung in French there is the latest Parlophone record of Lily Pons (RO20153), which I praised so recently as October, 1931 ; or if you are pining for German versions of *Now your days* and *And so, my lord, you'd fain dance*, they are to be had in the admirable examples of Gerhard Hüsch (Parlo. R1122). At the same time I can once more express appreciation of the refreshing vigour of the two Figaro airs as sung by Mariano Stabile (on Col. L1285) ; or, if you vote for English, the alternative versions of *Non più andrai* presented by Peter Dawson (*Now your days*, H.M.V. C1401) and John Brownlee (*So, Sir Page*, H.M.V. D1396). Between these last four records there is little to choose, though for actual beauty of tone I prefer the Stabile.

And now we come to *Don Giovanni*. I need not reiterate my praises of Chaliapine's *Madamina, il catalogo*, either for what it was in 1925 or for the splendid re-recording (H.M.V. DA994) that was issued in January, 1929 ; anyhow, you would select the latter. Peter Dawson's has disappeared, along with the *La ci darem* of Farrar and Scotti and a long string of *Batti, battis* and *Vedrai carinos*, of *Il mio tesoros* and *Dalla sua paces*, etc., which it would take too long to enumerate here. Elisabeth Schumann has, I am glad to say, replaced her former German versions of *Batti, batti* and *Vedrai carino* with up-to-date Italian ones (H.M.V. DB946 and DA845) which are in every respect an improvement. The *Fin ch'an del vino* and *Serenade* of Tita Ruffo find a satisfactory substitute in those of Mariano Stabile (Col. D1612), although the brand of origin is changed ; and, truth to tell, I consider the latter's *Serenade* far more in accord with tradition. In the same category, yet standing absolutely alone, is the superb rendering of Donna Anna's *Or sai chi l'onore* by Frida Leider (H.M.V. D1547), which had not, I think, been previously recorded. I reviewed it in March, 1929, together with the air from Gluck's *Armide* on the same disc, and have nothing further to add to the eulogium which I wrote then.

Otherwise it must be regretfully admitted that the recording of *Don Giovanni* is not making the further progress that it ought to. Of the familiar but ever-exquisite *La ci darem* there are only English versions by Miriam Licette and Dennis Noble (Col. 9503) or Alice Moxon and Stuart Robinson (H.M.V. B3430) ;

while the two airs of Don Ottavio are similarly reproduced by the solitary efforts of Heddle Nash (Col. 9880), or, going abroad for others, the smooth German specimen of Max Hirzel (Parlo. E10918). I must not omit the artistic *Mi tradì* of Miriam Licette (Col. 9911), which so few sopranos have a true idea about ; and there must not escape notice two other capital *Madaminas* besides Chaliapine's—to wit, those of Julian Giuliani (Parlo. E10963) and Gerhard Hüsch (Parlo. R1165).

I pass on to *The Magic Flute*. It will be remembered that Mozart's operatic swan-song, produced only three months before he died, was composed to a German libretto, and it was for that reason that I wrote (in February, 1926), " I would under all circumstances advise my readers to lend a willing ear to gramophone records of this opera sung in the German language." The pick of the available group—no longer available, alas !—were records by Frieda Hempel, Maria Ivogün, Pol Plançon, Emmy Bettendorf, Delia Reinhardt, Lotte Lehmann, Elisabeth Schumann, Selma Kurz, Emma Eames, Emilio Gogorza, Leo Slezák, Friedrich Schorr, Paul Bender, and Heinrich Schlusnus (what a constellation !) ; others were by Evelyn Scotney, Sabine Meyen, Luella Melius, Zenaida Jurjevskaya, Tudor Davies, Robert Radford, Marcel Journet, Alfred Jerger, and Ernesto Badini. I will not for a moment pretend that we can beat this to-day either numerically or for individual excellence. I only wonder that there should not have been some re-recordings by artists still on the active list ; for, with the exception of Robert Radford's *O Isis* (H.M.V. E78) and Tudor Davies's *Loveliness beyond compare* (H.M.V. E401), the whole collection seems to have " gone by the board." Which is the greater pity because, speaking generally, it is in the singing of *The Magic Flute* that the present compares least favourably with the past.

The new records in current circulation I have only space left just to enumerate. Thus, in the H.M.V. catalogue will be found recent recordings by Ewald Böhmer (*Papageno* airs in German, B3781) ; by Ivar Andrésen (*O Isis and Osiris* and *Within these sacred walls* in German, C1625) ; and Ezio Pinza (*Possenti Numi* in Italian, DB1088), all three good. In the Columbia are those of Anna Guglielmetti (*Gli angui d'inferno*, L2045), clever and brilliant ; of Heddle Nash (*Tamino* airs, 9228), smooth and well sustained ; of Norman Allin (*Within this hallowed dwelling*, 9802), broad and dignified ; and the duet *Manly heart*, by Miriam Licette and Dennis Noble. In the Parlophone are comprised those of Lily Pons (*Queen of Night*, RO20153, and *Pamina's* air, R20163), both splendid ; of Gerhard Hüsch (*Papageno* airs, R979 and E11046), quite unsurpassable ; of Ivar Andrésen (*Sarastro* airs, E10574), ditto ; of Emanuel List (*O Isis*, R1215), first-rate ; and, lastly, of Michael Szekély (*In diesen heiligen Hallen*, E10939), " jerky and explosive." But in these, after all, there is a redeeming proportion of superlatives.

Caruso Redivivus

The announcement made exclusively in THE GRAMOPHONE for October regarding the resuscitation of the old Caruso records, with amplified tone and modern orchestral accompaniments, has been promptly verified and followed up by an issue from the H.M.V. factory of the new record itself. The resulting effect is truly marvellous—something on which to congratulate everyone concerned. It is curious that this fulfilment of a long-existing wish of mine should have come almost simultaneously with the publication of the above series of articles, and I sincerely hope that some of the past recordings therein mentioned will be treated to the same clever method of reproduction. The success of the Caruso example in many respects exceeds my highest expectations.

The first point to observe is that the voice, whilst retaining all its old beauty of quality, is now brought out with abundant power. The balance between it and the orchestra is carefully preserved and discreetly graduated so as to be strong when the well-remembered tones are at their loudest ; and then they are very rich and resonant indeed. They may sound less powerful, less noisy than the modern recordings give us, but on this very account I infinitely prefer them. At any rate, they are pure Caruso ; about that there can be no mistake, and the effect of reticence is not unwelcome.

In *M'appari* (formerly numbered 052121* but now DB1802) all his wonted grace and suavity of phrasing is conspicuously manifested ; while in *Vesta la giubba* (formerly DB111, but now coupled with *M'appari*) one hears adequate force and fire in every salient passage. In both cases another great point that strikes one is the total absence of scratching or blasting or any of the mechanical blemishes of the early days. On the whole, therefore, this valuable experiment should lead to important consequences, and I look forward to listening at an early date to the suggested revivals of records by Patti, Melba, Tamagno, and other famous singers.

The Opera Merger

A few days after the issue last month of the official statement with reference to the agreement reached between the various operatic organisations, I had a conversation with Colonel Eustace Blois, who had just returned to town from Edinburgh. There he had been listening to what he described as the finest performance of *Tristan* that he had ever heard given in English. He expatiated on the extraordinary energy and spirit which Sir Thomas Beecham had thrown into his conducting and the splendid singing of Miss Florence Austral and Mr. Walter Widdop. He thought that Sir Thomas had recaptured all and more of his youthful vigour, and for that reason was doubly glad that he would be joining the Covent Garden Opera Syndicate as its Artistic Director. He did not anticipate the least trouble about obtaining from the Court of Chancery the authority for the release of the funds subscribed for the Imperial League of Opera. All the preliminary negotiations had been settled for linking up these organizations with those of the Old Vic-Sadler's Wells and, he also hoped, the Carl Rosa Company. I put no indiscreet questions, however, about the precise part that the B.B.C. would play in the maintenance of the so-called State subsidy for opera ; but I gather that the Broadcasting Corporation, and not the Treasury, will take over the entire liability, and furnish whatever financial support the new " National Opera Council " is likely to obtain from extraneous sources. The contributions of the B.B.C. for operatic relays have now, indeed, become absolutely essential for the vitality of the whole united undertaking.

With regard to the share of the provinces in all this, I can only repeat what I said when I originally proposed in these columns the fusion of the various operatic interests, namely, that the Carl Rosa Company, as the oldest and best known of the whole group, should be allowed its fair proportion of big towns, and so enabled to pursue uninterruptedly the long and honourable work which it has carried on since the days of Carl Rosa and more especially under its recent efficient management. The Vic-Wells enterprise so ably directed by Miss Lilian Baylis has a sufficiently heavy task to perform in London. HERMAN KLEIN.

CARUSO

*Actually, 052121 was the HMV single-face number for a 1906 recording. The recording which Victor used for the new dubbing dated from 1917, a version issued in the United States, but never in England. Ed.

The Gramophone and the Singer

A ROSSINIAN REVIVAL

by HERMAN KLEIN

IT is certainly the turn of Rossini. In the years since the war, revivals of Mozart and Verdi, or even of Meyerbeer in the countries where he is appreciated, have been finding a place more and more regularly in the active repertory of the big opera houses. We are no longer the leaders in these matters that we were at one time, but only followers of fashion at a respectful distance, imitating a foreign success now and then when opportunity occurs, which is rather seldom. Mozart, of course, is a trump card whenever played (at the right moment); his, however, is a limited suit, and, as Sir Thomas Beecham proved long ago, not more than three of his masterpieces, well performed, could be counted upon to draw good houses. His lovely *Seraglio*, for instance, has still to appeal as it deserves to modern British audiences, though popular enough in Central Europe. Verdi revivals, on the other hand, have been proving attractive in Italy as well as in Germany, Austria, Hungary, and Czechoslovakia, not to mention America.

But you cannot go on ringing the changes on the early Verdi operas for ever. There is too much similarity between them—I mean from a musical point of view, of course—for them to provide the necessary amount of variety. In these circumstances it would appear to be a refreshing contrast to turn from Verdian melodrama to Rossinian comedy, from the heavy tragedies of Busseto to the diverting *buffo* farces of the Swan of Pesaro. Until he composed *Falstaff* Verdi never wrote a humorous opera, though he showed there plainly enough what a genius he had for the task. But Rossini, with comparatively few exceptions (*Tancredi*, *Otello*, *Semiramide*, and *William Tell* the most conspicuous), did naught but set to music the most amusing comedies he could find, some of them positively side-splitting in their laughable qualities. That was in his younger days, we know, when his melodic and inventive resources were simply overflowing; and happily it is amongst that portion of his rich legacy that, according to all accounts, the Continental seekers after forgotten musical treasure have lately been rumm.ging to good purpose.

What, after all, does the present generation of this country know of Rossini? That he wrote a number of jolly overtures and a *Stabat Mater*, in addition to a mighty clever and amusing opera entitled *The Barber of Seville*; really that is about all. Yet he was the master whom Fétis described as "the most illustrious, the most popular of all the *compositeurs dramatiques* that Italy brought forth in the nineteenth century." I would humbly venture to add that, albeit by nature one of the laziest men who ever lived, he was also one of the most prolific, resourceful, and successful musicians of all time. Moreover, he was a reformer, though he seldom gets the credit for it. Not satisfied with the simple harmonies used by contemporary Italians, he introduced new modulations and dissonances that sounded strange at first, but in time grew lovable (note those in the overture to *William Tell*, for example). In fifteen years he had entirely transformed the taste of his countrymen. But, apart from his genius as a composer, he was a great all-round musician. He was also a marvellous accompanist, and those who heard him sing declared that his vocal art was amazing. According to Auber, "he had a beautiful baritone voice, and he sang the *Largo al factotum* with a spirit and *verve* which no one—not even Lablache—could approach."

But it is not so much of Rossini's own transcendent gifts as of his early operas that I wish to speak now; and the two in which I feel more especially interested at the moment—for the reason that, if report may be trusted, one or both are "earmarked" for revival in the near future—are *L'Italiana in Algeri* and *La Cenerentola*. The choice is good, inasmuch as they belong to Rossini's best *opera buffa* period. *L'Italiana in Algeri* was produced at Venice in 1813, *Cenerentola* at Rome in 1817—the latter only a year after *Il Barbiere* and a few weeks before *La Gazza ladra*, which was still a favourite at Covent Garden when Patti and Scalchi added *Semiramide* to their Rossinian répertoire after the death of Tietjens in 1877. I never heard either of the first two operas mentioned in this group, but both were popular in London in their day, and I fancy *L'Italiana* was done at Covent Garden so late as the 'sixties. As the date indicates, it belongs to a less matured style than the *Barbiere*; it was, indeed, the last of the pure *buffa* type that the master wrote.

Altogether *L'Italiana in Algeri* is a delightful opera, and I cannot wonder that it found its way all over Europe. Coming immediately after *Tancredi*, a serious work, it fully shared its popularity, and I may note the same important innovation in both, namely, that remarkable *crescendo* device so peculiar to Rossini, alike in his overtures and his concerted finales. He is said to have borrowed this effect from Paisiello, but, whether he did or not, it is certain that he made far finer use of it and went on employing it, despite the fact that in Paris later on they satirized and caricatured him under the name of "Signor Crescendo." The plot, a mixture of comedy and farce, breathes a genuine spirit of gaiety and liveliness. It deals with the adventures of a young Italian girl who is stranded on the shores of Algeria and there, by miraculous luck, encounters in the hour of need her faithful lover, who has become the favourite slave of the Bey, and is constantly refusing the most attractive offers of marriage. Ultimately they contrive to escape together and of course all ends happily, but not until after the story has run through a highly amusing series of cross-purposes. The score teems with melody and clever writing, a famous example of the latter being the trio *Pappataci*, in the second act, for the three men, Lindoro (not he of the *Barbiere*), Mustafà, and Taddeo, which used to be recognized as a classic in its particular *genre*. (It is worth while to procure Ricordi's vocal score for the pleasure of studying this quaint, characteristic number.) As a French critic has truly observed, " Nulle part, peut-être, la bouffonnerie italienne n'est exprimée avec plus de verité et de liberté." But, whilst praising the delicious comic features of the music, he also admires the elegance of some of its more serious touches ; as, for instance, in the duet for Lindoro and the Bey and the tenor's *cavatina*, *Languir per una bella*. As for the overture, it is simply one of Rossini's gems.

La Cenerentola, or *Cinderella*, was composed to a libretto based upon the old nursery legend, as treated for the stage by a French author, named Etienne, in a comedy that differed in many details from the panto-mime story of our childhood. I need not go into that, but may say that the plot is ingenious as well as amusing, while the principal part, like Rosina in *Il Barbiere*, was written for a contralto or low mezzo-soprano, in accordance with Rossini's custom. Hence it was that in later years so many of the principal airs for female voice had to be transposed to a higher key. This was naturally not the case when the part of Cenerentola was taken by the great contralto Alboni, who achieved in it one of the most remarkable triumphs that ever fell to an opera singer by her rendering of the famous *rondo-finale*, *Non più mesta*, as I had occasion to recall not long ago when it was so brilliantly recorded by Conchita Supervia. It was upon this theme, if I am not mistaken, that the illustrious Paganini wrote a series of variations for the violin that at the time he alone was capable of playing. There is altogether an extraordinary wealth of tuneful and often expressive melody in *Cenerentola*, which explains how it was that, taken in conjunction with its humour, vivacity, and rare musical ingenuity, its score was placed upon an even higher level than that of *L'Italiana in Algeri*, if not that of *Il Barbiere* itself.

We are told, however, that on its first production at Rome during the Carnival of 1817 it did not excite the same degree of enthusiasm. Only afterwards, when the public began to know it, did it begin to draw big houses—a story that has been repeated in connection with dozens of other operas. Again Rossini, like Handel, used to make use of material already used in previous works that had ceased to draw, and the score of *Cenerentola* contains quite a number of such excerpts, which (owing probably to their strong family likeness)

neither the critics nor the public happened to recognize. As the late Sutherland Edwards once wrote, " It is known to have been Rossini's custom when an opera of his fell, to pick up the pieces, and the score of *La Cenerentola* was adorned throughout with fragments saved from the ruins of his earlier works." This custom, as we know, was not a bad one, since it enabled Handel to put together the music of the *Messiah* and Rossini to " collect the fragments " for the score of the *Barber of Seville* in the incredibly short space of three weeks. The wonder of it is that in neither case has the music lost an iota of its freshness. Rossini once told a friend that he feared much of what he had written must one day pass out of fashion, but that he believed the second act of *William Tell*, the last act of *Otello*, and the whole of *The Barber* would survive the rest. As regards two out of the three, at any rate, time has proved him right.

I wonder whether *Cenerentola*, either whole or in part, may yet be added to this group ? I have formed the opinion that it might be well worth reviving, and I put that opinion forward with some confidence, because I have just been going over the music again from a copy of the original piano score (folio size), which I was fortunate enough to pick up many years ago, together with several other of Rossini's operas, at a music shop at Bayeux, in Normandy. I had been gazing with admiration at the celebrated tapestry depicting the events of the Conqueror's invasion of England, and was on my way back to my hotel when I passed this shop, and, seeing a pile of old scores in the window, I went in and purchased the lot. The title-page of this particular example describes it as follows : " Partizione della *Cenerentola*, opera buffa in due atti, musica di Rossini, ridotta pel Piano Forte. Prezzo 36f., à Paris, chez Carli, éditeur et m^d de Musique, Boulevard Mont-martre, No. 14." I may add that it advertised on an inner page the issue of six favourite operas by Rossini in full score at a total subscription price of 180 francs (then about £7), and the date for the appearance of the first was January 1st, 1824.

On one point alone do I feel some doubt—more strongly, perhaps, regarding *Cenerentola* than *L'Italiana in Algeri*—and that is, the likelihood of securing singers capable of doing justice to this extremely difficult florid music. In any event, they would have to be Italians fully conversant with the traditions of the *buffo* school and, if possible, in the habit of performing these very operas together. I heard such a company at the Lyceum Theatre when I was quite a youth, and I daresay there are such companies touring in Italy to-day, but am not sure. It does not follow, because *Il Barbiere* is familiar everywhere, that the artists who sing it (very badly, some of them) would be capable of undertaking operas by Rossini which they have never seen or heard. And it is quite certain that, unless those operas were done in the right way and with all the necessary executive ability, it would be absurd to think of reviving them.

HERMAN KLEIN.

The Gramophone and the Singer
THE OUTLOOK FOR OPERA IN ENGLAND
by HERMAN KLEIN

NOT being rash by nature or an inspired prophet by profession, I have no intention of signalizing my return to the subject of contemporary opera by indulging in any of the prognostications that flow so readily from the pens of my colleagues on the daily Press. I find it hard enough to say exactly where we stand, *vis à vis* of opera, in this wretched transitional state that music is passing through, without attempting to raise the curtain on the future, immediate or otherwise. And yet, to achieve the knowledge of the present position, like getting outside a wood in which we seem to have become hopelessly lost, is the only means whereby we can obtain some sort of reliable outlook that will restore our sense of orientation. One thing we do know. When we lost our way we lost the subsidy also ; and, even should we regain the one, there is absolutely no likelihood of our recovering the other. Not that I feel particularly sorry on this last account. The allocation of the subsidy (such as it was) was too indirect to be regarded as a State subvention : too " peculiar " in its handling to escape the doubts that attached to the methods of the Heathen Chinee. It was well meant, of course, but it did not work very satisfactorily.

The situation at the present juncture is definitely worse than it was this time a year ago. Not only does opera remain without a permanent home in Central London, but the moment when Covent Garden must be razed to the ground is so close at hand that the one more " international " season now arranged must positively be the last held there. And then—what ? Is the Vic-Wells to be the only organization left to remind opera-lovers of the " vanished glories " whereof *The Times* spoke in a recent article on this topic ? If that were so, with all respect for the good work that is being done under the management of Miss Lilian Baylis, I should be sorry for the disparity that would continue to exist between the reminder and the reality. Betwixt the extremes of opera sung in English, precariously carried on by three companies in North and South London and in the provinces, and high-class opera of the type represented by the traditions of Covent Garden, there is " a wide gulf fixed." When I hailed as a blessing the proposed amalgamation between the Syndicate and Sir Thomas Beecham's Imperial League, I trusted that it might somehow provide the requisite material for bridging the gulf in question, if not actually filling it up. It may yet be going to do so ; but, until the outlook in that direction has become clearer, we cannot see ahead far enough to boast that we are completely out of the wood.

Two important questions that have been previously asked in these pages still remain to be answered : Has this country as a whole ceased to care for all but certain types of grand opera—Wagner, Mozart, Verdi, Puccini, Mascagni, Leoncavallo, and one or two more ? And, secondly, is it beyond the resources of a great capital like London, where theatre after theatre, cinema after cinema, is being built, to provide itself with a worthy opera house capable of holding four to five thousand persons and erected within a few hundred yards of Charing Cross ? My own reply to these questions is distinctly in the negative. I believe that, allowing for changes of taste, the love of opera is as firmly ingrained in the British nature as it was a century ago. Recent experience of bad houses in the provinces proves nothing to the contrary. There has been excessive competition at an unfortunate period. The world depression affecting big towns such as Leeds, Birmingham, Liverpool, Manchester, and Nottingham has not —to quote only a single instance—prevented packed houses from assembling night after night in a mining district like Hanley. In the Metropolis we have evidence that there is always a reliable public for good, cheap opera, quite apart from the one which supports the short *saisons de luxe* that we shall soon be seeing exemplified, perhaps for the last time, at the dear old historic building in Bow Street. But the big public that wants to go to hear opera on a first-class scale at moderate prices at least once a week all the year round has yet to be trained, educated, and brought up to the mark in this land of ours.

Six weeks, or even three months, of " international " opera in the course of a whole year may be ridiculously inadequate, but it is a great deal better than none at all. It has, moreover, a certain propaganda value, besides keeping up our standard of judgment and appreciation. The true love of opera, the genuine understanding of the art that is embodied in the union of drama and music, cannot be acquired elsewhere than in the theatre. All these wonderful wireless relays and admirable gramophone reproductions are, when all is said and done, no more than so many convenient and pleasing substitutes for the real thing. They cannot, no matter how excellent in themselves, create for the listener an equivalent experience or make the same identical impression upon the human faculties as an actual stage performance. They can help to accustom the ear to particular sounds and become familiar with catchy melodies—when positive tunes are vouchsafed us. But the difficulty of following the words when sung in recitative, or indeed when sung anywhere, and even when aided by a synchronized perusal of the printed text, still remains a serious difficulty ; while the problem of guessing at the dramatic action will never be solved until fireside television is no longer a costly luxury, and perhaps, for the gramophone, not even then.

Nevertheless, the cultivation of the operatic habit in the English mind is an absolute essential, and some day it must be implanted there as a part of the national education. In the meantime, the country is in no mood to spend money on art of any description. Parliament grudged, as we have seen, the outlay of a few thousands a year from the profits of the B.B.C., which, after all, are not yielded by taxation but by appropriation for the benefit of the Treasury, as if they were derived from a schedule of the Income Tax. The indirect support of the B.B.C., by payment for relays of occasional performances, will do little permanent good to opera or towards creating a widespread taste for it. What is really needed is another national building like the palace in Portland Place—what an ideal site!—to be used, not as a radio headquarters, but as the central home of opera in London. Such a blessing is only a dream, of course. But then who would have dreamt ten years ago that British broadcasting was about to evolve and proudly own such a home for itself?

I had proceeded thus far with this article when I received, as a subscriber to the Imperial League of Opera, the circular requesting my consent to the new "practical scheme" for preventing its disintegration. Put forward as it was by three such good men and true as Mr. Reginald McKenna, Lord Esher, and Sir Hugh P. Allen, I had no hesitation in signifying my compliance. After all, the £60,000 already subscribed is of no use to anybody so long as it is lying *perdu* in the coffers of the Court of Chancery; while, if wisely applied by the administration now to be called the "London Executive Committee"—consisting of representatives of the Imperial League of Opera, the Covent Garden Opera Company, the Sadler's Wells Theatre, the Old Vic Theatre, and the British Broadcasting Company—it can, when "pooled with the resources of the co-operating units," be utilized to the utmost advantage for carrying out the original purpose of the League, namely, "to begin to function as an opera-producing institution." In that case, Sir Thomas Beecham will be the "Artistic Director and chief conductor" of the combined organization, exactly as he is to be of the forthcoming international season which is announced to begin on May 1st. In addition to agreeing to the scheme, the subscribers are duly reminded that they are reviving their original undertaking to pay 10s. a year for five years, and are thus liable for any "instalments that may be due to complete their five years' membership when the scheme is in full operation."

As one of the first, if not the very first, to suggest (in the pages of THE GRAMOPHONE) this fusion of operatic interests, I feel a particular interest in the outcome of the present experiment—for experiment it must still be called, seeing that nothing of the kind has ever been attempted before in connection with opera. On the whole I cannot see why it should not prove a success, even allowing for the various considerations put forward in the first part of this article. Obviously, the Vic-Wells will continue to bear no more than its fair share of the onus resting upon the English opera branch of the combined institution. One only thinks of what is to happen if and when Covent Garden Theatre has been pulled down. It is then that the real test will come. It is then that the vital necessity will become urgent—namely, to provide a suitable and worthy home for opera in London. Much as we may regret it, Covent Garden will have to go. It is wanted for the Market, and, since it can only be carried on at a loss in its present shape, it is a hindrance rather than a stimulant to the progress of opera in our midst. That it should be rebuilt is unthinkable, even were it feasible; the neighbourhood, the approaches, the costliness of the site—everything is dead against it. Equally to be opposed would be the idea of taking some already-existing theatre like Drury Lane or the Palace, or some more modern structure, with a view to converting it into an opera house big enough to accommodate an audience of five or six thousand at prices ranging from a shilling to eight or, at most, ten shillings. Even if the transformation could be effected, which is more than doubtful, the question of rental would again be likely to prove an insuperable obstacle. The only true remedy, as I have said more than once before, will be to follow the example of the cinema theatre-builders—pull down a few houses, form an island site in some central district, and build your new opera house there. Easier said than done? Yes, I know; and so have many other drastic reforms been that eventually proved the best road to prosperity.

HERMAN KLEIN.

THE SINGING OF BRAHMS

by HERMAN KLEIN

WHY did Brahms never write an opera ? No one quite knew. He had all the necessary capacity, all the technical resource, but somehow the idea did not appeal to him. Once, after a friend had alluded to it, he remarked jestingly, " To a first opera and a first marriage I could never bring myself." He was not of a very confident or trustful disposition, and though he could write good tunes when he chose—tunes like those in his " Hungarian Dances " that could be readily picked up and hummed or whistled despite their uncommon rhythms—he may have feared that he could not write a comic opera and perchance not have cared to try his hand at a serious one. It was on this account that his music took so long to become popular with the Viennese public. In the end they " learned to know and admire the compositions of Brahms and to take such an interest in the middle-sized, powerfully-built, long-bearded, blue-eyed musician that, when the first signs of his serious illness appeared and his strong frame shrank visibly from month to month, it was the talk of all classes from the highest to the poor professional musician." Yet, when his noble *Requiem* was produced years before, it had been hissed !

In England it was much the same story. Only by degrees did the illustrious Joachim, Brahms's greatest friend and champion, succeed in teaching the audiences of the Monday Pops how to understand and appreciate his chamber music. He began by introducing in 1867 the sextet in B flat for strings ; but six years elapsed before it was played for the second time, and only then did the name of Brahms begin to crop up in the Pop programmes. One after another the choicest of the quintets and quartets were discreetly brought forward, until at last in 1877 the full revelation came at Cambridge, where the first symphony, the now familiar C minor, was performed on the occasion when Brahms received his doctor's degree (*in absentiâ*). But there was something else in that same year that helped most of all to swell the flowing tide. The novelty I refer to, the sensation of the moment as it proved to be among amateurs of good music, was not actually an instrumental but a vocal one. It was the first set of the *Liebeslieder-Walzer*, Op. 52, for four voices with four-hand pianoforte accompaniment—a masterpiece of its kind, a gem surely of sparkling and spontaneous originality, if ever there was one.

Now at this particular juncture I knew exactly one solitary specimen of Brahms's songs, namely, the *Wiegenlied*, " Guten Abend, gute Nacht," which I had heard sung by Mme. Albani, who was said to have studied it with the composer in Germany. But it had

not prepared me for aught so enchanting as these clever but difficult waltz-quartets, with their picturesque pianoforte background ; neither could I have realised at the time, or rather after hearing the second set, that the biographer of Brahms in *Grove's Dictionary* would one day assert (with truth) that " These two sets of vocal quartets were among the first things that made for Brahms's real popularity with the English public, and since the date of the second set [November 26th, 1877] it has never declined."

I may add that the four singers who introduced the earlier set were Frl. Sophie Löwe, Frl. Redeker (afterwards Lady Semon, wife of Sir Felix Semon), Mr. William Shakespeare, and Mr. Henry Pyatt. Individually they were good artists, without being exactly great, though the ladies were first-rate lieder-singers, and Shakespeare, who started from the R.A.M. as a pianist and composer, had only just returned from his vocal studies with Lamperti at Milan. But what a quartet they made ; what an ensemble ! Careful study had enabled them to master and bring out all the freshness and originality of the music, to preserve a perfect balance with faultless intonation ; and their instantaneous changes from *pp* to *ff* and vice versa created effects that sounded entirely new. No wonder the audience felt, as they applauded the various numbers with growing enthusiasm, that nothing quite like it had been heard before. No wonder, either, that amateurs wanted to repeat the delightful experience, and that they at once began to ask what other music for the voice had been written by this excellent composer of chamber works, of difficult piano pieces and concertos, and at least one symphony, which had just been produced at Karlsruhe with great success and was shortly to be done by the Cambridge University Musical Society under Stanford. It did not take long to learn that he had already written dozens of beautiful songs, duets, trios, and choruses, not to mention the already famous *German Requiem* and the *Songs of Triumph* and of *Destiny*, both just on the point of being heard here.

But what had been made evident by the *Liebeslieder-Walzer* was that the mode of rendering these things was distinctly a speciality, the secret whereof was only to be acquired by those who had gone through a course of studying the lieder of Brahms's great precursors, Schubert and Schumann. Fortunately, there were singers at hand and on the way who had conquered the method and were equal to the task. I need not name now more than three or four—vocalists well known at the period I speak of such as Thekla Friedländer, Marie Fillunger, and Mr. and Mrs. Henschel, besides occasional recitalists from abroad like Gura and Von zur Mühlen and others who used to supply the vocal relief at the Pops. I was reminded of this novel feature (as it appeared to us) in the higher art of song-interpretation when I read the other day some criticisms of a wireless performance of Brahms's *Zigeunerlieder*, or *Gipsy Songs* for vocal quartet and pianoforte, Op. 103, which had originally excited as much admiration as the *Liebeslieder-Walzer* when they appeared at a later date. Who the singers were does not matter, but I think they were English, and their rendering of the wonderful collection of pieces was so far from being *à l'hongroise* as to suggest very little notion of the true way in which Brahms should be sung. How much they had under-rehearsed them one could hardly guess. The real point was that the essential snap and vitality, the true spirit and style, were completely lacking.

Let it be conceded once for all that, notwithstanding the purity of his melodic line and the rare vocal quality of his writing, the art of singing Brahms as he should be sung is an extremely elusive one. But it is to be acquired if diligently studied. Poor Shakespeare had the gift in him to the finger-tips; and he could also communicate it to or share it with all who sang with him. Hence the monopoly of the tenor part in these quartets that he enjoyed so long as the Pops continued to exist. I can recall a fresh distribution of the parts in the season of 1879–80, when his companions were Thekla Friedländer, Hélène Arnim, and Mr. Frank Ward; and that produced as nearly as possible an ideal performance. Two good "classical" English singers of the same period, soprano and contralto, were Miss Louise Phillips and Mrs. Isabel Fassett, both of whom succeeded in mastering the secret in their admirable duets. Miss Santley, Mrs. Hutchinson, Miss Carlotta Elliott and Miss Liza Lehmann, all refined and accomplished sopranos, were likewise constant favourites, but they rarely, very rarely, included a song by Brahms in their selections. English male singers were nearly as hesitant, as if afraid of burning their fingers with the unfamiliar stuff; though I seem to remember on one occasion a particularly good beginning on the part of Mr. Plunket Greene with *Feldeinsamkeit*. Sir George Henschel, ever in the van with novelties at his London Symphony Concerts in the '80's and '90's, was one of the pioneers in the vocal recital field at that period and gradually included more Brahms in his programmes; for he foresaw the day when the Hamburg master would hold his own with Schubert and Schumann in the estimation of the English public.

Still the progress was slow until after the turn of the century. There was, of course, no lack of material to draw upon; the difficulty was rather to know where to begin, for Brahms wrote in all some two hundred songs, and the early prejudice against them could only be overcome by selecting the more attractive. It seems odd to read in the latest edition of *Grove* that they used to be pronounced "unvocal"; but so it was, and "it is within the memory of many that the average English singer would not attempt to sing anything by him." The "absurd falsity" of the accusation was disproved when sopranos began to perceive and portray the classic beauty and symmetry of *Von ewiger Liebe, An die Nachtigall, Die Mainacht, Vergebliches Ständchen* and *Immer leiser wird mein Schlummer*; contraltos to revel in the *Sapphische Ode, Auf dem Kirchofe, Liebestreu*, and *Der Schmied*; tenors and baritones (or basses) to discover the charm of *Wie bist du meine Königin, Ständchen, Sonntag, An ein Veilchen, Ruhe, Süssliebchen*, and the dramatic quality of *Verrath*. It took time to win favour even for these in the concert room, and still longer to persuade a British gramophone company to venture to allow a record to be made of a single example. Besides, only a small minority cared twenty years ago to hear Brahms sung in the original German, and the English translations were so bad that no one wanted either to sing or to listen to them. (Hence the fact, I suppose, that I included a volume of new Brahms translations of my own in the collection of *Lieder in English* which Metzlers brought out before the War.)

The complete revelation of the art of singing Brahms in this country ought unquestionably to be dated from the arrival of Mme. Elena Gerhardt. That was in 1906, whilst I was yet a resident in New York, so I cannot be sure whether it was in that year or the next that I first heard her at a recital at Queen's Hall with her accomplished teacher, Artur Nikisch, at the piano. Subsequently she used to have the clever Paula Hegner for her accompanist, and in latter years, of course, it has been Mr. Coenraad van Bos. But this I do know: that no singer ever combined in herself the arts of vocalization and diction, as Elena Gerhardt has done, to the amazing degree that has enabled her, with her immense intelligence, truthfulness, and variety of treatment, to lay bare for us everything that there is to know and feel in Brahms's vocal compositions. Whatever the character of the song, and above all, perhaps, in those based upon the *Volkslied* which was so deeply ingrained in the master's nature, she has never once failed to grasp and interpret every nuance of colour or light and shade in what seems to be absolutely the right manner. The present generation has special reason to be grateful for her electrical gramophone records of Brahms, because they are not only technically perfect, but authoritative and unique. They have, I believe, been made exclusively for His Master's Voice, and I have only recently had occasion to speak of the *fine fleur* of the collection issued as part of the Connoisseur's Catalogue.

The present-day popularity of Brahms in every aspect of his genius requires no insistence from anyone. It speaks for itself from every concert notice-board and musical advertisement page. The name is among the select few that can be found worth relying upon for a one-composer programme, such as I observe, for instance, in the enterprising scheme for the current series of Sunday Concerts at the Grotrian Hall.

HERMAN KLEIN.

COLUMBIA ALBUM OF MASSENET'S "MANON"

by HERMAN KLEIN

IT will be fifty years next January since *Manon*—the best in my opinion of all Massenet's operas—was first given on the stage of the Opéra-Comique, Paris. Exactly a twelvemonth later (January 17th, 1885) it was produced in English by Carl Rosa at the Court Theatre, Liverpool; and in the following May I enjoyed my initial hearing of that English version at Drury Lane, with Marie Rôze and Joseph Maas in the two principal parts, which they sang splendidly. In 1891 it was mounted in French at Covent Garden by Augustus Harris for the début of the famous Belgian tenor, Ernest van Dyck, and the part of Des Grieux remained to the end of his career one of his finest characters. Unfortunately his co-débutante, Miss Sybil Sanderson, an American soprano, had little beyond her good looks to recommend her as Manon, and so completely dissatisfied Joseph Bennett that he "forgot" even to mention her in his criticism. Quite otherwise was it with an even lovelier woman and artist, Marie Heilbron, who created the part in Paris subsequently to her one visit to London (returning specially to the stage to do so); while her successor, Miss Mary Garden, made an outstanding impression in it on her Covent Garden début in 1902.

Since those days London has consistently lagged behind other centres, European and American, in the appreciation of this delightful opera—why, I cannot exactly say. The story, based by Meilhac and Gille upon the celebrated novel of the Abbé Prévost, may take rank with the really good operatic libretti, while its treatment of the subject is justly preferred to that adopted by Domenico Oliva in Puccini's version, which I have never liked so much as Massenet's. As for the music, comparisons apart, the French is so rich in Gallic grace and charm, so essentially dramatic where drama is needed, that the opera never fails to please wherever it is given. Only find the right Manon, and, as in the case of *Carmen*, if you can hit upon the right singer for the heroine, the opera with a good ensemble may be trusted to take care of itself. Hence the fact that even in this country, where it is so seldom performed in the theatre, every page of *Manon* is more or less familiar, thanks to innumerable band selections, concert excerpts, and airs constantly sung by well-known vocalists, both in person and on gramophone records.

It was high time, however, for the appearance of a complete and authentic recording of Massenet's opera such as is now issued in eighteen records by Columbia (Masterworks Portfolio No. 114. LX 202-219). And nowhere save in Paris could its stage realism or dramatic continuity have been communicated to the gramophone with the perfect mastery of tradition and executive finish associated with the work of the Opéra-Comique. This has meant presenting the whole opera in the original French text, and sung with irreproachable accent and style by artists and a chorus accustomed by actual stage performances to infusing life and dramatic significance into every scene. It was doubly necessary because the story of *Manon* is essentially one of quick action quickly told; and the music, written at a time when Massenet was feeling strongly the influence of the Wagnerian methods that were just beginning to stir the world, follows with unusual closeness the progress of the incidents of the plot. The listener who would follow them in turn will find himself enabled to do so quite easily by reading beforehand the English synopsis of the story, and then carefully perusing page by page, as the numbers indicate, the complete copy of the French libretto that accompanies each album. With the further aid of the wonderful diction of the singers this should be by no means a difficult task.

The quality of the rendering, like that of the recording, may be described in a word as of the highest excellence. The well-known conductor, M. Elie Cohen, has collected for his purpose a wholly first-rate ensemble, the principal parts being distributed as follows :—Manon, Mlle. **G. Feraldy**; Des Grieux, M. **Rogatchewsky**; Lescaut, M. **G. Villier**; Comte des Grieux, M. **L. Guénot**; Guillot de Morfontaine, M. **de Greus**; Brétigny, MM. **Gaudin** and **Vieuille**.

The busy opening scene in the courtyard of the hotel at Amiens is cleverly suggested. The lively dialogue of the gay noblemen and the sparkling passages for the trio of actresses are in effective contrast with the self-important utterances of Lescaut. When Manon enters upon the scene and, again, when her romantic lover-to-be, Des Grieux, declares his passion and proposes the elopement, we hear many of the motives that play their part in the subsequent development of the story. It will be noted, too, that the whole of the dialogue (there is not a great deal) takes the form of spoken *mélodrame*, without interrupting the flow of the orchestra; it is clearly enunciated and quite easy to follow. All the duets are well sung by the tenor and soprano, especially the big one in the seminary of St. Sulpice (Act 3), where M. Rogatchewsky also wins admiration for his splendid *Ah! fuyez, douce image.* Despite the thin texture of her voice, Mlle. Feraldy is such an accomplished singer that everything she does, in solo and ensemble alike, gratifies the ear and dominates the picture. The simple pathos of *Notre petite table*, the brilliant music of the scene in the Cours-la-Reine, the tragedy of the final meeting on the road to Havre—each in turn is depicted with the unfailing skill of a thorough artist.

The cuts are judicious and not too numerous.

M. Elie Cohen has seen to it that the "breaks" for the change of records occur at convenient places, and his excellent orchestra always maintains the right degree of prominence, together with a delightful delicacy in the rendering of the old-fashioned dances in Act 3. Another privilege is the co-operation of the distinguished artists who undertake the secondary but important male parts, and the exquisite balance of the charming trios sung by the three girls. *Manon* given in this perfect fashion will be a joy to all who hear it.

HERMAN KLEIN.

★　　★　　★

THE SINGER AND THE MICROPHONE
by HERMAN KLEIN

HAVING myself been guilty of referring to what is known as the "Technique of the Microphone," I confess to a certain amount of hesitation when declaring, as I now must, that the term is either a misnomer or else susceptible of too many interpretations. No technique that I know of connected with singing either for broadcasting or the gramophone, and no microphone yet invented for the capture of vocal sounds, could produce between them all the strange results that are now being attributed to their use. Under the headline "An Unprofitable Servant," the music critic of *The Times* wrote the other day these words : "We surely need a more scientific analysis than has yet been forthcoming of what the microphone actually does reproduce and what it ignores. Perhaps such an analysis has been made [I doubt it]. If so, it is time that its results were placed clearly and succinctly before musicians, and particularly before teachers of singing " [I agree].

Now, whilst waiting for this valuable analytical guidance, let us see if we can make a tolerable guess at the real *fons et origo mali*, the troublous cause which has given rise to the recent controversy on this subject. One must give it a name, of course ; but is it in reality the microphone alone that is to blame ? I venture to doubt it. So far as I am aware, that useful instrument is responsible only for what reaches it and is transmitted through it to the Control Room, whether situated in Broadcasting House or in a gramophone recording *atelier*. The whole mystery, then, may be summed up in the question : What happens in the Control Room ? Interference of some sort, naturally ; for the moment never mind what. Enough that it can not only affect and alter volume, quality, carrying

power, purity, verisimilitude, etc., but, as we now learn, it can also dictate the method, otherwise the technique, upon which the work and art of the singer are to be based. For it is with an eye to this controlling medium that the B.B.C., through its representative, Mr. Roger Eckersley, has declared that "the needs of microphone and concert platform are not identical " ; that, although "an artist who is experienced and fully master of technique usually makes a satisfactory microphone artist, even this is not invariably the case."

It comes to this, then. The new Frankenstein, which for the sake of argument we will call the Microphone, is invested with powers that can make it either a great friend or a great enemy. It is capable of doing both good and harm ; it is yielding every day abundant and convincing proof of its capacity for usefulness as well as misuse and abuse. In the right hands it may be very helpful ; in the wrong it may—as recent events in Germany and Russia have shown—prove nothing less than a curse. So far, certainly, it has contributed nothing beneficial to the art of singing. Wireless listeners have heard only too many instances of well-known voices sounding pinched and otherwise distorted through no fault of the artist. It is argued with some reason that this disparity may react in favour of a renewed demand for good singers in the concert room, and thus compensate for the "limited opportunities of engagement" which compelled the B.B.C. to send out its circular letter to "the very large number of artists on its lists." But meanwhile the Microphone remains where and what it is. We have to abide by two standards of criticism—one based upon the long-recognized traditions of the art, the other fixed by the Broadcasting Corporation within its own walls. In a word, consideration of the requirements of the Microphone comes first.

I object further to the interference of the Control Room on account of its tendency to use amplification to excess. It should be employed only for the legitimate purpose of reinforcing tone, not for the illegitimate purpose of creating the impression that a small voice is a big one ; which is both misleading and unfair. Where is the sense of increasing or reducing all voices to the same common denominator ? They simply lose individuality in the process. On the other hand, what a blessing it would be if control of some sort could eliminate the " bleat," the *voix blanche*, the wobbling tremolo, the super-nasal, the throaty, and all the rest of the irritating blemishes that we know so well ! These are the things that the amplifier may magnify but is powerless to conceal. Now and then a really good voice—a new one, I mean—makes its " first appearance " by wireless, but very rarely ; and now and then, but seldom, one hears a good voice from some foreign station, and wonders who the singer may be. On the whole, this vocal aspect of radio transmission is a disappointing business.

Just as there are voices that naturally record well for the gramophone, so are there some that are especially adapted by nature for wireless work. In neither case should the intervention of the Control Room modify or detract from this innate quality, which ought to be better recognized than it is by the magnates who sit in judgment on new-comers at auditions. Here is where the ability to judge and the right standard to judge by really come into play. I often ask myself as others do who these gentlemen may be. The B.B.C. standard in music ought to be settled by the motto, " Nothing but the best." If its own peculiar requirements demand something that the first-rate performer, known or unknown, cannot supply, then I predict a speedy renascence for the popular pleasures of the *viva voce* concert platform.

HERMAN KLEIN.

✦ ✦ ✦

The Gramophone and the Singer
GRAMOPHONE STARS AT COVENT GARDEN
by HERMAN KLEIN

UNCERTAINTY as to the future of Covent Garden Opera-house invests with a peculiar interest the season now in progress there, for it may be the last time that those historic walls will re-echo to the sounds of lyric drama or the voices of famous lyric artists, German, Italian, or otherwise. Let us continue to hope, whilst the powers that be are making up their minds, that the long-threatened end may not be yet. If, however, the cry of " Wolf ! " should prove this time to be well founded, there will at least be some satisfaction in reflecting that the season which " ends this strange, eventful history " was among the best of recent years, and that it witnessed a welcome union of the forces upon which (and whom) the whole future of opera in this country now depends.

For another thing, it has again convinced me that the right executive material—inclusive of a judicious admixture of native talent—is to be found available in bad times even more readily than in good, when competition is keener and big artists demand more unreasonable fees. I have been given to understand that the " stars " of the German performances just concluded were content to accept slightly lower *cachets* than in previous years ; and there were assuredly emphatic reasons for their so doing—reasons purely financial, of course, and in no one instance due to a diminishing scale of artistic value. I failed, indeed, to detect any sort of falling-off in the work of those whose admirable records have made their names as household words to the gramophone world. Like the records themselves, their voices are resisting wear-and-tear in a manner that is simply astonishing. Take as examples Lotte Lehmann, Frida Leider and Maria Olszewska, or, among the men, Lauritz Melchior, Friedrich Schorr, Herbert Janssen, Eduard Habich, and Otto Helgers. Never have they declaimed Wagner with such a wealth of wonderful tone and perfected art.

Disappointing Sir Thomas Beecham's *Rosenkavalier* was in many respects, but chiefly through no fault of his own. No one could have expected him to re-duplicate the performance of 1913 minus the cast to work the miracle ; he had not the Eva von der Osten for Oktavian, the Claire Dux for Sophie, the Paul Knüpfer or the Richard Mayr for Baron Ochs, though he had an even finer Marschallin than Margarete Siems in Lotte Lehmann. Comparisons may be futile in a sense, but to a certain extent they are unavoidable. Lotte Lehmann is one of those great artists who satisfy as completely whether seen *and* heard or heard only without being seen. She is an extraordinarily good actress ; therefore in order to appreciate and enjoy her embodiment of the Marschallin in the fullest degree, one must see her in the part. Adela Kern simply had the wrong idea of the character of Sophie, and her singing failed to match the merit of her records ; while Eva Hadrabova, whose records I have never heard, was even farther from suggesting either the personality or the voice of an Oktavian. As for Alexander Kipnis, a singer *par excellence*, but no actor for the rôle of the old Viennese *roué*, I would sooner have listened to one of his Mozart airs or his lieder than the whole of his efforts in Strauss's opera. The real joy of the evening was the Marschallin. It will dwell in the memory as a classic.

On the other hand, there will be other Sieglindes to equal Lotte Lehmann's moving impersonation, beautiful as it is. It helped materially to impart distinction to the *Walküre* performance ; but the strength of the cast as a whole was the *clou* there. I find no sign of deterioration in Schorr's Wotan or Olszewska's Fricka ; and little, if any, in Frida Leider's Brünnhilde, that is, till the fatigues of *Götterdämmerung* at last begin to tell their tale. Comparing in my mind the efforts of these artists with their best records of the same music, the freshness and stamina of their voices gave one more proof that Wagner in reasonable doses will never injure those who know how to sing him. It was the same with Lauritz Melchior's Siegfried, especially in the fearless hero's more youthful aspect. His splendid ringing notes here suggested the boy, not his figure ; whereas in the final drama it was Melchior's manly height and dignity of gesture that fitted the picture even better than his vigour, which for minutes enabled him to ward off the effects of a fatal stab in the back. At this point we all enquired with the chorus, " Hagen, was thu'st du ? " The new Mime, Hanns Fleischer, made a decidedly favourable impression, and the new Erda, Mary Jarred (a German-trained Yorkshire contralto), won golden opinions with her noble organ and pure declamation. But Herbert Janssen's Gunther was surely good enough to have deserved a less strident, tremulous Gutrune than Miss Odette de Foras. Of the rest, Fritz Wolff's Loge and Siegmund and Habich's Alberich were outstanding in this first cycle which Robert Heger conducted so well.

Sir Thomas Beecham's first *Tristan* of the season was partly spoiled through the illness of Frida Leider. That *contretemps* upset everyone except the orchestra, which was unsurpassable throughout. It appeared to drive Lauritz Melchior into forcing his voice terribly ; it certainly urged Maria Olszewska to seek the limelight as a melodramatic Brangäne that was quite at variance with tradition. Happily the other men were up to their wonted mark, and the soprano who flew from Cologne to replace the absent one at least acquitted herself creditably. I cannot honestly say that Frau Henny Trundt's voice or singing yielded any thrills ; she probably experienced more herself whilst in the air on her way to Croydon. But she is a sound artist, and her facial expression denotes intelligence, notwithstanding that her frown and her smile look dangerously alike for an angry princess who unwittingly swallows a love-potion. You cannot tell exactly which emotion is coming to the surface. Most of the singing in this *Tristan* was below the level that we are accustomed to in the records of the work.

Happily Mme. Frida Leider was able to appear and distinguish herself in the repetition of *Tristan und Isolde*, but that performance I did not hear. Those who were present were loud in their praises of Walter Widdop's Tristan, which big part the Yorkshire tenor then sang in German for the first time. His reputation as an operatic and a Wagnerian singer is obviously growing apace. The northern county further supplied a splendid Fricka No. II in Miss Mary Jarred, and her future career can hardly fail to be a brilliant one. A successor to Kirkby Lunn is badly needed. The *Parsifal* performance attained on the whole a higher level than usual. Fritz Wolff did well in the title-rôle, which, owing to the previous omission of his name, I feared was going to be sung by Mime in the person of Hanns Fleischer ! But the pleasantest surprise of all was the excellent Kundry, Gertrud Rünger, another unexpected new-comer whose name is quite unfamiliar. Her rich tones should record extremely well, and, as she is unlikely to have another chance of appearing here in opera for some time, I advise her to send us some gramophone samples of them as quickly as may be. It were needless to dwell on the fine singing of Friedrich Schorr as Amfortas or of Alexander Kipnis as Gurnemanz ; each in turn was a delight. The orchestra, too, under Robert Heger, added yet one more to its triumphs during this brief but memorable Wagner season.

The death of Colonel Blois on May the 16th aroused the sincere regret of all who knew him personally, in addition to the vast crowd of opera-goers who had profited by his zeal and energy in the management of Covent Garden during the last two Syndicates. He was a clever amateur musician and had a *flair* for discovering good singers. He once told me he felt sure the day would come when our native tongue would reign supreme amid the polyglot *mélange* known as " international opera." He also had faith in the future of the present fusion—with Sir Thomas Beecham in the forefront of the scheme. What a pity he should not have lived to witness its realisation !

The Gramophone and the Singer

THE ROYAL OPERA FINALE

by HERMAN KLEIN

THE three weeks of Italian opera, which followed the German season at Covent Garden and completed our miserable allowance for the year, brought forth neither interest of a high order nor artistic merit of the first class. To be quite candid, not one of the several well-known artists who took part in the six operas seemed capable of yielding the same thrill from the footlights that I have experienced at various times whilst listening to their gramophone records. There was no trace of unity of spirit in the atmosphere, no *Stimmung*, no evidence that the artists were really heart and soul in their task. Unlike the German performances that had for the most part given pleasure, we got a three weeks' spell of unequal and perfunctory labour from nearly everyone concerned.

In *Aïda* Eva Turner returned with distinction to her old part; no greater charm, perhaps, but voice and method as telling as ever. A new Amneris, Nini Giani, displayed, both here and as the naughty princess in *Don Carlos*, the kind of melodramatic upper tones that Verdi required from his female villains, but with medium well-nigh non-existent. Nervousness proved very nearly the undoing of Francesco Battaglia in *Celeste Aïda*; but his organ is indisputably a fine one when under proper control, and I would like to give him another chance, should he ever be allowed one. The Amonasro of Armando Borgioli impressed less favourably than did that of our own Dennis Noble later in the season—on the same night, by the way, that Muriel Brunskill proved herself a better Amneris all-round than her Italian predecessor. Ramfis was perhaps the least interesting of the clever studies presented by Fernando Autori; but his delineation of Philip II was unquestionably the pick of the series. If his voice only equalled his art he would be almost supreme in his line.

Do prima donnas invariably choose the parts that suit them best? I am certain they do not. Rosetta Pampanini sings the third act of *La Bohème* beautifully; but she no longer suggests the moribund Mimi any more faithfully than Melba did. Rosa Raisa has altered surprisingly little since she was here before the War; yet whereas her Countess in *Figaro* and Elena in *Mefistofele*—sedate ladies both—dwell vividly in the memory, her unemotional Tosca will chiefly be recollected as a graceful personality. A third " square peg " was the Marguerite of Gina Cigna in the stage version of Berlioz's *Damnation of Faust*. In my estimation the rôle fitted her no better than the fine work itself fits the opera house, for which it was never intended. I enjoyed the lovely music, as I always have done, but the Goethe story in this fragmentary form holds no dramatic interest whatever. Cesare Formichi's Mephistopheles suffered through his faulty French, and compared ill with his easy Scarpia of two nights before. Minghetti sang and acted well as Cavaradossi. Two of the three ladies mentioned above did infinitely better in the Verdi operas. Gina Cigna really did help to relieve some of the irretrievable monotony of *Don Carlos*, a feat now apparently beyond the power of the Greek tenor Lappas, or of the baritone Rimini, whose stage tremolo was as objectionable here as it is conspicuous by its absence from his splendid gramophone Falstaff.

Rosetta Pampanini's sympathetic Desdemona, which displayed her pure legato singing to every advantage, brings me to the consideration of Lauritz Melchior's Otello. I had looked forward to this impersonation with considerable hope, and to a certain extent my expectations were realised, though only in a histrionic and declamatory sense. Neither the tremendous vocal power of Tamagno nor the irresistible beauty of Jean de Reszke's *cantilena* formed a sufficient part of Melchior's equipment to enable him to present, let us say, an Otello comparable with his Tristan or his Siegfried. There is not sufficient charm or fascination of colour in his voice for the love passages; neither can he exert the tone to its utmost strength without making it sound forced and harsh; and, after all, Italian does not come to him so naturally as German, so that both language and music proceed from his mouth with an effect which is entirely strange. He had his imposing moments, of course; but apart from these his Otello was convincing in no greater degree than the pale Iago of Giacomo Rimini, a delineation about equally replete with good intentions. With a word of eulogy for the conducting of Sir Thomas Beecham, Antonio Votto, and John Barbirolli, I conclude this brief retrospect of some creditable, if far from satisfying, performances.

As to the future of Covent Garden, we know little more to-day than when I first gave warning of the demolition of the opera house some three years ago. Only now a decision one way or the other seems imminent. It is, of course, purely a question of finance, and the owners of the property are anxious to sell forthwith to the highest bidder. The sentimentalists are no less anxious to save a place so rich in cherished associations; but there are some who definitely want to see it pulled down and a fine modern opera house erected in its stead, either on the same site or elsewhere. I can understand both points of view, but I do not care even yet to predict which of them will ultimately prevail.　　　　HERMAN KLEIN.

The Gramophone and the Singer
SUPREME VALUE OF THE PERSONAL TOUCH
by HERMAN KLEIN

THE loss of personal contact between singer and audience is now being increasingly recognised as among the more detrimental influences induced by the vogue of what a certain authority is fond of describing as "mechanised music." For the moment the singers are feeling it far more keenly than the music-loving public ; for myself, I perceive it chiefly in the gradual disappearance of the style of vocal interpretation that was at one time the pride of the English concert platform. This is not to proclaim, as might easily be suspected, any definite inferiority in the quality of the singing *per se*. There is little music of any period that our present-day vocalists are not technically capable of rendering with the skill that it should be rendered. It is not there that they lag behind their forefathers.

It is not, either, in the calibre of the vocal programmes of to-day that any serious deterioration excites alarm ; they are as a rule besprinkled even more liberally than of yore with lieder and songs of the classical or higher type. But what is disappearing almost before our very eyes is the peculiar gift for presenting, with all the attraction of personal charm, new lyrics such as those which flowed in a steady stream from the British song-writers of the last quarter of the nineteenth century.

They relied for their successes, not only upon the talent of the singer, but upon the effect which the singers produced through immediate contact with the audiences before whom they appeared. This was a supremely important factor in the achievement. So much depended in the first instance upon the authentic interpretation of the composer's ideas as communicated by him or herself ; and, in the second, upon the individual quality of artists to whom their audiences as often as not were devotedly attached.

Nowadays this personal touch barely exists. That the undying charm of the music remains is proved by the fact that in B.B.C. programmes we find constantly group after group of favourite songs by Sullivan, Stanford, Parry, Goring Thomas, Mackenzie, Cowen, Liza Lehmann, or Edward German. In a later category also stand many honoured names of living composers who, however, are much less indebted for profitable royalties to the personal appeal of their interpreters. The latter may have been listened to by millions, but they have never been seen in the flesh by more than a small percentage of their admirers. In yet another category may be reckoned the vast repertory of good old English songs and ballads which depend largely for their unbroken popularity upon the manner in which they are sung. This art of a bygone period is remembered by very few ; and fewer still are the singers of to-day who can be trusted to render them after the manner of the school to which they belong. Would-be imitators are plentiful as blackberries, but rarely indeed does one come across a singer who knows how to impart to them the right turn of phrase, accent, idiom, or shade of expression.

It follows from what has been said that I should rejoice in a return of the demand for concerts of a purely vocal type at which only our best singers would be heard. If, for instance, we could have the old ballad concerts over again minus the ballads, substituting in their stead modern English songs of the highest order, one important step towards the preservation of mutual contact and renewed prosperity for the singer would be assured.

I have spoken before now of the marked degree in which the presence of an audience reacts upon the sensations of the experienced singer. There can be no question that it produces an infinitely more spontaneous state of feeling, and consequently a freer play of the emotions on the part of the artist. If the microphone —which we have now been told on the best authority requires a technique of its own—exercises a restraining influence, as it inevitably must, then there must also be a deeper, a more human quality in the singing heard in a concert room than we can possibly obtain through the wireless or mechanical mediums. I do not say this in disparagement of the latter, but to encourage recollection of the fact that there is a something extra, to be enjoyed with profit on both sides, when artist and audience are facing each other, that cannot be obtained otherwise. Why should not the concrete value of the two experiences, each in its own separate sphere, be more widely recognised and exploited ?

What is sauce for the goose is sauce for the gander. If the B.B.C. can give us ideal orchestral concerts at and from Queen's Hall and delightful chamber concerts in and from the studio, it is equally in its power to organise and provide for the musical world vocal concerts of as super-select a character as the present age can possibly furnish. HERMAN KLEIN.

The Gramophone and the Singer
THE PENALTIES OF EXAGGERATION
by HERMAN KLEIN

AS the regular readers of this page are aware, I have always been a firm believer in the utility of the gramophone for imitative purposes; that is to say, down to a certain point, when the model is a good and reliable one. It was for this reason that I invented years ago the " Phono-Vocal Method," which I once described in full in the columns of THE GRAMOPHONE, and which, as I then explained, was originally intended (1) as an aid to the teacher, (2) as a guide for the lonely student in those parts of the world where capable teachers are not to be had.

My faith in the system remains unshaken. But a new fear of consequences that may result from a too slavish and exact imitation of the vocal sounds extracted from modern electrical records has been awakened by something that I actually heard in my own studio one day last month. I had arranged to give an audition to a young man, who wrote to me from a remote town in the West Riding of Yorkshire, saying that he would be coming to London on a certain date expressly for me to hear him and give an opinion of his voice. He duly arrived, and, inasmuch as the interview was a confidential one, I naturally withhold names or facts which were given me only for my personal information.

My visitor began by informing me that, although he had brought some songs with him, he was unable to read them; for he did not know a note of music and had never had a lesson in music or singing in his life. His age, he told me, was twenty-seven, and he seemed very relieved when I assured him that that was not too old for him to begin learning singing, provided his voice was good enough to justify the outlay, and had not been injured in any way. He said that at school he had only sung among the other boys, that his voice had never " broken " so far as he knew, and that when it had matured he had been told he was a tenor (which I subsequently found to be true). I enquired where and how he had picked up his songs. It was then that I learned that he had a gramophone, and had been in the habit (greatly to his credit) of spending most of his spare cash on the purchase of records of the latest type, sung by Caruso and other favourite operatic tenors, but mostly by Caruso.

It was now time for him to let me hear him sing. He was obviously very nervous, so I left the choice of piece to him and, having done my best to restore his courage with one or two comforting remarks, I sat down to the piano and began the accompaniment. What followed is not quite easy to describe. The young man, after fully inflating his chest, started by letting out a series of stentorian notes, which he sustained at high pressure, his face distorted by glaring eyes and dilated nostrils, in an evident effort to reproduce (when the enunciation of the words did not actually choke him) the gigantic sounds which he had heard issuing from his gramophone. It was tremendous: it was awful; it was also pitiful. For, amidst the noisy din of crude, vociferous human tones, was plainly to be discerned here and there, when the vowel served, the unmistakable timbre of a really fine tenor voice. Only, the revealing gleams of beauty were rare. Nor did the whole of the strenuous, exhausting display last very long. Suddenly, after less than a dozen bars, the singer stopped and asked me to excuse him from continuing, as his nerves had given way and he could not keep either his voice or his body under control. It was true; he was shaking like an aspen leaf. I asked him to sit down and drink a glass of water.

Later on the poor fellow sang (i.e. bawled) something else, and proved that his previous exhibition had not been caused by nervousness only. Nature had been kind to him in its gift, but not in leaving him unprovided with the knack for using it. His endeavour to copy the amplified Caruso had merely resulted in a disastrous reduplication of the actual sounds that had penetrated his ear, and he had imagined that no amount of physical effort could be excessive to gain his object. His imitations had not extended to the language for he had never tried to sing in Italian. He thought, however, that he might manage *La donna è mobile* if I did not mind his using the English words. He did not get to the end of the first couplet. Here, again, one could see that the Caruso loudness had been the tempting model, while some English tenor (I need not name him) had furnished the dreadful but necessary English version; only, unluckily, the " fickle jade " had been too much for my untutored visitor, and he relinquished his brave effort in despair. Therewith ended his audition. He went back to Yorkshire knowing the truth—not wholly discouraged, but warned to be careful how he spent his hard-earned money on learning to sing.

Now here was undeniably a sad, an exceptional case —a case where the lack of imitative faculty had led the possessor of a strong, resonant voice to mistake blatant shouting for sounds similar to those which he *thought* he was hearing. Poor fellow, he was just the wrong sort of person to try to sing by the aid of the gramophone. He had been fascinated and led astray by the glorious sonority of the tones that had filled his ears, and which he had unluckily supposed to be of the normal strength given out by the average singer. I have related his story as a warning for those unsuspecting beginners who might be liable to commit the same fatal error of mistaking the doctored article for the real thing. The danger is there; and it is ever present, because the microphone voice has ceased to be identical in volume and quality with its original. It is a danger that must be avoided at all costs.

HERMAN KLEIN.

THE ENGLISH METROPOLITAN OPERA

by HERMAN KLEIN

THREATENED opera houses live long. Not long before the world financial depression seized America in its grasp, we were told that the Metropolitan Opera House in New York was coming down and a much larger, costlier building going up in its place. At about the same period we in London began to hear that nothing could possibly delay the demolition of Covent Garden beyond the termination of the lease in July 1933. Yet in neither instance has prophecy been verified by the event. Both theatres still remain standing, and seem likely to continue where they are for a considerable time to come. In New York a fresh season will be starting a few weeks hence, and at Covent Garden, after certain internal alterations have been made, the house will reopen for dancing under the direction of Mr. Bertram Mills, to be followed next year by one or more seasons of opera, " international " and otherwise, under the aegis of a reconstituted syndicate.

Meanwhile, an entirely separate and independent enterprise has provided occupation for those English artists—strengthened by notable additions—who had recently been touring the provinces under the misleading name of " The Covent Garden Opera Company." For this newer troupe its director, Mr. Robert Parker, has made bold to appropriate the more fitting title of " The Metropolitan Opera Company (London) Ltd." This has a good ring to it ; it could mislead no one (in this country at least), and it could hardly be mistaken for aught beyond a distant relative of the august institution on the other side of the Atlantic. By a curious chance, the present year happens to mark the fiftieth anniversary of the building of the New York Metropolitan, which was, I may mention, erected in order to meet the growing demand for Italian Opera, and also to supply adequate accommodation for the two classes of Society—the *nouveaux riches* of the German regime and the staunch supporters of the old school—which the long-popular Academy of Music no longer sufficed to furnish. The fine house on Broadway has had a distinguished history, and one hopes that the company which now bears its name over here may prove even in a partial degree worthy of it.

At the outset, however, Mr. Robert Parker's venture is being limited to a campaign in the provinces. What will follow must depend upon the success of that test. For the time being he has the field to himself. The once-honoured Carl Rosa Company appears to be in a state of suspended animation, or may perhaps—no one exactly knows—have ceased active operations altogether ; anyhow, some of its late members have now associated themselves with the new combination.

Thus the latter, by uniting the pick of the talent of the two leading British companies and reinforced by the notable addition of the gifted English soprano Miss Florence Easton, has been able to start off with a really powerful and attractive ensemble. Moreover, it has an unusually strong quartet of conductors in Messrs. Albert Coates, Aylmer Buesst, Charles Webber, and Robert Ainsworth. The Wagnerian fare provided for the opening weeks cannot fail, in the actual state of popular taste in the big provincial towns, to prove another good drawing card. Happily, Mr. Parker promises that when he comes to London at Christmas he intends to enlarge his repertory with other favourite operas, " ancient and modern " ; but for the moment it is too early to talk about that. I only trust that when the time comes he will exercise a discreet choice, and that he will make improved translations and clear, comprehensible English diction a *sine qua non* of his performances. On this last point, however, more anon.

The season started on September 11th with visits to each of the twin theatre suburbs, Streatham Hill and Golder's Green ; they are sufficiently part of London to justify the attendance of the Metropolitan music critics. I went over to Streatham for the opening representation of *Die Meistersinger*, regarding that difficult opera as a tolerably conclusive test of the new company's working calibre. To the advantage of being conducted by the talented and experienced Albert Coates, it added the further gain of a cast comprising artists who have been used to singing together in the past—with the co-operation of a well-trained chorus and orchestra, the latter consisting of fifty players led by Robert Carrodus. All things considered, it was a highly creditable performance. Despite roughness here and there, it went with a smoothness that disguised even the indispensable " cuts," the paucity of numbers in the big ensembles, and other less excusable blemishes that have since no doubt been overcome. As usual with these English opera organisations, greater stress was laid upon the importance of the musical interpretation than the rendering of the text. I could recline in my stall and thoroughly enjoy the former ; but, after half an hour's vain endeavour to catch the words of more than one or two of the characters, I simply gave it up. I need not single out the chief offenders; it would do no good if I did, for they were all "much of a muchness."

The fact is that in this matter of operatic diction the majority of our native singers are making no improvement whatever ; indeed, they are going from bad to worse. Either they are blind to the self-evident truth that their audiences long to hear and understand what they are talking about, or else they simply do not care, and think only of getting their voices into the foreground. They are too proud to be taught (as I know from personal experience) when once they have reached the stage ; and apparently the opera director of to-day does not feel himself strong enough to insist upon the autocracy of a " word-producer," if I may coin the expression, which he grudgingly allows to a strong conductor or to a masterful *régisseur*. It is the same with that other crying need, the employment of less stupid, commonplace, illiteral libretti. The fault does not lie with the impresario or manager so much as with the artists, who are not industrious enough or imbued with the requisite *esprit de corps* to take the trouble of learning new words, to replace the sometimes arrant nonsense that they have been in the habit of using. So long as this difficulty persists, it will be hopeless to look for better versions of the old operas.

But, under any conditions, audiences are entitled by bare right to be able to distinguish the words that are being sung, and the fact that they are not as a rule granted that right is one of the principal reasons why opera in English is not enjoying more nation-wide popularity. Mr. Robert Parker has told us that he is out to catch the reawakened yearning for opera in the vernacular, and if he is earnest about it, he must encourage the rising movement by every means in his power, even to the extent of compelling his singers to be corrected when their words are inaudible at rehearsal. Had something of this kind been done with *The Master-singers* I think I should have found myself listening to it with less divided feelings. As it was, splendid voices and occasionally splendid singing failed of their proper effect because—not of inferior articulation and diction alone—but because of a lack of sustained equality in the tonal beauty and technical excellence of the work. In other words, everyone could have done better had they not consistently tried so hard to do things in their own way and often with much exaggeration or excess of energy, instead of subordinating their powers to the will and direction of a recognised leader.

One conspicuous example of this common tendency to over-emphasise was the Beckmesser of William Michael, who sounded to me as though he were afflicted with a foreign accent. Others were the Fritz Kothner of Bernard Ross, the Magdalena of Gladys Parr, and the Eva of Miriam Licette, all three too restless and self-assertive for these parts. At the other extreme stood the unimaginative Walther of Parry Jones, concerned only with his audience in the theatre, and the sadly dull Pogner of Philip Bertram. Yet all of these are artists who can at their best be quite excellent. But, to be candid to the end, I must declare that the only two who did themselves and their tasks absolute justice were Arthur Fear as Hans Sachs and Browning Mummery as David. With increasing sonority and power of *sostenuto* Arthur Fear will one day give us a glorious embodiment of the poet-cobbler, for he sang beautifully and was the only actor of them all who appeared to have any idea of the value and importance of facial expression.

HERMAN KLEIN.

The Gramophone and the Singer

VOCAL RECORDING — THEN AND NOW
by HERMAN KLEIN

READERS of THE GRAMOPHONE last month must have been, like myself, deeply grateful to our Editor-in-Chief for expressing his " ardent hope that the problem of vocal recording will be seriously taken in hand, and that this unnatural amplification will be abolished once and for all." I cannot think that his weighty and timely behest will fall upon ears as deaf as those few that are supposed to revel in this concession to the fashionable demand for noise. As he truly added, " Once upon a time the reproduction of the human voice was the triumph of the gramophone. It should be worth while to restore it to the position it formerly held."

The reminder has especial value because, as Mr. Compton Mackenzie pointed out, it was suggested by the reinforced Tetrazzini record of *Una voce* and *Caro nome* lately issued by H.M.V. There are doubtless many other discs awaiting similar treatment, and what one wants to know is whether they are all going to be wound up to the same degree of amplified power as these Tetrazzini and Caruso records. If so, a mistake will be committed. It is not wise to take for granted that the present fashion is going to last. For my own part, indeed, I am prepared to see it die out as quickly as it came in, at any rate after tonal reinforcement has once more arrived at its proper level—that is, equality of strength with the original vocal organ. In saying " once more " I do not mean to imply that mechanical reproduction has ever yet succeeded in giving us an exact dynamic equivalent of the human voice. In pre-electric days it was too weak; it sounded too distant, too remote, often as though heard through a curtain. Now it goes to the opposite extreme. Yet of the two systems, as has been so frequently declared, it was the older that yielded the truer result, the greater beauty of timbre when the voice had beauty, the greater clarity of execution when the technique was flawless.

Ought this really to be so ? Surely it would be under-estimating the value of the microphone to assert that it is incapable of producing an exact replica of the voice, equal in every way to that of pre-electric recording, plus the added volume. When we come to think of it, the advantage to the singer is immeasurably in favour of the later method. The exigencies of the ancient horn used to put to a severe test one's coolness and self-control ; it could create " nerves " in artists who never knew what it was to lose a heart-beat in the presence of the largest and most critical audience. There was the constant fear of blasting, which could only be avoided by increasing the distance from the horn or turning the head aside or upwards when taking a high note. Imagine the discomfort and the disturbance inseparable from that sort of thing. Then there were the frequent repetitions of the same piece until a satisfactory record had been obtained. I believe I am correct in saying that the necessity for these occurs much less constantly than before. Nor was the singer always responsible. The trouble was very often caused, in the early days, through the lapses of the strange conglomeration of synthetic instruments that did duty for an orchestra.

My experience of the original Edison phonograph goes back to the period when it was first introduced into this country. In fact, I have good reason to believe that I was among the very first persons in London to make a vocal record, though I never received a copy of it, and if I did it got lost long ago. It must have been in 1881 or 1882, and the place where the deed was done was on the first floor of a shop in Hatton Garden, where I had been invited to listen to the wonderful new invention. To begin with, I heard pieces both in song and speech produced by the friction of a needle against a revolving cylinder, or spool, fixed in what looked like a musical box. It sounded to my ear like someone singing about half a mile away, or talking at the other end of a big hall ; but the effect was rather pleasant, save for a peculiar nasal quality wholly due to the mechanism, though there was little of the scratching which later was a prominent feature of the flat disc. Recording for that primitive machine was a comparatively simple matter. I had to keep my mouth about six inches away from the horn and remember not to make my voice too loud if I wanted anything approximating to a clear reproduction ; that was all. When it was played over to me and I heard my own voice for the first time, one or two friends who were present said that it sounded rather like mine ; others declared that they would never have recognised it. I daresay both opinions were correct.

Anyhow, all those early records were quite devoid of characteristic tone or nuance, and the difficulty of distinguishing clearly the individual voice of the singer was not to be overcome for many years. Of the great artists who recorded for the Victor Company, Melba was, I think, the first whose voice came out in its natural pure timbre, and that was chiefly due to the perfect ease of her production and the unartificial means by which she obtained her remarkable resonance. Then, also, the vagaries of the horn never gave her the slightest trouble. She was one of the coolest customers that ever made a gramophone record.

The Gramophone and the Singer

THE RIGHT TO BE A TEACHER OF SINGING

by HERMAN KLEIN

MANY years have passed since the suggestion was first made that teachers of singing, like lawyers, doctors, *et hoc genus omne*, should have to undergo examination before becoming legally entitled to practise their various professions publicly and for profit. That desirable reform has never been formally put before Parliament in this country, though I believe it has been seriously debated by Congress in the United States, where a Bill to enforce certification was promoted by the National Association of Teachers of Singing, of which the present writer was the first chairman (1906-7). Among those who favoured the scheme was the late Andrew Carnegie, who gave it his warm support. The main obstacle to carrying it into effect was the difficulty of specifying the exact nature of the proposed examinations and of acquiring the certainty that the candidate was in every way competent to exercise his or her functions as a teacher. And therein to this day lies the *crux* of the whole business : who is or is not a fully qualified person to undertake the training of the human voice, at the risk of training it badly or maybe of ruining it for ever ?

One solution has always been : " the proof of the pudding is in the eating." Let them teach for a certain period and then let us judge them by their pupils. Yes ; but under what conditions is the instruction to be given, and what of the unfortunate pupils thus submitted, as it were, to the chances of vocal vivisection ? The difficulties and the dangers are alike too great. In the end the remedy might prove worse than the disease. The result of this has been that the field has remained open to all comers, without restriction of any sort, and, alas, without the slightest means of legal protection or redress to shield the public from the impositions of the charlatan or the incompetent. Anybody can teach singing !

But for the moment I am not concerned with " anybody," nor even with those " somebodies " of the musical world who are obliged to eke out a living in these hard times by giving a few lessons now and then, here and there. One can as readily forgive the fools who " rush in where angels fear to tread," or smile as one used to in the benighted past on reading a provincial or suburban brass plate bearing the inscription, " Pianoforte Tuner and Teacher of Singing." With such as these I have no quarrel. But, on the other hand, I do find serious cause for concern in the continued lowering of the vocal standard among professional artists of native birth who have received or are receiving their instruction in Great Britain. (I speak, naturally, of the average singer, not of those few exceptions who stand at the top of the tree, though even they are far from being beyond the criticism that judges from the loftiest standpoint.) On every side we have evidence that young singers splendidly endowed by nature are coming before the public hampered by faults of technique, of method, of style, that have never been corrected because they were, in most instances, contracted during the period of tuition. It is seldom one reads a reliable notice of new-comers without coming across one or more particular items in the equipment of a vocalist—whether it be production, breathing, intonation, blending of registers, equality of scale, articulation of consonants, vowel tone, diction, or what not—that should be mastered during the early study of the art.

Now who but the teacher can be held responsible for any of these elementary shortcomings ? For those of a later type, connected with expression, tone-colour, contrast, and interpretation generally, the responsibility may lie elsewhere. It is a notorious fact that students not tied down to some particular institution (and not always then) do not remain loyal to the same good teacher, if they have been lucky enough to hit upon one, but flutter from studio to studio in search of what *they* consider to be the right kind of vocal instruction or of the hints and the coaching that will help to fill up the gaps in their store of knowledge.

Precisely here is it that the greatest danger may await them. As often as not it is for them a case of " out of the frying-pan into the fire." Let us consider for a moment what are likely to be the qualifications as vocal teachers of the majority of these coaches and " finishing " professors. As a rule, they are people with names acquired in different spheres of musical labour—as accompanists at concerts ; as *maestri al piano* in an opera house ; above all, as conductors who are in a position either to offer or secure engagements for them. It is the glitter of names constantly appearing on programmes, especially when combined with the advantage of being able to procure paying engagements, that renders the attraction of these (by no means inexpensive) teachers irresistible. What they know of the voice, of the real art of singing, may be summed up as a smattering of traditions of various grades ; and, when they are allowed or take upon themselves to interfere with the organ and the technique of the singer, then it is that the danger-point is touched, then the moment to hearken to the cry, *Cave canem !*

Quite recently, too, another class of vocal instructor has arisen in our midst, whose presence must, I fear, be largely attributed to the lack of concert engagements, to the diminution in the number of choral societies, the growing dearth of oratorio performances, and so forth. I refer to the singer of merit who has made something of a name, but who is anxious to add to his income by turning an honest penny in whatever direction he can. He sings for the B.B.C. as a matter of course ; he sings in opera, serious or light, if it comes his way ; he makes gramophone records ; he will even accept a *cabaret* engagement if the terms be good enough ; he is likewise ready in his spare hours to give singing lessons to all and sundry. Now here again, of course, the pupil must be said to be taking a chance. Not every good singer necessarily makes a good teacher. For one thing, he or she—let us say they, since both sexes are involved—may not possess the gift of imparting to others what they can do themselves. For another, it is almost certain that they have had no experience whatever in the work of judging, diagnosing, training, and cultivating to the best advantage the various kinds of voices that float into their purview. There are so many classes and types of voices, and each requires to be handled with knowledge in its own particular way to bring about the right results. In this delicate process it is so easy to take the wrong turning.

Experience must be earned somehow, I know ; and where singing is in question it is too often at the expense of the pupil who pays the fees. But a great master, Manuel Garcia, was wont to declare that " no one should set up as a teacher who had not studied for ten years and begun by charging nothing for instructing others."

What would the vocal practitioner say if he had to imitate his medical prototype in that respect ? Yet I am constantly encountering cases even more flagrant than those of the artist-teacher sort which I have described—I mean, one's own pupils of a year or two, or even less, who leave off before reaching the half-way stage of their normal tutelary period, and whom one next hears of as teaching on their own account. They do not as a rule omit to make known the source whence they have derived their limited knowledge, but I may add that that generally marks the extent of their gratitude. One outcome of this multiplication is, of course, that there are now thousands of vocal teachers (save the mark !) where there used only to be hundreds.

The only remedy for the glut lies in legislation : in the enforcement of a law requiring registration and the possession of a teacher's certificate, to be obtained only after due and proper examination. Will this ever come ? Speaking with a vivid recollection of what happened when it was tried in New York nearly thirty years ago, I fear not. But meantime I am extremely anxious to see our English vocal standard kept up, both as regards singing and teaching, and, not least of all, our standard of Press criticism maintained at the very highest level.

HERMAN KLEIN.

✱   ✱   ✱

The Gramophone and the Singer
THE VOICE, THE RECORD, AND THE RADIO*
by HERMAN KLEIN

THE latest contribution to vocal literature is comprehensive in content as well as title. It is also American; by which I mean to imply that it is analytical and thorough, whilst set forth in language that is sometimes difficult for the English reader to follow. There is such a thing as being right (or thereabouts) in idea, but over-technical, too elaborate and involved in statement. This is essentially a book written by experts for experts. Even so, however, I fancy that teachers of singing, to whose notice it is specially commended, will often find themselves compelled to read a sentence over and over again in order to arrive at a true sense of its import. Nor will they find it easy, without the aid of a glossary, to keep pace with the remarkable growth of terminological puzzles and novel nomenclature which the modern "technic" imposes upon the student. For more elementary and purely musical questions one is referred to an earlier book by one of the authors, entitled *The Science of Voice*; but that book I have not seen.

In this work the teacher and the scientist have joined hands very much as our own authorities, Emil Behnke and Lennox Browne, did fifty years ago in their well-known book, *Voice, Song, and Speech*, but with the addition of those factors which later mechanical inventions and devices have brought into the picture. Were all of these to be employed and consulted, the studio of the up-to-date vocal teacher would, it seems to me, be made to resemble the laboratory of a medical specialist. He could hardly, for example, dispense with a large and complex instrument called the "oscillograph," used for the purpose of tracing on paper or on a film the zig-zag lines formed by the vibrations of the human voice. It enables you to ascertain and measure quality, pitch, intensity, steadiness, etc. A few years ago I tested it once to please an American doctor who was a lecturer in Vienna and was anxious to possess a diagram made by a pupil of Garcia; but I never dreamed of utilizing a similar machine myself, any more than I would use a laryngoscope to examine my pupils' vocal cords. Other machines, such as the "electric harmonic analyzer," the "sound meter," the "level recorder," the "reverberation meter," etc., may have a scientific value, but in my opinion they do not form part of the equipment of the ordinary voice-trainer.

However, when we come to the main portion of this book we are at once told that its chief object is "to bring together the sciences of acoustical engineering and of vocal technic." We thus realize that fresh ground is being opened up, and that teachers and singers may learn important facts which they were not sufficiently familiar with before. They have been able to recognize effects, but they could not always explain their causes. It would take too long to follow Mr. Douglas Stanley through his extended observations on the subject of voice production, apart from the terminological obstacles that there beset our path. When his meaning is clear, however, he says much that is full of commonsense and also occasionally a good deal with which the present writer finds himself not quite able to agree. The latter certainly does not include Mr. Stanley's many strong and convincing arguments with regard to "crooning," which he justly describes as "an inartistic and most vicious form of voice production." Highly interesting are his definitions of the methods employed for this distortion and misuse of the art of singing: of the ways in which the microphone and the control-engineer have been jointly responsible for the practical application and ultimate glorification of this most objectionable monstrosity.

Nor does he stop at the "mere crooners." He refers to those radio singers with voices of infinitesimal volume, who broadcast "good, or passably good music," or else sing near the microphone in a soft *mezza voce* that would not travel half-way across a small concert room. Happily he thinks that their day is nearly over. The voice which, as he puts it, is "built on the soft," the "sweet" voice, the crooner, the "light, effeminate, throaty tenor," and the "squeaky coloratura" only last a few years. "The full, free, ringing voice which is technically well produced endures!" Here, needless to say, I heartily re-echo Mr. Stanley's sentiments. I am not equally at one with his views on subjects like the registers (or "registration," as he prefers to call it), the modes of dealing with "uncoordinated" and mixed voices (tones), the so-called *falsetto*, the range and compass of the various voices, and other important matters.

Again, I am not sure that I perceive the wisdom of applying the term "vibrato," even though technically correct, to a normal, steady sustained tone, whilst reserving the word "tremolo" for its opposite. The distinction may be allowable since it actually exists; but custom and long habit render it difficult to speak of legitimate good tone as "vibrato." I feel in saying this that it is only the word that I object to, not the "phenomenon" itself, as Mr. Stanley elects to call it. The first duty of one who instructs or criticizes is to make himself understood. The "vibrato" as a factor in singing is by no means a new one, and, knowing this, I do not fear being included in the

* *The Voice, its Production and Reproduction;* by Douglas Stanley and J. P. Maxfield. Pitman Publishing Corporation, New York and London. Price 10s. 6d. net.

American author's category of "vocal teachers who have remained impervious to the march of scientific knowledge." As for the term "falsetto," it was used by Manuel Garcia nearly a century ago in his famous Treatise on the Art of Singing—and used in its true sense—when he applied it not only to a man's head voice (now taboo), but to the medium register of the female voice. But then Mr. Stanley refuses to recognize the existence of a medium register ; and, among the many authorities whom he quotes (chiefly to expose their mistakes), he has not a word of either admiration or blame for Garcia, whom he does not even mention.

The real merit of this book lies, I think, in its endeavour to make clear to the student the secrets of the microphone and everything connected with its use, whether for recording or broadcasting. Sifting the wheat from the chaff, and eliminating the superfluities and peculiarities which I began by complaining of, there remains in its pages a vast amount of valuable information that will repay careful study. I wish I had had space to quote from Mr. Maxfield's chapters on "Reproduction," with its apt observations on acoustics in the studio and the functions of the pick-up. But these and many other valuable hints will be the reward of the reader who cares to spend half-a-guinea upon a clever book. HERMAN KLEIN.

★　　　★　　　★

Part III
ANALYTICAL NOTES
AND
FIRST REVIEWS

Operatic & Song Recordings
Reviewed by
Herman Klein

REVIEWS PUBLISHED IN 1925

OPERATIC

H.M.V.—D.B. 813 (12in., 8s. 6d.).—**Amelita Galli-Curci** (soprano): **Come d'aurato sogno (Tacea la notte)** and **Timor di me? (D'amor sull' ali rosee)** from **Il Trovatore** (Verdi).

H.M.V.—D.B. 758 (12in., 8s. 6d.).—**Chaliapine** (bass): **They guess the truth, Susannin's Aria,** and **Recitative** and **Finale of Susannin's Aria** from **A Life for the Tzar** (Glinka).

H.M.V.—D.B.834 (12in., 8s. 6d.).—**Apollo Granforte** (baritone):**Largo al Factotum** from **Il Barbiere de Siviglia** (Rossini) and **O Lisbona** from **Don Sebastiano** (Donizetti).

H.M.V.—D.A. 714 (10in., 6s.).—**Michele Fleta** (tenor): **Amapola** (Lacalle) and **Bimba, non t'avvicinar** (Cortesi-Bettinelli).

H.M.V.—D.10424 (12in., 6s. 6d.).—**Evelyn Scotney** (soprano): **Dearest Name (Caro Nome)** from **Rigoletto** (Verdi) and **Ave Maria** from **Otello** (Verdi).

BRUNSWICK.—10166 (10in., 4s. 6d.).—**Elisabeth Rethberg** (soprano): **Au Printemps** (Gounod) and **Ye who have yearned alone** (Tchaikovsky).

BRUNSWICK.—30110 (12in., 6s. 6d.).—**Mario Chamlee** (tenor): **Hosanna** (Granier) and **Open the Gates of the Temple** (Knapp).

BRUNSWICK.—15096 (10in., 5s. 6d.).—**Edith Mason** (soprano): **Ancora un passo** from **Madama Butterfly** (Puccini) and **Air des Bijoux (Jewel Song)** from **Faust** (Gounod).

VOCALION.—A.0241 (12in., 5s. 6d.).—**Luella Paikin** (soprano): **Il dolce Suono,** the Mad Scene from **Lucia di Lammermoor** (Donizetti).

COLUMBIA.—7370 (12in., 8s. 6d.).—**Dame Clara Butt** (contralto): **Cleansing Fires** (Proctor and Gabriel) and **She wore a wreath of Roses** (Bayley and Knight).

COLUMBIA.—X.328 (10in., 6s.).—**Stracciari** (baritone): **Prologue** from **Pagliacci** (Leoncavallo).

COLUMBIA.—L.1667 (12in., 6s. 6d.).—**Frank Mullings** (tenor): **Kathleen Mavourneen** (Crawford and Crouch) and **The Snowy-brested Pearl** (de Vere and Robinson).

COLUMBIA.—D.1525 (10in., 4s. 6d.).—**Norman Allin** (bass): **Tavern Song** (Fisher) and **See the way you Rogues** from **Il Seraglio** (Mozart).

IMPERIAL.—1481 (10in., 2s.).—**Luigi Cilla** (tenor): **Lolita** (Buzzi-Peccia) and **Manon** (Massenet).

FARLOPHONE.—E.10362 (12in., 4s. 6d.).—**Margarethe Siems** (soprano): **Dies einzige Wörtlein,** and **Fritzi Jokl** (soprano): **Song of the Page** from **Les Huguenots** (Meyerbeer).

Amelita Galli-Curci.—This latest example of what is perhaps the most successful phase of Mme. Galli-Curci's art conquers in spite of the hackneyed nature of its subject. I am not sure whether the "Diva of Coloratura" reckons the Leonora of *Il Trovatore* among her active rôles, but after hearing this well-executed record I should certainly consider it as among the possibles. And, if we must have *Tacea la notte* yet once again, by all means let us have it sung as cleverly and authoritatively as it is here, with all imaginable ease, flexibility, and *verve*. Let it even begin, as this does, with that lovely *coda* of the recitative, *Come d'aurato sogno*, just to give it a new title and make it sound like something fresh; until we turn the disc over and there find our old friend the *Baletta*, as familiar and brilliant as ever, but superbly sung by Galli-Curci, with her *blanche* but characteristic tone, and ending up on a marvellous E flat in *alt*.

Chaliapine.—The great Russian basso in the great air from the greatest of Russian national operas, Glinka's *Life for the Czar*. A *magnum opus*, truly, for everything is on the biggest possible scale. The air of Soussannine (as it ought to be written) is a wonderful piece of music and gives Chaliapine unlimited scope for the exercise of his art. No matter if you do not understand the language. The tremendous significance of accent, the tragic melancholy alternating with the animated outburst, the infinite variety of the treatment and contrast of colour, all combine to make up an overflowing measure of dramatic interest. And then the fullness and rotundity of the wonderful Chaliapine tone—perfectly recorded and excellently accompanied—you could have nothing better, no matter which side of the disc you play!

Apollo Granforte.—Use a half-tone needle for this record, which is powerful alike as a rendering and a reproduction. The voice is typically Italian; not

absolutely steady, but nearly so; a shade throaty and over-darkened for so joyous, light-hearted an air as the *Largo al Factotum*. More comedy is needed and more contrast. The diction, however, is clear, even when the tone is at its loudest I mean, when it is truly *granforte*. This sombre, funereal organ is much better suited by Donizetti's melancholy *O Lisbona*, in which it sounds remarkably well.

Michele Fleta.—It is the singer that is operatic, not the song. He presents two very ordinary Italian ditties, rather Neapolitan in cast, but in reality requiring a great deal more life and spirit, less "fading away" on every other note, than this tenor imparts to them. His style is tasteful and sympathetic, but not exactly inspiring. The accompaniments are quite prettily done.

Evelyn Scotney.—I have previously had occasion to write nice things about this artist in connection with the Vocalion, and therefore have positively nothing fresh to note concerning her *Caro Nome*, as sung for the H.M.V., except that it is in English, an American translation, and somewhat difficult to make out at that. The *Ave Maria* is also given in our native tongue, and even less distinctly, which is a pity, for the singing of both pieces is quite on a high level.

Elisabeth Rethberg.—The lovely quality of this singer's voice is her most precious asset, whether on the stage or the gramophone. Her art, to my thinking, is not so wholly irreproachable—judging it of course, from the standard of Elena Gerhardt and Julia Culp. In the Tchaikovsky song I find her a trifle monotonous, and it lies low for her. Moreover the pathetic accent is more apparent in her rich medium timbre than in the diction of Goethe's glorious lines. It should be equally touching and profound in both. Gounod composed *Au printemps* at Rome in 1840, when he was a passionate youth of 22. His graceful *chanson* calls for the *joie de vivre;* he marked it to be sung *animé et avec entraînement.* I wonder whether Miss Rethberg took this sufficiently into account. For, after all, she is a very conscientious artist.

Mario Chamlee.—After hearing these two records I feel that I have heard the man himself. He is evidently used to filling vast spaces, and he gives you of his opulent tone without stint or reserve. It is a gigantic organ, and he knows it. Also it is a genuine tenor, and the *ff* high A is to him a mere trifle; but one wishes that there were just a little less "scooping" on the way to it. The *Hosanna* by Granier, sung in English, is a telling sort of semi-sacred song, and no doubt Mr. Chamlee's powerful rendering of it will be as popular as that of Knapp's *Open the gates*, which has the stirring march rhythm (and "then some") of *Onward Christian Soldiers*.

Edith Mason.—This accomplished soprano gives us a welcome change from the sempiternal *Un bel dì*, in the shape of *Ancora un passo*, the ever-rising strain of gracious melody wherewith Madame Butterfly climbs the last bit of hill and announces her arrival at Lieut. Pinkerton's Nagasaki dwelling. She delivers it here with a clearness and purity of penetrating tone that would be lost at the back of the stage (indeed generally is), and winds it up with a faultless D flat as required by the score. The orchestral accompaniment is not equally beyond criticism, being quite discordant here and there. In the *Jewel Song* (without recitative) Miss Mason's vocalisation is no less artistic, while her tone is a model of steadiness.

Luella Paikin.—Yet another brilliant specimen to be added to the lengthy list of Mad Scenes. This one being from *Lucia* and extending the full length of both sides of a 12in. disc, is decidedly reasonable at 5s. 6d., for on the whole it is quite an admirable piece of work and amply justifies its issue. (I will not say "release," first, because I hate the word in its filmy sense, and, secondly, because poor Lucia was far too mad to have earned any but that which we know as the "happy" one.) Miss Paikin possesses a pleasing light soprano of considerable power, bright and clear in the head register, and displayed with a great deal of technical skill. Her scales are neat and accurate, she has an unusually good staccato; in fact, all the accessories essential for giving due effect to the *fioriture* of Donizetti's demented heroine. The orchestral accompaniment is well balanced and the recording praiseworthy.

Dame Clara Butt.—The two old ballads with which the popular contralto enriches the Columbia catalogue are not unworthy of the honour. *Cleansing fires* suits her the better; it brings out the broad, resonant quality of her chest tone. On the other hand *She wore a wreath of roses*—properly speaking, a man's song—lies in a higher *tessitura,* and the effort thereby entailed imparts a pinched quality to the medium notes. In every way, therefore, I prefer the side of the disc which reminds me of that "remote star" of my youth, Virginia Gabriel. Her "cleansing fires" are still burning.

Riccardo Stracciari.—How well Stracciari sings the *Prologue* from *Pagliacci* our readers must by this time be fully aware. He has done it afresh for the Columbia on two sides of a 10in. disc, and put into the task all that is best of his excellent voice and method.

Frank Mullings.—I rather like these old ballads sung by favourite vocalists with voices of gigantic amplitude. It reminds of one of the use of the Nasmyth steam hammer to crack a nut. But the result is good, especially when the well-known *tenore robusto* follows in the wake (and the style) of John McCormack and shows us how smooth and subdued and sustained he can be in things like *Kathleen Mavourneen* and the *Snowy-brasted* (pardon, *breasted*) *Pearl.*

Norman Allin.—Here the versatile English bass displays his command of worthy material. Treating his powerful organ discreetly, he achieves a crisp, humorous reading of the Mozart aria, with tolerably distinct words, and a really happy, jolly rendering of the *Tavern Song,* including capital low notes, all in the good old-fashioned drinking-ditty style. There are three verses, and the swinging triple rhythm is positively irresistible.

Luigi Cilla.—Lolita, being presumably Spanish, the veteran Buzzi-Peccia naturally endowed her with a lively *bolero* tune in the minor, to which the singer here imparts the no less natural strain of love-lorn sentiment. In the *Manon* the latter is a trifle more energetic and not quite so steady. But he has a charming voice, and altogether the record is well worth the price asked for it.

Margarethe Siems and Fritzi Jokl.—Comment upon these excerpts from *Les Huguenots,* sung in German by the above artists, appears in my current article on Meyerbeer's opera.

HERMAN KLEIN.

OPERATIC

BRUNSWICK.—30100 (12in., 6s. 6d.).—**Giuseppe Danise** (baritone) : **Panis Angelicus** (Franck) and **Pietà Signore !** (attributed to Stradella).

BRUNSWICK.—10174 (10in., 4s. 6d.).—**Maria Ivogün** (soprano) : **Tales from the Vienna Woods** (Strauss) and **Lo, here the gentle lark** (Bishop).

BRUNSWICK.—15095 (10in., 5s. 6d.).—**Giacomo Lauri-Volpi** (tenor) : **Di quella Pira** and **Ah sì, ben mio** from **Trovatore** (Verdi).

ACTUELLE.—15202 (12in., 6s.).—**Ninon Vallin** (soprano) : **Le Nil** (Leroux) and **Ave Maria** (Gounod).

HOMOCHORD.—P.5002 (12in., 4s.).—**Karin Branzell** (mezzo-soprano) and **Björn Talén** (tenor) : **Softly awakes my heart** from **Samson and Delilah** (Saint-Saëns) and the duet from **Act 4 of Carmen** (Bizet).

VOCALION.—K.03189 (12in., 4s. 6d.).—**Frank Titterton** (tenor) : **Your tiny hand is frozen** from **La Bohème** (Puccini) and **Strange harmony of contrasts** from **La Tosca** (Puccini).

H.M.V.—D.A.733 (10in., 6s.).—**Jeanne Gordon** (contralto) : **Voyons que j'essaie** (**Card Song**) and **Près des remparts de Séville** (Séguidille) from **Carmen** (Bizet).

VOCALION.—A.0245 (12in., 5s. 6d.).—**M. Murray-Davey** (bass) : **Was duftet doch** from **Meistersinger** (Wagner) and **Ella giammai m'amò** from **Don Carlos** (Verdi).

VOCALION.—K.05197 (12in., 4s. 6d.).—**Malcolm McEachern** (bass) : **Sperate, o figli** from **Nabucodonosor** (Verdi) and **Song of the Seraphs** (Urquhart Cawley).

VOCALION.—K.05196 (12in., 4s. 6d.).—**Phyllis Archibald** (contralto) : **Habañera** from **Carmen** (Bizet) and **Ah ! mon fils** from **Le Prophète** (Meyerbeer).

COLUMBIA.—L.1665 (12in., 6s. 6d.).—**Miriam Licette** (soprano) : **Thy call me Mimi** from **La Bohème** (Puccini) and **Waltz Song** from **Romeo and Juliet** (Gounod). Orchestra conducted by Sir Hamilton Harty.

PARLOPHONE.—E.10373 (12in., 4s. 6d.).—**Fritzi Jokl** (soprano) : **Der Hölle Rache kocht in meinem Herzen** (Queen of the Night aria) from **The Magic Flute,** and **O Säume länger nicht** from **The Marriage of Figaro** (Mozart).

PARLOPHONE.—E.10372 (12in., 4s. 6d.).—**Emmy Heckmann-Bettendorf** (soprano) : **Elizabeth's Greeting** from **Tannhäuser** (Wagner), and **Max Hirzel** (tenor) : **Lohengrin's Farewell** (Wagner).

Giuseppe Danise.—Neither of the songs recorded by this excellent baritone comes strictly within the domain of operatic music. He brings to them, however, the style and experience of an operatic singer, and both are really essential to serious " Church " airs like *Pieta, Signore !* and the *Panis Angelicus* of Franck. Signor Danise brings to Stradella's prayer a broad tone, a religious spirit, and the full measure of urgency that it demands. In the other piece he sings with great suavity of tone and phrasing against a rather assertive violin obbligato, but is tempted at times to attack with excessive energy. His chief weakness, though, is a tendency to frequent *rubatos,* especially in the even quaver passages of the *Pietà.*

Maria Ivogün.—The charming soprano who dazzled Covent Garden with her brilliant vocalisation in 1924 is heard, like most of her *genus,* to good advantage on the gramophone. I am glad, therefore, to recommend her records even though, as in the above instance, it is the singer alone who is operatic. For an old-fashioned Strauss waltz such as this she has the true Viennese touch, and I can imagine that the delight of the immortal Johann would have been as great as my own at listening not only to the wonderful lilt, but the sweeping grace and entrain of Maria Ivogün's warbling of the tune, and the clever vocal decorations with which she has ornamented it. In *Lo ! here the gentle lark* she is very nearly as bird-like and fascinating ; but not quite.

Giacomo Lauri-Volpi.—These well-worn airs from *Il Trovatore* will be welcome to lovers of the opera, who somehow never tire of comparing the different *tenori robusti* that attempt them. It is a pity—as I thought when I heard him at Covent Garden last season—that Signor Lauri-Volpi does not seek more for sweetness and less for strident tone ; also for steadiness and charm and a pure *sostenuto.* For he has a fine voice and plenty of power, as his *Di quella pira* amply demonstrates. The *Ah sì, ben mio* is susceptible of much greater refinement alike as to vocal treatment and diction.

Ninon Vallin.—These are vocal pieces by operatic composers, both sung with orchestra and violin obbligato. I prefer the singer's head register to her medium, which is rather nasal and tremulous, due to faulty production. Otherwise her voice is of agreeable quality and she is obviously an intelligent artist. *Le Nil* is a beautiful song, worthy of the pen which wrote that clever opera *Le Chemineau,* which Sir Thomas Beecham produced in London some years ago. In the more familiar *Ave Maria* the soloist is not quite so successful. Her style is not broad enough ; she " scoops " up too many notes ; and all the more acute vowels are made unpleasantly prominent.

Karin Branzell and *Björn Talén.*—Two earnest and capable Scandinavian artists, mezzo-soprano and tenor, who sing these duet selections with as much spirit and realism as if they were enacting the characters to the appreciative crowds that throng the opera-houses at Stockholm and Copenhagen. Both have good voices ; the pity is that they do not mingle so well as they might, which is a fault of timbre, not of singing. It is pleasant, however, to hear *Softly awakes* with the ending that Saint-Saëns wrote and a good B flat from the Samson instead of a scrape from the substituted violin. In the *Carmen,* too, one feels the atmosphere of the drama just prior to the fatal deed, where the tone of the Don José, if spasmodic and somewhat forced, is at least energetic and appropriate. But why such roughness in the orchestra ?

Frank Titterton.—The excerpt from *La Bohème* is taken too fast and lacks both tenderness and contrast. Again, in the passage from the first act of the *Tosca* this singer gives us one timbre, one colour, one jerking method of delivering his phrases throughout. If he used his voice with a less unsparing breath-pressure it would not vibrate so much or sound forced ; moreover, the *legato* would be smoother. It is worth while to tell Mr. Titterton these things, for he has a nice pure tenor voice and can sing artistically when he takes sufficient care.

Jeanne Gordon.—This singer has the true " mezzo " quality for Carmen and sings her music as though to the manner born. The rhythm, style, and diction are just right. But for her inequalities of scale and vowel tone, especially in the *Card Song,* there would be little room here for adverse criticism.

M. Murray-Davey.—I like the calm, sedate opening of Hans Sachs's first monologue, the steady sostenuto, and the genial sentiment. The consonants might be more distinct, and the final " en " of the German betrays an English tongue, but on the whole the record is a creditable piece of work, with smooth orchestration. In the air from *Don Carlos* Mr. Murray-Davey declaims his Italian even better than his German and gives a good traditional rendering, though his ebullitions of feeling are a trifle spasmodic. One thing, he has the voice and the manner of the typical *basso cantante.*

Malcolm MacEachern.—In this Antipodean singer the voice is superior to the style, or, rather, the latter is generally sacrificed to the former, while the diction is too often at the mercy of an unmistakeable dialect. On the other hand, those who admire a huge bass tone and a wonderful low C to end up with will like the early Verdi, even though their opinions may differ concerning the *Song of the Seraphs,* which to my ears sounds more demoniacal than seraphic.

Phyllis Archibald.—Here, again, we have to contend with a pronounced " overseas " dialect. And what a pity that such a superb contralto organ should not have the advantage of a more refined method. In *Ah ! mon fils* one finds the singer making all the customary " points," but wholly oblivious to the impurity of her French vowels and the inequalities of the tone wherein they emerge. There is no real charm, either in this or the jerky, shaky *Habañera* (American translation) which fills the other side of the disc, and I hope the day will come when Miss Archibald will make much better records.

Miriam Licette.—Both her latest efforts denote the experienced gramophone artist, and both are familiar as well as popular. The waltz-air from *Romeo* has the merit of steady tone, accurate text, and a bright, joyous, rhythmical reading. The Mimi auto-biography (" I'm always called Mimi," she truly says) sounds clear, ingenuous, and well recorded.

Fritzi Jokl.—I honestly dislike *Deh, vieni* in German, particularly when sung *minus* a single *appoggiatura* and *plus* that top B flat which isn't Mozart. It isn't Bach either, though *O säume länger nicht*, as here given, has both the title and the ring of a church cantata. Miss Jokl is heard to infinitely greater advantage in the Queen of Night's second aria, which she transposes down a half or even a whole tone. Her notes *in alt* are very pretty and neat.

Max Hirzel and *Emmy Bettendorf.*—On a single 12-inch disc *Lohengrin's Farewell* and *Elizabeth's Greeting*, which is tolerably good measure. But, alas, only a routine performance. The tenor is throaty, and the soprano has no good head notes, just missing the strong G necessary for the excerpt from *Tannhäuser*.

HERMAN KLEIN.

OPERATIC

MARIA SCHREKA (soprano).—**Weh' mir, ich fühls** and **Man nennt mich Mimi** from **Bohème** (Puccini). Polydor 65809, 12in., 5s. 9d.

SIGRID ONEGIN (contralto).—**Ach, ich habe sie verloren** from **Orpheus und Eurydike** (Gluck) and **O schöne Jugendtage** from **Evangelimann** (Kienzl). Polydor 72720, 12in., 6s. 9d.

DELIA REINHARDT (soprano).—**Einsam in trüben Tagen** from **Lohengrin** (Wagner) and **Sie sass mit Leide** from **Otello** (Verdi). Polydor 72775, 12in., 6s. 9d.

FRIEDA HEMPEL. (soprano).—**Voi che sapete** from **Figaro** and. **Hark! the Vesper Hymn is stealing** (arr. J. Stevenson). H.M.V., D.A.675, 10in., 6s.

MARIA IVOGÜN (soprano).—**Martern aller Artern** from **Die Entführung aus dem Serail** (Mozart) and **Geschichten aus dem Wiener Wald** (Johann Strauss). Polydor 85303, 12in., 6s. 9d.

G. MARIO SAMMARCO (baritone).—**Toreador Song** from **Carmen** (Bizet) and **Cavatina di Figaro** from **Il Barbiere di Siviglia** (Rossini). Actuelle 15205, 12in., 6s.

EVELYN SCOTNEY (soprano).—**Deh, non varcar quell'onda** and **To sorrow now my days are fated** from **The Magic Flute** (Mozart). H.M.V., D.1035, 12in., 6s. 6d.

MIRIAM LICETTE (soprano).—**Ave Maria** and **Salce (The Willow Song)** from **Otello** (Verdi). Col. L.1683, 12in., 6s. 6d.

Th. I. CHALIAPINE (bass).—**Nor sleep nor rest** and **How goes it, Prince?** from **Prince Igor** (Borodin). H.M.V., D.B.799, 12in., 8s. 6d.

HAROLD WILLIAMS (baritone).—**Gazing around** from **Act II, Tannhäuser** (Wagner) and **Confutatis Maledictis** from **Requiem** (Verdi). Columbia 9061, 12in., 4s. 6d.

CECIL SHERWOOD (tenor).—**'Tis the day (Mattinata)** (Tosti) and **Recondita armonia** from **Tosca** (Verdi). Zonophone G.O.66, 10in., 3s. 6d.

G. LENGHI-CELLINI (tenor).—**O Lola (Siciliana)** and **Brindisi (Drinking Song)** from **Cavalleria Rusticana** (Mascagni). Parlophone E.10386, 12in., 4s. 6d.)

LUELLA MELIUS (soprano).—**Ah! lo so (Pamina's Aria)** and **Gli angui d'inferno (Der Hölle Rache—from Magic Flute)**. H.M.V., D.A.723, 10in., 6s. 6d.

MICHAEL BOHNEN (baritone).—**Invocation** from **Robert le Diable** (Meyerbeer) and **Sei vendicata assai** from **Dinorah** (Meyerbeer). Brunswick 15097, 4s. 6d.

TUDOR DAVIES (tenor).—**Oh, voice of magic melody** and **Oh, loveliness beyond compare** from **The Magic Flute** (Mozart). H.M.V., E.401, 10in., 6s. 6d.

ELISABETH SCHUMANN (soprano).—**Neue freuden, neue Schmerzen** and **Ihr, die ihr Triebe** from **Le Nozze** (Mozart). Polydor 65654, 5s. 9d.

Maria Schreka.—The name of this German soprano is not unfamiliar to me, although she has never yet appeared in this country. She has a sympathetic voice, but, like so many of her countrywomen, she is prone to over-sentimentalise modern operatic airs generally and Puccini in particular. In *Un bel dì*, whereof we have here the German version, she represents a vastly sorrowful Butterfly instead of the still hopeful creature who is depicting to Suzuki the joyful scene of Pinkerton's anticipated return. Her tears also induce much slurring and scooping, which is a pity, because her tone is very pleasant, and the orchestral accompaniment is unusually good. The singer's subdued method sounds less out of place in Mimi's "autobiography " and it pleases accordingly.

Sigrid Onegin.—New features are not precisely to be looked for in fresh records of well-known pieces, but rather beauty of voice and style and an intelligent adherence to traditional rendering. These things will be found in adequate measure in Sigrid Onegin's quiet delivery of the great air from Gluck's *Orpheus*—grief that is tenderly peaceful but never for a moment passionate, as Giulia Ravogli used to make it for us ; anguish well under control, but minus the wonderful ending that Pauline Viardot-Garcia introduced. The contralto song from Kienzl's tedious opera, *Der Evangelimann*, begins on some lovely low notes, but they do not last long, worse luck ; for they are smoothly and deftly managed, with good breathing. This opera in 1897 was all the rage in Vienna, but when done at Covent Garden in the same year it sent most people to sleep, myself included. Both excerpts, by the way, are very clear and without scratch.

Delia Reinhardt.—This artist was the charming Oktavian of the *Rosenkavalier* revival at Covent Garden in 1924, and also sang *Madam Butterfly*. Neither opera is illustrated on the present disc, and it seems to me that her capacity for displaying animal spirits is less in evidence here. True, she wakes up towards the end of each, and there is the excuse that both Desdemona and Elsa are at the moment very much "down in the dumps." But that is not sufficient reason for the prevailing atmosphere of dullness—correct and dignified, if you like, but distinctly monotonous—whilst Elsa is relating her dream and Othello's unhappy spouse is giving us a German account of poor Barbara's betrayal. "Willow " or "Salce," I suppose it is all the same thing when translated into a foreign tongue ; and both records are at least worth hearing.

Frieda Hempel.—The *Voi che sapete* of this singer is dealt with (from another version, I fancy) elsewhere in the present number. The *Vesper Hymn* on the reverse side of the disc (bell included, gratis) will at least furnish an eloquent souvenir of one's childhood. I know I played it on the piano at the age of six, but now I can only ask, What is it doing in this *galère* ?

Maria Ivogün.—Once more "part heard," like a case at the Law Courts ! The waltz of Johann Strauss I mentioned last month in connection with *Lo ! here the gentle lark*. This time it appears in conjunction with an air from Mozart's *Seraglio* : and the latter shall be duly noticed when I come to that opera in my February article.

Mario Sammarco.—There can be little need to describe how this popular baritone disports himself in the discussion of such hackneyed items as the *Toreador's Song* and Figaro's *Largo al factotum*. Enough that he is lively and vivacious as ever in both, and that his voice, so far as my Sonora Model will allow me to do justice to a Pathé record, sounds surprisingly fresh and strong.

Evelyn Scotney.—Two Mozart pieces, which I shall deal with later. The *Magic Flute* air is sung, I think, to an American translation, and not a very good one. Anyhow, the quality of the voice comes out much more true and sympathetic in the other—an Italian—record.

Miriam Licette.—With the *Willow Song* and the *Ave Maria* on the two sides of the same disc we get the whole of Desdemona's pathetic opening to the last act of Verdi's *Otello*, now very familiar to most gramophone lovers of opera. Pathos in its saddest expression is needed here, and I fear it is somewhat defeated by an obvious effort to hurry the tempo so as to "get it all in." However, the words are clearly enunciated and the phrasing is sufficiently neat to satisfy a fastidious ear, while the tone, if unsteady at times, comes out pure and unadulterated in the natural timbre of the artist. Altogether it must be accounted an extremely well-made record, alike in its vocal and orchestral aspects.

Chaliapine.—These two excerpts from Borodin's opera, *Prince Igor*, exhibit the talent of the great Russian basso in its most impressive light. The massive voice is, as usual, finely employed and with a degree of sustained dramatic power that seems to interpret every shade of emotion. We can almost follow the story without understanding a word. The tone is magnificent ; the enunciation clear as a bell ; better recording could hardly be wished for. In the second section—the quicker movement—with its characteristic bold rhythm, the artist simply revels in his task and brings in a diabolical laugh with wonderful effect. The accompaniment is ably done, but at the end the singer " beats the band."

Harold Williams.—One an admirable rendering of the bass air, *Confutatis maledictis,* from Verdi's *Requiem,* particularly good for its devotional feeling and expressive, steady tone in the lovely passage, " Oro supplex et acclinis." The other less interesting on the whole, but nevertheless a quite acceptable performance of Wolfram's so-called fantasy from *Tannhäuser.*

Cecil Sherwood.—The name of this tenor is new to me. He has a bright, telling voice and uses it in a manner that tells of modern

Italian training. There is plenty of sonority in the air from *Tosca,* where accepted models are carefully followed. Tosti's ballad on the reverse side is tastefully sung to a piano accompaniment.

G. Lenghi-Cellini.—In these two pieces from *Cavalleria Rusticana* one perceives that the climate of England agrees very well with the Italian tenor, who has chiefly won his reputation here. His voice is free from *tremolo* and he invariably uses it to the best advantage. Both the *Siciliana* and the *Drinking Song* are given with any amount of spirit and well-directed energy, while the recording is first rate.

(The rest of these records will be noticed in my next Mozart article.)   HERMAN KLEIN.

REVIEWS PUBLISHED IN 1926

OPERATIC

RICCARDO STRACCIARI (baritone): **Brindisi** and **Il Sogno** from **Otello** (Verdi). In Italian. Col. X.332, 10in., 6s.

KEDROFF MALE QUARTET (unaccompanied): **Church Bells of Novgorod** (Russian folk-song) and **Introduction to A Life for the Czar** (Glinka). In Russian. Col. D.1530, 10in., 4s. 6d.

ARISTODEMO GIORGINI (tenor).—**Ridi, Pagliacci** from **Pagliacci** (Leoncavallo) and **In povertà mia lieta** from **La Bohème** (Puccini). Actuelle 15209.

LYSE CHARNY (contralto).—**Air des Larmes** from **Werther** (Massenet) and **Seguidille** from **Carmen** (Bizet). Actuelle 15209.

HERBERT TEALE (tenor).—**Lohengrin's Narration** from **Lohengrin** (Wagner) and **Lend me your aid** from **La Reine de Saba** (Gounod). Beltona 7001, 12in., 4s. 6d.

LOTTE LEHMANN (soprano) and **HEINRICH SCHLUSNUS** (baritone).—**Reich mir die Hand** from **Don Giovanni** (Mozart) and **So lang hab ich geschmachtet** from **Le Nozze di Figaro** (Mozart). Polydor 72933.

AMELITA GALLI-CURCI (soprano) and **TITO SCHIPA** (tenor).— **Un dì, felice, eterea** and **Parigi o cara** from **La Traviata** (Verdi). H.M.V., D.A.711, 10in., 6s.

Riccardo Stracciari.—Verdi's *Otello* is gradually but surely winning its way to the place it deserves in the hearts of opera-lovers in this country. All the best things in the score are now to be heard on the gramophone, and here we have two of Iago's few detachable pages, apart from the *Credo*—namely, the *Brindisi,* or Drinking Song, in Act I., and the passage from the duet with Otello in Act II., where the Moor's traitorous " ancient " first awakens the " green-eyed monster " by his story of what he overheard Cassio mutter in his dream about Desdemona. Both are short, but full of colour. The Drinking Song, a *macabre* sort of ditty, trolled forth by Iago amid the gathering storm, primarily to encourage Roderigo to get tipsy, is sung with abundant spirit. The *Sogno,* or dream, is related with the right degree of subtlety and a striking contrast in the voices of the two speakers. In each Stracciari shows what an artist he is.

Kedroff Male Quartet.—These are not in any sense operatic records, but I have been asked to say a word about them. The quartet is now well known here, and this disc will make still wider the appreciation of its magnificent tone and intensely Russian singing, thanks to excellent recording and a faultless interpretation of two of the quartet's choicest numbers. The imitation of deep, booming church bells by human voices is extraordinarily realistic, particularly towards the end, where they slowly die away. The Glinka *Introduction* from his famous opera, *A Life for the Czar,* combines a tenor solo in a plain-song chant with some fine four-part harmony sung by voices of amazing amplitude and richness, always in perfect tune. The effect is simply overpowering.

Aristodemo Giorgini.—There can be no doubt concerning the claims of this tenor—a Greek, apparently, with an Italianised *nom de théâtre*—to an attentive hearing. He possesses an abundance of tone of telling quality and sings with a lot of dramatic fire, besides commanding a capital high C. But his records puzzle me, especially the *Ridi, Pagliacci,* which floats off the pitch and on again in the strangest way. I have tried it over two or three times and always

with the same disagreeable result. On the other hand, the *Bohème* excerpt comes out fairly well and shows off the singer's *sostenuto* to decided advantage.

Lyse Charny.—These are superior examples of Actuelle–Pathé handiwork to those just noticed. They bring out the true timbre of Mme. Charny's voice, which is a rich, strong mezzo-soprano of undeniably French origin. It lends adequate intensity of expression to Charlotte's sad reflections in the duet, *Va ! laisse couler mes larmes,* with her sister Sophie (Massenet's *Werther,* Act III), one of the more interesting pages of an opera that I have always found rather tedious. On the reverse side of the disc is the *Seguidille* from *Carmen,* also sung in French. In this there is more rhythm than animation.

Herbert Teale.—If the singing of big, exacting tenor music comprised nothing more than the employment of a loud, robust tone, then these two records would fulfil every requirement. They represent nothing beyond what any ordinary Yorkshire chorister, with orders to " start *f* and keep it up," could do with the utmost ease. Only the Yorkshire chorister would do something more. He would now and then sing *p,* make a *cres.* or *dim.* and even introduce an occasional *nuance.* This singer does not trouble himself about anything of that sort ; he simply keeps his noisiest stop out from beginning to end ; and it saves him a lot of trouble. As for his dialect—well, least said soonest mended. But are we really so badly off for decently-trained tenors ?

Lotte Lehmann and *Heinrich Schlusnus.*—Two delightful Mozart duets which, had they come to hand a month earlier would have been gladly welcomed to a place in my first article on the master's operas. We know them best, of course, by their Italian titles as *La ci darem* and *Crudel perchè ;* but for the Polydor they are respectively given (in German) as *Reich mir die Hand* and *So lang hab' ich geschmachtet.* This does not really affect their charm, because they are sung here with admirable refinement, grace, and sense of their dramatic significance. The voices blend well, too, and the diction of both singers is irreproachable. For the careful recording praise is due, and the accompaniments, when they are distinguishable, sound excellent.

Amelita Galli-Curci and *Tito Schipa.*—These duets from *La Traviata* should arouse curiosity. In style they are quite unconventional—nothing like the *Parigi o cara* or the *Un dì, felice* of tradition. I should call them studies in staccato ; few of the phrases are sustained " so that you could notice it," and the tone of both singers throughout is strangely " white " for such serious personages as are Violetta and Alfredo when meeting and parting in Verdi's opera. The good points are that the voices are always in tune and that, being produced here on the same model, they blend well.   HERMAN KLEIN.

OPERATIC

MICHAEL BOHNEN (baritone).—**Wotan's Abschied** and **Der Augen leuchtendes Paar** from **Walküre** (Wagner). Polydor 85277, 12in., 6s. 9d.

ROBERT BURG (baritone).—**Leb wohl du Kühnes herrliches Kind** and **Der Augen leuchtendes Paar** from **Walküre** (Wagner). Parlophone E.10409, 12in., 4s. 6d.

FRITZI JOKL (soprano).—**Mit starrem Angesicht** from Act I.,

Lasst ab mit Fragen from Act IV. of **Un Ballo in Maschera** (Verdi) and **Titania ist Herabgestiegen (I am Titania)** from **Mignon** (Thomas). Parlophone E.10410, 12in., 4s. 6d.

EMMY HECKMANN-BETTENDORF (soprano).—**Mein Herr, was dachten Sie von mir** and **Czardas** from **Die Fledermaus** (Johann Strauss). Parlophone E.10411, 12in., 4s. 6d.

LUELLA PAIKIN (soprano).—**Non so più cosa son, cosa faccio** from **Nozze di Figaro** (Mozart) and **Je veux vivre (Waltz Song)** from **Roméo et Juliette** (Gounod). Vocalion A.0251, 12in., 5s. 6d.

RICHARD MAYR (bass).—**Hier im ird'schen Jammertal** from **Freischütz** (Weber) and **Porterlied** from **Martha** (Flötow). Polydor 62389, 12in., 5s. 9d.

JENNY SONNENBERG (contralto).—**Il mio core** from **Orfeo ed Euridice** (Haydn) and **When I am laid in earth** from **Dido and Aeneas** (Purcell). Polydor 66083, 12in., 5s. 9d.

ARMAND TOKATYAN (tenor).—**Amor ti vieta di non amar** from **Fedora** (Giordano) and **Siciliana** from **Cavalleria Rusticana** (Mascagni). Vocalion B.3121, 10in., 4s.

KATHLEEN DESTOURNEL (soprano) and **FRANK TITTERTON** (tenor).—**Lovely maiden in the Moonlight** from **La Bohème** (Puccini). **DESTOURNEL** and **HARDY WILLIAMSON** (tenor): **Dear love of mine** from **Nadeshda** (Goring Thomas). Vocalion K.05213, 12in., 4s. 6d.

GÖTA LJUNGBERG (soprano).—**Dich teure Halle** from **Tannhäuser** (Wagner) and **Elsa's Gesang an die Lüfte** from **Lohengrin** (Wagner). H.M.V., D.A.724, 10in., 6s.

M. MURRAY-DAVEY (bass).—**Nonnes qui reposez** from **Robert le Diable** (Meyerbeer) and **Si la rigueur** from **La Juive** (Halévy). Vocalion A.0254, 12in., 5s. 6d.

ROY HENDERSON (baritone).—**Duet from Act II., Scene I,** of **Falstaff** (Verdi). Vocalion K.05205, 05206, 12in., 4s. 6d. each.

RICCARDO STRACCIARI (baritone).—**Su questi Rose** and **Canzone della Pulce** from **La Dannazione di Faust** (Berlioz). Columbia X.333, 10in., 6s.

HAROLD WILLIAMS (baritone).—**Prologue** from **Pagliacci** (Leoncavallo). Two parts. Columbia 3843, 10in., 3s.

MIRIAM LICETTE (soprano).—**Vissi d'Arte (Love and Music)** from **La Tosca** (Verdi) and **Elisabeth's Prayer** from **Tannhäuser** (Wagner). Columbia L.1706, 12in., 6s. 6d.

ULYSSES LAPPAS (tenor).—**My love, get married** and **Old Demos** (Greek folk songs). Columbia L.1703, 12in., 6s. 6d.

Michael Bohnen.—It is probable that the name of this distinguished German baritone will appear before long in the list of artists who sing at Covent Garden. In other words, it will be possible for us then to appraise his vocal qualifications in the flesh, which is even more reliable than through the medium of a gramophone record. Meanwhile, judging by the latter, it seems to me that he possesses an organ of exceptional beauty and that he is an extremely fine artist ; but, *nous verrons !* His latest Polydor record is Wotan's wonderful closing scene from *Die Walküre*, complete on two sides of the disc, and on the whole given with a better handling of the instrumentation than Berlin sends out as a rule. For sheer vocal artistry the *Abschied* is superior to the second part, *Der Augen leuchtendes Paar*, which is marred by excessive inclination to "scoop" and yet the conclusion reflects with admirable truth the paternal sentiment and poignant sorrow of the impotent god, as his farewell to Brünnhilde dies away into silence. The record is certainly well worth having.

Robert Burg.—Here is the same selection from an artist with a more powerful voice, who doubtless makes a telling if truculent Wotan in the theatre, but a more brutal one than Bohnen's in his scolding of the disobedient Valkyrie. Here, too, we perceive the characteristic Wagnerian training in accent and declamation, coming down on every syllable like a sledge-hammer. He relents somewhat towards the end, or maybe it is rather self-pity than a forgiving spirit that moves him. Anyhow, he expresses himself in a rich nasal tone that would travel miles and overcome any ordinary orchestra, more especially if the sounds of the latter were blurred, as they are in the present instance. Altogether, though, a typical Teutonic and authentic rendering.

Fritzi Jokl.—This young soprano appears to have succeeded her famous namesake, Fritzi Scheff, as the popular *soubrette* of grand opera. Here she is, to begin with, the Page of the *Ballo in Maschera*, and includes his two short airs on one side of the disc. Her staccato method and pretty tone suit them very well, while her enunciation is excellent. Miss Jokl is, however, somewhat overweighted in the *Titania* air from *Mignon* (reverse side), wherein there is a good deal of "blasting" and the voice lacks brilliancy. Her vocalisation has a curious Hungarian flavour and is not always remarkable for its accuracy. The shake is good and the cadenza effective, but on the whole I should not call it a satisfactory performance of the air.

Emmy Bettendorf.—Neither in the preceding examples nor in these two numbers from *Die Fledermaus* can it be said that the Parlophone recording shows off the singer to real advantage. The voices sound distinctly dull. I am familiar enough wit Emmy Bettendorf's work to know that she is a first-rate gramophone artist, and it is not her fault, I fancy, that these delightful excerpts from the masterpiece of the immortal Johann should not be of finer texture than they are. Otherwise the rendering of the *Mein Herr, was dachten Sie* is extremely spirited and that of the *Czardás* duly sentimental and lively by turns. In fact, they are sung as they ought to be sung.

Luella Paikin.—There is nothing distinctive in style or character about the treatment of these oddly-contrasted solos. In each one finds a faithful replica of the Tetrazzini method, but without either the impulse or the spontaneity of the older singer. The waltz-air from *Roméo et Juliette*, sung in French, is neatly phrased ; but the *Non so più* lacks rhythmical energy and suggests a rather doleful, lackadaisical Cherubino.

Richard Mayr.—The two most popular drinking-songs in German opera, sung by our talented friend the Baron Ochs von Lerchenau, of *Rosenkavalier* fame, ought to be a real attraction to his English admirers. The Baron in this case is that fine artist, Herr Richard Mayr, to whom evidently the Plunkett of *Martha* and the Caspar of *Freischütz* are long-standing associates. It is pleasant to hear the old melodies so splendidly sung.

Jenny Sonnenberg.—The foreign singer who would do justice to Purcell needs a command of the pure English style that is rarely heard nowadays. This one, a mezzo-soprano described as a contralto, has a pleasing voice and knows our language, but not the peculiar Purcell touch. For the rest, she takes *When I am laid in earth* too fast and imbues it with too little dignity of utterance. She is heard to much better advantage, even though her sympathetic tone is apt to tremble, in the air *Il* (not *Del*) *mio core*, from Haydn's opera, *Orfeo ed Euridice*, which was written in London and performed at the Haymarket Theatre in 1793, the score being taken away to Germany by the composer and never published here. It is a charming old aria, nevertheless, and writ Haydn all over.

Armand Tokatyan.—I like this tenor better in these pieces from *Fedora* and *Cavalleria* than I did in his previous attempts. His style is up-to-date Italian and, but for a vibrato, his bright, resonant voice would be as well worth hearing in opera as many another.

Kathleen Destournel, Hardy Williamson, Frank Titterton.—The duet from the last act of Goring Thomas's beautiful opera, *Nadeshda*, is smoothly sung, with the usual cut, for it is very long. That from the first act of *La Bohème* (reverse side) is also an adequate and agreeable bit of work.

Göta Ljungberg.—Creditable vocal examples of the most familiar soprano pieces in *Lohengrin* and *Tannhäuser*, but by no means perfectly accompanied.

Murray-Davey.—This well-known bass has done good work for the Vocalion by adding to their repertory two worthy examples of Meyerbeer and Halévy—the evocation of the nuns in *Robert le Diable*, and the famous air for the Cardinal from *La Juive*. Both are capitally sung in French, and the vibrant basso *timbre*, if a trifle monotonous in colour, is admirably suited to the music.

Roy Henderson.—An ambitous *tour de force* is embodied here, in an endeavour to reproduce (on two 12in. discs) by a single voice, with orchestral accompaniment, the long duet between Falstaff and Ford from the second act of Verdi's ultimate opera. The effect of it is to make manifest that Mr. Henderson might prove an excellent representative of either personage, but that he cannot, on the gramophone, satisfactorily delineate both. His declamation is improving, so is his diction ; and he employs his fine voice without stint everywhere during the lengthy scene, which, I may add, is divided into four parts and sung in English. But neither sense of character nor the most intelligent changes of manner can enable the singer to depict for us the separate and distinct personalities that are required here. They sound too much like the same man ; nor can Ford's frequent Mephistophelean laugh persuade us—and it is very frequent—that he is not himself another Falstaff in disguise.

Riccardo Stracciari.—Of the Columbia novelties for the month which follow, this is by far the most interesting. Berlioz' *Damnation de Faust* is now in the regular operatic repertory in Italy and America ; hence these splendid records of two of Mephistopheles' solos, one from the chorus of sylphs whilst Faust lies sleeping, the other the *Song of the Flea.* Both are sung in Italian, the former in the languid manner dictated by the music, the latter with equally fitting alertness and spirit. Voice and orchestra alike come out perfectly.

Harold Williams.—A capital English rendering of the sempiternal *Prologue to Pagliacci*, with dark vowels but clear articulation and a broad, genial tone. The feeling is sincere, while passion is expressed in huge sweeps of *portamento*.

Miriam Licette.—Lovers of *Elizabeth's Prayer* and *Vissi d'Arte* who do not object to a little *vibrato* occasionally, will enjoy Mme. Licette's artistic rendering of both. She always sings sweetly, though one wishes that her English consonants came out more strongly.

Ulysses Lappas.—Greek folk-songs given in the original tongue by a popular Greek tenor. Excellent combination, truly. The tunes in minor mood and the language have a curiously Russian twang, and sound quite modern ; still, they are all Greek to me ! That " augmented " high note ending each stanza of *Old Demos* has an extraordinary effect, and Lappas sings it superbly. *My love, get married !* is a strange lament, more redolent of misery than joy.

HERMAN KLEIN.

OPERATIC

TH. I. CHALIAPINE (bass) and **FLORENCE AUSTRAL** (soprano), with Symphony Orchestra and chorus, conducted by Albert Coates.—**Seigneur, daignes permettre** and **Quand du Seigneur le jour luira,** the Church Scene from **Faust** (Gounod). H.M.V., D.B.899, 12in., 8s. 6d.

ROSA PONSELLE (soprano).—**Suicidio** from **La Gioconda** (Ponchielli) and **O Patria mia** from **Aïda** (Verdi). H.M.V., D.B.854, 12in., 8s. 6d.

BENIAMINO GIGLI (tenor).—**Tombe degl' avi miei** and **Tu che a Dio spiegasti** from **Lucia di Lammermoor** (Donizetti). H.M.V., D.B.870, 8s. 6d.

RICCARDO STRACCIARI (baritone).—**Vien Leonora** and **A tanto amor** from **La Favorita** (Donizetti). Col. X.334, 10in., 6s.

WILLIAM HESELTINE (tenor).—**On with the Motley** and **No, Pagliacci, no more** from **Pagliacci** (Leoncavallo). In English. Col. 3873, 10in., 3s.

OTTO WOLF (tenor).—**Siegfried's Tod** from **Götterdämmerung** and **Waldweben** from **Siegfried** (Wagner). Polydor 65696, 12in., 5s. 9d.

CLAIRE DUX (soprano) and **JOSEPH SCHWARZ** (baritone).—**Befreit, o welche Seligkeit** from **Trovatore** (Verdi), and **CLAIRE DUX : Musetta's Waltz** from **La Bohème** (Puccini). Polydor 70691, 12in., 5s.

LOTTE LEHMANN (soprano).—**Ohne Mutter bist du Kind gestorben** and **O Blumen, di ihr Gift im Ketch** from **Schwester Angelica** (Puccini). Polydor 72900, 12in., 6s. 9d.

EMMY HECKMANN-BETTENDORF (soprano).—**Ein Schönes war** and **Mit seinem Stab regiert er die Seelen** from **Ariadne in Naxos** (R. Strauss). Parlo. E.10421, 12in., 4s. 6d.

ROBERT BURG (baritone).—**Abendlich strahlt der Sonne Auge** from **Rheingold** and **Als du in kühnem Sange** from **Tannhäuser** (Wagner). Parlo. E.10422, 12in., 4s. 6d.

MIRIAM LICETTE, MURIEL BRUNSKILL, FRANK MULLINGS, KINGSLEY LARK, THORPE BATES, and GRAND OPERA CHORUS, with orchestra conducted by Sir Hamilton Harty : **King's Prayer** and **Finale, Act 1,** from **Lohengrin** (Wagner). In English. Col. L.1714, 12in., 6s. 6d.

Th. I. Chaliapine and Florence Austral.—The Church Scene from Gounod's *Faust*, sung by these artists and conducted by Albert Coates, is more interesting for the personality of its interpreters than for the interpretation itself. The idea was, I suppose, to allot the familiar strains to two big voices and a very full orchestra. The result is rather disappointing. The singers sound too distant and small in relation to the heavy band and chorus, and the effect of " atmosphere " is destroyed by the crowding and confusion of sounds in a limited space. It would have been better, I think, to let the organ do its customary work instead of relegating it to so many instruments. This may be Chaliapine's voice (frequently sharp, too), but it is not his commanding Mephistopheles ; while Miss Austral's French is inaudible and her voice has grown unexpectedly thin.

Rosa Ponselle.—This soprano has a voice which records perfectly, and, being an accomplished lyric artist, her work on the whole gives unalloyed satisfaction. Hers is essentially a dramatic style, and she has the rare ability to express temperamentally through the medium of the gramophone. This *Suicidio !* is the best that has yet appeared—full of effective contrasts, from a delicate *mezza voce* to a rich *plena voce*. On the reverse side, and very nearly if not quite as admirable, is her *O patria mia* from *Aïda*, better known, perhaps, as *O cieli azzuri*. Both are finely recorded.

Beniamino Gigli.—Quite a modern Edgardo is an interesting phenomenon, but somehow he reminds me of the new-fangled notion of dressing up the old operas in twentieth century costumes. Gigli has a glorious voice, unquestionably, but his methods sound just a shade too up-to-date Italian for the pure Donizetti school of the graveyard scene from *Lucia*. Still, significant declamation, stirring energy, and a trumpet tone on the high notes count for a good deal in things like the immortal *Tu che a Dio*, even though the timbre be a trifle nasal. In the *Tombe degl' avi miei* (really *Fra poco mi ricoverò*) the orchestration is capitally done. But why this new idea of disguising well-known arias under the title of the recitatives ?

Riccardo Stracciari.—Here is a singer who does not put old wine into new bottles. He gives you Donizetti exactly as the Swan of Bergamo intended that he should be given. No Puccini or Mascagni or Leoncavallo in the wrong places. In the present instance I find the two lovely airs for the King in *La Favorita* sung with delicacy, reserve, and just the right measure of suppressed passion. The voice is suave and the phrasing done with a pure legato, even when one or two superfluous ornamentations are introduced.

William Heseltine.—Here at least we have the square peg in the square, not the round hole. The rage and jealousy of Canio, no less than Leoncavallo's music, justly calls for all the strenuous utterance that the land of Mussolini seems to be capable of. And behold, here it is cleverly simulated by a modest, retiring Englishman, both outbursts complete on an economical 10in. disc. Well, he has a good, powerful voice and plenty of robust vigour ; and, after all, it is chiefly a question of these attributes.

Otto Wolf.—I know no harder task for a typical Wagnerian tenor than to have to deliver the whole of Siegfried's long and elaborate narrative in the last act of *Götterdämmerung* into the mouth of a recording horn. This singer was not equal to it in the degree that others might have been, because plastic vocalisation and the delineation of subtle shades of feeling are not in his line. His voice is hard, and from the moment at the start when he imitates Mime, it seems to suggest Mime all through rather than Siegfried. Still, the " Forest murmurs " are there, and very well the orchestra murmurs them too.

Claire Dux and Joseph Schwarz.—The *Trovatore* duet is well sung by both artists. It will be welcomed by gramophonists who do not mind the German text in Italian operas, and a similar remark applies to Claire Dux's neat rendering of the Musetta air from *La Bohème*, though the half-serious sentiment with which she invests it is not really appropriate to an exhibition of Parisian coquetry.

Lotte Lehmann.—Another eminent soprano giving us Puccini in her native tongue ! Nevertheless, I am fain to admit that *Suor Angelica* would be tiresome in any language. In the trilogy it comes between *Il Tabarro* and *Gianni Schicchi*, and is equal to neither. I regard this as Lotte Lehmann's memorial tribute to the composer rather than to *Suor Angelica*. Poor sad, dreary creature !

Emmy Bettendorf.—Two long-drawn melodies from Richard Strauss's *Ariadne in Naxos*, both beautifully sung and excellently accompanied. One of them, *Ein schönes war*, recalls at moments *Der Rosenkavalier*—tender, sweet, and sympathetic, and delivered with impeccable breath-control.

Robert Burg.—I described this singer last month. In his latest records he is somewhat rough for Wolfram and too Alberich-like for Wotan, but he declaims distinctly.

Columbia Operatic Ensemble.—The *Prayer* and the *Finale* from Act I. of *Lohengrin*, filling each side of a large disc, form a substantial test of the holding capacity of the modern phonograph for an extensive " concourse of sweet sounds." The result in this instance is, on the whole, vastly creditable, and even more so in the case of the *Finale* than that of the *Prayer*. In the latter the soloists are so close and loud that they virtually obliterate the orchestra and chorus. One feels that they might have evinced a little more discretion and reticence without danger to their deservedly high reputations. The error of judgment only occurs where all the voices unite to " do their darndest," as the Americans say, and then it is rather suggestive of Babel. But Mr. Thorpe Bates enunciates the *Prayer* solo with fitting dignity ; and both Mr. Frank Mullings and Miss Miriam Licette celebrate Lohengrin's victory over Tetramund with the right ring of jubilation.

HERMAN KLEIN.

OPERATIC

ENID CRUICKSHANK (contralto).—**The years roll by, no comfort bringing (Recit. et Aria de Lia)** from **L'Enfant Prodigue** (Debussy), and **Card Song** from **Carmen** (Bizet). Voc. K.05221, 12in. (4s. 6d.).

LUIGI CILLA (tenor).—**Addio Mignon** from **Mignon** (Thomas), and **Romanza** from **La Favorita** (Donizetti). Imperial 1565, 10in., 2s.

LUIGI CILLA (tenor).—**Romanza** from **Mignon** (Thomas), and **Questa o Quella** from **Rigoletto** (Verdi). Imperial 1564, 10in., 2s.

MAARTJE OFFERS (contralto).—**Erbarme dich mein Gott** from **Matthäus Passion** (Bach). H.M.V., D.B.907, 12in., 8s. 6d.

ELISE VON CATOPOL (soprano), **ELSE KNEPEL** (soprano), and **GRETE MANCKE** (contralto).—**Weiha, Waga, Woge,** and **Lugt Schwestern** from **Rheingold** (Wagner). Parlo. E.10432, 12in., 4s. 6d.

EMMY BETTENDORF (soprano).—**Ma dall'arido stelo, Act 2,** and **Morrò, ma prima in grazia, Act 3, Un Ballo in Maschera** (Verdi). Parlo. E.10431, 12in., 4s. 6d.

ELDA DI VEROLI (soprano).—**Ardon gl'incensi (Mad Scene)** from **Lucia di Lammermoor** (Donizetti), and **Dov'è l'Indiana bruna (Bell Song)** from **Lakmé** (Delibes). Duo. G.S.7002, 12in., 5s. 6d.

ELDA DI VEROLI (soprano).—**Ombra leggera** from **Dinorah** (Meyerbeer), and **Quì la voce** from **Puritani** (Bellini). Duo. G.S.7001, 12in., 5s. 6d.

IFOR THOMAS (tenor).—**Vesti la giubba** from **Pagliacci** (Leoncavallo), and **Che gelida manina** from **La Bohème** (Puccini). Duo. G.S.7003, 12in., 5s. 6d.

GERTRUDE KAPPEL (soprano).—**Brünhildes Schlussgesang** from **Götterdämmerung** (Wagner). Polydor 66099, 12in., 5s. 9d.

MARIA OLCZEWSKA (contralto).—**Höre mit Sinn** and **So sitzt er** from **Götterdämmerung** (Wagner). Polydor 72982, 12in., 6s. 9d.

SELMA KURZ (soprano).—**Caro Nome** from **Rigoletto** (Verdi), and **Addio** from **La Traviata** (Verdi). Polydor 72845, 12in., 6s. 9d.

ALICE RAVEAU (contralto).—**Habañera** from **Carmen** (Bizet), and **Handel's Largo**. Actuelle 15218, 12in., 6s.

RICCARDO STRACCIARI (baritone).—**Te Deum** from **La Tosca,** and **O tu bell'astro** from **Tannhäuser** (Wagner). Col. 7372, 8s. 6d.

L. BORI (soprano) and **T. SCHIPA** (tenor).—**Death Scene** from **La Bohème** (Puccini). Two parts, **Sono andati** and **O Dio, Mimi.** H.M.V., D.B.911, 12in., 8s. 6d.

HEBDEN FOSTER (baritone).—**Even bravest heart** from **Faust** (Gounod), and **Song of the flea** (Moussorgsky). Beltona 6039, 10in., 3s.

Enid Cruickshank.—A deservedly popular singer, whose excellent work at the Old Vic. and with the Carl Rosa Company has long been recognised, here gives us in English a couple of familiar extracts. The voice sounds best in the *Card Scene* from *Carmen*, where she is, of course, quite at home ; but even there Miss Cruickshank shows little sign of overcoming the tremolo which is her only serious defect. Apart from that the records deserve all praise.

Luigi Cilla.—Here are two discs at the very reasonable figure of 2s. each, that may be listened to with a certain amount of pleasure. In one *Wilhelm Meister's farewell to Mignon* is associated with the *Romanza* from the first act of *La Favorita* ; in the other the air from the last act of *Mignon* with the lively *Questa o quella* from *Rigoletto.* Signor Cilla has a pleasant voice and sings without effort. He may not be among the great tenors, but he is also not among the expensive ones. The text, of course, is Italian.

Maartje Offers.—One is glad to welcome so notable an addition to the repertory as the beautiful contralto air from the *St. Matthew Passion*, sung in German by a capable artist. To be ideal, Bach's wonderful music demands more repose and a steadier voice, while the violin obbligato, well played by Isolde Menges, is at times too loud. Still, the style in both cases is traditionally correct and pure, which is saying a great deal, and the recording on both sides of the disc leaves nothing to be desired.

Elise von Catopol, Else Knepel, and Grete Mancke.—The tuneful music of the three Rhine-daughters is far from being so easy as these ladies make it sound. They are obviously in the habit of singing it together whilst floating gracefully beneath the sunlit waters—a feat that Wagner's imagination could alone have conjured up. Flosshilde is a trifle shaky, but the Woglinde and Wellgunde are both excellent, and all three are well in tune and rhythmical. The orchestration, too, receives careful attention, though the lower strings are weak. Thanks to numerous cuts and the complete elimination of Alberich (whom nobody misses), the two sides of the disc furnish pretty nearly all that one wants to hear of the opening scene from *Rheingold*.

Emmy Bettendorf.—The unlucky heroine of Verdi's *Un Ballo in Maschera* has two beautiful airs allotted to her, one in the second and the other in the third—not the fourth—act of the opera. I can hardly conceive a more tender and expressive rendering than they are here vouchsafed by Emmy Bettendorf. Her sweet legato phrasing, the musical quality of her tone, and her flawless intonation lend the utmost charm to singing replete with all the requisite touches of pathos, passion, and remorse. Both pieces are well accompanied.

Elda di Veroli.—The soprano who is responsible for these additions to the Duophone catalogue possesses a pretty and well-trained voice, more remarkable, perhaps, for a neat, facile technique than variety of colour or positive brilliancy of style. What she does, however, is done without effort and satisfies the ear, and that much, in hackneyed pieces that have been recorded by the world's most famous singers, amounts to a very creditable achievement. I note more especially admirable breath control, a first-rate staccato, and nice crisp scale passages. The *Bell Song* from *Lakmé* and the *Shadow Song* from *Dinorah* are the best of the group.

Ifor Thomas.—Tenors are at liberty to imitate the modern Italian method as much as they please so long as they avoid the *vibrato*. Apart from this blemish, the reproductions of *Vesti la giubba* and *Che gelida manina* on this disc will be found quite up to the average in every respect.

Gertrude Kappel.—There can be no need to tell frequenters of recent *Ring* cycles at Covent Garden how splendidly the part of Brünnhilde is portrayed by this gifted artist. She compares it with more than one of the great sopranos who won encomiums from Wagner himself, in virtue not only of fine acting but breadth and nobility of conception and magnificent declamation. Such are the qualities (it is a pleasure to be able to say it) reflected to a great extent in these new records (one disc, two parts) of the sublime closing scene from *Götterdämmerung*. Happily, moreover, the combination of voice and instruments is skilfully accomplished, the latter being sufficiently yet not too much in evidence. A capable conductor is obviously at work in this, and the general effect impressively realises the heroic grandeur of the final climax.

Maria Olczewska.—Almost identical with the words just written must be my criticism of the earlier scene from *Götterdämmerung*, wherein Waltraute, one of the Valkyries, visits Brünnhilde and implores her to give up the ring. This fine episode, wherein Waltraute describes the decay of the gods in Valhalla and the doom and despair of their father, Wotan, is, perhaps, the most pathetic in the whole of the tetralogy. Mme. Olczewska, with her superb voice, declaims it superbly and invests it with extraordinary interest and significance.

Selma Kurz.—This clever singer is more at home in *Caro nome* than the touching passage in the *Traviata*, where the dying Violetta bids farewell to her stormy past. Still, we owe her thanks for recording the *Addio*—a really beautiful bit of Verdi, in which the famous composer declared that Patti used invariably to make him weep. Selma Kurz certainly puts a tinge of tender melancholy into it.

Alice Raveau.—Quite a contrast, again, the two sides of this Pathé disc ! Yet the same agreeable contralto sounds equally well in the *Habañera* from *Carmen* and Handel's *Largo* ; and saying that is equivalent to a high compliment. It sounds rather odd to hear the *Largo* sung in French, but after all why not ? Altogether the record is an interesting one.

Riccardo Stracciari.—Fine tone and plenty of it characterises the finale to the first act of *Tosca*—bells, orchestra, all complete, but without chorus, which really does not matter. Less negligible, though, is the faintness of the accompaniment to the *Tannhäuser* extract. At times it cannot be heard at all. Fortunately, the soloist does not seem to mind. He goes on comfortably without apparent support and with all imaginable suavity and opulence of tone.

L. Bori and *T. Schipa.*—A complete and absolutely adequate vocal representation of the scene of Mimi's death. What little there is for the tenor to do is capitally done ; but the honours on both sides of the disc are unquestionably carried off by La Bori, who, being a first-rate artist and an Italian to her finger-tips, knows how to make the most of every bar of Puccini's music.

Hebden Foster.—I find much more artistic merit, alike as regards singing and characterisation, in the performance of Moussorgsky's song *The Flea* than in that of Valentine's air from *Faust*. The sardonic humour of the Russian ditty is quite cleverly conveyed, and on that account, therefore, I warmly recommend this 10 in. record.

HERMAN KLEIN.

OPERATIC

PETER DAWSON (bass-baritone).—**Prologue, Parts 1 and 2, Pagliacci** (Leoncavallo). H.M.V., C.1259, 12in., 4s. 6d.

RICHARD MAYR (bass).—**Höre du alter Mantel** from **Bohème** (Puccini) and **So schwärmet Jugend** from **Barbier von Bagdad** (Cornelius). Polydor 62391, 10in., 4s. 6d.

JOSEPH SCHWARTZ (baritone).—**Blick' ich umher** and **Lied an den Abenstern** from **Tannhäuser** (Wagner). Polydor 72674, 12in., 6s. 9d.

ALFRED JERGER (bass) and **EMMY BETTENDORF** (soprano).—**Guten Abend** and **Hat einst ein Weib** from **Die Meistersinger** (Wagner). Parlo. E.10443, 12in., 4s. 6d.

LAURITZ MELCHIOR (tenor).—**Das der mein Vater nicht ist** and **Du holdes Vöglein** from **Siegfried** (Wagner). Parlo. E.10442, 12in., 4s. 6d.

EMMY BETTENDORF (soprano)—**Habañera** and **Card Scene** from **Carmen** (Bizet). Parlo. E.10441, 12in., 4s. 6d.

JOHN PERRY (tenor).—**The Prize Song** from **Die Meistersinger** (Wagner) and **Your tiny hand is frozen** from **Bohème** (Puccini). V.F. 531, 12in., 4s.

TATIANA MAKUSHINA (soprano).—**Elizabeth's Prayer** from **Tannhäuser** and **Isolde's Liebestod** from **Tristan und Isolde** (Wagner). V.F.630, 12in., 4s.

LUELLA PAIKIN (soprano).—**Voi che sapete** from **Figaro** (Mozart) and **Ah ! lo so** from **The Magic Flute** (Mozart). Voc. A.0263, 12in., 5s. 6d.

CLARA SERENA (contralto).—**O don fatale** from **Don Carlos** (Verdi) and **Voce di donna o d'angelo** and **La Gioconda** (Ponchielli). Voc. K.05227, 12in., 4s. 6d.

MAARTJE OFFERS (contralto).—**Mon coeur s'ouvre à ta voix** and **Amour, viens aider** from **Samson et Dalila** (Saint-Saëns). H.M.V., D.B.912, 12in., 8s. 6d.

BIANCA SCACCIATI (soprano).—**Voi lo sapete** from **Cavalleria Rusticana** (Mascagni) and **Vissi d'arte** from **La Tosca** (Puccini). Col. D.1542., 10in., 4s. 6d.

Tacea la notte placida and **D'Amor sull'ali rosee** from **Trovatore** (Verdi). Col. D.1543, 10in., 4s. 6d.

FRANCESCO MERLI (tenor).—**Dai campi dai prati** and **Giunto sul passo estremo** from **Mefistofele** (Boito). Col. D.1545, 10in., 4s. 6d.

Celeste Aïda from **Aïda** (Verdi) and **Cielo e mar** from **La Gioconda** (Ponchielli). Col. D.1546, 10in., 4s. 6d.

FRANK MULLINGS (tenor) and **NORMAN ALLIN** (bass).—**Love and War** and **Gendarmes' Duet** from **Geneviève de Brabant**. Col. L.1735, 12in., 6s. 6d.

Peter Dawson.—An earlier record of the *Prologue* to *Pagliacci* by this singer was reviewed by me in an article on Leoncavallo's opera which appeared in September, 1924. The present one, which takes its place, corrects what few defects I then pointed out ; it also embodies a far superior example of up-to-date recording, the vocal tone being marvellously close to nature, while the distinctive qualities of the instruments in the accompaniment come out with similar truthfulness. I will not say that Mr. Dawson has sung the *Prologue* better than before, for he sang it very well then, nor do I think he could materially improve upon his reading of it. I still feel, however, that he might assimilate his vowel tones a little more neatly and that he need not sound every final " y " as though it were written " ee "—i.e., " storee," " mem'ree,'' etc.

Richard Mayr.—The popular German bass whom we know best as the Baron Ochs of *Der Rosenkavalier* (the opera, not the film), will be displaying his versatility in more than one part during the coming season at Covent Garden. For the Polydor he has recently sung on a 10in. disc a couple of excerpts that form an excellent contrast—one the touching farewell which Colline addresses to the beloved garment that he is about to pawn ; the other, a clever air concerning love from Cornelius's opera, *The Barber of Bagdad.* The latter, being genuinely comic, with its constant repetition of the word " Liebe " on the lower bass octave, furnishes, as I say, an effective contrast to the pathetic page of Puccini, while both are quite admirably interpreted.

Joseph Schwartz.—Here we have Wolfram's familiar airs from *Tannhäuser,* sung in German and in the traditional Teutonic fashion by the experienced baritone who was giving recitals in London not very long ago. He has a fine voice, is a thorough master of Wagnerian methods, and succeeds, especially in the upper register, in imparting considerable grace and vibrant timbre to the melody of the *Star of Eve*. The harp is prominent, of course, but on the whole, the orchestral accompaniment sounds rather thin ; nor can I speak very highly of the recording, which sounds to me blurred and frequently unsteady.

Alfred Jerger and *Emmy Bettendorf.*—All lovers of the scene between Hans Sachs and Ev'chen in the second act of *Die Meistersinger*—one of the most remarkable for its fine imaginative feeling and subtlety in the whole opera—will be ready to welcome so artistic a rendering as the one here presented. There is no blending of voices in this duet ; it is merely a conversation full of smart repartee set to snatches of gracious melody with a background of suggestive orchestral motives. The latter, unfortunately, is not on a level with the smoothness and adequacy of the singing. Nevertheless, it is not poor enough to offend, and the ear finds sufficient to enjoy in the two voices, which are just perfectly fitted for what they have to do. Not a note is cut, yet the two sides of the large disc suffice to take in the whole duet.

Lauritz Melchior.—This capable tenor sang Siegmund in the second cycle of the *Ring* at Covent Garden two years ago, and he will again be doing one of the great Wagner rôles this month. His latest Parlophone record indicates that he will probably show himself to be an exceptionally good Siegfried. The colloquy with the Waldvogel embodies some very difficult music for the singer and demands some marked varieties of style. Melchior meets every requirement with the alertness and spirit of an artist who knows every point there is to be made. His *Sprechgesang* may at times be a trifle rough and jerky, but this is evidently intentional, for his voice can be sweet and musical enough when he likes, as, for instance, in the beautiful passage, " Wie sah meine Mutter wohl aus," which is sung with exquisitely tender feeling. The violins execute the flowing " forest murmurs " tolerably well, but the instrumentation as a whole does not come out so clearly and neatly as it ought.

Emmy Bettendorf.—The *Habañera* from *Carmen* lies rather low for this gifted soprano and she takes it at a slower tempo than Bizet intended, besides making it too serious, without *insouciance* or a touch of hidden devilry. The *Card Scene* suits her better ; there she keeps her tone delightfully steady and assumes with it the right dramatic and significant character. Altogether, the record is interesting, and one accepts the German text without question, because the artist pronounces it so musically.

John Perry.—A bright penetrating tone of true tenor quality, a free, manly style, and a natural feeling for rhythm impart a welcome liveliness to the singing of this artist. But in the use of his breath-pressure he is more powerful than discriminating, and it prevents his obtaining effects of colour or contrast. He must acquire refinement both in his singing and his diction—especially the latter. It is not " refaned " to put the accent on the last syllable in " mo*ment* " or in " mai*den*," or even in " frozen." Otherwise her " tinee hand " is quite acceptable.

Tatiana Makushina.—The delivery of *Elizabeth's Prayer* requires more repose, greater steadiness of vocal line, than I find here. In *Isolde's Liebestod* the vocalist, thanks to her clever declamation and careful phrasing, gets away, so to speak, with her main defect little noticed. She sings both pieces in German, and, on the whole, quite artistically. These V.F. records are well made, but the orchestra should stand out more clearly.

Luella Paikin.—It is given to few artists, however gifted, to sing Mozart really well, be it on the stage, the concert platform, or the gramophone ; and of these three perhaps the most difficult is the gramophone. Without being too critical, therefore, I may fairly remind Miss Paikin that it does not do to sing *Voi che sapete* with a *voix blanche* or *Ah ! lo so* with a timbre of haunting misery that induces persistent flatness. Both defects are due in a measure to her faulty attack and feeble adjustment in the medium register. The head notes suffer less and are of a pretty quality, though surely it ought not to be necessary to take so many breaths.

Clara Serena.—Here is a mezzo-contralto with a fine voice who makes too little use of her chest tone and of the muscles that regulate breath-control. The medium is pushed down too far ; which is nearly as bad as taking the chest quality too high. On the other hand, Miss Serena infuses a good deal of dramatic energy into her style and evidently knows her Verdi and Ponchielli airs well. But with such a pretty Italian name, it is not a little strange that her Italian vowels should be so redolent of Cockaigne ! The recording in each case is excellent.

Maartje Offers.—The only serious fault in these two familiar excerpts from *Samson et Dalila* is that apparent paradox, a steady *tremolo*. Frankly, it detracts appreciably from the charm of a sympathetic voice (lovely low notes) and capital singing. One also misses in *Amour, viens aider*, the sense of gloating assurance that should characterise Dalila's appeal to her love-god. It sounds too agitated and anxious. Yet the singer's style is unimpeachable, and her enunciation is that of a well-trained, intelligent artist. The difficult accompaniment to *Mon cœur s'ouvre* is well played, while the record itself is generally beyond reproach.

Bianca Scacciati.—This name is, I think, new here. It belongs to a typical Italian soprano of the modern school—voice inclined to be pinched and tremulous whenever vigour and pressure are employed. Evidently Signora Scacciati is intelligent, and it is a pity her tone is not so musical as she seems to be herself. At the same time one also feels that her readings of the hackneyed *Trovatore* airs are not quite in accordance with tradition ; the tempi are dragged, the pauses too lengthy. The best of the four efforts is the *romanza* from *Cavalleria*.

Francesco Merli.—A robust tenor of undoubted merit ; has a splendid voice, with only a slight occasional vibrato, and phrases with dignity as well as dramatic sentiment. His scale mounts evenly and comfortably to the B flat which he requires in both the airs from *Aïda* and *Gioconda*, and he is always in tune. The examples from *Mefistofele*, quite in another vein, are equally to be commended, though the *Dai campi* is rather too declamatory and forceful for a peaceful Faust at Eastertide.

Frank Mullings and *Norman Allin.*—Making this disc must have been great fun. Fancy the opportunities for sheer caricature in these old duets ! Well, neither singer has lost a chance anywhere, and the result is distinctly amusing.

HERMAN KLEIN.

OPERATIC

TH. I. CHALIAPIN (bass) with Symphony Orchestra and Chorus, conducted by Albert Coates.—**Coronation Scene** from **Boris Godounov** (Moussorgsky). H.M.V., D.B.900, 12in., 8s. 6d. (See also Orchestral reviews.)

MARCEL JOURNET (bass).—**Devant la maison** from **La Damnation de Faust** (Berlioz) and **Quand la flamme de l'amour** from **La Jolie Fille de Perth** (Bizet). H.M.V., D.A.759, 10in., 6s.

IFOR THOMAS (tenor).—**La Donna è Mobile** from **Rigoletto** (Verdi) and **E lucevan le stelle** from **La Tosca** (Puccini). Duo. G.S.9001, 10in., 3s. 6d.

ELDA DI VEROLI (soprano).—**Air and Variations** (Proch) and **Caro nome** from **Rigoletto** (Verdi). Duo. G.S.7007, 12in., 5s. 6d.

OLIVE JENKIN (soprano).—**In quelle trine morbide** from **Manon Lescaut** (Puccini) and **Voi che sapete** from **Figaro** (Mozart). Duo. B.5145, 10in., 2s. 6d.

H.M.V. Chorus and Orchestra.—An interesting addition to the group of selections from *Boris Godounov* is furnished by this *Revolutionary Scene*, sung in English by a chorus that evidently knew the whole thing by heart. Only so could it have been dashed off, so to speak, with the abundant life, vigour, and *élan* of a stage performance. The attack is excellent, the brief passages reflecting the changing moods of the Russian crowd are capitally contrasted. The scene fills both sides of the disc, and in part 2 there are some solo bits interspersed with the choruses, in which the " local colour " is rather well imitated. The recording, too, is admirable.

Marcel Journet.—On this 10in. disc the distinguished French basso reproduces a couple of his less hackneyed *morceaux*. One is the serenade of Mephistopheles from Berlioz's *Damnation de Faust*, and I like it exceedingly, though not better, perhaps, than de Gogorza's. The curious rhythm of the air and the bizarre imitation of a guitar accompaniment—just such a one as the devil would play !—are effectively combined. The sardonic character of this contrasts well with the swaying, semi-inebriated manner of the serenader in Bizet's early opera *La Jolie Fille de Perth*. To the latter Marcel Journet imparts a richer tone, however, as well as a delightful serio-comic humour that will hardly escape the attentive listener. Altogether, the record possesses unusual characteristics and is well worth having.

Ifor Thomas.—It is well to hear a good Welsh tenor singing popular Italian solos with a fairly correct accent and plenty of volume. It is a pity therefore that this artist does not maintain an invariably steady tone, as he shows at times that he can—for instance, in the later *cantabile* phrases of *Lucevan le stelle* and the higher passages of *La donna è mobile*. He must be careful not to tolerate, much less cultivate, an objectionable vibrato. But for the latter I should prefer his Puccini to his Verdi, which needs more lightness and a crisper diction. The orchestral accompaniments are quite creditable.

Elda di Veroli.—These are also welcome additions to the Duophone repertory, not by any means because they are unfamiliar, but because they are both excellent examples of brilliant and pleasing florid singing. The voice is a bright, pure soprano of extended compass, and the execution of the fioriture, especially in the Proch *Variations*, is notably clean and facile.

Olive Jenkin.—Much is expected from this singer, who is the possessor of a very sympathetic and musical organ. To realize her ambitions completely she will have to devote herself to further study, particularly if she wishes to sing Mozart and in Italian, which she has so far encompassed only with the aid of English (or is it American ?) vowels. Possibly she has not yet had much experience at recording, and will achieve better results in the near future.

HERMAN KLEIN.

OPERATIC

ELSA ALSEN (soprano).—**Isoldes Liebestod** from **Tristan and Isolde** (Wagner). Parlo. E. 10453, 12in., 4s. 6d.

ALFRED JERGER (bass).—**Wahn ! Wahn !** and **Doch eines Abends spät** from Act 3 of **Die Meistersinger** (Wagner). Parlo. E.10463, 12in., 4s. 6d.

MAX HIRZEL (tenor).—**Prize Song** from **Die Meistersinger**

(Wagner), and **Cavatina** from **Faust** (Gounod). Parlo. E.10462, 12in. 4s. 6d.

AMELITA GALLI-CURCI (soprano).—**Ai vostri giuochi** and **Ed ora a voi canterò una canzone,** the Mad Scene from **Hamlet** (Thomas), in Italian. H.M.V., D.B.927, 12in., 8s. 6d.

MARCEL JOURNET (bass).—**La calunnia è un Venticello** from **Il Barbiere di Siviglia** (Rossini), in Italian, and **Vous qui faites l'endormie** from **Faust** (Gounod), in French. H.M.V. D.B.921, 12in., 8s. 6d.

JOHN CHARLES THOMAS (baritone).—**Vision fugitive** from **Hérodiade** (Massenet) and **Eri tu che macchiavi** from **Ballo in Maschera** (Verdi). Brunswick 50071, 12in., 8s.

SELMA KURZ (soprano).—**Ah non credea mirarti** and **Rondo finale** from **La Sonnambula** (Bellini). Polydor 72953, 12in., 6s. 9d.

FRIDA LEIDER (soprano).—**In deines Kerkers tiefe Nacht** and **Es glänzte schon das Sternenheer** from **Il Trovatore** (Verdi). Polydor 72975, 12in., 6s. 9d. In German.

UMBERTO URBANO (baritone).—**Ora per me fatale** from **Il Trovatore** (Verdi) and **Buona Zaza del mio buon tempo, Romanza,** from **Zazà** (Leoncavallo). Polydor 70708, 10in., 5s.

Elsa Alsen.—Novel themes seem as difficult to discover as new ideas. It is to the treatment rather than the subject-matter that the patient reviewer must look, if he would find anything interesting to talk about in this month's issue of discs fresh from the matrix. Parlophone seems to have been busy adding to its Wagnerian collection and incidentally making a genuine effort to improve its orchestral accompaniments. It has certainly succeeded in doing this for Fr. Alsen's smooth performance of *Isolde's Liebestod,* and, being executed in two parts, it does not suffer from undue haste as so many do. The recording seems to me extremely good and does justice to a really excellent interpretation of the great final scene from *Tristan.*

Alfred Jerger.—Here, in the *Wahn, wahn !* I am not equally sure that the tranquil beauty of the deep string passages are equally well realised ; they sound thin and poor in quality, especially at the outset, though later on in the loftier regions there is not much fault to be found. But as to the merit of the vocal part there is no question whatever. The voice, being exceedingly sympathetic, is ideally suited for expressing the genial, kindly nature of Hans Sachs, and gives out phrase after phrase with a *legato* smoothness and a certainty of intonation that are peculiarly welcome in the poet-cobbler's monologue. After all, it is only the start that is feeble. The rest is entirely satisfying.

Max Hirzel.—A very pleasant tenor here gives us yet a third Wagnerian excerpt from the same *atelier* in the shape of the *Prize Song.* He keeps well in tune and has a nice even scale to bridge over the passages from the medium to the head register. One wishes that the rendering had moments of greater brilliancy and vigour ; a less apologetic Walther would be preferable. The other side of the disc has the same singer's idea of the *Cavatina* from Gounod's *Faust.* It is not my idea, even after making allowance for an inappropriate German version of the *Salut, demeure* we know so well. Does Herr Hirzel really imagine that the various turns and ornaments and other variations which he plasters so thickly over this lovely air would ever be tolerated for a moment by, let us say, a Parisian audience ? I fancy we should scarcely put up with them in London. The only desirable feature in the whole piece is the pretty *falsetto* high C, which Gounod intended.

Amelita Galli-Curci.—A characteristic interpretation of the Mad Scene for Ophelia from Thomas's *Hamlet,* sung in Italian by the " record " record-artist of our day will not be unwelcome to collectors of her wonderful H.M.V. productions. The tone and the manner are alike unmistakable ; you would guess who was singing a hundred yards away. The neatness and *maestria* of the *coloratura* are as amazing as ever, and the long cadenza adds one more to the many flute and voice duets for which this accomplished vocalist is responsible.

Marcel Journet.—Two excellent H.M.V. examples of the French basso's talent—familiar enough, goodness knows, but well worth having. He is most at home, perhaps, in the *Faust* serenade, and his style therein is notable for its sheer *diablerie,* with true rhythm and all the old richness of timbre. Contrast, too, and

sardonic touches are plentiful. In the *Calunnia* we perceive a reading quite different to Chaliapin's, more traditional, more purely vocal ; but in its way it is just as cleverly humorous, significant, comic in spirit, and giving free rein to exaggeration within artistic limits.

John Charles Thomas.—A capable baritone, who, if I am not mistaken, was heard at some concerts in London two or three years ago ; and presumably of American nationality. He pronounces Italian rather better than French ; his style is robust and dramatic, but on the whole too ponderous and somewhat lacking in distinction. His *Vision fugitive* is good, but might easily be more imaginative and display less of the brutal side. The singer's attack is further emphasised by palpable evidence of what is known as the *Coup de la glotte* and he often disfigures his phrase with a " scoop." Into *Eri tu* he puts a lot of sentiment, but is apparently unaware of the funny effect produced by the accompanying orchestra with a joyous, tripping reading of the triplets which Verdi meant to be intensely tragic in their measured slow rhythm.

Selma Kurz.—The famous Austrian soprano has no difficulty in coping successfully with the *coloratur* demands of the *Ah ! non giunge,* and even supplies additional obstacles of her own to add to its brilliancy, without reckoning the amazingly long shake at the end. In the still more exacting *Ah ! non credea,* which, of course, precedes the *caballetta,* her pure style and clever breathing enable her to give full effect to the long, beautiful *cantilena* passages and achieve on the whole a good legitimate rendering of the whole aria. The recording is satisfactory.

Frida Leider.—Our old friend *Trovatore*—Germanised as *Troubadour*—is apparently as popular as ever with the audiences of Central Europe ; otherwise I imagine we should not find singers of Frida Leider's stamp turning their attention every now and then to operas which their native high-brows are supposed to look down upon with contempt. There is not anything to choose between the Polydor samples here exhibited, both being splendidly sung, while the only difference compared with other records of the same pieces, to the critical ear, at least, lies in the variations of breathing and phrasing brought about by the substitution of German for the Italian text.

Umberto Urbano.—The words just written apply equally to the *Per me ora fatale* (not *Ora per me fatale*) from the same opera by this powerful baritone, whose accent proclaims his Teutonic nationality. The *Zazà* extract is also good.

HERMAN KLEIN.

CHORAL

HANDEL FESTIVAL (CRYSTAL PALACE), 1926.

Messiah (Handel).—**Choir and Orchestra of 3,500,** conducted by Sir Henry J. Wood : **Behold the Lamb of God** and **And the Glory of the Lord.** Col. L.1768, 12in., 6s. 6d.
　　He trusted in God and **Let us break their bonds.** Col. L.1769, 12in., 6s. 6d.
　　Lift up your heads, two parts. Col. D.1550, 10in., 4s. 6d.

Royal Choral Society with Royal Albert Hall Orchestra under Dr. Malcolm Sargent : **Behold the Lamb of God** and **Hallelujah Chorus** from **Messiah** (Handel). Recorded at the Albert Hall, April 2nd. H.M.V., D.1108, 12in., 6s. 6d.

Irmler Ladies Choir.—**Good Night, Good Night, Beloved** (Pinsuti) and **Laudate Dominum** (Mozart). Parlo. E.10475, 12in., 4s. 6d.

The Handel Festival.—The recording of the choral wonders inherent to this great triennial gathering forms the realisation of a dream which the present writer began to indulge in directly the achievement began to loom up as a scientific possibility. Happily the Columbia Company has grasped the magnitude of the undertaking with such accuracy that it has proved a complete success at the first attempt. There is no need for comparisons, but it is only fair to say that it is quite on a par with the unimpeachable excellence of the reproductions of certain episodes (noticed in another column) of the recent opera season at Covent Garden. Only for me, with my recollection of half a century of Handel Festivals, I am bound to add that this embodies the more precious and wonderful achievement of the two. To have thus gathered in and stored up in such concentrated fashion, within the tiny superficial area of a gramophone disc, that gigantic combination of sounds which can be heard nowhere else on earth save once every three years in the Centre Transept of the Crystal Palace, seems to me little short of miraculous. The wonder of it does not cease, but only increases, when you remember that you can turn this flood of sound on and listen to it with undisturbed enjoyment, within the comfortable but restricted space of your own drawing-room.

What strikes me as the most marvellous and perhaps most touching feature about these three records of *Messiah* choruses is the instantly recognisable sensation of that unique *timbre*, that peculiar conglomerate of sounds, which we associate with the triennial product of the Handel Orchestra and with no other musical combination in the world. There it is. You hear and distinguish it all without an effort—the 3,000 voices, the 500 instrumentalists, compact in one trained body, held under perfect rhythmical sway by a single conductor, and, what is being imparted to it in the process—namely, the extraordinary influence of the vast surrounding space which nothing can imitate, much less equal, outside of the place itself. The total result, as demonstrated by a good machine, is almost as overwhelming and thrilling on the gramophone as it is at the Crystal Palace ; and a higher compliment than that it is beyond human power to convey. The tribute emphasises itself, so to speak, in the echoes of the applause as it hits against the huge glass roof at the end of each chorus ; and not more in one case than another, for all are alike superb, the four 12-inch records and the two part 10-inch record of *Lift up your heads*. These will rejoice the soul of every musical listener, whether he or she has ever attended a Handel Festival or not.

Royal Choral Society (Albert Hall).—Here is more " actuality " of a similar kind and only a degree less charged with emotional effect. Two of the noblest choruses in the *Messiah* are nobly sung by a choir that has never been surpassed in the history of the Albert Hall. The tone is magnificent, the steadiness, power, and clearness of the performance, conducted by Dr. Malcolm Sargent, beyond praise ; and the recording in each instance a triumph of which the H.M.V. have every right to feel proud. They have, by the way, secured the exclusive right of recording the Albert Hall performances.

Irmler Madrigal Choir.—There is no notable volume of sound in these Parlophone examples of choral singing. The voices appear to number a double quartet or not many more ; but they manage delicate effects very prettily, their tone is sweet, and their *nuances* of light and shade are artistic, not abrupt or overdone. The solo in the *Laudate Dominum* is neatly sung by Gertrude Baumann.

HERMAN KLEIN

OPERATIC

FEODOR CHALIAPINE (bass).—**Ridda e fuga infernale** and with chorus, **Son lo spirito che nega** from **Mefistofele** (Boito). In Italian. Recorded at Covent Garden, May 31st. H.M.V., D.B.942, 12in., 8s. 6d.

DAME NELLIE MELBA (soprano).—**Donde lieta from Act III.** of **La Bohème** (Puccini) and **Farewell Speech**. Recorded at Covent Garden, June 8th. H.M.V., D.B.943, 12in., 8s. 6d.

MARION TALLEY (soprano).—**Caro Nome** from **Rigoletto** (Verdi) and **Una Voce** from **Barber of Seville** (Rossini). In Italian. H.M.V., D.B.936, 8s. 6d.
Comin' thro' the Rye and **Home, sweet Home** (Bishop). In English. H.M.V., D.A.783, 10in., 6s.

FRITZI JOKL (soprano).—**Cavatina de Rosina (Una Voce)** from the **Barber of Seville** (Rossini). In German. Parlophone E.10461, 12in., 4s. 6d.

ROBERT BURG (baritone).—**My Soul is sad** and **I have attained to power** from **Boris Godounov** (Moussorgsky). Parlophone E.10473, 12in., 4s. 6d.

EMMY BETTENDORF (soprano).—**Sie entfloh, die Taube, Romance of Antonia** from **Tales of Hoffmann** (Offenbach) and **Melodie, La Serenata** (Tosti). Parlophone E.10474, 12in., 4s. 6d.

GERTRUDE KAPPEL (soprano).—**Brünhildes Schlusgesang** from **Götterdämmerung** (Wagner)—**Starke Schelte, O ihr, der Eide**

ewige Hüter, Flieget heim, ihr Raben—three sides, and **Pace, Pace, mio Dio** from **La Forza del Destino** (Verdi). Polydor 66099 and 66100, 12in., 5s. 9d. each.

MARIA OLSZEWSKA (contralto) and **EMIL SCHIPPER** (bass).— **Ha ! dann begriff ich sein Verbot** (Ortrud-Telramund duet) from **Lohengrin** (Wagner), in three parts, and **Liebst du mich treu und innig** (with chorus) from **Carmen** (Bizet). In German. Polydor 72989 and 72990, 12in., 6s. 9d. each.

ULYSSES LAPPAS (tenor).—**Celeste Aïda** from **Aïda** (Verdi) and **Cielo e mar** from **La Gioconda** (Ponchielli). In Italian. Col. L.1762, 12in., 6s. 6d.

HEDDLE NASH (tenor).—**Una furtiva lagrima** from **L'Elisir d'Amore** (Donizetti) and **O Paradiso** from **L'Africana** (Meyerbeer). In English. Col. 9104, 12in., 4s. 6d.

LAURI-VOLPI (tenor).—**Racconto di Rodolfo (Che gelida manina)** from **La Bohème** (Puccini) and **Quando nascesti tu** from **Act II.** of **Lo Schiavo** (Gomez). In Italian. Brunswick 50073, 12in., 8s.

Feodor Chaliapin.—The practical application of the new method of electrical recording at any distance is already resulting in achievements that are calculated, to put it mildly, to take one's breath away. (Not a good thing for singers, I know, but not particularly harmful to the listener.) I was much struck, a few weeks ago, at the amazing qualities of the organ record made by the H.M.V. of Mr. Herbert Dawson's performance at Kingsway Hall (fifteen miles away !) of Boëllman's *Suite Gothique* ; but until the present month I had never been called upon to criticise records of the human voice made from a similar distance. It is indeed a new and wonderful experience, for it so happens that in each of these instances I had heard the actual performance itself, and without having the smallest notion of what the microphone was enabling the instrument and its manipulator to accomplish in the recording room. One can only ask oneself, " What limit is there going to be to this sort of thing ? "

It was a good idea to attempt the reproduction from a Covent Garden performance of a musical episode so characteristic and individual, and also in a sense elusive, as that of the Brocken Scene in Boïto's opera, *Mefistofele*. Knowing its difficulties and complexities as I do, I should have been quite prepared to predict failure for this experiment, instead of which here it is (H.M.V., D.B.942), a gorgeous and unqualified success, a triumph of realism and " atmosphere " that would have been utterly unattainable under any other conditions. It gives you Mefistofele's pæan of self-glorification, *Son lo spirito che nega*, with the demon Chaliapin, so to speak, in his own dæmonic element, and as he alone *when there is* capable of delivering it. Need I say more ? Only that, after he has finished it, you can turn your disc over and hear him pitching his strange ejaculations and shouts of encouragement into the midst of the dance of witches and devils, the tremendous *Ridda e fuga infernale* which succeeds it. The effect of this terrific dance and fugue, as executed in rhythmic chorus with untiring energy, is simply indescribable. Nothing like it has ever been heard viâ the gramophone before.

The Melba Farewell.—Here is another miracle—and an amazing contrast into the bargain. It has far less musical value, of course, but, on the other hand, it provides a most welcome souvenir of a highly interesting occasion. We have first of all the actual sounds of Melba's voice singing for the last time at Covent Garden the suave and silvery utterances of Mimi (H.M.V., D.B.943) from the third act of *La Bohème* ; also, on the reverse side, the intensely emotional little speech of thanks, broken by irrepressible sobs, wherein the artist acknowledged the more formal address of Lord Stanley of Alderley, and not omitting the storm of applause that followed. The floral display alone is missing !

Marion Talley.—This unfamiliar Anglo-Saxon name connotes a new prima donna of American birth (? and training) who made her début amid much local excitement at the Metropolitan Opera House last winter. Her records of *Una voce* and *Caro nome* (H.M.V., D.B.936) prove her to be the possessor of a very pure, strong soprano voice, running easily up into *alt* with a clear, vibrant tone and showing flexibility alike in scales, shake, and staccato. The method, however, is perceptibly of the machine-made order and it gives a distinct impression of frigidity. The Italian is " choice " and easily distinguishable, and on the whole I prefer it to her English, which the same singer makes manifest in *Comin' thro' the rye* and *Home, sweet home* (H.M.V., D.A.783). Her tone in these old songs suggests that she sang them without a suspicion of a smile.

Fritzi Jokl.—As an exemplification of the same *bravura* school of singing this Parlophone record of *Una voce* is the exact antipode of that just noticed. Fritzi Jokl's voice does not seem to reach us through some mechanical agency ; it is the voice itself. It is human, it rings true, it is musical in its natural sweetness and pellucid clearness. Technically it is also impeccable ; the attack is clean ; all the *fiorituri* and scales are faultlessly executed ; the staccato is like a shower of pearls. Really I have seldom heard a more delightful rendering of this hackneyed aria. What is also important, the German words flow lightly and easily—for a wonder ! —and the long sustained high C at the end is quite lovely. The *Caro nome* is equally perfect in its way.

Robert Burg.—Personally I have not the slightest objection to the clever imitations of Chaliapin furnished by the German *basso cantante* in his two selections from *Boris Godounov*. He could not have taken a more inspiring model whereby to display his own fine organ or to realise the dramatic impressiveness of a historical character that Moussorgsky's opera has enabled the great Russian singer to make his own. Robert Burg has caught the peculiar tone of forlorn and hopeless misery to perfection, and except when he gives us a touch of that jerky, grunting creature, Alberich, his style is the identical thing. By the way, the recording and accompanying of the above four excerpts are creditable to the Parlo. *atelier.*

Emmy Bettendorf.—Neither Antonia's monotonous air from the *Tales of Hoffmann* nor the well-known *Serenata* of Paolo Tosti was calculated to show this admirable artist to the best advantage. She does her best with them, and that is all I can say. Patti's (H.M.V.) record of *La Serenata* still remains the only authentic rendering.

Gertrude Kappel.—It seems to me that these latest examples of the new electrical recording bring the voice into brighter relief than the orchestra, which for the most part sounds somewhat opaque and blurred in quality. We have just had at Covent Garden a splendid sample of Gertrude Kappel's mastery of Brünnhilde's music, and I think that with a little stronger support she would be capable of an even finer interpretation of the *Closing Scene* from *Götterdämmerung* than that exhibited in the present triple record. Nevertheless, it is quite adequate, whilst the air from *La Forza del Destino* on the reverse side of Part III. forms a welcome supplement.

Maria Olszewska and Emil Schipper.—Lovers of *Lohengrin* (in German) will doubtless be glad to get this faithful reproduction by two excellent singers of that long duet in the dark between Ortrud and Telramund, which some people used to regard as a rare opportunity for " forty winks." It occupies three sides of two discs, with a rousing contrast on the fourth in the shape of the choral entry of the Toreador and the succeeding gem of brief duet from the last act of *Carmen.* Olszewska is irresistible as usual, but Dr. Schipper seems more at home vocally in Telramund's penitential garb than in the gorgeous satin and gold of the bullfighter, who needs a lighter touch.

Ulysses Lappas.—The singing of *Cielo e mar* is very fine—finer on the whole than that of *Celeste Aïda.* The full, round tone of the Greek tenor (who made his début here in 1919) never came out so clear and strong, so reminiscent of the Caruso richness, before. His B flat is not phenomenal, but up to A natural he has a splendid scale and his breath-control is first rate. The recording of both airs is unexceptionable.

Heddle Nash.—This young tenor, who has been singing a good deal and with invariable success at the "Old Vic," has a voice of such natural beauty and power and a style so pleasing that a distinguished career seems certain for him. He must, however, beware of a slight *tremolo* (a fault that is apt to grow) when in sentimental mood; and his enunciation of English is decidedly imperfect, the consonants being especially defective. The air from *L'Africaine* is the better of the two.

Giacomo Lauri-Volpi.—Yet another operatic tenor who has sung at Covent Garden and in his big moments is well worth listening to. His rendering of Rodolfo's air from Act I of *La Bohème* is excellent, but less interesting, because more familiar, than that of the *Quando nascesti tu* from *Lo Schiavo,* an opera by Gomez that was produced at Rio de Janeiro in 1889. This has some effective snatches of melody in the modern Italian style and they show the singer's voice to advantage, particularly his high B natural, when, as in this case, he happens to have a good one.

HERMAN KLEIN.

OPERATIC

WILLIAM MARTIN (tenor) and **MARCEL RODRIGO** (baritone).— **O Mimi, tu più non torni** from **La Bohème** (Puccini) and **Solenne in quest' ora** from **La Forza del Destino** (Verdi). In Italian. Col. L.1763, 12in., 6s. 6d.

JOSEPH HISLOP (tenor) and **APOLLO GRANFORTE** (baritone).— **O Mimì, tu più non torni** from **La Bohème** (Puccini) and **Solenne in quest' ora** from **La Forza del Destino** (Verdi), sung in Italian. H.M.V., D.B.939, 12in., 8s. 6d.

PETER DAWSON (bass-baritone).—**O Star of Eve** from **Tannhäuser** (Wagner) and **Even bravest hearts** from **Faust** (Gounod). In English. H.M.V., C.1267, 12in., 4s. 6d.

META SEINEMEYER (soprano).—**Wie nacht mir der Schlummer** and **Alles pflegt schon längst der Ruh'** from **Der Freischütz** (Weber). In German. Parlo. E.10484, 12in., 4s. 6d.

ROBERT BURG (baritone).—**Wenn mich für Häus lichkeit auf Erden** and **Ist dies denn Wirklich die Tatjana** from **Eugen Onégin** (Tchaikovsky). Parlo. E.10485, 12in., 4s. 6d.

ELISABETH SCHUMANN (soprano).—**Batti, batti** from **Don Giovanni** (Mozart) and **Voi che sapete** from **Le Nozze di Figaro** (Mozart). In Italian. H.M.V., D.B.946, 12in., 8s. 6d.

CHORUS AND ORCHESTRA conducted by **VINCENZO BELLEZZA**, recorded during actual performance at Covent Garden, May 31st.—**Prologue—Finale** from **Mefistofele** (Boito). Sung in Italian. H.M.V., D.1109, 12in., 6s. 6d.

SELMA D'ARCO (soprano), with Aeolian Orchestra.—**O che volo d'augelli, Ballatella** from **Pagliacci** (Leoncavallo), in Italian, and **Depuis le jour** from **Louise** (Charpentier), in French. Vocalion A.0265, 12in., 5s. 6d.

EMMY BETTENDORF (soprano) and **WERNER ENGEL** (tenor).— **Duet from Act 2** of **The Flying Dutchman** (Wagner). In German. Parlo. 10478, 12in., 4s. 6d. See Orchestral Reviews, September, page 164.

AROLDO LINDI (tenor).—**Ora e per sempre addio** and **Morte d'Otello** from **Otello** (Verdi). Sung in Italian. Col. L.1773, 12in., 6s. 6d.

LUELLA PAIKIN (soprano).—**Air de Nannette** from **Falstaff** (Verdi) and **Saper Vorreste** from **Un Ballo in Maschera** (Verdi). In Italian. Voc. A.0267, 12in., 5s. 6d.

MAY HUXLEY (soprano).—**Ah ! Fors' è lui** from **La Traviata** (Verdi). Two parts. Sung in Italian. Beltona 7006, 12in.

MANUEL HEMINGWAY (bass-baritone).—**Vecchia zimarra** from **La Bohème** (Puccini) and **Vous qui faites l'endormie** from **Faust** (Gounod). In English. Beltona 1040, 10in., 2s. 6d.

William Martin and *Marcel Rodrigo.*—In the singing of vocal duets the first consideration is that the two voices shall be well matched and the balance of strength tolerably even. Without that it is hopeless to think of arriving at a satisfactory result, whether the attempt be made on the stage, on the concert platform, or on a gramophone disc. In the present instance we have a tenor and a baritone of the lightest and the heaviest calibre respectively, the former continually forcing his voice to compensate for his weakness as compared with a companion who makes not the slightest effort to moderate the powerful sonority of his tone. Whether it be in Verdi or Puccini, the effect of the disparity is equally noticeable and unpleasant ; but the argument against it is perhaps strongest in the duet from the fourth act of *La Bohème,* where at one moment Marcel has taken the liberty of joining in Rodolfo's little tune, for the apparent purpose of lending him a helping hand. He must have fancied no one would notice it !

Hislop and Granforte.—Here are precisely the same two duets from *La Forza del Destino* and *La Bohème,* sung by artists with voices well matched in timbre and strength. It is scarcely recognisable as the same music. One perceives the complete understanding between the two men, the intention to support each other where the voices unite, the effort to make them blend rather than spoil their quality by shouting. The result is an excellent record of both pieces, alike in the singing and the making, while the orchestral accompaniment is quite on the same level of merit.

Peter Dawson.—It is curious, though, how the same orchestra can vary in different specimens of workmanship ; almost as much, in fact, as the tones of the singers themselves. In these accompaniments to *O Star of Eve* and *Even bravest hearts may swell,* the instruments strike one as too near and noisy ; they intrude upon the voice and blur the general effect. It should be remembered that with this wonderful electrical recording every sound registers. The greater the need, therefore, for a careful adjustment of values and distances. So, again, with the soloist. He has to beware of curious variations of timbre, of a *mezza voce* that sounds as though it proceeded from some other mouth than his—like a ventriloquial effect, and not very pretty at that. If Mr. Peter Dawson takes my advice he will re-make these two records and at the same time, as an artist fond of writing letters to the press on the important subject of diction and pronunciation, take greater pains with his own vowel-formation and clearness of utterance. Only a foreigner can be excused for saying " theenk " and talking about his " seester."

Meta Seinemeyer.—Goodness knows there are enough existing records of the *Freischütz* aria—*Softly sighs*, as we always call it—without any necessity for this very unsatisfactory Parlophone version. Scarcely anything about it is right ; and when I say that I think that here in England we may claim, through the great Jenny Lind and the scarcely less great Theresa Tietjens, to possess the accurate tradition, direct from Weber himself (who was so much in this country) of the manner in which the famous air should be interpreted. Apart from the singer's hollow, grief-stricken medium tone, doubtful intonation and lack of real joy, hope, or animation, she slurs too many of her phrases and, of course, follows the mistaken modern German method of ignoring the *appoggiatura*, in flat opposition to the custom of Weber's time. This last national error ought now, I feel, to be brought before the League of Nations.

Robert Burg.—As usual, this popular German baritone produces a delightfully clean, pure record of whatever he sings, and these two excerpts from Tchaikovsky's *Eugen Onegin* seem to reflect the pleasure that he takes in so doing. His voice is very steady, his words are distinct, and there is abundant contrast in his varied shades of expression. The selection from the ball-room scene is energetic and passionate, and it winds up with the orchestral dance motive that follows it in the opera, which makes a capital ending.

Covent Garden Chorus and Orchestra.—My remarks anent the H.M.V. records of the Brocken Scene from *Mefistofele*, executed during the performance of the opera at Covent Garden, apply with equal force to these of the Prologue which opens the same work. It was a case of giving us " the cart before the horse," but there may have been reasons for that, which do not really concern us. I will only say that I am glad the Prologue has not been overlooked, because it is one of the features of Boito's masterpiece, and he himself chose it for performance and conducted it in person at Cambridge in 1893, when the University conferred upon him the honorary degree of Mus. Doc. If the opening passages sound rather faint and distant, the full volume of the voices and orchestra quickly bursts forth with splendid tone and thereafter is maintained with imposing effect to the end.

Selma d'Arco.—If every part of this soprano's compass were as steady and satisfying as her head register, and if art had done as much as nature to make her a good medium for gramophone work, then there would be another tale to tell about these solos from *Louise* and *Pagliacci*. As it is, she requires further study to get rid of her tremolo, to improve her phrasing and her shake, to correct her faulty French and her cloudy enunciation, in short, to make herself the finished vocalist that she is capable of being. Neither *Depuis le jour* nor Nedda's *Ballatella* is exactly easy, of course, and both call for a technique superior to this. The recording and the accompaniments are highly creditable.

Parsifal and *The Flying Dutchman.*—The association on one disc of stray excerpts from Wagner—youth and age—as here exhibited is not what one might term convenient. Apparently Parts I. and II. of *Klingsor's Magic Garden* have been issued previously, as this is Part III. Anyhow, it is that portion of the second act of *Parsifal* which finishes up with the flower maidens and starts the duet between the hero and Kundry (Max Lorenz and Gema Guszalewicz). It is thus head and tail without much body, but such a charming sample that one can only wish there were more of it. Similarly, the reverse side gives only the middle section of the beautiful duet between Senta and the Dutchman, sung in irreproachable fashion by Emmy Bettendorf and Werner Engel. So far as they go, both records are welcome.

Elisabeth Schumann.—Our readers will be glad to be able to obtain excellent records of these two familiar Mozart airs, sung in Italian by the accomplished artist who has been heard in them both at Covent Garden and Wigmore Hall. Her style, alike in *Batti, batti* and *Voi che sapete*, is lively, free, and vivacious, her tone singularly pure. If I prefer her German to her Italian it is because the vowel tone of her mother tongue comes more naturally to her, whereas this occasionally suggests the foreigner. However, that is

but a tiny blemish, and will not interfere with the enjoyment of her artistic singing.

Aroldo Lindi.—I rather suspect this to be an American tenor —Mr. Harold Somebody—but that does not really matter. The real point is that he has adopted the Italian manner with sufficient skill to make the question of nationality unimportant and that he uses a fine robust voice with much freedom and power. His phrasing is a trifle jerky, and one misses true nobility of utterance and diction in his excerpts from *Otello*, notably in the *Ora e per sempre addio*, which requires a Tamagno to do it justice. I like better the death scene, wherein the singer is genuinely pathetic. Not satisfied with pouring forth his soul in the wonderful *Un bacio ancora*, he pours out a few extra dying sighs as well, after the music has ceased ! You must listen carefully and you will hear them.

Luella Paikin.—Quite an agreeable contrast—the melancholy air for Nannetta (not Nanette—no, no, *not* Nanette, please !) from the last act of *Falstaff*, and the pretty song for the page from *Un Ballo in Maschera*. Both are sung smoothly and in tune ; but I object to the interpolation of a long and wholly unsuitable cadenza into the latter. I think Verdi, if he had heard it, would have cut short the singer's career with language that is unprintable. I will not evoke it here.

May Huxley.—On a 12in. disc we might very well get the whole of *Ah, fors' è lui* when done in two parts. The cut before the *Sempre libera* here is doubly wrong, because the orchestra begins at the bit which precedes the repeat, then waits for the voice to go back to the *Follie, follie*, which of course makes nonsense of the dramatic idea. This singer has a charming voice, and uses it with plenty of *entrain* or " go." But sometimes, unfortunately, it goes off the key, as for example in the delicious *A quell'amor*, which sounds consistently flat so long as the melody remains in the medium. Also many liberties are taken with text, the values being altered so as to lengthen high notes, and so forth. The cadenza is a not too effective *mélange* of many I have heard, and the ending shake is not sustained on the exact notes. I fancy Miss Huxley can do better than this.

Manuel Hemingway.—This cheap Beltona record gives good value. The voice is a sonorous low baritone of sympathetic quality, which comes out particularly well in the farewell to the old coat from *La Bohème*, sung with plenty of natural expression. The words are also very clear, but the singer must look to his vowel tones, which are often loosely formed and liable to mislead the listener. The Mephistopheles laugh in the Serenade is executed on a combination of vowels that (very properly, no doubt) suggests something derived from a special Satanic vocabulary.

HERMAN KLEIN.

OPERATIC

EVELYN SCOTNEY (soprano): **Mi tradì, quell 'alma ingrata** and **Non mi dir** from **Don Giovanni** (Mozart). In Italian. H.M.V., D.1119 (12in., 6s. 6d.).

AMELITA GALLI-CURCI (soprano): **Carceleras (Prison Song)** from **Las Hijas del Zebedeo** (Chapi) and **Serenata** (Tosti). In Italian. H.M.V., D.A.805 (10in., 6s.).

META SEINEMEYER (soprano): **Sie sass mit Leide auf öder Haide (Willow Song)** from **Otello** (Verdi) and **Und ob die Wolke** from **Der Freischütz** (Weber). In German. Parlophone E.10506 (12in., 4s. 6d.).

ELDA DI VEROLI (soprano): **Ah! non credea mirarti** and **Ah! non giunge uman pensiero** from **La Sonnambula** (Bellini). In Italian. Duophone G.S.7008 (12in., 5s. 6d.).

MAY HUXLEY (soprano): **O Luce di quest'anima** from **Linda di Chamonix** (Donizetti), in Italian, and **Scenes that are brightest** from **Maritana** (Wallace), in English. . Beltona 7007 (12in., 4s. 6d.).

BENIAMINO GIGLI (tenor): **Mandulinata a Napule** (Tagliaferri), in Neapolitan, and **Quanto è bella** from **L'Elisir d'Amore** (Donizetti), in Italian. H.M.V., D.A.797 (10in., 6s.).

ENID CRUICKSHANK (contralto): **Connais-tu le pays** from **Mignon** (Thomas) and **Divinités du Styx** from **Alceste** (Gluck). In English. Vocalion K.05255 (12in., 4s. 6d.).

NICOLO FUSATI (tenor): **Addio alla Madre** from **Cavalleria Rusticana** (Mascagni) and **Morte d'Otello** from **Otello** (Verdi). In Italian. Velvet Face 691 (12in., 4s.).

GWLADYS NAISH (soprano), **EDITH FURMEDGE** (contralto), **DAN JONES** (tenor) and **NORMAN WILLIAMS** (basso cantante): **The Garden Scene** from **Faust** (Gounod). In English. Four parts. Velvet Face 1187 and 1188 (10in., 2s. 6d. each).

GOTA LJUNGBERG (soprano) and **WALTER WIDDOP** (tenor): **Du bist der Lenz** (**Love Duet**) from **Die Walküre** (Wagner). In German. Two parts. H.M.V., D.B.963 (12in., 8s. 6d.).

GIOVANNI MARTINELLI (tenor) and **ROSA PONSELLE** (soprano): **O Terra Addio** from **Aïda** (Verdi). Two parts. In Italian. H.M.V., D.A.809 (10in., 6s.).

WILLIAM MARTIN (tenor): **Che gelida manina** from **La Bohème** (Puccini), in Italian, and **Salut, demeure** from **Faust** (Gounod), In French. Columbia L.1789 (12in., 6s. 6d.).

WILLIAM HESELTINE (tenor): **Lohengrin's Narration** and **Lohengrin's Farewell** from **Lohengrin** (Wagner). In English. Columbia 9127 (12in., 4s. 6d.).

CECIL SHERWOOD (tenor): **M'Appari** from **Marta** (Flotow) and **Questa o Quella** from **Rigoletto** (Verdi). In Italian. Columbia 4074 (10in., 3s.).

HENRY SCHLUSNUS (baritone): **Wolfram's Eulogy of Love** and **The Evening Star** from **Tannhäuser** (Wagner). In German. Polydor 66408 (12in., 5s. 9d.).

THEODOR SCHEIDL (baritone): **The term is past** and **Angel of God, who, in my desolation** from **The Flying Dutchman** (Wagner). In German. Polydor 66414 (12in., 5s. 9d.).

EMIL LEISNER (contralto): **Hört ihr Augen auf zu weinen** and **Ohne Trost** from **Julius Caesar** (Handel). Polydor 73019 (12in., 6s. 9d.).

Evelyn Scotney.—It is always a pleasure to listen to tone so pure and recording so wonderful as we get in this disc. Moreover, the airs from *Don Giovanni* are two that are least frequently recorded, for the ostensible reason that they are the most difficult in the opera. Technically, Miss Scotney is quite equal to them, as she is, no doubt, to the most terrifying example of *coloratura* music that has yet been devised. At the same time it cannot with truth be asserted that she gets completely to the heart of *Non mi dir*, or that she suggests very vividly the underlying tragedy of *Mi tradì*. Each demands a fuller measure of dramatic feeling, greater variety of colour and a timbre that savours less of *voix blanche*. Nevertheless, even without those magnificent attributes, one can still enjoy the clean, impeccable singing of it all, the lovely head notes, the excellent, well-defined scale. Only two questions : in *Non mi dir*, where the return to the subject of the *larghetto* occurs, why shorten so much the *point d'orgue* or pause in order to do the whole in a single breath ? There are times when the singer takes more breaths than she needs. Again, in *Mi tradì*, if she sings the *appoggiatura* in the majority of cases, why not in all ? The accompaniments are played with clearness, precision and due regard for balance.

Amelita Galli-Curci.—Although not operatic, these records will be interesting to operatic admirers of the famous Italian *cantatrice*, whose mastery of her particular art has made the whole world marvel. As an example of mordant Spanish patter the *Prison Song* (*Las Hijas del Zebedeo*) is simply phenomenal ; I cannot recall anything so tremendously rapid and yet so absolutely distinct ; voice and words stand out vividly against the essential piano accompaniment ; the tone is pure Galli-Curci, and the Spanish flavour dominates even to the final turn of the *cadenza*. In the *Serenata* of Tosti which Patti helped to make popular, the rendering is not altogether so happy, because it is taken too fast and overladen with slurs ; besides, one misses that charming ending which Patti introduced and sang in her wonderful record of this song. But, on the whole, the new *Serenata* is worth listening to for qualities—the easy-going *dolce far niente* touch—which Galli-Curci alone has the secret of.

Meta Seinemeyer.—I like this soprano better in the second than in the first of the *Der Freischütz* airs, though the voice still has a sorrowful ring which is incompatible with the hopefulness that Agathe has to express, and it trembles slightly all the time. Despite the admiration of my Editor and the defence of someone else, I fear I cannot quite share the one or allow the justice of the other. If every succeeding generation of singers were to introduce different treatment and make a few more alterations in the original text or the *known* intentions of the composer, a good many vocal pieces that I could name would gradually lose some of their most characteristic features. This very artist supplies a further example at the back of *Und ob die Wolke* with an interpretation of the *Willow Song* (in German) from Verdi's *Otello* that manifestly presents several rhythmical points of departure from the *scena,*

as taught by Verdi himself to at least two Desdemonas I have heard.

Elda di Veroli.—A simple, unaffected rendering, without too many embroideries or "trimmings" of the divine *aria* and *caballetta* from the sleep-walking scene in Bellini's *La Sonnambula*. The F in *alt* at the end is unusually clear and the voice and style are pleasing throughout.

May Huxley.—The well-worn airs from *Linda di Chamounix* and *Maritana* imparted to this disc are sufficiently popular to justify their repetition at a figure that makes them easy to acquire. The singing of them here is quite effective, though open to criticism on the score of a certain lack of elegance and distinction in the execution of the *fiorituri* in Donizetti's piece. Neither of the long recitatives is very interesting, while faulty breathing causes the singer occasionally to force her voice and make it tremble. Yet it is a good voice and well worth listening to.

Beniamino Gigli.—The American popularity of this Italian tenor is due partly to his stage work, with which we on this side are unacquainted, and partly to his splendid records, which we are now pretty familiar with. The present example, a 10in. disc by the way, does not represent him at his very best, at least in the air from *L'Elisir*, where his tone is disproportionately nasal. In the Neapolitan ditty this fault matters less—indeed, may hardly be considered a fault at all. His tone has breadth and power, and I like his free manly delivery, which gives full value to every syllable. The *Mandulinata*, besides being tender and amorous, has a capital rhythmical swing.

Enid Cruickshank.—It is hard to say whether the tonal dulness of this record is to be attributed chiefly to the singer or to the recording. Perhaps each must bear some of the blame ; anyhow, I have heard both to greater advantage. Gluck's noble air requires abundant contrast of colour and expression, added to a clear, ringing tone and plain diction. Miss Cruickshank gives us forcible declamation and her customary intelligence without sufficient of these qualities ; moreover, her fine organ has never recovered from an early tendency to the *vibrato*, which, in the case of so good an artist, is a fact to be greatly deplored. On the whole the *Connais-tu* is less cloudy, more musical, and has greater charm.

Nicolo Fusati.—I do not remember to have heard any previous record by this tenor, but he is certainly a performer to be reckoned with. He reminds me somewhat of Zenatello, and his rendering of the *Morte d'Otello* compares favourably with the one by that artist recently noticed in this column, including the expiring gasps, which in this instance sound *ante-* and not *post-mortem*. The voice is a genuine *tenore robusto* of broad, telling quality, with a free, steady production, bold declamation, and exemplary enunciation. The *Addio alla Madre* from *Cavalleria Rusticana* is equally well done, though musically less interesting. The orchestral accompaniments to both are faithfully portrayed.

Garden Scene from *Faust*.—Two small discs (four parts) suffice to cover the ground for the immortal Gounod picture outside Marguerite's modest dwelling. We have here an adequate rather than a highly-finished interpretation by four competent British artists, Gwladys Naish, Edith Furmedge, Dan Jones, and Norman Williams. To all of them, as to ourselves, the delicious music is intensely familiar. All that it requires, I fancy, are the signs of more careful rehearsal, of a more sedulous regard for *nuance* and balance. Sheer beauty of singing is of far greater value in a scene such as this than all the ear-marks of individual self-identification. We can, or should, recognise our old friends without the need for special assistance on their part.

Göta Ljungberg and Walter Widdop.—This is the best record of the wonderful love duet in the first act of *Die Walküre* that I have yet heard. Indeed, I doubt whether any quite so good has yet been made. To say so much should be to say enough ; but I would add that to attain absolute perfection it needs a wholly steady Sieglinde, which Miss Ljundberg, for all her lovely tone and phrasing, does not quite give us. The defect, however, is relatively slight, and, thanks to Mr. Widdop's smooth, expressive *concours*, the whole scene is replete with impassioned feeling. The instrumental share of the record is also splendidly done.

Rosa Ponselle and *Giovanni Martinelli.*—Another magnificent duet in two parts on a single disc—this one a 10in. It embodies the final scene from *Aïda* and is a worthy rendering of that inspired page. Two superb voices, without a shadow of a tremor in either, are here blended with exquisite purity, with a plenitude of charm and an elegance of phrasing that could not be surpassed. The impression and the joy of it are irresistible. I feel inclined to declare that the possession of these last H.M.V. records should constitute a privilege for the gramophile.

William Martin.—A nice singer and evidently an artistic one.

The French is well pronounced—if anything better than the Italian, which is unusual from British lips. The high notes in *Salut, demeure* are not very striking, but the whole is neatly phrased and well in tune.

William Heseltine.—Although he imparts little variety of colour to Lohengrin's " few remarks " before leaving, the artist declaims easily and sustains his sympathetic tone comfortably to the end. One wishes, however, that it were a trifle less shaky ; for the intonation is faultless, the English words are fairly distinct, and the style is manly, frank, and heroic. As with the previous disc, this is an admirable example of new Columbia recording, and the accompaniments are quite clear.

Cecil Sherwood.—The name may be Anglo-Saxon, but the voice, the style, the delivery, the pronunciation, all are up-to-date Italian, including something of the atmosphere of the stage. *M'appari* is not unduly sentimental, and the tone is that of a powerful tenor ; while *Questa o quella* is full of go, with all the necessary dash and *abandon*.

Heinrich Schlusnus.—The Wolfram pieces, part of the best music in *Tannhäuser*, must have been tempting this capable singer for a long time. Anyhow, here they are, finely rendered in his pure baritone voice, with fitting expression and ample sonority and

breadth of tone as well as the ideal Wagnerian type of *cantilena*. The instrumentation is nicely brought out, the harp *arpeggi* being clearly executed. There is a strange effect at the beginning of the *Abendstern* melody. For two or three bars it sounds like another and much softer voice ; but the heavier tone quickly returns and remains till the close.

Theodor Scheidl.—In the last pieces and in this the Polydor orchestra shows evidence of improvement. Here especially, in the *Flying Dutchman* airs, it gives excellent support to a bass soloist of unusual distinction, richness, and power. One could hardly desire to hear a more characteristic rendering, or a voice better suited to the spirit of weary longing for rest that animates the unhappy Holländer. His diction, too, is amazingly good—duly lugubrious, but always dramatic.

Emmi Leisner.—Handel's *Julius Cæsar* has, I believe, been recently revived in Germany. Hence probably the recording of these extremely sorrowful excerpts from that opera, which contains more interesting examples of the master's genius. It must be admitted that they find an exact counterpart in the intensely lachrymose tones of this well-known contralto of the Berlin Staatsoper. The two airs are both in the same sad vein and offer no contrast whatever.   HERMAN KLEIN.

REVIEWS PUBLISHED IN 1927

OPERATIC

THEODOR SCHEIDL (baritone): **Als du in kühnem Sange** from **Tannhäuser** (Wagner) and **Oh, dürfte ich es glauben** (**Per me ora fatale**) from **Trovatore** (Verdi). In German. Polydor 62543 (10in., 4s. 6d.).

THEODOR LATTERMANN (baritone): **Hüll' in die Mantille** from **Tiefland** (D'Albert) and **So schwärmet jugend** from **Barber of Bagdad** (Cornelius). In German. Polydor 62542 (10in., 4s. 6d.).

AMELITA GALLI-CURCI (soprano): **Ombra leggiera** (**Shadow Song**) from **Dinorah** (Meyerbeer). Two parts, in Italian. H.M.V., D.A.817 (10in., 6s.).

THEODOR CHALIAPINE (bass): **Song of the Flea** (Moussorgsky), in Russian, and **La Calunnia è un venticello** from **Il Barbiere di Siviglia** (Rossini), in Italian. H.M.V., D.B.932 (12in., 8s. 6d.).

HOWARD FRY (baritone): **O Star of Eve** from **Tannhäuser** (Wagner) and **Credo** from **Otello** (Verdi). In English. Beltona 7008 (12in., 4s. 6d.).

LAURITZ MELCHIOR (tenor) and **EMMY BETTENDORF** (soprano): **Bridal Chamber Scene** (**Das süsse Lied verhallt** and **Wie hehr erkenn ich uns'rer Liebe Wesen !**) from **Lohengrin** (Wagner). In German. Parlophone E.10515 (12in., 4s. 6d.).

RACHEL MORTON (soprano): **Vissi d'Arte** from **Tosca** (Puccini) and **Habañera** from **Carmen** (Bizet). In English. H.M.V., E.440 (4s. 6d.).

GRAND OPERA CHORUS: **Soldiers' Chorus** and **'Gainst the Power** from **Faust** (Gounod). In English. Regal G.8704 (10in., 2s. 6d.).

THE B.B.C. CHORUS: **Soldiers' Chorus** and (with **HAROLD WILLIAMS**, tenor) **'Gainst the Power** from **Faust** (Gounod). In English. Columbia 9143 (12in., 4s. 6d.).

JOHN O'SULLIVAN (tenor): **Ora e per sempre addio** and **Monologo** from **Otello** (Verdi). In Italian. Columbia L.1806 (12in., 6s. 6d.).

PERTILE (tenor), **FERRARIS** (soprano), **RIGHETTI** (bass), **BAROMEO** (bass): **La rivedra nell'estasi** and (with **BERTANA**, mezzo-soprano) **E scherzo od è follia** from **Un Ballo in Maschera** (Verdi). In Italian. Parlophone R.20007 (12in., 7s. 6d.).

BROWNING MUMMERY (tenor): **On with the Motley** from **Pagliacci** (Leoncavallo) and **Your tiny hand is frozen** from **La Bohème** (Puccini). In English. H.M.V., C.1300 (12in., 4s. 6d.).

TUDOR DAVIES (tenor): **Legend of Kleinsack** from **Tales of Hoffmann** (Offenbach) and **Onaway ! awake, beloved** from **Hiawatha** (Coleridge-Taylor). In English. H.M.V., D.1142 (12in., 6s. 6d.).

Theodor Scheidl.—The combination of Wagner and early Verdi furnished by this record is probably the outcome of a demand. At any rate, it is evidence of the German liking for tunes which they enjoyed in their youth—as did their fathers before them— and which they still continue to enjoy. In this country we have thousands of opera-lovers who are not ashamed to admit that they still love every note of the *Trovatore*, while a good proportion of them, I dare say, are familiar enough with *Tannhäuser* to recognise and love (as I do) the melodious strain with which Wolfram welcomes his old companion back to the valley of the Wartburg. To all such I can recommend this capital record, especially that side of it which gives us the Count di Luna.

Theodor Lattermann.—Both operas here represented have been mounted at Covent Garden, but failed to " catch on." Personally I did not care for *Tiefland*, despite the genius of Emmy Destinn ; but *The Barber of Bagdad* is a delightful work and deserves to be better known. The present singer has a rough but not unpleasant voice, and his rendering of the *Liebe* air from the latter opera reveals a distinct sense of humour.

Amelita Galli-Curci.—The Italian *diva* here gives us the *Shadow Song* from *Dinorah* complete in two parts. It is more welcome so than in the cut version, even if it does not display the artist at her very best where intonation is concerned. As a piece of brilliant vocalisation it is sufficiently wonderful, and the final cadenza with the flute could scarcely be matched by any living singer.

Theodor Chaliapine.—These are re-recordings of pieces that were previously to be had only on different records. They come cheaper, therefore, to anyone who wishes to possess the two most remarkable examples of the *genre* wherein Chaliapine is unapproachable. For no one else in the world can sing the *Song of the Flea* or the *Calunnia* air from the *Barbiere* as he does, and it would be difficult to imagine a more perfect recording of either. They are simply marvels of characterisation, and they hit you, as Don Basilio says, like a *colpo di cannone !*

Howard Fry.—This baritone has a fine voice, his declamation is clear and forcible, and his style is marked by intelligence. It is a pity, therefore, that his breath-control does not enable him to conquer a persistent tremolo such as mars his delivery of *O Star of Eve*. The trouble is naturally much less apparent in the *Credo* from *Otello*, and I greatly prefer it in consequence.

Lauritz Melchior and *Emmy Bettendorf.*—One can only derive profound and unqualified pleasure from the singing of these two eminent artists in the bridal-chamber duet from *Lohengrin*.

Wagner wrote no lovelier music than this, and the excerpts are the gems of the whole scene. What strikes me most is the artistic restraint that characterises the tone of both voices. The quality is delicious, the intonation impeccable, the breathing and phrasing perfect. From first to last there is complete understanding between the two singers, and the accompaniment and recording are alike beyond criticism.

Rachel Morton.—Somehow something seems bound to be lost in an English version of *Vissi d'Arte*. The whole idea is so essentially Italian that it is practically untranslatable. Yet I am bound to say that Miss Morton has done better in this than in the *Habañera* from *Carmen*, from which the element of seductive fascination is altogether missing, and with it the lilt of the Spanish rhythm. Yet one cannot but admire the bright, telling quality of the voice, the purity of the head notes, and the unusually clear enunciation in both pieces. A singer of decided accomplishment, from whom we ought to get some first-rate records.

Grand Opera Chorus.—A good half-crown's worth for those who want two of the best choruses in *Faust*, sung with lots of " go," sonorous tone, rhythmical energy, and the right sort of spirit.

The B.B.C. Chorus.—The same numbers on a 12-inch disc at 4s. 6d., but without being shortened, and given with an amplitude of volume that suggests the numbers and spaciousness of an opera house. The gradual crescendo at the beginning of the *Soldiers' Chorus* conveys the idea of Valentine's comrades entering the town, and, on the other side, he himself (in the person of Mr. Harold Williams) starts off 'Gainst the Power with a vigour—seconded and carried by the aforesaid comrades—that fully accounts for Mephistopheles' haste to twist magic circles with his sword and step neatly out of harm's way. Both choruses are well recorded and the military band is excellent.

John O'Sullivan.—The easy sustained power here shown in two of the most trying moments for the hero of Verdi's *Otello* suffice to justify the singer's ambition in attacking them. His accent, without being faultless, is correct enough to satisfy exigent ears, and his declamatory style fairly choice Italian, as Hamlet would say.

La Scala Singers.—The famous ensembles in the first and second acts of *Un Ballo in Maschera* (Verdi again !) are so seldom really well sung on the stage that it was quite a good idea to have them recorded by these Milanese artists. Would they were all of the calibre of Signor Pertile, a tenor not unjustly held to be the equal of Caruso ! He has a magnificent voice and sings with extra-ordinary elegance and dash. I will not deny that he overdoes the laugh in *E scherzo od è follia*, but he does it cleverly and carries the whole quintet along with an irresistible swing. The Page is only moderate ; the Gipsy and the two basses are adequate ; the chorus growls confused interjections in the background. But Pertile dominates the situation, and he, like Eclipse, is a joy even when the rest are " nowhere."

Browning Mummery.—As a criticism of these English versions of the most hackneyed airs in *Pagliacci* and *La Bohème* I would this excellent Antipodean singer to study carefully the record just noticed or even the one which follows. If he does not take a lesson therefrom, I fancy the intensification due to the possibilities of electrical recording will compel his otherwise admiring listeners to keep some cotton-wool handy, in addition to a supply of extra soft needles.

Tudor Davies.—Two interesting selections, and neither overdone nor oversung. The *Legend* is, to my thinking, Hoffmann's best page in Offenbach's opera, even as *Onaway ! awake* is Hiawatha's best in Coleridge-Taylor's masterpiece. Both of them, to use a common phrase, take a lot of singing, and the popular Welsh tenor rises fully to the occasion. I have naught but praise for the vocal and technical merits of this record.

HERMAN KLEIN.

Records of Turandot *(Puccini)* and La Forza del Destino *(Verdi)*

(i) **Marcia del Ministri e Mandarini** from **Turandot** and **Battle-Music** and **Tarantella** from **La Forza del Destino : The State Opera Orchestra of Dresden,** conducted by **Fritz Busch.** Polydor 66430 (12in., 5s. 9d.).

(ii) **In questa Reggia, or son mill' anni e mille** and **Del primo pianto si, straniero, quando sei giunto** from **Turandot : Anne Roselle** (soprano), in German. Polydor 73024 (12in., 6s. 9d.).

(iii) **Terzetto dei Ministri (Ping, Pang, Pong).** Two parts, in German. **Paul Schöffler, Heinrich Tessmer, Otto Sigmund,** and **Orchestra of the State Opera, Dresden,** under **Fritz Busch.** Polydor 66429 (12in., 5s. 9d.).

(iv) **Overture to La Forza del Destino : State Opera Orchestra, Dresden,** conducted by **Fritz Busch.** Two parts. Polydor 66431 (12in., 5s. 9d.).

THE first records of Puccini's posthumous opera, *Turandot*, to be brought out in this country, are two double-sided twelve-inch discs issued this month by the Polydor Company. This opera was mounted at La Scala, Milan, in April last under Toscanini, and subsequently given with success in America, Austria, and Germany. At Dresden it was performed at the State Opera House under the direction of Fritz Busch, and it is from that source that we have the present admirable recordings. It is an extremely difficult work—by far the most elaborate of all Puccini's operas—and does not lend itself readily to the provision of gramophone excerpts. So much the greater credit to the Polydor executants, from the arranger downwards, for the ability with which these pieces have been selected, prepared, and performed. They will form a highly valuable guide for all who propose to hear *Turandot* at Covent Garden during the coming season of the London Opera Syndicate ; while gramophonists generally who love their Puccini will rejoice at the possession of these new wonderful examples of his fertile inventive genius.

Having recently had opportunity for studying the handsome vocal score published by Ricordi, I am in a position to appreciate more readily the characteristic and grandiose features of this music —so often reminiscent of *Madam Butterfly*—in its illustration of the picturesque old Chinese legend. It consists for the greater part of ensembles, choruses, and orchestral work, both stately and bizarre, lively and severe, enhancing the pageantry or colouring the comedy and tragedy of the stage drama. There is not a single separate number in the opera, but its absence will not evoke complaint so long as one can get a large slice of vocal drama such as that presented here in Turandot's splendid exhortation to the conquering Prince when they meet in the second act (record 2).

This is, however, preceded and almost led up to by the *March of Ministers and Mandarins* in record 1, which in turn is preceded by the extra-ordinarily novel and exciting *Terzetto of the Ministers* (Ping, Pang, and Pong) given on record 3. The fact that they stand in inverse order in the opera matters not ; they sound equally effective in any order.

The so-called March accompanies the change of scene from the first to the second tableau of Act 2, and includes some choral fragments that are not given in the record. It is genuine Eastern highly-coloured descriptive music, in the true Puccini vein, extremely well played by the Dresden Orchestra and very clearly recorded.

Turandot's address to the Prince, *In questa Reggia*, is perhaps the most exacting piece of declamation to be found in modern Italian music. It is in two parts and again the chorus is dispensed with. It has, I fancy, more dramatic than musical interest, but, whatever its effect in the opera, Anne Roselle (singing in German) does it abundant justice in this record. Her voice, albeit a trifle thin in quality, is a bright and telling soprano and the high notes, of which there are any quantity, come out clear and strong. By the way, I wonder how Jeritza will impress us in this long-sustained tirade.

I am not quite sure, of course, but I should not wonder if the *scherzando Gianni Schicchi*-like trio of the Masters of the Household, Ping, Pang, and Pong, proved to be the hit of the opera. It is certainly an amazing combination of quaint and rapid ejaculations, queer harmonies, and strange dissonances alternating with moments of reposeful beauty and absolute charm, the whole set off to the fullest advantage by varied and masterful orchestration. The three German artists sing it superbly, the baritone, Paul Schöffler, being especially fine ; while here, again, the orchestral playing shows the Dresden conductor, Fritz Busch, to be a first-rate conductor. Altogether this Chinese puzzle of Puccini's comes out surprisingly well under the Polydor auspices.

I can only refer briefly to the selections from *La Forza del Destino*. It is rumoured that Verdi's mid-period opera is only just " catching on " in Germany after all these years ; hence, I imagine, this very careful and adequate issue of the hitherto neglected *Overture, Battle-Music*, and *Tarantella*. The former, on a separate two-part record, is representative of Verdi in a mood that reminds you alternatively of Meyerbeer and Auber, and very pleasantly at that ; it is played with immense spirit and *verve*. The other two pieces, divided by a narrow space over which the needle must be lifted, occupy the reverse side of the disc containing the march from *Turandot* and, on the whole, leave one decidedly impressed by the greater interest of the clever *chinoiserie* invented by Puccini.

HERMAN KLEIN.

OPERATIC

EMMY BETTENDORF (soprano) : **Ocean, thou mighty Monster** from **Oberon** (Weber). Two parts, in German. Parlophone E.10525 (12in., 4s. 6d.).

ANNE ROSELLE (soprano) : **Ma dall' arido stelo divulsa** and **Morrò, ma prima in grazia** from **Un Ballo in Maschera** (Verdi). In German. Polydor 73025 (12in., 6s. 9d.).

ELISABETH RETHBERG (soprano) : **O Patria mia** and **Ritorna vincitor** from **Aïda** (Verdi). In Italian. Brunswick 50084 (12in., 8s.).

MARGARET SHERIDAN (soprano) : **Ave Maria** from **Otello** (Verdi) and **Un bel di vedremo** from **Madame Butterfly** (Puccini). In Italian. H.M.V., D.B.881, 12in., 8s. 6d.

SIGRID ONEGIN (contralto) : **Brindisi** from **Lucrezia Borgia** (Donizetti) and **Stride la vampa, Act II, Scene 2,** from **Il Trovatore** (Verdi). In Italian. Brunswick 15110 (10in., 5s. 6d.).

TINO PATTIERA (tenor) : **Che gelida manina** from **La Bohème** (Puccini) and **Flower Song** from **Carmen** (Bizet). In Italian. Parlophone E.10526 (12in., 4s. 6d.).

AROLDO LINDI (tenor) : **Ah sì, ben mio** from **Il Trovatore** (Verdi) and **Flower Song** from **Carmen** (Bizet). In Italian. Col. L.1816 (12in., 6s. 6d.).

ERIC MARSHALL (baritone) : **Nemico della patria** from **Andrea Chénier** (Giordano) in Italian, and **O Star of Eve** from **Tannhäuser** (Wagner) in English. H.M.V., D.1146 (12in., 6s. 6d.).

HEINRICH SCHLUSNUS (baritone) : **Death of Valentine** from **Faust** (Gounod) and **Lullaby** from **Mignon** (Thomas). In German. Polydor 66435 (12in., 5s. 9d.).

LAURITZ MELCHIOR (tenor) and EMMY BETTENDORF (soprano) : **Love Duet** from **Lohengrin, Act 3** (Wagner), **Atmest du nicht** and **Höchstes Vertrauen**. In German. Parlophone E.10527 (12in., 4s. 6d.).

GRAND OPERA CHORUS : **Miserere** from **Il Trovatore** (Verdi) and **The Angelus** from **Maritana** (Wallace). In English. Regal G.8728 (2s. 6d.).

EVA TURNER, E. RUBADI, F. CINISELLI, L. PACI, B. CARMASSI and LA SCALA CHORUS : **Finale, Act III,** from *La Gioconda* (Ponchielli) and (La Scala Chorus of Milan only) **Prologue** (Chorus of Angels) from *Mefistofele* (Boito). In Italian. Col. L.1817 (12in., 6s. 6d.).

Emmy Bettendorf.—Thanks to the improvements wrought by electrical recording, this is by a long way the best realisation of Frau Bettendorf's talent that the gramophone has yet yielded. Perhaps also the finest rendering of *Ocean, thou mighty Monster* heard through the same medium from the lips of a modern soprano. It is, indeed, a welcome example of the " grand style," with the voice of broad, noble proportions, the exceptional declamatory power, and the dignity of phrasing essential for the piece. The " nearness " of the voice is not its least surprising feature, while every word comes out with irreproachable clearness. The exciting *coda*, made so familiar by the *Oberon* overture, is the better for not being hurried, and the orchestra is excellent throughout.

Anne Roselle.—Apparently this is not a new piece of recording. Anyhow the " scratching " sounds like a reminder of old days ; nor does the tone represent the singer on the same level, or anything like it, that one perceives in her new *Turandot* records (noticed elsewhere). She may be an artist of " moods," yet that would not account for a marked tremolo, lack of breadth in the style, or a weak medium register contrasted with those bell-like headnotes of hers that never fail. In spite of which, one feels that she is the right singer for the unhappy heroine of *Un Ballo in Maschera*—emotional, dramatic, tense, and impassioned.

Elisabeth Rethberg.—Again I turn to my stock of superlatives, for these up-to-date recordings of the two great *Aïda* solos far surpass any yet attempted. Concerning the singer there is little that is fresh to be said. She is a " star " of the first magnitude, with an orbit that includes, I believe, the U.S.A., and ought to include this country ere many moons have passed. Her voice is a pure dramatic soprano, her breathing impeccable, her smooth *cantilena* an object-lesson, her high C in *O Patria Mia* a really beautiful note. Add to these things intense expression, a wonderful *diminuendo*, unlimited power, dramatic colour, true artistic perception, and, thanks to realistic recording, you have a fair idea of how Elisabeth Rethberg sings *Aïda*. The *Ritorna vincitor* is equally glorious, and I am thankful to say she does not drag the " Numi pietà " at the end.

Margaret Sheridan.—The *Ave Maria* from the last act of Verdi's *Otello* requires on the whole more repose, more complete steadiness of tone than Miss Sheridan brings to bear upon it. The tone itself is beautiful and charged with deep feeling ; the words are very distinct. However, the drawbacks that one perceives all too plainly in this exquisite piece are scarcely faults calling for criticism in *Un bel di* ; indeed, oddly enough, they hardly seem out of place. Here the Irish soprano is heard to much greater advantage, and her Italian diction, particularly as regards purity of vowel tone, is far more satisfactory. Both excerpts are recorded and accompanied faultlessly.

Sigrid Onegin.—This fine contralto would do well to study her effects a little less. She makes them too obvious and often sacrifices artistic discretion to a longing for sensation. Knowing that she has a grand organ and unlimited sustaining power, she overdoes her pauses and, as for instance in her cadenza to the *Brindisi* from *Lucrezia Borgia*, salutes your ear with a prolonged note that (honestly !) resembles the warning of an L.M.S. engine approaching Euston. The " new process " does not permit this sort of thing, even with the softest of needles. The best German contralto that ever sang the *Brindisi* to her countrymen (who are very fond of it) was Schumann-Heink, and Sigrid Onegin is just as sprightly and staccato in it as *she* was, that is, when she once gets off her long notes. In her splendid *Stride la vampa* she is more restrained, yet with a positive torrent of gorgeous tone.

Tino Pattiera.—Although one cannot help admiring this tenor's luscious quality and engaging style, it seems wrong somehow to sing *Che gelida manina* with the same dark, passionate tone that he puts into the *Carmen* song. Surely they call for utterly different modes of colouring and expression—the one ingenious, ingratiating, the other half appeal, half pent-up ecstasy. But Tino Pattiera never varies his vocal complexion, which is essentially Southern. He has a good voice, though, and is very clearly recorded.

Aroldo Lindi.—A tenor of quite another colour, this ; extremely bright, telling, and powerful. In some respects I prefer his *Flower Song* to that just noticed, while his *Ah si, ben mio* quite smacks of the old Tamagno school. Altogether a very satisfying disc.

Eric Marshall.—I am convinced that if this excellent baritone would cultivate deeper breathing he could wholly overcome the annoying tremolo that afflicts him at odd moments. His natural tone is frank and unspoilt, his timbre extremely sympathetic ; but both would gain from darker " covering " and thus facilitate stronger contrasts. In effect his rendering of *Nemico della patria* (*Andrea Chénier*) is too indulgent and sentimental for a monologue of that sort ; but on the other hand his *O Star of Eve* is quite appropriately poetic and refined. The H.M.V. accompaniments and recording are beyond praise.

Heinrich Schlusnus.—This time the popular Polydor baritone gives a couple of old favourites that will be highly appreciated in their improved (i.e., increased) degree of dynamic energy. Valentine's act of shuffling off this mortal coil seems a rather lonely business without the aid of either his sister or a chorus. Still, he does very well for a dying man, and fills the stage-gramophone with huge volumes of sound. A nice contrast to this is the smooth, tender performance of the old man's *Lullaby* from *Mignon*.

Lauritz Melchior and *Emmy Bettendorf.*—A continuation of the love-duet from the bridal chamber scene in *Lohengrin*, a portion of which was noticed in this column last month. The whole makes a singularly fine performance of the scene, sung with admirable art by two accomplished interpreters and ably supported by the orchestra.

Grand Opera Chorus.—Here is more for the money. A good well-filled disc for half a crown containing the *Miserere* from the *Trovatore* capitally sung in English by a strong, well-drilled chorus with competent soloists—anonymous, it is true, but undeniably there—bells, orchestra, and everything complete. In *The Angelus* from *Maritana* the tone and the equipment are no less adequate.

La Scala Chorus.—Although the Finale to the third act of *La Gioconda* is not what I consider an ideal choice for gramophonic purposes, yet it gives good opportunity for showing how the new process brings the separate solo voices into clear relief, and as such this fine Columbia record is quite a success. If I prefer the *Prologue* to *Mefistofele* it is first of all because I think it a finer piece of music, and secondly, because the deep, rich volume of the Italian voices in the Scala Chorus produce an impression, aided by the brass of the orchestra, of something grand and noble, which is what Boito's stupendous opening really is. Altogether there is material here both for enjoyment and admiration.

HERMAN KLEIN.

OPERATIC

RACHEL MORTON (soprano): **By the Ramparts of Seville,** Seguidilla, from " Carmen " (Bizet) and **He loves me** from " Faust " (Gounod). In English ; orch. acc. H.M.V., E.447 (10in., 4s. 6d.).

AIDA POGGETTI (soprano).—**Musetta's Song** from " La Bohème " (Puccini), in Italian, and **Le Toreador** from " Don Cézar de Bazan " (Adam), in French. V.F. 699 (12in., 4s.).

LAURITZ MELCHIOR (tenor): **Winterstürme wichen dem Wonnemond** (Siegmund's Love Song) from Act I. of " Die Walküre " (Wagner) and **Prize Song** from Act III. of " Die Meistersinger " (Wagner). In German ; orch. acc. Brunswick 50085 (12in., 8s.).

CECIL SHERWOOD (tenor).—**Una furtiva lagrima** and **Quanto è bella** from " L'Elisir d'Amore " (Donizetti). In Italian ; orch. acc. Columbia 4198 (10in., 3s.).

CECIL SHERWOOD (tenor): **Serenata** and **Sogno soave** from " Don Pasquale " (Donizetti). In Italian ; orch. acc. Columbia 4219 (10in., 3s.).

JOHN O'SULLIVAN (tenor): **O Paradiso** from " L'Africana " (Meyerbeer) and **Celeste Aïda** from " Aïda " (Verdi). In Italian ; orch. acc. Columbia L.1828 (12in., 6s. 6d.).

JOHN O'SULLIVAN (tenor): **Arioso** from " Pagliacci " (Leoncavallo) and **E lucevan le stelle** from " La Tosca " (Puccini). In Italian ; orch. acc. Columbia D.1564 (10in., 4s. 6d.).

DAME NELLIE MELBA (soprano) and **JOHN BROWNLEE** (baritone): **Dite alla giovine** from " La Traviata " (Verdi), in Italian, and **Un ange est venu** (Bemberg), in French ; piano acc., Harold Craxton. H.M.V., D.B.987 (12in., 8s. 6d.).

MARY OGDEN (mezzo-soprano) and **WILLIAM HESELTINE** (tenor) in **Home to our Mountains** and **GERTRUDE JOHNSON** (soprano) and **WILLIAM HESELTINE** with grand opera chorus in **Miserere** from " Il Trovatore " (Verdi). In English ; orch. acc. Columbia 9168 (12in., 4s. 6d.).

CHARLES HACKETT (tenor): **All hail, thou dwelling** from " Faust " (Gounod) and **Down her pale cheek** from " L'Elisir d'Amore (Donizetti). In English ; orch. acc. Columbia L.1832 (12in., 6s. 6d.).

G. ARANGI-LOMBARDI (soprano) and **LA SCALA CHORUS.**— **Madre pietosa Vergine** and **La Vergine degli Angeli** from " La Forza del Destino " (Verdi). In Italian ; orch. acc. Columbia L.1883 (12in., 6s. 6d.).

ARTHUR JORDAN (tenor): **Ah! Yes, thou'rt mine** from " Il Trovatore " (Verdi) and **Turiddu's Farewell** from " Cavalleria Rusticana " (Mascagni). In English ; orch. acc. Columbia 9180 (12in., 4s. 6d.).

ANNE ROSELLE (soprano): **Dio Madre** from " Madame Butterfly " (Puccini) and **Ritorna Vincitor** from " Aïda " (Verdi). In Italian. Orch. acc. Polydor 73026 (12in., 6s. 9d.).

BOHNEN (Sachs) and **SCHUTZENDORF** (Beckmesser): **Oh, ihr boshafte Geselle** and (Schützendorf only) **Den Tag sch' ich erscheinen** from Act II. of " Die Meistersinger " (Wagner). In German ; orch. acc. Parlophone E.10542 (12in., 4s. 6d.).

BOHNEN (Sachs), **BETTENDORF** (Eva), **OEHMANN** (Walther), and **SCHUTZENDORF** (Beckmesser): **Geliebter spare den Zorn** and **Jerum, jerum**, from " Die Meistersinger " (Wagner). In German ; orch. acc. Parlophone E.10541 (12in., 4s. 6d.).

EMMY BETTENDORF (soprano) and **LAURITZ MELCHIOR** (tenor): Duet, **Hörtest du nichts? vernamst du kein Kommen** from " Lohengrin " (Wagner) and (Bettendorf, with chorus) **Ich scheide nun aus Eurer Hitte** from " Undine " (Lortzing). In German ; orch. acc. Parlophone E.10540 (12in., 4s. 6d.).

TINO PATTIERA (tenor): **Recondita armonia** and **E lucevan le stelle** from " La Tosca " (Puccini). In Italian ; orch. acc. Parlophone E.10538 (12in., 4s. 6d.).

Rachel Morton.—This promising vocalist continues to do good work, but she has not yet mastered all the secrets of the art of recording. If she succeeds better in one piece than another, she should listen carefully for the point of difference and strive to take a lesson from them, making use only of the best qualities of tone that her voice can be made to yield. For example, this excerpt from " Faust " is better than that from " Carmen," because she succeeds more easily in producing a dark, sustained timbre, full of sympathy and passion, than when suggesting the sly, provocative utterances of the Sevillese damsel who warbles the *Seguidilla.* The latter, as a matter of fact, possess neither smoothness nor charm, though the words of the old English version come out clearly enough. By the way, I like hearing that lovely orchestral bit at the end of the Garden Scene in " Faust." It is generally either cut off by applause or by the descent of the curtain.

Aïda Poggetti.—The evident inexperience of the singer accounts for a great deal that is wrong about this record. Possessing a naturally fine soprano voice, she has failed as yet to obtain control of it. Her breathing is very faulty and permits of a marked tremolo, which shows badly in a gramophone record ; while her accent and enunciation are unsatisfactory both in Italian and French. Then she takes Musetta's lively, mischievous song literally at the pace of a funeral march—for all the world as though she had never heard it in " La Bohème " or anywhere] else. The air with variations known as " Le Toreador " is given in such slovenly fashion that I advise the artist for her own sake to re-record it. I am convinced she could sing it much better.

Lauritz Melchior.—Another welcome instalment on account from the excellent tenor who is going to sing Siegmund (but not Walther) at Covent Garden this season. He certainly has a fine voice and uses it in the heroic manner. His tone is more " covered " and refined in the *Prize Song* than the " Walküre " piece, but he sustains and phrases well in both, while his German diction might truly serve as a model. The sole fault worth pointing out is the audible gasp for breath. It might escape notice in the theatre, but on the gramophone it is palpable and irritating.

Cecil Sherwood.—There is a veritable spate of tenor records this month—not a single baritone ! Such an *embarras de richesses* is trying to one's powers of discernment ; for tenors formed and trained upon the modern Italian model sound so much alike that it is really difficult at times to tell one from the other. What is more, their average merit is very high, which only makes the task of discrimination harder still. In these new records by Cecil Sherwood the voice comes out big, clear, and resonant ; it only needs a little more variety of colour and occasionally, too, of steadiness, which in the case of this singer only means avoiding over-pressure. On the whole he sings Donizetti exceptionally well and each of his efforts has genuine merit to recommend it.

John O'Sullivan.—The Columbia Company would appear to be preoccupied with the immediate necessity for re-roasting the " chestnuts " or re-hashing the hackneyed. And a very good idea, too, when the right material is at hand, the demand self-evident, and the recording so amazingly improved. The old operas are, of course, the least expensive ; but then they are the ones we like best, and a voice with the Caruso-like quality and robustiousness of John O'Sullivan's has all the resisting power essential for the big " battle-horses." Hence the *Recitar* aria from " Pagliacci," the *Lucevan* from " Tosca," the *Paradiso* from " L'Africana," and *Celeste Aïda*—a sort of " clean sweep while you are about it." Well, truth to tell, they are all magnificently sung, well accompanied, and admirably recorded. Our Italo-Hibernian tenor is an artist to be reckoned with at Covent Garden next June. I would give him only one piece of advice—to beware of uniting into a single sentence phrases which *ought* to be divided by breaths that serve for exclamation or punctuation.

Dame Nellie Melba and *John Brownlee.*—Although the Bemberg duet is not one of his best efforts, it goes very well with the Verdi-like specimen from the second act of " La Traviata " as a suitable and effective theme for Dame Nellie and her talented countryman to exploit. Their voices mingle pleasantly, the quality of the famous prima donna's being still wonderfully pure. Harold Craxton's accompaniments are, as usual, quite perfect.

Mary Ogden, Gertrude Johnson, and *William Heseltine.*—More duets of the familiar but ever-popular sort, brought up to date by all the accessories that modern recording can furnish good singing withal ! The *Miserere* is the better example of the two ; the voices blend agreeably, although the soprano controls her medium more efficiently than her head register, and the tenor soloist is

often a trifle more modest than he need be. The chorus is adequate and well in tune. In *Home to our Mountains* some neat work is done by both singers.

Charles Hackett.—So far as the purely vocal side is concerned there is little fault to find with this tenor's performances. One might prefer a slightly less nasal production, and so strong an organ could well dispense with that extra " diapason." Still, there is no getting away from the fact that it is a fine tone. What is far more open to criticism is Mr. Hackett's distortion of English vowels and all the exaggerations—evidently unconscious in an American singer—to which it leads. Really some kind friend should point these errors out to him ! No amount of beauty of tone and sentiment will compensate (to English ears) for sounds that are a mere mockery of our glorious language. I have animadverted upon these things *ad nauseam,* but this singer is so good that he ought to be told of his mistakes—such, for instance, as that of singing the cadenza in the *Furtiva lagrima* upon a word like " ever."

G. Arangi-Lombardi.—With the Scala chorus in the background this clever Italian soprano makes a sufficiently picturesque affair of these two selections from *La Forza del Destino.* The *tremolo* is rather prominent, of course ; but then, *que voulez-vous* ? If you desire the real Italian article of to-day, you must take it as it comes, especially if, apart from that little defect, you have here a couple of highly dramatic and musically perfect records.

Arthur Jordan.—Rather doleful, I fear, the impression left behind by these solos. The singer is always artistic ; but in the present instance his style suggests oratorio rather than opera, and all of Turiddu at least dwells on the same wailing sentimental note. There is nothing really big or traditional either about this unmanly Manrico, though he is pleasing enough, I allow. Rather a pity, when the English words are so pure and distinct in both cases.

Anne Roselle.—The voice in this disc sounds small and obscured. I have tried it over two or three times with different needles, with the same result. Nevertheless, both records are interesting and, but for the singer's persistent *vibrato,* would worthily represent her art and her intelligence ; both of which are becoming celebrated. Perhaps some day she will get rid of the only objectionable blemish in her work and then we shall welcome in her a great Verdi-Puccini artist.

Bohnen and *Schützendorf.*—They are beginning to send us from the Continent some delightful Wagner " tit-bits " that have not hitherto been deemed worth the trouble of recording, or perhaps were too awkward to present under the old conditions. The consequence is that gramophonists will soon be able to claim a complete acquaintance with scores like that of that " Die Meistersinger." We have here scenes from the second act admirably sung by men who are obviously fine in their respective parts—Bohnen as Hans Sachs and Schützendorf as Beckmesser—and the recording gives a result astonishing in its realistic excellence.

Bohnen, Bettendorf, Oehmann, and *Schützendorf.*—The words just written apply exactly to this record, which reproduces the delicious episode in Act II. where Beckmesser endeavours to serenade Eva, but is interrupted by Hans Sachs with his noisy Cobbler's ditty, *Jerum, jerum* ; whilst Eva and Walther von Stolzing pursue their flirtation undisturbed beneath the shadow of the elder-tree. Even the quaint voice and horn-call of the night-watchman are included.

Emmy Bettendorf and *Lauritz Melchior.*—On one side of this disc the accomplished German artists continue and, I fancy, conclude their series of duet records from " Lohengrin," the complete set of which is well worth having. On the other side the soprano with chorus furnishes a tuneful selection from Lortzing's " Undine," an opera very popular in Germany that deserves to be known in England. It was first mounted at Hamburg in 1845, and the story is founded upon an Eastern story of a water-nymph without a soul, who obtained one by marrying a mortal, but acquired with it all the pains and penalties of humanity.

Tino Pattiera.—I wrote last month about this powerful tenor's " dark, passionate tone " and the invariable use that he makes of it. This monotony of colour matters less, perhaps, in the " Tosca " arias than it would elsewhere, the consequence being unqualified admiration for the breadth and sonority of the performance. The high notes are round enough, but one can enjoy even more the baritonal richness of the middle voice.

HERMAN KLEIN.

405

OPERATIC

ZENATELLO (tenor) and **NOTO** (baritone).—Duet, **Mio signore (No, my lord)** and **Ora e per sempre** (Addio) from **Otello** (Verdi), recorded from Covent Garden during actual performance, June 17, 1926. In Italian. Conducted by Vincenzo Bellezza. H.M.V., D.B.953 (12in., 8s. 6d.).

MAARTJE OFFERS (contralto).—**Printemps qui commence** from **Samson et Dalila** (Saint-Saëns) and **Connais-tu le pays ?** from **Mignon** (Thomas). In French. H.M.V., D.B.913 (12in., 8s. 6d.).

CHORUS AND ORCHESTRA OF THE STATE OPERA, BERLIN, conducted by Leo Blech.—**Da zu dir der Heiland Kam** and **Wach auf' es nahet gen den Tag** from **Die Meistersinger** (Wagner). In German. H.M.V., D.1211 (12in., 6s. 6d.).

ROSINA TORRI (soprano).—**Tu che di gel sei cinta**, Act 3, and **Signore, ascolta !** Act 1, from **Turandot** (Puccini). In Italian. H.M.V. B.2409 (10in., 3s.).

ELISA STÜNZER (soprano).—**Ah, lo so** from **Il Flauto Magico** (Mozart) and **Euch Lüften, die mein Klagen**, Elsa's Air from **Lohengrin** (Wagner). In German. Polydor 95015 (12in., 5s. 9d.).

HERBERT SIMMONDS (baritone).—**Prologue** from **Pagliacci** (Leoncavallo). In English. Regal G.8779 (10in., 2s. 6d).

LA SCALA CHORUS, conducted by **CAV. CARLO SABAGNO**.—**Gli aranci olezzano** from **Cavalleria Rusticana** (Mascagni) and **Coro delle compare** from **Pagliacci** (Leoncavallo). In Italian. H.M.V. C.1317 (12in., 4s. 6d).

LAURITZ MELCHIOR (tenor): **O Paradiso** from **L'Africaine** (Meyerbeer) and **Als ich erwachte**, Act III, Sc. 3, from **Tannhäuser** (Wagner). In German. Polydor 66439 (12in., 5s. 9d.).

CARL MARTIN OEHMANN (tenor): **Prize Song** and **Am stillen Herd** from **Die Meistersinger** (Wagner). In German. Parlophone E.10552 (12in., 4s. 6d.).

SIGRID ONEGIN (contralto): **Mon cœur s'ouvre à ta voix** from **Samson et Dalila** (Saint-Saëns), and **Chanson Bohême** from **Carmen** (Bizet). In French with orchestra. Brunswick 50077B. (12in.).

EVA TURNER (soprano): **Vissi d'arte** from **La Tosca** (Puccini and **Voi lo sapete** from **Cavalleria Rusticana** (Mascagni). In Italian. Columbia L.1836 (12in., 6s. 6d.).

APPLETON MOORE (baritone): **So, Sir page**, from **Figaro** (Mozart), and (a) **Serenade**, (b) **Drinking Song** from **Don Giovanni** (Mozart). In English. V.F. 703 (12in., 4s.).

BETTENDORF (Eva), **BOHNEN** (Sachs), **OEHMANN** (Walther), **GOMBERT** (David) and **LÜDERS** (Magdalena).—**Quintet** from Act III of **Die Meistersinger** (Wagner). In German. Parlophone E.10544 (12in., 4s. 6d.). (See under Orchestral Reviews : **Good Friday Music** from Parsifal).

JAN KIEPURA (tenor): **Recondita armonia** and **E lucevan le stelle** from **La Tosca** (Puccini). In Italian. Parlophone R.20008 (12in., 6s. 6d.).

Zenatello and *Noto*.—To those who, like myself, happened to be present at Covent Garden on June 17th last year, when Verdi's *Otello* was given, it will be peculiarly interesting to hear a portion of it over again, thanks to the unsuspected presence of a microphone and the necessary connection with an electric recording machine at Hayes, Middlesex. Wonderful are the ways in which things like this can be done. What an agreeable surprise, too, to hear the best part of the fine duet between Otello and Iago, which Messrs. Zenatello and Noto sang to such admiration, presented once more by the same two artists for our own especial benefit, as it were. It seems to me that this record brings with it every imaginable quality of the drama which is being enacted—the atmosphere, the text, the music, the splendid singing of the two men, the orchestral effects—everything, in short, that the ear could possibly take in. Zenatello's voice is in particularly first-rate order, his declamation imposing, his sense of climax and colour unerring. Bar the B flat, which Tamagno dwelt on with such ringing power, this might be the original Otello over again.

Maartje Offers.—The air from *Samson* is the better of the two. *Connais-tu le pays ?* is taken as if the sole idea were to get it

over and done with—audible gasps for breath and hurried, spasmodic phrasing. One asks, why such excitement over a request for a little geographical information ? And one adds, what a lovely quality of voice, if only it did not tremble ceaselessly !

Berlin Opera Chorus and Orchestra.—Often have I felt sorry when the overture to *Die Meistersinger* broke off at a " full close," instead of merging into the glorious chorale which is sung on the rising of the curtain by the congregation in the Katrinenkirche at Nuremberg. Well, here we have it now in sonorous volume, performed by the executive forces of the Berlin State Opera-house at the Singakademie under Dr. Blech. The whole effect is very satisfying, the quality of the voices being especially good ; and the orchestral bit at the end, where the burghers emerge from the interior of the church, is admirably played. Equally fine, in every sense, is the rendering of the choral hymn for St. John's Day sung by the crowd in the final scene on the banks of the Pegnitz.

Rosina Torri in Turandot.—The part of the slave, Liù, in Puccini's posthumous opera may not be nearly so prominent as that of the wicked heroine herself, but for all that it takes a first-class singer to do it justice. Maria Zamboni was the original, but, judging from this record, Rosina Torri must be extremely good, too, and I commend her effort to all who are endeavouring, with the aid of the H.M.V., to make acquaintance with this elaborate work before Signor Forzano mounts it at the Royal Opera. Of the two airs—if they may be so designated—sung by Liù, the one in the third act is the more interesting. It recalls most distinctly the touching dramatic passage in A flat minor, "That your mother should take you," sung by Madame Butterfly in the second act. It also sounds intensely dramatic here, and the clear, bright soprano of the singer rings true in every note of it. One could hardly wish to hear these pieces better sung or the result more accurately recorded.

Elisa Stünzer.—These are both records that " scratch " loudly enough to offend the ear ; and, to be quite candid, the singer is not one who can afford to put up with mechanical deficiences of that kind. Her voice is by no means remarkable, her style dull and lachrymose, her tendency to " scoop." If you can distinguish any words, you will find that she is singing *Ah, lo so* in German, not Italian. On the whole, she is to be preferred in the excerpt from *Lohengrin*, which lies more comfortably within her range.

Herbert Simmonds.—Cheap editions of good musical literature are always acceptable. Why not cheap records of popular operatic pieces ?—the *Pagliacci Prologue*, for instance. The present example is sung with good, honest, pleasing tone, plain enunciation, and freedom from exaggeration of any sort. Being in two parts, there is no need for hurry. Only now and then the vowels are not so correct and well defined as they ought to be. The gentleman before the curtain wants to deny that the actor " has no heart to feel," and makes it sound as if he said " has no hat to fill." Evidently he can't go round with one to make his collection.

La Scala Chorus.—The first thing that strikes the listener on hearing this record is the immensity of the volume of tone. It is simply tremendous. The next is the extraordinary clearness of the separate voices as they pursue their parallel harmonic lines. More often than not this *Pagliacci* " bell " chorus sounds on the stage a muddled and confused outpouring of vocal noise. Here it is the very opposite. The musical quality of the voices is preserved throughout just as surely as the rhythm of the *canzone popolare*, the ding-dong of the bell, and the rich colour of the orchestration. In short, it is another addition to the mechanical wonders that the new electrical recording is daily adding to the gramophile's store.

Lauritz Melchior.—The tenor who can sing Meyerbeer well is not essentially the one to shine as a Wagnerian artist, and *vice versa*. If the fact were not notorious there would be ample evidence of it in the records that fill each side of this disc. There is a whole world of difference between the merit of Melchior's singing of the *Africaine* air, its constrained manner, its lack of elegance and breadth, compared with his easy—I had almost said breezy—declamation in Tannhäuser's narration of his pilgrimage to Rome. The latter reveals the German tenor at home and at his best ; as Vasco de Gama on a voyage of discovery he sounds quite out of his element, and southern passion plays no part therein. Otherwise the singing is artistic and the orchestration neatly brought out.

Carl Martin Oehmann.—Here is another German robust tenor, but of a very different stamp. The voice is of vast dimensions, open and somewhat crude in quality, lacking in refinement and reticence, always well on the note and supported by rare breathing capacity, yet without poetry or tenderness of expression in the rendering of Walther's familiar show pieces. Obviously the artist knows his music thoroughly (he gives you more of *Am stillen Herd* than has ever been heard on a gramophone before), and delivers it with amazing freedom from effort, considering the amount of tone he brings out. Still, the quantity is more striking than the quality.

Sigrid Onegin.—This industrious artist continues to add constantly to her repertory, and all that she does is pretty nearly on the same level of excellence. Her voice, a mezzo-contralto of superb quality and power, is so easily produced that every kind of music from Opera to Lieder seems to lie comfortably within her reach. Her steadiness and breath-control are well exemplified in the air from *Samson et Dalila*, and the French text, both in this and the *Chanson bohême* from *Carmen*, serves as an aid to telling nasal resonance even when the words themselves are slightly indistinct. The top B flat ending to *Mon cœur s'ouvre* is neatly done, and the semiquaver turns in the *Carmen* are clear, whilst given with extraordinary *verve*.

Eva Turner.—The *Vissi d'arte* is sung very slowly, with much slurring of descending intervals, and therefore drags a good deal. In *Voi lo sapete* there is more freedom and *abandon*, consequently a livelier suggestion of misery, if I may so put it. The voice is strong, dramatic, and well-managed, the intonation correct, while the recording leaves nothing to be desired.

Appleton Moore.—Three Mozart airs on a single disc, and all three sung in a jolly animated sort of way which seems to fit them well enough. The style reminds me somewhat of the good old days of ballad opera ; the pronunciation of the English words certainly does ; and a tremulous, breathless energy adds to the general boisterousness of the whole thing. The record will please many.

Bettendorf, Bohnen, Oehmann, Gombert, and *Lüders.*—The quintet in the third act of *Die Meistersinger* is one of the musical wonders of the world, and it is also one of the most exacting *ensemble* pieces to perform. Even the finest artists cannot succeed in revealing its true loveliness and exquisite harmonic progressions save by dint of a perfect dynamic balance, in addition to every other recognized quality of vocal excellence. This combination is pretty hard to attain, and the five singers above named have only partially achieved their aim. When the voices unite they are too loud, too " thick," and their course is difficult to follow with precision. They are in tune, but the effect is noisy and rough, especially towards the end, thus marring the beauty of the wonderful climax. Altogether I would have expected a finer result from such artists.

Jan Kiepura.—" Save me from my friends," might well be the present motto of the young Polish tenor who made his London début at a B.B.C. concert at the Albert Hall last month. Happily I am not called upon to criticize here what he did on that occasion. Enough that I did hear him then (through my excellent loudspeaker) in the same two passages from *Tosca* that he has also recorded, and the results are singularly identical. Jan Kiepura possesses a magnificent organ, as yet only partially trained, but fraught with the greatest possibilities. If he will quit public life for a couple of years and devote himself seriously to hard study, he may even justify in the long run his alleged resemblance to a certain deceased tenor. So far, as these records show, he is only a creature of infinite promise.

HERMAN KLEIN.

OPERATIC

MARIA JERITZA (soprano).—**Agatha's Prayer** from " Der Freischütz " (Weber). Two parts. In German. H.M.V., D.B.982 (12in., 8s. 6d.). (Translated in THE GRAMOPHONE, July, 1926, p. 86.)

ELISABETH SCHUMANN (soprano).—**Deh vieni, non tardar** from " Le Nozze di Figaro " (Mozart) and **L'Amerò sarò costante** from " Il Rè Pastore " (Mozart). In Italian. H.M.V., D.B.1011 (12in., 8s. 6d.).

GERTRUDE JOHNSON (soprano).—**Waltz Song** from " Roméo et Juliette " (Gounod) and **Jewel Song** from " Faust " (Gounod). In English. Columbia 9193 (12in., 4s. 6d.).

SIGRID ONEGIN (contralto).—**Amour, viens aider** from " Samson et Dalila " (Saint-Saëns) and **Ah, mon fils** from " Le Prophète " (Meyerbeer). In French. Brunswick 50076 (12in., 8s.).

M. G. THILL (tenor).—**Je suis aimé de toi** from " La Traviata " (Verdi) and **Air de Jean** from " Hérodiade " (Massenet). In French. Columbia L.1964 (12in., 6s. 6d.).

FERNAND ANSSEAU (tenor).—**Salut, tombeau sombre et silencieux** and **Ah, lève-toi, Soleil !** from " Roméo et Juliette " (Gounod). In French. H.M.V., D.B.951, 12in., 8s. 6d.

MARIA ZAMBONI (soprano).—**Signore, ascolta** and **Morte di Liù** from " Turandot " (Puccini). In Italian. Columbia D.1572 D.1571 (10in., 4s. 6d.).

FRANCESCO MERLI (tenor).—**Non piangere Liù** and **Nessun dorma** from " Turandot " (Puccini). In Italian. Columbia (10in., 4s. 6d.).

BIANCA SCACCIATI (soprano) and **FRANCESCO MERLI** (tenor).—**In questa reggia** from " Turandot " (Puccini). Two parts. In Italian. Columbia D.1570 (10in., 4s. 6d.).

JOHN O'SULLIVAN (tenor).—**Di quella pira** and **Ah si, ben mio** from " Il Trovatore " (Verdi). In Italian. Columbia D.1573, (10in., 4s. 6d.).

MARIANO STABILE (baritone).—**Monologo dell'Onore** and, with Natalia de Santis, **Quando ero paggio** from " Falstaff " (Verdi). In Italian. Columbia L.1970 (12in., 6s. 6d.).

MARIANO STABILE (baritone) and **La Scala Chorus.**—**Te Deum** from " La Tosca " (Puccini) and, with **A. VENTURINI** and **G. NESSI, Brindisi** from " Otello " (Verdi). In Italian. Columbia L.1969 (12in., 6s. 6d.).

LA SCALA CHORUS OF MILAN.—**Chorus of Cigarette Girls** from " Carmen " (Bizet) and **O Signore che dal tetto natio** from " I Lombardi " (Verdi). In Italian. Columbia D.1568 (10in., 4s. 6d.).

Maria Jeritza.—It will be understood, of course, that this is the great air in *Der Freischütz* which we know best under the title of *Softly Sighs*, and which in the original German is called *Leise, leise.* I cannot say whether Agathe is in Maria Jeritza's répertoire, or indeed, whether she has ever essayed it at all ; but in any case it is not a character that would bring out the strongest side of her talent, and the music does not seem greatly to appeal to her. In spite of there being plenty of room to spare on the disc, she takes the whole piece at record speed (no pun intended !), sings it perfunctorily and without a trace of religious fervour. The tone is frequently hard, but the diction irreproachable throughout.

Elisabeth Schumann.—Two admirable bits of Mozart singing by an artist who always shines to advantage in the music of the immortal master. The voice is delightfully steady. But on a 12-inch disc we ought, I think, to get the recitative *Giunse alfin*, which precedes *Deh vieni*. The violin *obbligato* in the *Rè Pastore* air is gracefully played by Marjorie Hayward.

Gertrude Johnson.—The waltz-airs from *Roméo et Juliette* and *Faust* are familiar enough, yet how seldom does one hear them really well sung ? Brightness and fluency alone do not suffice ; they demand brilliancy and technical finish as well, and here, I fear, is where the present efforts fall short. The chromatic flourish that begins the Roméo ought never to be sung *staccato* ; while the *acciaciaturas*, or little grace notes, in the principal waltz theme are not all alike, as the singer seems to suppose. Most of them rise instead of falling to the main note, and Gounod was very particular about this being accurately done. The cadenza is smoothly executed, but, on the whole, the performance of the *Jewel Song* is the neater of the two.

Sigrid Onégin.—Just the right sort of alluring voice, of course, for a Dalila, but with little if any trace of the *diablerie* essential to *Viens aider ma faiblesse*, where the Philistine woman, revealing her real self, calls upon her gods to aid her in her seductive arts. The vocal tone is lovely, but too sentimental, and all the liberal " slurring " is quite out of place. In *Ah, mon fils*, as a pitiable, pleading mother, the gifted Sigrid is much more at home, and takes her high A sharp " like a bird."

M. G. Thill.—This tenor is at the Paris Opéra, but his name indicates a Belgian or Flemish rather than French origin. Anyhow,

407

he has a remarkably fine voice, powerful, resonant, and agreeable in quality, if now and then just a trifle rough. The traditions of the school are well displayed in both airs—a broad, dramatic style and untiring *sostenuto* in that from *La Traviata*, best known as *De miei bollenti spiriti*, and clear, strong declamation in the *Air de Jean* from Massenet's opera, in which Jean de Reszke first earned fame as a tenor in Paris. The latter is from the prison scene in the third act, and contains some effective but rather fragmentary phrases.

Fernand Ansseau.—It is a pleasure to hear two of the finest tenor moments in Gounod's *Roméo et Juliette* so grandly realised as they are by Fernand Ansseau in these records. He says to himself—or his voice—" laissez aller "—and it goes, with all imaginable strength, purity, and beauty of tone. One might easily, of course, hear *Ah, lève-toi, Soleil* as powerfully sung in the opera, but not often the salutation to the tomb of his ancestors wherewith Romeo bids farewell to life. He is, as a rule, somewhat fatigued by the time that climax arrives and less fit to do it justice. Here the gramophone gets the pull, for in this record you may hear Ansseau just as fresh as when he started. The recording is admirable.

Maria Zamboni.—The Columbia Company, with fitting enterprise, are helping to complete the selections from *Turandot* in time for the promised production of Puccini's opera at Covent Garden next month. Here are some from Milan that form a welcome addition to the H.M.V. collection already noticed by me ; welcome more especially because they are sung by the artists who created the rôles at La Scala last year. There is a pathetic quality in Maria Zamboni's voice that is peculiarly adapted for the music of the slave Liù ; a certain fatalistic manner, the lassitude of a creature tired of life, yet who does not depart from it without protest, that is reflected in every phrase. The music itself tells us nothing new, but the singer makes it descriptive and interesting. The recording, as in all these excerpts, is exceedingly clear.

Francesco Merli.—Generally speaking, there seems little about the Prince in *Turandot* to distinguish him vocally from other Puccini heroes. He gives you, in the best modern Italian tenor manner, bar after bar that reminds you of old friends—Rodolfo, Cavaradossi, F. B. Pinkerton, and the rest. In these passages he is trying to comfort Liù and to flatter himself that he is bound to overcome the resistance of the wicked Turandot. Both are excellent in their way.

Bianca Scacciati and *Francesco Merli.*—The soprano will, I understand, sustain her original rôle at Covent Garden and then will be the time to judge between her and Maria Jeritza, who is also to sustain the part here, as she did in New York. (I hope, at least, that we shall hear both Turandots.) The Italian soprano proves herself in this record a highly dramatic artist, and although her head notes are distinctly less sweet than those of Anne Roselle in the same music, her medium is far pleasanter and more free from tremolo. Her appeal to the Prince not to persevere in his ordeal is boldly declaimed, and his refusal to obey her wish makes the scene dramatically complete.

John O'Sullivan.—Here is a foretaste, and a good one, of the coming *Trovatore* revival. Both airs are splendidly given, with no lack of generous and powerful tone. The same tenor is also down for the Prince in *Turandot* and Raoul in the *Huguenots*—I beg pardon, *Gli Ugonotti*.

Mariano Stabile.—Simply perfect in his records, even as he was in his wonderful embodiment of Falstaff at our Royal Opera last season ! I cannot conceive anything finer than Stabile's rendering of the " Honour " monologue, and here it comes out absolutely " according to plan." Note, moreover, that the exquisite *Quand' ero paggio* is preceded by the whole of the masterly scene with Mistress Ford—musically represented by Natalia de Santis. The entire record, in fact, is a flawless treat. The second disc, giving the selections from *Tosca* and *Otello*, does not stand upon the same high plane. We have had the *Te Deum* much more effectively done by Formichi, even minus the Scala chorus. On the other hand, the drinking song of Iago is given with rousing spirit and *entrain*, well supported by Venturini, Nessi, and the aforesaid chorus.

La Scala Chorus.—The Cigarette Girls sing smoothly and in tune. The next thing will be a device for wafting the " smoky " atmosphere of Seville from the gramophone whilst they are doing it. The chorus of slaves from Verdi's forgotten opera, *I Lombardi*, was scarcely worth reviving. It sounds now like Donizetti-and-water. The one in *Aïda* a quarter of a century later simply knocked it into the proverbial " three-cocked-hat."

HERMAN KLEIN.

OPERATIC

EVA TURNER (soprano).—**O cieli azzurri** from " Aïda " (Verdi) and **Suicidio** from " La Gioconda " (Ponchielli). In Italian. Orch. acc. Columbia L.1976 (12 in., 6s 6d.).

ELISABETH SCHUMANN (soprano).—**Venite, inginocchiatevi** and **Non so più** from " Le Nozze di Figaro " (Mozart). In Italian. Orch. acc. H.M.V. D.A.844 (10 in., 6s.).

ELISABETH RETHBERG (soprano).—**Dich, teure Halle** from " Tannhäuser," Act 2 (Wagner), and **Euch Lüften, die mein Klagen** from " Lohengrin " Act 2 (Wagner). In German. Orch. acc. Brunswick 15116 (10 in., 5s. 6d.).

LOTTE LEHMANN (soprano).—**Auf Flügeln des Gesanges** (Mendelssohn) and **Von ewiger Liebe** (Brahms). In German. Orch. acc. Parlophone R.20013 (12 in., 6s. 6d.).
In questa reggia and **Del primo pianto** from " Turandot " (Puccini). In German. Orch. acc. Parlophone R.20014 (12 in., 6s. 6d.).

ROBERTO D'ALESSIO (tenor).—**Ecco ridente in cielo** from " Barber of Seville " (Rossini). and **Ay ! Ay ! Ay !** (Perez). In Italian. Orch. acc. Columbia D.1575 (10 in., 4s. 6d.). See also under *Songs*.

AURELIANO PERTILE (tenor).—**Non piangere Liù** and **Nessun dorma** from " Turandot " (Puccini). In Italian. Orch. acc. Parlophone RO.20010 (12 in., 4s. 6d.).
Vesti la giubba and **No, Pagliaccio non son** from " Pagliacci " (Leoncavallo). In Italian. Orch. acc. Parlophone R.20012, (12 in., 6s. 6d.).

CECIL SHERWOOD (tenor).—**La Donna è mobile** and **Questa o quella** from " Rigoletto " (Verdi). In Italian. Orch. acc. Actuelle 15244 (12 in., 3s. 6d.).

JAN KIEPURA (tenor).—**La Donna è mobile** and **Questa o quella** from " Rigoletto " (Verdi). In Italian. Orch. acc. Parlophone R.20016 (12 in., 6s. 6d.).

MARIANO STABILE (baritone).—**L'Onore** and **Prima di tutto** from " Falstaff " (Verdi). In Italian. Orch. acc. Parlophone R.O.20011 (10 in., 4s. 6d.).

FERNANDO AUTORI (bass).—**La Calunnia** from " Barber of Seville " (Rossini) and **Abbietta zingara** from " Il Trovatore " (Verdi). In Italian. Orch. acc. Parlophone R.20015 (12 in., 6s. 6d.).

ALEXANDER KIPNIS (baritone).—acc. by State Opera Orchestra, Berlin.—**Wotan's Abschied** from " Die Walküre " (Wagner). In German. H.M.V. D.1225 (12 in., 6s. 6d.).

Eva Turner.—One hears a good deal of this English soprano's success in Italy and remembers with equal pleasure the promise of her more modest labours at home with the B.N.O.C. or the Carl Rosa Company—I forget which. She is now also making records of the usual more ambitious operatic solos which dozens of other sopranos have made before her, and these from *Aida* and *Gioconda* are fairly up to the average mark. I would, however, warn Signorina Turner against the prevailing Italian habit of " forcing," because it is already beginning to harden her voice and invest it with a decided tremolo ; lots of power, of course, and all the usual dramatic effects, but no real beauty either of voice or style. The tone, when not forced or even pressed, is delightful.

Elisabeth Schumann.—These two airs from *Le Nozze* sound well in the Italian, albeit not perhaps quite so perfect as they would in the German text with this gifted artist as the singer. Happily, too, both are unhackneyed, and I am not at all sure that she has ever essayed the rôle of Cherubino, though *Non so più* is of course in the repertory of every Mozart soprano. So much the more interesting. The Susanna excerpt—*Go down upon your bended knees* in the English version—is particularly sweet and tuneful ; also capitally recorded and a model of clearness. The orchestra in both is perhaps a trifle too much in the background.

Elisabeth Rethberg.—Oh these Elisabeths, how clever they all are ! Well do they know also exactly what suits them ; and I daresay they are right in imagining that their admirers in every land where the gramophone flourishes (and where does it not ?) are never tired of hearing them perform upon the same old *chevaux de bataille*. These from *Tannhäuser* and *Lohengrin* seem to be as inevitable and popular as the solar eclipse that is due this month, only far more frequent. This Elisabeth, too, is an exquisite artist, and her *mezza voce* in *Euch Lüften* is even more wonderful than her declamation. The contrast of both in *Dich, teure Halle* is unusually marked.

Lotte Lehmann.—Not even Goethe's Charlotte (whereof Lotte is the diminutive) could have spread the butter on her bread more smoothly and finely than our favourite Marschallin has spread her mellifluous tone over the surface of the *Lieder* records which I am here permitted to review. The heavenly melody of *Auf Flügeln des Gesanges* is quite divinely phrased, i.e., without the slightest seeking after effect, sustaining it with a clarity and steadiness of tone that puts something of unwonted charm into Mendelssohn's immortal song. Again, in that of Brahms perfection is attained through simplicity, fervour, sincerity, and true sense of contrast. In the *Turandot* pieces one notes great depth of sentiment, growing passion cleverly brought out, irreproachable intonation, and a noble style throughout.

Roberto d'Alessio.—The name of this new Italian tenor is identical with that of the unbelieving hero of *La Sonnambula*, but his voice does not bring back memories of bygone tenors who used to warble the inspired Bellini melodies in equally bygone days. No, d'Alessio is fashioned, like all up-to-date Carusos, upon a certain recognized pattern of which contemporary Italian teachers have unquestionably mastered the peculiarities, and which I, for one, am as unquestionably not in love with. The style is equally unmistakable in each of the singers whose records I am noticing after this. The rendering of *Ecco ridente* reveals first-rate breath-control (one of the good qualities of the school) in a pleasing voice, but by no means immaculate *fioriture*.

Aureliano Pertile.—The La Scala favourite is to be heard at Covent Garden this month, so I will confine myself now to praising his obvious realization of Puccini's intentions in the two examples from *Turandot*. In those from *Pagliacci* the notable points are the tremendous vocal power employed, the fearless outbursts of anger, violent passion, and despair in which Canio can now indulge before the microphone, and which would formerly have resulted in hopeless " blasting." The effect of sonority is truly gigantic. If he can only keep down his tendency to a strong *vibrato* my impression is that he will prove to be the best robust tenor heard since Tamagno.

Cecil Sherwood.—The gramophonist who is not on the look-out for names will probably find as much satisfaction in this cheap Actuelle disc as in that recording the same two airs from *Rigoletto* noticed in the succeeding paragraph. Both are cut to pattern. The voices are different, the individual qualities different ; but the style, the phrasing, the ornaments and flourishes—these are absolutely identical. And the surprising part of it is that the foreigners appear to assimilate the familiar characteristics of timbre and method every bit as naturally and readily as the Italians themselves. Be they American, Polish, Irish, what you will, they all lay hold of the " pattern " with the same exactitude. Cecil Sherwood does this and something besides : he puts into his singing intelligence and a certain measure of individuality, and he always keeps perfectly in tune even on his loudest notes.

Jan Kiepura.—The same *Questa o quella* and *La donna è mobile*, imitated from the same model, only with a bigger tone and a few more liberties in the treatment of the design, and—at very nearly double the price. Personally I do not lay great stress on names or sensational methods. Hence I would for once prefer the cheaper article, because on the whole it is the better one. The more expensive record certainly furnishes more resonance for the money, more variety of rhythm and cadence, and a good high B at the end. *Voilà tout !*

Mariano Stabile.—Here, again, you have remarkably good value in a remarkably fine record. Stabile's rendering of these two scenes from *Falstaff* is quite unique, and it is gratifying to find that they have been made available for the gramophone in all their perfection. The orchestration sounds thin ; but, where the voice, the amazing diction, the endless varieties of colour and nuance are so completely satisfying, one does not feel the need for more. Indeed, it brings back the whole picture for those who have seen it, and faithfully suggests it for those who have not. As he trolls forth his contemptuous views of " honour " and his triumphant boasting to Ford, you can positively visualize the " fat man " strutting about the inn parlour at Windsor. Stabile is truly the ideal Falstaff.

Fernando Autori.—Creditably sung, but no more, and, of course, adequately recorded, are these familiar excerpts. Don Basilio in *La Calunnia* and Ferrando discoursing of the past to the Count's retainers, in the first scene of *Il Trovatore*, are early Rossini and Verdi of a purely characteristic type and always worth hearing.

Alexander Kipnis.—This is by a long way the finest record (two parts) of *Wotan's Abschied* that has come under my notice. Kipnis is a *basso cantante* with a glorious voice of enormous volume, yet capable of investing the long farewell with all the delicate and strongly contrasted shades of expression of which it is susceptible. But for his recent engagement at the Metropolitan Opera House, New York, Kipnis would doubtless have been heard in the *Ring* cycles just concluded ; but anyhow he was announced to be the Marcel in the revival of *The Huguenots*, and that would afford him a sufficient chance of proving his worth to begin with. His singing and declamation in this record must be described as magnificent, and in it he is worthily supported by the orchestra of the Berlin opera house. The recording, too, is extremely fine.

HERMAN KLEIN.

OPERATIC

ANNA MARIA GUGLIELMETTI (soprano).—**Regnava nel silenzio** and **Quando rapita in estasi** from **Lucia di Lammermoor** (Donizetti). In Italian. Col. L. 1959, 12in., 6s. 6d.

MARIA JERITZA (soprano).—**Il est doux, il est bon** from **Herodiade** (Massenet) and **Adieu, forêts** from **Jeanne d'Arc** (Tchaikovsky). In French. Orch. acc. H.M.V. D.B.1041, 12in., 8s. 6d.

GWLADYS NAISH (soprano).—**Shadow Song, Ombra leggiera** from **Dinorah** (Meyerbeer) and **Gli angui d'inferno, Queen of the Night Song**, from **The Magic Flute** (Mozart). In Italian. Orch. acc. Velvet Face 708, 12in., 4s.

ARTHUR JORDAN (tenor).—**Flower Song** from **Carmen** (Bizet) and **O vision entrancing** from **Esmeralda** (Goring Thomas). In English. Col. 9204, 12 in., 4s. 6d.

LUCIEN MURATORE (tenor).—**Amor ti vieta** from **Fédora** (Giordano) and **Air de la fleur (Flower Song)** from **Carmen** (Bizet). In French. Orch. acc. Actuelle 15245, 12in., 6s.

TINO PATTIERA (tenor).—**O Lola** and **Turiddu's Farewell** from **Cavalleria Rusticana** (Mascagni). In Italian. Orch. acc. Parlo. E.10584, 12in., 4s. 6d.

TITO SCHIPA (tenor).— **Fantaisie aux divins mensonges** from **Lakmè** (Delibes) and **Pourquoi me reveiller ?** from **Werther** (Massenet). In French. Orch. acc. H.M.V. D.A.870 10in., 6s.

CECIL SHERWOOD (tenor).—**Calma il tuo cor** from **Mefistofele** (Boito) and **A te o cara** from **I Puritani** (Bellini). In Italian. Col. 4365, 10in., 3s.

ALESSANDRO VALENTE (tenor).—**Non piangere Liù** and **Nessun dorma** from **Turandot** (Puccini). In Italian. Orch. acc. conducted by Manlio di Veroli. H.M.V. B.2458, 10in., 3s.

GIUSEPPE DANISE (baritone).—**Nemico della patria**, Act 3. Andrea Chénier (Giordano) and **Credo** from Otello (Verdi), In Italian. Orch. acc. Brunswick 50079, 12in., 8s.

CARLO GALEFFI (baritone).—**Largo al factotum** from **Barber of Seville** (Rossini) and **Dio possente** from **Faust** (Gounod). In Italian. Orch. acc. Col. L.1980, 12in., 6s. 6d.

IVAR ANDRESEN (bass).—**O Isis and Osiris** and **Within this hallowed dwelling** from **The Magic Flute** (Mozart). In German. Orch. acc. Parlo. E.10574, 12in., 4s. 6d.

SPANI (soprano) and **ZENATELLO** (tenor).—**Otello** Love Duet. Finale Act I.—**Quando narravi** and **Venga la morte** (Verdi). In Italian. Orch. acc. H.M.V. D.B.1006, 12 in., 8s. 6d.

LA SCALA CHORUS AND ORCHESTRA.—(a) **Gravi, enormi, venerandi**, Act 2, Sc. 2, and **O Divina ! nella luce mattutina** Act 3, Sc. 2 from **Turandot** (Puccini). In Italian. H.M.V. D.1241, 12in., 6s. 6d.

CHORUS AND ORCHESTRA OF THE STATE OPERA HOUSE, BERLIN, conducted by Oscar Fried.—(a) **Easter Hymn** from **Cavalleria Rusticana** (Mascagni) and **Bridal Chorus** from **Lohengrin** (Wagner). In German. Brunswick 80000, 12in., 6s. 6d. (b) **Spinners' Chorus** from **The Flying Dutchman** (Wagner) and **Hunters' Chorus** from **Der Freischütz** (Weber). Brunswick 80003, 12in., 6s. 6d. (c) **Grand March** and **Pilgrims' Chorus** from **Tannhäuser** (Wagner). Brunswick 80004, 12in., 6s. 6d.

EMMY BETTENDORF (soprano) with **CHORUS AND ORCHESTRA OF THE BERLIN STATE OPERA HOUSE,** conducted by Eduard Moerike : **Easter Hymn** and **Regina Coeli** from **Cavalleria Rusticana** (Mascagni). In German. Parlo. R.20017, 12in., 6s. 6d.

CHORUS AND ORCHESTRA OF THE BERLIN STATE OPERA HOUSE, conducted by Eduard Moerike :

Triumphal March, Act 2, Sc. 2, from **Aïda** (Verdi). In German. Parlo. R.20018, 12in., 6s. 6d.

Anna Maria Guglielmetti.—This *soprano leggiero* made her debut at Covent Garden recently in *Gli Ugonotti*, otherwise *Les Huguenots*, in the part of Margherita di Valois. The agreeable voice and vocal skill which she then displayed under trying circumstances are heard to better advantage in the present record. We may all be getting rather tired of the solo itself (and of a good many more like it), but it serves its purpose, presumably, for those chiefly interested, apart from its place in Donizetti's well-worn opera. Anyhow, it is nicely sung in a purely mechanical fashion, and every note of it is strictly in tune ; which is something to be thankful for when you can get a steady tone in addition.

Maria Jeritza.—If we did not have the pleasure of hearing Jeritza *in propriá personá* this season, we can at least have the satisfaction of listening to her voice in a couple of new records, which bring out with faithful accuracy her ringing tone and the effortless spontaneity of an unforced production. They are both sung in French, and " pity 'tis " that the accent should not be purer. (Truth to tell, it is very Austro-Hungarian indeed.) But both the airs are intelligently sung, and at least the right dramatic accent is always noticeable. Otherwise there is only Jeritza to distinguish their rendering from many others already in the catalogues, except that the recording is admirably clear and well defined.

Gwladys Naish.—If the *coloratur* work in the *Shadow Song* were on a level with the *staccato* and the runs in the *Magic Flute* air, this would be a highly creditable example of what a British singer with a naturally fine voice is capable of accomplishing. As it is, she has not been taught the right tempo for the *Ombra leggiera* and it drags so heavily along that all the lightness and charm disappear. Surely the conductor ought to have perceived the error, if only by the excessive length of the disc. The voice is clear and strong, especially in the declamatory tone towards the end of the Mozart ; while the facility in the head register should have been accompanied by a more accurate shake.

Arthur Jordan.—Surely this excellent tenor can stop his *tremolo* before it goes further and spoils a really good voice. At the same time he should refrain henceforth from slurring nearly every downward progression to an extent that is almost as bad as " scooping " in the other direction. How can one fail to notice these defects if watched for in a " test " record? It always goes against the grain when one hears a pleasing voice, solid diction, good intonation, and artistic intelligence practically spoilt by shortcomings of the kind I have indicated. The tone of the orchestra, too, does not balance well with the solo voice, Of the two pieces I prefer the *Vision entrancing*, which is elegantly phrased.

Lucien Muratore.—This disc produces such powerful sounds that I find it bearable only with an extra soft needle. The tone then is fairly sweet and pure. Here, in contradistinction to the record just noticed, I prefer the *Flower Song* from *Carmen*, although Muratore's French is inferior to his Italian. He makes a rather dull, monotonous thing of the air from *Fédora*, and I am bound to say it lends itself rather to that result ; there is not an iota of variety in tone, colour, or style, and the constant *portamento* is irritating.

Tino Pattiera.—Originally a fine tenor voice, its owner has acquired such a habit of emitting it with breathy gasps and jerks that he is fast depriving it of all its beauty. I have often begged for " atmosphere " in these operatic records, but cannot agree that it is to be arrived at by such means. The dark tremulous tone may fairly depict Turiddu's state of suppressed excitement during the tragic interviews with Lola and his mother ; but the same ejaculatory style all through is really too much—a little of it goes quite a long way. If Tino Pattiera wants to imitate a good model for well-controlled passion he should listen to Aureliano Pertile.

Tito Schipa.—These charming examples from operas by Delibes and Massenet are welcome, not only for their own sake, but because they exhibit the talent of the singer in its most favourable light—that is to say, under the soothing influence of a soft needle for the drawing room. Gramophones are getting so powerful in these days that Italian tenors with a *mezza voce* or even a *piano* like Tito Schipa's have no further need to put forth their full strength in refined French music. Nevertheless the artist phrases both airs with elegance, and engenders a wish to hear him on the stage both in *Lakmé* and *Werther*. The recording, too, is irreproachable.

Cecil Sherwood.—I have ascertained that this tenor is by birth an Australian who has lived in Italy for fifteen years. Hence the impeccable accent and the ultra-Italian method. For lovers of the latter doubtless nothing could be more acceptable than Mr. Sherwood's vocal concept of these airs by Bellini and Boito—the white open tone, the tolerably constant *vibrato*, the prevailing tendency to shout every phrase. Personally I am somewhat disappointed with the record, because it is not nearly up to the singer's usual level, as evidenced in several instances ꝗhat have won unqualified praise in this column.

Alessandro Valente.—The titles of the *Turandot* solos, like the music itself, are beginning to grow familiar. These are the two principal tenor excerpts, ably accompanied by an efficient orchestra and well conducted by Manlio di Veroli. The soloist has a sympathetic voice, a smooth scale, and a comfortable, easy style which he does not spoil by excess of energy. Both pieces are performed in a manner that does Puccini entire justice as heard apart from the stage.

Giuseppe Danise.—Here, again, a soft needle is advisable, the penetrating power of the vocal tone being extraordinary. This baritone is influenced, whether unconsciously or otherwise, by Chaliapin, notably in the manner of his declamation, and luckily he is intelligent enough to employ his imitative faculty to good advantage. His words are clear, his voice of splendid quality and good all through the scale ; while in both airs he shows himself master alike of the significance and beauty of the music. Altogether the record is well worth possessing—an excellent specimen of good work all round.

Carlo Galeffi.—The record of the *Largo al factotum* is unusually good. It bears all the traces of being accented by a well-trained Italian comedian—patter crisp and distinct, humour everywhere, plenty of lively *entrain*, resonant tone in a capital voice. As usual, the comedian succeeds less completely in the more sentimental mood of a Valentine ; for these new artists are not all Cotognis and Santleys ; and I care less accordingly for the *Dio possente* on the reverse side. Still, taken for all in all, there is sufficient good work in or on this disc to justify my recommending it.

Ivar Andresen.—A typically benevolent German High Priest peeps benignly through these reproductions of the two famous airs from *The Magic Flute*. The very style of the singer has a " bless you my children ! " touch, as he slowly drawls out the gracefully tender old music. He is a bass rather than a *basso profondo*, since he declines to descend to the low E at the end. But the quality of the voice is genuine and agreeable.

Spani and Zenatello.—There is an abundance of emotional feeling to be noted in these excerpts from Verdi's *Otello* ; and really there is not much more that is fresh to be said about them. Evidently the Desdemona and the Otello are vocally on the best of terms, and their voices, when they have to blend, do so most satisfactorily. The recording is bright, musical, and true.

La Scala Chorus and Orchestra.—With the advent of these magnificent selections the reproduction of *Turandot* for gramophone purposes must surely be approaching completion. Never before has a new opera been so swiftly recorded, so entirely at the disposal of a curious public. The next thing, I suggest, will be to ask the Italian marionettes at the London

Scala Theatre to mount this Chinese story and act it in their own way to Puccini's music, played by H.M.V. records on a first-class H.M.V. machine, as performed by the company of La Scala at Milan. It would be very appropriate and interesting. These choruses from the second and third acts bring to my ears the precise effects that I experienced recently at Covent Garden. They could not well be more sonorous or more impressive.

Berlin State Opera Chorus and Orchestra.—Here is a marvellous *réchauffé* of familiar stuff with a vengeance! It represents, I suppose, the apex of the triumphs achieved by the new recording process—for the present at any rate. By the time another total eclipse, visible in England, comes along, I dare say there will be gramophone records of choral singing to eclipse these; but the contingency seems a long way off. Alike for volume and fidelity of tone they are unsurpassable. You can enlarge or reduce dimensions—whereof there would appear in these reproductions to be a fourth—but you cannot very easily go beyond the actuality of the original. Like the records taken at our own Covent Garden or in the transept of the Crystal Palace during a Handel Festival, these choral sounds impinge upon your ears, not as if produced in the apartment where you are listening, but as if heard amid the vast spaces of the auditorium in which they were actually performed and recorded. To my ears, therefore, they are of that supreme excellence which cannot be transcended. The singing itself is of a nature to create this impression. Certainly I cannot remember to have ever heard the Easter Hymn from *Cavalleria Rusticana* or the choruses from Wagner's earlier operas so perfectly rendered in any opera house. The sonority is almost overwhelming, yet utterly free from opacity or confusion; clear enough to be dazzling, like the *feux d'artifice* of a great *coloratura* singer. The slowness of the *Bridal Chorus* from *Lohengrin* makes it one of the loveliest things imaginable, instead of the commonplace tune that it very often sounds. Oscar Fried is a conductor with imagination, and his forces faithfully reflect his refinement and intelligence, even as these records reflect their splendid efforts.

Emmy Bettendorf with Ditto.—Every word just written applies equally to the *Easter Hymn* conducted by Eduard Mörike with Emmy Bettendorf singing Santuzza's solo; and it fills both sides of the disc. The tone is, if anything a trifle more subdued and even more musical. The sense of space is again amazing, while the grandeur of the ending, with the full organ and the addition of the solo voice, produces a superb effect. The same forces, minus the soprano solo, of course, furnish yet another wonderful record in the great march and chorus accompanying the triumphal return of Radamès in the second act of *Aïda*. Here, again, gigantic volume is by no means the sole meritorious feature; but on the other hand slowness is a distinct disadvantage, and the prolonged, measured blare of the Egyptian trumpets becomes tedious. Besides, their quality is not equal to that of our British-made instruments, which were specially manufactured for the production of Verdi's opera in London fifty years ago.

HERMAN KLEIN.

OPERATIC

MICHELE FLETA (tenor).—**Celeste Aida** from **Aida** (Verdi) and **Una vergine** from **La Favorita** (Donizetti). In Italian. Orch. acc. H.M.V. D.B.1053, 12in., 8s. 6d.
FERNANDO AUTORI (bass).—**Serenata di Mefistofele** from **Faust** (Gounod) and **Ballata del fischio** from **Mefistofele** (Boito). In Italian. Orch. acc. Parlophone R.20020, 12in., 6s. 6d.
SPANI (soprano) and **GRANFORTE** (baritone).—**Decidi il mio destin** and **No, più non m'ami** from **Pagliacci** (Leoncavallo). In Italian. La Scala Orchestra, conducted by Carlo Sabajno. H.M.V. D.B.1046, 12in., 8s. 6d.
LA SCALA CHORUS.—**Inneggiamo al Signor** from **Cavalleria**

Rusticana (Mascagni) and, with **ANNA MARIA TURCHETTI** (soprano), **La vergine degli angeli** from **La Forza del Destino** (Verdi). In Italian. H.M.V. B.2445, 10in., 3s.

Michele Fleta.—Previous records by this typical specimen of the modern Italian tenor have elicited favourable comment, and so must the present examples. Personally, I am much less tired of listening to a solo from Donizetti's *La Favorita* than to the eternally celestial *Celeste Aida*. The trouble with a disc is that you cannot halve it with anybody. Otherwise, I would say to my best friend, "You shall take the *Celeste Aida*, which Michele Fleta sings quite excellently, and I will take the *Una vergine, angiol divina*, which he sings better still." Both, I admit, are slightly nasal, but not disagreeably so, and the singing is robust and tender by turns; while the recording is wonderfully clear. Well, as we can't toss for the half, you had better take them both.

Fernando Autori.—When I heard this useful artist at Covent Garden recently, I came to the conclusion that he was reliable in all things—including steadiness and intonation; but somehow I was driven to the conclusion that he does not add distinction of style to the possession of a fine voice. In a word, his methods are those of the good *routinier*. There is a certain amount of Mephistophelean flavour, both in the *Faust* serenade, which everybody knows, and in the boastful *ballata* which the same personage sings in the Brocken scene of Boito's opera. But there is nothing commanding or Chaliapin-like about either; the sardonic touch is not kept up enough. In fact, the sympathetic quality of the voice does not lend itself effectively to the music, despite the effort of the singer to make it do so. The laughs sound forced, and the extra one at the end could have been dispensed with, while the whistle after each verse would not suffice to start a train, much less attract the notice of a policeman.

Spani and *Granforte.*—The duet between Nedda and Silvio from the first act of *Pagliacci* is here given complete in two parts. It is, on the whole, remarkably well done. The soprano is not the exceptional artist that the baritone is; but from Italy at the present epoch that would have been too much to expect. Anyhow, her voice is adequate and she puts energy into her singing at the right moments. Granforte's is a really beautiful organ, with splendid compass and power, and a timbre that reminds me singularly of that great artist Cotogni, who shared the chief baritone parts with Faure or Graziani at Covent Garden years ago. It sounds young, fresh, resonant, and firm as a rock. Granforte does most of the work in the first record and throws abundant passion into Silvio's pleading. The Scala Orchestra brings out with praiseworthy clearness and finish the familiar features of Leoncavallo's scoring, the balance with the voices being quite irreproachable. The individuality of the different timbres is indeed marvellously depicted. When all unite towards the end in a strenuous outburst, the musical effect is splendid—a wonderful reproduction of a familiar portion of this opera that has never before been adequately recorded.

La Scala Chorus.—The first thing that strikes me about these records of ensembles from *Cavalleria Rusticana* and *La Forza del Destino* is the surprising quantity of music which they concentrate within the limits of a 10in. disc. (price 3s.). It is indeed what the auctioneers, in their own elegant jargon, describe as "a cheap lot." And also a good one. If the young lady who represents Santuzza and Donna Leonora only possessed a less "wobbly" voice, the quality of the solo bits might be described as equal in value to the quantity *and* quality of the other parts. Happily, she has not a great deal to sing. As for the rendering of the choruses, it reaches the very highest level of operatic excellence, being not only distinct and well-defined in execution, but impressively sonorous without any accompanying roughness or approach to shouting. The body of tone in the *Cavalleria* number is not less extraordinary than the steadiness of vocal line preserved in the other, and once more I pay a tribute to the rare merit of the recording.

HERMAN KLEIN.

OPERATIC

PAGLIACCI (Leoncavallo), recorded in the Scala Theatre, London, and sung in English by the Principals, Chorus and Orchestra of the British National Opera Company, conducted by Eugene Goossens, Senr. Complete in album, 36s. Columbia 4347–4358, twelve 10in. records.

OTHER RECORDS.

EVA TURNER (soprano).—**Ritorna vincitor** from **Aida** (Verdi). Two Parts. In Italian. Orch. acc. Col. D.1578, 10in., 4s. 6d.

M. G. THILL (tenor). **Flower Song** from **Carmen** (Bizet) and **Cavatina** from **Roméo et Juliette** (Gounod). In French. Orch. acc. Col. L.1985, 12in., 6s. 6d.

BENIAMINO GIGLI (tenor).—**Recondita armonia** from **Tosca** (Puccini) and **Donna non vidi mai** from **Manon Lescaut** (Puccini). In Italian. Orch. acc. H.M.V. D.A.856, 10in., 6s.

ROBERT EASTON (bass).—**Vulcan's Song** from **Philémon et Baucis** (Gounod) and **I'm a Roamer** from **Son and Stranger** (Mendelssohn). In English. Orch acc. Col. 9210, 12in., 4s. 6d.

BONCI (tenor) with Ensemble and Chorus.—**Di tu se fedele**, canzone with chorus and orchestra : and, with **RETTORE** (soprano), **RUBADI, BACCALONI** and **MENNI, E scherzo od è follia**, quintet with chorus and orchestra, from **Un Ballo in Maschera** (Verdi). In Italian. Col. L.1960, 12in., 6s. 6d.

LA SCALA CHORUS OF MILAN.—**Soldiers' Chorus** from **Faust** (Gounod) and **Anvil Chorus** from **Il Trovatore** (Verdi). In Italian. Orch. acc. Col. D.1576, 10in., 4s. 6d.

META SEINEMEYER (soprano).—**Son giunta, grazie O Dio** and **Non m'abbandonar** (**Madre, pietosa Vergine**), with chorus, from **La Forza del Destino** (Verdi). In German. State Opera Orchestra. Parlo. E.10605, 12in., 4s. 6d.

The Complete "Pagliacci."—The benefits of electrical recording are especially felt when it comes to a test like this. All the old risks and obstacles are no longer there to be overcome ; and, after laying out the score into the necessary convenient sections, so as to bring the whole opera within the scope of so many records, there remains only to go ahead with the performance in the ordinary way. Nothing could be simpler ; nothing more calculated to transfer to the whirring matrix the absolute actuality of tonal art combined with normal human effort. We hear in these twelve 10in. records the entire music of Leoncavallo's universally popular opera, exactly as we might be listening to it inside the Scala Theatre, London, where it was sung and played and mechanically recorded. It is not a reproduction, but the thing itself. Perfect in every detail ; the last word, so to speak, in gramophonic achievement, it is open to just so much criticism, and no more, than one would be able to level at the living representation. It is therefore a joy to listen, in spite of the brief interruptions, and take in the beauties of the whole opera at one sitting.

How different were the conditions under which I first made acquaintance with this work ! I do not allude to the first performance at Covent Garden in 1893 (with Melba, de Lucia, Ancona, and Richard Green in the cast), but to a private hearing from the vocal score, with my friend Enrico Bevignani at the piano, given for my benefit the previous year at Craig-y-Nos Castle, whilst I was staying there with Mme. Patti-Nicolini. So, if I was privileged to be the first to hear *Pagliacci* in this country, I now feel an additional pride in being the first writer to review this wonderful recording by the Columbia Company of the admirable B.N.O.C. performance at the Scala Theatre, under the baton of another eminent conductor and friend in the person of Mr. Eugene Goossens, senr. It would, I think, be superfluous to enter into details concerning each of the twelve discs, seeing that they vary very little, if at all, in merit. Suffice it to say that the singing of Miss Miriam Licette as Nedda, of Mr. Frank Mullings as Canio, of Mr. Harold Williams as Tonio, of Mr. Dennis Noble as Silvio, and of Mr. Heddle Nash as Harlequin touches and maintains with very little deviation the high level associated with their art at its best. The various scenes are carried on to their climax with unflagging energy and vigour, while the choruses throughout are amazingly sonorous and spirited. On the whole, the words come out rather more clearly than usual ; Mr. Williams being especially commendable in this respect. Yet I would fain reserve my warmest tribute for a quarter where I am as a rule least able to bestow it—I mean the orchestra. Mr. Goossens must have taken enormous pains to secure such a clear, vivid, and crisp yet refined rendering of Leoncavallo's clever instrumentation. Exquisitely balanced and always sufficiently audible, it imparts the requisite solidity of tonal foundation to the whole performance.

Eva Turner.—This excellent English soprano continues to bear aloft the banner of her country from end to end of Italy without any Fascist interference that I have yet heard of. In fact, she is now very nearly Italian herself ; and one adds with pleasures that the local *vibrato* which she was beginning to acquire shows distinct signs of abating. I have listened with relief, therefore, as well as satisfaction to her really splendid rendering of *Ritorna vincitor* (*Aida*) here embedded in a fairly cheap two-sided 10in. disc. The fine quality of the vocal tone deserves particular attention.

M. G. Thill.—The familiar qualities of the French school are "writ large" over both these airs. I am not sure as to M. Thill's nationality, but I do know that his accent is pure, his style free from tricks or mannerisms, and his powerful tenor voice fairly steady ; also that he is engaged at the Paris Opéra, where he sang the excerpts from *Carmen* and *Roméo* under the direction of M. Philippe Gaubert. His sole shortcoming of any importance lies in his method of producing his high notes. They are not clear and ringing ; he obviously forces them by employing a greater breath-pressure than they will stand. After all, loudness without beauty of tone is not enough for the enjoyment of a tenor's head register. By the way, the spelling of the French title on the *Carmen* label is incorrect. It should not be *La fleur que tu m'avis*, but *que tu m'avais jetée*.

Beniamino Gigli.—The well-managed voice of this young Italian tenor seems to improve as time goes on. It must be considered now as approaching its prime. Of all the imitators of Caruso (and they do not include Pertile, whose style is his own) it is Gigli, in my opinion. who gets nearest to the famous original, and notably so in the singing of Puccini. These selections from *Tosca* and *Manon Lescaut* are both of the highest excellence, alike in the vocal and the mechanical sense. Electrical recording having eliminated the dangers of " blasting," one perceives here the natural opulence of the tone throughout an even scale, enhancing the resonant power of the high notes, the beauty of the dark timbre, the absence of tremolo, and the ease of the *sostenuto*. The phrasing of Puccini has become such a mere convention that it is a pleasure to be able to point out these individual redeeming features.

Robert Easton.—The two records on this disc present a singular contrast—the same fine bass voice in both pieces, but a difference of style and effect that is simply astonishing. It is, however, no mystery, no problem beyond solution.

The singer knows how to make every point in *I'm a roamer*. He gets away with it from the starting-gate, and from that point is a winner as well as a roamer—tone, rhythm, words, humour, everything pat and perfect to the finish. With *Vulcan's Song* it is otherwise. Here too slow, there too fast ; now too deliberate and heavy ; nearly always too lugubrious—the true significance of Vulcan's allusive remarks and the satire of his own ugliness and deformity, showing what a mistake it is for him to quit Venus and his own fireside to go on nocturnal adventures—the humour of all this is utterly lost, thanks partly, perhaps, to the fatuity of the English translation. That, I suppose, is why Santley always insisted on singing this song in French.

Bonci with Ensemble and Chorus.—These concerted numbers from the second tableau of *Un Ballo in Maschera* present much the same features as those I have pointed out in previous (new) recordings. The tendency is to overload them with tone ; that is, for everybody to sing as loudly and noisily as if they had to fill a big auditorium. Even the gifted Bonci, who was once a model of refinement, is beginning to lose his velvety touch (presumably on account of " wear and tear ") and shout a bit at times ; whilst that laugh of his in the delightful quintet, *E scherzo od è follia*, is even more persistent and aggressive than Pertile's—it is positively annoying. Neither Jean de Reszke nor Caruso suffered " spasms " such as these ! Otherwise both records give a spirited idea of the scene in Ulrica's hovel.

La Scala Chorus of Milan.—Simply beyond criticism, of course ! Should a relentless destiny compel you to listen once more on the gramophone to the *Soldiers' Chorus* from *Faust* and the *Anvil Chorus* from *Il Trovatore*, I can conceive no more perfect medium than you will find here.

Meta Seinemeyer.—This excerpt from Verdi's *Forza del Destino* (last part with chorus) is magnificently sung by the German soprano, but not over well accompanied by the orchestra or heard to advantage through the recording. It is difficult, indeed, to imagine that this is a typical example of what the Parlophone can accomplish with the new process. Frau Seinemeyer is such a thoroughly first-rate artist that we ought to be afforded a much truer idea than this of the lovely quality of her tone and the tenderness as well as the dramatic power of her singing. As it is, it only sounds like a faint suggestion of either.

HERMAN KLEIN.

A SCHUMANN SONG CYCLE.

PARLOPHONE.

Frauenliebe und Leben, " Woman's Love and Life," Schumann, op. 42. Parlophone E.10696–8, three 12in. records with descriptive leaflet and words in German and English, 13s. 6d. Sung by **Emmy Bettendorf** (soprano) with piano accompaniment.

Song-cycles, like operas and symphonies, require to be heard in their entirety if we are to form an exact idea of what the composer intended when he laid out the plan of his work. Schubert did not, for reasons best known to himself, complete his so-called " Unfinished " symphony (neither did he, I fancy, expect anyone else to " finish " it for him) ; but when he invented the song-cycle he certainly intended the singer to perform the entire group whenever it was possible, though no great harm might be done by the omission of any. Even more urgently did Schumann demand this, because he employed the accompaniment to furnish a kind of *trait d'union* between the various numbers, and so made each an integral part of the whole. It is therefore all to the good that we should find gramophone records of a complete song-cycle such as *Frauenliebe und Leben* coming in for review, as it were, in the ordinary course of business.

The Parlophone Company deserves great credit for an artistic venture on the lines that I was advocating in THE GRAMOPHONE earlier in the year in connection with " The Singing of Lieder." It has even gone so far as to engage a soprano of the distinction of Frau Emmy Bettendorf to interpret the vocal part ; and right well, I may add, has she acquitted herself of the task. But beyond this, I am sorry to say, there is little to be offered in the way of praise, for the outcome as a whole must be pronounced very disappointing. The recording is so inferior that it is difficult to believe it to be done by the electrical process. The voice during most of the time sounds muffled and dull ; whilst the piano gives the impression of being one of those ancient silk-fronted instruments that the children of the early Victorian era practised their five-finger exercises upon. There are times, I admit, when these effects are less noticeable than at others, but such variableness ought not to occur when the material is there for a perfect all-round performance of a very beautiful set of songs.

Allowing for the fact that the *Frauenliebe und Leben*—there is no need for me to describe it again—was written for a mezzo-soprano, Emmy Bettendorf imparts all imaginable poetry and charm to Schumann's love-saturated melodies. *Du Ring an meinem Finger* lies conspicuously low for her ; but she phrases it with exquisite tenderness, and her *mezza-voce* here is delicious. *Er der herrlichste* sounds stronger because it lies higher ; yet it could be made more impressive by a long way. *Seit ich ihn gesehen* satisfies by its *Stimmung* and deep expression rather than any audible volume of tone. *Ich kann's nicht fassen* suffers from excessive waits and pauses in the halting middle section, though the last part is a dream of tender sentimentality. *Süsser Freund* begins lazily and dull, but brightens up as it goes on. The words need careful listening for, and the piano at moments is dreadful. *Nun hast du mir den ersten* starts with much more vigour, clearness, and musical quality. The effect of the quiet declamation in this final number, so full of reproachful pathos, is more satisfying than anything else in the cycle. Would that the whole had been equally beautiful ! HERMAN KLEIN.

OPERATIC

CHALIAPINE (bass).—**Farewell of Boris** and **Death of Boris** from **Boris Godounov** (Moussorgsky). In Russian, orchestra conducted by Eugene Goossens. H.M.V. D.B.934, 12 in., 8s. 6d.

CHALIAPINE (bass).—**In the Town of Kazan** from **Boris Godounov** (Moussorgsky) and **Song of Prince Galitsky** from **Prince Igor** (Borodin). In Russian. Orch. acc. H.M.V. D.A.891, 10in., 6s.

MARTINELLI (tenor).—**Celeste Aida** from **Aida** (Verdi), and **Che gelida manina** from **La Bohème** (Puccini). In Italian. Orch. acc. H.M.V. D.B.979, 12in., 8s. 6d.

MARTINELLI (tenor).—**La donna è mobile** from **Rigoletto** (Verdi) and **E lucevan le stelle** from **Tosca** (Puccini). In Italian. Orch. acc. H.M.V. D.A.842, 10 in., 6s.

SCHIPA (tenor).—**Chiudo gli occhi** (The Dream) from **Manon** (Massenet) and **O Colombina, il tenero fido** from **Pagliacci** (Leoncavallo). In Italian. Orch. acc. H.M.V. D.A.875, 10in., 6s.

GRANFORTE (baritone).—**O santa medaglia** from **Faust** (Gounod) and **Toreador Song** from **Carmen** (Bizet). In Italian. Orch. acc. H.M.V. D.B.938, 12in., 8s. 6d.

413

LOTTE LEHMANN (soprano).—**Ocean, thou mighty monster** from **Oberon** (Weber). In German. Orch. acc. In two parts. Parlophone R.20024. 12in.

PERTILE (tenor), **PAMPANINI** (soprano), and **GIULIO FREGOSI** (bar.).—**O soave fanciulla** from **La Bohème** and **Addio, fiorito asil** from **Madame Butterfly** (Puccini). In Italian. Orch acc. Parlophone R.20023, 12in., 6s. 6d.

SEINEMEYER (soprano) and **PATTIERA** (tenor).—**Du kommst daher** and **O wunderbare Schönheit**, duet from Act 3 of **Andrea Chénier** (Giordano). In German and Italian. Orch. acc. Parlophone E.10619, 12in., 4s. 6d.

DANISE (baritone).—**Avant de quitter ces lieux** (**Even bravest heart**) from **Faust** (Gounod) in French, and **Di Provenza il mar** from **Traviata** (Verdi). In Italian. Orch. acc. Brunswick, 50083, 12in., 8s. 6d.

SASSONE-SOSTER (soprano).—**Signor, ascolta** and **Tu che di gel sei cinta** from **Turandot** (Puccini). In Italian. Orch. acc. Actuelle 11459, 10in., 2s. 6d.

VOLTOLINI (tenor).—**Non piangere, Liù** and **Nessun dorma** from **Turandot** (Puccini). In Italian. Orch. acc. Actuelle 11460, 10in., 2s. 6d.

EVA LEONI (soprano).—**Bell Song** from **Lakmé** (Delibes) and **Le Rossignol et la Rose** from **Parysatis** (Saint-Saëns). In French. Orch. acc. Col. L.1988, 12in., 6s. 6d.

HEDDLE NASH (tenor).—**O Loveliness beyond compare** and **O Voice of magic melody** from **The Magic Flute** (Mozart). In English. Orch. acc. Col. 9228, 12in., 4s. 6d.

THEODORE RITCH (tenor).—**Dream Song** from **Manon** (Massenet), in French, and **E lucevan le stelle** from **La Tosca** (Puccini), in Italian. Orch. acc. Col. D.1590, 10in., 4s. 6d.

GENTILE, BORGIOLI, VANELLI, BACCALONI, NESSI, MANNARINI and **LA SCALA CHORUS.**—Sextet from **Lucia di Lammermoor** (Donizetti): and **GENTILE, BORGIOLI, PEDRONI, MANNARINI** and **LA SCALA CHORUS.**—**D'un pensiero** from **La Sonnambula** (Bellini). In Italian. Orch. acc. Col. L.1992, 12in., 6s. 6d.

ALFANI-TELLINI, CINISELLI, PACI and **LA SCALA CHORUS.**—Concerted Finale from Act 3 of **La Traviata** (Verdi): and **EVA TURNER, RUBADI, CINISELLI, PACI, CARMASSI** and **LA SCALA CHORUS.**—Concerted Finale from Act 2. of **Aïda** (Verdi). In Italian. Orch. acc. Col. D.1580, 10in., 4s. 6d.

Chaliapine.—With the magic name and no less magic art of Feodor Chaliapine is associated the most important contribution to the gigantic task of re-recording old successes yet accomplished by the H.M.V. I have not troubled to ascertain the dates of the original issues, but I am sure of one thing, and that is, that they stretch far back enough to constitute a flattering tribute to the freshness and staying-power of the singer's voice. He is now 54, and has been before the public well over thirty years. Yet his forces remain in all respects undiminished ; while the magnifying power of the new process would appear, if anything, to strengthen and enhance the individual qualities and volume of his tone until they equal those of the living organ. Here we have, to begin with, two excerpts from *Boris Godounov*, the opera in which he made in 1913 his first appearance at Drury Lane, and which, in my opinion, remains the finest of all his creations. Chaliapine is, in most things that he does, unique and unapproachable,

and in the *Farewell* and the *Death* of Boris he furnishes eloquent proof of the fact. He has also repeated an incomparable piece of bizarre comedy in *Vaarlam's Song, In the Town of Kazan*, the tremendous ditty which Moussorgsky put into the mouth of the beggar at the inn ; and he not only trolls it forth magnificently, but as though he were singing something he loved. (By the way, this is the scene and this the song of Vaarlam that Chaliapine is to give at the Albert Hall, when he appears there this month in a mixed operatic programme of novel design.) For Chaliapine was born at Kazan. Wonderful, again, are the tone and rhythm achieved in the *Song of Prince Galitsky* from Borodin's *Prince Igor*—another extraordinary piece of characterization, wherein each (Russian) word stands out clearly and conveys every iota of dramatic significance. The excellent orchestral accompaniments, directed by Eugene Goossens the Younger, show a vast improvement upon the old ones. Their strength is just in the right proportion to that of the solo voice.

Giovanni Martinelli.—These re-recordings of *Celeste Aïda* and *Che gelida manina* are also very welcome. Since he became an American favourite Martinelli has been heard here only at rare intervals, but he is now in his prime, one of the greatest living Italian tenors, and most of his older records scarcely do him justice. His beautiful voice remains fresh, unworn, pure in quality, and free from *vibrato*. He has marvellous breath control, a steady flow of opulent tone, and an effortless, ringing high C. In the new records his *Celeste Aïda* comes out better than ever, and will bear comparison with the finest that the gramophone can reproduce. For *Che gelida manina* the voice sounds almost too big, yet so suavely phrased that I fancy Puccini himself would have applauded it ; and what more can one say ? On a par with these are the *Lucevan le stelle* and *La donna è mobile* done on the 10in. disc. The sustained tone of the former and the tremendous spirit of the latter are quite splendid.

Tito Schipa.—These selections from *Manon* and *Pagliacci* complete the H.M.V. issue of re-recordings for the present month. They confirm the impression that, in fairness to everybody and everything, the whole of the pieces in demand should be similarly renewed whilst the artists are available to renew them. When Tito Schipa sang at Queen's Hall last season he proved himself to be gifted with unusual versatility ; and he shows it in these records by the vivid contrast between two styles—the quiet tenderness with which Des Grieux relates his *Dream* to Manon and the Neapolitan swing of the serenade that Arlecchino addresses to his flighty Colombina. Both are charming.

Apollo Granforte.—Having on previous occasions spoken highly of this baritone's work, I feel entitled to say that he can do better things than either of these familiar excerpts from *Faust* and *Carmen*. Valentine's song is taken too slowly ; there are alterations or errors, or both, in it that one feels inclined to resent, while the voice is none too steady. The *Toreador's Song* is less faulty and given with abundant spirit ; but here again the singer takes liberties with the time that a true artist ought to avoid and no student to imitate.

Lotte Lehmann.—I approached this latest record of *Ocean, thou mighty monster* in the critical spirit of one who heard the great Tietjens sing it at least half-a-dozen times. It was one of her famous *chevaux de bataille*. The greater, therefore, was my pleasure when I found myself listening to the finest rendering of Weber's glorious air that has come my way in modern days. It is the more wonderful when one remembers that Lotte Lehmann's voice, smooth, silken, lovely in quality though it be, is not that of a powerful dramatic soprano in the literal sense of the term. Tietjens's was nearly twice as big ; Ternina's probably half as big again. But for all the requirements of the noble *scena* from *Oberon*, Lotte Lehmann here proves herself a more than adequate interpreter. Her declamation, superb in its dignity, intelligence, clearness, and dramatic vigour, could not be surpassed. From the opening apostrophe, *Ozean, du Ungeheuer*, to the exciting climax where Rezia perceives and cries out to Sir Huon, it affords a magnificent example of this romantic school of singing, admirably supported as it is by the orchestra and exhibited to the best advantage by the electrical process of recording.

Pertile, Pampanini, and *Fregosi.*—Gladly will lovers of *La Bohème* and *Madam Butterfly* welcome these duet passages from either opera, if only for the reason that they are comparatively unhackneyed. Pertile's voice at its best reminds me not a little of Caruso's, and it records just as perfectly, which is saying much. The scene from *La Bohème* is the close of the first act, where Rodolfo and Mimi, having realized that they are in love, walk arm in arm out of the studio, singing as they go, to join their friends at the restaurant round the corner. The voices of soprano and tenor blend agreeably, if in favour of the latter until towards the end, where they share the parting high note. The other duet is nearly all Pinkerton; and none the worse for that, as embodied by Pertile in a farewell of glorious volume and intense expression, because, after all, nothing becomes the sentimental American better than his departure from the scene of misery that he has caused. Fregosi, alias Sharpless, just "chips in" where he gets a chance, and does it very nicely. The record is interesting.

Seinemeyer and *Pattiera.*—Another duet—the final scene from *Andrea Chénier,* where Madeleine joins the condemned poet in his dungeon and they ride off together to the guillotine. Here full steam is on from the first note to the last, and right well do the ecstatic exclamations of the lovers come out in the voices of these two soulful artists. They sound as if magnified to immense size, yet without detracting in the smallest degree from their fine quality. The words are less easily distinguished, because the lady is apparently singing in German and the gentleman in Italian.

Danise.—Gramophonists with a partiality for one of those huge deep baritone voices that emerge from the French school every now and then will assuredly find what they want here. The quality is somewhat reedy and not a little inclined to nasality; hence the fact that Danise may not be hailed as a second Lassalle or Plançon. Nevertheless it is an imposing, well-trained organ, and the singer has a spirited style, well adapted for the kind of piece he sings.

Sassone-Soster and *Voltolini.*—It is to be noted that these Actuelle records, issued by Pathé Frères Pathéphone, Ltd., are what are termed "needle cut," so that there is no necessity for—nor, indeed, possibility of—playing them with the Pathé sapphire ball. They comprise four items from Puccini's posthumous opera, *Turandot*, the titles whereof will absolve me from any fresh criticism of the music, while comparisons are equally uncalled for from the executive standpoint. Enough that both soloists are competent Italian artists, possessing good voices and an intimate acquaintance with the task they are set to perform. The orchestral work is also satisfactory and the recording of the best.

Eva Leoni.—A *soprano leggiero* who can do justice to the *Bell Song* from *Lakmé* must be exceptionally good. She is also the right singer for the "delightful fantaisie, all trills and roulades," which is about the only number that remains in the repertory of Saint-Saëns's music to the drama of *Parysatis*, composed by him in 1902 for performance in the open-air theatre at Béziers and first put on paper by him at a Greek café in Alexandria. Both pieces are rendered with a sweet, musical tone and remarkable ease and purity of execution.

Heddle Nash.—The unperfected technique which has so far detracted from complete enjoyment of this tenor's singing continues to betray itself in Mozart efforts such as the two airs from *The Magic Flute*. They are creditable efforts, but nothing more; whereas with a voice of such pleasing quality and undoubted artistic intelligence they would, if supported by correct breathing, a true *legato*, and a proper avoidance of

slurs in the wrong places, result in something really first-rate. Otherwise, for ordinary purposes the record will unquestionably "do."

Theodore Ritch.—A tenor whose voice, like his nationality, is unknown to me. The two sides of the present disc might have been sung by different persons, so unlike are they in almost every detail. The one I like is *E lucevan le stelle*, which in its dark vowel quality, manly, unaffected style, and easy powerful command of the loftier passages, is definitely redolent of the best modern Italian teaching. On the other hand, despite an equally good French accent, but inferior diction, the well-known *Rêve* from *Manon* is sung in a white nasal tone and, for the first half of the air, with unpleasantly flat intonation. Mr. Ritch might now try his hand at singing in English.

La Scala Ensembles and *Chorus.*—The facilities created by the new electrical process continue to enrich the Columbia catalogue with surprisingly clear and sonorous records of the big operatic ensembles, obtained for the most part at La Scala, Milan. The present selections include some of the most celebrated in 19th century Italian opera, representing Bellini, Donizetti, and Verdi at their most characteristic and effective moments. The sextet from *Lucia* on the whole, is too noisy, lacking in contrast and refinement. The famous *D'un pensiero*, embodying the situation in the second act of *Sonnambula*, which Sullivan so cleverly parodies musically in *Trial by Jury*, is much better balanced; the soprano is more in command and her E flat in *alt* at the end is quite good. The *Traviata* again is distinctly on an inferior level to the *Aïda*, where the voice come out splendidly and Eva Turner reigns supreme in virtue alike of her music and her voice.

HERMAN KLEIN.

OPERATIC AND GERMAN LIEDER

ELENA GERHARDT (mezzo-soprano).—**Mariae Wiegenlied** Op. 76, No. 52 (Reger) (translated June, 1925, Vol. III. p. 51) and **Geistliches Wiegenlied** (Brahms). In German, piano acc. H.M.V. D.B. 1030, 12in., 8s. 6d.

JOSEPH HISLOP (tenor).—**Salut, demeure chaste** from **Faust** (Gounod) and **Pourquoi me réveiller** from **Werther** (Massenet). In French, orch. acc. H.M.V. D.B. 944, 12in., 8s. 6d.

MAARTJE OFFERS (contralto).—**O du Fröhlicher** (Christmas Hymn, traditional) and **Stille Nacht, heilige Nacht** (Gruber) (translated Jan., 1925, Vol. II., p. 296). In German, organ acc. H.M.V., D.A. 768, 10in., 6s.

A. M. GUGLIELMETTI (soprano).—**Come per me sereno** and **Sovra il sen** from **La Sonnambula** (Bellini). In Italian. Orch. acc. Col. D.1583, 10in., 4s. 6d.

NORMAN ALLIN (bass).—**Tho' faithless men** from **La Juive** (Halévy) and **Little cattle, little care** (Jackson). In English. Orch. acc. Col. L.1996, 12in., 6s. 6d.

MME. McCORMIC and **GEORGES THILL.**—**Duet from Act 1** of **Manon** (Massenet). In French. Two parts. Orch. acc. under M. Frigara. Col. L.1953, 12in., 6s. 6d.

Elena Gerhardt.—In including for the first time in this page reviews of newly-recorded Lieder (chiefly sung by foreign artists), I regard myself as fortunate to be able to begin with something by that distinguished interpreter, Elena Gerhardt. The music she offers for our delectation may not be elaborate, but it is seasonable—eminently so—and it affords a most interesting example of different treatment of the same theme by two eminent German composers. The titles are not the same, but the traditional folk-tune is; being the famous cradle song of mediaeval days known as the *Geistliches Wiegenlied*. Only here it does not quite retain its original simple shape. Exactly when it was that Max Reger, a modern of the moderns, took it in hand I am not quite sure; nor does it greatly signify. Enough that he included it in his six books of "simple melodies for voice and pianoforte," Op. 76, which would indicate a tolerably recent date, long after it had been treated by Brahms and, as *Grove* tells us, "expanded and developed with consummate art." Which do I like the better of the two? That is really hard to say, for Mme. Gerhardt sings them so perfectly and invests them with such exquisite charm that it is a genuine relief to know they are both upon the same disc. In a word, you cannot acquire one without having the other also. And it will be doubly worth while for the sake of useful comparisons: if only to note how simply the complex Reger has used the tuneful old melody as a counter-theme in his piano accompaniment, whereas Brahms has handled it in the form of an effective viola or violin obbligato (here the former), as though,. having "first say" in the matter, he intended doing everything there was to be done. As a composition, therefore, the Brahms version must be accounted the more elaborate. For beauty of delivery and faultlessness of recording there is nothing to choose between them, though for my own part I must say that for once I prefer the obbligato accompaniment. It will be observed that an English translation of the text was published in Vol. III. of THE GRAMOPHONE in June, 1925.

Joseph Hislop.—It is gratifying to find a Scottish tenor pronouncing his French so accurately, on the whole, as it is in these two operatic pieces. That makes two languages besides his own that Joseph Hislop can utilize to advantage, in countries where his splendid vocal gifts are even more practically appreciated, apparently, than on this side of the Channel. His recent successes in Brussels and Paris have been duly reported, nor can I wonder at them if his Faust and Werther have been as fine as is indicated by these two records; and of course they have been. The opening of *Salut, demeure* (minus the recitative) is the loveliest example of *mezza voce* that has been heard from a British tenor since the palmy days of Edward Lloyd. The whole air is supremely well sung and the high C at the end is magnificent. The selection—"Ossian's song"—from Massenet's *Werther* (Act III.) is one of the most touching pages in an opera that suffers more from its dull libretto than its music, a good deal of which can be thoroughly enjoyed. Jean de Reszke once sang this *Pourquoi me réveiller* divinely, and its melancholy charm is abundantly realized in the present instance, thanks to Joseph Hislop's reposeful method and fine tone, supported by the graceful *arpeggiando* accompaniment of an excellent harpist. The entire record is mechanically faultless.

Maartje Offers.—This is another seasonable product of the kind noticed above. Familiar specimens of Old German music for Christmas again provide the subject-matter, presented with precisely the up-to-date accessories of gramophone mechanism, such as bells and organ, that are calculated to lend picturesqueness and colour to the general effect. Both hymns are introduced with loud, joyful chimes, followed by a few bars from the organ, which, of course, accompanies throughout, giving the desired ecclesiastical touch to the performance. Maartje Offers, with her powerful contralto voice, imparts a steadier flow of tone than usual to the simple phrasing of these glorious old tunes. She fairly revels in the well-known refrain of the traditional Christmas Hymn *O du Fröhlicher*, and lends it the requisite religious fervour. So, again, in the *Stille Nacht, heilige Nacht*, albeit her enunciation of the words is not quite so pure and distinct as it might be.

A. M. Guglielmetti.—This clever soprano verifies exactly on the gramophone the opinion I expressed about her when she appeared recently as the Queen in the *Huguenots* at Covent Garden. She is what I may term a highly-mechanized vocalist. Her voice, a sweet, ingratiating one, has been carefully trained to follow in the wake of Mme. Galli-Curci, to imitate her methods, copy her cadenzas, phrase as she does, breathe where she does, and execute her *fiorituri* in the same well-prepared, deliberate manner. The outcome is evident in extreme neatness akin to the sounds of a musical box, and with the same absolute lack of spontaneity. Every note is in tune and clearly heard. The whole thing supplies an accurate

model for the use of students, and I recommend it in consequence to vocal teachers.

Norman Allin.—A good record of the famous air from *La Juive* (*The Jewess*) is one of those achievements that every *basso profondo* is desirous of having to his credit. Norman Allin has certainly not failed in his endeavour, for this is an exceedingly good performance on the part of himself and all others concerned. It is vigorous and broadly phrased, without being unnecessarily heavy or lugubrious. But I cannot say as much for the doleful ballad, *Little cattle, little care*, which occupies the other side of the disc. Whence or why this pessimistic, mournful strain, I cannot tell. It is replete with misery.

Mme. McCormic and *Georges Thill.*—What a joy to turn from the preceding dirge to anything so enlivening and gay as this admirable record of the duet which terminates the first act of Massenet's *Manon*! Being in two parts it gives us the whole of the scene, with an irreproachable orchestral accompaniment conducted by M. Frigara. The tenor has the finer voice of the two, but nevertheless the young French soprano with the Irish name is bound to please with her pure diction, her sprightly manner, and the captivating *espièglerie* of her oft-repeated invitation, *Nous vivrons à Paris tous les deux*. No wonder that Des Grieux fell in love at first sight, poor fellow! His music is splendidly sung by Georges Thill, whom I have had previous occasion to eulogize. He is beyond question one of the best tenors singing at the Opéra-Comique at the present time. The electrical recording is quite first-rate.

HERMAN KLEIN.

OPERATIC AND FOREIGN SONGS

FLORENCE AUSTRAL (soprano) and **BROWNING MUMMERY** (tenor).—**Miserere** and **Home to our mountains** from **Il Trovatore** (Verdi). In Italian. Orch. acc. and chorus. H.M.V. D.1302, 12in., 6s. 6d.

NINON VALLIN (soprano).—**Jewel Song** from **Faust** (Gounod) and **Solveig's Song** from **Peer Gynt** (Grieg). In French, Orch. acc. Actuelle 11470, 10in., 4s.

FELICIE HÜNI-MIHACSEK (soprano).—**Ich soll ihn wiedersehen** from **Der Postillon von Longjumeau** (Adam) and **Alles teile unser Glück** from **Alessandro Stradella** (Flotow). In German. Orch. acc. Brunswick 50102, 12in., 8s.

SIGRID ONEGIN (contralto).—**Habañera** and **Seguidilla** from **Carmen** (Bizet). In French. Orch. acc. Brunswick 15128, 10in., 5s. 6d.

TOM BURKE (tenor).—**O vision entrancing** from **Esmeralda** (Goring Thomas) and **My dreams** (Tosti). In English, piano acc. Col. L.1951, 12in., 6s. 6d.

TOM BURKE (tenor).—**E lucevan le stelle** from **La Tosca** (Puccini) and **Nessun dorma** from **Turandot** (Puccini). In Italian. Orch. acc. Col. D.1593, 10in., 4s. 6d.

LUCREZIA BORI (soprano).—**Ciribiribin**, waltz song (Pestalozzi) and **Il Bacio** (Arditi). In Italian. Orch. acc. H.M.V. D.A.900, 10in., 6s.

EMILIO DE GOGORZA (baritone).—**O Sole mio** (di Capua) and **Santa Lucia** (Cottrau). In Italian. Orch. acc. H.M.V. D.A.903, 10in., 6s.

GIUSEPPE DANISE (baritone).—**La Paloma** (Yradier) and **Torna a Surriento** (de Curtis). In Italian. Orch. acc. Brunswick 30117, 12in., 6s. 6d.

ALFRED PICCAVER (tenor).—**Mattinata** (Leoncavallo) and

Lolita (Buzzi-Peccia). In Italian, orch. acc. Brunswick 15129, 10in., 5s.-6d.

RICHARD TAUBER (tenor).—**Die Lotosblume** (Schumann) and **Ungeduld** (Schubert). In German. Orch. acc. Parlo. R.O.20028, 10in., 4s. 6d.

RICHARD TAUBER (tenor).—**Lenz** (Hildach) and **Das zerbrochene Ringlein** (Kuhe). In German. Orch. and piano acc. Parlo. R.O.20029, 10in., 4s. 6d.

LOTTE LEHMANN (soprano).—**Murmelndes Lüftchen** (Jensen) and **Von Blut gerötet war meine Schwelle**, Madeleine's Aria from Act 3 of **Andrea Chénier** (Giordano). In German. Orch. acc. Parlo. R.20025, 12in., 6s. 6d.

AURELIANO PERTILE (tenor).—**Un grande spettacolo a venitre ore** and **Un tal gioco, credentemi** from **Pagliacci**, Act 1 (Leoncavallo). In Italian. Orch. acc. Parlo. R.20026, 12in., 6s. 6d.

BARDONE (soprano), **FREGOSI** (baritone), **PERTILE** (tenor), and **MINGHINI-CATTANEO** (mezzo-soprano).—**Bella figlia dell' amore**, quartet, and **V'ho ingannato**, duet, from **Rigoletto** (Verdi). In Italian. Orch. acc. Parlo. R.20027, 12in., 6s. 6d.

EMMY BETTENDORF (soprano).—**Mondnacht** (Schumann) and **Der Lindenbaum** (Schubert). In German. Piano violin and 'cello acc. Parlo. E.10629, 12in., 4s. 6d.

EMMY BETTENDORF (soprano).—**Allerseelen**, Op. 85, No. 3 (Lassen) and **The Last Rose of Summer** (Flotow). In German. Same acc. Parlo. E.10630, 12in. 4s. 6d.

ELIZABETH SCHUMANN (soprano).—**Wiegenlied** (Strauss) and **Freundliche Vision** (Strauss). In German. Piano acc. H.M.V. D.B.1065, 12in., 8s. 6d.

ALESSANDRO VALENTE (tenor).—**Vesti la giubba** from **Pagliacci** (Leoncavallo) and **Recondita armonia** from **La Tosca** (Puccini). In Italian. Orch. acc. H.M.V. C.1387, 12in., 4s. 6d.

TITO SCHIPA (tenor).—**Ombra mai fù**, Largo, **Xerxes** (Handel) and **M'appari** from **Marta** (Flotow). In Italian, orch. acc. H.M.V. D.B.1064, 12in., 8s. 6d.

Florence Austral and *Browning Mummery*.—It is a pleasure to find the names of these talented Australian singers coupled in good gramophone work, even though it be such well-worn duets as the *Miserere* and the *Home to our mountains* from *Il Trovatore*. The voices blend agreeably, and in tune ; they are clear and powerful. The chorus in the *Miserere* is inclined to "growl." Miss Austral discards the high C usually interpolated in place of the A flat on the repetition of "I'm thine for ever" ; but one can do without it. The record of *Home to our mountains* must surely have been made in the Albert Hall. There is in it an Echo which follows the voice of Azucena with most remarkable fidelity. It is amusing rather than disturbing ; and anyhow it is not stranger than hearing Verdi's contralto music so well sung by a soprano. It is a popular sort of record and for a 12in. not dear at 6s. 6d.

Ninon Vallin.—Cheaper still at 4s. is this young lady's Actuelle record of the *Jewel Song* from *Faust* and *Solveig's Song* from Grieg's *Peer Gynt* music. The waltz-air only is given without any of the recitative. The French accent and diction are worthy of a native, the voice fairly sympathetic, and the execution pleasantly neat. In the *Solveig* air the words may be less distinct, and there is a tendency to slur up to high notes ; but the tone in the refrain is charming.

Felicie Hüni-Mihacsek.—Adam's delightful light opera *Der Postillon von Longjumeau* is very popular in Germany, where they know how to appreciate these tuneful old things to-day as much as we in England did fifty years ago. Hence the recording of the principal soprano air by a well-known artist, and, I suppose, the rather high figure charged for the disc. The piece is sung with a musical tone—the first part with rich, generous soprano quality and expressive phrasing, the florid sequel with neat, pretty *coloratura* and plenty of animation. The same experienced touch is perceptible in the conventional air from *Alessandro Stradella*, though with a suspicion of doubtful intonation, particularly in the cadenzas. The music is not so good as that of *Martha*, yet the melodious swing and vocal effectiveness are quite worthy of Flotow.

Sigrid Onegin.—Always welcome in such a voice as this artist possesses are the most familiar operatic excerpts. There is no need to describe how she sings the two *Carmen* airs. Enough that her French is satisfying, her feeling and rhythm in the right Bizet mood, and her tone throughout superbly opulent. The *Seguidilla* is the more captivating of the two.

Tom Burke.—Save at certain moments in *O vision entrancing*, you would hardly recognise the Tom Burke singing in English as the same *tenore robusto* who holds forth with Pucciniesque vigour and amplitude the airs from *Tosca* and *Turandot*. I like him best in the latter because he sings Italian as to the manner born. In *My dreams* he sounds for all the world like a mild replica of John MacCormack. In that and the Goring Thomas air the tinkle of the piano accompaniment suggests prehistoric recording.

Lucrezia Bori.—Here are a couple of showy encore pieces brilliantly sung by one of the most accomplished Italian sopranos of her time. What a musical timbre, and what marvellous neatness and precision of execution ! Patti never knew *Ciribiribin*; but she made *Il Bacio*, and I have never heard it to such perfection since she sang it.

Emilio de Gogorza.—And here are a couple of Neapolitan "chestnuts," which, despite the cold season, I do not propose to "roast." As a matter of fact, the Hispano-American baritone converts them into such sugary *marrons* that they are bound to "go down," like the *portamento* with which they are so liberally bestrewn. The general effect is *très-chic*.

Giuseppe Danise.—Neapolitan again, with lots of local colour and the characteristic flavour of a good strong "Barbera." The resonance is powerful enough for outdoor use, and maybe a shade too strong for indoor. The classic version of *La Paloma* is that of de Gogorza, whose clever wife, I remember, used to tell the story of a lady friend of hers who thought she knew how to sing it. But this record of Danise's is, at any rate, quite in the approved manner.

Alfred Piccaver.—One might almost say "Ditto, ditto" here too, but somehow there is more charm in the seductive tones and languorous warbling of this tenor, who is Italian to the finger-tips, whatever may be said about his nationality. Both songs have their good points and Piccaver makes the most of them.

Richard Tauber.—German tenors of the calibre of this artist are extremely rare. He is a Lieder singer of the first rank. The voice is, despite a slightly nasal tinge, extremely sweet and sympathetic and under perfect breath-control. His diction, too, has a quiet beauty that reminds one of Leo Slezák at his best. In *Die Lotosblume* the resemblance is particularly striking, though the many original touches that enrich his phrasing show the singer to be no mere plagiarist. As a contrast, the energy displayed in *Ungeduld* is very welcome, especially on account of the quick enunciation required for Schubert's song, which is seldom to be heard to such advantage. Similar spirit and animation pervade the rendering of Hildach's *Lenz*, with its lively themes and effective climax ; while a lovely *pp. mezza voce* once more comes to the fore in Kuhe's sentimental old ditty, which loses nothing by being sung to a piano accompaniment. I hope to hear more records by Richard Tauber.

Lotte Lehmann.—The gifted soprano displays her admirable art in one of Jensen's best-known Lieder—one, moreover, that is seldom perfectly interpreted. Her tones are modulated with consummate skill and good recording brings them out in all their native purity. In the German version of *La mamma morta*, from *Andrea Chénier* we get the dramatic Lotte Lehmann of *Rosenkavalier*, and who could desire anything finer than that ? The phrasing of the big passages is broad and noble, their sweep most impressive.

Aureliano Pertile.—Judging by these efforts, Canio should be one of Pertile's big parts, and when he comes to Covent Garden again I hope we shall see him in *Pagliacci*. In both airs he follows effortlessly in the wake of Caruso and recalls many qualities of the tenor whom two Continents adored.

Bardone, Fregosi, Pertile, and *Minghini-Cattaneo.*—The famous quartet from *Rigoletto* is coupled here with the oft-omitted duet which concludes the opera, where the Jester discovers that the occupant of the sack is no other than his unlucky daughter. The latter—I mean the duet—receives the better rendering on the present record, being notable for the delightful tones of an exceptionally sweet Gilda—Wanda Bardone. In the quartet all shout at the top of their voices from first to last. The contrast between the four voices and the balance of the parts are completely spoiled.

Emmy Bettendorf.—I would beseech the Parlophone Company to think seriously before it continues its present system of performing the great Lieder of Schubert and Schumann with accompaniments arranged for string quartet or violin and 'cello with or without a piano. The reason for doing it is, presumably, that a group of stringed instruments produces better tonal effects on the gramophone than a pianoforte—especially the inferior instruments that appear to be used for this purpose in the land that can evolve a Blüthner or a Bechstein. But what aggravates these acts of desecration is the new plan of thrusting into the foreground a manufactured and aggressive violin obbligato, extracted from the composer's accompaniment, and invested with an importance in the harmonic scheme that was never intended to be conveyed by the modest pianist. Listening to these performances in the latest records, I find the whole piece deprived of symmetry

and balance—sometimes almost unrecognisable—while the precious obbligato suggests to my ears nothing so much as the acrobatic feats of the mobile leader of a Hungarian band. Please stop it !

Nothing, of course, can wholly disturb the equable temperament or classical interpretations of an Emmy Bettendorf. She pursues the even tenor (pardon—soprano) of her gracious way, undisturbed by the medley of sounds, and she alone succeeds in persuading us that we are hearing the divine melody of *Mondnacht* or the exquisite beauty of the *Lindenbaum*. But positively the sweet simplicity of Lassen's (not Strauss's) *Allerseelen* is gone from the old song entirely, though not to the same extent from *The Last Rose of Summer*, with its Flotow-like reminiscences of *Martha*. Otherwise these are four excellent examples of Emmy Bettendorf's quiet, finished art.

Elizabeth Schumann.—To wind up a month of nearly all the talents, there remains a faultless H.M.V. record of two of Strauss's most captivating Lieder by an artist who never fails to appeal and enthral. The smooth, even flow of lovely tone all through the *Wiegenlied* is just what the music needs. So, too, the charm of *Freundliche Vision* is caught with rare felicity, every phrase delivered in a delicious *mezza voce* with a perfection of *legato* that may serve as a model for any singer. Both, in fact, exemplify the ideal rendering.

Alessandro Valente.—This typical Italian tenor has no fresh points to make, but he has the voice and the style for scoring all the old ones. His *Vesti la giubba* (*On with the motley*) is a robust and dramatic performance and the recording does him complete justice. Of the two records the *Recondita armonia* is the finer, even though the voice is less steady.

Tito Schipa.—I have enjoyed listening to this tenor in things that suited him better. His *Ombrai mai fù* will only please the few—those, I mean, who will accept even the Italian concept of Handel. In *M'apparì* he is much more at home, and yet the voice does not sound altogether at ease or at its best. It is too white and a shade too coarse in quality.

HERMAN KLEIN.

REVIEWS PUBLISHED IN 1928

OPERATIC AND FOREIGN SONGS

MARIA GENTILE (soprano).—**Alfin son tua** and **Sparge un amaro pianto**, Mad Scene from **Lucia di Lammermoor** (Donizetti). In Italian. Orch acc. Col. L.1971, 12in., 6s. 6d.

GITTA ALPA (soprano).—**Couplets du Mysoli** from **La Perle du Brésil** (David), in French, and **Il Re Pastore** (Mozart), in Italian. Orch acc. Parlo. 10642, 12in., 4s. 6d.

LOTTE SCHÖNE (soprano).—**Wie melodien zieht es mir** (Brahms, Op. 105, No. 1) and **Die Forelle** (Schubert). In German. Piano acc. Parlo. R.20031, 12in., 7s. 6d.

NINON VALLIN (soprano).—**Connais-tu le pays ?** from **Mignon** (Thomas) and **Air des bijoux** from **Faust** (Gounod). In French. Orch. acc. Parlo. R.20032, 12in., 7s. 6d.

FELICIE HÜNI-MIHACSEK (soprano). Recitative and Aria, **Nun eilt herbei** from **The Merry Wives of Windsor** (Nicolai). In German. Orch. acc. Brunswick 50105, 12in., 8s.

MISS STILES ALLEN (soprano).—**One fine day** from **Madame Butterfly** (Puccini) and, with **ED HALLAND** (bass) and

ED. LEER (tenor), **Finale Trio** from **Faust** (Gounod). In English. Orch. acc. Electron O.178, 10in., 3s.

MAARTJE OFFERS (contralto).—**Agnus Dei** (Bizet), in Latin, and **Noël** (Adam), in French. Organ acc. (Herbert Dawson) and orch. H.M.V. D.B.980, 12in., 8s. 6d.

EDITH FURMEDGE (contralto).—**The Flower Song** and **When all was young** from **Faust** (Gounod). In English. Orch. acc. Electron O.181, 10in., 3s.

MARIO CHAMLEE (tenor).—**Vesti la giubba** from **Pagliacci** (Leoncavallo) and **E lucevan le stelle** from **La Tosca** (Puccini). In Italian. Orch acc. Brunswick 15130, 10in., 5s. 6d.

WILLIAM HESELTINE (tenor).—**Recondita armonia** and **E lucevan le stelle** from **La Tosca** (Puccini). In English. Orch. acc. Col. 4497, 10in., 3s.

AURELIANO PERTILE (tenor).—**Scendi ! sul Sognator** and **Queste ad un lido fatal** from **Nerone** (Boito). In Italian. Orch. acc. Actuelle 11491, 10in., 4s.

AURELIANO PERTILE (tenor).—**Recondita armonia** and **E lucevan le stelle** from **La Tosca** (Puccini). In Italian. Orch. acc. Parlo. R.20030, 12in., 7s. 6d.

HEINRICH SCHLUSNUS (baritone).—**Toreador's Song** from **Carmen** (Bizet) and **Nun ist's vollbracht** from **Undine** (Lortzing). In German. Orch. acc. Brunswick 50103, 12in., 8s.

IVAR ANDRÉSEN (bass) and **GOTTHELF PISTOR** (tenor).—**Vom Bade kehrt der König heim** and **Transformation Music** from **Parsifal**, Act 1 (Wagner). In German. Orch acc. Parlo. E.10641, 12in., 4s. 6d.

THE COVENT GARDEN SINGERS.—**Soldiers' Chorus** from **Faust** (Gounod) and **Pilgrims' Chorus** from **Tannhäuser** (Wagner). In English. Orch acc. Electron O.176, 10in., 3s.

LA SCALA CHORUS OF MILAN.—**Humming Chorus** from **Madame Butterfly** (Puccini) and **Festa e pane** from **La Gioconda** (Ponchielli). In Italian. Orch. acc. Col. D.1591, 10in., 4s. 6d.

Maria Gentile.—The "Mad Scene" from *Lucia* holds a perennial attraction for the light soprano and for the multitudes that love to hearken to her vocal fireworks. Here is what I take to be the very latest specimen. Its *raison d'être* is comprised in a voice of delightful sweetness, an easy mastery of all the *coloratura* that the music demands (duet-cadenzas with flute included), and irreproachable recording. Experience and control peep out at every bar; brilliant certainty in every scale and staccato group. Of the two sections I prefer the *Sparge in un amaro pianto*, because it evinces greater refinement and is not so disfigured by extravagant slurring as the *Alfin son tua*.

Gitta Alpa.—There is something wrong with this record. Probably the singer stood too far from the microphone. Anyhow, the voice sounds weak and distant, though one can hear enough to perceive that the vocalization is neat and accurate and may even be called brilliant. The whole thing seems to be *en miniature*. The *Couplets du Mysoli* (from *La Perle "du" Bresil*, please !) are prettily sung; and the violin obbligato fills its rightful place of prominence in the orchestral accompaniment to the *Re Pastore*. But are the trills really trills ?

Lotte Schöne.—The singing of these well-contrasted *Lieder* is completely satisfying. The charming Marzelline of last season's *Fidelio* displays here the art that can differentiate utterly in voice and manner a romantic melody of Brahms from a sprightly tune by Schubert. The former, whilst tender and graceful, is phrased with the utmost distinction. (Should the breath, however, in the opening sentence be taken before or after the word *mir* ? I have generally heard it after, I fancy, if at all; but the best plan is to do without altogether.) The humour and spirit of *Die Forelle* are caught to perfection.

Ninon Vallin.—Coldness and correctness personified ! This well-trained soprano, with her lovely French diction, her true intonation, her resonant tone and admirable breathing sadly needs "waking up." She starts off like a clever piece of mechanism, sings *à pleine voix* throughout, and never suggests the smallest touch of contrast. Such regularity of beat is worthy of Greenwich. Her shake in the *Jewel Song* is immaculate. But her Marguerite, like her Mignon, lacks humanity, the only sign whereof will be found in a rather weak B natural at the end of the waltz air. Otherwise, as a model for technique the whole thing is excellent.

Félicie Hüni-Mihacsek.—This superb performance of the big soprano air for Mistress Ford from Nicolai's *Merry Wives of Windsor*—shamefully neglected in this country, but adored in Germany—must be my "best of the month." I have

never heard it better sung. The entire interpretation, apart from the faultless management of a well-modulated voice, is replete with the true spirit of comedy, alternating with the tenderest sentiment, with intelligence, significance of meaning, and power of expression.

Stiles Allen.—A capital three shillings'-worth, this. The growing reputation of the English soprano would grow faster still if her style were invested with a little more artistic refinement and real interpretative feeling. As is shown here in *One fine day*, she relies overmuch on sheer robustness of tone and manner. There is little dramatic suggestion or joyful anticipation, still less underlying depth of passionate longing welling up as she draws the picture of Butterfly's day-dream. The voice itself, as usual, has ample volume and purity, except on the very last note—the high B natural—of the trio from *Faust*, where it unaccountably misses fire. Messrs. Leer and Halland are both good in this.

Maartje Offers.—This gifted Dutch artist is nothing if not seasonable in her gramophone efforts. Nor could her rich contralto tones be employed to better advantage than in Bizet's *Agnus Dei* and Adam's famous old song *Noël*, except perhaps, that she might have sung the latter a tone higher. The low notes are lacking in power, and not so steady as the "medium" passages which come out so well in the Bizet. The record is well worth having for the latter alone, with its fine organ obbligato played by Mr. Herbert Dawson and all the other orchestral effects in the bargain. These make a very imposing piece of a composition that is too often unworthily presented.

Edith Furmedge.—The two Siebel airs from *Faust* do not often fit the same voice well. The *Flower Song* lies in a lofty *tessitura*, the other in a low one; nor is the disparity quite straightened out by transposing the former down to A (a minor third), as Miss Furmedge has done. But *When all was young* suits her admirably, and she puts a pleasing, sympathetic quality into it. Her enunciation still requires a little more study to make it "get over" distinctly.

Mario Chamlee.—This starts a series of Puccini tenor records that I propose to deal with very briefly. The English language does not supply a poor reviewer with sufficient words for describing afresh these eternal repetitions. The present example is tearful and vigorous by turns, always dramatic, always robust.

William Heseltine.—Here a slight lisp imparts a trace of boyish weakness to a Mario Cavaradossi who might have been brought up in an English public school. Yet, for the British listener who likes to hear his native tongue in the most modern of Italian operas, the pure, bright tenor voice of this artist will render it doubly acceptable. The tremolo is less welcome.

Aureliano Pertile.—This, I need scarcely premise, is the real thing—the same two *Tosca* excerpts (taking the Parlophone first) sung quite *à la* Caruso by the most popular tenor in Italy. What more need be said ? One point only will I make, and that a matter of taste : one could have dispensed with the heartrending sobs after the magnificent climax that ends *E lucevan le stelle*. Such realism is very excusable on the stage; but on the gramophone it sound out of place, unmanly, in short, "tuppence coloured."

The Actuelle record by the same singer gives two scenes from Boïto's posthumous opera *Nerone*, and should prove of special interest to those who have not yet had an opportunity of hearing the work. The first, *Scendi ! sul Sognator* is an impressive invocation to the gods from the second act, consisting of a broad, long-sustained melody, supported by chords in the orchestra; the second, *Queste ad un lido fatal*, a tragic passage for Nero, tragically sung, from the moving scene with Simon Mago in Act I. Both are finely delivered, while the recording alike of the voice and the instrumentation is quite first-rate.

Heinrich Schlusnus.—There is a suspicion of heaviness

about the *Toreador's Song* (with chorus) that may be pardoned, I suppose, in a German baritone with a notably heavy voice. But of animation and rhythmical energy there is no lack. Schlusnus possesses a tone of glorious opulence, even when he is inclined to be nasal. He is heard to greater advantage, however, in the air from Lortzing's *Undine*, because there he is thoroughly at home ; his style fits the older-fashioned music exactly and his declamation is exemplary. Nothing could be better, either, than his expressive singing in the melodious second part, " O kehr zurück," where he has the support of a tuneful chorus.

Ivar Andrésen.—This is as fine a bass as Schlusnus is a baritone, and that is saying much. The two sides of the disc contain one episode from *Parsifal*—namely, the tremendous orchestral passage in the first act where, after King Amfortas has been conveyed across the stage in his litter, on the way from his bath to the Hall of Monsalvat, the whole scene (at Bayreuth anyhow) moves solidly away to effect the transformation. There is little here for the voices to do, but that little is adequately done, while the instrumental portion receives entire justice. Andrésen should be an ideal Gurnemanz.

Covent Garden Singers.—The lower voices rumble a bit incoherently in these familiar choruses, and in the *Tannhäuser* with a momentary departure from the key to which one is always resigned at the particular point where it occurs. Still, the voices have a manly ring, and they are strong enough for anything.

La Scala Chorus of Milan.—Here is an excellent specimen of up-to-date recording. It is wonderful how the electrical process enhances the resonance of the *bouche fermée* tone in the chorus from *Butterfly*. The effect is, if anything, louder than Puccini intended, because it eliminates that of distance. It is, in the opera, a clever and imaginative bit of suggestion ; here it rather becomes a *tour de force*. On the other hand, nothing could be better than the brightness and vigour shown in the opening chorus from *La Gioconda*, on the reverse side of the same disc.

HERMAN KLEIN.

OPERATIC AND FOREIGN SONGS

FLORENCE AUSTRAL (soprano).—**Ritorna vincitor** from **Aida** (Verdi). Two parts. In Italian. Orch. acc. H.M.V. E.474, 10in., 4s. 6d.

CLAIRE DUX (soprano).—**Serenade** (Strauss) and **The Virgin's Slumber Song** (Reger). Brunswick 10251.
  I would weave a song for you (Adams–O'Hara) and **Lullaby** (Rossetti–Scott). Brunswick 10252.
  To-morrow (Strauss) and **Moonlight** (Schumann). Brunswick 10253. Three records, 10in., 4s. 6d. each.

ELISABETH RETHBERG (soprano).—**Largo** (Handel) and **Rendi'l sereno al ciglio** (Handel). In Italian. Orch. acc. Brunswick 30119, 12in., 6s. 6d.

DUSOLINA GIANNINI (soprano).—**Vissi d'arte** from **Tosca** (Puccini) and **Voi lo sapete** from **Cavalleria Rusticana** (Mascagni). In Italian. Orch. acc. H.M.V. D.A.892, 10in., 6s.

LUELLA PAIKIN (soprano).—**Ah ! I loved him** from **Il Seraglio** (Mozart) and **Air and Variations** (Mozart). In Italian. Orch. acc. H.M.V. D.B.1057, 12in., 8s. 6d.

G. ARANGI-LOMBARDI (soprano) and **FRANCESCO MERLI** (tenor).—**O terra addio** and **Nel fiero anelito** from **Aida** (Verdi). In Italian. Orch. acc. Col. L.2039, 12in., 6s. 6d.

LUCREZIA BORI (soprano) and **LAWRENCE TIBBETT** (tenor).—**Night of Love,** Barcarolle from **Tales of Hoffmann** (Offenbach) and **Calm as the night** (Goetze). In English. Orch. acc. H.M.V. D.A.912, 10in., 6s.

GIUSEPPE GARUTI (tenor).—**Celeste Aïda** from **Aïda** (Verdi) and **Ah sì, ben mio coll'essere** from **Il Trovatore** (Verdi). In Italian. Orch. acc. Parlo. E.10657, 12in., 4s. 6d.

GOTTHELF PISTOR (tenor).—**Finale to Act 3 of Siegfried** (Wagner). In German. Orch. acc. Parlo. E.10658, 12in., 4s. 6d.

WILLIAM HESELTINE (tenor).—**Ah ! fairest sun** and **'Tis there ! All Hail !** from **Romeo and Juliet** (Gounod). In English. Orch. acc. Col. 9276, 12in., 4s. 6d.

BROWNING MUMMERY (tenor).—**Flower Song** from **Carmen** (Bizet) and **No, Pagliacci, no more** from **Pagliacci** (Leoncavallo). In English. Orch. acc. H.M.V.C.1419, 12in., 4s.6d.

MARIO CHAMLEE (tenor).—**On yonder rock reclining** from **Fra Diavolo** (Auber) and **Then you'll remember me** from **The Bohemian Girl** (Balfe). In English. Orch. acc. Brunswick 10227, 10in., 4s. 6d.

FRIEDRICH SCHORR (baritone).—**Sachs' Monologue** from **Die Meistersinger** (Wagner). Two parts, in German. Acc. by Berlin State Opera Orchestra under Dr. Leo Blech. H.M.V. D.1351, 12in., 6s. 6d.

CESARE FORMICHI (baritone).—**Credo** from **Otello** (Verdi) and **Ella verrà** from **La Tosca** (Puccini). In Italian. Orch. acc. Col. L.1949, 12in., 6s. 6d.

*****PETER DAWSON** (bass-baritone).—**Room for the factotum** from the **Barber of Seville** (Rossini) and **Toreador Song** from **Carmen** (Bizet). In English. Orch. acc. H.M.V. C.1400, 12in., 4s. 6d.
  Credo from **Othello** (Verdi) and **Now your days of philandering** from **Marriage of Figaro** (Mozart). In English. Orch. acc. H.M.V. C.1401, 12in., 4s. 6d.

THEODORE CHALIAPINE (bass) and **OLIVE KLINE** (soprano).—**The Death of Don Quixote** from **Don Quixote** (Massenet). Two parts. In French. Orch. acc. H.M.V. D.B.1096, 12in., 8s. 6d.

LA SCALA CHORUS OF MILAN.—**Chorus of Gipsies** from **La Traviata** (Verdi) and **Il bel giovanetto** from **Mefistofele** (Boito). In Italian. Orch. acc. Col. D.1595, 10in., 4s. 6d.

Florence Austral.—This is in all respects an improvement upon Miss Austral's earlier record of *Ritorna vincitor* sung in the English version. It gains enormously by the new recording, by being sung in Italian, by being spread over two sides of a 10in. disc, by a full orchestral accompaniment, and, last, but not least, by the advance that the artist has made in her art. The quality of her voice is quite beautiful, and despite a certain amount of echo, the purity of the sound as heard on the gramophone is that of the living singer. Only one little criticism : the little grace notes towards the end, on the " Numi pietà " passage, ought not to be treated as long *appoggiature*, thus converting the group of semiquavers into a regular " turn." Verdi meant the notes to be sung precisely as he wrote them, with a graceful *acciaccatura* to precede the triplet.

Claire Dux.—The three 10in. records just completed by Claire Dux for the Brunswick company offer a pleasant selection of short Lieder from various sources, the only doubtful one of which is a song of musical comedy ballad type called *I would weave a song for you*, by " O'Hara." It gains by association with Cyril Scott's well-known *Lullaby*, but is otherwise thoroughly out of place. However, this particular record would not be my choice. I recommend rather the other two— the delicious combination of Max Reger and Strauss, both exquisitely sung ; the soothing Strauss and Schumann, equally perfect in their way. The latter pair are with orchestral accompaniment.

* Re-recordings.

Elisabeth Rethberg.—For the sake of the beauty of tone such as this singer possesses the familiar Handelian airs here presented may be unhesitatingly welcomed. It is nice to hear such a lovely voice in such lovely melodies. Otherwise, if I may venture to say so, they appertain to a class of composition that German singers understand and interpret less accurately than our own. Both pieces are to an Italian text, it is true, but that does not prevent the gifted Frau Rethberg from applying to them untraditional reading and sentimentally-slurred *portamentos* such as are happily not allowed in the English concert-room. Which is a pity, so far as she is concerned.

Dusolina Giannini.—Comparisons here must at all points be in favour of the singer, because she is in her right element, sings Puccini and Mascagni just as they ought to be sung, and profits fully by all the improvements that can help her to outshine her predecessors. Her rich tone is well sustained both in *Vissi d'arte* and *Voi lo sapete*, and depicts with abundant colour the sufferings and miseries of the unlucky Tosca and the distraught Santuzza.

Luella Paikin.—One of those bird-like sopranos to whom airs with variations and vocal fireworks generally come so naturally as nursery songs. As a display of mechanical facility nothing could be more interesting. The first part of the air from the *Seraglio* is sung with a lovely tone, but insufficient pathos, and a trifle too quickly. The rest is quite charming, and the well-made record altogether embodies some clever vocalization.

G. Arangi-Lombardi and *Francesco Merli.*—These are the two great final duets from the third and fourth acts of *Aida*, sung by artists of ability and experience, who despite an occasional roughness and inequality of tone, give out their music with good effect.

Lucrezia Bori and *Lawrence Tibbett.*—It seems rather a waste to expend two such magnificent voices upon material so flimsy and unimportant. One asks, does *le jeu vaut la chandelle?* Well, not altogether; and yet the result of the combination is to produce effects above the average. For my own part, I prefer the *Barcarolle* sung by two women's voices as Offenbach intended. The Goetze duet comes out better.

Giuseppe Garuti.—The tenor voice here revealed in airs from *Aida* and *Il Trovatore* is of the strident and powerful type that distinguishes the modern Italian school—only, if anything, rather more so. The microphone process tends to intensify the penetrating nature of such a tone, and one derives only partial pleasure from the outcome. I fear I shall have to do a lot of warning before I get these gentlemen to understand that there is a limit to the capacity of the human *tympanum*.

Gotthelf Pistor.—Now this is a Wagnerian specimen, and he is, if anything, rather more stentorian than the Italian. The redeeming feature lies in the softer passages, which he mercifully grants us where he can; and they occur quite often, fortunately, in the course of the two colloquies between Siegfried and the Voice of the Wood-bird. Otherwise, where Siegfried is strenuous he shouts with a vengeance. But what a privilege to get a record which is such a clever combination of the two most beautiful episodes (not the Finale alone, as described) from the Forest Scene in *Siegfried*, and with orchestration so splendidly recorded! I have enjoyed it thoroughly. And, by the way, whose is the charming voice of the *Waldvogel?*

William Heseltine.—An English tenor of whom it may be said that he has only to get rid of his *tremolo* (and also his lisp) to attain a leading place in his profession. But, so long as he indulges in over-pressure of breath that makes every note vibrate as if it were a "trill," he will certainly not attain his ambition. He has a beautiful quality of voice, and there is not the least necessity for him either to sing *ff* all the time he is recording or to stand so close to the instrument. Loudness ought not to be the *summum bonum* of these new productions.

Browning Mummery.—The familiar excerpts from *Carmen* and *Pagliacci* sung by the Australian tenor reap the full advantage of up-to-date recording and the singer is too wise to give his power a too free rein except once now and then on the highest notes. His declamation is dramatic and there is no lack of emphasis or just expression. The tone is splendid. But is the "surface" all right? It seems to scrape a little.

Mario Chamlee.—A couple of old-fashioned favourites from the English opera repertory of my youthful days—none the worse for that, of course. Both are robustly rendered by the American artist, particularly the "yonder rock" of Auber's delightful opera, with its stern and menacing oft-repeated "diavolo." In the Balfe ballad the accent is on the "Me!"

Friedrich Schorr.—In *Die Meistersinger* Hans Sachs has to sing two monologues, and this is the first of them—*Was duftet doch der Flieder*—sung in the second act by the poet-cobbler when he emerges from his dwelling to breathe the peaceful air of Nuremberg. It begins gently but a trifle confusedly in this admirable record, and the effect persists for a few bars longer than seems requisite. But when Friedrich Schorr settles down to his task there is little to find fault with, and then the fine Staatsoper orchestra under Leo Blech plays up to its best form, the combined effort producing a marvellously good record of this beautiful piece of music. Being in two parts, it proceeds in leisurely fashion to its sublime conclusion, without hurry, but with a glorious sense of "space."

Cesare Formichi.—Here we get the difference. A record made in a broad space like the Scala Theatre by an artist with the huge voice and vast experience of Cesare Formichi. He overdoes nothing; exaggerates neither tone nor manner because his medium imposes no restrictions. The voice sounds rich and natural, is vibrant without trembling, and every word is distinct. The orchestra, conducted by Sir Hamilton Harty, is excellent both in execution and effect, and is always with the singer save at one point in the *Credo*, where the brass start off too quickly with their triplet chords.

Peter Dawson.—These re-recordings of four popular pieces from the repertory of Mr. Peter Dawson require no comment beyond the recognition of a notable advance, almost as remarkable in the case of the singer as of the electrical process. I should imagine that all who possess the old records will immediately want to replace them with these.

Theodore Chaliapine.—The incomparable Russian was in magnificent voice on the day when he made the record of the death scene from Massenet's *Don Quichotte*. The mind can conjure up nothing more wonderful, more realistic, more supreme. The voice alone carries one back to Chaliapine's best days, so strong, so clear, so robust is it. It enables you to picture the whole of the dying scene and the vision (where *Olive Kline* supplies the soprano voice), with all the characteristic interjections and ejaculations, in addition to some of the most dignified and noble passages that only Chaliapine could interpret in such fashion. On the whole, I think this by far the best record that he has ever made and perhaps the finest piece of voice recording that H.M.V. has ever issued to the public.

La Scala Chorus of Milan.—Very *staccato* and tripping is the familiar gipsies' chorus from *La Traviata*. One can almost see the dancers at it. Equally good is the *Kermesse* chorus from *Mefistofele*. The tone and precision are admirable.

HERMAN KLEIN.

ORATORIO

MASTER JOHN BONNER (treble).—**With verdure clad** from **The Creation** (Haydn). Two parts. Organ acc. Col. 9277, 12in., 4s. 6d.

DORA LABBETTE (soprano).—**Comfort sweet, my Jesu comes** (J. S. Bach). Two parts: flute obb. by **ROBERT MURCHIE**. Orch. acc. Col. L.2005, 12in., 6s. 6d.

Master John Bonner.—This boy would properly be described as a treble or soprano, but his *timbre* is that of a contralto, and when he sings *With verdure clad* you think you are listening to one, which sounds odd in this essentially soprano air. Nevertheless, you hear a tone of remarkable depth and power for a boy (who will probably be a tenor one day), and his scale is fairly even right up to the B flat. The piece is sung too slowly and he takes too many breaths, some of them because he dwells or makes a *tenuto* pause on every phrase where the cadence gives him a chance. This is a pity, because it creates an impression of breathlessness and destroys the true reading. The organist, also, "drags," and has a poor instrument. But the boy is greatly gifted and, properly taught, if there be time, should do better when he tries again.

Dora Labbette.—The Bach air sung in this record—I fancy it is from one of the church cantatas—is very beautiful and very difficult to sustain with perfect ease. It has also a delightful *obbligato* for flute, faultlessly executed by Mr. Robert Murchie. The soloist, Miss Dora Labbette, has the right voice for the piece and sings it with artistic taste and expression, though not invariably with the purity of vowel tone or clearness of enunciation that it demands. She sustains better in the short phrases than the long ones.

HERMAN KLEIN.

OPERATIC AND FOREIGN SONGS

AMELITA GALLI-CURCI (soprano).—**Parla! Valse** (Arditi) and **The Gypsy and the Bird** with flute obbligato (Benedict). Orch. acc. H.M.V. D.A.928, 10in., 6s.

A. M. GUGLIELMETTI (soprano).—**Gli angui d'inferno** from **The Magic Flute** (Mozart) and **Air with Variations** (Proch). In Italian. Orch. acc. Col. L.2045, 12in., 6s. 6d.

ELISABETH RETHBERG (soprano).—**Elsa's Dream** from **Lohengrin** and **Elisabeth's Prayer** from **Tannhäuser** (Wagner). In German. Orch. acc. Bruns. 50109, 12in., 8s.

MARGHERITA SALVI (soprano).—**Cavatina di Rosina** from **Il Barbiere di Siviglia** (Rossini). Two parts. In Italian. Orch. acc. Parlo. E.10669, 12in., 4s. 6d.

LOTTE LEHMANN (soprano) and **JAN KIEPURA** (tenor).— **Qua l'occhio al mondo** from Act I and **Amaro sol per te m'era il morire** from Act III of **La Tosca** (Puccini). In Italian. Orch. acc. Parlo. R.20048, 12in., 6s. 6d.

MIRIAM LICETTE (soprano) and **DENNIS NOBLE** (baritone). —**Can it be? Dare I believe thee?** from Act I of **Il Barbiere di Siviglia** (Rossini). Two parts. In English. Orch. acc. Col. 9290, 12in., 4s. 6d.

MAARTJE OFFERS (contralto).—**Les tringles des sistres tintaient, Chanson Bohème,** and **Voyons que j'essaie, Card Song,** from **Carmen** (Bizet). In French. Orch. acc. H.M.V. D.A.824, 10in., 6s.

ENRICO DI MAZZEI (tenor).—**Recondita armonia (O des beautés égales)** from **La Tosca** (Puccini) and **Siciliana** from **Cavalleria Rusticana** (Mascagni). In French. Orch. acc. Parlo. R.O.20043, 10in., 4s. 6d.

E lucevan le stelle (Le ciel luisait d'étoiles) and **O dolci mani (O douces mains)** from **La Tosca** (Puccini). In French. Orch. acc. Parlo. R.O.20044, 10in., 4s. 6d.

La donna è mobile from **Rigoletto** (Verdi), in Italian, and **Romance de Nadir** from **The Pearl Fishers** (Bizet), in French. Orch. acc. Parlo. R.O.20045, 10in., 4s. 6d.

Vesti la giubba (M'habiller) from **Pagliacci** (Leoncavallo) and **O celeste Aida** from **Aida** (Verdi). In French. Orch. acc. Parlo. R.20046, 12in., 6s. 6d.

M. VILLABELLA (tenor).—**Le Rêve** from **Manon** (Massenet) and **Je pense à vous** from **Maître Pathelin** (Bazin). In French. Orch. acc. Actuelle 15248, 12in., 4s. 6d.

M. GOAVEC (tenor).—**Flower Song** from **Carmen** (Bizet) and **Pauvre Paillasse** from **Pagliacci** (Leoncavallo). In French. Orch. acc. Actuelle 15249, 12in., 4s. 6d.

ALFRED PICCAVER (tenor).—**Siciliana** from **Cavalleria Rusticana** (Mascagni) and **Questa o quella** from **Rigoletto** (Verdi). In Italian. Orch. acc. Bruns. 15131, 10in., 5s. 6d.

IVAR ANDRÉSEN (bass) and **E. HABICH** (baritone).— **Gott grüss Euch** from Act I, Sc. i, and **Mein Herr und Gott** from Act I, Sc. 3 of **Lohengrin** (Wagner). In German. With orchestra and chorus. Parlo. E.10670, 12in., 4s. 6d.

ROSA PONSELLE (soprano).—**Elégie, Song of Mourning** (Massenet), in French, and **Ave Maria** (Gounod) in Latin. Orch. acc. H.M.V. D.B.1052, 12in., 8s. 6d.

EVELYN SCOTNEY (soprano).—**Elfenlied** (Wolf), in German, and **Song of the Nightingale** (Saint-Saëns). Piano acc. H.M.V. E.481, 10in., 4s. 6d.

SIGRID ONEGIN (contralto).—**Sapphische Ode** and **Auf dem Kirchhofe** (Brahms). In German. Orch. acc. Brunswick 10255, 10in., 4s. 6d.

WILLY FASSBÄNDER (baritone).—**Die beiden Grenadiere** (Schumann) and **Die Uhr** (Loewe). In German. Orch. acc. Parlo. E.10668, 12in., 4s. 6d.

Amelita Galli-Curci.—This sparkling contribution comes like a ray of sunshine from the south—or the west, I am not sure which. But, no matter where it was sung, it is genuine Galli-Curci sure enough, and of her best at that. The intonation is impeccable, the voice as usual, and the technical display up to the customary level of marvellous virtuosity. More need not be said, since both the pieces are merely pegs whereon to hang dazzling *feux d'artifice à la* Amelita; and I leave it at that.

A. M. Guglielmetti.—I have more than once written my estimate of this clever soprano. Her dazzling accomplishments are not likely to diminish under the influence of the new recording, seeing that it broadens her tone and gives increased effect to her "fireworks." She is simply a marvellous machine. Her staccatos are amazingly accurate, and they hit the nail on the head literally with the steely clang of a hammer. This metallic quality has never been so illustrated in a record before. In *Gli angui d'inferno* (the label at present has it *angeli*, but that would be too quaint!) the effect is even more striking than in the *Proch* variations, where the cadenza with flute is quite remarkable.

Elisabeth Rethberg.—Both the familiar Wagner excerpts are slightly hurried, as though the gifted singer had been anxious to get her work done. But, otherwise, one could not wish for a richer, more poetic tone, a clearer diction, a more individual reading, or a more exquisitely touching *mezza voce* than that which concludes the *Prayer*. In contrast to this, note the strength of the rhythm wherewith Elsa foretells the coming of her champion. It is a genuine declaration of confident faith. Excellent orchestral effects pervade both records.

Margherita Salvi.—A new Italian *soprano leggero*, and one whom I certainly prefer to others I have heard of late. The voice sounds extremely youthful and is of charming quality. Her execution is extraordinarily brilliant, and, after a somewhat quiet start, does entire justice to a very elaborate version of *Una voce*.

Lotte Lehmann and *Jan Kiepura.*—These duets are respectively from the Church scene and the final tableau at the Castle of St. Angelo in *Tosca*. They are welcome because not too hackneyed, both well sung and splendidly recorded. The soprano voice is pre-eminently superior throughout, but for sheer volume the balance is nicely maintained, even in the concluding unisonal passage, which winds up the duet—and the opera.

Miriam Licette and *Dennis Noble.*—This duet, an English version of the famous *Pronta io son* from *Il Barbiere*, offers a very different proposition from that just noticed, but here again the soprano is the infinitely superior partner. She has never done anything better, as regards either charm or facility of vocalization. If the words were as clear as the notes it would be simply perfect. On the other hand, Mr. Noble possesses neither the lightness nor the agility requisite for this music. His slurred runs may pass muster upon the stage, but here they are unpleasantly and obviously in evidence. He should try to improve this defect.

Maartje Offers.—I cannot see the wisdom of asking the Dutch singer to do something worthy her reputation in music so unsuited to her as that of *Carmen*. She has not the life or vivacity for the *Chanson bohémienne*, and she is too cold for the *Card Song*. In the few words that are audible the French accent sounds faulty.

Enrico di Mazzei.—Here are eight records on four Parlophone discs sung by the Italian tenor who appeared at a recent Sunday concert at the Albert Hall. I purposely postponed listening to them until I had heard him at the concert in order the better to compare the reproductions with the reality; and they did not disappoint me. It seems that Di Mazzei is a favourite at the Opéra-Comique in Paris. Hence his singing so much in French, I suppose. True, he makes himself understood in that language and gets out his powerful tones on French vowels by cleverly Italianizing them. Still, I prefer him both on the platform and the gramophone when he is employing his own mother-tongue. He has a fine voice, absolutely free from *tremolo*, and a great command of sustained head notes, while his breathing powers are nothing less than remarkable. Altogether, Di Mazzei is a tenor to be reckoned with, and any of these records will be found to exhibit his talent in a fair and favourable light.

M. Villabella.—There is barely average merit to be found in this record of the overdone *Rêve* from *Manon*. It is tastefully sung with an exceedingly nasal tone, which only consents to subside where it is compelled to—namely, on the " half voice." The words are fairly distinct, but the general vocal effect is " foggy." The other piece I do not know, and it sounds very dull.

M. Goavec.—The two principal airs from *Carmen* and *Pagliacci*, sung in French by a capital tenor with a steady telling voice. The style is as robust as the tone, and there is plenty of power available for the high notes, especially the B flat. *On with the motley*, well sung in good French, is worth listening to, particularly as the recording is satisfactory.

Alfred Piccaver.—One admires as much as hitherto the warm, round, sympathetic quality of this Continental favourite of British origin, and that " gift of the gods " he will not lose in a hurry. But I do hope he is not going to cultivate the lifeless, free-and-easy method that characterizes his rendering of the *Siciliana* from *Cavalleria* and the *Questa o quella*. The latter needs a rest, it is true, but both sound in this instance as though they had issued from an easy chair fitted with very soft cushions. The careless *insouciance* of the whole effort would be called a feat by some, and the singer's breath-control is certainly remarkable; but, on the whole, I prefer more animation, more contrast, in music of this sort.

Ivar Andrésen and *E. Habich.*—The spacious atmosphere discernible in these *Lohengrin* excerpts (with a trifle of echo occasionally superadded) is matched by the magnificent voices of King Henry the Fowler and his Herald. I cannot remember having heard any voice since Edouard de Reszke's give out the *Prayer* with such combined beauty and volume of tone. Ivar Andrésen is, perhaps, the finest of living basses and his glorious organ derives enhanced grandeur from the

new process. Habich, as we know, is quite first-rate also, while the orchestral and choral effects in both selections are fully up to the mark.

Rosa Ponselle.—With her rich, fascinating quality of voice, this artistic soprano does easy justice musically to Massenet and Gounod. Her *cantilena* is a model of purity (if her French is not) and the 'cello obbligato in the *Elégie* blends agreeably with her dark timbre. The *Ave Maria* is sung in A flat, which is unusually high ; but the singer makes the curious mistake almost throughout of omitting the third beat on the tied minims. This abbreviation spoils the rhythm not only of Gounod's melody, but, what is even worse, of Bach's *Prelude* ; and oddly enough, the harp, violin, and harmonium all give way to her. If you ignore the error, the placid beauty of the singing will delight all who forgive Gounod's vandalism and love his music.

Evelyn Scotney.—Two very clever exhibitions of finished vocalization. The *Elfenlied* of Hugo Wolf, rather " blanche," but sprightly and graceful. The *Rossignol* imitation, written by Saint-Saëns for a drama taken from a Persian legend, sung with clear, unforced musical tone and enriched by some remarkably good trills.

Sigrid Onégin.—Two of Brahms's most beautiful Lieder, sung with rare poetry and charm of style in the most generous and opulent of mezzo-soprano voices. There is naught here to criticize adversely, and columns of praise could not tell you more.

Willy Fassbänder.—An excellent baritone, this, with a pleasant and fairly powerful voice. A soft Southern accent betrays itself in his distinct enunciation, but he can " wake up " when he likes to and become quite bold and vigorous. On the whole, he makes a fine straightforward thing of *Die beiden Grenadiere.*   HERMAN KLEIN.

ORATORIO

MASTER E. LOUGH (treble).—**I know that my Redeemer liveth** from **Messiah** (Handel). Two parts. Organ acc. G. Thalben Ball.   H.M.V. B.2656, 10in., 3s.

ELSIE SUDDABY (soprano).—**Let the bright Seraphim** from **Samson** (Handel) and **O Sleep ! why dost thou leave me ?** from **Semele** (Handel). Orch. acc. H.M.V. C.1437, 12in., 4s. 6d.

BARRINGTON HOOPER (tenor).—**Sing ye praise** from **Hymn of Praise** (Mendelssohn) and **How vain is man** from **Judas Maccabaeus** (Handel). Organ acc. Zono. A.333, 12in., 4s.

Master E. Lough.—Seeing that something of a sensation was created by the Temple boy soprano's record of *Hear my Prayer*, it is hardly surprising to find H.M.V. hankering after another " best-seller " from the same source. Whether they have discovered it in his *I know that my Redeemer liveth* cannot be postulated with any certainty. The new record is sure, nevertheless, to be largely in demand, for it holds a good deal of the same charm, the same indescribable quality of tone and natural beauty of expression and phrasing. *Hear my prayer* was easier to sing, however, and the reading of the *Messiah* air is in many details less correct. The omission of the *appoggiatura* is quite indefensible here ; the *tempo* is unnecessarily hurried ; some of the vowels are mispronounced—the short *a* in " latter " and " stand," for instance. The final cadence suggests that some old forgotten octavo score was followed. And so on. Otherwise, it is a delight as before to listen to the boy's ineffable purity of tone and utterance, and his exquisite simple proclamation of faith. The organ (G. Thalben Ball) is well subdued, if too much in a hurry.

Elsie Suddaby.—Even more marked here is the " craze for speed." Never in my long experience have I heard *Let the bright seraphim* sung at this express rate. The old-time dignity is lost ; the trumpet passages in the voice part are all " rushed " ; and I could not detect a single Handelian *rallentando*. Perhaps some " spiritual medium " has caught Handel

423

objecting to any more. Anyhow, this is not my idea of the *Samson* air. In *Sleep,why dost thou leave me?* Miss Suddaby employs a thin tone, rather unsteady in the medium, and with diction none too clear. Her breathing and her consonants require attention. The record *per se* is beyond criticism.

Barrington Hooper.—Mendelssohn and Handel both demand greater virility of utterance and delivery than they receive from this painstaking tenor, who employs a "white" nasal tone and lachrymose sentiment much too constantly. True, he receives little to support him save misty crashes from the organ in *Sing ye praise*; but that does not excuse the other defects, or the tendency to deteriorate as well as diminish in all slowing-down passages. *How vain is man* happily urges him to greater vigour, and even inspires him to a little realism; for he declaims with much feeling and significance the lines :—

> And dreams not that a hand unseen
> Directs and guides this weak machine.

Surely this can't have been intended as a reflection on the new recording process! Besides, the record is well worth its price.   HERMAN KLEIN.

SCHUBERT'S WINTERREISE

Twelve Songs from Schubert's song-cycle *Winterreise* (*Winter Journey*), recorded on six Parlophone–Odeon Records by Richard Tauber. Piano acc. by Mischa Spoliansky. (Parlo. R.O.20037–42.) 4s. 6d. each double-sided 10in. record or complete in Album, 30s.

These records, we are told, form a first instalment of the exclusive programme of Schubert Centenary issues upon which Parlophone is at the present time engaged. It is certainly a most creditable beginning to what is sure to prove a highly interesting series. The album form is convenient and handsome. The songs are one and all beautiful, and not the most hackneyed examples of a group that is familiar to all lovers of Schubert's Lieder. Some of them came under notice in the articles on "Modern German Lieder" that appeared in THE GRAMOPHONE a few months back, and I am gratified to find that my plea for making these lovely things better known over here should, by a happy chance, have begun to be realized in this manner—so to speak from the "fountain head."

Nothing more typical of Schubert's genius—in its later and sadder aspect—could have been chosen than the song-cycle known as *Winterreise*. Little, if anything, tells here of the joyful spirit that dominates the *Schöne Müllerin*, whose author, Wilhelm Müller, wrote the poems of both. But they are glorious in their garb of melancholy, and Schubert's naturally lively disposition asserts itself, wherever it can peep out, in his tripping figures of accompaniment. I have not space, though, to dwell upon the settings; the singing claims all that can be spared.

The interpreter in this instance is Richard Tauber, a lyric tenor who has shown that he possessed both the voice and the temperament for the task. His rich, solemn tone breathes sadness; his style, subdued and refined, imparts an additional quiet melancholy to Schubert's melodies. In the *timbre* one could do with a shade less of nasal resonance; but, if it made neat phrasing easier and enhanced the "Tauberisch" quality of elegant lassitude, far be from me to complain, since here both are in the right place. In the matter of style I feel that there is a sameness of treatment, an absence of strong contrasts and varied tone-colour, that would tend to cause monotony were it not for the singer's rare musical feeling and sense of rhythm. You feel that he presents Schubert's phrase precisely as it was intended, and he charms you with his neatness and art even when you wish he would be a bit more virile and not make sudden *dims.* and let his voice die away at every note or two. Altogether, then, Herr Tauber's is not a faultless interpretation or a great one, but it is very lovable in its vocal grace, very artistic, and, let me add, thoroughly enjoyable. It also owes much to the refined and tasteful playing (on a poor instrument) of the piano accompaniments by Mischa Spoliansky; while the electrical recording enables the listener to take in every sound with the utmost ease and receive a clear, vivid impression of each song in turn.

Herewith are appended my notes of Herr Tauber's individual records, written down as I listened to them :—

No. 1. *Gute Nacht.*—Smooth, velvety tone; pure *cantilena*; poetic sentiment. Strikes the sad keynote.

No. 2. *Der Lindenbaum.*—The right feeling of weariness, but somewhat dull for lack of contrast. Consonants share the general lassitude.

No. 3. *Wasserflut.*—Sung in E minor—Schubert's own lower key. Nice expression; fitting dreariness.

No. 4. *Rückblick.*—A splendid rendering. The singer "wakes up" and stretches himself. Energy and rhythm admirable; voice masculine, strong, and less "white."

No. 5. *Frühlingsträume.*—A simple melody simply sung, yet rich in effective contrasts.

No. 6. *Die Post.*—A characteristic reading, full of sweetness and grace, though the voice glides up and down a good deal.

No. 7. *Die Krähe.*—Certainly an unusual rendering of this remarkable song. Constant changes of feeling and manner : apprehension, fear, pitiful appeal.

No. 8. *Stürmischer Morgen.*—The singer's Southern dialect comes out rather prominently here; a darker tone, in keeping with the stormy morning, would have been more desirable.

No. 9. *Der Wegweiser.*—Intense expressiveness; a wealth of sadness and mystery; a presentiment that the end of the road is near.

No. 10. *Das Wirtshaus.*—Very much the same blending of mixed emotions pervades this well-known Lied, and it is equally well sung.

No. 11. *Mut.*—A welcome "bright interval," as the weather forecasts put it. Naturally, therefore, a brief one, to make way for

No. 12. *Der Leiermann.*—Another Schubertian gem, exquisitely sung as a *bonne bouche* to finish with.

HERMAN KLEIN.

OPERATIC AND FOREIGN SONGS

FLORENCE AUSTRAL (soprano).—**Traum durch die Dämmerung, Dream in the Twilight,** and **Cäcilie** (R. Strauss). In German. Piano acc. H.M.V. E.491, 10in., 4s. 6d.

LOTTE LEHMANN (soprano).—**Ave Maria** and **Serenade** (Schubert). Parlo. R.20050, 12in., 6s. 6d.

An die Musik and **Du bist di Ruh'** (Schubert). Parlo. R.20051, 12in., 6s. 6d.

Sei mir gegrüsst and **Auf dem Wasser zu singen** (Schubert). Parlo. R.20052, 12in., 6s. 6d. All in German. Orch. acc.

MARIA OLCZEWSKA (contralto).—**Ja, die liebe hat bunte Flügel (Habañera)** from **Carmen** (Bizet) in German, and **Printemps qui commence** from **Samson et Dalila** (Saint-Saëns), in French. Orch. acc. H.M.V. D.1386, 12in., 6s. 6d.

KARIN BRANZELL (contralto).—**Träume, Dreams** (Wagner) and **Still wie die Nacht, Still as the Night** (Carl Bohm). In German. Orch. acc. Parlo. E.10679, 12in., 4s. 6d.

JOHN BROWNLEE (tenor).—**So, Sir Page,** from the **Marriage of Figaro** (Mozart) and **Sirs! Your toast! Toreador Song,** from **Carmen** (Bizet). In English. Orch. acc. H.M.V. D.1396, 12in., 6s. 6d.

ALFRED PICCAVER (tenor).—**For you alone** (Geehl), in English, and **La Donna è mobile** from **Rigoletto** (Verdi). In Italian. Orch. acc. Brunswick 15132, 10in., 4s. 6d.

GIUSEPPE COSTA (tenor).—**Addio alla madre** from **Cavalleria Rusticana** (Mascagni) and **Che gelida manina** from **La Bohème** (Puccini). In Italian. Orch. acc. Brunswick 148, 10in., 3s.

De' miei bollenti spiriti from **La Traviata** (Verdi) and **E lucevan le stelle** from **Tosca** (Puccini). In Italian. Orch. acc. Brunswick 149, 10in., 3s.

CARL MARTIN OEHMAN (tenor).—**Tannhäuser's Pilgrimage to Rome** from **Tannhäuser,** Act III (Wagner). In German. Orch. acc. Parlo. E.10681, 12in., 4s. 6d.

ROBERT BURG (baritone).—**Wotan's Farewell** from **Die Walküre,** Act III (Wagner). In German. Orch. acc. Parlo. E.10680, 12in., 4s. 6d.

THEODORE CHALIAPINE (bass).—**Song of the Volga Boatmen** and **The Prophet,** Op. 49 (Rimsky-Korsakov). In Russian. Orch. acc. H.M.V. D.B.1103, 12in., 8s. 6d.

MARIA GENTILE (soprano) and **ENZO DE MURO LOMANTO** (tenor).—**Son geloso del Zeffiro,** duet from Act 1 of **La Sonnambula** (Bellini). In Italian. Orch. acc. Col. D.1599, 10in., 4s. 6d.

AURELIANO PERTILE (tenor), and **IRENE MINGHINI CATTANEO** (mezzo-soprano).—**Mal reggendo** and **O giusto cielo** from **Il Trovatore** (Verdi). In Italian. Orch. acc. Parlo. R.20047, 12in., 6s. 6d.

FANNY HELDY (soprano) and **FERNAND ANSSEAU** (tenor).—**Parle-moi de ma mère** and **Qui sait de quel démon** from **Carmen** (Bizet). In French. Orch. acc. H.M.V. D.B.1115, 12in., 8s. 6d.

CHORUS AND ORCHESTRA OF THE OPERA-COMIQUE, PARIS.—Opening Chorus, **O doux parfums que promène l'aurore** from **Cavalleria Rusticana** (Mascagni) and **Choeur du Cortège,** Act IV, from **Carmen** (Bizet). In Italian. Parlo. E.10684, 12in., 4s. 6d.

Florence Austral.—It is at once a duty and a pleasure to encourage the singing of *Lieder* by British artists, especially in the case of one who owns the lovely voice of Miss Florence Austral. I trust, therefore, that I shall not be charged with hypercriticism if I point out that in these two Strauss songs the singer fails because she has not placed the same importance upon the text that she has upon the music. I would say to her, Use the original German words by all means, but pronounce them distinctly enough for us to be able to recognize the identity of the language. It may be a difficult task for you, but it is scarcely fair to impose such a difficult one upon us who listen. Neither the reposeful dreaminess of the *Traum durch die Dämmerung* nor the impulse and animation of the *Cäcilie* should be restricted to beautiful tone alone; for neither can suffice unaided to convey the poetic message of the song. The piano accompaniment is welcome.

Lotte Lehmann.—I note with sincere pleasure the increasing attention that this accomplished singer is giving to *Lieder.* It is as much her *métier* as opera, for she is very nearly, if not quite, the equal of Elena Gerhardt both as vocalist and interpreter, and to say that is to pay the highest tribute in my power. In any case this is the psychological moment for re-recording Schubert. The electrical process and the centenary year alike demand it, and I predict that this selection of gems will soon be selling " like hot cakes " both in German and English-speaking lands ; and, happily, a gramophone record is one of those cakes that form an exception to the rule. You can " eat " it and still have it ! These are all presented with orchestral accompaniment, and the ineffable *An die Musik* rather profits by the arrangement ; much more so than *Du bist die Ruh'* where the harp and violin are aggressively loud. The singer's lovely medium notes impart a wonderful charm to the *Ave Maria,* and it is long since I have heard *An die Musik* rendered with such exquisite tenderness and beauty of expression.

Maria Olczewska.—One feature of an Olczewska record can always be counted on as a foregone conclusion, and that is beauty of vocal tone. The rest matters less, of course ; and yet to achieve the perfect result in everything is also worth while, for we expect no less from an artist of Olczewska's calibre. The German text in the *Carmen* air does not aid the music as it does in the case of Wagner or Strauss ; rather it seems to impede the onward movement, and the singer does nothing to smooth it out. Hence some of the charm of the *Habanera* gets lost in the process. The bit of introductory chorus for the men as Carmen descends from the bridge is a welcome innovation. In Dalila's first air the timbre of the voice in the melody is more fascinating than the phrasing, which is merely straightforward and lacks the guile of the Philistine courtesan. There are moments here when we hear less of the orchestra than we should, and the same fault, I fear, applies to the French words all through.

Karin Branzell.—A rich, smooth contralto voice, with an even and unbroken range of at least an octave and a half, is something of a rarity in these days. This singer has chosen her pieces well, seeing that she depends largely upon beauty of tone and a nice *legato* style, and there is no fault to be found with her rendering of *Träume* and *Still wie die Nacht* unless it be a tendency to melancholy that might find greater relief now and then. Deep sentiment can sometimes lead to lifelessness if not relieved by sufficient contrast. Still the voice is always pleasing, the reading intelligent, the words audible ; while the support of orchestral colour in both instances is not out of place.

John Brownlee.—There is not much to praise or, for that matter, to blame in the presentation of these well-known airs from *Carmen* and *Figaro.* One hears a good honest voice, rather on the small side, with very little animation and absolutely no variety of any sort. The rhythm is steady and marked, but sounds mechanical, while the diction lacks vigour. Yes, on the whole, I fear there is more to blame here than to praise.

Alfred Piccaver.—It is nonsense to say that a person cannot forget how to pronounce his own language. Here is evidence of what life-long residence in Italy have done for Alfred Piccaver in that respect. His Italian is perfect ; his English— well, amusing. *For you alone* should be addressed more especially to his Teutonic or Fascist admirers, who will not trouble to argue with him over his accent, seeing that his voice is sumptuously rich and generous in volume. His *Donna è mobile* flows more easily, and if anything, betrays a shade too much of the *dolce far niente.* But what a glorious tone !

Giuseppe Costa.—I have come across more than one good

singer in my time named Costa; but this is the first Giuseppe "of that ilk," and he is distinctly the reverse of a good one. A persistent, palpable *vibrato*, superimposed upon a vicious method, puts him completely out of count for this public. Originally, it may have been brought about by an effort to increase the tone, but, whatever the cause, the result is extremely unpleasant. I dare not recommend these records lest some unwary singer should want to imitate them.

Carl Martin Oehman.—This tenor, who, if I am not mistaken, is a newcomer, has a bright, penetrating voice without the customary metallic harshness of the type, and has fairly mastered the Wagnerian art of declamation, his diction being noticeably clear. He gives here a capital account of the monologue known as Tannhäuser's *Pilgrimage to Rome*, and makes it as interesting as one can fairly expect it to be out of its place in the opera. The instrumentation is also well brought out.

Robert Burg.—The German operatic stage is singularly well off for fine baritones, as, indeed, it always has been in my recollection, and Robert Burg stands in the front rank of them. He ought, perhaps, to be called a *basso cantante*, seeing that his voice gathers strength and volume as it descends the scale, which is the reason why he sings the music of Wotan so superbly. But for the fault of slurring up to many of his notes, his method would leave no loophole for criticism, and the quality of the tone reminds me in its roundness and purity of Wiegand's, a famous Wotan of the early Bayreuth days. His rendering of the *Abschied* or *Farewell* on this fine record is truly magnificent, and I am glad to say it is well matched by the orchestral performance, which ought to be and is its not least noble feature. Since the new recording began I have heard none quite so satisfying.

Theodore Chaliapine.—A shade more truculent, maybe, yet not without the old touch of Tartar pathos, this new edition of the well-known Chaliapine record of the *Song of the Volga Boatmen*. Musically, it is superior in every way; dramatically, it tells the story far more effectively. The gradual approach, the noisy refrain in the middle, the slow departure, the weird, defiant spirit of the whole thing—all comes out with a clarity and force hitherto impossible of attainment. The chance has inspired the singer, who certainly "knows his job" better to-day than when he made the cancelled D.B.105 a few years ago. Like that, the new record is completed with Rimsky-Korsakov's fine descriptive song *The Prophet*, and once more I find it gloriously declaimed.

Maria Gentile and *Enzo de Muro Lomanto.*—Within the borders of this 10in. disc, using both sides, the Italian singers named have contrived a very pretty and pleasing record of the duet sung by Elvino and Amina, as they take farewell of each other in the twilight of the opening scene. For those who love Bellini—and Richard Wagner was one of those who did—

the simple charm and grace of the music are irresistible; and the two singers, when they keep their vocal ardour within bounds, manage to bring out all its lovable qualities. It is good to hear excerpts from *Sonnambula* now and again. There may yet be a generation that will want to hear the old opera once more.

Aureliano Pertile and *Irene Minghini Cattaneo.*—Lovers of the *Trovatore* will be able to derive ample enjoyment from the singing of these artists of the scene between mother and son in the second Act. It needs a tenor of Pertile's calibre to create fresh interest in the old, familiar tunes, and somehow he manages it. The Azucena is an equally dramatic singer, which is saying much, and the possessor of a powerful mezzo-soprano voice, well under control and tolerably free from tremolo. Of its kind, therefore, the record must be considered well above the average.

Fanny Heldy and *Fernand Ansseau.*—This record contains a page or two of the *Carmen* score that we never hear in this country, and chiefly on that account is exceptionally interesting. I should describe it as the duet for Micaela and Don José, from the First Act of the opera, given in its complete form and divided into parts covering each side of the disc. It is the portion always omitted here that begins the second part and starts off with *Qui sait de quel démon*, the familiar duet passage being afterwards resumed. The whole is delightfully sung, with remarkable steadiness of tone and clearness of diction, by the two French artists, who will be heard in Bizet's opera at Covent Garden during the coming season. Their voices blend well; there is no Italian exaggeration either of speed or phraseology; and the whole thing boasts the perfect simplicity and refinement that befit alike the music and the dramatic situation. Recording faultless!

Opéra-Comique Chorus and Orchestra.—We are getting on. Paris is now adding its quota to the specimens already provided by Milan, Berlin, and London (Covent Garden). Opera houses at other big musical centres will doubtless follow soon, and ultimately we shall be in the happy position of being able to study and compare the various authoritative renderings of all these familiar excerpts. It is a most instructive achievement and much ought to be learnt therefrom. I am rather at a loss to explain why the Opéra-Comique chorus should sing *Cavalleria Rusticana* in French and *Carmen* in Italian, though the former fact is not beyond comprehension, seeing that everything done at the Opéra-Comique is supposed to be sung in the French language. But, apart from this paradox, nothing about these choruses is open to question. The voices are of good quality and well balanced. There is a delightful *dolce far niente* atmosphere about the Sicilian number, while a no less striking measure of vivacity and "go" marks the entry of the bullfighters.

HERMAN KLEIN.

426

OPERATIC AND FOREIGN SONGS

TINKA VESEL-POLLA (soprano).—**Caro nome** from **Rigoletto** (Verdi),and **ZLATA GJUNGJENAC-GAVELLA** (soprano).— **Aria Mimi** from **La Bohème** (Puccini). Orch. acc. Electron X.527, 12in., 4s. 6d.

MARGHERITA SALVI (soprano).—**Caro nome** and **Tutte le feste** from **Rigoletto** (Verdi). In Italian. Orch. acc. Parlo. E.10691, 12in., 4s. 6d.

EMMY BETTENDORF (soprano).—**Die Loreley** (Silcher) and **Abendempfindung, Nightfall,** (Mozart). In German. Orch. acc. Parlo. E. 10690, 12in., 4s. 6d.

BELLA BAILLIE (soprano).—**Voi che sapete** and **Deh ! vieni non tardar** from **Marriage of Figaro** (Mozart). In English. Orch. acc. Col. 9373, 12in., 4s. 6d.

LOTTE LEHMANN (soprano).—**Leonore's Aria (Komm Hoffnung)** from **Fidelio** (Beethoven). In German. Orch. acc. Parlo. R. 20053, 12in., 6s. 6d.

Die Zeit, die ist ein sonderbar Ding from **Rosenkavalier** Act I (R. Strauss) and **Heil'ge Quelle reiner Triebe** from **Marriage of Figaro,** Act 2 (Mozart). In German. Orch. acc. Parlo. R.20054, 12in., 6s. 6d.

ELISABETH SCHUMANN (soprano).—**Im Abendroth, Die Vögel, Die Post** and **Wohin** ? (Schubert). In German. Piano acc. H.M.V., D. 1411, 12in., 6s. 6d.

ELENA GERHARDT (mezzo-soprano).—**Von ewiger liebe,**Op.43, No. 1 (Brahms) and **Immer leiser,** Op. 105, No. 2 (Brahms). In German. Piano acc. H.M.V., D.B.1021, 12in., 8s. 6d. Re-recorded.

LILIAN STILES-ALLEN (soprano).—**Santuzza's Song** from **Cavalleria Rusticana** (Mascagni) and, with **DAN JONES** (tenor), **Finale** from Act I, **Madame Butterfly** (Puccini). In English. Orch. acc. Electron X.523, 12in., 4s. 6d.

MARGARET SHERIDAN (soprano) and **AURELIANO PERTILE** (tenor).—**Bimba dagli occhi** and **Io t'ho ghermita,** Love Duet from Act I, **Madame Butterfly** (Puccini). In Italian. Orch. acc. H.M.V., D.B.1119, 12in., 8s. 6d.

JOHN McCORMACK (tenor).—**Die liebe hat gelogen,** Op. 23, No. 1 (Schubert), in German, and **Who is Sylvia ?** (Schubert), in English. Piano acc. H.M.V., D.A.933, 10in., 6s.

AURELIANO PERTILE (tenor).—**L'Ultima Canzone** (Tosti) and, with **IRENE MINGHINI-CATTANEO** (mezzo-soprano).— **Miserere** from **Il Trovatore** Act 4 (Verdi). In Italian. Orch. acc. Parlo. R.20055, 12in., 6s. 6d.

GIUSEPPE NESSI (tenor), **EMILIO VENTURINI** (tenor) and **ARISTIDE BARACCHI** (baritone).—**The Ministers' Trio** from **Turandot** (Puccini). In Italian. Orch. acc. Parlo. R.20056, 12in., 6s. 6d.

CARL MARTIN OEHMAN (tenor).—**Im ferner Land, Lohengrin's Narration,** and **Nun sei bedankt** from Act I of **Lohengrin** (Wagner). In German. Orch. acc. Parlo. E.10692, 12in., 4s. 6d.

ALFRED PICCAVER (tenor).—**Amor ti vieta** from **Fedora** (Giordano). In Italian, and **Pour un baiser** (Tosti). In French. Orch. acc. Brunswick 15133, 10in.

ERIC MARSHALL (baritone).—**The Two Grenadiers** (Schumann) and **Who is Sylvia ?** (Schubert). In German. Piano acc. Brunswick 20060, 12in.

IVAR ANDRESEN (bass).—**Heil König Heinrich** and **Wo weilt nun der, den Gott gesandt** from **Lohengrin,** Act 3, Scene 3

(Wagner). In German. Orch. acc. Parlo. E.10693, 12in., 4s. 6d.

MARCEL JOURNET (bass).—**Le père, la victoire** (Ganne) and **La Marche Lorraine** 'Ganne). In French. Orch. acc. H.M.V., D.A.930, 10in., 6s. Re-recorded.

Tinka Vesel-Polla and *Zlata Gjungjenac-Gavella.*—You might not think it, but the fair owners of these unpronounceable names are the possessors of exceptionally beautiful voices, both sopranos. The first named is a clever *coloratura* artist, and her *Caro nome* shows her not to be so acrobatic as some we know, nor quite so strictly accurate and precise in her execution ; but, on the other hand, a perfect mistress of all her effects, with a deliberateness of method that never leaves us for a moment in doubt as to her intentions. Her *tempo,* indeed, is too slow, but she compensates for that by the loveliness of the high notes which she lingers on so caressingly. It is delightful to hear a voice produced so naturally and with such absence of effort, with every note unfailingly in tune, notably in a head register that extends to the E in *alt.* The other Czecho-Slovakian *cantatrice* has a soprano of deeper, richer timbre, more lyrical in character yet possessing the same clarity and purity of timbre, the same steadiness and appreciation of tonal effect. She also is a natural singer and seems to be sublimely unconscious of standing before a microphone. *Mimi's Song* suits her well, also because her quality is sympathetic and she throws unaffected tenderness and sentiment into the simple things she says. So far as the language permits me to judge, both ladies represented in this record employ a smooth, clear, easy method of diction, and it is a pleasure to listen to their singing. The recording certainly affords them every chance.

Margherita Salvi.—The fresh, youthful quality, natural production and flexibility of this Italian voice cannot fail to give pleasure. The words are a trifle indistinct, but, after all, in *Caro nome* that does not matter much. It is nice to listen to such clean execution, steady tone, and pure intonation.

Emmy Bettendorf.—The old original tune of the *Loreley,* with its seven or eight verses, will appeal more to German than English listeners ; but the lovely Mozart song is " treasure trove," and ought to be better known in this country. It could not be better sung than it is by Emmy Bettendorf, that is certain. She poises the exquisite melody in the right vocal atmosphere, though she rather neglects the text. The flowing arpeggio accompaniment seems to anticipate a later school.

Bella Baillie.—The best feature of these airs from the *Marriage of Figaro* is the voice of the, to me, unknown singer. It is a pure, clear, well-trained soprano, always in tune, and smooth throughout its compass. The English words are not at all distinct, and there is no variety in the colour and expression of either piece ; but, on the whole, it is very pleasant singing.

Lotte Lehmann.—The amazing versatility of this artist reminds me of famous bygone sopranos such as Lilli Lehmann, Klafsky, and Ternina. They could have gone, as she does, from the great *Fidelio* aria to the *Porgi amor* (sung in German here) from *Figaro,* and thence to the scene from the first act of *Rosenkavalier*—had it been composed. The omission of the wonderful recit. " Abscheulicher," is to be regretted, but the air is magnificently rendered ; and there is no need to describe how Lotte Lehmann sings the music of the Marschallin. Her tone and the orchestral effects are faultlessly recorded.

Elisabeth Schumann.—Four beautiful Schubert songs, with well-played piano accompaniments and deliciously sung by a vocalist who has the art of it all in perfection. Can I say more ? The sprightliness of *Die Vögel* and *Wohin* is simply fairylike ; the tender sentiment of *Abendroth* and *Die Post* a love-dream.

Elena Gerhardt.—These are admirable re-recordings of two of Brahms's most characteristic *lieder.* The voice is less steady and resonant than of yore, but in point of volume the slight loss is more than counterbalanced by the increased sonority of the new process. For diction, phrasing, intonation and poetic feeling, both records are models.

Stiles-Allen and *Dan Jones.*—When, through sheer merit, a singer's work at last obtains wide recognition, I, for one, feel peculiar pleasure. Lilian Stiles-Allen has been a public vocalist for years, but only quite recently have her services come into general request, notwithstanding her fine dramatic soprano voice and legitimate oratorio style. She is a thorough artist, especially fitted for gramophone work, and, in order to complete her fitness in this direction, has only to set seriously about improving her enunciation, which is weak, flaccid, and indistinct. It is the only real fault in her share with Dan Jones in this abbreviated version of the *Love Duet* from *Madame Butterfly*. In *Santuzza's Song* her words are rather better, and she interprets it, of course, with all the necessary emotional feeling. The voice never wavers, while the accompaniments by John Barbirolli's orchestra, if occasionally a trifle cloudy, are refined and nicely balanced.

Margaret Sheridan and *Aureliano Pertile.*—This is the real thing. You get here an up-to-date Italian rendering, at high pressure throughout, of the complete, "uncut" version of the duet for Butterfly and Pinkerton. You feel it winding up the first act of Puccini's Japanese opera amid a blaze of temperamental glory. Pertile's voice is magnificent, and his outbursts of passion are of that fiery kind which suggests the commander of a South American submarine rather than a prim lieutenant of the U.S. navy, which is the sort that Pinkerton never comes near resembling. But never mind. The effect of the duet is soul-stirring, thanks also to the fact that "la Sheridan," as they call her in Italy, has never used her naturally fine voice with so much care, judgment, and histrionic ardour. I hope she will sing like this at Covent Garden ; and Pertile as well.

John McCormack.—*Who is Sylvia?* requires no more introduction than does the Irish tenor himself, but I question whether one Schubert-lover in a thousand knows *Die Liebe hat gelogen*. It is the sorrowful, dejected protest of a disappointed and betrayed lover ; and John McCormack has caught his sensations to a nicety, making you feel that there is nothing more vexing on earth than a naughty, deceitful coquette. I don't greatly admire his German accent, because it has an American flavour ; but it sounds fluent, while the dark colour of the voice is welcome. The Shakespeare song is sung as an *allegro* and Schubert marked it *moderato*. I suppose it is another phase of the prevalent craze for speed ; but it detracts somewhat from the sense of both words and music.

Aureliano Pertile.—Tosti is in demand. He must be, when popular tenors like Pertile and Piccaver utilize his Italian or French ditties for "the other side." He provides, I suppose, an agreeable contrast. Pertile is, as usual, very serious and strenuous in the *Miserere* from—I need not say what. He is light and almost airy in *L'Ultima Canzone*, which I trust will not be *his* last song. It rather suggests the Nasmyth hammer crushing a Neapolitan chestnut. The Leonora, the chorus, and the bell in the *Miserere* are not only all good, but all there !

Giuseppe Nessi, Emilio Venturini and *Aristide Baracchi*. If the music of Liù is the most touchingly melodious in

MARIA GENTILE

Turandot, the trio of the Ministers of State is assuredly the cleverest in its humour, its rhythmical spirit, its bizarre comicality. As sung by these lively Italians, who, if I mistake not, were the three originals in the production at La Scala as well as at Covent Garden, the whole thing is so musically funny that it makes you want to laugh outright. Its very blatant noisiness, which makes you also want to have a soft needle handy, adds to the mirthful qualities of this amazing record. When at full blast it can be first cousin to a steam-organ at a country fair.

Carl Martin Oehman.—The name of this excellent German tenor has been added to the Covent Garden list. His top notes are inclined to waver under pressure, but he sustains without apparent effort, and, judged by this record, he should make a good Lohengrin. However, he will not be heard in that part this season—only later Wagner.

Alfred Piccaver.—The Anglo-Italian tenor chooses a French example of Tosti, *Pour un baiser*, and warbles it with distinction rather than distinctness. I fail to catch the real accent as I do when he sings Italian. The voice, as usual, is superb in the "short and sweet" excerpt from *Andrea Chénier*, and for this the record is worth having.

Eric Marshall.—I have always thought Mr. Marshall had a big voice, and now electrical recording makes it sound huge. But he should beware of standing too close to the microphone. The proceeding is as risky as a "close up" in a film ; it is a bit of a test. He goes for dramatic realism in *The Two Grenadiers* and not without success, especially in the "Marseillaise" section. The note of adoration is missing from *Who is Sylvia?* which is pronounced "How is Sylvia?"

Ivar Andrésen.—Two more selections from *Lohengrin*, this time for King and chorus. And very fine both are.

Marcel Journet. — Welcome re-recordings, these, of two popular marches by Ganne, with solos by a Frenchman who knows how to do them justice.

HERMAN KLEIN.

H.M.V. OPERATIC SUPPLEMENT

LOTTE SCHOENE (with **HERBERT JANSSEN**).—**Tutte le feste al tempio** and (with **JOSEPH HISLOP**) **E il sol dell' anima**, from **Rigoletto** (Verdi). In Italian. Orch. acc. D.B.1127, 12in., 8s. 6d.

FANNY HELDY (soprano).—**Ah je suis seule** and **Ah! Tais-toi** (D.B.1129, 12in., 8s. 6d.) and **O messager de Dieu** and (with Marcel Journet) **Baigne d'eau mes mains** (D.A.940, 10in., 6s.) from **Thaïs** (Massenet). In French. Orch. acc.

AURELIANO PERTILE (tenor).—**Guardate, pazzo son** from **Manon Lescaut** (Puccini) and **Quando le sere al placido** from **Luisa Miller** (Verdi). In Italian. Orch. acc. D.B.1111, 12in., 8s. 6d. **Vesti la giubba** from **Pagliacci** (Leoncavallo), and **Un di all'azzurro** (Improvviso) from **Andrea Chénier** (Giordano). In Italian. Orch. acc. D.B.1118, 12in., 8s. 6d.

THEODORE CHALIAPINE (bass).—**Song of the Viking Guest** from **Sadko** (Rimsky-Korsakov) and **How goes it, Prince?** from **Prince Igor** (Borodin). In Russian. Orch. acc. D.B.1104, 12in., 8s. 6d.

FERNAND ANSSEAU (tenor).—**Vesti la giubba** and **No Pagliaccio non son** from **Pagliacci** (Leoncavallo). In Italian. Orch. acc. D.B.1097, 12in., 8s. 6d.

La fleur que tu m'avais jetée and **Je suis Escamillo** from **Carmen** (Bizet). In French. Orch. acc. D.B.1098, 12in., 8s. 6d.

LOTTE SCHOENE (soprano).—**Signore, ascolta** and **Tu che di gel sei cinta** from **Turandot** (Puccini). In Italian, acc. Berlin S.O.O.E.503, 10in., 4s. 6d.

MARIA OLCZEWSKA, ELSE KNEPEL and **GENIA GUS-ZALEWICZ.**—**Card Scene** from **Carmen** (Bizet). In German. Orch acc. D.1363, 12in., 6s. 6d.

Below are brief reviews of the second instalment of new records issued in the H.M.V. Operatic Supplement on the 1st of this month :—

Lotte Schoene, Herbert Janssen, and *Joseph Hislop.*— These duets from *Rigoletto* confirm my impression that the voice of Lotte Schoene is peculiarly adapted for gramophone work. In addition, she is a thorough artist and a charming singer. Her companions here are also of the first-class, as Covent Garden will shortly be making manifest. Herbert Janssen has the right sort of appealing voice for a Rigoletto, while Joseph Hislop we know all about. Both examples are well up to the new recording level.

Fanny Heldy.—The gifted soprano of the Paris Opéra will appear here this season as soon as the Wagner-lovers have had their turn. Alike as songstress and actress, she is said to be a wonderful Thaïs—far superior in the former capacity to Mary Garden, as these records indisputably prove. She ought to be singing the part in London, but will not do so this year. The proper title for D.B. 1129 is " *Dis-moi que je suis belle*, in two parts," and not as printed in the list and on the label. Anyhow, she sings it with splendid grace and entrain, while the duet with Journet is simply a gem.

Aureliano Pertile.—There is little to choose between these four records. All are interesting and consist of that intensely dramatic stuff which Pertile loves and declaims so well. They make you want to hear him in each of the operas represented— in this order for choice : *Luisa Miller, Manon Lescaut, Andrea Chénier* and *Pagliacci.* You may hear him in the last three, but never in the first. Never mind, you can listen to all their tales of human suffering through the passionate crescendos of these splendidly-executed records.

Theodore Chaliapine.—Here I can make a choice between two numbers because both are on the same disc, and if you go for the one that I prefer you must also take the other. Well, both are magnificently interpreted à la Chaliapine, and both are faithful examples of up-to-date recording ; but I like the jolly, lively, characteristic tunefulness of the *Prince Igor* song,

with all its abundant contract, much better than the *Song of the Viking Guest* from *Sadko*, which is as dreary as the " Steppe " that another Russian composer has written a song about. I need scarcely say that each is sung in masterful fashion.

Fernand Ansseau.—The spelling of titles on labels is again becoming careless. *Vesti la giubba* is easy because invariable. But the word *pagliaccio* comes not within the British " ken " ; while the correct title *Pagliacci*, minus the prefix " I," seems altogether beyond comprehension. Yet both these things stand plainly enough in the vocal score, though the title is wrong in the first edition of *Opera at Home*! And now, with apologies to Monsieur Ansseau, I will proceed to express my admiration for his singing of these familiar pieces—if pieces they can be called. His tone, so distinctively French and dark in timbre, is just right for the tearful outburst of *Vesti la giubba,* less so for the *No, pagliaccio non son*, because it lacks the sudden white-heat rage of the poor maddened clown whose despairing invective it embodies. Somehow it wants more of the frenzied Italian energy that Caruso used to impart to it.

Lotte Schoene.—The two passages allotted to Liù form the happiest inspirations in the opera of *Turandot*. They are genuinely original. Puccini has invested them with a world of tenderness and pathos, and Lotte Schoene brings this out fully in the present instance. Her tone is very pure ; her phrases have the ring of true feeling. The orchestral playing is most refined.

Maria Olczewska, Else Knepel, and *Genia Guszalewicz.*— If one cares for a German setting of *Carmen*, no better version of the *Card Scene* could be desired than this. First, the two girls with their careless rapture over the fortune-telling, *pour passer le temps*, and then the dark fatalism of Carmen herself, with its striking sense of contrast, as she reflects upon the uselessness of striving against the sentence of her dreaded enemy—" *spades.*" Wonderfully has Bizet depicted the episode in music which these three artists so admirably interpret. The record is in every respect adequate.

HERMAN KLEIN.

TRISTAN AND ISOLDA. ACT III

H.M.V., D.1413–1417 (five 12in., in album ; £1 2s. 6d.)
- D.1413. **Prelude** (London Symphony Orchestra under Albert Coates). **The Shepherd's plaintive piping awakens Tristan,** (Widdop, Fry, McKenna and L.S.O.).
- D.1414. **Kurwenal tells Tristan how they came to Kareol** and **Tristan awaits Isolda impatiently** (Widdop, Fry and L.S.O.).
- D.1415. **Isolda's ship appears in sight** (Widdop, Victor and L.S.O.) and **Tristan dies in Isolda's arms** (Ljungberg, Widdop and L.S.O.).
- D.1416. **Isolda weeps over the dead Tristan** (Ljungberg and L.S.O.) and **King Mark arrives. Kurvenal is slain.** (Andrésen, Habich, Noe, Guszalewicz and Berlin State Opera Orchestra under Dr. Leo Blech).
- D.1417. **King Mark grieves over the tragedy** (Andrésen, Guszalewicz and Berlin S.O.O.) and **Isolda dies of grief for Tristan** (Ljungberg).

This H.M.V. Album of the third act of Wagner's immortal music-drama, sung in German, consists of five double-sided discs, cleverly contrived so as to embody, with a minimum of interruption, the salient episodes of the tragic final scene in the courtyard of Tristan's castle. It represents a worthy effort to realize through the gramophone one of the most exacting musical pictures that the lyric stage can furnish. Nothing has been left undone to attain this end ; and, where Mr. Albert Coates and the London Symphony Orchestra drop for a moment the thread of their discourse, it is taken up for a couple of records by Dr. Leo Blech and the Berlin State Opera Orchestra, to be completed as to the death of Isolde by an English orchestra (unnamed) under the guidance of Mr. Lawrance Collingwood.

So, with the exception of a few pages that concern only Tristan and Kurwenal, nothing in the act is omitted—a very notable achievement in ten records.

My sole criticism is this. If the work had to be sung in German—and very properly too—it ought to have been sung entirely by German artists. I agree *in toto* with a well-known American critic who said the other day that he preferred even Chaliapine when singing in Russian; "he was himself and at home." Furthermore, the same writer added, "I am inclined to accept the view that German opera is best when presented in German. At the same time I consider that this holds good only when the singers of Wagner are themselves Germans." To the majority of listeners I daresay it will make no difference, because, once the language is not English, the question of accent will not trouble them very seriously.

It can also be argued that if the job could be given to English singers it was all to the good. I agree. At the same time the fact remains that the expert ear can detect the difference immediately in this otherwise splendid performance. Messrs. Walter Widdop (Tristan), Howard Fry (Kurwenal), Kennedy McKenna (the Shepherd) and Charles Victor have all acquitted themselves creditably, more especially Mr. Widdop, who had by far the most difficult task. But neither in the important matter of style nor for beauty of voice or purity and breadth of declamation could these artists be compared with an Isolde like Göta Ljungberg, a magnificent King Marke like Ivar Andrésen, or such a Brangäne as Genia Guszalewicz. And that is all, positively all, that I have to urge in the way of adverse opinion.

Otherwise there is naught save gratitude and admiration to be expressed for a marvellous example of what can be accomplished with the aid of the electrical process, when exploited in a true spirit of thoroughness and artistic enterprise. The conductors and the orchestras deserve the warmest praise; so far as their splendid share of this Album is concerned I feel that detailed criticism is not called for. I can only wonder what Wagner would have thought of it all had he been alive.

HERMAN KLEIN.

ORATORIO

THE CHOIR OF ST. MARYLEBONE PARISH CHURCH
(RONALD G. TOMBLIN, organist and conductor).—Stainer's *Crucifixion*, recorded in the church.

Columbia 9315. *The Procession to Calvary.*
9316. (a) Recit. *And as Moses lifted up the serpent.* (b) *God so loved the World.* (c) Recit. *Is it nothing to you?* (d) *The Appeal of the Crucified.*
9317. (a) *The Appeal of the Crucified* (contd.). (b) Recit. *After this.* (c) Hymn, *All for Jesus*, last verse. (12in., 4s. 6d. each).

Sir John Stainer's Cantata or Oratorio, *The Crucifixion*, is the most popular and widely-known of his many contributions to the repertory of church music. I remember well his taking me with him to the parish church of St. Marylebone in February, 1887, to its very first performance, in the presence of an overflowing congregation. I remember also that I enjoyed every note of it. The text of this "Meditation on the Passion of the Holy Redeemer" (to give it its full title) was selected and written by the Rev. J. Sparrow-Simpson, and the setting is for two solo voices (tenor and bass) and chorus, interspersed with hymns in which the congregation is or should be at liberty to join. The whole work occupies about forty minutes, and studied simplicity characterizes the music throughout. The performance on the occasion I refer to, was conducted by the composer (who, by the way, resigned his post as organist of St. Paul's in the following year), and I recollect that an address was delivered by Canon Barker in the middle of the Cantata—an interruption rather resented by the musicians who were present. Some of the best portions of the composition are reproduced in these three discs, and the recording of them is on a level with the finest records of organ and choral work that I have heard *via* the new process. The accompaniments, which are for organ throughout, are splendidly handled by Mr. Ronald G. Tomblin, who shows great discretion both in this detail and in the handling of his excellent choir. The solos are also ably sung, especially the recit. *Is it nothing to you?* and the air which follows. The boys are very good in the unaccompanied chorus, *God so loved the World*; while a really fine effect is obtained in *The Appeal of the Crucified*, where the resonance of the full ensemble is powerful and imposing and the true "church atmosphere" pervades the entire presentation of the music. Only in the last number—where the baritone recitative with choir *After this*, merges into the closing hymn *All for Jesus*—have I the complaint to make that the words are not pronounced incisively enough to be distinguished above the combined forces of choir and organ. Otherwise the whole selection has been admirably done.

HERMAN KLEIN.

OPERATIC AND FOREIGN SONGS

MASTER E. LOUGH (treble).—**Hark ! Hark ! the Lark** (Schubert) and **Who is Sylvia ?** (Schubert). In English. Piano acc. H.M.V., B.2681, 10in., 3s.

ELISABETH RETHBERG (soprano).—**Dich teure Halle, Elisabeth's Greeting** from **Tannhäuser** (Wagner) and **Einsam in trüben Tagen, Elsa's Dream** from **Lohengrin** (Wagner). In German. Orch. acc. H.M.V., D.1420, 12in., 6s. 6d.

NINON VALLIN (soprano).—**Depuis le jour** from **Louise** (Charpentier) and **Le roi de Thulé** from **Faust** (Gounod). In French. Orch. acc. Parlo. R.20059, 12in., 6s. 6d.

AMELITA GALLI-CURCI (soprano).—**Air and Variations** (Proch), in Italian, and **La Fauvette** from **Zémire et Azor** (Grétry). In French. Orch. acc. and flute obb. H.M.V., D.B.1144, 12in., 8s. 6d.

BARBARA KEMP (soprano).—**Kann mich auch ein Mädel erinnern** and **Die Zeit sie ist ein sonderbar Ding**, the Monologue of the Marschallin, from **Der Rosenkavalier** (Richard Strauss). In German, Orch. acc. H.M.V., D.1431, 12in., 6s. 6d.

EMMY BETTENDORF (soprano).—**Senta's Ballad** from **The Flying Dutchman** (Wagner). In German. Orch. acc. and chorus. Parlo. E.10706, 12in., 4s. 6d. Re-recorded.

ADELE KERN (soprano).—**Voices of Spring** (Johann Strauss). In German. Orch acc. Parlo. E.10707, 12in., 4s. 6d.

ALFRED PICCAVER (tenor).—**Flower Song** from **Carmen** (Bizet) and **Salut, demeure**, from **Faust** (Gounod). In French. Orch. acc. Brunswick 50110, 12in., 8s.

GOTTHELF PISTOR (tenor).—**Forging Song, Nothung--Nothung** and **Schmiede, mein Hammer, ein hartes Schwert**, from **Siegfried** (Wagner). In German. Orch. acc. Parlo. E.10708, 12in., 4s. 6d.

LUDWIG HOFMANN (baritone).—**Hymn of Johnny** and **Blues Song** from **Johnny Strikes Up** (**Jonny spielt auf**) (Krenek). In German. Orch. acc. Parlo. E.10698, 12in., 4s. 6d.

BENIAMINO GIGLI (tenor) and **GIUSEPPE DE LUCA** (baritone).—**Enzo Grimaldi** from **La Gioconda** (Ponchielli) and **Del tempio al limitar** from **I Pescatori di Perle** (Bizet). In Italian. Orch. acc. H.M.V. D.B.1150, 12in., 8s. 6d.

GALLI-CURCI, HOMER, GIGLI, DE LUCA, PINZA and BADA.—**Chi mi frena**, sextet from **Lucia di Lammermoor** (Donizetti), and **GALLI-CURCI, HOMER, GIGLI and DE LUCA.**—**Bella figlia dell'amore**, quartet from **Rigoletto** (Verdi). In Italian. Orch. acc. H.M.V. D.Q.102, 12in., 16s.

G. ARANGI-LOMBARDI (soprano) and **FRANCESCO MERLI** (tenor).—**Miserere** from **Il Trovatore** (Verdi), and **MERLI** and **TANCREDO PASERA** (bass), **Nume custode e vindice** from **Aïda** (Verdi). In Italian. Orch. acc. and chorus. Col. L.2066, 12in., 6s. 6d.

SIR GEORGE HENSCHEL (baritone).—**Das Wandern** and **Der Leiermann** (Schubert). In German. Piano acc. Col. D.1621, 10in., 4s. 6d.

Master E. Lough.—Very careful discrimination is needed in the choice of pieces for the Temple boy with the ethereal voice, whose record of *Hear my Prayer* made the hit of the year. It is not to be taken for granted, because of that, that he will sing Schubert as well as he sings Mendelssohn. This record proves the contrary. The self-same emotional quality that made such an appeal in *Hear my prayer* is out of place in a joyous outburst like *Hark, hark the lark*, or an adult proclamation of rapturous devotion like *Who is Sylvia ?* The sweet boyish Loughian tenderness cannot breathe the kind of rapture that is needed here. If he must do Schubert *Lieder* in this centennial year, why not try him with good English versions of *Du bist die Ruh* and *Frühlingsglaube ?* They would suit him perfectly.

Elisabeth Rethberg.—A rare combination is to be found in these fresh records of well-worn Wagnerian pieces. The glorious tone, the fine phrasing, the beautiful *cantilena*, together with the spacious amplitude of the new recording, make an ensemble not easily to be resisted. Elsa's "dream" will keep you awake, I am certain ; while the *Tannhäuser* is a greeting full of delightful enthusiasm, from Elisabeth herself. She fills the Hall of Song with every note.

Ninon Vallin.—The high opinion of the French singer already expressed in these columns is emphatically confirmed by the present selections from *Louise* and *Faust*. Many sopranos have essayed *Depuis le jour* without approaching this all-round success. The rich, full timbre of the medium is especially notable, and it has a characteristic quality of which you never tire. I do not say that the head notes are equally beautiful, nor is the union of both registers quite perfect, the result being that the intonation is not invariably impeccable. But the blemishes are slight in comparison with the good features ; and I admire the "Thulé" air from *Faust* all the more because both verses are sung, and in the opera we never get more than one.

Amelita Galli-Curci.—Here is a re-recording of the Proch variations, formerly in the H.M.V. catalogue under the number D.B.265. The improvement is manifest in the wonderful clearness and resonance alike of the voice, the *fiorituri*, and the orchestral accompaniment. The flute obbligato also takes a prominent part in the air from Grétry's opera, *Zémire and Azor*, which is very suggestive of Mozart, the Frenchman's great contemporary. Originally termed a *comédie-féerie*, this charming piece was first staged at Fontainebleau in 1771, and the subject is identical with that of *Beauty and the Beast*. Judging by this air, so exquisitely sung under the title of *La Fauvette* (*The Warbler*) by Mme. Galli-Curci, it would be eminently worth while to mount it on the English stage some Christmastide. A lovely record !

Barbara Kemp.—This fine reproduction of the concluding portions of *Der Rosenkavalier* was made in Berlin with the orchestra of the State Opera under the direction of Dr. Leo Blech. It includes the Marschallin's *Monologue* and parts of her final duet with Oktavian ; and very beautiful it all is. The soloist has a high reputation in her native land and deserves it. With her exceedingly pure, sympathetic tone and her exemplary diction, she reminds one not a little of Mme. Lotte Lehmann in the same role. The orchestral work comes out well—clear, strongly defined, yet subdued—and supports the singer admirably. I hope to hear more records by Barbara Kemp, and perhaps one day the lady herself.

Emmy Bettendorf.—Being among those who are fond of Wagner's *Flying Dutchman*, I welcome the re-recording of *Senta's Ballad* by the peerless Emmy Bettendorf. She sings the whole of it (in two parts), rather slower than Richter used to conduct it and to a distinctly higher pitch than ours— trifles which cannot detract from the beauty of a fine broad rendering full of contrast and tonal charm. The sonority of the record is amazing, and at 4s. 6d I call it a distinct bargain. Of course, it includes the chorus of Norse maidens. But in it I fancy I can distinguish some male voices *au fond* ; why is this ?

Adèle Kern.—A neat interpretation of Johann Strauss's famous waltz-song, but nothing very remarkable. The voice, albeit pretty and always in tune, is rather thin. The staccato is nice and crisp ; the trill excellent.

Alfred Piccaver.—Our friends abroad are not wise to let this splendid Anglo-Italian tenor sing in French. I have pointed out before, and I say it again, his French accent is as bad as his Italian is excellent, and, what is even worse, it is terribly indistinct. It imparts a lackadaisical aspect to his otherwise robust singing, if it cannot lessen the richness and power of his wonderful high notes. I do not "enthuse" over the latter as I once did, but the B flat in Piccaver's *Flower Song* and the semi-*falsetto* high C in his *Salut, demeure*, are really beautiful tones. Besides, the perfect ease with which he produces them is an added joy.

Gotthelf Pistor.—This German tenor has a good honest voice, well fitted for hard work, but not very refined in quality. In these two records he sings Siegfried's *Schmiedelieder* with lots of power and rhythmic energy and the right emphasis. He does it all, however, very mechanically, very deliberately, and without the inspirational impulse that I associated with the youthful Siegfried. The *Nothung* is too slow; the other gets a better accent and is fast enough to be lively.

Ludwig Hofmann.—Here are the first records I have heard of Krenek's celebrated "jazz" opera, *Jonny Spielt Auf* (*Johnny strikes up*). Lovers of jazz will revel in them. They are stuffed with cleverness—the cleverness that belongs to music of their type—and its admirers can rejoice not only in the human saxophone (a capital baritone, Ludwig Hofmann) who obliges from time to time, but in the most exquisitely spasmodic syncopated orchestration that was ever devised. How faultlessly the latter is executed by the band of the Berlin State Opera House I need scarcely say.

Beniamino Gigli and *Giuseppe de Luca.*—Operatic duets that are neither hackneyed nor dull are particularly welcome when sung, as in this case, by first-rate artists. I do not recollect ever hearing finer voices or better style in the scene from the first act of *La Gioconda*, where the spy Barnaba warns Enzo that he is recognized and his purpose in Venice known. The music is magnificent, notably that last big phrase for the tenor, so gloriously sung by Gigli. I wonder how it is that Ponchielli's masterpiece remains only a gramophone and not a stage favourite in England! The two voices also blend well in the melodious duet for Nadir and Zurga from *I Pescatori di Perle*, which is a good deal cut towards the end, yet without lopping off the best. This is another instance of fine singing finely recorded.

Lucia and *Rigoletto Ensembles.*—I name the pieces instead of the artists because the latter are so numerous, and also because they are given in the list above. Your breath will not be taken away by the price of this record *de luxe*, seeing who the singers are. They were probably expensive; or, what is the same thing, their royalties are fixed at a high figure. The point is that their united efforts, vividly and faithfully realized by the electrical process, have achieved a superb rendering of these familiar ensembles. Merely to express an opinion, I will say that I consider the balance between the voices better preserved in the sextet than in the quartet, and that while Galli-Curci is supreme in the one Gigli dominates the situation in the other. Was not this, after all, inevitable?

G. Arangi-Lombardi, Merli and *Pasera.*—I have already had occasion to praise the new Italian soprano in the May number (new Columbia List) and have nothing to add here, because she is only associated with Francesco Merli in the *Miserere*. Both voices are pleasing to listen to. The chorus comes out better in the *Trovatore* than in the *Aïda* Temple scene, where the body of sound is imposing but the parts are not always accurately sung. Again I say of Pasera—a splendid *basso*, if only his excessive breath-pressure did not cause a *vibrato*.

Sir George Henschel.—It is very wonderful—perhaps altogether without precedent—that a singer, who was giving recitals in London more than half a century ago, should still be capable of sitting down to the piano and accompanying himself in a couple of Schubert *Lieder*, as Sir George Henschel can. No one, of course, has ever accomplished such a feat for the gramophone before. The result is still more amazing, because the characteristic quality of the voice remains recognizable, unmistakable in all essentials, while the diction and the self-accompaniment are as perfect as ever. The record of *Der Leiermann* is simply lovable.

HERMAN KLEIN.

The New H.M.V. "Opera at Home"

When first this volume came before the public eight years ago the aptness of the title was far from being as appreciable as it is to-day. The growth in the supply of drawing-room or fireside music of every species has been simply beyond calculation. During the interval in question the gramophone has been supplemented—not superseded, thank goodness!—by the wireless; and between them they have encouraged a demand for and a love of music in the home, the like of which has never been known in the history of the art. Of the original edition of this book in 1920 "H.M.V." issued 20,000 copies. In the following year they printed a library edition of it, revised and enlarged, that probably doubled the earlier issue. Beyond that figures disappeared, and I only know that annual reprints continued, with enlargements and addenda, until now we have what is termed the "Fourth Edition, Completely Revised and yet Further Enlarged" for 1928.

How many millions of copies it is expected will be sold of this new edition I am again without information; and guesswork is not my strong point. But if I expect something very wonderful, it is because a copy of the latest *Opera at Home* lies before me, the most remarkable six shillings' worth of its kind that I have ever set eyes upon, and because I regard it as an indispensable adjunct to every house where there is a decent gramophone on the face of the globe. It does something more than fill a want. It enables you to complete your operatic education. There was a time, within easy recollection, when ignorance concerning opera and opera stories was believed to be so universal that the manufacturers of gramophones, especially in America, used to deem it essential to paste a printed descriptive key to the meaning of the record on the back of the disc, where at that time, of course, nothing was stamped but the number of the matrix. But it was a clumsy arrangement at best, and nowadays the vacant wasted space is no longer available for the purpose, even were it required. Which happily it is not.

Thanks to the gramophone, more than to any other existing medium or instrument, the human race is now musically much better educated, and it knows also a good deal better than it did, say twenty years ago, the utility and value of a book of reference of the type I am dealing with. Turn to its pages and you will find something far more interesting and informative on the subject of opera than the contents of an ordinary musical dictionary. As the editors justly claim in the preface, they have "tried to steer a course between the two extremes of over-elaboration and over-simplification. . . . Under each Opera the date of production, a list of the principal rôles, and, in most cases, a few introductory remarks are given. Then follows an outline of the plot, and this is in turn followed by a list of the excerpts which have been 'recorded,' with particulars of the records available of each. With each excerpt is given a brief description of the dramatic situation."

Such is the plan upon which *Opera at Home* is based. On the whole I find it carried out with intelligent care—perhaps with greater accuracy in some details than heretofore, though I frankly admit that I have not yet read through every plot and every accompanying or analytical description of the orchestral pieces *verbatim et literatim*. Maybe I never shall. However, I have scanned enough of the beautifully printed letterpress to be able to perceive that it is ably written, clear and concise in style, and accurate as to the spelling of names and other important details. The editors, aware of their fallibility when handling the various delicate and controversial topics connected with Opera, have perhaps been at greater pains than was actually necessary to forestall criticism. Indeed, they think " it would be impossible to produce a book on Opera that should be completely free from error "; and, further to justify their modest attitude, they jubilantly declare that the very authorities whom they consulted for this compilation were themselves in many instances at loggerheads " on some matter or other." At present my verdict is " not guilty "; and I trust I may continue to remain of that opinion.

Wisdom has been shown in eliminating from the present edition a great many of the operas included in the previous issues, and substituting in their places works that have been recently introduced into the repertory. I find that, out of a total of about 150, twenty-one have now been omitted and seventeen—the majority of a more modern type—selected for inclusion in the fresh list. As an indication of the direction in which tastes are moving, it will be of interest to give the names of these operas. The following have been dropped out :—

Cristoforo Colombo (Franchetti), *Dafne* (Peri), *Daughter of the Regiment* (Donizetti), *Don Sebastiano* (Donizetti), *Le Donne Curiose* (Wolf-Ferrari), *Il Duca d'Alba* (Donizetti), *L'Enfant Prodigue* (Debussy), *Il Guarany* (Gomez), *Isabeau* (Mascagni), *Le Jongleur de Notre Dame* (Massenet), *Lodoletta* (Mascagni), *Macbeth* (Verdi), *Manon Lescaut* (Auber), *Nero* (Rubinstein), *Polly* (Gay), *Quo Vadis* (Nouguès), *Reine de Saba* (Gounod), *I Vespri Siciliani* (Verdi), *La Wally* (Catalani), and *Zampa* (Hérold).

The following take their place :—

Ariadne at Naxos (R. Strauss), *Bartered Bride* (Smétana), *The Bat* or *Die Fledermaus* (J. Strauss), *Benvenuto Cellini* (Berlioz), *Don Quixote* (Massenet), *Goyescas* (Granados), *Life for the Tsar* (Glinka), *Love of the Three Oranges* (Prokofieff), *Mozart and Salieri* (Rimsky-Korsakov), *The Nightingale* (Stravinsky), *Pelléas et Mélisande* (Debussy), *The Perfect Fool* (Holst), *Phoebus and Pan* (Bach), *Russalka* (Dargomishky), *Sacred City of Kitesh* (Rimsky-Korsakov), *Turandot* (Puccini), and *The Violin-maker of Cremona* (Hubay).

Among the deleted ones are three or four that I personally would not have removed—as, for example, the Verdi pair, *Macbeth* and *I Vespri Siciliani*, the former of which has lately been revived at Berlin on a scale of remarkable magnificence. Excerpts from the earlier Verdi scores are frequently being recorded, especially on the Continent, and one can never say of any of them that it is definitely laid on the shelf for ever. From Gounod's *Reine de Saba* at least three numbers are in constant request, best known by their English titles of *Lend me your aid*, *Far greater in his lowly state*, and *She alone charmeth my sadness* ; and these ought surely to have sufficed to justify the retention of the opera, apart from the chance of its early revival when the " renascence of melody " reaches our slow-moving lyric stage.

In conclusion I may add that the new edition of *Opera at Home* is not less elegantly got up than its predecessors, while the new photographic reproductions furnish a delightful series of pictures in costume of the popular leading stars who have sung for H.M.V. during recent years.   HERMAN KLEIN.

NEW STRACCIARI RECORDINGS

The Columbia July supplement brings in its train a splendid series of new recordings by the famous baritone, Riccardo Stracciari, replacing the same items in the old list. They come under the Light Blue Label group, the 12in. double-sided being now numbered from L.2129 to L.2133 (price 6s. 6d. each), and the 10in., D.1625–6 (4s. 6d. each), and they constitute the " last word " in up-to-date electric process achievement. My chief impression in going through them has been one of amazement that a singer with such a superb voice and limitless power, such an artist of distinction and experience, should not have been heard at Covent Garden for so many seasons. I forget how many, but I know that Signor Stracciari made his début here in 1905 as the Conte di Luna in *Il Trovatore*, and he was here again later ; but then his visits ceased, and it is only through the medium of the gramophone that he has since been listened to and enjoyed—on this side of the Atlantic.

A trifle flattered it may be by the new process, but, even allowing for that, I am of opinion that Stracciari's voice is finer now than it ever was, while his management of it unquestionably evinces a higher order of *maestria*. Truly masterful in their variety are the contrasts of tone, colour, and character that he puts into the ten or a dozen airs of this collection. I may almost say that each is a model of its kind alike for the traditional rendering and the vocal characterization of the piece ; and I do say without the slightest hesitation to the young baritones who may read these lines—let all imitate them who can ! Even if the imitators cannot go the whole way with a phenomenal bit of singing like the *Largo al factotum*, they will at least perceive what Rossini meant and what Stracciari has accomplished, and that is something. The same joy and the same assistance are to be derived from the two wonderful *Rigoletto* excerpts (L.2130), from the *Eri tu*, from the *Credo*, and the *Prologue*.

The resonance, albeit tremendous, is not overdone or unbearable, and the voice sounds pure as well as big—big enough, of course, to fill the largest hall. In the singing there is, taking it all round, an immense amount of gusto and spirit, of sustained energy and power. It even lends interest and importance to a melody like Tosti's *Ideale*, which is coupled for some unknown reason with the *Credo* (Verdi and Tosti were great friends, certainly, so I hope the " misfit " will not create inharmony in " another place"). Among the fine ensembles for the soloist with chorus, nothing could be more imposing than the *O sommo Carlo* from *Ernani* or the finale to the first act of *Tosca*, dignified by the incongruous title of a *Te Deum*. These things are on a veritable big scale and encourage the belief that the whole lot were recorded in Milan, the voices, the language, and the style being obviously " choice Italian." Hence also, I surmise, the same old unsatisfactory conclusion to the

Toreador's Song that Vincenzo Bellezza provides at Covent Garden. My friend Ernest Newman has recently been complaining, as I did long ago, of the omission of the solo bits for the three women and Escamillo, which should impart the finishing touch to the ensemble. Yet all the rest, chorus included, is sung in this record, so there is no excuse. I can only add that the blemish is a small one beside the many points that call for unqualified admiration in this excellent reproduction of the Stracciari series.

HERMAN KLEIN.

OPERATIC AND FOREIGN SONGS

MARGHERITA SALVI (soprano).—**O d'amor messagera** from **Mirella** (Gounod) and **Ardon gl' incensi** from **Lucia du di Lammermoor** (Donizetti). In Italian. Orch. acc. Parlo. E.10718, 12in., 4s. 6d.

MAVIS BENNETT (soprano).—**Ave Maria** (Schubert) and **Serenade** (Schubert). In English. Orch. acc. H.M.V. C.1481, 12in., 4s. 6d.

LOTTE LEHMANN (soprano).—**Geheimes** (Schubert) and **Death and the Maiden** (Schubert). In German. Orch. acc. Parlo. R.O.20061, 10in., 4s. 6d.

EVELYN SCOTNEY (soprano).—**Caro nome** from **Rigoletto** (Verdi), in Italian, and **Je veux vivre dans le rêve**, waltz song from **Roméo et Juliette** (Gounod). In French. Orch. acc. H.M.V., D.1435, 12in., 6s. 6d.

KARIN BRANZELL (contralto).—**Voce di donna** from **La Gioconda**, Act 1 (Ponchielli) and **Condotta ell' era in cepp** from **Il Trovatore** Act 2 (Verdi). In Italian. Orch acc Parlo. E.10719, 12in., 4s. 6d.

GOTTHELF PISTOR (tenor).—**Ein Schwert verhiess mir der Vater** and **Was gleisst dort hell in Glimmerschein** from **Die Walküre** (Wagner). In German. Orch. acc. Parlo. E.10720, 12in., 4s. 6d.

JAN KIEPURA (tenor).—**Nessun dorma** and **Non piangere Liù** from **Turandot** (Puccini). In German. Orch. acc. Parlo. R.20057, 12in., 6s. 6d.

ENRICO DI MAZZEI (tenor).—**Que cette main est froide**, and **NINON VALLIN** (soprano).—**On m'appelle Mimi** from **La Bohème** Act 1 (Puccini). In French. Orch. acc. Parlo. R.20060, 12in., 6s. 6d.

AURELIANO PERTILE (tenor).—**Mercè, mercè, cigno gentil** and **Da voi lontan in sconosciuta terra** from **Lohengrin** (Wagner). In Italian. Orch. acc. H.M.V., D.B.1107, 12in., 8s. 6d.

BROWNING MUMMERY (tenor).—**Recondita armonia** and **E lucevan le stelle** from **Tosca** (Puccini). In Italian. Orch. acc. H.M.V., B.2724, 10in., 3s.

JOHN BROWNLEE (baritone).—**Prologue** from **Pagliacci** (Leoncavallo). In English. Orch. acc. H.M.V., D.1385, 12in., 6s. 6d.

HEINRICH SCHLUSNUS (baritone).—**Heimliche Aufforderung** (Richard Strauss) and **Heimweh** (Wolf). In German. Piano acc. Brunswick 7004, 10in., 4s. 6d.
   Ich grolle nicht (Schubert) and **Der Musensohn** (Schubert). In German. Piano acc. Brunswick 7005, 10in., 4s. 6d.

ROBERT BURG (baritone).—**Als du in kühnem Sange** and **O du mein holden Abendstern** from **Tannhäuser** (Wagner). In German. Orch. acc. Parlo. E.10721, 12in., 4s. 6d.

GIOVANNI INGHILLERI (baritone).—**The Credo** from **Otello** (Verdi) and **Pari siamo** from **Rigoletto** (Verdi). In Italian Orch. acc. Parlo. R.20058, 12in., 6s. 6d.

FOSTER RICHARDSON (bass), with chorus—**Soldiers' Chorus** from **Faust** (Gounod) and **Gypsies' Chorus** from **Il Trovatore** (Verdi). In English. Orch. acc. Zonophone 5105, 10in., 2s. 6d.

LA SCALA CHORUS.—**Soldiers' Chorus** from **Faust** (Gounod) and **Anvil Chorus** from **Il Trovatore** (Verdi). In Italian. Orch. acc. Parlo. R.138, 10in., 3s.

Margherita Salvi.—The waltz-air from Gounod's opera, *Mireille*, is difficult to sing really well, and the rendering of it on this disc betrays much faulty execution. It is not nearly so good, for example, as the *Caro nome* by the same soprano reviewed in the May number or the much easier *Ardon gl' incensi* coupled with the present record. There are signs of effort in the breathing ; the runs are inaccurate ; there is too much staccato ; the intonation is occasionally wrong ; and there is a general lack of the brilliancy that results from entire ease. The *Lucia* air seems to come better within the singer's means.

Mavis Bennett.—The singing of the Schubert *lied* is a study that requires especial care in every direction. When British singers attempt the task they should bear in mind what it imposes upon them and not treat it lightly. A pretty voice is only the beginning ; the artistry is the thing. Here is a method that has neither artistry nor the thought that should inspire it. The words, so vastly important, are sadly inaudible, and the diction is without charm. The rhythm of the *Ave Maria* is frequently uncertain. That of the *Serenade* is also faulty, the phrasing detached ; while the pizzicato string accompaniment suggests a very sleepy lot of players. Altogether one would imagine that Miss Bennett can do much better.

Lotte Lehmann.—Here, surely, in the singing of these two Schubert gems, is the model for the artistry that I was referring to above. Note the purity and simplicity that reigns in every bar, the meaning and distinctness in every syllable, the neatness and elegance that distinguishes every phrase. The combination of these qualities enables you to get to the heart of the song whilst you are revelling in the music and the exquisite tone of the singer. My sole criticism is that the rich low notes required for the utterances of Death in *Der Tod und das Mädchen* are not possessed by Lotte Lehmann ; and the words alone do not suffice. Perhaps, after all, the song were best left to the contraltos. But the other example—*Geheimes*—is simply delicious.

Evelyn Scotney.—An English *Caro nome* by Evelyn Scotney (D.1024) is the only one that has hitherto figured in the H.M.V. catalogue. This Italian specimen is an improvement upon it in every way—voice, style, brilliancy of execution, *e tutti quanti.* The waltz from *Roméo* matches it in all respects save one : respect for the composer's wishes as interpreted in the past by Patti, Melba, Eames and others. He would never allow a long pause on the A natural (key F major) nor the triplet ornaments introduced in the following bar. But with this exception there is naught save appreciation to be set down for a couple of charming records.

Karin Branzell.—A genuine contralto, this, with a glorious timbre both in the medium and chest registers and complete mastery of the *bel canto* as exemplified in the schools of Verdi and Ponchielli. The blind woman's air in *La Gioconda* needs just this sympathetic treatment and ingratiating quality, quite as much as the Azucena narrative from the scene with Manrico requires a bold dramatic manner to express the thirst for vengeance. And both are forthcoming in this remarkably fine record.

Gotthelf Pistor.—There is much less of the "rough and ready" in the German tenor's interpretation of Siegmund, telling us about the wonderful sword provided for his hour of need, than there was (as I pointed out last month) about the joyous songs that his son Siegfried carols whilst forging the broken pieces of that same weapon. I know not whether the extra delicacy here is due to the presence of the fair Sieglinde, whose infatuation grows with every sentence he utters, but assuredly the whole scene (in two parts, by the way) shows off Gotthelf Pistor to a degree of advantage that I had not previously suspected. His tone is clear and steady, with the fine strong middle notes requisite for a Siegmund, and his declamation is first-rate. The orchestral work and the recording are also excellent.

Jan Kiepura.—*Turandot* in German sounds nearly as odd as the *Bohème* in French, and the same exaggeration of vocal tone prevails, necessitating an urgent call for the softest fibre or other needle available. The pressure remains at " full steam " almost throughout, and, but for that trying circumstance, I should award the young tenor warm praise for a splendidly sustained effort. As it is, those who know and like his voice will be pleased to be able to get this record. His command and amplitude of breathing force are quite wonderful.

Enrico di Mazzei and *Ninon Vallin.*—This is the duet from the first act of *La Bohème* and sung in French. Personally I prefer Puccini in Italian, particularly when the tenor is an Italian—even though engaged at the Opéra-Comique in Paris. But the main defect of this record is its excessive loudness, and I find the same fault with most if not all of the Parlophone records I have heard this month. The resonance is so bright and metallic that it makes the voice sound strident. Ninon Vallin has more delicacy and sense of contrast, and di Mazzei might sound less mechanical, less noisy ; for both are excellent artists.

Aureliano Pertile.—There is a distinct difference between the reverberant calibre of these pieces from *Lohengrin.* In the short farewell to the swan one hears a suave, steady flow of ringing tone (suggestive of an empty theatre) ; in the Narration, on the contrary, a curiously subdued level of power, broken only by sudden shafts of penetrating light, contrasts of bright and sombre quality. It is for the most part singing full of distinction, rather heroic and defiant in manner, as though the Knight of the Grail were objecting to the revelation of his name and station, but on the whole far above the average of work done by present-day Italian tenors.

Browning Mummery.—Here is a British tenor who can generally be relied on for purity of tone and a good *sostenuto.* He displays both characteristics to advantage in the familiar excerpts from *La Tosca,* because they are sung in Italian, which is a language that compels him to greater purity than his own—at least as he pronounces it. Since he invariably sings with intelligence and feeling, and knows how to emotionalize love and despair as any decent Cavaradossi should, it follows that these solos represent Puccini and Browning Mummery at their best.

John Brownlee.—This is another effort by a singer from overseas ; and a good one at that. The Prologue done in two parts usually means the inclusion of the whole of the orchestral introduction to *Pagliacci,* as this does, and so makes the excerpt more complete. Happily the instrumental share is capitally played, while the vocal does infinite credit to the soloist, not only as regards colourful expression, but also for clear, crisp enunciation and broad, energetic phrasing.

Heinrich Schlusnus.—For a deep baritone with a rather big organ to control, it is wonderful what rare tenderness and profound sentiment Heinrich Schlusnus can infuse into his singing. He is certainly one of the most accomplished German lieder-singers of our time. His breathing method is irreproachable and his diction clarity itself. If fault there be, it is a certain monotony of tone-colour induced by over-prevalent nasal resonance ; but on the other hand the singer's beauty of style, his sense of rhythm, his variety of expression are gifts that " leap to the ears " in these four examples of Schubert, Wolf, and Richard Strauss. The piano accompaniments are excellent, especially in the more modern songs.

Robert Burg.—The two most beautiful strains of melody allotted to Wolfram in *Tannhäuser* are these ; and I can frankly add that they are completely matched for beauty of voice and style by the present singer. Robert Burg reminds me more than any living German baritone of Reichmann, the most ideal Wolfram of the Wagner era, whom I heard both at Bayreuth and in London. I need say no more to make it clear that the rendering of these two excerpts is exceptionally fine. The power of the voice, too, is restrained and delicate to a degree that should afford an eloquent example for the noisy male stars who now sing for Parlophone. At the same time the clean attack, free from a suspicion of " scooping," the perfect enunciation and phrasing—all these things go to show that the right method is attainable, if you only know how.

Giovanni Inghilleri.—The eminent new baritone who is now singing at Covent Garden has evoked the eulogies that he obviously deserves, but unfortunately (owing to circumstances over which I have no control) I have heard very little of him, and my remarks must therefore be confined purely to criticism of his records. He has a magnificent voice, with a particularly lovely tone in the middle register, but less breadth and power in the higher notes above E and F. His rendering of the *Credo* from *Otello* could hardly be surpassed for grandeur, though the ending, " E poi ? La Morte è il Nulla," is rather spoiled by the pauses being too short and the final phrase too hurried. The *Pari siamo* is dramatic and vocally beyond reproach.

La Scala Chorus.—Under the new conditions these old favourites seem to recover a lost interest and one can listen to them, splendidly sung as they are, with actual pleasure.

English Chorus with *Foster Richardson.*—The above, in Italian costs three shillings, the home product only half-a-crown ; so you can make your own choice. For bright vigorous tone, jovial singing, and good recording there is nothing to choose between them.

HERMAN KLEIN.

OPERATIC AND FOREIGN SONGS

EVA TURNER (soprano).—**In questa reggia** and **O principe che a lunghe caravane** from **Turandot** (Puccini). In Italian. Orch. acc. Col. D.1619, 10in., 4s. 6d.

Ritorna vincitor from **Aida** (Verdi). In Italian. Orch. acc. Col. D.1578, 10in., 4s. 6d.

ROSETTA PAMPANINI (soprano).—**Un bel dì** from **Madame Butterfly** (Puccini) and **Sì, mi chiamano Mimi** from **La Bohème** (Puccini). In Italian. Orch. acc. Col. L.2116, 12in., 6s. 6d.

EMMY LAND (soprano).—**Einsam in trüben Tagen, Elsa's Dream** and **Euch Lüften die mein Klagen** from **Lohengrin** (Wagner). In German. Orch. acc. Parlo. E.10732, 12in., 4s. 6d.

MARGHERITA SALVI (soprano).—**Violetta's Aria** from **La Traviata** (Verdi). In Italian. Orch. acc. Parlo. E.10731, 12in., 4s. 6d.

TOTI DAL MONTE (soprano).—**Lo dice ognun** and **La ricchezze ed il grado** from **La Figlia del Reggimento** (Donizetti). In Italian, La Scala orchestra and chorus. H.M.V. D.B.1152, 12in., 8s. 6d.

FLORENCE AUSTRAL (soprano).—**Porgi amor** from **La Nozze di Figaro** (Mozart), in Italian, and **Ave Maria** (Kahn) in Latin with violin obbl. by Isolde Menges. H.M.V. D.1446, 12in., 6s. 6d.

ELISABETH RETHBERG (soprano).—**Du bist wie eine Blume** (Rubinstein) and **Murmelndes Lüftchen** (Jensen). In German. Piano and strings acc. Brunswick 10260, 10in., 4s. 6d.

AMELITA GALLI-CURCI (soprano) and **GIUSEPPE DE LUCA** (baritone).—**Dite alla giovine** and **Imponete** from **La Traviata** (Verdi). In Italian, Metropolitan Opera House Orchestra. H.M.V. D.B.1165, 12in., 8s. 6d.

APOLLO GRANFORTE (baritone) and **HILDA MONTI** (soprano).—**Rivedrai le foreste imbalsamate** and **Su'dunque !** duet from Act 3 of **Aida** (Verdi). In Italian. Orch. acc. H.M.V. D.B.1153, 12in. 8s. 6d.

ALESSANDRO VALENTE (tenor) and **EMMA LATTUADA** (soprano).—**Tu, tu, amore** and **O tentatrice** from **Manon**

Lescaut (Puccini).   In Italian.   Orch. acc.   H.M.V. C.1503, 12in., 4s. 6d.

FAUSTO RICCI (baritone).—**Prologue** from **Pagliacci** (Leon-cavallo).   In Italian.   Orch. acc.   Parlo. R.10733, 12in., 4s. 6d.

GEORG A. WALTER.—Du bist die Ruh' (Schubert) and **Nacht und Träume** (Schubert).   In German.   Piano acc. H.M.V. B.2772, 10in., 3s.

Eva Turner.—The phenomenal success of the fair Bristolian at Covent Garden should as a matter of course draw renewed attention to her Columbia records. Their merits were dis-covered in these columns long before she returned to her native land with all the *éclat* of a " prodigal daughter." Nevertheless we take no particular credit to ourselves for perceiving gifts so obvious ; they were as palpable as our recent long spell of brilliant July sunshine. The contributions now " released " from *Turandot* and *Aïda* worthily represent Eva Turner in the two operas wherein she most distinguished herself recently. Both are magnificent specimens of her extraordinary power of *sostenuto* on the loftiest *tessitura*—head tone at highest pressure all or most of the time, without strain or deviation from the straight line of perfect intonation, and always clear, pure singing. The slightly " open " quality of the tone, without a trace of vulgarity, singularly recalls (as I have said before) that of Emmy Destinn.

Rosetta Pampanini.—The nne *Un bel dì* of this soprano I have already praised in noticing her Butterfly, and this fine record does it and her ample justice. A touch of melancholy underlies the happiness of the picture, which is drawn with broad vocal lines and no trace of affectation. I care only a trifle less for the Mimi air, and that because it is too much recited—rather heavy and precise, not quite spontaneous enough.

Emmy Land.—The hollow-sounding quality of this voice quickly becomes monotonous, despite careful phrasing and an expressive manner. It is more human—that is, less suggestive of a wood-wind instrument—in the *Dream* than in Elsa's soliloquy, but in neither are the words quite distinct enough.

Margherita Salvi.—On the whole, I can recommend this performance of *Ah! fors' è lui*, though at the outset it is rather diminutive and unimpressive. It improves as it goes along, until ultimately it becomes brilliant and the E natural in *alt* at the end is tremendous. The voice is fairly steady, but the vocalization more showy than refined or finished.

Toti dal Monte.—Familiar but always pleasing are these airs from the *Daughter of the Regiment* ; and their rendering exemplifies exactly what I mean by refined *coloratura*. The Italian translation is of recent date, I fancy, and it is enunciated with splendid rhythm and dash. The Scala orchestra and chorus, conducted by Gabriele Santini, are heard to the utmost advantage, for what they are called upon to do.

Florence Austral.—Voice lovely, as usual, but not employed in the ideal Mozart fashion for *Porgi amor*, though satisfactory enough in the *Ave Maria*. The violin obbligato in the latter is exquisitely played by Isolde Menges. Excessive breath pressure is doubly a fault when brought to bear on Mozartian melody.

Elisabeth Rethberg.—To avoid the blemish just pointed out, I would recommend a careful study of this record, where nothing is in excess and a delightful sense of proportion and artistic reticence marks the entire effort. The tone is lovely through-out these oddly-neglected *Lieder*, and though I will not say I have never heard the Jensen better sung, it is quite beautiful enough to be enjoyed without reservation. Even the violin repetition of Rubinstein's popular melody after the singer has left off is not unwelcome.

Amelita Galli-Curci and *Giuseppe de Luca.*—It would be difficult to imagine anything better of its kind than this per-formance of the duet between Violetta and her lover's father, from the second Act of *La Traviata*. Apart from the fact that the famous prima donna is at her best, it owes not a little of its charm to the admirable restraint of the baritone, who preserves the right balance in the numerous " thirds " and " sixths " by keeping his voice down to a tranquil *mezza voce*. The Metropolitan Opera House orchestra, under Giulio Setti, is worthy of its reputation.

Apollo Granforte and *Hilda Monti.*—Another example from La Scala, under Carlo Sabajno this time, but not quite so good as the preceding one. The father here is too powerful—too *granfortissimo* to be exact—even for the swarthy Amonasro, while the Aïda is not the steadiest that ever crossed the Nile or got crossed in love in the attempt. Yet in the old days we should have considered it a wonderfully good record of the duet.

Alessandro Valente and *Emma Lattuada.*—Yet another celebrated couple in a celebrated duet. The tenor, whose voice strongly resembles Alfred Piccaver's, is especially fine in the long scene from the second act of Puccini's *Manon Lescaut* ; he holds out as though he knew not the meaning of the word fatigue. The soprano, on the other hand, has a voice rather like Eva Turner's, but without her marvellous steadiness. Are these imitations or only accidents ? Anyhow, they are capable singers both, and intensely dramatic.

Fausto Ricci.—A fairly good rendering of the *Prologue*, but nothing at all out of the common. The voice is some-what nasal, and the singer's intelligence is manifest in the control of the dramatic rather than the vocal effects which this now-hackneyed piece demands. Nor is the high A flat quite flawless enough to " ring up the curtain."

Georg A. Walter.—The style of this latest addition to the ranks of Lieder-singers suggests a careful imitation of the methods of Leo Slezák. Only the voice is not very steady, the rapid intake of breath with its half startled gasp is too audible ; the command of tone-colour is not extensive enough. Yet I like the quality of the organ, the diction, and the intelli-gent phrasing. Here is an artist who should improve with further experience at the microphone.

HERMAN KLEIN.

" RIGOLETTO "

Complete H.M.V. Recording

(C1483-1494, 12in., 4s. 6d. each ; complete in album £3 7s. 6d.)

Here is a choice that incurred no possible risk of blame. There is not a country in the world where opera is sung that has not witnessed an amazing growth in the popularity of *Rigoletto* during the past five-and-twenty years. Unlike that of *Il Trovatore*, which instantly took every city in Europe by storm and had its tunes played on every barrel-organ and whistled in the streets by every butcher's boy, this was a case of comparatively slow advance to favour with the multitude. Real connoisseurs and *dilettanti* loved it from the first because they perceived the evidence of increased refinement and beauty, of a deeper and stronger dramatic vein running through the music, an altogether superior type of orchestration, in *Rigoletto* as compared with Verdi's previous scores. But the verdict of Italy in 1851 and of Covent Garden two years later took a little time to penetrate to the masses ; and so did the tunes.

But once they did get through it was wonderful how they "stuck." *Il balen* and *Di provenza* may have got the best of the start, but *La donna è mobile* quickly got on terms with them, and have been racing them hard ever since to a finish that is still centuries from being in sight. The gem of *Rigoletto* is, of course, the quartet, *Un dì se ben* ; and yet I suppose *Questa o quella* and *Caro nome* would beat it hollow if it came to a question of gramophone record sales. The fact is, however, that the whole opera overflows with gorgeous streams of Verdian melody at its " mid-way period " best ; grateful for the singer, delightful for the listener. This, allied to another eloquent fact, namely, the intensely dramatic nature of Victor Hugo's play, *Le Roi s'amuse*, upon which the story is founded, con-

436

stitutes an unanswerable argument for its suitability to "complete opera" presentation through the medium of the gramophone. It is a drama that comes over well. You can not only understand it, but *feel* it. The realism of the new recording process is the principal factor in making that result a certainty.

The H.M.V. announcement of this issue justly concludes that "the public is acquiring a taste for the better forms of music," seeing that "the average buyer of records is choosing over a far larger field than formerly"; and hopes that *Rigoletto* "will stimulate still more strongly that new passion of discovery on the part of the public." Undoubtedly it will. Furthermore, we are reminded of the reasons for omitting certain passages in the opera where action, etc., overshadows the music and which would only add to the expense without being essential to the completeness of the reproduction. To be exact, however, there is extremely little left out in this case. It never would be missed!

The fifteen 12in. records in which the opera is now made available were made in Milàn with the co-operation of the orchestra of La Scala under the direction of Carlo Sabajno, and to my thinking their share of the work constitutes one of its best features. The instrumental balance is faultless, the tone splendid in quality, the playing clear and true in colour and *nuance*, the style definite and authentic. The few choral passages are crisply sung and with abundant spirit. For the rendering of the solo parts I find, after listening carefully to every note of every record, very much to praise and little to blame. It is a typically Italian performance, such as one might hear in any first-class Italian theatre, but without embodying vocalization such as one expects from the "stars" who appear at Covent Garden or the Metropolitan Opera House, New York. Nor is it much the worse for that, seeing that it is consistently creditable, efficient, and traditional.

Signor Piazza, the Rigoletto, has a fine voice and sings with evident dramatic feeling and intelligence, though he is rather unequal—more impressive in some scenes than others, but always dignified and strong in the duets with Gilda; quite first-rate also in the appeal to the courtiers. The quartet is nicely balanced and goes with admirable spirit. The tenor, frankly speaking, I do not care for; his is the routine without the quality. The soprano, L. Pagliughi, is a capable singer, and her execution in *Caro nome* is commendably neat without being at all remarkable. She knows the part of Gilda "inside out;" the only thing I object to in her voice is its excessive *blancheur* and its persistently languorous tone. It is, however, exceedingly steady, and I may add that all the voices in this reproduction, with the unimportant exception of the Sparafucile, are unusually free from tremolo.

HERMAN KLEIN.

OPERATIC AND FOREIGN SONGS

THEODORE CHALIAPINE (bass).—**Vi ravviso** from **La Sonnambula** (Bellini) and **Ave, Signor**! from **Mefistofele** (Boito). In Italian. Orch. acc. H.M.V. D.A.962, 10in., 6s.

MARIA OLCZEWSKA (contralto).—**Mon coeur s'ouvre à ta voix** from **Samson et Dalila** (Saint-Saëns), in French, and **Lascia ch'io pianga** from **Rinaldo** (Handel). In Italian. Orch. acc. H.M.V. D.1465, 12in., 6s. 6d.

BENVENUTO FRANCI (baritone).—**Credo in un Dio crudel** and **Era la notte** from **Otello**, Act 2 (Verdi). In Italian. Acc. by La Scala Orchestra. H.M.V. D.B.1154, 12in., 8s. 6d.

ELIZABETH RETHBERG (soprano).—**Ritorna vincitor** and **O patria mia** from **Aida** (Verdi). In Italian. Orch. acc. H.M.V. D.1451, 12in., 6s. 6d.

ROBERT PRIMOZIC (baritone).—**Cavatina Figaro** from **Barber of Seville** (Rossini) and **Aria Rigoletto** from **Rigoletto**, Act 2 (Verdi). In Italian. Orch. acc. Electron X.532, 12in., 4s. 6d.

NANNY LARSON-TODSEN (soprano)—**Starke Scheite schichtet mir dort** and **Wisst ihr wie das ward?**—Brünnhilde kindles the pyre from **Götterdämmerung** (Wagner). In German. Orch. acc. under Dr. Weissmann. Parlo. E.10756, 12in., 4s. 6d.

MARIA VON BASILIDES (mezzo-soprano).—**Ombra mai fù, Largo** from **Serse** (Handel) and **Komm' süsser Tod** (J. S. Bach). In German. Organ and harp acc. Parlo. E.10757, 12in., 4s. 6d.

NINON VALLIN (soprano).—**Chanson du Chagrin d'Amour, Chanson du Feu Follet** (Parlo. R.20064) and **Danse du Jeu d'Amour**, all from **L'Amour Sorcier, Love the Magician** (de Falla), with orchestra, and **Seguedille Murcienne** (de Falla) (Parlo. R.20065) with piano. Sung in Spanish. 10in., 4s. 6d. each.

HEINRICH SCHLUSNUS (baritone).—**Epiphanias** (Hugo Wolf) and **Ständchen** (Richard Strauss). In German. Orch. acc. Brunswick 80033, 12in., 6s. 6d.

LA SCALA CHORUS OF MILAN.—**La tempesta** and **Fuoco di gioia** from **Otello** (Verdi). In Italian. Orch. acc. Col. 9483, 12in., 4s. 6d.

HEDDLE NASH (tenor).—Recit., **Ella mi fu rapita,** and air, **Parmi veder le lagrime**, from **Rigoletto** (Verdi). In English. Orch. acc. Col. 4986, 10in., 4s. 6d.

Theodore Chaliapine.—No matter what other paths he may stray into, M. Chaliapine never deserts for long his early love —Italian Opera. Like the discerning artist that he is, he prefers Rossini for the comic mood, Bellini for the sentimental, and Boïto for the bizarre. This time he provides examples of the last two, and, candidly speaking, I can make no attempt to choose between them. I love his *Vi ravviso* because it embodies something of the true *bel canto* with just that touch of cynicism in certain inflections which differentiates his Conte Rodolfo, condescending and anxious not to offend, from your ordinary Italian nobleman revisiting the scenes of early boyhood. The voice is clear and steady, and on the whole surprisingly fresh; the singing is agreeably free from dodges or devices of any sort. The *Mefistofele* air is masterly as usual, superb in declamatory power, demoniacal energy and defiant impudence. I always think it the gem of the "Prologue in Heaven"—certainly the most original bit—especially when the great Russian basso interprets it.

Maria Olczewska.—This admirable contralto is never heard to such advantage when singing in French as in the German or Italian language. With her round, opulent voice she could easily arrive at a finer rendering of Delilah's big air—if she took the pains. Still, this is a thoroughly artistic performance and quite free from the customary exaggerations. So, again, in Handel's famous aria, the quick *tempo* is not what we in the land of oratorio are accustomed to, neither is the phrasing nor the diction. But the beauty of the voice atones for all other shortcomings.

Benvenuto Franci.—The two sides of this disc sound like recordings under different conditions. The *Credo* somehow lacks the very brightness and resonance that the *Era la notte* could very well do without. I cannot account for this, but the fact remains. I remember the singer at Covent Garden as an excellent artist, a capital high baritone, but without much individuality or, for that matter, intellectuality in his style; and that is precisely what he demonstrates in these records. Each in its way demands greater subtlety of tonal colouring, more wealth of contrast. The voice itself suffices to please the ear; but is that enough? The Scala Orchestra is, of course, irreproachable.

Elizabeth Rethberg.—These well-known excerpts from *Aïda* were recorded by the same soprano for Brunswick and reviewed by me in this column in our number for February, 1927 (Vol. IV, p. 376). The present disc stands upon the same high level;

which is all that it is necessary to say because the other was absolutely flawless in all respects. I cannot imagine a rendering that would more nearly approach the ideal—that is to say, the model set by Teresina Stolz, who created the rôle of Aïda and whom I heard in Verdi's *Requiem* when she sang it here at the Albert Hall under the master's direction in 1875. From first to last the two airs are beautifully sung and worthily recorded.

Robert Primozic.—These are the first efforts I have heard by this baritone, and they lead me to the conclusion that he would make an impressive if gloomy Rigoletto, but a rather dull Figaro. I like his *Cortigiani* extremely. The tragic tone and the beseeching, despairing manner are quite what are needed. In the *Largo al factotum* one perceives facility and routine without either lightness or elegance. Still it is a fairly cheap record at 4s. 6d., because the voice is a fine one.

Nanny Larson-Todsen.—With the able support of a first-rate orchestra, under Dr. Weissmann, this talented Wagnerian soprano has achieved a magnificent rendering of Brünnhilde's final monologue in *Götterdämmerung*. To my thinking, it is a veritable privilege to be able to hear on the gramophone so marvellous a realization of the colossal closing scene, which on the stage is often (though not always) sung by a tired and hungry (yes, hungry) artist. This is a voice for which nature and art alike have done great things. The blending of delicacy with power is superb, while the grief-stricken tone suggests the farewell of one who is no longer the goddess, but the woman who hails the moment of reunion even whilst she deplores the tragedy that has led to it. It is just that mixture of contending emotions which it ought to be.

Maria von Basilides.—The appealing timbre and broad, dignified phrasing exhibited by this mezzo-contralto both in the Handel and the Bach will please most listeners. Yet, with all its sympathetic quality, her voice runs the risk of being thought monotonous because of a certain somnolence of manner, added to a fixed habit of slurring nearly every downward progression. For the rest, we are accustomed to hearing the *Largo* attain a stronger climax, while *Komm' süsser Tod*, if infused with due fervour of devotional feeling, is susceptible of more contrast. The accompaniments are well played on the organ and harp.

Ninon Vallin.—This clever vocalist, who has been singing lately at 2LO, proves herself more than ever in her interpretations of Manuel de Falla to be *tout ce qu'il y a de plus espagnole*. If the music in intensely Spanish, so, happily, is the performance. Even the accompaniments, whether for orchestra or, as in the *Seguidille*, for the piano, are calculated to win the approval of the gifted and exacting composer whom I dub the "Wizard of Granada." When, I wonder, are we to see *L'Amour Sorcier* performed in this country ?

Heinrich Schlusnus.—In a highly original song by Hugo Wolf like *Epiphanias* you need the interpretative skill of a true artist, and that, precisely, is what Schlusnus deserves to be called. Observe the art with which he differentiates between the changing moods whilst preserving the wonderful swing, the humour, the finesse, and the spirit of jollity. The march-like tread of the accompaniment, as it approaches and departs, recalls somewhat the famous "Turkish Patrol" of Michaelis. The same singer in Strauss's *Serenade* is just a trifle heavy ; but I heartily approve his sober *tempo*, and, after all, it is a man's song, not a woman's, though a man rarely sings it.

La Scala Chorus of Milan.—Practice makes perfect, and the two choruses from the First Act of *Otello*, which used to be regarded as almost impossible to do justice to, are here executed with the utmost ease, dash, and vigour allied to abundant life and rhythmical energy. These features never flag for a moment, while the body of tone is simple amazing. The solo bits in the Tempest scene and the orchestration come out with unfailing clearness and accuracy.

Heddle Nash.—This is a clean, effective rendering of the air which opens the Second Act of *Rigoletto*. The voice is pure and steady enough, but many of the vowels are distorted.

HERMAN KLEIN.

CHRISTIAN SCIENCE HYMNS

It may be regarded, I think, as axiomatic that people love most the hymns that they know best. Nevertheless, not only Christian Scientists, but all to whom the simple tunes of American hymnology yield sincere pleasure, will welcome gladly the four records (two 12in. discs, 9465–6, 4s. 6d. each) which have just been sung for Columbia by George Parker. Selected from the Christian Science Hymnal, the words of all four are by Mary Baker Eddy, and are especially valued by her followers on that account, as well as for the association of religious thought and feeling which the union of text and music must in this case inevitably bring to mind. For the interpretation of such themes no more suitable or more capable singer could have been found than Mr. George Parker. He evidently knows them well ; he invests them with just the right depth and intensity of devotional feeling—that and no more. His simplicity and beauty of expression imparts to each hymn the degree of sentiment and charm that it requires. His sympathetic voice and perfect diction maintain their smoothness and equality throughout, and impeccable recording makes the best of each. The organ, of course, is used for the accompaniments. There should be a wide demand for these Christian Science records.

HERMAN KLEIN.

NEW JEWISH VOCAL RECORDS

The love of the Israelitish race for music, which has come down from the ages, suffices to account for the increasing demand now being experienced on both sides of the Atlantic for gramophone records of Jewish music made by Jewish singers. This is no longer being limited to compositions, traditional or modern, heard only in the synagogue, such as, for instance, formed the staple of the *Jewish Chronicle* Competition Festival held in Kingsway Hall last June. There is also a growing demand, especially among the large American communities, for specimens of secular Hebrew song that bear about the same relation to the religious as music-hall ditties do to the anthems and hymns of the Church of England. To satisfy an equally strong liking for them over here, the British Brunswick, Ltd., have now added to their previous issue by putting on the market quite a representative batch of these up-to-date recordings.

Separate or detailed description is hardly called for, the family likeness in most cases being very strong. The singers, almost without exception, employ that peculiar *voix nasillarde* which is characteristic of their type. It lends itself to a quaint, amusing sort of humour, as the male French exponents of *opéra-bouffe* discovered years ago. Here that quality is enhanced by the fact that the text is nearly all in Yiddish, a language (or rather *patois*) which is always printed in Hebrew letters though based upon German spelling. Consequently, we get on the whole a most extraordinary mixture of philological and musical peculiarities, whilst at the same time listening to something which is essentially and characteristically Jewish and belongs to no other nationality.

Among the new recordings will be found one serious selection by the Cantor Israel Schorr (tenor), the titles of which, translated, run *And to Jerusalem, Thy city*, and *Therefore we are indebted* (12in., 45005 A and B, price 4s. 6d.), sung in pure Hebrew. The first is a genuine chant in a notably individual ornamental setting, full of Eastern colour and demanding great flexibility of technique. The second has an admixture of the operatic style with moments of serio-comic treatment that lend it amusing contrast. The scales and runs in this are executed, like the trills, with the natural facility redolent of the born Cantor and which few can imitate. Another fine double-sided record is that sung in Russian (40131, 10in., 3s.) by Isa Kremer, the clever Jewish soprano who not long since enjoyed quite a " vogue " at the London Coliseum, and who records exclusively for Brunswick. The Yiddish songs, however, form her speciality and the four present examples of these (40003-4 A and B, 10in., 3s.) are quite in her most humorous and characteristic manner. In the Russian things she is—like others ; in the Yiddish—like Isa Kremer. The records bring these features out with absolute truthfulness to the original, and that is all they need to recommend them.

The remainder (all 10in., 3s.) are sung in Yiddish. Morris Goldstein presents his with chorus (40002 A and B) in a merry display of noisy good humour. Aaron Lebedeff (40001 A and B) recalls certain touches of early Offenbach by his Hebrew wail of sorrow in a kind of Slavonic *volkslied* (nearly everything in D minor), with a polka rhythm that would do for a two-step sounding strangely like jollity in a minor mood. His mixture of tragic and comic is undeniably clever. The same sort of thing, only rather more commonplace, is heard in D. Medoff's *Mein Shikzal* (40006 A). In addition, there are two instrumental records (40007 A and B) done by Abe Katzman's Bessarabian Orchestra, one a Jewish *potpourri*, the other entitled *Erinerung fun Kishnev*. Both are lively and brimming over with local colour.

The new Jewish records now issued by Columbia stand in a different category. They are most of them reproductions of serious or synagogue music, whilst including several traditional pieces sung in Yiddish that are among the most interesting to be heard to-day. In the forefront of these I place the four records made on two discs (9453 and 9455, 12in., 4s. 6d. each) by Cantor G. Sirota, whose magnificent tenor is worthy of comparison with some of the finest voices on the operatic stage. He manages it, moreover, like an artist ; while his cultured style is as pure in its tradition as the music he sings—ornaments of every description being executed with the utmost sureness and ease. On the first disc the *Eili, Eili*, is given in Yiddish with orchestra; the *Hatikvah* in Hebrew with choir and organ—this last, with its strong rhythmical beat, a delicious old tune. The orchestral settings of *Schomoch vatismach Zion* and the *Reitsch* on the second disc, also conducted by S. Alman, are quite modern, but extremely fine, the solo effects in the latter displaying the Cantor's powers to the fullest advantage. These are also, of course, sung in Hebrew ; while a vivid contrast to them is afforded by the two folk songs (9458, 12in.) rendered in Yiddish with a telling, bright tenor voice by Cantor Mordechay Hershman, which are unmistakably of Polish origin. The first of these is an amusing polka melody with a quaint refrain ; the second also a lively dance tune, in course of which the singer contrives at least once to touch a high C. The recording of all these items is faultless.

The others of the group are performed by a body known as the London Jewish Male-Voice Choir, excellently trained and led by Isadore Berman. Precise and accurate in all their numerous " effects," they are invariably in tune and steady as a rock. One notes the many quaint passages with *bouche fermée* and the characteristic solo bits in the traditional Yiddish piece entitled *The Eternal Question* (9456, 12in., 4s. 6d.), coupled with which is another humorous one called *Rabbi*—apparently a story of school routine. Both are admirably done. Another contrast is revealed in 9457, a beautiful Hebrew prayer, very sad and plaintive, for the New Year, with it being associated a curious old joyful anticipatory chorus, *When the Messiah comes*. Quite a delightful number is this last, and especially noticeable in it is the frequent *bouche fermée* effect that seems to be peculiar to the Yiddish as distinguished from the purely Hebrew method. Two 10in. discs (4925-6, 3s. each) of four pieces, in Yiddish and unaccompanied, are likewise of extraordinary interest. They

are mostly serious, but all are characteristic in the extreme, while the last, *The Rabbi's Dance*, with verse after verse of singularly varied treatment and *bizarre* contrasts, is one of the most fascinatingly weird things I have ever listened to. Altogether a wonderful series !

HERMAN KLEIN.

OPERATIC AND FOREIGN SONGS

FLORENCE AUSTRAL (soprano).—**Ocean, thou mighty monster** from **Oberon** (Weber). Two parts. In English. Orch. acc. H.M.V. D.1504, 12in., 6s. 6d.

MARGHERITA SALVI (soprano).—**Bell Song** from **Lakmé** (Delibes) and **Shadow Song** from **Dinorah** (Meyerbeer). In Italian. Orch. acc. Parlo. E.10770, 12in., 4s. 6d.

EVA TURNER (soprano).—**Vissi d'arte** from **Tosca** (Verdi) and **Voi lo sapete** from **Cavalleria Rusticana** (Mascagni). In Italian. Orch. acc. Col. L.2118, 12in., 6s. 6d. Re-recorded.

Ritorna vincitor from **Aida** (Verdi). Two parts. In Italian. Orch. acc. Col. L.2150, 12in., 6s. 6d.

O patria mia from **Aida** (Verdi) and **D'amor sull' ali rosée** from **Il Trovatore** (Verdi). In Italian. Orch. acc. Col. L.2156, 12in., 6s. 6d.

In questa reggia and **O Principi, che a lunghe Carovane** from **Turandot** (Puccini). In Italian. Orch. acc. Col. B.1631, 10in., 4s. 6d. Re-recorded.

GOTTHELF PISTOR (tenor).—**Nur eine Waffe taugt** and **Amfortas, die Wunde** from **Parsifal** (Wagner). In German. Orch. acc. Berlin State Opera Orchestra. Parlo. E.10771, 12in., 4s. 6.d

EDMOND RAMBAUD (tenor).—**Air de Jean** from **Hérodiade** (Massenet). In French. Orch. acc. Actuelle 15265, 12in., 4s. 6d.

ALEXANDER KIPNIS (bass).—**Le Veau d'Or** and **Vous qui faites l'endormie** from **Faust** (Gounod). In French. Orch. acc. Col. 5044, 10in., 3s.

ARANGI-LOMBARDI (soprano) and **CARLO GALEFFI** (baritone).—**Mira, di acerbe lagrime** and **Vivrà! contende il giubilo**, duet from Act 4 of **Il Trovatore** (Verdi). In Italian. Orch. acc. Col. L.2157, 12in., 6s. 6d.

GIOVANNI MARTINELLI (tenor) and **GIUSEPPE DE LUCA** (baritone).—**Invano, Albaro** and **Le minaccie, i fieri accenti**, duet from Act 4 of **La Forza del Destino** (Verdi). In Italian. Orch. acc. H.M.V. D.B.1172, 12in., 8s. 6d.

LUCREZIA BORI (soprano).—**Quando men vo**, Musetta's Waltz Song from **La Bohème** (Puccini), in Italian, and **Valse d'oiseau** (Varney) in French. Orch. acc. H.M.V. D.A. 981, 10in., 6s.

NINON VALLIN (soprano).—**L'heure exquise** and **Si mes vers avaient des ailes** (Reynaldo Hahn). In French. Piano acc. Parlo. R.O.20068, 10in., 4s. 6d.

CIDA LAU (soprano).—**Voices of Spring** and **Tales from the Vienna Woods** (Johann Strauss). In German. Orch. acc. H.M.V. C.1539, 12in., 4s. 6d.

MARIO CHAMLEE (tenor).—**Si vous l'aviez compris** (Denza) and **Serenade française** (Leoncavallo). In French. Orch. Brunswick 15136, 10in., 5s. 6d.

ANTONIO NOTARIELLO (tenor).—**Bird Songs at Eventide** (Eric Coates), in English, piano acc., and **Ideale** (Tosti). In Italian. Violin and piano acc. Witton W.6001, 12in., 5s.

Twilight (Glen), in English, piano acc., and **Inverno triste** (Tosti). In Italian. Violin and piano acc. Witton W.6002, 12in., 5s.

Agnus Dei (Bizet), in Latin, 'cello and piano acc., and **Teach me to live** (Liddle). In English. Piano acc. Witton W.6003, 12in., 5s.

Rimpianto, Serenade (Toselli), in Italian, violin and piano acc., and **Vale** (Kennedy Russell). In English. Piano acc. Witton W.6004, 12in., 5s.

439

Vaghissima sembianza (Donaudy), in Italian, 'cello and piano acc., and **For you alone** (Geehl). In English. Piano acc. Witton W.6006, 12in., 5s.

NORMAN ALLIN (bass).—**Der Leiermann** and **Der Tod und das Mädchen** (Schubert). In English. Piano acc. Col. 5019, 10in., 3s.

THEODORE CHALIAPINE (bass).—**Der Doppelgänger** and **Der Tod und das Mädchen** (Schubert). In Russian. Orch. acc. H.M.V. D.B.1184, 12in., 8s. 6d.

Florence Austral.—The big air from *Oberon, Ocean, thou mighty monster,* is a task not to be lightly undertaken. It demands the resources of a genuine dramatic soprano, and that is precisely what Miss Florence Austral can claim to be. It fits her like a glove ; she skims easily and securely over its troubled waters whilst affording a clear idea of the depths beneath. Thanks to the division into two parts, there is no sign of hurry, and the glorious voice has time to give a clear definition of Weber's majestic phrases as they sweep up and down from one end of the scale to the other, winding up with a climax that has the true ring of excitement and joyfulness in every note. Only one little flaw can I observe, and that is in some of the earlier and softer passages : the intonation is now and then a shade below the exact pitch, the intervals are not invariably perfect. Probably the only most sensitive ear will notice this, and I only point it out because there is no other fault to find.

Margherita Salvi.—Both airs are extensively " cut," and in the case of the *Shadow Song* we could have done with a shorter and less elaborate cadenza and a bit more of Meyerbeer's valse. After listening twice to this I have come to the conclusion that the singer would do well to listen to it carefully herself, and consider the advisability of re-recording it. It is undoubtedly brilliant, but in several ornamental passages neither accurate nor precise. The *Bell Song* is much more correctly sung, the tone always clear as crystal, faultlessly in tune, and with a wonderful staccato in the bell refrain.

Eva Turner.—As in her opera singing so in her record making, this talented artist never varies, never deviates from what Lassalle used to call *la grande ligne,* and always, therefore, up to the standard that has won for her her present enviable reputation. Really, I know not how to differentiate between these several specimens of her skill, for all are quite first rate. They reflect, yet without echoing, the ample spaces of the Central Hall, Westminster, and the orchestral accompaniments come out splendidly, those in the re-recordings being, I fancy, conducted by Sir Thomas Beecham. The fine quality of the vocal tone asserts itself to supreme advantage in the *Aida* selections ; its unflagging *sostenuto* marvellous as ever in the *Turandot.*

Gotthelf Pistor.—I can speak only of the first of the two *Parsifal* records here named, that is to say, the selection from the " Good Friday " scene. It is on the whole a sound rendering, done in the right spirit of devotional feeling and with customary observance of traditional values, though without any notable vocal charm. The complete combination would, I suppose, be too much to expect. The work of the Berlin State Opera orchestra could not, of course, be improved upon.

Edmond Rambaud.—Presumably made in Paris and with the support of one of the big opera orchestras, this is an admirable record so far as it goes. But I am bound to confess that I consider it a waste of time for any tenor, however accomplished (and this is undeniably a capable tenor), to devote his energies to such arid, uninspired stuff as Massenet put into this *Air de Jean,* from *Hérodiade.* Even Jean de Reszke used to admit that he could make nothing of it, though the French loved to hear him sing it and the part was the one in which he first made his name in Paris. The solo voice in this instance is guilty of a constant " sagging " from the forward resonance and one *diminuendo* after another, the result of too much nasality. Yet it can be vigorous and penetrating when the

singer chooses ; and the orchestra, with its full, deep body of strings, is quite first rate.

Alexander Kipnis.—Here our friend the German Mephistopheles, singing in the easy-going French of the Rhineland, fairly lets himself go, and we get as the outcome a *Veau d'Or* and a *Serenade* that would have made Gounod open his eyes with astonishment. " What ! " he would have asked, " did I write such devilish, such truly. satanic music as that ? Does the earth nowadays produce such tremendous voices as this Kipnis has ? And is such a diabolical laugh really to be heard out of —," but no, I proceed no further. Purchase this amazing record, and judge for yourself.

Arangi-Lombardi and *Carlo Galeffi.*—Seldom can the hackneyed duet from the fourth act of *Il Trovatore* have been heard on the stage to such advantage as it is in this record ; on the gramophone, never. The voices are both fine, even when at their most strenuous, and the dramatic energy of it all is powerful and vivid to the final note.

Martinelli and *De Luca.*—Here, again, the electrical mechanism seems to impart fresh beauty to the old Verdi strains. The duet for the two men from *La Forza del Destino* is not hackneyed, truly ; far from it. But Caruso and Amato in their record did not contrive to get anything like the " atmosphere " into it that Martinelli and de Luca have done in this, while the reproduction of their voices approaches much more nearly to nature itself. Remember, Verdi was here on the point of advancing into his *Aida* period, and the dramatic quality of the music touches a higher level of refinement. This is superbly realised by both singers in a record that leaves nothing to be desired.

Lucrezia Bori.—The Musetta air is nicely sung, but does not represent the purely vocal talent of this excellent soprano so advantageously as the *Valse d'Oiseau,* with its really clever bird-imitations, set to an accompaniment wherein the celeste figures conspicuously. The French composer had evidently been listening to the song of the blackbird, for he has reproduced it with unusual exactitude and skill, even as his human interpreter has done in her turn. The effect of the trills, the clean octaves and scales, and the vocal acrobatics generally, all recorded to perfection, is quite charming.

Ninon Vallin.—I have no adverse criticism to offer concerning the singing of these two well-known songs by Reynaldo Hahn ; it is elegant, refined, and tender, and tone is vibrant, clear, and sympathetic. The sole drawback lies in the metallic quality of the piano and the heavy *marcato* touch of the accompanist. In *L'heure exquise* he treads over the keys without delicacy or imagination, but in *Si mes vers* he is more considerate.

Cida Lau.—A Viennese *soubrette,* apparently, and a charming one, I am sure. She has a very pretty voice, a pure soprano, and of the right coloratura timbre. Moreover she sings with wonderful dash, and carries off her characteristic effects in these two Strauss waltzes with a sparkle that it is difficult to resist. Her staccato is more accurately done than her shake, which is generally on the wrong note ; while, truth to tell, there is a certain wildness about her vocal flights that needs her doubtless attractive personality to compensate for it entirely. But she is undeniably clever.

Mario Chamlee.—The most agreeable feature of this tenor's records is the natural quality of his voice. He has also a style of his own, but I do not care for it ; he overdoes the sentiment of a song to the *n*th degree. Both of these are sung in French, and although the composers were Italians I cannot imagine that they would have altogether approved Mr. Chamlee's accent, which has a strong touch of the American about it.

Antonio Notariello.—I understand that this new tenor has been residing in London for nearly a year, which would account for his fluent conversational method of pronouncing English. He was to make his début at Queen's Hall last month, too late for me to hear him *in propria persona* before reviewing his records, just issued by the pianoforte firm of Witton and Witton.

They are, on the whole, good to listen to, especially with the aid of a soft needle. They introduce a characteristically Neapolitan tone and method, coupled with no small power of passionate utterance which is in need now and then of a trifle more restraint. Naturally, Notariello is most at home in the songs of his own native land, notably Tosti's *Ideale*, which he sings really well. The temptation to be tearful is too strong for him in Toselli's *Rimpianto*, and it betrays him into some Caruso-like sobs. But his tone when he darkens it sufficiently is very pleasing.

Norman Allin.—Seldom does the ample voice of this popular bass allow itself the degree of reticence that it does in the present Schubert record. A soft needle no doubt helps, but anyhow, there is reason to be thankful, for the result is a rendering of *Der Leiermann* that can be thoroughly enjoyed. It breathes just the right spirit of desolation, and the management of breathing and tone are alike excellent. In *Der Tod und das Mädchen* I perceive less merit because the necessary contrast is not attained. The voice that is full and heavy enough to represent Death is rarely light and juvenile enough to suggest the Maiden.

Theodore Chaliapine.—Nor is the great Russian basso, clever as he is, able to surmount the self-same obstacle. He tries singing the whole song at a quicker tempo, but that does not help matters. On the other hand, his reading of *Der Doppelgänger* is simply magnificent—impressive, charged with fear and apprehension, and climbing up to a wonderful climax.

HERMAN KLEIN.

OPERATIC AND FOREIGN SONGS

FRIDA LEIDER (soprano).—**Leonora's Aria** from **Fidelio** (Beethoven). In German. Orch. acc. H.M.V. D.1497, 12in., 6s. 6d.

MARIA OLCZEWSKA (contralto).—**Che farò senza Euridice** from **Orfeo ed Euridice** (Gluck) and **Ombra mai fù** from **Xerxes** (Handel). In Italian. Orch. acc. H.M.V. D.1490, 12in., 6s. 6d.

ENZO DE MURO LOMANTO (tenor).—**Questa o quella** and **La Donna è mobile** from **Rigoletto** (Verdi). In Italian. Orch. acc. Col. 5060, 10in., 3s.

ALFRED PICCAVER (tenor).—**Addio alla Madre** from **Cavalleria Rusticana** (Mascagni) and **Che gelida manina** from **La Bohème** (Puccini). In Italian. Orch acc. Brunswick 50114, 12in., 8s.

THEODORE CHALIAPINE (bass).—**In questa tomba oscura** (Beethoven), in Italian, and **When the King went forth to war** (Koenemann), in Russian. Orch. acc. H.M.V. D.B.1068, 12in., 8s. 6d.

MIRIAM LICETTE (soprano) and **DENNIS NOBLE** (baritone). —**Give me thy hand, O fairest** (La ci darem) from **Don Giovanni** (Mozart) and **The Manly Heart** (La dove prende) from **The Magic Flute** (Mozart). In English. Orch. acc. Col. 9503, 12in., 4s. 6d.

ANDRÉ BAUGÉ (baritone).—**Pour plaire aux femmes** and, with **LUCIENNE LESEVE** (soprano), **Térésa-Lavarenne** from **La Térésina** (Oscar Straus). In French. Orch. acc. Actuelle 11570, 10in., 3s.

MARIO CHAMLEE (tenor) and **RICHARD BONELLI** (baritone).—**Solenne in quest' ora** from **La Forza del Destino** (Verdi) and **Solo Profugo** from **Martha** (Flotow). In Italian. Orch. acc. Brunswick 50112, 12in., 8s.

DINO BORGIOLI (tenor) and **GINO VANELLI** (baritone).— **Nel cieli bigi** from Act 1 and **O Mimi, tu più non torni** from Act 4 of **La Bohème** (Puccini). In Italian. Orch. acc. Col. D.1634, 10in., 4s. 6d.

LOTTE LEHMANN (soprano).—**Der Nussbaum** (Schumann) and **Aufträge** (Schumann). In German. Piano and violin acc. Parlo. R.O.20071, 10in., 4s. 6d.

DAVID DEVRIES (tenor).—**Rêverie de George Brown** from **La Dame Blanche** (Boieldieu) and **Salut, demeure chaste et pure** from **Faust** (Gounod). In French. Orch acc. Parlo. R.20069, 12in., 6s. 6d.

NINO EDERLE (tenor).—**Addio, Mignon** from **Mignon** (Thomas) and **Chiudo gli occhi** from **Manon** (Massenet). In Italian. Orch acc. Parlo. E.10781, 12in., 4s. 6d.

GIOVANNI INGHILLERI (baritone).—**Prologue** from **Pagliacci** (Leoncavallo) and **Largo al Factotum** from **Barber of Seville** (Rossini). In Italian. Orch. acc. Parlo. R.O.20070, 10in., 4s. 6d.

META SEINEMEYER (soprano), **SIGISMUND PILINSKY** (tenor), **ROBERT BURG** (baritone), **HELENE JUNG** (soprano) and **Chorus.**—**Durch Gottes Sieg**, Finale from Act 1, and **PILINSKY, Lohengrin's Farewell** from Act 3 of **Lohengrin** (Wagner). In German. Orch. acc. Parlo. E.10782, 12in., 4s. 6d.

HERMANN FLEISCHMANN (Obercantor).—**Toras Haschem T' Mimoh** (Lewandowsky) and **Jaaleh** (Lewandowsky). In Hebrew. Organ, choir and orch. acc. Parlo. E.10784, 12in., 4s. 6d.

Frida Leider.—It is impossible to have too many records of a good thing, and, in these days of re-recording, it is the plain duty of the reviewer to welcome repetitions from every source of music that we love to hear, provided that it be well and worthily performed. I shall not mind how many *Abscheulichers* I have to listen to, if they equal or even approach the supreme excellence of Frida Leider's. From the first note to the last it is absolutely beyond reproach. In the pathos of the tone-quality, the touching, measured accents of a sublime trust, the unhurried elegance of the phraseology, in a word, the all-pervading nobility of style and expression, this is the true "Invocation to Hope" that Beethoven placed in the mouth of his glorious heroine. The difficulties of the piece I have too often pointed out for it to be necessary to expatiate further upon the merit of this achievement. Add to it all the utterance of another "hope"—that our own singers will strive to imitate the same effortless command of technique, combined with the same ease and simplicity of delivery, which alone can bring about that actuality of atmosphere that every gramophone artist aspires to attain.

Maria Olczewska.—Once more the popular German contralto gives us new versions of items peculiarly familiar to English concert-goers—items that belong more or less to the category referred to in the preceding paragraph. Only here we are brought face to face with previous defects, to wit, wrong readings of music with traditions that long use has made English musicians respect, together with serious mispronunciations of the Italian language. These are the more to be regretted because Maria Olczewska has a voice admired in this country by all who have heard her, and which she imprints upon a record with singular skill and fidelity. It is a thousand pities that the faults in question are not pointed out to her. Has no one "in authority" the courage to do so?

Enzo de Muro Lomanto.—The singer puts plenty of what his compatriots call *slancio* into the two favourite tenor airs from *Rigoletto*. He has a good telling voice and knows how to use it with unexaggerated dash and vigour. My sole objection is that he indulges in the too-liberal slurring which is the bane of present-day Italian singing. It seems to be getting more and more prevalent.

Alfred Piccaver.—This is one of the talented and presumably expensive British artists whom Sir Thomas Beecham has alluded to as owning bigger reputations abroad than in their own country, which rarely, if ever, hears them. He has, as we know, a truly beautiful voice. It reminds me as no other can or does of the exquisite timbre that was wont to delight everybody who heard that wonderful English tenor of the 'eighties, Joseph Maas. But *he* was never lackadaisical, never lethargic with sudden outbursts of generous tone, never given to slurring (forgive the colloquialism) all over the place.

And there is really no reason why Alfred Piccaver should do these naughty things.

Theodore Chaliapine.—It is good to have upon one disc these two widely-contrasted examples of the Chaliapinesque style. The Russian song is, as would be expected, utterly beyond criticism, full of life, descriptive power, and vivid detail. The Beethoven, which for no sufficient reason is generally associated with contraltos, is remarkable for a sober purity of style, intense expression, and a wonderfully subdued, reproachful pathos. None but a great artist could have so realized the marvellous change in the middle passage of the song, where the troubled spirit pleads no longer, and hurls out the command that its earthly remains shall no more be watered with tears, but allowed to rest in peace. This Etna-like outburst is a master-stroke.

Miriam Licette and *Dennis Noble.*—It would be unfair to ask for better voices or a nicer blending of tones than we get in these familiar Mozart duets. The *La ci darem* requires lighter singing, however. Mme Licette depicts Zerlina vocally as a serious, ladylike personage, and Mr. Noble suggests Don Giovanni rather as a clergyman in search of a living. On the other hand, the sentimental touch is quite in place in *La dove prende,* or *The manly heart,* where Papageno is serious for once and Pamina is her natural self—a " real lady." Indeed, the disc is well worth having for the sake of that side of it which yields one of the gems of *The Magic Flute.*

André Baugé.—A pleasing baritone does full justice to a pretty waltz tune and to his share of a tasteful melodious duet. I cannot say, though, that I care particularly for Oscar Straus sung in French ; there seems to be something awkward about the combination. Otherwise, considering the insignificant outlay, there is a fair amount of pleasure to be derived from the record.

Mario Chamlee and *Richard Bonelli.*—My last remark could not honestly be applied to these duets from *La Forza del Destino* and *Martha,* which (albeit I do not as a rule concern myself with prices) seem to me rather costly. The voices are ample and agreeable, well in tune, and Flotow's well-remembered stanzas are warbled with welcome smoothness. But both singers ought to improve their diction.

Dino Borgioli and *Gino Vanelli.*—Capitally sung are both these duets from *La Bohème,* that from Act I crisply and with abundant vivacity, the more dramatic one from Act III with just the right measure of feeling. It is quite a treat to hear good Italian voices that do not " dig in " with slurs.

Lotte Lehmann.—Not even a hopelessly metallic pianoforte can altogether counteract the charm of such singing as may be heard in these records of two of Schumann's loveliest *Lieder.* The *Nussbaum* is dainty and delicate ; its whispered secrets are full of fascinating mystery. The *Aufträge,* which no English soprano dares apparently to attempt, is simply exquisite in its breathlessness, its sense of impatience, the love and longing " writ large " on every phrase. Yet nothing disturbs the even flow of tone, with every word distinct, not so much music and voice as atmosphere and a message wafted in deepest confidence. The ending is especially delightful.

David Devries.—In the course of Boieldieu's famous *opéra-comique, La Dame Blanche,* which has held the stage in France for just over a century, there occurs an air for the tenor-hero known as the *Rêverie de George Brown*—that being the name of the gentleman in question, a young officer devoted to the cause of the Stuarts. The story, taken by Scribe from one of Scott's novels, is laid in Scotland in 1759 ; hence the fact that Boieldieu in his charming score made use of more than one well-known Scottish air. The particular one quoted in this *Rêverie* is *Robin Adair,* which haunts the hero because he associates it with a certain young lady, and, not knowing the words, he sings it to his own " la, la," with an earnestness that betokens the utmost enjoyment. Such is the piece that M. Devries has here recorded, and which he sings with such consummate elegance and skill. His series of shakes, ending upon a high C, sung *falsetto,* might make many a soprano green with envy. Although less interesting, his rendering of *Salut, demeure,* is given in the best French manner, and confirms the impression that the singer is an accomplished artist.

Nino Ederle.—Here we find the opposite extreme—an Italian drawing-room tenor with a sugary tone which never departs from its unsteady, monotonous level. A style so affected and spasmodic may please certain hearers, but I fear I must not be counted among them.

Giovanni Inghilleri.—This excellent baritone, one of the newcomers at Covent Garden last season, has only to avoid a growing tendency to cultivate the *vibrato* to take his place among successful record-makers. He possesses the right kind of voice for the work, considerable variety of expressive colour, and any amount of dramatic impulse. Hence a capital specimen of the *Prologue* (all on one side of the disc) and an equally good one of the *Largo al factotum,* bright, lively, busy, and inspiriting.

Pilinsky, Seinemeyer, Robert Burg, etc.—Neither of these excerpts from *Lohengrin* is worthy of the source whence it emanates. If we are to get such entirely false interpretations of Wagner as the *Finale* to the first act here presented, the sooner they are laid by the heels the better. The mania for speed results simply in hustling the music out of all recognition and depriving it of all breadth and meaning. The poor soprano does her best to keep up with the rest, but finds herself speedily obliterated. Pilinsky, evidently a courageous *Heldentenor,* has a better chance, of course, and puts in some powerful strokes ; but amid the noise and confusion Robert Burg employs his stentorian notes in vain—even he gets completely lost. Pilinsky's *Adieu to the Swan* is a far more fortunate effort.

Hermann Fleischmann.—This distinguished German *Ober-cantor* has a tenor voice of superb quality and is a past-master of his art. In Lewandowsky's fine settings of the Hebrew text he is admirably supported by choir, organ and orchestra, and the general musical effect of the combination is extraordinarily fine. The recording, too, is beyond reproach.

HERMAN KLEIN.

REVIEWS PUBLISHED IN 1929

OPERATIC AND FOREIGN SONGS

FLORENCE AUSTRAL (soprano) and the **ROYAL OPERA CHORUS AND ORCHESTRA, COVENT GARDEN.**— **Spinning Chorus** and **Senta's Ballad** from **The Flying Dutchman** (Wagner). H.M.V. D.1517, 12in., 6s. 6d.
Inflammatus from **Stabat Mater** (Rossini) in Latin, and **The Night is calm** from **The Golden Legend** (Sullivan). In English. H.M.V. D.1506, 12in., 6s. 6d.

DENNIS NOBLE (baritone).—**Largo al factotum** from **Barber of Seville** (Rossini) and **Il balen** from **Il Trovatore** (Verdi). In English. Orch. acc. Col.9556, 12in., 4s. 6d.

AMELITA GALLI-CURCI (soprano).—**La Paloma** (Yradier) in Spanish, piano acc., and **La Capinera** (Benedict), in Italian, orch. acc. H.M.V. D.A.1002, 10in., 6s.

EMILIO DE GOGORZA (baritone).—**La Sevillana** (Yradier) and **El Relicario** (Padilla). In Spanish. Orch. acc. H.M.V. D.A.998, 10in., 6s.

MARGUERITE d'ALVAREZ (mezzo-soprano).—**Près des remparts de Seville** (**Seguedille**) from **Carmen** (Bizet) and **Mon coeur s'ouvre à ta voix** from **Samson et Dalila** (Saint-Saëns). In French. Piano acc. H.M.V. D.A.1000, 10in., 6s.

MARIANO STABILE (baritone).—**Se vuol ballare** and **Non più andrai** from **Marriage of Figaro** (Mozart). In Italian. Orch. acc. Col. L.2185, 12in., 6s. 6d.

PETER DAWSON (bass-baritone).—**Song of the Flea** (Moussorgsky) and **Oh! my Warriors** from **Caractacus** (Elgar). In English. Orch. acc. H.M.V. C.1579, 12in., 4s. 6d.

GRAND OPERA CHORUS.—Vocal Gems from **Pagliacci** (Leoncavallo) and **Cavalleria Rusticana** (Mascagni). In English. Orch acc. H.M.V. C.1583, 12in., 4s. 6d.

JOSEF LINDLAR (baritone).—**Sachs' Aria** from **The Mastersingers**, Act 3 (Wagner). In German. Orch. acc. Parlo. E.10793, 12in., 4s. 6d.

THEODOR CHALIAPINE (bass).—**Madamina** and **Nella bionda egli ha l'usanza** from **Don Giovanni** (Mozart). In Italian. Orch. acc. H.M.V. D.A.994, 10in., 6s.

GIOVANNI MARTINELLI (tenor).—**Vesti la giubba** and **No, Pagliaccio non son** from **Pagliacci** (Leoncavallo). In Italian. Orch. acc. H.M.V. D.B.1139, 12in., 8s. 6d.

TOTI DAL MONTE (soprano).—**Carnevale di Venezia** (arr. Benedict). In Italian. Orch. acc. H.M.V. D.B.1004, 12in., 8s. 6d.

RICHARD TAUBER (tenor).—**I kiss your hand, Madame** (Erwin-Rotter) and **I'd like to kiss the ladies** from **Paganini** (Lehar). In German, orch. acc. Parlo. E.20072, 12in., 4s. 6d.

Florence Austral, Royal Opera Chorus and Orchestra.—The *Spinning Chorus*, followed by *Senta's Ballad*, forms the opening portion of the second act of *The Flying Dutchman*; hence the association of the two pieces in the present record, and they should be played in that order. Mr. John Barbirolli takes the chorus, with its quaint " Old Dutch " lilt, just at the right tempo; the women's voices sound bright and crisp, and Mary's bit of solo is charmingly sung by Nellie Walker. In the *Ballad* Florence Austral's clear and telling soprano is heard to great advantage; she declaims it with fine emphasis and imparts the necessary dramatic energy to the outburst which comes at the end, after the women with hushed voices have repeated the refrain. The *Inflammatus* from Rossini's *Stabat Mater* and the emotional ensemble, *The Night is calm*, from Sullivan's *Golden Legend*—another appropriate selection—appear to have been recorded at Covent Garden on the same occasion and with equal success. Miss Austral has the requisite physique for the quasi-operatic *Inflammatus*. She would have done better, however, not to hurry the middle

section; for afterwards she fails to relax her speed, loses dignity in the chain of trills, and conveys towards the end a " get it over quick " sort of feeling. The Sullivan is also on the fast side; and here the exquisite quality of the soloist's medium register is twice offset by a forcing of the top B flat and doubtful intonation of intervals in the *voix mixte*. Except for these slight blemishes the performance is a satisfactory one, while the recording is irreproachable.

Dennis Noble.—This improving baritone has achieved a mastery of the art of patter that might almost make Mr. Plunket " Greene " with envy. His *Largo al factotum* skips along (in English) at a pace and with a distinctness which remind me of Santley in the early Carl Rosa days. The comedy is effective without being overdone, and there is a generous flow of good tone throughout. Turning the disc over, I find I like this Figaro better than the Count di Luna—I mean, of course, the air, not the man. Maybe the Italians know better how to combine a smooth *cantabile* treatment with a less sugary tone than Mr. Noble's, and so suggest more cleverly the unmitigated scoundrel that Manrico's brother is. Otherwise the record is wholly first-rate.

Amelita Galli-Curci.—Why singing in Spanish should generally induce an extra liberal supply of *portamento* I have often failed to understand. No doubt *La Paloma* suggests the *dolce far niente* in stronger measure than *La Capinera*, and that is the only excuse for the up-and-down swing of the hammock which Mme. Galli-Curci indulges in a Latin language other than her own. At the same time she endows both airs with delicate touches galore, and *La Capinera* in particular with a tone deliciously soft, sweet, and restrained. What an object-lesson for some singers I could name in the avoidance of mere loudness and noise!

Emilio de Gogorza.—The peculiarity just pointed out does not emerge from the Spanish singing of the American baritone who has made a life-study of this kind of thing. His style is as pure as his pronunciation, which is saying a good deal. His voice has lost none of its freshness and vigour; the accent is rhythmical and the tone conveys plenty of character and colour. These songs seems to demand a dance with castanets, and, when the gramophone is reinforced by television, we shall doubtless be enabled to see Mr. de Gogorza doing this " song and dance " in the appropriate Andalusian costume.

Marguerite d'Alvarez.—It is rather difficult to realize that the two familiar operatic pieces here presented are sung by the same artist, so animated, subtle, and engaging is the *Seguedille*, so dull and lifeless the air from *Samson*. In the *Carmen* she appears to forget the microphone and sing with all the requisite verve and abandon. In *Mon coeur s'ouvre* she reveals the later d'Alvarez of the concert-room, including *tremolo*, *portamento*, and a steady disregard for the pitch. Why should these things be?

Mariano Stabile.—If this admirable artist could be induced to regard Figaro—the valet of Mozart's opera, not the barber of Rossini's—as a less ponderous personage than Sir John Falstaff he would, I am certain, treat his music in a lighter vein. As it is, the magnificent voice which everyone admires so much in Verdi's last opera sounds decidedly heavy in these airs from the first act of *Le Nozze*. (It was the same to some extent with his singing in *Don Giovanni*.) *Non più andrai* comes out better than *Se vuol ballare* because it is taken at a livelier pace; but the latter is marked *allegretto*, and should really be much the quicker movement of the two. Yet, after all, it is a pleasure to hear the well-worn melodies sung with such richness of tone and clarity of diction.

Peter Dawson.—Here, in the company of Moussorgsky and Elgar, we certainly get clean away from the conventional run of things. For I would not dare to hint that the *Song of the Flea* has yet grown hackneyed, or that the artist who sings it must essentially be accused of attempting to imitate Chaliapine—least of all the present interpreter, who as a rule proves himself possessed of ideas of his own. Anyhow, one could not wish to hear a more characteristic rendering of the song or a chuckle more sardonic than Peter Dawson provides through the medium of an English text. He is likewise dignified and sonorous in the splendid Lament from Elgar's early cantata, *Caractacus*, a solo that deserves to be better known than it is, though, to achieve its full effect, it needs to be heard against a choral background. The picturesque orchestration is, however, shown in full relief.

Grand Opera Chorus.—Lovers of *Pagliacci* and *Cavalleria Rusticana* are sure to welcome these vocal and instrumental *potpourris* from the most popular of short operas of our day. They comprise as many favourite tit-bits as two sides of a disc will conveniently contain—snatches from solos and choruses, well performed, lasting quite long enough for recognition.

Josef Lindlar.—This is the closing scene on the banks o the Pegnitz, where Hans Sachs not only claims but insists (on behalf of Wagner no doubt) upon respect for the achievements of the old masters of music. Admirably interpreted by the forces of the Berlin State Opera, under Dr. Weissmann, it constitutes an exceedingly fine reproduction of the imposing finale. Its sole drawback, to my mind, is the over-loud, over-tremulous Hans Sachs of Josef Lindlar. His may be the right manner and the right tradition—that I do not question, but the delivery is so noisy as to submerge everything else, bar the chorus, who take a splendid revenge at the very end, when the sopranos mount gracefully to their high C and the orchestra finishes off the opera as it began, with the imposing theme of the overture.

Theodor Chaliapine.—The famous Russian was in capital voice when he sang this record of Leporello's great air, and that is really to say enough, for there is no need to tell *how* he sings it. The comedy is masterly, of course ; the variety of colour and expression inexhaustible ; the patter unique. But what is perhaps as noteworthy as anything is the dark timbre of the voice in the *Nella bionda* section, where Chaliapine gives you a piece of "straightforward" *cantilena* surprisingly free from tricks and quite in the style of twenty years ago. The orchestra is ably conducted by John Barbirolli.

Giovanni Martinelli.—The *Vesti la giubba* is, I may mention, a re-recording, and anyhow it is magnificent. The *Pagliaccio non son* is a new and extended version of Canio's still finer outburst in the scene where comedy turns so pitifully to tragedy. The excerpt is now complete, for Nedda starts it with her few preceding bars, the comments of the chorus are heard, and even Arlecchino puts in an observation or two. But the main thing, of course, is the glorious voice and declamation of Martinelli, sustaining and prolonging the whole episode with a maximum of dramatic power and feeling. The record was made in New York with the co-operation of the Metropolitan Opera chorus.

Toti dal Monte.—That this gifted *soprano leggiero* is the best singer of her class Italy has produced since Tetrazzini there can be no manner of doubt. I advise anyone who feels inclined to question the assertion to make an early purchase of the present record. No other artist now before the public could have matched it for quality of voice and perfection of execution in a showpiece like Benedict's arrangement of the *Carnevale di Venezia*. It is practically without blemish. The *cantabile* introduction is sung with astonishing purity and smoothness of tone—the clear, round, full-throated tone which it is customary though not always legitimate to compare with that of the nightingale. This is done on one side of the disc ; on the other come the variations—curtailed if I mistake not, but a triumph of *coloratura* including some amazing cascades of chromatic scale-work, followed by no less extraordinary imitations of the harmonics of a violin (echoed by the flute)

attacked and held with a neatness and certainty such as one might imagine the great Paganini himself to have achieved on that magic Cremona of his. And he composed the tune, you remember, besides dazzling our forefathers when he played it. Well, Toti dal Monte can dazzle you with it too.

Richard Tauber.—The "Tango Song" here embodied is a catchy refrain which doubtless forms the *bonne bouche* of the latest Viennese *chef-d'oeuvre* of its type. Very pretty and tuneful, it cannot fail to prove irresistible to waltz-lovers, and to the many thousand admirers of the popular vocalist who warbles it.

HERMAN KLEIN.

NEW JEWISH RECORDS

If supply be the evidence of demand, then must the popularity of Jewish records be well on the up-grade. The fact is easy to comprehend. These things are inimitable of their kind. Only by sheer reproduction can they be placed before their connoisseurs with the actuality of detail that is essential to their individual nature and style of treatment. Nothing less true to the original than the original itself could possibly satisfy. So here once more, in the latest batch of Columbia mid-month records, we have the outcome of the accomplished efforts of **Cantor G. Sirota**, with choir and organ, under the direction of Mr. S. Alman, and also a further selection of the less serious pieces sung in Yiddish by various "stars" familiar to the frequenters of New York's Second Avenue Theatre, etc.

The Cantor's contribution is contained in three discs (9546–48, 12in., 4s. 6d. each), the most welcome of which will perhaps be the famous *Kol Nidrei* that ushers in the service on the eve of the Day of Atonement. Sung, of course, in Hebrew and recorded in two parts, its delivery is marked by intense devotional feeling as well as beauty of voice and expression. One does not recognize the principal theme as identical with that which Max Bruch employed for his well-known arrangement for violoncello with orchestra, but the general form and character of the ancient melody are undoubtedly there for the careful listener to hear, enriched in the second part with much florid ornamentation, and also with occasional turns and cadences that lend it something of an operatic character. The music consists largely of short phrases for the soloist, most of which (leaving out the solemn flourishes) are immediately repeated in rich harmony by the voices of the boys and men. In the other pieces Mr. Sirota is, if possible, even more prominent, notably in the *Havdallah* and in the *Psalm 55* (both 9547), wrongly described as a *Meditation*. This is actually set to the celebrated *Pietà Signore* of Stradella, and therefore partakes more of the nature of an appeal to the Deity, very urgent and full of anguish, which the tenor singer, growing more strenuous as he proceeds, ends with effect upon a high A. The melody used in the *Havdallah* is traditional ; and so, again, is that of 9548, the *Adonoi, Adonoi* (pronounced "Adoshem" to avoid using the holy name in any but religious worship) being extensively decorated with elaborate florid embellishments. Finally, in the reverse record, *Vechol hachaiyim*, there emerges a still more remarkable example of loud and urgent appeal (with choral responses) given out in powerful declamation, covering a high and extended *tessitura* that includes numerous high B flats. In the way of Jewish records none more interesting or more strikingly characteristic than these have yet been issued.

The same group includes a couple of instrumental selections played by the **Menorah Symphony Orchestra**, each on a single disc and in two parts. These may best be described as superior ballet music of an Eastern type, yet modern in character, and revealing certain unmistakably Hebrew touches suggestive of the nationality of their composer, an American Jew named Goldfaden. It is bright, melodious, straightforward music, strongly rhythmical, yet entirely free from jazz, and scored with skill by an adept in the use of effective up-to-date devices. The *Shulamith* and the *Bar Kochba* would either or both of them afford appropriate material for a splendid Oriental ballet.

The Yiddish items are as usual clever and amusing. In accent they are somewhat Americanized, which is only natural, seeing that their interpreters presumably derive their origin from the cosmopolitanism of the " melting pot " rather than the actual purlieus of Vilna, Kovno, or Warsaw. But anyhow, they are vividly true to life—and ear. The serio-comic qualities of **Irving Grossman**, with or without chorus, find their feminine counterparts in the lively ditties of **Nina Sheikewitz** and **Molly Picon** (seven 10in. discs at 3s. each, 5089–95) ; while their subjects, ranging from " grave to gay, from lively to severe," cover the whole gamut of jazz and other rhythms, including two-step, polka, ordinary waltz, and old-fashioned galop. The accompanying band is mostly redolent of pre-war German, plus lots of American " go " ; but the saxophone raises its impertinent head here and there, just to remind the listener that this is the twentieth century, and I need scarcely add that perfect electrical recording serves to drive the nail home. Herman Klein.

OPERATIC AND FOREIGN SONGS

MAVIS BENNETT (soprano).—**They call me Mimi** from **La Bohème** (Puccini) and **Shadow Song** from **Dinorah** (Meyerbeer). In English. Orch. acc. H.M.V. C.1614, 12in., 4s. 6d.

MLLE. FERALDY (soprano).—**Adieu, notre petite table** and **Fabliau** from **Manon** (Massenet). In French. Orch. acc. Col. L.2227, 12in., 6s. 6d.

SIGRID ONEGIN (contralto).—**Che farò senza Euridice** from **Orfeo ed Euridice** (Gluck) in Italian, and **Ah ! mon fils !** from **Le Prophète** (Meyerbeer). In French. Orch. acc. H.M.V. D.B.1190, 12in., 8s. 6d.

CONCHITA SUPERVIA (Mezzo-soprano).—**Cavatina di Rosina, Una voce poco fà** from **The Barber of Seville** (Rossini). In Italian. Orch. acc. Parlo. R.20074, 12in., 6s. 6d.

META SEINEMEYER (soprano).—**Entrance of Butterfly**, Act 1 and **Un bel dì**, Act 2 from **Madame Butterfly** (Puccini). In German. Orch. acc. Parlo. E.10805, 12in., 4s. 6d.

LAURITZ MELCHIOR (tenor).—**Höchstes Vertrau'n hast du mir schon zu danken** from Act 3, Sc. 2, and **O Elsa, nur ein Jahr an deiner Seite** from Act 3, Sc. 3, of **Lohengrin** (Wagner). In German. Orch. acc. H.M.V. D.1505, 12in., 6s. 6d.

FRANCESCO MERLI (tenor).—**Celeste Aida** from **Aida** (Verdi) and **Cielo e mar** from **La Gioconda** (Ponchielli). In Italian. Orch. acc. Col. L.2208, 12in., 6s. 6d.

CARLO MORELLI (baritone).—**Cortigiani vil razza** and **Miei signori** from **Rigoletto** (Verdi). In Italian. Orch. acc. Col. 5169, 12in., 4s. 6d.

COSTA MILONA (tenor).—**Ah mon mi ridestar** from Act 3, **Werther** (Massenet) and **Di tu se fidele** from Act 1, **Un Ballo in Maschera** (Verdi). In Italian. Orch. acc. Parlo. E.10802, 12in., 4s. 6d.

ALFRED PICCAVER (tenor).—**Ah ! si ben mio** from **Il Trovatore** (Verdi) and **O tu, che in seno agli angeli** from **La Forza del Destino** (Verdi). In Italian. Orch. acc. Brunswick 50115, 12in., 8s.

APOLLO GRANFORTE (baritone).—**Era la notte** from **Otello** (Verdi) and **Eri tu che macchiavi quell' anima** from **Un Ballo in Maschera** (Verdi). In Italian. Orch. acc. H.M.V. D.B.937, 12in., 8s. 6d.

MARIA GENTILE (soprano) **Tutte le feste** and **ENZO DE MURO LOMANTO** (tenor).—**Parmi veder le lagrime** from **Rigoletto** (Verdi). In Italian. Orch. acc. Col. 5147, 10in., 3s.

ROSETTA PAMPANINI (soprano) and **GINO VANELLI** (baritone).—**Decidi il mio destin** and **E allor perchè** from

Pagliacci (Leoncavallo). In Italian. Orch. acc. Col. L.2214, 12in., 6s. 6d.

NESSI (tenor), **VENTURINI** (tenor), **BARACCHI** (baritone) and **INGHILLERI** (baritone), with **LA SCALA CHORUS.**— **Uragano** and **Brindisi** from **Otello** (Verdi). Parlo. R.20075, 12in., 6s. 6d.

CERNAY (mezzo-soprano), **LEBARD** and **FENOYER** (sopranos) of the Opéra-Comique.—**Card Scene** from **Carmen** (Bizet). In French, in two parts. Orch. acc. Parlo. E.10803, 12in., 4s. 6d.

CAMBON (baritone), **DALLERAND** (bass) **H. FERRER** (soprano) and Chorus of the **Theâtre National de l'Opéra, Paris.**—**Prologue**, in three parts, and **La Polonaise** from **Boris Godounov** (Moussorgsky). In French. Col. 9589, 9590, 12in., 4s. 6d. each.

LOTTE LEHMANN (soprano).—**Ave Maria** (Bach-Gounod) and **Largo, Ombra mai fù** (Handel). In German. Orch. acc. Parlo. R.O.20076, 12in., 6s. 6d.

M. PANZÉRA (baritone).—**Claire de Lune** (Fauré) and **Chanson triste** (Duparc). In French. Orch. acc. H.M.V. E.519, 10in., 4s. 6d.

Mavis Bennett.—With her delightfully bird-like voice, this clever soprano might fairly allow her words about double their present value without fear of deducting in the smallest degree from the precious purity of her notes. She would thereby afford her listeners far more satisfaction, since her vocalisation yields not a jot to her words, and yet, in its care for brilliancy, fails to achieve entire accuracy with the " small notes," especially in the initial attack of a group. A careful ear readily perceives these defects in a familiar *cheval de bataille* such as the *Shadow Song*, and the merits of an otherwise charming record cannot truthfully be said to counterbalance them. Faulty diction, sad to relate, is permitted to wreak much damage in the training of our native singers. *They call me Mimi* in the present instance is at least sung so that we know what the story is about, but the colloquy between the mad Dinorah and her shadow is " wropt in mystery."

Mlle. Feraldy.—Well, here is the perfect model for the French method of getting the words over. Not so much as a syllable or even a consonant missing ! If you admire Massenet's *Manon* (and surely you must like a very great deal of it) you will take infinite pleasure in listening to the rare perfection of an art such as Mlle. Feraldy's, which seems to combine every possible quality of excellence. You will want to play *Adieu, notre petite table*, over and over again, just as Romeo found parting such sweet sorrow that he could say good-bye until it were morrow. A delicious record !

Sigrid Onegin.—Here the same model recurs in a Scandinavian's Italian, the ravishing contralto tone persisting throughout, and never at the expense of the words. We hear the true *legato*, happily free from slurring, in phrases that are both elegant and expressive, coupled with a dignity that *Che farò* does not invariably receive. I note only one mistake—the pronunciation of " Euridice," which is sung in the German instead of the Italian manner, that is to say, with the first syllable like the German *eu* in " *Euch*." The rendering of *Ah ! mon fils* in French is very nearly as fine, but not quite. The vocal production and the phrasing are equally pure ; but in the exacting middle passage on the high notes the voice loses something of its penetrating power, and the A sharp does not yield its expected thrill. The noble cadenza written for Viardot-Garcia is admirably sung, and the slowness of it is not excessive. The orchestra, like the recording, leaves naught to be desired.

Conchita Supervia.—The name no less than the method of this mezzo-soprano (all but a contralto, by the way) point to a Spanish origin. Her voice has the individual *timbre* that one chiefly hears in the Andalusian women and sounds as though it owed more to natural gifts than to the refining influence of art. Nevertheless her *bravura* is singularly flexible and sometimes even brilliant. A curious feature of it is an extremely marked *coup de la glotte*, so audible that again and again in this adroit rendering of *Una voce* there seem to emerge *due voci* instead of one. Seriously, the anticipation of the note in the throat of the singer can be distinctly heard on the gramophone—a phenomenon that I have never encountered before.

Meta Seinemeyer.—A pleasing record this—limited, so far as my judgment is concerned to the *Entrance of Butterfly*. The girls sing well in tune, while the geisha-bride's progress towards her ill-fated dwelling is very sweetly announced, if with a trifle more tremulousness than even so trying an occasion can be said to warrant. *Un bel di* has apparently not yet dawned.

Lauritz Melchior.—Welcome excerpts from *Lohengrin*, particularly so because they embody two of the least hackneyed pages of Wagner's early opera ; moreover, they are sung by a tenor who has no mannerisms, whose voice is musical and sympathetic, whose declamation is clean and unforced, his enunciation clear and his German very pure.

Francesco Merli.—This is an improving tenor, and one who deserves to be heard at Covent Garden more frequently. His voice sounds wonderfully well in these familiar airs from the masterpieces of Verdi and Ponchielli, and in the recording of them there is no trace of tonal exaggeration.

Carlo Morelli.—Italy no longer counts her Rigolettos by the score, but by the hundred. And they are all so good, too ! If they resemble each other closely no one need be astonished ; for these are the days of records galore, and the Italians are a race of born imitators. Yet somehow Carlo Morelli, both in denunciation and appeal, sounds like an artist who thinks for himself. His contrasts are as swift as they are vivid, and obviously his concept of the Jester is shaped by intelligence no less than feeling. What is more, he has an exceptionally fine voice.

Costa Milona.—This tenor also has a voice of fascinating quality. It resembles Piccaver's just as Piccaver's recalls that of the lamented Joseph Maas ; in other words, there is a *soupçon* of English throatiness that I for one do not find objectionable. Costa Milona's accent and vivacity of style proclaim the genuine Italian, and his tone, if less round than Piccaver's, likewise reflects a less marked tendency to " fade away " or become lackadaisical. The chief difference, however, lies in the middle voice, which is really powerful, while the aforesaid Italian character also distinguishes the ringing head notes. The *Werther* air is thoughtfully interpreted but I like the new tenor even better in that from *Un Ballo in Maschera*, which demands a higher degree of elegant vocal finish—and gets it.

Alfred Piccaver.—After the remarks just made it becomes doubly interesting to compare these records. So far the superiority of the Anglo-Italian, alike as regards richness of tone and *maestria* of technique and style, must be ungrudgingly conceded. His *Ah ! si ben mio* has the ease and distinction of a true artist, of a singer with an amazing breath-control, if lacking the variety of tone-colour that would characterize a great artist. I can forgive him for not being able to make more of the air from *La Forza del Destino*. It is not one of Verdi's happiest inspirations - and, despite many typically Verdian passages, it sounds to me always a dull and monotonous piece. Piccaver has done nothing to relieve this impression.

Apollo Granforte.—To establish the presence—the atmosphere —of Iago it is necessary to preface *Era la notte* with a few bars of the preceding conversation with Otello. Granforte does this, and is thus enabled to produce a striking contrast when he starts his tissue of lies about the dream and proceeds to imitate the voice of the sleeping Cassio in a whining *mezza voce*. The effect, which is wonderful, was originated by Maurel when he created the part, but I have not heard it so well done since, either on the stage or the gramophone, though I have often deplored its absence. The present singer cannot be equally praised for his *Eri tu*. It is useless, to my thinking, to give this air without the recitative, and for the reason just mentioned—that it is essential to the atmosphere of the scene, which it absolutely foreshadows. Altogether the rendering conveys a wrong idea of Renato's emotions when he stresses the anguish of his bygone happiness and his picture of " past delights." The manner is tragic, but the voice here is not sufficiently musical.

Maria Gentile and *Enzo de Muro Lomanto.*—I cannot altogether see the wisdom of uniting separate records by two artists upon a single disc. The duet from the second act of *Rigoletto* would be another story—as, indeed, it often is. But different airs from different scenes, such as these are, have no mutual *raison d'être*, and it were best for them to be kept apart. Otherwise each on its own merits is worth hearing.

Rosetta Pampanini and *Gino Vanelli.*—Here, in the duet from *Pagliacci* between Nedda and Silvio, we have a case in point—an appropriate union which only creates trouble when it occurs in the opera itself ; and then the results are very tragic, as we all know. My sole criticism of this record is a trifling one : it is that the baritone throughout is rather too loud. He causes his companion to sound less prominent than she should ; yet Rosetta Pampanini really has a powerful voice. Apart from that, both sing well together and they make an impressive effect with their impassioned bursts of melody. The recording is particularly clear.

Nessi, Inghilleri, and others.—To lovers of *Otello* this opening scene of the storm and Iago's drinking-song is always interesting, both for its own sake and because the gramophone is beginning to increase their familiarity with its musical complexities. The present example is not so good as one I have heard that came from La Scala. It sounds at times quite blurred, being badly hurried and rushed all through. I imagined the great Faccio, the friend of Verdi, had set the tempo for this music for all time.

Cernay, Lebard, and *Fenoyer.*—An Opéra-Comique trio of clever ladies in the Card Scene from *Carmen* should be quite the right thing, should it not ? It certainly is so in this version, which brings out in the two parts all the vivacity of the smuggler girls at their game, and the fatalistic presentiment of Carmen when she seeks to learn her future from the cards. The entire episode is given with admirable spirit, extremely well sung, and ably accompanied.

" *Boris Godounov* " (*Paris*) Selection.—Although the names of certain French soloists are very properly inscribed on the labels, they have actually but a small part in the execution of these notable Columbia selections from *Boris*. They are taken from a performance at the Paris opera-house, and the chorus and orchestra of that establishment are the principal forces therein. Nothing more imposing, more sonorous, or on a grander scale could well be imagined. I doubt whether Moscow or Petersburg in the " palmy days " of the Romanoffs could have yielded anything like the superb moments of Moussorgsky's opera (even had they performed it, which I don't fancy they did) that are embodied in these two discs. The French text is not the same as that printed in the Oxford University Press score, but it can be quite easily followed. The " cuts " in the opening passage of Part I are effectively done, and the two solo voices are well defined. The Coronation scene is magnificent, the ensemble being grandiose while the bell effects complete the realistic body of sound. Equally spirited is the orchestral *élan* of the sparkling Polonaise, with its pretty solo rendered by the pretty voice of Mlle. Ferrer.

Lotte Lehmann.—None but the rabid highbrow will object to the Bach-Gounod *Ave Maria* as heard through the lovely voice of the popular German soprano ; and the sole blemish to be noted in the Handel *Largo* is the excessively quick speed at which it is taken. Both are beautifully phrased.

M. Panzéra.—These songs of Gabriel Fauré and Duparc are agreeably sung by a French baritone with a voice of very pleasing quality, sweeter and rounder in its middle than in its higher register.

HERMAN KLEIN.

NEW OPERA ALBUMS

"RHINEGOLD" AND "SIEGFRIED" (H.M.V.)

It is curious as a coincidence, but otherwise scarcely surprising, that the choice of *Siegfried* as the winning item in our " Big Works Competition " should have synchronized with the publication by H.M.V. of an album containing an extensive selection from the score of Wagner's music-drama. Personally, I have been unable to ascertain whether a specially-retained foreteller of coming events is kept upon the premises at Hayes, or even at Oxford Street, for the purpose of anticipating the results of our GRAMOPHONE competitions ; but such an individual should evidently prove useful, and I might even be induced, if a vacancy occurred, to offer myself for the post. Meanwhile, *Siegfried* (or, rather, a goodly portion of it) has come to hand, in company with some scenes from *Rhinegold*, the whole forming a welcome instalment on account of that complete recording of the *Ring* which will no doubt one day be our proud possession. As entertainment for a single *séance*, however, the instalment plan in this instance provides ample material. It occupies well over an hour and it comprises many of the salient features of the first and third sections of the tetralogy.

On the inside cover of the album will be found some useful general remarks and, following these, a running commentary upon the story, as it develops in these selected passages, together with a few sparse references to the music and the *motiven*. The corresponding pages of the Schott edition of the **vocal** score are also given for the benefit of those who need them to follow the music. With the records themselves, as with their arrangement, there is little, if any, fault to be found. The fact that the whole sixteen sides, in spite of their all bearing the hall-mark of H.M.V., do not emanate from a single source does not interfere in the slightest degree with the average excellence of the collection. It might be of interest for the expert to compare the relative merits of the three orchestras engaged, viz., the London Symphony Orchestra under Albert Coates, the Berlin State Opera Orchestra under Leo Blech, and the Vienna State Opera Orchestra under Karl Alwin ; but for my part I consider that little would be gained by what must necessarily be a very subtle and complex proceeding, and consequently I leave it to others.

The essential points to be emphasized here are the high standard of the recording as a whole, the obvious care which the three eminent conductors have shown in the execution of their respective tasks, and the highly satisfactory interpretation both of the vocal and the instrumental portions of Wagner's gigantic work under discussion. The four excerpts from *The Rhinegold* (D.1546–1319) present so to speak, the head and tail of the introductory drama. At first we hear the English voices of Arthur Fear as Alberich, Misses Trenton, Suddaby and Nellie Walker (only for a moment) as the Rhinemaidens ; and later on Walter Widdop as Loge with Arthur Fear as Wotan. The scenes in which they appear are the stealing of the gold, dawn over Valhalla, and the descent into Nibelheim ; and the language they sing, like that which follows, is German. That splendid artist, Friedrich Schorr, enters with the Berlin contingent in the *Rhinegold* finale and shares honours with Leo Blech in the grandiose entry of the gods into Valhalla. Here he is the solitary soloist, and we could not wish for a better.

Into the six *Siegfried* discs (D.1530–35) a large quantity of magnificent music has been compressed. It starts off fittingly with the big Forging ditty of the " fearless hero," declaimed with tremendous spirit by Rudolf Laubenthal—every note, every word as true as the hammer-stroke that goes with it. The subsequent " meditation " affords a delightful contrast in tender filial yearning, with many notable themes accompanying in the orchestra. Then come two sides replete with the lovely " Forest Murmurs," their delicate charm a veritable triumph for Dr. Leo Blech and his players, and succeeding these another which contains the beautiful soliloquy

for Siegfried after he has killed the dragon and well delivered by Rudolf Laubenthal. Next we have a disc devoted to the glorious interview between Erda and Wotan (superbly rendered by Maria Olczewska and Emil Schipper), including the latter's farewell to the world, but omitting his scene with the defiant youth. Finally, of course, there comes the great closing duet between Brünnhilde and Siegfried, wherein Laubenthal has for a companion the incomparable Frida Leider. Needless to say that both, working their hardest, achieve their best, and worthily crown a very admirable and praiseworthy piece of work.

"PELLÉAS ET MÉLISANDE" (Col.)

An authentic record of Debussy's opera, based upon the no less famous play by Maeterlinck, and produced in 1902 at the Opéra-Comique, Paris, has been long and eagerly awaited. It was, if anything, more pressingly wanted than the *Carmen* album brought out last month, for the reason that, whereas *Carmen* sounds well in any language (and is performed in many), *Pelléas et Mélisande* only sounds right when sung in French and only quite perfect when rendered by artists possessing the accent, the method, and the tradition of the company by whom it was originally represented. Certain of those singers took part in the performances of *Pelléas* at Covent Garden and the Manhattan Opera House, New York, both of which I witnessed ; and the principal parts will always remain associated in my memory with the consummate artistry of Mary Garden, Jean Périer, and Hector Dufranne. It will thus be taken for granted that nothing less than the very best could satisfy me in a gramophonic reproduction of this opera, and I am proportionately gratified to have found my ideal realized in the Columbia album just issued. Comparatively little of the score is omitted ; the whole of the essential parts are there ; and the recording all through maintains the highest order of up-to-date excellence. In the *brochure* which accompanies the album the story is succinctly told, act by act, supplemented by a description of what happens in each record.

Six two-sided discs (12in., L.2233–38) suffice for the allotted reproduction. The orchestra is conducted by Georges Truc, and the rôles are distributed as follows : Pelléas, Alfred Maguenat ; Golaud, Hector Dufranne ; Arkel, M. Narçon ; Mélisande, Marthe Nespoulous ; and Geneviève, C. Croiza. It would be impossible to imagine diction more perfect or musical dialogue more exquisitely conveyed than will be found in these twelve records. There is no need for me to describe them in detail. The sequence of the various scenes can be followed without the slightest difficulty, particularly by those who have seen Debussy's opera on the stage, absorbed in the scenic fascination of the setting and the weird, uncanny creatures whom a Maeterlinckian fate buffets through it. The strange yet lovely music " comes over " with singular fidelity of *nuance*, colour, and effect ; the singing keeps throughout at a high level ; while the wonderful instrumentation is interpreted with all the requisite delicacy and refinement. On the whole, I am inclined to express the opinion that *Pelléas* is the finest recording of a French opera that Paris has yet sent us.

HERMAN KLEIN.

OPERATIC AND FOREIGN SONGS

FRIDA LEIDER (soprano).—**Or sai chi l'onore** from **Don Giovanni** (Mozart), in Italian, and **Ah ! si la liberté** from **Armide** (Gluck). In French. Orch. acc., conducted by John Barbirolli. H.M.V. D.1547, 12in., 6s. 6d.

GIOVANNI MARTINELLI (tenor).—**Un di all' azzurro spazio** and **Come un bel dì di Maggio** from **Andrea Chénier** (Giordano). In Italian. Orch. acc. H.M.V. D.B.1143, 12in., 8s. 6d.

ROSA PONSELLE (soprano), **GIOVANNI MARTINELLI** (tenor) and **EZIO PINZA** (bass).—**Io muojo ! Confessione !** and

Non imprecare, umiliati a lui from **La Forza del Destino** (Verdi). In Italian. Orch. acc. H.M.V. D.B.1202, 12in., 8s. 6d.

SOPHIE BRASLAU (contralto).—**Romance (La Nuit—Night)** (Rubinstein, Op. 44, No. 1). In Russian; and **Come to me, O beloved** (Cantata) (Bassani-Malipiero) in Italian. Orch. acc. Col. L.2226, 12in., 6s. 6d.

DINO BORGIOLI (tenor).—**Dei miei bollenti spiriti** from Traviata and **MARIO GENTILE** (soprano) in **Addio del passato** from **Traviata** (Verdi). In Italian. Orch. acc. Col. D.1639, 10in., 4s. 6d.

LOUIS GRAVEURE (tenor).—**E lucevan le stelle** from **Tosca** (Puccini) and **La donna è mobile** from **Rigoletto** (Verdi). In Italian. Orch acc. Col. 5211, 10in., 3s.

META SEINEMEYER (soprano) and **TINO PATTIERA** (tenor).—**Già nella notte densa** and **Eddio vedea fra le tue tempie oscure** from **Othello** (Verdi). In Italian, with Orchestra of the State Opera House, Berlin, conducted by Dr. Weissmann. Parlophone E.10816, 12in., 4s. 6d.

MARGHERITA SALVI (soprano).—**Cavatina di Zerlina, Part I, Or son sola, alfin respiro** and **Part II, Domani il r to cava compito** from **Fra Diavolo** (Auber). In Italian, with State Opera House Orchestra, Berlin, conducted by Dr. Weissmann. Parlophone E.10817, 12in., 4s. 6d.

NINO PICCALUGA (tenor).—**Ridi Pagliacci** and **No, pagliaccio, non son** from **I Pagliacci** (Leoncavallo). In Italian. Orch. acc. Parlophone E.10819, 12in., 4s. 6d.

IVAR ANDRESEN (bass).—**O Isis and Osiris** and **Within these sacred walls** from **The Magic Flute** (Mozart). In German. With orchestra and chorus. H.M.V. C.1625, 12in., 4s. 6d.

Mlle. DENYA (soprano).—**Un si grand et secret amour** and **Toi, froide fière statue** from **Turandot** (Puccini). In French. Orch. acc. Col. D.1645, 10in., 4s. 6d.

ALESSANDRO GRANDA (tenor).—**Nessun dorma** and **Non piangere, Liù,** from **Turandot** (Puccini). In Italian. Orch. acc. Col. D.1644, 10in., 4s. 6d.

AURORA RETTORE (soprano).—**Saper vorreste** and **Volta la terrea fronte alle stelle** from **Un Ballo in Maschera** (Verdi). In Italian. Orch. acc. Col. D.1643, 10in., 4s. 6d.

FRANCESCO MERLI (tenor).—**Donna non vidi mai** and **Ah! non v'avvicinati** from **Manon Lescaut** (Puccini). In Italian. Orch. acc. Col. D.1642, 10in., 4s. 6d.

EBE STIGNANI (contralto).—**Condotta ell'era in ceppi,** in two parts, from **Il Trovatore** (Verdi). In Italian. Orch. acc. Col. D.1641, 10in., 4s. 6d.

DORIS VANE (soprano).—**They call me Mimi** from **La Bohème** (Puccini) and **One fine day** from **Madame Butterfly** (Puccini). In English. Orch. acc. Col. 9652, 12in., 4s. 6d.

Frida Leider.—Even with no more than a few bars of the important recitative which precedes Donna Anna's great air of the first act, one welcomes warmly such a fine rendering as this, because it proceeds altogether upon classical lines and bespeaks in every phrase the presence of a singer of the front rank. The transition from the key of the recitative to that of the aria is so cleverly done as to be negligible, and makes a useful cut for purposes of gramophone length; otherwise it would be unpardonable. Besides, what follows is in the grand declamatory manner of the old school and big enough to rouse to action the most somnolent of Don Ottavios. On the reverse side another treat is in store. The beautiful *Ah, si la liberté*, thus beautifully sung, affords a worthy souvenir of the revival of Gluck's *Armide* at Covent Garden last season. Unluckily, Frida Leider is not at her happiest when singing in French, and her words fail now and then to *sauter aux oreilles* just as they did in the opera. Otherwise criticism has not a point to urge against the making of this record—towards which, by the way, John Barbirolli and his orchestra have contributed a creditable share.

Giovanni Martinelli.—I confess that many tenors bore me to extinction in the music of *Andrea Chénier*. As a rule, it is because their only idea is to shout it. Not so Martinelli. He really sings every note of these two airs, putting into them a wealth of glorious tone and an intensity of passion which is overwhelming without being overdone. The gusts nearly sweep you off your feet, yet without damaging your tympanum or causing any other sort of discomfort due to loss of equilibrium. For the tone never loses its rich, dark quality, never diminishes its untiring stamina or sustaining power, and makes you feel that this is the right singer for such music.

Rosa Ponselle, Martinelli and Ezio Pinza.—This is a capital recording of the splendidly dramatic trio which constitutes the finale of Verdi's *Forza del Destino*. It is in two parts, and the first recalls the outbursts of rage and fury made familiar in *Il Trovatore* by our old friends Manrico, Leonora, and the Conte di Luna. In the second we hear a suave melody started by the bass and taken up by the other voices in turn, rather in the *Otello* manner, then leading up to a strenuous climax. The ending is very tragic and comes out well here. Altogether the three artists make of it an exceptionally fine record.

Sophie Braslau.—A female bass or a lady tenor—which ought we to call this clever Russian vocalist ? The quality of the timbre, especially when you hear the first notes, is very hard to distinguish from a man's (and that man a tenor); but she can go down too, and the quality there is even more arresting in its sonorous breadth. To what extent the voice has been magnified by mechanical means I know not; but its power is almost superhuman, while I could wish that the tone-colour varied a little more. These songs suggest misery, anguish, and pleading, nothing else; hence their suiting the singer so well. The Malipiero is less tedious than Rubinstein's weak imitation of Gounod, but it also recalls the early Italian style of Stradella's *Pietà Signore*, without, however, its depth and sincerity of feeling. The record, nevertheless, is quite unique in its way and well worth having.

Dino Borgioli and Maria Gentile.—These are, of course, separate pieces, not duets, but, being from the same opera, are not unfittingly associated on the same disc. Both are admirably sung; for here we have Borgioli at his exuberant best, and Maria Gentile in her most touching mood, with a voice that even brings back the indescribable, unforgettable sighs wherewith the greatest of all Violettas, Adelina Patti, was wont to linger over her " farewell to the past." Even the smallest re-awakening of such a memory is something to be thankful for.

Louis Graveure.—I think I have heard this singer somewhere, but cannot quite remember where. Nor do I recognize his voice in this record, which has developed it into a noisy tenor of amazing hugeness (large halls and soft needles indispensable !). The *Tosca* air is given with expression; the *Rigoletto* with more *brio* than elegance or sureness of phrasing. The Italian, too, requires polishing, both as to accent and grammar. The Duke, when he talks about the *donna* who is *mobile*, should not refer to her as *muti* but *muta d'accento*.

Meta Seinemeyer and Tino Pattiera.—The voices of these two singers blend very harmoniously in the love duet which terminates the First Act of Verdi's *Otello*—one of the most beautiful and original of the many inspired pages that enrich the score of that opera. It was, indeed, the number over which the critics " raved " loudest when *Otello* was first produced at La Scala forty years ago. Unfortunately, it is the custom nowadays to hurry the tempi; and Dr. Weissmann does not avoid the common mistake of modern conductors. Otherwise there is little fault to find, while the exquisite *mezza voce* effects of Meta Seinemeyer are worth a journey to listen to. The tenor is also good in his softer moments, though his " Un bacio ancora " does not equal Tamagno's in tenderness and warmth.

Margherita Salvi.—Auber's charming opera *Fra Diavolo* is never, alas, done here now, albeit on the Continent it still holds its own. The aria presented in this record was not, I fancy, in the original score, but added subsequently; anyhow

I cannot remember hearing Pauline Lucca sing it at Covent Garden, and the part of Zerlina was one of her most fascinating creations. It is a difficult show-piece, quite in the Italian style, and Margherita Salvi makes a brilliant thing of it. There is more repose and certainty about her vocalization now than when she first stood before the microphone. She obtains a sweeter tone, a smoother *cantilena*, and her execution in the *cabaletta* (Part II) is notably easy, flexible, and dashing.

Nino Piccaluga.—Much might be said in recommendation of this *Pagliacci* record, did occasion call for it ; but the fact remains that the subject is trite and its treatment in the present instance quite ordinary. The high notes are mostly forced and tremulous, thanks to a throaty production of them, but the middle register is rather pleasant and the diction very nearly " choice Italian."

Ivar Andrésen.—It may reasonably be doubted whether the two Sarastro airs from *The Magic Flute* have ever before been delivered with such a gorgeous abundance of phenomenal tone—certainly in front of a microphone. Better still, I can perceive here no internal evidence of the " magnifying " process. I am gathering expert experience on the point, so that I begin to be able to distinguish the natural from the exaggerated, and my conclusion is that the organ of Ivar Andrésen, being of too colossal proportions to require enlargement, is wisely left entirely to itself. The result is a tone of supreme grandeur that will not " split the ears of groundlings," but prove infinitely gratifying to the critical listener.

Mlle. Denya.—With a voice of penetrating power allied to faultless diction, the French soprano imparts all the necessary tone of authority to the commanding utterances of Turandot, and makes them proportionately interesting. She is the only singer besides Eva Turner who has succeeded in doing this. As a whole, the record could not be improved upon.

Alessandro Granda.—It takes a first-rate tenor to do justice to the two solo bits sung by the Unknown Prince in Puccini's last opera, and, as made manifest by the present record, Alessandro Granda answers to that description. He possesses an exceptionally fine voice, sustains with ease, and betrays no effort in mounting to the higher regions. His head notes are just as steady and pure as those in the middle register, and he phrases like an artist. The instrumentation comes out with clear definition, thanks to careful recording.

Aurora Rettore.—The Page's songs from *Un Ballo in Maschera* are getting increasingly popular, and one could hardly wish to hear them sung in a prettier tone or more sprightly fashion than they are here.

Francesco Merli.—Those who prefer early to late Puccini will heartily welcome the tenor airs from *Manon Lescaut* as proffered by such a capable and versatile artist as Merli. His voice records admirably because naturally produced and requires no artificial aid to render it imposing, while in the matter of style he seems able to adapt himself to any composer.

Ebe Stignani.—This accomplished contralto has deservedly won a high reputation in Italy, and is there considered to be the best Azucena of the day. It is more than probable that the verdict is a just one, if we may judge by her singing of the gipsy's great air, *Condotta ell'era in ceppi*. By dividing it into two parts she has gained the necessary time and space for a highly dramatic and full-blooded performance.

Doris Vane.—After French and Italian versions, we come to Puccini in English ; and happily with little, if any, loss of musical effect. Words and melodies sound equally pleasing and familiar, for the singer imparts the same consistent value to both in an excellent record.

HERMAN KLEIN.

OPERATIC AND FOREIGN SONGS

DUSOLINA GIANNINI (soprano).—**Madre, Pietosa Vergine** from **La Forza del Destino** (Verdi). In Italian, with chorus. Orch. acc. Conducted by John Barbirolli. H.M.V. D.B.1217, 12in., 8s. 6d.

BENIAMINO GIGLI (tenor).—**Dei miei bollenti spiriti** from **La Traviata** (Verdi) and **Tombe degl' avi miei** from **Lucia di Lammermoor** (Donizetti). In Italian. Orch. acc. H.M.V. D.B. 1222, 12in., 8s. 6d.

MARYSE BEAUJON, F. BORDON and CHORUS.—**Scène de l'Eglise** from **Faust** (Gounod). In French. Orch. acc. Columbia 9669, 12in., 4s. 6d.

NAZARENO DE ANGELIS (bass).—**Serenade** from **Faust** (Gounod) and **Ecco il mondo** from **Mefistofele** (Boito). In Italian. Orch. acc. Columbia L.2247 12in., 6s. 6d.

ARMANDO BORGIOLI (baritone).—**Prologue** from **Pagliacci** (Leoncavallo). In Italian. Orch. acc. Columbia 5248, 10in., 3s.

AURELIANO PERTILE (tenor).—**Non t'amo più** (Tosti) and **Mattinata** (Leoncavallo). In Italian. With members of La Scala Orchestra, Milan, conducted by Carlo Sabajno. H.M.V. D.B.1008, 10in., 6s. 6d.

A. M. GUGLIELMETTI (soprano).—**Sempre libera** from **La Traviata** (Verdi) and **Ah! non giunge** from **La Sonnambula** (Bellini). In Italian. Orch. acc. Col. D.1646, 10in., 4s. 6d.

ARANGI-LOMBARDI, EBE STIGNANI, A. BARACCHI, G. NESSI, G. NENNI and CHORUS.—**Voce di donna o d'angelo** and **E un anatema** from **La Gioconda** (Ponchielli). In Italian. Orch. acc. Col. L.2277, 12in., 6s. 6d.

MARGHERITA SALVI (soprano).—**The Carnival of Venice** (Anonymous) and **Por un pajaro** (F. Orejon). In Italian. Orch. acc. Parlophone E.10828, 12in., 4s. 6d.

META SEINEMEYER (soprano).—**Liebestod** from **Tristan und Isolde** (Wagner) and **IVAR ANDRESEN** (bass) **Tatest du's wirklich** from **Tristan und Isolde** (Wagner). In German, with Berlin State Opera House Orchestra, conducted by Dr. Weissmann. Parlophone E.10829, 12in., 4s. 6d.

AUGUSTO GARAVELLO (bass).—Basilio's Aria, **La Calunnia** from **The Barber of Seville** (Rossini) and **Son lo spirito** from **Mefistofele** (Boito). In Italian. Orch. acc. Parlophone E.10830, 12in., 4s. 6d.

CONCHITA SUPERVIA (soprano) and **INES FERRARIS** (soprano).—**Presentation of the Rose** from **Der Rosenkavalier** (R. Strauss). Orch acc. Parlophone Odeon R.20078, 12in., 6s. 6d.

Finale, Act III, from **Der Rosenkavalier** (R. Strauss). Orch. acc. Parlophone Odeon R.20079, 12in., 6s. 6d.

CONCHITA SUPERVIA (soprano).—**Voi che sapete** and **Non so più cosa son, cosa faccio** from **The Marriage of Figaro** (Mozart). In Italian. Orch. acc. Parlophone Odeon R.20077, 12in., 6s. 6d.

MLLE FERALDY (soprano).—**Tu m'as donné le plus doux rêve** (Delibes) and **Blanche Dourga** (Delibes). In French. Orch. acc. Columbia D.1649, 10in., 4s. 6d.

BERLIN STATE OPERA.—**Ich weiss auch nix . . . gar nix** and **Closing Scene, Act 3** from **Der Rosenkavalier** (R. Strauss). Actual performance at the Berlin State Opera, recorded in 1928. H.M.V. D.1629, 12in., 6s. 6d.

Dusolina Giannini.—It is always a pleasure to hear a new record by this singer—one of the few Italian sopranos now prominently before the public who knows how to use a beautiful voice in the right way. She is, moreover, developing into an interpretative artist of a high order, and I am sorry to observe that she will not be repeating her last year's visit to Covent Garden, for I had no opportunity of hearing her then *in propriâ personâ*. Meanwhile she consoles us with a really touching performance of the best solo in *La Forza del Destino*, an effort full of pleading pathos and tender expression. Seldom does one find nowadays such a pure, even scale and freedom from tremolo in a voice of this sweet and sympathetic timbre, wherein no suggestion of " registers " seems to obtrude itself and the head notes are as round as the lower ones. The orchestra is kept well in place by John Barbirolli, and the bit of chorus is there at the right moment.

Beniamino Gigli.—Here is another excellent Italian artist—a tenor, however, of whom London knows nothing save through the medium of his gramophone work. His voice is beginning to take on a darker hue, and is all the better for it, as I think everyone will agree who cares for these familiar examples of Verdi and Donizetti sung as Caruso and Campanini used to sing them. This record affords ample justification for every word of adverse criticism that I write about certain tenors whom contemporary Italian audiences are content to applaud.

Maryse Beaujon, F. Bordon and Chorus.—This complete record in French of the Church Scene from *Faust* is far and away the best that has been done, to my knowledge. The two protagonists have splendid voices ; they are perfect both in declamation and diction, making every syllable as clear as daylight in summer. The chorus, too, is exceptionally good—fresh, powerful, and well balanced. As for the organ, of course we never hear anything like it outside a cathedral or a big hall ; when it comes with that wonderful Gounodian coda, where poor Marguerite sinks down in a faint, the effect is almost overpowering. On the whole, the ensemble, in a musical sense, both for clarity and imposing grandeur, beats any experience attainable in an ordinary opera house.

Nazareno de Angelis.—It was a capital idea to couple as a contrast Mephisto's most characteristic numbers from the operas of Gounod and Boito. Only a *basso* with the experience and *savoir faire* of a Chaliapine or a De Angelis would have the ability to drive home the contrast by extracting the maximum of dramatic realism from each. The round quality of the Italian's voice remains exceedingly well preserved ; the sardonic thrill of old likewise.

Armando Borgioli.—I am ready, nay glad, to listen to the sempiternal *Prologue* as often as may be necessary, provided it be sung as artistically and with the same vocal finish as the (baritone) Borgioli delivers it in this record.

Aureliano Pertile.—The only excuse for employing a steam hammer to crack a nut is the " curiousness " of the thing. The droll idea of Pertile spreading his huge voice over ballads by Tosti and Leoncavallo can be best explained by two facts, viz., the surprising delicacy and charm with which he does it, and the vast extent of a popularity that will ensure a keen demand for the outcome. I wonder if this will be as large in England as, say, in Italy or America, where Pertile is an idol and by no means a lineal descendant of Nasmyth.

A. M. Guglielmetti.—(By the way, can anyone inform me what these initials stand for ? It seems hard lines that a surname too long for the ordinary record label should deprive a clever vocalist of her just nomenclature. Or can it be that she objects to being called Annamaria ?) The pieces here recorded are the two *caballetti*, or quick concluding sections, from well-known airs—*Ah! fors' è lui* and *Ah! non credea.* Justice is seldom done to either, so perhaps it was as well that a light soprano so faultless in her *coloratura* as A. M. G. should for once give us the tails without the heads. You see, it is not her names only that get decapitated !

Arangi-Lombardi, Ebe Stignani, and others.—It is really the two ladies who are supreme here. The men and the chorus only complete the brief ensemble, never heard out of the opera, which comes in towards the end of *Voce di donna.* That lovely contralto air is finely rendered in this instance by Ebe Stignani, who also shares honours with the soprano in the exciting quarrel scene from the second act of *La Gioconda.* It is the moment when the guilty Laura, wife of the Venetian Duke Alvise, catches her fair rival waiting to keep a rendezvous with the man whom they both love. Ponchielli's strong, picturesque music makes it one of the most striking incidents in the opera—indeed, very nearly the most striking in actual fact, so far as the two ladies are concerned. Both artists sing admirably in this record, particularly Ebe Stignani in *Voce di donna.*

Margherita Salvi.—I have heard variations on the *Carnival of Venice* calling for more brilliant *bravura* than this version contains, but, for what they are, Sgra. Salvi finds in them an effective vehicle for the display of her art. She has a bird-like quality when she rises to *alt,* or even *altissimo,* and her technique is very sure, very finished. The Spanish song *Por un pajaro* charms by its melodic grace and piquant fanciful rhythm, whilst owing much to neat, animated execution of the singer.

Meta Seinemeyer and *Ivan Andrésen.*—Here we have an unusual combination—a *Tristan* record with Isolde's *Liebestod* on one side and King Marke's equally famous reproach, *Tatest du's wirklich,* on the reverse. The former is complete, but the latter stops after it has proceeded about half way, which is regrettable, because Ivar Andrésen sings it so beautifully that one would gladly hear the remaining half. The better plan, in my opinion, would have been to devote two discs to the job, allowing King Marke to finish his speech on the other side and Isolde to present one of the glorious passages from her tirades in the first act. Both the selections given here suffer from lack of balance between the voices and the orchestra, which is that of the Berlin State Opera House and ought, therefore, to be vouchsafed its proper prominence in the reproduction. I fancy the microphone was not well placed. Meta Seinemeyer does not know how to be over-loud, and she sings the *Liebestod* with exquisite smoothness and restraint, but there are moments when the orchestral background fades into faintness because the balance is wrong. In the Marke excerpt the trouble is less noticeable, because the greater part of it consists of a kind of duet between the King and the bass clarinet (superbly played), and Andrésen, like the great artist that he is, employs his marvellous *mezza voce* with precisely the same degree of loudness that the *obbligato* player does his instrument.

Augusto Garavello.—The voice is resonant and well in tune, but not of notable beauty. The diction is excellent. The reading of *La Calunnia* suggests a rather careful study of Chaliapine's. There is more of the artist's own individuality and less of his Russian prototype's in the *Son lo spirito* from *Mefistofele.* His tone sounds broader and rounder here, whilst fully preserving the necessary sardonic colour. I am glad it is not described as the *Aria del Fischio.* Such a poor whistle would not in the old days have served even to bring a four-wheeler off the rank.

Conchita Supervia and *Ines Ferraris.*—Evidently great pains have been taken over these selections from *Der Rosenkavalier,* for they are of undoubted merit. Consisting as they do chiefly of the scenes between Oktavian and Sophie, the two soprano voices are to the fore most of the time, together with that fascinating " silver rose " *motif* which Strauss tinkles so sweetly with his combination of harp, celeste, and violins high up on the E string. Each singer charms us in turn, and more especially the Oktavian, whose voice is of rare sweetness. The orchestra, though unnamed, is also thoroughly competent and the recording very good indeed.

Conchita Supervia.—Seekers after the unconventional will find plenty of it and to spare in the singing of the Cherubin's airs by this impulsive Spanish soprano. She overdoes the liveliness at the expense of what we are apt to recognize as the traditional " points " and all the varieties of expression and Mozart purity of style. What is more, she misses most of meaning, while her Italian positively bristles with faults. I much prefer her Oktavian.

Mlle. Feraldy.—These are respectively the airs for the Indian heroine from the first and third acts of *Lakmé,* and each has its distinct individual charm, a natural expression of feeling which differs entirely from that embodied in the Franco-Hindoo show-piece known as the *Bell Song.* This singer appears to be an ideal *Lakmé*—vocally, at any rate. Her voice is clear and steady, her style musical and elegant, her diction quite faultless. The romance, *Blanche Dourga,* could not be more perfectly rendered, while the other air, short and sweet, is equally well done and affords an exquisite contrast.

Berlin State Opera.—Some people regard the last few pages of *Der Rosenkavalier* as the culminating peak of its exotic beauty and intriguing originality of masterful orchestral treatment. The trio is assuredly a *chef-d'œuvre* of the first rank. For recording purposes, however, it demands more delicate handling from the singers than it receives here. For most of the time the voices are terribly ill-balanced, that of the Marschallin predominating entirely too much all through, while the Oktavian sounds coarse and tired, and, except on her high notes, the Sophie is submerged to the point of being inaudible. How much better the last-named could be heard is amply proved in the final duet (reverse side), which is a triumph not only for the lovers, but for the Berlin State Opera Orchestra. Oh, those silver wedding bells, how they haunt one !

HERMAN KLEIN.

STAINER'S "CRUCIFIXION"

I can predict without hesitation a wide popularity for this latest addition to the Columbia Masterworks Series. It is an admirable recording of Stainer's best-known church composition, and I hope that its appearance just before Easter has been in time to satisfy the wide demand which it is sure to create. The records—twelve in number, on six discs, Nos. 9675–9680—were made in the Central Hall, Westminster, where there is not only a vast space available, but an organ possessing exceptional breadth and power of tone. It may go without saying, therefore, that the familiar music attains in this reproduction an unusual grandeur of effect, the solo voices especially being extremely vibrant and penetrating, unless the softest available needle be used.

Little did Sir John Stainer, most modest of musicians, dream of the world-wide favour that was in store for what he termed his " Meditation in the Sacred Passion of the Redeemer." His previous oratorios, notably his setting of *The Daughter of Jairus*, had met with acceptance, but it was *The Crucifixion* that made his name known as a church composer wherever Protestant worship is carried on in the English tongue. He was the organist of St. Paul's Cathedral at Easter, 1887, when it was my privilege to be his guest at the St. Marylebone Parish Church for the first performance of this beautiful work. I was immensely interested, for oratorio singing in London churches was not the common occurrence then that it has since become, and, as it proved, this simple composition of Stainer's was to do more than any other work of the kind to popularize the new experiment. He conducted it himself, in the presence of a crowded congregation, and told me afterwards how much the rendering had delighted him. I may say here that the hymns in which the whole assemblage joined on that occasion with remarkable spirit are necessarily omitted from the present recording.

Just as it would be quite superfluous to describe the music here, so is there as little need for me to enter into a detailed account of the manner in which it has been recorded for the Columbia album. Enough that the solo parts are ably sung by Mr. Robert Easton (Jesus), Mr. Francis Russell (Narrator), Mr. Robert Carr, and Mr. Randal Jackson ; while the choruses are given with noteworthy refinement of tone and style and accuracy of intonation by the B.B.C. choir under the direction of Mr. Stanford Robinson. Another feature of importance and deserving of unqualified praise is the restrained and artistic organ playing of Mr. R. Tomblin. Altogether the reproduction seems bound to fulfil a practical purpose of universal utility.

HERMAN KLEIN.

OPERATIC AND FOREIGN SONGS

ENZO DE MURO LOMANTO (tenor).—**E lucevan le stelle** and **Recondita armonia from La Tosca** (Puccini). In Italian. Orch. acc. Col. D.1656, 10in., 4s. 6d.

TANCREDI PASERO (bass).—**O Re del ciel from Lohengrin** and **ARMANDO BORGIOLI** (baritone)—**Grazie Signore** from **Lohengrin** (Wagner). In Italian. Orch. acc. Col. D.1653, 10in., 4s. 6d.

GERTRUDE JOHNSON (soprano).—**Fondly within my heart enshrined** from **Traviata** (Verdi) and **Shadow Song** from **Dinorah** (Meyerbeer). In English. Orch. acc. Col. 9709, 12in., 4s. 6d.

J. ROGATCHEWSKY (tenor).—**Les adieux au cygne** and **Récit du Graal** from **Lohengrin** (Wagner). In French. Orch. acc. Col. L.2300, 12in., 6s. 6d.

ALESSANDRO GRANDA (tenor).—**Cielo e mar from Lohengrin** (Wagner) and **TANCREDI PASERO** (bass)—**Si morir ella dè** from **La Gioconda** (Ponchielli). In Italian. Orch. acc. Col. L.2301, 12in., 6s. 6d.

A. M. GUGLIELMETTI (soprano).—**Variations on a theme by Mozart.** In Italian. Orch. acc. Col. D.1650, 10in., 4s. 6d.

GEORGES THILL (tenor).—**La Caravane** and **Il est des Musulmans** from **Marouf** (H. Rabaud). In French. Orch. acc. Col. L.2289, 12in., 6s. 6d.

LUCREZIA BORI (soprano).—**Connais-tu le pays ?** and **Me voici dans son boudoir** from **Mignon** (Thomas). In French. Orch. acc. H.M.V. D.A.1017, 10in., 6s.

A. PERTILE and **A. TELLINI** (tenor and soprano).—**Cessaro i canti alfin** and **A. PERTILE** and **E. FANELLI** (tenor and soprano)—**Di, non t'incanta.** Both from **Lohengrin** (Wagner). In Italian, with members of the La Scala orchestra, under Carlo Sabajno. H.M.V. D.B. 1218, 12in., 8s. 6d.

STILES ALLEN (soprano).—**They call me Mimi** from **La Bohème** (Puccini) and **Ritorna vincitor** from **Aida** (Verdi). The first side in English, the second in Italian. Orch. acc. Edison Bell Electron X.542, 12in., 4s. 6d.

MORLAIS MORGAN (baritone).—**Recit—Rise, I say. This I grant thee** and **Aria—It is thou who hast blighted** from **Un Ballo in Maschera** (Verdi) and **Credo** from **Otello** (Verdi). In English. Orch. acc. Edison Bell Electron X.545, 12in., 4s. 6d.

EMMY BETTENDORF (soprano) and **KARIN BRANZELL** (contralto).—**Barcarolle** from **Tales of Hoffmann** (Offenbach) and **KARIN BRANZELL**—**Chanson Hindoue** from **Sadko** (Rimsky-Korsakov). In German. Parlo. E.10836, 12in., 4s. 6d.

META SEINEMEYER (soprano), **JARO DWORSKY** (tenor) and **EMANUEL LIST** (bass).—**Church Scene, Act 4** and **Prison Scene, Act 5** from **Faust** (Gounod). With Grand Organ and the Berlin State Opera Chorus and Orchestra, under Dr. Weissmann. In German. Parlo. E.10835 and E.10834 respectively, 12in., 4s. 6d. each.

CHORUS AND ORCHESTRA OF LA SCALA, MILAN.—**Introduction** to **Cavalleria Rusticana** (Mascagni). In Italian, conducted by Ettore Panizza. Parlo. E.10843, 12in., 4s. 6d.

GERHARD HUSCH (baritone).—**Wohl wusst' ich hier sie im Gebet zu finden** and **O du mein holder Abendstern** from **Tannhäuser** (Wagner). In German, with the Berlin State Opera Orchestra, under Dr. Weissmann. Parlo. E.10839, 12in., 4s.

MARIO CHAMLEE (tenor).—**Thy lips are like crimson berries** and **Drinking Song** from **Cavalleria Rusticana** (Mascagni). In Italian. Orch. acc. Brunswick 10272, 10in., 4s. 6d.

LOTTE LEHMANN (soprano).—**Morgen** (R. Strauss) and **Mit deinen blauen Augen** (R. Strauss). In German, with violin and piano. Parlo. Odeon R.O.20081, 10in., 4s. 6d.

Enzo de Muro Lomanto.—Most of the virtues and few of the

defects of the modern Italian tenor are discernible in this record of the two *Tosca* airs—the head and tail, I might say, of Mario Cavaradossi's offending. If they are to be presented yet once more before an obedient microphone, let it be with as much unaffected charm of style and breadth of manly tone as they are given here. The singer is a great favourite, of course, in America.

Tancredi Pasero–Armando Borgioli.—It is not inappropriate to associate on one record these two excerpts from the first act of *Lohengrin*, because there they follow closely on each other. The bass delivers the broad theme of King Henry's Prayer, and from the lips of Tancredi Pasero it sounds very broad indeed, despite that rapid vibrato of his (due to excessive breath-pressure) which is his only serious fault. Otherwise, he is in the front rank of Italian "singing basses." The fine baritone of Armando Borgioli needs no "amplifying," but gets it—too much of it. A little restraint would make him an ideal Telramund, and his articulation is exemplary.

Gertrude Johnson.—*Ah! fors' è lui* does not sound very inspiring when translated into *Fondly within my heart enshrined*, does it? What nonsense, too! Mr. Compton Mackenzie comes much nearer the mark with his *Ah, perhaps this is he*, etc., only it would not quite fit the music—which is the English translator's eternal trouble. Anyhow, this particular Violetta (and Dinorah, too, for that matter) suffers from too close an intimacy with the colloquialisms of her mother-tongue, at any rate in her singing of them. I would love to encourage the singing of opera in English, but how few there are who can avoid sacrificing the beauty and poetry of the music to the exigencies of their own individual mode of speech. Here are an excellent voice, perfect intonation, and much technical flexibility, to be sure; but the fond heart that enshrines Alfredo does not beat in the bosom of Dumas' heroine, nor is the *Shadow Song* much more than a neat vocal exercise.

J. Rogatchewsky.—An interesting voice, this, and an interesting artist. Whether a Frenchman or a Pole, or a little of both, his tone on first hearing sounds strangely like a contralto's, and only displays real power on the high notes. Hence it seems odd to hear the suave phrases of the Knight of the Swan—bidding his legendary bird farewell or revealing his stupidly-concealed name and identity to Elsa and her family—issuing forth in a charming lady-like *cantilena*, which is, nevertheless, so fascinating that you cannot resist its appeal. My impression is that a less nasal method would vastly improve M. Rogatchewsky's tone, but even as it is he is a charming singer.

Alessandro Granda–Tancredi Pasero.—Here the Milanese basso shares responsibilities with the hero of Ponchielli's *La Gioconda*, that opera forming what the French would term the *trait d'union*. Both are splendid voices, and *Cielo e mar* is always worth hearing from a singer with Granda's wonderful animation and natural declamatory power.

A. M. Guglielmetti.—(I have concluded that the initials are to distinguish this lady from P. M. Guglielmetti, who sings best in the afternoon.) The Mozart variations add another triumph of brilliant *coloratura* execution to this soprano's collection. Call it mechanical if you will; it is like the achievement of a clever acrobat whom you can never catch tripping—and about whose safety you never experience a moment's fear. You sit in wonder and listen, instead of looking, that is all.

Georges Thill.—I trust we shall soon be hearing the whole of Rabaud's operatic allegorical legend—originally produced at the Paris Opéra and quite recently mounted with success at the Cologne Festival. The music is, of course, extremely up-to-date, but by no means aggressively high-brow or difficult to grasp, while the orchestration is a superb sea of colour. These two pieces suggest at once that wealth of Eastern *couleur locale* which is the main characteristic of the work, and their original interpreter at the Opéra sings them with delightful expression and purity of style. By the way, *La Caravane* is very reminiscent of *Turandot*, and cleverly like it into the bargain.

Lucrezia Bori.—When an eminent high soprano takes to singing mezzo-soprano airs it is not essentially a sign of weakness, but merely means agreeable little "stunts" that she takes, so to speak, "in her stride." Anyhow, her *Connais-tu* and *Gavotte* from *Mignon*—usually sung by a mezzo-soprano if not by a contralto—may be regarded as a tribute to the loveliness of her medium register, which is irresistible. No need to add that she invests the two pieces with the exquisite pathos and the sparkling crispness which they respectively demand.

Pertile-Tellini; *Pertile-Fanelli.*—Here for the very first time we come across a Lohengrin with two Elsas; only, as it would appear, Elsa No. 2 does not enter the Bridal Chamber until after Elsa No. 1 has taken her departure, which is perhaps a fortunate thing for the preservation of the peace. The trick is done by turning over the record. On one side you will find the first half of the so-called love duet, with Pertile singing beautifully, rather pleased with himself and quite hopeful about Elsa in her ingratiating mood; not as yet too inquisitive, you know. But on the reverse side it is palpable that he is less comfortable with his bride, whose voice as well as her feelings have undergone a change. There is something rather vivid about the contrast, though whether it justifies the new device I am not quite sure, feeling as I do that the immortal Richard would certainly have objected to it. Nevertheless, Pertile is superb, and his pair of Elsas possess, vocally speaking, about equal degrees of merit. Happily the orchestra proves likewise equal to the test.

Louisa Stiles-Allen.—The clear, ringing tone of this well-known soprano comes out well in her English rendering of *Mi chiamano Mimi*; less so somewhat in her Italian *Ritorna vincitor*, which also requires greater varieties of contrast; for, after all, Aida is an impulsive Ethiopian, and quite the opposite of Mürger's modest little *grisette*. For the former, however, the prevailing quality of sad, dark tone seems wholly appropriate. The recording is clear enough, but the same can scarcely be said of the words. The best feature is the smoothness of the singer's *legato* throughout.

Morlais Morgan.—Here, again, I find a distinction *with* a difference. The *Credo* suffers less from a poor English translation than *Eri tu*, and can be made to do with declamation in lieu of *bel canto*. The secret of the latter is not within this singer's grasp (a pity, because he has a splendid voice), and someone should explain to him that angry baritones ought not to lisp, because it detracts from the dignity of their speech.

The recording of big airs like these carries with it a certain measure of responsibility. Besides, *Eri tu* needs to be treated, not in a martial spirit, but with a subtle combination of suppressed rage, disappointment, misery, and grief for departed joys. This is too much of a free-and-easy, go-as-you-please handling.

E. Bettendorf–Karin Branzell.—If the duet from the *Tales of Hoffmann* has palled upon you, no matter how long ago, this German record is calculated to revive your bygone liking for its gentle, swaying two-part harmony. Two beautiful voices, faultlessly in tune with each other and blending as it were into a single timbre, convert it into a rare and delicious exotic, whose perfume will delight you whenever you care to transfer it from its envelope to the table of your machine. The *Sadkó Song* is phrased with elegance and grace, but if sung by a woman it does not well bear transposing down from the original tenor key, in spite of nicely-modulated chromatic groups like these.

Meta Seinemeyer–Jaro Dworsky–Emanuel List.—The evergreen freshness of Gounod's *Faust* is once more demonstrated in these admirable records of the Church and Prison Scenes. They are done on the grand scale, so that a little judicious " amplifying " of the voices—and such voices, too—does not sound amiss. Making full allowance for the reinforcement, it is evident that Dr. Weissmann has big forces at his disposal and that he knows how to get the utmost dynamic power out of them. In the Church Scene a very imposing ensemble is achieved. It should come out splendidly in an auditorium of corresponding magnitude, and makes me feel that I would like to see and hear this Marguerite and Mephistopheles in the flesh. The Prison trio is cut slightly, but in revenge the final choral epilogue is sung intact.

La Scala Chorus and Orchestra.—Apart from unusual sonority and refinement, one finds in this opening of *Cavalleria Rusticana* that atmospheric touch which the music depicts and which well-trained Italian voices alone can impart. It is well worth having the record for that, apart from its other merits.

Gerhard Hüsch.—Here again we have the stamp of high-class work by the Berlin State Opera *personnel* under the baton of Dr. Weissmann. The soloist is evidently built for the part of Wolfram. His voice diffuses poetry and a good deal of charm; he sings with restraint; he phrases expressively and with an artist's delicacy. One cannot well ask for more.

Mario Chamlee.—This American tenor shows decided signs of improvement. His voice is under better control and there is less exaggeration about his style. The Turiddu songs sound really well on this record and will repay the modest outlay asked for the investment. They are given with the necessary spirit and rhythmical energy and, so far as I can judge, without the artful aid of amplification.

Lotte Lehmann.—There is really nothing to be said about this rendering of Strauss's *Morgen* that would not smack of "painting the lily." Everything on the subject has been written already. If the reader is desirous of hearing a beautiful song sung just in the way that it should be, let him or her procure this specimen. The other song may be on the "other side," but it is on the same high artistic level.

HERMAN KLEIN.

OPERATIC AND FOREIGN SONGS

ROSA PONSELLE (soprano).—**Ernani ! Ernani ! involami** from **Ernani** (Verdi) and **Pace, pace mio Dio** from **La Forza del Destino** (Verdi). In Italian. Orch. acc. H.M.V. D.B.1275, 12in., 8s. 6d.

DUSOLINA GIANNINI (soprano).—**Un bel dì vedremo** from **Madame Butterfly** (Puccini) and **In quelle trine morbide** from **Manon Lescaut** (Puccini). In Italian with Berlin State Opera Orchestra, conducted by Clemens Schmalstich. H.M.V. D.B.1264, 12in., 8s. 6d.

META SEINEMEYER (soprano).—**Cantate** (with chorus) and **Vissi d'arte, vissi d'amore** from **La Tosca** (Puccini). In Italian with Berlin State Opera Orchestra, under Weissmann. Parlophone E.10851, 12in., 4s. 6d.

GITTA ALPAR (soprano).—**Bird Song** from **Pagliacci** (Leoncavallo) and **Voi che sapete** from **Marriage of Figaro** (Mozart). In German. Orch. acc. Parlophone Odeon R.20082, 12in., 6s. 6d.

Reading the stars on high from **Ballo in Maschera** (Verdi) and **Couplets du Mysoli** from **The Pearl of Brazil** (F. David). In German. Orch acc. Parlophone Odeon R. 20083, 12in., 6s. 6d.

MARIA OLCZEWSKA (contralto).—**Du meine Seele, du meine Herz** (Schumann. Op. 25, No. 1.), with piano accompaniment by George Reeves, and **Nur wer die Sehnsucht kennt** (Tchaikovsky) with piano (Alwin), Violin (Dauber), and 'cello (Kvarda). In German. H.M.V. E.534, 10in., 4s. 6d.

COSTA MILONA (tenor).—**Siciliana " O Lola "** from **Cavalleria Rusticana** (Mascagni) and **Romance de Nadir** from **The Pearl Fishers** (Bizet). In Italian with orchestra under Weissman. Parlophone E. 10853, 12in., 4s. 6d.

RICHARD TAUBER (tenor).—**O Sole mio** (di Capua) and **Ay-Ay-Ay** (P. Freire). In German. Orch. acc. Parlophone Odeon R. 20084, 12in., 6s. 6d.

ALESSANDRO VALENTE (tenor).—**Or son sei mesi** and **Ch'ella mi creda libero** from **La Fanciulla del West** (Puccini). In Italian with members of La Scala Orchestra, under G. Nastrucci. H.M.V. B.3015 10in., 3s.

LENGHI CELLINI (tenor).—**Addio Mignon** from **Mignon** (Thomas) and **La donna è mobile** from **Rigoletto** (Verdi). In Italian. Orch. acc. Piccadilly 250, 10in., 1s. 6d.

FRANCIS RUSSELL (tenor).—**Erik's Song** and **Steersman's Song** from **The Flying Dutchman** (Wagner). In English Orch acc. Col. 9746, 12in., 4s. 6d.

EDWARD HALLAND (bass).—**Calf of Gold** and **Mephisto's Serenade** from **Faust** (Gounod). Sung in English. Edison Bell Electron O. 288, 10in., 3s.

CANTOR MORDECHAY HERSHMAN (tenor).—**Ismach Moisheh** (S. Gozinsky) and **Menasheh** (Rund and Jaffe). In Hebrew, Col. 9713, 12in., 4s. 6d.

ROSA PONSELLE (soprano) and **MARION TELVA** (contralto).—**Mira, o Norma** from **Norma** (Bellini). In Italian with Metropolitan Opera House Orchestra, conducted by Giulio Setti. H.M.V. D.B.1276, 12in., 8s. 6d.

GUIDO AGNOLETTI (tenor) and **AMELIA ARMOLLI** (soprano).—**Duet from Act 1 " Si "** and **Duet from Act 2 " Si "** (Mascagni). Italian. Orch. acc. Edison Bell Electron X.549, 12in., 4s. 6d.

EMMY BETTENDORF (soprano) and **KARIN BRANZELL** (contralto).—**Entweihte Gotter** from **Lohengrin** (Wagner). In German, with Berlin State Opera House Orchestra under Weissmann. Parlophone E.10852, 12in., 4s. 6d.

MARIA GENTILE (soprano), **ALESSANDRO GRANDA** (tenor) and **CARLO GALEFFI** (bass).—**Prelude and Duke's Song** from **Rigoletto** (Verdi), and the same singers with **EBE STIGNANI** (contralto).—**Quartet, Bella figlia d'amore** from **Rigoletto** (Verdi). In Italian. Orch. acc. Col. L.2310, 12., 6s. 6d.

CHORUS AND ORCHESTRA OF THE PARIS OPERA HOUSE. — **Soldiers' Chorus** and **La Kermesse** from **Faust** (Gounod). In French and recorded in Paris Opera House. Col. 9747, 12in., 4s. 6d.

FRANCESCO VADA (tenor) and **EDGAR THOMAS** (bass). — **Ah ! Mimi ; you will never come back** from **La Bohème** (Puccini) and **Be mine the delight** from **Faust** (Gounod). In English. Orch. acc. Broadcast Twelve 5073, 2s.

STILES ALLEN (soprano) and **EDITH FURMEDGE** (contralto).—**Duet from Act 2 of Aida** (Verdi). In English. Orch acc. Electron X.546, 12in., 4s. 6d.

Rosa Ponselle.—The fact that *Ernani, involami* has once more been recorded, this time by the soprano who is known to be the most popular *cantatrice* of Italian descent since Tetrazzini or Galli-Curci stirred the American multitude, is eloquent proof of the life that still survives in certain examples of early Verdi. Fifty years have gone by since *Ernani* ceased to be a favourite opera in this country. Not even Patti, in her prime, could keep it alive here ; but she liked singing *Ernani, involami* (don't ask me why!) and so did many other *prime donne*, including Frieda Hempel, who recorded it for H.M.V. The air is effective, you see ; though not nearly so eminently Verdian of the superior type as *Pace, mio Dio*, which fills the ear with glorious tone on the reverse side of this same disc, and which belongs to an opera that came some eighteen or twenty years later. With a warm, penetrating voice, a true, even scale, steady, vibrant tone, admirable scales, clear articulation, accurate intonation and artistic phrasing, Rosa Ponselle imparts to both airs every quality of vocal and dramatic distinction whereof they are susceptible. Under the perfect recording conditions of our time, it is a pleasure to listen to such singing.

Dusolina Giannini.—The *Un bel dì* is somewhat disappointing, in the sense that it is so surcharged with emotion as to give a false idea of the picture that Butterfly is conjuring up for her faithful Suzuki—and herself. So emotional is it that one almost expects her to faint, or at least, to burst into tears at any moment. Now the idea of Pinkerton's return is one of joy, not of heartrending concern. This is not yet the miserable, disillusioned Butterfly who ultimately commits suicide ; why not differentiate, therefore ? The voice quivers a great deal, in fact, approaches nearly at times to a decided tremolo ; while the varying tone-colours, interesting though they are, sound too deeply tinged with

ROSA PONSELLE AS GIOCONDA

tragedy. The same characteristics are just right for the volcanic Puccini, of *Manon Lescaut*, and the singer's rendering of *In quelle trine morbide* could not possibly be bettered. The appealing timbre touches you in the right way ; it plays on one strong satisfying chord, and the Berlin Orchestra supports it with unfailing efficiency.

Meta Seinemeyer.—Versatility is evidently among the virtues possessed by this clever German soprano, in addition to the beauty of voice in the interpretation of Wagner that has distinguished her recent work at Covent Garden. As regards this record, the excerpt from the second act of *Tosca* allows her little scope, being mainly a choral episode during Scarpia's supper, yet so graceful and purely Italian that I welcome its transfer to the gramophone. In *Vissi d'arte*, however, she comes very near indeed to the ideal established in this overworked piece by the illustrious Ternina, who created the rôle of Tosca in London. Would that every would-be imitator of that great artist were so successful as Meta Seinemeyer. The touching quality of her plaintive reproach is really exquisite ; her breath-control and vocal technique generally, beyond praise.

Gitta Alpar.—The young lady in pink and silver who sang Sophie in *Der Rosenkavalier*, has a pretty voice and uses it deftly enough ; but I confess that in one way and another, there is a great deal in her singing that is open to criticism—too much, indeed, for detailed comment here. For one thing, she varies tremendously, now rousing admiration, now disappointing with some blemish or *faux pas* that ought never to have been allowed to happen. Of the four pieces in these records, the two that suit her best are *Nedda's air* and the *Charmant oiseau*. Neither is positively of striking merit, but both are sung neatly and well in tune ; whereas in the staccato passages of the Page's song from *Un Ballo*, there are serious lapses from correct intonation. The *Voi che sapete* is that of a schoolboy, a love-lorn callow youth, not of an extremely knowing and experienced young generation, full of mischievous humour, as it ought to be.

Maria Olczewska.—Although little known yet as a Lieder-singer, the talented contralto has only to make a few records well fitted to her voice and style to make sure of earning a reputation in this direction. But she needs to be careful in her choice. For instance, Schumann's *Widmung* (the real title of *Du meine Seele*) is not a happy one, being devoid of life, impulse, inspiration. On the other hand, Tchaikovsky's setting of *Nur wer die Sehnsucht* just evokes all that is lovely in the Olczewska tone and manner of delivery, succeeding in spite of the noisy *obbligati* whom no one looked for or wanted.

Costa Milona.—A *tenore robusto*, this, of undoubted merit, with a fine voice, excellent method, and full, broad Italian style. The clear singing tone and absence of tremolo, together with a powerful *sostenuto*, enable him to do justice to the *Serenata*, while a rich middle register stands out well in the air from the *Pêcheurs de Perles*. Unlike some that I am coming to directly, there is no evidence of excessive amplifying in this record.

Richard Tauber.—But here there is enough and to spare—of amplification, I mean. To be candid, I do not recognise the voice at all. The manipulating operator, functioning at his will presumably, has simply exaggerated a pleasant tenor into an aggressively nasal baritone. Even if Herr Tauber be really a light baritone, the interference, combined with the languid nature of these Southern ditties, only serves to make his recording heavy and distort his otherwise irreproachable diction. Happily the sentiment and the elegance are there.

Alessandro Valente.—Puccini-lovers who are not to be persuaded that *The Girl from the Golden West* did not inspire another *Butterfly* or *Tosca* will be glad to get these two airs, capitally sung, well accompanied by a portion of the Scala Orchestra, and admirably recorded.

Lenghi-Cellini.—Except that the singer's voice has been amplified out of all recognition—and we have known it now for a very long time—this " Piccadilly " record seems worth the price asked for it. The strong emphasis, *affettuoso* style, and sudden contrasts are, after all, only Italy up-to-date.

Francis Russell.—The *Steersman's Song* in *The Flying Dutchman* is sufficiently accentuated by Wagner's music, and there was no need for the singer to exaggerate it by an extra *marcato* on every note ; it rather spoils the intended effect of an improvisation. *Erik's Song* is more intelligently treated and suffers less from the same method. But what a fine voice it is !—one of those pure English tenors that might be made equal to the most exalted tasks, were it only cultivated in the right manner and to the necessary degree.

Edward Halland.—The words just written apply with exactly the same force to this promising bass. His is a splendid organ, but he uses it too roughly, even for a cruel, sardonic Mephistopheles. The (English) traditions of both songs have been carefully studied and observed ; the enunciation is distinct ; and there is a good sense of rhythm.

Cantor Mordechay Hershman.—The first of these Hebrew melodies has more of the character of a folk-song than the second. It is lively and rather modern and would make a capital dance tune. The other is redolent of the synagogue, and the Cantor, who rejoices in a well-trained tenor voice of ample power, has known how to deal with it in the approved orthodox fashion. This contrast makes the record a doubly interesting one.

Rosa Ponselle and *Marion Telva.*—This is a super-record of the famous duet sung by Adalgisa and Norma in the second act of Bellini's opera, where the former pleads with the High-Priestess for the lives of her (Norma's) children. There was a time when you would hear it warbled by sweet voices in every drawing-room, strummed on every piano, and murdered by every German band that played at the street corner. Here you have the original tune in two parts—a charming strain of melody harmonised principally in thirds and sixths, and rendered with infinite precision by voices that blend very well indeed, though not perhaps, to absolute perfection. Indeed, the Norma has a quality of tone that would be difficult to match. The slow tempo of the Andante is the right one, and very delightful it is.

Guido Agnoletti and *Amelia Armolli.*—Mascagni's recent opera *Si*, presents an entirely unploughed field for the gramophone artist, and, judged by these tuneful duets, an exploration of it may prove profitable. I know nothing about the dramatic situation in either, but I do know that the music is surprisingly fresh, well-invented, and bubbling over with lively spirit. Moreover, it is nicely sung by two singers who understand each other perfectly and infuse into their repartee plenty of smartness, rhythmical contrast, and variety of colour.

Emmy Bettendorf and *Karin Branzell.*—Another duet—a magnificent one this time—and sung by two artists of the first rank. The scene between Elsa and Ortrud in the second act of *Lohengrin*, is to my thinking, one of the gems of the opera, and the whole of it can now be easily done on the two sides of a single disc, as it is in this instance. The effect would, however, have been much more satisfying if the sympathetic voice of Emmy Bettendorf had not been so badly distorted. It sounds hollow, and of a timbre quite different from that

which made us love so many of her earlier records. Manipulation again, of course ! Well, I can only say that this kind of thing is not going to increase the sale of records among gramophonists who know how to distinguish a natural voice from one heard through a megaphone. And this is a very bad sample of the new system.

Maria Gentile, Alessandro Granda, Carlo Galeffi : Ebe Stignani.—This excellent record embraces all the opening portion of the last act of *Rigoletto*, including, naturally, the immortal quartet, which is the *clou* of the present excerpt, with one of the loveliest D flats at the end that I have heard since Melba was a youthful Gilda. There are moments of roughness, especially on the part of the *Rigoletto*, that could easily have been avoided ; but, apart from these, little fault can be found with the treatment of the ensemble. It is my considered opinion that not nearly enough authoritative restraint and control are imposed nowadays upon the individual efforts of singers when contributing to these big operatic numbers. They probably imagine that they know all there is to know about it, and that the conductor has got quite enough to do to attend to his orchestra.

French " Faust " Chorus.—As might be expected, the chorus of the Paris Opéra, provides an ideal rendering of the selection from the *Kermesse* scene here presented. There are points in it that British choristers should imitate—matters of reading and tradition, I mean, not mere singing. The men's voices are a trifle over-loud at times, but with this exception the balance in front of the microphone has been carefully preserved and the rhythm is quite wonderful. The recording, too, is first-rate.

Francesco Vada and *Edgar Thomas.*—His *nom de théâtre,* notwithstanding, the tenor sounds no less British than the bass, and both have capital voices. With a little more experience in the art of recording and perhaps a shade more self-denial on the part of the more powerful organ, they should do good work together. Their singing needs greater smoothness and they do not possess the Italian art of dialogue. The *Faust* excerpt, being the more familiar, comes out much better than that from *Bohème*, where they had to use a vile translation. The orchestra, too, requires to be better balanced and have a few more players in it.

Stiles Allen and *Edith Furmedge.*—It is good to hear two such fine English voices as these worthily united in the duet for *Aida* and *Amneris*. The contrasts of tone and emotion are definitely portrayed, and there is a dramatic ring in the rounding of the phrases that suggests the atmosphere of the scene— by now a familiar one to most listeners. The words stand out clearly, while the orchestral touches all make their due effect. On the whole, a decidedly successful record.

HERMAN KLEIN

OPERATIC AND FOREIGN SONGS

ROSA PONSELLE (soprano).—**Casta diva** from **Norma** (Bellini). In Italian with Metropolitan Opera House Orchestra and Chorus, conducted by Giulio Setti. H.M.V. D.B. 1280, 12in., 8s. 6d.

MARIA JERITZA (soprano).—**L'amour est une vertu rare** from **Thais** (Massenet). In French with orchestra. And **Vissi d'arte, vissi d'amore** from **Tosca** (Puccini). In Italian with orchestra. H.M.V. D.A. 972, 10in., 6s.

AMELITA GALLI-CURCI (soprano).—**Last rose of summer** and **Home, sweet home** (Bishop). In English with piano. H.M.V. D.A. 1011, 10in., 6s.

EMMY BETTENDORF (soprano).—**Solveig's Song** from **Peer Gynt** (Grieg) and **Know'st thou the Land** from **Mignon** (Thomas). In German with orchestra. Parlophone E.10867, 12in., 4s. 6d.

GERTRUDE JOHNSON (soprano).—The Blue Danube (J. Strauss) and The Voices of Spring (J. Strauss). In English with orchestra. Regal G.1068, 12in., 4s. 6d.

JOSEPH HISLOP (tenor).—Che gelida manina from La Bohème (Puccini) and Addio alla madre from Cavalleria Rusticana (Mascagni). In Italian with orchestra, conducted by John Barbirolli. H.M.V. D.B. 1230, 12in., 8s. 6d.

LENGHI CELLINI (tenor).—Here's to the sparkling cup from Cavalleria Rusticana (Mascagni) and Una vergine from La Favorita (Donizetti). In Italian with orchestra. Piccadilly 251, 10in., 1s. 6d.

RUDOLF BOCKELMANN (baritone).—Toreador's Song from Carmen (Bizet) and Mirror Song from Tales of Hoffmann (Offenbach). In German with Berlin State Opera House Orchestra, conducted by Clemens Schmalstich. H.M.V. C.1680, 12in., 4s. 6d.

NINO PICCALUGA (tenor).—Salve dimora from Faust (Gounod) and Il fior from Carmen (Bizet). In Italian with orchestra Parlophone E.10866, 12in., 4s. 6d.

JOSEPH FARRINGTON (baritone).—Largo al factotum from The Barber of Seville (Rossini) and Vulcan's Song from Philémon et Baucis (Gounod). The first in Italian, the second in English. Both with orchestra. Metropole 1137, 10in., 3s.

MARCEL JOURNET (bass).—Les deux Grenadiers (Schumann) and La Marseillaise (De l'Isle). In French with orchestra. H.M.V. D.B. 924, 12in., 8s. 6d.

F. LEIDER (soprano) and E. MARHERR-WAGNER (soprano). —Doch nun von Tristan and Er schwur mit tausend Eiden from Tristan and Isolde (Wagner). In German with Berlin State Opera House Orchestra, conducted by Dr. Leo Blech. H.M.V. D.1667, 12in., 6s. 6d.

AMELITA GALLI-CURCI (soprano) and GIUSEPPE DE LUCA (baritone).—Piangi, piangi, fanciulla and Ah! Veglia, o donna from Rigoletto (Verdi). In Italian with Metropolitan Opera House Orchestra, conducted by Giulio Setti. H.M.V. D.A.1028, 10in., 6s.

BESSIE JONES (contralto) and BARRINGTON HOOPER (tenor).—Now I will dance but to please thee and with GLADYS COLE (soprano) Speak to me of my mother from Carmen (Bizet). Zono. GO.87, 10 in., 3s. 6d. With FOSTER RICHARDSON (bass) Hate and Rage from Il Trovatore (Verdi) and with FOSTER RICHARDSON and ESTHER COLEMAN—I'm your slave, sweet girl, believe me, quartet from Rigoletto (Verdi). All in English with orchestra. Zono. GO.88, 10in., 3s. 6d.

G. NESSI (tenor), A. BARACCHI (tenor), E. VENTURINI (baritone).—Ping, Pong, Pang from Turandot (Puccini). In Italian with orchestra. Col. D.1663, 10in., 4s. 6d.

META SEINEMEYER (soprano), GRETE MERREM-NIKISCH (soprano), and EMANUEL LIST (bass).—Nicht dort, dort ist das Vorzimmer and Bin von so viel Finesse charmiert from Der Rosenkavalier (R. Strauss). In German with Berlin State Opera House Orchestra under Weissmann. Parlophone E.10864, 12in., 4s. 6d.

META SEINEMEYER (soprano), ELSA STUNZNER (soprano), and GRETE MERREM-NIKISCH (soprano).—Mein Gott, s'war mehr wie eine Farce and Hab' mir's gelobt ihn Lieb zu haben from Der Rosenkavalier (R. Strauss). In German with Berlin State Opera House Orchestra, conducted by Weissmann. Parlophone E.10865, 12in., 4s. 6d.

LOTTE LEHMANN (soprano), KARIN BRANZELL (contralto), GRETE MERREM-NIKISCH (soprano), RICHARD TAUBER (tenor), and WALDEMAR STAEGEMANN (bass).—Finale of Act 2 from Der Fledermaus (J. Strauss). In German with the Berlin State Opera House Orchestra, conducted by Weissmann. Parlophone Odeon R.20085, 12in., 6s. 6d.

LA SCALA CHORUS OF MILAN.—Invocazione alla luna and Gira la cotè from Turandot (Puccini). In Italian, orchestral accompaniment. Col. 9725, 12 in., 4s. 6d.

MARIO CHAMLEE (tenor).—La Donna è mobile from Rigoletto (Verdi) and Com' è gentil from Don Pasquale (Donizetti). In Italian with orchestral accompaniment. Brunswick 10275, 10 in., 4s. 6d.

ROSETTE ANDAY (Contralto).—Dank sei dir Herr from Cantate con Stromenti (Handel) and Erbarme dich mein Gott from St. Matthew Passion (Bach). In German, with the Vienna State Opera Orchestra, conducted by Karl Alwin. The second air has a Violin Obbligato by Franz Malrecker. H.M.V. D.1664, 12 in., 6s. 6d.

BENVENUTO FRANCI (Baritone).—O, Monumento and Ah ! Pescator, affonda l'esca from La Gioconda (Ponchielli). In Italian with members of La Scala Orchestra, conducted by G. Sabajno. H.M.V. D.B.1117, 12 in., 8s. 6d.

Rosa Ponselle.—This record of *Casta diva* is unique for many reasons, one of which, however will suffice : namely, that no other exists that can for a moment be compared with it. If there be no other *Casta diva* record, then it is more than ever unique ; and I take leave to prognosticate that it will remain for many a day unrivalled as a perfectly ideal specimen of the art with which this difficult air should be sung. The feature that strikes one most, not only from the outset but all through the piece, is the extraordinary beauty of the tone, as the result of an all-pervading sense of restraint, imparting to the voice an individual quality, a purity, steadiness, and withal a richness of volume, such as I have not heard from half a dozen throats in the whole of my experience. On a par with the loveliness of the voice is a mastery of technique which the trying opening phrase of *Casta diva* at once reveals in full measure—the faultless breathing of that heavenly phrase, the even *legato* of the scale, the clean, precise *fiorituri*, the impeccable chromatic descent, and the genuine Italian art of the phrasing of each passage. Then, following after the aria, comes the contrast of the *Cabaletta*, sung with great decision and definiteness of rhythm, in its way equally admirable, though, of course, not half so exacting in a purely vocal sense. On the whole, therefore, the Ponselle *Casta diva* is a delightful achievement as well as a unique one, and I recommend it accordingly.

Maria Jeritza.—Of the two airs here recorded by the Viennese soprano, I have no hesitation in "plumping" for *Vissi d'arte*, though even in that familiarity has made her careless with a note here and there, as, for example, the B flat thrown into the " santi tabernacoli sall." But she feels the life and drama of the music, and it suits her voice and style better than the dull, semi-religious chant that Thais sings in her scene with Athanael just before bidding farewell to Alexandria. In both pieces the voice comes out clear and strong.

Amelita Galli-Curci.—When a popular Italian prima donna warbles *The last rose of summer* and *Home, sweet home*, she merely revives a fashion of bygone days, and doubtless there are many who will be grateful to her for her condescension (which should also prove extremely profitable). The Galli-Curci touch is unmistakable even in simple things like these, and it is a pleasure to listen to her appealing tone, to a delivery free from affectation, and her neat phrasing of the old melodies with the quaintest of accents, quite in accord with accepted tradition. Happily, too, there is little if any interference with the musical text, though the words might be a trifle more distinct.

Emmy Bettendorf.—It is good to be able to welcome this delightful singer back to the fold in an unexaggerated and truthful reproduction of even well-worn things like *Solveig's Song* and *Connais-tu* (both sung in German). Her rendering of both is simply exquisite in its poetic suggestion, romantic feeling, and that wonderful personal touch whereby the singer conveys the idea that she is singing for you and you alone. The *mezza voce* is worthy to be compared in its sustained delicacy with that of Rosa Ponselle, and it was precisely with such a tone that Grieg taught his wife to sing Solveig's refrain.

What a contrast to the " amplified " Elsa of last month !

Gertrude Johnson.—I am sorry, but I cannot somehow care for *The Blue Danube* as a vocal waltz. *Voices of Spring* was intended to be one, and became a favourite all over the world years ago. Both are in the present instance sung with abundant spirit and " go."

Joseph Hislop.—Listening to such records as these of hackneyed airs by Mascagni and Puccini, I feel more than ever constrained to join the chorus of astonishment that our talented Scots tenor is persistently kept out of the Covent Garden combine. True, his repertory may be somewhat limited, but I prefer his Rodolfo to Pertile's any day, and the rich, dark quality of his voice to that of most of the lyrical tenors now on the boards. They can take a good lesson from him in breathing as well as in variety of tone-colour and freedom from nasality. His *Che gelida* is about the best I know, and one does not tire of it before the end.

Lenghi Cellini.—I wrote about this excellent tenor last month. Much the same characteristics are made manifest in the present examples of his method, which, if it were a trifle less jerky and not so subject to sudden contrasts of impetuous vigour and sentimental smoothness, would give his genuinely dramatic qualities a better chance. The pleasant tone and old Italian *affettuoso* manner in the Donizetti air are, of course, wholly appropriate.

Rudolf Bockelmann.—I am not sure, but I fancy this is the first music I have heard, other than Wagner, from the lips of the new German *basso cantante* who recently made such a hit at Covent Garden. He has splendid resonance and power in every part of his extended compass, the high notes up to E being particularly bright and telling. His delivery of the *Toreador's Song* may be less realistic and descriptive than the French Escamillos have accustomed us to expect, but, on the other hand, he equals the best of them in rhythmical spirit and energy. The ending with the girls' voices—generally cut here, as I have oft complained—is included in this capital performance. The air from *Hoffmann* is sustained with notable smoothness and ease, while the recording in both instances is irreproachable.

Nino Piccaluga.—Voice seems to be chief consideration here. Seldom have I heard *Salve dimora* given in such an unvarnished matter-of-fact manner, minus a suspicion of grace or elegance, but with lots of heavy tone everywhere. In the middle section there is a bad deviation from the right key, but after a bar or so the singer contrives to slip back on to the proper track ; hence, I suppose, its escaping notice. The *Carmen* air, sung in D major (a semitone up) exhibits the *parlante* style out of place and carried to an extreme. The voice is a real tenor and could be used to better purpose.

Joseph Farrington.—There is life as well as character in the singing of Figaro's *Largo*. The voice, too, is clear and of good honest quality. Curiously enough, the Italian seems to convey this impression more convincingly than the English text of *Vulcan's Song*, which might even be accused of a modicum of dullness. The tone here is too dark and, as I have previously pointed out, there is more subtle humour in Gounod's air than " meets the eye."

Marcel Journet.—It was, we may be sure, by intention and not by accident, that the famous French basso associated on the same disc the *Marseillaise* of Roget de l'Isle and the *Deux Grenadiers* of Schumann. It affords the opportunity for comparing the latter version with the original, and incidentally for noting how much more *brio* Journet throws into the real thing (by which I mean his country's national anthem) than the abbreviated arrangement so successfully employed by Schumann. In any case, both are finely sung, and, therefore, eminently worth listening to.

Frida Leider and *K. Marherr Wagner.*—We are beginning to take it for granted now that there is no longer such a thing as indifferent or bad recording. All we need to know is that the material at disposal has been good and made good use of ; that alone is what we look for in the result, and if not forthcoming the operator is not to be blamed. With regard to such records as this of Isolde's *Narrative*, it will suffice to give their names ; they tell their own story. There is no finer Isolde in the world than Frida Leider, while the orchestra of the Berlin State Opera House, under Dr. Leo Blech, would be hard to beat anywhere. With such aid, the significance of the scene with Brangäne stands out as it never has done on the gramophone screen.

Amelita Galli-Curci and *G. De Luca.*—There is a welcome atmosphere of refinement about these two duets from *Rigoletto* that is too often absent from them alike on the stage and elsewhere. Something has to depend, of course, upon the nationality and taste of the audience, and I can think of theatres abroad where the interpretation of these scenes between father and daughter, even by artists of such distinction as Galli-Curci and De Luca, would be thought many degrees too mild and subdued. My own opinion of them is quite the reverse. It is precisely when sung with delicacy and restraint that they sound best ; that every note comes out clearly and is perfectly in tune. Rarely of late, either, have I heard two voices, soprano and baritone, blend so harmoniously—a pleasant relief from the modern tendency towards noise and speed.

Carmen in English.—The four records included in this group are all of them open to serious criticism, thanks to the want of care and capable supervision shown in their preparation and rehearsal. Here was evidently no guiding spirit to prevent mistakes and set wrong right. I have said before, and I fear I shall have to say it again, that no matter how clever singers may be (or think themselves), it is quite useless to collect them in a studio when they have never met before or have never sung together on the stage, and expect them to perform difficult ensemble music correctly, with unity of spirit, finish, or the most ordinary effects of light and shade. Their pronunciation of their own language, to begin with, differs in nearly every case, and they even sing wrong notes and with faulty rhythm, yet have no one apparently endowed with authority to pull them up or the ability to set them right. This kind of inefficiency is never perceptible in operatic excerpts that come to us from foreign *ateliers*, and it is about time that it was stopped over here. Ambitiousness is all very well, but Bizet and Verdi are not composers whose music can be treated in the same cavalier fashion as jazz or revue stuff.

Seinemeyer, Merrem-Nikisch, and *Stünzner.*—In these excerpts from the *Rosenkavalier* and the succeeding items in this column is provided an exact illustration of the argument that I have just been laying down. Music more difficult or exacting in every way than that of Strauss's opera does not exist, and I should rather like to know, though not perhaps to experience, what would be made of the same selections by a heterogeneous collection of our own native singers. Well, it would do them good, anyhow, to take a lesson from these admirable records, performed under the able and experienced direction of Dr. Weissmann. I will not say I have not heard the wonderful trio in the last act more beautifully done, but it is an excellent performance none the less, while the orchestral support is particularly praiseworthy.

Turandot Trio.—Yet another vocal trio of extraordinary originality, about as unlike the female specimen just referred to as the *Rigoletto* quartet is unlike the *Meistersinger* quintet. Of the three Italians who sing it G. Nessi was in the original cast of *Turandot*, and his companions, A. Baracchi and E. Venturini, if I am not mistaken—one or both of them—were in the Covent Garden cast. Anyhow, they are all three accomplished singers of this highly fantastic, fascinating music, which constitutes for many the *clou* of the *Turandot* score.

A more colourful and authentic rendering it would be hopeless to look for.

Fledermaus Finale.—This seems to be the kind of gala performance combination that Vienna or Berlin would concoct in honour of the Johann Strauss Centenary; otherwise I cannot imagine how it was ever got together, even for that most popular of all popular comic operas, *Der Fledermaus.* Everybody, of course, knows the finale to the second act (or at least they will the moment they hear it) with its glorious waltz theme, second only in inspiration to that of the immortal *Blue Danube.* In the record under notice you can have the privilege of hearing an amazing combination, viz., Lotte Lehmann, Karin Branzell, Grete Merrem-Nikisch, Richard Tauber, and Waldemar Staegemann. The result is naturally ideal, and unparalleled in a piece of this sort. Mind you don't let it escape your eager grasp.

La Scala Chorus.—The two choruses from *Turandot* here reproduced are on the same level of executive merit as the *Ping, Pang, Pong* mentioned above, and I cannot say more than that in their favour. The *Invocazione alla luna* is given with rare breadth of tone, character and colour, imparting full effect to the sweep of the unisonal melody which is its main feature. The well-drilled Scala chorus is nowadays a treat to listen to. In the other number, *Gira la cotè*, the singing is remarkable for its crispness and animation, and both are delightful examples of the latest phase of Puccini's genius.

Mario Chamlee.—A decided improvement is to be noted in the production of this tenor's voice. It is less open and "white" than it was, and the darker colouring has added richness as well as power to a naturally fine organ. His higher middle notes are still his best, and he wisely sings *La donna è mobile* in B flat instead of B major. The real point is that he sings it with confidence in addition to the necessary *entrain.* The *Com' è gentil* is distinguished by tasteful feeling and graceful phrasing. The downward *portamento* is prettily done.

Rosette Anday.—This well-known German contralto spoils some highly artistic work by a persistent tremolo such as in this country would never be tolerated for a moment in an oratorio singer. Happily she does not wholly spoil it. One can listen with pleasure to her broad, dignified phrasing of Handel and Bach, and enjoy the devotional feeling that she puts into these airs, of which the one from the *St Matthew Passion* is, of course, the more familiar here. The violin obbligato is finely played by Herr Franz Malrecker, and in both instances Kapellmeister Karl Alwin secures the best results from his famous Viennese orchestra.

Benvenuto Franci.—Seeing that this is the most powerful Italian baritone now on the operatic stage—his voice is nearly double as big as Stabile's—it was really a work of supererogation to " amplify " him to the extent observable in the recording of these airs from *La Gioconda.* Sounds naturally ample in resonance have been exaggerated into vociferousness, as can be perceived at once by the noisiness of the orchestra and chorus. This can be remedied by the use of a soft needle, but the toning-down ought not to be necessary, while it only accentuates the *vibrato* effect caused by the slight pinching of the high notes. Otherwise, in a big auditorium Franci's huge voice and magnificent singing should create something of a sensation.

HERMAN KLEIN.

Cobbett's Cyclopedic Survey of Chamber Music*

Already has the attention of readers of THE GRAMOPHONE been drawn to the colossal compilation whose title appears above, and I devoutly re-echo our Editor's expressed hope that those of our readers who cannot afford to buy it outright will make a point of asking for it and studying it through their libraries. Obviously a work on such a stupendous scale is not to be absorbed by occasional reference or a cursory perusal. Like *Grove's Dictionary*, it needs to stand close at hand upon one's own bookshelf, to be taken down as required, or read page by page for sheer pleasure, until the whole of its fascinating and immensely instructive contents have been mastered. I think the plan of this *Cyclopedic Survey*, apart from the authority and critical knowledge shown in most of the articles, is simply wonderful. It is unlike that of any other dictionary of the kind—original in lay-out as well as content, clear in statement, definite and accurate as to facts, sensible and judicial in analysis

* Compiled and edited by Walter Willson Cobbett; with a Preface by Sir Henry Hadow. In two volumes, price £5 5s. Vol. I, A to H. Oxford University Press; London: Humphrey Milford.

and delivery of opinion. Most remarkable of all, there is the continuous chain of interesting post-scripts from Mr. Cobbett's own pen, enriching every or nearly every article with some thoughtful comment of his own, and so linking together the whole with one pervasive individual expression of feeling or appreciation. It is like taking in a vast panorama amid the guiding observations of a cicerone who knows it all from personal experience.

I am writing here about the *magnum opus* of a very old friend, of whose friendship I am to-day more than ever proud. I used to meet Mr. Cobbett frequently in the early days of those unforget-table Monday Pops. that I have written about, at his gracious re-quest, for the second volume of this book. I knew him first as a keen, ardent lover of chamber music ; then as an enthusiastic amateur quartet-player ; and finally as a valuable far-seeing patron of the art that he adored. The fact that he cared little about vocal music *per se* could not alienate my affections from him, be-cause, in reality, I loved chamber music as much as he did ; though, not being a rich man, but only a humble critic, I could not help with purse, but only with pen, to achieve what he did to advance the cause we both had at heart. And now, after en-dowing our young native composers and executants with prizes, medals and money to encourage them to write works and perform " phantasies " side by side with the masterpieces of chamber music, see what Walter Willson Cobbett has done ! He has devoted his latest years — time, labour, energy, capital (to be well recouped, I hope)—to the pro-duction of this great lexicon, which is going to prove a mine of information to lovers of chamber music for generations to come. All honour to the man who has performed this triumphant achievement.

WALTER WILLSON COBBETT

Sir Henry Hadow has struck the right keynote in his Introduction. He truly says that this work is " the first systematic attempt to collect in orderly arrangement all the relevant facts which bear upon its theme ; it has drawn upon a wide range of expert knowledge and opinion ; it has every prospect of being a definitive and permanent contribution to the literature of music." As such, to begin with, it ought to make an irresistible appeal to all genuine lovers of chamber music, including that newer generation whose admiration for the master-pieces of three centuries has been largely awakened by means of the gramophone and the helpful guidance of this Magazine. It should be un-derstood that the *Cyclopedic Survey* is no mere dry-as-dust compilation. I do not know exactly how many thousand articles it contains, but I do know that I have not come across one that is not replete with useful inform-ation concisely put, while many are in-tensely interesting—such, for instance, as Professor Donald Tovey's essays on " Brahms," and " Chamber Music " ; M. Vincent d'Indy's " Beethoven " and " César Franck " ; Professor Sourck's " Dvořák," and Mr. Cobbett's own delightfully anecdotal article on " The Chamber Music Life." This last gives some of the Editor's views and experiences on the general subject, and traces back to the revelation of first hearing Joachim lead a Beethoven quartet at the Pops that " limit-less enthusiasm which has reigned in his heart for the study of chamber music during the greater part of his life." The outcome and the reward are alike evidenced in two flattering letters from M. Vincent d'Indy, one printed on page 284, the other received since the publication of the present volume.

HERMAN KLEIN.

OPERATIC AND FOREIGN SONGS

AMELITA GALLI-CURCI (soprano).—**Chanson Solveig** (Grieg) and **Lo ! here the gentle lark** (Bishop). In English, orchestral accompaniment. H.M.V. D.B.1278, 12 in., 8s. 6d.

SUZANNE BERTIN (soprano).—**Caro nome** from **Rigoletto** (Verdi) and **Rêves de Printemps** (J. Strauss—R. Genée). In Italian, orchestral accompaniment. Metropole 1153, 10 in., 3s.

SYDNEY DE VRIES (baritone).—**Prologue** from **Pagliacci** (Leoncavallo). In English, accompaniment by Schauspiel Orchester. Metropole 1148, 10 in., 3s.

HAROLD WILLIAMS (baritone) and **FRANCIS RUSSELL** (tenor).—**I lay with Cassio** and **Witness yonder marble heaven** from **Otello** (Verdi.) In English, orchestral accompaniment. Col. 9827, 12 in., 4s. 6d.

MAVIS BENNETT (soprano) and **JOHN TURNER** (tenor).— **Miserere** from **Il Trovatore** (Verdi), and **Vocal Gems** from **Il Trovatore** sung by the **GRAND OPERA COMPANY.** In English, orchestral accompaniment. H.M.V. C.1692, 12 in., 4s. 6d.

OLGA OLGINA (soprano).—**The Bell Song** from **Lakmé** (Delibes) In French, orchestral accompaniment. Decca S.10002, 12 in., 6s. 6d.

GERARD MAINE (baritone).—**Prologue** from **Pagliacci** (Leoncavallo). In English, orchestral accompaniment. Broadcast Twelve 5083, 2s.

ELISABETH FEUGE-FRIEDERICH (soprano).—**Dich teure Halle** and **Allmächtige Jungfrau, Elisabeth's Prayer** from **Tannhäuser** (Wagner). In German, orchestral accompaniment. Parlophone E.10877, 12 in., 4s. 6d.

RICHARD TAUBER (tenor).—**Indian Love Call** and **O, Rose Marie, I love you** from **Rose Marie** (Rudolf Friml). In German, orchestral accompaniment. Parlophone Odeon R.20086, 12 in., 6s. 6d.

M. MICHELETTI (tenor).—**Ah ! lève-toi, soleil** from **Romeo and Juliet** (Gounod) and **Elle ne croyait pas** from **Mignon** (Thomas). In French, orchestral accompaniment. Parlophone E.10881, 12 in., 4s. 6d.

META SEINEMEYER (soprano) and **HELEN JUNG** (mezzo-soprano).—**Hast du es gehört** and **Juchhei, nun ist die Hexe tot** from **Hänsel and Gretel** (Humperdinck). Parlophone E. 10870, 12 in., 4s. 6d.

MARGARET SHERIDAN (soprano) and **AURELIANO PERTILE** (tenor).—**Tu ! tu ! Amore** and **O Tentatrice !** from **Manon Lescaut** (Puccini). In Italian, orchestral accompaniment. H.M.V. DB.1281, 12 in., 8s. 6d.

LIGHT OPERA COMPANY.—**Vocal Gems** from **Maritana** (Wallace). In English, orchestral accompaniment. H.M.V. C.1693, 12 in., 4s. 6d.

ERIC MARSHALL (baritone).—**Sometimes in my dreams** (d'Hardelot) and **Prologue** from **Pagliacci** (Leoncavallo). Brunswick 20082, 12 in., 4s. 6d. In English, piano accompaniment.

STILES ALLEN (soprano).—**Vissi d'arte** from **La Tosca** (Puccini) and **Musetta's Waltz Song** from **La Bohème** (Puccini). The former in Italian, the latter in English, orchestral accompaniment. Electron 0294, 10 in., 3s.

DAN JONES (tenor).—**The Flower Song** from **Carmen** (Bizet), and **Onaway, awake beloved** from **Hiawatha** (Coleridge-Taylor). In English, orchestral accompaniment. Electron 0291, 10 in., 3s.

Amelita Galli-Curci.—I wrote only last month in justification of a record of *Home, sweet home* and *The last rose of summer* made by this accomplished vocalist, urging as a good reason the fact that there were many illustrious examples of foreign *prime donne* warbling old English airs like these. Nevertheless, I did not mean that I was fond of listening as a rule to melodies presented with a strong foreign accent, no matter how popular the artist who presents them. Besides, Mme. Galli-Curci studies and records these things in America, and I am not at all sure that that is the best place in the world for acquiring the true traditions for the treatment of pieces like *Lo ! here the gentle lark,* or even for *Solveig's song* as presented through the medium of a French (and very nearly inaudible) translation. Bishop's ballad even comes off the better of the two, thanks to clean, clever vocalisation and highly effective acrobatics in conjunction with an excellent flautist. But I can safely say that I never before heard the song from *Peer Gynt* rendered in this lackadaisical comatose manner, with such an excess of *portamento,* and the refrain sung so sadly out of tune. Speaking quite candidly, I would advise the gifted Amelita to return to operatic coloratura work and leave these ill-advised special *plats du jour* severely alone—for consumption in this country at least.

Suzanne Bertin.—One listens here to an imperfect, because rather slovenly, technique, but a very pleasing voice with a bright, penetrating tone, always in tune, and managed with an amount of adroit dash that makes you ignore the aforesaid technical defects. The staccato and shake are both exceptionally good, obviously because they come easily to the singer, and in fact all her ornaments shine to better advantage amidst the comparative freedom of the Strauss waltz than within the narrower and more exquisite lines of *Caro nome.* Still there is life and *entrain* everywhere, and the head notes are nicely attacked. Perhaps a little more care in the scale and rapid passages would have made all the difference.

Sydney de Vries.—Although he belongs to the opera house at Mannheim and is accompanied by the "Schauspiel Orchester," this interpreter of the *Prologue* is unquestionably of British origin ; his words leave no doubt on that point, and they are happily plain for all to hear (bar the sibilants, which are weak). The tone is full and big—I fancy naturally so—and the quality has a certain distinction that one cannot help admiring. Also there is no lack of dramatic intelligence in the singer's delivery, while his breath-control is good, except in the production of a slightly-forced A flat.

Francis Russell and *Harold Williams.*—Notwithstanding the handicap of the English translation of Verdi's *Otello,* which is exceptionally colloquial and commonplace, these excerpts from the duet in Act II are entirely welcome. A subdued Iago atones for a somewhat blustering Othello, and so a fair balance is struck. Both have good voices and the orchestra supports them splendidly.

Trovatore Selections.—The *Miserere* fares well at the hands of Miss Mavis Bennett and Mr. John Turner, and the choral " gems " receive ample justice at the hands of the unnamed " Grand Opera Company." Which is about all that it is necessary for me to say concerning music and efforts so wholly familiar.

Olga Olgina.—If I am not mistaken, this is the first record from the Decca *atelier* that I have been called upon to deal with. On the whole it is a very creditable specimen. The artist is, I understand, from Warsaw, and she sings the *Lakmé* air in tolerably good French—when you can contrive to catch her words, which is not so frequently as it should be. But she owns a bright, telling voice of extended compass and sings well " on the note." Her head register is particularly clear, her staccato admirable, her style generally most effective. The top F is easily taken and held without effort, so that one feels this is the right kind of singer for the refrain of the *Bell Song.* The introductory cadenza is transposed up a semitone to allow of that high F being exploited, and the return to the key of B minor has been neatly managed.

Gerard Maine.—Another addition to the now-lengthy list of *Pagliacci Prologues* sung in English. It proceeds from a powerful and agreeable, but as yet slightly unwieldy, organ; a true baritone with a real dramatic timbre. The heaviness is due to a throaty production and should be overcome without much difficulty. Improvement in this direction would also lead to purer vowel formation and perhaps even to a less abrupt and jerky utterance of the words. In spite of these faults the record reveals features of promise, and I have not failed to note the fact that it costs only two shillings.

Elisabeth Feuge-Friedrich.—A clear resonant soprano of refined texture and exactly of the right pleading quality for *Elisabeth's Prayer*; a rendering which, if it were not taken at such an accelerated tempo, I might almost describe as ideal. In *Dich, teure Halle*, one looks as a rule, for a bigger tone: though in saying this I hope I may not be understood to be asking for the cheap assistance of that modern bugbear, the "amplifier." I mean rather that voice as well as delivery should be on a broader declamatory scale; yet, so much having been said, I can find naught but praise for the singer's expressive style, her intelligent phrasing and strong rhythmical feeling. The accompaniments and recording also command approval.

Richard Tauber.—The popular German light tenor, with his facile grace and charm both of voice and delivery, is, naturally, the right singer for the singing melodies of *Rose-Marie*, and I recommend this record as a faultless example of its kind. Fortunately there is a certain manliness about the passionate sentiment that relieves the music of some of its saccharine element.

M. Micheletti.—Here is a French tenor with a voice more robust than Richard Tauber's but not nearly so artistically controlled. The breathing method of the latter is practically irreproachable; M. Micheletti's results in an over-emphatic glottic attack and a gasping termination to almost every note. What a pity it is! The Frenchman's voice, as displayed in the excerpt from *Roméo*, is positively of a beautiful quality, but he is obviously not comfortable on his high notes and cannot sustain them without undue effort. Besides, one listens in vain for a *soupçon* of the tenderness in making love, a touch of the poetic feeling and infinite grace, that Jean de Reszke was wont to infuse into these same phrases. Ah, well, maybe I am asking for too much; and yet one feels about this record that it might easily have been made so much more satisfying than it is.

Meta Seinemeyer and *Helen Jung.*—Both voices are exceptionally sweet, yet somehow they do not blend perfectly, nor is their *legato* so wholly immaculate as some that I can recall in the days when *Hänsel and Gretel* was a genuinely popular opera. Truth to tell, the *Evening Prayer* has been better sung. Even the gifted Meta Seinemeyer is not blameless in this instance; her upper tones occasionally develop a decided *vibrato* and she sings too loudly for an even balance to be attained. Both singers are heard to better advantage (though they have much less to do) in the joyful waltz which the two children sing and dance after they have consigned the Witch to her own well-heated oven. The duet here sounds crisp and vivacious both in the voices and the orchestra, and is altogether extremely well given.

Margaret Sheridan and *Aureliano Pertile.*—As Puccini's *Manon Lescaut* becomes better known it becomes more appreciated, though in this country, as elsewhere, it suffers the disadvantage of having to overtake the long-standing popularity of Massenet's *Manon*. That success it may never quite achieve, nor am I altogether certain that it deserves to. The two operas are too unlike in treatment for comparisons between them to be fair and there is a great deal to admire in each. The duet for Manon and Des Grieux in the second act is one of Puccini's most dramatic pages and of its type far more advanced and "gripping" than anything in *La Bohème*. It fits Pertile, of course, to perfection, and brings out in

Margaret Sheridan's voice qualities not always perceived there. Altogether they make of it an unusually interesting and attractive record. The work of the Scala orchestra, under Sabajno, could not be bettered.

Light Opera Company.—The anonymous participants in these *Gems* from *Maritana* are quite good enough not to be compelled to conceal their light with their names " under a bushel." The reason is presumably that they are too numerous for mention. Each gem apparently has a different setting— by which I mean a different interpreter—and all are of creditable excellence. The old favourites, such as *Yes, let me like a soldier fall, Turn on, old Time,* and *Scenes that are brightest,* are naturally very much in evidence. The voices sound smooth and agreeably British, while the recording leaves nothing to be desired.

Eric Marshall.—It is always the voice of this popular singer, not his method or his style, that fixes your attention. It is the natural beauty of the organ that wins your admiration, notably as compared with his phrasing and diction, which (in English particularly) strike the critical ear as being incredibly careless. One feels that there is here the material (and no doubt the intelligence) for a magnificent rendering of the *Prologue*, yet somehow nearly every opportunity is missed. And in saying this I am not unmindful of the good points, as displayed in Guy d'Hardelot's effective ballad. Only you cannot quite judge the *Prologue* by the same standard.

Stiles Allen.—I heartily wish that some of the Italian recorders of *Vissi d'arte* would take this as an example of how to sing with a beautiful legato tone and engaging simplicity of delivery—not the over-dramatised manner that so many of them employ. On the other hand, it would be good for our English soprano if she could listen more attentively to their pronunciation of Italian consonants and vowels. Her English diction in *Musetta's Song* would also gain immensely by increased strength and emphasis of utterance. It would assuredly add to the charm of this slightly sad rendering of a piece that ought to be full of subtle spirit and " go."

Dan Jones.—A bright, pure, steady tenor, used with vigour coupled with discretion, invariably in tune, and most agreeable to listen to. There is an animated sentiment and sincerity of expression about the *Onaway, awake* that is especially meritorious, while in the *Carmen* air the voice is, on the whole, admirably managed. The recording in each instance is excellent.

HERMAN KLEIN.

OPERATIC AND FOREIGN SONGS

LOTTE LEHMANN (soprano).—**Frauenliebe und Leben, Woman's Love and Life,** Op. 42 (Schumann). In German, orchestral accompaniment. Parlophone RO.20090-3, four 10in. records, 4s. 6d. each, or in album with German words and English translation, 18s.

GÖTA LJUNGBERG (soprano), and **WALTER WIDDOP** (tenor), with London Symphony Orchestra under **Albert Coates.**—**Herzeleide** from **Parsifal,** Act 2 (Wagner). Four Parts. H.M.V. D.1651, 1652, 12in., 6s. 6d.

SIGRID ONEGIN (contralto).—**Alleluja** from the motet **Exultate** (Mozart) in Latin and **Il segreto per esser felice,** Drinking Song from **Lucrezia Borgia** (Donizetti). In Italian, orchestral accompaniment. H.M.V. DA.1046, 10in., 6s.

LENGHI-CELLINI (tenor).—**Una furtiva lagrima** from **Elisir d'Amore** (Donizetti) and **Questa o quella** from **Rigoletto** (Verdi). In Italian, orchestral accompaniment. Piccadilly 252, 10in., 1s. 6d.

461

NINA KOSCHETZ (soprano).—**Kaddish, Mourn Prayer** (traditional) and **Eili, Eili,** (traditional) in Hebrew, orchestral accompaniment, H.M.V. DB.1205, 12in., 8s. 6d.

Lotte Lehmann.—This is in every way a vast improvement upon the first recording of Schumann's song cycle, *Frauenliebe und Leben*, issued by Parlophone and reviewed by me in this magazine in September, 1927. Without entering into minute comparisons that would serve no practical purpose, I may say definitely that I prefer Lotte Lehmann in this music to Emmy Bettendorf; and I would by far rather put up with a fussy orchestral accompaniment (which the composer did not write, of course) than the tinkling of a wretched piano such as offended our ears in the version of two years ago. A great advance has been made in every direction since then (the new electrical process had only just been introduced), and albums sung or played by a single artist are no longer a novelty. It may be remembered that the whole plan was first advocated in these columns, and, so far as cycles of songs are concerned, had never been thought of until it was suggested in my articles on "The Singing of Lieder" earlier in the same year. I am glad to think that it has taken such a hold upon the gramophone public; it affords only one more proof of the extent to which their artistic perception and appreciation have gone forward.

In the present Parlophone version one feels throughout—what is most needed—the all-pervading charm of the singer's art; the pleasant sensation that nothing of it is obscured or made less beautiful in the course of transmission. Every sound stands out in bold relief; every syllable, every murmur, every tiny utterance, down to that particular sound whereof one would willingly hear less—I mean the constant hiss of the intake of breath—the only blemish upon the perfection of an exquisite achievement. Obviously, Mme Lehmann has made a careful study not only of Schumann's wonderful music but of Chamisso's intensely sentimental poem, and she has brought to bear upon both the light of her artistic intelligence and ripe experience. Fortunately the music does not lie too low for her, seeing that her middle and lower notes have recently acquired a new depth of richness and capacity for expressing profound emotion. Those who have heard her bring out the full intensity of such moments in, let us say, the closing monologue as she sits before her mirror in the first act of *Der Rosenkavalier*, will readily undertsand how she has contrived to impart the same lovely *mezza voce* quality, the same intimate effects of delicate, half-whispered secrecy to passages such as those in *Ich kann's nicht fassen, nicht glauben* and *Süsser Freund, du blickest*. The broader tone is easily available, of course, for *Er, der herrlichste von Allen* and *Du Ring an meinem Finger*; but more remarkable, because reserved for quite the end, is the complete change of colour and feeling in the final number, *Nun hast du mir*, with its restrained outburst of disappointment, grief, and inconsolable misery. These are the touches to which you can listen with unqualified pleasure. And don't be angry with the meddlesome obbligato violinist—he is not to blame !

Göta Ljungberg and *Walter Widdop.*—There are some parts of *Parsifal* that never seem to repay the trouble of recording, and the so-called *Herzeleide* scene between Kundry and the youthful hero in Klingsor's magic garden is one of them. The music does not lend itself to the purpose . It needs the stage and the subtle spell of personality to sustain its interest; to make clear the complete working of the minds of these two creatures—one striving under the baleful infiuence of a sorcerer. the other resisting the woman's wiles by sheer strength of innocence, pity, and spiritual grace. Göta Ljungberg has the right attributes of voice and artistic feeling and knows her part backwards; but not even she can suggest the character or motives of the unwilling Kundry in this episode, especially through a maze of thick, cloudy, enharmonic progressions, woven into a web of heavy instrumentation such as even Albert Coates cannot present in clarified atmosphere. As for Walter Widdop, what little he has to accomplish on two of

these four records conveys but the vaguest notion of what Parsifal is thinking, saying, or doing. His singing, like his German, is very faulty and open to criticism from more than one standpoint. Yet nobody in particular is to blame for the failure. It is due to the utter unsuitability of the theme itself for this medium, and the effort to overcome it was bound to result in a waste of time and energy. On the stage, and notably at Bayreuth, it is an ineffable delight.

Sigrid Onegin.—Here is another kind of *tour de force* that was not worth while. Mozart's *Alleluja* was never intended for a spacious contralto voice, however lightly and adroitly employed. It reminds one too much of that amusing experience of one's circus days, when the massive pachyderm condescended to execute a waltz upon a tub. Naturally Mme Onegin sings the *Alleluja* with facility and rhythmical sense as well as vocal skill, and her B natural at the end ought to persuade you that she was meant for a soprano. But she is far more lovable as a contralto, which she really is and, I hope, will continue to remain. Her rendering of *Il segreto* follows the hallowed German tradition of Schumann-Heink, with certain flowery ornamentations in addition; long pauses and shakes on high notes, and so forth, which help to make the record worth having.

Lenghi-Cellini.—The first point to be noted about this Piccadilly product is that it costs you only eighteen pence; for which modest sum you acquire a genuine moving interpretation of *Una furtiva lagrima*, by a popular tenor who is too clever to miss a chance in a Caruso aria of this lachrymal type. The sobs are not alone, however. They are accompanied by excellent singing in a tone much darker and rounder than it was once of yore. It is perhaps a shade too dark for *Questa o quella*.

Nina Koschetz.—Two very pathetic and beautiful excerpts from the Hebrew liturgy, familiar to all who are acquainted with them, and bound to win admiration from all who have yet to know them. The solo voice is exceedingly well trained and fits the touching music like a glove. The diction is clear; the phrasing, now subdued and mournful, now loud, strong and replete with the spirit of desolation, is pure and intensely picturesque. Altogether a fine example of Jewish cantillation.

META SEINEMEYER (soprano).—**Liebesträume No. 3** (Liszt) and **Die Nacht** (Rubinstein). In German, with orchestra conducted by Dr. Frieder Weissmann. Parlophone E10901, 12in., 4s. 6d.

EMMY BETTENDORF (soprano).—**Largo** (Handel) and **Ave Maria** (Schubert). In Italian with organ accompaniment. Parlophone E10902, 12in., 4s. 6d.

RICHARD TAUBER (tenor).—**Legend of Kleinsach** and **Hoffmann's Aria** from **Tales of Hoffmann** (Offenbach). In German, with orchestra. Parlophone Odeon R20089, 12in, 6s. 6d.

EMANUEL LIST (bass).—**Hagen summons the Vassals** from **Gotterdämmerung** (Wagner). In German, with Berlin State Opera Orchestra and Chorus, conducted by E. Moerike. Parlophone E10904, 12in., 4s. 6d.

META SEINEMEYER (soprano) and **TINO PATTIERA** (Tenor).—**Finale Duet** from Act 3 **Aïda** (Verdi). In Italian, with orchestra. Parlophone E10905, 12in., 4s. 6d.

ROY HENDERSON (barytone).—**O Star of Eve** from **Tannhäuser** (Wagner) and **Toreador's Song** from **Carmen** (Bizet). In English with chorus and orchestra. Broadcast "Twelve" 5100, 2s.

GÖTA LJUNGBERG (soprano).—**Salomé and the Head of Jokanaan, Finale** from **Salomé** (Richard Strauss). In German, orchestral accompaniment. H.M.V. D1699, 12in., 6s. 6d.

CLARA SERENA, DORIS VANE, FRANCIS RUSSELL and **DENNIS NOBLE.**—Vocal Gems from **Maritana** (Wallace). In English, with orchestra. Col. 9872, 12in., 4s. 6d.

HAROLD WILLIAMS (barytone).—**O Star of Eve** from **Tannhäuser** (Wagner) and **Toreador's Song** from **Carmen** (Bizet). In English, with orchestra. Col. 9873, 12in., 4s. 6d.

HEDDLE NASH (tenor).—**Il mio tesoro** and **Dalla sua pace** from **Don Giovanni** (Mozart). In Italian, with orchestra. Col. 9880, 12in., 4s. 6d.

Meta Seinemeyer.—I need not dwell on the sensations that one experiences on hearing anew the voice of a singer who has just passed on. It is one of those strange phenomena that the gramophone alone can create—an impression far more touching in its realism than any that the camera can convey ; for, after all, the sound of the human voice is like the reflection of life itself and therefore as it were, part and parcel of the living being. But enough of that ! To listen to the quiet charm the exquisite vocal quality of these records of songs by Liszt and Rubinstein is not only to enjoy music made doubly beautiful by its rendering, but to deplore with a profounder regret the premature passing of a most delightful singer. The sincerity of her work was among her many rare merits and it stands forth plainly for all to hear in these pieces, the orchestral accompaniments to which (never intended or provided by the composers) were, pathetically enough, conducted by the singer's husband of a month, Dr. Frieder Weissmann.

Emmy Bettendorf.—The well-worn melodies are sung in the soloist's most refined and graceful manner. The organ accompaniment to *Ombra mai fù* seems entirely *à propos,* because somehow the familiar air sounds more at home on that instrument than it possibly could on either the piano or an orchestra. But the same cannot be said of Schubert's *Ave Maria.* The tune itself could not have been more perfectly phrased by Heifetz, or even the redoubtable Kreisler himself. But the simple, flowing arpeggios of the accompaniment were never meant to be swallowed up in the enveloping chords of the Parlophone *grand orgue.* All that can be said in favour of it is that the new effect is imposing and by no means inappropriate to the religious purport of Scott's prayerful lines. Besides, Emmy Bettendorf's tones sound equally lovely under most conditions, and the recording here is admirable.

Richard Tauber.—Hoffmann's airs suit this popular German tenor exceptionally well, and he accordingly does them something more than justice. There is a romantic quality about his voice and style that inevitably fascinates the listener, even when the timbre and volume have undergone extensive amplification. Moreover, his singing is just what Offenbach wanted—crisp, rhythmical, spirited, quasi-fantastic ; and you can hear every word he utters.

Emanuel List.—Hagen's call to the Vassals is to the powerful German *basso cantante* something like the proverbial rag is to a well-bred English bull-pup. He gets it between his teeth, holds on to it, and, the harder you pull, the harder he bites and grips and chews it. But there is more than the mere summons in this welcome excerpt from *Götterdämmerung ;* and Emanuel List, with his huge voice and Gargantuan declamation, gets out of it every ounce of the the effect that the Bayreuth master intended. The chorus, too, is splendid, while the Berlin State Opera Orchestra shines to advantage throughout.

Meta Seinemeyer and *Tino Pattiera.*—Even when divided in two parts, the duet between Aïda and Radamès in the Nile scene of Verdi's opera, is rather a long selection to get on to a single disc. The effort in this instance has meant hurrying the tempi from first to last, and the music suffers in proportion. The reading sounds wrong. The effect on the singers was less marked in the case of Meta Seinemeyer than in that of the tenor, who loses dignity directly he is forced out of his gentle canter (I had nearly said his *bel canto*) into something like an agitated gallop. Despite this the record is an exceedingly good one and well worth having for the sake of the lamented soprano who so recently took part in it.

Roy Henderson.—I find here a highly commendable specimen of Broadcast Twelve recording at the very reasonable figure of two shillings for the 10in. disc. A shilling each for *O Star of Eve* and the *Toreador's Song,* both well sung by Roy Henderson, sounds fairly cheap, doesn't it ? I do not even grumble at the old Hersee words being used ; they offend much less in this than in other parts of *Carmen.*

Göta Ljungberg.—Those who witnessed this artist's magnificent performance as Salomé at Covent Garden in 1924, *and enjoyed it,* will gladly seize the opportunity to renew some of their pleasure with the present fine recording of the final scene—hypnotic as it is horrible—where she gloats over the decapitated head of John the Baptist.

Clara Serena, Doris Vane, Francis Russell, Dennis Noble and Chorus.—Vincent Wallace's old favourite, the evergreen *Maritana,* has its public, and a very large one too. To such as revel in its *Vocal Gems* through the medium of the gramophone this choice collection, gathered by Columbia British artists, will come as an unalloyed source of joy. Excellently sung and recorded, the *Gems* could not well be improved upon.

Harold Williams.—Comparisons being—well, what they are, I will not institute any between this record and the one done by Roy Henderson of the same two airs. Both attain much the same high level, and I hope both will create the same demand. Choice between them is very much a question of taste.

Heddle Nash.—Here are the two tenor airs from *Don Giovanni* which won for the singer such warm praise when he sang them at Covent Garden last season. Neither presents an easy task, but to the former Old Vic " star " they apparently offer no sort of difficulty. He takes the long phrases, the high notes, the extended runs, etc., without turning a hair ; and had he done otherwise the microphone would certainly have told the tale. The record, therefore, represents a highly creditable achievement.

HERMAN KLEIN.

OPERATIC AND FOREIGN SONGS

FANNY HELDY (soprano).—**Jewel Song** in two parts : **Les grands Seigneurs** and **Achevons la metamorphose** from **Faust** (Gounod). In French, with orchestra, conducted by Piero Coppola. H.M.V. DA1051, 10in., 6s.

ELSIE SUDDABY (soprano).—**Ave Maria** (Bach–Gounod). In Latin, with violin obbligato by Marjorie Hayward, and **Though reviling tongues assail us** (Bach). In English, with orchestral accompaniment. H.M.V. C1733, 12in., 4s. 6d.

ROSE CARDAY (soprano).—**Chanson Hindoue** from **Sadko** (Rimsky–Korsakov) and **Couplets du Charme** from **L'Amour Masqué** (Messager). In French, with orchestral accompaniment. Dominion B20, 10in., 1s. 9d.

LAURITZ MELCHIOR (tenor).—**Rome Narration** from **Tannhäuser**, Act III. (Wagner), two parts. In German, with London Symphony Orchestra, conducted by Albert Coates. H.M.V. D1675, 12in., 6s. 6d.

ORESTE DE BERNARDI (tenor).—**La Donna è mobile** and **Questa o quella** from **Rigoletto** (Verdi). In Italian with orchestral accompaniment. Dominion B.17, 10in., 1s. 9d. And **Non piangere liù** from **Turandot** (Puccini) and **E lucevan le stelle** from **La Tosca** (Puccini). In Italian, with orchestral accompaniment. Dominion B16, 10in., 1s. 9d.

GUIDO VOLPI (tenor).—**Dai campi, dai prati** from **Mefistofele** (Boito) and **Cigno fedel** from **Lohengrin** (Wagner). In Italian, with orchestral accompaniment. Dominion B18, 10in., 1s. 9d.; and **Donna non vidi mai** from **Manon Lescaut** (Puccini) and **S'ei torna alfin** from **Lohengrin** (Wagner). In Italian, with orchestral accompaniment. Dominion B19, 10in., 1s. 9d.

TOM BURKE (tenor).—**Vesti la giubba** from **Pagliacci** (Leoncavallo). In Italian, with orchestral accompaniment. And **Sea Rapture** (Coates). In English, with orchestral accompaniment. Dominion B15, 10in., 1s. 9d.

LOTTE LEHMANN (soprano).—**Love and music, these have I lived for** from **La Tosca** (Puccini) and **They call me Mimi** from **La Bohème** (Puccini). In German, with the Berlin State Opera Orchestra, conducted by Dr. Weissmann. Parlophone Odeon R20095, 12in., 6s. 6d.

NINON VALLIN (soprano).—**L'Automne** (Fauré-Sylvestre) and **Clair de Lune** (Fauré-Verlaine). In French, with piano accompaniment. Parlophone Odeon RO20094, 10in., 4s. 6d.

EMMY BETTENDORF (soprano) and **KARIN BRANZELL** (contralto).—**'Neath the chances of battle** from Act II. of **Aida** (Verdi). In German, with orchestral accompaniment. Parlophone E10916, 12in., 4s. 6d.

MAX HIRZEL (tenor).—**Bande der Freundschaft** and **Tränen vom Freund getrocknet** from **Don Juan** (Mozart). In German, with orchestral accompaniment. Parlophone E10918, 12in., 4s. 6d.

EDITH FURMEDGE (contralto).—**Amour, viens aider** from **Samson and Delilah** (Saint-Saëns) and **O del mio amato ben** (S. Donaudy). The former in French, the latter in Italian, both with orchestral accompaniment. Edison Bell Electron X552, 12in., 4s. 6d.

STILES ALLEN (soprano) and **EDITH FURMEDGE** (contralto).—**Flower Duet** from **Madame Butterfly** (Puccini) In English, with orchestral accompaniment. Edison Bell Electron 0282, 10in., 3s.

BRUNO SARTI (tenor).—**O Sole mio** (di Capua) and **Tango des Roses** (Schreier-Bottero). In Italian, with violin obbligato played by Di Vito. Edison Bell Electron 0301, 10in., 3s.

EDWARD HALLAND (bass).—**O Star of eve** from **Tannhäuser** (Wagner) and **O ruddier than the cherry** from **Acis and Galatea** (Handel). In English, with orchestral accompaniment. Edison Bell Electron 0297, 10in., 3s.

ROYAL CHORAL SOCIETY.—**Chorale Act I.** and **Finale Act III.** from **The Mastersingers** (Wagner). In English, recorded at actual performance under Dr. Malcolm Sargent, at Royal Albert Hall, on February 2nd, 1929. H.M.V. B3122, 10in., 3s.

ARTHUR FEAR (baritone).—**The Page song** from **Falstaff** (Verdi) and **Woo thou thy snowflake** from **Ivanhoe** (Sullivan). In English, with orchestral accompaniment. H.M.V. B3123, 10in., 3s.

BROWNING MUMMERY (tenor).—**The dream** from **Manon** (Massenet) and **No, Punchinello, no more**, from **Pagliacci** (Leoncavallo). In English, with orchestral accompaniment. H.M.V. B3121, 10in., 3s.

GIOVANNI INGHILLERI (baritone).—**Largo al factotum della città** from **The Barber of Seville** (Rossini) and with **OCTAVE DUA** (tenor) and **LUIGI CILLA** (tenor)—**Brindisi —Inaffia l'ugola** from **Otello** (Verdi). In Italian, with chorus and orchestra. H.M.V. D1698, 12in., 6s. 6d.

LAURITZ MELCHIOR (tenor) and **FRIEDRICH SCHORR** (baritone).—**Hast du, Gunther ein Weib** and with **TOPASWATSKE** (bass).—**Was nahmst du am Eide nicht teil** from **Götterdämmerung** (Wagner). In German, with Berlin State Opera Orchestra, conducted by Leo Blech. H.M.V. D1700, 12in., 6s. 6d.

IVAR ANDRÉSEN (bass). — **Hagen's watch** from **Die Götterdämerung** (Wagner) and **Pogner's address** from **Die Meistersinger** (Wagner). In German, with orchestral accompaniment. Col. L2341, 12in., 6s. 6d.

RICHARD MAYR (bass) and **ANNI ANDRASSY** (contralto).—**Final scene** from **Act II.** of **Der Rosenkavalier** (Richard Strauss). In German, with orchestra, conducted by Bruno Walter. Col L2340, 12in., 6s. 6d.

Fanny Heldy.—A good French rendering of the *Jewel Song* is always acceptable, if only because it gets you away from the commonplace English version of Henry Chorley. And this one is further made acceptable by the spirited singing of an artist whose first thought when she stands before the microphone is to remember that she is Marguerite, not a young soprano practising *solfeggi* in E major. Hence the atmosphere ; also the life and animation requisite for Gounod's waltz air. The voice is over-loud, yet not sufficiently to be objectionable, and the lady gives full value to every word, especially the French vowel tones. I like best her medium register ; the head is not always sweet ; but she runs up a pretty scale and has a neat shake. Another thing : you cannot hear her taking a single breath.

Elsie Suddaby.—Bach and Bach–Gounod are two very different things. In her air from the Bach cantata Miss Suddaby is more than at home—she is giving a lovely example of calm, pure, religious expression, phrased in the authentic manner and replete with quiet charm. On the other hand, in the impassioned Southern melody which Gounod embroidered like a wonderful piece of *appliqué* work upon Bach's prelude, the singer forgets her pure style, begins to " scoop " in the second bar on the second syllable of " Maria," and thereafter repeats the same error too frequently for the good of the music. Her Latin words, however, come out more clearly than her English, which are surprisingly inaudible. The voice throughout is clear, but the climax is rather mild.

Lauritz Melchior.—Although I fear I am somewhat solitary in my opinion that Tannhäuser's account of his pilgrimage to Rome is extremely dull—out of the opera, at least—still I can always find musical enjoyment in such a delivery of it as this. Lauritz Melchior is that *rara avis*, an intellectual tenor ; and here he makes one feel and understand every shade of the emotions which the unlucky victim of the Venusberg experiences, as the punishment for his dire offence against the morals of the Wartburg. His voice, his manner, his phrasing— all admirably recorded, together with Albert Coates's masterful reading of the orchestral part—combine to create in you a thoroughly sympathetic attitude of mind and ear, which, after all, is the most that any honestly repentant Tannhäuser has a right to expect.

Rose Carday.—This is the first of a numerous group of 10in. discs bearing upon them the new device, " Dominion," and which I am interested to observe are issued at the reasonable figure of 1s. 9d. each. Except for over amplification there is no serious fault to be found with the mechanical side of the new records ; they bear all the evidence of up-to-date methods. I have never heard Miss Rose Carday before, but she is a very competent vocalist, and I prefer her in the sustained music of the *Sadko* air. There her voice is steady and musical, despite an occasional lack of refinement ; but in Messager's Parisian ditty she unconsciously lowers her style to the level of the music, and warbles it with a naughty tremolo. It is curious how singers will permit themselves lapses of this sort.

Oreste di Bernardi.—The strident tone of this tenor's voice is to be attributed to nothing but excessive amplifying. In reality it has a very pleasing, sympathetic timbre, essentially Italian in character, and naturally quite powerful enough without artificial reinforcement. The orchestral accompaniment is also too noisy and strepitous at the beginning of each piece, but fortunately softens down when the soloist comes in. The best of the group is *E lucevan le stelle* ; it is the least

464

oppressive and the most musical. I hope the singer will now give us some specimens of his repertory that are not quite so hackneyed.

Guido Volpi.—Here is another excellent tenor who is not altogether the *robusto* that the Dominion operator would have us believe. In *Dai campi* he makes the common mistake —common, I mean, where this air is concerned—of using open vowels and a white tone. Yet the quality can be agreeable and manly too, as we may perceive in the excerpts from *Lohengrin* and the *Donna non vidi mai* from *Manon Lescaut*. These last suffice to place Guido Volpi in the light of an intelligent singer, while his articulation is singularly clear and distinct.

Tom Burke.—It is only ten years since the Lancashire tenor made his début at Covent Garden, and, considering what great things were then promised, we ought to have heard more of him in the interval. These two records prove, anyhow, that his fine organ keeps in good condition. He has also lost little if aught of his breezy style or, for that matter, his old tendency to overdo the *portamento*—a habit for which *Vesti la giubba* certainly offers every temptation. The Italian quality of the voice is as pure and noticeable as ever.

Lotte Lehmann.—Nothing that this great artist does can be other than well done. But, being " a little lower than the angels," she cannot be expected to shine in everything alike. She gives us *Vissi d'arte* and *Mi chiamano Mimi*—both in German, which is not to my thinking the right lingual medium for them. Now Ternina—unforgettable Tosca !—was a Croat with a faultless German accent, and, so far as I know, she never made the mistake of singing Puccini in anything but Italian, the only language in which his music sounds exactly as he meant it to. That is the point. The two airs here recorded are beautifully rendered (bar the " breaths " perhaps), but they do not sound quite as they ought because the words seem to interfere with the vocal line instead of forming part of it. Yet that may be an individual criticism that no ears but mine would heed.

Ninon Vallin.—One often hears these songs of Fauré's sung over the wireless, but seldom if ever with such purity of voice and style as in this record. Every detail is perfect, save the tone of the piano, and that is downright bad—not so metallic as it is wooden. Yet somehow it cannot spoil the singing.

Emmy Bettendorf and *Karin Branzell.*—This is the now familiar, not to say hackneyed, duet for Aida and Amneris, sung with plenty of vocal power and dramatic energy by two voices of fine quality. Verdi stands a German version much better than Puccini, so there is nothing to complain of on that account ; but I cannot help wishing that Karin Branzell had put a little more subtlety into the colouring of her glorious voice, which is a contralto (unadulterated), and consequently a trifle weak on head notes that were written for a mezzosoprano. The vibrant, sympathetic quality of Emmy Bettendorf's tone is well brought out in a very successful record.

Max Hirzel.—In this performer I salute a German tenor who sings Mozart really well. There need be no mistake about it. Our own Heddle Nash may beat him for equality of resonant tone in these very same Don Ottavio airs, but in many other respects he could take a lesson from him. Without going into details or comparing language effects, I will put the matter into a nutshell by advising lovers of good Mozart singing to procure this record and listen to it very carefully. I think they will enjoy it. The voice is sweet, natural, and— unamplified.

Edith Furmedge.—It would be as well if the last word of the preceding paragraph could be applied to the present example of Edison Bell recording, because in all other respects it is a highly satisfactory production. It is, I think, an error of judgment to use the new device for voices that are already " big," and Miss Furmedge's is certainly that. Her French is fairly good, but requires further correction, and I advise her next time she essays the air from *Samson* to sing the G to which

Saint-Saëns limited the cadenza originally—not the B flat, which he himself never liked. I wonder who recommended to her the tiresome imitation of Handel with the Handelian title, *O del mio amato ben*, by the modern Sicilian composer, Donaudy. It is melodious without being effective or really beautiful.

Stiles Allen and *Furmedge.*—I am sorry, but here again I have to temper my praises with criticism. The *Flower duet* from *Butterfly* requires, above all things, smoothness, delicacy, swing, and charm. This recording of it gets the *desiderata* in question from neither voices nor orchestral accompaniment, the main cause being an oversight which I have often had occasion to point out, namely, lack of sufficient preparation and rehearsal. The two voices, moreover, would have blended better had the right balance been insisted on. I would advise a re-recording of the duet.

Bruno Sarti.—I suppose I might compare *O Sole mio* to one of those shilling-shockers that are " best sellers " in the book world. It is always selling. Well, here is a new edition of it by a real Italian tenor, who is very pleasant to listen to when his voice is not allowed to get white or nasal ; and for best part of the time he keeps it nice and dark. Bar the tendency to fade away, he is also very acceptable in another tango tune called the *Tango des roses* ; and the combination provides the " best buyers " with quite a profitable three-shillings' worth.

Edward Halland.—This is a baritone-bass of the good old vigorous school, and for the present writer the attraction of his record is *O ruddier than the cherry*, which may be described as a bit of fine realistic work. He rages, he melts, he burns—all three at once—and, as my friend the late W. A. Barrett would have declared, he nearly imitates (unconsciously) the great basso, Carl Formes, by imploring someone to " make a *ba-ab* for my *gapacious ma-ut*." Only the same sort of thing is not quite so appropriate to *O star of eve*. An amplified business-like Wolfram is scarcely a poetic Minnesinger, which by rights he ought to be.

Royal Choral Society.—The performance of *Die Meistersinger* which was given at the Albert Hall in February last, under Dr. Malcolm Sargent, has found a welcome souvenir in these excellent records of the opening chorale and the final chorus of Nurembergers. There are moments when the microphone does not seem to have caught the sound-waves with the usual equality of volume and evenness of strength ; but they are probably due to the familiar acoustic eccentricities of the *locale*, which, as everybody knows, are as unreliable as the *piume al vento* in *La donna è mobile*. On the whole the two choruses come out very well indeed.

Arthur Fear.—Can it be that Mr. Fear has never heard *Falstaff* ? If he has, it is strange that so painstaking an artist should have committed the error of delivering the *Page's song* (which is actually Falstaff's reminiscence of the days when he was a slim, lively page to the Duke of Norfolk) in trumpet-tones suitable for the worthy Knight's tirade concerning *Honour*. Maurel, who was Verdi's chosen Falstaff, was wont to sing it from first to last in a delicious *mezza voce*. In *Woo thou thy snowflake* the singer is almost as badly at sea. A shaky start in the recitative only just escapes carrying him into the wrong key ; notes and words are alike hazy ; the s's are lisped ; there is plenty of tone, but no atmosphere of passion, and the rendering generally is mechanical. Mr. Fear can do much better than this.

Browning Mummery.—The last " n " in Manon should not be pronounced ; it is included in the sound of the whole syllable. Otherwise this tenor's words are always accurate, as well as distinct. The *Dream* is sweetly phrased with a pleasing timbre, and the telling quality of the voice is effectively displayed in the passage from *Pagliacci*. The tone, moreover, is steady and clear, and every note in tune.

Giovanni Inghilleri.—I know of no Italian baritone at

the present day, with the possible exception of Mariano Stabile, who could have recorded these pieces so well as Giovanni Inghilleri. His *Largo al factotum* is a model of all that it ought to be—free from exaggeration, superb in voice and manner, the patter simply amazing for speed and clarity. Equally fine in its way is the *Brindisi* from *Otello*, and faultlessly recorded into the bargain.

Lauritz Melchior, Fried. Schorr, and *Topas-Watske.*—Two of these names speak for themselves, and the third is that of a first-rate Hagen. There should also be a fourth singer, the soprano who contributes the few bars allotted to Gutrune ; but she is not mentioned on the label, so I cannot give her name. Anyhow, the two selections from *Götterdämmerung* are admirably done by the above artists, under Dr. Leo Blech, with the *concours* of the Berlin State Opera orchestra, and they add two more useful items to the H.M.V. collection, which is growing very quickly. The standard is well maintained.

Ivar Andrésen.—Curiously enough, this magnificent rendering of *Hagen's Wacht* starts exactly where the preceding record leaves off, and would form a worthy pendant to it, even though from a different source. With it, on the reverse side, is coupled *Pogner's address*, from *Die Meistersinger*, and to that Ivar Andrésen does equal justice, which is really saying all that is necessary. Altogether the record is one of the best that has recently been issued from the Columbia *atelier*.

Richard Mayr and *Anni Andrassy.*—Here, again, is a reproduction that is beyond criticism. As everyone knows, at the close of the second act of *Der Rosenkavalier* the naughty old Baron, Ochs von Lerchenau, after the duel with Oktavian, has a glorious scene nearly all to himself. How marvellously Richard Mayr portrays the quick recovery and hums his fascinating Viennese waltz need not be told. It is all here, with Bruno Walter to complete the ensemble.

HERMAN KLEIN.

OPERATIC AND FOREIGN SONGS

MARIA NEMETH (soprano).—**Ozean, du Ungeheuer** from **Oberon** (Weber). In German, with the Vienna State Opera Orchestra, conducted by Karl Alwin. H.M.V. D1717, 12in. 6s. 6d.

TOTI DAL MONTE (soprano).—**Polonaise, Io son Titania** from **Mignon** (Thomas) and **O, luce di quest' anima** from **Linda di Chamonix** (Donizetti). In Italian, with orchestral accompaniment. H.M.V. DB1318, 12in., 8s. 6d.

ELISABETH SCHUMANN (soprano).—**O hätt ich Jubals Harf** (Handel) and **Die heiligen drei Könige aus Morgenland** (R. Strauss). In German, with orchestral accompaniment. H.M.V. D1632, 12in., 6s. 6d.

FRIDA LEIDER (soprano) and **LAURITZ MELCHIOR** (tenor).—**Love Duet** from **Tristan and Isolde** (Wagner). In German, with orchestral accompaniment. H.M.V. D1723-4, 12in., two records, 13s.

LOUISE HELLETSCHUBER (soprano).—**There was a king in Thule** and **Jewel Song** from **Faust** (Gounod). In German, with orchestral accompaniment. Parlophone E10932, 12in., 4s. 6d.

LOTTE LEHMANN (soprano).—**Ständchen** and **Traum durch die Dämmerung** (R. Strauss). In German, with orchestral accompaniment. Parlophone Odeon RO20096, and **O Sanctissima** and **Stille Nacht, heilige Nacht.** Old hymns, in German, with orchestral accompaniment. Parlophone Odeon RO20098.

META SEINEMEYER (soprano), **SIGISMUND PILINSKY** (tenor), **ROBERT BURG** (bass), **HELEN JUNG** (mezzo-

soprano), and **FRITZ DUTTBERND** (baritone).—**Procession to the Minster** from **Lohengrin** (Wagner). In German, with orchestral accompaniment. Parlophone E10933, 12in., 4s. 6d.

Maria Nemeth.—Readers of this journal who are also readers of *Vox*—and I trust there are already many of them—will have seen in the new weekly a notice which I gave there of a radio performance by Maria Nemeth of *Ocean, thou mighty monster*. The libretto of *Oberon* was originally English, but as in this case the singer is a Viennese she naturally sang it in German. And very finely she did it ; being a dramatic soprano of the genuine stamp, with a voice equal to all ordinary requirements and a little more—as she proved on the same occasion by a remarkably fine rendering of *Marten aller Arten*. On the whole, I think her best in the great Weber air. She contrives to bring out its dramatic meaning, which is more than most sopranos can do away from the stage ; while her resonant organ and declamatory vigour enable her to do justice to music that is susceptible of real grandeur. Hence am I in a position to recommend without qualification her admirable record of it.

Toti dal Monte.—It may be said with truth that the clever and accomplished Toti dal Monte sings nothing that she does not adorn. That is, indeed, her business in life : to find fresh ornaments for hackneyed airs, and to present both old and new under as new a guise as possible, together with the added charm of a singularly sweet, pure, light soprano tone. In these examples she demonstrates all her wonted skill alike in "changes" and cadenzas, whilst proving also that acrobatics are not everything. She cannot thrill you with the *Linda* air as Patti used to—who could ?—but she persuades you to acknowledge its tuneful prettiness. She cuts the *Polonaise* (without good reason so far as I can see), but in the end she makes you admit that she has a marvellous technique and all the requisite brilliancy for tackling this sort of thing.

Elisabeth Schumann.—This is a German version of *O had I Jubal's lyre* (minus the second part) and a semi-sacred song by Strauss which I had not heard before, though it does remind me in character now and again of the *Rosenkavalier*. Both pieces are sung with Frau Schumann's accustomed taste and purity of style, and for once I prefer her in the modern to the classical or oratorio school. The accompaniments are well played by the Vienna State Opera orchestra under Karl Alwin.

Frida Leider and *Lauritz Melchior.*—Here, on two discs (four sides), we have the entire love duet from the second act of *Tristan and Isolde*, superbly sung by two of the greatest Wagnerian artists now living. Albert Coates conducted the whole excerpt, but with two different orchestras— the first half with the Berlin State Opera, the second with the London Symphony. If I refuse myself the indulgence of minute comparisons, it is because neither time nor space will allow of it. Besides, the average merit of the whole achievement is far too high for it to be necessary. Only occasionally— in the first of the two English records—does one perceive that the balance between voices and instruments is imperfect, the former being louder in proportion than the latter. The singing of both protagonists is magnificent, with a final climax that makes you long for more.

Louise Helletschuber.—Which should take our fancy the more, a German Marguerite who realises the Teutonic conception of Goethe's Gretchen, or a French Marguerite who brings with her the language and the Gallic charm of Gounod's heroine ? Well, really I cannot say, having liked each in turn during a long experience in the opera house. But when it comes to the gramophone the personality counts less, the voice and art of the singer more ; and here is a case where I am wholly unacquainted with the former and find the latter delightful. This is the reading of the *Jewel Song* that used to stir our emotions so tremendously when Pauline Lucca sang it—so intensely *schwärmerisch*, so bubbling over with passionate sentiment, yet so neat and artistic was it. I have enjoyed listening to this record very much, and could have declared it blameless but for two things—both in the *coda*—(1) that intrusive G sharp stuck in where one never heard it before, and (2) the extremely feeble B natural (Gounod's) at the very end. Surely such a fresh, clear soprano could command a better specimen of head tone than the microphone caught here.

Lotte Lehmann.—The vocal Christmas gifts enshrined in these four records are quite well worth purchasing—the sacred because they are old German hymns that the children wlli love, the secular because if there is any modern composer whom our ideal Marschallin sings beautifully it is Richard Strauss. Otherwise there is not much to say except to praise the nicely-restrained orchestral accompaniments and the recording, which is excellently done.

Meta Seinemeyer, Robert Burg, etc.—The two sides of this disc embody the final scene of the second act of *Lohengrin,* and it is an error to label it *The Procession to the Minster,* because during the greater part of it there is no procession. The *cortège* has been broken up by those naughty people, Ortrud, Telramund and Co., long before the first record starts ; while the wind-up, as everybody knows, is merely a kind of *chassez-croisez à trois,* hand-in-hand, performed by the King and the bride and bridegroom. The voices of poor Meta Seinemeyer and Robert Burg come out well and the chorus is first-rate. The Lohengrin is also evidently competent ; but the shock of the interrupted wedding march has apparently reduced him to tears. His penetrating tone is lachrymose throughout. Yet, all said and done, lovers of Wagner's early opera will be rather glad to have this tit-bit.

SIGRID ONÉGIN (contralto).—**O mio Fernando** from **La Favorita** (Donizetti) and **O don fatale** from **Don Carlos** (Verdi). In Italian, with orchestral accompaniment. H.M.V. DB1292, 8s. 6d.

CONSTANCE WILLIS (contralto).—**Softly awakes my heart** from **Samson and Delilah** (Saint-Saëns) and **Habañera** from **Carmen** (Bizet). Broadcast Twelve 5114, 2s. In English, with orchestral accompaniment.

JOSEPH HISLOP (tenor).—**To the children** (Rachmaninov) and **The Grey House** from **Fortunio** (Messager). In English, with orchestral accompaniment. H.M.V. B3154, 10in., 3s.

ALESSANDRO VALENTE (tenor).—**O Paradiso** from **L'Africana** (Meyerbeer) and **Addio fiorito asil** from **Madam Butterfly** (Puccini). In Italian, with orchestral accompaniment. H.M.V. B3141, 10in., 3s.

GUIDO VOLPI (tenor).—**L'Anima stanca** from **Adriana Lecouvreur** (Cilea) and **Amor ti vieta** from **Fedora** (Giordano). In Italian, with orchestral accompaniment. Dominion B25, 10in., 1s. 9d.

ORESTE DE BERNARDI (tenor).—**Che gelida manina** from **La Bohème** (Puccini). Two parts. In Italian, with orchestral accompaniment. Dominion B24, 10in., 1s. 9d.

RICHARD TAUBER (tenor).—**Song of the Volga Boatmen** and **Stenka Razin.** In German, with chorus and orchestral accompaniment. Parlophone Odeon RO20097, and **Roses and Women** (Franz Grothe) and **Little mother of my dreams** (J. Cowler–K. Schwabach) RO20099, 12in., 6s. 6d. each. In German (free leaflet of words), with orchestral accompaniment.

Sigrid Onégin.—I think I have previously observed that this accomplished contralto is not heard at her best in Italian music and the Italian language. Her voice is glorious enough to sound well in anything, but it is positively unkind of her to treat *O mio Fernando*—a combined outpouring of tragic sorrow and outraged dignity if ever there was one—as though it were a trivial, lively Panofka study ! The interpretation of *O don fatale* gives the same impression exactly—of the singer never having played the rôle and knowing absolutely nothing of the story of *Don Carlos.* Approached in this manner, you cannot expect to infuse into records atmosphere or *Stimmung* or anything else (tradition included) save the beauty of your own wonderful voice.

Constance Willis.—Experience with the B.N.O.C. has made a dramatic singer of this artist and taught her to bring some of her stage instincts with her into the recording studio. In such cases let me assure the Broadcast Twelve operator that there is no need for indiscriminate over-amplifying ; the voice and the style are quite big enough without his artful aid. The only other criticism I would make concerns the descending chromatic phrases of the *Habañera* ; and there Miss Willis is too inclined to " slither " down from note to note when a clean scale is absolutely essential.

Joseph Hislop.—It is pleasant to hear the Scottish tenor in something besides Italian opera, especially Verdi and Puccini. The association of Rachmaninov and Messager may seem curious at first glance, but the music explains it. Both are suitable songs for a Christmas audience of children and, sung in this charming manner, they should be able to attract as big a crowd of youngsters as the Christmas-tree itself—or nearly so. The voice is delicately modulated, and in the Russian song assumes a truly touching quality.

Alessandro Valente.—" A little less robust and a trifle more restrained " would make all the difference in this tenor's method. Even allowing for a certain amount of excessive amplification, one can feel as well as hear that he attempts too much. Neither Vasco di Gama nor F. B. Pinkerton in these melodies is out to beat the record in a hundred-yard sprint. The voice may be Tamagnoesque, if you will, but it ought not to be *vox et praeterea nihil.*

Guido Volpi.—The records by this singer reviewed in last month's GRAMOPHONE were on the whole superior to the present examples from the ultra-modern school of Cilea and Giordano. Candidly, I have little admiration for the music or for the vocal exaggerations which they superinduce.

Oreste di Bernardi.—Here the Dominion makes a worthier show, albeit the labels are misleading. The two sides actually embody the whole of *Che gelida manina,* not two separate pieces ; and so much the better, for the voice is by far the best of this Italian group, and Rodolfo's confession of love at first sight is a highly creditable outpouring.

Richard Tauber.—It seems rather odd, perhaps, for a tenor to be singing the *Song of the Volga Boatmen* after one has got used to Chaliapine and all the baritone-basses that follow in his wake. But if you are popular you can dare anything, and Richard Tauber is nothing if not popular. On the whole, he comes very well out of the ordeal (if ordeal it may be called) and gives a very good idea of how a Danube boatman would lay back on his oars to the same old river-chanty tune. The Tauber-like *insouciance* is there if the realism of Chaliapine is not, while the chorus helps to put in the touches of local colour. In the other ditties the singer is slightly more at home ; which, being freely translated, means that " Richard is himself once again." HERMAN KLEIN.

OPERATIC AND FOREIGN SONGS

LOTTE LEHMANN (soprano).—**Träume** (Wagner) and **Schmerzen** (Wagner). Sung in German with orchestral accompaniment. Parlophone Odeon RO20100, 10in., 4s. 6d.

VALENTINA AKSAROVA (soprano).—**Pleurez, mes yeux,** from **Le Cid** (Massenet), in French, and **All for you** (Tchaikovsky), in Russian. With piano accompaniment. Decca F1561, 10in., 2s.

RICHARD TAUBER (tenor).—**O Mädchen, mein Mädchen** and **Sah ein Knab ein Röslein steh'n** from **Friederike** (Lehar-Horzer-Lohner). Sung in German with orchestral accompaniment. Parlophone Odeon R20101, 12in., 6s. 6d.

FRANK TITTERTON (tenor).—**Strange harmony of contrasts** and **When stars were brightly shining** from **Tosca** (Puccini). Sung in English with orchestral accompaniment. Decca M97, 10in., 3s.

ORESTE DE BERNARDI (tenor).—**Torna a Surriento** (De Curtis) with guitar and violin accompaniment, and **TOM BURKE** (tenor).—**O primavera** (Tirindelli). In Italian with orchestral accompaniment. Dominion B32, 10in., 1s. 9d.

ORESTE DE BERNARDI.—**Addio alla madre** from **Cavalleria Rusticana** (Mascagni) and **Recondite armonie** from **La Tosca** (Puccini). In Italian with orchestral accompaniment. Dominion B33, 10in., 1s. 9d.

MICHAEL SZEKELY (bass).—**The Landgrave's Speech** from **Tannhäuser** (Wagner) and **Within this hallowed dwelling** from **The Magic Flute** (Mozart). In German with orchestral accompaniment. Parlophone E10939, 12in., 4s. 6d.

RICHARD WATSON (bass).—**Slander's Whisper** from **The Barber of Seville** (Rossini) and **When a maiden takes your fancy** from **Il Seraglio** (Mozart). In English with orchestral accompaniment. Decca M95, 10 in., 3s.

Lotte Lehmann.—Wagner's "studies" on *Tristan* are unquestionably the most beautiful of his none too numerous songs. And here they are quite beautifully sung—as, indeed, only a true Isolde could sing them ; with all the requisite sense of pent-up emotion and restrained passion, even to the very intake of breath whose sound you would seriously object to in anyone but a Lotte Lehmann or a Gerhardt. There is a subtle difference of timbre here between the *Träume* and the *Schmerzen ;* a contrast of qualities that sounds just right for each. In one the singer suggests her impatient yearning ; in the other the deeper, mezzo-like tones of one to whom love has meant a full measure of suffering. The vocal technique in either instance is supremely fine, the control absolute. On second hearing they sounded even more exquisite than before. The accompaniments are well played.

Valentina Aksarova.—A Russian singer rarely seems to go far astray when portraying sorrow and misery, but her lack of contrast often leaves something to be desired. It is so in the present case. One feels all the sadness of *Pleurez, mes yeux*, minus the trace of consolation and hope that a French-woman would somehow get into the language, especially if her pronunciation of it were distinct as well as pure. In Tchaikovsky's song Mme. Aksarova does better, because she is naturally more at home in her native tongue and also yields something more satisfying than mere voice. Her efforts are painstaking and intelligent, but not invariably interesting.

Richard Tauber.—I am told that the indefatigable Richard is becoming nearly as popular with gramophonists in this country as he is in his own. The reasons for it are plain to all who hear his records ; and he never commits the error of singing music that does not suit him or that lies beyond his means. He is fond of Franz Lehar ; and I doubt not for a moment that Franz Lehar is fond of him. At any rate the " Light Opera King " knows how to write for him music that fits his voice like a glove. Take, for example, these highly pleasing airs from *Friederike*. The *Mädchen, mein Mädchen*, will haunt you for a week at least, while the new tune that Lehar has invented for Goethe's *Haidenröslein* is so entirely different from Schubert's (thank goodness !), yet so insinuatingly pretty, that I fancy you will approve my vote of forgiveness to the Hungarian composer for his audacity in venturing to re-set the great poet's lines. Richard Tauber's no less insinuating voice and manner do the rest.

Frank Titterton.—One cannot help admiring the enterprise of the new Decca Company in bringing out records by an English tenor (in English, of course) of the well-worn *Tosca* airs (which you will only recognise by their Italian titles). Comparisons are odious, so I make none—I mean between Mr. Titterton and the favourite native Cavaradossis of the day. But I would point out that in these capital records he has not achieved the necessary contrast between the two pieces. *E lucevan le stelle* is exactly right in spirit and character ; it is the melancholy retrospect of an unhappy lover at the point of execution. But *Recondite armonie* may not be " tarred with the same brush," for it should be the joyous reverie of a lover waiting at the trysting-place for the woman he adores. Why, then, sing it with the same solemn, sombre tone that is employed for the other ? With this exception, I can award hearty praise to both efforts.

Oreste de Bernardi and *Tom Burke.*—Here we have precisely the same trouble illustrated—only at a relatively much cheaper figure, in a Dominion 10in.—by a capable Italian tenor. He, too, sings *Recondite armonie* as an expression of tearful regret at the state of things in general, and couples with it, not *E lucevan*, but that genuinely lachrymose bit from *Cavalleria Rusticana*, the *Addio alla Madre*. So again we have, in an artistic sense, one wrong and one right reading combined in the work of a competent artist with a naturally fine organ. His Neapolitan folk-song is really better, because more truly characteristic, though the guitar accompaniment is scarcely loud enough. Again I find that the Dominion operator over-amplifies the voice at the expense of every other consideration. It is certainly so in the case of the Tirindelli serenade sung by Tom Burke on the reverse side of the same disc. On the whole, however, these records attain a good standard and are marvels of cheapness.

Michael Szekely.—This singer, presumably a Hungarian, is strictly speaking a *basso cantante*. He has a powerful, resonant voice, and delivers the Landgrave's address with becoming dignity. It is a pity, therefore, that his method should be so jerky and explosive, or that he should unsteady his tone by forcing it. Obviously these faults are not inevitable, for in the Sarastro air—sung in F instead of E major—they are not nearly so conspicuous.

Richard Watson.—Here, again, Mozart brings out the best that is in a bass (a good sign, anyhow), while the faults once more are such as time and care will eradicate. The voice is a clear, bright steady one, and reminds me rather of Robert Radford's in his youthful days, especially in *When a maiden takes your fancy*. The mistake in *La Calunnia* (with the awkward English title of *Slander's Whisper*) is the excessive exaggeration of the *staccato*. Rossini never meant Don Basilio to jerk out those quavers as if he were dancing an egg-dance or imitating Mime tapping on his anvil. It is doubly irritating because it completely obliterates the words. Nevertheless, Richard Watson has all the makings of a good singer.

HERMAN KLEIN.

The London Opera Festival.

Not for many a day has so much interest been compressed into a short winter opera season as Mr. Robert Stuart has managed to concentrate in the month's " Festival " at the Scala Theatre, which is beginning practically as this number is published. He is giving us a most fascinating series of revivals, or rather reproductions of new-old operas, most of them unheard in London for years, one or two not within living memory. Fancy being able at last to listen to the *Orpheus* of that pioneer of the operatic art-form, Monteverde (properly spelt, for a wonder), which was first written and performed some 320 years ago for Gonzaga, Duke of Mantua.

That privilege I hope to enjoy and shall certainly never forget. A double bill, consisting of Locke and Gibbons' masque *Cupid and Death*, with Purcell's *Dido and Æneas*, will form the great early-English item of the menu. Handel's opera *Julius Cæsar*, done recently in Germany ; Mozart's early effort, *La Finta Giardiniera* ; and Gluck's *Alcestis* further represent 18th century masters, and are quite unknown over here to the present generation. Weber's *Der Freischütz* one used, of course, to hear regularly at Covent Garden, at any rate whilst Pauline Lucca came to delight us with her exquisite Agathe ; but that was going on for 40 years ago. *Hansel and Gretel* and a short opera by Gervase Hughes will also figure in the scheme ; and many well-known singers and conductors are to take part in this extremely creditable campaign.   H. K.

OPERATIC AND FOREIGN SONGS

MARIA NEMETH (soprano).—**Der Freund ist dein** from Act 1 and **Doch eh' ich des Todestal** from Act 3, **Die Königin von Saba** (Goldmark) With chorus. In German with orchestral accompaniment. H.M.V. D1720, 12in., 6s. 6d. Words and English translation on p. 430.

OLGA OLGINA (soprano).—**Una Voce** from **Il Barbiere di Siviglia** (Rossini). In Italian with orchestral accompaniment. Two parts. Decca M92, 10in., 3s.

LOUISE HELLETSGRUBER (soprano).—**They call me Mimi** and **Musetta's Waltz Song** from **La Bohème** (Puccini). Sung in German with orchestral accompaniment. Parlophone E10945, 12in., 4s. 6d.

MIRIAM LICETTE (soprano).—**Batti, batti** and **Mi tradì quell' alma ingrata** from **Don Giovanni** (Mozart). In Italian with orchestral accompaniment. Col. 9911, 12in., 4s. 6d.

MARGARET SHERIDAN (soprano) and **AURELIANO PERTILE** (tenor).—**Vicino a te** and **La nostre morte**, final duet from Act 4, **Andrea Chénier** (Giordano). In Italian with orchestral accompaniment. H.M.V. DB1289, 12in., 8s. 6d.

FRANCIS RUSSELL (tenor).—**Prize Song** from **Die Meistersinger** (Wagner) and **Sound an Alarm** from **Judas Maccabaeus** (Handel). In English with orchestral accompaniment. Col. 9924, 12in., 4s. 6d.

SIGISMUND PILINSKY (tenor).—**The Prize Song, Part I.**, from **Die Meistersinger** (Wagner) and with **META SEINEMEYER** (soprano), **Part II.** In German with orchestral accompaniment and chorus. Parlophone E10947, 12in., 4s. 6d.

JOSEPH HISLOP (tenor).—**Prize Song** from **Die Meistersinger** and **Lohengrin's Narrative** from **Lohengrin** (Wagner). In English with orchestral accompaniment. H.M.V. DB1351, 12in., 8s. 6d.

Maria Nemeth.—It is not surprising that the new Viennese *diva* should have made records of excerpts from Goldmark's *Queen of Sheba*, seeing that that tuneful and picturesque opera is *à la-maison* or *chez elle* (whichever you prefer) at the Vienna Staats-Oper, where it was first performed in 1875. Personally I have never heard it in London, but I remember a splendid representation of it at the Metropolitan Opera House, New York, and am aware that the Carl Rosa Company did it well at Manchester in 1910. Why it never got into the regular repertory at Covent Garden it is hard to say, unless it be that Biblical subjects (bar *Samson and Delilah*) do not catch on at that august establishment. For gramophonists who have never heard Goldmark's opera the interest of the present record, apart from the winning grace of the melodies, lies in the beauty of the solo voice and its smooth blending with those of the female chorus, which are also unusually sweet and refined. The recording operator seems, if I may say so, to have focussed both with the skill of a clever photographer, the balance of the ensemble, with Karl Alwin's Staats-Oper orchestra in the background, being beyond reproach. I need scarcely add that Maria Nemeth's pure, steady soprano, with its limpid, translucent timbre, floats easily and with dominant power above them all.

Olga Olgina.—As might have been expected, this accomplished young Polish soprano gives a brilliant account of *Una voce* (10in., in two parts, price 3s.), and the record is worth having for its purity of tone and neatness of execution. It is her habit to begin nervously and she does so here ; then settles down, and—all is well for the rest of the journey. The " changes " are familiar and tolerably Rossinian, the scales and trill laudably accurate.

Louise Helletsgruber.—To amateurs who prefer their *Bohème* in German this record may be recommended without hesitation. Whether as Mimi or Musetta the vocalist exhibits a beauty of tone and delicacy of expression that one cannot help admiring. The waltz-song is perhaps treated a shade too " soberly," as the French would put it ; for, after all, Musetta is not precisely a modest Gretchen, you know. Still, it makes up in charm for what it lacks in *verve*, and the recording is obviously fidelity itself.

Miriam Licette.—Versatility cannot be denied to the singer who is equally at home as Donna Elvira and Zerlina—equally Mozartian in *Mi tradì* and *Batti, batti*. Artistry marks the interpretation of both airs, as well as welcome steadiness and purity of voice. The orchestral accompaniments and the recording also call for unqualified praise.

Margaret Sheridan and *Aureliano Pertile.*—In these days of studied amplification it is advisable not to dwell much on the question of vocal power, especially if one is not familiar with the recording (or recorded) voice. I thought Pertile sufficiently robust already, but here he is a veritable giant ; while, unless Margaret Sheridan has changed lately from a light into a dramatic soprano, the metamorphosis here indicated is equally untrue to nature. Anyhow, a certain amount of discretion is needed in this matter. According to some ideas this may be a superbly penetrating reproduction of the final duet from *Andrea Chénier*. According to others it may be a mere duel of strength, with the advantage on the side of the male protagonist. Anyhow it is gloriously Italian up-to-date, of the kind that the French call *laissez-aller* !

Francis Russell.—When a powerful young English tenor bubbles over with energy and high spirits it seems almost a shame to ask him to curb either ; nor would I do so once more but for the fact that, in the *Prize Song* at least, the *quantum* is excessive and therefore misplaced. In *Sound an alarm* there is another story to tell. The ringing tone and agitated movement are right enough, even though the declamation suffers from careless enunciation and silent sibilants. But must one always be boisterous, bustling, and breathless ? Surely not in the *Prize Song*, at any rate.

Sigismund Pilinsky.—Presumably a Polish tenor; anyhow a well-trained artist with a capital voice of the heroic type. His rendering of the *Preislied* from the scene on the banks of the *Pegnitz* would furnish a famous object-lesson for impulsive young singers like the one above referred to. The few bars for Eva so exquisitely sung by poor Meta Seinemeyer only awaken a longing for more. The chorus and orchestra of the Berlin State Opera contributed a worthy share to the excellence of this record, but I regret to add that the amplifier put in *his* work only too generously.

Joseph Hislop.—This Wagner record deserves an exalted place among the Hislop collection. Of his many meritorious efforts in this direction I recall none so completely satisfying. The *Prize Song* becomes in his hands a veritable love-song, glowing, like the morning it celebrates, with the warmth of sunshine and newly awakened passion. The tone is vibrant and full, the feeling well controlled, the diction such that one hears every syllable. In the *Lohengrin Narrative* a more sedate note is properly struck, but with a voice no less haunting in its beauty. In both pieces the *cantilena* is sustained with effortless smoothness and an art free from needless *portamento* or any other kind of exaggeration. The orchestration is admirably treated, under the careful guidance of John Barbirolli.

HARDY WILLIAMSON (tenor).—**La donna è mobile** and **Questa o quella** from **Rigoletto** (Verdi). In English with orchestral accompaniment. Homochord D1447, 10in., 2s. 6d.

WALTER WIDDOP (tenor).—**Lend me your aid** from **Queen of Sheba** (Gounod). Two parts. In English with orchestral accompaniment. H.M.V. D1742, 12in., 6s. 6d.

RENATO ZANELLI (tenor).—**Dio! mi potevi scagliar** from Act 3 and **Niun mi tema** (**Death of Othello**) from Act 4, **Otello** (Verdi). In Italian with orchestral accompaniment. H.M.V. DB1173, 12in., 8s. 6d.

EMANUELE SALAZAR (tenor).—**Monologo** from Act 3 and **Niun mi tema** from Act 4, **Otello** (Verdi). In Italian with orchestral accompaniment. Col. L2365, 12in., 6s. 6d.

NINO PICCALUGA (tenor).—**Ah! si ben mio coll' essere** from **Il Trovatore** (Verdi) and **Death of Othello** from **Otello** (Verdi). In Italian with orchestral accompaniment. Parlophone E10946, 12in., 4s. 6d.

ARMAND CRABBÉ (barytone).—**Prologue** from **Pagliacci** (Leoncavallo). In French with orchestral accompaniment. Two parts. H.M.V. DB1128, 12in., 8s. 6d.

HEINRICH SCHLUSNUS (barytone).—**An die Musik** and **Am Meer** (Schubert). In German with piano accompaniment. Polydor 62644, 10in., 4s. 6d.

FRIEDRICH SCHORR (barytone).—**Wahn Monolog** from Act 3, **Die Meistersinger** (Wagner). In German with orchestral accompaniment. H.M.V. D1734, 12in., 6s. 6d.

GIOVANNI INGHILLERI (barytone).—**La povera mia cena** from Act 2 and, with **OCTAVE DUA** (tenor), **Tre sbirri, una carrozza** from Act 1, **Tosca** (Puccini). In Italian with orchestral accompaniment. H.M.V. D1701, 12in., 6s. 6d.

THEODORE CHALIAPINE (bass).—**Le Cor** (Flegier), in French, and **The Old Corporal** (Dargomijsky), in Russian, with orchestral accompaniment. H.M.V. DB1342, 12in., 8s. 6d.

IVAR ANDRÉSEN (bass).—**Tom der Reimer** (Loewe, *Op.* 135). In German, two parts, with orchestral accompaniment. Col. L2372, 12in., 6s. 6d.

Hardy Williamson.—The Italian titles are misleading, but, I suppose, requisite for the purpose of identification. The singing would be the better for a label of the same sort, being really too tame and dull for association with the naughty Duke of Verdi's *Rigoletto*.

Walter Widdop.—Another case of superfluous amplification! Can it be that the singer himself was responsible? It is quite possible, of course, that he addressed himself, not to the microphone, but to the amplifier, forgetful of the fact that the latter would be utterly unable to resist the force of his sublime appeal, as expressed in *Lend me your aid*. Well, aid was absurdly unnecessary; for tones more resonant and convincing were never put into Gounod's air by Edward Lloyd or Ben Davies in their prime. Then, again, when Mr. Widdop began his recitative by asserting the frailty and weakness of man, it struck me that he must really be trying to impose upon the credibility of the amplifier, which (or who) naturally knew better but nevertheless " obliged." In spite of this slight misunderstanding, there is no escaping the fact that this is an extremely fine record.

Renato Zanelli.—When an Otello—of Verdi's creation, I mean—is capable of imparting through the microphone the atmosphere of an actual stage performance, he must be a very good Otello indeed. Such, judging from these records of the two big monologues, I should imagine Renato Zanelli to be. His is a tenor voice of the genuine *robusto* type, carrying all the necessary weight and stamina for the task, together with the declamatory vigour, energy, and sense of contrast. He depicts here all the tortures of jealousy and remorse: in the first record, beginning calmly with suffering, resignation, restraint, and no little poetic feeling, afterwards working up to the tempest of savage outbursts natural to the Moor. The crescendo is splendidly done, even if the B flat at the end be not perfect. Then in the second record we get a no less artistic rendering of that touching lament beside the couch of the murdered Desdemona, rich in strong, expressive notes, mournful sobs, and the wonderful reminiscence of past joy in the great phrase, " Ancor un bacio," followed by all the realistic sighs and gasps of the dying warrior. Altogether a splendid reproduction.

Emanuele Salazar.—Now here I shall have to repeat myself almost word for word; that is, unless the intelligent reader will be good enough to spare me the trouble by accepting my assurance that Salazar is as good as Zanelli, and that the present selections from *Otello* are every bit as satisfying as the identical pair just noticed. Such an occurrence is very rare indeed—two recordings of the same magnificent scenes, each of the same supreme merit, and practically nothing to choose between them, excepting my own individual impression that the tones of Emanuele Salazar recall more closely those of the illustrious Tamagno, while on the other hand he may be a trifle less pathetic and lachrymose than his living rival. But he is every whit as strong and impressive, and for my own part if I wanted one man's record I would take care to possess myself, as a curiosity, of the other.

Nino Piccaluga.—Yet another exponent of Othello's death scene! It never rains but it pours; and this time it pours tears and misery by the bucketful. The trouble is that there is nothing manly or dignified about these ebullitions of grief. Can it be right, either, to address poor innocent Desdemona in scolding tones, as though it were her fault that she was a corpse? The whole business sounds to my ears dreadfully overdone. Signor Piccaluga's fine voice is employed to much better purpose in the *Ah! si ben mio*, which is very good indeed.

Armand Crabbé.—Artistic as he is, this clever French baritone somehow fails to persuade us (in his language) that the *Pagliacci Prologue* is really a melodramatic preface to a tragi-comedy. His story pursues its course evenly, but without contrast; where he should be lively he is dull, and where he should throw in a touch of colour he has none handy because he has used up his pigments *en masse*. As usual, his enunciation is faultless.

Heinrich Schlusnus.—Apparently this singer is as much at home in Lieder as in opera. At any rate, here are two of Schubert's choicest examples, rendered with tone of rich, round, satisfying quality, broad, intelligent phrasing, and a goodly measure of manly charm. The diction, too, is a delight. I wish I could say the same of the tone of the piano.

Friedrich Schorr.—The vocal characteristics of this double record of the " *Wahn* " *Monologue* are wholly irreproachable, and so are the orchestral, thanks to the self-evident care of Dr. Leo Blech, well supported by his men of the Berlin Staats-Oper. I love the leisurely, reposeful manner in which Hans Sachs here reflects good-humoredly upon the crass obstinacy and stupidity of his fellow Nurembergers, who refuse to acknowledge a genius when they see and hear one. My sole adverse criticism is that the accent with which some of the phrases are delivered sounds a trifle too refined, too pedantic and *précieux*, from the mouth of the worthy poet-cobbler. He may have thought like a poet, but he certainly must have spoken like an ordinary member of his Guild.

Giovanni Inghilleri.—Scarpia has no solos to sing, in the strict sense of the term ; but here are two excerpts, each long enough for one side of a disc, and vocal enough to show him off to advantage. Moreover, they contain (in the finale to the first act) the most grandiose and imposing music in an opera that has only his one ensemble, namely, the procession through the church whilst Scarpia, forgetful of his devotions, is hurling his " Va, Tosca," at the unsuspecting victim of his villainy. This tremendous combination of solo, chorus, organ, orchestra, and clanging church bells is pandemonium while it lasts ; but that is not very long, and I will admit that it comes out nearly as clear and comprehensible in this fine record as it does in the opera house. Signor Inghilleri sings forcibly and well in both items, but naturally gets his best chance in the page from the supper-table scene, when he informs the unlucky *cantatrice* of the nature of his price for sparing her lover.

Theodore Chaliapine.—These are two of the songs which, if I am not mistaken, the singer has more than once included in his Albert Hall recitals. How he sings them need not, therefore, be told. Enough that he seems to have been in splendid voice when he recorded them, and that all the well-known " effects " are realistically reproduced. The tone in the French song is of amazing clarity ; in the other there is an extraordinary variety of character and sentiment, while the *Old Corporal's* words of command are crisp and smart as ever.

Ivar Andrésen.—The basso with the big voice has exactly the right organ and manner for one of Loewe's old ballads. *Tom der Reimer* is one of the best of them (did you ever hear Sir George Henschel sing it ?), and in this record are contained all the poetry and romance, together with the swing and vigour of delivery that it demands. The tone is glorious, of course ; and one can imagine that it was with some such musical narrative, with lute accompaniment, that the troubadours and trouvères of old used to fascinate their listening multitudes.

HERMAN KLEIN.

※　　※　　※

ABRIDGED OPERAS

Polydor 95234–7 (four 12in., 26s.). *Der Freischütz* (Weber).

Polydor 95313–7 (five 12in., 32s. 6d.). *Die Fledermaus* (J. Strauss).

There was at one time such a run on " potted operas " that two or three of our leading publishers found it worth while to bring out special concert editions of certain vocal scores to meet the growing demand. No doubt they are still selling well. I may point out, however, that the nature of their condensation

lay in the dropping out of a number here and there, and the utilising of all " cuts " sanctioned by custom rather than the *potpourri* plan adopted in these latest Polydor records. Of the two methods I am inclined to prefer the latter. It calls for some ingenuity, as everyone knows who has listened to those popular American *mélanges* of favourite airs that lead into one another with a similarity which often proclaims their mutual indebtedness, and without respect to composers who may range from Handel to Haydn Wood. In an opera this plan facilitates the process of abbreviation in a wonderful way ; the short cuts enable one to cover the ground as it were on musical skis. Before you know it almost, the end of the second disc has brought you to the end of the first, and sometimes even the second, act of the opera ; and in less than half an hour, there you are, at the end of the whole affair. If you have missed a good deal, never mind ; presumably you had not time for more, and you can comfort yourself with the reflection that you have only missed the non-essentials. If you want the whole work (as I personally should) you can wait for the inevitable album. Only the wait may be a long one.

Polydor has issued in this way Weber's *Der Freischütz* and Johann Strauss's *Die Fledermaus*—a very excellent choice, too ! Both sung in German, they will naturally appeal most strongly to German ears, to which every note of the music and, indeed, every word of the spoken dialogue (there is quite a lot of it, by the way) are as familiar as are, let us say, the *Bohemian Girl* and *Maritana* over here. Nevertheless, the delightful music, despite its abbreviation, combined with the first-rate German singing, the equally good orchestral accompaniments, and the efficient (if occasionally over-amplified) recording combine to make these " Abridged Operas " a decidedly attractive feature. In view of the recent revival of *Der Freischütz* at the New Scala Theatre (noticed by the writer in another column) its arrival in this form at the present moment is something of a coincidence. Anyhow, it is welcome. Herein will be found a particularly fine Caspar, a vigorous and not too throaty Max, a charming Aennchen, a dramatic Agathe (with *Leise, leise* most amusingly curtailed), and quite a striking condensation of the weird music in the Wolf's Glen. In its no less consecutive shape the *Fledermaus* version reproduces all the gems of the " Waltz-King's " immortal operette, brimful of the most fascinating triple rhythms that the brain of dancing man ever conceived.

HERMAN KLEIN.

OPERATIC AND FOREIGN SONGS

LOTTE LEHMANN (soprano).—**How like a flower thou bloomest** and **Widmung, Dedication** (Schumann). In German with orchestra. Parlophone Odeon RO20102, 10in., 4s. 6d.

EMMY BETTENDORF (soprano).—**Ich liebe dich** (Grieg) and **Serenade, Leise flehen meine Lieder** (Schubert). In German with orchestra. Parlophone E10962, 12in., 4s. 6d.

JOHN McCORMACK (tenor) and **SALON GROUP** (male voices). —(*a*) **Holy Night,** (*b*) **The Trout,** (*c*) **Impromptu,** (*d*) **To the Lyre,** and (*a*) **Hark, hark the lark,** (*b*) **Hedge-Roses,** (*c*) **Who is Sylvia ?** (Schubert). Sung in English with orchestral accompaniment. H.M.V. DB1383, 12in., 8s. 6d.

JULIAN GIULIANI (barytone).—**Bartolo's Aria** from **The Barber of Seville** (Rossini) and **The Catalogue Song** from **Don Juan** (Mozart). Sung in Italian with orchestra. Parlophone E10963, 12in., 4s. 6d.

LOTTE LEHMANN (soprano), **RICHARD TAUBER** (tenor), **HANS LANGE** (tenor), **WALDEMAR STAEGEMANN**

(baritone), **KARIN BRANZELL** (contralto), **GRETE MERREM-NIKISCH** (soprano).—**Er ist Baron** and **Ein Fürstenkind** from **The Gypsy Baron** (J. Strauss). Sung in German, with chorus and orchestra conducted by Dr. Weissmann. Parlophone Odeon R20104, 12in., 6s. 6d.

ZONOPHONE LIGHT OPERA COMPANY.—Vocal Gems from **Maritana** (Wallace). In English with orchestral accompaniment. Zonophone A377, 12in., 4s.

FRANCESCO VADA (tenor).—**The Dream** from **Manon** (Massenet) and **La Danza** (Rossini). In English with orchestral accompaniment. Broadcast Twelve 5136, 10in., 2s.

Lotte Lehmann.—The accomplished Berlin soprano is continuing to record her well-chosen series of Lieder. This month she gives us two of Schumann's shortest and most popular favourites, both with orchestral and obbligato trimmings of the usual *ad captandum* order. *Du bist wie eine Blume* has a long prelude for violins and horn which does nothing beyond anticipating the singer and lengthening out the record. The *Widmung*, taken a trifle slower than usual, restores some of the piano accompaniment, and is all the better for it. Both Lieder are exquisitely sung—the first with a tender, wistful expression, the second in a vein of warmer passion and a very effective contrast in the E major passage, while the richness and depth of the low notes is quite surprising.

Emmy Bettendorf.—Here, again, we have familiar Lieder. The peerless Emmy no doubt feels as much at home in these as in opera, but for my own part I must confess to admiring her most in the latter. Take, for instance, her rendering of *Ich liebe dich*. It reveals little, if any, of the singer's customary sense of climax; the big phrase has no real crescendo, while the dotted note on the second syllable of *dich* is hurried and slurred over in the most unfortunate manner. The composer's wife used to broaden this out with an effect that was almost overwhelming. Much better, happily, is Fr. Bettendorf in the Schubert *Serenade*. She begins it with a strangely sweet and caressing *mezza voce*, accompanied by harp and the inevitable violin, which pops in and out like a clown in the harlequinade. Then in the second verse we get, I fancy, an oboe *obbligato* providing a not unwelcome change. Finally, the real Schubert emerges at last, with the singer at her very best, and one feels that for the sake of this moment the whole record has been worth while. Only, you must be prepared to wait for it.

John McCormack and the *Salon Group.*—I can only imagine that this perversion or *potpourri*, or whatever you care to call it, was suggested by *Lilac Time*. The two sides of the disc, sung by our Irish tenor with the complicity of his American friends (surely on the other side of the Atlantic, not at Hayes ?) contain exactly four short, familiar Schubert songs, separated by obtrusive interludes by the band and a (very) occasional murmuring of mysterious chords in the background by the Salon Group. These last also appear here and there in the songs, after the manner of those improvised " seconds " that used in my childhood to embellish the refrain of a sentimental ballad, as interpreted by the local vocalist at a Saturday " sing-song." Very nice and saccharine, of course ; but not even up to the *Lilac Time* level.

Julian Giuliani.—An excellent recording, this, of airs for Don Bartolo and Leporello that require first-rate singing to do them justice. Of the two, *Vi manca un foglio* comes off rather the better, because the singer—a low baritone with a telling, resonant organ—is more at home in Rossini than Mozart, whose glorious *Catalogo* demands a richer low register. Moreover, the quaint little leaps into *falsetto* that suit Don Bartolo and belong to the good old *buffo* style would be out of place in the mouth of Leporello ; and it is in the former that our soloist excels. He seems, indeed, to be a genuine

buffo artist, and for that reason I welcome the present record on at least the Rossinian side of it.

Johann Strauss Ensembles.—The art of " assembling " operatic parts to good practical purpose is well exemplified in these comic opera finales by the Viennese Waltz-King. They bring in all and sundry members of the cast, whom it pays to distribute among distinguished popular favourites. The better the singers the better the concrete evidence of their employment. Most of them in turn get a little bit of solo, wherein we at once recognise their voices—Lotte Lehmann's and Richard Tauber's, for instance. Then, when the whole of them get into full swing, the total effect is really big enough to carry you away. The *Zigeunerbaron*, which I saw at Vienna many years ago, was one of the best of the Strauss group of comic operas after the *Fledermaus* ; it contains fewer waltz tunes, but the polka and galop rhythms are irresistible.

Zonophone Light Opera Company.—In these *Vocal Gems from Maritana* we get another turn of the operatic kaleidoscope —rather a crude one, it is true, but still calculated to prove acceptable to the humble gramophonists who are not ashamed to own their admiration for Vincent Wallace. Identification of the cast is neither necessary nor desirable, as they say in France about the *recherche de la paternité* ; that being *chose défendue*. Enough that the dear old melodies, or as much of them as can be enclosed in the two sides of a 12in. record, emerge from their pigeon-holes with becoming promptness and fit into each other with the accuracy of a mosaic. The singing, on the whole, is quite creditable, the recording first-rate.

Francesco Vada.—Apparently an English tenor with an Italian name and training—a combination that used to be more common in the old days than it is now. He has a pleasant voice, not absolutely steady, but fairly clear and sympathetic ; diction being distinct and intonation accurate. The style is too heavy and ponderous to make the most of the *Dream* from *Manon*, while in *La Danza* it sounds rather halting and breathless. But the voice and the spirit are both there, and the Broadcast Twelve only costs you a couple of shillings.

HERMAN KLEIN.

OPERATIC AND FOREIGN SONGS

MARYSE BEAUJON (soprano).—**L'amour est une vertu rare** and **Dis-moi que je suis belle** from **Thais** (Massenet). Sung in French with orchestral accompaniment. Col. LX8, 12in., 6s. 6d.

OLGA OLGINA (soprano).—**The Nightingale (Solowej)** (Alabieff), sung in Russian, and **Caton** (Rozycki), sung in Polish, both with piano accompaniment by Leslie Heward. Decca M83, 10in., 3s.

SUZANNE BERTIN (soprano).—**Caro nome** from **Rigoletto** (Verdi) and **Jewel Song** from **Faust** (Gounod). The former sung in Italian and the latter in French, with orchestral accompaniment. Piccadilly 5005, 10in., 2s.

MURIEL BRUNSKILL (contralto).—**Gypsy Song, Act 2,** and **Card Song, Act 3,** from **Carmen** (Bizet). Sung in English with orchestral accompaniment. Col. DB30, 10in., 3s.

BENIAMINO GIGLI (tenor).—**Maria, Mari** (Di Capua) and **Quanno 'a Femmena Vo'** (V. de Crescenzo). Sung in Neapolitan with orchestral accompaniment. H.M.V. DA763 10in., 6s.

HEDDLE NASH (tenor).—**Shall I tell thee the name of thy lover ?** and **Dawn with her rosy mantle** from **The Barber of Seville** (Rossini). Sung in English, the former with harp accompaniment, the latter with orchestral accompaniment. Col. DX18, 12in., 4s. 6d.

Maryse Beaujon.—In the two principal airs sung by Thais Massenet strove with his accustomed sincerity to give fitting expression to the dramatic situation and the flow of the text. He succeeded much better, however, in the first than in the second—to name them in their present order, which is not that of the opera. I mention this because *L'amour est une vertu rare* is one of those semi-religious commentaries that create a sort of "goody-goody" feeling without really convincing one that the converted Egyptian courtezan could have "changed her spots" quite so suddenly. On the other hand, *Dis-moi que je suis belle* is a spontaneous outburst, and has genuine charm as well as melodic grace, altogether in the spirit of the lovely heathen praying to Venus to prolong her beauty into old age. It also affords a good chance to the singer, whereof Maryse Beaujon has availed herself as a sensible Thais should. She warbles it delightfully, with the purest of French diction and vocal style, and with none of the over-accentuation that disfigures the *vertu rare* of the conversion air. The recording is first-rate.

Olga Olgina.—Two very pretty songs, Russian and Polish respectively, sung with combined delicacy and dash by an accomplished soprano who is improving as she gets more used to the microphone. Leslie Heward's sure touch at the piano gives her confidence, and a bell-like voice skilfully used does the rest. *The Nightingale* is especially effective. The composer, Alabieff, flourished a century ago, and his song was made popular by great singers like Viardot, Patti, and Sembrich, who introduced it as a show-piece into the "Lesson Scene" in the *Barber of Seville*. *Caton* is an elegant air in waltz-time, with lots of pauses on high notes which the vocalist prolongs till she makes the listener feel as if out of breath from trying to "help her."

Suzanne Bertin.—Cheapness stands for nothing inferior in the way of quality in these reproductions of *Caro nome* and the *Jewel Song*. On the contrary, both are up to standard in most if not all respects. The singer's voice and style are typically French, and free from the least affectation, while being sufficiently brilliant to satisfy all reasonable requirements. The scale and head notes are pure and even, the shake is clear and neat, and the general effect is pleasing, with—in the *Jewel Song*—a good high B for the penultimate note.

Muriel Brunskill.—Average merit and careful vocalisation mark these records of the *Carmen* airs, which are sung, if I mistake not, to the old Hersée translation. The feature that most attracts is the lovely natural quality of the tone.

Beniamino Gigli.—Until this tenor, now so popular with American audiences, shows us what he is like at Covent Garden next month it is impossible for me to say how much or how little his seeming power is due to the aid of the amplifier. But I can at least perceive that he has a glorious voice and knows how to sing Neapolitan songs as one to the manner born. Both these specimens have a loud castanet and orchestra accompanying them, and the rhythms (triple in one case, tarantella-like in the other) are of the type dear to the Italian ear. So they will be, doubtless, to many British ears before they are much older.

Heddle Nash.—Lindoro's airs in the opening scene of the *Barber of Seville* demand great elegance and *aplomb*, allied to all the technique and control that the art of the singer can bring to bear. I am not sure that the former star of the Old Vic has yet thrown off certain little mannerisms of the old days sufficiently to realise the full beauty of the Rossinian school; but he is unquestionably moving in the right direction. Considering what a dreadful version of the text he has employed in order to sing these airs in English, he has perhaps acquitted himself of a difficult task rather better than might have been expected. At any rate, he phrases with tolerable

freedom whilst preserving a metronomic regularity of tempo, and sings with taste as well as expression and impeccable intonation. His ornaments are fairly traditional, though not always correctly turned; but altogether I fancy the balance of these critical remarks weighs in favour of the artist.

FRANK TITTERTON (tenor).—**Your tiny hand is frozen** from **La Bohème** (Puccini) and **Flower Song** from **Carmen** (Bizet). Sung in English with orchestral accompaniment. Decca K505, 12in., 3s. 6d.

FRITZ WOLFF (tenor).—**Der letzte Grub** (Levi-Eichendorff) and **Mädele, guck' raus** (Vollmer-Grimmiger). Sung in German with orchestral accompaniment. Polydor 90082, 10in.

HEINRICH SCHLUSNUS (baritone).—**Lacrimae Christi** (Carl Bohm) and **Das Herz am Rhein** (Hill-Dippel). Sung in German with orchestral accompaniment. Polydor B2275, 10in.

SYDNEY DE VRIES (baritone).—**Prologue** from **Pagliacci** (Leoncavallo). Sung in English with orchestral accompaniment. Piccadilly 5009, 10in., 2s.

JOSEPH FARRINGTON (baritone).—**Song of the flea** (Moussorgsky) and **Vulcan's song** from **Philemon et Baucis** (Gounod). Sung in English with orchestral accompaniment. Piccadilly 5011, 10in., 2s.

ARTHUR FEAR (bass-baritone).—**It is now (Eri Tu)** from **The Masked Ball** (Verdi) and **Your honour ! Ruffians ! (Honour Song)** from **Falstaff** (Verdi). Sung in English with orchestral accompaniment. H.M.V. C1822, 12in., 4s. 6d.

FRANK TITTERTON (tenor) and **ROY HENDERSON** (bass).—**Ah ! Mimi, tu più non torni** from **La Bohème** (Puccini) and **Solenne in quest' ora** from **La Forza del Destino** (Verdi). Sung in Italian with orchestral accompaniment. Decca K506, 12in., 3s. 6d.

ENRICO CARUSO (tenor).—**Deh ! ch'io ritorni** from **L'Africana** (Meyerbeer) and **Addio** (Tosti). Sung in Italian with orchestral accompaniment. H.M.V. DB1386, 12in., 8s. 6d.

ZONOPHONE LIGHT OPERA COMPANY.—**Vocal Gems** from **Les Cloches de Corneville** (Planquette). Sung in English with orchestral accompaniment. Zonophone A384, 12in., 4s. 6d.

Frank Titterton.—An improvement is to be noted in the recording art of this tenor, and I do not hesitate to attribute it to the more careful regard for important *nuances* of delivery and diction that has been suggested at various times and by various critics, including myself. The voice is fine enough to deserve only the best of treatment, the most refined of methods; and both seem to be coming along, though a suspicion of the old roughness may crop up occasionally. The sibilants must be made yet stronger, the vowels pronounced with fewer diphthongs; while a climax like that towards the end of the *Flower Song* should have the ring of true passion, spontaneous and irresistible, not a mere calm flow of nice steady tone. Recording excellent.

Fritz Wolff.—An extremely pleasant voice and not too German method came out well in these songs, to which the manly tone is pure and musical enough to lend a certain charm. I like the Swabian serenade, with its pretty, love-pleading *volkslied* tune; while the music of the *Letzte Grub*, if not particularly high-class, is at least melodious and taking.

Heinrich Schlusnus.—Here, again, Polydor employs an artist of high rank to impart distinction to ordinary music. Carl Bohm is not precisely another Carl Loewe, but his imitations of the old German ballad have the same rhythmical, diatonic, free-and-easy flow, and they are doubly enjoyable to those familiar with the national legends of romantic mediæval times upon which they are mostly based. In other words, they tell a good story to appropriate music, and a thorough tist like Heinrich Schlusnus makes them sound even better an they are.

Sydney de Vries.—The whole of the *Prologue* for two shillings does not sound dear. On the contrary it may be recommended as good value, seeing that the piece is dramatically sung, with a successful attempt at contrast and colourful expression. The enunciation is on the whole clear, but it could be made better still if the r's were more strongly rolled where they are required to join words or syllables together. There is also plenty of time to make everything heard at the leisurely pace (wisely) adopted by the singer. He has a capital organ and gives out a good G to ring up the curtain. The orchestral accompaniment is quite well done.

Joseph Farrington.—Also from Piccadilly come these capital reproductions of popular bass airs, both of which I seem to have heard from the same singer on a previous occasion, perhaps on the wireless. Of course they are none the worse for that. One can always enjoy the bizarre Mephistophelean flavour that he puts into the satirical laugh in the *Song of the Flea*. The humour of *Vulcan's Song* is not yet quite cynical enough—it is too straightforward and matter of fact. On the whole, however, both are admirably sung.

Arthur Fear.—At present it strikes me that Mr. Fear is a too variable artist. Certain things he does wonderfully well ; others he does equally badly. In this instance he exemplifies his variability by an extremely feeble, uninteresting performance (in English) of *Eri tu*, and follows it up with a no less vigorous, subtle, masterful interpretation of the *Honour Song* from *Falstaff*. The latter part he has done on the stage, I know ; but I am not sure that he has ever attempted Renato. If he has, it is the more astonishing that he should appear to have so inadequate an acquaintance with the dramatic purport of the scene. Even the singing is feeble and devoid of significance. Yet would I gladly buy the record for the sake of the splendid Falstaff.

Frank Titterton and *Roy Henderson.*—The voices blend exceedingly well in the duet from *Bohème;* less well in that from *La Forza del Destino*. It is curious how one misses the authority and decision of the reading that Italians can give of this mid-Verdi music. I make no comparisons between the two singers, beyond saying that the tenor sounds more at home in the Puccini duet, while the baritone is equally alert in both. The hand of *Destino* is nevertheless decidedly lacking in the necessary *Forza*.

Enrico Caruso.—This air from *L'Africaine* follows directly after the *Paradiso* in the fourth act, but is not nearly so beautiful or so hackneyed. Its robust style suited Caruso exactly, and I am glad he made a record of it—particularly one so finely phrased and characteristic of the lamented tenor as this is. Presumably he made it in New York, and the present issue is an electrical re-recording of it. The declamatory power of the high B's and B flats is simply astonishing. The chorus is eliminated, and no one would miss it who was not familiar with the opera, wherein Caruso was wont to prove himself a superb Meyerbeerian singer. This welcome record happily survives to demonstrate the fact. On the reverse side is an Italian version of Tosti's *Good-bye*, but about that the less said the better.

Zonophone Light Opera Company.—The voices in this selection from Planquette's *Cloches de Corneville* might be of better quality without being too good for the music. I find them on the whole rather coarse, and the diction in one or two conspicuous instances is lacking in refinement. The

Serpolette and the chorus and orchestra are fairly satisfactory ; the men are the sinners. The still-popular tunes will doubtless please, but my impression is that 4s. is a somewhat stiff price to ask for a record that does not begin to compare with the German *operette* selections. The British article stands no chance of competing successfully with superior foreign examples of the same kind of thing.

CONCHITA SUPERVIA (soprano).—**Know'st thou the land** and (with **V. Bettoni**) **The Swallow Duet** from **Mignon** (Thomas). Sung in Italian with orchestral accompaniment. Parlophone Odeon R20105, 12in., 6s. 6d.

NINON VALLIN (soprano).—**Solveig's Song** from **Peer Gynt** (Grieg) and **Chant Hindou** from **Sadko** (Rimsky-Korsakov). Sung in French with pianoforte accompaniment. Parlophone Odeon R20106, 6s. 6d.

EMMY BETTENDORF (soprano).—**The Merry Widow** (Lehar and (with female chorus) **Tarrying gently** (Schubert). Sung in German with orchestral accompaniment. Parlophone E10974, 12in., 4s. 6d.

META SEINEMEYER (soprano) and **TINO PATTIERA** (tenor). —**Sweetest maid in the moonlight** from **La Bohème** (Puccini) and **Say not so** from **Andrea Chénier** (Giordano). Parlophone E10976, 12in., 4s. 6d.

MARCEL WITTRISCH (tenor).—**O Maiden, my maiden** (Lehar) and **A boy saw a rose-bush** (Lehar). Sung in German with orchestral accompaniment. H.M.V. C1843, 12in., 4s. 6d.

Conchita Supervia.—The Mignon has such an extremely pretty voice that it seems a pity she cannot keep it steadier ; but what I might term a " permanent vibrato " is a hard defect to overcome. She records a lovely timbre, though, and does it with any amount of emotional atmosphere, which makes her *Connais-tu* more than acceptable in its Italian guise. In the *Swallow Duet* the baritone takes a creditable part.

Ninon Vallin.—French is a wonderful singing language in the mouth of such an artist as this. She achieves the ideal union of voice and words, and thus imparts a certain freshness of charm even to old friends like *Solveig* and *Sadko*. If there be a fault in the Grieg song it is that the refrain is not sufficiently warbled—as, for instance, is that of the Rimsky-Korsakov, which sounds simply adorable. The tone in the former is over-dark and the D natural covered too much.

Emmy Bettendorf.—Whatever its actual source, the Schubert solo with chorus of female voices is a delightful *trouvaille*, and we ought to be very grateful for it—certainly I am. Anything more exquisitely fairylike in its lightness and delicacy it would be impossible to imagine. But for certain characteristic modulations I should have been as ready to attribute it to Mendelssohn as to Schubert. Anyhow its charm is undeniable, and the added grace and refinement of Emmy Bettendorf and her companions make it wholly irresistible. After—or even before—such a jewel as this, even the lively *Merry Widow* loses something of her sparkle and fire.

Meta Seinemeyer and *Tino Pattiera.*—The *Andrea Chénier* is the more successful of these two duets. Even Meta Seinemeyer, with all her talent, which we so much admired, could make the mistake of treating Mimi as a doleful, tragic young person ; while the painter whom she loved was, according to Tino P., an excessively throaty young man. Yet, turn from Giordano to Puccini, and all is changed. Both voices come out in their true colours, and you have a positively splendid rendering of the scene, with Meta Seinemeyer quite at her best, which, as you are aware, was a treat worth enjoying.

Marcel Wittrisch.—Inasmuch as the good German tenors are all trying their hands (profitably, I imagine) at the masterpieces of Franz Lehar, no apology is necessary for reviewing these H.M.V. examples in a column so appreciative as mine. Indeed, of their kind they are extremely satisfying, and I have not the slightest hesitation in recommending them accordingly. HERMAN KLEIN.

OPERATIC AND FOREIGN SONGS

ELISABETH SCHUMANN (soprano).—**Mein Herr Marquis** from Act 2 and **Spiel' ich die Unschuld vom Lande** from Act 3 of **Die Fledermaus** (Johann Strauss). In German, with orchestral accompaniment. H.M.V. E545, 10in., 4s. 6d.

MARIA OLCZEWSKA (soprano).—**Sapphische Ode** and **Die Mainacht** (Brahms). In German, with piano accompaniment (George Reeves). H.M.V. E546, 10in., 4s. 6d.

FANNY HELDY (soprano).—**Je veux vivre,** Waltz Song from **Roméo et Juliette** (Gounod) and **Depuis le jour** from **Louise** (Charpentier). In French, with orchestral accompaniment. H.M.V. DB1304, 12in., 8s. 6d.

BENIAMINO GIGLI (tenor).—**O Paradiso** from **L'Africana** (Meyerbeer) and **M'appari** from **Marta** (Flotow). In Italian, with orchestral accompaniment. H.M.V. DB1382, 12in., 8s. 6d.

RENATO ZANELLI (tenor).—**Improvviso**—**Un dì all' azzurro spazio** and **Si fù soldato** from **Andrea Chénier** (Giordano). In Italian, with orchestral accompaniment. H.M.V. DB1339, 12in., 8s. 6d.

FRIEDRICH SCHORR (baritone).—**Die Frist ist um!** from **Der Fliegende Holländer** (Wagner). Two parts, in German, with orchestral accompaniment. H.M.V. D1813, 12in., 6s. 6d.

IVAR ANDRÉSEN (bass).—**Ansprache des Königs** from **Lohengrin** (Wagner) and **Ansprache des Landgrafen** from **Tannhäuser** (Wagner). In German, with orchestral accompaniment. H.M.V. C1853, 12in., 4s. 6d.

Elisabeth Schumann.—Like a breath of fresh spring air wafted through an open window is the refreshing sound of these tuneful numbers from *Die Fledermaus,* the famous operette of Johann Strauss which is so soon to be revived at Covent Garden with the more or less Viennese star cast now on the spot. To hear Elisabeth Schumann sing *Mein Herr Marquis* and *Spiel'ich die Unschuld vom Lande* is to understand how impossible it is for this sort of thing to be well and truly done by any but natives initiated and trained in the Viennese school. Her rendering of them is simply delicious. The first is a genuine specimen of the Strauss waltz, warbled with bird-like tone—a saucy, railing, mocking-bird tone—and garnished with a hundred different embellishments. The other a merry tune in a swinging six-eight rhythm, with runs, scales, staccatos, elegant *fiorituri,* rippling laughs and sly *portamenti,* all executed in a clear musical voice with the perfection of neatness. Karl Alwin's accompaniments are worthy of the singer, and the recording is equally so.

Maria Olczewska.—Here are two of Brahms's most celebrated songs, interpreted by an artist whom we all love to listen to. Whilst the voice is beautiful and the shading of *nuances* delightfully smooth, one longs sometimes for a warmth of feeling that plumbs more deeply still the depths of intense passion—in the *Sapphische Ode* even more than the *Mainacht.* The words, too, often lack graphic utterance, and the distinctive grip of the German consonants, being mostly enunciated

with the soft Slavonic glide of the Polish accent. One admires the clean-cut phrasing; forgives the breath being *before* instead of *after* the *mich* in the second verse of the *Ode;* and asks why the important long-sustained E flat in the *Mainacht* should not be as perfectly in tune as the rest of the song? Yet the record as a whole is an admirable example of liedersinging.

Fanny Heldy.—Clarity and a pure, penetrating tone are always to be expected from this talented French soprano, together with a highly-finished vocal technique. Variety of dramatic expression does not emerge so generously from her gramophone as from her stage work. Nevertheless it is a pleasure, even a privilege, to listen to oft-ill-used pieces like the valse air from *Roméo* and *Depuis le jour* when sung with the faultless execution of a Fanny Heldy. I, for one, do not ask for more than what seems to me the maximum of charm and effect.

Beniamino Gigli.—Everything it is necessary to say about the new tenor's records has already been written in these pages. The next thing will be to judge of the man himself. Meanwhile his *M'appari* affords a good idea of the reasons that have led to the promised revival of *Marta* during the forthcoming Italian season. His tone sounds nearly if not quite as glorious as Caruso's, and there are points of close resemblance in the timbre as well as in the mode of enunciating the language. This last similarity is even more noticeable in the *Paradiso* air, which Gigli sings and phrases very finely indeed.

Renato Zanelli.—The model here is not Caruso but Tamagno, though I don't think the latter ever sang in *Andrea Chénier,* the two best tenor airs from which are included in this record. Like his distinguished prototype, Zanelli is a genuine *tenore robusto di forza,* possessed of untiring energy and an organ capable of resisting any amount of strain. His production is more "open" than Gigli's, and consequently less refined in quality; but it is admirably adapted for music like this of Giordano's, and, notwithstanding a liberal dose of "amplifying," the net result is tolerably free from exaggeration. Anyhow it produces a vivid sample of strenuous and splendid declamation.

Friedrich Schorr.—The part of Vanderdecken is generally reckoned to be among this artist's very best. His most important solo in Wagner's Dutch opera is that which he has here recorded with such perfect realisation of the conflicting emotions that beset the unhappy hero, when he steps ashore after his prescribed interval to search for the woman who shall prove "faithful unto death." The style is noble and elevated, the expression tragic and impressive in its significance, the diction broad and measured. The voice suggests the stormy mood and the hungry yearning for peace and rest; in a word, it reflects alike the man and the music. Schorr is a great artist.

Ivar Andrésen.—Both these familiar excerpts from *Lohengrin* and *Tannhäuser* receive an interpretation full of beauty and contrast, the latter being, if anything, the quality that one gets most rarely in their rendering. I have nothing fresh to say about the voice and art of this accomplished basso, who, as I think I have previously remarked, reminds me in many respects of the incomparable Edouard de Reszke. Certainly there is no other singer now living or before the public who comes so near to the level of that lamented artist or indeed to the level, for grandeur of sonority and warm richness of the organ, exemplified by Ivar Andrésen himself. He is in a class by himself, a singer *hors ligne,* with an altogether marvellous control over a huge volume of tone. He uses it in a darker timbre for the Landgrave than for Henry the Fowler—an effect that is new to me; but gradually it becomes more genial and in the end it softens into a tender *mezza voce* that is quite lovely.

475

FERNANDO AUTORI (bass).—**Slander's Whisper (La Calunnia)** from **Barber of Seville** (Rossini) and **Catarina, while you play at sleeping (Vous qui faites l'endormie)** from **Faust** (Gounod). In English, with orchestral accompaniment. H.M.V. C1842, 12in., 4s. 6d.

HERBERT JANSSEN (baritone).—**Valentin's Gebet (Even bravest heart)** and **Valentin's Tod (Death of Valentine)** from **Faust** (Gounod). In German, with orchestral accompaniment. H.M.V. C1852, 12in., 4s. 6d.

ROSA PONSELLE (soprano).—**Tu che invoco** and **O Nume tutelar** from Act 2, **La Vestale** (Spontini). In Italian, with orchestral accompaniment. H.M.V. DB1274, 12in., 8s. 6d.

ROSA PONSELLE (soprano).—**Songs my mother taught me** (Dvorak) and **Since first I met thee** (Rubinstein, arr. Watson). H.M.V. DA1023, 10in., 6s.

BENIAMINO GIGLI (tenor) and **EZIO PINZA** (bass).—**Giusto Cielo! Rispondete** and **Tu che a Dio spiegasti** from Act 4, **Lucia di Lammermoor** (Donizetti). In Italian, with orchestral accompaniment. H.M.V. DB1229, 12in., 8s. 6d.

IRENE MENGHINI CATTANEO (mezzo-soprano).—**Aprile foriero (Printemps qui commence)** and **Amor! i miei sini proteggi (Amour, viens aider)** from **Samson et Dalila** (Saint-Saëns). In Italian, with orchestral accompaniment. H.M.V. DB1332, 12in., 8s. 6d.

GIOVANNI INGHILLERI (baritone).—**Pari siamo** from **Rigoletto** (Verdi) and **Eri tu** from **Un Ballo in Maschera** (Verdi). In Italian, with orchestral accompaniment. H.M.V. D1823, 12in., 6s. 6d.

BIANCA SCACCIATI (soprano) and **FRANCESCO MERLI** (tenor).—**Vicino a te** and **La nostra morte** from Act 2, **Andrea Chénier** (Giordano). In Italian, with orchestral accompaniment. Col. LX12, 12in., 6s. 6d.

IVA PACETTI (soprano).—**Pace, mio Dio** from **La Forza del Destino** (Verdi) and **La mamma morta** from **Andrea Chénier** (Giordano). In Italian, with orchestral accompaniment. Col. LX11, 12in., 6s. 6d.

Deh! non volerli vittime from **Norma** (Bellini). Two parts, in Italian, with orchestral accompaniment. Col. LB1, 10in., 4s. 6d.

Fernando Autori.—Neither the intelligence of the artist nor the ease that comes of long experience can altogether hide the faults of his English accent, which—he being merely human —frequently betrays his Italian origin. The drawback is slight, however, when weighed against the amount of enjoyment that is to be derived from listening to such a sympathetic voice and excellent singing. The *Calunnia* (*Slander*) air is especially good.

Herbert Janssen.—Over-amplification has resulted here in a rather rough, noisy Valentine, with a degree of prolonged resonant power in the death scene that is decidedly phenomenal in a soldier who has been mortally wounded. *Even bravest heart may swell* under such circumstances; and it does so. The singer uses a bold dramatic method, but Gounod would have objected to the number of notes that he alters to suit his voice

Rosa Ponselle.—Recent revivals in New York, Milan, and elsewhere have drawn attention to Spontini's remarkable opera *La Vestale*, the masterpiece of the Roman composer who was practically the inventor of real grand opera as developed by Meyerbeer, Halévy, Rossini, and Wagner (*Rienzi*). Spontini was favoured by the protection of Napoleon and the Empress Joséphine, and under their auspices *La Vestale* was produced at the Paris Opéra in 1807. The airs sung by Rosa Ponselle are the most beautiful things in the score. They demand precisely the qualities that she exhibited in her singing of *Casta Diva* and the rest of the *Norma* music; and they receive it in opulent measure. Nothing could well be more delightful or satisfying than her tone and phrasing in these long-drawn melodies which seem to contain in them the very essence of the Bellini school. In the songs by Dvorak and Rubinstein on the smaller disc her art is notable for its charm and grace, but not for a similar perfection of classical purity, elegance and refinement. In a word, she seems less at home and at her ease in the Slavonic lied than in the old Italian aria. But her voice in either or any is a never-ending joy.

Beniamino Gigli and *Ezio Pinza.*—As everyone knows, the final scene in *Lucia di Lammermoor* represents the family graveyard whither Edgardo hies him to commit *hari-kari* upon the tombs of his ancestors. The tenor is Gigli; while Pinza and the chorus of the Metropolitan Opera House impersonate the faithful servitor and the sedate gentry of the surrounding neighbourhood who calmly watch his last moments. They also revel in some of the most familiar but ravishing melodies that Donizetti ever penned, and regale their ears with notes of the same glorious quality. All who listen to this faultless record can do likewise.

Irene M. Cattaneo.—A good mezzo-soprano voice, deprived of much of its naturally rich, velvety timbre by an incessant *vibrato*. More than once already have I had occasion to notice this annoying defect in the same artist's gramophone work, and it is doubly regrettable because she is experienced and dramatic in a more than common degree. Indeed, few Italian Dalilas know so well how to declaim her invocation to the Philistine gods; while Mr. John Barbirolli's reading of the orchestral part is admirable in both airs.

Giovanni Inghilleri.—Here we have not only a splendid singer, but the real traditional rendering of *Eri tu*. It may well serve as a model, to be studied and imitated by the many bold and adventurous baritones who "fancy themselves" in Verdi's exacting air, and approach it in the light, cheerful spirit that I have so often had reason to deprecate. If they listen "with all their ears" and a modest resolution to profit thereby, I for one promise to accord them the fullest credit for any and every faithful imitation that comes my way. Let them notice in particular the dramatic intensity and truthfulness of the whole thing, and the many individual touches that lend an enhanced significance to the wonderful changes of mood which it portrays. The *Pari siamo* is also quite first-rate.

Bianca Scacciati and *Francesco Merli.*—The final duet for the hero and heroine is one of those straightforward but strenuous pieces that make the popularity of Giordano's opera in Italy easy to understand. You can follow the diatonic idiom of the music and hear your protagonists exerting themselves without the smallest effort on your own part—*dolce far niente* personified, in fact. The singers are both splendid workers, and a disc with two fine records is the result.

Iva Pacetti.—A typical up-to-date Italian soprano with all the *défauts de ses qualités*. She scoops, she slurs, and she trembles; but she has a voice that appeals to and attracts you. What a pity that all things are not equal in this case! But at any rate, they move on the up-grade. The *Norma* is indifferent; the *Forza del Destino* good; the *Andrea Chénier* quite up to "top-notch."

HELENE CALS (soprano).—**Il Bacio** (Arditi), in Italian, and **Je suis Titania, Polonaise** from **Mignon** (Thomas) in French, with orchestral accompaniment. Parlophone E10990, 12in., 4s. 6d.

SUZANNE BERTIN (soprano).—**Rêves de Printemps** (Johann Strauss) in Italian, and **Waltz Song** from **Roméo et Juliette** (Gounod) in French, with orchestral accompaniment. Piccadilly 5018, 10in., 2s.

MARIA VON BASILIDES (mezzo-soprano).—**Ave Maria** (Bach-Gounod) and **Geistliches Wiegenlied** (Brahms). In German with instrumental accompaniment. Parlophone E10989, 12in., 4s. 6d.

ERIC ENDERLEIN (tenor).—**Forging Song** from **Siegfried** (Wagner) and **Spring Song** from **Die Walküre** (Wagner). In German, with piano accompaniment. Piccadilly 5020, 10in., 2s.

LENGHI CELLINI (tenor).—**O Colombina** and **Vesti la Giubba** from **Pagliacci** (Leoncavallo). In Italian, with orchestral accompaniment. Piccadilly 5019, 10in., 2s.

IVAR ANDRESEN (bass).—**Ein feste Burg** from **Les Huguenots** (Meyerbeer) and **Ein furchtbares Verbrechen** from **Tannhäuser** (Wagner). In German, with orchestral accompaniment. Col. LX13, 12in., 6s. 6d.

Mlle FERALDY (soprano) and **GEORGES THILL** (tenor).—**Le Tombeau Scene** from **Roméo et Juliette** (Gounod). In French, with orchestral accompaniment. Col. LX14–15, 12in., 6s. 6d. each.

ELISABETH KUHNLEIN (soprano), **ALFHILD PETZET** (soprano), and **PAULA LINDBERG** (mezzo).—**Prelude and Song of the Rhine Daughters** from **Götterdämmerung** (Wagner). In German, with orchestral accompaniment. Parlophone E10987–88, 12in., 4s. 6d. each.

Sir GEORGE HENSCHEL (baritone).—**Wait thou still** (traditional) and **By the waters of Babylon** (Dvorak). Accompanied by himself. Col. LB3, 10in., 4s. 6d.

CARLO MORELLI (baritone).—**Il Sogno (The Dream of Cassio)** and **FRANCESCO MERLI** (tenor) **Ora e per sempre addio** from **Otello** (Verdi). In Italian, with orchestral accompaniment. Col. LB2, 10in., 4s. 6d.

Hélène Cals.—A German *soprano leggiero* of ability, and evidently proficient in all the mechanical arts associated with her *métier*. She uses her flexible voice with skill and neatness, and she climbs her heights with unflagging energy. The *Titania* air is the better varied and cleverer effort of the two.

Suzanne Bertin.—A French soprano of the same type, but a more vivacious and brilliant executant. She also offers a couple of effective examples well recorded on a smaller disc at less than half the price, which is worth consideration. Her head notes are birdlike, and her staccato crisp and clear, but she also might display more contrast.

Maria von Basilides.—The singing of this lady is unfortunately dull; her manner hesitating and nervous; her breathing obviously faulty. Yet her voice sounds sweet and sympathetic enough to merit superior treatment. In the Brahms *Wiegenlied* one perceives intelligence, but little else; while in the *Ave Maria* the violin obbligato steps into the foreground and you hear less than you should of the actual soloist. Why this lack of discretion?

Eric Enderlein.—No matter how cheap the article, it is a mistake in these days to record Wagner, or any sort of big operatic music, with only a piano accompaniment. It is an even worse mistake to issue inadequate and incorrect labels. The *Spring Song* is not from *Siegfried* but from *Die Walküre*, and the *Forging Song* (whereof this represents about one-third) is sung so slowly to its tinkling piano accompaniment that it almost escapes recognition. Herr Enderlein is evidently of the genuine *Heldentenor* species, and good enough to insist on fairer treatment.

Lenghi Cellini.—It is always safe to rely on this artist for an individual reading as well as a dramatic one. He goes straight to the heart of the matter, and his experience enables him to surmount most of his difficulties. His *Vesti la giubba* is as earnest as his Harlequin's song is light.

Ivar Andrésen.—Once more our old friend the Landgrave, but at a later juncture in the story, just after Tannhäuser's "unpardonable crime" in offending the susceptibilities of the modest dames at the Wartburg. He starts off in angry mood with tones sufficiently stentorian to quell a Gandhi crowd caught in the act of making salt, then softens down into his lenient sentence of a year's exile as a Roman pilgrim. Equally fine is Andrésen in the Meyerbeer setting of Luther's immortal hymn. Altogether an interesting combination, and well recorded in the bargain.

Feraldy and *Georges Thill.*—The Tomb Scene in *Roméo* is one of Gounod's happiest inspirations and in its way as dramatic, to my thinking, as the Prison Scene in *Faust*. The duet takes two discs and four sides to hold it; but the investment is eminently worth while when recorded by two such splendid singers as these.

Elisabeth Kuhnlein, Alfhild Petzet, and Paula Lindberg.—This excerpt from *Götterdämmerung* also requires a double allowance of space. It comprises the whole of the scene between Siegfried and the Rhinemaidens in Act III., with the part of the hero neatly eliminated. The fine orchestra of the Berlin State Opera, under Max von Schillings, atones for that omission, but unluckily it cannot make amends for the refusal of the three female voices to blend harmoniously. Particularly noticeable is the nasal, reedy tone of the Flosshilde (the mezzo-soprano), who upsets the balance of the trio by using a forced chest quality and singing slightly sharp most of the time. This might be excusable whilst swimming about in the Rhine, but from the calm waters of the Berlin Opera House one expects a smoother adjustment of timbres. Otherwise it is a pleasure to hear the glorious music so worthily played.

Sir George Henschel.—The label tells us that Sir George was 79 years old when he sang and accompanied himself in these two songs. It is certainly a remarkable achievement as well as a welcome souvenir of a unique talent. The voice is clear and steady, the enunciation wonderfully distinct, and the interpretation—notably of the Dvorák—artistic in the extreme.

Carlo Morelli and *Francesco Merli.*—The Dream, of course, is not really Cassio's, but the fabrication of Iago's wicked mind, invented for the purpose of increasing Othello's jealousy. Maurel originated the vocal rendering, just as Tamagno created the style of delivery for his great outburst in the *Ora e per sempre addio*. Present-day singers can only hope to approach, but not surpass, those memorable efforts of a past epoch; and the two represented by this record have contrived, like good golfers, to manage their "approach" very well indeed.

HERMAN KLEIN.

NEW JEWISH RECORDS

The **Jewish National Choir** of New York has recently made some half a dozen 10in. records of traditional and other folk-songs which appear to be of Polish provenance, and therefore form a suitable addition to the collections of the same sort already published in this country by the Columbia Company. The most interesting of the group are the more serious numbers, in which the voices of the choir take a prominent part. Though sung in Yiddish, they are nevertheless of a purely Hebrew type, devotional or quasi-devotional in character, and full of those touching Eastern cadences that appeal to the general musical ear as much as to the Jewish. The first example, *Fregt die Welt* (DB64) is made striking from the opening bar by its curious staccato effect of repeated chords, with a real silence in between. This is executed with great precision, faultless intonation, and clever nuances of light and shade. The second, on the reverse side, begins with a melancholy soprano solo of typical Hebrew character (drawn-out melody, sudden sforzandos, and so forth), sung by **Sophie Kemper** in a clear, plaintive tone, marred by the customary tremolo. This is called *Moischelach un Shloimelach*, and is given in the distinctive Yiddish intonation, which is largely nasal.

The Passover Chant *Chad-Gad-Yo* (DB65) is an old but not precisely ancient tune, sung mostly in unison by female and male voices in turn and with a capital swing. On the other side is a folk-song with a long title, and another soprano solo, which a young lady named **Sonia Gladstone** warbles in a voice and style very much akin to that of Miss Kemper. But happily the solo work is not the predominant feature of the more interesting of these records, and they can be thoroughly enjoyed for the sake of their individual beauty as specimens of true Hebraic folk-song. As for the efforts of the Vilna comic artist, **Peisachke Burstein,** they will doubtless appeal (DB66–8) to lovers of the strident and noisy, and even more to ears that are able to grasp the meaning of the humorous language which the singer pronounces with such gusto. Some have a choral refrain, some have not ; but all are very lively in their different dance-rhythms, wherein the quick 2–4 polka is the prevailing strain.

Of another type altogether are the two fine old traditional tunes reproduced on the last disc (DB69). These obviously belong to the purest type of Jewish liturgy, and, declaimed (or cantillated) as they are with intense devotional expression by **Cantor A. Fuchsmann** (piano accompaniment), they are well worth listening to. The *Zadik Katomor* is especially touching, for the singer has a voice of excellent quality when not too throaty, with the racial facility for employing a beautiful trill and strong, clear declamation. The recording of the whole selection is irreproachable.

HERMAN KLEIN.

H.M.V. "PAGLIACCI" ALBUM

The continued popularity of Leoncavallo's one successful opera rests upon a solid and safe foundation. Thirty-eight years have elapsed since it was first produced at the Teatro del Verme, Milan, and one year less since it was first given at Covent Garden in the presence and with the co-operation of the composer. Well do I recall the curiosity which it excited. The idea of " a play within a play " was at least as old as " Hamlet," if not a good deal older ; but the treatment in this instance was novel, on account of the fact that the time-worn Italian stage story of the deception of Pagliaccio by Columbine and Harlequin had been varied by making a handsome outsider the lover, and thus importing into the mock action the elements of a real tragedy. To add to its dramatic force, Leoncavallo, who was his own librettist, brought into prominence the secret passion of Pantaloon (Tonio) for Canio's spouse, with the motives of jealousy and revenge that lead to the discovery of her intended elopement and the final catastrophe which follows. Swift, picturesque melodrama such as this is of the very essence of effective Verdian opera.

The H.M.V. recording of this work fulfils the ideal that the present writer has more than once insisted upon, namely, that it should be executed by Italian performers amidst a thoroughly Italian colouring and atmosphere. Not that an equally perfect English rendering would not answer the same purpose in a purely musical or even vocal sense (an achievement I have yet, however, to come across), but that it would still be lacking in the indefinable something which we recognize as the native touch. Operas as rich in local colour as *Pagliacci*, *Cavalleria* and *Tosca*, for instance, absolutely require this, just as much as an opera like *Hugh the Drover* demands the personality and accent of British interpreters. It is therefore a wise policy on the part of the leading gramophone companies to go for these albums to the country from which the original work emanated. The present example comes from Milan, where it was performed by the chorus and orchestra of La Scala, under the direction of Maestro Sabajno, with the following cast : Nedda, Adelaide Saraceni ; Canio, Alessandro Valente ; Tonio, Apollo Granforte ; Peppe, Nello Palai ; Silvio, Leonildo Basi. It is recorded on nine double-sided plum label, 12in., discs (Nos. C1829–37), and also is available coupled in sequence (Nos. C7049–57) for use with H.M.V. automatic models.

In detail there is little to be said, and in that little still less save by way of praise. Italian women singers nowadays are so inferior on the whole to the men that no surprise will be felt if I say that I do not care so much for the Nedda as for her companions, who are one and all first-rate. The Prologue lends the key-note of distinction to the rest ; for Apollo Granforte has a superb organ, whose power he neither abuses himself nor permits the presiding mechanical genius to amplify or distort out of recognition. His style throughout is marked by greater ease and refinement than that of Alessandro Valente, who nevertheless possesses a very fine tenor voice and the requisite amount of dramatic energy, coupled with poignant feeling, for an adequate interpretation of the part of Canio. But I need not go on making comparisons, since each artist in turn contrives to shine to advantage at the right moment. With her pretty head notes and crisp, vivacious vocalization, the Nedda gives charming effect to her *Ballatella* and comes out well also in the duets with Tonio and Silvio ; only in the final scene with unhappy clown does she slightly spoil her tone by forcing it. The dramatic episode in question goes with immense spirit, and both here and elsewhere Cav. Sabajno has done splendid things with the Scala orchestra. As for the chorus, I can only say that it beats, alike for tone, precision, contrast, and refinement, any that I have ever heard in Leoncavallo's opera.

HERMAN KLEIN.

OPERATIC AND FOREIGN SONGS

SOLOISTS AND CHORUS OF THE OPÉRA-COMIQUE, PARIS.—Abridged version of **Carmen** (Bizet), with **Lamoureux Orchestra** under **Albert Wolff**. In French. Polydor 95328–32, five 12in., 32s. 6d.

CHORUS AND ORCHESTRA OF THE STATE OPERA HOUSE, BERLIN.—**Benediction of the Poignards** from **The Huguenots** (Meyerbeer). In German. H.M.V. C1861, 12in., 4s. 6d.

GRAND OPERA COMPANY.—Vocal Gems from **Die Fledermaus** (Johann Strauss). In German. Orch. acc. H.M.V. C1847, 12in., 4s. 6d.

ENRICO CARUSO (tenor).—**Première Caresse** (de Crescenzo) and **Bois épais** (Lully). In French. Orch. acc. H.M.V. DA1097, 10in., 6s.

LEO SLEZAK (tenor).—**Morgen, Op. 27, No. 4,** and **Ständchen, Op. 17, No. 1** (Richard Strauss). In German. Piano acc. **Michael Raucheisen.** Polydor 23017, 10in., 4s. 6d.

CONCHITA SUPERVIA (mezzo-soprano) and **INES FERRARIS** (soprano).—**Dance Duet** from **Hansel and Gretel** (Humperdinck). Two parts, in Italian. Orch. acc. Parlo. R20111, 12in., 6s. 6d.

ELISABETH SCHUMANN (soprano).—**Sei nicht bös** from **Der Obersteiger** (Zeller) and **Nightingale Song** (Zeller). In German. Orch. acc. H.M.V. E552, 10in., 4s. 6d.

MARGARET SHERIDAN (soprano) and **RENATO ZANELLI** (tenor).—**Già nella notte densa** and **Ed io vedea fra le tue tempie** from **Otello** Act I (Verdi). In Italian. Orch. acc. H.M.V. DB1395, 12in., 8s. 6d.

ADELE KERN (soprano).—**Air of Marzelline** from **Fidelio** (Beethoven) and **Air of the Page** from **Les Huguenots** (Meyerbeer). In German. Orch. acc. Polydor 66946, 12in., 6s. 6d.

THEODOR SCHEIDL (baritone), with **VIENNA-SCHRAMMEL QUARTET.**—**Grüss mir mein Wein** from **Countess Maritza** (Kalmán) and **Wien wird bei Nacht erst schön** (Stolz–Sterk). In German. Polydor 90148, 10in., 4s. 6d.

OLGA OLGINA (soprano).—**Splendon le sacre faci** from **Lucia di Lammermoor** (Donizetti) and **Caro nome** from **Rigoletto** (Verdi). In Italian. Orch. acc. Decca T126, 12in., 4s. 6d.

FRANK TITTERTON (tenor).—**Spring Song** from **Die Walküre** and **Prize Song** from **Die Meistersinger** (Wagner). In German. Orch. acc. Decca K516, 12in., 3s. 6d.

GIOVANNI INGHILLERI (baritone) and **TINA POLI RANDACCIO** (soprano).—**Mira d'acerbe lagrima** and **Vivra! contende il giubilo** from **Il Trovatore** (Verdi). In Italian, Orch. acc. Parlo. R20110, 12in., 6s. 6d.

MARGARETE BÄUMER (soprano).—**Von einen Kahn** and **Den als Tantris unerkannt ich entlassen,** from Act 1, Scene 3, **Tristan and Isolde** (Wagner). In German. Orch. acc. Parlo. E10996, 12in., 4s. 6d.

ELISABETH GERÖ (soprano).—**Chanson Espagnole** (Delibes) in French, and **L'Estasi** (Arditi) in Italian. Orch. acc. Parlo. E10994, 12in., 4s. 6d.

M. MICHELETTI (tenor).—**Salut, demeure** (Cavatina) from **Faust** (Gounod) and **Flower Song** from **Carmen** (Bizet). In French. Orch. acc. Parlo. E10999, 12in., 4s. 6d.

SYDNEY DE VRIES (batitone).—**Cortigiani, vil razza dannata** from **Rigoletto** (Verdi) in Italian and **Eri tu (It is thou)** from **Un Ballo in Maschera** (Verdi). In English. Orch. acc. Piccadilly 5033, 10in., 2s.

LENGHI-CELLINI (tenor).—**Ah! si ben mio** and **Di quella pira** from **Il Trovatore** (Verdi). In Italian. Orch. acc. Piccadilly 5032, 10in., 2s.

RICHARD WATSON (bass).—**Vecchia zimarra** from **La Bohème** (Puccini) and **Infelice** from (Verdi). In Italian. Orch. acc. Decca F1749, 10in., 2s.

Artists and Chorus, Opéra-Comique (Paris).—I consider this abridged version of *Carmen* a model of what such things should be. If we are to have concert arrangements of popular operas, we want them to preserve at any rate some continuity of action and so give a comprehensible idea of what the musical fuss is all about. These records not only do so by means of very clever dovetailing and abbreviating of the whole of the salient numbers, but by including all the essential portions of the spoken dialogue as it is audibly uttered by the singers of the Opéra-Comique. It is quite admirably done, and when cinema-photography comes to the aid of the gramophone the illusion of a real stage performance will be made complete. Six records instead of five would, however, have prevented much hurrying of *tempi* in certain places ; and doubtless M. Albert Wolff, the eminent conductor of the Lamoureux Orchestra, was no more the guilty cause of this than was Mr. Stanford Robinson in the recent *Elijah* album. If economy be at the root of the matter, I protest. But here is the sole tiny flaw in a splendid piece of work ; for the recording is excellent, the voices, principals and chorus alike, are typically admirable in all respects, and the Bizet orchestration receives entire justice. Added to which we get the charm of faultless French, a perfect style, and the authentic reading of the Opéra-Comique. English performers, please copy !

Chorus and Orchestra, State Opera, Berlin.—This is the first record I can remember of the impressive scene from the Conspiracy act of the *Huguenots,* where the iniquitous priests and friends of the Comte de St. Bris come to his house to plot the Massacre of St. Bartholomew, to bless their poignards and distribute their distinctive white armlets. The broad unisonal passages are vigorously rendered, with a due effect of contrast in the *staccato pp* bits, where we can almost perceive the " cat-like tread " ridiculed by Mr. Bonavia in his biography of Verdi and referred to in my preceding article of this number. If justification for such treatment of the episode be needed, here it is. The chorus evidently sings it much more frequently than the Meyerbeer-revilers in this country would care to tolerate ; but it is very fine for all that.

Grand Opera Company.—Personally I am too fond of *Die Fledermaus* and the waltzes of Johann Strauss to do anything but hail with unalloyed satisfaction the new lease of life that they have entered upon. I use the word "satisfaction" because, as a matter of fact, I have been predicting the revival all through the dark period of (artistically) unprofitable jazz-making, ever since the vogue of *Der Rosenkavalier* with which it started. Herein we are only following in the wake of Vienna and Berlin, the latter of which provides this delightful selection of gems from the operette that caught on so strongly at Covent Garden. Their life and swing compel response.

Enrico Caruso.—I wonder whether the famous tenor would have felt exactly proud of these French records of his. To my mind they represent his style at its very worst. Even the vocal quality is inferior, and as for the accent and the exaggerations of the familiar mannerisms I can only describe them in a word as execrable. It would have been much wiser, in my opinion, not to have put such posthumous efforts on the market at all.

Leo Slezak.—It is quite a relief to turn to the consummate art of the Moravian tenor as displayed here in two of Richard Strauss's most popular and melodious songs. His treatment of the *Ständchen* is peculiarly distinctive, being sung for the greater part in a delicate and ethereal *mezza voce* little louder or more substantial than that used for the *Morgen*. The effect is simply thrilling—sweet, tender, inviting, yet manly throughout without being either noisy or fast. The diction, as usual, is exquisitely pure and musical.

Conchita Supervia and Ines Ferraris.—I had no idea until I heard this record of the duet for the children from the first act of *Hansel and Gretel* that it could be made to sound better in Italian than it does in German. It is seldom, indeed, that vocal music of any kind gives greater pleasure in a foreign than in the original tongue ; but if there be one to do the trick, it is Italian. We listen, as it were, to two veritable children barking and snapping at each other, not a couple of vicious grown-ups. The whole thing is crisp, spirited, and full of humour; it preserves withal the quaint, lively rhythm and old-fashioned *volkslieder* grace of the German tunes.

Elisabeth Schumann.—This accomplished soprano is achieving quite a reputation as a warbler of waltz-airs, and with very good reason. She is intensely musical, and she has an extraordinary sense of rhythm, in the display whereof her voice never for an instant loses its roundness or purity of *timbre*, being always the faithful servitor of its theme and the most engaging of interpreters. The well-known *Sei nicht bös* is deliciously phrased in the lightest of veins; while the no less popular *Nightingale's Song* reveals an unsuspected gift in the art of the *siffleuse* that makes it very taking indeed. The English pronunciation as a rule is wonderfully good, but I do wish someone had warned Mme. Schumann against giving the Cockney diphthong to the vowel sound on the "Once again." We of course make it sound more like "agen."

Margaret Sheridan and *Renato Zanelli.*—The love duet which terminates the first act of Verdi's *Otello* constitutes one of the most beautiful moments in that glorious opera, and it is a pity, perhaps, that it should always bring to my recollection the singing of Jean de Reszke and Dame Melba in preference to that of Tamagno and Signora Cataneo, who created it for London at the Lyceum Theatre in 1889. The artists who made this record resemble the latter more than the former, especially the tenor, who has based his method upon the Tamagno traditions. His high notes are unsteady, but his middle voice is rich and sonorous; whilst, on the contrary, his fair (Irish) colleague is shaky in the medium and strong as well as captivating in the region of her head tone. The balance is therefore right, and an efficient orchestra completes an adequate ensemble.

Adele Kern.—This Viennese singer is engaged at the opera house at Charlottenburg, and there, with the aid of its orchestra, she recorded these two strongly contrasted pieces. Listening first to the calm, sedate air of Marzelline from the "ironing" scene in *Fidelio*, you would hardly suspect the lively spirit and energy essential for the dashing Page in the first act of the *Huguenots*. Yet both characteristics are there in abundant measure, exhibited with a voice and style that you cannot help but admire. The *bravura* passages in the Meyerbeer air are neatly and skilfully executed, though the clear tone often echoes very palpably in what appears to have been an empty theatre. Could this not be avoided by inviting a local crowd to come in and listen without payment?

Theodor Scheidl.—The voice is that of a *basso cantante*, not a baritone; yet, forsooth, the owner is such an artist that he can do whatever he pleases with it. Well accompanied by the Vienna Schrammel Quartet, he sings his waltz-tunes with a grace so fascinating, a style so light and refined, that one wonders what kind of repertory he sings as a rule at the Berlin State Opera. His rich, vibrant tone is quite suitable for Wolfram or even Wotan; but here, as it happens, he is making your feet dance to his insinuating 3–4 time, warbled with a charm that ought to make his records "sell like hot cakes" in other countries besides Germany.

Olga Olgina.—As she gains in confidence, the organ of this agreeable young vocalist likewise grows in steadiness and individuality. The flute *obbligato* in the *Lucia* air is less obtrusive than usual and the effect proportionately more legitimate. The singing is on the whole better here than in the *Caro nome*, where it is neat enough, but not marked either by the highest degree of finish or by absolute purity of intonation on certain of the prominent pause notes. The *cadenza* is the usual one and quite brilliantly sung.

Frank Titterton.—This is also a creditable Decca production. and slightly cheaper than the Polish lady's, being the work of a rising and improving English tenor. The latter is still at his best in passages that call for robust handling; he sustains well and with passionate utterance, his words as a rule being now very distinct indeed. Thus his *Prize Song* has understand-

ing as well as power, and the tenacity with which he holds on to his high A's shows that they have no terrors for him. Altogether I welcome this record as an evidence of decided artistic growth.

Giovanni Inghilleri and *Tina Poli Randaccio.*—There is nothing to say about this familiar duet between Leonora and the Count di Luna from the last act of *Trovatore* except that it is exceedingly well sung by both artists. None of the customary dramatic effects is either misplaced or lacking, and there is plenty of animation and impulse in the efforts of two voices that blend admirably throughout.

Margarete Bäumer.—We are obviously listening here to an Isolde of some distinction. The voice is mellow and sympathetic rather than resonant or penetrating, and—*tant mieux!* The trying phrases of the narration to Brangäne emerge with ample power and unmistakable dramatic intelligence, while the orchestral part is worthy of Dr. Weissmann and his well-trained men. The whole conveys the necessary poignant feeling.

Elisabeth Gerö.—The piece by Delibes is the one we know best as *Les Filles de Cadix*, and it is brilliantly sung in French (with the Berlin Orchestra just mentioned) by a light soprano who possesses an unusually pretty voice of abnormal compass. Both in the Delibes air and in the well-remembered *Estasi* of Arditi she touches without the least effort a bell-like F sharp in *alt*. Her execution includes all the conspicuous features of the old Italian florid school, notably a singularly perfect shake neat scales, and a delicately crisp *staccato*.

M. Micheletti.—A capable and interesting tenor, evidently French by birth and training. His smooth voice rises easily to the requisite range for the *Faust* and *Carmen* airs, but in the former he uses a lovely falsetto for the high C and in the *Flower Song* the customary B flat from the chest. He has a pure accent, clear enunciation, and passionate warmth of sentiment, and he phrases with elegance.

Sydney de Vries.—Again I ask, why use English for *Eri tu?* Otherwise, apart from over-amplification, these records of Verdi airs are quite acceptable. The *Rigoletto* is sung with pathos and dramatic power as well as assurance.

Lenghi-Cellini.—Besides sticking to the "chestnuts," this excellent tenor certainly contrives to pull them out of the fire. His *Di quella pira* (wrongly labelled *O quella pizi*, whatever that may mean) is particularly telling, despite noisy amplifying.

Richard Watson.—A good baritone, with a dramatic style, sonorous voice and evidently Italian experience. Again the artificial increase of volume offends my ear, but it cannot altogether spoil a capital record.

HERMAN KLEIN.

McCormack in a Fox Film

At the beautiful new Prince Edward Theatre in Greek Street, close to our London Office, "Song o' my Heart" has been shown since Tuesday. This is the film which has been built round the voice and personality of Count John McCormack, and was made in Ireland and at Hollywood.

H.M.V. records of three out of the new songs that he sings are already available. On one (DA1111, 10in., 6s.) McCormack sings his own *Fairy Story by the Fire* to Merikanto's setting (and Roger Quilter's familiar *Now sleeps the crimson petal*). In both Edwin Schneider, who went to Hollywood with him, plays the piano accompaniment. On the other record (DA1113) he sings two rather unworthy film songs, *I feel you near me* and *A pair of blue eyes*, with orchestral accompaniment. These last are also issued at half the price (B3434) sung with great feeling and with more rhythm by Lilian Davies, who although she does not follow McCormack's wonderful last phrase in *A pair of blue eyes*, gives a distinguished performance of both songs.

Other songs of McCormack's which are already in the H.M.V. list and are sung by him in the film are *Little Boy Blue*, *I hear you calling me*, *Just for to-day* and *Then you'll remember me*.

THE H.M.V. ALBUM OF "TOSCA"

" Le jour succède au jour," said Alfred de Musset; and even so one *Tosca* succeeds another *Tosca*, not on the stage only, but inside the covers—the elegant covers—of the gramophone album. As a matter of fact, the cover plays an important part in these H.M.V. productions, since it embraces all, or nearly all, of the printed matter concerned with the history and the interpretation of the opera. You may look in vain for the actual words of the text, either in the original form or a translation. The difficulties connected with the latter are solved by taking for granted that you know the story already, or that you can follow the words so distinctly enunciated by the singers; or else that you can, if you like, easily procure a copy of the libretto from Messrs. Ricordi. But what you will find here is an admirable résumé, signed with the familiar initials " H.W.L.," containing all the facts and details about Puccini's popular opera that you are likely to require, together with a certain amount of critical comment of the kind that cannot fail to interest as well as instruct. It was a happy idea to refer by number to the records which give some of the salient portions of the first act, and, on the other hand, a pity not to have followed the same plan systematically all through. In these albums either an index or a separate heading for each record would seem so useful as to be almost indispensable.

Since memories are short and the " lives " of records (electrically produced) are likely to be long, it is distinctly good that " H.W.L." should have recalled two of the more famous *Tosca* casts, dating from the first performance at the Constanz Theatre, Rome, in January, 1900. On that occasion Darclée created the rôle of the heroine, De Marchi that of Cavaradossi, Giraldoni that of Scarpia, Galli that of Angelotti, and Borelli that of the Sacristan, Mugnone being the conductor. At Covent Garden, six months later these parts were undertaken respectively by Ternina, De Lucia, Scotti, Dufriche, and Gilibert, with Mancinelli as conductor. The latter cast has never been surpassed, at any rate so far as regards the Tosca and the Scarpia; for Ternina, " one of the greatest operatic artists in living memory," was absolutely ideal, and I quite agree that Scotti's Scarpia was " unique."

An excellent ensemble now secures a worthy permanent performance for the H.M.V. album. It is essentially a Milanese achievement, and, I might say, redolent of La Scala, whose able maestro, Carlo Sabajno, has associated with him the chorus and orchestra of that establishment and the following cast: Floria Tosca, Carmen Melis; Mario Cavaradossi, Piero Pauli; Scarpia, Apollo Granforte; Angelotti, Giovanni Azzimonti; Sacristan, Antonio Gelli; Spoletta, Nello Palai; Sciarrone, G. Azzimonti.

To go *seriatim* through the fourteen double-sided records (Nos. C1902—1915) would involve the repetition of an oft-told tale. Suffice it to say that the calibre of the workmanship and artistry revealed in them is of the highest order. Consequently, there is no need for comparisons. I cannot perceive any shortcomings either in the interpretation of the score or the quality of the recording. Each scene stands out clearly, strongly, effectively; and let me add that the necessary interruptions or divisions have been extremely well devised. It should, therefore, be easy to provide with this material a thoroughly realistic and comprehensible musical representation of Puccini's opera. After the quieter moments of the Church scene, the playful love duet and the Sacristan with his boys, comes a singularly fine rendering of the imposing finale, as the Cardinal's procession crosses the stage and Scarpia hurls out his defiant " Va! Tosca." In still stronger contrast, however, comes the lurid drama of the second act, and here Carmen Melis and Granforte are at their very best. Their characterization of the two protagonists in the unequal struggle is so vivid as to be perfectly thrilling; while the graphic orchestration furnishes a background that seems fully to compensate for the absence of stage effects, of

visible personalties and dramatic gestures. The voices, unlike that of the Cavaradossi, which is rather over-amplified, are always well in the picture, and the progress of the tremendous scene *à deux* can be followed without the slightest difficulty. The final act, again, is portrayed with sure and skilful touches that convey a full sense of the tragedy enacted upon the platform of the Castle of Sant' Angelo.

HERMAN KLEIN.

OPERATIC AND FOREIGN SONGS

AMELITA GALLI-CURCI (soprano).—**Russian Nightingale Song** (Alabieff) and **Clavelitos** (Valverde) and **Estrellita** (Ponce). The first sung in English, the others in Spanish. With piano acc. by Homer Samuels. H.M.V. DA1095, 10in., 6s.

LOTTE LEHMANN (soprano).—**Elsa's Dream** and **Elsa's Song to the Breezes**, from **Lohengrin** (Wagner). Sung in German with Orch. Parlophone Odeon RO20113, 10in., 4s. 6d.

EMMY BETTENDORF (soprano).—**It is a wondrous sympathy** (Liszt) and **How like a Flower thou bloomest** (Liszt). Sung in German, with Orch. Parlophone E11011, 12in., 4s. 6d.

FRANK TITTERTON (tenor).—**On with the Motley** from **Pagliacci** (Leoncavallo) and **Siciliana** from **Cavalleria Rusticana** (Mascagni). Sung in English, with Orch. Decca F1739, 10in., 2s.

RICHARD TAUBER (tenor).—**A Garland of Apple Blossoms**; and with **VERA SCHWARZ** (soprano) **Who has implanted this love in our hearts?** from **The Land of Laughter** (Lehar), accompanied by the Orchestra of the State Opera House, Berlin, and conducted by the composer. Parlophone Odeon R20112, 12in., 6s. 6d.

GEORGE BAKLANOFF (baritone).—**In vain the sad and heavy heart seeks after peace** and **And in restless mood** from **Prince Igor** (Borodin). Sung in Russian, accompanied by Orchestra of the State Opera House, Berlin. Parlo. E11014, 12in., 4s. 6d.

IVAR ANDRESEN (bass).—**Der selt'ne Beter** (C. Loewe), ballad in two parts. Sung in German with Dr. Franz Hallasch at the piano. Col. DX65, 12in., 4s. 6d.

CHORUS AND ORCHESTRA OF THE STATE OPERA HOUSE, BERLIN.—**Huntsmen's Chorus** from **Der Freischütz** (Weber) and **Sailor's Chorus** from **Der Fliegende Holländer** (Wagner). Both in German. H.M.V. E557, 10in., 4s. 6d.

BARBARA KEMP (soprano) and **TINO PATTIERA** (tenor).—**'Tis thou! 'tis I** and **Whither now?** from **Carmen** (Bizet) Act IV. Sung in German, with Orchestra and Chorus of the State Opera House, Berlin. Parlo. E11013, 12in., 4s. 6d.

Amelita Galli-Curci.—The familiar poignant tone remains fresh and penetrating; the wonted charm continues to prevail; and so long as the artistic individuality of the singer is still there to permeate the whole effort, so long will records by the famous Italian soprano command a sale all the world over. Alabieff's *Nightingale* is a sweet bird, and he could not ask for a more eloquent human representative. Happily, the intonation in this instance is impeccable; nor could one ask for greater clarity of tone and diction. The staccato in the cadenza with flute is equally beyond reproach. On the reverse side the two songs by Ponce are so unlike, yet so Spanish, that the contrast is doubly striking. In one the speed of the patter is simply amazing; the hammer-blows can only be likened to the percussion of a gentle hailstorm. In the other you find the fascination of the sentimental slow jota warbled in the true Galli-Curci manner, which is always worth hearing.

Lotte Lehmann.—For their perfect rendering Elsa's two solos demand the exercise of a high order of vocal art, in conjunction with tone possessing great natural beauty. Qualities such as these they unquestionably obtain in the present instance, and I need say no more to recommend to gramophonists one of the very finest *Lohengrin* records that it has ever been my lot to listen to. Happily, too, the breathing is freer than usual from "inspiratory murmur," while every note is exquisitely in tune.

Emmy Bettendorf.—It seems rather a long time since we had anything of importance from this talented soprano, who unfortunately reserves her stage efforts entirely for home consumption and cannot be accused of lack of industry in that direction. She sends us here two lovely specimens of poetic Lieder-singing, such as might well have entranced the impressionable old Abbé who composed the songs, though I am not equally sure that he would have approved the orchestral trimmings, violin *obbligati, vorspiele,* and *nachspiele,* etc., with which the Wizard of the Parlophone has endowed them. (However, Liszt was himself an " arch-meddler," so perhaps he deserves his posthumous penalty.) Very sweet and tender do both songs sound from the lips of the gifted Emmy, for she murmurs them in her most honeyed *mezza voce* and with *n*th degree of refinement and delicacy.

Frank Titterton.—Once more I would venture to suggest that over-amplification does not enhance the value of even the cheapest of Decca records. Nor has Mr. Titterton any prescriptive right to this misleading sort of aid because he happens to be rounding out into a real *tenore robusto.* The whole principle of the thing is wrong; these records would be quite good enough to appeal on their own merits minus an artificial reinforcement which makes them unpleasantly strident.

Richard Tauber and *Vera Schwarz.*—Both extracts are extremely tuneful and Leharesque, though I like the solo rather better than the duet. The slow waltz rhythm of the latter should make it highly acceptable for dance purposes.

George Baklanoff.—Here is another case of exaggerated amplifying—as though a superb organ like this really needed fictitious enlargement! Baklanoff is as great a singer of the *Prince Igor* music as Chaliapin any day, and no reasonable person could ask for more than that. It is a delight to hear fine music sung with such splendidly dramatic declamation. Why overdo the sonority?

Ivar Andrésen.—In this case we get another atmosphere and no evidence of undue interference. The glorious voice tells its own tale whilst telling that of the "Man who seldom prayed." The ballad is not one of Loewe's best, but I never heard it sung like this before, and such a rendering makes all the difference. Wonderful, indeed, can be the effect of a simple musical narrative related with such noble tone, profound sentiment, depth of contrast, and faultless management of voice and nuance. The accompaniment is well played by Dr. Franz Hallasch.

Berlin S.O. Chorus and Orchestra.—There can be no need to describe how these familiar items from *Freischütz* and the *Holländer* are done by such a body of executants. The resonance, of course, is phenomenal; the smartness, precision and vigour amazing.

Barbara Kemp and *Tino Pattiera.*—An interesting and effective German reading by two clever artists of the final duet from *Carmen.* Observe the subtle gradual growth of the long crescendo to the climax of the tragedy. Observe also the slow change from his despair and her contempt to blind rage and equally blind fear. The whole scene is splendidly depicted and admirably recorded.

HERMAN KLEIN.

THE H.M.V. PINAFORE ALBUM.

It should, of course, be *H.M.S. Pinafore;* we all know that. But in the present instance the above title serves to indicate a version for which "His Master's Voice" is responsible and so to differentiate the gramophonic reproduction from the Savoy original, which has never yet, so far as I am aware, been sanctified by inclusion in the official Navy List. In his *Bab Ballads,* from which Sir W. S. Gilbert borrowed the idea of the story of the *Pinafore* (it being his own property), the name of the vessel commanded by Captain Reece was, doubtless for the sake of the rhyme, given as the *Mantelpiece;* but, once mentioned there, we hear of it no more; whereas immortality, safe almost as that of Nelson's *Victory,* awaits the name of Captain Corcoran's *Pinafore.*

It was performed for the first time at the old Opera Comique Theatre, after the withdrawal of *The Sorcerer,* on May 28th, 1878, and ran for about two years. Its popularity during that period amounted to a "craze." Nothing like it has been known since, either in England or America, where it remains to-day the greatest favourite of all the Gilbert and Sullivan operas, not excluding even *The Mikado.* Mr. Arthur Lawrence has truly said in his *Life of Sir Arthur Sullivan,* "It was not an uncommon thing for one individual to have seen the piece, say, a dozen times; church choirs added it to their repertoire; thousands of sturdy Puritans, who had never been inside a theatre before, went to see one or other of the performances. It is on record that a hundred thousand barrel-organs were constructed to play nothing else." I wonder how many gramophones will now be sold on purpose to play this Album, which they will not only do a hundred thousand times better, but therewith evoke the most perfect reproduction of the authentic Savoy performace that has yet been achieved.

There was only one way to arrive at this result, and that was to go to the fountain head for it; which is what H.M.V. has invariably done for its recordings of these operas. In other words, they have placed the entire direction of the business in the able and responsible hands of Mr. Rupert D'Oyly Carte, the son of the famous Richard whom it was my privilege to know from the days when he built the first Savoy Theatre. It goes without saying, therefore, that the present Album offers a complete and faithful replica of the performance recently witnessed at that newly-constructed house. The cast is as follows: Sir Joseph Porter, (Sir) Henry A. Lytton; Captain Corcoran, Mr. George Baker; Ralph Rackstraw, Charles Goulding, Dick Deadeye, Darrell Fancourt; Josephine, Elsie Griffin; Hebe, Nellie Briercliffe; and Little Buttercup, Bertha Lewis. In certain concerted pieces Sydney Granville and Stuart Robertson also take part.

To state that the whole interpretation of the opera was carried out under the bâton of Dr. Malcolm Sargent is to give assurance that the true Savoy traditions have been accurately preserved. His *penchant* for brisk *tempi* is no drawback here; rather the contrary, in fact. He maintains the lively atmosphere that the music demands and yet never neglects its delicious sentimental aspects. At one point only do I notice a conspicuous departure from the right Sullivanesque reading, namely, in failing to observe the classic pause before the Captain's "Hardly ever," upon which Sir Arthur absolutely insisted. The work of the chorus and orchestra could not in any way be improved upon; it is simply perfect, and the *timbre* throughout adapts itself admirably to the exigencies of the recording instrument. The names of the soloists speak for themselves. There is no need to praise either the dry, unctuous humour or the faultless diction of Sir Henry Lytton, who renews in his delightful art all that was so individual and alert in the methods of the famous George Grossmith. Of the others, Miss Bertha Lewis comes nearest in voice and style to Miss Everard or Rosina Brandram; but as Josephine Miss Griffin might perhaps have sung with a trifle more liveliness and spirit.

HERMAN KLEIN.

482

OPERATIC AND FOREIGN SONGS

DUSOLINA GIANNINI (soprano).—**O Sole mio** (Di Capua) and **Mannella mia** (Neapolitan Folk Song) (trans. : Giannini). Sung in Neapolitan with Orch. H.M.V. DB1247, 12in., 8s. 6d.

ELISABETH SCHUMANN (soprano).—**Warnung** (Mozart) and **Wer hat das Liedlein erdacht** (Mahler) and **Wiegenlied** (Mozart). Sung in German, the first with George Reeves at the Piano, the second with Orch. H.M.V. E555, 10om., 4s. 6d.

MARGHERITA CAROSIO (soprano).—**Polonaise** from **Mignon** (Thomas) and **Spargi d'amaro pianto** from Mad Scene, Act 3. **Lucia di Lammermoor.** In Italian with Orchestra of the State Opera House, Berlin. Parlo. E11024, 12in., 4s. 6d.

JOHN McCORMACK (tenor).—**None but the weary heart** (Tchaikovsky) and **To the children** (Rachmaninov). In English. Piano and 'cello acc. H.M.V. DA1112, 10in., 6s.

RICHARD TAUBER (tenor).—**Thou art my star** (Eisemann Mihaly) and **Mary** (Robert Katscher—Austin Egen). In German with Orch. acc. Parlophone Odeon RO20114, 10in., 4s. 6d.

VILLABELLA (tenor).—**In vain do I ask** from Act 1; and **ROUARD** (baritone).—**Sword Scene** from Act 2 **Faust** (Gounod). In French. Chorus and Orchestra. Parlo. E11026, 12in., 4s. 6d.

HORACE STEVENS (baritone).—**Wotan's Farewell** from **The Valkyrie** (Wagner). In English. Orch. acc. Four parts. Decca K527, 12in., 3s. 6d.

ALICE MOXON (soprano) and **STUART ROBERTSON** (bass-baritone.—**Give me thy hand, O fairest** from **Don Giovanni** (Mozart) and **Lightly, lightly** from **Monsieur Beaucaire** (Messager). In English. Orch. acc. H.M.V. B3430, 10in., 3s.

Dusolina Giannini.—If one is not too utterly tired of *O sole mio*, a new pleasure may be derived from hearing it sung by a soprano, and that soprano one with the pure Italian tones of Dusolina Giannini. She puts into it every essential grain of sentiment without vulgarising it, as so many tenors have done, with ounces of *portamento*. It sounds, indeed, almost like good music ; while the Neapolitan ditty on the reverse side pleases because it is so wonderfully tender and graceful without descending to commonplace. All this can be done with ordinary material by a charming singer.

Elisabeth Schumann.—Here we realise what another type of charming singer can accomplish with material that is worthy of her talent. No need to tell how this little lady sings Mozart. Her crisp yet delicate treatment of both the songs is a delight for the refined ear to listen to ; the clear, strong accentuation of the words a model for any singer. The quaintly archaic runs in the Mahler lied are exquisitely done, and, best of all, one can be grateful for the artistic reticence of a tone unspoilt by over-amplifying. The orchestra sounds well in the *Wiegenlied,* and the piano accompaniments in the other songs are beautifully played by Geo. Reeves.

John McCormack.—Have you seen and heard the McCormack film? If not, I have ; and this record will give you a vivid idea of how our "County" tenor sounds when you are not actually listening to him in the flesh. No reproduction however perfect, can quite convey the thrill of the artist himself, but meanwhile the familiar characteristics gleam brightly enough through this electrical medium. I cannot say that the two Russian songs—especially *None but the weary heart*, which was written for a mezzo-soprano—are particularly well adapted to show off this tenor's voice ; but there can be no question that he knows how to make them effective. N.B.—The word "firmament" is not pronounced in English as if the first syllable were sounded like *fear*.

Margherita Carosio.—Undeniably a clever coloratura soprano. Yet her voice sounds hard, glottic, and at times even unsympathetic. Everything is bright, glittering, mechanical. As I have remarked before, Italian teachers appear to be encouraging the cultivation of this type of florid singer ; and, frankly speaking, it affords me no enjoyment to listen to their throaty acrobatics. They are wondrously rapid and dazzling, like the tricks of a gymnast in a circus, but you fear every moment lest they should terminate in a débacle.

Richard Tauber.—This prolific warbler of *operette* ditties is here at his best in a couple of those urgent appeals for "love, love, love" that make him the darling of the fair sex in Berlin, Vienna, and every other Continental city where his name and voice are known. His persuasive pleading to *Mary, Mary, Mary* is one of the most pathetic things I ever listened to. Who could say "no" to such a pitiful petition from a fascinating and fashionable vocalist?

Villabella-Rouard.—This is not one singer, but two, a tenor and a baritone respectively, and their excerpts from *Faust* have at the least the merit of being unhackneyed. With their fine voices and experienced style, they impart welcome interest to Faust's apostrophe from the opening scene, where he summons the aid of the Spirit of Evil, and to the episode in the Kermesse act, where Valentine defies the powers of the same Satanic personage. Both are well sung in French, and in the second the chorus duly takes part.

Horace Stevens.—It is good to find two complete discs (four sides) devoted to the rendering of a big piece like *Wotan's Farewell*, virtually the entire closing scene from the music-drama of *The Valkyrie*. As declaimed by Horace Stevens (in plain understandable English) and excellently played by a first-rate orchestra, it represents wonderful value for the price at which it is issued, and I feel I ought warmly to congratulate the Decca firm upon its enterprise. The whole thing is splendidly done.

Alice Moxon and *Stuart Robertson.*—The style that suits Messager and *Monsieur Beaucaire* is not exactly the one that is needed for Mozart and *Don Giovanni*. Which fact is abundantly illustrated by the satisfaction that can here be derived from the first of these pieces and the sense of inadequacy that pervades the second. The short, jerky, *staccato* method will not serve for the latter any more than the modern Oxford diction which is supposed to denote the amorous (Oxford) Don.

HERMAN KLEIN.

H.M.V. ALBUM OF PUCCINI'S "MADAMA BUTTERFLY" IN ITALIAN

Selections in Italian from *Madama Butterfly* have had a place in the H.M.V. catalogue from the days when the Victor Company began recording them in New York from the lips of Caruso and Scotti, Emmy Destinn and Geraldine Farrar, Alda and Martinelli, Farrar and Homer and Caruso, not to mention Joseph Hislop and Dinh Gilly and an *Un bel dì* from Amelita Galli-Curci herself. But these were all isolated examples and, supremely interesting though they were, they were pre-electrical and consequently destined to vanish into the *Ewigkeit*. A fate less merciless assuredly awaits the "Complete Opera in English," a product of later date very favourably reviewed by me in this magazine, and which has already, I believe, enjoyed a world-wide sale. With Rosina Buckman, Nellie Walker, Tudor Davies and Frederic Ranalow for its leading quartet, the version last mentioned will have no difficulty in holding its own in the estimation of such gramaphonists as prefer their operas in the vernacular.

Here we have *Madama Butterfly* issued, for the first time under the auspices of H.M.V., in the original "choice Italian" whereof Hamlet made mention when revealing the authorship of his play to the King. (Columbia did it in that language not many months ago.) It is a well-planned Album of some sixteen double-sided 12in. discs (numbered C1950 to C1965) and comes with all the distinction of cachet attaching to a performance executed with the orchestra and chorus of La Scala under the able direction of **Maestro Carlo Sabajno.**

From such an illustrious source one expects nowadays perfect results ; and, so far as the mechanical features—i.e., the quality of the recording, bar over-amplification—and the work of the aforesaid orchestra and chorus are concerned, the general rendering of Puccini's popular opera is quite up to standard. But where it falls below the expected level—not throughout by any means, but here and there, and more especially in the case of certain characters and scenes—is in the quality of the voices and the singing. From the very opening scene for Goro, Pinkerton, and Sharpless, a certain note of coarseness, nay of harshness, is struck ; and it prevails steadily until the "hail, Columbia" and the whisky have given place to the geishas.

Now this impression, which is very palpable, is largely due to the fact that the amplifier has taken charge from the start. These three men's voices are none of them natural ; they all sound more or less distorted, notably the principal tenor's ; and his, I may further add, undergoes a certain amount of over-amplification every time he opens his mouth, except perhaps during a few bars of the love duet, where *gentillesse oblige* and you immediately perceive the difference. (I have declared before that I could not explain what claim tenors possess to this special treatment, and I cannot explain it now. Do they consider that it converts them forthwith into Carusos?) Happily a more normal effect is produced when the girls make their up-hill climb to the Pinkerton dwelling. Neither here nor elsewhere, I am glad to say, is the voice of Miss **Margherita Sheridan** submitted to an unreasonable amount of this sort of thing. I do not say that it is not occasionally distorted, for it is. But on the whole her tone is allowed to retain its natural

timbre, and it is very fortunate that it should be so ; for the heroine in *Butterfly* has a tremendous lot of music to sing and, as we have heard *viva voce* at Covent Garden, Miss Sheridan is quite at her best in this opera. At the outset her head tones may be a trifle unsteady, but she quickly gains control, displays plenty of vivacity and entrain, attacks well, throws passion into the love duet, and in due course brings dramatic resource and pathetic sentiment into the portrayal of her delineation. Altogether a very picturesque and satisfying Butterfly.

I would that it were possible to award equal praise to the F. B. Pinkerton, at any rate in a vocal sense. Ere now I have found much to commend in the records of this half-English, half-Italian, **Lionello Cecil,** whom I have never heard in the theatre : but his voice continues to grow whiter and more tremulous as he becomes more popular in Italy, and his sense of contrast, like his *mezza voce*, has vanished. Fortunately, his best moments occur in the love duet, or rather in the early part of it, until rising passion induces him to shout the well-amplified ending, where gramophonists will find a soft needle a *sine qua non*. Really one does not feel inclined to share Butterfly's grief over her husband's absence during the second act.

The singing of the second act, indeed, affords the most enjoyable moments of the performance. Butterfly's duets with Suzuki and Sharpless are both conceived in the true spirit of the drama ; the right atmosphere pervades them ; the quaint charm of the music produces its full effect as record after record unfolds the story. So, too, with the picturesque comedy of the scene where the wealthy Yamadori renews his fruitless wooing, and poor Butterfly emphasizes her quiet refusal with subdued peals of laughter. The close of the act, from the reading of the letter, the flower duet with Suzuki, down to the *bouche fermée* of the distant chorus as the women begin their long vigil, is admirably done, the just balance between voices and orchestra being more delicately preserved here than anywhere else in the opera.

The Intermezzo preceding the third act occupies one whole disc and it could not be more nobly phrased. Then, when the action is resumed, one perceives abundant—sometimes too abundant—energy reinforcing it, especially in the very fine trio that marks Pinkerton's return. (There is more time for physical recuperation when making records than during the brief interval between acts in a dressing-room.) But it is an Italian, not an American, much less a British Pinkerton who hurls his tears and sobs at us in the "Addio." The tragedy of the final episode is vividly brought out. Miss Sheridan is very artistic in her slow, gradual development of the terrible climax, from her eloquent silences to the moment when she bids farewell to the child and hurries off to her death. There is a reward in all this for a great deal that was not so satisfying before. The thrill is rather late in coming, but when it does come it grips you.

The following is the full cast : Cio-Cio-San, **Margherita Sheridan** ; Suzuki, **Ida Mannarini** ; Lt. Pinkerton, **Lionello Cecil** ; Kate Pinkerton, **Elena Lorni** ; Sharpless, **Vittorio Weinberg** ; Goro, **Nello Palai** ; Yamadori, **Antonio Gelli** ; The Bonze, **Guglielmo Masini** ; The Imp. Commissioner and the Official Registrar, **Antonio Gelli.** HERMAN KLEIN.

OPERATIC AND FOREIGN SONGS
(SEPTEMBER AND OCTOBER ISSUES)

ELISABETH RETHBERG (soprano) and **FRIEDRICH SCHORR** (baritone).—**Sieh' Ev'chen! Dächt' ich doch** and **Hat mann mit dem Schuhwerk** from Act 3, Sc. 1 of **Die Meistersinger** (Wagner). In German. Orch. acc. H.M.V. DB1421, 12in., 8s. 6d.

ELISABETH RETHBERG (soprano).—**Zigeunerlied** from Act 1 **Gypsy Baron** (Joh. Strauss) and **Heilige Quelle** from Act 2 of **Marriage of Figaro** (Mozart). In German. Orch. acc. Parlo. RO20115, 10in., 4s. 6d.

EMMY BETTENDORF (soprano).—**Caro mio ben** (Giordani) in Italian and **Melody in F** (Rubinstein), in German. Organ and orch. acc. Parlo. E11044, 12in., 4s. 6d.

   Love Waltz (Heymann-Liebmann) and **Speak not of Love eternal** (Granichstädten—Marischka). In German. Organ and Orch. acc. Parlo. E11045, 12in., 4s. 6d. Leaflets of words.

ROSE PAULY-DREESEN (soprano).—**Leonora's Aria** from Fidelio (Beethoven). In German. Orch. acc. Parlo. E11036, 12in., 4s. 6d.

MARGARETE BÄUMER (soprano).—**O Hall of Song** and **Away from him!** from Act 2 of **Tannhäuser** (Wagner). In German. Orch. acc. Parlo. E11035, 12in., 4s. 6d.

JOVITA FUENTES (soprano).—**One fine day** and **Death of Butterfly** from **Madame Butterfly** (Puccini). In Italian. Orch acc. Parlo. E11047, 12in., 4s. 6d.

MAY BLYTH (soprano), **HENRY WENDON** (tenor) and **RICHARD WATSON** (bass).—**Finale** from Act 3 of **Aida** (Verdi). In Italian. Orch. acc. Decca K533, 12in., 3s. 6d.

   Garden Scene from Act 3 of **Faust** (Gounod). In French. Orch. acc. Decca K535, 12in., 3s. 6d.

Elisabeth Rethberg and *Friedrich Schorr.*—It is good to be able to begin the autumn reviews under this head with something superlatively excellent. No less could fairly be said of this faultless rendering of the "footstool duet" from the third act of *Die Meistersinger.* It brings out in full glory one of the loveliest inspirations that Wagner ever put into a score; in other words, it is a perfect musical realisation of the scene, with the clear, silvery tones of the impulsive Eva and the sly humour of the mischievous Sachs everywhere intact. Both voices fall gratefully on the ear; the melodious repartee is a joy throughout; and the words—ye gods! what a lesson to some of our thick-speaking native singers! Who was responsible for the instrumental recording deponent knoweth not, but it is admirable.

Elisabeth Rethberg.—The all-round nature of the German operatic training—one night tragedy, the next comedy or even farce—explains the capacity for contrasts such as versatile women like Elisabeth Rethberg and Lotte Lehmann can furnish. From Wagner to Johann Strauss and back to Mozart seem to be entirely natural transitions. The gifted Elisabeth demonstrates it in this interesting record (that is, if you don't miss her Eva) by her bird-like, brilliant singing of the *Zigeunerlied,* so suggestive of the pent-up energy of the canary; followed by a turn to the serious in the air for the Countess which we know best under its Italian title of *Porgi amor.* This last is quite beautifully phrased, slow without being dragged, minus appoggiaturas, of course (as is the modern fashion), and always simple, unaffected, touching in its pathos. The tone is immaculate and ravishing throughout.

Emmy Bettendorf.—To the genius who invents orchestral accompaniments for Parlophone, as I have frequently observed, all popular music of the past is fair game for manipulation. I know not whether the same mind that invents new harmonies for *Caro mio ben* furnished an entirely fresh and elaborate vocal version of Rubinstein's famous *Melody in F*; but here is Emmy Bettendorf accepting both in their new dress and, what is more, singing them in her most delightful manner. Even Giordani himself would have found it difficult to resist the fascination of the extra touches and the intensely Teutonic sentiment. But as to Rubinstein I am not so certain. He was a man of leonine moods, and would have roared his loudest when that superfluous, intrinsic male chorus "chips in" in the *coda,* and converts the whole thing into a cheap *operette* number. The lovely voice of the soloist, adding a double charm to the well-known tune, has nearly saved the situation when this catastrophe occurs, albeit the *tessitura* is low for her. In the end she conquers; but even then one feels inclined to ask, "Was it really worth while?" The companion disc contains less familiar material. Love is the eternal theme of both songs (we should term them ballads), and the accomplished vocalist idealizes them, as she does everything, by her graceful, artistic singing. Her waltz rhythm in the first is irresistible, and in the second she balances accounts with what is apparently a high-class jazz orchestra. Why not try it and hear what it sounds like?

Rose Pauly-Dreesen.—This soprano's tone is somewhat pinched and thin at moments, and, despite her obvious artistic qualities, does not altogether enable her to satisfy in Fidelio's great air, *Abscheulicher.* She seems to be more of a lyric than a dramatic singer, and her style reveals little charm. Her diction, too, lacks the dignity that is so wonderfully embodied in the rhythm of Beethoven's tremendous theme, "Ich folg' dem innern Triebe, ich wanke nicht." The accompaniments are well played under Dr. Weissmann.

Margarete Bäumer.—The pieces given in this record represent the most declamatory portions of Elisabeth's task in *Tannhäuser,* and on the gramophone one seldom hears them to such advantage as in the present instance. Frl. Bäumer has an organ of full, round proportions and her methods are undeniably impressive. *Dich theure Halle* tells us nothing particularly new; but the effect of the outburst where the heroine protects the misguided champion of the Venusberg from the anger of the outraged Minnesingers is singularly fine.

Jovita Fuentes.—Evidently a sweetly attractive Spanish Butterfly. She really sounds like the charming little geisha who had the misfortune to arouse the infatuation of Pinkerton and fall genuinely in love with him. Her voice is by no means powerful, but it is exceedingly pretty and very carefully trained. Her *One fine day* is conceived in the right spirit, while in the scene preceding the suicide she is just emotional enough, without being over-tearful. Her intonation is absolutely correct.

May Blyth, Henry Wendon, Richard Watson.—Why English artists should sing operatic excerpts for the gramophone in a foreign language, when there is no need to do so, passes my comprehension. They may be assured that no foreign singer (especially French) would ever think of using an English text except under the strongest compulsion. The kind of Italian and French displayed in these excerpts from *Aida* and *Faust* offers no excuse for deserting the mother-tongue, which is quite beautiful enough when properly treated. What increases my objection is the indistinctness that results from inferior pronunciation. The *Aida* selection is in every way better than the *Faust.* The latter ought hardly to be entitled the "Garden Scene," since it only begins at Mephistopheles's invocation to the night and the flowers, and concludes with his promise of Marguerite's avowal at the window, which, under the circumstances, Faust is not allowed a chance of over-hearing. Much lovely music is thus omitted.

SIGISMUND PILINSKY (tenor).—**Arise then, mighty Rome, anew** from **Rienzi** (Wagner) and **Lord, in the starry spheres** from **The Prophet** (Meyerbeer). In German. Orch. acc. and chorus. Parlo. E11037, 12in., 4s. 6d.

RICHARD TAUBER (tenor).—**I live for your love** and **Wonderful, so wonderful** from **Frederica** (Franz Lehar). In German. Orch. acc. Parlo. RO20116, 10in., 4s. 6d. Leaflet of words.

VILLABELLA (tenor).—**Paresseuse fille** from Act 1 and **Duel Trio** from Act 4 of **Faust** (Gounod). In French. Orch. Acc. and chorus. Parlo. E11033, 12 in., 4s. 6d.

ALESSANDRO VALENTE (tenor).—**Si, fui soldato** from **Andrea Chénier** (Giordano) and **Serenata** (Mascagni). In Italian. Orch acc. H.M.V. B3486, 10in., 3s.

ALFRED PICCAVER (tenor).—**Am stillen Herd** and **Prize Song** from **Die Meistersinger** (Wagner). In German. Orch. acc. Polydor 95351, 12in., 6s. 6d.
　　Torna a Surriento (de Curtis) and **Di te** (Tirindelli). In Italian. Orch. acc. Polydor 90150, 10in., 4s. 6d.

KARL AUGUST NEUMANN (baritone).—**Largo** (Handel) and **Die Himmel rühmen** (Beethoven). In German. Organ acc. Polydor 23029, 10in., 3s.

ALEXANDER KIPNIS (bass).—**Mondnacht** (Schumann) and **Traum durch die Dämmerung** (R. Strauss). In German. Piano acc. Col. LB4, 10in., 4s. 6d.

KATE HEIDERSBACH (soprano) and **MAX LORENZ** (tenor). —**Das süsse Lied verhällt** and **Ist dies nur Liebe**, Love Duet from **Lohengrin** (Wagner). In German. Orch. acc. H.M.V. C1899, 12in., 4s. 6d.
　　O Fürstin and **Doch welch ein seltsam neues lieben** from **Tannhäuser** (Wagner). In German. Orch. acc. H.M.V. C1897, 12in., 4s. 6d.

MARIA LUISA FANELLI (soprano), **PIERO PAULI** (tenor) and **G. MASINI** (bass).—**Forma ideal** and **Amore, mistero**, from Act 4 of **Mefistofele** (Boito). In Italian. Orch. acc. and chorus. H.M.V. DB1440, 12in., 8s. 6d.

GERHARD HÜSCH (baritone).—**Pari siamo** and **Cortigiani, vil razza dannata** from **Rigoletto** (Verdi). In German. Orch. acc. Parlo. E11034, 34in., 4s. 6d.
　　Blick ich umher from Act 2 of **Tannhäuser** (Wagner) and **Papageno's Song** from Act 2 of **The Magic Flute** (Mozart). In German. Orch. acc. Parlo. E11046, 12in., 4s. 6d.

BEATE MALKIN (soprano), **TINO PATTIERA** (tenor), **HELENE JUNG** (mezzo-soprano) and **PAUL SCHÖFFLER** (baritone), with orchestra and chorus of the State Opera House, Berlin, conducted by **DR. WEISSMANN.**—**Operas in Brief** No. 1, **Il Trovatore** (Verdi). In German. Parlo. E11048-50, 12in., 4s. 6d. each.

Sigismund Pilinsky.—A robust Polish tenor with a resonant if not invariably steady tone. He is better in early Wagner than in Meyerbeer. The Prophet's spirited appeal to his followers sounds like a lachrymose bit of special pleading; it requires much more energy and animation to give it due effect. The ringing high notes are, however, well sustained, while the choruses add interest to these uncommon selections.

Richard Tauber.—Two airs from Franz Lehar's new light opera *Frederica*, recently done in English at the Palace Theatre. I have not heard Joseph Hislop sing them, so I cannot possibly make comparisons. I only know that they are perfectly suited to Richard Tauber's unique style and that he infuses into them rather more masculine vigour and *entrain* than is his wont. He has, moreover, the able support of the orchestra of the Berlin State Opera House.

Villabella, Rouard, Billot, with *Chorus.*—Two excerpts from *Faust*, capitally sung by French artists in their own language. They have the resonant clang of the theatre, and

the duel trio goes with abundant spirit, as does also the Easter hymn of the first act.

Alessandro Valente.—An excellent tenor, this, who declaims well without shouting. His fine voice does easy justice to the *Si fui soldato* (*Andrea Chénier*) and lends a certain charm to Mascagni's *Serenata*, which is not the one heard from behind the curtain in the *Prelude to Cavalleria Rusticana*. The orchestra of La Scala, under Carlo Sabajno, plays the accompaniments.

Alfred Piccaver.—With his magnificent voice and facile, listless manner, this notable tenor makes Wagner sound like mere child's-play. The sole drawback lies in the fact that he does not convince us he is in dead earnest. Nevertheless, it is a double pleasure to listen to Walther's songs when mastered with such consummate ease and this proving that Wagner knew exactly what the human voice was capable of doing. Piccaver sings admirably in German and maintains an amazing flow of vibrant, steady if slightly nasal tone. The two Neapolitan ditties on the companion disc are equally effective of their kind.

Karl August Neumann.—A marked tremolo is scarcely the right adjunct for the interpretation of Handel's *Largo* and Beethoven's *Creation's Hymn*. Otherwise, a fine baritone voice and unusually good organ accompaniment impart value to this effort.

Alexander Kipnis.—This accomplished basso never disappoints; he sticks to the lofty standard that has won him his great reputation as an interpreter of opera and *lieder*. Schumann's *Mondnacht* is a difficult song for a man with a heavy voice to sing, but we find it here given with a refinement and restraint, a depth of expression, a beauty of tone, that a Gerhardt or a Hempel might envy. The Strauss *lied* is sung and enunciated with the same meticulous care.

Kate Heidersbach and *Max Lorenz.*—Evidently an inexperienced Lohengrin and a talented Elsa. Both possess the kind of bright, musical voice that tells well in the love duet, and the only actual blemish is the excessive speed at which they occasionally press on the *tempo*. Love duets ought not to be hurried. The instrumental part is beautifully executed by the Berlin State Opera orchestra under Clemens Schmalstich. Even better, though, is the general rendering of the scene from the second act of *Tannhäuser*, because here impetuosity and pure feeling go hand in hand without marring the musical symmetry.

Maria Fanelli, Piero Pauli, and *G. Masini.*—These highly original ensembles, sung with the Scala chorus, from the episode of the Classical Sabbath in Boito's *Mefistofele*, should please all admirers of that most interesting and (in this country) much-neglected opera. The three solo voices have all the necessary distinction, and there is a dramatic breadth of treatment such as I have seldom heard in this music.

Gerhard Hüsch.—Yet another sympathetic, clever German baritone! In Wolfram's *Fantasy* he displays ripe intelligence and undoubted artistic feeling; in the Papageno air a style replete with crisp, merry, comic spirit, enhanced by the tuneful charm of a celeste accompaniment. What more would you have? For my part I would like only to see as well as hear Hüsch.

Operas in Brief, No. 1.—Apparently Berlin is going to send us a series of the capital *potpourris* of popular operas which it knows so well how to manufacture. It starts with that well-worn evergreen, *Il Trovatore*—a greater favourite still by a long way in Germany than it remains over here—and all the tit-bits are nicely dovetailed into the sample mosaic. Who devises these things is not stated, but they are very skilfully assembled, and Dr. Weissmann and his forces are not ashamed to put their best work into them, for they get their *quid pro quo* not only in the pecuniary sense, but in the knowledge that the Germans positively adore good *potpourris*. The whole opera is boiled down into three records. I can assure you it is all quite excellent and most amusing.

HERMAN KLEIN.

OPERATIC AND FOREIGN SONGS

EMMY BETTENDORF (soprano) and **HANS CLEMENS** (tenor).—**Rose Songs** (Phillip zu Eulenburg). (1) Monthly Roses; (2) Briar Roses; (3) Rambler Roses; (4) Water Roses. Chorus and Orch. acc. In German. Parlophone E11060, 12in., 4s. 6d.

CONCHITA SUPERVIA (mezzo-soprano).—**Seven Popular Spanish Songs** (De Falla). (1) El Paño Moruno; (2) Sequidilla Murciana; (3) Asturiana; (4) Jota; (5) Nana–Canción; (6) Polo. In Spanish. Piano acc. by Frank Marshall. Parlophone RO20117–9, 10in., 4s. 6d. each.

MAY BLYTH (soprano).—**They call me Mimi** from **La Bohème** (Puccini) and **Elsa's Dream** from **Lohengrin** (Wagner). In English. Orch. acc. Decca K538, 12in., 3s. 6d.

NINON VALLIN (soprano).—**D'une Prison** and **L'Air** (Reynaldo Hahn). In French. Piano acc., the second by the Composer. Parlo. RO20120, 10in., 4s. 6d.

CHARLES ROUSSELIERE (tenor).—**The death of Siegfried** from **The Twilight of the Gods** (Wagner) and **The Forging Song** from **Siegfried** (Wagner). In French. Orch. acc. Polydor 561011, 10in.

LULA MYSZ-GMEINER (contralto).—**Auf Flügeln des Gesanges** (Mendelssohn) and **Das Veilchen** (Mozart). In German. Piano acc. Polydor 23107, 10in., 3s. Also **Schwesterlein** (Brahms) and **Heimweh** (Hugo Wolf). In German. Piano acc. Polydor 23108, 10in., 3s.

ALFRED PICCAVER (tenor).—**Non piangere, Liù**, and **Nessun dorma!** from **Turandot** (Puccini). In Italian. Orch. acc. Polydor 95352, 12in., 6s. 6d.

Emmy Bettendorf, Hans Clemens and Chorus.—Not so very long ago, we should have heard a tuneful cycle of *Rose Songs* for two solo voices and chorus, such as this, disdainfully described as "*vieux jeu.*" The style, in fact, is redolent of the mid-Victorian period and not even so advanced as that of Liza Lehmann's *In a Persian Garden*, which in treatment it somewhat resembles. I have often remarked that honest, straightforward melody is nowhere more appreciated than in the home of the *Volkslied*, and Phillip zu Eulenberg was doubtless as well aware of this as I am; anyhow, his music can be regarded as a welcome reaction from the modernistic tendencies of the age. The outcome is an extremely pleasing set of pieces, and I am glad to see that Wagnerian singers of the calibre of Emmy Bettendorf and Hans Clemens have not deemed it beneath their notice. To them the task was mere child's play, but they have lent it a certain measure of distinction. The pretty effects come off without a single miss. Sometimes the solo voices alternate, and at others they unite with the chorus in telling ensembles, everything being very musically rendered. Oddly enough, the theme of the *Monthly Roses* bears a close resemblance to *The last rose of summer*, which would distinctly recommend it to the Germans, who adore *Martha*.

Conchita Supervia.—It must be about ten years since I first came across the wonderfully clever set of *Seven Popular Songs* by Manuel de Falla here recorded. And they are as delightful as they are clever. It takes a born Spaniard to do them justice; nor can I imagine a rendering more true to the composer's intentions, more redolent of the genuine national style, than that achieved by Conchita Supervia, who not only possesses a phenomenal voice, but is in her own particular way a phenomenal artist. Her rich, penetrating tone varies constantly with the changing moods of the music and her contrasts seem quite as natural and appropriate. Take that

between the *Asturiana* and the *Jota*—the acme of melancholy tenderness followed by the very spirit of the intoxicating dance—nothing could be more striking. The accompaniments are well played by Frank Marshall, but I do not care for the piano, though it cannot spoil the general effect.

May Blyth.—Not once, but many times already, have I had occasion to point out the inferiority of Miss May Blyth's enunciation to the other features of her vocal equipment. It is a pity she does not amend this defect, because in her case it is a rather serious one. For me, and I fear also for many of her gramophone admirers, it detracts considerably from the pleasure of listening to her records. She has a very fine voice; she knows it; and she concentrates on her tone to such an extent that only a few of her words " come over." If the two factors were more completely blended the result would be a greater command of the variety of timbre and expression that comes naturally in speech. That is the secret of the mastery so evident in the work of the Spanish singer above referred to. As it is, there is in these records by the English soprano little or nothing to differentiate *Mimi's Song* from *Elsa's Dream*, which, of course, is quite wrong.

Ninon Vallin.—Here we return to the perfect union of song and speech—an art that, to my thinking, can be fairly easily imitated and ought at any cost to be acquired. It is a literal joy to hear words so beautifully pronounced as they are in these two lovely songs by Reynaldo Hahn (with the composer himself at the piano in the second one). It is not the voice in this case that is the singer's main consideration, nor is it the element from which the listener derives his sole satisfaction. But then the French school regards this matter in a very different light—unfortunately neglected far more than it should be by English teachers—and until it is more widely imitated on this side of the Channel the consequences will remain discreditable to makers of British records. The recording *per se* may, as it is here, be worthy of the singer.

Charles Rousselière.—No longer is it remarkable, apparently, for a robust French tenor to take a few pages of Siegfried's music as it were " in his stride." Personally, as my readers are by this time aware, I prefer to hear it sung in German; but, apart from that, there are plenty of enjoyable points to be discerned in the present excerpts, not forgetting the remarkable feat of squeezing the *Forging Song* from *Siegfried* and the episode of the hero's death into the two sides of a 10in. disc. The singer's declamation might be more impressive if it were not quite so jerky and mechanical; but his rhythm is admirable and he is always in tune. The Opéra orchestra is finely kept together by M. Albert Wolff.

Lula Mysz-Gmeiner.—Surely the well-known interpreter presented in these four lieder ought not to be described as a contralto. Her light, delicate tones sound much more like those of a soprano, though she might certainly pass for a "mezzo." Anyhow, she uses throughout a very charming *mezza voce*, and is a fascinating singer to listen to, whatever her category. Here, again, is the kind of diction and phrasing that would serve as a healthy model for some of our native singers.

Alfred Piccaver.—The *Turandot* pieces suit this tenor because they sound best when sung with an easy Eastern *insouciance*; that is, with the kind of placid sentimentality wherein—until he gets excited—Mr. Piccaver excels. For one thing, he can declaim forcibly and with a splendid tone without suggesting that he is making the slightest effort, and I like that better than the over-amplified *tours de force* that modern Italy so often sends us for the heroes of the Puccini operas. Still, there is no need to go to sleep just as you are saying *Nessun dorma*, because the statement contradicts the fact; neither should the contemplative suavity of that passage (scarcely an air, is it?) partake of the melancholy spirit of consolation and sympathy embodied in *Non piangere, Liù*. The two ideas are distinctly different and require a contrast.

ALFRED PICCAVER (tenor).—**Dispar vision** from **Manon** (Massenet) and **Ossian's Song** from **Werther** (Massenet). In German. Orch. acc. Vienna State Opera conducted by Julius Prüwer. Polydor 95353, 12in., 6s. 6d.

RICHARD TAUBER (tenor).—**Vienna, Town of my Dreams** (Sieczynski) and **On the Prater the trees are in blossom again** (Stolz). In German. Orch. acc. Parlo. R20121, 12in., 6s. 6d.

ALFREDO RUBINO (baritone).—**Toreador Song** from **Carmen** (Bizet) and **Di Provenza** from **La Traviata** (Verdi). In Italian. Orch. acc. Parlo. E11061, 12in., 4s. 6d.

THEODORE CHALIAPINE (bass).—**Vous qui faites l'endormie** from Act 4 of **Faust** (Gounod) and with **COZETTE** (tenor). —**Le Veau d'Or** from Act 3 of **Faust**. In French. Orch. acc. H.M.V. DB1437, 12in., 8s. 6d.

ALESSANDRO VALENTE (tenor).—**Il fior che avevi a me** from Act 2 of **Carmen** (Bizet) and **E lucevan le stelle** from Act 3 of **Tosca** (Puccini). In Italian. Orch. acc. by members of La Scala Orchestra, Milan, cond. by Carlo Sabajno. H.M.V. B3487, 10in., 3s.

MARCEL WITTRISCH (tenor).—**Nothing by Laughter** and **Thine is my whole heart** from **Land of Laughter** (Lehar). In German. Acc., Marek Weber and his Orch. H.M.V. B3583, 10in., 3s.

EDITH FURMEDGE (contralto).—**Oh, my heart is weary** from **Nadeshda** (A. Goring Thomas), in English, and **Nobles seigneurs** from **Les Huguenots** (Meyerbeer), in French. Orch. acc. Electron X560, 12in., 4s.

RICHARD WATSON (bass).—**O Isis and Osiris** and **Within these sacred bowers** from **The Magic Flute** (Mozart). In English. Orch. acc. Decca F1889, 10in., 2s.

MIRIAM LICETTE (soprano).—**Thou, oh love** from **The Marriage of Figaro** (Mozart) and **Alleluiah** from **Exultate** (Mozart). In English. Col. DX130, 12in., 4s. 6d.

DORIS VANE (soprano).—**Cradle Song** from **Bronwen** (Holbrooke). In English. Orch. acc. Col. LX78, 12in., 6s. 6d.

JOHN COATES (tenor).—**Bran's Answer to Matholoe** and **The Bard's Song** and **Taliessin's Song** from **Bronwen** (Holbrooke). In English. Orch. acc. Col. LX77, 12in., 6s. 6d.

GRAND OPERA COMPANY in Vocal Excerpts from **Il Trovatore** (Verdi). With orch. cond. by Stanley Chapple. In English. Broadcast Twelve 5187–8, 12in., 2s. each.

GEORGES THILL (tenor).—**Recit du Gräal** from **Lohengrin** (Wagner) and **Air d'Admète** from **Alceste** (Gluck). In French. Orch. acc. Col. LX71, 12in., 6s. 6d.

NORMAN ALLIN (bass).—**Honour and Arms** from **Samson** (Handel) and **She alone charmeth my sadness** from **Queen of Sheba** (Gounod). In English. Col. DX125, 12in., 4s. 6d.

Alfred Piccaver.—The wisdom of this choice is not to be questioned. Massenet suits the floating tones and easy methods of Piccaver better than any other composer ; and the combination in *Manon* and *Werther* is simply irresistible. No wonder that Vienna (whose opera orchestra shares in this) grows " fanatical " and calls Alfred before the curtain twenty times when he sings such rôles. The recording, too, is exceptionally smooth and noiseless.

Richard Tauber.—Two exceedingly pretty and piquant ballads of the waltz-haunting Viennese type. There is no particular need to say how they are sung in this instance. The voice and manner of Richard Tauber are as unalterable as the laws of the Medes and Persians.

Alfred Rubino.—The *Toreador's Song* is nearly as hackneyed as *Di Provenza*, and yet baritones go on singing both, for all the world as though they—the baritones—had just arrived on the scene and regarded everything as new. The voice, however, has a genuinely sound ring and does full justice to the music, which is saying a good deal.

Theodor Chaliapine.—The latest evidence of the great Russian's gramophone activities takes the form of the two airs for Mephistopheles from Gounod's *Faust*. Despite their

manneristic rendering—and the manner is original in the extreme—I must confess that they interest one intensely and even secure forgiveness for all the liberties with the time and the text. With the *Veau d'Or* is included the preceding encounter with Wagner during the Kermesse, thus making the scene more complete. Then comes a genuine reading of the satanic song, subtle, daring, devilish, and flamboyant, sung as it ought to be and as Chaliapine alone knows how to sing it.

Alessandro Valente.—With a fine dramatic voice and style to match, this excellent tenor finds himself thoroughly at home in the airs from *Carmen* and *Tosca*. He makes all the customary points, and his natural tone is so resonant that it does not cry aloud for amplification to the extent that this operator seems to have thought necessary.

Marcel Wittrisch.—These ultra-sentimental ditties from Lehar's *Land of Laughter* require a certain artistic touch to make them acceptable, and they obtain it from Herr Wittrisch, who possesses a neat, effective method in addition to an agreeable organ. He may be considered an ideal interpreter of the Viennese-Tauberesque school.

Edith Furmedge.—For the price at which it is issued this record should stand in a higher class than it does. Truth to tell, I find in it little to admire. The vocal tone is coarse, the diction lacking in distinction and refinement. The *Nadeshda* air is better rendered than the *Page's Song*, where the French is faulty and the *cadenzas* are poorly done. Even the playing of the accompaniments is rough.

Richard Watson.—Here is better value for your money, even though the size be smaller and the quality not tip-top. The mistake of this singer is that he lisps and unduly hurries— both serious shortcomings in so dignified a personage as Sarastro. The voice, too, ought to be much steadier

Miriam Licette.—Contrasting styles in the same composer are vividly exemplified here by the Countess's first air from *Figaro* and the *Alleluia*, which every ambitious soprano has latterly taken to singing. Fortunately, Miss Licette has not miscalculated her powers, and she is quite admirable in both pieces. Her *Porgi amor* (to give it the Italian title) is known to everyone ; but not so the florid religious aria, wherein I find her runs clean, smooth, and full of the necessary jubilant spirit. *Tant mieux !*

Doris Vane and *John Coates.*—These two artists have been singing for Columbia selections from Josef Holbrooke's *Bronwen*, the third and as yet unperformed section of his trilogy (words by Lord Howard de Walden), whereof we have already heard *The Children of Don* and *Dylan*. I do not propose to discuss the music apart from its context, but may say that it sounds both clever and interesting as here recorded, particularly that portion of it for which the still-active John Coates is responsible. He lends dramatic value to whatever he sings and his enunciation is splendid. A striking *Funeral March* is coupled with the *Cradle Song*.

Grand Opera Excerpts.—By a strange coincidence, the *Trovatore* selection just issued by Broadcast Twelve is almost identical with *potpourri* noticed by me last month, which came as No. 1 of *Operas in Brief* from the Parlophone studio. Well, you can never have too much of a good thing, and this one is an English specimen for those who prefer the vernacular.

Georges Thill.—This artist may fairly be considered the best " heroic " tenor now singing at the Paris Opéra, and that opinion finds confirmation in his new record of the *Grail Narrative* from *Lohengrin* and the no less trying air of Admète from Gluck's *Alceste*. Both are superbly given, the power and vibrant quality of the *sostenuto* throughout being amazing. I only hope that Thill will not be allowed to overwork.

Norman Allin.—This is a re-recording of one of our English basso's best known efforts under the old conditions. It has given me real pleasure to hear it. The tone, without over-amplification, is wonderfully fresh and clear ; it sticks to the traditional style of the great oratorio and opera singer, Foli, who used to render the Gounod air particularly well ; and the Handelian " divisions " are executed with accuracy and ease.

RICCARDO STRACCIARI (baritone).—**La Mattinata** (Leoncavallo) and **O Sole mio** (di Capua). In Italian. Orch. acc. Col.DB264, 10in., 3s.

SIGRID ONEGIN (contralto).—**Alto Rhapsody** from Goethe's **Harzreise im Winter** (Brahms). In German, with **Berlin State Opera Orchestra** and **Berlin Doctors' Choir.** H.M.V. DB1442–3, 12in., 8s. 6d. each.

FRIEDRICH SCHORR (baritone).—**Blich ich umher** from Act 2 of **Tannhäuser** (Wagner), with **New Symphony Orchestra** under **Coates**, and **Jerum! Jerum!** (Schusterlied) from Act 2 of **Die Meistersinger** (Wagner), with **London Symphony Orchestra** under **Coates.** In German. H.M.V. D1846, 12in., 6s. 6d.

HEINRICH SCHLUSNUS (baritone).—**Caro mio ben** (Giordani), in Italian, organ acc., and **Largo** from **Xerxes** (Handel), in Latin, orch. acc. **Berlin State Opera,** conducted by **Julius Prüwer**: violin, **Paul Godwin.** Polydor 66984, 12in., 6s. 6d.

HEINRICH REHKEMPER (baritone).—**The Firerider** (Wolf) and **The Stork's Message** (Wolf). In German. Piano acc. by **Michael Raucheisen.** Polydor 27186, 12in., 4s. 6d.

THEODORE SCHEIDL (baritone).—**Come, throw your mantilla** from **Lowland** (D'Albert) and **The prancing steed** from **Cavalleria Rusticana** (Mascagni). In German. Orch. acc. **Berlin State Opera** conducted by **Weigert.** Polydor 90165, 10in., 4s. 6d.

BERLIN STATE OPERA SOLOISTS, CHORUS AND ORCHESTRA conducted by **Hermann Weigert.**—Abridged Version of **La Bohème** (Puccini). In German. Polydor 95362–6, 12in., 6s. 6d. each.

Riccardo Stracciari.—Another re-recording apparently. Without comparing it to the old one, which I have forgotten, I can only say that the connoisseurs for whom Tosti's *Mattinata* and *O sole mio* constitute a delight will look in vain for a baritone rendering of them to beat this. If Stracciari is singing as well as this to-day, how comes it that he is no longer heard in London?

Sigrid Onégin and *Male Choir.*—Brahms's *Rhapsody* for alto solo and male voices—one of his smaller masterpieces—is a difficult work to sing and must be still more difficult to record. Nevertheless it should fare better than it has in this instance. Its abstruse character does not bring out the best of Sigrid Onégin's glorious voice; she is uncomfortable in the long-leaping intervals, and her tone does not stand out well when the noisy, heavy male voices once start. With the Berlin State Opera orchestra supporting him, it seems to me that Dr. Kurt Singer might have secured greater refinement and a more perfect balance. As it is, the ensemble often sounds confused and obscure, especially towards the end, when the music approaches its climax.

Friedrich Schorr.—Space fails me this month to comment at length upon such familiar examples as we have here of a great Wagnerian artist's talent. Enough that they are in every way worthy of the perfect Wolfram and the ideal Hans Sachs. Moreover, the orchestra, under Albert Coates, blends superbly with the singer and shares his triumph in the fullest degree.

Heinrich Schlusnus.—Although terribly exaggerated by the amplifier, the voice of the famous German baritone is still recognizable amid the din of organ or orchestra. Both the fine old melodies are grandly delivered, and by the discreet use of softening treatment they can even be made to sound beautiful in their stentorian surroundings.

Heinrich Rehkemper.—The feature of this artist's singing lies in his extraordinary powers of characterization, and to hear it exhibited as it is in two of Hugo Wolf's most exciting songs, together with a faultless piano accompaniment, should provide a magnificent treat for others besides the undersigned. The effect of the *Firerider* is simply terrific, and the suggestion of Mime will not escape those who have heard Albert Reiss.

Theodor Scheidl.—I heard d'Albert's opera *Tiefland* twice in New York and well remember the effective baritone solo embodied in this record. It is a kind of *serenade* with imitation guitar accompaniment, and the singer infuses into it a tremendous amount of gusto. He has a vigorous yet sympathetic style and a splendid voice. These he also displays to great advantage in *Alfio's Song*, which sounds almost humorous when sung in German.

Berlin State Opera Troupe.—The forces brought to bear upon this abridged version of *La Bohème* were quite superlative enough to ensure a first rate performance. The able conducting of Hermann Weigert and careful recording have done the rest. The arrangement of the opera for the purpose is highly ingenious and brings it within the category of a popular *potpourri* such as is now greatly in demand. There are five closely-packed double-sided discs, all of them interesting. Who the singers are I cannot say, though I might make a good guess; but they are undeniably in the front rank.

HERMAN KLEIN.

NEW COLUMBIA JEWISH RECORDS.

MORDECAI HERSHMAN (tenor).—**Hymns** (Gozinsky), **UMIPNEI CHATOEINU** and **OVINU MALKEINU.** In Hebrew. Orch. acc. Col. DX108, 12in.,
Hymn (J. Rapaport), **Eilu devorim,** and **Mizratzeh B'rachmim** (traditional). In Hebrew. Orch. acc. Col. DX109, 12in.,
Songs, Duets, and **Monologue.** In Yiddish. Piano or Orch. acc. Col. 232–35, 10in.,

Apart from the absence of choral items, the supply of which has hitherto been sufficiently liberal, the new group of Jewish records issued last month by Columbia should satisfy all current requirements. After all, the public for this sort of gramophonic speciality is bound to be more restricted in this country than in the United States, where it is, I believe, in very large demand, thanks to the extent of the Jewish communities in every city and their flourishing social position.

Still, there should be many thousands of the Hebrew race in London alone for whom the music and the language of these records have a deep meaning and significance, as well as the attractiveness of centuries of familiar association. If the words be old to the point of archaism—and in the so-called hymns or serious numbers they certainly are so—the new settings here provided are only new in a sense; for they betray most of the turns of phrase, the ornaments, the vocal embellishments and *tours de force* peculiar to the Jewish liturgy of Eastern Europe, and therefore dear to the " chosen people " all the world over. Hence the suitability of the settings so finely and powerfully rendered in his pure, robust tenor voice by Cantor Mordecai Hershman. To him all their formidable flourishes and intricacies come naturally and easily, for to him they present none of the difficulties that would make them impossible of execution to the ordinary singer. The modern facilities for true and faithful recording have done good service in bringing such wonderful displays within reach of all who possess a gramophone; whilst in the synagogue they may also find as fitting a place as in the home.

The comic records stand, of course, in a different category. For their full enjoyment they require a knowledge of Yiddish; but with that advantage they can be very entertaining indeed. A monologue spoken by Jehuda Bleich, comic duets by Gus Goldstein and Clara Gold, and songs by the " Vilner Komiker," Peisachke Burstein, are comprised in the series, and they are sure of a ready appreciation among the alert audiences to whom they appeal.

HERMAN KLEIN.

"CAVALLERIA RUSTICANA"
HIS MASTER'S VOICE ALBUM

Among the modern operas that record well I would certainly include *Cavalleria Rusticana*. The action is close, easy to follow, and not too tightly packed with incident, yet dramatic and charged with a strong emotional quality. One misses the Sicilian colouring inherent in the picture and the characters, just as in *Carmen* one misses the Spanish and in *Butterfly* the Japanese; but this is compensated for in other ways, while for all who have seen the opera there can be nothing easier than to recapture both the picture and the atmosphere when listening to the gramophone reproduction. In furnishing a fair measure of those important attributes the H.M.V. Album released last month fulfils its purpose. It ought to do so, for it comes stamped with the *cachet* of La Scala, whose orchestra and chorus, conducted by the talented Maestro **Carlo Sabajno**, may be counted on to live up to their reputation.

The names in the cast are not equally familiar over here, though I take it that the artists are or have been members of the Scala troupe. Here is the distribution: Santuzza, **Delia Sanzio**; Turiddu, **Giovanni Breviario**; Lucia, **Olga de Franco**; Alfio, **Piero Basini**; Lola, **Mimma Pantaleoni**. Their work is contained in nine double-sided 12in. discs (Nos. C.1973–81), also available coupled in sequence for use with H.M.V. automatic models. The inside cover of the case provides an interesting account of Pietro Mascagni's career and that of his work, which seems to be correct in all details except as to the year in which it reached this country. *Cavalleria Rusticana* was first performed in London (at the Shaftesbury Theatre) in 1891, not 1893, and it was produced at Covent Garden, not in 1894, but in 1892, which was the year of that tremendous double season when Sir Augustus Harris gave no fewer than 150 representations of 30 operas, and Gustav Mahler made his début as the conductor of the German series. The new opera created such a sensation (Calvé making her début as Santuzza) that it was given eleven times between May and July and twenty-one times during the autumn season between October and December. Not even *Carmen* or *Pagliacci* achieved such instant popularity here.

Curiously enough, the voice of the tenor in the new album bears an extraordinary resemblance to that of Francesco Vignas, the Turiddu of Signor Lago's performances at the Shaftesbury and, incidentally, of the representation given at Windsor Castle by command of Queen Victoria, at which I had the honour of being present. Rarely have I heard two voices so similar in timbre; only Breviario's is not so steady as his predecessor's, though of equally good quality and perhaps quite as powerful. This last point I could not decide without hearing him in the flesh, inasmuch as the recorded tone sounds very much amplified, especially in the bigger numbers, and might therefore be misleading; but there are in it many moments that make me think I am again listening to Vignas. When he begins the Siciliana during the *Prelude*, giving a clever effect of distance, then gradually coming nearer, the similarity to my ears is quite startling. Altogether Breviario is decidedly the star of this cast and shares honours with the Scala band and chorus. Personally, I find little to admire in the work of the others. They all suffer from a palpable *tremolo*, and their singing is not distinguished in any instance by true refinement. The Santuzza is clearly a dramatic singer (and so, for that matter, are they all), but, except in the lowest register, which is beautiful, her tone is thin and strident. She is at her best in the prayer and the duet with Alfio, a baritone who wobbles along huskily suggesting a waggon unprovided with tyres. The Lola has a fine voice and her name of Pantaleoni makes me wonder whether she is descended from the gifted family bearing that cognomen. The recording throughout leaves nothing to be desired.

HERMAN KLEIN.

COLUMBIA "RIGOLETTO" ALBUM

Welcome, little stranger! As usual, *Rigoletto* slips in quietly, making his modest entry without fuss, preceded by his betters —if his betters they really be. He was always a weakling at the start. Says Arthur Pougin: "It was not without trouble that *Rigoletto* succeeded in seeing the footlights; for a moment it was despaired of." Censured by the Austrian Government on account of its political allusion (the subject was derived from Victor Hugo's *Le Roi s'amuse*), it only squeezed its way into the Fenice at Venice with the aid of a changed title and the well-kept secret of the tune of *La donna è mobile*, which the tenor Mirate had sworn not even to hum or try at rehearsal until the last moment before the production. Then, of course, came "a perfect triumph, as spontaneous as possible," with the public on leaving the theatre humming the words and the music of the *canzone*, and, next day, "all Venice mad over it."

That was in 1851. In fact, *Rigoletto* got to most places in the fifties, but at Paris only to the Théâtre des Italiens. Not until years after the production of *Aida* was it admitted to the stage of the Grand Opéra (1885), with Lassalle and Krauss as the Jester and his daughter. By then it had been a favourite of thirty years' standing at Covent Garden. Given a fair chance and left to itself, *Rigoletto* can be relied upon to hold its own with any of Verdi's operas. Similarly, this newest Columbia album may be trusted to equal in popularity the *Traviata*, the *Trovatore*, and *Aida*, which have preceded it (though I am not sure that I ought to include *Trovatore* among the "complete operas"). Speaking for my own part, I will only say that I consider the story of Rigoletto, like that of *Cavalleria Rusticana*, as peculiarly adapted for gramophonic purposes; it is easy to follow, clear and straightforward in dramatic treatment, and should not even be puzzling as to the final scene, where the principal characters are supposed to be separated by a garden wall.

The opera has been recorded at Milan (on fifteen 12in. discs, DX139–153) under the direction of Cav. Lorenzo Molajoli, with the co-operation of the entire orchestra and chorus of La Scala. The principal parts are distributed as follows:—Rigoletto, **Riccardo Stracciari**; Gilda, **Mercedes Capsir**; Duca di Mantova, **Dino Borgioli**; Sparafucile, **Ernesto Dominici**; Maddalena, **Anna Masetti Bassi**; Giovanna, **Ida Mannarini**; Il Conte di Monterone, **Duilio Baronti**; Marullo, **Aristide Baracchi**; Borsa, **Guido Uxa**; Conte di Ceprano, **Eugenio Dall'Argine**; Contessa di Ceprano, **Ida Mannarini**.

A glance at these names will suffice to indicate an unusually strong ensemble, and happily the recording is, on the whole, worthy of the performance. I have said before and I once again reiterate my opinion that the Italians are quite exceptionally gifted in the art of maintaining the continuity, the vitality, the atmosphere of a living drama, amid the uninspiring environment of an empty hall or theatre and in front of the tell-tale microphone. The sole fault I have to find with this otherwise fine reproduction is one that the ordinary listener would not be likely to observe, much less find detract from his complete enjoyment: I refer to the vagaries, human or mechanical, imposed by that strange instrument, the amplifier. It reminds me of the "spot light" in a ballet or a revue. It follows the star performers when they come into prominence, and at other times relegates them to the comparative naturalness which I infinitely prefer. Rigoletto and the Duke, with Gilda here and there, are especially selected for this kind of treatment, and it is curious to note how the voice changes character as the "spot light" is put on or taken off. I could name the instances in which these contrasts occur, but it is scarcely worth while; they are not marked enough to interfere seriously with one's enjoyment of some very first-rate singing.

The opening scene is efficiently and consistently done, Dino Borgioli and Stracciari coming out especially well.

The subsequent colloquy between Rigoletto and Sparafucile is heightened in effect by the unusual clarity of the accompanying 'cello solo. The *Pari siamo* is splendid all through, the last part of the scene with Gilda inaugurating a series of duets that are of unusual excellence. Mercedes Capsir sings *Caro nome* delightfully, reminding me of her best work in the *Traviata* album. Her D flat is a lovely note. The chorus, *Zitti, zitti*, owes much to the absence of the amplifier, and the whole of the Abduction finale is equally fortunate, with resultant good effect. The idea of Rigoletto's interpolated calls for Gilda was a capital one, imparting realism to the episode. In Act II Stracciari sings very finely throughout the long scenes with the courtiers and his daughter; one often wishes that the latter's attack of high notes were as clean and sure as his. Bar this, her *Tutte le feste* is admirable. But the real gems of the performance are reserved for the last act. After Borgioli's superb *La donna è mobile* we get the famous quartet (on two discs) and, by dint of carefully following the text, the individual dramatic intent of each of the various voices can be clearly perceived. (A soft needle here will, however, vastly improve the tone quality and the dynamic effect.) The music of the tempest and the trio, with a glorious Maddalena to the fore, lead up splendidly to the ultimate catastrophe. We never hear this music to equal advantage in the theatre; nor do we often get at all the beautiful duet for the father and daughter after he has opened the sack and ascertained the full tragedy of his belief in Monterone's curse. The whole scene caps the climax on a highly creditable achievement.

HERMAN KLEIN.

OPERATIC

LEILA BEN SEDIRA (soprano).—**Bell Song** from **Lakmé** (Delibes). In French. Orch acc., conducted by Maurice Frigara. Parlo. E11074, 12in., 4s. 6d.

LOTTE LEHMANN (soprano).—**Du bist der Lenz** from **Die Walküre** and **Isoldes Liebestod** from **Tristan und Isolde** (Wagner). In German. Orch. acc., conducted by Dr. Weissmann. Parlo. R20122, 12in., 6s. 6d.

ELISABETH RETHBERG (soprano).—**Michaela's Air** from **Carmen** (Bizet) and **One Fine Day** from **Madame Butterfly** (Puccini). In German. Orch. acc., conducted by Dr. Weissmann. Parlo. R20123, 12in., 6s. 6d.

DANIELLE BRÉGIS (soprano).—**Mon coeur soupire** and **Air de Suzanne** from **Les Noces de Figaro** (Mozart). In French. Orch. acc. Decca T133, 12in., 4s. 6d.

MARION ANDERSON (contralto).—**Love, come to my aid** and **Softly awakes my heart** from **Samson and Delilah** (Saint-Saëns). In English. Orch. acc., conducted by Lawrance Collingwood. H.M.V. C2047, 12in., 4s. 6d.

KOLOMAN VON PATAKY (tenor).—**Fairer than the lily** from **The Huguenots** (Meyerbeer) and **Like a dream** from **Martha** (Flotow). In German. Orch. acc., conducted by Julius Prüwer. Polydor 95373, 12in., 6s. 6d.

ALFRED PICCAVER (tenor).—**Come un bel dì di Maggio** from **Andrea Chénier** (Giordani) in German, and **Ingemisco** from **Requiem** (Verdi), in Latin. Orch. acc., conducted by Julius Prüwer. Polydor 95354, 12in., 6s. 6d.

JOSEF VON MANOWARDA (baritone).—**Die Fussreise, Wandering** (Wolf) and **Verborgenheit, Secrecy** (Wolf). In German. Piano acc., Arpad Sandor. Polydor 23160, 10in., 3s.

WALTER WIDDOP (tenor).—**All hail, thou dwelling pure and lowly** from **Faust** (Gounod) and **Yes, let me like a soldier fall** from **Maritana** (Wallace). In English. Orch. acc., conducted by Lawrance Collingwood. H.M.V. D1887, 12in., 6s. 6d.

Leila Ben Sedira.—I should surmise that this new singer is, like her name, of Eastern origin, and that, like her voice, she is extremely youthful. Neither supposition prevents her accent and method from being absolutely French nor her art from fascinating you by its delicacy and charm. Her head register has an outstanding sweetness and purity, well displayed as to its extraordinary compass by the *Bell Song* from *Lakmé*, in which part she must be wonderful. A slight *tremolo* is to be noticed all through the medium, but not sufficiently to be objectionable. Her technique is brilliant; her *staccato* and shake impeccable; the ease and facility of it all amazing. She sings two F's in *alt*, one of them at the end a miracle that ought to be performed by the Queen of Night. The record, presumably from Paris, is remarkable for a total absence of the over-amplifying that mars more than one of the examples reviewed below.

Lotte Lehmann.—Every Wagnerian excerpt recorded by this accomplished artist has a special value of its own that will one day be treasured as a precious model. *Verb. sap.* (Would that some of her gifted predecessors, half forgotten now, I fear, had enjoyed the same privilege!). Of these two sides, I declare a slight preference for the Sieglinde, which is an unrivalled and unique specimen. The Isolde is good too; but I have heard it equally well done.

Elisabeth Rethberg.—Michaela's air sung in German compares moderately with the same given in the original French, and, despite her refined, elegant delivery, I doubt whether it can be said that Elisabeth Rethberg overcomes the obstacle of language in this instance. Still, her tone is of exquisite quality, and the *mezza voce* which she employs so generously both here and in *One Fine Day* lends a peculiar charm to each theme in turn. Anyhow, though, her singing sounds more free, more dramatic, in the Puccini air than in the Bizet, and perhaps it is as well that, as in the case of the preceding record, by buying one disc you buy both pieces.

Danielle Brégis.—Here one listens to a Cherubino and a Susanna with a pretty voice and nice expression, but not a very strong sense of style. Nor is the tone quite steady or even or free from roughness. The French words are accurately pronounced, but they might be more distinct.

Marion Anderson.—The advertisements describe this exponent of the Dalila airs as a "new contralto." I recognise the fact whilst wishing that she had brought to her task a trifle more variety of colour and feeling for contrast. It is the old story: a splendid organ and a tone that records beautifully, but, beyond *p*'s and *f*'s or an occasional *cres.*, not the slightest hint of the drama that lies behind these highly significant melodies. Singers with such fine voices have no right to take things so easily. And why do the strings always scrape so mercilessly through those introductory bars of *Love, come to my aid*? They sound dreadful!

Koloman von Pataky.—Although the syllables of his presumably Hungarian name sound all awry, his combination of tone and words have anything but the same effect. In fact, his imperturbable smoothness constitutes one of his most conspicuous attributes, and with it is allied no small measure of power and sweetness of tone. He sings, moreover, with freedom and distinction, and masters cleverly the very real difficulties of Raoul's air with viola *obbligato* from the first act of *Les Huguenots*. He has an extended range and finishes comfortably on the high A and B flat. In *M'appari* he is even more animated and effective, yet not over-sentimental. Altogether, a highly welcome addition to the Polydor list of robust tenors.

Alfred Piccaver.—Concerning the rendering of the air from *Andrea Chénier* there is nothing fresh to be said. The beautiful *Ingemisco* from Verdi's *Requiem* receives the luscious Italian tone-colour that it demands, but scarcely the requisite amount of religious fervour. The style in each example is essentially Piccaveresque, and readers are beginning to know exactly what that means.

Josef von Manowarda.—This new baritone-bass strikes me as being a pleasing rather than a highly accomplished singer. His voice may or may not be as big as it sounds (and it might rival Andrésen's for volume, but certainly not for actual beauty or perfect control) ; anyhow, the style is sympathetic and fairly interesting. Of the two Wolf songs, *Verborgenheit* is the one in which the singer seems most at home. The tone of the piano is metallic.

Walter Widdop.—The Yorkshire tenor is quite at his bste in these two old favourites. Thank goodness, he sings them both in his mother tongue and, what is more, leaves you in no doubt as to the identity of the language or the text. You hear his " hail " tumbling gently upon the roof of Marguerite's dwelling, and you realise that his breast has expanded for the ball on a high A of singular beauty, prior to his soldierly fall " upon some open plain." (*Vide* the late Mr. Fitzball, who meant no pun on his own name.) One's mind boggles at the suggestion that these things could be better rendered, or even better recorded.

HERMAN KLEIN.

REVIEWS PUBLISHED IN 1931

OPERATIC AND FOREIGN SONGS

ELISABETH RETHBERG (soprano).—**The King of Thule** and **The Jewel Song** from Act 2 of **Faust** (Gounod). In French. Orch. acc. H.M.V. DB1456, 12in., 8s. 6d.

STILES ALLEN (soprano).—**Softly sighs,** from **Der Freischütz** (Weber), sung in English, and **In quelle trine morbide,** from **Manon Lescaut** (Puccini), sung in Italian. Orch. acc. Edison Bell Electron X566, 12in., 4s. 6d.

ADELE KERN (soprano).—**The Doll Song** from **Tales of Hoffman** (Offenbach) and with **ALFRED STRAUSS** (tenor), **Good day, my dearest child** from Act 1 of **Vienna Blood** (Strauss). In German. Orch. acc. Parlo. E11081, 12in., 4s. 6d.

ISOBEL BAILLIE (soprano).—**The Doll Song** from **Tales of Hoffman** (Offenbach) and **Dream of Home** (**Il Bacio**) (Farnie and Arditi). In English. Orch. acc. Col. DX165, 12in., 4s. 6d.

SUZANNE BERTIN (soprano).—**Ah ! fors' è lui !** from **La Traviata** (Verdi) and **Je suis Titania** from **Mignon** (Ambroise Thomas). In French. Orch. acc. Piccadilly 5100, 10in., 2s.

CONCHITA SUPERVIA (mezzo-soprano).—**Seguedille** and **Gipsy Dance Song** from **Carmen** (Bizet). In French. Orch. acc. Parlo. R20127, 12in., 6s. 6d.

DINO BORGIOLI (Tenor).—**Caro mio ben** (Giordani) and **Princesita.** In Italian. O.ch. acc. Col. DB340, 10in., 3s.

ENRICO AMANDI (tenor).—**Vesti la giubba** from **Pagliacci** (Leoncavallo) and **M'appari tutt'amor** from **Marta** (Flotow) In Italian. Orch. acc. Decca F1942, 10in., 2s.

RICHARD TAUBER (tenor).—**Once upon a time there was a love dream** and **Red is your mouth** from **The Target** (Tauber). In German. Orch. acc. Parlo. RO20124, 10in., 4s. 6d. And **May I ask for the nex tango** (Rotter-Jurmann) and **Drink your health, dear, with me** (Rosen-Schwabach). In German. Orch. acc. Parlo. RO20126, 10in., 4s. 6d.

JAN ZALSKI (tenor).—**O Paradiso** from **Africana** (Meyerbeer) and **E Lucevan le Stelle** from **La To ca** (Puccini). In Italian. Orch. acc. Piccadilly 5103, 10in., 2s.

HAROLD WILLIAMS (baritone).—**Recit and Aria, Eri tu,** from **Ballo in Maschera** (Verdi) and **Iago's Credo** from **Otello** (Verdi). In English. Orch. acc. Col. DX158, 12in., 4s. 6d.

RICHARD WATSON (bass).—**Tho' faithless men,** cavatina from **The Jewess** (Halévy), and **Nazareth** (Gounod). In English. Piano acc. Decca F2040, 10in., 2s.

OLGA OLGINA (soprano) and **FRANK TITTERTON** (tenor).—**Love Duet** from Act 1 of **Madam Butterfly** (Puccini). In Italian. Orch. acc. Decca K549, 12in., 3s. 6d.

Elisabeth Rethberg.—This is the first record sung in French by Elisabeth Rethberg that I remember to have heard, and her accent, for a German, is strikingly free from the customary blemishes. It is a pleasure, moreover, to listen to her rich, warm tones, to the elegant, assured sweep of her phrasing, in such a hackneyed piece as this *Faust* excerpt, lifting it out of the ruck of the ordinary commonplace rendering to the level of a really beautiful performance. Observe the note of sustained melancholy in the *King of Thule* ballad, and how it changes suddenly to an outburst of joyful surprise and delight when the jewel casket has been opened—a voice that might be proceeding from another Marguerite altogether. Seldom is this done so well to-day. The *shake* in the waltz is smooth, but not beyond reproach ; the high B at the end, a lovely note, held not a moment too long. The playing of the orchestral accompaniment is superb.

Stiles Allen.—Congratulations are due to this conscientious artist for the great improvement manifest in her recording. The purity of her timbre in the *cantabile* melody from Puccini's *Manon Lescaut* is as nearly as possible ideal. On the other hand, whatever the merit of her *Softly sighs*, it is completely nullified by the injustice done to a great piece of music. Less than half of it is there, and even that is sung at an absurdly fast rate. Yet there was plenty of room for more on the disc.

Adèle Kern and *Alfred Strauss.*—It cannot be said that the German lyric stage suffers from a lack of good *coloratura* singers. They simply abound ; and this young lady is one of them. Her voice has charm as well as range, and she takes her head notes with conspicuous ease. Her *shake* and *staccato* are models of neatness. Her *Doll Song* gives the idea that it is being sung by an automaton, which is something to be thankful for ; on the other hand, it is taken much too slowly, and the numerous alterations in the florid passages were superfluous. Offenbach's *fiorituri* were good enough for anybody, and much prettier. This piece is not a mere vocal study. In the duet f om Johann Strauss's *Wiener-Blut* (why the ugly title of Vienna-Blood?) both singers do justice to the graceful waltz and their voices blend well.

Isobel Baillie.—Here, oddly enough, is an English soprano's version of the *Doll Song*. It might almost be called an exact reversal of the one just referred to. The music is rendered note for note as Offenbach wrote it ; the *tempo* is as fast as the German one is slow ; and it gives the impression of being sung by a lively maiden who is playing with her doll rather than impersonating it, being full of human animation and not the least bit mechanical. Well, I suppose we must not expect every point to be right on both sides of a disc. On the other, in this case, *Il Bacio* gets all the smoothness and spirit that can be desired.

Suzanne Bertin.—The *Traviata* aria and the Polonaise from *Mignon* will both stand a little judicious cutting, though not quite so much, perhaps, as is inflicted on them in this record. The time is coming, I fancy, when it will be necessary to state on the label that the version used is an abbreviated one ; otherwise the present custom may grow more and more unfair to the purchaser, even at the low figure of 2s., which actually represents half-price for half the piece. Miss Bertin's execution is neat, bright and sparkling, if rather breathless; and her voice comes out well in an impeccable French accent.

Conchita Supervia.—This gifted mezzo-soprano should be a perfect Carmen, and it is a pity, therefore, that she should have had to scamper through the Gipsy air with the tambourine as if Lilas Pastia were waiting to announce "closing time." The speed somewhat spoils the rendering. Happily the *Seguedille* (also in French) fares somewhat better, particularly because sung in its entirety with the aid of an unidentified Don José, who peeps into the record as in the opera just at the psychological moment. The fine voice and Spanish *élan* of Conchita Supervia are alike irresistible.

Dino Borgioli.—Treated as a modern Italian love-song, Giordani's famous *Caro mio ben* seems to be growing upon the ear of the Latin public. It can certainly be made very attractive in its way when sweetly rendered as it is here by a sympathetic tenor like Dino Borgioli, who knows how to avoid the sickly sentimentality of over-saccharine phrasing. He is equally at his ease in the other song, which seems to be of Spanish origin and is undeniably taking. The music is a cross between the Andalusian and Neapolitan lilts, with plentiful allusions in the text to things like *Mariposa* and *mañana*. You may possibly want to dance to it.

Enrico Amandi.—This tenor's method is faulty. Despite a good organ of sympathetic quality, his upper notes fail to resist the strain of a consistently high *tessitura*. His *Vesti la giubba* is dramatic enough in intention, but vocally inadequate, and there is a persistent *vibrato* all through it. *M'appari* comes better within his means, but even here the tone is often thick and throaty, apart from incorrect phrasing and lack of contrast.

Richard Tauber.—In the first of these records the popular light tenor appears as composer as well as singer. Whatever *The Target* may be, he certainly knows how to write music *à la* Lehar that is well suited to his own voice and individual style, which, if I may say so, could make effective anything in waltz-rhythm that was ever yet inscribed on Viennese music-paper. The other two songs are no less picturesque and—Tauberesque; for the sempiternal 3–4 prevails throughout, or nearly so, and the insinuating charm of the singer spreads a glamour over all.

Jan Zalski.—There is nothing to distinguish this singer—presumably of Polish origin—from the dozens of operatic tenors who nowadays frequent the gramophone studios, but the record may at least be recommended because its quality is passable and its price reasonable. Smoothness, combined with a certain measure of sweetness and intelligence, may be very acceptable, but, after all, one begins rather to wonder whether there can continue to be a profitable demand for these oft-repeated things. *O Paradiso* and *E Lucevan le Stelle* are no doubt desirable enough in their way and highly necessary in their place, but, unless the interpretation be exceptional, might it not be for their good to give them a rest?

Harold Williams.—Here you may welcome what I venture to consider the best records of two difficult Italian airs ever attempted in English by a contemporary British artist. I do not say they are absolutely beyond criticism, but they come very near to being so. In *Eri tu* Mr. Williams almost hides with his artistic treatment the deficiencies of a poor English version, whilst making every word clear and rounding off his dramatic phrases like a finished artist. Only one little defect: he sings the *gruppetti* or "turns" slowly, as if they formed an integral part of the melody, whereas they are merely ornaments to be done rapidly but clearly. Iago's *Credo* is rendered as it should be, like a true soliloquy, with an abundance of colour and contrast; consequently it has the right significance and is an "atmospheric" reading, replete with malice, jealousy, hate, and everything devilish.

Richard Watson.—Once again this resonant bass fills our ears with ringing tone, but disappoints by his want of refinement and his curious way of enunciating his words. Sometimes he drops off his sentences at the end with an effect that is unwittingly comical; as, for example, in the famous air from *The Jewess* when he prays, "Let Thy voice, O Lord, lead them home to *tea*," meaning, of course, "home to *Thee*"! Otherwise he is the undeniable possessor of a splendid recording voice. In Gounod's *Nazareth* he is quite good.

Olga Olgina and *Frank Titterton.*—Italian being the universal language of singers, I suppose it was thought to be for the best that these two artists should make it their medium for a record of the love duet from *Madam Butterfly*. Unfortunately the words of the Japanese bride are almost wholly inaudible, while Mr. Pinkerton, U.S.N., has still to take a good many lessons before he can claim to pronounce Italian vowels correctly. Apart from this the duet, which fills both sides of the record, is interpreted with abundant spirit and most of the growing passion of which it is susceptible; also the musical beauty that two fine voices can bring to their task.

HERMAN KLEIN.

"TANNHÄUSER" from BAYREUTH

THE Bayreuth Festspiel has imparted its *cachet* to a good many people and things since it first came into existence 55 years ago. Never before, however, has the impression been so clear, so vivid, so authoritative, as in the gramophone reproduction of *Tannhäuser* just issued by Columbia, in an album of eighteen discs, numbered LX81-98. This brings Bayreuth to our very doors—nay, our very parlours, seeing that it was actually recorded in the theatre during the Festival of 1930. *Tannhäuser* was not mounted at Bayreuth until well on in the 'eighties, or even the early 'nineties; but ever since then it has been as much in request there as *Tristan* and *Die Meistersinger*, which come next in order to *Parsifal* and the *Ring* cycle.

The original German text being the one sung, it behoved the Columbia Company to associate with it in their printed leaflet the best available English translation. They did well, therefore, to utilise that given in the Breitkopf und Härtel vocal score, which is from the accomplished pen of Mr. Ernest Newman. The voluminous stage directions should be read beforehand, together with an account of the opera and its eventful career in Paris, for which the version of 1861 was prepared. The latter, of course, has always been in use at Bayreuth (as it is now everywhere), and a note informs us that it was "abridged for recording purposes under the supervision of Ernest Newman and the late Siegfried Wagner." The cuts, however, are neither extensive nor of a kind to which any reasonable critic would be likely to take exception. The performance, conducted by Karl Elmendorff, was given with the following cast:— Tannhäuser, Sigismund Pilinszky; Elisabeth, Maria Müller; Venus, Ruth Jost-Arden; Hermann (the Landgraf), Ivar Andrésen; Wolfram, Herbert Janssen; Walther, Geza Belti-Pilinszky; Biterolf, Georg von Tschurtschenthaler; Heinrich, Joachim Sattler; Reinmar, Carl Stratendorf; Ein Hirte, Erna Berger.

The overture and Venusberg music take up the first five sides, and the immensity of care revealed in the rendering of the wonderful orchestration is faithfully reflected in the recording. I have never heard finer. The tempi are the Bayreuth *tempi*—measured, sober, dignified, correct: an object-lesson for the conductors who pin their faith to speed as a means of effective and characteristic interpretation. The tenor is excellent, if a trifle nasal; the Venus unusually superb, with a glorious tone; the chorus of sirens calculated to delight the most sensitive ear. That good beginning is only a foretaste of joys to come. I shall have to be economical with my superlatives if I want them to last out the whole of this very remarkable presentation. The sole blemish that I feel constrained to point out is a slight excess here and there of amplification, with a certain amount of resultant echo where the music stops suddenly. The amplifying being directed to the sonorous voices of Tannhäuser and his male friends, it is precisely there that the effect of the device is chiefly noticeable. Examples of this are to be found in the almost overpoweringly grand finales of the first and second acts.

The voices of the principals, taken for all in all, are not only of exceptionally fine quality, but singularly free from tremolo. The Elisabeth, Maria Müller, has one of those gorgeous soprano organs that impress from the first note, and her *Greeting to the Hall of Song* is quite splendid. Good, too, is the succeeding duet, though Herr Pilinszky makes me wish occasionally that his pleading were a trifle less lachrymose. The whole of the Tournament of Song is rendered on what may be justly termed the "grand scale"; and for my part I am fain to admit that I have here enjoyed the purely musical hearing without missing to any appreciable degree the scenic and sartorial accessories of the spectacle. Another point: I think the supreme touch of beauty, individually at any rate, comes from the singing of the part of Wolfram by that admirable artist Herbert Janssen; it is not less replete with poetic than vocal charm. Hereabouts is it that the most substantial cuts have been made, yet so as to leave a minimum sense of loss. We feel quite content to dispense with the tedious tributes of Walther and Biterolf, and get on to the magnificent outburst of Elisabeth on behalf of her unworthy knight, which constitutes, as it ought, the *clou* of the whole performance. Needless to add what a noble pendant to this is furnished by the judgment of the Landgraf, *Furchtbares Verbrechen*, as delivered by Ivar Andrésen.

To dwell on the familiar features of the last act would also be superfluous. One notes the excusable omission of the introduction known as *Tannhäuser's Pilgrimage*, but revels in the loveliness of the *Prayer*, of the *Star of Eve*, and the splendid male voices in the *Pilgrims' Chorus*. Satisfactory also is it to find the tenor's best effort in the long narrative of Tannhäuser's journey to Rome; it suits him well because it calls for the expression of repentance and grief, and he utters it in sufficiently manly fashion. His final scene with the disappointed Venus and Wolfram is exceedingly well done by all three singers, and winds up the opera with fitting impressiveness. One so seldom has an opportunity of listening to this trio and the grand choral finale. Congratulations, therefore, to all concerned!

HERMAN KLEIN.

OPERATIC AND FOREIGN SONGS

ELISABETH RETHBERG (soprano).—**Senta's Ballad** from **The Flying Dutchman**. In German. Orch. acc. H.M.V. DA1115, 10in., 6s.

CONCHITA SUPERVIA (mezzo-soprano).—**Card Scene** from **Carmen** (Bizet). In French. Orch. acc. Parlo. R20131, 12in., 6s. 6d.
Granada (Albeniz-Cuenca), orch. acc., and **Dance No. 5** (Granados-Munzo Lorenia), piano acc. In Spanish. Parlo. R20130, 12in., 6s. 6d.
La Paloma (Yradier) and **De la Serrania** (Romero–Machado). In Spanish. Orch. acc. Parlo. RO20129, 10in., 4s. 6d.

OLGA OLGINA (soprano).—**Musetta's Valse Song** from **La Bohème** (Puccini) and **Un bel dì vedremo** from **Madama Butterfly** (Puccini). In Italian. Orch. acc. Decca K559, 12in., 3s. 6d.

EMMY BETTENDORF (soprano) and **JOHN GLÄSER** (tenor).—**Garden Scene** from **Faust** (Gounod). In German. Orch. acc. Parlo. E11092, 12in., 4s. 6d.

TOMMASO ALCAIDE (tenor).—**Mi par d'udir ancora** from **Pescatori di Perle** (Bizet) and **Spirto gentil** from **La Favorita** (Donizetti). In Italian. Orch. acc. Col. LX108, 12in., 6s. 6d.

PEPE ROMEU (tenor).—**Serenade** (Toselli) and **Ay Ay Ay** (Freire). In Spanish. Orch. acc. Col. DB368, 10in., 3s.

GERHARD HÜSCH (baritone).—**Hat dein heimatliches Land (Di Provenza)** from **La Traviata** (Verdi) and **Sonst spielt ich mit Szepter und Krone** from **Csar und Zimmermann** (Lortzing). In German. Orch. acc. Parlo. E11091, 12in., 4s. 6d.

ARTHUR FEAR (bass).—**The elder's scent** from **The Mastersingers** (Wagner) and **It is enough** from **Elijah** (Mendelssohn). In English. Orch. acc. H.M.V. C2072, 12in., 4s. 6d.

Elisabeth Rethberg.—When the whole of *Senta's Ballad* is sung without a cut, as I am glad to say it is in this case, the wisdom of recording the complete piece on both sides of a 10in., instead of one side of a 12in. disc, is quite obvious. It just fills the former and is rather too long for the latter; and this artist is not one to follow the prevalent example of suiting her *tempi* to her recording time-limit. She invests the familiar but always slightly difficult air with her customary warmth and sincerity of expression as well as the necessary abundance of opulent tone alike in the slower passages and in the strong rhythmical melody that begins each verse of the ballad. The outburst which forms the coda is magnificently sung.

Conchita Supervia.—This eminent Spanish mezzo-soprano provides in her latest records an interesting sample of her peculiar art—an art which in its purely vocal aspect is open to criticism, but as a vehicle for the effective interpretation of Spanish music is unrivalled at the present time. She has all the defects of her qualities, yet, despite that, it is wonderful how she grips your attention and, I may add, commands your admiration. More than ever does she make you feel that, after Conchita Supervia, you will never be satisfied with, or even want to listen to, the rendering of a Spanish song by a woman of another nationality. A Calvé, perhaps, or a De Lussan, might have given you something of the same kind; but they are Frenchwomen, and they are silent. A Galli-Curci may be the nearest approach now, but hers is only a clever imitation; for the Italian and the true Spanish are miles asunder. For similar reasons Supervia is less convincing in her *Carmen*. At least I have heard the Card Scene—her share of it—more finely sung than it is by her in this record (where, by the way, she has two charming companions for the smuggler girls); whereas, frankly speaking, I have never heard any colouring so vivid or passion so intense or contrasts so tremendous as she puts into Albeniz and Granados, or even into that worn-out Mexican ditty, *La Paloma*.

Olga Olgina.—It occurs to me that these two pieces might have been more suitably recorded on a 10in. disc. They are rather short for a 12in., and in *Un bel dì*, which is by far the more satisfactory of the singer's efforts, the orchestra is accorded excessive space for prelude and postlude. Musetta's air is a piece of graceful vocalization, and the voice in it delightfully pure; but one could wish somehow for a trifle more suggestion of the sly meaning in the girl's words. So, too, with *Butterfly*: one would never dream what a world of yearning lies beneath her picture of her husband's longed-for return. Meanwhile Miss Olgina bids fair to become quite a "recording angel." She has a lovely tone.

Emmy Bettendorf and *John Gläser.*—This may be described as an ideal record of the love duet from *Faust*. It breathes the very atmosphere of the Garden Scene, minus even the sulphurous presence of Mephistopheles to direct the behaviour of the moon. When two such admirable singers blend beautiful voices in the perennial melodies of Gounod, be their mother-tongue what it may, the effect is irresistible. Enough that John Gläser is a tenor worthy of association with the peerless Emmy, here at her very best. One could not wish to hear a more perfect rendering of the entire excerpt.

Tommaso Alcaide.—Quite acceptable, these souvenirs of Bizet and Donizetti, not alone for their own sake, but as specimens of very good Italian singing coupled with equally pure Italian tenor tone. The long diminuendos now so much in vogue are here exhibited at fullest length.

Pepe Romeu.—Here is another pleasing Italian tenor, though not altogether what my actor friends would describe as an exemplar of the "legitimate" school. He eschews the operatic aria, and, like Richard Tauber, goes in more for the "manly saccharine." Yet is he by no means lacking in robustness or power—that is, if I may trust my ears to distinguish between real volume and the amplified article. He certainly records well, and his intimate mode of expression (Tauberisch again) makes his singing rather fascinating.

Gerhard Hüsch.—It is gratifying to find here full confirmation of the opinion I formed recently of this German baritone's capabilities. He has a voice of exceptional beauty, and a natural charm of style that lends distinction to the simplest melody—melody of the kind exemplified in both the straightforward operatic airs that he gives us here. He even contrives to impart some freshness to the well-worn *Traviata* song, while in that from *Csar und Zimmermann* (still popular wherever German is sung) the suavity and grace of the music are fully brought out.

Arthur Fear.—This record is bound to give pleasure, because its vocal quality is supremely sympathetic and the singing that of an artist. If the same freedom and variety of treatment noticeable in *It is enough* had been extended to Hans Sachs's monologue, there would have been nothing left to desire.

HERMAN KLEIN.

Abridged Version of Faust

Among the Polydor records from Messrs. Keith Prowse is a newly-recorded version in French of Gounod's *Faust*, contained in five 12in. discs which comprise practically all the salient numbers of the opera. The names of the (? Opéra-Comique) artists are not disclosed on the labels, for the probable reason that room could not be found for them in the limited space ; but one gathers from this source that the chorus is that of the Paris Opéra and the orchestra that of the Concerts Lamoureux, the whole being directed by that admirable *chef-d'orchestre*, M. Albert Wolff. The work of compression—a champion piece of dovetailing—was done by MM. Weigert and Maeder, and the ten sides are crowded to the last sixteenth of an inch. The excellence of the Faust and Mephistopheles is clearly established in their opening duet, that of the Valentine in his Kermesse solo and death scene, that of the Marguerite in the jewel episode and love duet ; and withal no haste or hurry anywhere, the *tempi* far more sober and correct than one hears them as a rule in London. The singing, generally speaking, is admirable on the part of principals and choristers alike ; yet on the whole this surprises me less than the continuity of the music and the extraordinary quantity of it that has been concentrated without apparent effort in this extremely clever mosaic. It may well stand as a model for things of the kind, and I sincerely hope it will be found possible to imitate it over here.

Columbia " Trovatore " Album

The collection of operatic albums done by electrical recording is, to quote a famous utterance, "swellin' wisibly." Scarcely a month passes without call for a notice of some fresh addition to the list of operas reproduced in this convenient form, with or without abridgment. The latest of the complete examples is the Columbia album of *Il Trovatore*, executed in Milan by a familiar ensemble and with a now equally familiar level of technical excellence. The choice of Verdi's most hackneyed opera for the kind of superfine treatment accorded it here is in itself proof that its popularity is still far from worn out. Evidently the old tunes continue to exercise their pristine fascination. I imagine the big gramophone companies maintain a pretty accurate touch upon the musical pulse of the world. They know what is in demand and likely so to remain. The Italian and American sales of this *Trovatore* album will probably be enormous.

Well, it deserves to be, for it is exceedingly good from every point of view. The quality of the recording is quite superb—little if any over-amplification ; fine voices ; and singing marked by that alert assurance which only goes with music that the singers know "backwards." And then the orchestra. I suppose I have heard the *Trovatore*—beloved of the barrel organ-grinders—accompanied in opera house and theatre by every species of instrumental combination that civilised musician ever put together ; well, so much the greater pleasure have I found in listening at close range to an absolutely refined, delicate rendering of Verdi's much-decried, much-belied orchestration such as you get here. I declare that, so far as my experience is concerned, it is a positive revelation. Blatant, noisy, rough, vulgar, were adjectives thought to be too good to apply to this vivid and realistic score ; but the hand of a skilful conductor, backed up by strings, wood-wind and brass of the noblest purity, together with playing simply perfect in its way, throws a new light upon the whole work. The chorus, too, is up to the best Scala standard. Instead, therefore, of feeling bored, as I might have thought myself entitled to feel after a lifetime of the old opera, I have listened for once to a performance that I thoroughly enjoyed.

The cast is as follows :—Leonora, Bianca Scacciati ; Azucena, Giuseppina Zinetti ; Manrico, Francesco Merli ; Conte di Luna, Enrico Molinari ; Ferrando, Corrado Zambelli ; Ines, Ida Mannarini ; Ruiz, Emilio Venturini. These names speak for themselves. The English translation is that provided in the Ricordi vocal score, and sufficiently answers its purpose. A useful account of the events related in Gutierrez's melodramatic romance (upon which *Il Trovatore* is founded and which here precedes the "Story of the Opera") will be appreciated by those who as a rule find it difficult to make head or tail of the bloodthirsty plot. This résumé concludes thus : "The Count's child cannot be found, but in the pile of cinders when the fire is exhausted the bones of a boy are discovered. The gipsy, Azucena, realising her awful mistake, decides to bring up the boy as her own son, and through him to have vengeance on his family. The Count before dying begs his elder son to endeavour to solve the mysterious disappearance of the boy." Well, to me it reads as though the boy had been reduced to cinders, whereby Azucena must have experienced some difficulty in "bringing him up." But of course Di Luna *père* did not know *that*, any more than he knew what a villain his elder son would turn out in the opera. But it always was, and always will be, a very puzzling business !

Old Vic and Sadler's Wells Opera

Alternate fortnights North and South of the Thames, for the supply of "Permanent Opera" to Londoners, constitute the first fruits of the excellent plan devised by Miss Lilian Baylis. The artistic value of the scheme is beyond cavil ; there will be ample time to compute its economic chances as soon as Islington and Finsbury have had a fair opportunity of proving that their love of music and the theatre vies with that of Kennington and the Elephant and Castle. And why should it not? If opera in English can be made to draw at Golder's Green and Streatham, then surely the taste for it must be spreading in this metropolis. As for drama, surely a fine roomy theatre built on the hallowed ground where Samuel Phelps trod the boards seventy years ago ought to be simply packed for a dozen nights in every month ! We are all proud of the manner in which Shakespeare is performed at the Old Vic, and the dwellers on the northern side must henceforward assert a proprietary right to a "King's share" in that pride as strongly as if it had been brought to their boroughs by the New River Company.

There is still manifest room for improvement in the quality of the operatic performances, but I am of opinion that it will come as soon as the means justify the heavier outlay. Permanent opera involves the necessity for a permanent company (or at least it should), the members of which must maintain, both individually and collectively, a certain high standard of excellence, while the provision for training and rehearsals must be on a generous scale. Thus alone can competition prevail against the forces of a subsidized Covent Garden or earn the right to share in the same benefits. I thought the opening representation of *Carmen* early in last month an extremely lively and spirited affair, whose chief merit lay in the efficiency of the ensemble.

More Opera in English

The Spring tour of the Covent Garden Opera Company will open on February 9th at the Empire Theatre, Liverpool, with *Die Fledermaus*, conducted by John Barbirolli, the musical director. A fortnight at Liverpool, a fortnight at Halifax, a fortnight at Birmingham, and then a week at the Hippodrome at Brighton will bring the tour to a close at the end of March.

The King's Theatre at Hammersmith has just had a week of Opera in English by the Royal Carl Rosa Opera Company, ending on Saturday the 31st with *La Bohème*.

HERMAN KLEIN.

496

THE H.M.V. "TROVATORE" ALBUM.

(H.M.V. D1952–66, in album, £4 17s. 6d.)

There can be no question about it. This latest H.M.V. Album is a remarkably fine reproduction of *Il Trovatore* and one of the best examples, if not the very best, of opera-recording that has been put forward since the electrical process came into use. To say that is to start, as I am fully aware, upon an exalted note ; but I am not afraid of being told that I am too venturesome, for the theme is worthy of the note, and if I were to set about applying to it my largest collection of superlatives I should not fear being told that I was overstating the case. Only I do not intend to waste time or bore the reader by any such proceeding. There is nothing to be said about a performance of Verdi's opera that has not been said a thousand times already, and " less than nothing " when it discloses no loopholes whatever for the shafts of criticism.

Still, there remain a few noteworthy impressions to relate, after promising that my expectations were roused to a lofty pitch by the unusual excellence of the Milan cast. This is as follows : Manrico, **Aureliano Pertile** ; Conte di Luna, **Apollo Granforte** ; Ferrando, **Bruno Carmassi** ; Ruiz, **Giordano Callegari** ; Old Gipsy, **Antonio Gelli** ; Leonora, **Maria Carena** ; Azucema, **Irene Minghini Cattaneo** ; Inez, **Olga de Franco.** The orchestra and chorus are those of La Scala, and the conductor the experienced **Carlo Sabajno.** You will admit it to be the kind of ensemble that would attract you, supposing that you wanted to hear a thoroughly representative performance of an Italian opera which you would otherwise think it simple torture to listen to if done, say at Covent Garden or La Scala, in mediocre fashion. Well, you would not be disappointed, any more than I was. Obviously, exceptional trouble has been taken over the filling of these fifteen 12-inch discs (numbered, by the way, D1952 to D1966), and I am glad to be able to add that there is little over-amplification to complain of throughout the whole of the four acts. The voices come out with an effect of musical purity that is, on the whole, far preferable to the excessive noise of the exaggerated tone. There are moments, it is true, when Pertile employs *sforzandos* and *parlatos* that rather grate upon the delicate ear ; but they are not actually trying, and somehow they seem to be part of the job in music like Manrico's. Besides, if the *Di quella pira* is a trifle stentorian, that is what every Italian would consider a point in its favour ; while, on the other hand, the *Ah ! si, ben mio* is a gem of smooth *cantilena*, and in the duets with Leonora and the old gipsy mother Pertile shows himself to be a model of gentle tenderness.

Granforte is the faultless artist throughout. I have heard shouted and ruined passages which he gives out with all the requisite dramatic force, yet without the slightest deviation from the pure vocal line. Moreover, he uses a beautiful *mezza voce* and his *Il Balen* almost reconciles you to the conventionality of the trite old melody. The Leonora deserves her Italian reputation. Her voice has a lovely timbre ; it is vibrant and penetrating, and the only fault is a tendency to over-press on the head notes when they occur in dramatic passages ; then out pops a tremolo. Otherwise Maria Carena's singing does not offend in this way, nor does Irene Cattaneo's to any appreciable extent. Listen carefully to the last two discs, and you will admit that the four artists just named have furnished some of the finest ensemble work ever heard in the final act of *Il Trovatore.* And I think that is about all I need say about this splendid Album.

HERMAN KLEIN.

OPERATIC AND FOREIGN SONGS

OLGA OLGINA (soprano).—**Ah ! fors' è lui** from **La Traviata** (Verdi). In two parts. In Italian. Orch. acc. Decca K570, 12in., 3s. 6d.

EMMY BETTENDORF (soprano).—**Morgen, Op. 27, No. 4,** and **Von ewiger Liebe, Op. 43, No. 1** (Richard Strauss). In German. Orch. acc. Parlo. E11100, 12in., 4s. 6d.

NINON VALLIN (soprano).—**La Delaissée** and **Lyde** (Reynaldo Hahn). In French. Piano acc. Parlo. RO20134, 10in., 4s. 6d.

   Casta Diva from **Norma** (Bellini) and **L'altra notte al fondo in mare** from **Mefistofele** (Boito). In Italian. Orch. acc. Parlo. R20133, 12in., 6s. 6d.

TOMMASO ALCAIDE (tenor).—**Siciliana** from **Cavalleria Rusticana** (Mascagni) and **Ah ! non mi ridestar** from **Werther** (Massenet). In Italian. Orch. acc. Col. L137, 10in., 4s. 6d.

ALESSANDRO VALENTE (tenor).—**Se quel guerrier io fossi !** and **Celeste Aida** from Act 1 of **Aïda** (Verdi). In Italian. Orch. acc. Members of La Scala Orchestra, Milan. H.M.V. B3682, 10in., 3s.

RICHARD TAUBER (tenor).—**Serenata** (Toselli-Bohm) and **Mattinata** (Leoncavallo). In German, acc. Dajos Bela Orchestra. Parlo. RO20135, 10in., 4s. 6d.
   Zigeunerweisen, Hand in hand (Borganoff-Schwabach) and **An der Volga, Night on the Volga** (Sab-E. Schubert). In German, acc. Dajos Bela Orchestra. Parlo. R20132, 12in., 6s. 6d.

DAVID LESLIE (tenor).—**Flower Song** from **Carmen** (Bizet) and **Walther's Prize Song** from **Die Meistersinger** (Wagner). In English. Orch. acc. Piccadilly 701, 10in., 1s. 6d.

CAV. JOSEPH DE VITA (baritone).—**Funiculi, funicula !** (Denza) and **Maria Mari** (di Capua). In Italian. Instru. acc. Imperial 2405, 10in., 1s. 3d.

MOSTYN THOMAS (baritone).—**Prologue** from **Pagliacci** (Leoncavallo). In English. Orch. acc. Col. DX213, 12in., 4s. 6d.

HEDDLE NASH (tenor) and **DENNIS NOBLE** (baritone).—**Come with me, no risk you run** from **Die Fledermaus** (J. Strauss) and **Ah Mimi, false, fickle-hearted** from **La Bohème** (Puccini). In English. Orch. acc. Col. DX212, 12in., 4s. 6d.

VERA SCHWARZ (soprano) and **MAX HIRZEL** (tenor).—**Love duet** from **Madame Butterfly** (Puccini). Two parts. In German. Orch. acc. Berlin State Opera Orchestra. Parlo. E11101, 12in., 4s. 6d.

Olga Olgina.—This is perhaps the best vocal record yet issued from the Decca studios. It is free from pretty nearly all the blemishes that I have hitherto had to complain of in that company's product. In fact, as a well-measured, faithful interpretation of *Ah ! fors' è lui,* sung at normal tempi and spread over both sides of the disc, it will compare favourably with any that I am acquainted with. Miss Olgina shares in the improvement. Her work has shown distinct progress of late and she has evidently been studying carefully the peculiar demands that the microphone makes upon the singer. The old hesitancy has disappeared ; the breath-control has become surer ; the naturally sweet, musical quality of the voice is allowed full sway. In the recitative there are longer pauses and more *portamenti* than a well-behaved Violetta ought to allow herself ; but, *per contra,* one hears more intelligent expression and real emotion than usual, while the *fiorituri* and *cadenzas* are executed with the ease and assurance of an accomplished vocalist. The *Sempre libera* is dashing and brilliant, the shake being remarkably good ; but I do not care greatly for the high E flat (or is it a sharp D natural ?) tacked on at the end. The orchestral accompaniment is extremely well played.

Emmy Bettendorf.—Sung with the now-customary violin *obbligato*, Strauss's poetic melody, *Morgen*, fits to a nicety the softer tones of Fr. Bettendorf's voice, and gives abundant scope for that intimately expressive feeling which she has at command. Nor is the timbre affected by over-amplification, as it is in the first part of Brahms's *Von ewiger Liebe*, particularly where the young man of the story grows a bit agitated—unnecessarily agitated in this rendering of the song. However, the exaggeration is atoned for by the calm, reposeful assurance of the final section, where the loving girl declares her devotion to be of the sort that will not melt, like iron and steel, but last for ever. Both *lieder* are interpreted with a rare sense of contrast, as well as with the utmost earnestness and sincerity.

Ninon Vallin.—The sorrowful mood always seems to bring out what is best in this singer. Not that her style is actually tearful; it is her voice that is pervaded with the moving quality of *tristesse*. These charming songs of Reynaldo Hahn (admirably accompanied by the composer) are exceedingly poetic, and the artist renders them with an exquisite vein of tender sentiment. No less affecting is her phrasing of the dungeon air from *Mefistofele*, which calls for similar treatment. There is less occasion for it in the *Casta diva* (opening movement only); but the glorious melody is nevertheless touchingly phrased.

Tommaso Alcaide.—Tenors are becoming more than ever a puzzling, intriguing race. I do not refer, of course, to their human qualities, which were pretty well ascertained, analysed, and described many years ago. But in their habits of thinking, their artistic idiosyncrasies, their modes of—shall I say?—allocating their voices, and so forth, they are certainly unique among mankind. In Italy at the present epoch they seem to be moulded "according to plan." They get tied, as a rule, to one end or the other of the rope that serves for the tug-of-war, and there is nothing between but a white handkerchief to separate their respective "pulls." They either laugh or cry, rejoice or weep, bless or curse, make love or take revenge. Their voices are unfitted for the happy medium, and very few seem capable of representing both sides in the "pull" with equal felicity. The singer whose name heads this paragraph has an organ whose timbre was apparently created for the expression of grief—that lachrymose tint which, one would imagine, appeals most strongly to the ear of the amorous heroine of present-day Italian opera. With his pure, resonant *tenore robusto* he could just as well be joyous; but he isn't. He prefers to portray a miserable Turiddu and an unhappy Werther, and, inasmuch as he does vocal justice to both (though with feeble diction and indistinct enunciation), the best thing is to purchase him at his own valuation and enjoy the wonderful smoothness of his *mezza voce* and his well-tempered scale.

Alessandro Valente.—I have heard *Celeste Aidas* that I liked much better than this, and I am not sure that A. V. has not produced one himself. The *parlato* style is all very well in the recit., *Se quel guerrier io fossi;* but, when everything is said and done, the opening air in *Aida* is as much a love-song in its way as Lindoro's serenade, *Ecco ridente in cielo*, at the beginning of *Il Barbiere*. It ought, therefore, to suggest some vein of tenderness in the bosom of the Egyptian warrior; whereas this rendering, for robustious vigour, may almost be said to out-Pertile Pertile. As to the beauty of the voice and the declamation there can be no question, but it is a beauty of volume rather than of charm or expression.

Richard Tauber.—Being unfamiliar with these modern and very much up-to-date arrangements for voice and orchestra *à la Hongroise*, I can only speak of them as I find them. The fact that they are sung by Richard Tauber gives a sufficient idea of their vocal quality. In the first he revels in a kind of sentimental fantasy spun around the melody of the *Volga Boatmen's Song*, with balalaika accompaniment; and the second, no less effective, is a kind of Hungarian *lassan*, or slow movement, quite in the gypsy style, rhapsodizing gently to the distant strains of a dulcimer and a violin. Both are rather sorrowful, but Richard Tauber is not the singer to overdo that side of life. His manner always suggests the lover who is too irresistible to be unhappy for long at a time.

The *Serenata* of Toselli and the *Mattinata* of Leoncavallo are things that enjoy universal popularity, and so, I might almost say, do the records of Richard Tauber. The former suit him perfectly, and as a matter of course he sings them with his customary elegant *insouciance*, combined with a manly yet delicate tone.

David Leslie.—Here is another singer, a tenor this one, who unites the gift of a capital, if insufficiently trained, voice to that of an unmistakable North of England accent. Listening to his animated delivery of the *Prize Song* (opening and concluding verses only), I am led to wonder whether his somewhat tight, throaty production would permit him to hold out if he sang the whole of the piece and in the right key—a semitone higher. But then it would be unreasonable, I allow, to expect "full measure and overflowing" (the latter the *Flower Song* from *Carmen*) for the modest sum of eighteenpence.

Joseph de Vita.—This record illustrates the brighter side of Italian tenor existence. The Cavaliere who sings it is such a happy-sounding individual that I fancy he must be somehow related to that other cavaliere mentioned by Mme. Galli-Curci (as Norina in *Don Pasquale*), when she reads about his glance in her romance and then proceeds to boast that she also understands a thing or two in her succeeding air, *So anch' io la virtù.* But *Maria Mari* and *Funiculi, funicula* are more popular with the Neapolitans of to-day than the liveliest ditty that Donizetti ever wrote, and no doubt sell many more thousands via the gramophone than he, poor fellow, ever dreamt of getting royalties for—or would have done had such things existed in his lifetime. Seriously, though, these songs could not well be sung with greater crispness and *aplomb* than they are here. And only 1s. 3d.

Mostyn Thomas.—Here you have the *Prologue* with a rich, fruity Northern Welsh cum North of England dialect that you could very nearly cut with a knife. Being powerfully amplified, the fine natural tone assumes proportions that would tell effectively at an open-air Eisteddfod, and it mounts easily at the end to a splendid A flat. This is a plain, rough Tonio, with a genial manner and a homely accent, whom it becomes ill to pronounce "certain" as if it were the feminine of the French adjective and then make "curtain" rhyme with it. Why, also, that tremendous Mephistophelean laugh interjected in the midst of the *Prologue*? I never heard it there before. But perhaps this Tonio was not quite so free from guile as his provincialisms might lead one to believe; and, after all, his fine voice is his best recommendation.

Heddle Nash and *Dennis Noble.*—A couple of interesting duets, brightly sung by two deservedly popular young English artists. There is nothing that would move (or bore) you to tears about either. The jollity of the excerpt from Johann Strauss's delightful waltz-opera is caught and conveyed with infinite spirit; while the seriousness of Marcel and Rodolfo's fourth-act reflections never descends to the level of the lachrymose. In short, a capital record.

Vera Schwarz and *Max Hirzel.*—The love duet from *Madam Butterfly* is evidently in demand. I hope it will not become more hackneyed than *Un bel dì vedremo*. Fortunately it is by no means easy to do justice to (I scarcely need promise not to waste compliments over a poor rendering), but this time the first German version that I have yet heard compels both attention and praise. The voices are excellent, the tone well under control, the *crescendo* of passionate utterance admirably managed. One could not wish for better diction or truer intonation than are here displayed throughout, and the soprano's high C at the end is an unforced, resonant note of bird-like sweetness.

HERMAN KLEIN.

OPERATIC AND FOREIGN SONGS

ELISABETH GERÖ (soprano).—**Bird Song** from **Pagliacci** (Leoncavallo) and **Lasst ab mit Fragen** from **Un Ballo in Maschera** (Verdi). In German, **Berlin State Opera Orchestra** conducted by **Dr. Weissmann**. Parlo. E11111, 12in., 4s. 6d.

LOTTE LEHMANN (soprano).—**There once was a King in Thule** from **Faust** (Gounod) and **Know'st thou that land?** from **Mignon** (Thomas). In German, **Berlin State Opera Orchestra** under **Dr. Weissmann**. Parlo. R20137, 12in., 6s. 6d.

LOUISE HELLETSGRÜBER (soprano).—**Ich weiss nicht wo ich bin** from Act 1 and **Ihr die ihr Triebe des Herzens kennt** from Act 2 of **Marriage of Figaro** (Mozart). In German. Orch. acc. Conducted by **Dr. Weissmann**. Parlo. R886, 10in., 3s.

EMMY BETTENDORF (soprano).—**Romance**, Op. 51, No. 5, (Tchaikovsky), and **Träumerei**, Op. 15, No. 7 (Schumann-Alfi). In German. Orch. acc. Conducted by **Otto Dobrindt**. Parlo. R887, 10in., 3s.

RICHARD TAUBER (tenor).—**Can it be possible ?** (**Kann es möglich sein ?**) and, with **VERA SCHWARZ** (soprano), **Tête-à-tête tea** (**Beim Tee en deux**) from **The Land of Smiles** (Lehar). In German. Orch. acc. Conducted by the Composer. Parlo. RO20136, 10in., 4s. 6d.

ARMAND TOKATYAN (tenor).—**Lolita** (Buzzi-Peccia) and **L'Ultima Canzone** (Tosti). In Italian. Orch. acc. H.M.V. DB1471, 12in., 8s. 6d.

BENIAMINO GIGLI (tenor).—**Notte Lunare** (Doda) and **Se** (Denza). In Italian. Orch. acc. H.M.V. DB1454, 12in., 8s. 6d.

Elisabeth Gerö.—This lady has a very nice soprano voice, situated somewhere between the light and the lyric kinds, and inclining rather to the latter ; her range of head tone is considerable, without any great brilliancy of execution beyond an even scale and a bell-like staccato. The medium is rich and warm and sounds pleasing enough in the *Page's Song* from *Un Ballo*, though the mood is a trifle sad and lacking in the necessary archness. Nedda's air is sung the better of the two ; the shakes are clear and accurate, and the only fault worth pointing out here is an inclination to " scoop."

Lotte Lehmann.—The accompaniments in this, as in the above and the next items, have to be credited to Dr. Weissmann and his Berlin State Opera Orchestra, who between them always achieve well-balanced and highly finished results. Not for a long while have I heard a record by Mme. Lehmann that I like so well as this. Only when hurried is the intake of breath audible, while the phrasing throughout denotes the highest intelligence and artistic feeling. Seldom, indeed, does one hear the much-sung *King of Thule* ballad endowed with the mystic charm, the romantic poetry, that here pervades voice and words from the first moment of the recitative. Such beautiful singing is indeed a pleasure to listen to. The same wonderful *mezza voce*, with occasionally a rounder, fuller quality of voice, is discernible in the *Mignon*, and it is charged with a rare measure of deep, restrained emotion. Oddly enough, the lines of Goethe, as re-translated from the French back into the German, are altered here and there so that they do not unite perfectly with the tune.

Louise Helletsgrüber.—If you want to reconcile your ear—trained most likely by Italian singers—to Mozart's *Nozze di Figaro* sung in German, you cannot do better than possess yourself of this record of the two Cherubino airs, as rendered by a young soprano who has evidently sat adoringly at the feet of the artist responsible for the preceding paragraph. I can pay no higher compliment than to say that it reproduces much the same expressive musical tone, clean attack, neat phrasing, and clear articulation of the text. In short, the imitation, if it be one, is extremely good ; and the *Non so più* is even better than the *Voi che sapete*, giving as it does the exact idea of the boy's bewilderment and unrest. Moreover, the B flat usually

interpolated at the end is omitted, and " trimmings " of every sort are severely discarded. Nothing could be better.

Emmy Bettendorf.—Here, on the contrary, are " trimmings " and to spare. One would imagine that this delightful singer has definitely forsaken the straight vocal composition for adaptations and adulterations such as no true artist should deliberately encourage. If the land were now barren and there were no more good music for the voice left to record, then it would be easier to understand Frau Bettendorf's recent thirsting after " fresh woods and pastures new," legitimate or otherwise. But for my part I do not believe this. Neither do I imagine that her admirers, at any rate in this country, are really anxious to hear her in all these paraphrases of melodies which were not written for the human voice. If the effect were a hundred times lovelier I still would not counsel readers to listen to one of Tchaikovsky's *Six Piano Pieces* in a futile arrangement for soprano solo, with orchestral accompaniment and intrusive passages for male chorus and violin obbligato. Who invented the words I know not ; but as they are nearly inaudible, it doesn't much matter. In the *Träumerei* there are fewer accessories ; nevertheless, the crime is equally blameworthy, and I am not going to defend it for a moment.

Richard Tauber.—Both these pieces from Franz Lehar's *The Land of Smiles* afford an indication that the creative resources of the pen which wrote *The Merry Widow* are as yet far from exhausted ; and that lively comic masterpiece dates from just over a quarter of a century ago. The " smiles " appear to have been intended for the attractive voice and method of the irresistible Herr Tauber, and he applies both with a thoroughness that is exceedingly " fetching." The solo, *Kann es möglich sein ?* is apparently a reproach in dramatic form and receives full value for its melodic charm. The duet, sung with Frl. Vera Schwarz, is a graceful colloquy after the manner of Johann Strauss ; rather like a strong flirtation.

Armand Tokatyan.—This surname looks Japanese, but is actually, I believe, Slavonic in origin. Anyhow, the record was made in New York by the Victor Co. and is one of several (noticed herewith) that H.M.V. is placing on the British market this month. The voice has a genuine tenor ring and is supported by abundant lung-power. The singer is likewise a well-trained artist. I met the composer of *Lolita* when in New York and Tosti was among my most intimate friends, so both songs are welcome for " auld lang syne." But, truly, *Lolita* is a bright *bolero* with a catchy refrain, while the Tosti suits Mr. Tokatyan equally well.

Beniamino Gigli.—I noticed in the last record and again in this that the American operator promises to be strong on amplification. I cannot see why he should not reserve his manipulative feats for voices that positively need fortifying ; he should remember the undeniable fact that whatever is added mechanically to the voice in loudness or penetrating resonance involves an equivalent subtraction of purity, sweetness, perhaps even beauty of tone. Gigli also sings here two modern Italian songs in the accustomed up-to-date style, with his wonted rich, dark tone ; and easy things for him to make an effect with they no doubt were. They are sure to be welcomed effusively.

MAX LORENZ (tenor).—**Fanget an !** (**Trial Song**) and **Am stillen Herd** (**By silent hearth**) from **Die Meistersinger** (Wagner). In German, **Berlin State Opera Orchestra** conducted by **Clemens Schmalstich**. H.M.V. C2153, 12in., 4s. 6d.

AURELIANO PERTILE (tenor) and **BENVENUTO FRANCI** (baritone).—**Invano, Alvaro !** and **Le minaccie i fieri accenti**, duet from Act 4 of **La Forza del Destino** (Verdi). In Italian. Orch. acc. Members of **La Scala Orchestra, Milan**, conducted by **Sabajno**. H.M.V. DB1219.

LAURITZ MELCHIOR (tenor) and **LONDON SYMPHONY ORCHESTRA** conducted by **ROBERT HEGER**.—**Was ruht dort schlummernd?** and **Das ist kein Mann !** (Siegfried discovers Brünnhilde on the fire-girt rock) from Act 3 of **Siegfried** (Wagner). H.M.V. D1836, 12in., 6s. 6d.

Wie end' ich die Furcht? (Siegfried awakens Brünnhilde with a kiss) from Act 3 of **Siegfried** (Wagner) and **Wohin nun Tristan scheidet** (Where Tristan now is going) from Act 2 of **Tristan und Isolde** (Wagner). H.M.V. D1837, 12in., 6s. 6d.

FRIEDRICH SCHORR (baritone) and **RUDOLF LAUBENTHAL** (tenor).—**Grüss' Gott, mein Junker** and **Mein Freund, in holder Jugendzeit** from Act 3 of **Die Meistersinger** (Wagner). In German. Orch. acc. **London Symphony Orchestra** conducted by **Coates.** H.M.V. D1990, 12in., 6s. 6d.

COVENT GARDEN OPERA COMPANY and **LONDON SYMPHONY ORCHESTRA** conducted by **John Barbirolli.**—**Finale** of Act 2 of **Die Fledermaus** (J. Strauss). H.M.V. C2107, 12in., 4s. 6d.

BENVENUTO FRANCI (baritone).—**Urna fatale dal mio destino** from Act 3 of **La Forza del Destino** (Verdi) and, with **G. MASINI** (bass), **Per me ora fatale** from Act 2 of **Il Trovatore** (Verdi). In Italian. Orch. acc. Members of **La Scala Orchestra, Milan, and Chorus,** conducted by **Sabajno.** H.M.V. DB1262, 12in., 8s. 6d.

M. ENDREEZE (baritone).—**Vision fugitive** from **Hérodiade** (Massenet) and **Voilà donc ce terrible cité** from **Thais** (Massenet). In French. Orch. acc. Parlo. E11110, 12in., 4s. 6d.

Max Lorenz.—The *Trial Songs* from *Die Meistersinger,* which Edward Lloyd so often sang at the Richter Concerts in the old days—and how superbly too !—have been left somewhat in the cold of late ; why, I have not the least idea, for they are among the most brilliant gems in Wagner's priceless Nuremberg collection. They are here presented by a typical " Heldentenor " with all the necessary stamina and Bayreuth mastery of style for doing them justice. His powerful voice, augmented by a discreet amplifier, is splendidly supported by the Berlin State Opera Orchestra, under Clemens Schmalstich, and the recording is first-rate. In a word, this record is wholly satisfying, and not unworthy the Walther von Stolzing who described himself as a pupil of Walther von der Vogelweide, a 15th century Minnesinger of the highest order. And, by the way, the latter Walter was in turn described by the *Evening Standard* the other day as a gentleman named " Walker," under which name he has, I believe, frequently appeared among the singing Knights in *Tannhäuser.* At any rate Wagner put him there.

Aureliano Pertile and *Benvenuto Franci.*—Among the best things in *La Forza del Destino* are the duets for the tenor and baritone and for the baritone and bass. Here is the former ; the other is noticed lower down in this column. If you hear both records you will observe some strange freaks of amplification in the voice of Benvenuto Franci. Sometimes he actually shouts down the colossal Pertile ; at others he comes out in the guise of a gentle baritone with an organ of normal timbre. Personally I prefer the normal. Some might prefer the riot of tone that ensues when the two men join forces ; if not, please have your softest needle handy. Anyhow, this duet is magnificently sung and must not be missed on any account.

Lauritz Melchior.—I congratulate the most heroic of heroic German tenors on having gone " one better," in this " Awakening of Brünnhilde," than any of the Siegfried records that

I have previously heard of his. Moreover, I am thankful to say that he has done it without the meretricious aid of the self-assertive amplifier. Therein lies one of its chief merits. We get the natural tone of Lauritz Melchior, in one of his most amazing efforts and without the slightest tinge of exaggeration, accompanied by the London Symphony Orchestra at its best, as manœuvred by Robert Heger with a perfect balance of dynamic force and refined tonal values. Really this interpretation of the glorious scene from *Siegfried* is supremely fine. Admirable, too, is the wonderful excerpt from *Tristan* on the reverse of the second disc—that great moment where he begins " O König, das kann ich dir nicht sagen ! " The voice is full of grief and despair, but no shame ; only the weight of sorrow that is yielding to the hand of destiny. Melchior has never done grander work for the gramophone than in these records.

Friedrich Schorr and *Rudolf Laubenthal.*—Here, again, are names that speak for themselves, with Albert Coates this time directing the London Symphony Orchestra. The morning confab between Sachs and Walther, amid the placid holiday atmosphere of St. John's Day, is another of those gems from *Die Meistersinger* to which I have already referred. It brings out all that is most genial in the natures of the poet-cobbler and his guest, and is brimming over with melody and harmonies that enchant the ear with their exquisite discourse. There may be here and there acidulated notes in the voice of the tenor, but from first to last Friedrich Schorr is ideal.

Covent Garden Opera Company.—This record varies noticeably in many ways, but chiefly from the now familiar effects of amplification—louder here, softer there, like the ebb and flow of irresponsible sound-waves. After the delightful impression created by the foreign artists in the same finale (*Die Fledermaus*, Act 2) it makes a poor showing. Plenty of energy and spirit, of course, lots of go, rhythmical vigour and all that ; but not a *soupçon* of refinement in music or words till we arrive at " Brother dear and sister dear," where confusion gives place to clearness and we no longer find the anomaly of dark, solemn voices trying to sing as though they were lively and gay. These faults do not show up so much in the theatre, but they do on the gramophone.

B. Franci and *G. Masini.*—I have practically dealt with this duet from the *Forza del Destino* in the similar one reviewed above. Here the baritone, like Richard, " is himself again," while the bass makes good use of a very sonorous voice and good dramatic style.

M. Endreeze.—The label tells us nothing about this tenor or his whereabouts beyond the fact that he sings his Massenet in French, which statement, on trying over the record, I find to be entirely accurate. What is more, it sounds like the French of a Frenchman, with operatic style to match and a purity of diction deserving of all praise. I ought perhaps to know where M. Endreeze is in the habit of appearing in *Hérodiade* and *Thais,* but can only declare with certainty that I think him good enough for the Paris Opéra, which is probably his artistic home. He is a baritone of unusual excellence, with a sombre but sympathetic voice of the sort that fits him for Massenet parts, and altogether he creates in one the desire to hear from him again.

HERMAN KLEIN.

OPERATIC AND FOREIGN SONGS

AMELITA GALLI-CURCI (soprano).—**Bolero**—**Les filles de Cadix** (Delibes) and **Chanson Indoue** from **Sadko** (Rimsky-Korsakov). In French. Orch. acc. H.M.V. DA1164, 10in., 6s.

LOTTE LEHMANN (soprano).—**Dich teure Halle (Elisabeth's Greeting)** from Act 2 and **Allmächtge Jungfrau (Elisabeth's Prayer)** from Act 3 of **Tannhäuser** (Wagner). In German. With the **Orchestra of the State Opera House, Berlin,** under **Dr. Weissmann.** Parlo. RO20139. 10in., 4s. 6d.

OLGA OLGINA (soprano).—**Addio** from Act 4 of **La Traviata** (Verdi) and **Mirella,** waltz (Gounod). In Italian. Orch. acc. Decca K574, 12in., 2s. 6d.

TOTI DAL MONTE (soprano).—**Ah! Non credea mirarti** from Act 3 of **La Sonnambula** (Bellini) and **Sul fil d'un soffio eterio** from Act 3 of **Falstaff** (Verdi). In Italian. With Members of **La Scala Orchestra and Chorus, Milan,** conducted by **Carlo Sabajno.** H.M.V. DB1317, 12in., 8s. 6d.

CONCHITA SUPERVIA (soprano).—**Aria and Rondo Finale** from **La Cenerentola** (Rossini). Orch. acc. Parlo. R20140, 12in., 6s. 6d.

TINA POLI RANDACCIO (soprano) and **GIOVANNI INGHILLERI** (baritone).—**Ciel! mio padre** and **Su, dunque, sorgette egizie coorti,** duet from Act 3 of **Aida** (Verdi). In Italian. Orch. acc. under **Albergoni.** Parlo. R20141, 12in., 6s. 6d.

MARGARETE BÄUMER (soprano) and **REIMER MINTEN** (tenor).—**Heil dir Sonne** and **Siegfried! Seliger Held** and **So berühre mich nicht** and **Ob jetzt ich dein?** duet, from Act 3 of **Siegfried** (Wagner). In German. Orch. acc. under **Dr. Weissmann.** Parlo. E11118, 12in., 4s. 6d.

RUDOLF BOCKELMANN (bass-baritone).—**Wotan's Farewell** and **Magic Fire Music** from **Die Walküre** (Wagner). In German. Orch. acc. **Berlin State Opera Orchestra** under **Schmalstich.** H.M.V. C2179, 12in., 4s. 6d.

HEINRICH SCHLUSNUS (baritone).—**Largo al factotum** from **Barber of Seville** (Rossini) and **Alla vita che t'arride** from **Un Ballo in Maschera** (Verdi). In German. Orch. acc. **Berlin State Opera Orchestra** under **Weigert.** Polydor 67012, 12in., 6s. 6d.

EWALD BOHMER (baritone).—**Der Vogelfänger bin ich ja!** from Act 1 and **Ein Mädchen oder Weibchen** from Act 2 of **The Magic Flute** (Mozart). In German. **The Berlin State Opera Orchestra,** conducted by **C. Schmalstich.** H.M.V. B3781, 10in., 3s.

Amelita Galli-Curci.—Almost one feels disposed to think it strange that the most successful of Italo-American recorders did not lay these *morceaux* under contribution before now. Few singers could do them so well or be so well suited by them. Had Delibes never written *Lakmé* or *Sylvia* his semi-Spanish ditty, *Les Filles de Cadix*, would still have made a name for

him; and, had Kreisler never made a violin solo out of the *Chant Indoue*, one or two sopranos (and tenors) of my acquaintance might yet have sufficed to inform the world that there was such an opera as *Sadko*, which, by the way, will most likely be seen in London before the season is much older. Mme. Galli-Curci, with the unique recording voice of yore, interprets these things in her own individual manner—that is to say, dotting all the i's and crossing all the t's until you feel that every tiny point has been made and not a chance missed. Is the method growing a trifle mechanical? Somehow I fancy it is. Are the delicate ornaments executed to the "pink of perfection" that we used to admire so—the chromatic semiquaver runs, the catchy *mordants* in the Delibes air, the descending figures in the *Sadko*, for instance? Perhaps not quite. But yet (the expression that Shakespeare's Cleopatra hated because it " allayed the precedence "), I must not put you off. If you are a collector of Galli-Curci records, you will not care to dispense with these.

Lotte Lehmann.—All who care to possess what may be termed " classical " renderings of Elisabeth's two solo pieces will find them on this disc. I find in them no loophole for adverse criticism. Even the sound of the intake of breath is not constant enough to trouble the meticulous listener, and it is only very slight when it is perceptible. On the other hand, the positive merits are very great indeed, seeing that they embody all that is precious in the art of this admirable singer. I note that both *Greeting* and *Prayer* are transposed down a semitone; that is, unless Dr. Weissmann has dropped his Berlin pitch since I last heard the State Orchestra. In any case it does not matter a bit, provided the *descensus Averni* proceeds no farther. You must not attempt to correct the disparity by raising the figure of your " speedometer." That might spoil the tone.

Olga Olgina.—It is surely by careless oversight that the label of this record calls the *Traviata* selection by the impossible title of *Addios* (sic) instead of *Addio del passato*, and, secondly, that it bears the objectionable " warning " about the disc remaining the property of the Decca Company which they promised the indignant Critics' Circle to affix no more to any records sent out for review. Both numbers are very sweetly sung and excellently recorded, though I am bound to say that the achievement as a whole is not upon the same high level as the same soprano's recent record of *Ah! fors' è lui.* The waltz-air requires greater lightness and brilliancy, also a stricter regard for rhythm. The staccatos halt; there are two many rallentandos ; and the coda is cut.

Toti dal Monte.—I think this is the most exquisite rendering of *Ah! non credea* I have ever heard on the gramophone ; and that is saying a great deal. The vocal tone is simply lovely. It is replete with the unaffected pathos of genuine injured innocence, and therein tells the whole story of *La Sonnambula.* Every note is beautifully sustained and clear. Instead of *Ah! non giunge*, which we can very well do without, the reverse presents an altogether delightful performance of one of the choicest pages in Verdi's *Falstaff*, to wit, the charming ballad which Nannetta (Sweet Anne Page) sings with her fairy companions in the Windsor Forest scene. The solo bit is a dream, while the young ladies of La Scala have subdued their voices to a faultless *mezza voce.*

Conchita Supervia.—The accomplished Spanish mezzo-soprano has here boldly attacked (on two sides, I may observe) the very difficult rondo-finale from *La Cenerentola* (Cinderella), which we knew best in my youth under the title of *Non più mesta* and on which Paganini composed and played some amazing variations. The piece itself was the *cheval de bataille* of the celebrated contralto, Alboni, who brought down the house every time she sang it. The opera was the one which Rossini composed immediately after *Il Barbiere*, and likewise comes next to it in point of melodic grace and charm. If its revival could be brought about through this showy record of Mme. Supervia's, I for one should be extremely grateful

501

Her embellishments and *bravura* generally display extraordinary flexibility and executive skill.

Tina Poli Randaccio and *Giovanni Inghilleri.*—In this *Aida*, whose name is not familiar, the powerful voice of Inghilleri, well amplified though it be, distinctly finds its match. Happily, however, it is something more than a competition of vocal strength. The modern Italian school is represented at its best by both artists; one could not reasonably desire to hear this fine *Aida* duet better sung. Neither in the singing or the recording is there a trace of exaggeration.

Margarete Bäumer and *Reimer Minten.*—A duet of a very different type, this—much longer, infinitely more exacting, four sides instead of only two—yet equally deserving in its way of unqualified praise. Fr. Bäumer possesses the qualities of the ideal Brünnhilde (I need not describe them) in so far as concerns their vocal and declamatory demands. Her rich, serious tone has just the right tragic timbre and dramatic colour for the glorious duet which triumphantly ends up *Siegfried*; while her companion here is (at least to the ear) the kind of *Heldentenor* that we associate with the part of the "fearless hero." Neither is a rarity nowadays, especially in the countries of *Mitteleuropa*, where every province rears its own tribes of *Nibelungen* personages and brings them up in the accepted Bayreuth traditions. Parlophone-Odeon, like H.M.V. and Columbia, chooses the pick of such protagonists, provides them with an orchestra like Dr. Weissmann's, and in the result we get tremendous slices of the *Ring* that not very long ago would have been looked upon as miracles. Here is one of them.

Rudolf Böckelmann.—This excellent basso-cantante is not, unfortunately, to be heard at Covent Garden during the present season, and it may be some consolation to his admirers to know that he has provided them with a singularly fine reproduction of his noble and manly rendering of Wotan's *Abschied*, which in this instance, I hope, means only Böckelmann's *Aufwiedersehen*. The sonority of his tone is not merely big, but natural and pleasing; its superb quality is not spoilt by artificial accessories. His expression is unforced and conveys just the right degree of pathos. For Wotan, loving father though he be, has to remember his promise to Fricka and assume a stern exterior, otherwise what would become of the business of the fire-girt maiden and all that follows? The Berlin Orchestra is magnificent, and Schmalstich is evidently a tip-top Wagnerian conductor. Altogether, this is the best separate record of the *Walküre* closing scene that I have yet encountered.

Heinrich Schlusnus.—In this record we find a capital German baritone and a first-rate artist, whom I have often praised for his good work, falling short of success because he is, or appears to be, out of his element. With the best of imaginable intentions, his attempt to do justice to *Largo al factotum* (in Italian too!) eventuates only in a pale and unconvincing reflection of the real thing. It may be vigorous and painstaking; but it is dull, heavy, without spontaneity, lacking in genuine life. The patter never flows freely, and when Figaro should call out " Uno alla volta," he is made to shout " Un 'altra volta," as if fearing to drive away his customers! The German version of the air from *Un Ballo in Maschera* (not one of Verdi's inspirations, anyhow) is merely insipid, and over-amplified at that.

Ewald Böhmer.—Quite in another category stands this effort of another German baritone—a newcomer, I fancy—who knows exactly what he ought to sing and how to sing it. In his quiet, easy manner he reminds me rather of Richard Tauber, though probably he is less expensive. His voice, moreover, has much of the same charm, and his diction is no less exemplary. But are these talents all concentrated upon Strauss or Lehar? Not a bit of it. He turns his attention to Mozart and, for a change, provides, together with Herr Schmalstich's orchestra, about the most delicious and perfect rendering of the Papageno airs from the *Magic Flute* that I have ever heard to the original text. It is a record that must not be missed.

HERMAN KLEIN.

H.M.V. "FAUST" ALBUMS

This month has brought us the "compleat" *Faust* of Gounod, issued by H.M.V. in two albums of ten discs each, or twenty double-sided records in all, numbered from C2122 to C2141 (automatic couplings C7109-28). As is only fitting and proper in the case of the most popular of French (if not of all) operas, the new recording has been done in Paris and the music sung in French by French artists. (I am not absolutely certain about the tenor, whose name is Vezzani; but, even if he be an Italian, his accent is quite good enough to justify his being taken for a Frenchman.) It can rightly claim to be an authentic reproduction of the full score as Gounod ultimately left it; a true interpretation of the spirit as well as the letter of the work; blameless in the matter of *tempi* and *nuances*, and alike vocally and instrumentally correct down to the smallest detail. For this satisfactory result M. Henri Busser, with orchestra and chorus of the Paris Opéra, is entitled to warm praise, as are also the following artists of the cast: **César Vezzani** (Faust), **Marcel Journet** (Mephistopheles), **Louis Musy** (Valentine), **Michael Cozette** (Wagner), **Marthe Coiffier** (Siebel), **Jeanne Montfort** (Marthe), and **Mireille Berthon** (Marguerite).

Speaking in a general sense, the beauty of the new *Faust* seems to me to be marred by one blemish, and one only—its all-pervading loudness. For the greater part of the time the singers give the impression that they are shouting at the top of their voices; yet of course they are doing nothing of the kind. The effect arises apparently from two causes. One is the excessive resonance of the empty concert-hall—the new Salle Pleyel—which, as I gather from collateral evidence, was the *locale* employed; and the other the mistaken use of additional amplification. Why this could not have been foreseen and provided against, goodness only knows. But there it is; and in the more delicate scenes of the opera—the love music of the garden, for example, where it cries aloud, not for noise, but for softness and sweetness—the feeling of excessive power is particularly noticeable. It can be modified by mechanical means, no doubt, and it may not sound so loud in a large room or a concert hall; anyhow, no amount of extra resonance can detract from the merit of the musical interpretation, which is splendid throughout. The voices are all of good quality, the singing is delightfully artistic, and the diction rarely if ever falls below the best French level.

An important and interesting feature of this Album is the inclusion of the picturesque Walpurgis Night music, which so seldom forms part of the opera as given in this country. Until the late Sir Augustus Harris mounted the act (at great trouble and expense) it had never been seen over here, despite the popularity of the lovely ballet-music, now so familiar to everyone. But there is much more in it than mere ballet, as Boïto so cleverly proved by his treatment of the Brocken scene in *Mefistofele*. Goethe's fantastic creation was not put into his *Faust* for nothing; indeed, it is absolutely essential if we are to be able to make head or tail of the Prison scene, which it immediately precedes. Gounod has put some highly characteristic music into his Walpurgis act, and to my thinking it is by far the most valuable contribution brought to the gramophone repertory by this H.M.V. performance. It is also among those portions of the opera—for instance, the Kermesse, the Soldiers' Return, the Church scene, the Death of Valentine, and the final Apotheosis of Marguerite—that suffer least on account of the excessive sonority. On the contrary, the sole fault complained of here becomes a virtue, and the fine organ of the Salle Pleyel, by adding its imposing effect to the ensemble, atones not a little for the unwelcome echo supplied by the acoustics of the empty hall at moments when it is not wanted.

Operas may come and operas may go, but *Faust*, well presented as it is in these Albums, probably stands a better chance than most of going on for ever.

HERMAN KLEIN.

Francis Toye's Life of Verdi*

There is a certain directness of style about Mr. Toye's critical writings that seems to proclaim his fitness to deal with the life and works of a master so abruptly candid and frank as was Giuseppe Verdi. Throughout the pages of this interesting book there stands out clearly the predominant characteristic of honesty and love of honesty, the passionate desire to do justice by his fellow man, that distinguished the Bard of Sant' Agata from the majority of his contemporaries. Connected with him there were no private mysteries to be laid bare, no *liaisons*, secret or otherwise, to be uncovered and analysed through the discovery of voluminous letters dealing more or less with matters of love and money. The correspondence quoted, some of it for the first time, in these pages relates almost exclusively to works as they are being projected or composed; and, if not precisely exciting, it is often amusing and at least free from the tinge of passion or eroticism. Even had such qualities been in Verdi's nature he could not have put his thoughts upon them down on paper. For his disposition was one of the most sensitive and retiring ever possessed by a great musician.

Hence it was that the world knew nearly all that there was to know about him. Only, to gather together the many strands of the story it was necessary to take the trouble of searching in various directions and of studying many accounts that did not always agree on points of detail. It is the outstanding merit of Mr. Toye's biography that it collects for us the whole of these facts and presents them in a single, well-planned volume. One half is devoted to the life-story, and that is by far the most interesting for its conciseness of treatment and freshness of viewpoint; while the other consists of a clear description and criticism of the plot and music of the twenty-six operas and the ecclesiastical and lesser works that came from Verdi's pen. Such a book was absolutely needed, and its compilation called for much patient research. Again, therefore, I say that its author, a writer imbued with enthusiasm and the appreciative faculty, was the right man for the job.

He enables us to trace better than anyone else has done that extraordinary process of development which manifested itself so strikingly in the musician, without any material change in the spirit or the inner nature of the man himself—a born peasant who "to the day of his death retained some characteristics, bad as well as good, of his class and upbringing." Again, Mr. Toye properly emphasises the originality of Verdi's genius and the fact, upon which I have so often ventured to insist, that he owed positively nothing to Wagner or Berlioz or any other innovator of his time for the successive phases of growth and above all of harmonic development that marked his

---

Giuseppe Verdi: his Life and Works. Wm. Heinemann Ltd. 495 pp. Price, one guinea.

later scores from the period of *Aida* and the Manzoni *Requiem*. Such changes, such progress in the technique and the artistic product of a musician long past the prime of life, will for ever be a standing reflection upon the common dictum that the mentality of old age is incapable of grand and noble and enduring creations. *Otello* and *Falstaff* afford living evidence to the contrary.

OPERATIC AND FOREIGN SONGS

LILY PONS (soprano).—**Ardon gl'incensi** and **Spargi d'amaro pianto**, the Mad Scene from **Lucia di Lammermoor** (Donizetti). In Italian. Orch. acc. H.M.V. DB1504, 12in., 8s. 6d.

VALERIA BARSOVA (soprano).—**Una voce poco fà (Cavatina di Rosina)** from **The Barber of Seville** (Rossini). In Russian. Orch. acc. Parlo. E11128, 12in., 4s. 6d.

META SEINEMEYER (soprano).—**Golden Moments (Und Susanna kommt nicht)** from **Marriage of Figaro** (Mozart). In German. Orch. acc. Parlo. E11130, 12in., 4s. 6d.

EIDE NORENA (soprano).—**Mad Scene** from **Hamlet** (Ambroise Thomas). In French. Orch. acc. Parlo. R20145, 12in., 6s. 6d.

OLGA HALEY (mezzo-soprano).—**When I am laid in earth** from **Dido and Aeneas** (Purcell, arr. Geehl) and **Where'er you walk** from **Semele** (Handel, arr. Geehl). Orch. acc. Parlo. E11121, 12in., 4s. 6d.

MARIAN ANDERSON (contralto).—**O don fatale** from **Don Carlos** (Verdi), in Italian, and **Plaisir d'amour** (Martini), in French. Orch. acc. H.M.V. C2065, 12in., 4s. 6d.

CLARA SERENA (soprano).—**O Love, from thy power** and **Fair spring is returning** from **Samson and Delilah** (Saint-Saëns). In English. Orch. acc. Col. DX245, 12in., 4s. 6d.

RICHARD TAUBER (tenor).—**Four Words, Vier Worte möcht' ich dir jetzt sagen** (Irwin-Rotter) and **When the lilac blooms again, Wenn der weisse Flieder wieder blüht** (Doelle-Rotter). In German. Orch. acc. Parlo. R20143, 12in., 6s. 6d.
Si vous l'aviez compris (Denza) and **Ideale** (Tosti). In German. Orch. acc. Parlo. R20144, 12in., 6s. 6d.

YVONNE PRINTEMPS (soprano).—**Le pot-pourri d'Alain Gerbault** (arr. Labis). In French. Orch. acc. H.M.V. D1996, 12in., 6s. 6d.

M. ENDREZE (baritone).—**Ballad of Queen Mab** and **Capulet's Lament** from **Romeo and Juliet** (Gounod). In French. Orch. acc. Parlo. E11129, 12in., 4s. 6d.

TINO PATTIERA (tenor).—**Danza, danza** and **Canzone alla mia bella viola** (Becce) from the film **Fra Diavolo**. In Italian. Orch. acc. Parlo. R926, 12in., 3s.

LOUIS v.d. SANDE (baritone).—**Prologue** from **Pagliacci** (Leoncavallo). In German. Orch. acc. Sterno 8009, 12in., 2s. 6d.

PETER DAWSON (bass-baritone).—**Pari siamo** from **Rigoletto** (Verdi) and **Il balen** from **Il Trovatore** (Verdi). In English. Orch. acc. H.M.V. B3698, 10in., 3s.

THEODORE CHALIAPINE (bass).—**Merry Butterweek** (Sieroff) with **Russian Opera Chorus**, and **Trepak** (Moussorgsky). In Russian. Orch. acc. H.M.V. DB1511, 12in., 8s. 6d.

Lily Pons.—The fact that the old operatic "Mad Scenes" continue to be recorded is sufficient indication that the demand for them continues to survive. The opera itself may no longer be an item in the popular repertory, at least in this

503

country, but that has no bearing upon the subject. Few people would stir a yard, apparently, to hear *Lucia di Lammermoor*, or even so far as that to listen to Ambroise Thomas's *Hamlet*. I do not at the moment perceive any haste on the part of our gramophone companies to secure first place with an album of either of these operas, rich as they both are in fine music and associations with the respective geniuses of Sir Walter Scott and William Shakespeare. But let some Continental star come forward with the Mad Scene from one or the other and what is the result ? A glad eye and a prompt " Open Sesame." Of course it has to be a really first-class performance, because anything second-class in this line may just as well not exist. It will be taken for granted, consequently, that the particular *Mad Scene* under notice demonstrates the fitness of Mme. Lily Pons for her purpose, which is that of a brilliant *coloratura* soprano seeking comparison with the very greatest. Her voice is pure and clear in quality, her range extensive, her head register well placed (including a high F at the end of the long flute cadenza), and her execution neat rather than phenomenal. On the whole, therefore, an excellent *bravura* performance.

Valeria Barsova.—Presumably this is a Russian artist. Anyhow she sings *Una voce* in that language and all the evidence points in the same direction. Although described as a soprano, I consider her more of a high mezzo, with a true compass limited to the two octaves from middle C upwards. The texture of the voice is slightly hard, with a tendency to undue nasal resonance in the higher medium, which is, for that matter, a not uncommon fault in Russian singers. The attack of these notes is, moreover, frequently a shade over-vigorous ; while a somewhat staccato method is relieved occasionally by well-sustained musical tones. The intonation is perfect at all times, and the *fiorituri* are very smoothly executed, being mostly of a familiar and not too ambitious order.

Meta Seinemeyer.—The lamented German soprano evidently made this record of the Countess's big aria before the days of " amplification " came to puzzle and mislead us. Yet, weak as the voice sounds by comparison, I prefer it for the sake of all the other good qualities that proclaim a sincere, refined, and conscientious artist. At any rate we have here genuine Mozart phrasing, supported by breathing as faultless as could possibly be imagined and a wholly perfect management of the voice in the longest passages. I like best the outpouring of grief in the andantino or slower part of the air ; the allegro might have been taken a trifle faster if only to secure the necessary contrast. The accompaniments were well played.

Eidé Norena.—Here is Mad Scene, No. 2, sung as it ought to be in the original French with diction and accent alike impeccable. I confess to a solid liking for the music of Ophelia's operatic soliloquy, and to my thinking it affords her on the stage a much better chance of enacting a poor damsel bereft of reason than mere words can. The gramophone limits her, of course, to the vocal display alone, and there she sounds (like her unfortunate friend Lucy of Lammermoor) quite as sane and reasonable as you or I who are listening. One cannot say in either case " That way madness lies." Anyhow the way in this instance is extremely pleasant, for the singer has a charming voice and style, her timbre being very sympathetic in the medium register and hardly less sweet and musical in the more elevated region. Her rhythm and diction are likewise excellent.

Olga Haley.—This is a thoughtful artist, whose work invariably commands respect. One hesitates, therefore, before condemning her for having appropriated Handel's well-known tenor air, *Where'er you walk*. What is sauce for the gander ought unquestionably to be sauce for the goose, and on that principle the lovely air from *Semele* might sound equally well when sung by a clever mezzo-soprano. The fact remains, however, that it does not. It expresses the adoration of a man for the simplest deeds of his lady-love in figurative language, not as ordinary daily happenings. All the tenderness is a-wanting, and, to make matters worse, the song is rushed through at a speed that no mere man ever yet indulged in. The other side of the disc presents Miss Haley in her usual favourable light. One could not desire a more unaffected, straightforward, dignified outpouring of grief and resignation than this farewell of Queen Dido to life and love. One can even overlook the over-amplification, for the tone is too rich and full to be spoiled.

Marian Anderson.—A similar exemption would apply to the recording of this superb contralto were the voice less " tight " in its throatiness. Cannot the fault be remedied ? It certainly ought to be ; and equally so the use of English vowels in the Italian *Don fatale* and the French *Plaisir d'amour*. As it is, all the beauty of the opulent tone and the innate dramatic power behind the utterance of the words is obscured by errors of method and of articulation. Which is a great pity, since the natural gifts of the singer are quite exceptional enough to win her a place in the front rank of her class.

Clara Serena.—The character of Delilah is perhaps easier to depict on the stage than in a gramophone record. On this account it has sometimes occurred to me that a good portrait of the singer in appropriate costume should if possible be inserted somewhere in the label of every record such as this. It would help in the present instance, for example, to get a better idea of what the Philistine courtezan was driving at in these two very different airs, instead of conveying the impression, as they do, that she was actuated by identical emotions in each. The colour of the voice as well as every inflection should realize the very opposite. *Fair Spring* is an outwardly innocent but inwardly sly and subtle suggestion ; *O Love from thy power* is an invocation, not to God but the devil, for the achievement of a nefarious purpose. Surely the contrast between the two should be very vividly portrayed !

Richard Tauber.—It seems years, and yet it is only months, in a way, since I began writing about the records of this very popular tenor, recommending them for what they were and endeavouring to appraise his talents from them for the benefit of my readers. They were all I had to go by, and let me add that it is not my fault if I have nothing more now, for although Herr Tauber was singing in London in a Lehar comic opera for some time, I was not afforded an opportunity of hearing him in person. Hence the fact that there is nothing fresh to observe about the latest specimens of his recording art ; they are up to his usual mark, and therefore pretty, taking, lively and tender by turns, sweet, insinuating, impulsive, and always pleasing.

Yvonne Printemps.—The talented actress who is the wife of Sacha Guitry is, as most of us are aware, a delightful singer and *diseuse*. What she seems to have recorded here is a genuine *pot-pourri* of tunes from opéra-bouffe and the repertoire of the Folies-Bergère allied to modern or rather up-to-date words more or less suggested by the world-cruising exploits of Alain Gerbault. How far I am correct in my surmise I am not altogether certain, but I do know that the *mélange* is very tuneful and its rendering extremely artistic and amusing. The comic touches are exquisite.

M. Endrèze.—Few baritones make a great success of Gounod's setting of the *Queen Mab* ballad ; and for various reasons. Somehow it never seems to come quite naturally from the Mercutio of the opera, as distinguished from the fantastic gentleman of Shakespeare's play. The gist of the poetic idea is too far-fetched and fanciful to ring true in an opera. Again, the music is exceedingly difficult ; the rhythms are catchy, the transitions rapid, and it needs a highly accomplished singer to do it justice. So much the greater credit, then, to its present interpreter for overcoming the difficulties of the piece with such skill and adroitness. His rich baritone voice and exemplary diction are likewise worthily displayed in the prosy but melodious homily pronounced by Capulet in expectation of poor Juliette's marriage with Paris. His pure legato is a model.

Tino Pattiera.—I can only speak of the talking film entitled *Fra Diavolo* by hearsay, and I believe its relationship to Auber's opera is of the slightest. Anyhow these Italian *canzone* (which are not by Auber) seem to be the right things in the right place, and they are sung by a tenor whose voice and style are eminently fitted to show them off to advantage.

Louis v.d. Sande.—The *Prologue*, much amplified, but admirably sung in German by a baritone who has a powerful and facile A flat at his disposal. His timbre is appropriately dark and full of menace, yet not lacking in a shade of tenderness when required. Even if you do not catch the meaning of his words, you feel that he is giving you ample warning of the tragedy to come.

Peter Dawson.—The English translation of *Il balen* reeks less of colloquial commonplaces than that of *Pari siamo*, but I cannot honestly say that I enjoy listening to either, even from the lips of this painstaking singer. (By the way, he has not overcome his disturbing lisp.) As it sounds to me, Verdi's broad cantilena calls for a more aggressive and forcibly dramatic treatment if these pieces are properly to express the feelings of Rigoletto and the Count di Luna.

Chaliapine.—Excuse the omission of the Theodore. There can be only one Chaliapine in this world—at a time—and at the moment of writing he is filling the Lyceum Theatre with enthusiastic audiences at a fee of £600 per night. Meanwhile let the modest gramophonist be grateful if he can obtain for much less than the price of a stall an even more enduring memory of Chaliapine's unique talent, in the shape of these two additions to his list of Russian songs as enumerated in the H.M.V. catalogue. Need I say how he sings them or how they are recorded? I trust not, for I have no more superlatives available for this month.

HERMAN KLEIN.

OPERATIC AND FOREIGN SONGS

LOTTE LEHMANN (soprano).—**Alone here doth she dwell** and **In the regal festal garments** from **Ariadne on Naxos** (Richard Strauss). In German. **Orchestra of the State Opera House, Berlin.** Parlo. R20147, 12in., 6s. 6d.

EMMY BETTENDORF (soprano).—**Ye now are sorrowful** from **A German Requiem** (Joh. Brahms). In two parts. In German, with **Chorus and Orchestra,** under **O. Dobrindt.** Parlo. E11138, 12in., 4s. 6d.

HEINRICH SCHLUSNUS (baritone).—**Die Himmel rühmen** (Beethoven) and **Arioso, Dank sei dir, Herr** (Handel). In German. Orch. acc. Polydor 95421, 12in., 6s. 6d.

RICHARD TAUBER (tenor).—**Will'st du?** and **Wolgalied** from **The Czarevitch** (F. Lehar, Jenbach-Reichert). In German. Orch. acc. Parlo. R20146, 12in., 6s. 6d.

VERA SCHWARZ (soprano).—**Born on the rosy wings of song** and with **MAX HIRZEL** (tenor) **Look with pity down on a soul fast fleeting** (Miserere Scene) from Act 4 of **Il Trovatore** (Verdi). In German, with **Chorus and Orchestra of the State Opera House, Berlin,** under **Dr. Weissmann.** Parlo. E11137, 12in., 4s. 6d.

MICHELE FLETA (tenor).—**La Dolores,** Madrigale (Breton) and **Ay, Ay, Ay** (Perez-Freire). In Spanish. Orch. acc. H.M.V. DB1483, 12in., 8s. 6d.

*****PAUL BENDER** (bass).—**Odin's Meeresritt,** ballad (text by Aloys Schreiber, music by Carl Loewe), and **Kleiner Haushalt** (Rückert and Carl Loewe). In German. Piano acc. Ultraphon E415, 12in., 6s. 6d.

WILHELM RODE (baritone).—**Credo** from **Otello** (Verdi) and **Ich, der Geist der stets verneinet** from **Mefistofele** (Böito). In German. Orch. acc. Ultraphon F525, 12in., 6s. 6d.

(*Sent for review by The Gramophone Exchange.)

Lotte Lehmann.—*Ariadne auf Naxos* has been heard in London at most half a dozen times; it is the opera of Richard Strauss with which we are apparently least anxious to renew acquaintance. Mounted at His Majesty's Theatre during the Beecham season of 1913—that is, barely a year after its first production at Stuttgart—it was again given in a new version in May 1924, this time by the Grand Opera Syndicate at Covent Garden, when Mme. Lehmann sustained the title-rôle and that delightful soprano, Maria Ivogün, made her début as Zerbinetta. Happily the elder artist has bethought her of the charming air in which Ariadne gives expression to her feelings when longing for the return of Bacchus to the desert island of Naxos, and she has here recorded it for the benefit of her thousands of admirers. The music suits her to perfection, and as it consists for the greater part of pure melody and graceful yet characteristic phrases elegantly turned, I need scarcely say with what pleasure it may be listened to in the hands of this gifted artist. I have gone over it more than once without being able to distinguish a flaw either in the voice or the recording. Even the exacting passage just before the end is comfortably managed and the whole piece beautifully done, including the important work of the State Opera House, Berlin. I should add that it occupies both sides of the disc.

Emmy Bettendorf.—Outside the domain of opera there is a long list of masterpieces awaiting the attention of the great German singers, and I am glad to find one so distinguished as the "peerless Emmy" setting a good example for once by choosing legitimate excerpts, rather than vocal solos manufactured out of popular piano pieces or Lieder embellished with violin *obbligati* and elaborate orchestral accompaniments. In the present instance we have a truly noble soprano air to which justice is seldom done. It is perhaps the gem—at any rate among the solos—of Brahms's superb *Deutsches Requiem*, and the more frequently you hear it—that is, the better you know it—the more you will enjoy listening to it. Mme. Bettendorf invests it with deep devotional feeling, whilst singing the suave phrases with all her accustomed beauty of tone and fervour of expression. The musical effect is enhanced when the conductor, Herr Dobrindt, brings in his well-balanced choir, whose words, oddly enough, can be more readily caught than those of the soloist.

Heinrich Schlusnus.—Here is a clear case of over-amplification. One wonders whether the record is intended only for use in a vast concert-room or the open air. It is unquestionably too strident and penetrating for ordinary purposes, though it might sound well enough from beneath the folds of a thick eider-down quilt. But who wants to hear the massive tones of Heinrich Schlusnus magnified to twenty times their natural volume? I for one do not. It is a pity, therefore, that he cannot be allowed to sing Handel and Beethoven in his own true voice, which obviously has no need of these megaphonic devices. Really, if Polydor took my advice, they would withdraw this sample, and give him a chance of proving how much better the unexaggerated specimen would sound. The songs could hardly be better sung.

Richard Tauber.—Although, as I write, this popular singer is back in London, I have still not heard him "in the flesh"; which is perhaps as well, since I have only to deal with his gramophone records and not with the stage performer. I have also only to judge of the effects that he produces and not the process of technical evolution whereby he has arrived at them. I mention this because I sometimes wonder whether the peculiar mixture of palatal and nasal timbres which, in the opinion of some people, constitutes the main attraction of his voice, was bestowed upon him by nature or brought about by a specific and diligent study of the method. One thing is certain: it has earned him a fortune. He is, moreover, a most intelligent singer of the kind of music that is adapted to his voice and style. The kind in question is supplied for him in prolific quantities by Franz Lehar, and two characteristic examples of it reside in these records.

Vera Schwarz and *Max Hirzel.*—Put briefly, we have on the two sides of this disc a very pleasing and competent rendering in German of Leonora's air, *D'amor sull' ali rosee*, followed by the *Miserere* scene from the *Trovatore*, all ably done by two excellent artists and a well-trained chorus.

Michele Fleta.—As might be expected from this highly priced (and prized) singer of Spanish songs, we have in this record something authentic, individual, striking. He uses his sympathetic tenor with ingratiating charm, for he knows how to make the very best of it without resorting either to mannerism or exaggeration. Breton, the composer of the *madrigale*, wrote the opera of *Dolores*, perhaps the most successful and popular of all modern Spanish operas. I thoroughly enjoyed listening to it during a month's stay at Barcelona, in 1896, and have often wondered why Londoners have never had a chance of revelling in its riot of Andalusian and other Iberian melodies. If I am not mistaken, this *madrigale* is from that same opera ; anyhow it is a gem of its kind, and I am glad that Fleta has now coupled it with his re-recording of the famous *Ay, Ay, Ay*, which chiefly owes its world-wide vogue to him.

Paul Bender.—Here are two of Carl Loewe's dear old dramatic ballads, with the correct piano accompaniments, sung just in the right manner by a celebrated German basso whose fine organ is as well preserved as his traditional style. His characterization is admirable, his patter in the *Kleiner Haushalt* without a blemish. Every syllable comes out clearly ; and the recording sounds quite first-rate.

Wilhelm Rode.—From the same " Ultraphon " source comes another good record, possessing the advantage of background supplied by tip-top German orchestras. The *Credo* is accompanied by that of the State Opera House, Berlin, under Selmar Meyrowitz ; the *Mefistofele* excerpt by the Berlin Philharmonic under the same reliable conductor. The vocalist, I scarcely need remind readers, is one of the leading baritones of the State Opera House at Vienna. He has an exceedingly fine voice, and though his style presents an absolute contrast to those illustrated by, let us say, the Iago of Maurel or Stabile and the Mefistofele of Chaliapine, it is nevertheless intensely powerful, melodramatic, and imbued with the strong, realistic colouring of the German and Austrian schools. This contrast is what makes it for me a highly interesting record. It is well worth listening to.

HERMAN KLEIN.

OPERATIC AND FOREIGN SONGS

LILY PONS (soprano).—**Bell Song** from **Lakmé** (Delibes). In French. Orch. acc. H.M.V. DA1190, 10in., 6s.

GERHARD HUSCH (baritone).—**The Heavens are telling** (Beethoven, Op. 48, No. 4) and **The two Grenadiers** (Robert Schumnan, Op. 49, No. 1. Text, Heine). In German with **Orchestra of the State Opera House, Berlin**, under **Dr. Weissmann**. Parlo. R972, 10in., 3s.

GITA ALPAR (soprano).—**Doll's Aria** from **Tales of Hoffmann** (Offenbach), in German, and **Villanelle** (Dell' Acqua), in French, with **The Berlin Symphony Orchestra** under **Dr. Felix Günther**. Parlo. E11146, 12in., 4s. 6d.

RICHARD TAUBER (tenor).—**Fair is the World** and **Dearest, trust in me** from **Fair is the World** (Franz Lehar, Ludwig Herzer, Fritz Löhner). In German. Orch. acc. Parlo. RO20148, 10in., 4s. 6d. And **One day we must say "goodbye"** (Fritz Rotter, Schmidt, Gentner) and **Every woman gladly sheds a tear** (Rotter, Dr. B. Kaper). In German. Orch. acc. Parlo. RO20149, 10in., 4s. 6d.

ANDRÉ GOUDIN (baritone). **Song of the Toreador** from **Carmen** (Bizet) and **Song of Ourrias** from **Mireille** (Gounod). In French, with the **Orchestra of l'Opéra-Comique, Paris**, under **Louis Masson**. Decca K584, 12in., 2s. 6d.

LIGHT OPERA COMPANY. Vocal Gems from **Rigoletto** (Verdi). In English with Orch. H.M.V. C2152, 12in., 4s. 6d.

Lily Pons.—This young lady is, I learn, a Belgian by birth. She received her musical training at the Liège Conservatoire, where she was "discovered" by the tenor Zenatello. He introduced her to the notice of the all-powerful Gatti-Casazza, and in due course she made her début at the Metropolitan Opera House, New York, where most of her brief and successful career has so far been spent. Her singing proclaims her a highly accomplished light soprano, while her finished rendering of the *Bell Song* recalls not only the style but the actual timbre of that gifted artist, Marie Vanzandt, whose charming creation of *Lakmé* I witnessed at the Opéra-Comique in 1883. Her execution is extraordinarily neat and agile, her staccato a miracle of delicate flexibility. Above all, the tone is sweet and sympathetic, while the diction is clear and precise. The record, quite a perfect thing in its way, was made in America.

Gerhard Hüsch.—With the aid of Dr. Weissmann and his orchestra, the admirable German baritone recently heard at Covent Garden endows with fresh interest a couple of well-worn themes. The broad, masculine quality of his voice finds ample scope in Beethoven's noble melody ; and I observe a new effect in the orchestral treatment of the second *motif*. The varied tone-colour and diction impart a novel reading to Schumann's great song—it is worthy to be compared with Plançon's, only far more German, more idealistic and true to Heine. I see no reason, though, why the closing bars should have been entrusted to the organ.

Gita Alpar.—The art of singing the *Doll's Song* from *The Tales of Hoffmann* as Offenbach intended it to be sung lies in the assumption of a tone and manner suggestive of a piece of mechanism and not a human being. The effect of this in an air which itself imitates the jerky movements of an automaton can be best appreciated in the theatre, where we can see the corresponding looks and gestures of Hoffmann's absurd "flame" as she displays her quaint little stock of vocal ornaments and gewgaws. Apart from the stage, in a gramophone record, the idea is most successfully realised by force of contrast, as we have it here, thanks to a clever artist who has known how to place it side by side with a thoroughly natural, human rendering of Dell' Acqua's well-known *Villanelle*. You can amuse yourself by comparing, as I have done, the dull, listless expression of the Doll (note that queer tumble of the voice when her machinery "runs down") with the bright and animated feeling which pervades her voice in the other piece. The florid singing in both is neat and accurate, without perhaps being exceptionally brilliant ; the staccato, for instance, is far superior to the shake, yet on the whole there is no serious blemish to be found anywhere. The Berlin Symphony Orchestra, under Dr. Felix Günther, has treated the accompaniments in the right delicate spirit.

Richard Tauber.—The labour of constant public work may have proved too trying for Herr Tauber's throat during his engagement at Drury Lane, but evidently it has not been onerous enough to prevent his pursuing at intervals the pleasant and profitable task of making comic opera records. Truly, the actual physical labour involved herein is not precisely of a strenuous nature, nor, judging by his tone-production, does the Tauberesque warbling at any time seem to involve a heavy outlay of strength. Yet it must be remembered that, when he presents himself before the microphone, the singer has perforce to be in what my athletic friends call "the pink of condition," and maybe has to repeat the same piece over and over again before the final faultless reproduction is achieved. In any case, I can perceive absolutely no technical faults in these four records. The singing is that of a supreme master of his own particular *métier*. The music, whether by Franz Lehar or Fritz Rotter, fits him like a glove, for it enables him to introduce all his favourite effects in the now-familiar manner. The most pleasing, I fancy, is the Viennese waltz measure exemplified in *Fair is the world*, which has many artistic touches and, just to remind us that Tauber is a real tenor, finishes up on a fairly powerful B flat. The other songs are less like Strauss and more redolent of modern jazz, with its saccharine harmonization and endless repetitions.

André Goudin.—Despite all temptations from across the Rhine, and notably from Berlin and Bayreuth, as presented in the well-performed masterpieces of the two Richards, Wagner and Strauss, France remains on the whole singularly faithful to her Gounod and her Bizet. You can see this for yourself, any time you may happen to be visiting Paris, in the enviable bills of the Opéra and the Opéra-Comique that help to adorn the kiosks which line the busy boulevards. There, among the all-the-year-round favourites, you will never fail to have your eye caught by such titles as *Faust* and *Carmen*, *Mireille* and *Les Pêcheurs de Perles*, *Roméo et Juliette* and *La Jolie Fille de Perth*. Alas, we have no national opera or operas here to draw us away from our firesides, where our sole consolation is to be found in the excellent substitutes that replace the real thing. Whether there is much demand just now for these Parisian samples I am not quite sure, but to me they are always welcome when they are competently performed. Otherwise there is not much to be said about this Decca specimen beyond the fact that M. Louis Masson has turned out, with the aid of his Opéra-Comique orchestra, some capital swinging accompaniments to M. André Goudin's airs from *Carmen* and *Mireille*. The singer possesses a resonant baritone voice and all the requisite traditions peculiar to his *genre*. His low notes have been sacrificed for his high ones, and his occasionally lethargic style may be in part attributed to his laboured breathing. But he sings the *Toreador* ditty and the particularly jolly ballad of the *bouvier*, Ourrias, with plenty of go and—well, you cannot expect every perfection at once in this fallible vocal world !

H.M.V. Light Opera Company.—Here is a brief but breezy selection from *Rigoletto*, whose only un-recommendable feature is that it is ridiculously dear. I cannot for the life of me see what there is in this quite ordinary collection of excerpts from a non-royalty opera by Verdi to make it worth 4s. 6d. In a vocal sense there is little if anything in the record to justify its costliness. It includes the opening chorus (bits only), the two tenor airs, part of the first duet for Gilda and her unfortunate father (much less prominent here than his daughter), and, to conclude, a frankly moderate rendering of the quartet. The words and the singers are English.

HERMAN KLEIN.

507

OPERATIC AND FOREIGN SONGS

LILY PONS (soprano).—**Voi che sapete** from **Marriage of Figaro** (Mozart) and **Queen of the Night Aria** from **The Magic Flute** (Mozart). In Italian. Orch. acc. Parlo. RO20153, 10in., 4s.

META SEINEMEYER (soprano).—**In quelle trine morbide** from **Manon Lescaut** (Puccini) and with **IVAR ANDRESEN** (bass) **Chi puo legger nel futuro** from **Force of Destiny** (Verdi). In German. Orch. acc. Conducted by **Dr. Weissmann.** Parlo. E11153, 12in., 4s.

RICHARD TAUBER (tenor).—**Across the seas I salute you, dear Homeland** (Krome-Rotter) and **Love brings the dawning** (Grothe-Wilcyzynski). In German, with **Dajos Bela Orchestra.** Parlo. RO20152, 10in., 4s.
Farewell, I kiss your hand in vain (R. Fall-Beda) and **Springtime reminds me of you** (Rotter-Jurmann). In German, with **Dajos Bela Orchestra.** Parlo. RO20155, 10in., 4s.

FRANZ VÖLKER (tenor).—**Death of Otello, Niun mi tema,** from **Otello** (Verdi) and **Flower Song** from **Carmen** (Bizet). In German, with **Berlin State Opera Orchestra** under **Hermann Weigert.** Polydor 95436, 12in.

HEINRICH KNOTE (tenor).—**Siegfried's Death** from Act 3, Sc. 2, **Götterdämmerung** (Wagner) and **Nur eine Waffe taugt** from Act 3, **Parsifal** (Wagner). In German, with **Berlin State Opera Orchestra** under **Dr. Weissmann.** Parlo. E11162, 12in., 4s.

HEINRICH SCHLUSNUS (baritone).—**Waldandacht,** Op. 211, No. 3 (Abt) and **Schäfers Sonntagslied** (Kreutzer). In German. Orch. acc. Conducted by **Joh. Heidenreich.** Polydor 90168, 10in.

GERHARD HÜSCH (baritone). **Era la notte** from **Otello** (Verdi) and **Papageno's Song** from **The Magic Flute** (Mozart). In German. With **Berlin State Opera Orchestra** under **Dr. Weissmann.** Parlo. R979, 10in., 2s. 6d.

LOUIS V. D. SANDE (baritone). **Toreador's Song** from **Carmen** (Bizet). In German; and **ALEXANDER KIRCHNER** (tenor): **Lohengrin's Narration** (Wagner). In German. Both with the **Berlin State Opera Orchestra** under **Karl Rockstroh.** Sterno 8015, 12in., 2s. 6d.

ALEXANDER KIPNIS (bass).—**Das schöne Fest, Johannistag** from Act 1 **Die Meistersinger** (Wagner) and, with **E. RUZICZKA** (mezzo-soprano), **Herr Kavalier, Letter Scene and Waltz** from Act 2, **Der Rosenkavalier** (R. Strauss). In German, with **Berlin State Opera Orchestra** under **Orthmann.** H.M.V. DB1543, 12in., 6s.

RUDOLF BOCKELMANN (bass-baritone).—**Verachtet mir die Meister nicht** from Act 3 and **Jerum ! Jerum ! (Cobbling Song)** from Act 2, **Die Meistersinger** (Wagner). In German, with **Berlin State Opera Orchestra** under **Schmalstich.** H.M.V. C2255, 12in., 4s.

Lily Pons.—The air of the *Queen of Night* sung in this record is the one known in the Italian as *Gli angui d'inferno* and is heard in the second act of the *Magic Flute.* The new Belgian soprano here uses the Italian text ; but, if I am not mistaken, she sings *Voi che sapete* in French, and there neither text nor melody falls so pleasantly upon the ear. In a word, it lacks the necessary smoothness and musical charm. I know not why it is, but so few singers have the true idea of how to sing *Voi che sapete* or how to express its real meaning. The vocal acrobatics in the florid air bring this artist's talent into more effective play, and we perceive once more the qualities that aroused admiration a couple of months ago in her *Bell Song* from *Lakmé.* Her *staccato* and her management of the head tone generally are exceedingly adroit, while the style is much more Mozartian. The occasional harshness in the timbre is due to over-amplification. When presented *au naturel* it is a sweet, telling voice.

Meta Seinemeyer and *Ivar Andrésen.*—I am glad to see that Parlophone have not yet come to the end of the interesting records bequeathed by a talented opera singer who was taken from us all too soon. This time we hear her in examples of Verdi and Puccini, which, though they may not represent either master at his best, nevertheless deviate agreeably from the beaten track and unmistakably show that Meta Seinemeyer possessed the gift of versatility. The attractive quality and admirable legato that were distinguishing features of her singing come out clearly and with irreproachable diction in her rendering of the passage from *Manon Lescaut.* It is delightfully free from any trace of exaggeration and yet abundantly expressive. The duet with Ivar Andrésen is cut clean out of the middle of the scene between Leonora and Padre Guardiano in the second act of *La Forza del Destino.* Being, therefore, without head or tail, it makes a somewhat shapeless specimen, and is in no sense worthy of the real Verdi. Both singers did their best in the execution of an ungrateful task which I fancy they might easily have spared themselves.

Richard Tauber.—These four songs were obviously written to suit the singer, whose particular methods now appeal strongly to a British as well as an Austro-German public. There is consequently little that calls for minute description. No opportunity is lost of making the usual effect with the sudden contrasts, abrupt transitions, and all the other clever devices that we now know so well. *Across the seas* is soft and pleasing ; its companion piece bright, dashing, and full of life ; also over-amplified. The *Farewell,* less noisy and infinitely touching in sentiment, is coupled with another lively Tauber-esque mosaic, concocted of subtle contrasts and sly murmurs. There will be a wide demand for both discs.

Franz Völker.—A Viennese *Heldentenor* with a fine, robust, powerful voice that curiously resembles Richard Tauber's in quality, but in nothing else save the ease with which it is produced. There are moments when you might really think you were listening to the light opera star ; but only moments. This is a genuinely big organ ; the style broad and straightforward and utterly free from tricks ; the phrasing marked by distinction and dramatic intelligence. I should much like to hear Franz Völker as Otello, and if the whole of his Don José is as good as his *Flower Song* it must be very good indeed. He has abundant feeling and his German diction at any rate is exemplary. Both these records were sung with the Berlin State Opera Orchestra, under Hermann Weigert, but Völker himself is engaged at the Vienna State Opera.

Heinrich Knote.—A splendid operatic veteran is Heinrich Knote—one of those who flourish under the weight of years and hard work. He is 61 this year, and it was thirty years ago last May when he made his début at Covent Garden as Siegfried. He was magnificent then ; and his voice is still wonderfully preserved and fresh after a lifetime of that " severe Wagnerian strain " which was once regarded as fatal to the longevity of the vocal cords. (What nonsense !) I have heard Knote many times—in London, at Bayreuth, and at the Metropolitan Opera House ; and I can positively assert that he now sings these selections from the *Götterdämmerung* and *Parsifal* with as much declamatory vigour and spirit as he did in the opening decade of the present century. The tone has all the old ring and very nearly all of the old charm, while the technique of the delivery remains impeccable. The orchestral work and the general merit of the recording, under Dr. Weissmann's able bâton, are no less praiseworthy.

Heinrich Schlusnus.—It is good to listen now and then to the old-fashioned German lieder of Franz Abt, whose songs at one time were fashionable everywhere, but are now unaccountably neglected. Welcome, too, from the lips of a Schlusnus, is a bit of broad religious melody such as you may hear in the *Schäfers Sonntagslied* of Conradin Kreutzer, whom, by the way, you will not confuse with that other Kreutzer (Rodolphe—violinist and composer—to whom Beethoven dedicated his famous sonata), although they were actually contemporaries. In my opinion there is an old-world grace, alike in these songs and their interpretation, that you cannot fail to appreciate and enjoy.

Gerhard Hüsch.—If the reading of Iago's lie to Otello, in pretending that he heard Cassio talking in his sleep about Desdemona, were always, like Verdi's music, an exact reflection of Shakespeare's meaning, we should be inflicted with fewer misinterpretations of it. I only wish it could have been recorded for the gramophone by the original operatic Iago, Victor Maurel; the true nature of the episode and its villainous suggestion could then have been imitated by later baritones without misconstruing the whole scene. As it is, very few contrive to do so; but Gerhard Hüsch is one of them, and I advise others to imitate his manner of singing it. Then, while they are about it, they can listen carefully to the other side of the disc, where they will find an equally ideal treatment of Papageno's *aria d'entrata*. The rôle was one of those undertaken here by the same excellent artist during the recent German season, and I liked him in it immensely. He records easily and naturally, infusing into word and tone alike precisely the sparkling vivacity and humour that the song ought to convey. No tricks, no trimmings here; only plain, straightforward honest singing.

Louis V. D. Sande and *Alexander Kirchner*.—I observe that this Sterno record costs only half a crown, and in consideration of that economical advantage I am not going to condemn it for the use of an excessive supply of amplification, which you would probably have the patience to try and soften down in virtue of its outstanding merits. I do not, as a rule, approve unrelated solos by different singers upon one and the same disc; but these certainly do not hurt each other, for both are sung in German, and each in turn will be found very good. The baritone who sings the *Toreador's Song* does so with a telling voice and plenty of go. His tenor companion gives a very acceptable account of Lohengrin's pedigree and knightly adventures, notwithstanding a certain lack of that delicacy of treatment which most Elsas expect at his hands until the cat is actually " out of the bag."

Alexander Kipnis.—The watchword of the illustrious maker of operatic records is naturally " Make hay while the sun shines." There is probably more money to be made out of them in these critical days of financial crisis than there is to be had out of engagements at leading opera houses, where fees and salaries are being ruthlessly cut down. Even busy men like Alexander Kipnis must find important compensation in their gramophone royalties, compared with which their broadcasting fees are probably negligible. Here is a record that deserves to sell largely over the whole world. The most blasé listener can find new joy in this amazingly good rendering of Pogner's address. Taken quicker than usual, yet not too fast, it is a natural, easy-going talk by a wealthy goldsmith to his fellow-townsmen, winding up with the generous offer of his own fair daughter as chief prize at the annual Nuremberg competition festival! Nothing could be more genial, more hearty, or vocally speaking, more glorious; nothing more completely in the right Wagnerian tradition. The excerpt from the *Rosenkavalier* amounts to a revelation; especially in the rich quality of the low notes, which beat those of Richard Mayr by yards. Kipnis as Baron Ochs must really be wonderful, and I hope we shall see him in the part next year. What a record this, for the new " Connoisseur Catalogue "!

Rudolf Bockelmann.—After Pogner, Hans Sachs and another brilliant example of what modern recording can accomplish with distinguished and well-balanced materials. The same Berlin State Opera Orchestra that accompanies Kipnis under Orthmann here supports Bockelmann under Schmalstich, and with equally fine results. Positively I am unable to conceive of anything to surpass Bockelmann's supreme effort. The youthful resonance, the roundness and purity of his manly tones, combined with the rare perfection of his phrasing and diction, lend an unwonted distinction to his delivery of Hans Sachs' defence of the old masters—his final warning to the Mastersingers at the end of the opera—the fresher here because declaimed without the fatigue entailed by all that comes before it. The volume and sonority of the *Cobbler's Song* are especially welcome because not due to adventitious aid.

HERMAN KLEIN.

Supplement *to* THE GRAMOPHONE, *October* 1931

THE H.M.V. CONNOISSEUR CATALOGUE

ANSSEAU, Fernand, Tenor

DB1364
- Duet with JOURNET—**Mais ce Dieu que peut-il pour moi ?** (If I pray, who is there to hear me ?)—" Faust " (*in French*) Gounod
- Duet with JOURNET—**Ici je suis à ton service** (Here I am at your service)—" Faust " (*in French*) Gounod

DB1384
- Duet with ORENS—**C'est toi; c'est moi ! l'on m'avait avertie !** (Is it you ? They told me to expect you)—" Carmen " (*in French*) Bizet
- Duet with ORENS—**Mais moi, Carmen, je t'aime encore** (But I, I love you still)—" Carmen " (*in French*) Bizet

These famous duets from *Faust* and *Carmen* are sufficiently well sung to merit their place in the new catalogue; the distinguished tenor who takes part in each is, or should be, guarantee enough for that. Still, much depended upon who was selected to support him, and happily the choice in either case was satisfactory. Fernand Ansseau could scarcely have wished for a better Carmen than Mme. Orens, or a more alert Mephistopheles than Marcel Journet. Bizet and Gounod are both well served by artists who know their job thoroughly; the diction and the singing throughout are superlatively good, and the orchestration in each instance comes out perfectly.

H. K.

DB1540 **Ye that now are sorrowful**—" Requiem " Op. 45. Pts. I and II Brahms

Brahms may be said to shine in his tenderest religious mood in this lovely air, which is one of the most impressive numbers in his inspired *German Requiem*. Most sopranos find it rather trying, but Florence Austral takes it easily, as it were, in her stride, and from every point of view accords it absolute justice. Her *sostenuto*, like her intonation, is impeccable; from first to last the soaring, lark-like tone floats aloft and never wavers. The whole effort constitutes a triumph for singer and mechanism alike. Praise must also be given for the smooth choral and orchestral features, executed under the bâton of John Barbirolli.

H. K.

BROWNLEE, John, Baritone

D2024
- **Vision fugitive** (Fleeting vision)—" Hérodiade " Massenet
- **Salomé! demandes au prisonnier** (Salomé! Go ask the slave set free)—" Hérodiade " Massenet

D2005
- **What the red-haired bosun says** Harrhy
- **Turn ye to me** arr. Lawson

Hérodiade was the opera by Massenet in which Jean de Reszke scored the phenomenal hit as John the Baptist at the

Théâtre-Italien, Paris, in 1884, which led to his no less successful début (as a tenor) three years later at Drury Lane Theatre, London. *Vision fugitive* is, however, the now-popular baritone air for the King that people most associate with this opera ; next to it, perhaps, coming the soprano solo, *Il est doux, il est bon*. It was natural, therefore, for it to be included in the new Catalogue as a specimen of the talent of John Brownlee, the Australian baritone, who is now one of the principal singers at the Paris Opéra. Needless to say that he is thoroughly at home in it, and makes the most of the effective phrases that Massenet's fertile inventive power never failed to provide. Accent and timbre have become entirely French in a degree rarely found in British vocalists.

The second piece from the same opera is not so well known, for the simple reason that it is infinitely less interesting. Why it should have been exhumed from the score for this occasion is not quite clear, when there must be so many other things in Mr. Brownlee's repertoire better worth hearing. All one can say is that the record will repay those who acquire it for the sake of hearing *Vision fugitive* well sung.

H. K.

CHALIAPINE, Theodore, Bass

DA1061
- **Maschenka** (Folk Song) (*in Russian*) (*unacc.*)
- **Down the Petersky** (Folk Song) (*in Russian*) (*with Petersky Balalaika Orch.*)
  arr. Chaliapine

DB1352
- **Siberian Prisoner's Song** (*in Russian, with piano*) arr. Karategen
- **She laughed** (*in Russian, with piano*) Lishin

No one who heard Chaliapine during the last Russian season at the Lyceum Theatre needs to be told that his voice is undergoing almost as little deterioration with the flight of years as his art, which, as a matter of fact, is greater now than it ever was. His rendering of the folk-songs is inimitable ; he gets down to the very pith and marrow of their meaning. His *mezza-voce* in the unaccompanied *Maschenka* is marvellous—more so, to my thinking, than the fortissimo that prevails over a big Balalaika orchestra in the Petersky piece. Yet even the latter ends up with a whispered tone as soft as any in the *Maschenka*. Then, again, if ever Siberian prisoners sing (with piano accompaniment), you would wish them to do so as Chaliapine does, even though you may not understand a word. You know that he gives you the spirit as well as the letter of everything. There is no great choice to be made between these records. They are all perfect in their way.

H. K.

CORTIS, Antonio, Tenor

DA1075
- **Non piangere Liù**—" Turandot " (*in Italian*) Puccini
- **Nessun dorma**—" Turandot " (*in Italian*) Puccini

DA1154
- **O Paradiso !** (Oh Paradise !)—" L'Africana " Meyerbeer
- **Credo a una possanza** (I believe in a power); **Io no ho amato** (I have not loved)—" Andrea Chénier " Giordano

The two tenor airs in *Turandot* were sung so recently at Covent Garden by this same singer that there is no need to describe in detail his rendering of them. It is declamation of the accepted Puccini type, very sustained and passionate, very sad and dolorous. Here, with the amplifier's artful aid, the voice of Cortis is made to sound much bigger than in the theatre, and consequently a few degrees less sympathetic. Still, the timbre is highly agreeable, the production not too open, the delivery free from a suspicion of effort or strain. I have always predicted a brilliant future for this young singer, and, after last season's experience he ought to be heard in London regularly. Gramophonists will be glad to find his records of the *Turandot* airs included in the " Connoisseur Catalogue."

H. K.

DE LUCA, Giuseppe, Baritone

DA1169
- **Per me ora fatale** (Thou bring'st, eventful hour)— " Il Trovatore " (*in Italian, with chorus*) Verdi
- **Aprila, bella, la fenestrella** (Serenata) (My loved one, open your casement) " I Gioielli de la Madonna " (*in Italian, with chorus*) Wolf-Ferrari

DB1436
- **Ah, Pescator affonda l'esca** (Fisherman, thy bait now lower)—" La Gioconda " (*in Italian with chorus*) Ponchielli
- Trio with TEDESCO and ANTHONY—**O sommo Carlo !** (O mighty Carlos)—" Ernani " (*in Italian, with chorus*) Verdi

Giuseppe de Luca was born at Rome in 1876 and has been on the operatic stage 34 years, during which period he has created several of the most important rôles in modern Italian opera. He is therefore an experienced as well as an accomplished artist, and his fine baritone voice remains to-day as fresh and strong as it ever was. The four records named above display his talent in the most favourable light. An ideal Count di Luna, he makes the episode from *Il Trovatore* an epitome of the whole story, the choral and instrumental accessories doing the rest. The same support, furnished by the Metropolitan Opera House, New York, and conducted by Giulio Setti, lends the soloist equal effect in the other three ensembles. I find the serenade from the *Gioielli della Madonna* particularly attractive—well sung and brightened by colourful orchestral touches. It will be remembered what a success poor Sammarco had in this scene when the opera was first given in London in 1912. The finale, *O sommo Carlo !* used to be one of the features at the Floral Hall Concerts (in what is now the potato market) at Covent Garden in the 70's and 80's of the last century, when the whole company would take part in it. De Luca is supported in this performance by a couple of good solo singers, which is the reason, I suppose, why it is described as a trio. Anyhow it is a capital record of Verdi's fine finale.

H. K.

FRANCI, Benvenuto, Baritone

DB1433
- Duet with LANDI—**Dunque ? All' opra** (What next ? To do it)—" Barbiere di Siviglia " (*in Italian*) Rossini
- Duet with LANDI—**All' idea di quel metallo** (The idea of that enchanter) " Barbiere di Siviglia " (*in Italian*) Rossini

The records on this disc are so sadly over-amplified that I hesitate to recommend it, save to people with insensitive ears who can stand plenty of noise. Franci has always indulged a tendency to shout, just as one or two good pianists I know make more use than they should of the soft pedal : but this fault is growing worse with the help and encouragement of the new recording, and he will soon become quite unbearable. Otherwise this sounds quite a good performance of the duet from the first act of the *Barbiere*—with the barber well in the foreground most of the time.

H. K.

GALLI-CURCI, Amelita, Soprano

DB1355
- **Polonaise—Io son Titania** (I'm fair Titania)— " Mignon " (*in Italian*) Thomas
- **Una voce poca fà** (A little voice I heard)—"Barbiere di Siviglia " (*in Italian*) Rossini

DB1477
- **Caro nome, che il mio cor** (Dearest name)— " Rigoletto " (*in Italian*) Verdi
- **Grand air de Catherine**—" Etoile du Nord " (*in French*) (*Flutes obbl.*) Meyerbeer

DB1516
- **O riante Nature** (O laughing Nature)—" Philémon et Baucis " Gounod
- **Cantata** Scarlatti, arr. Van Leeuwen

The nature of the technical demands that the *Polonaise* from *Mignon* makes upon the *soprano leggiero* are not only peculiarly suited to the genius of Mme. Galli-Curci, but are such as she can easily comply with. Hence a rendering brilliant at all points and in strict accordance with the composer's text. One may hear more " showy " attempts, but few if any so closely accurate or marked by the same facility of accomplishment. The *Polonaise* is now the most popular piece by a long way in Thomas's opera, and it has been a favourite of mine since I first heard it sung by Bianchi at the Promenade Concerts (Covent Garden) in the late seventies. There is no fear of its becoming hackneyed so long as gramophonists insist upon the Galli-Curci standard and nothing lower. Two such *tours de force* as the *Polonaise* and *Una voce poco fà* offered upon a single record by the same gifted singer must be regarded as a rare opportunity for the seeker after bargains.

Barely less desirable for good value and artistic merit is the combination of *Caro nome* with Catherine's elaborate air with the two flutes from *L'Etoile du Nord*. Only one tiny blemish occurs in the *Rigoletto* number, and that just at the close, where the high B starts off a trifle below pitch—only, however, to rise to its proper level as the *messa di voce* presses to its finish. On the other hand, Meyerbeer's extraordinarily difficult cadenza with the flutes, if slightly modified in shape, remains the almost impossible feat that Patti and Sembrich used to surmount ; and now Galli-Curci conquers it with apparently the same consummate ease. I could not pay her a higher compliment.

H. K.

GERHARDT, Elena, Mezzo-Soprano

D2009	Feldeinsamkeit (In Summer Fields) (*with piano*) Brahms Nachtigall (The Nightingale) ; **Ständchen** (Serenade) (*with piano*) Brahms
DB1544	Suleika's zweiter Gesang (Suleika's second Song) (*with piano*) Schubert Zum Schluss (Conclusion) ; **Frühlingsnacht** (A Spring Night) (*with piano*) Schumann
D2007	Auf dem Kirchhofe, Op. 105, No. 4 (In the Church-yard) (*with piano*) Brahms Vergebliches Ständchen (The vain Suit) ; **Das Mädchen spricht, Op. 107, No. 3** (The Maiden Speaks) (*with piano*) Brahms
D2008	Wie komm' ich denn zur Tür herein (And if I come unto your door) ; **Mein Mädel hat' 'nen Rosenmund** (My maiden has a mouth of red) (*with piano*) Brahms Feinsliebchen, du sollst mir nicht barfuss geh'n (My darling shall never with bare feet go) ; **Erlaube mir, Feinsliebchen** (Allow me) (*with piano*) Brahms
DA1219	Wohin ? (Whither) **Op. 25, No. 2** (*with piano*) Schubert Verborgenheit (Secrecy) (*with piano*) Hugo Wolf

The five discs contributed to this catalogue by Elena Gerhardt comprise fifteen of her most famous lieder. Ten are by Brahms, two by Schumann, two by Schubert and one by Wolf—a disparity in selection for which there were doubtless good reasons. But all are beautiful, faultlessly interpreted, and no less perfectly accompanied on the piano by the singer's talented coadjutor, C. V. Bos. There is really no need to enter into details, even if one could, concerning Mme. Gerhardt's rendering of each of these songs. To choose between them would be an invidious if not impossible task. What is chiefly important for the connoisseur to know is that when these records were made the singer was in better voice than I have heard her for years. Her tone sounds fresh, bright, pure, and steady, as in the golden days when her great teacher, Nikisch, accompanied her at their Queen's Hall recitals. Her breathing has righted itself once more ; only the fact, not the sound of it, can be noted. She gets to the heart of every song. She creates the impression that her readings are absolutely authentic and right, that they never ought to be presented in any other way. There are sufficient items here for an entire short recital—one from which a truly musical audience can derive the utmost pleasure.

H. K.

GIANNINI, Dusolina, Soprano

DA1029	Allerseelen (All Souls' Day), **Op. 10, No. 8** R. Strauss Zueignung (Devotion), **Op. 10, No. 1** R. Strauss
DB1265	Gretchen am Spinnrade (Margaret at Spinning Wheel) Schubert Ungeduld (Impatience)–"Dieschöne Müllerin" Schubert

Beyond the sheer beauty of the voice there is little to excite admiration in these records. One feels inclined to ask what the peerless Dusolina came to be doing *dans cette galère ?* Evidently she was not aware that the German *lied* was not altogether in her line ; at any rate not that of Richard Strauss. She has neither caught its spirit nor penetrated its meaning. The same tame inadequacy of feeling and monotony of colour pervades both songs. In the Schubert she is somewhat more successful, notably *Gretchen am Spinnrade*, where her dramatic instinct finds greater scope and the accentuation of Goethe's lines is excellent. The only serious fault in the *Ungeduld* is that there are too many rallentandos ; they only serve to break up the persistent rhythm, the irresistible impulse of the main theme. Curiously enough, the head notes in all these pieces are thin and disappointing.

H. K.

GIGLI, Beniamino, Tenor

DB1296	Santa Lucia luntana (Santa Lucia, I long for you) (*in Italian*) Mario Voce 'e notte ! (Voice of the Night) (*in Neapolitan*) Curtis
DB1499	Cielo e mar ! (Heaven and Ocean !)—" Gioconda " (*in Italian*) Ponchielli Viva il vino spumeggiante (Brindisi) (Here's to the sparkling cup)—" Cavalleria Rusticana " (*in Italian, with chorus*) Mascagni

There is no need to differentiate between these two imitations, or adaptations, of the Neapolitan folk-song style which Beniamino Gigli reproduces so effectively. Both are quite up to his best mark, frankly engaging in their pathetic appeal, after the manner of expectant Italian lovers, yet never breathless or gasping in the utterance thereof. Gigli is an artist as well as a tenor, and his lovely voice is combined with a style that can lend distinction even to lachrymose love-sick plaints of the Neapolitan type.

Quite another thing, of course, is the effect upon the more critical ear of the two operatic records. There you get the same luscious tone (somewhat amplified, I admit), but a far more interesting Gigli. A touch of melancholy there is in whatever he sings, even when it is a toast or a drinking-song, such as this from *Cavalleria*, with its chorus sparkling almost as much as the *spumeggiante* " Asti " when the cork is just drawn. But Turiddu feels that this after all, may be his last drink on earth ; while Enzo, when he indulges in *Cielo e. mar*, is joyfully awaiting the advent of his fair but naughty Laura ; and it is in this fine aria that Gigli, I fancy, does himself most justice. His *sostenuto* in it is quite amazing, and his B flat at the end a note to thrill you if ever one could.

H. K.

HELDY, Fanny, Soprano

DB1512	Oh ! la pitoyable aventure !—"L'heure Espagnole" (*in French*) Ravel Restons ici puisqu'il le faut (Yes, I will do as I am told)—" Manon " (*in French*) Massenet
DB1513	On m'appelle Mimi (They call me Mimi)—" Bohème " (*in French*) Puccini Sur la mer calmée (One fine day)—" Madame Butterfly " (*in French*) Puccini

This is about the only page from Ravel's clever opera *L'Heure Espagnole* that will permit itself to be separated from the score with anything like a profitable vocal effect. Such as it is,

Mlle. Fanny Heldy makes the most of it. Her tones do not grow less acidulated than of yore, nor, at the same time, does her art diminish in sureness, purity, or mastery of touch. Her intonation, like her execution, is impeccable, and one only wonders whether she might not now and then impart to her phrasing a greater degree of heart-felt expression. Were there in her singing as much variety of feeling as there is authority, all would be well. The brief selection from Massenet's *Manon* suits her on this account better than those from the Puccini operas; and yet there is much to admire in all three. I know no other French woman whose diction is quite so distinct, whose words catch the ear quite so instantaneously; she makes you like Puccini as well in French as in Italian, and that is saying something. The best singing in this group comes out in the air from *Butterfly*, the best orchestral results attained by M. Piero Coppola are manifested in the excerpt from *L' Heure Espagnole*.

H. K.

HISLOP, Joseph, Tenor

DA890	**Mens jeg venter** (*in Norwegian, with piano acc. by Percy Kahn*)	Grieg
	En Svane (*in Norwegian, with piano acc. by Percy Kahn*)	Grieg

Joseph Hislop is by now probably known to thousands of admirers abroad as against hundreds in his native land. That is wrong, of course; but what are we going to do about it? Such things have happened before, and they are not creditable either to managers or artists. In Stockholm, where the Scots tenor made his début and also in Italy and South America, he has long been a favourite. He sings Grieg's songs in the original Norwegian, and sings them well. Here are two that are known everywhere and lose nothing of their delicious local colour at his hands. Yet, whilst admiring the refinement of his style, I find his tone at times too soft and veiled in proportion to the amount of its carrying power. His *mezza voce*, for instance, does not travel like that of Slezák or Schipa. Nevertheless I would not have the entrancing *Swan* sung with less contrast than it is by Hislop, who evidently revels in its gentle sweetness. It shows him to be a greater artist than he was when I last heard him, and I prefer his musical whisper in music such as this to all the sonorities of the heavy type that the microphone is often made to convey.

H. K.

INGHILLERI, Giovanni, Baritone

E590	**Il balen del suo sorriso** (Tempest of the Heart)— " Trovatore "	Verdi
	Di Provenza il mar (Thy home in far Provence)— " Traviata "	Verdi

I do not personally see the necessity for—nor even the advantage that was to be gained by—including these ancient Verdian " chestnuts " in a collection bearing the title of " The Connoisseur Catalogue." I may be wrong, but to my thinking they have had their day, having served their purpose of tickling the ears of the groundlings; and they might now very well be omitted from a selection primarily intended to tickle the ears of a more cultured class of listeners. Let Inghilleri sing them never so well, he cannot make such barrel-organ ditties sound other than tiresome, whether it be on the gramophone or on the stage. I would really like to know why they were chosen for this list, in preference to things such as the *Honour* passage from *Falstaff* or the *Credo* from *Otello*, which are so much worthier of the real Verdi and which this excellent baritone can at least sing equally well. And, like Brutus, I shall pause for a reply.

H. K.

JOURNET, Marcel, Bass

DB1457	**Pro peccatis** (For his people)—" Stabat Mater "	Rossini
	La Procession	Franck

Marcel Journet wears as well as some of the music that he sings; which is saying a great deal. How long both will last is a question that does not concern the writer. I only know that the French basso seems to stand the onslaughts of time with extraordinary success; and that is perhaps more than can be said of Rossini's *Stabat Mater*, which, when I was young, was regarded as standing next in popular estimation to the *Messiah*, *Elijah*, and *The Hymn of Praise*. The *Pro peccatis* shows off Journet's imposing tones to rare advantage; it lies well within his range, and he imparts to it all the breadth and dignity that it needs. The same remark applies to his effective delivery of Franck's *Procession*.

H. K.

KIPNIS, Alexander, Bass

DB1551	**In diesen heil' gen Hallen** (Within these sacred halls)—" Magic Flute "	Mozart
	Duet with ELSE RUZICZKA—**Rache Arie** (I'll have vengeance)—" Marriage of Figaro "	Mozart
E 591	**Porterlied** (Porter Song)—" Martha "	Flotow
	Hier im ird'schen Jammertal (Caspar's Drinking Song)—" Der Freischütz "	Weber
E 592	**Ständchen des Mephistopheles** (Mephistopheles' Serenade)—" Faust "	Gounod
	Rondo vom goldenen Kalb (Calf of Gold)—" Faust "	Gounod
DA1218	**Wer ein Liebchen hat gefunden** (If a sweetheart one has met with)—" Die Entführung (" Il Seraglio ")	Mozart
	O Isis und Osiris (O Isis and Osiris)—" Magic Flute "	Mozart

With his ample (not amplified) tones and extended compass, Alexander Kipnis can do effortless justice to all those bass solos we know so well as having been favourites with the operatic audiences of a past era. And they can be favourites still when sung by artists of the Kipnis stamp; we may be sure of that. Here is a group of the kind I allude to. I recommend to the notice of budding Norman Allins the airs of Sarastro and Don Bartolo. Observe the restrained yet satisfying volume and noble phrasing of the one; the mixture of cunning, rage, and subtle contrasts of colour in the other; the amazing clarity of the articulation of the consonants in both. There is inimitable —yet not unattainable—art in all this, together with strangely little that the student would do well to avoid, or rather, not to copy.

Particularly good are the two drinking-songs, because Kipnis sings them strictly according to the traditions of the German school to which they belong; he refuses to differentiate his praises of wine and beer, though the modern conductor, in his craze for analysing scores, would doubtless deem that possible. On the other hand, I do perceive on the singer's part a disposition to yield to the temptation of exaggerating the sardonic humour of Mephistopheles. He sings both airs magnificently; but the variegated laughs at the end of the *Serenade* are overdone and too prolonged. Again, his Satanic majesty should recollect that he cannot afford to vociferate in the *Calf of Gold* before a microphone as he can in an opera-house. Beyond that I would have naught other than what Kipnis has done.

Regarding Osmin's air from *Die Entführung* and Sarastro's *Isis und Osiris* only the same high admiration can be expressed, since they stand in a precisely similar category. Each number calls for the same irreproachable Mozart singing, and yet they are wholly different in character. In the power to realise this, as we have seen in the items previously dealt with, lies the secret of the versatility that makes the German basses such wonderful all-round artists and Kipnis perhaps the greatest of them all. Let me add that the recording of the whole series is superlatively good.

H. K.

KOCHETZ, Nina, Mezzo-Soprano

DB1204 {
Berceuse—" Sadko "   Rimsky-Korsakov
Arioso of Iaroslavna—" Prince Igor " Borodin
}

Lovers of Russian opera will doubtless be glad to renew by these records pleasant memories of the recent season at the Lyceum. Apart from those of M. Chaliapine there might well have been more of them. If these be a fault to find in the work of Nina Kochetz, it concerns only the production of her voice, which is too tight and throaty. She sings with a persistent *vibrato* and abandons it but for a moment in the softer passages of the *berceuse* from *Sadko* (which in its way is as fascinating as the more familiar air of the Persian merchant). This is to be regretted, for Nina Kochetz has the style of the Russian school in her veins, romantic sentiment and all, and if you can forgive the wobble you will be delighted with her rendering of these things.

H. K.

LEIDER, Frida, Soprano

D2025 {
Starke Scheite schichtet mir dort (Pile on pile of mightiest logs)—" Götterdämmerung " Wagner
Duet with ELFRIEDE WAGNER—**Schweigt eures Jammers jauchzenden** (Silence the grievous wail)—" Götterdämmerung " Wagner
}

D2026 {
O ihr, der Eide heilige Hüter ! (O ye, of vows the heavenly guardians !)—" Götterdämmerung " Wagner
Fliegt heim, ihr Raben ! (Fly home, ye ravens !)—" Götterdämmerung " Wagner
}

DB1553 {
Träume (Dreams) Wagner
Schmerzen Wagner
}

We have here a very complete and more than adequate performance of the piece of music that is at once the *crux* and the climax of Wagner's greatest music-drama. For protagonist it has that noble Brünnhilde, Frida Leider, the one best known to the present generation of Wagner-lovers in this country and, I think I may add, the most admired. There is no need to tell how she declaims this final scene of the *Götterdämmerung*. From first to last it is a sustained effort of the highest order and its reproduction in these discs stands in a like category. The balance between voice and orchestra sounds to me perfect in a degree that is seldom equalled in the opera house, even when that opera house is at Bayreuth. The vocal tone is beyond reproach, while Dr. Leo Blech and the Berlin State Opera orchestra have done their portion of the excerpt supremely well. The few bars interpolated by Elfriede Wagner as Gutrune can scarcely be said to constitute a " duet," but for what they are quite satisfactory.

The *Träume* and *Schmerzen* must not be listened to after the great closing scene, nor, for that matter, just before it. At any other moment Wagner's familiar *Tristan* studies, as he termed them, can be heard with entire acceptance. To Frida Leider, their rightful interpreter (being as great an Isolde as she is a Brünnhilde), the two songs come as child's-play : but we do not enjoy them a whit the less for that.

H. K.

LJUNGBERG, Göta, Soprano

D2019 {
Nur die Schönheit (I lived for music and love)—" Tosca " Puccini
Duet with JOSEF SCHMIDT—**Nur dein etwegen wollt' ich nicht sterben** (The sting of death I only felt for thee)—" Tosca " Puccini
}

D2020 Duet with WALTER WIDDOP—**Love Duet,** Pts. I and II—" Lohengrin " Wagner

Göta Ljungberg is the fortunate possessor of an idea recording voice. The sole drawback is that its glorious resonant timbre is not sufficiently relieved by variety of colour. She may sing for you by the hour and you will go on listening for the sheer enjoyment of absorbing that one unchanging tone, as you might that of the *charmant oiseau* which Félicien David made so famous. But you will wonder why a singer obviously gifted with temperament should have so few colours on her palette to paint the picture with. For this reason you would probably prefer her Turandot to her Tosca ; I certainly should, though I have not seen her in either part. Her notion of *Vissi d'arte* (which you may have recognised under its German title) is not emotional enough, not sufficiently indicative of disappointment and torment. On the other hand the mere singing of the air is satisfying. So is the duet with Cavaradossi in the last act ; and it would be still more so were the efforts of the unlucky painter a trifle less nasal.

In the love duet from *Lohengrin* the Scandinavian soprano is thoroughly at home. She knows how to interpret Wagner, at any rate in this bridal-chamber scene, with just the right amount of dramatic spirit, and to imbue its melodious phrases with as much passion as Elsa is commonly imagined to possess. The Lohengrin, too, as presented by Walter Widdop, is manly as well as tender, anxious yet assured, and obviously able to express both in voice and words (German, of course) all the shades of hope and longing and misery that the gallant Knight goes through during that trying half-hour. His tone is refined and musical, his phrasing invariably dignified. Altogether this record is well worth the two sides that are devoted to it.

H. K.

McCORMACK, John, Tenor

DA1170 {
Anacreon's Grab (Anacreon's Grave) (*with piano*) (*in German*) Wolf
Schlafendes Jesuskind (Sleeping Christ Child) (*with piano*) (*in German*) Wolf
}

Frankly speaking, I do not greatly care for Count McCormack's rendering of these two Wolf songs. Their placid religious mood, intensely serious yet never deviating from their simple straight line, does not seem somehow to bring into relief the best aspects of his talent. Neither does the German accent, accurate as it may be, bring into play the most sympathetic timbre that he possesses. All commendation is due to the artist for associating his gifts with such austere examples of the German lied, but, on the other hand, the question of suitability always arises, and in my opinion he can do both himself and his theme better justice than he does in the present instance.

H. K.

DA1172 {
Three Aspects (*with piano*) C. H. H. Parry
There (*with piano*) C. H. H. Parry
}

DA1175 {
The bitterness of love (*with piano*) Dunn
Love's secret (*with piano*) Bantock
}

DA1178 {
Far apart (*with piano*) Schneider
Fairy Tree (*with piano*) O'Brien
}

If songs are to find, through this Connoisseur Catalogue, their proper place, which the gramophone has denied them all this time, the first of these three McCormack records, DA1172, is of vital importance. Once and for all, if we don't support it at least as well as the far more luxurious symphonies, we shall deserve no more. It is the very type of song record we want, and need, so badly ; and possibly the finest English song record yet issued. There are getting on for a hundred of Parry's *English Lyrics* in print ; English musicians, let alone the general public, know little enough about them ; few of us are in a position even to say that we think them all poor. These two, to noble poems of Mary Coleridge (the whole Set, the Ninth, is Mary Coleridge), will, for what they say and their eloquence in saying it—all that really counts—stand up to pretty well any of the German *Lieder*. McCormack's singing of them is that of a master-singer. Of his voice, and his use of it, all I must say is that its fulness and sympathetic quality have never struck me more. No composer, probably, has ever given more full and meticulous directions than Parry ; for instance, there are six independent markings over " Shining in every colour of the sun." Possibly there may be one, even more, not observed exactly by McCormack ; but he is a master, he has assimilated each song, he just *sings*, and most certainly the *spirit* of every single mark of Parry's is there. Above all (in significance for most singers) there is nothing that Parry has *not* directed. Perhaps there are one or two great interpretative artists whose singing of such songs could not be put below this ; but certainly this could not be put below any other.

There is perhaps not on the level of *Three Aspects ;* but it is a good song. Again, McCormack's excellence eclipses one or two slight faults.

Love's Secret is one of Bantock's best settings. Before I knew it, I thought Bantock the last man to set this little lyric, best known probably by its first line : " Never seek to tell thy love." I still find it not ideal ; but the least to be said is that it is interesting, clever, amusing in such sense as a setting at all apt of this can be called amusing. Actually I fear there is little beneath the ingenuity ; but it is a song for the connoisseur to exercise his judgment on. *The bitterness of love* I recognised instantly, though I am not aware that I have heard it more than once before, and then six months ago on a review record. This confirms its strong feeling and atmosphere. It is scarcely sterling, but (to mix metaphor and literalism) infinitely more worth listening to than the usual scrap-iron.

The Fairy Tree is somewhat similar, though not in subject or precise treatment ; the music has some quality, and interest, and aptness, though not quite equal to the very good little poem. *Far apart* is not so easy to praise.

C. M. C.

MELBA, Dame Nellie, Soprano

Recorded during Melba's farewell performance at the Royal Opera House, Covent Garden, June 8th, 1926

DB1500 { **Canzone del Salce** (Willow Song)—" Otello " (*in Italian*) Verdi
Addio di Mimi (Mimi's Farewell)—" Bohème " (*in Italian*) Puccini

Reference has already been made on more than one occasion in the pages of THE GRAMOPHONE to these highly interesting and successful efforts to capture the actual tones of Melba's voice on the night—the memorable 8th of June, five years ago—when she bade farewell to the operatic stage at her beloved Covent Garden. They possess an historic value, and my sole regret is that other " great women-singers " before Melba were not allowed the same privilege of bequeathing to posterity, through an invisible microphone, the sound of voices that were at least as beautiful as hers. But from first to last Dame Melba was what the world calls a " lucky person." The Connoisseur who listens with careful attention to these early stage recordings, and compares them with those made recently at Bayreuth, will not fail to observe the marked advance that improved science and experience have enabled the operators to accomplish. Yet the Melba records remain a remarkably true and faithful reproduction of the voice and method of the last of the Victorian prima donnas ; and as such they are bound for all time to command grateful appreciation.

H. K.

MELCHIOR, Lauritz, Tenor

D2037 { **Gott ! Warum hast du gehauf dieses Elend** (Heav'n had it pleased thee to try me)—" Otello " Verdi
Jeder Knabe kann mein Schwert mir entreissen (Do not fear me)—" Otello " Verdi

D1838 { Duet with OTTO HELGERS—**Mime heiss ein mürrischer Zwerg** (Mime was a crabbed old dwarf)—" Götterdämmerung " (*in German*) Wagner
Duet with OTTO HELGERS—**In Leid zu dem Wipfeln** (In grief to the branches)—" Götterdämmerung " (*in German*) Wagner

D1839 { **Brünnhilde ! Heilige Braut !** (Brünnhilde ! Holiest Bride !)—" Götterdämmerung " (*in German*) Wagner
Wie sie selig (Full of Grace)—" Tristan und Isolde " (*in German*) Wagner

D2022 { **Ein schwert verhiess mir der Vater** (A sword, my father foretold me)—" Walküre " Wagner
Duet with GENIA GUSZALEWICZ—**Siegmund heiss' ich und Siegmund bin ich** (Siegmund call me for Siegmund)—" Walküre " Wagner

Here is a goodly representative collection of the gramophonic triumphs of Lauritz Melchior. They are chiefly Wagnerian, of course, as befits a *Heldentenor* whose career, so far as the English public is acquainted with it, has been almost exclusively restricted to the embodiment of Wagner's greatest heroes. Yet we have not, I think, witnessed here his impersonation of the great Verdian hero, two of whose finest scenes head the above list ; and now, having listened to the records, I confess to a strong desire to hear him sing the rôle of Otello itself. At Covent Garden he would almost certainly have to undertake it in Italian in an Italian season ; still I do not see much difficulty about that, and, for my own part, I would prefer to hear him sing it in the original tongue. Nevertheless, the two excerpts come out splendidly enough in the German as Melchior interprets them ; while the orchestral parts, executed by the New Symphony Orchestra under John Barbirolli, are admirably clear and refined. The second, which is the Death scene, is especially well done.

The fine selections from *Götterdämmerung* and *Die Walküre* add another instalment towards the complete recording of Herr Melchior's share in the *Ring*. They are well worth having. The *Walküre* disc was made in Berlin with the State Opera Orchestra under Dr. Leo Blech ; the others were done here with the co-operation of the London Symphony Orchestra, conducted by Prof. Robert Heger, who also took part in the excerpt from the third act of *Tristan*. Individual comment concerning these is hardly necessary, if I say that they stand on a level with the previous Wagnerian records from the same source. And beyond a doubt they do !

H. K.

NEMETH, Maria, Soprano

D2023 Martern aller Arten (Thou may'st learn to hate me) Pts. I and II—" Il Seraglio " (*in German*) Mozart

The " great bravura song," as Otto Jahn called it, is not only the most difficult vocal piece in *Il Seráglio*, but perhaps the most exacting that Mozart wrote for the soprano voice, not excepting even those for the Queen of Night in the *Magic Flute*. It is not merely the florid passages but the declamatory—in fact, the combination of the two—that make it trying for the most " voluble " of vocalists. I am bound to say that my admiration for Maria Nemeth is pushed a degree higher by this splendid rendering of *Martern aller Arten* (I may wish she had not omitted the " r " in the second syllable of the first word, but that, after all, is but a tiny defect.) The singing may truly be described as an exhibition of the "grand manner." The life and energy of the whole thing is astounding; as refreshing as it is rare. Maria Nemeth has a voice of singularly bell-like ring and resonant power. She never deviates an iota from the key, her scale is wonderfully even, and her technique does not at any point betray the slightest inaccuracy or trace of effort. I only wish that the same could be said of some of our own bravura singers; but then I do not know how many more years Maria Nemeth studied than they did. It is the ease, the *aplomb*, the sense of masterfulness, that strikes you as so wonderful. There only remains to add that the singer has received every possible assistance from the orchestra of the Vienna State Opera, under Karl Alwin, and that the recording leaves no loophole for criticism.

H. K.

OFFERS, Maartje, Contralto

DB1286 { Komm' süsser Tod! (Come, sweet death) (*in German, with piano*) Bach
Du lieber Heiland (O blessed Saviour)—"St. Matthew's Passion" (*in German*) Bach

In these two lovely Bach airs we hear a Maartje Offers with a steadier tone than of yore, and not alone steadier but of a richer, rounder contralto timbre, unspoilt, I am glad to say, by over-amplification. The noise of the intake of breath has not yet gone the way of the tremolo, but happily it does not intrude itself too much upon the ear. What one loves in these pieces is the sense of peace, the restful spirit of meditation, the undisturbed flow of reflective and religious feeling. The quality and charm of the voice provide an unceasing glow of beauty for the glorious settings yielded by the genius of the Leipzig cantor. The delicious rippling of the two flutes in the air from the *St. Matthew's Passion* creates its customary marvellous effect of something ethereal in the highest spiritual sense—a point beyond the ordinary musical concepts of this world. The short notes of the basses, however, both here and in the recitative, are too much inclined to imitate a grunt. Perhaps Mr. Barbirolli ought not to be blamed for this.

H. K.

OLSZEWSKA, Maria, Contralto

E589 { Der Tod und das Mädchen (Death and the Maiden) (*with piano*) Schubert
Aufenthalt (My resting place) (*with piano*) Schubert

Some of the words in *Der Tod und das Mädchen* are not very distinct. Certain consonants, particularly those pronounced with the tip of the tongue, are "slithered" over in a way that smothers the sound of the whole syllable, whether at the beginning, middle, or end of the word. The vowel tone is pure and luscious; but, to my ear, slovenly enunciation detracts from the beauty of the sweetest singing. The softer the voice the stronger the words should be; and in this matter the talented contralto might take a lesson from the records of Elena Gerhardt and Elizabeth Schumann. She will there find that a diminuendo on a note, where the word ends with a consonant, does not, and should not, entail the disappearance of the latter. The rendering of *Aufenthalt* is an altogether better piece of work. The music demands more vigour, and the singer in consequence imparts greater vigour to her text, making it clearly audible. To become a really first-rate lieder-singer she must perfect her art by thinking about her words quite as much as she does about her glorious voice. Her natural dramatic temperament will then assert itself with fuller sway even where the tone itself has to be held strongly in check.

H. K.

ONEGIN, Sigrid, Contralto

DB1484 { Der Erlkönig (The Erl King) (*with piano*) Schubert
Das Lied im Grünen (Song of the Open) (*with piano*) Schubert

DB1485 { Von ewiger Liebe, Op. 43, No. 1 (Eternal Love) (*with piano*) Brahms
Ruhe Süsseliebchen im meinem Schatten, Op. 33, No. 9 (Rest thee, my darling) (*with piano*) Brahms

If a woman is to sing the *Erlkönig* then by all means let it be a contralto. If a good one she commands as a rule more shades of tone-colour than a soprano, and can thus supply the necessary varieties of characterization. Sigrid Onégin, with her phenomenally rich, powerful voice, fulfils the requisite vocal purpose, and her art and intelligence do the rest. Two blemishes only will I note: the words are not so clear as they might be and the accompaniment is played so fast that the triplets lose their identity except when the father's galloping steed slows down. When he takes a "breather" we distinguish the patter of his hoofs. In *Das Lied im Grünen* the atmosphere of peace and joy in the "open" is delightfully suggested; the quality of the tone is beautiful, the rhythm quite faultlessly maintained, the whole feeling one of pure happiness and enjoyment. To this good impression the piano touch of Clemenz Schmalstich contributes not a little.

The two songs by Brahms are among his most treasured gems, and I, for one, am grateful to the gifted Sigrid Onégin for recording them so splendidly. Her wonderful tone comes out deliciously in both. Her accompanist, Franz Rupp, does clearer and more delicate work here than in the *Erlkönig*.

H. K.

PINZA, Ezio, Bass

DA1134 { Fin ch' han dal vino calda (Let wine flow like a fountain)—"Don Giovanni" (*in Italian*) Mozart
Deh vieni alla finestra (O come unto thy window, love)—"Don Giovanni" (*in Italian*) Mozart

These excellent reproductions of the two short solos allotted to Don Giovanni—the only ones, indeed that he has to sing—are good enough to prove that we ought to hear Signor Pinza in the entire rôle. They give the impression that he was not allowed a full chance at Covent Garden last season. True, his superb organ has more of the *basso cantante* than the pure baritonal quality; but if he can sing the Don's serenade and his song about wine with this degree of lightness, this impulsive *élan*, then I see no reason why he should not be able, like the great Fauré—the original Mephistopheles of *Faust*—to do equal justice to the whole music of the part. There is also present here the essential contrast of colour between the two aspects of Don Giovanni's nature—the rattling, devil-may-care spirit of the *brindisi* and the impassioned if half-mocking entreaty of the serenade. The singer has known just how to establish this difference; and it makes his records valuable as a model for other things besides tone and enunciation.

H. K.

PRINTEMPS, Yvonne, Soprano

E550 { Que soupirer d'amour (Ariette de Cloris) (*in French, with piano*) Lully
Dites-lui qu'on l'a remarqué (The Declaration), "Grande Duchesse de Gerolstein" (*in French, with piano*) Offenbach

Admirers of the talented French actress who is much more of a *diseuse* than a singer, would very properly resent severe criticism of these records on purely vocal grounds. I shall not, therefore, offer any. Suffice it to say that she has a pleasing voice and that there is something fascinating even about the "scoops" and slurs of her ultra-Parisian mannerisms. One is listening to Yvonne Printemps, and that fact covers a multitude of sins.

H. K.

RETHBERG, Elisabeth, Soprano

DB1461 {
Morrò, ma prima in grazia (I die, yet first implore thee)—" Un Ballo in Maschera " (*in Italian*) Verdi

Ma dall' aride stelo divulsa (When at last from its stem)—" Un Ballo in Maschera " (*in Italian*) Verdi
}

The first of these airs forms part of the duet between Renato and Amelia, which opens the third act of *Un Ballo in Maschera*. In it the sinning wife pleads to be allowed to see her child again, and it is in reply to this prayer that Renato sings the recitative which immediately precedes *Eri tu*, one leading into the other. One can easily overlook the fact that the tempo is a shade slower than usual, because the tone is exceptionally beautiful and the phrasing worthy of the Verdian soprano whose Aida is among the best now to be heard. The whole piece is replete with tenderness and pathos.

The second air as here enumerated really occurs at an earlier stage of the unhappy Amelia's career, when she is awaiting her lover by night at the agreed rendezvous. It is perhaps musically the finer air of the two and certainly the more dramatic, being in fact quite equal to the now-popular *Pace, mio Dio* in *La Forza del Destino*. There is no need to say how Elisabeth Rethberg sings it, since she is an acknowledged past-mistress in this kind of operatic music; while the slight altera-tion of the words in the final cadence is all to the good. The oft-recurring obbligato phrase for the oboe (or English horn) is delightfully played, as are, indeed, the whole of both accom-paniments. The clearness of the recording, too, is remarkable.

H. K.

RUFFO, Titta, Baritone

DB1397 {
Adamastor, re dell' acque (Adamastor, ruler of the ocean)—"L'Africaine " (*in Italian*) Meyerbeer

Nemico della Patria? (The enemy of his country ?) —" Andrea Chénier " (*in Italian*) Giordano
}

Notwithstanding the obloquy that modernistic musical criticism aims at the genius of Meyerbeer, his operas continue to be sung and his melodies recorded. His posthumous opera, *L'Africaine*, contains some of his finest airs, and among the most striking of them is this *Adamastor* in which Nelusko, the fanatical adorer of the African queen, Selika, reveals his savage nature. Titta Ruffo here realises with tremendous power its strong rhythm and rugged feeling. His contemptuous laugh has something more than a Mephistophelean touch ; it is actually diabolical in its sardonic flavour. As an example of the singer's gift for characterization it is unique.

The excerpt from *Andrea Chénier* stands more in the line of present-day Italian declamation and calls rather for sheer sonority, sustained vigour, beauty of tone. These qualities the famous baritone brings to bear in equally satisfying measure, with the result that one of the most coherent passages in Giordano's opera—and one of the most impressive—is made highly attractive as a theme for gramophonic display. The mechanical treatment in both these records is beyond criticism.

H. K.

SCHIPA, Tito, Tenor

DA974 {
Nina (Canzonetta) (*in Italian*) Pergólesi, arr. Bourdon

A Vucchella (A little posy) (*in Neapolitan*) Tosti
}

DB1079 {
La Partida (The Departure) (*in Spanish*) Alvarez

Alma de Dios (The Spirit from Heaven) (*in Spanish*) Serrano
}

DB1387 {
Ave Maria (*in Italian*) Mascagni

Una furtiva lagrima (Down her cheek a pearly tear)—"Elisir d'Amore " (*in Italian*) Donizetti
}

One wishes that all the slurring, portamento-loving modern Italian singers would imitate the economy shown by Tito Schipa in the use of decorative detail. It is precisely that which makes him such a master of pure phrasing, apart from the sweetness of his delightful tenor voice. *Nina*, of course, is only short for *Tregiorni son che Nina*, one of the loveliest melodies that Pergolesi ever wrote. The arrangement does not err in the direction of " grace notes," but Schipa makes it exquisitely graceful without them. The Neapolitan *canzone* is a pleasant enough specimen, admirably sung and recorded with orchestra. The Spanish items are no less to be commended for their characteristic charm—the *Partida* not so much a parting in sorrow as a lively *au revoir* with castanet obbligato ; the *Alma de Dios* a tender salutation, set to a martial tramp that begins more tragically than it ends.

The *Ave Maria* was set by Mascagni many years ago as a kind of counter-melody to the tune of his celebrated Intermezzo in *Cavalleria Rusticana*, and I fancy that Mme. Calvé was the first to sing it in London. So that by this arrangement you get the whole of the Intermezzo (if you are not too tired of it) *plus* a dozen bars or so of an *Ave Maria* that may just as well be sung by a man as by a woman. But what would alone suffice to make the record worth having is Schipa's exquisite rendering of *Una furtiva lagrima*. It is sung with the restraint, the delicacy of feeling, the soft beauty of expression, that so few tenors since Gardoni have brought to bear upon this simple air.

H. K.

SCHOENE, Lotte, Soprano

D1562 **Nun eilt herbei** (Aria of Mistress Ford) Pts. I and II—" Merry Wives of Windsor " (*in German*) Nicolai

D2004 **Der Hirt auf dem Felsen** (Shepherd on the rock) Pts. I and II (*in German*) Schubert

Thanks are due to this singer for giving us a very fine ren-dering of Mistress Ford's air, from Nicolai's opera, *The Merry Wives of Windsor*, which once upon a time Carl Rosa succeeded in making nearly as popular in this country as it is to-day in Germany. It belongs, however, to the romantic school of Weber, and that unfortunately is rather under a cloud at the present time. More than half of the air in question consists of a lengthy recitative, quite after the *Freischütz* manner (then nearly twenty years old), liberally decorated with elegant florid passages that demand exceedingly neat and brilliant execution. There it is, apparently, that Lotte Schoene has found her true *métier*. She has improved and her voice has grown immensely since she appeared here a few seasons ago ; it is now a real delight to listen to her clear, rich, opulent tone through a full soprano compass of over two octaves and a half, allied to a technique unusually correct, facile, and finished. Well accom-panied by the Berlin S. O. O., under Leo Blech, this strikes me as being a record of exceptional interest and value. It will make me keep a good look-out for further efforts from the matured Lotte Schoene.

A Schubert song of " heavenly length " as the critical Schumann would have observed—that being what he remarked concerning the great Symphony in C. It is here wisely divided into two parts, and let me gratefully add that the ever-im-proving art of Lotte Schoene, the abiding freshness of her sweet soprano, and the exquisite neatness of her execution, abundantly suffice to maintain interest until the lonely shepherd on the rock has reached the conclusion of his tuneful soliloquy. You will have noticed that these musical shepherds are generally proficient performers upon some woodwind instrument, preferably the *cor anglais*, whereof Wagner made such marvellous use in the last act of *Tristan*. Schubert, like Weber, had a greater *penchant* for the clarinet, and in this song our pastoral youth is evidently meant to show that he can sing his graceful *roulades* as cleverly as he can play them. One feels sure that the talented Lotte Schoene could do both if she tried, as it is, her vocal share in the record is so charming that there is nothing more to be said, unless it be to compliment the unnamed clarinettist of the Berlin State Opera Orchestra on his smooth and masterly rendering of the aforesaid *obbligati*.

H. K.

SCHORR, Friedrich, Baritone, and New Symphony Orchestra (cond. by **Albert Coates**)

D2017
- **Es ist genug** (It is enough)—" Elijah " (*in German*) Mendelssohn
- **Ist nicht des Herrn Wort wie Feuer** (Is not His word like a fire ?)—" Elijah " (*in German*) Mendelssohn

E 586
- **Hermit's Air**—" Der Freischütz " (*in German*) Wagner
- **Als du in kühnem Sange** (As thou in dauntless song)—" Tannhäuser " (*in German*) Wagner

E 587
- **Traum durch die Dämmerung** (Dream in the twilight) (*in German*) R. Strauss
- **Ich grolle nicht** (I'll not complain)—" Dichterliebe " (*in German*) Schumann

It is good to have in one's oratorio collection examples of famous airs sung to the original text, such as these, for instance, from *Elijah*, by an accomplished singer like Friedrich Schorr. More than that, it is a treat to hear them given with the beauty of voice, the nobility and distinction of style that characterize his delivery of *It is enough ;* the tremendous yet not excessive vigour and power of his *Is not His word like a fire ?* In the reading there are a few points that differ from those we are accustomed to in the English version; but in every instance they are interesting, apparently inevitable, not objectionable. The tempi are in the Mendelssohn tradition handed down through Staudigl and Santley.

The *Hermit's Air*, not very familiar in the rare performances of *Der Freischütz* that we hear in England, and the passage wherein Wolfram welcomes Tannhäuser on his return from the Venusberg adventure are also welcome items—strains of broad melody that no one better than Schorr knows how to lend the necessary grandeur of tone and diction. For the two lieder I must confess I care less. The Strauss plods along too heavily and sleepily even for a gentle stroll in the twilight; while *Ich grolle nicht* was surely never intended to be taken at this funereal pace—it makes it too dull for words.

H. K.

SCHUMANN, Elisabeth, Soprano

D1824
- **Er ist's** (Spring) ; **Aufträge** (Messages) (*in German, with piano*) Schumann
- **Schneeglöckchen** (Snowdrops) ; **Der Nussbaum** (The hazel tree) (*in German, with piano*) Schumann

D1951
- **Schlechtes Wetter** (Bad weather) ; **Ständchen** (Serenade) (*in German, with piano*) R. Strauss
- **All mein Gedanken** (All the fond thoughts) ; **Hat gesagt, bleibt's nicht dabei** (My father said) (*in German, with piano*) R. Strauss

E532
- **Marienlied** (Song of St. Mary) (*in German*) Marx
- **Muttertändelei, Op. 43, No. 2** (A mother's dallying) (*in German*) R. Strauss

It is a mistake to make comparisons between Elisabeth Schumann and other lieder-singers. She has a style, an individuality of her own, that separates her completely from the most distinguished of her rivals. That style must be suited by the music, naturally ; but as she seldom if ever makes a wrong choice, the danger of an unfavourable comparison can scarcely occur. For the same reason her gramophone work almost always possesses certain *nuances* that shed an interesting—perhaps even a novel—light upon the composition, in addition to the vocal charm and grace of her interpretation. For example, the crisp lightness of her touch, her delicate staccato, her sure, unswerving intonation, the exquisite sentiment of her phrasing, the clarity of her diction— all these, and other good qualities as well, are here in evidence. Space will not allow of a detailed analysis ; enough that each of the ten songs is a gem, faultlessly recorded and admirably accompanied. If I had to award a prize for one in particular I would give it to Strauss's *Schlechtes Wetter*, though the *Muttertänderlei* runs it close. By the way, the latter and the *Marienlied* are accompanied by the Vienna State Opera orchestra under Karl Alwin.

H. K.

TARASOVA, Nina, Mezzo-Soprano (Diseuse)

B3844
- **Folk Song**—A New Volga Song (*in Russian, with piano acc. by Milne Charnley*)
- **Black eyes** (*in Russian, with piano acc. by Milne Charnley*)

The natural open production of this Russian mezzo-soprano would have sounded pleasanter without the reinforcement of an amplifier. She is classified as a *diseuse*, but for that matter she is just as truly a singer—of the type of folk-song illustrated here. Over-refinement in such cases would be equally undesirable. Perhaps the kindest thing I can say, to be truthful, is that she suggests a sort of female Chaliapine by her faithful imitation of the voice and manner of the Volga boatman or the Muscovite *moujik*—when they happen to be musical. *Ergo*, her records may be regarded as curiosities in their way.

H. K.

ZANELLI, Renato, Tenor

DB1439
- **Ora e per sempre addio, sante memorie!** (Now and for ever, good-bye, sacred memories !— " Otello " (*in Italian*) Verdi
- Quartet with ROGGIO, PALAI and MASINI— **Storm and Entrance of Otello** (Uragano ed Esultate)—" Otello " (*in Italian*) Verdi

These pieces ought to be played in opposite order to that in which they are here placed. The quartet comes in Act I and the *Esultate*, splendid but short, should not follow but precede that wonderful outburst, inspired by Shakespeare-Boito, where Otello bids farewell for ever to the " tranquil mind," farewell to " the plumed troop and the big wars, That make ambition virtue." Both are magnificent, and Zanelli declaims them magnificently, but it seems to me that the concerted choral number must—if they are to be sung together at all—be taken first. The *Esultate* after the *Ora e per sempre* has the effect of an anti-climax. Anyhow, it is a joy to hear them so splendidly given as they are in these records.

H. K.

THE H.M.V. CONNOISSEUR CATALOGUE
(Concluded)

CORTIS, Antonio, Tenor

DB1468 { **Che gelida manina** (Your tiny hand is frozen)— Act I " Bohème " (*in Italian*)   Puccini

Salve, dimora (All hail thou dwelling)—Act 3 " Faust " (*in Italian*)   Gounod

The pieces by which Signor Cortis is represented in this catalogue may be regarded as a decisive test of any operatic tenor's claim to stand among acknowledged masters of his particular class or craft. The fact that he sings them well is, so to speak, his justification ; and these are exceedingly well sung. I do not object in the least to their being given, both of them, a semitone lower than they were written. They probably suit him the better for it, and consequently sound better, particularly the excellent high B's, which are much to be preferred to pinched or shaky high C's. The voice of this singer is incomparably finer than it was when I first reviewed his records a few years ago ; it was pleasant enough then, but it is a splendid organ now, and in all probability has attained the full height of its beauty and power. The *Salve, dimora* is elegantly phrased, while *Che gelida* rings with just the right intensity of growing passion.

H. K.

KIPNIS, Alexander, Bass

D2018 { **Als Bublein klein an der Mutter-Brust** (When that I was as a tiny boy) " Merry Wives of Windsor "   Nicolai

Fünftausend Thaler (Five thousand thaler) " Der Wildschütz "   Lortzing

This is an air with chorus, sung by Falstaff in Nicolai's delightful opera, *The Merry Wives of Windsor*—another of those tuneful, characteristic numbers that make one marvel at the neglect that Nicolai's masterpiece has long undergone at English hands. Had we a few more singers of the type of Lotte Schoene and Alexander Kipnis I think we should soon find it in the Covent Garden repertory. It was in the Carl Rosa fifty-three years ago. A still more striking example of the basso's versatility is heard in the air from Lortzing's opera *Der Wildschütz*, one of those ultra-Teutonic ditties of the old-fashion *volkslied* sort that distinguishes the ballads of Carl Loewe. I need scarcely add that the singer revels in both to his heart's content. The chorus takes a prominent part in the Falstaff number, but in the other he has the field to himself and his humorous patter will evoke from you something more than a smile.

LJUNGBERG, Göta, Soprano

D2036 { **Eines Tages sehen wir** (One fine day)—Act 2 " Madam Butterfly "   Puccini

Als euer Sohn einst fortzog (Mother, you know the story) " Cavalleria Rusticana "   Mascagni

There is a wistful charm in the rendering of these familiar airs that explains their choice for the new catalogue, apart from the interest of an individual reading in a text to which we are not accustomed where Puccini is concerned. The clear, bright Northern voice comes out refreshingly in both cases, if with no great variation of tone-colour, and the necessary dramatic feeling pervades each in turn. I cannot remember to have seen Miss Ljungberg either as Cho-cho-San or as Santuzza, even if she has sung them at Covent Garden ; but it is obvious from these records that the music of both characters suits her well.

SPANI, Hina, Soprano

E588 { **Montanesa**   J. Nin

El Majo Discreto (The Discreet Lover)   Granados

I have only one fault to find with these fascinating songs : they are too short. Rarely will you hear voice and music in combination to such perfection from the lips of a purely Spanish singer. The only way to compensate for the brevity of the display is to avail yourself of the gramophonist's privilege and grant yourself as many encores as you please to take. There will be no one to object. The voice is, truly speaking, more of a mezzo-soprano than a soprano ; hence the richer quality of the medium notes. Anyhow we have here a charming singer, with a style peculiarly her own and an art that is unimpeachable in its essentially Iberian nationality and depth of sentiment. I have often heard the delicious *Discreet Lover* of Granados, but never quite so deliciously sung.

H. K.

"MARITANA" ABRIDGED

Columbia DB613–8 (10in., 2s. 6d. each ; in album with booklet giving words of songs, 17s. 6d.).

Abridged version of Wallace's *Maritana*, sung by **Miriam Licette, Clara Serena, Heddle Nash, Dennis Noble,** with **Grand Opera Company** and orchestra conducted by **Clarence Raybould.**

The latest addition to the Columbia operatic list is welcome for more than one reason. To begin with, it was high time a popular English work found its way into the select group of opera albums. The Milanese *ateliers* have gradually been acquiring a monopoly of this kind of thing, and they naturally are wise enough to deal exclusively with Italian operas and Italian artists—in fact with the native product that they understand and perform best. What is more, they have set the right example in sparing neither trouble nor expense over their executive material, that is to say, in securing first-rate singers for the principal parts, an eminent conductor, and the finest available orchestra and chorus. This plan has been found to pay—I hope, well—in the long run, and I am glad to think that, if we want to imitate it with operas of our own, there need no longer be any fear of our having to go to Milan or Paris or anywhere else abroad for them. Indeed, the new Columbia *Maritana* is proof to the contrary. It shows that, provided the right artistic stuff be employed, we can do the thing as well as anybody.

Nor is it any the worse for being an abridged version. Who wants the whole of *Maritana* at a single sitting minus stage equipment and the good old scenes to fill and please the eye ? The faithful admirers of Vincent Wallace—a British musician, mind you, of whom this country still has every reason to feel proud—are not likely to clamour for more via the gramophone than a reproduction of the favourite airs, concerted pieces, and choruses. Well, here they all are, from '*Tis the harp in the air* and *Of fairy wand had I the power* down to *Scenes that are*

brightest, Sainted Mother, and the final emsemble, *What mystery does thus control ?* Even the note of interrogation is not forgotten. But the great point is that the whole twelve selections from first to last are really admirably done. Even the slight over-amplification contrived, no doubt, in view of large provincial audiences in halls of fair size, is not serious enough to matter, since it can always be reduced for performances in small rooms. The solo quartet could not easily have been improved upon, seeing that it comprises accomplished and experienced artists such as **Miriam Licette** (Maritana), **Clara Serena** (Lazarillo), **Heddle Nash** (Don Cæsar de Bazan), and **Dennis Noble** (Don José), with Clarence Raybould as conductor. The entire series of excerpts moves along with unflagging spirit and energy, and I may add that the recording, like everything else, merits unequivocal praise.

HERMAN KLEIN.

THE H.M.V. "TRAVIATA" ALBUM

It seems only the other day (though it was a couple of years ago) that the Columbia Album of *La Traviata* came out, together with a new prose translation of the text from the pen of Mr. Compton Mackenzie, which lent an added interest and value to the Italian recording. I pointed out at the time the obvious advantage that was gained by enabling the listener to see at a glance the general purport of an utterance in its entirety, instead of being asked to follow each separate sentence word by word. The latter plan will not even help one to learn Italian, since the translation (or, rather, adaptation) does not render the literal meaning of the words, save in rare instances, and scarcely in a single case when the text is being displaced or transmogrified to make it fit the music. Yet, in the *Traviata* Album just issued by H.M.V., what do we find ?—the old device over again of providing for each line, as it is sung in the Italian, an intervening line of English text taken from the vocal score (Ricordi's) and placed underneath it. Thus you are expected to do three things at once : hear the Italian words, read the corresponding English sentence, and listen to the singing and playing of Verdi's music. Only the expert auditor who knows the opera well can be expected to do that. Moreover, the difficulty was scarcely to be lightened by the necessity for printing all the repetitions in which the characters and the chorus have to indulge.

Apart from this secondary consideration—which is what it is, after all, and no more—I have nothing but praise for the new Album. It has been prepared with exceptional care under the direction of Maestro **Carlo Sabajno,** whose great experience in this kind of work is no doubt responsible for the increasing average of excellence to be observed in the purity of tone and perfect dynamic balance that distinguish the recording. The conventional cuts having been made, the whole opera as we now know it has been comfortably reproduced in thirteen double-sided discs, numbered C2214 to C2226. The chorus and orchestra are those of La Scala, upon whose merits, like those of their conductor, there is no need for me to dilate. The cast is as follows : Violetta Valéry, **Anna Rozsa ;** Flora Bervoix and Annina, **Olga de Franco ;** Alfred Germont, **Alessandro Ziliani ;** George Germont, **Luigi Borgonovi ;** Gaston, **Giordano Callegari ;** Baron Duophol, **Arnaldo Lenzi ;** Marquis of Obigny and Doctor Grenvil, **Antonio Gelli.**

The names of the artists singing the parts of the two lovers are unknown here, and judging by their photographs in the book of words as well as by their voices, I should say that both are quite young. *Tanto meglio!* They suggest all the better the types of the 1830's depicted by Alexandre Dumas *fils* in *La Dame aux Camélias ;* and their contemporary costumes, which so annoyed the romance-loving Venetians in 1853, do not affect us here in the slightest degree. It is the singing that matters ; and that, I may assure you, is of unwonted excellence. Wonderful to relate, it is from first to last delightfully free from the prevailing blemish of a tremolo ; the voices, not only of the soprano and tenor, but of the baritone also, are actually as steady as a rock, besides possessing that attractive and pleasing quality that you do not tire of listening to long before the opera is ended. The men's are rather, perhaps, of the regular Italian sort that we are accustomed to nowadays, particularly that of the Alfredo —I beg pardon, plain Alfred in this version, though no relation to our gay young friend in *Die Fledermaus ;* and anyhow a very nice tenor indeed, for all his *bollenti spiriti.* But both of them occupy a back row when compared with the fascinating Violetta, Anna Rozsa, whose pure soprano has just the girlish hue of a fresh young English or Scots voice lately arrived from somewhere in the North of England or beyond the Tweed. And her singing is no less charming than her organ. Her *Ah! fors' è lui* stamps her as a well-trained, accomplished vocalist, her share in the duet with the elder Germont as an exponent of strong emotional and dramatic feeling, her portion of the finale in Act III sufficiently powerful, and her pathos in the dying scene alike touching and beautiful. I have made a note of this artist's name, and shall look forward to hearing her in London *in propria persona.* The minor characters are adequately represented ; and with that I think everything has been said.

HERMAN KLEIN.

OPERATIC AND FOREIGN SONGS

THEODORE CHALIAPINE (bass).—**Elégie (Song of Mourning)** (Massenet). In Russian. Piano and 'Cello acc. And **Persian Love Song** (Rubinstein). In Russian. Orch. acc. H.M.V. DB1525, 12in., 6s.

BENIAMINO GIGLI (tenor).—**Vecchio Ritornello (The Old Refrain)** (Kreisler). In Italian, and **Carmela** (de Curtis) in Neapolitan. Orch. acc. H.M.V. DA1195, 10in., 4s.

LOTTE SCHOENE (soprano) and **WILLY DOMGRAF-FASSBANDER** (baritone).—**Pronta io son,** Duet from Act 1 of **Don Pasquale** (Donizetti), in Italian, two parts. **Berlin State Opera Orchestra** under **Orthmann.** H.M.V. DB1546, 12in., 6s.

LAWRENCE TIBBETT (baritone).—**Largo al factotum** from Act 1, **Il Barbiere di Siviglia** (Rossini) and **Eri tu** from Act 3 **Un Ballo in Maschera** (Verdi). In Italian. Orch. acc. H.M.V. DB1478, 12in., 6s.

FRIEDRICH SCHORR (baritone) and **GOTA LJUNGBERG** (soprano).—**Gut'n Abend, Meister** and **Ich seh ! 'swar nur,** Duet from Act 2, **Die Meistersinger** (Wagner). In German, **London Symphony Orchestra** under **L. Collingwood.** H.M.V. D2001, 12in., 6s.

RICHARD TAUBER (tenor).—**Prologue** to **Pagliacci** (Leoncavallo). In German. Orch. acc. Parlo. RO20161, 10in., 4s. See also under Miscellaneous Reviews.

CONCHITA SUPERVIA (mezzo-soprano).—**El Relicario** (J. Padilla-Oliveros Y. Castelloi) and **Lagarteranas** (J. Guerro-Luca de Tena-E. Reoyo). In Spanish. Orch. acc. Parlo. RO20158, 10in., 4s. And **La Farruca** (Turina) and **Clavelitos** (J. Valverde). In Spanish. Orch. acc. Parlo. RO20154, 10in., 4s.

C. E. KAIDANOFF (bass).—**Varlaam's Song, In the town of Kazan,** from **Boris Godounov** (Moussorgsky) and **Song of the Flea** (Moussorgsky). In Russian. Orch. acc. H.M.V. B3928, 10in., 2s. 6d.

LOTTE LEHMANN (soprano).—**The May-Night (Wander silberne Mond)** Op. 43. No. 2. (Brahms) and **The Vain Suit (Guten Abend, mein Schatz).** Op. 84. No. 4. (Brahms.) In German. Acc. by Instrumental Trio. Parlo. RO20159, 10in., 4s.

LILY PONS (soprano).—**Pamina's Aria** from **The Magic Flute** (Mozart) and **Bionda's Aria** from **Il Seraglio** (Mozart). In French. Orch. acc. conducted by **C. Cloëz.** Parlo. R20163, 12in., 6s.

EIDE NORENA (soprano). **Gilda's Aria** from **Rigoletto** (Verdi) and **Waltz Song** from **Roméo et Juliette** (Gounod). In French. Orch. acc. conducted by **H. de Fosse.** Parlo. R20162, 12in., 6s.

Theodore Chaliapine.—The genius of the great Russian bass is exhibited in these days under three separate and distinct aspects, each in its way equally striking and remarkable. They consist of his stage work, his concert appearances, and his recording for the gramophone. In the first he reigns supreme alike as actor and singer ; the second limits him in the matters of costume and movement, but neither in gesture nor facial expression ; the third, which is the one that I am at present dealing with, limits him only to the things that can be expressed through the medium of the human voice. Yet even here in this last he is all-comprehensive, complete, and unique—unique in the literal sense, because he gives us more of himself and his many-sided art than does any other person who sings in front of a microphone. He is a living proof of the fact that I have been seeking to establish for three decades, namely, that the true " Mastersinger " should be capable of putting the drama as well as the character of the operatic scene into the gramophone record. If no one approaches Chaliapine in this respect it is partly, of course, because no one else exclaims *toujours l'audace !* or dares to take the liberties that he takes. Yet his effects never fail to come off. Therefore they must be right ; and in saying that I do not suppose for a moment that they are such as the composers of the music ever dreamed of, though I am perfectly sure that they would never have protested against the artist's reading. For example, in the records under notice, Massenet would probably have cried with joy to hear his *Elégie* delivered with such a sustained ecstasy of sorrow, such a torrent of overwhelming misery, such amazing contrasts of sonority and softness. Similarly, the leonine Rubinstein would have been breathless with astonishment at hearing his *Gelb rollt mir zu Füssen* converted into a *Persian Love Song* that is a half-whispered appeal *ad misericordiam,* illustrated with real (or nearly real) tears, and accompanied by *pizzicato* strings and a whining oboe. Then at the end, that idea of murmuring the Persian refrain which rightfully belongs to the piano alone—why, it is a veritable master stroke ! And I leave it at that.

Beniamino Gigli.—We come now to the simpler things of life. They take the form of songs of the type that Tosti and Denza were wont to turn out by the dozen, at any rate in their " salad days," and which Beniamino Gigli warbles *a piena voce* as befits the legitimate successor of Caruso. When I say that they are likewise strongly amplified I hope I have prepared you for the orgy of tone that they furnish withal. The familiar triple rhythm and *dolce far niente* swing of the *Carmela* call up visions of Posilippo and the Bay on a moonlight evening, while the voice of Gigli (heard for choice at a distance) is a treat not readily to be despised.

Lotte Schoene and *Willy Fassbänder.*—Seldom do we have the opportunity of hearing German artists giving such a good account of pieces belonging to the Italian *buffo* school as may be enjoyed in this rendering of the famous duet from Donizetti's *Don Pasquale.* Patti and Cotogni used often to sing it at Covent Garden, and I heard them in it not only there, but at the Floral Hall Concerts next door. I institute no comparisons, but I mean a real compliment when I declare that the critic must be hard to please who will ask to hear it better done than it is in this performance with the Berlin State Opera orchestra under Orthmann. Lotte Schoene has a bird-like quality of tone, and Fassbänder a baritone that is sympathetic as well as flexible, while both display acquaintance with the traditions of the best Italian school. In fact, I consider this quite equal, if not actually superior, to the H.M.V. record of pre-electric days sung by Bori and De Lucia.

Lawrence Tibbett.—It is so long since I received a record by this American singer that I had almost began to wonder whether he had ceased to find time for gramophone work in the intervals between his visits to Hollywood and the opera houses of Chicago and New York. Evidently not, for his present effort shows him to be in good vocal training at the microphone. His *Largo al factotum* reveals a resonant, flexible voice, together with an abundance of life and vigour not unworthy of Titta Ruffo (it has his high spirits) and a speed in patter that might emulate the doughty deeds of a Malcolm Campbell or a Stainforth. The Italian accent is unusually good, and altogether the song may be said to give us the immortal barber in capital style and up-to-date. The *Eri tu* is sung with sustained power and tragic vehemence; with more of menace than of melancholy. One would welcome a moment or two of Chaliapine's wonderful sense of contrast and his exquisite *mezza-voce*; moreover, the strength would be enhanced in effect by a few touches of pathos. Nevertheless, it is an artistic interpretation, and the vocal quality is refined throughout. The accompaniments, too, betray the guidance of an alert and experienced hand.

Göta Ljungberg and *Friedrich Schorr.*—If asked to explain why the scene between Hans Sachs and Eva in the second act of *Die Meistersinger* is so frequently recorded, I should reply, "Because it is one of the most charming and melodious episodes in the opera." It contains no opportunity for display, being little more than a dialogue of musical repartee that ends just as abruptly as it begins. But how clever; how full of sly suggestion; how illuminating in the clear light that it throws upon the characters of the poet-cobbler and the goldsmith's daughter! I need not enlarge upon the consummate art of these two singers or the perfect understanding wherewith they delineate every point in their delightful confab. It could not be surpassed.

Richard Tauber.—Of all singers this is perhaps the last from whom one would have anticipated so essentially baritonal an achievement as the *Prologue*. And yet, when all is said and done, it is only the natural corollary of my argument, frequently suggested if not expressed, that Tauber's voice belongs to the category of those low tenors who are, in point of fact, virtually high baritones. It is in reality well fitted for Leoncavallo's cleverly-written and melodious music, which touches neither extreme, yet shows off a dramatic singer to the best advantage. Hence its extraordinary popularity. Slightly but not excessively amplified, it makes his organ sound more opulent of tone than usual, but without depriving it of the smooth, velvety timbre that is its chiefest charm. It is also quite a manly rendering and fairly free from tricks, and therefore pleases as well as satisfies the captious listener.

Conchita Supervia.—Where modern Spanish music is concerned it would be futile to ask for more realistic and colourful interpretations than those provided by Conchita Supervia. I would also like to acknowledge her industry in seeking out and studying the latest songs composed by the recognised successors of Albeniz and Granados, and the encouragement that her art gives younger men to strive to follow in their footsteps. For, truly her singing of these things is an inspiration as well as a joy; her intensely Spanish character, with its amazing vivacity and piquant flavour, pervades every bar; her rhythm, taste, and feeling are allied to technique of a very high order; her voice, even when she forces the chest tone, seems created by nature for this kind of work and it records splendidly. The songs are all extremely original; I should really find it hard to choose one before another for emphatic admiration.

C. E. Kaidanoff.—Another specimen of the genuine Russian bass and a talented singer to boot. I like immensely his robust patter and free delivery in *Varlaam's Song*, which shows off well the volume and range of his voice. Better still,

though, is the variety of his tone-colour and ironic humour in the *Song of the Flea*. It is sung as only a Russian can sing it, and I might almost say a Chaliapine at that; for there is an unmistakeable similarity between this artist's voice and that of his illustrious countryman, upon whom he seems to have modelled method, tone, style, and everything else. He sounds to me like a " find."

Lotte Lehmann.—In some matters the Parlophone " arrangers " are incorrigible. I have complained again and again of their partiality for stentorian tone and obtrusive instrumental accompaniments; but they do not seem inclined to mend their ways. These two lovely Brahms lieder, beautifully sung by a gifted vocalist, are in my opinion made almost unrecognizable under a disguise of clumsy, elaborate decoration of a sort that the music was never intended to bear. The idea of overloading Brahms with obbligatos and counterthemes is worse than a superfluity—it is an impertinence; and it is about time, in my opinion, that such interferences with the compositions of a great master were brought to a stop. His pianoforte accompaniments, well played upon a good instrument, are quite good enough for his admirers in this country, and they ought to sell the record as readily as the spurious versions adopted by any " instrumental trio."

Lily Pons.—The new Belgian soprano may not surround Mozart with the true atmosphere (*Stimmung*, if you like) that one properly associates with these airs from the *Magic Flute* and the *Seraglio*; but she certainly invests them with a charm that is quite her own. Her style is eminently pure and artistic, and every note has music in it. Her even scale and excellent breathing enable her to cope easily with the exacting phrases of Pamina's air. Her expression of grief is so unforced and touching that it is a pity when she tarnishes its flawless perfection with an un-Mozartian addition to the concluding cadence. In Bionda's aria the tone sounds at moments a trifle thin, like the French text to which it is allied, but the phrasing is correct and the F *in alt* as resonant as a bell.

Eidé Norena.—Here is another French rendering of something we generally hear in Italian, but let me assure you that a French *Caro nome*, if as delightful as we get it in this instance, may be very welcome indeed. The waltz from *Roméo* is equally irreproachable.

HERMAN KLEIN.

OPERATIC AND FOREIGN SONGS

ROSA PONSELLE (soprano) with **EZIO PINZA** (bass).—**May Angels guard thee** from Act 2 **La Forza del Destino** (Verdi) and with **GIOVANNI MARTINELLI** (tenor) **Miserere** (**Again the wail of sorrow**) from Act 4 **Il Trovatore** (Verdi). In Italian, with Chorus and Orchestra of the Metropolitan Opera House under **Giulio Setti**. H.M.V. DB1199, 12in., 6s.

THEODORE CHALIAPINE (bass).—**Rondo of Farlaf** (Patter Song) from Act 2 **Russlan and Ludmila** (Glinka) and **Aria of the Miller** from Act 1 **Roussalka** (Dargomijsky). In Russian. Orch. acc., under **M. Steimann**. H.M.V. DB1530, 12in., 6s.

BENIAMINO GIGLI (tenor).—**Your tiny hand is frozen** from Act 1 **La Bohème** (Puccini) and **All hail, thou dwelling pure and lowly** from Act 3 **Faust** (Gounod). In Italian. Orch acc., under **Eugene Goossens**. H.M.V. DB1538, 12in., 6s.

LOTTE LEHMANN (soprano).—**Sanctuary of the heart** (Ketelbey) and **Three horsemen came riding** (arr. Dr. Römer). In German, with chorus, organ and orchestra under **Dr. Römer**. Parlo. RO20166, 10in., 4s.

NANNY LARSEN TODSEN (soprano).—**Senta's Ballad** from

The Flying Dutchman (Wagner). In German, with **Chorus and Orchestra of the State Opera House, Berlin** under **Dr. Weissmann.** Parlo. R1079, 10in., 2s. 6d.

Before starting on my monthly " quota " (the word of the moment suggested by a recent Verdian headline, "Music and Agriculture ") I would like to express my gratification at being able to base upon up-to-date conditions all notices of new records appearing now and hereafter in these columns. I will not say I have not been fortunate hitherto. Both my H.M.V. and my Columbia models have done me right good service this many a day ; nor should I have felt myself qualified, with less efficient means at my disposal, to discharge in adequate fashion the responsible duties entrusted to me. But these are days of constant progress where mechanical devices are concerned, and the suspicion had for some time been growing upon me that some at least of the faults I was in the habit of pointing out were of a kind that recent improvements could, and actually did, either modify or obliterate altogether. For example, I find that the new His Master's Voice Electrical Reproducer, model 551D, not only yields a magnificently pure and truthful quality of tone, but enables me to regulate the use of every adjustment with the utmost speed, promptitude, and accuracy. In a word, I can rely upon every part of the machine to do its intended work properly and perform its allotted share towards producing the finest results. I can even reduce my *bête noire*, the over-amplified record, to reason by a turn of the knob which governs the " Volume Control " ; and that is a great gain indeed. I need not occupy further space with the description of improvements that have probably long ago received their due acknowledgment in the more technical pages of THE GRAMOPHONE. Let me only add that I am extremely grateful for the change and am hoping that my readers will in turn receive their full share of benefit from it.

Rosa Ponselle—Ezio Pinza—Giov. Martinelli.—The first record gives the closing episode of the second act of *La Forza del Destino*, the second the *Miserere* scene from *Il Trovatore.* The former has been sung by the same artists at Covent Garden, but the second only, I fancy, at the Metropolitan Opera House, New York. There is no need, at this hour, to enlarge upon the American soprano's interpretations of Verdi. Her voice, like his music, is steeped in emotion, and directly the two elements meet they set up an equivalent current of feeling in those who listen. The connection and the response are equally instantaneous ; the contrasts are no less striking. The stately and dignified phrases of the Padre Guardiano provide the effective background as well as do the suave, mellifluous tones of the imprisoned Manrico (happily unable here to emerge through a thick wall to bow his applause) ; and I take the same serene pleasure in listening to the sonorous Pinza as to the evergreen Martinelli. It is satisfactory moreover to know that you can buy the record holding these three fine voices, together with good choral and orchestral accessories, for the sum of 6s.

Theodore Chaliapine.—I am glad that the unique Chaliapine has lost no time in recording two of his cleverest efforts in the Russian operas that were heard here for the first time at the Lyceum Theatre last summer. It was hard enough to do them justice in print then ; to make a second attempt now is scarcely worth while. Only let me warn you that these are more normal renderings—though no less interesting on that account—than the extraordinary reading of Rubinstein's *Persian Love Song* to which I drew attention last month. No one knows better than Chaliapine where to draw the line. His rapid patter in the Glinka air is of an amazing fluency. In the song of the old miller from the first act of *Roussalka* he imparts inimitable character to a thoroughly Russian theme, and sustains the lively, tuneful spirit of the piece with a youthful freshness that is simply marvellous.

Beniamino Gigli.—For what they lack in novelty these latest samples of the periodical Gigli output certainly make up in perfection of quality. The *Che gelida* is indisputably

faultless. It provides an object-lesson in refinement of vowel-tone and ease of production. Both in this and the *Salve dimora* there is a high C that might make even Welsh tenors turn green with envy. The sole fault in the *Faust* air is an excess of *portamento* which is foreign to the school. Otherwise it is a wholly artistic and impressive rendering.

Lotte Lehmann.—It all depends, of course ; but for my own part I should have preferred to hear a tenor soloist in these pieces to a soprano. This is especially so with regard to the *Three Horsemen came riding*, a traditional German ballad with a hunting theme for horns of the kind that Weber made use of in *Der Freischütz.* The male chorus sings this with approved Teutonic gusto, but the delicate voice of Lotte Lehmann scarcely copes with it so effectively. She is better suited, assuredly, by the Ketelbey piece, a simple diatonic melody nicely arranged by Dr. Römer for solo, chorus, and orchestra. You may observe in this a " second subject " which consists of the opening phrase of the famous *Kol Nidrei* tune that Max Bruch arranged for 'cello solo. On the whole, however, the record is well put together and welcome for its seasonable attributes.

Nanny Larsen Todsen.—The telling voice of this admirable Wagnerian soprano lends all the requisite effect to *Senta's Ballad*, in conjunction with the efficient support of Dr. Weissmann, his splendid Berlin orchestra, and a well-trained group of Norwegian spinster—no, spinning choristers. One recognizes the earnestness and conviction that the Senta throws into her narrative of the curse hanging over the poor Dutchman whose fate has so aroused her sympathy that she can think of naught else. Wagner never wrote music more characteristic than this ; and I note with approval that the singer refuses to consider it complete without the outburst at the end, which we always hear in the opera but not invariably in a concert rendering.

RICHARD TAUBER (tenor).—**O Sanctissima** (O du fröhliche) and **Silent Night, Holy Night.** In German, with **Church Organ and Bells.** Parlo. Odeon RO20164, 10in. 4s.

BELLE BAKER.—**Eili, Eili**, and (with **Choir**) **David Hamelech** (Jewish Folk Songs). With **The Brunswick Concert Orchestra.** Brunswick 104, 12in. 4s.

MARCEL WITTRISCH (tenor).—**La Paloma** (Yradier) and **O sole mio** (De Capua). In German. Orch. acc. H.M.V. B3767, 10in., 2s. 6d.

VALERIA BARSOWA (soprano).—**Along my pathway** from **Les Noces de Jeannette** (Massé) and **Charmant Oiseau** from **The Pearl of Brazil** (David). In Russian, with **Orchestra of the State Opera House, Berlin** under **Dr. Weissmann.** Parlo. E11176, 12in. 4s.

BJORN TALEN (tenor).—**The Prize Song** from **The Master-singers** (Wagner) and **Winterstürme wichen dem Wonne-mond**, from **Die Walküre** (Wagner). In German, with **Orchestra of the State Opera House, Berlin** under **Dr. Weissmann.** Parlo. E11177, 12in., 4s.

FLORICA CHRISTOFOREANU (mezzo-soprano).—**O Aprile foriero** from **Samson and Delilah** (Saint-Saëns) and **Farewell to the little table** from **Manon** (Massenet). In Italian. Orch. acc. Parlo. E11178, 12in. 4s.

CONCHITA SUPERVIA (mezzo-soprano).—**Ay, Ay, Ay** (Freire) and **Carceleras** (Chapi). In Spanish. Orch. acc. Parlo. RO20165, 10in. 4s.

MIRIAM LICETTE (soprano) and **HEDDLE NASH** (tenor) with male chorus.—**Miserere Scene** from **Il Trovatore** (Verdi), and with **MURIEL BRUNSKILL** (contralto) and **DENNIS NOBLE** (baritone).—**Fairest daughter of the Graces** (Bella figlia dell' amore) from **Rigoletto** (Verdi). In English. Orch. acc. Col. DX302, 12in., 4s.

STILES ALLEN (soprano).—**O rejoice that the Lord has arisen** from **Cavalleria Rusticana** (Mascagni), and with **HARDY WILLIAMSON** (tenor).—**Miserere Scene** from **Il Trovatore**

(Verdi). In English, with **London Concert Orchestra** under **Orazio Fagotti** and chorus. Winner L5397, 10in., 2s.

PIERRE FOUCHY (tenor).—**Aubade de Mylio** from **Le Roi d'Ys** (Lalo) ; and **ANDRE GAUDIN** (Baritone).—**Air** from **Werther** (Massenet). In French, with the **Orchestra of L'Opéra-Comique, Paris** under **Louis Masson**. Decca F2601, 10in., 1s. 6d.

Richard Tauber.—Here is another seasonable contribution in the shape of a couple of familiar carols, with organ and bells (plenty of bells) all complete. But their chief recommendation lies in the fact that they are well and worthily rendered by that prince of amorous ballad-singers, Herr Richard Tauber. Herewith he proves himself a versatile no less than a fascinating artist, and, like the oratorio vocalists of another day, as much at home in the church as in the concert-room—as successful with a merry hymn-tune as with the engaging melody of a sly Viennese waltz. Both carols are sung in the same quiet, devotional style, and with an absolute freedom from affectation or "tricks" of the theatrical sort. One imagines that they have only to become known to achieve a wide popularity, especially when Christmas bells are wanted to assemble the family circle. These are loud enough to be heard up in the top attics.

Belle Baker.—Apparently this singer is a lady ; but she might easily be mistaken for a tenor of Semitic origin recording these quaint Jewish folk-songs under the Wailing Wall at Jerusalem, so abundantly tearful are they, so redolent of that abject misery which the daughters of Israel, sitting by the waters of Babylon, must have felt in the very act of weeping. It seems almost a pity that their modern imitator should have been quite so nasal, for we know how beautiful these weird old traditional melodies can sound when intoned by a properly-trained Cantor. But in this instance the soloist has sacrificed beauty for mere realism, and very disagreeable realism at that. Her method lacks even the redeeming quality of quaintness ; indeed, I cannot think of the Hebrew congregation that would endure it, at any rate in this country. The "Shemang" at the end of the *Eili, Eili* is an "inspiration" (in the physical sense) rather than an outpouring ; and in the *David Hamelech* one regrets that the brief lilting refrain of the female chorus did not silence the solo altogether.

Marcel Wittrisch.—German versions of our old acquaintances, *La Paloma* and *O sole mio*, should prove not unacceptable to the student who is fond of comparing linguistic influences on voice and style. Besides, half-a-crown is not dear for such a good baritone specimen as this.

Valeria Barsowa.—Much the same argument applies to these Russian renderings of a couple of florid French airs, one of which is the somewhat hackneyed but always effective *Charmant Oiseau*. The other is from a charming little one-act opera, *Les Noces de Jeannette*, that deserves to be better known over here than it is. Victor Massé wrote it for the Opéra-Comique in Paris, where it was produced in 1853, with the celebrated original Marguerite of Gounod's *Faust*, Mme. Miolan-Carvalho, in the part of the heroine. So popular did it become that it was performed there for the 1000th time so long ago as 1895. Jeannette's vocal display is supposed to imitate a nightingale, here represented by the flute ; and a very pleasing duet they make of it. The voice is essentially a girlish light soprano of unforced natural timbre, and controlled with abundant technical resource.

Björn Talén.—Norwegians have never struck me as being a people inclined to hurry ; but this tenor is an exception to the rule, judging by the careless rapture with which he dashes off the *Preislied*. A trifle less carelessness and a little more rapture might have been advisable ; for the voice is a fine one, and I am surprised that so experienced an "old hand" as Dr. Weissmann should have allowed himself to be run away with in this fashion. Both singer and conductor had themselves better in hand in the *Walküre* air, and it has fared better

accordingly—a more "sober" rendering, with some tenderness and sense of *nuance* in it.

Florica Christoforeanu.—Yet another new singer and a different nationality—Roumanian, I presume. Anyhow, a powerful, sympathetic organ, an assured dramatic style, and unquestionably a real mezzo-soprano—not soprano—character. In the last respect the label is wrong, whatever the authority may have been. None but a mezzo-soprano could have infused such a rich and resonant quality into the middle and lower notes of the *Printemps qui commence*. Maybe a little less grief in the tone and more suggestion of the scheming Philistine woman would have made it even more meritorious. The air from *Manon* needs a rather lighter voice and not quite so much of the tragic mood. Manon Lescaut was a sentimental young person, but ready and on the look-out for adventure ; nor were her eyes brimming over with tears or her voice gasping with sobs when she bade farewell to Des Grieux and the *petite table*.

Conchita Supervia.—In this consummate artist we have living proof that a genuine contralto, or even an acknowledged mezzo-soprano, need not lose her identity as such because her voice is capable of soaring to heights more generally associated with the high soprano or even the *soprano sfogato*. Malibran, one of the greatest Rosinas that ever lived, was a singer of that stamp ; so was Trebelli. I am merely mentioning the fact to point a moral. In the present instance the talented Conchita Supervia does not "pull out her top notes," but confines herself to the part of her expressive voice that is requisite for a couple of her most attractive national numbers. As a matter of course, she sings them adorably—in a word, as she alone can.

M. Licette, M. Brunskill, Heddle Nash, and *Dennis Noble.*—These are names that speak for themselves. The realm of English opera could not provide a stronger team for the performance of things like the *Miserere* from *Trovatore* and the quartet from *Rigoletto* ; nor do I intend embarking upon the invidious task of picking holes or making comparisons. One criticism only will I allow myself, and that concerns the chorus in the *Miserere*. It is too small, too loud, too self-assertive ; and it upsets the balance every time.

Stiles Allen and *Hardy Williamson.*—There is a run on the *Miserere* this month—exactly why or wherefore I should be much interested to learn. Perhaps it is in demand ; or can it be the name of a "runner" in another Irish sweepstake ? If so, the inevitable bell which begins it must be the signal for the start. No ; this is happily the "finish" ; and, as it only costs 2s., inclusive of the *Prayer* from *Cavalleria Rusticana*, maybe the touch of excitement in the tones of the Leonora-Santuzza will be thought worth so modest a figure. Seriously, though, it is a capital record, and equal to many that cost more.

Pierre Fouchy and *André Gaudin.*—It is a good thing there is no nationality in art, otherwise I fear the cry of " Buy British ! " might deter many from interesting themselves in a record which is French from *alpha* to *omega*. But that is not the real trouble. I doubt whether the record would really interest them, cheap as it sounds at eighteenpence ! Surely this kind of thing is intended only for the French market. Music and singers are good enough in their way, but utterly unfamiliar here ; and, as it so happens, the pieces selected by M. Louis Masson from *Le Roi d'Ys* and *Werther* are among the dullest in those dull operas.

HERMAN KLEIN.

REVIEWS PUBLISHED IN 1932

OPERATIC AND FOREIGN SONGS

LOTTE LEHMANN (soprano).—**Mein Herr, was dächten Sie von mir ?** from Act 1 and **Klänge der Heimat** from Act 2 of **Die Fledermaus** (Joh. Strauss). In German. Orch. acc. Parlo. RO20171, 10in., 4s.

RICHARD TAUBER (tenor). **I loved you more** (Jurmann and Rotter) and **My Greetings** (Wilczynski and Grothe). In German. Orch. acc. Parlo. RO20170, 10in., 4s.

LILY PONS (soprano). **Pourquoi dans les grands bois ?** from Act 1, and **Dans la forêt près de nous** from Duet Act 2, of **Lakmé** (Delibes). In French. Orch. acc. Parlo. RO20169, 10in., 4s.

FRIEDRICH SCHORR (baritone). **Aha ! Da streicht die Lene schon um's Haus** from Act 3 of **Die Meistersinger** (Wagner). With the **London Symphony Orchestra** conducted by **Albert Coates.** And **E. SCHUMANN** (soprano), **MELCHIOR** (tenor), **SCHORR** (baritone), **PARR** (contralto) and **WILLIAMS** (tenor). **Selig, wie die Sonne meines Glückes** from Act 3 of **Die Meistersinger.** In German. With the L.S.O. conducted by **John Barbirolli.** H.M.V. D2002, 12in., 6s.

VALERIA BARSOWA (soprano). **I am Titania** from Act 2 of **Mignon** (Thomas) and **Song, jest, perfume and dance,** from Act 1 of **Romeo and Juliet** (Gounod). In Russian. With **Orchestra of the State Opera House, Berlin.** Parlo. E11186, 12in., 4s.

HEINRICH SCHLUSNUS (baritone).—**Dass doch gemalt all' deine Reize waren** and **An die Geliebte** (Hugo Wolf). In German, piano acc. Polydor 91079, 10in., 4s.

MARGIT ANGERER (soprano) and **ALFRED PICCAVER** (tenor).—**Ah, quegli occhi** (Act 1) and **Amaro sol per te m'era il morire** (Act 3) from **La Tosca** (Puccini). In Italian. Orch. acc. Polydor 95462, 12in., 6s.

Lotte Lehmann.—It was inevitable that sooner or later we should have these songs from *Die Fledermaus* sung by their most ideal living interpreter. To the best of my knowledge she has never recorded them before ; though why not, is something of a mystery. Anyhow here they are, ready to serve as a model for all willing imitators who execute these pieces to English words in the fond belief that they are doing so in the manner that Johann Strauss intended them to be sung The art of Lotte Lehmann distinctly proves that it is not merely, as so many imagine, a matter of voice *plus* energy and dash, and no more. On the contrary, you will find that in every bar you get, not only perfect management of tone, but the real Viennese rhythm, so indescribably subtle in its national individuality, together with the clearest possible diction, true purity of accent, and the right undercurrent of satirical humour where wanted, as in the *Mein Herr, was dächten Sie.* Above all, you recognize in these records the characteristic contrast between the *haut ton* of the mistress and the insolent perkiness of the maid, otherwise the inimitable Viennese *soubrette.* Again, in the *Klänge der Heimat,* the *lassan* and *frischka* of the real Hungarian tune, as embodied by Liszt in his famous Rhapsodies, are vocalised with the grace and spirit of an accomplished singer. Too seldom can you hear this music rendered in such fashion.

Richard Tauber.—I am constantly being asked whether in my opinion Richard Tauber's voice is a genuine tenor. I think I answered that question more or less directly when I first began writing about it, and I think now, as I did then, that it is a light high baritone. This fact does not make it a whit less pleasant to listen to, unless it is "forced" or *abused* (as Garcia termed it) by being pushed beyond its natural *tessitura,* or allied to the music of opera that is too heavy, too continuously strenuous, to come within its compass and power. I am also of opinion that this is the true explanation of the reason why Herr Tauber suffers from a delicate throat and suffers from the kind of throat nervousness that leads to disappointments such as occurred recently at the Albert Hall. The singer who fears ordeals of that description (and he is not the first to be afflicted with misapprehensive dread at the prospect of standing before an audience of seven thousand in the huge building at Kensington Gore) is, of course, a totally different personage from the calm, collected artist who stands before the microphone after a long experience of the triumphs that he can achieve through that medium. Why he should not have the sense to realize that he can attain precisely the same result in the Albert Hall without exercising one degree more of effort, is quite beyond my comprehension, unless it be attributable to the sort of nervousness I have above indicated. Regarding these records there is only one word to be said : of their special class and in their particular way they are perfect.

Lily Pons.—These tuneful excerpts from *Lakmé,* so charmingly sung by the clever Belgian soprano whose name and talent must now be growing familiar to our readers, will serve to increase one's surprise that Delibes' delightful opera has not been restored to the Covent Garden repertory. If the right English singer could be found to do the music of the heroine justice, it would certainly add to the attractions of the company, even though better suited to a smaller *locale* than our leading opera house. A Marie Vanzandt may not crop up every day—an American girl she was, and quite ideal in the part which she created at the Opéra-Comique in Paris—but Noel Eadie would, I think, be admirable in it and I would gladly see her making the essay. Meanwhile, it would also be very pleasant to hear Lily Pons herself. She has the perfect voice for this music, and she records it with a purity of timbre, a smoothness of legato, a musical feeling, added to just the faultless intonation and diction that Delibes—a very fastidious Frenchman—welcomed so gladly in Vanzandt. I cannot say more in recommendation of this excellent record.

Friedrich Schorr and Others.—The selection here presented from the third act of *Die Meistersinger* is welcome not alone for the sublime quintet, but for the portion of the scene that leads up to it, especially because rendered in irreproachable fashion by the best Hans Sachs of our time. The quintet itself deserves equal praise, and I make my best bow to Mr. John Barbirolli and the London Symphony Orchestra for their share in this achievement. The balance of voices and instruments is kept with remarkable skill, and I can scarcely remember an instance where a more beautifully sustained pianissimo, held with such exemplary reticence or crowned with such a level crescendo, has been heard from the gramophone. Only in the final climax is one permitted to feel that the voice of Elisabeth Schumann, so ethereal until that moment, might have been brought out with greater power and sonority. But there is no other tiny spot on the sun of this unusually fine performance.

Valeria Barsowa.—I have had something to say in a previous review about this new Russian singer, and she confirms my estimation of her by revealing the same unequal traits in these solos. It seems a pity that a *coloratura* soprano of her undoubted talent should not have pursued her training to a higher degree of accuracy and finish. She has a very impulsive musical temperament, and when indulging in headlong flights of *bravura* is apt to commit all sorts of faulty bits of execution that greater care and study in preparation might easily have prevented. There is no need to point these out in detail; they occur chiefly in descending scales and passages of ornamentation; while the staccato is faulty, or else introduced where it should not be, as for instance in the cadenza that introduces the waltz from *Roméo* and which Gounod always required to be sung *legatissimo*. Then, again, the over-long high note disagreeably held at the end of the waltz is almost as unpardonable as are the many breaks and tiny pauses that disfigure the *fioriture* both in this and the Titania air. All these things are regrettable and, I repeat, point to inadequate drilling or supervision. Yet the gifts are too obviously precious to be wasted, and I hope the young soprano will forthwith turn her attention to serious work and study. She might also learn to record in other languages besides her own. By the way, I hear she is to give a recital in London in the spring.

Heinrich Schlusnus.—It is customary in these enlightened days to eulogise Hugo Wolf at the expense of other accepted masters of the art of lieder-writing, but I fail to see why this should be altogether necessary. Surely one can perceive the extraordinary genius for truthful and felicitous musical expression that Hugo Wolf possessed, without derogating by means of doubtful comparisons from the work of composers who were at least equally gifted. On the other hand, it is eminently desirable that Wolf's songs should be more widely known and appreciated than they are in this country, and for that reason I have cordially welcomed the good news that the newly-formed Hugo Wolf Society is practically what they call in the City " over-subscribed "—that is, if it ever really can be where adherence to a good cause is in question. That cause, in the meantime, can only be helped by the issue of splendid examples such as Heinrich Schlusnus has here furnished through Polydor. Both are lovely songs and worthy of the same attentive thought and study on the part of the listener that they have obviously received from the interpreter. The first is notable for its energy and depth of feeling; the second reveals moments of greater tenderness and yearning, but also of power, together with fine contrasts of tone-colour. I would note that the piano accompaniments, excellently played by Franz Rupp, are rendered precisely as the composer wrote them, without the meddlesome co-operation of violin or other tiresome *obbligati*.

Margit Angerer and Alfred Piccaver.—Good voices, both, and capital singing in a couple of *Tosca* duets whose only shortcoming lies in their brevity. Their genial mood reflects precisely as it should two of the rare instances of happy converse between the unlucky hero and heroine of Sardou's bloodthirsty drama, namely, in the church scene and on the platform outside the Castle of Sant' Angelo when the lovers are indulging in their false hopes of future joy. (During this last episode I have always longed for a chance of warning them that Scarpia's wretched bullets have *not* been drawn from the guns as he had promised. It would make the *dénouement* so much less unpleasant.) N.B. The velvety tones of Piccaver's voice are at last beginning to acquire a more sturdy, manly quality.

HERMAN KLEIN.

OPERATIC AND FOREIGN SONGS

FRIDA LEIDER (soprano).—**Ich sah' das Kind** (" Herzeleide ") from Act 2 of **Parsifal** (Wagner) and **Isolde's Liebestod** from Act 3 of **Tristan und Isolde** (Wagner). In German. With the **London Symphony Orchestra**, conducted by **John Barbirolli**. H.M.V. DB1545, 12in., 6s.

LAWRENCE TIBBETT (baritone).—**Votre Toast, je peux vous le rendre (Toreador's Song)** from Act 2 of **Carmen** (Bizet), in French, and **Tre sbirri, una carrozza** (Finale, Act 1) from **Tosca** (Puccini). In Italian. With **Metropolitan Opera House Chorus and Orchestra**. H.M.V. DB1298, 12in., 6s.

RICHARD TAUBER (tenor).—**Have pity!** (Bakalainikow) and **Im Rolandsbogen** (Mania, Ritzel). In German. Orch. acc. Parlo. RO20172, 10in., 4s.

LEILA BEN SEDIRA (soprano).—**Trahir Vincent** and **Non, jamais, jamais** from Act 2 of **Mireille** (Gounod). In French. Orch. acc. Parlo. R1123, 10in., 2s. 6d.

NINON VALLIN (soprano). **Serenade** (R. Strauss—Masset) and **Dream in the Twilight** (R. Strauss—L. Hettich). In French. Piano acc. Parlo. RO20173, 10in., 4s.

LOTTE LEHMANN (soprano).—**Styrienne (A gypsy lad I well do know)**, from Act 2, Scene 1 of **Mignon** (Thomas), and **There with him is she now**, from Act 2, Scene 2. In German. Orch. acc. Parlo. RO20174, 10in., 4s.

GERHARD HUSCH (baritone).—**If you are after a little amusement** and **Now your days of philandering are over** from Act 1 of **The Marriage of Figaro** (Mozart). In German. Orch. acc. Parlo. R1122, 10in. 2s. 6d.

JOSEPH SCHMIDT (tenor).—**Strange harmony** from Act 1, and **When the stars were shining** from Act 3 of **La Tosca** (Puccini). In German. Orch. acc. Broadcast Twelve 5263, 10in., 2s.

GEORGES THILL (tenor).—**Your tiny hand is frozen** from Act 1 of **La Bohème** (Puccini) and **Lohengrin's Farewell to the Swan** from Act III of **Lohengrin** (Wagner). Orch. acc. Columbia LX159, 12in., 6s.

THE CARL ROSA OPERA COMPANY, conductor **ARTHUR HAMMOND**.—Vocal Selection from **Faust** (Gounod). In English. Orch. acc. Crystalate Z113, 12in., 2s.

Frida Leider.—Whether it be heard in a soprano or a contralto voice is immaterial, the *Herzeleide* holds for you the same quality of fascination that it was intended to hold for *Parsifal*, provided it be sung with the same full measure of soothing smoothness and ingratiating charm. But to do this requires very great art, added to a clear understanding of the sort of hypnotic influence that the magician Klingsor is exercising over Kundry and she in turn is endeavouring to convey to the " pure fool " whose innocence makes him immune from the wiles of them both. Never shall I forget how two of Wagner's finest interpreters, Materna and Rosa Sucher, contrived to realize that strange scene in the early days at Bayreuth, by infusing into their tones precisely the suggestion of hypocritical sympathy, of false yet unexaggerated expression, which betrayed that the whole thing was a lie. After that you did not feel the least bit surprised when the garish foliage of the magic garden came tumbling down at the touch of the holy Spear, a heap of decayed ashes. Well, it is that same atmosphere of unreality that I can feel in Frida Leider's delightful, unbroken flow of vocal utterance in this *Herzeleide* record. Exquisitely sung, it is also flawlessly supported by Wagner's wonderful undercurrent of orchestration conducted by John Barbirolli. The *Liebestod* on the other side of the disc moves me less, perhaps; but it is a harder nut to crack both for singer and players, and I rather doubt whether either could have achieved a finer result or a more satisfying one.

Lawrence Tibbett.—In a leading journal I read the other day a notice of a film in which this American baritone was criticised for sounding as if he had made a bet with himself that he would attain the maximum both of loudness and continuity in his share of the performance. The criticism was probably well earned. At any rate, his rendering of the *Toreador's Song* gives that impression of a big voice that could go on, like Tennyson's brook, " for ever "; which is, after all, I admit, the kind of impression that a Toreador ought to give. As for the loudness, I make no complaint since my new H.M.V. Electrical Reproducer enables me so easily to moderate the ardour of even a Lawrence Tibbett; and the quality of the timbre is certainly pleasing. Still more palpably is the employment of such an organ appropriate in Scarpia's " Va! Tosca," the reiterated menace of which pervades the thundering crashes of brass and bells in the finale of the Church scene. It rings in your ears long after the noise and turmoil of the other sounds have ended.

Leila ben Sedira.—The air from *Mireille* is here labelled under two titles, but in reality it is the same one divided into two parts, thus enabling the singer to avoid making the usual cut in the section which begins after *Non, jamais*, at the words *A toi mon âme*. It is all melody of the purest Gounod type, and this charming vocalist with the Arabic cognomen has been trained in the right school to invest it with the requisite fluency and grace. Obviously French is to her as her native tongue ; she pronounces it with a refined accent, and her style has the authority of one who derives her traditions from " headquarters," which in this instance I take to be the Opéra-Comique. It is a pleasure to listen to scales and *fiorituri* so crisply and accurately executed, without the smallest departure from the composer's own notation, even to the F in *alt* which occurs (without undue prolongation) at the end of the piece. I have not heard this air so well done since Emma Nevada (Mignon's mother) sang it in a revival of Gounod's pastoral opera at Covent Garden—first time there, however—during a Mapleson season in 1887.

Richard Tauber.—Evidently we are not to reach the end of Herr Tauber's repertoire yet awhile. For that matter, how can we when he is always adding to it ? I make no pretence at keeping count of all the ballads and light opera solos that he enriches the gramophone (and himself) withal, especially as they sound to my ear so much alike that it is hard to distinguish one from another. I only know that they are very attractive in their Tauberesque way ; that Parlophone records them faultlessly, and that they are infinitely more reliable than the singer's own promised appearances at the Albert Hall or on the stage. You can at least make sure of hearing him, and hearing him at his best, by possessing yourself of this latest disc. In that respect I resemble the touts of the racing editions : I like to recommend " certainties." By the way, the *Rolandsbogen* implies a distinct invitation to join Richard in a quiet stroll along that lovely shore of the Rhine where the wine comes from.

Ninon Vallin.—It was Alfred de Musset, if I remember aright, who inspired Sir F. Paolo Tosti (a genuine British Knight !) with the poem that begins " Ninon, Ninon, que fais-tu de la vie ? " But surely de Musset never meant the query to be addressed to this busy and industrious recorder of Richard Strauss *à la française*. He was upbraiding an idle female (forgive the word !) for whom one day succeeded another and the hours flew by without her learning the true meaning of love. I cannot include the fair Ninon Vallin *dans cette galère*. Being an artist to the finger-tips, she is a hard worker ; and she must have worked particularly hard to make these familiar lieder sound as sweetly in French as Elena Gerhardt or Frieda Hempel has made them sound in German. What the translations are like I have made no effort to find out. I only know that they seem to fit the music well, and that " *Je vais à pas lent* " is a very happy rendering of " *Ich gehe nicht schnell*." The piano accompaniments are nicely played and recorded.

Lotte Lehmann.—We ought to be grateful in these days for any attempt to get out of the rut of hackneyed operatic pieces. The *Styrienne* sung by Mignon when she dresses up as a boy in the naughty Filina's room is one of the gems of Ambroise Thomas's opera, and in bygone days, when the famous Christine Nilsson trolled it forth in her own inimitable manner, her audiences would go wild with delight. Hers was just the true Tyrolean touch (though she was a Swede) that it required, and Minnie Hauk (the great Carmen) imitated her nearly enough to please most people. The only previous record of it that I can trace is one by Geraldine Farrar (DB854, pre-electric, of course) which, however, I have never heard. And now comes the gifted Lotte Lehmann with her own entirely novel reading of this quaint folk-song of the Eastern Alps—novel because she mysteriously half-whispers the first part of the tune and reserves her full voice for the jodelled refrain.

The effect is charming, like a girl telling her childish secret, and therefore the greater contrast to the subsequent outburst (reverse side) when the jealous Mignon, a woman at last, perceives her Wilhelm Meister in close converse with the flirtatious Filina. Altogether a most welcome record !

Gerhard Hüsch.—Having exhausted *The Magic Flute*, this artist has now turned his attention to *The Marriage of Figaro*, and, on the whole, with equally good results. And yet—somehow I should have been better pleased with these songs from the first act had the pitch been raised instead of being lowered a trifle, as they undoubtedly are. It makes the voice on the lower notes sound rather dull. For the interpretation there can be naught but praise, above all, the surprisingly clear enunciation of the words, which stand out as distinctly as if they had been carved out of the music. *Now your days* in particular is sung with any amount of animation and *brio*.

Joseph Schmidt.—Half-price may be reckoned cheap for any record that can claim to possess average merit, and in the present instance I should have been prepared to make still greater allowances at the reasonable figure of 2s. " for the lot." As a matter of fact there is not much to excuse beyond a little roughness in the quality of the recording. The singer's tone if somewhat nasal and in need of greater variety of nuance, is a pure tenor, rich and strong in timbre, and always well on the note. The over-full amplification gives rise to some distortion, but not to any great extent. There is abundant emotional expression all through.

Georges Thill.—Here, on the other hand, one perceives at once the very characteristics the absence of which was noted in the previous example. The Frenchman (or Belgian, I am not sure which) demonstrates beyond question that it is possible to sing Puccini with tenderness and Wagner with charm. No sudden or violent contrasts, as though one portion of the tiny hand were freezing and another burning up ; but the smooth, sensitive legato of a poet in love and used to expressing himself in melody as delicately as he does in words. The voice, moreover, proclaims unmistakably that nasal resonance and nasality mean two very different things ; and in singing French that is extremely important. The *Lohengrin* theme is beautifully sustained and the diction quite wonderful.

Carl Rosa Company.—Mr. Arthur Hammond has put together an admirable *pot-pourri* of gems from *Faust*, and the company which he conducts so ably have done them complete justice. More than that I cannot and need not say, unless it be to draw attention to the small outlay by which you can procure ten minutes of thoroughly delightful music.

HERMAN KLEIN

OPERATIC AND FOREIGN SONGS

EIDÉ NORENA (soprano).—**Hymn to the Sun** from **Le Coq d'Or** (Rimsky-Korsakov) and **Mathilde's cavatina** from Act 2, **William Tell** (Rossini). In French. Orch. acc. under **Defosse.** Parlo. RO20177, 10in., 4s.

NINON VALLIN (soprano).—**Comme autrefois dans la nuit sombre** and **C'est lui! mes yeux l'ont reconnu**, Air, Act 2 from **The Pearl Fishers** (Bizet). In two parts. In French. Orch. acc. under **G. Cloëz.** Parlo. RO20178, 10in., 4s.

GITTA ALPAR (soprano) and **HERBERT ERNST GROH** (tenor).—**One day a rapture ethereal** from Act 1 and **Let us fly from these walls** from Act 3 of **La Traviata** (Verdi). In German. Orch. acc. under **Dr. Weissmann.** Parlo. RO20176, 4s.

LAURITZ MELCHIOR (tenor) and **FRIEDRICH SCHORR** (baritone).—**Abendlich glühend in himmlischer Gluth** and **FRIEDRICH SCHORR.**—**Euch macht ihr's leicht** from Act 3 of **Die Meistersinger** (Wagner). With L.S.O. H.M.V. D2000, 12in., 6s.

CHALIAPINE (bass) and **POZEMKOVSKY** (tenor).—**Mad**

Scene and **Death of the Miller** from Act 3 of **Roussalka** (Dargomizhsky). In Russian. Orch. acc. H.M.V. DB1531, 12in., 6s.

GEORGES THILL (tenor).—**La Marseillaise** (Rouget de l'Isle) and **Le Rêve Passe** (Krier and Haimer). In French. With Chorus and Garde Républicaine Band of France. Columbia DB745, 2s. 6d.

BIANCA SCACCIATI (soprano), **FRANCESCO MERLI** (tenor) and **NAZZARENO DE ANGELIS** (bass).—**Trio, Qui posa il fianco** and **Qual voluttà trascorrere**, from Act 3 of **I Lombardi** (Verdi). In Italian. Orch. acc. under **Cav. Lorenzo Molajoli**. Columbia LX162, 12in., 6s.

HELENE GALS (soprano).—**Piangerò** from **Julius Caesar** (Handel), in Italian, and **Vidit suum** from **Stabat Mater** (Pergolesi), in Latin. Instr. acc. Parlo. E11195, 12in., 4s.

Eidé Norena.—Singers are not half careful enough, I find, about the tone-colour that they use for their pieces, or, should I say, the choice of pieces that are suitable for their vocal limitations. Miss Norena possesses not only a charming voice, but remarkable facility, added to the capacity for singing high notes exquisitely in tune. The trouble is that she seems to have only one dark, serious tone, like an organ with no more than a single stop (if such a thing existed in these days) ; and she employs that one alone for the rendering of two airs of such opposite character as are sung in this record. The very name in the original French of Mathilde's air, *Sombres forêts* (known in the Italian as *Selva opaca*), would suffice to indicate which of the two gains most by the fitness of the singer's solitary timbre. Despite several little alterations and embellishments—happily not in the simple Rossinian cadenza—the interpretation of this lovely song is wholly delightful. On the other hand, I cannot for the aforesaid reason, honestly say that I am quite content with the *Hymn to the Sun,* from *Le Coq d'Or.* It sounds too much like a solemn vocal exercise in chromatic descending passages, very clever and interesting technically, but utterly lacking in the note of joy and radiant happiness that it demands. So gifted and pleasing a vocalist ought surely to be able to give a little more thought to this important question of contrast.

Ninon Vallin.—The air sung by Leila in the second act of Bizet's opera, *The Pearl Fishers,* cannot be regarded as one of that composer's happiest inspirations. Yet the fault was scarcely his, as I think you will agree on examining the subject-matter of the poem. It has, for instance, none or scarcely any of the dramatic motive contained in the more familiar Michaela's song in *Carmen.* There you get fear and anxiety mingled with the quiet resolution that comes of trust in the aid of Providence, whereas in this piece (recorded in two parts) one finds little beyond the young lady's self-comforting reflection that she is about to retire for the night with the protection of her watchful lover in close proximity to her chamber. No excitement, therefore, and little change of mood ; but a graceful and ingratiating melody which Mme. Ninon Vallin, with her opulent tone, admirable method, and flawless purity of style, knows exactly how to make the most of. The accompaniment is well played by the orchestra under M. Cloëz and the recording leaves nothing to be desired.

Gitta Alpar and Herbert E. Groh.—If anything can reconcile the exigent listener to hackneyed Italian music sung in German, it will be when it is so artistically performed as are these duets for Violetta and Alfredo from the first and third acts of *La Traviata.* Both voices are of smooth and agreeable quality, while the singing is delightful because refined, easy, and unaffected. In their way they could not be improved upon.

Lauritz Melchior and Friedrich Schorr.—Once more these trusty comrades give us a selection worth having from their rich Wagnerian store. It is nothing new, and probably would not be so welcome if it were ; yet I doubt whether they have recorded it before. It is the concluding portion of the duet for Walther and Hans Sachs from the third act of *Die Meistersinger,* with (on the reverse side) the noble passage in

which Sachs acknowledges the salutations of the guilds after their procession to the banks of the Pegnitz. In the latter it is Friedrich Schorr who appropriates the lion's share—in fact, the whole of the honours. In the duet Lauritz Melchior has the best of the bargain, seeing that his share includes the full statement of the *Preisleid* in all but its final glorified form, which is of course reserved for the open-air competition, or Nuremberg Eisteddfod, with the hand of the fair Eva for prize. Both artists sing splendidly, as usual ; and the London Symphony Orchestra takes the honours for a sonorous yet discreet rendering of the instrumentation, the name of the conductor not being stated.

Chaliapine and Pozemkovsky.—There is much solo and very little duet in this excerpt—the former appropriated with our ready consent by the most distinguished of all Russian singers. He made a sensation at the Lyceum last summer with the *Mad Scene* and *Death of the Miller* in the third act of *Roussalka,* and I for one am grateful that H.M.V. did not miss the opportunity of recording an episode so intensely dramatic and musically striking. Only a great actor like Chaliapine could have conceived it and only a singer of his calibre could have contrived to put into a gramophone record the amount of atmosphere and descriptive realism that he has here invested it with. It is simply astonishing from every viewpoint, and only the electrical process could have allowed of such an achievement. Note above all the pathetic melody of the final theme and the quaint little touches where the tenor interjects a remark here and there. And it is all so essentially Russian.

Georges Thill.—Singing for the multitude viâ the gramophone is evidently regarded in France as a patriotic duty. (It may also be a highly profitable proceeding ; but never mind that. There was a time, I believe, when our illustrious tenors, Braham and Sims Reeves, used to sing British nautical ballads for the same reason.) This is the first time, I fancy, that a leading tenor of the Paris Opéra has recorded the *Marseillaise* and a " quick-step " ditty of the military type. Without enquiring further into the object I may say unhesitatingly that the result is calculated to reconcile several thousand French conscripts to their year or years of military service. No voice can be too good for Rouget de l'Isle's inspiring national air, and no living French tenor that I know of could sing either this or the lively marching song that goes with it more superbly or with greater entrain than Georges Thill. A good chorus and the band of the Garde Républicaine just make the thing perfect. As Hortense Schneider used to sing in *La Grande-Duchesse,* " Ah ! que j'aime les militaires."

Bianca Scacciati, F. Merli, and N. de Angelis.—These three excellent artists have raked up, for the benefit of Verdi-lovers, a highly effective trio from his early opera, *I Lombardi,* and if you are fond of the pre-*Trovatore* style it cannot fail to give you a good deal of pleasure. The only number that I know in the opera is the tenor air, *La mia letizia,* which I used to warble in my youthful days ; but this trio is no less characteristic of the growing maestro, and, though I cannot explain why the tenor sings mostly in the subdued tone of a hero at the point of death (perhaps he is), the three voices between them manage to make out of its ingredients a very dramatic dish *à la* Verdi.

Hélène Gals.—Rarely does one come across so accomplished a Handelian artist among German singers as this soprano. I consider her voice and style ideal for 18th century music, and can discover no flaw, unless it be a slightly excessive speed, in her rendering of the sublime air, *Piangerò,* from Handel's opera of *Julius Caesar.* A few of the harmonies differ from those to which English ears were accustomed in the past and the sudden irruption of a modern piano in the quick middle passage is rather disturbing. But this cannot spoil the beauty of the music or the expressive melancholy of the singing. Fr. Gals displays a like perfection of phrasing and intonation in the lovely air from Pergolesi's *Stabat Mater,* together with the same faultless attack and *sostenuto* and not a suspicion of a quiver in the tone. Wireless sopranos, please imitate !

HERMAN KLEIN.

THE FIRST DECCA-POLYDOR LIST

OPERATIC AND SONGS

HANSEL AND GRETEL (Humperdinck, arr. Weigert). Abridged Opera. Soloists, chorus and orchestra, **Members of the Berlin State Opera**, conductor **Hermann Weigert**. In German. CA8000-8003, four 12in., 20s.

An abridged version of *Hansel and Gretel*—especially so good a one as this—would be welcome enough for its own sake at any time, but just now it synchronizes aptly with the revival of *The Miracle*, for which Humperdinck wrote music that is not unworthy to be compared, in its "incidental" way, with the best pages in his first children's opera. In saying this, I do not leave out of consideration his second opera, *Königskinder*, an unfairly neglected work which many regard as containing finer music than either of the others. But for my own part I have never lost any of my love for *Hansel and Gretel*, and I fully realized that fact whilst playing over the four discs (eight sides) of this well-arranged Decca-Polydor version. Its melodic beauty is a joy for ever; its harmonic skill on a par with its orchestral loveliness. In less than an hour you get practically the entire opera. I do not seem to have missed any of its salient features; yet when it was over I found myself wishing for more. That feeling was, of course, largely due to a performance that rises very nearly, if not quite, to perfection. Delightful singing from the choicest voices of the Berlin State Opera, supported by their own admirable orchestra under Hermann Weigert, the constructor of the version. What more could there be to desire?

ELISABETH OHMS (soprano), **ADELE KERN** (soprano) and **ELFRIEDE MARHERR** (soprano).—Trio from **Der Rosenkavalier** (R. Strauss), **I made a vow to love him** and **'Tis a dream of Heaven**. In German. Orch. acc. under **Julius Prüwer**. CA8021, 12in., 5s.

Here again, as in the recording of the *Hansel and Gretel* abridgment, we find ourselves upon a high plane of excellence. If it does not altogether arrive at the same level of perfection, there are good reasons why. The music is infinitely more difficult; the voices are not quite evenly balanced at the most delicate moments; and last, but not least, one has listened to more ideal interpretations (gramophonic and otherwise) of this most exacting and elaborate of trios for female voices. Yet, all said and done, it is a satisfying and in most respects a first-rate performance. Elisabeth Ohms is the possessor of one of the most beautiful dramatic soprano voices now to be heard on the German operatic stage, and she is not wholly to blame if it comes into the foreground more conspicuously than those of her two companions. Moreover, she is the Marschallin; and that imperious if amorous lady has intentionally been made conspicuous by the composer in this scene as everywhere else. The climax, therefore, provides the most successful part of the trio, while in the last part we get some very pleasing legato singing from the Oktavian and the Sophie in conjunction with a faultless rendering of the fascinating Rose theme which Strauss has orchestrated in such a quaintly original manner. The recording alike of this and the vocal portions cannot be over-praised.

ELISABETH OHMS (soprano).—**Ocean, thou mighty monster!** from **Oberon** (Weber). In German. Orch. acc. under **Manfred Gurlitt**. CA8022, 12in., 5s.

After many years of neglect, the gorgeous air from Weber's *Oberon*—best known under its English title of *Ocean, thou mighty monster!*—has latterly found its way back into the active repertory of all the leading dramatic sopranos. I am glad of it, for it is a genuine test of their powers and bound to find any unsuspected weak places in their Valkyrian armour—particularly if there be no Siegfrieds and Nothungs about. But Elisabeth Ohms has nothing to fear from any of them. Her vocal armour is unpuncturable. Nature and art alike have exactly fitted her for such a rôle as Rezia, and one would

give something to hear her sing the whole of it on this side of the North Sea. Until our operatic situation clears, however, amateurs may well be content to listen to a record of this calibre; it will afford them intense satisfaction from every point of view. The broad, rich tone all through an extended range, the rare nobility of the declamation, phrasing that is impeccable both in purity and clearness of diction—these and other exceptional qualities combine to lend the *Ozean* of Elisabeth Ohms the supreme interpretative powers that Weber has demanded, and I do not hesitate to rank it among the finest renderings that I have heard since Tietjens sang it. Manfred Gurlitt's orchestra is splendid too.

ALFRED PICCAVER (tenor).—**Di te** (Tirindelli) and **Torna a Surriento** (de Curtis). In Italian. Orch. acc. under **Julius Prüwer**. DE7001, 10in., 4s.

If Piccaver records did not sell they would not be made, and if they did not sell well they would not appear in this list. I see nothing, however, in the above record to justify its inclusion here. The Anglo-Italian tenor is much too *insouciant* in style—lackadaisical is the nearest English equivalent I know for it—to be a good singer of Neapolitan ditties. He does not even suggest so much underlying energy as Richard Tauber; though both exemplify the same type and school of vocalist. Your born Italian is the right man for these things.

MARGIT ANGERER (soprano) and **ALFRED PICCAVER** (tenor).—**No eyes on earth** and **The bitterness of death** from **La Tosca** (Puccini). In Italian. Orch. acc. under **Manfred Gurlitt**. CA8026, 12in., 5s.

Here in the duets from *Tosca* we find Alfred Piccaver at his true *métier*—opera—and working with the sort of "half-character" soprano, in Margit Angerer, for whom such music as Puccini's was written. The result is eminently satisfying. Their voices blend harmoniously on the rare occasions that they have to sing simultaneously and their intonation is strictly on the note. He throws unusual animation into the music of Cavaradossi, particularly in the duet that comes just before the shooting; and the Tosca, despite her inclination for the tremolo, has a voice of so much natural charm, besides her tenderness of expression, that one listens to her with real pleasure. If the records have a fault it is that they are a trifle short.

ALFRED PICCAVER (tenor).—**Kashmiri Love Song** (Woodforde-Finden) and **For you alone** (Geehl). In English. Piano acc., **Julius Prüwer**. CA8030, 12in., 5s.

Alfred Piccaver's quaint foreign accent imparts a piquant flavour to his singing of English words, but, truth to tell, there is something more interesting than that about his rendering of the *Kashmiri Love Song*. The real point of it is that it suits him marvellously well. His languorous delivery is precisely adapted to the *Pale hands* of Amy Woodforde-Finden's murmurous melody, with its flavour of sensuous Eastern feeling. Indeed, I doubt whether the right tone and manner for this best-known of the *Indian Love-lyrics* has ever before been heard on the gramophone; and, after all, Piccaver's voice, when he uses it appropriately, has a richness of volume and a certain charm of its own that I should be the last to deny him. In Geehl's *For you alone* he invokes, of course, immediate comparison with another popular tenor; but I do not propose to choose between them. Forgive me if I quote the old saying for once—"You can pay your money," etc.

FRANZ VÖLKER (tenor).—**You are my heart's delight** and **Patiently smiling** from **Land of Smiles** (Lehar). In German, acc. **Vienna State Opera Orchestra** under **Melichar**. PO5015, 10in., 2s. 6d.

As in the case of Alfred Piccaver and the ballad *For you alone*, any encroachment upon the Tauber repertoire is subject to comparisons which may be favourable or the reverse, according to the individual taste of the listener. In this instance, I can only say that while Franz Völker is the better tenor and has the support of the Vienna S.O. orchestra conducted by Alois Melichar, he only just manages to hold his own with the redoubtable Richard on his own ground. Still, it is something to be able to do that. What he does not do, I am glad to note, is to give us a slavish imitation of the Tauberisms with which we are so well acquainted. Nor was there any need for him to do so. Franz Völker has a sturdy reputation of his own, and, when it comes to acting as well as singing Franz Lehar on the light opera stage, I am told that the Viennese like him very nearly if not quite as much as they do the elusive Herr Tauber. At any rate, I am going to recommend readers to purchase this selection from *The Land of Smiles*, provided they get a record on which the needle does not "scrape," as mine does somewhat.

FRANZ VÖLKER (tenor).—**An Operatic Medley** (Mark. graf). In German. Orch. acc. under **Melichar.** PO5001, 10in., 2s. 6d.

All who are fond of *potpourris* will doubtless like this new departure in vocal records. Speaking for myself, I cannot pretend to care for mixtures or hotchpotches of the kind, no matter how pleasantly sung ; but I do know that they are nearly as popular in foreign restaurants and on board Atlantic liners as are the surprise selections given by our co-Editor from one of the broadcasting stations. Consequently, this record of Franz Völker's has a certain *raison-d'etre* ; and, for the information of all who are interested (at the risk of spoiling the element of surprise), I may mention that the principal material is derived from Flotow's *Martha*, followed by *Una furtiva lagrima*, and the sempiternal *O Paradiso*. The last-named wins by a couple of lengths.

ELSA KOCHHANN (soprano) and **FRANZ VÖLKER** (tenor).—**Trinke liebchen, trinke schnell,** from **Die Fledermaus** (Johann Strauss) and, with **EMMA BASSTH** (contralto).—**Ha seht, es winkt** from **Der Zigeunerbaron** (Johann Strauss). In German. Orch. acc. under **Joseph Snaga.** PO5002, 10in., 2s. 6d.

I have now begun to despair of finding anything new to say about selections from *Die Fledermaus*. That is the worst of resuscitations resulting from "crazes" like the Johann Strauss. The Waltz-King has only recently been discovered by the present generation, and I can well understand the joy that it affords them to revel in his masterpieces. There was a time when I loved nothing more than dancing to them myself ; I can take a similar pleasure in listening to them now ; but, if you ask me to *write* anything fresh about them, I cry *peccavi!* and retire discomfited. So regarding this spirited duet and trio from *Fledermaus* and *Zigeunerbaron* I can only say that they are both sung and recorded with a degree of executive merit that cannot fail to win entire approbation. I like the trio best because it has an infinite amount of "go," and when the contralto (a fine voice, by the way) creeps in quite unexpectedly the relief furnishes a delightful contrast.

JULIUS PATZAK (tenor).—**Siciliana** from **Cavalleria Rusticana** (Mascagni) and **Lebwohl, mein Blütenreich** from **Madame Butterfly** (Puccini). In German. Orch. acc. under **Melichar.** PO5007, 10in., 2s. 6d.

For the faithful interpretation of Mascagni and Puccini a slightly more robust voice than Julius Patzak's might be desirable. Also I should advise him not to try and imitate Richard Tauber, unless in the solos of light opera or ballads of the Tauberesque species. Still, this tenor with the Czech name obtains sufficient sonority for doing justice to these short excerpts from *Cavalleria* and *Madame Butterfly* without having recourse to undue amplification, a fact that is distinctly to his credit. Naturally the *Siciliana* shows him off to better

advantage than the quieter melody of Pinkerton's farewell, which I do not much care for without the other voices to "carry on " ; or is it that I find no particular pleasure in the American's lonely exhibition of belated grief and remorse. But the theme is effective, certainly, and that is no doubt the reason why it appears on this record.

FRITZ WOLFF (tenor).—**By silent hearth** from **The Master-singers** (Wagner) and **Do'st thou breathe the sweet incense** from **Lohengrin** (Wagner). In German. Orch. acc. under **Manfred Gurlitt.** CA8023, 12in., 5s.

This is not the epoch of a dearth in good Wagnerian tenors. It existed once but it has passed, and they are now plentiful as the proverbial blackberries. Anyhow Fritz Wolff is one of them—nay more, somewhat better than the average, being free from most of the conventional habits that they imitate in each other. It follows, therefore, that little fault can be found with these excerpts. The *Probelied* from *Die Meister-singer* is notably well sung. The tone is sympathetic without lacking power ; the attack of high notes clean and effortless ; the flow of the *cantilena* unusually pure and smooth. Through all one feels the true dramatic sense, which here means the fervour of a knightly troubadour who has fallen in love. So again, in Lohengrin's poetic strain there is just enough of passion and not too much ; plenty of power without a scintilla of forcing. In both records the quality and right balance of Manfred Gurlitt's orchestra deserve attention and favourable comment.

HEINRICH SCHLUSNUS (baritone).—**Toreador's Song** from **Carmen** (Bizet) and **Undine's Return** from **Undine** (Lortzing). In German. **Berlin State Opera Chorus and Orchestra.** CA8038, 12in., 5s.
Caro mio ben (Giordani), organ acc., and **Largo** from **Xerxes** (Handel), orch. acc. In Italian. CA8024, 12in., 5s.

This eminent singer never forgets what is due to the patrons of his art who do not claim to be among the high-brows, and such is his versatility that he can meet the wishes of either class with equal proficiency. If the present record is to be a best-seller, or anything approaching one, it will be by means of the *Toreador's Song*, which may well be in universal demand ; for I have rarely if ever heard a better sung in other than the French or Italian tongue. On the other hand, the air from Lortzing's old-fashioned opera *Undine* is probably meant rather for home consumption, being little known beyond the Central European frontiers, though it may be welcomed elsewhere for the sake of the singer.

The two popular Italian airs are made the most of by Herr Schlusnus, alike as regards amplitude of tone and beauty of voice and style. In *Caro mio ben* the organ lends a grandiose effect to Giordani's simple melody, but I am not sure which feature would most astonish the old composer, the submerging prominence of the "king of instruments" or the modern flavour of the harmonization in the massive chords that it introduces. The tune is broadly given out by the singer, and so is that of the *Largo*, which on the whole escapes with less unwonted embellishment.

HEINRICH REHKEMPER (baritone).—**Kindertotenlieder** (Mahler). In German. Orch. conducted by **Jascha Horenstein.** CA8027-9, 12in., 5s. each.

These intensely sad but beautiful songs were written by Gustav Mahler in 1902 to words by Ruckert. There are five of them in all, recorded on three discs. The singer is the celebrated Munich baritone, Heinrich Rehkemper, and the name of the able conductor is Jascha Horenstein, to whom hearty compliments are due for his delicate rendering of Mahler's exquisite symphonic score. It would be impossible to flatter so distinguished, so highly poetic an artist as Herr Rehkemper, for he is simply beyond criticism. In these songs he gives us the veritable voice of mourning, of subdued lamentation that is the true expression of grief combined with dignity; a quality of tone rarely heard and extremely touching. It is singularly sombre and tragic in timbre, and, in contrast with the prevailing *mezza voce*, wonderfully restrained in an organ that is really powerful, we hear rare outbursts of sorrow that arise apparently from the very depths of misery. On the whole, I can conceive of no finer interpretation than this. It is strangely atmospheric throughout, replete with the poetry of a spiritual mind, and governed by masterly art. The recording happily does justice to these qualities and keeps them distinctly in view.

VIENNA MALE CHOIR, conducted by **ALOIS MELICHAR.**— **Wine, Women and Song** (Johann Strauss, arr. Dahms). LY6016, 12in., 4s.

The organization responsible for this excellent piece of work is presumably the Vienna Männergesangverein, whom I remember well from the occasion of their first visit to London many years ago. I thought then, and I still think, that it is far and away the finest male voice choir in the world. Other countries have followed suit, but without being able to surpass this splendid body of singers, every one of whom is in effect a picked soloist. The task set them in this record must have been regarded by them as mere " child's-play "; but, Strauss's waltzes being just now all the rage, it represented a good popular choice, and is doubly so because none but a choir of this order could have reproduced to such perfection in a vocal form all the characteristic attributes of a Strauss waltz originally written for orchestra. It is in this that it is remarkable—probably unique. What other choir could have sung the familiar tunes of *Wein, Weib, und Gesang* with such amazing elasticity of rhythm, such *élan*, or such unity of style and sense of contrast? I know of none.

HERMAN KLEIN.

OPERATIC AND FOREIGN SONGS

EIDE NORÉNA (soprano).—**Micaela's Air** from **Carmen** (Bizet). In French. Orch. acc. under **G. Cloez.** Parlo. RO20181, 4s.
HERBERT ERNST GROH (tenor).—**Farewell Mignon** from Act 2 of **Mignon** (Thomas) and **Harlequin's Serenade** from Act 2 of **Pagliacci** (Leoncavallo). In German. Orch. acc. under **Dr. Weissmann.** Parlo. E1166, 2s. 6d.
GERHARD HUSCH (baritone). **The Register Aria** from Act 1 of **Don Juan** (Mozart). In German. **Grand Symphony Orchestra** under **Dr. Weissmann.** Parlo. E1165, 2s. 6d.
EMMY BETTENDORF (soprano).—**Salut d'amour** (Elgar, Klingenfeld) with chorus and Orchestra and with **JARO DWORSKY** (tenor). **'Tis but a love song** from **Tales of Hoffmann** (Offenbach). Orch. acc. conducted by **O. Dobrindt.** Parlo. E11200, 12in., 4s.
CELESTINO SAROBE (baritone).—**La Mantilla** (Alvarez) and **La Paloma** (Yradier). In Spanish. Orch. acc. under **Manfred Gurlitt.** DE7000, 10in., 4s.
SYDNEY DE VRIES (baritone).—**It is thou** from **Un Ballo in Maschera** (Verdi). In English. And **Cortigiani, vil razza dannata** from **Rigoletto** (Verdi). In Italian. Orch. acc. by the **Schauspiel Orchester.** Piccadilly 907, 1s. 1d.
THE CARL ROSA OPERA COMPANY, Vocal Selection from **Tales of Hoffmann** (Offenbach), acc. by **Carl Rosa Orchestra** under **Richard Austin.** Imperial Z119, 12in., 2s.
RICHARD CROOKS (tenor).—**Walther's Prize Song** from Act 3 of **Die Meistersinger** (Wagner) and **Lohengrin's Narration** from Act 3 of **Lohengrin** (Wagner). In German. Orch. acc. H.M.V. DB1598, 12in., 6s.

Eidé Noréna.—As the majority of us are aware, *Micaela's Air,* one of the most original and clever of the numbers that Bizet introduced into the score of *Carmen* without immediate bearing on the plot or action of the opera, is frequently made dull and uninteresting by poor vocalization. In this record the very reverse is the case. The singer and the singing are alike on a level with the theme, and seem to convince us that there could be no other way of interpreting it. The voice has an individuality of timbre that has by now grown familiar, and one could go on for a very long while listening to a tone so pure and limpid, so easily produced. Another point: Eidé Noréna is an artist who takes pains with her diction, and you have no difficulty in catching every syllable of her perfect French pronunciation. To acquire all this she must have worked very, very hard, for such artistry is not cheaply won.

Herbert Ernst Groh.—The pieces are both well chosen to show off to advantage an agreeable light tenor. This is not one of the vocal instances where " vaulting ambition o'erleaps itself "; on the contrary, thanks to efficient breathing and careful management of the voice, you feel the artist to be eminently safe wherever he goes. I note also the resonant clang of the double basses in the *pizzicato* accompaniment to *Harlequin's Serenade,* which my new H.M.V. machine brings out with wonderful strength and clearness. Dr. Weissmann's is a good orchestra and the microphone enables him to use it with the utmost effect. Altogether a capital record.

Gerhard Hüsch.—I wonder to whom occurred the brilliant idea of calling Leporello's song *Madamina,* by the title of "The Register Aria." Was it meant to refer to a cash register, a stove, an organ stop, or a section of the human voice? A more complete misnomer I have rarely come across. If intended as a translation of the Italian original, *catalogo* or catalogue, nothing could have been more inept or commonplace. Still, happily it does not affect the merit of the record, which presents a curiously intimate rendering of a *buffo* song, minus any of the broad comedy that Chaliapine and the Italian basses generally invest it with. The only explanation is that Hüsch is a baritone—a first-rate one, too—and that the Leporello music is not altogether in his line. Yet he sings it in the original key; and to German ears the German text will not, of course, sound strange. The clearness of the enunciation and the reticence shown in the delivery are exemplary.

Emmy Bettendorf and *Jaro Dworsky.*—The popular Elgar trifle makes an effective ditty, though the words so kindly fitted to it by Herr Klingenfeld are too indistinct for the present reviewer to know whether they help to raise it to a higher plane of poetic excellence. Anyhow, it is sure to please, while the duet from the last act of *Hoffmann* is equally bound to evoke applause from the diners.

Celestino Sarobe.—As I have often remarked, it takes a Spaniard to give the right touch to Spanish music. (But then the same rule applies in greater or lesser degree to music of every nationality.) If the reasons are stronger in the case of the country on the other side of the Pyrenees it is only because the music there has characteristics more definitely marked than that of almost any other European land, not excluding even Scotland, Hungary and Russia. I know a good many singers who imagine they can sing a Spanish song like a native; but they are mistaken—they cannot. The voice, of course, has nothing to do with it; it is the manner, the style, the instinctive rise and fall of the inflections and the nuances that are everything. Here is a baritone with a rather heavy organ who warbles his well-worn *Paloma* with the lightness of a bird and handles his *Mantilla* with the grace of a woman. He satisfies your ear because the whole thing is ineffably Spanish. You cannot ask for better of its kind.

Sydney de Vries.—It will be noted that the *Eri tu* is sung in English and the *Cortigiani* in Italian; and of the two I prefer the latter because the pronunciation sounds easier and more distinct. Mr. de Vries labours under a throaty production and smothers his tone when using his native tongue. His style bespeaks the experienced artist and is essentially dramatic.

It seems a pity that he cannot overcome his other faults. At the same time we must not lose sight of the fact that this is not an expensive record. Indeed, at the reduced price of 1s. 1d. it is decidedly cheap.

Carl Rosa Opera Company.—Here is another low-priced record—one that is well worth a couple of shillings. It provides a really first-rate selection of *The Tales of Hoffmann*, by executants who are constantly performing the opera and therefore know every note of it by heart. It sounds just like that. Truncated though they be, the various excerpts are given with the same spirit and *entrain* as if they were being sung upon the stage. It is no part of my duty to guess at the cast, but I fancy I could name them as they emerge in succession from their obscurity, and I can assert without hesitation that they are all admirable. The *Doll Song*, the *Barcarolle*, and the trio of the last act are especially good. And then, you see, everyone is inspired by the presence of the regular Carl Rosa conductor (or at least one of them), Mr. Richard Austin. The recording is excellent.

Richard Crooks.—The portrait of this young American tenor has figured on the H.M.V. envelopes for a sufficient length of time to make me familiar with his features, but as it so happens this is the first of his records that has come my way. Better late than never. I find that nature has endowed him generously in a vocal sense, and time and further study should enable him to develop into an artist to be reckoned with. His voice has abundant power and vibrant quality and he uses it with no slight skill. The attack may be improved; it is not invariably clean; while the downward portamento occurs too frequently. Still more important is the need for less nasal resonance, an abuse of which not only deprives the head register of its bright ringing timbre, but tends to limit its strength and range. These and other indications point to the conclusion that Mr. Crooks has been taught in the modern Wagnerian school, and his good German accent confirms that belief. Nevertheless the method has its drawbacks—for example, the shortening of the compass, which we do not observe in the best Italian tenors; likewise the ease with which they produce their A naturals, B flats, and high Cs. On the other hand, the German or Austrian tenors, even when their tone is nasal, can generally make their words well heard. Welcome features in this singer are his steady tone, his intelligent phrasing, his pure intonation, and his remarkable stamina, thanks to which he is able to sustain the test of the *Preislied* to the very end without sign of effort or fatigue. His *sostenuto* betokens correct breathing and a strong throat—both necessary attributes for a robust tenor. He can also put charm and expression into his work, as I note more particularly in the opening phrases of Lohengrin's *Narration*, while his declamation towards the end has all the requisite dignity. On the whole, therefore, Mr. Crooks may be hailed as a singer of unusual promise, and, if he will get rid of at least some of his nasality, I feel inclined to predict for him a brilliant future.

HERMAN KLEIN.

[The Celestino Sarobe record has strayed from the Decca-Polydor reviews and the Richard Crooks record was issued in February.—LONDON ED.]

OPERATIC AND FOREIGN SONGS

BENIAMINO GIGLI (tenor).—**O dolce incanto** from Act 2 of **Manon** (Massenet) and **Mi par d'udir ancora** from Act 1 of **The Pearl Fishers** (Bizet). In Italian. Orch. acc. H.M.V. DA1216, 4s. 6d.

HELGE ROSWAENGE (tenor).—**The only woman** and **Thou art my dream** from **The Song of Love** (Johann Strauss, arr. Korngold Herzer). In German with **State Opera Orchestra, Berlin**, under **Alois Melichar**. Decca-Polydor PO5024, 10in., 2s. 6d.

HELGE ROSWAENGE (tenor) and **HEDWIG VON DEBITZKA** (soprano). **Oh, Joy beyond comparing** from **The Tales of Hoffman** (Offenbach). In German with the **Berlin State Opera Orchestra** under **Hermann Weigert**. And **FELICIE HUNI-MIHACSEK** (soprano) and **WILLI DOMGRAF-FASSBAENDER** (baritone).—**Barcarolle** from **Tales of Hoffmann** (Offenbach). In German. With **Orchestra and Chorus of the Berlin State Opera** under **Julius Prüwer**. Decca-Polydor CA8057, 12in., 5s.

FRANZ VOELKER (tenor).—**Santa Lucia** (Gordigiani, arr. Charmile), Neapolitan Folk Song, and **Schönau, that's my paradise** (Kutschera). In German. Orch. acc. Decca-Polydor PO5022, 10in., 2s. 6d.

JULIUS PATZAK (tenor).—**In my gondola** (Johann Strauss) from **A Night in Venice** with the **State Opera Orchestra, Berlin**, under **Hermann Weigert** and **Sweetest Lady** (Offenbach) from **The Goldsmith of Toledo**. With **Chorus and Orchestra of the State Opera, Berlin**, under **Julius Prüwer**. Decca-Polydor PO5021, 10in., 2s. 6d.

ALFRED PICCAVER (tenor).—**Lohengrin's Narration** and **Farewell** from Act 3 **Lohengrin** (Wagner). In German, orch. acc. under **Manfred Gurlitt**. Decca-Polydor CA8058, 12in., 5s.

Beniamino Gigli.—It will be noticed that these airs from French operas are sung in Italian. That is because the singer is wise enough to be aware that his voice sounds best when he is using his native tongue. The matter is a more important one than might appear at first sight, for few Italians sing French really well, and Enrico Caruso, for one, used to fancy that he was an exception to the rule. He was wrong. The foreign language invariably robbed his tone of much of its natural breadth, depth, and charm; and the effect used to remind me of the white kid gloves that he wore in the garden scene of *Faust*. Happily Gigli is not under a similar false impression, the consequence being that his beautiful voice imparts an unwonted fascination to the languorous *berceuse* lilt of the romance from Bizet's *Pêcheurs de Perles*. He sustains it almost all through in an easy *mezza voce*, taking the high B in the same manner instead of the customary French *falsetto*. Others will prefer this as I do. The air from *Manon* is similarly treated, and sounds the better for it. The dark timbre of the voice in both selections is quite lovely. One admires the reticence and the delicacy of pressure exercised over the powerful organ, as well as the art shown in the soft, tender legato which pervades the phrasing throughout. In many respects these two records display the ability of Gigli in a new light.

Helge Roswange.—I observe here a Scandinavian addition to the growing ranks of light tenors who impart a Tauberesque flavour to their Johann Strauss and Viennese opera generally. Really there is need for some supplement to the biographical dictionaries to be issued occasionally by the gramophone companies for the purpose of keeping ignorant English writers up to date in the *provenance* of all these new singers. I know it does not affect the merit of their records, but it cannot fail to be useful as a guide. The singer under notice is thought none the worse, I dare say, for the slight throatiness perceptible in his middle register, especially as it is compensated for by excellent high notes, good diction, and a steady, sympathetic tone everywhere. Both these excerpts from *The Song of Love* are nicely treated alike by the arranger and the singer, and of their kind are deserving of cordial recommendation. The same tenor is also associated, on another Decca-Polydor disc, with a soprano (*Hedwig von Debitzka*) in a portion of the duet from the last act of *The Tales of Hoffmann*. Here he is free from the hampering defect of imitating a particular style and sings much more naturally. His Antonia has a fresh, pleasing voice that is well produced and admirably trained. It is clear and pure, and, though her method is a trifle staccato, her intonation of head notes is unusually true and musical. One would like to hear more from this young couple.

Mihacsek and *Fassbänder.*—This arrangement of the *Barcarolle* from *The Tales of Hoffmann* for soprano and baritone, instead of two female voices, is on the reverse side of the disc just referred to ; and more's the pity. Unlike the other duet, the two timbres refuse to blend properly, while the male voice is much too loud and heavy for his partner's, which can only be distinguished clearly now and then. This experiment of allotting the music of Nicklausse to a male voice can only be regarded as a failure. (It was written by Offenbach for the famous Marguerite Ugalde, and I heard her in it when I saw the opera in Paris a couple of years after its production at the Opéra-Comique, with the equally famous Adèle Isaac in *all three* of the soprano rôles.) Let us hope the present experiment will not be attempted again.

Franz Völker.—Having written last month about this excellent tenor, whose natural voice and facile delivery it is a pleasure to listen to, I have only to observe now that he does entire justice to the popular melodies set forth in the present records. If you are not too tired of *Santa Lucia* (as I believe a good many Neapolitans of to-day are), you can play it once, say, to three or four repetitions of the more sentimental *Schönau*. By the way, *Santa Lucia* has its exact rhythmical (mazurka) counterpart in the *Traviata* duet, *Parigi o cara*, and also in *La donna è mobile*.

Julius Patzak.—I like Patzak much better in these light pieces than I did in his selections from *Cavaleria* and *Butterfly* reviewed last month. His voice is less hard and nasal, his tone less amplified. Evidently he has not earned a high reputation in his own country for nothing. He is a genuine tenor and his high notes are not forced ; also I am glad to observe that he can dispense with downward slurs and certain other Tauberisms that were noticeable in his previous efforts, though the latter, oddly enough, were from serious operas and these are not. Offenbach's *Goldsmith of Toledo* is quite unknown here, but judging by *Sweetest Lady* it must be in the line of *Hoffmann* rather than the earlier *opéras-bouffes*, of which *La Belle Hélène* is, of course, a typical specimen. The accompanying chorus can just be distinguished in the " background " of this record, but only very faintly ; it should have been sung more loudly or nearer to the microphone. Still, the general effect is very harmonious and pleasant.

Alfred Piccaver.—The latest message from our Anglo-Austro-American tenor must, on the whole, be entered to the credit side of his account. Nasal his voice has always been, and nasal, I suppose, he will keep it to the end. But apart from that peculiarity he is capable of variation to a degree that is as astonishing as it can be welcome. So here, in these examples from the last act of *Lohengrin*, he pulls out his finest declamatory " stop " and therewith rises to the full height of his argument. If only his diction were as clear and strong as his delivery of Lohengrin's beautiful strains of melody, the total result would be splendid. As it is, it is far in advance of the kind of thing that Piccaver gives us in his records as a rule. The style is robust, animated, dramatic—in a word, Wagnerian. Under Manfred Gurlitt the orchestra comes out well.

HEINRICH SCHLUSNUS (baritone).—**Serenade** (Ständchen) and **Welcome** (**Sei mir gegrüsst**) (Schubert). Decca Polydor CA8040, 12in., 5s. Also **Silent Love** and **Song to Spring** (Hugo Wolf). Decca Polydor DE7002, 10in., 4s. All in German with piano acc. by **Franz Rupp.**

JEANNE GATINEAU (soprano) and **GEORGES SERRANO** (tenor).—Duet from **The Servant turned Master** (Pergolese). In French, with orch. acc. Decca Polydor LY6014, 12in., 4s.

JOHN MOREL (baritone).—**Ay, Ay, Ay** (Perez-Freire, Gartman, arr. Leslie). In Spanish. And **Water Boy**, Negro convict song (arr. Robinson). In English. Piano acc. **Ella Morel.** Parlophone R1191, 10in., 2s. 6d.

YVONNE PRINTEMPS (soprano).—**Plaisir d'amour** (Martini) and **Au clair de la lune** (Lulli). In French. Harpsichord acc. H.M.V. DB1625, 12in., 6s.

CONCHITA SUPERVIA (mezzo-soprano).—**Musetta's Waltz Song** from Act 2 of **La Bohème** (Puccini) and **Gentle Flower in the dew** from **Faust** (Gounod). In French. Orch. acc. under **G. Cloez.** Parlophone RO20180, 10in., 4s.

RICHARD TAUBER (tenor).—**Come Gipsy** and **Greetings! Vienna!** from **Countess Maritza** (Kalman, Brammer, Grunwald). In German. Orch. acc. under **Dr. Weissmann.** Parlophone RO20183, 10in., 4s.

LOTTE LEHMANN (soprano).—**Cradle Song** (Weber, Hiemer) and **I do not grieve** (Schumann). In German. Instrumental acc. Parlophone RO20185, 10in., 4s.

W. AMERIGHI-RUTILI (soprano) with **LINA LANZA** (mezzo-soprano) in **Hear me, oh Norma** from Act 2, Scene 1 of **Norma** (Bellini), and with **G. COLOMBO** (tenor) **Ah, thou cruel one** from Act 2, Scene 2 of **Norma**. In Italian. Orch. acc. under **A. Albergoni.** Parlophone E11203, 12in., 4s. 6d.

KOLOMON VON PATAKY (tenor) and **HEINRICH SCHLUSNUS** (baritone).—**O Mimi, tu più non torni** from **La Bohème** (Puccini) and **Solenne in quest' ora** from **The Force of Destiny** (Verdi). In Italian. Orch acc. under **Joh. Heidenreich.** Decca-Polydor CA8061, 12in., 5s.

HEDWIG VON DEBITZKA (soprano).—**O del mio dolce ardor** (Gluck). In Italian. With piano acc. by **Julius Prüwer.** And **Hark, then, to the soft chorus of flutes** (Bach). In German with acc., two flutes and piano. Decca-Polydor CA8060, 12in., 5s.

Heinrich Schlusnus.—The qualities of a very fine lieder-singer are palpably evident in the rendering of these well-known songs by Schubert and Hugo Wolf. From every point of view they sound exactly right. Each in turn catches the spirit of the composition whilst reflecting in many minute details the poetic thought and individuality of the artist. I will not say I have not heard greater beauty of voice in the *Serenade* ; indeed, I have, a good many times ; but more depth and intensity of feeling I have seldom heard expressed in those inspired phrases. *Sei mir gegrüsst* rather suffers from the number of its verses (and they are all here), but Herr Schlusnus puts a surprising amount of variety into them. No less varied in another way are the changes of tone-colour that he infuses into the two Wolf songs, and especially, despite an almost continuous *mezza voce*, in the *Verschwiegene Liebe*, where the frequent touches of *rubato* are wonderfully well done both by singer and accompanist. The latter, Franz Rupp, has an altogether exceptional genius for this work— a talent that I do not hesitate to place on a level with that of Conrad van Bos. The piano, too, sounds like a good one.

Jeanne Gatineau and Georges Serrano.—We have here something of a novelty, combining speech with voice ; that is to say, the merits of a French " talkie " with good French singing. The baritone describes the plot of the scene from time to time, while the accompaniments are played by a piano and string trio. The actors in the piece consist of an old gentleman, his saucy servant, and a deaf mute (who does not appear in this version !). *La Serva padrona*, as it is entitled, is Pergolese's stage masterpiece. It was first played at Naples in 1733 and at Paris in 1746, the composer being only twenty-one when he wrote it. The music is of enchanting tunefulness and grace. The story concerns the successful devices whereby the naughty maid contrives to turn the tables on her master and become mistress of the house. Although in acting the duet takes an hour to perform, its interest never flags for an instant, and, as shortened for this disc, it is no less absorbing. Both singers are accomplished artists. Their clever characterization and faultless diction are allied to most admirable singing, and the whole effort affords an unqualified treat.

John Morel.—I must give this singer every credit for being no less at home in the all-too-familiar *Ay, ay, ay* than in the hardly less appealing negro ditty known as *Water Boy*. Except in the childlike tearfulness of their pathos they have little in common, but the same voice somehow provides a *trait d'union*, and the English of the negro convict sounds as good as the Spanish of the other gentleman. The singing, I almost forgot to say, is equally characteristic in both.

Yvonne Printemps.—It is well to realize that the gifted Mme. Sacha Guitry (for such is her name in private) has made decided improvement as a vocalist. I believe she used to be called a charming *diseuse*, but now she is also a charming singer ; and the qualities of each are delightfully combined in her recording of these beautiful old 18th century songs. The long *cantilena* of the *Plaisir d'amour* is perhaps a trifle too spun out, particularly in the final repetition, where just at the end a sob is introduced that is too "stagey" for the piece. Otherwise no flaw can be perceived in the rendering.

Conchita Supervia.—Having often pointed out that the real meaning of Musetta's *Waltz Song* (bad title !) is not made clear enough, I suppose I ought not to complain if it is underlined, as in this case, to the *n*th degree. But that does not matter so much as the over-marking of the musical rhythm by accenting every note in every bar. I do not think that so good an artist as Mme. Supervia would have done this had she thought the matter out more thoroughly ; neither would she have allowed her tone, which sounds so wonderfully in her native Spanish tunes, to have become so hard and devoid of contrast as it is in this piece. I am also of opinion that she has had the Siebel air transposed too high; it is here in D flat, and that is a semitone higher than Gounod wrote it. As a rule, the transposition is in the other direction, down to B flat. However, it flows easily and without effort. All that we miss is the rich opulence of the true Supervia tone.

Richard Tauber.—There can be, I imagine, no more industrious vocal gramophonist at work to-day than Herr Tauber, and the best of it is that in this particular sphere he is completely reliable. He can choose his own hour and mood for visiting the *atelier*, and that is always a comfort. The question is one which does not concern listeners ; and where there is no visible appearance there can be no "disappearing act." I do not mind admitting that it must be extremely enjoyable to see as well as hear this popular singer in *Countess Maritza*, provided he warbles his Hungarian *Come, gipsy* and his tuneful Viennese *Greetings* as captivatingly in the opera as he does in his latest records. The number and variety of the variations that can be based upon an agreeable theme, no matter how familiar, is simply amazing.

Lotte Lehmann.—Here is a record worth having for the sake of one side of it alone, counting the other as what the bakers call "make-weight." Dealing with the latter first, I protest against the choice by so accomplished a soprano as Lotte Lehmann of a song like *Ich grolle nicht*, written by Schumann for a man's voice, and that man a baritone. The most divine singing to be heard out of heaven could not make it suit her. On the other hand (meaning side), Weber's *Wiegenlied* may be placed among those exquisite things of beauty that are "a joy for ever." On no account ought it to be missed.

W. Amerighi-Rutili with *Lina Lanza* and with *G. Colombo.*—Two duets from *Norma* that should have a strong appeal for all who agree with Wagner that *Norma* was the masterpiece of an inspired writer of melody. Listening to them, it is good to realize that Italy can still produce fine natural voices and pure, steady singing. The lady who sings the music of Norma,

and who consequently takes part in both duets, possesses an organ of exceptionally vibrant, noble quality, the upper notes of which are wholly free from shrillness. She is always in tune, and delivers her phrases with mingled grace and authority. In each piece the voices blend quite pleasantly.

Koloman von Pataky and *Heinrich Schlusnus.*—Here, again, we have duettists who are well matched and capable of doing full justice to their familiar tasks. Beyond that there is really nothing to say. As a rule, it is a good plan to leave these things to the Italians : but, when their language is as distinctly and accurately pronounced and their beloved Verdi and Puccini are as faithfully interpreted as in the present instance, an exception to the rule may be even welcome.

Hedwig von Debitzka.—I have already mentioned above the attractive voice and method of this new singer, whose portrait —no less attractive, certainly—has a place in the Decca-Polydor Book, No. 2, so ably edited by my friend Robin Legge. Therein you can glean much information about the Bach cantata from which this lovely air with the flutes was derived, and to which I may add my meed of praise for its rendering by Miss von Debitzka. One wishes that there were more Bach sopranos of her stamp in this country. In the wonderful air of Gluck from *Elena e Paride (Helen and Paris)* her style is just a shade less irreproachable, but the flaws are far from being serious and, you know, the universal *portamento* is so fashionable !

HERMAN KLEIN.

OPERATIC AND FOREIGN SONGS

ELISABETH OHMS (soprano). **Thou monstrous Fiend** from **Fidelio** (Beethoven). In German. Orch. acc. under **Manfred Gurlitt**. Decca-Polydor CA8086, 12in., 5s.

ALFRED PICCAVER (tenor). **By silent hearth** and **The Prize Song** from **Die Meistersinger** (Wagner). Decca-Polydor CA8087, 12in., 5s.

LUDWIG HOFMANN (bass). **Calf of Gold** and **Mephistopheles' Serenade** from **Faust** (Gounod). In German. Orch. acc. under **Julius Prüwer**. Decca-Polydor DE7004, 10in., 4s.

ADELE KERN (soprano). **Love Songs Waltz** and **Tales from the Vienna Woods** (Johann Strauss). In German. Orch. acc. under **Hermann Weigert**. Decca-Polydor LY6021, 12in., 4s.

HEINRICH SCHLUSNUS (baritone). **The Drummer Boy** and **Rhine Legend** from **Des Knaben Wunderhorn** (Mahler)r In German. With **The Berlin State Opera Orchestra** unde **Hermann Weigert**. Decca-Polydor CA8082, 12in., 5s.

LILY PONS (soprano).—**Les Variations de Proch** and **Parysatis** (Saint-Saëns). In French. Orch. acc. under **G. Cloez**. Parlo. RO20187, 10in., 4s.

EMANUEL LIST (bass).—**O Isis and Osiris** from Act 2 of the **The Magic Flute** (Mozart) and **The Calf of Gold** from Act 2 of **Faust** (Gounod). In German. Orch. acc. under **Dr. Weissmann**. Parlo. R1215, 10in., 2s. 6d.

TINO PATTIERA (tenor).—**Di tu se fedele** from Act 1 of **Ballo in Maschera** (Verdi) and **Brindisi** from **Cavalleria Rusticana** (Mascagni). In Italian with **Chorus and Orchestra of the State Opera House, Berlin,** under **Dr. Weissmann**. Parlo. R1216, 10in., 2s. 6d.

JOSEPH SCHMIDT (tenor).—**La Donna è mobile** from **Rigoletto** (Verdi). In German. And **Lolita** (Buzzi-Peccia). In Italian. Orch. acc. Broadcast Twelve 3191, 1s. 6d.

Elisabeth Ohms.—I begin my reviews this month with another batch of Decca-Polydor records. I might even more appropriately express wonder as to how long the new issue is to continue, for the *embarras de choix* resulting therefrom for all but the wealthiest enthusiasts is increasing all the time with this steady output. Having given us an ideal *Ocean, thou mighty monster*, Elisabeth Ohms now adds to the list one that comes within a degree or two of the same perfection in another sort of monster, taking the fiendish adjectival shape that the translator of *Fidelio* has applied to Beethoven's *Abscheulicher*. Fiendishly difficult it assuredly is, that tremendous aria of which Tietjens and Ternina, alas! left behind only memories, not records. The present example is, I think, as fine as any that has been made since the electric days, and, in regard to purity and beauty of tone-quality, clarity of diction and orchestral values, and recording generally, perhaps the finest. The effect of the recitative is so delicately chiselled by voice and instruments that it is touching in the extreme. The only tiny blemish, scarcely audible perhaps to any but the most sensitive ear, may be discovered in the intonation of the final B natural.

Alfred Piccaver.—From *Lohengrin* to *Die Meistersinger* is for the *Heldentenor* a natural and easy step. Edward Lloyd of old took it in his stride, and with all my heart I wish that inventive science had been advanced enough to enable him (for the sake of posterity) to record the result as faithfully as the modern microphone has conveyed it here for Mr. Piccaver. Strict regard for truth compels me to admit that I am growing just a little tired of this singer's monotonous timbre and still more monotonous style of delivery. That is where he is different from the other English tenor whose Wagner singing Richter so greatly loved and admired. You cannot always paint in one shade of colour without running the risk to which I refer. A trifle more or less of energy and wakefulness will not achieve all the requisite variety. It is like the minister who preaches sermon after sermon on the same nasal note, as the Puritans used to; sooner or later his efforts produce the inevitable doze and the possible snore. Only heaven forbid that I should predict similar consequences in this case!

Ludwig Hofmann.—I had the good fortune to hear this (to me) new baritone-bass on the stage before listening to the Mephistophelean airs here offered; and I prefer his voice considerably in the *Faust*. As stated elsewhere in this number, I did not admire the production or quality of much of the tone that he used for the singing of Wotan in *Das Rheingold*. He sounds much more pleasant and genial, not nearly so jerky or snappy, when dealing with French currency—as a matter of fact, Gounod's own radiant *Calf of Gold*! Again, he is much more acceptable in the latter than in the Serenade from the same opera, which he has vulgarised by shouting sardonically the greater part of it and then winding up with a guffaw worthy of a transpontine costermonger.

Adele Kern.—The waltzes of Johann Strauss provide agreeable opportunity for the display of this soprano's very pretty and musical voice. She sings sweetly and with great technical precision, though I fancy I have heard records of hers that show more life and *élan*, as well as a more liberal measure of Viennese rhythm and character. She is said to "carry her audiences away." Perhaps that is because they inspire her more than the microphone does. But I would encourage her to try again. She certainly has a lovely E flat in *alt*.

Heinrich Schlusnus.—More songs by Gustav Mahler! Well, the more the merrier, so long as they have artists like Rehkemper and Schlusnus to interpret them poetically and light our way into their profoundest meaning. These examples are from the *Lieder des Knaben Wunderhorn*, which Mahler was setting to music so long ago as 1890, a couple of years before his first visit to London, when no one even guessed that he was a composer as well as a Wagnerian conductor. Now few people remember the splendid performances that he secured of *Tristan* and *The Ring* at Drury Lane, whilst French and Italian opera was being given at Covent Garden under the same indefatigable impresario, Sir Augustus Harris. I like immensely both these records—*The Drummer Boy* with its martial rhythm and drum-taps from beginning to end, rather anticipating Ravel's *Bolero*, and the no less striking *Rhine Legend*,

based upon a charming slow-waltz theme, replete with original ideas and masterful treatment. In fact, all of it is highly interesting music, intelligently sung and delicately played under Hermann Weigert.

Lily Pons.—What are known as "vocal fireworks" are rather gone out of fashion, but in all probability they will always remain acceptable so long as the display is brilliant and artistic, which the examples here presented certainly are. It was only a year or so ago that I first acclaimed this Belgian soprano as a first-rate singer and she continues to give me no reason for altering my opinion. On the contrary, her voice improves as it goes on maturing, while her technique is even surer and more finished than heretofore. She puts fresh animation into the *rococo* Proch variations, and does a wonderful piece of bird imitation in the clever fantaisie, *The Nightingale and the Rose*, from the elaborate music which Saint-Saëns wrote for the drama *Parysatis* on its production in the arena at Béziers in August 1902. The record is worth having for the sake of the latter example alone, embodying as it does the perfection of pure tone and delicately flexible vocalization.

Emanuel List.—Here is an interesting contrast: on one side the religious sacerdotal Sarastro; on the other the noisy tribute of Satan to the power wielded by the *Calf of Gold*. For vocal merit there is not much to choose between them; yet I cannot help feeling that the quality of the organ itself, so dignified, sonorous, and solemn, is more completely suited to Mozart's broad melody than to Gounod's outburst of devilish glee as he quaffs his wine from the necromancer's cask. But the point is that each is admirably recorded, and sounds equally well in its way.

Tino Pattiera.—Here is an Italian tenor of the old-fashioned *robusto* pattern from whom very few records seem to make their appearance on the English market. The reason is probably that he sings most of the time in his own country and in the class of opera that is popular there. His production is slightly throaty, but not sufficiently so to deprive the voice of its resonance, while its carrying power in a theatre must be considerable, especially the higher notes, which are of splendid timbre and well on the right pitch. His style betokens an artist of distinction, his diction is clear and intelligible, and he has a capital *mezza voce* for use in tender moments. The air from *Un Ballo in Maschera* goes with lots of spirit and the *Brindisi* from *Cavalleria Rusticana* receives abundant rhythmical energy.

Joseph Schmidt.—In spite of a faulty disc (apparently due to inefficient packing, not careless handling in this office), I obtained a very definite idea of the quality of this singer's voice and recording. Both are good enough to be considered cheap at eighteenpence, particularly by our friends of the Italian colony, whom I understand to be pretty accurate judges of the value of a gramophone record. They may, of course, object to *La donna è mobile* being sung in German, but they ought not to, since Mr. Schmidt sings it quite as well as he does *Lolita*, and that, in his "choice Italian," sounds very well indeed. He has a fine voice, and probably most European languages come alike to him.

HERMAN KLEIN.

New "Connoisseur" Issues

To continue this month, I signalize the issue of an H.M.V. Album containing Berlioz's popular *chef-d'œuvre*, *La Damnation de Faust*. Slightly abbreviated, the great work is finely done in ten 12in. discs (C2399–C2408), with a line-by-line English translation of the French text to which it is sung. Of the four soloists, two are artists of the Paris Opéra and two of the Opéra-Comique, which is equivalent to saying that their share of the rendering bears the closest criticism. The St. Gervais choir, and the orchestra of Concerts Pasdeloup, under Piero Coppola, complete an executive combination of the highest excellence. That the Album will be warmly appreciated wherever Berlioz's dramatic legend is known I feel convinced.

A highly artistic rendering by Thom Denijs of Schumann's *Dichterliebe* fairly earns its place in this collection. The 16 songs are done on three 12in. discs (D2062–4) with the aid of a capable but anonymous accompanist ; and the singer—a most agreeable tenor with baritonal middle notes—has obvious intelligence in addition to a refined style, poetic feeling, and an unusual command of contrast. Two well-known examples of modern Italian opera, in *Suicidio* and *La mamma morta* (C2347), are dramatically sung by Maria Luisa Fanelli, a soprano who possesses a sympathetic voice, and the right attributes for this kind of task. Quite in another vein are a couple of pieces from Weinberger's opera *Schwanda the Bagpiper*, sung by Karl Hammes (10in., B4124). The music is tuneful and pleasing, with only a few modern touches, and I can imagine it very much to the taste of Viennese audiences, especially as given in the dark, manly tones of this excellent baritone. The second air, *Ich bin der Schwanda*, has the support of a chorus and is probably *the* popular number of the opera. Karl Alwin conducts. I bracket together three discs (10in., B4118, 4119, 4121), the first and last sung by C. E. Kaidanoff (bass), the second by H. A. Sadoven (mezzo-soprano), which will make an especial appeal to amateurs of Russian music. Well sung and recorded, they are all worth hearing, particularly B4119, wherein the two voices unite pleasantly with the Balalaika orchestra in Dargomijsky's brief but irresistible *Vanka-Tanka*. "Sounds like Chaliapine," is the first thing you will say on hearing Alexander Kipnis in two Russian folk-songs (10in., E585); indeed, the similarity is almost startling both as to voice and manner. The *Soldier's Song* has plenty of martial swing, but for infectious spirit and *entrain* it is beaten by *Kalinka*, which pulsates with a more purely Russian character and rhythm. The same admirable bass also provides (10in., two sides, E599) a splendid rendering of Leporello's *Madamina* or *Catalogue Song* from *Don Giovanni* (I refuse to degrade it with the title of *Register Arie*) ; and I conclude for the present with a good word for the two Mexican songs, *Serenata* and *Estrellita*, by Ponce (10in., DA1005), both given with the true national flavour, plus a peculiar charm of her own, by Nina Kochitz.

Herman Klein.

P.S.—I thank the correspondents who have reminded me that Ludwig Hofmann made records of selections from *Parsifal* and *Jonny spielt auf*. I had overlooked the fact.

OPERATIC AND FOREIGN SONGS

RICHARD TAUBER (tenor). **The Stars were shining** and **Strange Harmony** from **Tosca** (Puccini). In German. Orch. acc. Parlo. RO20189, 10in., 4s.; and **The Song of Love** from **Tales from the Vienna Woods** (Joh. Strauss, Korngold, Herzer)—Orch. acc. under **Erich Wolfgang Korngold**—and **Frau Luna** (Lincke, Backers)—Orch. acc. under **Ernst Hauke**. In German. Parlo. RO20190, 10in., 4s.

TINO PATTIERA (tenor). **Di tu se fedele** from **Ballo in Maschera** (Verdi) and **Brindisi** from **Cavalleria Rusticana** (Mascagni). In Italian. **Chorus and Orchestra of the State Opera House, Berlin,** under **Dr. Weissmann**. Parlo. R1216, 10in., 2s. 6d.

FERNANDO GUSSO (baritone). **O sole mio** (Capua, Capuro) and **Visione Veneziana** (Brogi, Orvleto). In Italian. Pianoforte acc. Decca M411, 10in., 2s. 6d.

HEINRICH SCHLUSNUS (baritone). **Man nennt mich den schwarzen Studenten** from **The Force of Destiny** (Verdi) and **O dürfte ich es glauben** from **Il Trovatore** (Verdi). In German. With Chorus and Orchestra under **Julius Prüwer**. Decca-Polydor DE7005, 10in., 4s.

LEO SLEZAK (tenor). **Night and Dreams** and **To Music** (Schubert). In German. Pianoforte acc. Decca PO4037, 10in., 2s. 6d.

MARIA VON BASILIDES (mezzo-soprano). **The Crusade** and **Night and Dreams** (Schubert). In German. Organ acc. Parlo. R1234, 10in., 2s. 6d.

GRETL VERNON (soprano). **The Blue Danube** and **Tales from the Vienna Woods** (J. Strauss). In German. Orch. acc. H.M.V. C2430, 12in., 4s.

Richard Tauber.—These two Parlophone records afford conclusive evidence of a fact which I have noted before—that there are two distinct Richard Taubers : one the comic opera hero now familiar to our Palace Theatre public, the other a singer of serious opera whom we know in London only by his sparse gramophone efforts in that direction. The latter, regarded in a purely artistic sense, have the most to recommend them. The former are bound to be the more largely in request, because they typify that special kind of art which has won for Herr Tauber his enviable position in the musical world that takes its cue from Vienna, Johann Strauss, and Franz Lehar. In the interpretation of such things as these, no matter what we may feel or think about certain phases of his method and style, it is beyond cavil that Tauber now stands *facile princeps*. One might prefer to hear plenty of other tenors sing the two airs of Cavaradossi from *La Tosca*, because they can invest them with more of the characteristic Puccini tone and feeling than this singer does. On the other hand, one cannot say that he fails to do them justice or that his rendering is not artistic ; while, of course, the very fact that they emerge in the well-known voice of the popular waltz-tenor will alone suffice to make his admirers want to possess them. I do not suggest a choice between the two discs, because that is eminently a matter of taste. Enough that the *Song of Love* and the *Frau Luna* could not be better sung or more faithfully recorded.

Tino Pattiera.—I have dealt so recently with the singing of this excellent tenor that it would be superfluous to describe it over again. He must be a prominent favourite in Berlin at the present time, otherwise the alert Dr. Weissmann, with the chorus and orchestra of the State Opera House at his disposal, would hardly be eager to exploit him in excerpts so oft repeated as the air from *Un Ballo* and the *brindisi* from *Cavalleria*. Anyhow they suit him to a nicety, for he has just the dash and *verve* that they require, together with the essential robustness of manly tone. I cannot remember to have heard a more spirited delivery of the *brindisi*, while the vigour of the chorus just supplies the right finishing touch.

Fernando Gusso.—A pleasant quality of baritone voice and an agreeable style that seems thoroughly at home in the Italian *canto popolare.* Accepting *O sole mio* as an "inevitable," I find certain enjoyable features both in the music and rendering of the Venetian ditty. I like its quaint turns of melody and its unexpected colourful harmonies deftly applied with a modern touch. These help to make the simple music interesting and a clever singer does the rest.

Heinrich Schlusnus.—The passion of German opera-lovers for early Verdi being one of the "signs of the times," I cannot say I am surprised at the appearance of these two specimens under the auspices of a singer like Heinrich Schlusnus, though the juxtaposition certainly does suggest setting a Nasmyth hammer to crack a nut. Not that the nut tastes any the worse for it. Whatever this artist does, he does well, and there is a measure of satisfaction in knowing that he does not consider the music of Ferrando, the too-faithful henchman of the wicked Count di Luna, as a task beneath his dignity. Seeing how admirably he acquits himself of it, I quite agree with him. The selection from the *Force of Destiny* could have been more easily spared. It was always a pure "pot-boiler."

Leo Slezak.—By a coincidence, both this well-known tenor and the equally well-known mezzo-soprano whose name follows below have chosen the same Schubert air, *Nacht und Träume,* for recording in different *ateliers* at approximately the same date. The result is somewhat notable, and I advise all who are interested in such things to possess themselves of both records. They will find illustrated in unusually striking fashion two successful attempts to interpret the same song in an identical manner. Each artist employs a *mezza-voce* consistently throughout together with much the same variety of *nuances,* endeavouring to impart the same weird effect of haunting fear, the same nightmarish impression of nocturnal unrest. Slezak, of course, excels in this sort of thing, and now, at the age of fifty-seven, is still a very accomplished singer. His *An die Musik* is good, but hardly on the same high level as the other.

Maria von Basilides.—Notice of this lady's *Night and Dreams* is included in the preceding paragraph. There is only to add that she displays in the *Kreuzzug* or *Crusade* a no less delightful charm of voice and style, combined with equal purity of diction.

Gretl Vernon.—This is the name of a Viennese *soubrette* who will remind you in a somewhat remarkable degree—only in her own essentially Austrian way—of Miss Gracie Fields. Yet I do not think it an imitation, or anything near one. The resemblance is simply in the bright, penetrating voice, and the use of it; in the sudden staccatos and echoings of a freakish octave or so above, on notes that are never off the key. Also in the *joie de chanter* that makes you think of a human bird, with all the forceful rhythm—waltz-rhythm, of course—that denotes the gipsy-like "ping" of a Balalaika player or a Hungarian band. Taught or untaught, it is a wonderfully individual example of voice production, with a few harsh notes here and there, especially in the medium, that somehow don't grate upon the ear, but rather the reverse. The whole process is obviously under complete control. Above all, in the singing of these delicious Strauss melodies you feel you are listening to an artist who is thoroughly in her element and whose infectious gaiety it is impossible to resist. When she sings the *Blue Danube* or the *Tales from the Vienna Woods* she sings about them as things that she knows and loves, and would gladly caress if she could. The *entrain* and effect of the whole display are, as I say, irresistible. The ordinary rules of vocal criticism do not apply here; in that respect Gretl Vernon seems to me to be, I repeat, another Gracie Fields, only as purely Viennese as our Gracie is North of England, with less comical spirit, perhaps, but with a *chic* that is quite her own. These records were, I understand, made at the new H.M.V. studio at St. John's Wood, and the orchestral playing of the accompaniments has a touch of heaviness that inclines me to believe it. Anyhow, you will not regret the outlay for purchasing them.

HERMAN KLEIN.

OPERATIC AND FOREIGN SONGS

ADELE KERN (soprano). **Solveig's Song** from **Peer Gynt** (Grieg) and **The Flower Song** from **Faust** (Gounod). In German. With the **Berlin State Opera Orchestra** under **Alois Melichar.** Decca-Polydor PO5031, 10in., 2s. 6d.

JULIUS PATZAK (tenor). **Serenade** (**Ständchen**), Op. 17, No. 2, and **Cäcilie,** Op. 27, No. 2 (Richard Strauss). In German. With the **Berlin State Opera Orchestra** under **Julius Prüwer.** Decca-Polydor PO5035, 10in., 2s. 6d.

LUCIEN VAN OBBERGH (baritone). **Bel enfant amoureux et volage** from **The Marriage of Figaro** (Mozart) and **Ah, madame, les exploits** from **Don Juan** (Mozart). In French. Orch. acc. under **A. Wolff.** Decca-Polydor LY6029, 12in., 4s.

CONCHITA SUPERVIA (mezzo-soprano). **Printemps qui commence** from **Samson and Delilah** (Saint-Saëns) and **Connais-tu le pays?** from **Mignon** (Thomas). In French. Orch. acc. under **G. Clöez.** Parlo. R20192, 12in., 6s.

RICHARD TAUBER (tenor). **Ich liebe dich** (E. Grieg—F. von Holstein) and **Last Spring** (E. Grieg-M. Lobedanz). In German. Orch. acc. under **Dr. Weissmann.** Parlo. RO20191, 4s.

HERBERT ERNST GROH (tenor). **Come in the Gondola** from **A Night in Venice** (Joh. Strauss). And with **EMMY BETTENDORF** (soprano). **Who tied the knot?** from **The Gipsy Baron** (Joh. Strauss). In German. With Chorus and Orchestra under **Otto Dobrindt.** Parlo. R1257, 2s. 6d.

TITO SCHIPA (tenor). **Napulitanata** (Costa) and **Chi se ne scorda occhiù** (Barthelemy). In Neapolitan. Orch. acc. H.M.V. DA1054, 10in., 4s.

GRETL VERNON (soprano). **Heut' Nacht hab'ich geträumt von dir** (Kalman) and **Das Lercherl von Hernals** (Ascher). In German. Orch. acc. H.M.V. B4215, 10in., 2s. 6d.

Adele Kern.—In the June number I had to speak in favourable terms of this young soprano's recording of Johann Strauss. I must now find similar praise for her singing of Grieg and Gounod; and I do so without reserve because I can hardly hold her responsible for the funereal pace adopted in the case of one if not both songs. Let me assure Herr Alois Melichar that Grieg, when he accompanied his wife in the *Peer Gynt* air, took it about half as fast again. I will not deny that the short introductory passage sounds rather fine on the violins of the Berlin Opera orchestra, but when the voice begins it should be at an altogether quicker tempo, with yet another acceleration on the refrain. Otherwise we are listening to Melichar and not to Grieg. Just the same fault is to be found with the rendering of Siebel's flower song, which I had always imagined to be in regular waltz rhythm, not the slow, ponderous tune that it is made into here. In spite of these errors of judgment on the part of the conductor, both pieces are sung with a good deal of charm, for Frl. Kern has one of those sweet, flexible voices that sound well in almost any kind of music.

Julius Patzak.—The same orchestra, under Julius Prüwer, is heard to advantage in two well-known songs by Richard

Strauss, of which the *Cäcilie* more especially bears clear evidence of having been conceived in the orchestral vein. I am not equally sure about the *arpeggiando* figuration of the *Serenade* (*Ständchen*) when transferred to the gramophone, because the piano can always make it sound more crisp than the violin. But about the *Cäcilie* there can be no doubt whatever, and a heroic tenor of Patzak's calibre proves that he is capable of making a very dashing and brilliant affair of it. I regard this song as in a different class to the Lieder with piano accompaniment composed by Schubert, Schumann, and Brahms, and the transfer to the orchestra which is utterly wrong with most of them is thoroughly justified in the present case. I liked the record so much that I played it over three or four times for the sheer pleasure of listening to it. The tenor quality, moreover, is singularly pure.

Lucien van Obbergh.—It is extraordinary to what an extent nationality and language can colour the presentation of our oldest musical acquaintances, making them, in fact, so different to their ordinary aspect that we can hardly recognize them. The very titles put one off the scent, to begin with ; none but the well-informed would guess at a glance that *Bel enfant amoureux et volage* is supposed to be the French equivalent for *Now your days of philandering*, or that *Ah, madame, les exploits* is only another way of starting off *Madamina, il catalogo è questo*. In short, the two most familiar solos sung by Figaro and Leporello in course of their respective operas, and here interpreted in the traditional French style by a worthy baritone whose Dutch or Flemish name I have never previously written. Whether to recommend our old friends to you in their strange guise I am not altogether certain. At least you will find them lively and full of high spirits, if rather fussy and in a hurry to get it over ; while the words are so well enunciated that you will not need to miss a single syllable. The voice, too, is of that pleasant, sympathetic timbre—not quite so nasal as usual, perhaps—which seems to be an innate adjunct of the school. Anyhow, if you are fond of Mozart sung in any language why not try him in French?

Conchita Supervia.—With Saint-Saëns and Ambroise Thomas the case is not the same. They were Frenchmen and their music is essentially French in character ; consequently the latter should be sung for choice in the text to which it was composed. The vocalist may even be of Spanish birth, but, if she can pronounce with as good an accent as this lady does, no harm will ensue. For my own part, if I wanted to hear her at her very best and enjoy the fruits of her genius in their most delightful aspect, I should unhesitatingly go in for one of her Spanish records, which are alike incomparable and irresistible. On the other hand, if I merely wished to possess a good record of Conchita Supervia in airs from *Samson* and *Mignon* I should certainly consider that I had it here.

Richard Tauber.—The versatile hero of the *Land of Smiles* turns his attention, now to one popular composer, now to another, and contrives to mete out to them all some measure of justice. The latest is Grieg, and, candidly speaking, I would as lief hear him sing the songs of the romantic Norwegian as those of any other acknowledged master. *Ich liebe dich* just suits him perfectly, of course, and he also infuses no small amount of grace and sentiment (of the right sort) into *Letzter Frühling*. I need not say more, unless perhaps to award a word of praise to Dr. Weissmann for the delicacy of his orchestral accompanying.

Herbert Ernst Groh and *Emmy Bettendorf.*—The first of these names belongs to an agreeable tenor whom I fancy I have already at some time or other described as a frank imitator of Richard Tauber. I daresay many people will think him none the worse for that, since, whether natural or assumed, the resemblance is so ridiculously close that it may be compared to that of Shakespeare's two Dromios, and might, if it were a case of listening and not looking as well, lend to complications as amusing as those presented in the *Comedy of Errors.* For example, a lady accepting this polite invitation to " come in the gondola " would probably do well to make sure beforehand whether her host was to be Richard Tauber or Herbert Ernst Groh, especially if it happened to be a very dark *Night in Venice*. Either, no doubt, might prove an especially pleasant companion, and the two voices would assuredly utter the same flattering confidences in the same fascinating manner. Hence the need for making sure. The duet from *The Gipsy Baron* brings to the fortunate tenor a very gifted vocal coadjutor in Emmy Bettendorf, who is, to my thinking, a good deal above the level of her task. I find it simply irritating to hear such an artist wasting her talent upon a dozen bars, and no more, of a comic opera duet.

Tito Schipa.—These Italian trifles make up a charming record. There is really nothing to say about them, except that they are of the lightest, prettiest Neapolitan kind, and just the type that the popular tenor, imitating others before him, likes to lend the attraction of his sympathetic voice and versatile art. The consequence is that they can be listened to with pleasure.

Gretl Vernon.—The new Viennese star whom I wrote about last month does not scintillate with quite so much sparkling coruscation here as she did in the efforts that led me to mention her in the same breath with our unique Gracie Fields. Nevertheless, she again impresses with the cleverness of her legitimate vocal tricks and enables you to admire in her the welcome qualities of a natural singer ; one, moreover, who possesses the true Slavonic instinct for rhythm. Her bell-like head tone does not offer so much variety as her medium, which is ideal for a perfect diction ; but it is always clear, bright, and penetrating, like that of the lark (why " larks " on the label?) whose song she adroitly imitates not only in her singing, but with her whistling.

HERMAN KLEIN.

New "*Connoisseur*" Issues (*H.M.V.*)

In resuming my review of this list with Lauritz Melchior's contribution, it will be convenient to include therewith the Third Set of selected passages from *Siegfried*, in which he plays the most conspicuous part. This Album constitutes, in fact, one of the most remarkable collections of the series, and I heartily commend it to all who like to have their Wagner *de luxe*, faultlessly recording the finest available vocal and instrumental interpretation of the great music-drama. The six 12in. discs (DB1578–1583) take in the major portion of the first act and a goodly slice of the second ; and in these generous excerpts Lauritz Melchior has the support in turn of Heinrich Tessmer (Mime), Friedrich Schorr (Wotan), and Eduard Habich (Alberich), together with the London Symphony Orchestra under Robert Heger. The explanatory notes provide, as usual, a reliable guide to the dramatic action, while the dates of production are quite correct, though I would remind " H.W.L." that at the time when *Siegfried* was first given in London (1882) we spoke of the old opera house in the Haymarket as " Her " and not " His " Majesty's Theatre. Apart from the Album, Melchior has done with the same orchestra (DA1227, 12in.) *Am stillen Herd*, one of the *Probelieder* from *Die Meistersinger*, and the *Lenzlied* from *Die Walküre*. Both are good, but the latter is the finer of the two.

The large proportion of foreign vocal recordings included in the new Catalogue will not have escaped notice, nor am I going to find fault with that which undeniably adds alike to its interest and variety. Take, for instance, the specimens provided by the Metropolitan Russian Church Choir in Paris and the Orfeo Catala de Barcelona. It is not so much on account of their musical beauty (though that is by no means to be despised) as of their characteristic national qualities that they are welcome, since they enable you to study at your ease the curious features of Russian Church music (B4131, 10in., and C2395, 12in.) ; or, again, a typically Spanish choir of boys and men in two cantatas by Bach (D2066–8 and D2075–6, 12in.), of which No. 4 is complete and No. 140 excerpts only. Some of the effects in the former are quite beautiful, and in the latter the famous *Sleepers, wake* is particularly well sung. A French *basso cantante*, M. Louis Morturier, displays a fine voice with admirable results in airs from Haydn's *Seasons* and Berlioz's *Enfance du Christ* (D2058, 12in.) ; while a Russian tenor, N. I. Nagachevsky, shines less brightly in a couple of songs (B4120, 10in.) that could easily have been spared from a connoisseur's collection. *En revanche*, the luscious tones of Sigrid Onegin are worthily employed in *Du bist die Ruh'* and Liszt's *Die Lorelei* (DB1291, 12in.), the pure, unaffected phrasing of Schubert's gracious melody calling for especial praise.   HERMAN KLEIN.

OPERATIC AND FOREIGN SONGS

LOTTE LEHMANN (soprano). **Pamina's Aria** from Act 2 of **The Magic Flute** (Mozart) and with **Chorus** the **Entrance of Butterfly** from Act 1 of **Madame Butterfly** (Puccini). In German. Orch. acc. Parlo. RO20194, 10in., 4s.

GABRIELE RITTER-CIAMPI (soprano). **Il Re Pastore** (Mozart) and **Il Pensieroso** (Handel). In Italian. Orch. acc. Decca CA8092, 12in., 5s.

RICHARD TAUBER (tenor). **Morgen** and **Heimliche Aufforderung** (Richard Strauss). In German. Orch. acc. Parlo. RO 20195, 10in., 4s.

HEINRICH SCHLUSNUS (baritone). **Let wine flow** and **O, come unto thy window** from **Don Giovanni** (Mozart). In German. Orch. acc. Decca DE7008, 10in., 4s.

LEO SLEZAK (tenor). **The Linden Tree** from **The Winter Journey** and **By the Sea** (Schubert). In German. Piano acc. Decca LY6032, 12in., 4s.

HEDWIG JUNGKARTH (soprano) and **HELGE ROSWAENGE** (tenor). **Selection** from **Les Huguenots** (Meyerbeer). In German. With **The Berlin State Opera Orchestra**. Decca LY6027, 12in., 4s.

THE CARL ROSA OPERA COMPANY. Vocal Selection from **The Flying Dutchman** (Wagner). Imperial Z130, 12in., 2s.

Lotte Lehmann.—Butterfly, slowly approaching the home she is to share with Pinkerton, here gives, with excited interpolations by her relatives, the tragic motive of the duet which comes later when she is left in peace with her husband. The other song is Pamina's sad air from *The Magic Flute*, when Tamino, her lover, passes her by without recognition, but only because he is under an oath of silence. These two end happily, unlike poor Butterfly. Both songs are, of course, exquisitely and movingly sung.

Gabriele Ritter-Ciampi.—*The Magic Flute* is Mozart's last opera, composed only a few months before he died, but *Il Re Pastore*, a " dramatic cantata," is a very youthful work which was produced when he was only nineteen. *L'Amerò, sarò costante*, which Gabriele Ritter-Ciampi sings with such lovely phrasing, enchants with its simplicity. The Handel aria is a good medium for this singer's brilliant coloratura. Her trill is amazing.

Richard Tauber.—It is difficult to write with moderation of *Morgen* as sung by Richard Tauber. My record will soon be showing signs of wear, so often have I played it, and each time with an added delight. This is perfection of song, voice and interpretation, all gathered into one side of a ten-inch record. It is backed by the passionate *Heimliche Aufforderung*. I have not heard Tauber in *lieder* records since he did some of Schubert's *Winterreise*, when his name was still unknown in England. Those records also got some very hard wear.

Heinrich Schlusnus.—Quality comes before quantity on this ten-inch record which is all finished in less than five minutes. *Let wine flow* sparkles for a minute and a half, and the favourite serenade fills up the rest. But no one could regret the price they pay for these two gems. They are of the first water.

Leo Slezak.—Two beautiful interpretations of Schubert by a tenor whose older Polydor recordings were so highly praised and prized.

Hedwig Jungkarth and *Helge Roswaenge*, with the *Berlin State Opera Orchestra*.—The bright spots from Meyerbeer's *Huguenots* have been collected here, and the soloists sing the two best-known airs admirably ; the tenor song with its viola obbligato is specially attractive. A first-rate record of its kind.

The Carl Rosa Opera Company.—A wonderful two-shillings' worth, which includes the Sailors' Chorus, Senta's Ballad, the Steersman's Song, the Dutchman's Aria, " Engulfed in Ocean's Deepest Wave," and the Duet between Senta and the Dutchman. The anonymous soloists acquit themselves well.

F ♯.

New " Connoisseur " Issues (concluded)

In the final instalment of my reviews of the H.M.V. collection that excellent French baritone Charles Panzera displays rare art in two songs (D2059, 12in.)—veritable tone-poems—by Duparc, *La Vie antérieure* and *L'Invitation au voyage*, both gems of their kind. Lily Pons reconciles us by her delightful treatment to yet another *Caro nome* (DB1597, 12in.). Her model phrasing, faultless intonation, and pure style are well matched by a lovely vocal quality. *Tutte le feste*, also from *Rigoletto*, worthily fills the other side. Those who enjoy the art of Yvonne Printemps as I do will welcome her in two airs from the comic opera *S.A.D.M.P.* (DB1607, 12in.) by Louis Beydts that are worthy of André Messager at his best. The " return to the subject," different each time, is unusually original, and the piquant elegance with which it is realized by the singer enhances its charm ; here we have the acme of grace.

I recommend also two trios from Verdi's early operas, *I Lombardi* and *Attila* (DB1506, 12in.), magnificently sung in Italian by Elisabeth Rethberg, Beniamino Gigli, and Enzo Pinza. They exemplify the *Trovatore* manner as only great artists who know the meaning of restraint are capable of presenting it. Conversely, the same gifted soprano gives us Verdi at his ripest in an ideal rendering of the *Salce* and *Ave Maria* from *Otello* (DB1517). I regard it as by far the most perfect that has ever been recorded. A couple of pieces contributed by the Russian Male Quartet (B4116, 10in.) are by no means remarkable, but characteristic enough to please. Lotte Schoene warbles very sweetly the *Farewell of Mimi* (DA1238, 10in.), and on the other side gives a somewhat subdued rendering of a *Bolero* of Rossini's, arranged by Schmalstich, both done with the Berlin Orchestra. Elsie Suddaby in Schumann's *Widmung* and Brahms's *Wiegenlied* (B4009, 10in.) is surprisingly off the mark as to tempi ; they are too utterly slow and somnolent for (even English) words ! Walter Widdop achieves two first-rate records (D2053 and DB1566, 12in., respectively) of *O vision entrancing* and the *Prize Song*, and the two beautiful tenor airs from Handel's *Acis and Galatea*, each worthy of the Yorkshire tenor in his most robust and intelligent mood. A Russian baritone, G. M. Youreneff, with a capital voice, does ample justice to *The lonely steppe* and *The Bells of the Kremlin*. And therewith, I may add, *Finis coronat opus*.

HERMAN KLEIN.

OPERATIC AND FOREIGN SONGS

ELISABETH SCHUMANN (soprano).—**Was i' hab**, Bavarian Folk Song (Bohm) and **Der Vogel im Walde** (Taubert, adapted by Karl Alwin). In German. Orch. acc. H.M.V. DA1274, 10in., 4s.

RICHARD CROOKS (tenor).—**O Lola, rosengleich blühn deine Wangen** from *Cavalleria Rusticana* (Mascagni). Piano acc. And **Wie sich die Bilder gleichen** from Act I of **Tosca** (Puccini). In German. With **The Berlin State Opera Orchestra** under **Clemens Schmalstich**. H.M.V. E601.

HEDWIG VON DEBICKA (soprano).—**Alleluia** and **Et incarnatus est** (**Mass in C minor**) (Mozart). In Latin. Orch. acc. under **Julius Prüwer**. Decca CA8099, 12in., 4s.

HEINRICH SCHLUSNUS (baritone).—**The Youth by the Brook** (Schubert) and **The Wanderer to the Moon** (Schubert). In German. With piano acc. by **Franz Rupp**. Decca DE7011, 10in., 2s. 6d.

BENIAMINO GIGLI (tenor).—**Canta pe' me** (De Curtis). In Neapolitan. **Marta** (Gilbert, Simons). In Spanish. Orch. acc. H.M.V. DA1279, 10in., 4s.

LOTTE LEHMANN (soprano).—**Freudvoll und Leidvoll**, Op. 84, No. 1, and **Die Trommel gerühret !** Op. 84, No. 2 (Beethoven, Text, Goethe). In German. Orch. acc. under **Manfred Gurlitt**. Parlo. RO20196, 10in., 4s.

RICHARD TAUBER (tenor).—**Melody in F** (Rubinstein) and **Simple Aveu** (Thomé, Klingenfeld). In German. Orch. acc. Parlo. RO20197, 10in., 4s.

GITTA ALPAR (soprano).—**Bell Song** from *Lakmé* (Delibes). In German. With **Orchestra of the State Opera House, Berlin**, under **Dr. Weissmann**. Parlo. E11214, 12in., 4s.

THEODOR SCHEIDL (baritone).—**How could I ever forget my beloved ?** and **I am Schwanda** from **Schwanda the Bagpiper** (Weinberger). In German. With the **State Opera Chorus and Orchestra** under **Hermann Weigert**. Decca-Polydor CA8104, 12in., 4s.

HEINRICH REHKEMPER (baritone).—**The Fire-Rider** and **The Stork's message** (Wolf). In German. Piano acc. by **Michael Raucheisen**. Decca-Polydor LY6022, 12in., 3s. 6d.

M. ENDRÈZE (baritone).—**Toreador's Song** from **Carmen** (Bizet) with **Chorus and Orchestra** under **G. Cloëz**. And **Lorsqu'à de folles amours** from **La Traviata** (Verdi) with Orchestra under **H. Defosse**. In French. Parlo. E11215, 12in., 4s.

Elisabeth Schumann.—The Germans take a pride in their folk-songs, and distinguished artists do not regard the singing of them as an act of condescension so much as a joy conferred upon themselves as well as those who listen to them. I am not quite sure that it is the same with us. What I hear of English songs and their singers throughout their various *media* of to-day does not exactly convince me that this art of interpreting folk-songs comes as to the manner born or by cultivation to the majority of British vocalists. More's the pity. The Scots, for example, keep their traditions alive far more tenaciously than the average Southerner does, but why should this be so ? An all-round mistress of her art like Elisabeth Schumann can sing *Volkslieder* with equal charm, no matter what corner of Central Europe they come from. Here are a couple of them, one from the Bavarian Tyrol, the other a famous old ballad by Taubert that Mme. Liebhart, a clever and artistic imitator of birds, used to delight people with when I was in my teens. Her successor does them with the same easy grace and unaffected, spontaneous sentiment. What is more, she executes the whistling refrain in each, if not like an accomplished *siffleuse*, at least prettily and well in tune. The Taubert ballad is not, of course, so much of a folk-song as the Bavarian, which has the characteristic dance-rhythm of a slow waltz.

Richard Crooks.—This is a very pleasing record of modern Italian operatic excerpts sung in excellent German by a tenor who has quality, ease of production, steadiness, a good *sostenuto*, and apparently ample power. Moreover, his measure of nasal resonance, if marked, is by no means excessive, he pronounces well, and his phrasing is artistic as well as intelligent. The recording, with the Berlin State Opera Orchestra under Schmalstich, is of customary excellence.

Hedwig von Debicka.—One misses in this rendering of Mozart's *Alleluia* precisely the spirit of jubilation and praise that the old Hebrew word was meant to convey. The voice is bright, but the manner is not, and the runs, though clear, sound just a wee bit laboured ; apart from which there is lacking that remarkable sense of rhythmical *entrain* so inspiriting, for instance, in Elisabeth Schumann's singing of the same piece. Quite different is the effect of Frl. von Debicka's delivery of the *Et incarnatus est* from the C minor Mass. Here her smooth, unwavering tones, rich in quality and depth, are displayed with truly devotional style and feeling in music that exactly suits her. She has a singularly even scale, ascending to a facile head register, where good breath-control and purity of intonation enable her to do justice to the really exacting high passages of this piece. All of which is finely brought out by careful recording, in combination with a faultless orchestral accompaniment under Julius Prüwer.

Heinrich Schlusnus.—Everybody knows by now how great an interpreter of Schubert lieder Heinrich Schlusnus is, and I cannot conceive of a solitary hypercritical soul finding aught save praise and admiration for his rendering of the two seldom-heard but lovely specimens encased within this Decca-Polydor record. It is worth every penny of the half-crown asked for it, and its value is enhanced by the perfect playing of the original piano accompaniment by Franz Rupp—the kind of thing which makes one thankful for the absence of an orchestra or any other interference with the composer's intentions. Imagine, then, two exquisite Schubertian melodies, sung with the sympathetic voice and simple, refined treatment such as only an ideal German singer can bring to a theme of this sort. You have it here.

Beniamino Gigli.—A Neapolitan song of the ecstatic type and a Spanish one of the quaintly emotional should be very welcome to thousands of this tenor's admirers who once owed fealty to the unforgettable Caruso. He, too, was fond of escaping now and then from the operatic fold and indulging in these quasi-national canzonettas. Gigli has the same undoubted *flair* for them and sings them attractively; that is to say, with abundant spirit and his wonted opulence of tone. His Spanish is a trifle difficult to follow, though he uses a nice sombre tone for it; but his Neapolitan is as plain and impeccable as the intensity of his passionate pleading.

Lotte Lehmann.—These are two of Beethoven's lesser known songs, but they will soon become familiar enough if heard through the medium of Mme. Lehmann's fine voice and ardent delivery. *Freudvoll und Leidvoll* in this key may be just a shade high for her (Beethoven was ever exigent with his sopranos), but *Die Trommel gerühret* suits her to perfection, and she renders Goethe's words with wonderful depth and beauty of expression. A capable orchestra, under Manfred Gurlitt, brings the accompaniment out well.

Richard Tauber.—I may not personally care much for vocal adaptations of the catchy *morceaux* that the restaurant orchestras delight the souls of diners withal, but they are consistently encored, so presumably they must be doubly in request when sung by vocalists who command the public ear in everything they do. Such an one is Richard Tauber, who, it goes without saying, has the art of this kind of thing at his fingers' ends. He takes the melodies of Rubinstein and François Thomé and colours and flavours them to his liking, as a clever painter or a masterful chef might respectively transfer a pretty love scene to canvas or an old *entremet* to a modern menu. In either case the result is something you can enjoy. The Tauber tone and style would cast a spell of its own over anything in the least singable.

Gitta Alpar.—It is long since one heard from this highly accomplished soprano. Her art seems, however, to improve with time, and her records ought to sell more widely than they do. She resumes with a singularly polished performance of the *Bell Song* from *Lakmé*, every feature of which is dealt with carefully, artistically, and well. Even the prevailing sombre hue of the tone is rightly chosen to suggest the melancholy spirit of the Indian maiden whom her father compels to sing before the crowds in the cities, so as to attract the attention of her English lover and reveal his identity. The voice is intensely sympathetic and lends itself well to the Eastern melody, besides producing clear and sparkling head tone and a faultlessly pure staccato in the Bell theme. The Berlin orchestra is directed by the experienced Dr. Weissmann, and that is saying enough.

Theodor Scheidl.—I fancy I have paid tribute previously to these selections from *Schwanda the Bagpiper*, a modern opera on the old lines if ever there was one. The Berlin State orchestra in this instance is under the baton of Hermann Weigert, and the singer is evidently at home in tuneful melodies that he has frequently sung upon the stage. The quality of his voice is naturally dark and manly, yet he changes it readily to the bright, joyous character that is called for in the second piece, *I am Schwanda*. Here the rich body of tone contributed by chorus and orchestra is admirably brought out in a record of exceptional merit. I wish we could hear more of Weinberger's opera over here.

Heinrich Rehkemper.—Not having as yet heard any of the Hugo Wolf Society's records, I am unable to institute comparisons, nor am I altogether sure that I want to. But I cannot help expressing the hope that when they do come along they may be all on a par with this magnificent specimen. Rehkemper's *Fire-Rider* is a masterpiece, and well-nigh equally so is *The Stork's Message*; while in both the playing of the piano accompaniment by Michael Raucheisen seems to me the ideal realization of the composer's meaning. From every standpoint the interpretation is perfect; and, seeing the technical difficulties that are involved, that is a great thing to be able to say. The singer's artistry is supreme throughout.

M. Endrèze.—Items like the *Toreador's Song* and *Di Provenza* necessarily find a place in the repertory of every French baritone, and the gramophile who would like to possess them in a first-rate recording by a free, resonant organ will discover them here. No fault can be found, either, with the diction, the intonation, or the steadiness of the sustaining power. The toreador of M. Endrèze is bold and lively in description, as he doubtless would be in the bull-ring; while the smooth *cantilena* of Germont *père* fitly typifies that highly respectable French gentleman. No wonder he makes poor Alfredo resign himself to his unhappy fate.

HERMAN KLEIN.

OPERATIC AND FOREIGN SONGS

EMMY BETTENDORF (soprano) and **GERHARD HÜSCH** (baritone).—Duets, **Reich 'mir die Hand, mein Leben** from Act 1 of **Don Juan** (Mozart) and **Bei Mäunem welche Liebe fühlen** from Act 1 of **The Magic Flute** (Mozart). In German. Orch. acc. under **Dr. Weissmann.** Parlo. R1320, 2s. 6d.

ELISABETH OHMS (soprano).—**Command yourself, Mignon** and **Did I not know a girl?** from **Der Rosenkavalier** (Richard Strauss). In German. Orch. acc. under **Manfred Gurlitt.** Decca-Polydor CA8108, 12in., 4s.

LEILA BEN SEDIRA (soprano).—**Waltz Song** from **Romeo and Juliet** (Gounod, Barbier, Carre) and **Waltz Song** from **Mireille** (Gounod, Mistral, Carre). In French. Orch. acc. Parlo. R1323, 2s. 6d.

JOSEF SCHMIDT (tenor).—**Fickle Fortune** from **1001 Nights** (Joh. Strauss—Bürger—Leopold Hainisch) and **Yes, on my honour** from **The Gipsy Baron** (Joh. Strauss). In German. **Orchestra of the State Opera House** under **Dr. Weissmann.** Parlo. R1330, 2s. 6d.

RICHARD TAUBER (tenor).—**Speak to me of love** (Lenoir, Grau) and **A Waltz Dream** (Oscar Straus, Dörmann, Jacobson). In German. Orch. acc. under **Franz Schonbaumsfeld.** Parlo. RO20199, 4s.

FRANK TITTERTON (tenor).—**Flower Song** from **Carmen** (Bizet) and **Lend me your aid** from **La Reine de Saba** (Gounod). In English. Orch. acc. Broadcast Twelve 3240, 1s. 6d.

HEDDLE NASH (tenor).—**Plume in the summer wind** and **In my heart all are equally cherished** from **Rigoletto** (Verdi, English words Macfarren). In English. Orch. acc. Columbia DB932, 2s. 6d.

WALTER GLYNNE (tenor).—**Such was life in my youth** and with **GARDA HALL** (soprano) **Who tied the knot?** from **The Gypsy Baron** (Joh. Strauss). Orch. acc. H.M.V. B4271, 2s. 6d.

Emmy Bettendorf and *Gerhard Hüsch*.—When two singers of this calibre combine to offer their simple tribute at the altar of Mozart we may make pretty sure that the gift will be worthy of the master whom they wish to honour. In the whole range of his operatic treasures there are none that enjoy a greater popularity than these duets from *Don Giovanni* and *The Magic Flute*. Played, sung, whistled, and hummed as they have been for nearly a century and a half, there is no music better known on the face of the globe, nor any that is better loved. In this country we have been used to hearing them sung in Italian more than in German, but really that makes no difference to the sum total of the charm that they exercise when rendered, as they are here, with unaffected grace and feeling. If there be a solitary loophole for criticism it is to be found, I think, in a tendency to over-seriousness in the tone and manner of the Don Juan. It seems to me that the darker colour of voice might well have been reserved for the reflective passages of Papageno, when for once he comes out of his comic shell and shows us that he is a philosopher as well as a bird-catcher. In the scene with Zerlina he is making love to a coquette and ought not to be too solemn; but his singing is fascinating enough, anyhow, to overcome all her scruples, while in both duets the voices blend delightfully. How divinely Emmy Bettendorf executes her share need hardly be stated. Her vocal colour is just right in both cases and there is not a suspicion of seeking after effect anywhere. Her phrasing, like that of Gerhard Hüsch, betokens the true artist. Hence the unalloyed joy of listening to such familiar gems for the thousandth time when performed and recorded in this faultless manner.

Elisabeth Ohms.—Excerpts from *Der Rosenkavalier* are not easy to discover nor easy to arrange, but when they do emerge they are very welcome and make us more than ever grateful that an uncertain quantity like Richard Strauss should have given the world such an undeniable masterpiece. Here are two—*the two*—pessimistic but lovely commentaries uttered by the Marschallin upon the fading joys of life and beauty, the inevitable advancing age and slow decay, that await even the *grandes dames* of the eighteenth century Austrian *noblesse*. There is a vein of sadness running through this music that has its exact counterpart in the poignant tones of Elisabeth Ohms, and that constitutes her an ideal singer for the part. The breadth and dignity of her style, the pathos of her expression, the musical charm of her phrasing, all are equally brought out by this admirable record, wherein may also be noted many masterful touches of orchestral colouring due to the skilful hand of Manfred Gurlitt.

Leila ben Sedira.—I recollect having to say very nice things about a previous record of this young lady's—for young she must be with a voice of such juvenile freshness of *timbre*. This she continues to possess, together with a neat, well-trained technique and considerable animation of style. She might, perhaps, have been allowed to sing both her valses a trifle faster. Both Patti and Melba used to adopt the tempo taught them by Gounod himself in the *Roméo* air, and that was decidedly quicker. On the other hand, neither of them sang it in the original key (G), because they found it too high for them; they always did it in F. This singer manages the higher key very comfortably. Her neat, facile vocalization

enables her to do entire justice to the much more difficult valse from *Mireille*, and she sings it with exactly the extra ornamentation that Gounod wrote for Emma Nevada, which not every soprano can do either. Altogether, therefore, this may be considered an exceptional record of its kind and consequently an interesting one.

Josef Schmidt.—An excellent Viennese tenor, whose name must by now be getting fairly well known over here. He sings Johann Strauss as though he enjoyed doing it; and small blame to him, say I. The two airs from *Der Zigeunerbaron* form a capital contrast, though both, of course, are based chiefly on waltz rhythms. *Fickle Fortune* is characteristically melodious in the genuine Strauss vein; the other begins with a bold phrase in quasi-patter style, then merges into the inevitable 3-4 measure, and winds up—according to the present singer—with a splendid high C from the chest. He has a clear ringing voice, with only a shade too much nasality here and there, while his style is at once manly, elegant, and telling. His diction, too, is beyond praise, every word being distinct.

Richard Tauber.—The first of these songs seems to be in need of a sequel. What does the young lady say to Herr Tauber when he asks her to speak to him of love? (he calls it *Glück*; the French version, which is the original, I believe, calls it *Amour*). Well, what can she say? We can only guess, and at that point we must leave it—hoping for the best. Meanwhile the popular tenor can go on asking for so long as his enticing tones will permit him, and when they cease to do so the gramophone will doubtless continue to do it for him. The record is a good one; the tunes are tender, sweet, and engaging; and, if some may not care for the *falsetto* ending to Lenoir's ditty, they will find ample compensation for it in the robust, jolly finale that winds up the Oscar Straus.

Frank Titterton.—What can only be described as the atmosphere of the theatre, the magic touch of the actor who lives his part, is about needed to impart the requisite dramatic quality to these operatic pieces. They are smoothly sung, and all that, and the vocal technique in both is creditably sure; and yet there is a something lacking—the something that belongs to the stage and not to the oratorio platform. In days gone by the oratorio soloists were mostly opera singers. In very few instances was it the other way about. To a certain extent I think these airs should be *acted* in front of the microphone, not necessarily with gesture, but better perhaps with than without, as I have observed Italians do when speaking at the telephone. "More life!" That's it. More life; even when the record costs only the reasonable sum of eighteen-pence!

Heddle Nash.—A good deal of the missing quality just referred to is present in these hackneyed *Rigoletto* airs, which, having been practically done to death by the foreigners, are now being steadily revivified by the English tenors. The stage has certainly done much for Mr. Heddle Nash, and—but no, I am not called upon to make comparisons. I will merely remark that his style has undeniably gained in freedom and energy, his voice in resonant power, *minus* amplification. There remains now for him to cultivate charm, refinement, and delicacy of expression—the things that make the real artist—and a shade more distinction as well as distinctness in his enunciation.

Walter Glynne and *Garda Hall*.—Here is a third English tenor whereof better things may one day be expected—and predicted. Only this one will learn that he cannot prosper for ever on a *voix blanche*. It becomes too tedious after a while. At the first sound of the duet I fancied it was Miss Garda Hall who had begun. Then I recognized my error; and soon the lady convinced me of it with her own pure notes. Her companion's words are much distorted. And is the style really supposed to be the Viennese *cachet* of Johann Strauss—*extra sec*?

HERMAN KLEIN.

541

THE H.M.V. CONNOISSEUR CATALOGUE
THIRD ISSUE
New "Otello," "Carmen" and "Siegfried" Albums

THE compilation of the Connoisseurs' Catalogue is growing apace. Its commercial value may not be profitably demonstrated until we experience the complete re-establishment of world-prosperity, but in the meantime, the artistic merit of the scheme is being everywhere recognized. The gramophone societies, we may be sure, are keeping a sharp look-out for interesting additions to their winter programmes, and, unless I am much mistaken, they will greedily seize upon one of real importance that is being made available this month—I refer to the H.M.V. Album fresh from La Scala of Verdi's glorious opera **Otello.** It was anything but an easy work to record ; in fact, look where you will in the current modern repertory, you will not find one more difficult to reproduce faithfully and accurately on a series of gramophone discs. It simply abounds with traps and pitfalls. It requires a combined art of stage and studio such as has not hitherto been attained ; though it might, I think, have been exemplified so long ago as the July of 1889 at our own Lyceum Theatre, had the microphone and the rest of the recording accessories been available then as they are to-day. For that performance of *Otello* for the first time in England, under the great Faccio, of Milan, with Tamagno and Maurel in their original rôles of Otello and Iago, was also very nearly as perfect, as free from blemish, as the one that now reaches us from La Scala through a different and much less expensive medium.

Happily this is one of the cases where there is no need to waste one's energy over comparisons with the past, since here, let me assure you, the present has in nearly every way the best of it. Happily, again, there is evidence in these sixteen records (H.M.V. C2413–28) that somehow bygone models have not been forgotten, much less ignored. How it has been managed I cannot say, but the tenor, Fusati, has unquestionably contrived to achieve the finest imitation of the voice and manner of Tamagno that I have yet heard. Nature and art alike have assisted him in the process, for he must be a great deal too young to have ever listened to the famous tenore robusto *in propriâ persona*, and I doubt whether the latter's few pre-electric records would have enabled him to do the trick. Anyhow, he revives the great Otello with amazing fidelity, and that is good enough for me. It would have been hardly short of miraculous had Granforte got so near to the Maurel tone and the ineffable style of the original Iago. He possesses, however, an admirable method and an intensely dramatic manner of his own which fulfil every needful purpose. Had his voice been more unlike Fusati's in quality a better contrast might have been the result. As it is, the ·"onesto Iago" sounds most of the time quite as honest as his master. Yet in spite of that, their scenes together carry a genuine air of conviction and the full measure of tonal grandeur that Verdi intended. The dramatic atmosphere is conveyed with wonderful power, more especially in big outbursts like the *Esultatevi,* the *Brindisi,* the *Credo,* the *Addio, sante memorie,* and the great climax of the third act.

But not the voices alone, the superb choruses and ensembles, or even the excellent diction of every singer, are responsible for this unfailing visualization of the tremendous drama that is being enacted. We feel it above all in the ceaseless under-

current of symphonic orchestration which is one of the marvels of this opera. I may say without hesitation that this admirable recording of the score under Carlo Sabajno unfolds hundreds of delicate touches and unsuspected devices that you might perceive by a perusal but that you could never grasp with your ears in a theatre. Listening to record after record in mute astonishment at their revelation, I have almost forgotten to pay adequate attention to the most ideal rendering of Desdemona's music that has come into my experience. For in this part, at any rate, Maria Carbone proves herself a great artist and gifted with a lyric soprano voice of extraordinary emotional quality. Melba may have sung the *Wil'ow Song* and the *Ave Maria* more beautifully ; but in the love music of Act I, the gentle pleading sweetness of the duets with Otello, or in the big ensemble that comes later on, no one has produced such clear, strong, luscious tone or soared above vast masses of sound in such enchanting fashion as this. The men may be very fine ; but, speaking for myself, I would procure this *Otello* Album for the charm of the Desdemona and the unique loveliness of the instrumentation alone. The whole thing is a triumph.

Here is the full cast :—

Otello	...	...	...	... **Nicolo Fusati**
Iago	...	...	...	**Apollo Granforte**
Cassio	...	...	...	... **Pietro Girardi**
Roderigo	...	...	...	**Nello Palai**
Lodovico	...	...	...	**C. Zambelli**
Montano	...	...	...	... **Enrico Spada**
Desdemona	...	...	...	... **Maria Carbone**
Emilia	...	...	...	**Tamara Beltacchi**

From the same reliable source comes a splendid Italian addition to the growing list of **Carmen** Albums. You may observe in it the same distinguishing features as in the *Otello* of reverent regard for the composer's meaning ; the same unity of treatment and intelligent reading everywhere ; the same correct tempi ; the same rare excellence in the work of the leading personages ; the same crisp, precise singing of the choral parts and ensembles ; last, but not least, the same firm, masterful handling of the orchestra, whether in the passages of utmost delicacy or those of immense sonority and power. Nothing is exaggerated, nothing overdone. The music of the opera is allowed from first to last to tell its tale in the clear, direct manner that it should. From the purely mechanical point of view it is equally above criticism. This Milanese recording is invariably clean cut ; there are no ragged edges. The smart, unanimous attack, the bold, strong rhythm, the definite staccato finish on the ultimate note—these evidences of faultless drilling that are characteristics of every choral number are symbolical of the amazing precision that marks the execution of the entire work. Mind, I do not pretend to discover anything new. I merely remark that in my opinion we have had nothing quite like this in the recording of opera before.

Talent is not spared in the distribution of the various rôles. Many of the names may be unfamiliar to opera-goers who, like myself, do not frequent the Scala in these days. But the artists are obviously in the first rank of contemporary Italian singers ;

while, for one thing, the Micaela of the *Carmen* performance is no other than the superb Desdemona of the *Otello*, Maria Carbone. The Carmen herself, Gabriella Besanzoni, albeit more contralto than mezzo-soprano, with a heavier voice than we are accustomed to hearing in the part, is evidently another artist *hors ligne*. I feel that I should love to see these two women *act*, if only to prove that their acting is as good as it *sounds*—as good, that is, as their singing. In the latter respect Carbone may be the more accomplished of the two. For sheer vocal technique her duet with Don José and her song in the mountain scene are simply delightful, apart altogether from the beauty of the organ. On the other hand, Besanzoni shows from the *Habañera* onward that she has her weighty tones under complete control, minus any tremolo or any harshness in the upper register, and that she knows how to adapt her voice to the expression of every kind of emotion in the gamut of Carmen's nature. Her booming notes remind me of Giulia Ravogli in this part. The warmth of the Latin race pervades every utterance. Her *Seguidilla* is just the right mixture of provocation and sensuous suggestion ; one can only murmur " Poor José ! "

On the whole, the men of the cast, without being equally remarkable, are extremely efficient. Pauli is a capital light tenor, yet capable of infusing plenty of vigour into his dramatic moments, and his scene with Carmen at Lillas Pastia's tavern brings him up to the level of his companion, which is saying much. The Toreador (whose name rather indicates that Ernesto Besanzoni is the husband in real life of the lady who sings Carmen) has a resonant, sympathetic baritone voice that enables him to do justice to his song as well as to the exquisite bit of duet in the last act. The smugglers' quintet goes with great spirit and not too fast, the voices being bright and well balanced. But I must not be tempted to enter too minutely into details. The whole of the second and third acts call for unreserved praise alike on the part of principals and chorus, with a special word for the impeccable rendering of Micaela's song. In saying "impeccable" I include everything but the interpolated B flat at the end, which I hope and believe is now done nowhere save in Italy. Well, they are welcome to it. I am glad to say that in France and over here all good Micaelas have learnt to dispense with the incongruity. There is not much more to be said about this most creditable production. The conclusion of the third act, the dramatic duo that ends the tragedy—all the salient features, in fact, are vividly portrayed ; and if the ballet (an excrescence anyhow) be omitted, the various preludes and intermezzi are there and faultlessly played.

The full cast is as given below :—

Carmen	...	...	...	**Gabriella Besanzoni**
Don José	...	...	...	**Piero Pauli**
Micaela	...	...	...	**Maria Carbone**
Escamillo	...	...	...	**Ernesto Besanzoni**
Zuniga	...	...	...	**Enrico Spada**
Frasquita	...	...	...	**Nerina Ferrari**
Mercedes	...	...	...	**Tamara Beltacchi**
Il Dancairo	...	...	...	**Nello Palai**
Il Remendado	...	...	...	**E. Venturini**
Morales	...	...	...	**Attilio Bordonali**

The nineteen records in this Album are numbered C2310–C2328.

The third **Siegfried** Album (166) issued this month furnishes the completion of the super-selections from Wagner's music-drama recorded by His Master's Voice. It consists of four discs (DB1710–13), seven sides of which are devoted to the great duet for Siegfried and Brünnhilde that ends the opera ; while on the eighth is the *Prelude* to Act I, describing the labours of the enslaved Nibelungs under the tyranny of Alberich and his magic ring. The whole forms a worthy addition to a wonderful piece of recording, done, if I mistake not, at the studio at St. John's Wood last summer under the capable direction of Prof. Robert Heger. The supreme excellence of the material employed will be realised when I say that the orchestra is that of the Royal Opera, Covent Garden, together with the German **Lauritz Melchior** and the English **Florence Easton** for the two protagonists. I have watched Miss Easton's career from its very start in America ; and her astonishing rise from the humblest beginnings with the Henry Savage Opera Company to her present exalted position at the Metropolitan Opera House is something of which we in this country ought to feel proud. She is quite magnificent in this duet, thanks to a beautiful and powerful voice and truly noble declamation, such as make her a fitting partner for the Siegfried who is, beyond any doubt, the finest *Heldentenor* of to-day.

The very latest additions to the third supplement of the **Connoisseurs' Catalogue** are not all to hand as I write this review, but I begin with what items I have of the vocal group that fall to my share. Their average grade is exceedingly high. That gifted young singer **Maria Ivogün** re-enters the field with a triumphant display of fireworks in Zerbinetta's difficult Recit. and Aria from Strauss's *Ariadne auf Naxos* (DB4405), a veritable *tour de force* that none but the " elect " may dare attempt. Our whilom Don José, **Piero Pauli**, is well suited by *Fenton's air* from Act IV of *Falstaff* (DB1648), on the reverse side being the duet *A Parigi andrem* from Massenet's *Manon*, well sung with **Adelaide Saraceni**. As a contrast, the other Manon sobs out *In quelle trine morbide* from Puccini's version (B4236), and this, I am bound to say, shows **Maria Luisa Fanelli** to much greater advantage than the *D'amor sull' ali rosee* with which it is associated. Worthier than either of their place in the Catalogue are the songs contributed by the accomplished French baritone, **Charles Panzéra**. In his particular line he stands quite at the top of the tree, and his four songs by Duparc (*Phydilé*), Guy Ropartz (*La Mer*), De Sevérac (*Chanson pour le cheval*) and Gabriel Fauré (*Les Berceaux*) on two discs (D2082 and E602) suggest a couple of fascinating cabinet gems. **Tito Schipa** reappears in the double capacity of soloist and duettist, and his singing is as refined as ever, notably in his Neapolitan ditties, *'A canzone d'e stelle* and *Mandulinata a Napule* (DA1090). Then with **Amelita Galli-Curci**—displaying all her old art—he sings two duets from *La Traviata* (DA1133) and others equally popular from *Rigoletto* and *Don Pasquale* (DA1161), both of which are about as free from blemish as one could well imagine. Finally, he also joins another " old hand," **Emilio de Gogorza**, in a couple of Spanish duets, *Los Rumberos* and *A la luz de la luna* (DA976), that should prove irresistibly attractive.

HERMAN KLEIN.

OPERATIC AND FOREIGN SONGS

ADELE KERN (soprano).—**Deh ! vieni, non tardar** from **The Marriage of Figaro** and **Con vezzi e con lusinghe** from **Il Seraglio** (Mozart). In German. With **The Berlin-Charlottenburg Opera Orchestra** under **Julius Prüwer.** Decca-Polydor CA8117, 12in., 4s.

LUDWIG HOFMANN (bass).—**The Porter Song** from **Martha** (Flotow) and with **ALBERT PETERS** (tenor) **Truth alone in wine** from **Undine** (Lortzing). In German. Orch. acc. under **Julius Prüwer.** Decca-Polydor DE7012, 10in., 2s. 6d.

ALFRED PICCAVER (tenor).—**Nessun dorma** and **Non piangere** from **Turandot** (Puccini). In Italian. Orch. acc. Decca-Polydor CA8116, 12in., 4s.

HEINRICH SCHLUSNUS (baritone).—**Epiphany** (Hugo Wolf) and **Serenade** (Johann Strauss). In German. Piano acc. by Franz Rupp. Decca-Polydor CA8109, 12in., 4s.

HEDDLE NASH (tenor).—**The Dream Song** from **Manon** (Massenet, English words Agate). In English. And **La Danza** (Pepoli, Rossini). In Italian. Orch. acc. Columbia DB961, 10in., 2s. 6d.

JAN KIEPURA (tenor).—**La Danza** (Rossini). In Italian. And **Love, I bring you my heart** (Spoliansky-Eyton). In English. Orch. acc. under **Dr. Weissmann.** Parlo. RO20201, 10in., 4s.

LILY PONS (soprano).—**Gilda's Aria** from **Rigoletto** (Verdi) and **They call me Mimi** from **La Bohème** (Puccini). In French. Orch. acc. Parlo. R20204, 12in., 6s.

NINON VALLIN (soprano).—**Adieu, notre petite table** and **Gavotte** from **Manon** (Massenet). In French. Orch. acc. Parlo. RO20203, 10in., 4s.

GITTA ALPAR (soprano).—**The Swallows Waltz** (Joh. Strauss-Knepler, arr. Lehnert). Two parts. In German. Orch. acc. Parlo. RO20202, 10in., 4s.

LOTTE LEHMANN (soprano).—**A Ship across the billows** and **There is a single blossom** (**Hymn to Our Lady**). In German. Organ acc. Parlo. RO20205, 10in., 4s.

SYDNEY RAYNOR (tenor).—**Ah ! fuyez, douce image** from **Manon** and **Désolation de Werther** from **Werther** (Massenet). In French. Orch. acc. Decca K685, 12in., 3s.

MEMBERS OF THE BERLIN STATE OPERA under **HERMANN WEIGERT.**—**Die Fledermaus** (Johann Strauss). In German. With Orch. Decca-Polydor CA8118–22, 12in., 4s. each.

Adele Kern.—This is the worst example of suppression of the *appoggiatura* that has yet reached this country. One by one have Mozart's ornaments been eliminated until not a single example remains. I can positively declare that I failed to recognise the recitative when it began, and only a little of it when it had ended. By what authority the German conductors are stripping beauty of its decorations in this way I know not. It seems to me like sheer vandalism, and the more barbaric because the German endings to the words, where the higher penultimate note was intended, suffer from its omission quite as badly as would the Italian to which the music was written. It is a great pity that Herr Julius Prüwer and his colleagues, as they would call themselves, should continue to send out to the world from an authoritative source wholly untraditional readings of the *recitativo secco* and destroy the charm of the Mozart touch into the bargain. I would again remind them that Mozart is not Sebastian Bach; that there is no justification whatever for treating their vocal writing on identical lines. In the present instance the method is doubly regrettable because the remarkable singing of *Adele Kern* reveals a Susanna of the highest quality. Yet she pleases me infinitely more with her rendering of the air from *Die Entführung*, best known by its German title of *Durch Zärtlichkeit und durch Schmeicheln*, since its virgin loveliness is unspoiled and the quality of the voice as pure and sweet as the vocalization is without blemish.

Ludwig Hofmann.—In these two old-fashioned favourites we gain a true idea of the bright, natural voice which our recent Covent Garden Wotan can bring out in the lighter type of German opera. It is a faculty that he shares with others, of course, and in the past one of the gems of a *Martha* performance was the hearing of this same " Porter " song from the lips of Edouard de Reszke. The vivacity and swing of the bucolic tune sound all the better when floating on the surface of a big voice, and the highest compliment I can pay this *basso cantante* is to say that in his combined lightness and vigour he reminds me of his distinguished precursor. The duet from Lortzing's *Undine* is much less familiar here than in Germany, but it is tuneful enough to please the average listener and enlists the support of a capable tenor.

Alfred Piccaver.—Those who expect to find Mr. Piccaver thoroughly at home and at his ease in the subdued atmosphere of the two airs from *Turandot* will not be disappointed. Their suavity and reflective *insouciance* appeal exactly to his natural mode of expression and show off his voice more effectively than the bright, lively strophes allotted to Verdi's naughty Dukes and careless heroes, who are not really as indifferent as this tenor makes them sound. However, in the Puccini pieces he is quite at his best and I award him full marks for a capital interpretation of both.

Heinrich Schlusnus.—It seems to me rather a pity that a song so cleverly written alike for voice and piano as Hugo Wolf's *Epiphany* (or *The Three Kings*, as it is also called) should have for its theme such poor stuff. One can understand a Friar Tuck trolling forth his " Ho, jolly Jenkin, I spy a knave in drinkin'," because carousing was his proudest boast. But who that has stood before some old Italian picture of the three Holy Kings, kneeling at Nazareth with their offerings of myrrh, frankincense, and gold, can imagine one of those staid, richly attired dignitaries telling us how on his journey thither he has eaten and drunk his fill, but with reluctance paid his bill. To me it sounds ridiculously coarse and, if I may say so, mediæval Teutonic. I turned to the *Serenade* of Strauss for a contrast and found it. But that is not to say that it suits Heinrich Schlusnus in the smallest degree, or, shall I say rather, that he has the least idea how to express it. If I were the Serenaded One, reposing on my comfortable bed and listening to this doleful outpouring of sentiment, I should remark, " Thanks. It must be raining in the sunlight. I don't think I'll trouble to dress and ' come out ' this morning ! "

Heddle Nash.—Manon's *Dream* is related with nice feeling, and the melody flows smoothly as well as easily, in the manner that the composer meant it to. The only point open to criticism, either here or in Rossini's lively *saltarello*—far more difficult for an Englishman to sing well—is a lack of " bite " in the enunciation of the words. It may not be a case of *vox et præterea nihil*, but there can be no question which comes foremost in the singer's mind. And the quality of the tone in both records is certainly charming.

Jan Kiepura.—By a coincidence the Polish and the English tenors have recorded the same piece, Rossini's *La Danza*, which appears now to have become the property of both sexes and all voices. I am naturally tempted to compare them—but not at each other's expense ; for both are good in their different ways. Kiepura's has the right Italian *verve*, but indulges in more *rubato* than usual, though only a dancer might fairly object to that. His words are perfectly distinct, and his voice has a splendid ring that is not due altogether to the amplifier. There are other *nuances* that characterise the two renderings and those I must leave to the listener to discover. Perhaps a choice may be dictated by the alternative piece, which in the Parlophone record is the popular *Love, I bring you my heart*, from the film *Tell me to-night*, in which Jan Kiepura figures as hero.

Lily Pons.—All who take a pleasure, as I do, in listening to this talented young Belgian soprano will like to hear her in the well-worn airs from *Rigoletto* and *La Bohème*, if only to learn how prettily she can make them sound in French and in her girlish musical voice. Our readers will not, in all probability, be disappointed if such be their aim. Her tempo for both is somewhat more sober than we are accustomed to now, but is actually about the same as prime donne employed in the years gone by, when operatic life was less strenuous. Needless to add, the vocalization in *Caro nome* is neatness itself ; mere child's play, in fact, for a singer of this calibre.

Ninon Vallin.—In these exquisite miniatures—French music as well as French words—you may feel more thoroughly at home, for the songs and the singer seem to fit. The public of Paris and Brussels have been enjoying their *Manon* in one form or another ever since Massenet wrote it half a century ago, but apparently without tiring of it in the least. Neither would I, if I could always hear *Notre petite table* and the *Gavotte* sung by a Ninon Vallin. Note, if you please, the wonderful contrast of colour between the sad and the gay Manon—the touch of genius there. And the miracle of purity in the diction and accent—note that too ! After all, there must be a good deal of virtue in the " fitness of things."

Gitta Alpar.—How much of this tuneful show-piece is unadulterated Strauss (the Johann), how much Knepler, and how much Lehnert I do not pretend to say ; nor does it really matter. Enough that the fundamental waltz is by the great Johann himself, which tells you at once that it is just as delightful to sing as to dance to ; also that the "trimmings," by whomsoever invented and arranged, are both appropriate and effective in their good old Viennese style ; and that the whole thing emerges from Dr. Weissmann's baton and Gitta Alpar's throat as a combination that would have sent our good friend Baron Ochs waltzing round the room with unmitigated joy. The introduction, with its pastoral theme for the clarinet and its bird-imitation (as if heralding the announcer from Trieste), prepares you at once for Gitta Alpar's deep-throated " Frühling " and the series of amazing upward *arpeggi*, sung staccato, which help to decorate and embellish the more or less familiar Strauss. The two sides of the 10in. disc are well filled with this kind of thing, and if you are fond of it (and Gitta Alpar) you could not find either in greater perfection.

Lotte Lehmann.—Here is Mme. Lehmann's annual contribution to her store of German Christmas music (for German it certainly is, *durch und durch*, words, tunes, singing, and everything else). The hymns belong probably to the modern rather than the ancient category, and the second one contains the well-known down-scale that Sims Reeves used to sing with such a flourish in *The Bay of Biscay*—or was it *The Death of Nelson*? Anyhow, here it is in these *Hymns to Our Lady*, and given out with all possible earnestness and vigour by singer and organist alike.

Sydney Raynor.—The artist who has made this record of airs from *Manon* and *Werther* is described on the labels as " Premier ténor de l'Opéra-Comique," and, whether his nationality be French or not, he is evidently worthy of that distinction. His voice is a pure high tenor, under good breath control, managed with skill, and capable of expressing emotions that call for strong dramatic feeling. Hence his excellent recording of two of the best scenes in the music of Des Grieux and Werther. His style and, indeed, his tone remind me not a little of Ernest van Dyck, whose *Ah! fuyez, douce image* was unforgettable. The *Werther* episode (Act II) is also finely done.

Members of Berlin State Opera.—I reviewed this capital abridged *Fledermaus* (February 1930, p. 412) before it was brought into the Decca catalogue of Polydor recordings. It is very welcome. I might almost call it the " authorized version " of Johann Strauss's immortal comic opera ; for, although the singers remain anonymous, there can be no question as to their supreme ability. In dialogue as well as music they proclaim the alert, unflagging mastery of every scene that distinguishes the favourite whom Berlin delights to honour ; and under the able direction of Hermann Weigert their work has all the spirit and sustained energy of a stage performance. The voices are quite first-rate ; the singing just what you would expect from the pick of the German Komische-oper. The five discs are not dignified with the title of " Album," but nevertheless they form one that is in every sense worth having.

HERMAN KLEIN.

REVIEWS PUBLISHED IN 1933

OPERATIC AND FOREIGN SONGS

DUSOLINA GIANNINI (soprano) and **BENIAMINO GIGLI** (tenor).—**What then, Santuzza?** from **Cavalleria Rusticana** (Mascagni). In Italian. With **Members of La Scala Orchestra, Milan,** under **Carlo Sabajno.** H.M.V. DB1790, 12in., 6s.

LOTTE LEHMANN (soprano).—**Die Lotosblume** (Rob. Schumann, H. Heine), Op. 25, No. 6, and **An den Sonnenschein,** Op. 36, No. 4, and **Marienwürmchen,** Op. 79, No. 14 (Schumann). In German. Instrumental acc. Parlo. RO20207, 4s.

JOSEF SCHMIDT (tenor).—**Your tiny hand is frozen** from Act 1, Scene 3, and **Mimi is a heartless Maiden** from Act 3 of **La Bohème** (Puccini). In German. With **The Berlin Symphony Orchestra** under **Dr. Weissmann.** Parlo. R1392, 2s. 6d., and **Strange Harmony** and **When the Stars were brightly shining** from **La Tosca** (Puccini). In German. Orch. acc. Broadcast International B101, 1s. 6d.

ALFRED PICCAVER (tenor).—**The Dream** from **Manon** (Massenet) and **Love doth forbid you** from **Fedora** (Giordano). In German. Orch. acc. under (*a*) **Manfred Gurlitt** and (*b*) **Julius Prüwer.** Decca-Polydor DE7015, 2s. 6d.

GEORGES THILL (tenor).—**Agnus Dei** (Bizet). In Latin. And with **Choir, Noël** (Adolphe Adam, de Roquemaure).

In French. With Orchestra and Organ. Columbia DX421, 12in., 4s.

LEO SLEZAK (tenor).—**Litany** and **Dusk** (Schubert). In German. Pianoforte acc. Decca-Polydor PO5053, 2s. 6d.

RICHARD TAUBER (tenor).—**The Golden Song** from **Lilac Time** (Schubert-Berté) and **The Mystery** (K. Blume-H. Löns). In German. Orch. acc. under (*a*) **Franz Schönbaumsfeld** and (*b*) **Dr. Weissmann.** Parlo. Odeon RO20208, 10in., 4s.

HERBERT ERNST GROH (tenor).—**Open your window, Spring is here** (Hans May, after Johann Strauss), and **Love's Dream after the Ball** (Czibulka). In German. With **Chorus and Orchestra** under **O. Dobrindt.** Parlo. R1368, 2s. 6d.

FERNANDO GUSSO (baritone).—**Silenzio cantatore** (Lama) and **Ave Maria** (Tosti). In Italian. Orch. acc. Decca M428, 2s. 6d.

MARCEL WITTRISCH, KATE HEIDERSBACH, and **WILLI DOMRAF-FASSBAENDER.**—**Lohengrin's Arrival** from **Lohengrin** (Wagner). In German. With the **Berlin State Opera Chorus and Orchestra** under **C. Schmalstich.** H.M.V. DB4400, 12in., 6s.

Dusolina Giannini and *Beniamino Gigli.*—When two artists of the first rank join forces with the determination to " put their shoulders to the wheel " it would be strange indeed were the outcome anything less than superlative. Here is the scene for Santuzza and Turiddu from *Cavalleria Rusticana* sung about as perfectly as it can be by two singers of supreme merit who, so far as I am aware, have not yet been heard in it together save on the other side of the Atlantic, and there only on the stage. In the H.M.V. list this duet does not figure as a separate item, but as part of the album of Mascagni's opera, where it is rendered by Della Sanzio and Giovanni Breviario. Comparisons are unnecessary in order to establish the excellence of the present record, but, if I say that the latter forms a worthy pendant to Dusolina Giannini's record of the romanza, *Voi lo sapete* (H.M.V. DA892), my testimonial is warm enough. Her tone, always clear, rich, and satisfying, is used throughout with fine dramatic perception, and, from a quiet but impressive beginning, works up to a really splendid climax. In this fitting crescendo she is seconded by an animated and vigorous partner in Beniamino Gigli, whose superb voice is never heard to greater advantage than in emotional music of this kind. The elimination of Lola is scarcely noticeable, her absence being atoned for by the repetition of her graceful theme on the flute just as it is when she takes her departure in the opera. Otherwise nothing is omitted and nothing lacking that can contribute to the perfection of the excerpt.

Lotte Lehmann.—Three of Schumann's most poetic and exquisite Lieder are enclosed in this disc, one on one side and two on the other. When she sang them the accomplished artist was in her happiest vein, her voice at its best, her phrasing and diction elegance itself. If there be a fault to find it is not with the singer, but with the "instrumental accompaniment" and that arch-meddler the solo violin, who is permitted to besmirch the purity of the *Lotosblume* with his superfluous arabesques. I have asked before, and I ask again, why does the Parlophone "arranger" think it necessary to "paint the lily" with this sort of stuff? Surely Schumann's piano accompaniment is good enough to be allowed to tell its own tale (as it does happily in the *Marienwürmchen*) without outside assistance!

Josef Schmidt.—There are distinct signs of an advance in the art of this German *tenore robusto*. His style is getting more refined and is now free from affectation or mannerism. The high notes seem to be produced with greater ease. He appears this month under the auspices of Parlophone and Broadcast Twelve, the former on a 10in. disc at 2s. 6d., the latter on a 10in. at 1s. 6d., and with the aid of both you can procure your fill of Puccini in German, so well sung and pronounced that you will not miss the original "choice Italian." The fine *sostenuto* is the more welcome because it is not marred by excessive *portamento*. Altogether, I think this is how Puccini ought to be rendered.

Alfred Piccaver.—Truly a wise selection, this, of a piece that threatens shortly to become hackneyed. The *Dream* of the dreamy Des Grieux sung by a dreamy tenor like Mr. Piccaver may, for once, be considered an ideal adjustment of means to an end. One only wishes that Massenet were alive to hear it. He would, I am certain, declare it to be precisely the mood and the manner in which he intended Manon's too trustful lover to relate that fanciful vision which soothed his agitated brain during his pre-prandial stroll. Its sentiment is quite akin to that of *Notre petite table* and fully as French, despite Mr. Piccaver's excellent German accent, which is as smooth as his tone—and Manon's spotless tablecloth. After it the air from *Fedora* sounds a trifle aggressive; but I like it very much because it is short, and the singer has not the time to rouse himself too completely from his visionary frame of mind. The vocal quality, seriously speaking, is quite beautiful.

Georges Thill.—The *Agnus Dei* of Bizet was, if I am not mistaken, written for a mezzo-soprano, and this admirable Parisian tenor has been heard in music that suits him better. He can, of course, do justice to the passages that lie high enough for him, but the lowest notes are not within comfortable reach. However, he compensates fully for that defect in his other piece, the familiar friend of one's boyhood days, the stirring *Noël* of Adolphe Adam, the gifted Frenchman who wrote *Le Châlet* and *Le Postillon de Longjumeau*, operas ever so popular at one time. *Noël* was here just in time for Christmas, and therefore seasonable; but as sung by M. Thill—despite memories of Plançon—it must always be welcome.

Leo Slezak.—These two Schubert songs present a strong contrast, made doubly vivid by the remarkable difference between the timbres in which the singer interprets them. Were he any other but the Leo Slezak of to-day—that is to say, the intellectual Lieder-singer and no longer (as I imagine) the active, robust operatic tenor of bygone years—one would feel inclined to criticize his tone in the *Litanei* as too muffled and husky. It may be mystical, I allow, but it is also too misty and confidential. On the other hand, *Im Abendrot* (*Dusk*) affords a peep at the old voice in all its beauty and strength, and the expressive power displayed in it is simply wonderful. I award all credit for the use of the composer's piano accompaniment, but would have preferred to hear it played on a better instrument.

Richard Tauber.—A capital record of one of the most popular numbers in *Lilac Time*, and another on the same disc of an ordinary but tuneful ditty that is doubtless a "best-seller" in the singer's native land. There is no need to describe how Herr Tauber warbles these things. His voice can sometimes lend an added charm even to Schubert, and that is saying much.

Herbert Ernst Groh.—This is the fifth tenor record in succession in the present series. *Quel embarras de richesses!* The last represents the Viennese order—Johann Strauss and Czibulka, both masters of the waltz rhythm that is once more enchanting the whole world. The singer in this instance has a bright, manly tone and a neat, clean attack, allied to a vivacious style. Both pieces are delightful waltzes either to listen or dance to, and they are unusually well scored. The chorus makes its entry each time in the usual effective way.

Fernando Gusso.—Until I saw this record I had no notion that Tosti had ever written an *Ave Maria*, and after I heard it I was quite sure he had not. As a matter of fact, it is only a commentary on one, and an exceedingly dull specimen at that, e.g., for such a lively writer as Tosti. It begins like *The Lost Chord*, but does not succeed in discovering the missing *Ave Maria*. Fernando Gusso is a painstaking singer, with an unusually dark, sombre voice that does not tend to brighten the music he is offering here. In fine, therefore, not a very inspiring record.

Marcel Wittrisch and others.—From Berlin via Hayes comes this exceptionally superior performance of the scene in the first act of *Lohengrin*, where the Knight of the Grail steps ashore on the banks of the Scheldt (probably at the "Old Swan Pier"), and after a tender adieu to his *compagnon de voyage*, takes the general situation in charge. You may note the effective contrast between the gentle tones used for the one and the ringing voice employed for the Brabantian folk, or, again, the solemn warning notes and the *Ich liebe dich* addressed to Elsa. Evidently trouble has been taken to lend the essential dramatic quality to this episode, which I always regard as the most moving and most replete with musical splendour in the whole of Wagner's opera. The three leading personages required for this excerpt are in skilful hands, while the band and chorus of the Berlin State Opera, under Schmalstich, have done their work excellently.

HERMAN KLEIN.

OPERATIC AND FOREIGN SONGS

RIA GINSTER (soprano).—**Voi che sapete** from **Le Nozze di Figaro** (Mozart). In Italian. Och. acc. under **Dr. Malcolm Sargent.** And **Martern aller Arten** from **Die Entführung aus dem Serail** (Mozart). In German. Piano acc. by **Gerald Moore.** H.M.V. DB1832, 12in., 6s.

ADELE KERN (soprano).—**Vedrai carino** and **Batti, batti, O bel Masetto** from **Don Giovanni** (Mozart). In German. With **Berlin State Opera Orchestra** under **Alois Melichar.** Decca-Polydor PO5059, 10in., 2s. 6d.

LEO SLEZAK (tenor).—**Tom the Rhymer** (Loewe). In German. Pianoforte acc. Decca-Polydor LY6060, 12in., 3s. 6d.

HEINRICH SCHLUSNUS (baritone).—**Caro mio ben** (Giordani). In Italian. Organ acc. by **Franz Rupp**. And **Largo** from **Xerxes** (Handel). In Italian. Orch. acc. under **Julius Prüwer**. Violin solo by **Paul Godwin**. Decca-Polydor CA8024, 12in., 4s. And **On the Water** (Schubert). With pianoforte acc. **By the Weser** (Pressel). In German. With **Berlin State Opera Orchestra** under **Herman Weigert**. Decca-Polydor DE7020, 10in., 2s. 6d.

GITTA ALPAR (soprano) and **HERBERT ERNST GROH** (tenor).—**Perchance she comes** from Act 1 of **Die Bajadere** (Kalman) and **Dearest friend, seek not to touch the stars** from Act 2 of **The Count of Luxembourg**. In German. Orch. acc. under **O. Dobrindt**. Parlophone RO20210, 10in., 4s.

MAGGIE TEYTE (soprano).—**Petite Dinde, ah ! quel outrage** and **Ma Foi ! pour venir de provence** from **Véronique** (Messager) and **Tu n'est pas beau, tu n'est pas riche** from **La Périchole** (Offenbach). In French. Orch. acc. Decca T201, 12in., 4s.

ARMAND CRABBÉ (baritone).—**La Jota** (de Falla) and **Rubia** (Crabbé). Orch. acc. Decca T202, 12in., 3s. 6d.

RICHARD TAUBER (tenor).—**I want to be loved once again** (Stolz-Gilbert-Robinson). In German. Orch. acc. under **Dr. Weissmann**. And **The Cherries in my neighbour's garden** (Hollaender-Freund). In German. Orch. acc. under **Franz Schönbaumefeld**. Parlophone RO20209, 10in., 4s.

SYDNEY RAYNER (tenor).—**Obstination** (Fontenailles). In French. And **A Vucchella** (Tosti) in Neapolitan. Pianoforte acc. Decca F3327, 2s.

FERNANDO GUSSO (baritone).—**Addio a Napoli** (Cottrau) and **Ncopp' 'a ll'onna** (Fassone). In Italian. Orch. acc. Decca M429, 2s. 6d.

JOHN TURNER (tenor).—**Woman's a fickle jade** and **When a charmer would win me** from **Rigoletto** (Verdi). In English. Orch. acc. H.M.V. B4251, 10in., 2s. 6d.

MAFALDA SALVATINI (soprano).—**An die Laute** and **Rastlose Liebe** (Schubert) and **Von ewiger Liebe** (Brahms), Op. 43, No. 1. In German. Piano acc. by **Michael Raucheisen**. Parlophone E11230, 12in., 4s.

Ria Ginster.—Here is a new soprano with a voice notable for its clarity and sympathetic charm, ease of production, and exceptional flexibility and sureness of execution. Her style in singing Mozart is nearly, but not quite, free from blemish ; however, with greater microphone experience, the tendency to harden the tone on crescendos and make it quiver should speedily disappear. The Italian pronunciation in *Voi che sapete* can also be improved and more contrast obtained. Far superior in every way is the rendering of the great air from *Die Entführung*. It has authority and distinction, while the runs are brilliantly sung. It ought, however, to be done again with an orchestra, though Mr. Gerald Moore's piano accompaniment is quite first-rate.

Adele Kern.—The two Zerlina airs are not often sung in the true Mozart tradition, as they are here ; and they are doubly welcome because of their rarity, though, as I have often said, I like them best in the original Italian text. The first section of the *Batti, batti*, is taken a shade too fast to begin with, but the tempo settles down afterwards. The voice is pleasing in quality, the intonation flawless, the phrasing neat and clean throughout ; and the Berlin S.O. Orchestra admirable as usual under Alois Melichar.

Leo Slezak.—I do not remember hearing Slezak before in a Loewe ballad, but so good is his rendering of *Tom the Rhymer* that I now hope to enjoy him in others. As usual nowadays, he depends largely for his effects upon contrasts of full tone and *mezza voce*, with the latter for choice. The sudden changes are almost startling, and so complete that one might be listening to a duet for tenor and mezzo-soprano. For those who understand German the story is brought out with wonderful vividness.

Heinrich Schlusnus.—I seem to have heard these old airs by Handel and Giordani sung before by the same singer, because I recollect not caring either for voice or accent in the Italian—a language that does not sound well through German vowels—or for the modern harmonization of the organ accompaniments played by Franz Rupp. I prefer the simpler diatonic chords of the composer's " figured bass." The melody of the Largo as a violin solo is another though less objectionable innovation. In the lovely *Am Meer* of Schubert and the old-fashioned *lied* by Pressel—intensely German, you know—the singer is more thoroughly at home and at his ease.

Gitta Alpar and *Herbert Ernst Groh.*—In these duets you will be able to appreciate the perfect union of two delightful voices. The sweetness of both timbres is matched by the delicate smoothness with which they blend. I need not dwell on the individual excellencies of these two artists ; suffice it to say that they are shown off to the rarest advantage by the graceful and flowing numbers that they sing.

Maggie Teyte.—I have often thought that Miss Maggie Teyte was designed by nature and art for the elegant, fanciful productions of the lighter French school a great deal more than for the serious lyric drama to which she habitually aspires. She should never attack anything heavier than *Pelléas et Mélisande*. Here in the sparkling gems of Messager and Offenbach—and not the over-hackneyed ones either—she is simply unsurpassable. Her diction is as usual beyond reproach, and I note the clever use to which she now puts her maturing chest tones, which come out most effectively in two splendid records.

Armand Crabbé.—This excellent baritone brings out all or most of the charm peculiar to Manuel de Falla's characteristic national rhythms, even though his Spanish be, like himself, either French or Belgian, I forget which. He warbles and patters his *Jota* like an artist, anyhow. In his own song there is much less to admire and infinitely less originality, but he sings that well, too.

Richard Tauber.—A couple of up-to-date waltz-airs submitted to the customary fascinating Tauberesque treatment. Despite his many imitators this popular tenor remains *facile princeps* in his own line ; and as he never departs from it, it is almost superfluous to add that in these examples " Richard is himself again " !

Sydney Rayner.—*Obstination* is a pretty song, if a trifle over-sung. It requires a special kind of gentle warbling *legato* that only a born Frenchman seems to achieve naturally. Again, the Neapolitan manner in voice and song is a gift that rarely comes to any save the Neapolitan, who imbibes it from the cradle. I fancy Mr. Rayner will do best to stick to opera.

Fernando Gusso.—Here we have the Neapolitan all right, but in what a dull mood ! Or is it the voice itself that is dull? It vibrates ; but there is in it no colour, no life, no ring, and no amount of amplification can replace these things.

John Turner.—These *Rigoletto* airs only serve to make manifest the fact that bad English translations can spoil the best music and the best vocal tone.

Mafalda Sabatini.—Rarely does one hear perfect German from Italian lips. I imagine this lady was either born in Germany or has studied there most of her life. She sings Schubert better than Brahms, and I doubt whether she has ever quite gathered the poetic meaning of *Von ewiger Liebe*, though she sings everything with evident intelligence. It is, moreover, a pity that one hears so plainly the hissing intake of every breath. These are all shortcomings that ought to have been nipped in the bud.

HERMAN KLEIN.

OPERATIC AND FOREIGN SONGS

CONCHITA SUPERVIA (mezzo-soprano).—**Spring Song** (Mendelssohn, A. G. Miranda). In Spanish. Orch. acc. And **Santa Lucia** (T. Cottrau). In Italian. Orch. acc. Parlophone RO20212, 10in., 4s.

ENRICO CARUSO (tenor).—**O Sole mio**, Neapolitan Folk-song (G. Capurro, E. di Capua), and **La donna è mobile** from Act 3 of **Rigoletto** (Verdi). In Italian. With **Symphony Orchestra**. H.M.V. DA1303, 10in., 4s.

JOSEPH SCHMIDT (tenor).—**Depart, fair vision**, from Act 3 of **Manon** (Massenet). In German. Orch. acc. under **Dr. Weissmann.** And **Rodrigue's Prayer** from Act 3 of **Le Cid** (Massenet). In German. Orch. acc. under **O. Dobrindt.** Parlophone R1443, 10in., 2s. 6d.

HEINRICH REHKEMPER (baritone).—**A Message** and **The Rat's Death Song** (Wolf). In German. Piano acc. by **Michael Raucheisen.** Decca-Polydor PO5063, 10in., 2s. 6d.

ALFRED PICCAVER (tenor).—**Torna a Sorriento** (de Curtis). In Italian. Orch. acc. under **Julius Prüwer.** And **Di te** (Tirindelli). In Italian. Orch. acc. under **Manfred Gurlitt.** Decca-Polydor DE7001, 10in., 2s. 6d.

FRANZ VÖLKER (tenor).—**E lucevan le stelle** and **Recondita armonia** from **Tosca** (Puccini). In German. Orch. acc. under **Julius Prüwer.** Decca-Polydor DE7021, 10in., 2s. 6d.

SYDNEY RAYNER (tenor).—**Au clair de la lune** (Leoncavallo) and **Elégie** (Massenet). In French. With Piano acc. and Violin Obbligato. Decca M433, 10in., 2s. 6d.

ARMAND CRABBÉ (baritone).—**Amoureuse** (Berger) and **Nele-Ay-Ay-Ay** (Crabbé). In French. Orch. acc. Decca M434, 10in., 2s. 6d.

MICHELE FLETA (tenor).—**Vainement, ma bien aimée,** from Act 3 of **Le Roi d'Ys** (Lalo). In French. And **Valse No. 15** (Brahms, Moreno). In Spanish. Orch. acc. H.M.V. DA1208, 10in., 4s.

RICHARD TAUBER (tenor).—**Maria, Mari !** Italian Folk-song (Edi Capua, Otto Stransky). In German. Orch. acc. under **Ernst Hauke.** And **Memories of Sorrento** (E. de Curtis, Eugen Matray). In German. Orch. acc. under **Dr. Weissmann.** Parlophone RO20211, 10in., 4s.

CHARLES KULLMAN (tenor).—**All hail, thou dwelling,** from **Faust** (Gounod), and **Flower Song** from **Carmen** (Bizet). In English. Orch. acc. Columbia DX442, 12in., 4s.

Conchita Supervia.—I have remarked before upon the extra charm that the use of her native tongue enables this singer to impart to her theme, whatever it may be, and now we can put her to the test in a melody that everyone knows, yet, in this country at least, no one sings. In other words, she creates a fresh interest in Mendelssohn's sempiternal *Spring Song* by transferring it from the piano-keyboard of the *Lieder ohne Worte* to the human medium of the *Lieder mit Worte* (or *Worten*, to be accurate). Let me for once confess that I find the liberty wholly justified by the result. The luscious tone, the easy, graceful poise of the phrasing, the unaffected simplicity of the whole rendering, reconcile me forthwith to a proceeding that will give pleasure to all who hear it, even though they don't understand a word of Spanish. The key is very wisely lowered from A to F major, and so fits the voice perfectly ; but for many reasons I would add the warning : " Imitators, beware ! You are not all Supervias." On the other side of this record is another old tune, much easier to sing, which the least cultured Neapolitan can warble without fear of failure. How the talented Conchita treats it—not in Spanish, but her very best Italian—I leave my readers to discover for themselves. For the rest, they will find, as I have done, almost a surfeit of Neapolitan folk-songs in the reviews of the month that follow, beginning with a most illustrious example.

Enrico Caruso.—We have here the second of the newly reinforced and reproduced records by Caruso, the first of which was brought out by H.M.V. with such extraordinarily good results a short time ago. The present issue is in my opinion even more successful than the earlier one. I had never heard Caruso's record of *La donna è mobile* before ; anyhow, it did not impress me as it does now. It sounds like the actual stage rendering brought to life again, and yet the original record—DA561, made in 1908 and no longer in the general catalogue, but transferred to No. 2 or " records of unique and historic interest "—was obviously, like a ship on the rocks, in danger of becoming a total loss. My thanks go out to the lifeboat crew for the rescue of a magnificent specimen of the great tenor's finest robust style. The voice rings out with astonishing clearness and purity as well as unlimited power, while the ending, with its *roulade* or flourish and a superb high B natural, brings back a something that no other tenor within my recollection ever surpassed or perhaps even equalled. *O sole mio* restores a somewhat later gramophone souvenir (DA103), and one that, if I mistake not, had more to do than any other with the world-wide popularity of di Capua's catchy Neapolitan ditty. Anyhow, here it is once more, and in an idealised shape that will unquestionably help to prolong its vogue. Congratulations to all concerned !

Joseph Schmidt.—Better known under its French title of *Ah ! fuyez, douce image*, the air sung by Des Grieux in the third act of *Manon* requires just the vibrant tone and sense of despair that it receives in this rendering. Also it strikes the listener as being a far finer example of Massenet's genius than the excerpt from *Le Cid* that is coupled with it. This is described as a Prayer, and, if so, is presumably addressed by Rodrigue to Saint Jacques de Compostello when he appears to him in a vision in his tent—not that that matters much. What is of greater interest is that *Le Cid* was the opera in which Jean de Reszke made such a hit when he created Rodrigue at the Paris Opéra after his rentrée there as a tenor in 1885. The passage is extremely well declaimed by the present singer, who has the requisite emotional equipment for it.

Heinrich Rehkemper.—I have yet to hear a record by this German baritone that does not increase my admiration for his vocal gifts and my wonder that he is not as much of a favourite at Covent Garden as Schorr or Bockelmann. He ought certainly to get the same chance. His powers of characterization are wholly exceptional, as I had occasion to point out last year in his interpretation of Mahler. Now in these widely contrasted songs by Hugo Wolf he displays equal intelligence and skill, coupled with the utmost realism and intensity of delineation. Especially fine is he in *Der Rattenfänger.* The speed of his incisive enunciation, the dramatic power and vocal quality of the whole rendering, are just right for the song ; while the difficult accompaniment is admirably played.

Alfred Piccaver.—All that can be said of these Neapolitan " die-hards " is that the present singer presents them in their most attractive guise, with great richness of tone, plenty of spirit, and much less than usual of his wonted somnolence of manner. In fact, I am bound to admit that the latter shortcoming is rapidly disappearing from Mr. Piccaver's style ; he is much more energetic and animated than of yore, and he now has the true Italian touch in sentiment as well as in voice and delivery.

Franz Völker.—Although the Italian titles of the two airs from *Tosca* are adhered to on the Decca-Polydor label, they are sung in German, and, I am glad to say, sound none the worse on that account, for the reason, no doubt, that there is nothing in their interpretation that a Toscanini or a Polacco could possibly object to. And, if the observance of tradition is right, so also is the timbre of the Frankfort tenor, whose excellent records are invariably much appreciated over here.

Sydney Rayner.—There was a time when one used to hear complaints about the dearth of good tenors; but now, surely, the shoe is on the other foot, and there seems a likelihood of our being told that the demand does not keep pace with the supply. More than half the records I am reviewing this month are by tenors, while the ladies, for once, are conspicuous with a single exception by their absence. Mr. Sydney Rayner, who is, I understand, an American, was in London recently and gave a recital at which he pleased quite a number of people, including the critics. He would appear to have found his true *métier* at the Opéra-Comique, but unfortunately we have no opportunity for testing his merit as a stage artist, save on a plane that he would not care to descend to. However, the chance for "comic opera" of the kind he sings in Paris may yet come, and meanwhile his records are meeting with favour. These songs by Leoncavallo and Massenet are sung with artistic feeling and adequate depth of expression. The familiar *Elégie* comes out especially well, the only fault there being the over-prominence of the violin obbligato, owing to the fact that it either runs note for note with the voice or else rises too conspicuously above it. Neither is the true function of an obbligato.

Armand Crabbé.—I may have been unlucky in my sample of this record, but the scrape of the needle is heard over the surface on both sides. The music does not greatly interest me either. *Amoureuse* begins too low and sometimes gets rather high for the singer; it is the sort of waltz air that might be better suited for a woman's voice. The other piece—M. Crabbé's own composition—has a nice *Ay-Ay-Ay* refrain of the usual type, with a somewhat foggy accompaniment for the lower strings *pizzicato*. Altogether not a first-rate record.

Michele Fleta.—Here is another tenor who in his time has done capital operatic work for the gramophone, but in the present instance he has not made a very happy choice. The melodious *Aubade* from Lalo's *Le Roi d'Ys* does not really suit him well. It needs one of those light French voices that can pursue a smooth, sweet course without having to depend so much upon the use of the *mezza voce*. The accent, too, could be superior, though the singer is not so distinct as he might be even in his own native tongue, as heard in the Spanish words which he uses in the arrangement of the Brahms waltz No. 15. Here, however, he is more robust and sings with more *abandon*—more like his natural self.

Richard Tauber.—It is interesting to compare this record of *Torna a Sorriento* (German version) with that by Alfred Piccaver noticed above, but not so easy to choose between them, for each has its good qualities. It depends chiefly upon which voice of the two you prefer. Curiously enough, the German tenor sings his a semitone higher than the Anglo-Italian, who as a rule sings much higher music; one is in E major, the other in E flat. In Piccaver's rendering, of course, you get the original language; in the other the Tauber charm plus a fascinating *Maria, Mari!* That may help you to decide between the two.

Charles Kullman.—Yet another American tenor, possessor of a strong, sympathetic voice and a capital high C, displayed to advantage in the *Faust* air. The newcomer appears to have studied in Italy and has acquired a telling *sostenuto* with a broad operatic style. His English requires further polish, and he must leave off pronouncing his short i's and y's as if they were ee's. Otherwise his rendering of the *Flower Song* has many excellent features and the tone throughout falls most pleasantly on the ear.

HERMAN KLEIN.

OPERATIC AND FOREIGN SONGS

LOTTE LEHMANN (soprano).—**O! Sacred Head** and **Christ's dear Mother stood in Sorrow.** In German. Organ acc. Parlo. RO20215, 10in., 4s.

VERA SCHWARZ (soprano).—Amelia's Aria **Here is the gloomy spot** from Act 2 of **Un Ballo in Maschera** (Verdi). In German. Orch. acc. under **Dr. Weissmann**, Parlo. R1466, 10in., 2s. 6d.

BENIAMINO GIGLI (tenor).—**Cujus animam** from **Stabat Mater** (Rossini). In Latin. And **Pietà, Signore!** (Stradella). In Italian. With **Members of La Scala Orchestra**, Milan, under **Carlo Sabajno**. H.M.V. DB1831, 12in., 6s.

SUZANNE BALGUERIE (soprano).—**O malheureuse Iphigénie** from **Iphigénie en Tauride** (Gluck, arr. D'Indy) and **Divinités du Styx** from **Alceste**. In French. Orch. acc. under **Albert Wolff**. Decca-Polydor LY6065, 12in., 3s. 6d.

ELISABETH OHMS (soprano) and **THEODOR SCHEIDL** (baritone).—**Versank ich jetzt in wunderbares Träumen** from **The Flying Dutchman** (Wagner). In German. Orch. acc. under **Julius Prüwer**. Decca-Polydor CA8150, 12in., 4s.

HEINRICH SCHLUSNUS (baritone).—**The Two Grenadiers** and **The Hidalgo** (Schumann). In German. Piano acc. Decca-Polydor CA8144, 12in., 4s.

RICHARD TAUBER (tenor).—**One likes to believe in woman's love and luck** and **You are my dream** from **The Song of Love** (Joh. Strauss, Korngold, Herzer). In German. Orch. acc. under **Erich Wolfgang Korngold**. Parlo. RO20216, 10in., 4s.

FRANCESCO VADA (tenor).—**La Donna è mobile** and **Questa o quella** from **Rigoletto** (Verdi) and **On with the Motley** from **Pagliacci** (Leoncavallo). In English. Orch. acc. Broadcast Twelve 3296, 1s. 6d.

SYDNEY RAYNER (tenor).—**Celeste Aida** from **Aida**, and **Ora e per sempre addio** from **Otello** (Verdi). In Italian. Orch. acc. Decca T204, 12in., 3s. 6d.

Lotte Lehmann.—A ready sale, both here and in Germany, of the records of sacred pieces sung by this artist has evidently encouraged a further search in the same direction, and for other religious seasons beside Christmas. With Easter at hand, there should be abundant opportunity for utilizing two *Kirchenlieder* (Church hymns with organ accompaniment) so beautifully sung as these. In form and character they recall nothing so much as the Lutheran chorales of Bach's *Passion* or his cantatas, the tune, of course, being limited to a solo voice, with harmonies supplied *ad libitum* by the organist—in this instance a very good one. The words *Christi Mutter stand in Schmerzen* will be recognized as a German translation of the opening line of the *Stabat Mater*, and it indicates at once the source whence the text of this particular hymn is derived. The words and tune of the other are no doubt equally traditional, and the recording of both cannot fail to satisfy the most exigent listener.

Vera Schwarz.—Somewhere about the middle of the big air for Amelia in the second act of *Un Ballo in Maschera* the clock of the neighbouring church is heard to strike midnight. How best to manage this lengthy process on a 10in. record that divides the air into two parts seems to have provided the Parlophone operator with the chance for a brilliant idea. He has simply made his clock strike six twice, first at the end of the opening part, and the second half at the beginning of the next. The pause in between the two half-dozens apparently makes no difference to Amelia, for she exclaims " *mezzanotte* " quite naturally, and goes on as though nothing unusual had occurred. As I have remarked more than once before, the aria in question is one of the best things in an opera that I consider among the finest of Verdi's second period. It is now as popular on the Continent as *Rigoletto* or *La Traviata*, and ought to be equally so here, despite the inconsistencies of the plot, which is no worse than those of *Trovatore* and *La Forza del Destino*. Ably supported by Dr. Weissmann's orchestra, Frl. Vera Schwarz gives a rendering of the air that is in the highest degree dramatic and full to the brim of colour and expression. Her top C may be a trifle thin, but her head notes as a rule are adequate and her middle register has a very individual quality.

Beniamino Gigli.—This admirable tenor seems to be following illustrious precedents by taking on the work of the concert room as well as the opera house, and it may be that he will find it pay him as well to appear at the Albert Hall as it paid Caruso and Chaliapin before him. Meanwhile he has started upon a new line in the recording of concert *morceaux* by giving us a couple of hardy old favourites, both of which suit him remarkably well. The *Cujus animam* from Rossini's *Stabat Mater* calls for robust, vigorous treatment and a bold martial swing, together with a liberal allowance of the rich tenor high notes that Gigli possesses in such unfailing plenitude. He supplies exactly what is needed without a symptom of effort, and never slackens power for a single bar. His ringing B natural towards the end is surmounted with the ease of a Grand National winner taking his final fence. In complete contrast with this are the serious timbre and devotional manner employed by the singer in the famous Stradella air, *Pietà, Signore*, transposed up to the key of E flat minor so as to bring it comfortably within his effective compass. Thus laid out it fits his voice far better than I should have expected, while one discriminating cut avoids unnecessary repetition and brings the long solo into the right proportions. The refined quality and playing of the Scala orchestra, under Carlo Sabajno, provides a perfect background for the entire effort.

Suzanne Balguérie.—Here is a new French soprano who has evidently been trained in the strict traditions of the Conservatoire and who knows how to handle the difficult music of Gluck (as arranged by Vincent d'Indy) according to the accepted canons of the school. But, whilst acknowledging her ability to fulfil these requirements, I cannot help thinking that she was guilty of an error of judgment in attempting for the gramophone the air from *Alceste*, *Divinités du Styx*, which was obviously intended for a mezzo-soprano or contralto and is generally sung by one or the other. Her stately tempo, her dignified, unhurried delivery, her faultless diction, may be just right for the piece, but the deep rich notes for the " Ministres de la Mort " and other low passages are conspicuously lacking. On the other hand, the newcomer is perfectly at home in the fine air from *Iphigénie en Tauride*, the higher *tessitura* of which fits her sympathetic voice in a way that definitely clinches my argument. This is well worth hearing; the *Divinités* is not,

in anything like the same degree; and I commend my verdict to M. Albert Wolff, the talented conductor of the Opéra-Comique, who with his excellent orchestra here represents the true Gluck traditions that I have referred to.

Elisabeth Ohms and *Theodor Scheidl.*—I know nothing of Wagner, whether in his earlier or his later works, more difficult to record to perfection than the duet for Senta and Vanderdecken from the second act of *The Flying Dutchman*. That, perhaps, is the reason why it is so seldom done. It is also the reason for my not wishing to be hypercritical in regard to the present effort on the part of two famous German singers. Yet I cannot honestly say that their voices blend really well or that they hit upon the ideal balance of strength wherever they join in the opening portion of the scene. The dreamy Senta and the hesitant Dutchman express their individual feelings in long and sustained passages with great artistic skill, so that the music exercises much of its familiar charm; but the real dramatic effect of the duet is not made apparent until the lengthy cadenza *à deux* has been sung, the tempo changes with the Dutchman's anxious enquiry, *Willst du dein Vaters Wahl nicht schelten?* and both singers begin to let themselves go. Then Scheidl's voice takes its proper place in the picture and later on Elisabeth Ohms gives us the full benefit of her lovely tone. Mind, I do not say that the strange episode of this Scandinavian meeting could be more faithfully portrayed outside the opera house. Yet vocally, perhaps, a closer approach to Wagner's intention might have been attained by two such accomplished artists as these with a more careful study of tone-values where perfect blending and intonation are of such vital importance to the general result. I wonder whether they, with Herr Julius Prüwer as adviser as well as conductor, would consent to " have another try " ? In the meantime the present record is quite good enough to stand.

Heinrich Schlusnus.—Two of Schumann's most characteristic lieder, sung with every attribute that art and experience can bring to bear. I need say no more.

Richard Tauber.—Equal brevity will suffice for dealing with these latest examples of the Strauss-Korngold combination. They are certainly very taking in their way, and a notable feature is that neither song is strictly in waltz rhythm. But the swaying, undulating elegance of the Tauber method makes sure that they shall be none the less attractive because of that. The Viennese influence is unmistakable, especially when *One likes to believe in woman's love*, as one title puts it.

Francesco Vada.—This singer, whose origin, despite his Italian name, is as Britannic as the text which he uses for his arias, has a capital voice and a free dramatic style that betokens a certain amount of stage training. He is most effective in *On with the Motley*, where tone, enunciation, and dramatic emphasis are alike good. In the *Rigoletto* songs the voice comes out equally well, but nothing will ever persuade me that " Woman's a fickle jade " can be made to sound a satisfactory substitute for " La donna è mobile," while a breath in the midst of the Caruso-like flourish at the end is one of the things that is *not* done.

Sydney Rayner.—The new American tenor is heard to much greater advantage in this Italian Decca than in the French ones recently noticed. The bright language and broad phrases of Verdi seem to release his voice and impart freedom to his declamatory energy. I may say frankly that I admire his *Celeste Aida* more than any I have heard for a long while. It indicates progress all along the line, and I have listened with pleasure to every word and note of it. The *Addio, sante memorie*, is likewise far above the average. I make no comparisons, but I begin to think that some of the Italian tenors basking in the centre of the limelight will soon have to look out for a serious rival in the person of Sydney Rayner. If good enough now for the Opéra-Comique he may ere long be acclaimed at La Scala, and then—what price Covent Garden ?

HERMAN KLEIN.

OPERATIC AND FOREIGN SONGS

MADELEINE GREY (soprano).—**Kaddish (Prayer for the Dead).** In Hebrew. **Méjerke,** in Hebrew and Yiddish, and **L'Enigme éternelle,** in Yiddish (Ravel). Pianoforte acc. by the composer. Decca-Polydor PO5066, 2s. 6d.

HEINRICH SCHLUSNUS (baritone).—**Minnelied,** Op. 71, No. 5, and **Ständchen,** Op. 106, No. 1 (Brahms). In German. Piano acc. Decca-Polydor DE7022, 2s. 6d.

JULIUS PATZAK (tenor).—**Una furtiva lagrima** from **The Elixir of Love** (Donizetti) and **La Danza** (Rossini). In Italian. With **The Berlin State Opera Orchestra.** Decca-Polydor PO5067, 2s. 6d.

GINA CIGNA (soprano) and **NAZZARENO DE ANGELIS** (bass).—**The Church Scene** from **Faust** (Gounod). In Italian. With Chorus and Orchestra. Columbia LX233, 12in., 6s.

GINA CIGNA (soprano).—**Suicidio** from **La Gioconda** (Ponchielli) and **Casta Diva, che inargenti** from **Norma** (Bellini). And **Ma dall' arido stelo** and **Morrò, ma prima in grazia** from **Un Ballo in Maschera** (Verdi). In Italian. Orch. acc. Columbia LX234 and 235, 12in., 6s. each.

CESARE FORMICHI (baritone).—**Monumento** from **La Gioconda** (Ponchielli) and **Cortigiani vil razza** from **Rigoletto** (Verdi). In Italian. Orch. acc. Columbia LX236, 12in., 6s.

ELISABETH FRIEDRICH (soprano) and **CARL HARTMANN** (tenor).—**The Bridal Chamber Scene** from **Lohengrin** (Wagner). In German. With **Berlin State Opera Orchestra** under **Dr. Weissmann.** Parlo. R1491 and 1492, 10in., 2s. 6d. each.

BIANCA GHERADI (soprano) and **BENVENUTO FRANCI** (baritone).—**Dunque io son, tu non m'inganni?** from **Il Barbiere di Siviglia** (Rossini). In Italian. Orch. acc. Columbia LB9, 12in., 6s.

CLAIRE DUX (soprano).—**Morgen** (Richard Strauss) and **Ave Maria** (Schubert). In German. With Piano and Violin. Parlo. RO20218, 10in., 4s.

RICHARD TAUBER (tenor).—**Serenade** and **The Phantom Double** (Schubert). In German. Orch. acc. Parlo. RO20217, 10in., 4s.

ROSETTA PAMPANINI (soprano) and **GINO VANELLI** (baritone)—**Decidi il mio destin** and **E allor perchè** from **Pagliacci** (Leoncavallo). In Italian. Orch. acc. Columbia LX238. And with **DINO BORGIOLI** (tenor)—**O soave fanciulla,** and with **AURORA RETTORE** (soprano), **BORGIOLI** and **VANELLI, Addio, dolce svegliare** from **La Bohème** (Puccini). In Italian. Orch. acc. Columbia LX237, 12in., 6s.

Madeleine Grey.—Two out of the three pieces on this record were composed by Ravel as long ago as 1914, and are given in the list of his published works under the title of *Deux Mélodies Hébraïques.* Of these the *Kaddisch,* or Prayer for the Dead, is here reproduced on one side; while the other, *L'Enigme éternelle,* follows on the reverse side after a later composition, a song to words half in Hebrew, half in Yiddish, entitled *Méjerke.* All three are highly characteristic. The *Kaddisch,* which is the best known, is very beautiful, and seems to be partly founded on the ancient orthodox chant that is generally intoned to this prayer, when sung at the graveside and in the synagogue or home to mark the anniversary of a parent's or near relative's death. Neither of the others is so solemn and touching as the *Kaddisch,* wherein the florid passages form but the essential Eastern ornaments, and add to rather than detract from the expression of grief whilst proclaiming the immortality of the soul. *Méjerke* is an exhortation from a mother to her son, and alternates, strangely enough, a lively tune with Yiddish and a declamatory phrase with pure Hebrew lines. *L'Enigme éternelle* is frankly in the manner of a folk-song with a bright, tuneful refrain. These pieces,

admirably recorded, are heard to the greatest possible advantage in the present interpretation. Her English name notwithstanding, the soprano soloist is obviously of foreign Jewish extraction. Voice, style, and manner leave no doubt whatever as to that; neither could a more perfect rendering possibly be imagined, since to the lovely tones of the singer is added the supreme attraction of M. Ravel's own personal piano accompaniment, which is as refined, modest, yet effective as his music is worthy of the composer of the *Shéhérazade* songs and *L'Heure Espagnole.*

Heinrich Schlusnus.—Never was Brahms so much in request, never were his works of every description so highly prized as in this, the year which marks the centenary of his birth. The actual date is the seventh of this very merry month of May, and I am bound to say that our musical *entrepreneurs* in most parts of the country are doing their best between them to furnish a fitting national tribute to the genius of the Hamburg master. If more of his instrumental than of his vocal compositions are claiming gramophonic attention, there are probably good reasons for it. The songs in particular have enjoyed their full share during the past decade—at any rate, from German singers; and now here is Herr Schlusnus with a couple of them that I do not remember to have heard from him before. I love the *Minnelied* sung by a baritone with his warmth of tone, his earnestness and depth of expression, his purity of diction. The metallic quality caused by over-amplification can be reduced by using a fibre needle, and the record as it stands certainly needs the softening influence. In the *Ständchen* the same fault is less perceptible; only this is a song that I somehow like better in a woman's voice, though the present singer very nearly succeeds in imparting to it the requisite measure of light and mischievous humour.

Julius Patzak.—Paradoxical as it may sound, I cannot help saying that Donizetti was in his happiest vein when he wrote that sorrowful, tearful ditty, *Una furtiva lagrima.* It has survived long after his amusing and sparkling opera *L'Elisir d'amore,* with the delightful quack, Dr. Dulcamara, made famous by the inimitable Lablache, has apparently descended into oblivion. It would strike you as being a very simple air and quite easy to sing, but I can assure you it is nothing of the sort. It requires a perfect *sostenuto* and a flawless legato, together with the utmost delicacy of phrasing and just that suggestion of " tears in the voice " which comes so naturally to a tenor of Patzak's racial descent. Altogether this is a first-rate recording of the song, and equally good in its way, as well as completely in contrast, is that of *La Danza* on the reverse of the disc. It is given with superb tone and *verve,* once more strengthening my conviction that Rossini's *tarantella* sounds best when sung by a man, whatever the words may hint at.

Gina Cigna and *Nazzareno de Angelis.*—The church scene from *Faust* does not seem quite complete without an organ in the background, nor is it easy to see what was gained by its omission from this otherwise admirable record of the impressive episode from the fourth act of Gounod's opera. Still, the orchestra acts as an efficient substitute, and by the imaginative listener I daresay the organ can for once be dispensed with. There is certainly a sufficiently imposing volume of tone without it. Both the Marguerite and the Mephistopheles hold their own against a powerful chorus of demons and a resounding orchestra, so that all the familiar points stand out in clear relief.

Gina Cigna.—The first record ever made of the *Suicidio* air from *La Gioconda* was that sung by the lamented Lillian Nordica for Columbia at New York nearly thirty years ago; and I was there to hear her make it. Alas! she did not enjoy the same mechanical advantages as fell to the present singer, who represents a later and different type of (Italian) soprano. The declamatory school that serves well for *Suicidio* is, of course, less helpful in *Casta Diva;* but there is no reason why the same artist should not be able to do justice to both, and, on the whole, Signorina Cigna, if not another Rosa Ponselle, uses her fine organ skilfully enough to justify the daring venture.

Anyhow, she imparts to the *Gioconda* excerpt all the dramatic emphasis and significance that it demands, which is saying much. The record is worth having for that alone, while the two airs from *Un Ballo* on LX235 not only show the artist in her true light, but are quite splendidly sung.

Cesare Formichi.—All who are looking forward to hearing this eminent baritone again during the coming season at Covent Garden may be recommended to possess themselves of this, his latest effort for the gramophone. Evidently his voice retains all its sonority, its richness, its capacity for passionate utterance. The *Cortigiani* is immensely strong without being overdone ; in the biggest outburst it loses not a jot of its rare quality. Barnaba's apostrophe to the Venetian " den of the Doges " is not wonderful as music, but it is effective for the singer, and brings out a dignified display of Formichi's declamatory powers, with a ringing A flat at the end.

Elisabeth Friedrich and *Carl Hartmann.*—The glorious bridal duet from *Lohengrin* here occupies the whole four sides of two 10in. discs, very discreetly divided up by Dr. Weissmann and rendered with notable tonal refinement by his excellent Berlin State Opera Orchestra. I cannot remember to have heard the instrumental beauties of the scene more vividly brought out. Equally to be praised are the two singers, of whom I fancy that the Elsa is a newcomer to the Parlophone studios. Her *mezza voce* is particularly to be admired, and her liberal employment of it something to enjoy and be thankful for. Hartmann has a genuine tenor voice, with the precise heroic yet suave timbre that a Lohengrin (or a Siegmund or a Tristan) should rightfully possess. Like Frl. Friedrich's soprano, it sounds very fresh and youthful, and one feels that it would be pleasant to see as well as hear both artists in these parts.

Bianca Gherardi and *Benvenuto Franci.*—This record of the immortal duet between Rosina and Figaro would be even further beyond criticism than it is were it not for a couple of peculiarities on the part of Signor Franci. He is during most of the time too loud ; and he has a habit of introducing a little chuckle after every witticism, as though obsessed with the cleverness of his own humour—a trick only permissible on the stage. On the other hand, his style has the right Rossinian flavour and his *fiorituri* are nearly as flexible as those of his fair companion. Hers is an extremely bright, resonant voice, well trained for florid music, and one can imagine her making a delightful Rosina.

Claire Dux.—It is a privilege to welcome once again a record sung by this accomplished artist. Just twenty years have elapsed since she made her début in London in Sir Thomas Beecham's first production of *Der Rosenkavalier* as Sophie to the Marschallin of Eva von der Osten and the Baron Ochs of Paul Knüpfer. There is still the same lovely purity and sweetness in her voice, while the perfection of her art remains unsullied by any kind of blemish. Needless to add, therefore, that she adorns with a fresh charm the familiar melodies of Schubert and Strauss. Neither has been more beautifully recorded, and the only pity is that she could not spare us a second verse of the *Ave Maria*.

Richard Tauber.—The *Serenade*, gracefully warbled, can be listened to with unqualified pleasure, even though the tempo be unusually fast. But *Der Doppelgänger*, if interesting, loses something of its mysterious quality when sung by a tenor, and when, moreover, it lacks variety of tone and inflection. But why this new English title ? *The Phantom Double* seems rather to suggest the experience of a disappointed backer after a vain pursuit of profit by means of the " Tote."

Rosetta Pampanini, Aurora Rettore, Dino Borgioli, and *Gino Vanelli.*—This is an *ensemble de luxe,* and when they all join in the quartet from the third act of *La Bohème* the result fulfils one's highest expectations. The duets are not less magnificently sung, and I question whether that for Nedda and Silvio has ever yet been recorded by two such fine voices or with such abundant realisation of the passionate scene. In the *Soave fanciulla* Dino Borgioli is simply irresistible.

HERMAN KLEIN.

Verdi's "Falstaff"—Columbia Album

By many good judges Verdi's swan-song is held to be his greatest opera ; and maybe they are not far wrong. In any case, it is beyond question his most difficult. Hard for singers, hard for an audience to follow, I cannot help attributing to its swift, tricky, complicated musical movement not a little of the slow growth of its popularity. Otherwise, it has everything in its favour—Shakespeare's delicious comedy of *The Merry Wives,* Boito's masterly moulding of it into operatic shape, and a setting by the grand old man of music (when well on in his eighties) that might well be termed a miraculous achievement.

Falstaff was first performed at La Scala—whence comes also this first complete gramophonic recording—on February 9th, 1893. In the following year it was mounted at Covent Garden with Pessina in Maurel's superb creation of the title part, Arimondi in his original rôle of Pistol, Giulia Ravogli (now Mrs. Harrison Cripps) as Mistress Quickly, Olga Olghina as Anne Page, and Mancinelli conducting. Both here and in Paris (where Verdi himself attended the *première*) the opera had a warm reception, and Stanford in an article in the *Fortnightly* expressed the opinion that it might meet with greatest success out of Italy, where " the masses were more or less taken aback by its novelty and uncompromising idealism." But this prediction, if in some measure verified, has not proved true with regard to the interpretation of *Falstaff,* wherein, as with *Otello,* the Italians have invariably won the highest laurels. It is a work that seems to have been written by an Italian for his own countrymen, and I know of no other nationality that could have approached for that reason the degree of all-round excellence attained in the Columbia album under notice. It has the very quality of " joyous lightness "—to use his own words—that Verdi found lacking in parts of the Paris performance. I cannot imagine his being other than amazed and delighted with the crispness, the sparkling brightness, the extraordinary speed and accuracy of this performance.

The opera, which is in three acts and six scenes, is reproduced on fourteen discs, numbered from LX241 to LX254, and the following is the cast :—John Falstaff, GIACOMO RIMINI ; Alice Ford, PIA TASSINARI ; Nannetta, INES A. TELLINI ; Quickly, AURORA BUADES ; Fenton, ROBERT D'ALESSIO ; Meg Page, RITA MONTICONE ; Ford, EMILIO GHIRARDINI ; Pistol, SALVATORE BACCALONI ; Dr. Caius, EMILIO VENTURINI ; and Bardolph, GIUSEPPE NESSI ; with the Milan Symphony Orchestra, conducted by CAV. L. MOLAJOLI. Nearly half of these names will be familiar to readers ; anyhow, the entire ensemble consists of artists thoroughly at home, not only in their parts, but in the technique of gramophone recording. The voices, too, are of genuine power and satisfying quality, while the aptness with which they have been selected is proved by the fact that they fit the music like a glove.

HERMAN KLEIN.

OPERATIC AND FOREIGN SONGS

ENRICO CARUSO (tenor).—**Celeste Aida** from Act 1 of **Aida** (Verdi) (in Italian) and **Je crois entendre encore** from Act 1 of **Les Pêcheurs de Perles** (Bizet). In French. Orch. acc. H.M.V. DB1875, 12in., 6s.

WALTER KIRCHHOFF (tenor) and **MARGARET BAUMER** (soprano).—**Vorspiel** and **Duet** in three parts (Act 1) and **Oath Scene** (Act 2) from **Götterdämmerung** (Wagner). In German. With the **Berlin State Opera Orchestra.** Parlo. R1523 and 1524, 10in., 2s. 6d. each.

WILHELM RODE (baritone).—**Wahn, wahn, überall wahn** and **Doch eines Abends spät** from **Die Meistersinger** (Wagner). In German. Orch. acc. under **Manfred Gurlitt.** Decca-Polydor CA8157, 12in., 4s.

JOSEF VON MANOWARDA (baritone).—**Wandering** and **Secrecy** (Hugo Wolf). In German. Piano acc. by **Arpad Sandor.** Decca-Polydor PO5068, 10in., 2s. 6d.

BENIAMINO GIGLI (tenor).—**Ombra mai fù** from **Xerxes** (Handel) and **Una furtiva lagrima** from **L'Elisir d'Amore** (Donizetti). In Italian. Orch. acc. H.M.V. DB1901, 12in., 6s.

RICHARD TAUBER (tenor).—**I would that my love might blossom** (Mendelssohn-Heine) and **Shimmering Silver** (Mendelssohn-Melchert). Duets sung by one voice. In German. Orch. acc. Parlo. RO20219, 10in., 4s.

JOHN HENDRIK (tenor).—**Gipsy Love** (Léhar-Willner-Bodansky) and **The Czarevitch** (Léhar-Jenbach-Reichert). In German. Orch. acc. Parlo. R1517, 2s. 6d.

Enrico Caruso.—This is the third of the cancelled Caruso discs to undergo post-electric treatment. On the whole, it comes through the test with the same surprising results, though not perhaps with the same all-round success. In the *Celeste Aida* the difference can be accounted for by two things—a slightly less resonant timbre in the voice, except on the splendid head notes ; and the general tendency of the added orchestral accompaniment to maintain a disproportionate loudness. Perhaps the latter defect can be set right, but the former might be difficult to improve. Bizet's air is sung, as usual, a tone lower than it was written, but that only serves to enhance the rich baritonal quality that was one of Caruso's characteristics. His French is, I fear, too hopelessly bad to derive any benefit from the process of resuscitation; but the record was worth rescue, if only for the sake of his unforgettable *legato* singing of a highly characteristic melody. The original records were respectively numbered H.M.V. DB144 and DB136.

Walter Kirchhoff and *Margaret Baumer.*—The labels of these *Götterdämmerung* excerpts are somewhat misleading. What they really consist of is the scene between Siegfried and Brünn-hilde which follows after the Norn scene at the opening of the music-drama. The so-called Vorspiel is merely the short orchestral passage heard during the change from night to morning. But never mind, it is all good to hear and, as a whole, very effectively performed. The brilliancy of Kirchhoff's voice atones in a measure for the lack of the same quality in his companion's, especially in the Oath scene, where her dramatic intelligence impresses more than her declamatory power. But then this is, at the best of times, exceedingly difficult music to do justice to through the microphone ; indeed, the orchestra has the best of it all the time. (Tautological, but true !)

Wilhelm Rode.—We have here, to put it concisely, the second of Hans Sachs's two monologues, divided into two parts. It is not marked by any notable variety of tone or expression, but I may fairly describe it as a thoroughly sound, traditional rendering. The voice has a curious hollow ring which seems to lose quality in the softer phrases ; but it is the right *basso cantante* type for the character, while the words are quite distinctly enunciated. Manfred Gurlitt's orchestra, as usual, is first rate.

Josef von Manowarda.—The weight of vocal tone and the singer's style alike contribute to a rather ponderous medium for the interpretation of Hugo Wolf. The two songs are among his best known, and they are sympathetically sung, with accurate intonation if not with impeccable steadiness. By the way, this company has yet to solve the piano problem ; it sounds like the same metallic instrument that I spoke about many moons ago.

Beniamino Gigli.—I recommend this disc for one side of it only—that which gives you *Una furtiva lagrima*. Gigli meets with ease all the difficulties that I recently indicated in connection with this air and really sings it beautifully, that is to say, with a delicious *legato* and all imaginable delicacy, tone and contrast galore, artistic in every sense. But what of *Ombra mai fù?* It is hard to believe that the same singer could have seriously intended so complete a reversal of all that Handel's famous Largo is supposed to convey. The martial recitative, the flamboyant delivery of the phrases, the noisy tone and the incessant *portamento*, in the style of a love-song rather than a tender tribute to the friendly shade of a leafy tree—all this simply converts Signor Gigli's version of the glorious air into something dangerously near to caricature.

Richard Tauber.—A duet for one voice is a decided novelty. It is also a curiosity that might, if frequently repeated, induce a sense of monotony, through the absence of those very elements of harmony in contrasted sounds that lie at the root of music. For people who are so enamoured of Herr Tauber's voice that they cannot have too much—or, should I say, too many—of it, this new presentation of two of Mendelssohn's well-known vocal duets will doubtless provide a welcome feast. It affords, when repeated three times, the delightful variety of listening first to the upper and afterwards to the lower line of the acrobatic Tauberesque combination, and finally to the ensemble of both. It is a clever device in its way if only because of the perfect synchronisation that it achieves ; but, as suggested, it is a joy that has its limitations.

John Hendrik.—Where were the ladies this month? I ask myself the question on approaching the conclusion of a task almost wholly concerned with efforts of the sterner sex. (Can it be a symptom of current supply and demand? Are the latter expected to sell better? I wonder.) My last record—a Parlophone which I notice is fitted with the automatic stopping groove hitherto restricted to H.M.V. discs—reveals yet another imitator of Tauberesque methods, in the person of a tenor with a Dutch name and a pretty voice whom I cannot remember to have heard before. He sings two characteristically Hungarian ditties from the prolific pen of Franz Léhar with appropriate Tzigàne accompaniment, and a very nice ensemble they make. The soloist is inclined to be slightly nasal, but his style is earnest and not without charm, albeit his *mezza voce* is not so pleasing as that of his model.

HERMAN KLEIN.

VOCAL

CHALIAPINE, Feodor, Bass

DB1699	**Prayer—Now let us depart** (*in Russian, with Choir of the Metropolitan Russian Church in Paris, under N. P. Afonsky*) Strokin
	Open to me the gates of repentance (*in Russian, with Choir of the Metropolitan Russian Church in Paris, under N. P. Afonsky*) Wedel
DB1700	**The Legend of the Twelve Brigands** (*in Russian, with Male Choir under N. P. Afonsky*) arr. S. Zharoff
	Down the Volga (Folk Songs of the Volga) (*in Russian, with Male Choir under N. P. Afonsky*) arr. Alexandroff

These are the first pieces sung by Chaliapine with the Paris choir of his native church to appear in this catalogue. Their resemblance to each other is only superficial. The solo voice is supreme in every instance, as it ought to be when the great Russian basso is the soloist, but M. Afonsky knows how to vary his treatment by subtle touches and how to obtain a maximum of effect from his well-trained voices. The Chant of Repentance is very solemn and devotional, as befits its grief-stricken character; and the lachrymose phrases delivered by Chaliapine are curiously contrasted with a still deeper voice sustaining a low D natural for bars at a time. The effect is strange and impressive. The Prayer has a more limited musical interest but plenty of variety, thanks to the amazing resource of the solo singer. In *The Legend of the Twelve Brigands* will be noticed the familiar theme of *Malbrouck s'en va t'en guerre*, but which of the two is the original I should not care to say. Here the solo and the choir alternate regularly and the latter sings *pp* nearly throughout. The former in the Volga folk-song dominates the mixed voices with stentorian utterances, and the rise and fall of the extremes of sound produce an extraordinary effect.

DENIS d'INES

DB4855 { Le Bourgeois Gentilhomme (Molière)—Act IV— Turkish Ceremony (Music of Lully)

It will be remembered that the first version of Strauss's opera *Ariadne auf Naxos* had for its framework this same scene in the fourth act of Molière's play, *Le Bourgeois Gentilhomme*. In the present record we have the original version of the Turkish Ceremony performed at M. Jourdain's entertainment, as given at the Comédie-Française with music by Lully, the famous Italian composer and innovator, who flourished at the court of Louis XIV at the period when Molière's brilliant genius was also in the ascendant. Here the whole of the diverting episode is in the nature of frank caricature or burlesque. The broad flatteries uttered by M. Denis d'Inés with so much unction are heard throughout the scene punctuating the no less absurd Turkish gibberish concocted or imitated by the chorus. Accompanying these are the delightful old-fashioned passages for the orchestra composed by Lully, whose dances as usual are the acme of fascinating grace and rhythm. It was a capital idea to entrust M. Charpentier, the able conductor, with the task of gathering this fragrant bouquet at "headquarters" and so preserving it for all time. The record is a most valuable example of what the gramophone can accomplish in this direction.

FLETA, Michele, Tenor

DB1746 { Jota—" La Bruja " (*with orch. and chorus*) Ramos Carrion–Chapì
Todo esta igual—" La Bruja " (*with orch.*)

The prominence given to the first—the author's—name on this label is rather misleading. The real hero is the composer, Ruperto Chapì, the gifted Spanish musician who died in 1909, leaving behind him, at the age of 58, the scores of some 170 works for the stage, operas, *zarzuelas*, and the like, whereof *La Bruja* is one of the best known. He won his reputation in the 'eighties before Albeniz rose to fame, and by many was accounted more genuinely entitled than the latter to the highest place in the Spanish music of that period. Although I hardly agree with this opinion, I confess to great admiration for Chapì's clever and ingenious use of the national idioms, a welcome example of which is forthcoming in these vocal selections from *La Bruja*. As sung with immense *verve* by Michele Fleta, and supported by the true type of Spanish vocal crowd as seen and heard in the *zarzuela* entertainment, they certainly create a desire for more from the same tuneful and characteristic source. By which, of course, I mean to indicate the works of Ruperto Chapì.

GINSTER, Ria, Soprano—

DB1870 { Zephyretten leicht gefiedert (Ye gentle breezes) (*in German*)—Act 3 "Idomeneo" (*Cond. Dr. Malcolm Sargent*) Mozart
Se il padre perdei (If I lost my father) (*in Italian*)—Act 2 " Idomeneo " (*Cond. Dr. Malcolm Sargent*) Mozart

Better known under its Italian title of *Zeffiretti lusinghieri,* the first of these numbers from Mozart's *Idomeneo* has long held a place in the hearts of soprano vocalists, if not in the catalogues of English gramophone firms. My first duty, therefore, is to thank so talented an artist as Frl. Ria Ginster for making good an important omission; my second, to assure her that her wellnigh faultless rendering of both airs will win for her a host of fresh admirers. My sole reason for not describing them as absolutely perfect is that I question the entire purity of her upward scale, and that in more than one instance: it is certainly inclined to slur. This slight fault is one to be corrected, and it is the more surprising in a singer whose technique on the whole is so free from blemish. Her tone is beautifully clear, musical, and steady; always clean on the note in an unfaltering attack. Her shake, too, is neat and even, her phrasing in the traditional Mozart style which one so seldom hears. I repeat, therefore, that it is a pleasure to find these *Idomeneo* airs, so admirably sung and recorded, occupying a place in the latest " Connoisseur's " list.

IVOGUEN, Maria, Soprano

DA4402 { (*a*) O, du liabs Aengeli (Volkslied); (*b*) Z' Lauterbach hab' i mein Strumpf verlorn (Volkslied)
(*a*) Gsatzli (Volkslied); (*b*) Maria auf dem Berge (Volkslied)

These exquisitely simple Volkslieder form a striking contrast to the astonishing vocal *tour de force* which the accomplished Hungarian soprano contributed to an earlier edition of the same H.M.V. catalogue. That was the enormously difficult Zerbinetta aria from Strauss's 1916 version of his *Ariadne auf Naxos*, in which she appeared when it was first given at Vienna and later in 1924 when she made her début in the same character at Covent Garden. Somehow I had begun to think that poor Zerbinetta was beginning to feel rather lonely among the " Connoisseurs "; but now she will be able to enjoy the companionship—free from all possible rivalry—of *Maria auf dem Berge* and the other heroines of Hungarian folk-song, including her of the Lost Stocking, who figure in this merry group. I cannot imagine specimens more enchanting of their kind nor a singer now living capable of interpreting them with an equal degree of enchantment. Maria Ivoguen's voice is, if possible, lovelier than ever, her diction and phrasing a greater miracle of charm. Her quaint staccato ornamentation right up at the top of the head register remind one of nothing so much as the unique arabesques on the walls of the Alhambra at Granada. She gave a recital at Wigmore Hall on April 8th, and sang a most interesting programme. She should have been heard at Covent Garden as well.

NEMETH, Maria, Soprano

D1717 { Ozean, du Ungeheuer! (Ocean! thou mighty monster!)—" Oberon," Pts. I and II Weber

Here is another of the exceptional sopranos for whom there seems to be no room at Covent Garden, unless (prior to the re-discovery of Eva Turner) for some abnormally high part like that of the Princess in *Turandot*. But Maria Nemeth is also a classical singer—witness her superb record of *Martern aller Arten* already in the present H.M.V. list (D2023). And now she contributes a magnificent one of *Ocean, thou mighty monster!* Hers is just the right voice for the Weber of this expansive mood, and, in addition to the strong, vibrant tone, attacking and sustaining lofty B flats that are plentiful as blackberries in autumn, she possesses the equally requisite command of a broad, noble style, variety of tone-colour, and true dramatic intelligence. Her breathing and vocal technique give her a confidence which stops at no sort of obstacle, cross-country or otherwise ; and her high C is a genuinely human outburst of jubilation, expressing precisely the joy and relief that Rezia feels when she perceives that the " mighty monster " is bearing Sir Huon to her side. That so good a singer should have provided this very necessary missing link to the sparse H.M.V. collection of *Oberon* items is distinctly a matter for congratulation.

TITO SCHIPA, Tenor

DB1723 { Sento nel cor — Scarlatti
Che farò senza Euridice (How shall I fare without Eurydice)—Act 3 " Orfeo ed Euridice " Gluck

This record is worth having for the sake of the lovely old air by Scarlatti which fills one side of it, and to which the Italian tenor imparts his well-known elegance of artistic handling. It exemplifies in a striking way, as it did in the case of Battistini, what perfect vocal training in the old school can still do to differentiate the classical type of singer from the powerful *robusto* who exploits his natural and other gifts in the melodramatic rôles of Puccini, Mascagni, and Leoncavallo. Turning to the other side of the disc I find myself out of harmony with Signor Schipa for the simple reason that I have been brought up to regard *Che farò senza Euridice* as a piece written for a contralto, like the part of Orpheus to which it belongs. That a tenor is capable of singing it I do not deny (especially if transposed up a third or a fourth, which utterly spoils it); but that no amount of careful phrasing will make it really suitable for a tenor, or indeed for any naturally cold, unemotional male voice imbued with artificial passion is clearly exemplified in the present instance. In other words, Gluck's inspired music does not fit the singer's organ, and nothing will make me believe for a moment that he is actually trying to realise the overwhelming nature of the tragedy that he is supposed to be depicting.

SCHNABEL, Therese, Soprano (*pianoforte accompaniments played by* **Artur Schnabel**)

DA1294 { Liebestreu (True Love) — Brahms
Nicht mehr zu dir zu gehen (To see you no more) — Brahms

DB1833 { Der Doppelgänger (The Wraith) — Schubert
Die Stadt (The Town) — Schubert

DB1834 { (*a*) Der Soldat (The Soldier's Execution) — Schumann
(*b*) Frühlingsnacht (Spring Night) — Schumann
Der Schatzgräber (The Treasure Hunter) — Schumann

DB1835 { Gruppe aus dem Tartarus (A group from Tartarus) — Schubert
Kreuzzug (Crusade) — Schubert

DB1836 { (*a*) An die Laute (To the Lute) — Schubert
(*b*) Der Musensohn (Son of the Muses) — Schubert
Der Erlkönig (The Erl-King) — Schubert

It is by no means easy to form an accurate judgment upon the merits and demerits—for there are both to be considered—of these interesting records. The fact that they are accompanied by Mr. Artur Schnabel and sung by his sister is, presumably, a sufficiently good reason for recommending them to the favourable notice of " Connoisseurs." Yet that alone would not be enough to "place" them without some definition of their qualities. The main point to be settled is how Miss Schnabel's

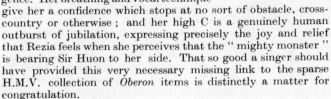

voice will strike the listener. If you like it you will like her record ; for you cannot fail to admire her art, which is thorough and absorbing in every sense. The timbre is curious—neither unsympathetic nor unpleasing, but decidedly nasal and inclined to be metallic, yet without being harsh ; in short, the kind of voice that is wholly individual and capable of intense human feeling. I ought perhaps to describe it as an acquired taste, for as I went on listening I found that it began rather to grow upon my ear ; and *that*, after all, is the supreme test. One technical defect is a prevailing tendency to pinch certain closed vowels and make them hard ; another, the almost total absence of variety in the tonal colouring, due chiefly to the dialectic twang which persists through the scale. The German, therefore, is not absolutely pure, whilst on the other hand the enunciation is so clear that every word can be plainly distinguished.

Coming to the interpretation, it must be said that Miss Schnabel is a born singer of Lieder, and gets to the heart of every song in this well-chosen group. At the same time it would be impossible to over-estimate the debt that she owes to her masterful, nay phenomenal, accompanist. The genius of the great pianist is apparent in a good deal more than mere flawless execution ; it is evident in the perfect sympathy and understanding that make him literally one with the singer. No less remarkable is the individuality that his amazing diversity of touch, now soft and caressing, now crisp and bright, now strong and commanding, enables him to impart to each of his readings. For it is, in truth, a definite reading that Mr. Schnabel brings to bear upon every song. We may have heard the *Erlkönig* and *Der Musensohn* so played before now, but never, certainly, such a rendering of the *Frühlingsnacht* or, more wonderful still, such a differentiation between right- and left-hand touch as in *An die Laute*—a gem, if ever there was one ! Such is the combination of brother and sister as I perceive it in these attractive records. They are well worth hearing.

SCHORR, Friedrich, and LEISNER, Emmi, Mezzo-Soprano

With London Symphony Orchestra cond. by John Barbirolli

DB1720 { Der alte Sturm, die alte Müh ! (The wonted Storm, the wonted Strife !) (*in German*) (In vain Fricka pleads with Wotan to avenge Hunding)—Act 2 " Walküre " — Wagner
So ist es denn aus mit den ewigen Göttern (Is all then at an end with the glory of godhood) (Fricka upbraids Wotan) (*in German*)—Act 2 " Walküre " — Wagner

With London Symphony Orchestra cond. by John Barbirolli

DB1721 { Mit tiefem Sinne, willst du mich täuschen ? (With darksome meanings would'st thou mislead me ?) (Fricka taunts Wotan) (*in German*)—Act 2 " Walküre " — Wagner
Was verlangst du ? (What demand'st thou ?) (Wotan yields to Fricka) (*in German*)—Act 2 " Walküre " — Wagner

Here on four sides we have in its entirety the scene between Wotan and Fricka from Act II of *Die Walküre*, which incidentally has for its outcome the unhappy orientation of the *Nibelungen* tragedy. If only Fricka had not interfered how differently her husband's plans might have worked out ! but she did, and so brought about all the rest of the consequences that make up the strange story of Wagner's tetralogy. Time was when this same scene of quarrelling and scolding used to be looked upon as a boring interlude. It is so no longer, especially when rendered by consummate artists like Friedrich Schorr and Emmi Leisner, with the able support of the London

Symphony Orchestra and John Barbirolli at the helm. Beyond this there is nothing fresh to be said. After Schorr's splendid work at Covent Garden last month, the gramophile will be more than ever eager to possess records of his share in the *Ring*, and I am certain that the opportunity now presented will not be neglected.

SCHUMANN, Elisabeth, Soprano

DB1845 { **Traum durch die Dämmerung** (Dream in the twilight); **Ich schwebe** (Suspense) (*in German, with piano*) R. Strauss
Mondnacht (Moonlight Night) (*in German, with piano*) Schumann

When Frau Elisabeth Schumann sings Strauss and Schumann to the piano accompaniment of her husband, Herr Karl Alwin, the result, as everyone is aware, approximates very nearly if not quite to perfection. To say so much is to say everything; there is no further need to paint the lily or gild refined gold, thereby committing a sin of which I believe myself rarely to be guilty. Only *Ich schwebe* is wholly new to me; and I commend the choice because it suits the singer extremely well. It is not a song *pour tout le monde*. As for her *Mondnacht*, which demands an absolutely faultless *cantilena*, I can only say that I have very rarely listened to such an ideal rendering. All these accompaniments are obviously done by a highly skilled artist.

ZENATELLO, Giovanni, Tenor

DB1007 { **Una vela !** (Ho ! a vessel !)—Act I "Otello" Verdi
Duet with GRANFORTE—**Si, pel ciel marmoreo giuro !** (Witness, yonder marble heaven)—Act 2 "Otello" Verdi

In this country at least Zenatello has done next to no work for the gramophone. One item only is left in the Columbia catalogue, and now this addition to the H.M.V. comes as a sort of "better late than never." For the Veronese tenor is well on in his fifties, and in October next it will be eight-and-twenty years since he helped to celebrate the 100th performance of *Un Ballo in Maschera* at Covent Garden by making his début in it. Two years later I heard him in New York at the Manhattan Opera House, where he met with even greater success. He was and still is a very fine *tenore robusto*, and, as he emphatically proves in these records, capable of investing the music of *Otello* with all the requisite power and vigour. In the first record (the opening scene of Verdi's opera) his effort is limited to the *Esultate*, which he declaims with all due energy. But better still is his spirited share in the duet of the second act, sung with Granforte; and between them the two artists make a really first-rate reproduction of the famous scene.

PHILHARMONIC CHOIR, cond. by C. Kennedy Scott
D1375 Psalm 86, Pts. I and II Holst

This fine setting of the 86th Psalm, "Bow down thine ear, O Lord," is one of two psalms for soli, chorus, strings, and organ that were published by Augeners in 1912. It belongs, therefore, to the period just preceding the appearance of *The Planets*, when the growing individuality of the young composer (already music-master at the St. Paul's Girls' School) was beginning to assert itself. Its form is practically that of an anthem, and it has an important organ solo following upon the opening choral passage. Then come short unaccompanied phrases for tenor solo and soprano choir, succeeded in turn by the soprano solo and male voices, the whole winding up with a coda for full chorus. The music represents the more orthodox style of the youthful days when Mr. Holst was under the benign influence of the Elizabethan masters, and the value of that influence is reflected in the contrapuntal skill, the pure part-writing, the easy flow, and the austere yet elegant ecclesiastical character of the whole setting. As usual, Mr. Kennedy Scott's choir is perfect, and both soloists acquit themselves creditably of a brief but delicate task.

BERLIN STATE OPERA ORCHESTRA and CHORUS

DA4405 { **O Isis und Osiris**—" Die Zauberflöte "
Mozart—L.B.
BERLIN PHILHARMONIC ORCHESTRA—Marsch der Priester—" Die Zauberflöte "
Mozart—L.B.

These two excerpts from Mozart's last opera are to be warmly commended, alike for the excellence of the instrumental and choral tone and as examples of the skill with which modern recording can be made to lend a fresh charm to old friends. Everyone knows the sedate and solemn tread of the *March of the Priests*. All Mozart-lovers, too, are familiar with Sarastro's *O Isis and Osiris*, whose broad melody delights the soul of every ambitious bass and which Norman Allin for one has enshrined with chorus in a capital Columbia record (DB9802). In the present instance the soloist is conspicuous by his absence, but the melody is all there in the voices of the chorus, precisely as we hear them in the opera, and thus Herr Leo Blech has contrived to reproduce on a single 10in. disc very nearly the whole of a familiar but lovely scene.

DONIZETTI'S " DON PASQUALE "

Don Pasquale was written by Donizetti expressly for the Parisian public and first produced at the Théâtre des Italiens on January 4th, 1843. The four principal characters were sung by four very great artists, namely, Grisi, Mario, Tamburini, and Lablache, and its success was instantaneous. The plot, of the genuine Italian *buffo* order exemplified in so many of Rossini's operas, was said to be founded on a still earlier piece, entitled *Ser Marc Antonio*, composed by Pavesi. Anyhow, the subject is familiar enough—the elderly would-be husband of a charming coquette, "beaten on the post" by a younger aspirant whom she happens to prefer. Donizetti's music is of delicious freshness and has a piquant grace that is quite irresistible. After Grisi had retired, the part of Norina was taken at Covent Garden by Patti; but the younger *diva* had previously played it at New York in 1860 (two years before) when she was a girl of seventeen. Music and character alike fitted her to perfection, and she used to revel in both. I saw her as Norina twice.

I am very pleased that H.M.V. should have secured such a splendid Scala recording of *Don Pasquale* as that now issued. It forms a worthy and important item in the new supplement to the Connoisseur's Catalogue, in which it is numbered C2519 to C2533 (twelve two-sided records). The cast is as follows: Don Pasquale, **Ernesto Badini**; Dr. Malatesta, **Afro Poli**; Ernesto, **Tito Schipa**; Notary, **Giordano Callegari**; Norina, **Adelaide Saraceni**. Chorus and orchestra of La Scala, Milan; Conductor, Carlo Sabajno.

For those who are able to follow the plot, as set forth on the covers of the album, it should be easy to appreciate the thoroughly Italian comedy of the dialogue contained in the duets and trios which, even more than the solo numbers, constitute the bulk of this delightful score. Almost without exception they are exceedingly well interpreted, and they communicate in a wonderful degree the spirit and humour of a stage performance. In this latter sense the recording is a very remarkable one. As a sample, I would instance the quartet that concludes the second act, which I have never heard more crisply sung. Don Pasquale's "patter" in this is one of Badini's gems. The tenor solos could hardly have been in safer hands than those of Tito Schipa, who is artistic in everything he does. His *Bella siccome un angelo* is particularly elegant. Adelaide Saraceni is, of course, thoroughly at home in a part like Norina; she is one of the leading *soprani leggieri* of the Italian stage of to-day and an extremely clever *comédienne* into the bargain. Her voice, if a trifle thin, is amazingly flexible, and it stands out clearly in all the ensembles. Her chief air, *So anch' io la virtù*, is not unworthy of comparison with the Galli-Curci recording; while the famous duet in the third act, *Tornami a dir* (DA1161) is here shared with the same excellent tenor in Tito Schipa. Altogether this album of *Don Pasquale* leaves nothing to criticise or be desired.

DEBUSSY'S "PELLÉAS ET MÉLISANDE"

One's first thought on glancing at this album was to regret that only "selected passages" of Debussy's opera should have been recorded ; one's second thought to approve the wisdom of the idea. The drama of Maeterlinck is no more conventional in form and treatment than Debussy's music, and, without the optical aid of the stage action, the combination could easily become monotonous before the end was reached. In the shape here presented it is anything but that ; for all the essential features, both of story and music, are compressed into the seven records, and the interest is cleverly carried on. Another point. The instrumental (10in.) and the vocal (12in.) records are kept separate, so that they can be played in turn as indicated in the note on the work printed on the album cover. (They are respectively numbered E603–5 and D2083–6.) Played in their proper order they really comprise a sufficiently complete sequence and afford a very satisfying idea of what this unusual opera is like. No airs ; no set pieces ; nothing but lovely tone-pictures and poetic dialogue allied to exquisitely colourful and expressive music. For my own part, I find the whole thing delightful, and all who know the opera well will, I am sure, agree with me.

Only three characters are represented, viz. : Mélisande, **Yvonne Brothier** ; Pelléas, **Charles Panzera** ; and Arkel, **Willy Tubiana** ; that of Golaud being omitted. It would serve little useful purpose to describe in detail the various scenes depicted in the selections. Suffice it to say that they have all the beauty and significance that could be derived from a flawless performance. I have never heard Debussy's realistic musical colloquies sung with greater delicacy, with greater purity of diction, or with a fuller measure of vocal charm. In some respects, indeed, the work of Mlle. Brothier and M. Panzera excels that of the original interpreters—and I could pay them no higher compliment. Equally admirable is the rendering of the instrumental excerpts under the experienced direction of M. Piero Coppola, while from first to last I have failed to discover any blemish in the recording.

Herman Klein.

OPERATIC AND FOREIGN SONGS

ELISABETH SCHUMANN (soprano).—**Heidenröslein, Lied im Grünen** and **Du bist die Ruh'** (Schubert). In German. Piano acc. by **Karl Alwin**. H.M.V. DB1844, 12in., 6s.

THEODORE CHALIAPINE (bass).—**Chanson du départ, Chanson du Duc, Chanson à Dulcinée** and **Mort de Don Quichotte** (Ibert), from the film "Don Quixote." In French. Orchestra conducted by the composer. H.M.V. DB1310 and 1311, 10in., 4s. each.

JAN KIEPURA (tenor).—**Ninon, smile at me just once,** and **O Madonna!** (Kaper-Jurmann-Rotter-Marischka) from the film "A Song for You." In German. Orch. acc. under **Dr. Weissmann**. Parlo. RO20221, 10in., 4s.

JOSEPH SCHMIDT (tenor).—**Why do you pass me by?** (Niederberger-Heller) and **Once I believed in your love** (Lewinnek-Karlick). In German. Orch. acc. under **Otto Dobrindt**. Parlo. R1528, 10in., 2s. 6d.

RICHARD TAUBER (tenor).—**Humoreske, Op. 101, No. 7** (Dvorak-Lengsfelder-Intrator) and **Le Cygne** (Saint-Saëns-Balan). In German. Orch. acc. under **Dr. Weissmann**. Parlo. RO20220, 10in., 4s.

GEORGES THILL (tenor).—**La Maison grise** from **Fortunio** (Messager-De Caillavet-De Flers) and **Elégie** (Massenet). In French. Orch. acc. under **Pierre Chagnon**. Columbia LB10, 10in., 4s.

BENIAMINO GIGLI (tenor).—**Lucia, Lucì** and **'A Canzone 'e Napule** (De Curtis). In Neapolitan. With **Members of La Scala Orchestra**, Milan. H.M.V. DA1292, 10in., 4s.

Elisabeth Schumann.—Disc space is well economised in the recording of the three Schubert lieder which Frau Schumann here sings with so much delicacy and taste. The chief faults to be pointed out, apart from a certain breathlessness here and there, concern the enunciation of the words, and these are due largely to the fact that in the singer's estimation vowels are all-important ; consonants have to take second place. Too many sibilants are clipped and glossed over or else missing altogether, while final letters like the "m" and "n" in *im Grünen* might as well not be there. The tone is lovely everywhere throughout, and so it ought to be, for everything is sacrificed to it, especially in *Du bist die Ruh'*. Happily, however, the exquisite purity of the phrasing remains immaculate, and the tone-colour is nicely varied to fit the poetic idea. Needless to say, Karl Alwin's accompaniments display his wife's art in its most favourable light.

Theodore Chaliapine.—The music of the *Don Quixote* film is not, in my opinion, its strongest feature, nor was it perhaps expected to be ; but it is exceedingly characteristic and clever, and wonderfully so, considering how quickly it had to be put together. (I have been told that Ibert was positively the only Frenchman who could have written it in the time.) The present records give the four principal pieces—I hardly like to describe them as songs—sung by Chaliapine, and I have no hesitation in saying that they gain immensely by being heard separately from the film. Their Spanish character, which is extremely marked, comes out far more strongly, as does also the bizarre quality of the orchestration, which can hardly be fully appreciated in a cinema theatre. The modernistic touch that flavours the whole setting also becomes more apparent in the gramophone version. It is not necessary to dwell on M. Chaliapine's rendering of these *morceaux*. Enough that they were written for him, that the style, like the voice, is peculiar to his genius, that he makes them as interesting as it is possible to make them. No one else could execute this music with the same mastery of exotic Eastern flourishes or the same wealth of Russo-Spanish sentiment. You must hear, too, the flamboyant martial rhythm and rugged emphasis that he bestows upon the declamation of the fascinating *Chanson du Duc*, which is far superior as music to the weird lament that inexplicably issues from the mouth of the departed Don Quixote after the burning of his beloved books.

Jan Kiepura.—Here is more vocal film music, this time from *A Song for You*, with the young Polish tenor for its protagonist. It is of a very different type from that just described, being entirely Viennese in character and of the up-to-date light opera sort peculiar to Léhar and his imitators. The tunes are sung with plentiful animation and purity, an abundance of energetic appeal being combined with the brighter *nonchalance* of the Duke in *Rigoletto*, particularly in the *Madonna* record, which winds up with a stirring *tra-la-la* refrain. Dr. Weissmann's orchestra is in support.

Joseph Schmidt.—Viennese music once more, of the same easily recognisable light opera sort. Neither air tells us anything new, therefore ; but the voice and mood of the singer seem to be exactly what is required, and the talent of the artist is too well known to need description. He is quite as much at home in light as in serious opera, and knows how to make the best of a Strauss-like waltz.

Richard Tauber.—I remarked recently that this popular singer had taken to fitting well-known instrumental melodies with words and giving them the benefit of his unique vocal touch. The device is now a favourite one with many artists, and I daresay it has proved quite a commercial success. Anyhow, the melodies are sure of warm acceptance and I imagine there are no royalties to be paid on their use—a double recommendation. Both Dvorak and Saint-Saëns would, I am sure, have appreciated the compliment had they been alive ; but then these tributes are only paid to the dead. In each case the Tauberesque method is delightfully employed.

Georges Thill.—Massenet's *Elégie* will soon need a rest. It has been somewhat overdone of late. Still, it is not often sung with such steady, sympathetic, musical tone as in this record, nor are the words as a rule enunciated so beautifully. The other song, from André Messager's graceful opera *Fortunio*, is very sweet and tender, and M. Thill brings out its charm with his customary artistic perception. I consider his record the best that I have heard this month.

Beniamino Gigli.—Often as he reminds me of Caruso, the gifted Beniamino never does so more than when he is singing the attractive Neapolitan ditties of De Curtis. These are, I fancy, the two latest specimens, and it is quite wonderful how they contrive to offer variations on themes that are " old as the hills." But, like the ancient Gaelic tunes played by the pipers, if you love them you never grow tired of them. Gigli is now the greatest living Neapolitan minstrel, and, as everyone knows, in things of this sort he is at once incomparable and irresistible. These two records will be heard on every self-respecting gramophone throughout the country, and I predict for them a tremendous vogue with B.B.C. listeners, who always lap up the cream of such examples when presented through the medium of certain popular recitals that I know of. The voice in them is beautiful, and should need no further amplification from the control room.

HERMAN KLEIN.

OPERATIC AND FOREIGN SONGS

SYDNEY RAYNER (tenor).—**Première Caresse** (Crescenzo) and **Mattinata** (Leoncavallo). In French. Piano acc. Decca M437, 10in., 2s. 6d.

BENIAMINO GIGLI (tenor).—**Santa Lucia,** Neapolitan Folk Song (Cottrau). In Italian. Orch. acc. under **John Barbirolli.** And **Mamma, quel vino è generoso,** Turiddu's Farewell from **Cavalleria Rusticana** (Mascagni). In Italian. With **Members of La Scala Orchestra, Milan,** under **Carlo Sabajno.** H.M.V. DB1902, 12in., 6s.

JOSEPH SCHMIDT (tenor).—**Santa Lucia** (L. Gordigiani) and **Mattinata** (Leoncavallo). In Italian. Orch. acc. under **O. Dobrindt.** Parlo. R1550, 10in., 2s. 6d.

Tell me to-night from the film **Tell Me To-night** (Spoliansky-Marcellus Schiffer) and **Good-night, pretty Signorina** (Niederberger-Heller). In German. Orch. acc. Parlo. R1565, 2s. 6d.

HÉLÈNE REGELLY (soprano).—**Invitation to the Waltz** (Weber-Emile André). In French. Orch. acc. Parlo. R1563, 2s. 6d.

RICHARD TAUBER (tenor).—**Ständchen** (Richard Strauss, A. F. Von Schack) and **Dream in the Twilight** (Richard Strauss, Otto Bierbaum). In German. Orch. acc. under **Dr. Weissmann.** Parlo. RO20222, 10in., 4s.

Sydney Rayner.—This is a month of tenors and doubles; and a very meagre display, too, for the delectation of readers of this column. I cannot say that the appetite for tenor records grows by what it feeds upon, but for the moment there would seem to be few other varieties in demand. I can only hope that the lull is purely a temporary one. Meanwhile, its strangest feature is the clash in different quarters between issues of well-known—and well-worn—Italian ditties like *Mattinata* and *Santa Lucia*. What is the reason, I wonder? Has our boasted development of musical taste and culture resulted, so far, in nothing better than a burning desire to revel in delights of the kind here illustrated? Surely not. Yet the demand must exist or the supply would not be forth-

coming. Well, be it so—until better times are again with us.

The Franco-American tenor, whose name stands at the head of our modest list, sings Leoncavallo's tuneful *canzone* in excellent French, and couples with it a taking *romance* by Crescenzo that is, I believe, very popular in Paris at the present time. He sings both with clear, vibrant tone; the voice is always sympathetic and in the middle of the note, while the violin obbligato is discreetly introduced. It is interesting to compare the French rendering of *Mattinata* with the Italian one by Gigli noticed below, and each has points to recommend it.

Beniamino Gigli.—A precisely similar difficulty awaits me in dealing with Gigli's *Santa Lucia* and that sung by Joseph Schmidt. (Really, it is too bad to have to enter into these invidious comparisons; but I am naturally not responsible for " doubles " when they occur in this provoking way; nor are they so profitable as a winning one on the " Tote.") The two renderings are quite unlike each other, and it is not to say that I do not care for Joseph Schmidt's because I have a preference for Beniamino Gigli's. The latter takes his *Santa Lucia* rather more *con moto*, as it ought to be, and the Italian tenor also lends it more variety than the Viennese because he sings each verse with a different kind of voice—the second with a curious sort of *falsetto* which I have never heard him use before. This contrast makes the old Neapolitan melody sound very attractive, while the sustained beauty of the Gigli tone does the rest. By the way, the old folk-song was not composed by two different people, as the names might suggest. Gordigiani was responsible for one version or arrangement and Cottrau for the other. That is, I believe, the correct explanation; and Cottrau wrote the orchestral accompaniment played under John Barbirolli. Turiddu's tearful appeal to his mother, which Gigli sings on the reverse side of the disc with a Scala orchestra under Carlo Sabajno, can seldom have had a more touching delivery. I cannot recollect ever hearing him in the part; indeed, he has never sung it here.

Joseph Schmidt.—I think there is no more to be said about *Santa Lucia* and *Mattinata*, as given in this artist's record. than has already been comprised in my preceding remarks. Both are capitally sung in Italian, with an orchestra conducted by O. Dobrindt. The second record contains melodies of the latter-day Viennese type now so tremendously in fashion. One of them is from the film *Tell me to-night*, to which I believe the song gives its name. Anyhow, it is extremely effective and the singer renders it with his customary *brio*.

Hélène Regelly.—At last it has occurred to an ingenious French musician to utilise for vocal purposes the fascinating *Invitation à la Valse* by Weber, which Berlioz orchestrated so cleverly nearly a century ago. The adaptation may not be equally masterful, but it has been done with skill and a good eye for variety of treatment—just enough singing to more or less appropriate words where the voice can tell best, alternating with a spoken line or two and then the orchestra alone. Altogether the soloist, who has a charming voice, makes a very pleasing impression with her " invitation."

Richard Tauber.—It is always gratifying to find evidence of reaching out to higher things in a singer of obvious intelligence and talent, whose methods, no matter how great the popularity they may have won for him, have ofttimes laid him open to serious criticism. In these two well-worn songs by Richard Strauss, as rendered by Richard Tauber, there is everything to be admired and little or nothing to find fault with. Indeed, I have never heard them better sung by a man, or with greater taste and delicacy by a woman either. We all know the charm of the voice and the easy control of varied gradations of tone-colour, but what is comparatively new is the beauty of the phrasing and the remarkable delicacy and reticence shown in the matter of *portamenti*. The strong contrasts recall the lieder style of Leo Slezák and the articulation of the syllables is equally distinct. I only hope there will be as wide a public for these as for Herr Tauber's long series of efforts in the region of Viennese light opera as exemplified by the older Strauss.

HERMAN KLEIN.

OPERATIC AND FOREIGN SONGS

LAURITZ MELCHIOR (tenor).—**Prize Song** from **The Master-singers** (Wagner). With **The London Symphony Orchestra** under **John Barbirolli.** And with **A. REISS** (tenor), **Siegfried forges the sword** from **Siegfried** (Wagner). In German. With **The London Symphony Orchestra** under **Albert Coates.** H.M.V. DB1858, 12in., 6s.

RICHARD TAUBER (tenor).—**The Ratcatcher's Song** (Neuen-dorff–Engelhardt) and **Ma Curly-headed Baby** (Clutsam-Henzen). In German. Organ acc. Parlo. RO20223, 4s.

JOSEPH SCHMIDT (tenor).—**A Song goes round the world** and **Don't Ask** from the film **A Song goes round the world** (May, Neubach). In German. Orch. acc. under **O. Dobrindt.** Parlo. R1582, 2s. 6d.

Lauritz Melchior.—Walther von Stolzing does not figure among the greatest of Lauritz Melchior's Wagnerian assumptions. Neither does *Die Meistersinger* fill anything near the prominent space in the H.M.V. Connoisseur's Catalogue that we find allotted to the *Nibelungen* generally and to *Siegfried* in particular. The only example by Melchior from the Nuremberg opera, so far, has been the first of the so-called Trial Songs—that which begins *Am stillen Herd in Winterzeit* (DA1227). If no newer record was available, it seems to me that the latter would have been a more appropriate selection to couple with the present recording of the *Prize Song* than the *Forging Song,* which (DB1690) forms part of the *Siegfried-*Melchior collection. This combination evoked unfavourable criticism from a correspondent who wrote so long ago as May 10th complaining that the reverse side of DB1858 was " merely a reprint of one part of a previous *Siegfried* set, with a very abrupt ending." He considered this " a little unkind " ; but I would point out, on the other hand, that the *Forging Song* is an unusually fine specimen of Melchior's talent, and, in a purely vocal sense, superior to his rendering of the *Prize Song,* which lacks both poetry and contrast. The smooth *legato* and pure, easy tone so essential for Walther's improvisation seem altogether beyond the singer's reach.

Joseph Schmidt.—There is no denying the efficacy of the film as a medium for spreading the popularity of songs such as these, or of the gramophone for " rubbing in " the tunes after the film has done its work. It is a sort of " Here they are, and you can go on repeating them if you want to till the record is as worn out as the melody." In essence there is little difference to be observed in the structure and character of all these things ; but now and then you come across a variation that is clever enough to lend a touch of novelty and so increase the chances of success. Of these two ditties sung by Joseph Schmidt, *Don't Ask* (a strange version of the German title, *Frag ich*) is notable for one or two up-to-date rhythmical changes as piquant as they are brief, but the other never gets beyond the limited confines of an ordinary military march, which a tenor of Schmidt's calibre easily makes effective, while a few added high notes do the rest. I will not say that the singer has much opportunity for the display of his real powers in either. What **there** is to be done with them, however, he certainly accomplishes.

Richard Tauber.—You must not look here for the redoubtable Richard in his superior or " lieder " mood, which I had occasion to draw attention to with some admiration a month ago. There is no scope for such display in the present instance. This particular *Ratcatcher's Song* is not of the Hugo Wolf species—far from it ; being nothing more than a sentimental ballad of ancient German type, wherein the melancholy *Rattenfänger* bewails his lowly and miserable lot. Evidently business was bad with him ; he had not had the good luck to come across a town like Hamelin, where the community happened to be worried by a plague of rats, musk or otherwise. One asks, why not try Shropshire ? Quite as little suited to the real Tauberesque genius is the negro lullaby entitled *Ma*

Curly-headed Baby. The best feature of it is the warbling of the refrain, and that because there are no words to it. For **a** German the term " curly-headed " is simply untranslatable.

Herman Klein.

COLUMBIA ABRIDGED OPERAS

Economy and convenience are highly important considerations in most things, but especially so where the collection of operatic albums is concerned. The possession of the entire work is a desirable luxury for the gramophile who can afford it, and he must not be discouraged from indulging his commendable hobby. On the other hand, there must be many who find the luxury in question too expensive to be frequently enjoyed, and it is, for such, more particularly that the abbreviated versions may be welcomed as a godsend. They contain the pick of the basket, and they represent a discriminating choice from among the salient features of the score. These remarks apply with peculiar aptness to the abridged editions of *Il Trovatore* and *Carmen* just issued by Columbia. In either case there is just enough to satisfy the cravings of the ardent opera-lover and as rich a feast as can reasonably be looked for in a dozen full records, and an hour of delightful reminiscences. The original albums were issued—*Il Trovatore* in February 1931, and *Carmen* in November 1932, and duly noticed in these pages. The respective casts included : (1) **Bianca Scacciati** as Leonora, **Francesco Merli** as Manrico, **Enrico Molinari** as the Conte di Luna, **Giuseppina Zinetti** as Azucena ; and (2) **Aurora Buades** as Carmen, **Ines Alfani Tellini** as Micaela, **Aureliano Pertile** as Don José, **Benvenuto Franci** as Escamillo, and **Aristide Baracchi** as Morales. These names require no further recommendation at my hands, and indeed the singing and recording in each instance are entitled to the warmest eulogies. I might, of course, give a list of the particular numbers that are included in the two selections, but it is hardly necessary to occupy space with these, because, as I have said already, they comprise the best and, if really needed, they can be found in the latest Columbia catalogue. There is only to add that both albums were prepared with the aid of the finest talent that Milan can supply, namely, the chorus of La Scala and the Milan Symphony Orchestra, under the admirable direction of **Cav. Lorenz Molajoli.**

Herman Klein.

✳   ✳   ✳

Metropolitan Opera Company.—The newly-formed Metropolitan Opera Co. (London) will open its tour at the Streatham Hill Theatre on September 11th. It is under the direction of Mr. Robert Parker, the well-known basso, and consists mainly of the principal artists recently associated with the English Covent Garden and Carl Rosa Companies. To these, however, must be added the names of several distinguished British singers whose co-operation will lend a tower of strength to the undertaking. Indeed, it may be fairly anticipated that the performances of the new troupe will surpass in all-round merit any that have been given in English either in London or the provinces in recent years. It will travel with an orchestra of 50 and a chorus of the same strength ; the conductors being Messrs. Albert Coates, Aylmer Buesst, Robert Ainsworth, and Charles Webber. The repertory at the outset is to consist of Wagner operas only, viz., *The Mastersingers, The Flying Dutchman, Lohengrin,* and all four dramas of *The Nibelung's Ring,* but later on it will be greatly extended. The highest price for seats will be 8s. 6d., and the scale downward in proportion, so that a strong bid is to be made for popular support. With an enterprising and energetic man like Mr. Parker at its head, there is every reason to anticipate a solid and permanent success for the new venture.

Herman Klein.

OPERATIC AND FOREIGN SONGS

LUISA TETRAZZINI (soprano).—**Caro nome** (from Act 1 of **Rigoletto** (Verdi) and **Una voce poco fà** from Act 1 of **Il Barbiere di Siviglia** (Rossini). In Italian. Orch. acc. H.M.V. DB1979, 12in., 6s.

BENIAMINO GIGLI (tenor).—**Chanson Indoue** from **Sadko** (Rimsky-Korsakov). In French. And **Triste Maggio** (V. de Crescenzo). In Italian. Orch. acc. H.M.V. DA1307, 10in., 4s.

LULA MYSZ-GMEINER (contralto).—**The Stars** and **Death and the Maiden** (Schubert). In German. Piano acc. Decca PO5077, 10in., 2s. 6d.

JOSEPH SCHMIDT (tenor).—**O Paradiso** from Act 4 of **L'Africaine** (Meyerbeer). In German. And **Penso** (Tosti). In Italian. Orch. acc. Parlo. R1593, 10in., 2s. 6d.

EMMY BETTENDORF (soprano).—**The Flower Waltz** from **The Nutcracker Suite** (Tchaikovsky). In German. With **Chorus and Grand Symphony Orchestra.** Parlo. R1605, 10in., 2s. 6d.

GITTA ALPAR (soprano).—**I Live for Love, A Girl Like Nina, Madeleine's Soliloquy** and **I think I'm in Love with my Wife** from **Ball at the Savoy** (Abraham, Grünwald, Beda). In German. Orch. acc. Parlo. RO20224 and RO20225, 10in., 4s. each.

RICHARD TAUBER (tenor).—**I've found my Heart** and **Give me your Heart** (Tauber, Faber). And **Don't Complain** and **At Every Time** from **Lilac Time** (Schubert). In German. Instrumental acc. Parlo. RO20226-7, 10in., 4s. each.

FERNANDO GUSSO (baritone).—**Luna d'estate** (Tosti). Piano acc. And **Dicitencello vive!** (Falvo-Fiore). Piano and violin acc. In Italian. Decca M443, 10in., 2s. 6d.

GIUSEPPE LUGO (tenor).—**Me grimer** from **Pagliacci** (Leoncavallo) and **O douces mains** from **La Tosca** (Puccini). In French. Orch. acc. under **Florian Weiss.** Decca DE7023, 10in., 2s. 6d.

ALFONSO ORTIZ TIRADO (tenor).—**Cancione, Florecita,** and **Te quiero dijiste** (Maria Grever). In Spanish. Orch. acc. H.M.V. B4497, 10in., 2s. 6d.

THE HABIMA PLAYERS.—**Elijah the Prophet** and **At the Wailing Wall, Jerusalem.** In Hebrew. Columbia DB1186, 10in., 2s. 6d.

SYDNEY RAYNER (tenor).—**Che gelida manina** from **La Bohème** (Puccini) and **Improvviso di Chénier** from **Andrea Chénier** (Giordano). In Italian. Orch. acc. Decca T205, 12in., 3s. 6d.

Luisa Tetrazzini.—A great deal of nonsense has been heard and written recently about the talented prima donna who set London and New York by the ears during the early years of the century. Candour compels one, however, to acknowledge that her day has gone, and all attempts to resuscitate it will be futile save with the aid of the gramophone. Tetrazzini is the first of her sex to be accorded the benefit of the revivying process that has brought fresh life and enhanced

vigour to the records of Caruso. Herein H.M.V. have, as usual, shown discretion in their choice ; and their field is large enough for mistakes to be easy. But the fair Luisa *did* sing *Caro nome* and *Una voce* with extraordinary *verve*, and with a splendid persistence in the finest traditions of the old Italian school—there can be no doubt about that. Hence the desirability of preserving in the one and only possible way these fine examples of her voice and skill at their best. The task of amplifying her brilliant tones and dazzling vocalisation has been well accomplished and the fresh orchestration fits, on the whole, with satisfying accuracy. The more successful of the two, if choice there be, is the *Una voce*, whereof the original (DB690) was recorded, according to the " historic " catalogue, in 1908. In this the grace and charm of the phrasing is remarkable, while the cadenzas and the *fiorituri* generally are executed with a clearness and purity rarely to be heard nowadays.

Beniamino Gigli.—It is a pleasure to hear the *Chanson Indoue* from *Sadko* sung by a tenor, for which voice it was originally written by Rimsky-Korsakov. It was so rendered, I remember, in the all-Russian performance at the Lyceum not long ago, though not altogether with the rare distinction of quality and vocal *maestria* that the Eastern air receives in this new Gigli interpretation. Had the popular Italian only taken the same pains to avoid slurring the principal melody (as Kreisler did in his paraphrase, for instance) that he has done to define with clearness the chromatic descent of all the semiquaver groups in the refrain of this lovely song, his rendering would have been absolutely ideal. As it is, it will most certainly delight your ear. The *Triste Maggio* of Crescenzo recalls the manner of Paolo Tosti. It works up through several melodious climaxes to a powerful ending, producing some characteristic examples of that rich, dark tone in which Gigli revels, in strong contrast to the lighter sort that he uses in the *Chanson Indoue.*

Lula Mysz-Gmeiner.—It is a very long time since we had any of the records of this eminent contralto, whose name suggests a Slavonic nationality of some sort. Her voice has a very individual quality, and her almost whispered *mezza-voce* (another of those that suggest Leo Slezák's) is used with clever effect in Schubert's *Death and the Maiden* to represent the friendly and soothing attitude of Death. One is not so familiar with *Die Sterne*, but it is delightful Schubert through and through and ought to be more widely known. In both lieder the singer is " atmospheric " and interesting.

Joseph Schmidt.—In spite of his marked nasal tendency, this singer's voice pleases most people, and I learn that the sale of his records in Great Britain is on the upward grade. His style is broad and free from affectation, his intonation pure both in the upper and lower registers. Evidence of this is palpable in the great air from *L'Africaine* (not *Africana*, please, if Meyerbeer had any say in the matter !), which has seldom had better justice done it since the days of recording began. There is likewise a high B in the Tosti song—orchestrated with an appropriate tambourine obbligato—that is well worth hearing. The air from Korngold's opera, *The Dead City* (yet to be heard in London, though quite popular abroad and in America) has a tender appeal that makes it rather touching, especially as Schmidt sings it, and the high *tessitura* throughout has no terrors for him. He cannot, however, rescue from dullness the quasi-religious piece, *Blessed are they who are persecuted*, from Wilhelm Kienzl's tedious opera, *Der Evangelimann*, which Augustus Harris's successors produced at Covent Garden in 1897. It fairly sent me to sleep then, and might easily do the same again.

Emmy Bettendorf.—Unfortunately the soloist plays but an insignificant part in this oddly-arranged version of the waltz from Tchaikovsky's *Nutcracker Suite*. As a whole I consider it a good idea spoilt in the execution. The noisy, assertive male chorus is wholly superfluous. For the greater part of the time it enters only to drown the solo voice—the enchanting tones of Emmy Bettendorf deserve better usage—and, were it not that the orchestration is Tchaikovsky's, intact from first to last, I should feel inclined to complain that it showed no consideration whatever for the singer. But, *voilà*, it was never intended to accompany a singer, or for any vocal purpose whatsoever, and it leaves you wholly unable to appreciate the co-operation of a gifted artist whose lack of opportunity here reduces her to silence most of the time. The male choir has far more to do ; and one only wishes it had not. " Alfy's " words are, of course, consistently inaudible. Nevertheless, those who love their *Nutcracker* waltz will probably admire and enjoy the whole thing.

Gitta Alpar.—Not having seen *Ball at the Savoy*, I am not in a position to appraise at their full value these four examples of the unique art of Gitta Alpar, but that does not prevent me from perceiving how clever, how fascinating they are. Her talent is of an order that admits of plentiful imitation, but none that really hits the mark. She possesses the *vis comica* in a supreme degree, and yet in her serious moments she can draw tears. Her control of vocal inflections is quite amazing, and they are some of them as quaint as they are characteristic, yet free from vulgarity. The open tone in the lower register and the utterance of the *parlato* bits provide both humour and contrast ; they surprise you and make you smile, nay, laugh outright. Everything is sung with tremendous *en train*. The sentimental songs, such as *Madeleine's Soliloquy*, are mostly tears and sighs, while the lively ones simply carry you away. Every word of the German text can be plainly distinguished, and as a whole the four pieces are examples of faultless recording. By the way, the title, *I think I'm in love with my wife*, seems to me mis-translated. The German words run " I have a husband who loves—and kisses me." How can this be ? But happily it does not really matter.

Richard Tauber.—Our *Lilac Time* visitor sings a couple of very pleasing songs which he appears to have composed himself, and I am glad to add that he interprets them with exemplary taste and feeling. The words, by Marianne Faber, discuss an ancient theme with simplicity and poetic sentiment, and are thoroughly adapted to the needs of the Tauberesque style alike musically and vocally. The rich, baritone timbre with which they are sung is all to the good. The two songs from *Lilac Time*, also given in German, are not of equal merit. *Don't complain* sounds exactly as it should—light, airy, and charming ; *At every time*, somewhat over-amplified, sounds ponderous and even strained, especially in the concluding phrases of each verse. We have been used to hearing this exquisite music sung, as the violins play it in its original shape, lightly, delicately, and without forcing the tone. What a blessing that Herr Tauber's command of effect can make his listeners forget even when he is overdoing things.

Fernando Gusso.—A baritone with a pleasant, sympathetic voice, whose manner only requires a little more animation to make him a highly agreeable singer. It is just this lack of life and vigour that results in a rather dull rendering of Tosti's *ballata*. The other song has more " go " and seems to benefit accordingly.

Giuseppe Lugo.—Why an Italian tenor, and an excellent one at that, should choose a French text for singing Puccini, I fail to understand. It may be true (as the label states) that he is engaged at the Opéra-Comique, but that fact does not make his French accent any better than it sounds in the mouths of most Italians. I feel sure that these excerpts from *Pagliacci* and *Tosca* would have been even more successful had Signor Lugo rendered them in his native language. Anyhow, he sings very sweetly and has an engaging manner.

Alfonso Ortiz Tirado.—Here is a Spanish tenor who sticks to his mother tongue and eschews the operatic in favour of the latest *Canciones* of his country. The present examples, by Maria Grever, are extremely piquant, being purely Spanish both in rhythm and character without being over-sentimental. The singer's organ is well trained and sufficiently flexible to do justice to melodies that punctuate the dance tunes after the fashion made familar to us by the broadcast band-warblers. Only Señor Tirado has a genuine voice, not a " whiffle," and his vocal efforts are well worth listening to.

Sydney Rayner.—This American-born French tenor continues to make progress. His voice, after deducting a goodly percentage for amplification, is gaining in power, volume, and resonance ; his style has more assurance and breadth than when we first heard him. He sings Rodolfo's air with considerable variety of tone-colour and very properly treats it as a declaration of love as well as of the pride that becomes a fully fledged poet. His high C has the right quality and is taken with ease. Truth to tell, his French in this seems to bring out a finer timbre of voice than his Italian in the *Andrea Chénier*. Such is the effect of the language which the singer is most accustomed to using—and Mr. Rayner's French is now, I must admit, unusually good. Altogether this is a capital record, and the *Che gelida manina* is particularly satisfying.

The Habima Players.—The monologue sung by Rowina by the Wailing Wall at Jerusalem is an interesting example of an Eastern survival that is not in itself beautiful. It cannot be described as music, for there is none in it ; but, as a prolonged outburst of well-nigh unbearable misery and despair, it constitutes a remarkable *tour de force*, and as such may possibly make a strong appeal to Hebrew ears. In olden times it might have induced a gentle application of the Egyptian lachrymal bottle. Quite otherwise is it with the "Folksong from the Golem," apostrophising Elijah the Prophet in a slow, mournful crescendo from a *pp* beginning to a powerful climax. This is a comparatively modern setting of a beautiful melody for women's voices, supported by a deep undercurrent of *bouche fermée* tone for the men. It is pure synagogue music, faultlessly intoned by the singers, quite admirably recorded, and achieving an effect of extreme beauty.

COLUMBIA ABRIDGED OPERAS

Trovatore and *Carmen* in abbreviated album form have been quickly followed by *Aida* and *Madame Butterfly*. The former pair were noticed by me last month, and the latter are now also available. The popularity of all four operas is so worldwide that the demand for them in this convenient shape is sure to be very large. There is nothing new for me to say concerning their merits, which have been abundantly attested by their success in the complete form. Enough that the present selections are from the same source, the casts and the records (six from each collection) being identically the same. Both the *Aida* and *Madame Butterfly* albums were issued at intervals of a month from each other towards the close of 1929, exactly four years ago, having been preceded shortly before by *La Bohème*. In each instance I gave an account of the history of the opera, and for those I can now only refer the reader to the back pages of THE GRAMOPHONE. The gem of the *Butterfly* recording remains in my estimation the Cio-Cio-San of Rosetta Pampanini, the best representative of the part in a vocal sense since Emmy Destinn. Her rendering of *Un bel dì* is irreproachable and completely fulfils Puccini's concept of that difficult air. The singing of the chief parts in *Aida* is no less worthy of unqualified admiration, and both operas are splendidly conducted by Cav. Lorenzo Molajoli.

HERMAN KLEIN.

ADDITIONS TO THE H.M.V. CONNOISSEUR CATALOGUE

VOCAL

BENDER, Paul

C2591	{ Erlkönig	Loewe
	Edward	Loewe

The quaint, masterly ballads of Carl Loewe, I am glad to see, continue to hold their own among the corner-stones of the edifice of German song. They are not forgotten; nor are they likely to be. My first acquaintance with them goes back to Eugen Gura; then came George Henschel and Reichmann; later on, Richard Mayr (of Baron Ochs fame) and Paul Bender. The last two are now probably the finest exponents of Loewe still active and before the public, and, as we are all allowed our preferences, I take Bender as the more subtle and impressive of this pair. His rugged tones seem to have been intended by nature for the interpretation of the weird and supernatural, albeit capable of softening their roughness when required to the expression of a deep and glamorous tenderness. These extremes he illustrates with his Kaspar in *Der Freischütz* and his König Marke in *Tristan*, and the same gift enables him to characterise as he does the different voices in the *Erlking* and *Edward*. The completeness of the changes is incredible in its swiftness and descriptive force. His control of breath and vocal colouring is marvellous; hence the singular picturesqueness and value of these records, enhanced as they are by the admirable piano accompaniments of Michael Raucheisen.

FRIJSH, Povla

DA1325	{ L'Hiver and	Koechlin
	La Pluie	Georges
	Pendant le bal	Tchaikovsky

DA1324	{ Med eu vandlitje	Grieg
	Dans les ruines d'une Abbaye	Fauré

By birth a Norwegian, Povla Frijsh is a soprano vocalist of unusual distinction. She owns a voice remarkable for its purity and sweetness, and her style is marked by an individuality that imparts new interest to her readings. She sings chiefly in a soothing *mezza-voce*, but can rise when occasion requires to a clear, penetrating volume of tone. Pleasant to relate, her French accent is irreproachable, so that in these songs of Fauré, Koechlin, and Georges the charm of her diction can exert its full sway. In Grieg's delicious *Water-Lily*, which she takes more slowly than the composer used to, one marvels at the smoothness of her sustained legato; and exactly similar criticism applies to her rendering of the familiar Tchaikovsky song. Yet with both she weaves a spell so potent that one regrets when the end comes and it has to be broken. Her accompaniments are played with the requisite delicacy, though now and then with a greater use of both pedals simultaneously than seems really advisable. A voice so lovely when it is *dans les nuages* has no need of extra cloudiness from the pianoforte. I predict an admiring crowd for this singer's records.

GIANNINI, Dusolina

DB1937	{ Von ewiger Liebe, Op. 43, No. 1	Brahms
	Immer leiser wird mein Schlummer, Op. 105	Brahms

DA1319	{ Heimliche Aufforderung, Op. 27, No. 3	R. Strauss
	Ständchen, Op. 17, No. 2	R. Strauss

Whether willed by choice or force of circumstances it is not for the writer to say, but the fact seems to be that Sgra. Dusolina Giannini is growing more and more a lieder singer and less and less of an opera singer. So much the greater opera's loss—a conclusion arrived at after hearing her in private a short time ago and strengthened by a study of the present H.M.V. records. German education and training could alone have helped her to acquire the ease and sureness with which she attacks Brahms and Strauss, pronouncing the text accurately, entering fully into its meaning and spirit, and phrasing her sentences with the freedom of the born native (which she is not). In these four songs one perceives, moreover, a strong sense of contrast; notably in *Von ewiger Liebe*, where it is indispensable and where it is cleverly allied with a strong dramatic element. The *Immer leiser* is neatly phrased, and its atmosphere of urgent, weary yearning is well reflected in a voice that retains its luscious beauty through every shade of passion, subdued or otherwise. These extremes are always admirably controlled, as witness the Strauss songs, the first of which is all *laissez aller*, while the second, the *Ständchen*, is just as light and delicate in texture until at the very end out comes the *grand jeu*.

GINSTER, Ria

DB1877	{ Die Mainacht, Op. 43, No. 2	Brahms
	Seligkeit and Rastlose Liebe	Schubert

DB1874	{ Wiegenlied, Op. 49, No. 4 and	Brahms
	Maria Wiegenlied, Op. 76, No. 52	Reger
	Wiegenlied, Op. 105, No. 2	Schubert

DB1926	{ Wiegenlied, and	Mozart
	Wiegenlied, Op. 98, No. 2	Schubert
	Treue Liebe, Op. 7, No. 1 and	
	Botschaft, Op. 47, No. 1	Brahms

DA1326	{ Ach ich fühl's, from Act 2 of "Die Zauberflöte"	Mozart
	Non so più, from Act 1 of "Le Nozze di Figaro"	Mozart

Here is a lieder singer whose work can only be judged by the highest standard—the standard of a Marcella Sembrich, an Elena Gerhardt, an Elisabeth Schumann. Her voice may be lighter in calibre than theirs, less beautiful when used at full pressure; but it has a sensuous charm of its own, an immaculate purity that never deteriorates when ranging from a *mezza voce* to a *mezzo forte*; it is always a pleasure to listen to her singing alike on the radio or at the gramophone. Her command of tone-colour and variety of *nuances* might be greater certainly; but she has well-developed powers of expression and undoubted interpretative skill. She is heard to best advantage in the lighter songs of Schubert, but, as will be seen from the present selection, certain lieder by other masters are thought to hold an equally prominent place in her repertory.

Thus the first group begins with *Die Mainacht* of Brahms, which receives an interesting rather than an ideal rendering. The opening is delightful, but the second passage, *Uber-hüllet vom Laub*, is sung loudly, instead of *piano* as Brahms marked it, and so nullifying the succeeding *crescendo*. Again, the long phrase on *Und die einsame Thräne* is taken too slowly to be sung (as it should be) in a single breath. Still, these are comparative trifles and they do not disturb the calm flow of profound sentiment, the significance whereof is enhanced by the refined articulation of every syllable of the poem. *Seligkeit* is not one of the most familiar of Schubert's songs, but *Rastlose Liebe* is; and both are gems, more particularly as presented here. The waltz theme of the former is so fascinating that one wonders how it escaped the net of *Lilac Time* (or did it? I am not sure); and the accompaniment of Gerald Moore is a joy.

The second might be called the *Wiegenlied* group, comprising as it does the little masterpieces in that form of Brahms, Reger, and Schubert. It does not, however, exhaust Frl. Ginster's list of treasures in that direction, seeing that in DB1926 she includes two that are even more famous. Whether Mozart ever wrote *Schlafe, mein Prinzchen*, is a question that need not trouble us at this time of day; probably he did not, but who cares? Still more entrancing in its simplicity and grace is Schubert's setting of *Schlafe, holder süsser Knabe* (words by Claudius), with which it is coupled on the same side of the record, the other being devoted to Brahms's *Treue Liebe* and *Botschaft*. How well the singer succeeds in lending the right qualities of delicacy, refinement, and feeling to all these songs that suit her so well may be gathered from what I said of her art at the outset.

In the singing of the two Mozart arias—or rather, perhaps, only in the supremely difficult *Ach, ich fühl's* (*Ah, lo so*)—may be discerned some tiny blemishes of style and treatment. For example, the *appoggiature* should have received a stronger accentuation; the important semitones in upward progression have not the clear definition that a violinist would give them; the descending intervals to notes in the medium register are not always as perfectly in tune as they might be. The timbre of the voice in *Non so più* is hardened nearly throughout by excessive amplification; still, that is not the singer's fault, whereas the mistake of pronouncing the Italian *e* like a German *i* can be laid only at her door. Yet, as I have said, these are but trifling spots on the sun of an admirable record. Excellent, too, are the orchestral accompaniments to both airs, conducted respectively by Oskar Holgar and Dr. Malcolm Sargent.

KIPNIS, Alexander, and Berlin State Opera Orchestra

D2088
{
Die Verleumdung, sie ist ein Luftchen, from "The Barber of Seville" Rossini
Il lacerato spirito, from "Simon Boccanegra" Verdi
}

It is to be hoped that gramophonists will recognise under its German title of *Die Verleumdung* our old acquaintance *La Calunnia*, that gem of vocal caricature wherein Don Basilio solemnly depicts for the benefit of Dr. Bartolo the horrible effects that can ultimately result from a mere breath of scandal. How wonderfully Chaliapine has realised the humour of Rossini's masterly setting everybody knows, but I am glad to be able to express the opinion that in this record Alexander Kipnis fairly runs a dead-heat with the great Russian. In the matter of voice there is nothing to choose between them, and we get the same amazing *crescendo* together with the same terrific *colpa di cannone* in its German equivalent. We even seem to behold, with the aid of a little imagina-

tion, Rosina's lanky tutor slowly rising from the ground with arms outstretched and the alarmed Dottore staring at him with bulging eyes. It is all so very realistic in a musical sense. The *Lacerato spirito* is one of the finest bass airs of Verdi's middle period, and Kipnis renders it with a rare wealth of tone and expression, supported by the half-whispered *Miserere* of a capital chorus swelling up to a telling climax. The whole record, therefore, is full of interest.

RETHBERG, Elisabeth, and Giacomo Lauri-Volpi

DB1341
{
Pur ti riveggo, mia dolce and La tra foreste vergini (from Act 3 of "Aida") Verdi
}

DB1458
{
Ah No! Fuggiamo! (from Act 3 of "Aida") and with Giuseppe de Luca Verdi
Ma divina (from Act 3 of "Aida")
}

It is generally agreed, I think, that Aida is the finest of the limited number of rôles in which Elisabeth Rethberg has been heard in London. Be that as it may, she is unquestionably entitled to rank with Adelina Patti, Teresa Stolz, Emmy Destinn, and Lillian Nordica among the greatest of all Aidas. So much the more valuable, then, are these records of her scenes, first with Radamès, afterwards with both lover and father, from the third act of the opera. I am delighted to welcome them at the present time as evidence that there is no falling off in the freshness and power of an exceptionally beautiful voice or in the control of an art that has found thousands of admirers on both sides of the Atlantic. In these days of perfect recording there is little more to be said, except on the technical side, and one imagines that Hayes would be willing to allow all credit in that respect to go to a trans-atlantic *atelier*. In any case, it is H.M.V. once more that we have to thank for a rich operatic treat; for here we have not only an unsurpassable Rethberg, but, in Lauri-Volpi and de Luca, a tenor and a baritone worthy in the fullest degree to be associated with her. They make a magnificent trio.

TASSINARI, Pia, PAULI, Piero, and Members of La Scala Orchestra, Milan

DA1322
{
Tardi si fà and
Sempre amar! (from Act 3 of "Faust") Gounod
}

TASSINARI, Pia, and Members of La Scala Orchestra, Milan

{
L'Altra notte in fondo al mare (from Act 3 of "Mefistofele") Boito
and with Piero Pauli
O soave fanciulla (from Act 1 of "La Bohème") Puccini
}

DB1933   The Jewel Song (from Act 3 of "Faust") Gounod

At first glance it seems odd to find a group (on four sides of two discs) of well-worn numbers from Gounod's *Faust* included in the select company of a Connoisseur's Catalogue. But on further reflection one asks, Is not this opera a *chef-d'œuvre* that will live; and, given a performance of quite exceptional merit, is it not that, rather even than the music itself, which entitles the new records to their place in this honourable list? To begin with, Italy owns at the moment no finer singers of their type than Pia Tassinari and Paolo Pauli, a lyric soprano and tenor both in the very foremost rank. To hear them sing Gounod's immortal love duet is no ordinary pleasure; for their voices, apart from their opulent richness and charm, are free from the blemishes that disfigure so many modern Italian efforts, and they blend to absolute perfection. Again, in the *Jewel Song* Pia Tassinari shows herself quite on a level with her most distinguished sisters of the French school. Which is saying a great deal, since it implies that everything in the armoury of her art is beyond reproach. The *King of Thule* ballad reveals a glorious tone, together with rare simplicity of delivery and faultless diction, while the vocalisation of the valse is brilliant in the extreme. Praise equally high must be bestowed upon her rendering of the dungeon air from *Mefistofele* —it has imagination and power, added to a full measure of tragic feeling that recalls the unforgettable genius of Christine Nilsson in this scene (would that that, too, could have been recorded for the gramophone !). Finally, the duet which ends Act I of *La Bohème*, given on the same disc, is lifted to an unwonted plane of excellence by the union of two artists who have the merit of appearing to be as inspired before the microphone as they are upon the stage. They are splendidly supported throughout these selections by the orchestra of La Scala, conducted by Franco Ghione.

LA MAÎTRISE DE LA CATHÉDRALE DE DIJON

DB4893 { **Ave Verum**
{ **Ave Coelorum Domina**

DB4894 { **Kyrie, Orbis Factor**
{ **In this Holy Temple.** Psalm 150

DB4895 { **Crux Fidelis**
{ **Ubi est Abel**

DB4896 { **Kyrie I** and **Christe** (from "Missa Assumpta est")
{ **Suite du Kyrie et Agnus** (from "Missa Assumpta est")

DB4897 { **Sanctus** (from "Missa Assumpta est")
{ **Benedictus** and **Hosanna** (from "Missa Assumpta est")

DA4846 { **Kyrie** (from "Messe pour le temps de l'Avent")
{ **O Benigne** (from "Prose Exulta felix Divio")

For the benefit of readers who may not be aware of it, let me state that the word *Maîtrise*, in the sense here used, means " a house where the children of the choir receive their lessons from the *Maître de Chapelle*." It also means, obviously, the choir itself—and a famous one, too ; for the rare qualities of the choir of the Cathedral of St. Bénigne, at Dijon, are known throughout the length and breadth of Catholic France. There, we are told, " the art of polyphonic singing has been raised to the utmost perfection " ; and in the minds of all who listen to these records there will be no doubt whatever about the truth of that statement. They were made, not in the cathedral itself, but in the Festival Hall of the old Palace of the Dukes, in the presence of the Bishop, the Mayor, the venerable Mgr. Moissenet (former director of the choir), and Monsieur J. Samson (a lay member), its present trainer and conductor.

I understand that the six 12in. records comprised in the above series are to be published separately in an album, and for this some very helpful and informative notes on the music have been prepared by the able pen of Mr. Peter Latham. With their aid the enquiring gramophonist can learn in a few lines the essential story of that marvellous growth and development of polyphonic church music whereto these choice examples from the sixteenth-century masters bear such eloquent witness. We have heard most or all of them at the Albert Hall, sung by the Sistine Chapel and other foreign choirs, but not, I am bound to say, with the same exquisite purity of tone, impeccable intonation, or wonderful clearness of detail, that emerges from the work of these Dijon singers. The full choir numbers 120, half of them boys from eight to ten years old, the other 60 young seminarists who take the lower parts. Their tone, as a whole, is less " dark " than that of our English boys, but not nearly so " open " as that of the Spanish and Italian children ; in fact, it presents a happy medium between the two types. The attack is precise and definite, the phrasing clean, the parts well balanced ; the flow of the counterpoint is smooth and unhalting, the gradual *diminuendos* from full voice to an ethereal pianissimo must be heard to be appreciated— nay, believed. These slow, measured *nuances*, breathing the essence of tranquil repose, occur nowhere else as in the incomparable early masterpieces of the schools here represented ; nor should I wish to hear them more ideally performed.

To particularise further would occupy too much space.

The selection is well made to illustrate the various styles embodied in the classical *répertoire* of the Dijon singers, and it rightly proceeds with an upward advance from the four- and five-part early examples of Josquin des Prés until the climax is attained in those taken from Palestrina's immortal Mass, *Assumpta est Maria*, all for six-part choir. Whatever follows music such as this must of necessity be in the nature of an anticlimax ; yet, in saying as much, I fancy M. Samson will not accuse me of being ungracious, in view of the eulogies that I have been compelled to lavish upon him and his wonderful boys. Their achievements will assuredly fill a prominent niche in the gallery of the Connoisseur's collection.

THE WESTMINSTER SINGERS

B4425 { **The splendour falls on castle walls** — Odell
{ **It's oh! to be a wild wind** and — Elgar
{ **Feasting I watch** — Elgar

The inclusion of English part-songs and their singers in this list has come none too soon. We are justly proud of both, having had good reason to be so since the Elizabethan days that saw their birth. As then, as now, they stand *hors ligne* in their own category. The present specimens, well sung by a representative and admired vocal quartet, constitute a modest but satisfactory beginning to what ought to be a numerous and worthy contribution, if the demand for such records proves as adequate as it should. For my own part, I can listen to this kind of unaccompanied singing with no less enjoyment than to the more elaborate product sent us by the Männergesangverein of Vienna, or even the Maîtrise of Dijon Cathedral. *The splendour falls on castle walls*, from the pen of Frank Odell, is a part-song written in the best traditions of the English school ; that is to say, it is musically, cleverly harmonised, and replete with adroit effects.

The Westminster Singers do it something more than justice, as indeed they ought, seeing that they faithfully prepare all their work under Mr. Odell's direction. At any rate, the " effects " all come off with unfailing certainty. The two Elgar pieces are executed in the same finished manner. They belong to the composer's Op. 45, a set of *Five Partsongs* for male voices, words from the Greek Anthology ; and although first published in 1922, really date from about the same year as the *Coronation Ode* (1902), which came not long after *The Dream of Gerontius*. They reflect the ripening vigour and individuality of the Elgar of that period. Alike in an artistic and a technical sense, these Westminster records allow no loophole for adverse criticism.

HERMAN KLEIN.

OPERATIC AND FOREIGN SONGS

LOTTE LEHMANN (soprano).—**O why so long delay?** from **The Marriage of Figaro** (Mozart) and **Psyche wandelt durch Säulenhallen** from **Die toten Augen** (d'Albert). In German. Orch. acc. Parlo. RO20229, 10in., 4s.

EMMY BETTENDORF (soprano). — **Stéphanie Gavotte** (Czibulka-Alfy) and with **HERBERT ERNST GROH** (tenor) **Autumn Song** (Tchaikovsky-Alfy). In German. With **Grand Symphony Orchestra.** Parlo. R1633. 10in., 2s. 6d.

STILES ALLEN (soprano).—**One fine day** from **Madame Butterfly** (Puccini) and with **EDWARD HALLAND** (tenor) and **EDWARD LEER** (bass), **Final Trio** from **Faust** (Gounod). In English. Orch. acc. Edison Bell 5603, 10in., 1s. 6d.

HEDDLE NASH (tenor).—**Your tiny hand is frozen** from **La Bohème** (Puccini) and **Serenade** from **The Fair Maid of Perth** (Bizet). Orch acc. In English. Columbia DX540, 12in., 4s.

RICHARD TAUBER (tenor).—**Every day is not Sunday** (Clewing-Ferdinands) and **I greet you, my beautiful Sorrento** (Waldmann-Heyse). In German. Orch. acc. Parlo. RO20228, 10in., 4s.

JOSEPH SCHMIDT (tenor).—**Yes, you alone** from **La Vallière** (von Mory-Bibo) and **The King's Page** (Goetze-Rheinberg). In German. Orch. acc. Parlo. R1634, 10in., 2s. 6d. And **Española** (Serrano). In Spanish ; and **Wenn du treulos bist** (Benatzky). In German. Orch. acc. H.M.V. B8033, 10in., 2s. 6d. And **O sole mio** (di Capua-Bock) and **La Paloma** (Yradier). In German. Orch. acc. Broadcast 3139, 10in., 1s. 6d.

HEDWIG VON DEBICKA (soprano), **ELSE RUZICZKA** (contralto), **HELGE ROSWAENGE** (tenor), **KARL NEUMANN** (baritone), and **The Berlin State Opera Orchestra and Chorus** under **Alois Melichar.** Excerpts from **The Tales of Hoffmann** (Offenbach). In German. Decca PO5079-81, 10in., 2s. 6d. each.

Lotte Lehmann.—Whether this distinguished artist has or has not ever undertaken the rôle of Susanna in *Le Nozze di Figaro* I am unable to say. Probably she has ; but certainly not since the youthful days of her operatic career, and then she must have made a delightful representative of the character. Anyhow here she is (as our London Editor would say) rendering with all her youthful charm the German equivalent of *Deh vieni, non tardar*, and giving a valuable lesson to some of her less experienced rivals in the art of true Mozart singing. The tone throughout is firm and clear ; the phrasing characterised by all her wonted purity of style and diction ; the reading replete with expressive fervour and the sense of longing that words and music so fully convey. I would add with satisfaction that nowhere is there a trace of the noisy intake of breath that used formerly to mar this singer's recording of sustained music. The shortcoming has entirely disappeared. The air on the reverse side is from Eugen d'Albert's opera *Die toten Augen*, a much later work then his better-known *Tiefland*, but on the Continent very nearly as popular. It was produced at Dresden in 1916. The piece is melodious and cast in quite a simple, orthodox shape, but not remarkable for its originality. As sung by Fr. Lehmann with her accustomed lyrical grace and feeling, it cannot fail to please.

Emmy Bettendorf.—When Czibulka brought out his *Stéphanie Gavotte* years and years ago—before "royalties" supplied the wherewithal for one's daily bread—he was probably rewarded with a few gold pieces for a piece that was to sell by the million copies in every corner of the habitable globe. The publishers must have made a fortune out of it until the copyright ran out. But little did Czibulka dream that one day his graceful tune would be warbled by a famous operatic soprano to words by an Austrian versifier devoted to this line of business. Such is, however, the fact ; and it is also true that the art of a gifted singer like Emmy Bettendorf redeems the whole thing from the level of a mere ordinary compilation. To many, I dare say, the old gavotte will thus reappear with all the charm of novelty, and a very pleasant experience they will find it. Personally, I like better still the other side of the disc, where the same artist introduces her delightful talent, in conjunction with that cf Herbert Groh, in an ingenious arrangement of Tchaikovsky's *Autumn Song*. The two voices mingle most agreeably, and the artistic quality of the whole combination is decidedly above the average. Even the irrepressible violin obbligato comes in at the right places and does not outstay its welcome. Altogether a well-made record.

Stiles Allen.—The impression gained from a careful hearing of this latest rendering of *One fine day* is that Miss Stiles Allen has looked upon it in the light of an ordinary operatic aria and completely ignored its descriptive nature. Which is a distinct pity, because if she had studied the text more closely she would have perceived that Butterfly's vision of Pinkerton's return (never to be realised) calls for absolutely dramatic treatment. As it is, the singer relies solely for her effect upon the intrinsic beauty of her tone, which is undeniably great, though scarcely sufficient in itself for the needs of this particular "fine day." The value of the disc will, I think, be chiefly discovered in the celebrated trio from the last act of Gounod's *Faust*, which occupies the other side. Here Miss Allen's powerful tones are heard at their best, and she has two admirable coadjutors in Messrs. Edward Halland and Edward Leer. Between them, save only as to the very last notes, they make the trio go with capital spirit.

Heddle Nash.—To the procession of recording tenors there is apparently no end. I think they must outnumber the sopranos and contraltos put together. There must be a reason for this ; but it would take too long to go into here. One can be the more grateful to those of the "elect" who find among their opera scores something fresh to sing, and Mr. Heddle Nash has provided a welcome quasi-novelty in the *Serenade* from Bizet's *Fair Maid of Perth*, which opera was produced at the Théâtre-Lyrique, Paris, in 1867, and for the first time in English at Manchester by Thomas Beecham in 1917. A foolish adaptation of Scott's novel and inequalities in a clever score are jointly responsible for the neglect into which the work has fallen ; but this is one of its most tuneful pages, and I am glad to find that it has been rescued from oblivion over here by a singer who can render it with effective smoothness and grace. It is in a minor key and the touch of Eastern colour will not fail to be noted. The much more familiar *Tiny hand* from *La Bohème* is likewise ably given, though, alas, the very finest vocalisation can no longer reimbue the delicate phrases with their pristine freshness.

Richard Tauber.—This singer sets his own standard and we measure him up accordingly. Whenever he is in serious mood his voice sounds dark and baritonal ; and it does so in these apparently very earnest love-ballads, which are quite of the Tauberesque type that has proved so acceptable to a large portion of the globe. They enable him to plead his cause with an irresistible appeal. At least one imagines that to the feminine heart it must prove so, especially when the degree of musical effect is not of inferior quality. The *mezza voce* ending to *Every day is not Sunday* suggests a delightful week-end when Sunday does arrive, and the greeting to Sorrento has tremendous swing.

Joseph Schmidt.—Since writing last of this tenor's records I have heard him in London in a short broadcast recital, but I must admit to no greater advantage than in his gramophone work, on which he would find it hard to improve. Of his present contributions I admire the two airs from *Tosca,* for the reason that his tone is, as usual, much purer when heard through the Italian than the German language. Otherwise there is little comment called for. I like particularly his *Recondita armonia* because he phrases it with an effortless breadth; and his *E lucevan le stelle* because of the absence of fuss in taking the more strenuous passages. But both are really well sung. So, too, are *O sole mio* and *La Paloma,* despite the touch of nasality which either the text or the tune, or both, bring in their train. But still it is something to be able to get a first-rate record of them for eighteenpence. It needs a singer of this calibre to do justice to a song with an extended *tessitura* such as *Yes, you alone.* The music also shows some attempt at originality; and there precisely is where it is superior to its very conventional companion piece with the long title. The German words are distinctly enunciated, but they are not apparently intended to depict matters of real importance.

In the H.M.V. record Joseph Schmidt provides further evidence of his versatility. *Española* is a sparkling *cachucha* of the joyous Spanish type that Sullivan has used so happily in *The Gondoliers.* In this sample, however, a genuine high tenor is required, for it simply bristles with B flats, and it is quite astonishing to hear the splendid ease with which they are reached and sustained by the singer. He enters thoroughly into the spirit both of this and of the sentimental Hungarian-Neapolitan ballad with the German title. Taken for all in all, you have here a full and "fruity" record that ought to give you satisfaction.

Berlin State Opera.—Although Offenbach wrote *The Tales of Hoffmann* for the Paris Opéra-Comique and not for a German or Austrian opera house, it is just as well that we should have an authentic gramophone performance of so popular a work from a first-class German source. It will be understood, of course, that the whole of it is not contained in these four Decca-Polydor discs; but they do actually give us as much as we want, their total content being very nearly the same as that of an ordinary abridged album. What is of even greater importance, the singing is of the high order to be expected from the Berlin State Opera, where the conductor, Herr Alois Melichar, has taken care to provide the best material at his disposal. The net result is some fine all-round work from singers of repute like Helge Roswaenge (tenor), Hedwig von Debicka (soprano), Else Ruziczka (mezzo-soprano), and Karl Neumann (baritone); in addition to the famous chorus and orchestra of the B.S.O. The excerpts include part of the *Prologue,* the *Doll's Song,* the *Barcarolle,* and nearly all the other tit-bits in the score, while the recording is fully up to the mark.

CHORAL

FESTIVAL OF ENGLISH CHURCH MUSIC.—**Coronation Anthem** (Parry) and **God Save the King.** Two hundred and sixteen choirs under **Dr. Sydney Nicholson.** Organ acc. by **Dr. Ernest Bullock.** Columbia DX541, 12in., 4s.

ST. GEORGE'S CHAPEL CHOIR.—**For all the Saints** and **The Church's One Foundation** (Descant by C. Hylton Stewart). Cond. by **Rev. E. H. Fellowes, M.A.** Columbia DB1206, 10in., 2s. 6d.

COLNE ORPHEUS GLEE UNION.—**The Pilgrims' Chorus** from **Tannhäuser** (Wagner) and **The Lord shall reign** from **Israel in Egypt** (Handel). In English. Cond. by **Luther Greenwood.** Regal-Zono. MR1045, 10in., 1s. 6d.

Church Music Festival.—The opportunity for a choral recording on what may be called the Handel Festival scale at the Crystal Palace last July was not likely to be missed by Columbia, who have given special attention in recent years to big events like this. In one sense the Festival of English Church Music, given under the direction of Dr. Sydney Nicholson, embodied a new undertaking—one that may have far-reaching effects upon the progress of choral music in the cathedrals and larger churches of this country. Otherwise, in its nature and character, the gathering of the 216 choirs, as represented to the number of 4,000 voices, achieved the climax of its labours upon a now-familiar plan, doing so, I may add, in a manner that was immensely creditable to all concerned. For the truth of that assertion the present record speaks emphatically enough. It exhibits alike in tone and execution an ensemble of the best traditions of English Choral training.

The work upon which these efforts are focussed was happily chosen for the purpose. It is the *Coronation Anthem* that the late Sir Hubert Parry wrote for the crowning of King Edward VII in Westminster Abbey on August 9th, 1902, and which was then conducted by Sir Frederick Bridge, the organist of the Abbey. The text is derived from Psalm 122, "I was glad when they said unto me," and the choral setting (here divided into two parts) is largely based upon these broad, noble phrases of which the composer of *Judith* was so consummate a master, interspersed with a liberal sprinkling of the "Vivats" which the boys are, according to custom, called upon to ejaculate at these solemn functions. The important orchestral portions of the score were, of course, allotted at the Crystal Palace to the organ only, and performed with splendid effect upon the new instrument by Dr. Ernest Bullock. I need not dilate upon the executive merits, much less the grand body of refined tone displayed by this magnificent choir, which the marvels of modern recording fortunately allow to be preserved upon this and the three discs reviewed on page 187 of our last month's number.

St. George's Chapel Choir.—Here again Columbia have to be thanked for a welcome addition to the collection of gramophone anthems and hymns that can be enjoyed for their own sake, as well as requisitioned for school and other religious services. They are based upon two of the best-known and best-loved hymns extant, to wit, *The Church's One Foundation* and *For all the Saints,* and the records were made in St. George's Chapel under the careful guidance of the Rev. E. H. Fellowes, M.A.,

Mus.Doc., the well-known writer and authority on Elizabethan vocal music. The treatment of the two hymns is virtually identical, the third verse in each instance being sung *pp* and *a cappella*, with a discreetly added " descant " by C. Hylton Stewart which can do little, however, to enhance the simple beauty of tunes such as these of S. S. Wesley and Vaughan Williams. I fancy the voices generally might have had a brighter ring, and the balance between men and boys is too frequently to the advantage of the former ; nevertheless, the observance of light and shade is worthy of the choir's reputation, as are also the accuracy of attack and intonation.

Colne Orpheus Glee Union.—Both ambition and creditable achievement are once more manifest in these records from the Colne Parish Church. To bestow unqualified praise would be stretching a point, since in each instance a larger body of voices is actually needed. *The Lord shall reign*, from Handel's *Israel in Egypt*, includes the gigantic double chorus *The horse and his rider*, which, as we know, is a task of Handel Festival proportions, though not essentially dependent upon an army of singers. Nor does excess of energy invariably compensate for lack of numbers, either in this or in the *Pilgrims' Chorus* from *Tannhäuser*, where it is impossible to conceal even the tiniest departure from the pitch. Still, the singing, if unequal, is everywhere meritorious.

ENGLISH SONGS, ETC.

BEN DAVIES (tenor).—**Tom Bowling** (Dibdin) and **Come into the garden, Maud** (Balfe). Columbia DB1205, 10in., 2s. 6d.

HAROLD WILLIAMS (baritone).—**When the Harvest's in** (H. E. Wright–T. C. Sterndale Bennett) and **The Merry-go-round** (E. Lockton–A. F. Tate). Columbia DB1204, 10in., 2s. 6d.

ROY HENDERSON (baritone).—**Leanin'** (Sterndale Bennett) and **The Fortune-Hunter** from **Bow Bells** (Dickson-Willerby). Piano acc. Decca F3665, 10in., 1s. 6d.

Ben Davies.—Following, not unworthily, in the footsteps of Sims Reeves and Edward Lloyd, the eminent Welsh tenor does well to give occasional proof at the microphone of his undiminished ability to show the world how those bygone heroes of English song were wont to treat their theme. In this instance he recalls a couple of Sims Reeves's most famous efforts, and I can pay him no higher compliment than to say that he does so faithfully and well, whilst adding here and there an individual touch of his own. His voice remains marvellously young and fresh and reveals not a little of its power and resonant timbre. No one now living can impart the old-fashioned flavour to these songs—notably *Tom Bowling*—in anything like the same degree.

Harold Williams.—Here are two jolly songs of their good British sort, which no doubt make as strong an appeal to-day as they ever did, especially in those distant homesteads of our far-flung Dominions where they bring back (" in the gloaming " and otherwise) a precious memory of unforgotten early days in the homeland. Mr. Harold Williams himself came from those parts, and he knows in a vocal sense exactly what such songs require.

Roy Henderson.—One criticism, however, I would offer which applies equally to Mr. Williams and Mr. Henderson. It is that they do not adopt a sufficiently easy, colloquial style for simple and unpretending ballads such as Sterndale Bennett (he of the " entertaining " present era, not his distinguished forbear) provides them withal. They never heard Santley, I know ; but if they had done, I fancy they would have imitated his natural, unaffected way of pronouncing his language in these ditties—with or without dialect. Their words are too solemn, their diction too ultra-refined, for anything below the level of oratorio. A love-song is not necessarily the story of a tragedy. Both in *Leanin'* and *The Fortune-Hunter* Roy Henderson's tone gives unalloyed pleasure.

TOM BURKE (tenor).—**My Moonlight Madonna** (Webster-Fibich) and **Gipsy Fiddles** (Wrubel). Orch. acc. Broadcast 3346.

ROBERT NAYLOR (tenor).—**I know a lovely garden** (d'Hardelot) and **Love is mine** (Gartner). Instrumental acc. Parlo. R1622, 10in., 2s. 6d.

JOHN McCORMACK (tenor).—**Love's Roses** (Broones). Piano acc. by composer. And **My Moonlight Madonna** (Fibich, arr. Scotti). Piano acc. by Percy Kahn. H.M.V. DA1341, 10in., 4s.

RICHARD CROOKS (tenor).—**Until** (Teschemacher-Sanderson) and **A little love, a little kiss** (Ross-Silescu). Orch. acc. H.M.V. DA1337, 10in., 4s.

WALTER GLYNNE (tenor).—**A Soldier's Farewell** (Kinkel) and **When other lips** from **The Bohemian Girl** (Balfe). In English. Orch. acc. H.M.V. B4340, 10in., 2s. 6d.

PETER DAWSON (baritone).—**Punjaub March** (Payne) and **With Sword and Lance** (Starke). Orchestra and Chorus. H.M.V. B8015, 10in., 2s. 6d.

PAUL ROBESON (bass).—**Blue Prelude** (Bishop) and **Swing along** (Cook). Piano acc. H.M.V. B8018, 10in., 2s. 6d.

Tom Burke.—In *My Moonlight Madonna* one may perceive signs of the influence of Richard Tauber ; but it may be due to the fact that Fibich's popular melody is the kind of Strauss-like waltz-air that the immortal Richard proffers so generously. It is none the worse for that ; only somehow I prefer *Gipsy Fiddles* because it evokes more of the manly, natural style that characterised the Tom Burke of the *Bohème* period.

Robert Naylor.—This young tenor deserves and wins hearty approbation, for his voice is as true and genuine as his style is unaffected and sincere. Moreover, he sings a nice type of ballad, if not precisely a new one, and the treatment of Guy d'Hardelot's *I know a lovely garden* with *obbligati* for violin and 'cello lends it a novel aspect. A similar arrangement of *Love is mine* adds to the effectiveness of a capital song.

John McCormack.—We are not getting so many records from this favourite tenor as of yore. So much the worse for his myriads of admirers, whose appetite will be whetted rather than satisfied by this latest addition to the list. It comprises exactly two songs of the ordinary modern ballad type. One of them is the *Moonlight Madonna*, by Fibich, which for some reason has caught the fancy of the waltz-loving crowd, but is obviously (in this key) much too low for Count McCormack to show off the beauty of any but his baritone register. On the other hand, his voice is happily resonant in every part of its compass ; and he knows it. His words, as usual, are faultlessly underlined, never a syllable being lost, and he has the skill to be able to impart significance even to poor stuff like *Love's roses*. But how much better it would be if he set the example of singing better songs !

Richard Crooks.—It is surprising that recital-givers and gramophone artists pay so little attention to the matter of key-contrast. These two songs, which cannot either of them afford to lose a grain of effect, are bound to suffer, if played together, through being in the same key. In other respects the singer brings out all that is effective in them. His voice in *Until* is turned on at the full. I observe that the words for *A little love, a little kiss*, were written by my old friend Adrian Ross, who died only the other day. I wonder whether the music was written to fit them or they to fit the music ? The latter, anyhow, sounds very Hungarian, and in that spirit, by turns lively and sentimental, it is brightly interpreted. But why, Mr. Crooks, go up a whole octave to produce a *falsetto* on the final cadence ? That sort of thing " isn't done."

Walter Glynne.—Two conspicuous faults have already more than once been pointed out in the singing of this promising tenor. And he has them still. One is the extreme " whiteness " of his *voix blanche*, the other his excessive distortion of his English vowels. Yet, with the aid of a little resolute study, both errors would be easily remediable ; and that should be well worth while for a clever artist who has the sense not to allow success to spoil him. To mispronounce the stilted words of the late Poet Bunn in *When other lips and other hearts* brings the whole thing dangerously near to caricature.

Peter Dawson.—These capital marches for military band have been neatly fitted with words that carry the tune, as our American friends say ; and the soloist's splendid voice and diction safely manage the rest. A large proportion of band, naturally ; but no one will grumble at that, because there is also a goodly amount of Peter Dawson.

Paul Robeson.—Gifted with a pure, rich, natural voice, and commanding a style of unsurpassable breadth and nobility, it is no wonder that this artist stands where he does in the esteem of the public of two hemispheres. There is no need to ask what he is singing ; he knows exactly what will suit him, and his choice is good enough for those who listen. Here, for instance, he has made no approach to a mistake. The tune of *Swing along* will haunt you long after that wonderful voice has finished it ; and so will the slow, even tread of the march-like *pizzicato* bass in the accompaniment of the *Blue Prelude*, against which the soloist steadily maintains his characteristic melody.

THE VICTORIAN QUARTETTE.—Kind is my Mary (Richardson) and **Eileen Alannah** (Marble-Thomas). Regal-Zono. MR1039, 10in., 1s. 6d.

NORMAN ALLIN (bass) and **RAYMOND NEWELL** (baritone). —**Descriptive Ballad, Shipmates o' Mine,** including **The Spanish Maid, Drake goes West, Sea Shanty, Hearts of Oak, Jutland, The Battle, Glory of the Sea, Hymn for Sailors** and **Finale.** With the **Debroy Somers Band and Chorus.** Columbia DX550, 12in., 4s.

The Victorian Quartette.—I would recommend these four singers still further to improve their work, which shows considerable ability and promise, by paying more attention to their balance of tonal strength. At present the soprano and tenor are unduly prominent—possibly because theirs are the best voices of the group. The words also need more careful and unanimous enunciation, while a real *pp* would be much appreciated. These improvements once effected (and they are worth trying for), I see no reason why four such good vocalists should not step confidently and successfully into the operatic arena, without, however, deserting their present line of repertory.

Norman Allin, Raymond Newell, etc.—Another novel combination, I believe ; with, for its immediate object, a vocal *potpourri* after the manner of the instrumental models popularised by Alfred Mellon, Jules Rivière, Arditi, Jimmy Glover, Herman Finck, and others. A capital notion, to be sure ! You will recognise many old friends in the course of this clever medley, which deserves a more distinctive title than *Shipmates o' mine,* a *Descriptive Ballad.* It has been neatly put together and the realistic wind effects are positively redolent of the ocean. As a matter of course, Mr. Norman Allin and his comrades throw themselves heartily into the spirit of the affair, and give it all the breezy life and vigour of stories appertaining to our gallant sailors. By the way, why not call it *The Yarn of the British Tar?*

COLUMBIA ABRIDGED OPERA ALBUMS

Proceeding with their issue of popular opera albums in abridged form, Columbia have this month added to the list *Rigoletto* and *Tosca.* Only a comparatively short period has elapsed since the complete editions were reviewed in these pages, and, so far as merits of reproduction are concerned, there is nothing to add to what was then written about them. The sole surprising feature is that the abridgment seems to be effected with so little disturbance to the consecutiveness of the music and so little apparent loss of indispensable numbers. The principal singers may be named once more—in *Rigoletto,* Mercedes Capsir, Ida Mannarini, Anna Masetti, Dino Borgioli, and Riccardo Stracciari ; in *La Tosca,* Bianca Scacciati, Alessandro Granda, Enrico Molinari, and Aristide Baracchi.

HERMAN KLEIN.

OPERATIC AND FOREIGN SONGS

VIORICA URSULEAC (soprano), **MARGIT BOKOR** (soprano), and **ALFRED JERGER** (baritone).—**Excerpts** from **Arabella** (Richard Strauss). With **The Berlin State Opera Orchestra** under **Clemens Krauss.** Decca-Polydor DE7024–5, 10in., 2s. 6d. each.

HERBERT ERNST GROH (tenor).—**To-morrow the sun will be shining** (Sieczynski) and **Lovely is the day** (Meisel). In German. Orch. acc. Parlo. R1655, 10in., 2s. 6d. And **Friends, give heed to the story** from **Der Postillon von Longjumeau** (A. Adam). In German. And **Italian Serenade** from **Der Rosenkavalier** (Richard Strauss). In Italian. Orch. acc. Parlophone R1674, 10in., 2s. 6d.

THE CARL ROSA OPERA COMPANY.—Selections from **Il Trovatore** (Verdi), **Maritana** (Wallace) and **Tannhäuser** (Wagner). Conducted by **Arthur Hammond.** And **Cavalleria Rusticana** (Mascagni) and **Madame Butterfly** (Puccini). Conducted by **Richard Austin.** Imperial Z146–50, 12in., 2s. each.

LONDON LIGHT OPERA COMPANY.—Selection from **The Mikado** (Gilbert-Sullivan). Edison Bell Winner W22, 10in., 1s.

BENIAMINO GIGLI (tenor).—**Occhi Turchini** (Denza) and **Serenata** (Schubert). In Italian. Orch. acc. H.M.V. DB1903, 12in., 6s.

STILES ALLEN (soprano).—**Vissi d'arte** from **La Tosca** (Puccini) and **Musetta's Waltz Song** from **La Bohème** (Puccini). Orch. acc. Edison Bell 5606, 10in., 1s. 6d.

ENRICO CARUSO (tenor).—**The Lost Chord** (Procter-Sullivan). In English. And **Ombra mai iù** from **Xerxes** (Handel). In Italian. Organ acc. H.M.V. DB2073, 12in., 6s.

RICHARD TAUBER (tenor).—**The Heavens are telling** (Beethoven) and **Netherland Hymn** (Weyl, arr. Kremser). With Chorus and Organ. Parlophone RO20232, 10in., 4s.

RICHARD CROOKS (tenor).—**Waltz Song** from **A Waltz Dream** (Oscar Strauss-Herbert) and **Castles in the Air** from **Frau Luna** (Lincke-Ross). Orch. acc. H.M.V. DA1328, 10in., 4s.

TITTERTON (tenor).—**Heartless** (Meisel-Hudson) with Piano acc. and **Throw open wide your Window** (May) from **Viennese Waltz,** with String Quintet. Decca F3694, 10in., 1s. 6d.

BERLIN STATE OPERA CHORUS AND ORCHESTRA.— **Triumphal March** from **Aida,** Act II (Verdi). Sung in German (2 parts). Parlophone R1673, 10in., 2s. 6d.

HEINRICH SCHLUSNUS (baritone).—**In Summer fields** and **Ah, Sweet my love, thou charmest me** (Brahms). In German. Piano acc. by **Franz Rupp.** Decca-Polydor LY6075, 12in., 3s. 6d.

JEAN PLANEL (tenor).—**The Childhood of Christ** (Berlioz). In French. With the **Orchestre Symphonique of Paris** cond. by **F. Ruhlmann.** Two Parts. Columbia DX514, 12in., 4s.

A. CAVARA (tenor), **K. A. NEUMANN** (baritone), **H. BATTEUX** (tenor), **F. FLEISCHER-JANCZAK** (baritone), **E.**

KANDL (bass), and E. BERGER (soprano).—Sie Flieh'n mich from Act 3 of Rigoletto (Verdi). And with ELSE RUZICZKA (contralto).—Nur Scherze sind's und Possen from Act 1 of The Masked Singer (Verdi). In German. With Chorus and Berlin State Opera Orchestra under Leo Blech. Decca-Polydor CA8168, 12in., 4s.

Strauss's "Arabella" Excerpts.—The first recordings of scenes from Richard Strauss's latest opera have now reached this country. The general verdict on *Arabella* was decidedly mixed, both as to Hofmannsthal's libretto and Strauss's music ; and, judging by the wireless relay of the *première* at Dresden vouchsafed by the B.B.C., I feel pretty sure that critical opinion has not erred about this work. The story read to me as too involved, and the music—so far as I could make it out without the aid of a score or a very satisfactory hearing over the ether —sounded too much like a laboured repetition of the patterns woven *ad infinitum* in the composer's preceding works. Still, in every plum-pudding there are, or ought to be, a few plums, and these, I fancy, have been adroitly seized upon in the present instance by the clever Viennese conductor, Clemens Krauss (in charge of the Berlin State Opera Orchestra), for recording on two 10in. discs issued by Decca-Polydor. Certainly they put what they exhibit in the best possible light. The duet from Act I is stamped all over with the *Rosenkavalier* hallmark, and it is admirably sung by Viorica Ursuleac and Margit Bokor. The former, who created the leading rôle, has a voice of unusual quality—a poignant intensity of charm and feeling not easy to resist. The two-part harmonies sung by the two sisters are exquisitely in tune, and they seem to recall the Marschallin and Oktavian over again with, towards the end, that dear old ruffian Baron Ochs in the background. The whole has an effect extremely refined and melodious. In the finale of Act II, Frl. Ursuleac starts off with a sort of lament, soaring into exalted regions. Her notes come out with tremendous power, but the phrases are of the meandering sort and very sustained, without saying much that is new, while here Herr Jerger's bass-baritone is at its roughest. Altogether, if I were going to choose between the two records, I should vote for the first (DE7024).

Herbert Ernst Groh.—Nowadays we expect the most accomplished tenors to devote their voice and talent to themes of the most ordinary description. That habit came in with the *Fledermaus* vogue, and, as it has turned out more profitable (I am sorry to say) than the serious work, we can hardly wonder that things are as they are in the vocal world. All the up-to-date Viennese touches and devices are conspicuous in these two songs, and what is not in the voice part, to which I am bound to say the soloist lends all possible grace and fluency (he being a first-rate artist), is compensated for by orchestral effects provided by every instrument in turn and by various unnamed singers backing up Herr Groh in thirds and sixths, all in nicely written effects that are well calculated to please the popular ear. The combination is so ingenious that it deserves to succeed. Adolphe Adam's tuneful opera *Le Postillon de Longjumeau* was, half a century back, one of the most popular in the lighter repertory everywhere ; and to-day in Germany it is still among the active favourites. There the tradition of the great tenor Wachtel is not forgotten, as the present singer emphatically proves. His rendering of the Postilion's celebrated air is splendidly animated and overflowing with energy. Equally good, in quite another style, is his warbling of the *Italian Serenade* which punctuates the proceedings of the Marschallin's hairdresser.

Carl Rosa Opera Company.—I, for one, am delighted that the apparently moribund phase of the Carl Rosa Company's sixty-years' career should not have been allowed to pass without gramophonic evidence of its sturdy condition in those dying moments. Indeed, this very evidence may ere long prove of value in resuscitating the body before it gets beyond the "suspended animation" stage. For, in spite of failure in other quarters, my faith in the name of Carl Rosa is so strong that I decline to believe in this stoppage as more than a temporary one. Anyhow, these five selections from favourite

operas, Italian and English, are not less welcome than would be a few good snapshots of scenes and people who may, for aught we can tell, be going to disappear from our ken for ever. They are, moreover, worth preserving for their own sake, because the familiar music is exceedingly well sung and played by everyone concerned ; while soloists whose voices can easily be recognised contribute their full share to the excellence of the ensemble under the able direction of Arthur Hammond and Richard Austin. At the price of two shillings each, these long records assuredly give value for the money.

London Light Opera Company.—Here, for half the price, we find a smaller allowance, but an efficient one, of *The Mikado.* I make no attempt to pierce the anonymity of the executants, but they are obviously well up to their job. The selection is tolerably representative, and the merit of the singing should satisfy all ordinary requirements.

Beniamino Gigli.—The Denza Song reintroduced in this record is not very well known, though among its composer's best. Its essentially Italian strain naturally calls also for the best of Gigli's native qualities, alike in voice and sentiment ; in a word, it suits him as though written for him. The same tender appeal serves appropriately for a very artistic rendering of Schubert's *Serenade,* wherein nothing is sacrificed to mere effect. The voice is lovely and we are especially grateful for it in its subdued aspect—notably the delicate *mezza voce* so correctly employed at the outset.

Stiles Allen.—As previously observed, this talented artist arouses admiration in music that is adapted to her voice and style. Here the fact is plainly illustrated. The poignant feeling of *Vissi d'arte,* its unrelieved sense of religious disappointment, she seizes upon with an unerring grasp and depicts Tosca's outburst with touching beauty for all it is worth. Nothing could be better. But the same characteristics are simply out of place in Musetta's frank acknowledgment of her naughty disposition. *Her* ideas, as you know, do not lend themselves to serious expression.

Enrico Caruso.—The third and latest resuscitation of early Caruso records is not up to the level of its precursors. At least, his share of them is not. The organ accompaniments make for improvement and the volume, of course, is increased. But neither the throatiness induced by his English in *The Lost Chord* nor his strange reading of Handel's *Largo,* as we generally call it, tends to exhibit the powers of the famous tenor in their most favourable light. I am aware that these things do not count in the estimation of his millions of "thick and thin" admirers. Nevertheless, I cannot help expressing the opinion that the choice in the present instance was not altogether wise.

Richard Tauber.—Poor Beethoven ! I wonder if he would recognise any of his handiwork in this sad caricature of the song that has always been known in the English version as *Creation's Hymn.* Even the title has been changed ; and, what is worse, is given that of one of the most famous choruses in Haydn's *Creation—The Heavens are telling.* What a mix-up, to be sure ! As for the music, it is nearly all chorus and very little Tauber. The soloist just starts it off and then speedily becomes submerged in a sea of German male-voice choral tone. Could anything be more inept ? The Dutch hymn offers a pleasant contrast ; at any rate it gives Herr Tauber a fair chance of displaying his versatile talent in his new devotional rôle.

Richard Crooks.—In spite of being over-amplified, this is a capital record. The voice reminds one now of Caruso, now of Richard Tauber, and, generally speaking, of the two combined —a mixture by no means to be despised. The music belongs to the Viennese waltz type so much in vogue, which will be a further recommendation to listeners who retain pleasant recollections of the two successful comic operas concerned.

Titterton.—It is almost a pity that Mr. Titterton should have decided—if he really has decided—to drop the "Frank." I thought that only pianists (like Paderewski and Solomon) were supposed to enjoy the privilege of dispensing with their "front names." Anyhow, frankness remains in the free, candid delivery of the English tenor, and he displays it with welcome *entrain* and rhythmical swing in both these foreign pieces. His vocal quality is improving all the time.

Berlin Chorus and Orchestra.—The demand for selections from *Aida* must be very extensive, if we may go by the variety of shapes in which they are being served up. In this case two sides of a 10in. disc are attractively filled with a sonorous performance of the "Triumph of Radamès," done by the chorus and orchestra of the Berlin State Opera House.

Heinrich Schlusnus.—There can be no need to describe how Heinrich Schlusnus interprets Brahms. He puts all his soul into the poetry, all his depth of expression, all his wealth of feeling and vocal *maestria* into the music. Lest you should be in doubt as to the identity of the songs under their quaint English titles, I may mention that *In summer fields* is *Feldeinsamkeit* and the other is *Wie bist du, meine Königin*. The piano accompaniment to each is faultlessly played by Franz Rupp.

Jean Planel and *Paris Orchestra.*—It was a happy idea to record this characteristic page from Berlioz's badly neglected oratorio *L'Enfance du Christ*. It depicts the *Repose of the Holy Family* on the journey to Egypt, and is a peaceful pastoral movement scored for orchestra in the French master's most picturesque manner. This receives a delicately suave rendering at the hands of the Orchestre Symphonique of Paris, under M. F. Ruhlmann. It has been recorded with sedulous care, the tenor solo being no less competently furnished by M. Planel, a singer of evident talent.

Berlin State Opera Performers.—These ensembles from *Rigoletto* and *Un Ballo in Maschera*, sung and played by executants to whom their difficulties present no obstacle, will prove highly acceptable to Verdi-lovers, who can seldom have the chance of hearing them given to such advantage.

ENGLISH SONGS, ETC.

ALFRED PICCAVER (tenor).—**Roses of Picardy** (Haydn-Wood). Orch. acc. And **Thank God for a Garden** (Del Riego). Piano acc. Decca M449, 10in., 2s. 6d.

ESSIE ACKLAND (contralto).—**O Divine Redeemer** (Gounod) and **My heart is weary** (Goring-Thomas). Organ and Orch. acc. H.M.V. C2611, 12in., 4s.

HEDDLE NASH (tenor).—**Annie Laurie** and **MacGregor's Gathering** (trad. arr. J. Batten). Piano acc. and **Male Quartette**. Columbia DB1199, 10in., 2s. 6d.

TOM BURKE (tenor).—**Parted** (Tosti) and **Song of Songs** (Moya). Acc. by **Charles D. Smart** on the Wurlitzer Organ. Broadcast Twelve 3354, 10in., 1s. 6d.

STUART ROBERTSON (bass-baritone).—**Dashing away with the smoothing iron ; Bobby Shaftoe ; A Farmer's Boy** and **I married a wife** (arr. Hely-Hutchinson). With piano and **Male Quartet**. H.M.V. B8006, 10in., 2s. 6d.

JOHN HENDRIK (tenor).—**My Darling** and **Two Eyes are Smiling** from **The Circus Princess** (Kalman) ; and **The Last Waltz** from **The Last Waltz** (Oscar Straus) and **Loving You** (Freeman-Lubbock). Orch. acc. under **Mark Lubbock**. Parlo. R1656-7, 10in., 2s. 6d. each.

RAYMOND NEWELL (baritone).—**The Demon King** (Newman-Charles) and **Top o' the House** (Haydon-Bowen). Acc. **Wolseley Charles**. Columbia DB1198, 10in., 2s. 6d.

MASTER THOMAS TWEEDY (treble).—**On Wings of Song** (Mendelssohn) and **Hark, hark! the lark** (Schubert). Piano acc. Decca F3704, 10in., 1s. 6d.

FERGUS KELLY (tenor).—**I'm away in Killarney with you** (King-Kennedy) and **Rose of Tralee** (Glover). Plaza P158, 8in., 6d.

JOHN McCORMACK (Tenor).—**As I sit here** (Sanderson) and **I know of two bright eyes** (Clutsam). Piano acc. by **Percy Kahn**. H.M.V. DA1342, 10in., 4s.

RICHARD TAUBER (tenor).—**A Brown Bird singing** (Barrie-Haydn Wood) and **I love the moon** (Rubens). Orch. acc. Parlophone RO20231, 10in., 4s.

DEREK OLDHAM (tenor).—**Roses of Picardy** and **Love's Garden of Roses** (Haydn Wood). Orch. acc. H.M.V. B8053, 10in., 2s. 6d.

INA SOUEZ (soprano).—**Love will find a way** from **The Maid of the Mountains** (Graham-Fraser-Simson) and **My Hero** from **The Chocolate Soldier** (Stange-Oscar Strauss). Orch. acc. Columbia DB1226, 10in., 2s. 6d.

RICHARD CROOKS (tenor).—**Nirvana** (Weatherly-Adams) and **How lovely are Thy dwellings** (words from Psalm lxxxiv) (Liddle). Orch. acc. H.M.V. DB1951, 12in., 6s.

CHARLES KULLMAN (tenor).—**Love, here is my heart** (Ross-Silesu) and **Vale** (d'Arcy-Russell). Orch. and Organ under **Joseph Batten**. Columbia DB1227, 10in., 2s. 6d.

NORMAN ALLIN (bass).—**A Lowland love-song** (arr. Senior) and **Molly Brannigan** (arr. Villiers Stanford). Piano acc. Columbia DB1225, 10in., 2s. 6d.

LEONARD C. VOKE.—**The Prodigal Son** (Stebbins) and **They were ninety and nine** (Sankey). Piano acc. Edison Bell Winner W44, 1s.

ENRICO CARUSO.—**A Dream** (Cory-Bartlett) and **For you alone** (O'Reilly-Geehl). With Symphony Orch. H.M.V. DA1349, 10in., 4s.

RICHARD HAYWARD.—**The Mud Cabin on the Hill** and **The Old Man of Killyburn Brae** (traditional, arr. Hayward). Orch. acc. Decca F3736, 10in., 1s. 6d.

MASTER RAYMOND KINSEY.—**Ave Maria** (Gounod) and **O for a closer walk with God** (Foster). Organ acc. H.M.V. C2629, 12in., 4s.

EDGAR THOMAS (bass-baritone).—**Ora pro nobis** (Piccolomini) and **The old rugged Cross** (Rev. G. Bennard). With **Chorus and Orchestra**. Rex 8060, 10in., 1s.

PETER DAWSON (bass-baritone).—**Auld Songs o' Hame** (Geehl) and **O sing to me an Irish song** (Geehl). With Chorus and Orch. H.M.V. C2597, 12in., 4s. And **The Sacred Hour** and **In a Monastery Garden** (Ketelbey). With Chorus, Organ and Orch. H.M.V. C2595, 12in., 4s.

Alfred Piccaver.—It is pleasant to reflect that English singers, no matter how long they study and stay abroad, feel sufficiently drawn to the old country to come back occasionally, if only for a short stay, and to add to their repertories native songs of the moment that happen to be in request. Far be it from me, therefore, to find fault with Alfred Piccaver for not looking higher this time. After all, *Roses of Picardy* and *Thank God for a garden* belong to as good a class of ditty as many of the Austro-Hungarian examples in waltz and other dance rhythms that are nowadays loaded upon us with such unending abundance. Moreover, Alfred Piccaver can sing them better than a good many tenors—that is to say, in a manly, unaffected style, without mannerism or exaggeration, and without that somniferous delivery that at one time marred his efforts. The quality of his voice is, what it always has been, round, robust, yet sympathetic, and possesses a power and volume that can afford to laugh at control-room amplification.

Essie Ackland.—This singer, who is by birth Australian, has lived "home" long enough to have earned for herself many admirers. Her voice must be described as a mezzo-contralto, whose chief strength and charm are to be found in its middle notes. The registers, though deftly blended, are still sufficiently discernible in their differences of timbre, and I am inclined to think that the chest might have been more fully developed without detriment to the higher part of the voice. Unquestionably, however, it is an exceptionally fine organ, and with further study its owner ought to achieve a distinguished career. *O Divine Redeemer* was written by Gounod for a soprano, and Goring Thomas added *O my heart is weary* to the score of his opera *Nadeshda* for a mezzo-soprano ; but Miss Ackland overcomes the *tessitura* of each with skill, whilst putting into both the full emotional content of a dramatic temperament. Two things she can improve in order to make herself a first-rate artist : one, her English diction, the other, her management of the breath in long passages ; and she might also avoid cutting off with a jerk the last word of each sentence in her recitative.

Heddle Nash.—Following the illustrious example of Sims Reeves, this rising young tenor has made an inroad in the domain of Scottish song by singing *Annie Laurie* and *MacGregor's Gathering.* He could not have chosen better. Doing entire justice to the music, which fits his bright voice perfectly, he should now venture upon a closer imitation of the true Scots dialect, so as not to mix ordinary Middlesex with his threat to " lay me *doon* and *dee.*" He may also with advantage infuse a trifle more of romantic sentiment into Mr. J. Batten's excellent arrangement of *Annie Laurie.* But the bold, martial declamation of *MacGregor's Gathering* is much to be praised, and the tone is splendid throughout.

Tom Burke.—Let me say at once that the Wurlitzer organ, whatever its merits as a solo instrument, is quite unfitted for accompanying songs of the type here presented. The undercurrent of noisy wind in the bass, persisting nearly all through, creates a disturbing effect and diverts attention from the singer. At the rate things are moving in this direction, the craze for " jazz variety " will very soon make accompaniments more important and prominent than the melody and the singer. Already the liberties taken with classical songs and Lieder, on certain gramophone records, are arousing both annoyance and resentment among the more cultured listeners who support the industry. In such a florid framework, Tosti's ballad seems entirely lost, despite Mr. Tom Burke's dramatic treatment and effective use of his telling voice.

Stuart Robertson.—In folk-songs of this description, where there is a " burden " or refrain to be sung, the interpolation of the male quartet should not be discouraged. As well might one wish to abolish the chorus of an old-time ballad. Admirably arranged by Mr. Victor Hely-Hutchinson, these four specimens are presented under just the right conditions, and, needless to add, Mr. Stuart Robertson has just the right voice and enunciative skill for a vivid handling of them.

John Hendrik.—If this singer's head notes were a trifle less pinched, they would possess more ringing quality, and the whole voice would thereby be improved. As it is, there is too great a tendency to concentrate upon the lower or baritone register, and the real tenor suffers in consequence. Otherwise here is an artist with precisely the right sparkling method for Kalman's Hungarian tunes or Oscar Straus's suave, swaying waltzes, and he brings out their salient points with unerring aptitude. *Loving you* has a taking two-step rhythm and will probably make the dancers' toes twinkle.

Raymond Newell.—The energetic baritone still loves his old-fashioned descriptive ballad. In this one the *Demon King* of pantomime revels in confession of his misdeeds on the stage ; yet, whilst admitting that his intentions there are deplorable, he prides himself upon his exemplary home conduct, and even declares that, like Longfellow's " Village Blacksmith," he " goes on Sunday to the church." There is plenty of " go " in the music of this, and also in the companion ditty, which repeats Tommy's customary " grouse " with all the requisite martial trimmings. Both are sung in crisp and spirited fashion.

Master Thomas Tweedy.—This boy has a pure, rich soprano voice, well worth the further training that it needs. At present his breathing is faulty ; he is much inclined to " scoop " ; and he has a habit of swelling on every long note, without, however, always sustaining the pitch. *On wings of music* betrays a somewhat self-conscious manner, and *Hark, hark ! the lark* is too doleful for a happy song. Nevertheless, Master Tweedy's unquestionably beautiful voice will enable him one day to make his mark.

Fergus Kelly.—It is astonishing what a quantity of music can be got on to a tiny 8in. record (price sixpence). This particular " Plaza " specimen provides two whole long Irish songs of the appealing type that figure all too seldom in modern programmes. The Hibernian tenor who sings them reveals the national character by his voice as well as his brogue, and is, therefore, the right man in the right " plaza." He and his melodies are both genuine.

John McCormack.—Songs of tender recollection make an unfailing appeal, in the first place to this singer, in the second to those who listen to him. And there are many who strive to imitate—though not with invariable success—the model that he offers of suavity, grace, and unforced sentiment. No one can make more than he does of an unpretentious ballad, and he demonstrates the fact plainly enough in these.

Richard Tauber.—Someone suggested the other day that Richard Tauber was an " Admirable Crichton " of his art. I agree, so far as the implication of versatility goes, but not when he descends from his pedestal to certain levels that the present writer has never yet approved. I allude, not to the songs, but to the treatment of them. If Herr Tauber can phrase German lieder carefully, there is no reason why he should slur English songs up and down the scale in this unpleasant way ; nor need he make ugly sounds on certain English vowels in one place and not in another. His oft-repeated " you " in Paul Rubens's little ballad offends the ear each time, because the tone and the vehemence are alike disagreeable.

Derek Oldham.—The last speaker—I mean singer—would do well to copy the natural, unadulterated English of Mr. Derek Oldham. Here are ballads sung as they should be sung— and pronounced. But then the Savoy school teaches lessons that are nowadays more honoured in the breach than in the observance. Haydn Wood must be thankful for such an interpreter.

Ina Souez.—When listening to this young soprano over the wireless, I have often regretted that she has never been taught the breathing that ensures a steady, un-tremulous tone ; for she has a voice of charming quality and of the bright, resonant type that Florence St. John, Ruth Vincent, and José Collins used to have. (They also knew the meaning of the word *nuance.*) Otherwise these souvenirs of *The Maid of the Mountains* and *The Chocolate Soldier* are very welcome.

Richard Crooks.—The qualities and defects attributed to Mr. Crooks in another column are also perceptible in these records of songs by Stephen Adams and Samuel Liddle. I will only repeat that his fine organ might be used with greater artistry and his English diction based upon other than foreign models. More reticence, more refinement, would aid in bringing him very nearly, if not quite, to the top of the tree. He ought to have heard Edward Lloyd sing *Nirvana* !

Charles Kullman.—Not without good reason do I persist in making these comparisons with bygone singers. It seems to me beyond dispute that the voices are as good as ever ; that it is rather the method and the style that show deterioration. Never in my experience have we had so many first-rate tenors ; and never before was there such a demand for tenor records. But why do they specialise so much ? Here is Mr. Charles Kullman, with his really sympathetic voice, concentrating on two melancholy songs, pleading in both of them as though the tears were flowing and his heart would break. A little contrast, one tiny suggestion of a happy mood, would have been such a relief ! Then, again, practically all the upper notes are sung in *mezza voce*, which likewise tends to monotony. Mr. J. Batten's orchestra and organ are most efficient.

Norman Allin.—Here at last is a reminiscence of the old school ! Foli himself could not have bettered these admirable specimens of Scots and Irish Song. Norman Allin is a true artist, and more than that I cannot say. Please note, if you will, the full round tone, better now than ever ; the complete control of resources ; the dignified yet spirited style ; the right manly sentiment ; the true sense of humour. You can want nothing to beat this.

Leonard C. Voke.—The well-trained " gospel singer " who has made these records will carry back those who can remember to the visit of Moody and Sankey many years ago, when all London went to their " revivalist meetings " at Her Majesty's Theatre in the Haymarket and also, I think, the Albert Hall. They sang not exactly negro spirituals, but something similar, uniting Biblical stories and sacred texts to the most tuneful of modern airs. Their sincerity of feeling is well reflected in these Edison Bell examples.

Enrico Caruso.—This re-recording appears in the H.M.V. issues for the current month in addition to the one noticed above in "Operatic and Foreign Songs"; which explains what Caruso is doing, after so many years, *dans cette galère.* He made many more important records, as all the world knows; but everything he sang he sang with all his "heart and voice," as we observe in the National Anthem. Hence the unmistakable Caruso touch in these popular ballads, which somehow fit him (or he fits them) better than Handel and *The Lost Chord*; moreover, I predict for them in their renovated condition a much larger sale. But there is no telling, and I may be quite wrong.

Richard Hayward.—Two old Irish airs, sung in the real traditional style by a genuine Irish minstrel of the type you expect to come across on the shores of the Lake of Killarney. (I have been there twice, so I know.) On these occasions you do not look for tenor, baritone, or bass; so you will not miss the descriptive label. A typical Irish voice, accent, and lilt, with every word as plain as a pikestaff, are all you want; and they are certainly to be found here.

Master Raymond Kinsey.—There is in this boy's voice a dark, rich colour and a beauty of texture that are quite exceptional. The same adjective applies to his breath-control, the evenness of his scale, the depth and maturity of his expressive power. His style is characterized by a degree of natural feeling that has the similitude of a passion which we know cannot be real in a boy, but which evidently induces his teacher to give him songs that call for strong underlying emotion. Such are the Gounod *Ave Maria* (English version) and Foster's *O for a closer walk with God.* He pleads for forgiveness in right good earnest and with every token of distress, enhanced by the loveliness of true *larmes dans la voix*; it is all most touching. It would be better, however, if his vowels were not so over-closed and his articulation so compressed by undue tightening. He has a good compass, reaching in the *Ave Maria* to a clear B flat—a semitone higher than written. By the way, did Mr. Foster ever hear the introductory phrase before Valentine's song in the second act of *Faust*? He must have done, I fancy.

Edgar Thomas.—The varied tastes of the multitude have perforce to be catered for and vocal records at a shilling have to be in stock when asked for. Still, it may fairly be questioned whether there is real need to revert for present material to such ultra-sentimental ballads of a past age as these. They did no credit to their own epoch and were not sung by first-rate ballad singers even then. Their revival to-day, largely as they may sell, will do nothing to encourage the improving taste of gramophonists. The ruggedness of their rendering almost rivals that of the Rev. Mr. Bennard's ancient cross. Surely Rex can do better than this!

Peter Dawson and Others.—Seemingly the vocal *potpourri* has come to stay. In these four records it is exemplified in its most elaborate form. To do justice to its cleverly devised material would be equivalent to describing an amusing yet by no means complex jig-saw puzzle of familiar tunes; and I have not a column left for the purpose. Enough that the whole combination is effective to the *n*th degree. I cannot see how anyone is going to resist Mr. Peter Dawson's gallant assault, supported as he is by every imaginable kind of musical fighting force, including choir, female soloists, organ, orchestra, instrumental *obbligati*, bells, and (in the *Monastery Garden*) a detachment of nightingales and other singing birds. Seeing that the leader is in first-rate form after his visit to Australia, and gives us in the Geehl selections the pick of his national Scotch and Irish melodies, followed by a vigorous *Kyrie Eleison* for the monks in the Monastery scene, climbing up to a tremendous climax for all the assembled forces, I feel convinced that this elaborate set-piece will go off with all the brilliancy it so richly deserves. HERMAN KLEIN.

CHORAL

THE BOYS OF ST. MARY'S OF THE ANGELS CHOIR SCHOOL.—While shepherds watched their flocks by night (N. Tate-Este's Psalter) and **Once in Royal David's City** (Alexander-Gauntlett). Organ acc. by **A. T. Batts.** Columbia DB1248, 10in., 2s. 6d.

B.B.C. WIRELESS CHORUS.—Fum, Fum, Fum (arr. Kurt Schindler), **Jolly Bachelors** (Eng. words Opdycke and Schindler, music Moya, arr. Schindler), and **Nightingale of France**, both from **Songs of the Spanish Provinces** (Catalonia); and **Silversmith** (Taylor-Schindler) from **Spanish Choral Ballads.** Conducted by **Cyril Dalmaine.** Columbia DB1202, 10in., 2s. 6d. **Good Friday Music in a Catalonian Church** (Opdycke-Nicolau, arr. Schindler). Soloist **GLADYS WINMILL.** In Latin and English. Conducted by **Cyril Dalmaine.** Columbia DX545, 12in., 4s.

MINSTER CHOIR.—A Garland of Hymns (No. 2). Organ acc. Regal-Zono. MR1114, 10in., 1s. 6d.

SALVATION ARMY WIMBLEDON AND CHALK FARM SONGSTERS.—Favourite Carols. Acc. by **Band of Salvation Army Supplies Department** under **A. W. Foot** and **E. Souter.** Regal-Zono. MR1112, 10in., 1s. 6d.

CELESTIAL HARMONY SINGERS.—The Lost Chord (Procter-Sullivan) and **The Holy City** (Weatherly-Adams). With Orchestra and Organ. Regal-Zono. MR1115, 10in., 1s. 6d.

YE OLDE-FASHIONED WAITS.—Hail, smiling morn (Spofforth) and **Nazareth** (Gounod). Orch. acc. Regal-Zono. MR1113, 10in., 1s. 6d.

ST. GEORGE'S CHAPEL CHOIR, WINDSOR.—Blest are the departed from **The Last Judgment** (Spohr) and **O Strength and Stay** (Ellerton-Hort-Bourgeois, arr. Harris). Conducted by **Dr. W. H. Harris** with Organ. Columbia DB1228, 10in., 2s. 6d.

COLNE ORPHEUS GLEE UNION.—Drink to me only with thine eyes (Jonson-Button) and **Annie Laurie** (arr. J. Cantor). Conducted by **Luther Greenwood,** with Organ. Regal-Zono. MR1081, 10in., 1s. 6d.

UNACCOMPANIED CHOIR.—Hark! the Herald Angels sing (Mendelssohn) and **God rest ye, merry gentlemen** (traditional). Cond. by **Arnold Goldsborough.** Decca F3726, 10in., 1s. 6d.

ST. MARTIN'S CHORAL SOCIETY.—Christians, Awake! (Wainwright) and **The First Nowell** (traditional). Conducted by **Arnold Goldsborough.** Decca F3725, 10in., 1s. 6d.

CHOIR OF ST. MARY-LE-BOW.—Hark! the Herald Angels sing, **Good King Wenceslas, O Come all ye Faithful, Christians, Awake!, The First Nowell,** and **While Shepherds watched their flocks by night.** Organ acc. by **J. E. Humphreys.** Rex X1001-3, 10in., 1s. each.

ROYAL CHORAL SOCIETY.—The Holly and the Ivy (arr. Stainer), **See amid the Winter's snow** (arr. Goss), **God rest you, merry gentlemen, I saw three ships** (arr. Stainer), **It came upon the midnight clear** (arr. A. Sullivan) and **Bethlehem** (Gounod). Organ acc. H.M.V. B8073-4, 10in., 2s. 6d.

Boys of St. Mary's Choir School.—Not too late, it is to be hoped, for the seasonal supply of sacred recordings, Columbia leads the way this month with a couple of highly acceptable numbers by the Boys of St. Mary's of the Angels Choir School, founded by the Rev. Desmond Morse-Boycott. The organist, Mr. A. T. Batts, who accompanies the lads, is, presumably, also their trainer, and as their voices are very sweet it seems a pity that there should not be more of them. The tone would be fuller as well as stronger in proportion. Meanwhile, they keep well together, and their intelligence is self-evident.

B.B.C. Wireless Chorus.—If not altogether new, here is something decidedly unusual and amusing. The arrangement by Kurt Schindler called for a good deal of accuracy and precision in execution, and congratulations are due to Mr. Cyril Dalmaine for the efficient training of his forces. In the "Songs of the Spanish Provinces," Catalonia, the land of Albéniz, is drawn upon for an extremely characteristic and lively chorus, full of variety and contrast. The title *Fum, Fum, Fum*, beaten out again and again as a sort of refrain, is made still funnier by being pronounced in a drum-like fashion to sound like *Pum, Pum, Pum*! The other piece begins more in an Elizabethan than a Spanish manner, but as soon as the guitar imitation comes in (recalling Debussy's *Mandoline*), the Iberian source of the whole thing is unmistakable. Male and female voices are both employed in a "merry roundelay."

In a different category stands the *Good Friday Music in a Catalonian Church*. It is purely devotional, and the mixture of Latin and English text seems unconventional, though the latter is probably a translation from the Spanish and is allotted (exclusively, I fancy) to the soloist, who finds in Miss Gladys Winmill an interpreter of rare refinement. The music is modern and suggests the influence of Verdi's *Requiem*, besides including in the earlier section a phrase that might have been lifted bodily from the *Miserere* in the same master's *Trovatore*. In other words, the Catalonian composer has favoured operatic as well as religious treatment, and shown in both an uncommon mastery of choral effects. From first to last this *Good Friday Music* is exquisitely sung.

Minster Choir, Salvation Army, etc.—In this collection of four 10in. discs, for which Regal-Zonophone is responsible, come anticipations of Christmas musical fare that should find (at eighteen pence apiece) ready acceptance everywhere. The *Garland of Hymns* (No. 2) introduces in Part I such favourites as *Jesu, lover of my soul, Hark, the herald Angels*, and *O God, our help in ages past*; while Part II comprises *Oh God of love, Come all ye faithful*, and *Lead, kindly light*. They are sung by carefully trained, well-balanced voices, and the words are distinctly heard. The organist's modulations leading from one hymn to another are quite nice. The *Celestial Harmonists* are rather upset for my ear by a too-assertive tenor, who was perhaps too near the microphone; but in the *bouche fermée* portions—an effect that is getting considerably overdone in these days—the balance is just right. The solo voices in each ballad are of good quality, and the orchestra and organ supply plenty of volume in support. On the other hand our old friends *Ye Olde-fashioned Waits* could do with less accompanying. In *Hail, smiling morn*, when I was a boy, we used to dispense with an accompaniment altogether, while Santley, the original singer of *Nazareth*, would have looked upon an intrusive violin as an insult. Why is the public being taught to expect all these superfluous ornamentations? In the carols sung by the Chalk Farm and Wimbledon Salvation Army singers there emerges a capital body of tone and the right spirit, but absolutely no trace of light and shade. If they had come from Yorkshire, what a difference there would have been!

St. George's Chapel Choir.—I would like, personally, to thank Dr. W. Harris for reviving in this form the beautiful and once-popular quartet *Blest are the departed*, from Spohr's neglected oratorio, *The Last Judgment* (*Die letzten Dinge*). I shall never forget hearing Henry Leslie's Choir sing it (many a time, indeed, ever so long ago), and I can pay the Windsor singers no higher compliment than to say that they here afford a worthy reminder of that eloquent achievement. The music is really beautiful. The piece coupled with it is by Louis-Thomas Bourgeois, a French composer who lived early in the eighteenth century and wrote a number of cantatas that were much in request. But that was not the era of copyright or royalties, and, according to Fétis, the unfortunate musician died in great poverty. All who hear this lovely rendering of his music will agree that he deserved a happier fate. Both pieces are skilfully conducted by Dr. Harris.

Colne Orpheus Glee Union.—Once more Mr. Luther Greenwood and his merry men are to the fore, this time with arrangements of old ballads that, so to speak, carry their passports in their portfolios. The singing is creditable; but it would be the better for a further reduction of individual zeal and energy and more regard for balance. Thus, if the exceedingly florid "descant" which overlays *Drink to me only* were sung at about half this strength, it would not disguise—nay, conceal—the glorious old melody as it now does. *Annie Laurie*, thanks to the powerful basses (at any rate in the first verse), remains much more consistently in view.

Unaccompanied Choir.—Its anonymity notwithstanding, this is a capital little choir, as might have been expected from any body of voices collected and trained by the able organist of St. Martin's-in-the-Fields. In fact, it is quite good enough to deserve a name, if not a christening. Christmas is coming, and so what more appropriate than a time-honoured announcement thereof! I can imagine none. This is the kind of music that all respectable "waits" of yore had in their repertory; only they did not invariably sing it with such delightful tone and precision. Thank you, Mr. Arnold Goldsborough!

St. Martin's Choral Society.—Here the choristers emerge from their anonymity and boldly proclaim themselves the St. Martin's Choral Society, with Mr. Goldsborough still at their head. The difference is that the body of tone sounds fuller and bigger, while the recording is labelled as having taken place in St. Martin's Church. Christmas carols again form the theme, and very well they sound, too, *Christians, Awake!* being sung with the organ and the *First Nowell* unaccompanied.

Choir of St. Mary-le-Bow.—Here are more additions to the seasonal influx of carols sung by metropolitan church choirs, which no doubt make a special appeal to the parishioners immediately interested, as well as to a wider circle of those who love old-fashioned musical observances. These in particular are notable for the prominence of solo voices alternating with the full choir of boys and men, and the plan is a good one to adopt where there are so many verses to be sung. The principal treble has a pleasing quality and the bass soloist is also excellent. Altogether the execution of these six numbers (on three discs, price 1s.), with Mr. J. E. Humphreys at the organ, is highly creditable.

Royal Choral Society.—Last, but not least, in the procession of Christmas carols, is a detachment from the Albert Hall that does honour to our premier metropolitan choral society, which nowadays devotes the whole of its mid-winter concert to a programme of these things. The selection has been carefully made, and the performance boasts a distinction that justifies the higher cost of the records. They reveal a splendid quality and body of tone, together with the utmost smoothness and precision of attack and a unanimity of light and shade that it is a pleasure to listen to. The arrangements by Goss, Sullivan, and Stainer are admirable; the organ accompaniment marked by conspicuous discretion. One notes many interesting points—in particular the fine crescendo leading to the triumphant ending of Gounod's *Bethlehem*. Altogether these are carols worth having as well as hearing.

HERMAN KLEIN.

REVIEWS PUBLISHED IN 1934

OPERATIC AND FOREIGN SONGS

E. BERGER and **A. KERN** (sopranos), **E. RUZICZKA** (contralto), **M. HIRZEL** (tenor), **K. A. NEUMANN** (baritone).—**Hm, Hm, Hm ! Der Arme kann von Strafe sagen** from **Die Zauberflöte** (Mozart) and **E. BERGER** and **A. KERN** (sopranos), **M. HIRZEL** and **C. JOKEN** (tenors), and **E. KANDL** (bass).—**Nie werd' ich deine Huld verkennen** from **Die Entführung aus dem Serail** (Mozart). In German. With the **Berlin State Opera Orchestra** under **Leo Blech.** Decca-Polydor CA8169, 12in., 3s. 6d.

CARL HARTMANN (tenor).—**Winter storms have waned** (**Spring Song**) and, with **ELISABETH FRIEDRICH** (soprano), **Thou art the Spring, A Love-dream wakes** and **Siegmund call me** from Act I, Sc. 4 of **Die Walküre** (Wagner). Four parts, in German ; **Orchestra of the State Opera House, Berlin,** conducted by **Dr. Weissmann.** Parlophone R1703-4, 10in., 2s. 6d. each.

HERBERT ERNST GROH (tenor).—**Surely you have laughed and cried together** from **The Bird Catcher** (**Der Vogelhändler**) (Zeller-Rotter) and **Vienna-Blood** (J. Strauss-Alfy) on Parlophone R1688 ; **Last Serenade** (Magnani-Alfy) and **Chanson Triste** (Tchaikovsky-Alfy) on Parlophone R1705. Each with chorus and orchestra, in German, 10in., 2s. 6d.

RICHARD TAUBER (tenor).—**Bella Venezia** (Schulenburg) and **I for you and you for me** (Lehar-Rebner-Stein). In German. Orch. acc. Parlophone RO20233, 10in., 4s.

LAWRENCE TIBBETT (baritone).—**Song of the Flea** (Goethe-Moussorgsky) and **Pilgrim's Song, Op. 47, No. 5** (Tolstoi-Tchaikovsky). Orch. acc. H.M.V. DB1945, 12in., 6s.

JOSEPH SCHMIDT (tenor).—**Lodern zum Himmel** from **Der Troubadour** (Verdi) and **Ach so fromm, ach so traut** from **Martha** (Flotow). In German. With the **Berlin State Opera Orchestra** under **Clemens Schmalstich.** H.M.V. B8036, 10in., 2s. 6d.

RICHARD CROOKS (tenor).—**En fermant les yeux** from **Manon** (Massenet) and **Angels guard thee** (Godard). Orch. acc. and violin obb. H.M.V. DB2093, 12in., 6s.

Berlin Artists and State Opera Orchestra.—If there is one branch more than another of gramophone recording in which the foreign organisations have definitely manifested superiority to our own, it is that of the big operatic ensemble. We have not gone ahead in this direction as we have, for instance, in the recording of orchestral and chamber works. The reasons for this seem obvious enough, though they may not be equally apparent to everybody. But the subject is too important to be dealt with briefly here, and I propose, therefore, to return to it at an early date in " The Gramophone and the Singer," to which page it properly belongs. A fitting example on which to hang comparisons will assuredly present itself in these selections from two of Mozart's most vocally exacting operas. They are seldom adequately sung on the stage, much less in front of the microphone ; and under the latter conditions I doubt whether they have ever been so well done before. All the greater, therefore, the credit due to Herr Leo Blech, a conductor who has evidently brought this kind of work down to the finest of fine points. I cannot conceive a higher degree of perfection, either in clarity of interpretation on the part of the singers or in smoothness and purity of technical reproduction.

We have, to begin with, the complete quintet from the first act of *The Magic Flute,* which begins with Papageno's comic supplication to be released from the useful contrivance (so badly needed when there are all-night sittings in Parliament) that temporarily " puts the lid " on his gossiping tongue. Tamino is powerless to relieve him of the padlock ; but the First Lady speedily does so, with a warning not to tell any more fibs ; and she next proceeds to hand Tamino the golden flute upon which so much depends, while the bird-catcher receives his no less magical chime of bells. Upon the mingled humour and seriousness of this situation Mozart has built up, as we know, one of his most delightful concerted pieces, replete with ingenuity and melodic charm ; and here one is grateful alike for the beauty of the voices and the delicate precision of the art lavished upon such music.

The excerpt from *Die Entführung*—curiously entitled a *vaudeville* on account, I imagine, of its comic blending of satire, spite, and satisfaction—is the closing number of the opera, and depicts the escape of the lovers and their attendants from the clutches of the nicely defeated Osmin. This glorious finale, which brings all the fine principal characters into action, together with the chorus of janissaries, is more difficult than the above quintet. It is, however, no less faultlessly rendered, and the secret of that is that the whole of the executants are accustomed to each other, besides having their task completely at their fingers' ends. If the bass is at moments a trifle rough, it may be claimed that the character demands it ; but that is a mere trifle. Once more a talented conductor is in entire control of admirably trained forces, and the outcome is a sheer joy for the listener.

Carl Hartmann and *Elisabeth Friedrich.*—Here, on two 10in. discs, is enclosed the whole of the beautiful love-duet from the first act of *Die Walküre,* which includes, of course, Siegmund's *Spring Song* and the grandiose passage in which he draws the sword Nothung from the trunk of the tree. The former he invests with only a moderate degree of grace or tenderness, but the more strenuous climax he declaims with all the power required of a genuine *Heldentenor,* which is what Herr Hartmann undoubtedly is. An undercurrent of deeper passion throughout the scene is, however, evinced in the unusually expressive singing of Fr. Friedrich, a soprano with just the kind of soft yet vibrant tone that I associate with a Sieglinde. She certainly offers the right womanly contrast to her companion's powerful outbursts, and her sense of dramatic fitness goes far to preserve the true atmosphere of the scene. Dr. Weissmann, with his customary skill, contributes a fine instrumental background—a reading worthy alike of the theme and the reputation of his Berlin players. Higher praise it would be difficult to bestow.

Herbert Ernst Groh.—It is rather to be regretted that this excellent tenor so frequently sacrifices the quality of his voice for the sake of getting his high notes. He may be able in consequence to put another semitone or two on to his naturally high compass, but what of that? The effort to finish, as he does, on a D flat is not good reason enough for spoiling, with his loud open tone, many of the notes that precede it. This is in the extract from *Der Vogelhändler,* which he otherwise sings in a bright, sparkling manner and with much infectious spirit. Both in this and the *Wiener-Blut* waltz he is supported by an energetic chorus, so that sonority shall not be lacking anywhere ; and even in the *Chanson Triste* of Tchaikovsky (with German words) is reinforced with choral and obbligato effects in harmony with the now inevitable pattern. But the solo voice of course predominates, and so easily that, where a true legato is needed, Herr Groh might well abandon his explosive style of attack for the gentler methods of the artist whom he imitates. His faults thus corrected, such pleasing and lively selections as these would be wholly welcome to the musical, as they are sure, anyhow, to be to the "groundlings."

Richard Tauber.—I do not care greatly for the spurious Venetian strains of Herr Schulenberg, despite their taking mandoline accompaniment and characteristic Tauberesque treatment. But in the Lehar song there is some genuine melody, besides opportunity for artistic vocal touches which not even the inevitable violin obbligato (what a nuisance it is becoming!) can prevent a clever singer like Herr Tauber from making effective.

Lawrence Tibbett.—The novel rendering of Moussorgsky's *Song of the Flea* is extremely amusing in its way. It may not be at all what the composer intended or what a Chaliapine would propose to adopt in his most burlesque mood. It is too deliberate, too much broken up by pauses, in a word, too unctuous to be altogether funny. On the other hand, it is skilfully handled in the vocal sense and the singer disguises his voice so completely that I for one should never have recognised it had I not known who he was. You can perceive this by comparing the noisy tone and the dozen varieties of tipsy guffaws with the serene, expressive phrasing and sonorous beauty of the *Pilgrim's Song* on the other side. The violent contrast certainly betokens versatility, but of the two efforts give me the Tchaikovsky air. Its broad phrases are finely sustained, with all the requisite breath capacity and richness of volume, ending up with a splendid crescendo and climax.

Joseph Schmidt.—Here are two good old *chevaux de bataille* of the robust tenor's repertory. Both are on the same disc, so there will be no occasion for anyone to dispute either preference or choice. Only please play *Lodern zu Himmel* (that being the German for *Di quella pira*) after you have enjoyed *M'appari* (beg pardon, *Ach so fromm*), otherwise you will not have Joseph Schmidt's superb high C's coming in when they can no longer cast everything else into the shade. As a matter of fact, though, his clear, ringing tones are equally impressive throughout. A little more variation in colour and phrasing would have made both efforts perfect.

Richard Crooks.—I wonder why both pieces on this record are so extremely over-amplified. Each is a soft, sweet, contemplative piece of music, yet, instead of respecting the composers' plainly expressed intentions, the impression is created that they are meant to be shouted as loudly as possible. However, there is no indication that it is the singer's fault; indeed, as regards both style and restraint, he is more reticent and careful than usual. Probably a soft fibre needle will, therefore, meet the case and give Mr. Crooks's admirers a chance of enjoying his capital French accent and diction in the "Rêve" from *Manon*. His English vowels, as displayed in the *Berceuse* from Godard's *Jocelyn*, require attention.

✹ ✹ ✹

H.M.V. ALBUM OF "DER ROSENKAVALIER"

Just in time for a cordial New Year's greeting, there arrived the long-expected album of Richard Strauss's masterpiece, *Der Rosenkavalier.*

ELISABETH SCHUMANN

Coming from Vienna via Hayes, I looked forward to the finest possible sample of up-to-date gramophone output; and I found it. The names on it guaranteed as much; there was really no room for fear or occasion for disappointment. Only in one matter did actual inspection bring relief. The recording was not too terribly long. No attempt had been made to reproduce the big score *verbatim et literatim* from the first note to the last. The whole opera practically has been recorded on thirteen discs or twenty-six sides (DB2060 to 2072); and, what is not less important, the cuts have been judiciously made. I miss one page that might possibly have been left in, the Italian serenade for the tenor in the first act. Yet, after all, it is only an exotic interpolation that has nothing to do with the story, and, away from the stage, its absence is scarcely likely to be deplored or even noticed. Moreover, the scene wherein it occurs has been shorn of most of Hofmannsthal's hairdressing and other trimmings and the rest of the sometimes lovely, always clever, music stands out in the stronger relief for it.

The credit for so much skilful dovetailing must, of course, be attributed to the talented conductor of this performance, Professor Robert Heger, whose admirable work we value more the more we see or hear of it. Thanks to his alert intelligence and the unsurpassable playing of the Vienna Philharmonic Orchestra, I can declare without hesitation that the present recording of Strauss's instrumentation affords me greater enjoyment than I have ever known it to give in the theatre; and that is saying a great deal, considering how often and where (Dresden included, with the original interpreters) I have heard *Rosenkavalier* given.

The names of the artists in the H.M.V. cast exonerate me from the obligation of dealing in detail with the singing. The principal characters are cast as follows:

The Feldmarschallin	... ...	**Lotte Lehmann.**
Ocktavian	... ...	**Maria Olszewska.**
Sophie	... ...	**Elisabeth Schumann.**
Marianne (the Duenna) ...		**Aenne Michalsky.**
Annina	... ...	**Bella Paalen.**
Baron Ochs von Lerchenau		**Richard Mayr.**

This may fairly be termed an ideal distribution. One can only feel grateful that such a combination should have been secured and preserved for posterity whilst these distinguished artists were still in possession of their full powers. Fortunately, they give ample evidence of this fact all through the opera.

HERMAN KLEIN.

CHORAL

Col. DX560 (12in., 4s.).—**The B.B.C. Wireless Chorus,** conducted by **Cyril Dalmaine : O Gladsome Light** from **The Golden Legend** (Sullivan) and **The Long Day Closes** (Chorley and Sullivan).

Regal-Zono. MR1150 (10in., 1s. 6d.).—**Colne Orpheus Glee Union,** conducted by **Luther Greenwood : Sunset** (**Abide with me**) and **Rossini** (Parker). Recorded in Colne Parish Church.

B.B.C. Wireless Chorus.—Two of the best examples of Sullivan's four-part writing have been happily chosen here by Mr. Cyril Dalmaine for exhibiting the quality of the B.B.C. Wireless Chorus. *O gladsome light* is the evening hymn sung by the villagers in *The Golden Legend,* and I retain a vivid recollection of the effect that it made when first rendered by the famous Yorkshire choir at the Leeds Festival of 1886. It had to be repeated then under the composer, as it was afterwards under Barnby at the Albert Hall, and as I daresay it always will be (when the encore is granted) in any future performance of this beautiful work. Sullivan's style is unmistakable in most of his music, but in none more than pure four-part writing such as this, of which he was an acknowledged master ; and *O gladsome light* happens to be a gem. *The long day closes,* composed to words by his friend Henry F. Chorley, was a much earlier effort, having been published by Novellos in 1868. But it is no less charming in its melodic grace and the easy flow of its delicate harmonies. Both pieces are reproduced on this record with praiseworthy balance and refinement alike of tone and execution.

Colne Orpheus Glee Union.—Mr. Luther Greenwood is indefatigable. Hardly a month passes but he makes some addition to the repertory of his excellent choir, and though I confess to not being familiar with the music of either of these last two, I hasten to acknowledge that it has given me decided pleasure to listen to them. Were the words enunciated with the same care that is bestowed upon the singing, even higher eulogy might have been earned. Those of *Abide with me* are, of course, too well known for a syllable to be left in doubt ; but in the case of *Rossini,* notwithstanding the conductor's own arrangement of them, I am fain to admit that three repetitions of as many verses still leave me puzzled. But never mind ; the simple tunes and straightforward harmonies come out with the utmost clearness and in a rich male-voice tone that is doubly welcome because it is so indubitably English.

HERMAN KLEIN.

OPERATIC AND FOREIGN SONGS

LOTTE LEHMANN (soprano).—Arabella's Aria **Mein Elemer** and **Erlist der Richtige.** And with **KATE HEIDERSBACH, Ich weiss nicht wie du bist** from finale, Act I, **Arabella** (Richard Strauss). Orch. acc. under **Richard Jäger.** Parlophone RO20237 and 6, 10in., 4s. each.

BENIAMINO GIGLI (tenor).—**Forbidden Music** (Gastaldon). In Italian. And **If my Mother only knew** (Nutile). In Neapolitan. Orch. acc. H.M.V. DB1385, 12in., 6s.

JOHN McCORMACK (tenor).—**Vespers** (Howard Fisher) and **South Winds** (Percy Kahn). Piano acc. by **Percy Kahn.** H.M.V. DA1343, 10in., 4s.

HERBERT ERNST GROH (tenor).—**Caro mio ben** (Giordani, arr. Guido Papini). In Italian. And **Elégie** (Massenet). Instrumental acc. Parlophone R1721, 2s. 6d.

Lotte Lehmann.—Once more I head this column with the name of one of the most diligent and consistently artistic workers in the gramophone world. I doubt whether there has ever been a singer since recording was invented who has main-

tained such a steady, regular output of high-class contributions to the repertory. For it must be borne in mind that Mme. Lotte Lehmann never descends to the level of the trivial or the commonplace. Her choice is guided by truly æclectic spirit, even when she sings a simple *volkslied* or a Christmas carol, just as surely as when she labours conscientiously over the latest conundrums of Richard Strauss. It is one of the latter that we find in these Parlophone records—difficult nuts to crack for the ordinary singer, but apparently quite easy tasks for our favourite Marschallin to accomplish. I say nothing about the music, because I have not yet heard the opera and have no particular desire to prejudice the listener for or against *Arabella.* The point about these excerpts is that they are both interesting and characteristic, and I cannot imagine their being more adequately rendered. The instrumentation comes out clearly and well, if not with exceptional refinement, while the fair Arabella holds her own against it with her accustomed steadiness, intelligence, and power. There are only a few bars of duet, but they are of the usual Straussian type and quite admirably sung.

Beniamino Gigli.—Experience teaches that it does not really matter what Gigli sings so long as he sings it and gives us the full benefit of his generous organ. When I first heard *Musica proibita* I understood it to be a soprano song expressing the feelings of a love-lorn Italian maiden, whose suspicious mother has forbidden her to listen to the serenading of the lover who ventures within earshot of her balcony. The tunefulness of Gastaldon's ballad made it extremely popular in the nineties, and it may well become so again, now that the leading Italian tenor has changed the import and genders of its text so as to render it suitable for his purpose. Anyhow, he puts into it any amount of tone, fire and passion, and that, *après tout,* is all that one really needs to bother about. The Neapolitan ditty suits him even better, and affords ample scope for displaying a characteristic style in addition to the glorious wealth of a magnificent voice.

John McCormack.—Here are two little songs of pleasing and unpretentious type, quietly interpreted by a tenor of a different calibre, who makes his own appeal in his own way, and is *facile princeps* at this particular kind of thing.

Herbert Ernst Groh.—Tenor No. 3 follows up the Italian and the Irish with a creditable illustration of the German method of treating familiar compositions not indigenous to the Hitlerian soil. In these I am glad to say that Herr Groh is content to do without unnecessary striving after abnormally acute excursions into the regions of *falsetto,* and proves himself in consequence a thoroughly good vocalist. He might perhaps have seen to it that modern harmonies should not be introduced into the accompaniment of *Caro mio ben,* and that a too muddy mixture of instruments did not obscure that of both pieces. But for the former my old friend Papini (a delightful fiddler in his day) was no doubt responsible ; while Massenet's *Elégie* simply clamours for the violin obbligato which Parlophone keeps on the premises. Altogether quite an amusing record.

EMMY BETTENDORF (soprano) with **HERBERT E. GROH** (tenor).—**The Garden Scene** from Act 3 of **Faust** (Gounod). In German. Orch. acc. under **Dr. Weissmann.** Parlophone R1736, 10in., 2s. 6d.

JAN KIEPURA (tenor).—**Di quella pira** from **Il Trovatore** (Verdi) and **Celeste Aida** from **Aida** (Verdi). In Italian. Orch. acc. Parlophone RO20235, 10in., 4s.

RICHARD TAUBER (tenor).—**Venetian Gondola Song** (Mendelssohn-Bartholdy) and **La Foletta** (Marchesi-Frey). In German. Orch. acc. Parlophone RO20234, 10in., 4s.

VLADIMIR ROSING (tenor).—**The Song of the Flea** from **Faust** (Moussorgsky). Piano acc. by **Ivor Newton.** And **The Song of the Volga Boatmen.** Balalaika acc. In Russian. Parlophone E11240, 12in., 4s.

PAUL O'MONTIS.—**Ghetto** (Erwin) and **Kaddisch** (Stransky-Robitschek). In German. Piano acc. Parlophone R1742, 10in., 2s. 6d.

ROBERT HOWE (baritone).—**Jan's Courtship** from **Songs of the West**, Devonshire Dialect Song, and **The Somerset Farmer**, Somerset Dialect Song (Brandon-Lane Wilson). Piano acc. Parlophone R1735, 10in., 2s. 6d.

EVA LIEBENBERG (contralto).—**Ave Maria** (Bach-Gounod) and **Ombra mai fù** (Handel). In English. With organ, harp and strings. Broadcast Twelve 3363, 1s. 6d.

Emmy Bettendorf and Herbert Groh.—Faust may be the hero (such as he is) of Gounod's opera, but Marguerite is as unquestionably the heroine of the garden scene, and never worthier of the distinction than when embodied by such a beautiful singer as Emmy Bettendorf. This record only accentuates my regret that we cannot hear her in the part at Covent Garden—for that matter, with the same Faust as her associate. The two artists are quite at the top of their form in this rendering of the famous love duet, which Dr. Weissmann has evidently taken very great pains over. The cuts are not too numerous, and the whole episode hangs coherently together. Restraint governs the singing of both interpreters ; their voices are heard to great advantage under the beneficent influence of melody that is replete with subdued yet intense passion.

Jan Kiepura.—Another notable operatic tenor ! I prefer his *Celeste Aida* to his *Di quella pira* in spite of the orgy of high C's that enriches the *Trovatore* outburst. In the latter his phrasing is slovenly ; his semiquaver groups dwindle into a mere slur of four notes made to sound like two. The singer is much more at home in *Celeste Aida*, in which his fine voice yields the right robust quality without doing injustice to the music.

Richard Tauber.—Thanks are due to the popular tenor who sings Mendelssohn's neglected songs *with* words, and rescues from oblivion a charming effort such as the *Venetian Gondola Song.* Herr Tauber here sings it most effectively with a mandoline accompaniment, and he employs similar means to lend local colour to Marchesi's *La Folletta* (spelt on the label with only one " l "). The record is in all respects first-rate, and exhibits the artist in his most acceptable light.

Vladimir Rosing.—If not altogether what it was, the voice of the Russian tenor certainly retains most of its old flexibility and power of characterisation. His reading of the Moussorgsky *Flea Song* is clever and in a certain degree original. It suffers from the usual fault—the excessive exaggeration of the mocking laugh, wherein each fresh singer apparently does his best to outdo his predecessor, with the result that what was originally meant for a chuckle is rapidly developing into a cacophonous cough. A warning on this point might well find a place in the spoken English explanation of the story wherewith Mr. Rosing precedes the song. How he declaims the now-hackneyed refrain attributed to the *Volga Boatmen* there can be no need to tell.

Paul O'Montis.—In these two selections from the store of modern Jewish serio-comic songs, one cannot but admire the extraordinary skill, the graphic realism, the sense of humour, the sudden changes from grave to gay, that mark their interpretation. To some listeners they might sound funny and elicit laughter ; from others their unaffected pathos might as easily bring forth a tear. The music is negligible ; but the total effect is wonderful, and, as a study of Hebrew character, well worth enjoying.

Robert Howe.—The baritone who sings these dialect ditties of Devon and Somerset conceals beneath his exterior of rough Western diction a really fine voice, and thus is able to impart capital musical effect to his amusing folk-songs. Their authenticity is beyond dispute, and the subtle differences between the dialects such as only a native could detect. They go with immense spirit and strength of rhythm, and the frequent interjection of spoken words is not their least notable feature.

Eva Liebenberg.—Although it makes no difference to the excellence of the record, I am sorry to see that the name of the composer who wrote the tune sung by the contralto soloist is omitted from the label. It is duly inserted in our list because we have put it there ; but there is no excuse for leaving out Gounod's name altogether, seeing that he really did invent the melody (and a beautiful one, too) which he ventured to impose upon Bach's celebrated Prelude. What is more, the singer in this instance successfully asserts the right to infringe upon a domain generally occupied by the sopranos. Albeit a contralto, she has an unusually rich, powerful voice, and does full justice to Gounod's noble theme, which he expressly intended to be sung " by all voices." The mixed instrumental accompaniment is less like what he meant, and is, I fear, equally unsatisfactory in the Handel *Largo* (*Ombra mai fù*) on the other side.

HERMAN KLEIN.

OPERATIC AND FOREIGN SONGS

DUSOLINA GIANNINI (soprano).—**Vergini degli angeli** from Act 2 and **Pace, pace mio Dio** from Act 4 of **La Forza del Destino** (Verdi). In Italian. Orch. acc. H.M.V. DB1228, 12in., 6s.

BENIAMINO GIGLI (tenor).—**Addio, Mignon** from Act 2 and **Ah ! non credevi tu** from Act 3 of **Mignon** (Thomas). In Italian. Orch. acc. H.M.V. DB1270, 12in., 6s.

FRANZ VÖLKER (tenor).—**Siegmund's Love Song** from **Die Walküre** and **Lohengrin's Farewell** from **Lohengrin** (Wagner). In German. Orch. acc. under **Joh. Heidenreich.** Decca-Polydor LY6080, 12in., 3s. 6d.

HEINRICH SCHLUSNUS (baritone).—**Frühlingsglaube** and **To Sylvia** (Schubert) and **Zueignung** and **Ich liebe dich** (Richard Strauss). In German. Piano acc. by **Franz Rupp.** Decca-Polydor DE7026-7, 10in., 2s. 6d.

*****ELISABETH SCHUMANN** (soprano).—**An die Nachtigall,** Op. 98, No. 1 ; **Liebhaber in allen Gestalten** (Schubert) ; **Loreley,** Op. 53, No. 2 ; and **Ständchen,** Op. 36, No. 2 (Schumann). In German. Piano acc. by **George Reeves.** H.M.V. DA1355, 10in., 4s.

ADELE KERN (soprano).—**Recitative and Air of Zerbinetta** from **Ariadne auf Naxos** (Richard Strauss). In German. With the **Berlin State Opera Orchestra** under **Alois Melichar.** Decca-Polydor LY6081, 12in., 3s. 6d.

HERBERT ERNST GROH (tenor) and **EMMY BETTENDORF** (soprano).—**Come sing the song of love** from Act 3 of **Tales of Hoffmann** (Offenbach). In German. And with **GERHARD HUSCH** (baritone)—**In this solemn hour** from Act 3 of **The Force of Destiny** (Verdi). In Italian. Orch. acc. Parlo. R1757, 10in., 2s. 6d.

FRIEDEL SCHUSTER and **ELISABETH FRIEDRICH** (sopranos).—**We're saved, freed for evermore** from Act 3 of **Hänsel and Gretel** (Humperdinck). In German. With Chorus and Orchestra. Parlo R1744, 10in., 2s. 6d.

ALESSANDRO VALENTE (tenor).—**Canta pe me** and **Du ca nun chiagne!** (de Curtis). In Italian. Orch. acc. by **Fred Hartley and his Quintet.** Decca F3871, 10in., 1s. 6d.

THE KARDOSCH SINGERS.—**Castles in the South** (Grothe-Hannes) and **Sonia from the Ural** (Steininger-Felder). In German. Parlo. R1760, 10in., 2s. 6d.

LOTTE LEHMANN (soprano).—**The Letter Scene** from **Werther** (Massenet, Kalbeck). In German. Orch. acc. Parlo. RO20240, 10in., 4s.

RICHARD TAUBER (tenor).—**Berceuse de Jocelyn** (Godard) and **Un Peu d'Amour** (Fysher, Silesu). In French. And **O Woodlands Far** (Mendelssohn, Bartholdy, Eechendorff) and **Ueber Nacht** (Wolf, Sturm). In German. Orch. acc. Parlo. RO20238-9, 10in., 4s. each.

SYDNEY RAYNER (tenor).—**La donna e mobile** from **Rigoletto** (Verdi). In Italian. And **O Paradiso** from **L'Africaine** (Meyerbeer). In French. Decca M453, 10in., 2s. 6d.

The two principal soprano airs from *La Forza del Destino* demand for a satisfactory rendering the qualities of a supreme Verdi singer. That is to say, they call for deep emotional expression, artistic restraint, immaculate purity of intonation and phrasing, allied with that strong dramatic sense which can bring to the studio the broader atmosphere of the stage. It is but just to acknowledge that Dusolina Giannini in her best moments gives evidence of the possession of these very gifts—a fact that has often led me to regret her continued absence from our leading, nay, our only opera house. A clever lieder-singer she no doubt is ; but greater still are her claims to shine in the front rank of operatic artists, and the proof of that statement lies in the present record. The contrast between the two airs is quite striking : the subdued devotional feeling, the smooth, delicate *cantilena* of the *Vergini degli angeli* ; then the stronger, more agitated phrases of the *Pace, mio Dio* ; nothing could be better. In the former we get the important background of the Scala orchestra and chorus, under Maestro Sabajno, faultless in tone and balance ; in the other a careful accompaniment conducted by John Barbirolli. Altogether the selection well deserves its place in a catalogue *de luxe*.

There are welcome signs that the amplification craze has at last entered upon the decline that I predicted for it. At any rate, it has begun in the recording of tenor solos of the better class, such as this of the two airs from *Mignon* sung by Beniamino Gigli. How much is due to the mechanical and how much to the vocal side is a matter of indifference to the lover of true *bel canto* ; yet I prefer to think that the singer is really getting the best of it and can use his full natural powers in front of the microphone without being accused of shouting. I am convinced that Caruso was never guilty of shouting when he recorded in pre-electric days, any more than he did in the theatre, though he has been charged with both offences. I am equally certain that Beniamino Gigli has often been misrepresented in the same manner. Anyhow, this record proves, beyond cavil, that his normal tone is a lovely *mezzo-forte* that he can sustain in *cantabile* passages without undue force or breath-pressure. It also shows that he knows how to rely upon his *mezza-voce* for his general effect when the nature of his piece requires it—as it does in both these songs from *Mignon*—rather than the use of big notes and huge volume. In short, he can be and is a thorough artist. The *fermate*, or long pauses on certain notes, are of no more than average duration, and anyhow one can forgive them for the sake of the sensuous charm of the voice that holds them. In the *Addio, Mignon* the feeling of gentle reproach is well conveyed in just the right colour and sombre quality and with obvious restraint. In the other air the colouring is much the same, only the climax is attained with a trifle more energy and power in the degree required by the music. On the whole, therefore, a most satisfying record.

Franz Völker.—There can scarcely be need to remind my readers of the pleasant things I have written about this Viennese tenor since he first came out in his native country three or four years ago. But, now that he is engaged for the coming season at Covent Garden, it is only fair to remember that he was first recommended for that distinction in the review columns of THE GRAMOPHONE. (A good many other foreign artists have benefited likewise on the strength of the ex-cellence of their records.) In this particular example of his talent Herr Völker appropriately heralds his advent with Siegmund's *Spring Song* from *Die Walküre* and rather prematurely bids us "Hail and Farewell" with the final narration from *Lohengrin*. I may add that he sings both very finely indeed. The predominant feature of his method is an unruffled ease ; he provides his imposing high notes with a minimum of effort, and their resonant, vibrant quality is the result of good breathing, coupled with a naturally perfect mechanical adjustment. Again, he has facile command of both light and dark timbres, while his enunciation and declamation are meritorious above the average. Nor does he betray distortion of the throat at any part of a singularly even scale ; which makes his

singing a real pleasure to listen to. In both these excerpts he shows himself an accomplished Wagnerian artist, and their attractiveness is enhanced by capital orchestral playing under the direction of Herr Joh. Heidenreich.

Heinrich Schlusnus.—A singer of remarkable ability he is and always must be, but I hope Herr Schlusnus will not risk weakening the sonority of his lower notes, with their rich baritone timbre, by transposing his songs into tenor keys or something very much like it. His head register is agreeable, but not worth the sacrifice. He sings *Frühlingsglaube* charmingly, but too fast for my liking. His *Who is Sylvia* is not only taken at the right tempo (moderato), but pleasantly varied by the middle verse being infused with a delicate softness. The two Strauss lieder are marked by notable impulse and energy, boldness of attack, and a splendid sense of rhythmical feeling. As usual, Franz Rupp's piano accompaniments are perfection itself.

Elisabeth Schumann.—Everything recovered from the more remote corners of store-houses packed wth Schubert and Schumann may fairly be accounted "treasure trove." I feel a kind of personal gratitude to this accomplished singer, first of all for her industry in the seeking and finding ; secondly, for her wonderful art in applying the perfect interpretation to a group of lieder so replete with delicate poetic charm. She has given us the double joy of listening to exquisite music, exquisitely sung, together with themes that for most ears must sound absolutely new. I do not propose to notice them separately, since all four alike are gems, yet unalike ; having the quality of precious stones upon a lady's fingers, that suffer naught from shining in close company. I cordially advise you to get this record.

Adèle Kern.—The over-elaborated, horribly difficult air for Zerbinetta is about all that survives in English memories of Strauss's opera, *Ariadne auf Naxos*, the revised version of which was given at Covent Garden ten years ago next May. Such a nondescript compilation could hardly be expected to catch on anywhere, least of all in a country like ours, where *Der Rosenkavalier* has absorbed the entire supply of admiration that we have to spare for exotic operas like those of Strauss. But I suppose this Zerbinetta air, which is nothing more than a display of vocal fireworks, will continue to emerge with the regularity of a set-piece at Brock's annual Crystal Palace benefit so long as there are light sopranos capable of giving effect to its awe-inspiring *coloratura*. Adèle Kern is one of these by right of her remarkable talent and all-round gifts. She delivers the portentous recitative with the requisite authority of dramatic accent, and she attacks vigorously, if somewhat breathlessly, the more *cantabile* phrases of the air. The brilliancy of her *fiorituri* in the showy *roulades* does not quite equal that of Maria Ivogün, nor is her trill so good or her scale passages so unlaboured, if I may use the word. Yet I repeat that her singing of this trying piece is adequate and effective, and leaves behind a sense of efficiency even where it does not dazzle. The Berlin State Opera Orchestra, under Alois Melichar, gives the instrumentation its full value.

Emmy Bettendorf, Herbert Groh and Gerhard Hüsch.—Two duets, and not a trio, make up the sum and substance of this record, the tenor having a share in each. He joins Fr. Bettendorf in a smooth rendering of the scene between Hoffmann and Antonia in the third act of Offenbach's now popular opera. He likewise takes part with Gerhard Hüsch in a no less admirable performance of the duet for Alvaro and Carlo—best known by its Italian title of *Solenne in quest'ora*. It is good to hear these familiar items from the lips of well-known German artists. The clear, dark tone of Fr. Bettendorf's Antonia is particularly suited both to the character and the music.

Friedel Schuster and Elisabeth Friedrich.—The final episode in *Hänsel and Gretel*, when the Witch's victims are restored to life and liberty, is made up musically of a charming collection of the leading motives heard during the opera and upon which the overture is based. Generally speaking it does not command the attention that it deserves, but, separately recorded, it can be listened to with unqualified pleasure, especially when the whole of it is as well sung and played as it is in this instance. The voices of both children are sympathetic and tuneful, and the choral bits for their resuscitated companions go with plentiful spirit. The Father's name is not given, but he is evidently a capable artist. That last phrase of the " Evening Prayer," as given by the combined forces, was Humperdinck's finest inspiration.

Alessandro Valente.—A couple of Neapolitan ditties by de Curtis, of the customary type, sung by a tenor with a well-amplified tone and the robust energy needed for a sustained fortissimo from the first note to the last. To those who love this kind of thing it will make an irresistible appeal.

Kardosch Singers.—I should call these character part-songs, founded chiefly upon *volkslieder* or national themes, having their origin somewhere in Eastern Europe. The singers, four male voices, well trained and cleverly used, might possibly be traced to the same neighbourhood. And yet their humour seems somehow to possess an American touch. The great point, however, is that they are amusing and that their work is marked both by crispness and humour.

Lotte Lehmann.—This month the indefatigable Marschallin contributes the Letter Scene from Massenet's *Werther*, and therein proves herself an ideal singer of the best page allotted by the French master to the young lady of " bread and butter " fame—Charlotte to wit—from whom Frau Lehmann derived her diminutive front name. She sings it most delightfully, with just the quietly emotional reflective air of the girl who is thinking hard whilst she reads, and is studying every up and down stroke of the letter from the man she secretly loves. I have heard many Charlottes in this strangely fascinating yet unsatisfactory opera, but not one who has realised the thoughts passing through the mind of the reader so perfectly as this. It calls irresistibly to one's recollection the scene before the

looking-glass in *Rosenkavalier* ; it is much less lengthy, but quite as interesting, and the artist's only rival in depicting this sort of incident is herself. Her tones lose not an iota of their freshness or their command of expressive colour, and it strikes me that she is a greater mistress than ever of the art of the microphone.

Richard Tauber.—A couple of interesting records supply the welcome assurance that this favourite singer is not forsaking his recent excursion into the realms of the " legitimate." He continues to remind his admirers that Mendelssohn wrote a good song or two in his time, and, though he wisely sings it in German, the English title, *O woodlands far*, will not conceal its identity as a familiar specimen. Hugo Wolf's *Ueber Nacht* calls for a steady *sostenuto* in addition to a nice sense of climax, and Herr Tauber brings both to bear upon its rendering minus the smallest trace of trickery. In short, he shows here how well he can sing when he likes. On the second disc, in similarly good style, he trots out a pair of well-worn French songs, apparently without the smallest fear of their being thought hackneyed. I doubt whether he throws a new light on their faded charms.

Sydney Rayner.—Better late than never I have heard an excellent record by this artist of the air from *L'Africaine* and *La donna è mobile*. The label announces the former as being sung in Italian, but actually it is given in the original French —a language whereof Mr. Rayner has now obtained a very creditable mastery. His voice, too, keeps on improving alike in sympathy and power, and one hopes that the day is not far distant when he will be heard here in opera. Also he might in the meantime help to enlarge the Decca repertory with selections from some of his newer rôles, other than those already recorded by him, instead of relying upon the eternal *chevaux de bataille* that every *tenore robusto* brings into the ring. Or is it merely a question of supply and demand? Gramophiles certainly love making comparisons.

HERMAN KLEIN.

Part IV

MISCELLANEOUS
ARTICLES
BY
HERMAN KLEIN

GRAMOPHONE CELEBRITIES
XV.—Emilio Eduardo de Gogorza
By HERMAN KLEIN

WHEN I went to New York towards the end of 1901, to take up a sojourn there that was to last between seven and eight years, I took with me a letter of introduction from the late Mrs. Ronalds—a great lover of music, a charming singer, the friend of Arthur Sullivan and Tosti—to her old teacher, Signor Emilio Agramonte, one of the few remaining *maëstri* of the true Italian school. He received me with the utmost cordiality. Agramonte was the principal vocal instructor of Emilio Eduardo de Gogorza, the subject of this article, and it was from him that the young baritone, a native of Brooklyn, N.Y., acquired the sound, irreproachable method that in the fullness of time was to win, for his voice and singing, admirers among gramophonists in every part of the inhabited globe.

But it was not in the United States that he learned the elements of his art. His parents were Spanish and the fact of his being born in Brooklyn was due to chance. He was only two months old when he was taken to Spain, where he received his early education and learned to speak Spanish and French like a native. At the age of eleven he was sent to England and sang there in various episcopal churches. Later on he gained further experience of the same kind in Paris, remaining in Europe until he attained his twentieth year. Here we have the explanation of de Gogorza's mastery of many languages and the

[*Bain's News Service, N.Y.*

purity of his accent in nearly all of them. He returned to New York in 1893 a veritable cosmopolitan, but with no desire to remain a Spanish subject, as his parents had registered him at the Spanish consulate at the time of his birth in Brooklyn. It took a considerable period of residence, however, before he could secure his final papers as an American citizen, which he proudly remains to this day.

Emilio de Gogorza completed his studies under Agramonte in 1897, and in the same year made his début as a concert singer in New York, under the auspices of that great artist, Marcella Sembrich. She thought highly of his talent and proved in many ways a valuable friend. The beauty of his voice, the neatness of his phrasing, the purity of his style generally, won high praise from critics renowned for their candour and severity. His public position was quickly won. By the time I landed in the United States four years later, he had become a finished artist, and I found a genuine pleasure in listening to him. We were introduced, and I found an equal pleasure in the discovery that he was a charming man. There is no need to say much about his career as a concert baritone, except that he sang and gave recitals everywhere in North America and won for himself a wide and enviable reputation.

Meanwhile—exactly at what date I am unable

to state, but it does not really matter—de Gogorza had started in a quiet way his long and useful connection with the Victor Gramophone Company. He was, I believe, their first " musical advisor " (is so still in fact) ; and that must have been rather before the period when I took up a similar position with the Columbia Company, which I held until I left America in 1909. (Anyhow he was more fortunate in the appreciation that his services evoked than I was.) But he was also to earn both reputation and wealth for the Victor people and himself, not alone as an impresario of distinguished record-makers from Sembrich and Caruso downwards, but as a singer of very fine and widely-saleable records himself.

To have achieved this at a time when the mechanism of the gramophone was vastly inferior to what it is to-day involved close and continuous study of the conditions. De Gogorza must have worked hard to learn how to display his consummate art in the making of records, and no less hard,

I am sure, to instruct and impart similar knowledge to the great artists who came under his charge in the recording-room or on the way to it. In the language of the day, " he knew his job." He knew which voices would record well and which would not ; and I can easily believe that he made few mistakes. A delightful singer under any circumstances, he has himself been a perfect model for reproducing his own voice and style, as Caruso reproduced his, in a wholly natural manner and without modification or change or effort of any sort.

In 1911 he married the famous operatic soprano, Emma Eames (widow of Julian Story), one of the most gifted and interesting singers that America ever brought forth. She was born at Shanghai, educated at Boston, and trained vocally by Marchesi at Paris. But then, you see, the old saying applies in both cases : " Art has no nationality."

H.K.

❧ ❧ ❧

MUSIC IN THE BALTIC STATES
By HERMAN KLEIN

I SPENT recently a delightful three weeks in as many of the Baltic States—Finland, Estonia, and Latvia. I visited in turn the cities of Helsingfors, Reval, and Riga, their respective capitals, and returned by the same route that I went, viz., Hull, Copenhagen, Helsingfors. It was a most interesting trip, restful, beneficial (including nine days there and back by sea in a comfortable steamer), and yet in a way exciting, for it was full of novelty and of sights and experiences that gave one "furiously to think." (Russia I approached by the Baltic years ago—to St. Petersburg and thence to Moscow—but felt not the smallest desire to enter there again now.) But the three republics that I have named, mere provinces before the war, are now new countries " in the making," and it was curious in the extreme to mark how they are striving to build up, out of a strange mixture of old and modern, of ancient and up-to-date, their independent, self-governing dominions that owe vassalage neither to Empire nor Bolshevism. The latter they hate even more than they fear it ; for the Soviet tyrants occupied their cities and homes and treated them cruelly until they gained their freedom in 1921. Meanwhile they are at peace with one another, and, in addition to trade and commerce, education and literature, I find that the foremost concern of each

country is to encourage, as substantially as its means will admit, the art of music.

That these people adore music may go without saying ; the age and wealth of their folk-lore is sufficient proof of the fact. The men may not sing in the streets as do the Italians or Spaniards, but they love opera no less intensely, and they enjoy good open-air music as thoroughly as the Germans or the Austrians. Of the latest musical inventions, sad to relate, the one that has made least headway in their midst is the gramophone. They appear to be just aware of its existence, little more. I can honestly say that the sounds of a decent gramophone—I bar the impertinent noises of the portable instruments that invaded the deck of our English boat—did not salute my ears half a dozen times during the entire pilgrimage. No, a really good gramophone, playing really good records, I never heard once. Which was a pity, because it would have indicated the probability of an early recording of some of the vastly interesting folk-songs, such as the wonderful old things that Mme. Wiegner-Grünberg, a popular and accomplished artist, unique in her rendering of the Latvian *Volkslieder*, was gracious enough to break her holiday in order to sing for me in her handsome flat at Riga. To make records of them she would have to travel as

584

far as Berlin and place herself at the disposal of the Polydor company.

In all three capitals there are choral bodies working with energy and enthusiasm, but August is their holiday time, so I was not fortunate enough to be able to hear any of them. On the other hand, Riga and Reval were both busy with preparations for opera seasons that were to last many months, and in the latter city, as I shall presently relate, I contrived to attend the opening performance whilst on my return journey to catch the boat at Helsingfors. At Riga I stayed six days, and thanks to the courtesy and hospitality of Dr. A. Bihlmans, one of the chiefs of the Latvian Foreign Office, and a man of great culture and distinction, I enjoyed every moment of the time. He introduced me to, among others, the head of the Conservatoire, Professor Vitols, a gifted Latvian composer, who lived many years at St. Petersburg in the old days and was the friend of Tchaikovsky and Glazounov (still alive and hearty, he informed me). Also Dr. Bihlmans kindly arranged for me to be present at a couple of the rehearsals at the fine opera-house, where they were preparing Rimsky-Korsakov's *Kitesh* for the opening representation of the season. Unluckily it was too soon for me to hear the combined forces on the stage, so that my acquaintance with this remarkable work was scarcely more complete than when it was given in concert form at Covent Garden last March, under the auspices of the B.B.C. Nevertheless, I preferred the splendid Latvian soloists and, still more, the amazing Latvian chorus; while the Latvian text was certainly not more cryptic or unmusical to my Western ears than the Russian had been. I had to make a little speech and compliment them all when I departed.

The new *chef d'orchestre*, no mean rival to Albert Coates, was no other than the talented Emil Cooper (spelt in English fashion), who for three or four years before the war was principal conductor of the Russian seasons given by Sir Joseph and Sir Thomas Beecham at Drury Lane. I had not met him then, but have heard much about him since, his reputation being nowadays of literally European proportions. He afforded me ocular and aural demonstration of his right thereto. Providing me with a vocal score, he sat or stood among his singers, beating time without a baton, his excellent *maestro al piano* placed behind him, and stopping to correct with unerring skill and judgment, he enabled me not only to estimate the qualities of conductor and "conducted," but to appreciate the beauties of *Kitesh* as I had not done before. Cooper is an astonishing little man, a genuine master of his "job," and I sincerely hope that it will be possible for Lt.-Col. Blois to give us an opportunity at Covent Garden of renewing acquaintance with him ere long. He told me he was full up with important engagements for another year at least, but he would dearly like to come to England again.

Riga, although it has not nearly recovered its pre-war glories, is a bigger and richer city than Reval, even as Latvia is a more developed and resourceful country than Estonia, though the latter is now working hard to escape from the fetters of Russian tradition and making up for lost time. To opera in Reval the same contrast applies. The State there is still too poor to allow it an adequate subsidy (in England the B.N.O.C. would be thankful for even so much—about £3,000 annually, at the present rate of exchange), and with that the director, Mr. Hanno Compus, finds it hard to make ends meet. Hence a company somewhat inferior to the Riga combination, as I proved for myself on the interesting opening night of the season. They gave a meritorious representation of Tchaikovsky's *Eugen Onegin* (a dull opera in spite of the many beautiful things that the score contains), but the only voice to arouse my admiration was that of the Tatiana, a young soprano named Marta Runge, who had come straight from the local Conservatoire. She was, I understood, a débutante; certainly her ideas of acting were quite elementary, and her vocal resources were not yet under perfect control. Still, there was all the talent for the making of a successful artist clearly in evidence, with half a dozen others of fair promise from the same institution among the remainder of the cast. Do you wonder, then, if I felt slightly envious of this little distant land, where native singers could be trained for opera in a competent school and then sent straight to the stage to gain their experience, their livelihood, and ultimately reputation and success both at home and abroad? The only trouble is that, as a rule, the geniuses, when they do come along, no sooner become finished artists than they quit their native heath and seek their fortunes in richer localities.

But if Reval cannot afford "stars," the other two capitals can, and to some extent do. I heard no opera, either actual or preparatory, at Helsingfors, but was told that the season's scheme there was tolerably ambitious and that among the expected "guests" was that fine Scottish tenor of rising fame, Joseph Hislop. Apart from his more recent triumphs, his education and early successes in the neighbouring city of Stockholm would account for Finland's interest in him. He is assured of a hearty reception in the more distant capital, where, by the way, he will not be called upon to sing in the local tongue, but in Swedish. I understand that in former times this indulgence was not granted to anyone, however distinguished, and that once long ago even the services of the great Chaliapin were refused because he could not oblige with the Finnish text. To-day I fancy the same objection would scarcely be forthcoming. On the whole, however, Finland is far behind both Estonia and Latvia in the matter of foreign language study. You hardly come across a soul who speaks English, or even German and Russian, except among the better classes, and, for a really go-ahead country in commercial matters, Finland is surprisingly self-centred and isolated in this respect. But of two things at least it can be proud—its music, national, symphonic, and vocal, which we in England already know so much of; and its architecture, which I find not alone strikingly original and characteristic, but noble and impressive in a marked degree.

HERMAN KLEIN.

Part V
SELECTIONS FROM THE CORRESPONDENCE SECTION OF *THE GRAMOPHONE*

PATTI AND HER GRAMOPHONE RECORDS

(To the Editor of THE GRAMOPHONE.*)*

DEAR SIR,—The quaint stories related by Sir Landon Ronald at a recent Press Club dinner, and reported in the *Daily Telegraph*, doubtless served their purpose. Mme. Calvé and Mr. Ben Davies are happily alive to read and comment upon them if they want to ; but Adelina Patti is dead and buried, and cannot therefore speak for herself. As the writer of her authorised biography, "The Reign of Patti," I should like to state through your columns that Sir Landon's account of what she said on hearing her own voice on a gramophone for the first time differs entirely from that given to me by one who was present, and the accuracy of which was confirmed by her husband, Baron Cederström, who saw the proofs of my book, and by her solicitor, the late Sir George Lewis.

The latter had arranged with H.M.V. for the making of the records at Craig-y-Nos Castle, and, as Patti had at first a rooted objection to doing so, this was not an easy job. However, all the difficulties were overcome and, to quote my own words, "Happily her feeling towards the gramophone changed from the moment when she heard her own records. This was two or three days after she had finished making them. The Baroness was coming down to déjeuner and descending the main staircase to the hall (where the instrument had cunningly been placed), when the tones of her own voice fell for the first time upon her ear. One who was present relates that she stopped, turned visibly pale, clutched at the banisters, and remained where she was standing until the piece was finished. Then she ran quickly down the stairs to the hall, and, exclaiming, 'Oh, you darling !' threw her arms round the horn of the gramophone. Her aversion had been cured by her own voice."

I wonder whether Sir Landon Ronald's memory can have played him a trick ? According to him, the *diva's* exclamation (on presumably the same occasion) was, "How magnificent ! What a great singer Patti is !" It may be, of course, that in the excitement of the moment she gave vent to some such utterance ; but my informant does not appear to have heard it. In any case, I can say of my own knowledge that, despite all the flattery she received, self-admiration was not one of her weaknesses. She knew exactly how divinely she sang ; but never once did I catch her praising herself for her own singing.

Yours faithfully,

HERMAN KLEIN.

✦ ✦ ✦

PATTI AND HER GRAMOPHONE RECORDS.
(To the Editor of THE GRAMOPHONE.*)*

DEAR SIR,—I read with interest Mr. Herman Klein's letter to you.

Unfortunately I did not read Mr. Klein's Biography of Patti, or I should have been tempted to have informed him that his account of that great singer's experience of making records for the first time was quite inaccurate.

He states that it was two or three days after she had finished making the records before she had heard one. This is not in accordance with the facts of the case. I can tell you exactly what did occur, as I happened to spend nearly a week at Craig-y-nos Castle for the purpose of accompanying Madame Patti when she felt inclined to attempt to make records.

It is quite true that she had a great prejudice against the gramophone, and even whilst I was staying with her she continually expressed astonishment that I should have any admiration for such an "abomination."

However, after I had been there a day or two, the good news came that she would consent to try and make a record.

The necessary apparatus had been fixed up in a small room, and from the moment that she began to sing there was not a single person present excepting myself at the piano.

After she had made the record she insisted on it being played back to her. It was explained to her that this would mean that the record would be destroyed and made useless, but she was adamant on the point.

Accordingly, it was played back, and it was at that moment (and not two or three days afterwards, as Mr. Klein asserts) that Patti turned to me and said : "Ah, mon Dieu ! maintenant je comprends pourquoi je suis Patti ! Mon cher, quelle voix ! Quelle artiste !"

Let me add at once that this was said in a very naïve manner, as if she were speaking of somebody else. There was not a touch of conceit to be traced.

She was such a great artist that she knew exactly what great singing was. This was the first time she had heard the voice and phrasing of Patti, and her expression of admiration was entirely due, to my mind, to the fact that she was listening to one of the very greatest artists of all time.

Even her husband, Baron Cederström, was not present on this occasion by her express desire. But the recorder was Mr. Fred Gaisberg, who was on the other side of the thin partition which divided the recording room from the machine, and he can vouch that my story is accurate and not exaggerated.

I have never repeated this little history without assuring my audience of Patti's habitual modesty, and I think everybody will agree that the emotion of hearing her own voice reproduced for the first time in her life was more than sufficient to cause her little outburst, which was really touching in its simplicity.

I do not know who Mr. Klein's informant was, but he or she was certainly not present on the occasion to which I refer. And, my dear Mr. Klein, my memory has not played me a trick !

Yours faithfully,

LANDON RONALD.

[Mr. Klein writes :—It was very wrong of my old friend Sir Landon Ronald not to have read my biography of Patti, because it was written at her reiterated request and she would not have liked him to be unacquainted with all the authoritative information which it contains. If he were to do so even now, he would perceive (as I have done since reading his letter) that the occasion of the exclamation which he has quoted both in English and French was entirely distinct from that referred to in my *Reign of Patti*. And evidently there were two such occasions—one immediately after she had made the record, when it was "played back" for her ; the other when, a few days later, she was descending the staircase at Craig-y-Nos Castle and there fell upon her ears the sounds of her own voice reproduced *from a gramophone for the first time*. By then Sir Landon had probably left the Castle and never heard the second exclamation at all. Anyhow, my informant was unquestionably present when it was uttered. The blame for the two being confounded rests entirely with Sir Landon Ronald—(1) for not having read my biography ; (2) for not having clearly indicated the occasion in his speech as he has done in the above letter ; and (3) for making no reference in the former to the naïve or jocular manner in which Mme. Patti spoke of her voice and her artistry. Had he hinted at this last even in the slightest degree, for the information of his innocent audience, I think, Sir, I should never have thought it necessary to address a letter to you on the subject. Both Sir Landon and I knew the *diva* too well for such a defence to be essential.]

LILLI LEHMANN, JULIA CULP, VICTOR MAUREL.

(To the Editor of THE GRAMOPHONE.)

DEAR SIR,—In connection with Mr. Klein's enthusiastic notice of the Lilli Lehmann records in last month's issue, some of your readers may be interested in the following reply, written in her own vigorous handwriting, to a request for information about her records made by my friend, Mr. Edgar Ailes, of Detroit, U.S.A. (to whom, rather than to myself, the present re-issue is ultimately due):—

> Salzburg; 10–8–1926.
> Mozarteum.
>
> DEAR SIR!
> Yes I sung many gramophone records long ago! . . . I cannot tell here what songs. But you could ask of: *Casta Diva, Norma.—fidelio aria.—Traviata aria* and *finale* very good,—many songs all nicely good. I know that the Company has spoiled many of mine records throwing the war, as they not had material; but there are enough good one you may order. . . . I and II aria from Belmont and Constanze (Entführung) *Schubert* and *Beethovenlieder*, Volkslieder : Kommt ein Vögerl geflogen, and english ones, *blue bells, Robin Adair*, etz.
> I am here in Salzburg for 2 months teaching, but I finish the 5th of September and shall only be at home : Berlin—Grunewald, Herbert-strasse 20—of the middle of October. Wishing you could get all you want with most kind regards, very sincerely yours very truly,
> LILLI LEHMANN.

I am informed that Mme. Lehmann also recorded, among other things, *Mi tradi* (Don Giovanni), *Porgi amor* (Figaro), Schubert's *Erlkönig, O hätt' ich Jubals Harf* (Handel), and Schumann's *Intermezzo* and *Mondnacht*; but up to date the Parlophone Company has not succeeded in tracing these.

After the success of the Lehmann issue, it would be interesting to know how many people wish to possess Victor Maurel's Odeon records from *Otello, Falstaff*, and *Don Giovanni*. Maurel was, of course, Verdi's idol, and the original Iago and Falstaff. Julia Culp's complete and unsurpassable Odeon *Frauenliebe und Leben* (four records) would also be welcomed by many; they make Lotte Lehmann's version sound sentimental and breathy, and they have the correct piano accompaniment. Yours faithfully,
DESMOND C. SHAWE-TAYLOR.
Greenlanes, Burnham, Bucks.

(To the Editor of THE GRAMOPHONE.)

DEAR SIR,—There are strong possibilities that the Columbia Phonograph Company and the Parlophone Company will soon be able to offer special pressings of very old records of great historical interest. At the present writing these two companies are looking up the master records of Victor Maurel, Jean and Edouard de Reszke, Ernest Van Dyck, Victorien Sardou and Joseph Jefferson (reciting selections from his famous *Rip Van Winkle*).

If there are any readers of THE GRAMOPHONE who are interested in securing pressings of such records I wish they would send me their names and addresses immediately. These names will be handed to the proper company officials or dealers, who in turn will write those interested should the pressings be made up. Yours faithfully,
WILLIAM H. SELTSAM.

318, Reservoir Avenue,
Bridgeport, Conn., U.S.A.

(To the Editor of THE GRAMOPHONE.)

DEAR SIR,—As anything written by Mr. Klein is of lasting value to music-lovers I trust he will pardon me for pointing out a slight yet important error which appears in his all-too-brief volume, " Great Women Singers of My Time," and is mentioned again in his dissertation upon the Lilli Lehmann records. (An appreciation, allow me to say, which adds vastly to the satisfaction of those who subscribed for them.) The error in question occurs on page 215, where it is stated that Madame Lehmann was born on May 15th. This, however, was her sister's birthday, she herself being born—according to her own autobiography—on November 24th, 1848. (The sister, Marie Lehmann, sang at the Vienna Opera, married Fritz Helbig, and had a daughter, Hedwig, who became her aunt's devoted companion and accompanist—which explains the similarity of tone noted by Mr. Klein.) The original error, I believe, was made by the late H. T. Finck in " Success in Music," and was quoted later by Mr. Legge in the *Daily Telegraph*, so that Mr. Klein was quite justified in repeating it.

And now may I venture to criticise the critic? He tells us that the singers of 1870-90 were unparalleled in their perfection, and speaks—as does Mr. Newman—most disparagingly of the modern prima donna; but I seem to recall the names of great singers who lived and triumphed *before* those enumerated, and I *have* heard of three or four golden-voiced women of later days: whose glories, doubtless, will be chronicled when Toscanini (for example) writes *his* reminiscences. He heard Lilli Lehmann in 1898, we know, and has listened to every celebrated singer since; indeed, his declaration that one of the youngest possesses " the loveliest voice in the world " has been quoted already in THE GRAMOPHONE. (She is renowned, also, for her fine musicianship.)

With regard to another subject, the " Press agents " derided so scathingly by Messrs. Klein and Newman, I think it can be admitted that they are used, and needed, only by inferior folk (of any profession), while no one will deny the fact that singers of former times would have welcomed thankfully the services of the " business managers " employed by their successors (some of whom, by the way, are quite as modest and dignified as any of the ladies lauded so deservingly by Mr. Klein).

To conclude, may I ask, with sincere respect, and without questioning in any way the authority of so great a master of his art, *why* the writing of reminiscences should be reserved for critics only? It is a matter of opinion, certainly, but I myself would give a thousand others for the autobiography with which that magnificent woman, Madame Lilli Lehmann, once " troubled the world." Yours faithfully,
N. MARSCHALL.

Northenden, Cheshire.

International Record Collectors' Club

Following his letter published last September, p. 128, Mr. William H. Seltsam writes :—

One of the strangest paradoxes of the gramophone business is the accumulation of a vast treasure of records of great historical importance which, when withdrawn from catalogues, do but gather dust on the shelves of company vaults. These "morgues of forgotten voices," as I call them, have often aroused my curiosity. Why are histories and biographies written about these great celebrities, and photographs displayed, yet the records which preserve their voices, forgotten? Some companies save these matrices; others destroy tons of them because, as they tell us, there is no present-day demand! Having many times questioned this excuse as highly illogical, I made a vow to dig down to the base of the matter.

To determine the extent of the demand for such recordings, I sent letters to typical leading periodicals as THE GRAMOPHONE, *Phonograph Monthly Review*, and the *New York Times*. The news of this activity spread. Then the fun began! In the deluge I received replies from Maine to California, from Ireland to Manchuria and Australia. Briefly, I am convinced that there is a demand for the historical record. To test my theory more fully, I am founding the *International Record Collectors' Club*, the policy being to unearth and offer special editions of these rarities.

I am pleased to announce that our committee in charge of monthly choices consists of the names of fourteen international authorities on historical records. That indefatigable historian Ulysses J. Walsh declares : " I am strongly of the opinion that your proposal to organize an International Record Collectors' Club, for the purpose of supplying special pressings of records of ' historical ' and other collectors' interest, is the most important development the phonograph world has known for years. In my estimation the whole idea is nothing less than a stroke of genius, and you may be sure that as one whose abiding passion for years has been for historically important records, I shall be glad to aid your plans in any possible way." In the *New York Times* Mr. Compton Pakenham (in his " Newly Recorded Music " column) wrote : " Here is another opportunity for collectors to prove that their inquiries for records no longer on the current lists were not merely frivolous."

While many very rare matrices are being traced in Europe, our first issue will be an American which I feel is especially valuable and timely. Most music lovers are aware that the 1931–32 season marks the farewell in the career of Geraldine Farrar. It was my idea to re-issue two of her older recordings, but good fortune showed favours in an unexpected manner. Two 10in. matrices of Miss Farrar's voice which have never been published or offered for sale in any form have been found. Both were recorded prior to 1923, and comprise the following selections :

Der Nussbaum (Schumann), in English with piano.

Ouvre Tes Yeux Bleus (Massenet), in French with orchestra.

Miss Farrar has given our club special permission to issue these recordings in a limited, numbered edition. Orders will be filled in numerical sequence as received. Collectors should thoroughly understand that this edition, when exhausted, will not be supplemented with additional pressings.

Overseas customers should place their orders with Mr. P. G. Hurst, Hamiota, Isted Rise, Meopham, Kent, England, who conducts the "Collectors' Corner" in THE GRAMOPHONE, and will act as the representative of our Club in England. The club number IRRC–1 should be stated in the order. While no definite price can be set on overseas orders, due to differences in duties, we feel that the double-faced pressing will be in the vicinity of about $2. We do know that the price will be considerably cheaper if ordered according to the above plan.

If successful with our first issue, announcements of further choices will be mailed monthly to those interested.

318, Reservoir Ave.,   WILLIAM H. SELTSAM,
Bridgeport, Conn., U.S.A.   *Secretary.*

" RUDDIGORE "

(To the Editor of THE GRAMOPHONE.)

DEAR SIR,—I hope Mr. Klein will allow me to call in question one small point in his delightful article on *Ruddigore*. He writes : " It is a treat to hear the Sullivanesque overture, with its sustained vivacity, its weird suggestions of the supernatural, its lightning runs for the violins, and its amazing mastery of form, so splendidly rendered." I think he will find that, as a matter of fact, the Overture recorded by H.M.V. is—so far as the arrangement goes—not Sullivan's at all. When the opera was revived after its long silence, several of the numbers were, for one reason or another, omitted. What satisfied the author and composer was, apparently, not considered good enough for this more enlightened generation ! Among the numbers so omitted were the duet *The battle's roar is over* and the second Finale. As, however, both these numbers figured in Sullivan's Overture, and as it would never have done for the Overture to contain tunes which were not heard again, it became necessary to re-write the work, and the task was committed to—I think—Mr. Geoffrey Toye, the then conductor of the D'Oyly Carte Company. This is the Overture now performed, and that it is an effective piece of work is evident to all who hear it. Sullivan's original Overture was, doubtless, not one of his best. It cannot be compared with those he wrote for *Iolanthe* or *The Yeomen*. Yet one cannot help regretting its complete disappearance. There is a characteristic charm about it, a smoothness in the writing, a naturalness in the transition from tune to tune, and withal a *unity*, which are not, I think, so apparent in its successor. That, of course, is largely a matter of taste. Whatever the rival merits of the two works, the fact remains that the present Overture is not by Sullivan, and the name of the arranger ought surely to be stated on the record, in justice to all parties concerned.

Yours faithfully,
H. H. E.

Sanderstead.

The above letter was submitted to Mr. Geoffrey Toye, who wrote as follows to Mr. Klein :—

" In the original Full Scores the Overtures to *Iolanthe* and *Yeomen* are in Sullivan's handwriting, including all the details of the scoring.

" With regard to the Overtures of the other operas, it is generally understood that these were left for Mr. Cellier, the conductor, to arrange—very often at the last moment before the date of the production. These Overtures therefore vary in merit and are generally considered to be inferior to the two mentioned above.

" When we revived *Ruddigore* an Overture of mine was substituted for the existing one, which incidentally contained a tune which was being omitted in our production of the opera.

" This Overture is the one now played before the opera, and is recorded on H.M.V. DB4005. I also substituted a new Overture for *Pirates*, which seemed to require it. Whether these Overtures have more merit than the old ones is a matter which posterity can judge for itself.

" I am aware that the suggestion of any alterations to the Gilbert and Sullivan Operas fills the purists with alarm and despondency, but I will not for a moment admit the ' untouchability ' of these excellent Operas as opposed to all others. If works such as Aïda, Carmen, Lohengrin, Hoffmann and many others can be and are habitually cut to meet modern conditions why not the Gilbert and Sullivan Operas ? Moreover, we know that Sullivan himself had the intention of ' making some changes when he had the time,' especially in the case of *Pinafore*, of which he said, later in life, that he had written some of the numbers and choruses in the wrong keys. As it turned out, however, he was always busy on some new production, and died before he had time to make the alterations.

"Perhaps I should add, for the benefit of the faithful, that I took the greatest trouble to satisfy myself about the writing of these operas, making the fullest enquiries from every available source, including people who were on the stage and in the orchestra in the opera companies in the time of Sullivan and Cellier."

"Yours faithfully,
"H. H. E."

Bardenstead.

The above letter was submitted to Mr. Geoffrey Toye, who wrote as follows to Mr. Klein:—

"In the original Full Scores the Overtures to Iolanthe and Yeomen are in Sullivan's handwriting, including all the details of the scoring.

"With regard to the Overtures of the other operas, it is generally understood that these were left for Mr. Cellier, the conductor, to arrange—very often at the last moment before the date of the production. These Overtures therefore vary in merit and are generally considered to be inferior to the two mentioned above.

"When we revived Ruddigore an Overture of mine was substituted for the existing one, which incidentally contained a tune which was being omitted in our production of the opera.

"The Overture is the one now played before the opera, and is recorded on H.M.V. DB4008. I also substituted a new Overture for Yeomen which seemed to require it. Whether these Overtures have more merit than the old ones is a matter whose posterity can judge for itself.

"I am aware that the question of any alterations to the Gilbert and Sullivan Operas fills the purists with alarm and despondency, but I will not for a moment admit the probability of these so-called Operas as opposed to all others. If works such as Aida, Carmen, Lohengrin, Hoffmann and many others can be and are habitually cut to meet modern conditions why not the Gilbert and Sullivan Operas? Moreover, we know that Sullivan himself had the intention of making some changes when he had the time, especially in the case of Yeomen, of which he said, later in the day, that he had written some of the numbers and choruses in the wrong keys. As it turned out, however, he was always busy on some

Mr. Klein writes:

"I would like to thank Mr. Geoffrey Toye for his very kind and helpful letter, which I can confirm on every point. I can also assure the enthusiasts that no one could have been more satisfied than Sullivan himself was nor more grateful for the assistance that he received in these matters."

Part VI
BOOK REVIEWS
(1925 TO 1933)

MUSICIANS AND MUMMERS
By HERMAN KLEIN.

(London: Cassel and Company, Ltd., 1925.) (Review by Compton Mackenzie, October, 1925)

But if you want really good musical reminiscences I suggest Mr. Herman Klein's new book *Musicians and Mummers* (Cassell & Co., 21s.), in which you will find any number of them. You will find a good deal more than mere reminiscence, and no book that I know of gives a clearer account of musical taste during the last half century. Incidentally, it is a valuable guide to dramatic taste during the same period. For some time readers of THE GRAMOPHONE have had the advantage of Mr. Klein's unrivalled knowledge of the opera, so that fortunately he needs no introduction in these columns. I read the book through at a sitting, which I venture to think is a tribute to the author's ability to be interesting, and as I learnt a number of facts of which I had hitherto been ignorant I have no doubt that most of our readers will benefit as much as I did from a course of Mr. Klein. The book is of particular interest to gramophonists for the account it gives of the " Pops " at St. James' Hall (need I explain to the present generation that " Pops " was an affectionate diminutive for the concerts of classical music provided every week by Messrs. Chappell at St. James' Hall, on the site of which Mr. De Groot nowadays provides music that is no doubt extremely popular, but not often classical ?) which represented the equivalent of the gramophone in those days. It is noteworthy that they came to an end just as the gramophone began to get going. Of course, I am not suggesting for a moment any sort of cause or effect, but it is interesting to see the way the time-spirit works sometimes. One asks oneself why after 1,600 concerts public support should begin to fall off. It was certainly not due to any increasing lack of interest in music. I wonder sometimes if we shall see the same kind of sudden unwillingness to support the promenade concerts at the Queen's Hall. I think that Mr. Klein convinces us that singing has deteriorated in the last twenty-five years. It is always difficult not to suspect an old playgoer when he writes about the wonderful past, because such a one is apt to forget that the zest of his own youth made those plays and books and pictures seem so much better in retrospect than those offered to his fatigued maturity. But singing is another matter, especially when it is judged by so accomplished a master of the art as Mr. Klein, because he has had to preserve a critical attitude towards it all his life and his condemnation of modern singing is not to be attributed merely to the enthusiasm of a youthful enjoyment he is no longer capable of feeling. My own experience of the gramophone has convinced me that singing is steadily deteriorating. I should be inclined to back McCormack even against Sims Reeves, but apart from him I have no one to put up against the giants of the past. I sometimes ask myself what we should think nowadays of my own grandfather as a comedian, and I say to myself that, after all, the Victorian age which produced and appreciated so many great men cannot be accused of not knowing what a good actor or singer was. Mr. Klein's attitude to contemporary iconoclasm is wonderfully suave, and it might be recommended as a model to some of our iconoclasts. Of course, I have inherited such a long, and if you like hide-bound, artistic tradition that I find myself as easily in perfect communion with Mr. Klein's point of view as if he were not thirty years my senior. When, for instance, he deplores the neglect of Meyerbeer I am entirely in sympathy with him. Of course, there will always come a time when we must destroy some of our rubbish, but I have noticed that whenever I have had what is called a good clear out of my papers or books, I always manage to destroy many papers and many books that I have afterwards wanted, and I feel convinced that the present fashion of lightening the ship of art will end in its turning turtle, if we are not careful. It must always be remembered that in art the minority has the loudest lungs, and that contemporary criticism is a minority report. Some years ago, in the course of a conversation with William Heinemann, I happened to remark that some book was a great success, whereupon he replied in a tone of the very profoundest contempt, " Oh yes, a great success with the little London clique, but what use is that to a publisher ? " The present attitude of the little London clique in matters of art much resembles that of a revolutionary tribunal, which is so eager to cut off the head of an aristocrat that it has no time to give him a fair trial. This is a Kruschen period, and women have even purged themselves of their hair and their petticoats ; but the dreadful thought occurs that the more they have put off, the larger presently will become their appetite to put on. Women always undress after a period of social agony like the great war. Their last undressing was followed by crinolines, and crinolines were followed by the fashions of the seventies and eighties, and so it will go on. A book like Mr. Klein's, written by an essentially wise and genial and tolerant personality, may serve to suggest to some of us that while we have been wringing the necks of a number of swans, we have all the while been mistaking a great many goslings for cygnets.

The following books are reviewed by Herman Klein in his *The Gramophone and the Singer* No. 43 (December, 1927), p. 208

Grove's Dictionary of Music and Musicians. Third Edition, in five volumes, edited by H. C. Coles. Vol. 1 (A to C) London: Macmillan & Co.

The Gentle Art of Singing, by Henry J. Wood. In four volumes, Vol. 1. London: Oxford University Press.

Sir Arthur Sullivan, his Life, Letters, and Diaries, by Herbert Sullivan and Newman Flower. London: Cassell & Co.

Some Memories and Reflections, by Emma Eames. London: D. Appleton & Co.

OPERATIC TRANSLATIONS

I am asked to say a word about the two small volumes of *Operatic Translations* just issued in THE GRAMOPHONE Library from the office of this Magazine. There is no need to tell our readers that they are from the accomplished pen of H. F. V. Little, or to describe the accessible " line upon line " form that makes them so easy of reference and perusal. There can be no doubt that they fill an absolute want, for they are at once educative and an aid to the understanding. How constantly does it happen that, listening to an operatic record sung in a strange tongue, you say to yourself, " Yes, very beautiful; but I wonder what it's all about! " And even if you know the language, you cannot, alas! always distinguish the actual words; or, again, if you can hear every syllable, you will find it very pleasant to have before your eyes, following every line of Italian or French, this free and compact translation of Mr. Little's. My advice, therefore, is that you provide yourselves immediately with these convenient volumes, which comprise translations of nearly every operatic record that you are likely to be listening to, both now and for a long time to come.

HERMAN KLEIN.

OPERA AT HOME*

The New H.M.V. " Opera at Home "

When first this volume came before the public eight years ago the aptness of the title was far from being as appreciable as it is to-day. The growth in the supply of drawing-room or fireside music of every species has been simply beyond calculation. During the interval in question the gramophone has been supplemented—not superseded, thank goodness!—by the wireless; and between them they have encouraged a demand for and a love of music in the home, the like of which has never been known in the history of the art. Of original edition of this book in 1920 " H.M.V." issued 20,000 copies. In the following year they printed a library edition of it, revised and enlarged, that probably doubled the earlier issue. Beyond that figures disappeared, and I only know that annual reprints continued, with enlargements and addenda, until now we have what is termed the " Fourth Edition, Completely Revised and yet Further Enlarged " for 1928.

How many millions of copies it is expected will be sold of this new edition I am again without information; and guesswork is not my strong point. But if I expect something very wonderful, it is because a copy of the latest *Opera at Home* lies before me, the most remarkable six shillings' worth of its kind that I have ever set eyes upon, and because I regard it as an indispensable adjunct to every house where there is a decent gramophone on the face of the globe. It does something more than fill a want. It enables you to complete your operatic education. There was a time, within easy recollection, when ignorance concerning opera and opera stories was believed to be so universal that the manufacturers of gramophones, especially in America, used to deem it essential to paste a printed descriptive key to the meaning of the record on the back of the disc, where at that time, of course, nothing was stamped but the number of the matrix. But it was a clumsy arrangement at best, and nowadays the vacant wasted space is no longer available for the purpose, even were it required. Which happily it is not.

Thanks to the gramophone, more than to any other existing medium or instrument, the human race is now musically much better educated, and it knows also a good deal better than it did, say twenty years ago, the utility and value of a book of reference of the type I am dealing with. Turn to its pages and you will find something far more interesting and informative on the subject of opera than the contents of an ordinary musical dictionary. As the editors justly claim in the preface, they have " tried to steer a course between the two extremes of over-elaboration and over-simplification. . . . Under each Opera the date of production, a list of the principal rôles, and, in most cases, a few introductory remarks are given. Then follows an outline of the plot, and this is in turn followed by a list of the excerpts which have been ' recorded,' with particulars of the records available of each. With each excerpt is given a brief description of the dramatic situation."

Such is the plan upon which *Opera at Home* is based. On the whole I find it carried out with intelligent care—perhaps with greater accuracy in some details than heretofore, though I frankly admit that I have not yet read through every plot and every accompanying or analytical description of the orchestral pieces *verbatim et literatim*. Maybe I never shall. However, I have scanned enough of the beautifully printed letterpress to be able to perceive that it is ably written, clear and concise in style, and accurate as to the spelling of names and other important details. The editors, aware of their fallibility when handling the various delicate and controversial topics connected with Opera, have perhaps been at greater pains than was actually necessary to forestall criticism. Indeed, they think " it would be impossible to produce a book on Opera that should be completely free from error "; and, further to justify their modest attitude, they jubilantly declare that the very authorities whom they consulted for this compilation were themselves in many instances at loggerheads " on some matter or other." At present my verdict is " not guilty "; and I trust I may continue to remain of that opinion.

Wisdom has been shown in eliminating from the present edition a great many of the operas included in the previous issues, and substituting in their places works that have been recently introduced into the repertory. I find that, out of a total of about 150, twenty-one have now been omitted and seventeen—the majority of a more modern type—selected for inclusion in the fresh list. As an indication of the direction in which tastes are moving, it will be of interest to give the names of these operas. The following have been dropped out :—

Cristoforo Colombo (Franchetti), *Dafne* (Peri), *Daughter of the Regiment* (Donizetti), *Don Sebastiano* (Donizetti), *Le Donne Curiose* (Wolf-Ferrari), *Il Duca d'Alba* (Donizetti), *L'Enfant Prodigue* (Debussy), *Il Guarany* (Gomez), *Isabeau* (Mascagni), *Le Jongleur de Notre Dame* (Massenet), *Lodoletta* (Mascagni), *Macbeth* (Verdi), *Manon Lescaut* (Auber), *Nero* (Rubinstein), *Polly* (Gay), *Quo Vadis* (Nouguès), *Reine de Saba* (Gounod), *I Vespri Siciliani* (Verdi), *La Wally* (Catalani), and *Zampa* (Hérold).

The following take their place :—

Ariadne at Naxos (R. Strauss), *Bartered Bride* (Smétana), *The Bat* or *Die Fledermaus* (J. Strauss), *Benvenuto Cellini* (Berlioz), *Don Quixote* (Massenet), *Goyescas* (Granados), *Life for the Tsar* (Glinka), *Love of the Three Oranges* (Prokofieff), *Mozart and Salieri* (Rimsky-Korsakov), *The Nightingale* (Stravinsky), *Pelléas et Mélisande* (Debussy), *The Perfect Fool* (Holst), *Phoebus and Pan* (Bach), *Russalka* (Dargomishky), *Sacred City of Kitesh* (Rimsky-Korsakov), *Turandot* (Puccini), and *The Violin-maker of Cremona* (Hubay).

Among the deleted ones are three or four that I personally would not have removed—as, for example, the Verdi pair, *Macbeth* and *I Vespri Siciliani*, the former of which has lately been revived at Berlin on a scale of remarkable magnificence. Excerpts from the earlier Verdi scores are frequently being recorded, especially on the Continent, and one can never say of any of them that it is definitely laid on the shelf for ever. From Gounod's *Reine de Saba* at least three numbers are in constant request, best known by their English titles of *Lend me your aid*, *Far greater in his*

lowly state, and *She alone charmeth my sadness*; and these ought surely to have sufficed to justify the retention of the opera, apart from the chance of its early revival when the " renascence of melody " reaches our slow-moving lyric stage.

In conclusion I may add that the new edition of *Opera at Home* is not less elegantly got up than its predecessors, while the new photographic reproductions furnish a delightful series of pictures in costume of the popular leading stars who have sung for H.M.V. during recent years. HERMAN KLEIN.

The following books are reviewed by Herman Klein in his *The Gramophone and the Singer* No. 52 (September, 1928), p. 235.

Clara Butt, Her Life Story by Winifred Ponder. London: George G. Harrap & Co. Ltd.
Music by John Redfield. N.Y.: Columbia University Press.
Long-Haired Iopas, or *Chapters from Twenty-five Years of Music-Criticism* by Edward Prime-Stevenson. Privately printed.
Foundations of English Opera by Edward J. Dent. Cambridge University Press.
Mozart by Dyneley Hussey. London: Kegan Paul.
Sullivan's Comic Operas by Thomas F. Dunhill. London: Edward Arnold & Co.
Bach by Charles Sanford Terry. Oxford University Press.

Cobbett's Cyclopedic Survey of Chamber Music
by Walter Wilson
Cobbett, Vol. 1 & 2. Oxford University Press.

See pages 458–459 and 598.

MR. COBBETT'S CYCLOPEDIC SURVEY: VOL. II.

WITH the issue by the Oxford University Press of the second volume of Mr. Cobbett's *Cyclopedic Survey of Chamber Music,* its indefatigable Editor has the full right to exclaim *Finis coronat opus!* For the finish does indeed crown a notable and noble achievement, which lights up with its brilliant success the twilight of a long and industrious life. Once again, as in the preceding half of the work, is one struck by the felicitous and comprehensive choice that is made manifest in the hundreds of articles comprising this valuable compilation. Nothing is omitted, and everything is in the fullest sense authoritative. Enthusiasts who read this Magazine will perhaps miss another such interesting and informative essay as that which appeared under letter " G "— I allude to Mr. Compton Mackenzie's article on " Gramophone Chamber Music "—which I venture to predict will be permanently regarded as both the first and the last word on that particular topic. A re-perusal of it impels me to say that the growing love for chamber music is bound to send gramophonists eagerly and constantly to the pages of Mr. Cobbett's *magnum opus,* if only for the reason that these contain such masses of instructive criticism concerning the masterpieces they have learnt to delight in and the gifted geniuses who created the works in question.

Let me try now to pick out a few of the plums for you as they come along. If you want to know all about the " International Society for Contemporary Music," read what Edwin Evans has to say. Regarding " Interpretation," study the rather short but helpful article by André Mangeot. Sydney Grew discourses attractively on the " Player-Piano and Chamber Music." Two very fine articles that I recommend to your especial notice (particularly the second one) are Alfred Casella's on " Italian Chamber Music," and J. B. Trend's on " Spanish Chamber Music " ; it is quite wonderful how they bring into relief the characteristic qualities of each in turn. Mention of contrasts reminds me that there are two separate articles on Schumann, one by Richard Aldrich, the American musical critic, the other, devoted more particularly to the interpretation of him, by Mme. Schumann's greatest surviving pupil, Fanny Davies. These should be studied and compared with careful attention, since they emphasize the fact that the best of judges will always differ in opinion where Schumann's music is concerned. The very reverse is the case in regard to Schubert, with whom Willi Kahl deals in a long and thoughtful essay, which the veteran Editor supplements with one of those pregnant and valuable " postscripts " that abound throughout his *Survey.* It has been said that the most vital point of certain letters lies in the postscript ; and very often it will be found so here, although the same editorial hand writes the P.S. in every case.

A truly magnificent article on " Mozart " is from the pen of Dr. Hermann Abert, who passed away shortly after he had written it in August, 1927. The P.S. in this instance reminds us that Abert rewrote Otto Jahn's *Life of Mozart* and made of it practically a new biography, but rightly takes him to task for comparing the great musician to Michelangelo rather than Raphael. I quite agree with Mr. Cobbett on this point. The article does full justice to all the more prominent chamber works, while a Russian critic's analysis of the glorious quintet in G minor, printed as an addendum in smaller type, can also be read with profit. A reference to the fact that this " superlatively beautiful " composition was played no fewer than forty-four times at the Popular Concerts (or Monday and Saturday " Pops ") seems the appropriate occasion for me to confess that I had the honour of writing, by Mr. Cobbett's request, the story of the " Pops " for this volume. One question I have not attempted to answer—Who was the favourite composer of the old " Pop " audiences ? Well, in the end I think it was Beethoven ; but, during the greater part of the half-century that the institution lived (truly does Mr. Cobbett observe that it should never have been allowed to die !) the suffrages of St. James's Hall were pretty evenly divided between Mozart, Beethoven, Mendelssohn, Schubert, Schumann and perhaps Haydn.

Concluding my notice of this amazing Survey, there is in it so much to praise and admire—it has been enthusiastically reviewed by the press of the whole world—that I hardly like to leave off on a discordant note. Yet I cannot help saying how heartily I disagree with every argument in Leigh Henry's article on " Jazz in Relation to Chamber Music." It is an able attempt to define and defend a proposition which I have neither time nor space to enlarge upon here. Enough that I do not believe " chamber music and jazz " to be in the smallest degree " connected by means of folk characteristics." There is positively nothing in common between the two unless it be the syncopated rhythm of certain negro dances that are more distinctive of the *cabaret* than the " chamber " of musical art ; and I am among those to whom, as Mr. Leigh Henry starts out by anticipating, the association " will appear little short of blasphemous."

HERMAN KLEIN.

"Fact and Fiction about Wagner" *

This is a book that only Ernest Newman could have written. He lays stress in the foreword upon his " double interest in Wagner and detective work," and admits that " the opportunity of gratifying two dominant passions simultaneously was too tempting to be missed." I can say without hesitation that the world is greatly indebted to him for undertaking the job; or, rather, for reducing to a succinct form the various speeches for the prosecution that he has made during the past twenty years or more, when pressing home his indictments against certain of Wagner's biographers. The mis-statements have been mainly of two sorts, deliberate perjury and the purely imaginary inventions due to simple vanity. In either case they have been extremely mischievous, because, stupid as most of them have been, they have generally found credence. For instance, I remember well the issue of Ferdinand Praeger's book *Wagner as I knew him*, than which, says Mr. Newman, " a clumsier piece of knavery and foolery could hardly be imagined." Yet at the time it came out in 1892 (Praeger had been a music-teacher living in London and had actually met Wagner), it was hailed as an excellent and reliable piece of work, nor could all the denials and refutations subsequently launched against the book dissuade people from believing that Praeger's stories were absolute truth.

This is but one example out of a hundred, and I am only led to single it out for mention because I happened to know the author personally and can agree with every word that our " detective " has written concerning him and his book. But there are many instances that are far more interesting, because they are far more elaborate in their fiction and have required subtler handling in order to expose them thoroughly. The manner need not be quoted here, though Mr. Newman, of course, gives them all and also deals with them in his customary fearless fashion; nor is there any need to add that in every instance he proves his case up to the hilt. As the result we have in *Fact and Fiction about Wagner* a book that was sorely needed and is bound to prove of the utmost value to all who really want to get at the truth about the inner life and history of that most extraordinary man.

HERMAN KLEIN.

---

* *Fact and Fiction about Wagner.* By Ernest Newman. 309 pp. Cassell and Co., London. Price 8s. 6d. net.

Puccini's Letters

By no stretch of the imagination could Puccini have been considered an accomplished letter-writer. He was wont to write as he spoke—in a simple, straightforward manner, without the least pretention to literary or rhetorical artifice. It is, therefore, solely regarding the man and his works that interest can be derived from the *Letters of Giacomo Puccini*, edited by Giuseppe Adami, and just published by George G. Harrap & Co. (London, price 12/6). From this viewpoint, the correspondence extending over forty years, addressed chiefly to the famous head of the house of Ricordi, becomes valuable on account of the light that it throws on the composition and production of operas now popular all over the world. Very interesting also is the collection of letters written by the maestro to the editor, Signor Adami, perhaps his most intimate friend, who in his introduction provides the most truthful and accurate analysis of Puccini's character and art that has yet been penned. Here we find clearly set forth the facts of that long struggle with adverse criticism which the composer of *Bohème* and *Butterfly* had to go through, especially in his own country, before his final complete triumph was achieved—at what cost only he himself could know and relate. The story is well worth reading.

HERMAN KLEIN.

THE GOLDEN AGE OF OPERA. By Herman Klein. (Routledge, 10s. 6d. net.)

I expect that many readers of this book will feel some curiosity as to what exactly is meant by the term " Golden Age," in the view of so unusually wide and lengthy an experience as that of Mr. Herman Klein; and that those with precious thirty-year-old memories may feel a certain nervousness lest they may be found to have lived in a fool's paradise. Each age may be expected to have its own views, and Mr. Klein's is that the period of operatic decline began to set in soon after the turn of the century; and that although several glorious seasons of opera followed, these were really more in the nature of a twilight, or, at the best, of an Indian summer. At the opening of the twentieth century, although Patti and Albani had recently made their farewells, Jean and Edouard de Reszke, Calvé, Tamagno, Plançon, Eames, Renaud, and Adams were still in full song, but their retirement shortly afterwards left many blanks, and was a heavy offset against the coming of Caruso, the continuation of Melba, and the occasional reappearances of Maurel, Battistini, and Ancona, all of whom were distinctly " getting on," though still singing superbly.

It is easy to see Mr. Klein's viewpoint, with such a vista of glorious memories behind him, but the Edwardian era did not depend entirely upon the remnants of the past. It witnessed the rise of *La Bohème*, in which Melba and Caruso made history, as did Destinn, Caruso, and Scotti in *Butterfly*. We can, however, see in retrospect that the beginnings of " operdämmerung " were apparent, and it must be admitted that Mr. Klein is right.

He has chosen the time for his publication well, as there are undoubted signs of a revival of interest, on both sides of the Atlantic, in the singers of the " Golden Age "; the very appearance in print of the famous names has been enough to arouse the memories of old opera-goers to something very like enthusiasm—a feeling which is shared to a highly significant extent by the post-war generation.

It is a work of art to have compressed so much information

into a comparatively small space, and at the same time to have retained the narrative form throughout. We have the impression, though it is not forced upon us, that Mr. Klein and the Opera were almost interchangeable terms : he was indispensable to it, both as an expert and a negotiator : he engaged Battistini, reconciled Patti and Jean de Reszke, and arranged Patti's farewell—achievements which leave us in no doubt as to the value of his services to Opera in general and to Augustus Harris in particular. At the age of seven he heard Jenny Lind, and he seemed to be in some way connected with all the milestones of operatic history : the Meyerbeer craze, Nilsson, Patti, Otello, the de Reszkes, Pagliacci, Ternina, Wagner, and Verdi. The procession of events and persons seems endless, and the author has something to say about all of them, to which his vast experience and obviously great tact give a personal touch that opera-lovers will not fail to recognise. I doubt whether I have ever heard of a more charming compliment being paid to any-

body than when on the eve of the realisation of Jean de Reszke's ambition to sing *Tristan* in German, Mr. Klein, being unable to be present on the following night, was invited to supper by Nordica to meet the brothers. "Supper over . . . Mr. Amherst Webber went to the piano, apparently as prearranged, and started the love scene from Act 2 of *Tristan*. Still sitting at the table, my hostess and Jean de Reszke began that marvellous duet, both singing in German ; and they never left off till they had finished it. This they did for me *con amore*—an act of friendship which I can never forget. . . ."

This book is a work of reference and a volume of memories ; it comes from the right source, and is written in the right way. That every reader of "Collectors' Corner" will want a copy is a foregone conclusion, and I can assure others that if they have been waiting for a book like this, they need wait no longer.

P. G. Hurst

The following reviews can be found earlier in this volume:

Part VII
BIBLIOGRAPHICAL NOTE

Herman Klein's books have been mentioned, together with publication details, in the Introduction. It was noted that these books are in one sense largely autobiographical, in so far as they recount the author's artistic life. Both the fact that he was very much involved "behind the scenes" in many important musical events, and enjoyed personal friendships with many of the important artists of his day have made works like *Thirty Years of Musical Life in London, 1870–1900* veritable gold mines of information for many biographers, e.g. Clara Leiser in her *Jean de Reszke and the Great Days of Opera* (N.Y., Minton, Balch & Co., 1934) and Ira Glackens' *Yankee Diva: Lillian Nordica and the Golden Days of Opera* (N.Y., Coleridge Press, 1963). Details, such as they are, of Klein's personal life, and biographical notes on members of his family have been largely drawn from brief passages and footnotes scattered through Klein's own works. His activities as an *impressario,* especially during the years 1908–1909, are documented in *The New York Times.* He made very substantial contributions in the form of detailed recollections of his old teacher, Manuel Garcia, in M. Sterling Mackinlay's *Garcia the Centenarian And His Times: A Memoir of Manuel Garcia's Life and Labours for the Advancement of Music and Science* (Edinburgh, W. Blackwood & Sons; N.Y. D. Appleton & Co., 1908).

Manuel Klein is the subject of an article, with photograph, in the Philadelphia edition of John Wanamaker's *The Opera News* for March 25, 1912 (Vol. IV, No. 13). This article includes a long list of songs and musical shows for which he was responsible while "Composer-Lyricist" of the New York Hippodrome, some of which are not listed in the 18 composer credits assigned him in Bloom's *American Song: The Complete Musical Theater Companion* (N.Y., Facts On File, 1985).

References to Manuel and playwright brother Charles are preserved in the works of New York critics of the day, i.e., see Arnold Schwab's compilation of critiques by James Gibbons Huneker in *Americans in the Arts, 1890–1920* (N.Y., AMS Press, 1985, pps. 231–33; 314).

Part VIII
OBITUARY

July 23, 1856—March 10, 1934

THE musical press and the press in general have dealt fully with the life and character of the man who has been the mentor and friend of us and our readers month by month ever since he wrote his first article for us at the beginning of our second year, in June 1924. At that time Herman Klein's short but invaluable monograph on " Bel Canto " had lately been added to the Oxford University Press series of Oxford Musical Essays, and in conjunction with the biographical and autobiographical books that he wrote subsequently, this forms a background to the teaching that he has given us in his monthly reviews and articles.

The value of that teaching cannot be exaggerated. In Herman Klein we were supremely fortunate in securing the ideal authority on operatic records. There was not, and is not, anyone whose qualifications for such a task of criticism were comparable. He was immersed in the tradition of the operatic stage and yet he was the president of the Critics' Circle by virtue of his long career as an all-round music critic. Moreover, he was one of the very first music critics to take notice of the gramophone and was appointed "musical adviser" to the Columbia Company as long ago as 1906 in New York, where he introduced David Bispham, Anton van Rooy, Lillian Blauvelt and Ruth Vincent, among others, to the recording studio. The story of those early days, and of the premature launching of his "Phono-Vocal Method" with Madame Nordica to illustrate his teaching, he has told in these pages; and it is safe to say that among music critics of his age he was unique in his wholehearted recognition of the musical importance of the gramophone, and unique in his fearless enthusiasm for it and determination that he would do all in his power to guide its progress on the best and most fruitful path. His recent warnings about the pitfalls of microphone recording were timely as well as authoritative.

His work, his spirit, his tradition, live on; but the man himself is gone from us, and it is of the friend who will nevermore come to the London office for an early

THE LATE HERMAN KLEIN

cup of afternoon tea and a talk about the article for the next number, whose regular handwriting on sheets of notepaper from a block—he knew exactly how many words he wrote to a page—I shall no longer read; whose spruce figure and courtly manners and beautiful speaking voice gave a rare quality to every meeting; it is of him and his personal charm that I am thinking most often.

This charm and kindliness were all the more endearing because he was by no means a merely genial and mellow old man when I first came to know him. The piercing eyes and protruding chin were eloquent signs of strong character and unflinching principle, and his bodily vigour was part and parcel of his unfailing mental and moral activity. Wisdom and courage were his constant companions, and he went his way with assurance.

But no man of his age and wide experience as musician and journalist could possibly have shown a more kindly and forbearing patience without the slightest trace of condescension towards the utterly untrained novice whom he found sub-editing THE GRAMOPHONE, and I am thankful to look back on these ten years of perfect accord. He taught me much in the friendliest way.

He once told me that he was the first professing Jew to become a Christian Scientist, and I have often thought that the implications in that conversion were a key to his character. He was also a prominent and devoted Freemason. His family came originally from Riga, and he was *au fond* a man with a cosmopolitan culture and a very strong English bias. His remarkable memory was allied to a certain precision of outlook; but it was by something latent in his outward achievements and position that his chief charm garlanded esteem with affection. This was, I think, his faithfulness in his inner life, and with it a wistfulness.

However that may be, all of us who are connected with THE GRAMOPHONE mourn the loss of one who gave us his best service to the end of his life and was content to spend his energies in the upholding of a great tradition.

CHRISTOPHER STONE.

NOTES ON THE INDEXES

The *Index of Extended Works* lists by *title* reviews of recordings of complete operas, musical comedies, oratorios or other collections.

The *Index of Record Reviews* lists by *artist* all records reviewed by Herman Klein under the monthly heading "Analytical Notes and First Reviews," which are found beginning on page 387 of this volume. In addition, the index lists all recordings specifically mentioned and identified by reference to catalog numbers found in the texts of Klein's "The Gramophone and the Singer" or other signed articles. These references can be identified as other than "first reviews," as their page numbers will fall between pages 63 and 387 of this volume.

The *General Index* includes subjects and persons mentioned in Klein's articles. Names dropped as rhetorical devices and authors of sources cited are not included. Passing mentions are omitted unless they embody some historical fact not treated in more detail in Klein's published works, or contain critical comment or comparisons thought by this editor to be of value to those engaged in research.

A note on *spelling:* During the period covered by the reviews in these pages, spellings of certain singers' names sometimes changed. Some erratic spellings are no doubt typographical errors; others are the result of changes which took place when these singers appeared for the first time in England. Where variations are found, this editor uses forms which have persisted on record labels, in record company catalogs, and in standard reference works.

Index of Extended Works

Index of Record Reviews

Herwin, Carrie 91, 92, 93, 361
Heseltine, William 212, 392, 401, 405, 419, 421
Heyer, Edwin 489
Hill, Carmen 199
Hirzel, Max 363, 389, 396, 465, 498, 506, 574
Hislop, Joseph 113, 169, 250, 398, 416, 429, 457, 467, 512
Hofmann, Ludwig 259, 432, 534, 544
Homer, Louise 91, 92, 93, 120, 361, 432
Hook, Ethel 82, 361
Hooper, Barrington 424, 457
Howe, Robert 211, 577
Hüni-Mihacsek, Felice 133, 150, 417, 419, 489, 532
Hüsch, Gerhard 363, 453, 486, 495, 507–508, 526, 530
Hutt, Robert 137
Huxley, May 399–400
Hyde, Walter 93, 212

Inghilleri, Giovanni 262, 358, 435, 442, 446, 465, 471, 476, 480, 502, 512
Irmler Ladies (Madrigal) Choir 397
Ivogün, Maria 131, 132, 363, 388–389, 543, 554

Jackson, Randell 311, 451
Jadlowker, Herman 126, 127, 133, 241
James, Lewis 91
Janni, Roberto 100
Janssen, Herbert 429, 476, 494
Jenkin, Olive 395
Jerger, Alfred 132, 138, 168, 394, 396, 569
Jeritza, Maria 85, 111, 112, 129, 219, 407, 410, 456
Jewish National Choir (of New York) 478
Jewish Vocal Records 438–439, 444–445, 478, 489
Johnson, Edward 107
Johnson, Gertrude 344, 405, 407, 452, 457
Jöken, Carl 574
Jokl, Fritzi 120, 169, 388–389, 391, 397–398
Jones, Bessie 102, 457
Jones, Dan 311, 400, 428, 461
Jones, Parry 293
Jordan, Arthur 92, 176, 203, 206, 405, 410
Jost-Arden, Ruth 494
Journet, Marcel 119, 120, 132, 135, 138, 141, 168, 219, 395–396,

428, 457 502, 512
Jung, Helene 442, 461, 467, 486
Jungbauer, Jenny 181
Jungkarth, Hedwig 489, 538
Jurjevskaja, Zinaida 128

Kaidanoff, Konstantin (C. E.) 521, 535
Kalter, Sabine 122
Kandl, Eduard 471, 528, 544, 570, 574
Kappel, Gertrude 168, 393, 398
Kardosch Singers 579
Kasenow, Gerald 489
Kedroff Male Quartet 390
Kelly, Fergus 571
Kemish, Ethel 199
Kemp, Barbara 120, 431, 451 (B.S.O.), 482
Kemper, Sophie 478
Kern, Adele 431, 471, 480, 492, 528, 534, 536, 544, 547, 574, 578
Kern, Leonhard 471
Kiepura, Jan 407, 409, 422, 435, 544, 557, 577
Kindermann, L. 259
Kinniburgh, Tom 211
Kinsey, Raymond 572
Kipnis, Alexander 136, 138, 240–241, 409, 440, 509, 512, 518, 535, 563
Kirchhoff, Walter 553
Kirchner, Alexander 509
Kirkby-Lunn, Louise 80, 92, 93, 133, 183, 205, 211, 213, 361
Klust, Herta 471
Knepel, Else 393, 429
Knote, Heinrich 508
Knupfer, Paul 120
Kochhann, Elsa 529
Korsoff, Lucette 71, 357
Koshetz, Nina 462, 513, 535
Kreisler, Fritz 176, 326
Kremer, Isa 439
Krumrey-Topas, L. 466
Kubelik, Jan 133
Kuhnlein, Elisabeth 477
Kullman, Charles 549, 571
Kurz, Selma 88, 122, 132, 168, 362, 394, 396

L'Opera Chorus and Orch, (Paris) 454
La Scala Chorus & Orch./ Sabajno &c. 222, 262, 406, 408, 410, 413, 420, 421, 435, 453, 458
Labbette, Dora 176, 202–203, 212, 422
Land, Emmy 436

Landi, Bruno 510
Landlar, Josef 444
Lange, Hans 472
Langley, Stephen 211, 213
Lanza, Lina 533
Lapelleterie, Rene (d'Opera Comique) 479
Lappas, Ulysses 99, 106, 168, 392, 398
Larsen-Todsen, Nanny 247, 522
Lattermann, Theodor 401
Lattuada, Emma 436
Lau, Cida 440
Laubenthal, Rudolf 259, 447, 500
Laurenti, Mario 86, 87
Lauri-Volpi, Giacomo 388, 398, 563
Lawson, Winifred 312
Lazaro, Hipolito 77, 124, 163, 226, 360
Lazzari, Carolina 86
Lazzari, Virgilio 136
Lebard, Henriette 446
Lebedeff, Aaron 439
Lehmann, Lilli 126, 327–328
Lehmann, Lotte 131, 144, 150, 167, 362, 390, 392, 408, 414, 418, 422, 425 427, 434, 442, 446, 453, 458, 462, 465, 467–468, 472, 482, 491, 499, 501 505, 521–522, 524, 526, 533, 538, 540, 545–546, 549, 565, 575, 576, 579
Leider, Frida 151, 363, 396, 441, 447–448, 457, 466, 513, 525
Leisner, Emmi 174, 401, 555
Lenghi-Cellini, Giuseppe 124, 137, 390, 455, 457, 462, 477
Leno, Dan 318–319
Lenzi, Arnaldo 519
Leoni, Eva 415
Leslie, David 498
Lewis, Bertha 312, 482
Lewis, Mary 129
Licette, Miriam 363, 389, 392–393, 412, 423, 442, 469, 488, 519, 523
Liebenberg, Eva 577
Lilley, Alice 311
Lindberg, Paula 477
Lindi, Aroldo 263, 361, 399, 404
Lipkovska, Lydia 161
List, Emmanuel 259, 363, 453, 457, 463, 534
Ljungberg, Göta 129, 169, 216, 259, 391, 400, 429, 462–463, 513, 518, 521
London Jewish Male Voice Choir/ Berman 439
Lorai, Elena 484
Lorenz, Max 399, 486, 500

613

General Index